ISBN 978-1-333-54956-5
PIBN 10518051

1 MONTH OF
FREE
READING

at

www.ForgottenBooks.com

By purchasing this book you are eligible for one month membership to ForgottenBooks.com, giving you unlimited access to our entire collection of over 700,000 titles via our web site and mobile apps.

To claim your free month visit:

www.forgottenbooks.com/free518051

English
Français
Deutsche
Italiano
Español
Português

www.forgottenbooks.com

Mythology Photography **Fiction**
Fishing Christianity **Art** Cooking
Essays Buddhism Freemasonry
Medicine **Biology** Music **Ancient**
Egypt Evolution Carpentry Physics
Dance Geology **Mathematics** Fitness
Shakespeare **Folklore** Yoga Marketing
Confidence Immortality Biographies
Poetry **Psychology** Witchcraft
Electronics Chemistry History **Law**
Accounting **Philosophy** Anthropology
Alchemy Drama Quantum Mechanics
Atheism Sexual Health **Ancient History**
Entrepreneurship Languages Sport
Paleontology Needlework Islam
Metaphysics Investment Archaeology
Parenting Statistics Criminology
Motivational

GARDNER ASAPH CHURCHILL.

(No. 1165, page 297.)

NATHANIEL WILEY CHURCHILL.
(No. 440, page 229.)

EDITOR'S PREFACE.

GEORGE M. BODGE.

In works of this kind the preface, though placed at the beginning and meant as an introduction, is understood to be the last word of the authors or compilers. As both my dear friends and colleagues in this work have died long before the completion of the volume, it devolves upon me, as editor and surviving member of the trio of compilers, to prepare this introductory word. It is not to be supposed that all who use this volume will read the preface, but I am sure that I speak the wish of my colleagues when I appeal to their kinsfolk of the name and blood to receive this word, and in their names (the names of Gardner Asaph Churchill, son of Asaph [No. 702], and Nathaniel Wiley Churchill [No. 440]) I send the greeting which they would have sent had they lived to this time.

A SKETCH OF THE PROGRESS OF THE WORK.

The work, the completion of which now results in this volume, entitled "The Churchill family in America," was begun, in the Plymouth branch, in 1852, by Charles M. S. Churchill, of Milton, Mass. [No. 704], who collected much information in relation to the Plymouth branch, which otherwise would have been lost. This was preserved in manuscript, but was not published until after many years later, when his nephew, Gardner A. Churchill, received the material and began to utilize and add to it, with the purpose of publishing a genealogy of the Plymouth branch of the family. The present writer's first acquaintance with this work was soon after this, about 1882, when Gardner A. Churchill, then a parishioner and intimate friend of the writer, came to advise with me as to the form and matter of a genealogical circular of inquiry to be sent out to the Churchill kindred in America. Mr. Churchill published

and sent out several thousands of these blanks, to Churchills all over
the country, and received answers from about one-third of those
who received them. About one-half of the answers received gave
the desired information, and many had to be appealed to again
and again before satisfactory accounts could be obtained. Yet small
as the returns were, the blanks then received have been, later, of
great service. Mr. Churchill in the following years put a great
amount of time, personal research, and money into the work of
gathering material. His research was mainly by correspondence,
searching of published historical works and records available in
Boston and vicinity. Soon after 1882 Mr. N. W. Churchill became
actively associated with him, and the work received in his person a
great impulse, because he was deeply interested in the pursuit, had
a remarkable memory and a marvellous capacity for gathering and
recording facts and statistics, and then his business for many years
was that of a travelling salesman, and as such he visited nearly all
the cities in the northern States. I have at hand some forty of
his business memorandum-books, which show that he filled in the
first part of each book with orders for goods, while the opposite
end was filled up with genealogical notes made at personal visits at
the homes of Churchills or allied families, or records copied at town,
church, and county offices. At the same time N. W. corresponded
with many whom he had visited and aroused to interest, who, later,
sent him the results of their personal inquiries. This friendly
partnership and coöperation of G. A. and N. W. went on for
many years, even until the death of G. A. in 1896; N. W. passing
over all the material he gathered to G. A., who recorded the same,
and, wherever possible, arranged it in order, but kept a copy of all
and returned the original notes and correspondence to N. W., and at
the same time submitted to him his own collections, so that each
had all the material, while G. A. had his mostly digested, arranged,
and indexed for use, and N. W. had his undigested, but partially
arranged in bundles of letters and note-books, numbered and labelled
so that he could refer at once to any family of either branch. For
many years the plan of the work had contemplated only the Plymouth
branch, while it was found that a vast amount of matter was collecting relating to the Connecticut branch. So it was decided to place
that in order so far as it could be readily collected, and publish it in
connection with the other. Some time before his death G. A. made
a statement of the progress and condition of the work, which he
intended as an outline of a preface to the volume, and which furnishes in part the material of this present sketch. That shows that
it was not intended to follow the female lines beyond the mention of

their names and marriages; and also that it was then thought that the Manhattan branch was an offshoot of one of the other branches, or of the Virginia family. In 1887 G. A. had compiled and published in pamphlet form a brief account of his own line of the Plymouth branch, for private distribution, and some time before his decease he had decided to publish the material already in hand and had arranged it in order for that purpose. For two years after his death the work ceased, except that the correspondence was kept up by N. W. with the families already interested.

In November the writer, having returned to the vicinity of Boston, at the wish of the family of G. A. Churchill, became actively engaged in the work as editor and assistant compiler, associated with Mr. Asaph Churchill, son of G. A., who became the business head of the enterprise representing his father's family, and with N. W. Churchill as colleague. Thus we joined in the design to arrange and publish the six generations of the Plymouth, and all the material in hand of the Connecticut branches; but after a brief survey of the field and the material, it was found that nearly all the living Churchill kindred belonged in the seventh to the tenth generations, and that, in order to make the book at all satisfactory, it would be necessary to add as much as possible of these generations. So the plan of the work was changed in extent, and it was also found to be desirable to add the families of the daughters as well as the sons of Churchills, as these allied families have been found in most cases more interested in their Churchill ancestry than many bearing the name. These changes vastly increased the work and of course extended the time and added immensely to the cost of the volume, the price of which, however, remains the same as for original subscribers. A prospectus of the volume was issued, with subscription-application attached, and subscriptions were soon received sufficient to warrant the issuing of the work, which it was supposed might be completed within a year, or two years, at least. But it was found necessary for N. W. to go all over his vast mass of letters and notes in order to bring the work to conformity with the new plans. He had to do all this personally, as no one understood his notes or correspondence except himself, and when the writer issued a new set of inquiry blanks and these were sent out to all of the name who could be reached, an enormous additional correspondence was at once imposed upon both N. W. and the editor. Mr. Churchill was conducting an exacting business in Boston, and could devote little time during the day, but worked late into the nights often, and far beyond his strength. This work went on thus until the summer of 1901, when Mr. Churchill's health broke down and he was obliged to abandon the work entirely, and the completion of the volume thus devolved upon the writer, with the irreparable loss to all of the vast amount of valuable personal information which Mr. Churchill held in his memory about the men and women, their places of residence, business, characters, etc., which he intended to give the writer, after the outline of the plan should be completed. He never prepared anything of biography, but gave the names and dates of birth, marriage, and death, in his manuscript, while many times in his conversations about the people he would give vivid and interesting descriptions of their homes, occupation, habits, and personal appearance. Thus the writer has been obliged to depend upon information derived from correspondence with later members of the families for sketches of the head of each family, which in many cases have not been obtainable.

The great mass of Mr. N. W. Churchill's notes and correspondence was turned over to me in the fall of 1901, and I was obliged to go over every note and letter, and arrange the same in indexed files, in order to make proper comparison, and to make additions and corrections. This proved to be a prodigious task and, together with the increasing correspondence and final preparation of the matter for printing, greatly delayed the work. For this delay also the members of the family, many of them, who have failed to respond to our earnest and repeated appeals for the simplest information about their own immediate families, are largely responsible. Our correspondence with the kindred in all the branches has been mainly pleasant, and both my colleagues greatly prized the cordial approval and ready help received from their kinsfolk. From some lines it has been learned that among them a profound indifference and ignorance as to their ancestry had prevailed till their interest had been excited by news of this enterprise. Some have, for a time, misled our compilers by returning as authentic information what afterwards was found to be only hearsay, and without any foundation in fact. G. A. Churchill speaks of the notion that he found prevailing in some directions, as to the descent of the emigrant Churchills, John of Plymouth, and Josiah of Connecticut, from the Duke of Marlborough, and points out the absurdity of the claims from the simple fact that the duke was not born until 1650, many years after the emigrants were settled and married in this country. After a very exhaustive search with the best heraldic authority in England and America he was satisfied that American Churchills, with the exception of the Virginia family, descendants of William, have no claims whatever to a coat-of-arms, even if it were possible for an American to receive an English coat-of-arms. Coats-of-arms do not descend

by inheritance, except to the heirs of the person to whom such coats
have been granted by the king. It is to be regretted that our senior
compiler was misled by an English correspondent, W. H. Churchill,
who sent him a book-plate copy of a coat-of-arms of a Churchill line,
which copy was photographed and sent out to many of the family.
Mr. Churchill sent it, he said, as a sample of what one of the
English connection had worn, and a reference to the committee on
heraldry very quickly showed it to be of recent granting, and of no
particular interest to American Churchills. Indeed, the photograph
shows it to be a composite, made up for some Churchill who had
married into a name having a coat-of-arms of more importance than
his own. Mr. G. A. Churchill, in the remarks on the family above
alluded to, says:

> Those who shall, from family interest or general curiosity, peruse the follow-
> ing pages will find little that is marvellous, brilliant, or grand, in the history of
> those whose names are recorded. They will find rather, illustrated, the virtues
> of the honest artisan, the peaceful tiller of the soil, the hardy seaman. They
> were mostly Christian men and women, self-reliant, courageous, and determined.
> In three wars our ancestors have borne an honorable part, and in the late Civil
> War many of the name or kindred have served with credit on land and sea. For
> myself, I am abundantly satisfied that the character of our ancestors in America
> needs no lustre borrowed from any foreign patent or title of nobility.

In addition to what our compilers have done in the Plymouth
branch, it may be stated here that in the Connecticut branch Amos
Churchill of Hubbardton, Vt. [see page 386, No. 105, Conn.], collected much material concerning his own line, from his grandfather
down to his own generation, and published a series of articles in
the "Vermont Historical Gazetteer" in 1851, containing much
valuable information about that line, though his traditions of the
ancestry back of his grandfather were entirely erroneous, showing
that he never consulted the records in Connecticut or elsewhere, and
depended solely upon his own memory of the traditions in his
father's family.

In the Manhattan or New York branch nothing has been published and no research had been made until N. W. Churchill discovered, about 1897 or '98, that this was a distinct branch; and as
the old records of that colony are very meagre and irregular, the
results of our investigations are rather unsatisfactory. At the time
of the death of N. W. he had made but little progress in the
compilation of this branch, and among his last words to me was
the charge "do the best you can with the papers, for there are
many excellent families whose records we have not yet filled." I
have tried loyally to fulfil that injunction, with what result may be
seen.

The movements of the generations of the Churchill family are illustrative of the migrations of the New England families in general. Three generations remained comparatively near the coast, while the fishing, lumbering, and ship-building interests afforded occupation sufficient for the rapidly increasing families of sons and daughters, and while the farming lands were yet plenty, near at hand; but when the old settlements were all taken up and it became necessary for the younger generations to purchase land, they began to reach out for free homesteads. Western Massachusetts became a goal for both the Plymouth and Connecticut branches, and later, when the lands of Vermont were opened up, we find both branches represented there; and then, a generation later, when Northern New York and a little later the rich lands of the "Holland Purchase" were offered, we find families from many lines of each branch among the settlers, and thence to the middle West went many sturdy settlers of the Churchill blood, after the War of 1812, in which they bore an honorable part. When the eastern timber lands of Maine and the cheap homesteads of Nova Scotia and New Brunswick were offered, many from the Plymouth branch removed thither and settled, as will be seen. Now descendants of all lines of the three great branches are scattered far over the continent, from ocean to ocean, and from Upper Canada to Mexico.

EXPLANATION OF PLAN; ARRANGEMENT OF MATTER, ETC.

The system adopted for this volume is that of the New England Historic Genealogical Society, in its regular publication, the "Register," slightly modified in the numbering to suit the needs of this more extensive work.

The emigrant ancestor in each branch is numbered 1, and his sons, 2, 3, and 4. The small figure at the right, and above these names, as in JOHN,[1] WILLIAM,[2] etc., indicates the generation of each. The names enclosed in parentheses, following the name of each head of a family, show his line of ancestry. The Roman numerals opposite the names of the children show the order of birth, while the Arabic numbers opposite some of these names show the possible heads of Churchill families, and, when so found to be, are carried forward with the names, to the proper place in the next generation. In some cases names have been found to represent families, after the general enumeration was completed, so that it was necessary to designate their place by adding the letters, a, b, c, etc., as, for instance, 260, 260a, 260b, etc. In a few cases, for the same reason, such numbers have been assigned to daughters, when their families have been found too late to be placed in the regular order. In general, as will be noted, the families of the daughters are carried one generation under the family of their fathers. In the exceptional cases above mentioned, they are assigned numbers and carried forward, like the sons, to the next generation. The index will rectify these irregularities. A very few abbreviations have been used, as *b.* for born, *bpt.* for baptized, *m.* for married, *d.* for died, *dau.* for daughter, etc. The effort has been to make the record the plainest possible, and the index has been prepared with the utmost care so as to involve the least confusion and trouble in the use of the book. The Connecticut and Manhattan branches have been marked along with the running title, to facilitate the work of tracing families.

ACKNOWLEDGMENTS OF ASSISTANCE.

Among the many whose courtesy and kindly help have greatly aided the making up of this volume, I make mention here of a few in behalf of my colleagues and the family of Mr. G. A. Churchill, who undertook the publication in respect to his memory and his known wishes, and express their gratitude to their kindred and friends throughout the country. I will say that many of those who may have assisted, by personal interviews, are now unknown to me, as no list was written down, but many were held by both the compilers in grateful memory. I have only the letters and notes to show the names of those most helpful up to the time of my association in the work. Some of these I will mention.

Norman Churchill, of Galesburg, Ill. [No. 148, page 418], and later his son-in-law, Professor Comstock; Mr. Isaac Bradford Churchill, Glen Ellyn, Ill. [No. 616, page 277]; Hon. John C. Churchill, of Oswego, N.Y. [475, page 239]; Mrs. Angeline J. (Churchill) Johnson, of Holden, Vt. [daughter of No. 607, page 268], and her brothers, Charles H. and Columbus C.; Mr. George D. Seymour [see under No. 140, page 410, and 360a, page 511]; Robert H. Churchill, Marinette, Wis. [No. 532, page 484]; Charles S. Churchill, Roanoke, Va. [No. 670, page 541]; Mrs. Almira (Churchill) Ross, Binghamton, N.Y., and her sister, Mrs. Lucy M. (Churchill) Hull, of Monroeton, Pa. [see No. 437, page 542]; Mr. Frank Farnsworth Starr, of Middletown, Conn., the well-known genealogist; Rev. Frank Churchill Scoville, Greenwich, N.Y. [see page 196, No. 377]; Mrs. Susannah Badger (French) Tenney, of Newmarket, N.H., great granddaughter of Thomas Churchill [No. 25, page 20] and wife of Perley W. Tenney; both of her grandmothers were

Churchills, viz., Lydia (Churchill) French, and Susannah (Churchill) Badger, her parents, Reuben French and Sally True Badger, being cousins. She was greatly interested in this volume and gave much valuable assistance. Mr. M. V. Tillson, South Hanson, Mass.; Miss Josephine Hill Churchill, daughter of N. W. Churchill, our senior compiler, who, since his death, has given much time and assistance to the work; Mr. James Wells Hull of Pittsfield, Mass., grandson of Rev. Jesse Churchill [No. 46, see page 360]; Mrs. Alice (Carter) Stephenson [page 110, under No. 181], of Portland, Me.; and Mrs. Mabel (Churchill) Jones [page 224, under No. 429], also of Portland; Mr. George W. Boyer, Hartland, N.B. [see No. 406b, page 212]; Mr. Calvin Churchill, Lakeville, N.B. [see No. 173, page 102]; William P. Churchill, Brooklyn, N.S. [page 253, under No. 526]; Rev. Anson Titus, Medford, Mass.; Mr. Alfred Cole, Buckfield, Me.; Marlborough Churchill, Sing Sing, N.Y. [No. 463, page 235]; Miss Agnes Fetters Churchill of Amesbury, Mass. [daughter of No. 202, page 121]. Many others deserve mention, and some have received notice in the body of the work, and the names of others were held only in the memory of my colleagues.

THE CHURCHILL FAMILY IN ENGLAND.

While the compilers of this genealogy of the Churchill Family in America wish to avoid the appearance of intention to claim near kinship with the lines of Churchills in England which have received and transmitted the titles and perquisites of nobility, they deem it proper, and indeed expedient, to embody the facts of the early history of the name, at least, which is an inalienable inheritance, in Anglo-Saxon usage. Both my colleagues devoted much time and careful study to this matter, and both were in substantial agreement in the accounts which each personally prepared. G. A. Churchill adopted entire the account by Lediard, the biographer of John Churchill, Duke of Marlborough; while N. W. carried the line a little farther back in the details of the earliest traditions, according to the English writers on heraldry, from whom Lediard made up his accounts, viz.: Guillim, Anderson, and Collins. Many critical works have been produced in later times, bringing the fallacies of early heraldic writers under the clear light of modern investigation, but I give the account practically as my colleagues prepared it. We have numerous letters from members of the Churchill kindred who seem to have exceedingly vague ideas of heraldry and the relations of American families to "coats-of-arms," and of what constitutes the proper right or claim of those whose ancestors, bearing a name which has been known in English heraldry, have yet no positive evidence of descent from any family to which "arms" have been granted. To such, who have not the opportunity to consult standard works on heraldry, I would suggest a careful reading of the article on this subject in the Encyclopedia Brittannica, and also the many references to John Churchill, Duke of Marlborough, under the latter title, "Domes-day Book," which contains the records of surveys in England up to 1086 A.D., showing the grants of "William the Conqueror" to his followers, with conditions of said lands, etc., contains the name of Roger de Courcil, who is said to have been the ancestor of the English and American Churchills. Armorial bearings or coats-of-arms were first known about 1120 A.D.

The name Churchill is found in English records as Courcelle, Courcil, Curichill, Chercile, Churchil, Churchall, Churchell, and Churchill, the last being the accepted form for many generations.

THE CHURCHILL COAT—OF—ARMS.

SABLE. *A Lyon rampant,* ARGENT, *debruised with a bendlet* GULES.

I have not been able to find just when or to whom this coat-of-arms was granted, but in "Collins' Peerage," Vol. I., page 365 (footnote), it is said to have been claimed by Sir John Churchill, son of Jasper, of Bradford, No. 16. The records of Herald's College, England, confirm this claim. He may have inherited it from ancestors generations back, for all evidence I have found, possibly from Bartholomew (No. 5), who was knighted under King Stephen.

ORIGIN OF THE NAME AND LINEAGE OF THE FAMILY OF CHURCHILL.

A township in France called Courcil, now Courcelles, in Lorraine, was given as a manor to Wandril De Leon, son of Gitto De Leon, of a noble family, and himself a famous soldier, as early as 1055 A.D. He had two sons, Richard and Wandril. The first became the feudal lord of Montalban ; married YOLAND, Countess of Luxemburg, and from them descended the noble house of De Leon in France, at the present day.

1. WANDRIL DE LEON took the name of his manor, and became Lord of Courcil; married ISABELLA DE TUYA, and had two sons, Roger and Rouland de Courcil, and thus became the founder of the Courcil (Churchill) family.

2. ROGER DE COURCIL followed William, Duke of Normandy, known as "William the Conqueror," into England in 1066 A.D., and when William became king, received for his services lands in the counties of Dorsetshire, Somersetshire, Wiltshire, and Shropshire. In "Domes-day Book," in the survey for Wiltshire, we read

"Roger De Courcelle holds Fisertone of the King. Bondi held it in the time of King Edward and it paid 10 hides. The land is 10 Carucates. Of this there is in Demesnes 5½ hides, and there are 3 Carucates; and there are 16 Villans and 12 Bordars and 14 Cottars with 7 Carucates. There is also a Mill paying 20 shillings, and 12 acres of meadow and 10 acres of wood. The pasture is half a mile long and as much broad. It was and is worth £25."

The meaning of the old words is somewhat obscure. Carucate means, in a general way, as much land as one plow would cultivate, varying with situation, soil, etc., from sixty to one hundred acres ; "hide" had about the same meaning, but without reference to the plow, meaning, perhaps, "a holding." "Demesnes," the feudal lord's own reservation, not held by his tenants ; Villans, Bordars, and Cottars were the tenants or serfs, of different classes, rated, I think, in the order of mention.

Roger de Courcil married GERTRUDE, daughter of Sir Guy de Torbay, and took up his residence in Somersetshire. He had three sons, John, Hugh-Fitz-Roger, and Roger-Fitz-Roger. These younger sons married into landed families and assumed the names of the lands or family-titles to which they succeeded, dropping the name Courcil.

4. JOHN DE COURCIL, eldest son of Roger, married JOAN DE KILRINGTON, by whom he had a son,

5. BARTHOLOMEW, who was knighted under King Stephen [1135–1154] as Sir BARTHOLOMEW DE CHERCHILE, and who was made Master of the Castle at Bristol, holding it for the king. He married AGNES, daughter of Ralph Fitz Ralph of Tiverton, and had son,

6. PAGAN DE CHERCHILE, who married (———) and had a son;

7. ROGER DE CHERCHILE, who married (———) and had a son,

8. ELIAS DE CHIRCHIL, who married the daughter of the ancient house of Columbers, and by her had three sons, *John* and *Giles*, neither of whom left male issue, and

9. WILLIAM CHURCHILL, the third son, who assumed that form of the name, resided at Rockbear in Devonshire, married (———) and had a son,

10. GILES CHURCHILL, who married (———) and had a son,

11. CHARLES CHURCHILL, who married MARGARET, only daughter and heiress of Sir William Widville, who brought him considerable estate. They had a son,

12. THOMAS CHURCHILL, who married GRACE, daughter of Thomas Tylle, of Tylle House in Cornwall, and by her had a son,

13. WILLIAM CHURCHILL, who married MARY, eldest daughter of Richard Creuse of Wicroft Castle in Devonshire. They had three sons: *Roger*, who settled in Catherston, *William* in Corton, both in the County of Dorsetshire, and *John*, who settled in Muston in the same county.

14. ROGER CHURCHILL, married JANE, widow of Nicholas Meggs, and daughter of Sir William Peverell, of Bradford, County of Yorkshire, by whom he had issue.

15. MATTHEW CHURCHILL, who married ALICE GOULD, daughter of James Gould of Dorchester, County of Dorsetshire, by whom he had issue.

16. JASPER CHURCHILL, of Bradford, married ELIZABETH CHAP-LET, daughter of John, of Harrington, in Dorsetshire, and had two sons, John and Jasper (the latter married and had four daughters).

17. JOHN CHURCHILL, eldest son of Jasper, became a celebrated lawyer, a member of the Middle Temple, and by an extensive practice considerably augmented his estate. His residence was at Mintern in Dorsetshire. He married SARAH WINSTON, daughter of Sir Henry Winston of Standon, in Lincolnshire, and his wife, Dionése Bond, daughter of Sir Thomas Bond. They had two sons, William and Winston. The latter succeeded to the title and estate.

18. SIR WINSTON CHURCHILL, born in 1620, had his residence at Wooten Basset, in Wiltshire, and married ELIZABETH DRAKE, daughter of Sir John Drake, of Ashe, in Devonshire, and had seven sons and four daughters, as follows: (1) *Winston*, b. 1646; d. in infancy. (2) *Arabella*, b. March 16, 1648; d. Feb. 23, 1714. (3) *John*, b. May 24, 1650; d. June 16, 1722. (4) *George*, b. Feb. 29, 1653; d. May 8, 1710, unmarried. He was Lord High Admiral of the British Navy. (5) *Charles*, b. Feb. 2, 1656; d. Dec. 29, 1714, married, but had no children. He was a general in the British Army, and was at the taking of Quebec, under Major-General Hill. (6) *Montjoy*, d. in infancy. (7) *Jasper*, d. in infancy. (8) *Theobald*, became a clergyman of the English Church, and died unmar-

ried Dec. 3, 1684. (9) *Dorothy.* (10) *Mary.* (11) *Barbara.* All three of these youngest children died in infancy.

19. JOHN CHURCHILL, second son of Sir Winston, was born May 24, 1650, at Ashe in Devonshire, and died near Windsor, June 16, 1722. He was the famous English general and statesman. He was educated in part at St. Paul's school. At the age of fifteen he was appointed a page in the household of the Duke of York, afterwards James II. of England. (His sister Arabella was maid of honor to the Duchess of York, where she became a court beauty of renown, and a favorite of King James II.)

By the favoritism of James, the influence of his sister, and his own ability, John Churchill was advanced to places of command in the army, by successive steps, until he became commander-in-chief, and one of the most renowned of British military generals, as well as an adroit and successful statesman. He received the highest rank in the peerage in 1702 as Duke of Marlborough. He married in 1678 SARAH JENNINGS, daughter of Richard Jennings of Sandridge, in Hertfordshire, the favorite attendant of Princess Anne, a lady of beauty and grace, and of energy and ambition equal to his own. They had children: (1) *Henrietta,* b. July 19, 1681 ; m. Francis, only son of Lord Sydney Godolphin; (2) *Anne,* b. 1683; m. Charles Spencer only son of Robert Spencer, Earl of Sunderland; (3) *John,* b. 1685, d. Feb. 20, 1703, aged eighteen years ; (4) *Elizabeth,* b. 1683 ; m. Scroop Egerton, Earl of Bridgewater · (5) *Mary,* b. 1688 ; m. Viscount Mountheimer, son of Ralph, Earl of Montague; (6) *Charles,* b. 1690, d. in infancy.

The duchess outlived her husband twenty-two years, in the enjoyment of the vast wealth which was left her by the duke. She was a person of power and great influence in the politics of England. Neither of the duke's sons lived to have children, so that the title would have passed to the son of the oldest daughter, Henrietta, wife of Lord Godolphin, had he lived, but he died before the duke's death, and so the title passed to the family of Anne, second daughter of the duke, and wife of Charles Spencer, the third earl of Sunderland. Robert, the first son of Anne, having died, the second son, Charles, succeeded to the title and became second Duke of Marlborough, in 1733.

The title was now held in the Spencer family name and the succession simply is given here.

George Spencer, third duke, born Jan. 26, 1739.

George Spencer Churchill, fourth duke, born March 6, 1766. He was allowed in 1807, upon petition to the crown, to assume the name *Churchill.*

George Spencer Churchill, fifth duke, born Dec. 23, 1793.

John Winston Spencer Churchill, sixth duke, born June 2, 1822, and succeeded to the dukedom July 1, 1857.

George Charles Spencer Churchill, seventh duke, born May 13, 1844.

Charles Richard John, eighth duke, born Nov. 13, 1871. He married Consuelo Vanderbilt, daughter of William K., of New York, granddaughter of Cornelius, the founder of the Vanderbilt family of New York in its present station of power and wealth.

Sir Randolph Henry Churchill, the third son of the seventh duke, was born Feb 13, 1849, became a leader in English politics of considerable note. He married Jennie Jerome, daughter of Mr. Leonard Jerome, of New York, April 15, 1874. Their son, *Winston Churchill,* achieved considerable notoriety in the Boer war, and was in 1902 a member of Parliament.

A CONJECTURE AS TO THE ANCESTRY OF AMERICAN CHURCHILLS.

Referring to William Churchill, No. 13, it is found that he made his will March 12, 1599, making his youngest son, John, his sole executor, though, of course, the estate and title passed to the eldest son. John Churchill, the youngest son, born, it is thought, between 1540 and 1550, married Elenor Meller, daughter of John Meller, of Kyme, in Dorsetshire, and settled at Muston in the same county, and was there a gentleman of respectable estate and position. They had nine sons and four daughters, viz.: (1) George; (2) Richard; (3) John, died soon; (4) John; (5) Robert; (6) Maximilian; (7) Thomas; (8) Jasper; (9) Matthew; (10) Edith; (11) Sarah; (12) Jane; (13) a child, died unnamed. The conjecture is that one of these nine sons was the father or grandfather of Joseph Churchill of London, who, in 1628, was a merchant in Fleet Lane, and was supplying Governor Endicott of Massachusetts Bay Colony with arms and other articles of outfit.

It is possible that this Joseph was the father of John of Plymouth, or Josiah of Connecticut, perhaps of both. Both these emigrant settlers named their oldest son Joseph, according to the old custom. There is no evidence of any relationship of Joseph of London to John of Muston, or of any connection between the emigrant settlers and the said Joseph, or of any kinship between the said settlers, one with the other.

FIRST GENERATION.

1.

JOHN CHURCHILL the emigrant ancestor of the Plymouth branch of the family in America, was born in England and first appeared at Plymouth in Massachusetts, in 1643, and died there Jan. 1, 1662/3.

It is a matter of regret that up to the completion of this volume nothing has been found to give even a clue to the birthplace, parentage, previous residence, or occupation of this emigrant ancestor of such a large posterity. He was not in the tax-lists of Plymouth in 1632, but appears in 1643 in the list of the male inhabitants between sixteen and sixty years old, who are "able to bear arms." Diligent research through many ways and for many years has failed to add any authentic information to the bare fact that he was at Plymouth in 1643. In addition we have the following items: He married Hannah Pontus, Dec. 18, 1644; bought a farm of Richard Higgins, Aug. 18, 1645; was propounded freeman, June 4, 1650, and admitted June 5, 1651. He bought, Oct. 20, 1652, of Nathaniel Masterson, then of Manchester, in Massachusetts, ten acres of upland lying at Wellingsley, in the township of Plymouth. In this deed Mr. Churchill is called "Planter." Mr. William T. Davis, in "Ancient Landmarks of Plymouth," page 331, has the following pertinent reference, which we quote verbatim:

> John Churchill, the progenitor of the Churchill family, who appeared in Plymouth in 1643, settled at Hobshole. His land was on the easterly side of the street, and extended from the southerly line of the field opposite to "Jabez Corner" to a point thirty feet distant from the southerly line of the estate of Branch Blackmer. Here he lived and died, but no tradition exists concerning the precise spot on which his house was situated. There are some indications, however, in the records, that the old house owned by Thomas B. Sears and Amos Leshure, which was built by Elkanah Churchill, the grandson of John, occupies the site of the ancient dwelling. After the death of Mr. Churchill, the estate fell into the hands of his son Eleazer.

In Mr. Churchill's will, given below, we note that he had acquired, by grant or purchase, quite a large land property. At his death, his eldest son, Joseph, was about sixteen years old. The widow, with her six children, lived, evidently, in the "new house," which he mentions as designed for Joseph, after the mother's death, while if Joseph marries before that event he is to have "the old dwelling-house." The widow was left the use of his whole property during her life. It is proper here to give some account of this wife and mother.

HANNAH (PONTUS) CHURCHILL was the daughter of William Pontus, who was at Plymouth as early as 1633, and was born in Holland or England in 1623. Very little appears in the records of Plymouth concerning William Pontus, although he was a land-owner and a citizen of some prominence and influence in the colony, and a member of the Court 1636–1638 inclusive. It is therefore gratifying to the editor of this volume to be able to add something to the sum of our knowledge of the parents of Hannah Pontus, the ancestress of the numerous lines of this Plymouth branch of the Churchills.

In the notes of Mr. Charles B. Richardson, gathered in his researches, in the Records at Leyden, and published in the "Historical Magazine," London and New York, December, 1859, Vol. III., page 358 — lists of the names and occupations of some of the company of the Pilgrims who did not embark in the "Mayflower" are found. Among these are John Robinson, minister, from England; William Pautes (Pontus), fustian-worker, from Dover. On page 263 of same volume William Brewster is mentioned a witness on behalf of "William Pautes, fustian-worker, from near Dover on his marriage with Wybra Hanson, maid, on the 4 December, 1610." Now Mary Pontus, the sister of Hannah, married, Oct. 31, 1645, James Glass, and in the Plymouth Colony Records, Vol. VIII., page 7, is found the birth of Wybra Glass, daughter of James and Mary, born Aug. 9, 1649. This name Wybra, so uncommon, would seem to indicate a close relation between Wybra (Hanson) Pautes (Pontus), of Leyden, and this granddaughter of William Pontus. The wife of Mr. Pontus was living in 1633, but she is mentioned as "Good-wife Pontus." See "Mayflower Descendants," Vol. I., page 160. They lived, probably, near the southwestern limits of the "Mile and a half tract," as by maps of 1701. He died Feb. 9, 1653, leaving his small estate by will of 1650 to his two daughters. Mrs. Hannah (Pontus) Churchill married, June 25, 1669, Mr. Giles Rickard, as his third wife, and survived him six years. She died at Hobb's Hole, Dec. 22, 1690, "in her sixty-seventh year."

THE ORIGINAL CHURCHILL HOMESTEAD.

From " Old Colony Memorial Deeds," Vol. VIII., p. 111.

Memorandum the 18th of August 1645. That Richard Higgins doth acknowledge, that for and in consideration of the sum of twelve pounds, to be payd in manner and forme following by John Churchwell, That is to say, five pounds the first of March next, fourty shillings that tyme twelve months, and fourty shillings the first of March 1647, and the remayning three pounds the first of March in the year of our Lord, 1648, all which payments are to be made in corne or cattell or other current payment of the country as they will then passe from man to man at the said time of payment, — Hath freely and absolutely bargained and sold unto the said John Churchwell, all that his dwelling-house, out-houses and buildings, with the garden and orchard situate neere Browne's Rock, together with the uplands thereunto adjoining, and all his lands at Woeberry together with his meddow at South Ponds and at Colebrook meddowes towards Agawam, and all the fencing in and about any part of the premises, and all his Right title and Interest of and into the said premises with their appurtenances and every part and parcell thereof, — To have and to hold, etc., etc.

Provided that it shall be lawful for the said Richard Higgins to take away the borůs that lyne the inward roome, and the bedstead and boards overhead, and some fruit trees in the said orchard, so that he leave the said John thirty good fruit trees in the said orchard, and the forsaid payments to be made at Plymouth.

October 29, 1649.

Received by me, Richard Higgins full satisfaction from John Churchwell upon all accounts from the beginning to the present.

RICHARD HIGGINS.

THE WILL OF JOHN CHURCHILL.

The Will nuncupative of John Churchill Senr., late deceased, exhibited before the Court held at Plymouth the 3^d of March 1662 attested upon oath as followeth.

Abigail Clarke, aged twenty three years, or thereabouts, being deposed saith that on Tuesday 24th of December last past before the date hereof, her kinsman, viz. John Churchill Senr, being ill at . . . but of perfect memory, did express himself in manner as followeth, that his mind and will was that his son Joseph Churchill and his son Eliezer Churchill shall have and enjoy all his lands both uplands and meadows within the township of Plymouth excepting only fifty acres of land granted to him by the Towne, lying at Mannonnett ponds, which he gave them unto John Churchill his son, moreover that his will was that his son William shall have his purchase land at Punckatusett, viz. his share towne's land there; further that he did express himself that his son Joseph shall have his new house at his wife's death and for the use of all the lands aforesaid that they shall bee for the use and improvement of his wife as long as she lives and that he also said that in case Joseph should marry or bee for himself, that then he should have the use of the old dwelling house and some land to make use of. And as for his estate remaining he said that he knew not whether there would be anything left when his children were brought up or not, but if his wife could spare it, then that Joseph should have a yoake of oxen, and Eliezer a yoake of oxen, and Hannah a cow if not two; and in case anything should be left at his wife's decease, that then such of his children as have nothing in particular as above given them should have what is left, in equable proportion, to equallize what is given them forenamed as far as it will goe.

The oath of Abigail Clarke taken in the Court held at Plymouth the third day of March 1662

Attested p^r me Nathaniel Morton

Att the Court of his Maj^{tee}, held at Plymouth in New England on the 2nd day of March anno Domini 1668, Joseph Churchill came before the said Court and allowed approved Rattifyed & confirmed the Will of his father John Churchill

deceased, above expressed in all and every the particulars; the said Will and
Testament to stand and remain and continue unalterable and inviolable forever.
Plymouth Ss., Oct. 20. 1652, a true copy from the Plymouth Colony Record
Book of Wills, Vol. 2ᵈ Part second Page 82
Attest Wᵐ. S. Russell, Keeper of Said Records.

AN INVENTORY OF THE GOODS AND CHATTELS OF JOHN CHURCHILL, LATE DE-
CEASED, APPRAISED BY THOSE UNDERWRITTEN, THE 11 FEBRUARY, AND
EXHIBITED TO THE COURT HELD AT PLYMOUTH THE THIRD OF MARCH, ONE
THOUSAND SIX HUNDRED AND SIXTY THREE AS FOLLOWETH,

	£.	s.	d.
Impˢ 4 oxen	16	00	00
Item, 2 cowes	05	00	00
" 2 heifers supposed to be with caif	05	00	00
" 2 steers of 2 yrs. old and one heifer of 2 yrs old	07	00	00
" a Yearling steer	01	00	00
" 2 steer calves	01	10	00
2 Sows & three Piggs	01	10	00
2 feather bed tickes not full	03	10	00
4 Blankets	01	10	00
3 Pair of Sheets	02	00	00
2 pillows and 4 pillow beers	01	00	00
5 napkins and a Tablecloth	00	06	00
his wearing clothes	06	00	00
Stokens and shoes & an home made coat	01	00	00
a hatt	00	08	00
3 Shirts	00	12	00
Bands and handkerchiefs	00	08	00
a great brass Kettle	01	00	00
a Bellmettle skillett	00	02	00
2 great iron Potts	01	10	00
an old Kettle and an iron skillett	00	05	00
Pothooks and pot hangers and an old iron ladle	00	04	00
1 plough share and Coultre	00	08	00
3 Scythes & 3 Sickles	00	10	00
a pair of tongs and a fire shovel	00	02	00
4 pewter platters	00	12	00
2 pewter basons & drinking pot and seven alcomy (Alchymy) spoons	00	05	00
on Earthen Ware	00	08	00
2 Trays, 7 trenchers & some other Wooden vessels	00	04	00
2 hogsheads, 4 Barrells	00	10	00
2 Beer Barrells & a churn & a Washing tubb	00	08	00
a trundle bedstead, 2 chairs & 2 old tables	00	10	00
2 axes, a morticing axe & 2 hatchetts	00	08	00
2 pickaxes, 3 hoes	00	06	00
2 Augurs and some other small iron tools	00	03	00
5 Wedges and a beetle-ring	00	05	00
2 guns	05	10	00
a sword and shot pouch, 2 lbs powder 4 lbs shot	00	12	00
2 spring wheels and 3 pair of cards	00	10	00
Meale baggs & sacks & a sifting trough	00	08	00
1 fan, 2 corn sieves, & 2 meal sieves	00	10	00
2 cow bells	00	01	00
a cart & wheels	01	00	00
2 chains, a bolt and shackle	00	08	00
1 Wainhead yoke, the ring & staple 2 Ring yokes with hooks and staples	00	10	00
in Books 00. 06. 00 in old Lumber 00. 05. 00	00	11	00

74 14. 06

Debts due from the Estate

	£	s.	d.
Item, to Robert Finney	6.	00.	00
" in other small debts	1.	00.	00.

Plymouth Ss. Oct. 20, 1652.

A true copy from the Book of Wills 2nd. Part Volume 2d, page 83

Attest   WM. E. RUSSELL
Keeper of the P. Colony Record.

JOHN CHURCHILL married at Plymouth, Dèc. 18, 1644, HANNAH PONTUS, the daughter of Mr. William Pontus, of Plymouth. She survived her husband and married a second husband, Giles Rickard (or Reccord), June 25, 1669.

Children of John and Hannah Churchill.

2   I. JOSEPH,[2] b.   1647; m. SARAH HICKS, June 3, 1672.
     II. HANNAH,[2] b. Nov. 12, 1649; m. JOHN DREW,   , 1672.

He was the son of William Drew, and was born in England in 1642. His grandfather was Sir Edward Drew, who was knighted by Queen Elizabeth. He appeared in Plymouth first in 1660. They lived in Plymouth.

Children of John and Hannah (Churchill) Drew.

1. Elizabeth Drew, b. Feb. 5, 1673.
2. John Drew, b. Aug. 29, 1676; m. Sarah Delano.
3. Samuel Drew, b. Feb. 1, 1678; m. 1st, Lydia (———); m. 2d, Ruth Delano.
4. Thomas Drew, b. May 1, 1681.
5. Nicholas Drew, b. Oct. 16, 1684; m. Rebecca Morton, April 19, 1716.
6. Lemuel Drew, b. Aug. 1, 1687; m. Hannah Barnes, Dec. 22, 1715.

3   III. ELIEZER,[2] b. April 20, 1652; m. 1st, MARY (———); m. 2d, MARY DOTY Feb. 8, 1685.
     IV. MARY,[2] b. Aug. 1, 1654; m. THOMAS DOTY, Feb. 8, 1688. •

They lived in Truro. He was a sea-faring man. Mary, the wife, died, and he married, 2d, Mary (———.), and he died Dec. 4, 1678. His will was proved March 8, 1679.

Children by First Wife.

1. Martha Doty, b. 1672.
2. Hannah Doty, b. December, 1675.

By Second Wife.

3. Thomas Doty, b. July 22, 1679.

4   V. WILLIAM,[2] b. 1656; m. LYDIA BRYANT, Jan. 17, 1683.
5   VI. JOHN,[2] b. 1657; m. REBECCA DELANO, Dec. 28, 1686.

SECOND GENERATION.

2.

JOSEPH [2] CHURCHILL (JOHN [1]). Born in Plymouth, 1647. He lived on the farm first owned by his father. Some time before 1700 he built the house which is still standing on the easterly side of the curve in the road opposite the " Sandy Gutter Road." Little is preserved of his life.

The following extract from Davis's " Landmarks of Plymouth," page 346, will throw some light upon his outward conditions:

It will be remembered that the southerly line of the mile-and-a-half tract was bounded by the farm of Joseph Churchill, lying on the southerly side of Wellingsley. This farm extended from Oberry or Woeberry, as it was some-times called in the early records, across the Chiltonville road near Sandy Gutter, to the harbor, and was owned first by John Churchill, the progenitor of the Churchill family, and afterward by his son Joseph. The house, built by Joseph Churchill before 1700, is still standing, on the easterly side of the curve in the road opposite the Sandy Gutter road. The house, with the land immediately surrounding it, was sold, in 1715, by Joseph Churchill to his son Barnabas. Lemuel Churchill, son of Barnabas, sold a part of the estate to Thomas Faunce, who sold it, in 1767, to Jonathan Churchill, by whom it was sold in the same year to John Faunce. In 1773 Charles Churchill and his wife Sarah, who had acquired an interest in the estate through her first husband, Isaac Churchill, son of Barnabas, sold the other part to John Faunce, making him the owner of the whole.

Passing through several hands, in 1822 the house was bought by Freeman Morton, and Mr. Davis continues,

At the time of its purchase by Mr. Morton the shape and character of the house were ancient. Its roof was afterwards raised by him, the chimney reconstructed, and the modern expression given to its exterior which it now wears. Its interior, however, still bears the marks of extreme age, and is worthy of a visit by the antiquarian. It is now (1883) owned by Alvin G. Morton, son of Freeman, who remembers the Dutch oven it once had, with its opening in the yard, covered by a small shed-like structure protecting it from exposure.

JOSEPH [2] CHURCHILL married at Plymouth, June 3, 1672, SARAH HICKS, daughter of Samuel and Lydia (Doane) Hicks, and grand-daughter of Robert Hicks, the first settler of the name.

Children born in Plymouth.

6   I. JOHN, [3] b. July 3, 1678; m. DESIRE HOLMES, Nov. 19, 1700.
     II. MARGARET, [3] b. Oct., 1684; m. SAMUEL BATES.

Children born in Plymouth.

   1. Thomas Bates, b. March 2, 1709; m. Lydia Savory.
   2. Samuel Bates, b. April 16, 1713.
   3. John Bates, b. Nov. 24, 1716.

4. Barnabas Bates, b. Jan. 15, 1719.
5. Job Bates, b. Oct. 14, 1721.

7 III. BARNABAS,[3] b. July 3, 1686; m. LYDIA HARLOW, Feb. 5, 1711.
   IV. MERCY,[3] b. 1689; d. soon.
8 V. JOSEPH,[3] b. Jan. 1692; m. ABIAH BLACKWELL, of Sandwich, 1716.

3.

ELIEZER [2] CHURCHILL (JOHN [1]). Born in Plymouth, April 20, 1652. Admitted freeman at Plymouth, 1683. He lived at Hobshole, upon a part of the original estate of his father, having come into possession of the first house built by him.

According to the provisions of his father's will, and later arrangements with the mother and other heirs, Eliezer Churchill came into possession of that part of the original Churchill homestead which contained the " old house." To this land was added a strip thirty feet wide lying next to Branch Blackmer, by grant of town, 1709. He died about 1716. In " Landmarks of Plymouth " Mr. Davis says : Eliezer Churchill

probably built and occupied as a residence the building, taken down within a few years, which for many years was occupied as a shop by Ichabod and Edwin Morton. The grant was made for Eliezer " to erect a warehouse upon." This warehouse, if ever built, occupied a part of the site of the house of the late Edwin Morton.

ELIEZER [2] married 1st, MARY ———; 2d, Feb. 8, 1688, MARY DOTY, daughter of Edward and Faith (Clarke) Doty. She died Dec. 11, 1715, aged 60 years.

Children of First Wife.
I. HANNAH,[3] b. Aug. 23, 1676; living unmarried in 1715.
II. JOANNA,[3] b. Nov. 25, 1678; living unmarried in 1715.
III. ABIGAIL,[3] b. 1680; m. 1st, FRANCIS BILLINGTON, May 17, 1703; 2d, NATHL. HOWLAND, as his second wife, 1725.

Children born in Plymouth.
1. Sarah Billington, b. Dec. 11, 1702.
2. Sukey Billington, b. Jan. 1, 1704.
3. Francis Billington, b. Feb. 16. 1708.
4. Jemima Billington, b. June 10, 1710; m. Joseph Bent, Oct. 17, 1728.
5. Constant Billington, b. Feb. 2, 1713; m. Francis Merrifield.
6. Abigail Billington, b. Oct 21, 1716.
7. Joseph Billington, b. Jan. 11, 1719.

9 IV. ELIEZER, Jr.,[3] b. Feb. 23, 1682; m. HANNAH BARTLETT, dau. Robert.
10 V. STEPHEN,[3] b. Feb. 16, 1685; m. EXPERIENCE ELLIS.
   VI. JEDIDAH,[3] b. Feb. 27, 1687; m. Dec. 1, 1709, THOMAS HARLOW, son of William.

Children of Jedidah and Thomas Harlow.
1. Thomas Harlow, b. July 25, 1712; m. Patience Tilson, of Plympton.
2. Elizabeth Harlow, b. March 14, 1715; d. 1718.

3. Jonathan Harlow, b. March 22, 1718; m. Sarah Holmes.
4. Lydia Harlow, b. June 4, 1721.
5. Eleazer Harlow, b. Dec. 13, 1723.
6. Jedidah Harlow, b. Oct. 3, 1726; m. Abner Sylvester.
7. Nathaniel Harlow, b. July 22, 1729.

Children of Second Wife.

VII. MARY,[3] b.1688; m. EDWARD STEVENS, Dec. 23, 1708.

Children born in Plymouth.

1. Mary Stevens, b. June 21, 1710; m. Joseph Cole.
2   Hannah Stevens, b. April 11, 1712; m. Benjamin Bartlett.
3. Sarah Stevens, b. May 25, 1715.
4. Lemuel Stevens, b. Dec. 25, 1716.
5. Elizabeth Stevens, b. April 30, 1719; m. Benjamin Harlow.
6. Edward Stevens, b. Sept. 19, 1721; m. Phebe Harlow.
7. Eliezer Stevens, b. Dec. 10, 1723; m. 1st, Sarah Sylvester; m.
    2d, Mrs. Susannah (Cobb) Sylvester.

11 VIII. ELKANAH,[3] b. March 1, 1691; m. SUSANNAH MANCHESTER, Dec. 24,
        1720.
    IX. NATHANIEL,[3] b. April 16, 1693; d. March 24, 1714.
    X. JOSIAH,[3] b. 1694.
12 XI. JOHN,[3] b. Sept. 12, 1698; m. 1st, MARY JACKSON, of Portsmouth,
        N.H.; m. 2d, MRS. ELIZABETH COTTON.

4.

WILLIAM[2] CHURCHILL (JOHN[1]). Born in Plymouth in 1656;
lived in Plympton and died there Oct. 5 1722. He inherited lands
in Punkatussett, now Plympton, and was among the first settlers in
that part of old Plymouth, and was the progenitor of the Plympton
branch of the family. Mr. Churchill and his wife were members of
the church in Plymouth.

From manuscript notes of Mr. Lewis Bradford, town clerk of
Plympton for many years, we have the following extract:

I made Mr. Isaac Churchill, Senior, a visit, who is grandson of the first
William, of Plympton, and, in 1826, is 85 years of age, to obtain information
of him about the first generation in Plympton, but did not obtain so much as I
had hoped, although his memory appears to be good for a person of his age. He
said that the father of the first William Churchill lived at Hobb's Hole, in
Plymouth, but did not recollect his given name. William lived in a house which
stood where the house of Mr. Isaac Churchill, Senior, now (1826) stands, as the
said Isaac says, and which appears very highly probable from an agreement
recorded in Book I., p. 40, Town Records.

Married in Plymouth, Jan. 17, 1683, LYDIA BRYANT, daughter of
Stephen and Abigail (Shaw) Bryant. She died Feb. 6, 1736, in the
74th year of her age.

Children born in Plympton.

13 I. WILLIAM,[3] b. Aug. 2, 1685; m. RUTH BRYANT, dau. of John.
14 II. SAMUEL,[3] b. April 15, 1688; m. 1st, JOANNA BRYANT; 2d, MRS.
        MERCY ——— ELLIS, widow.

III. JAMES,[3] b. Sept. 21, 1690; m. MARY McFARLIN, Dec. 27, 1716.

They had no children. He died in Plympton, Dec. 25, 1754, and his widow died there June 9, 1770, in her 81st year. He left his property to his nephew David Churchill. They lived where Caleb Stetson lived in 1827, below the nail factory, by the road west side of the meadows. He was one of those who used to pray at noon at the meeting-house during the ministry of Rev. Jonathan Parker.

15 IV. ISAAC,[3] b. Sept. 16, 1693; m. SUSANNAH LEACH.
16   V. BENJAMIN,[3] b. 1695; m. MARY SHAW, Dec. 5, 1717.
      VI. LYDIA,[3] b. April 16, 1699; m. JOHN LOVELL, Nov. 8, 1727.
17 VII. JOSIAH,[3] b. Aug. 21, 1702; m. JEMIMA HAMBLEN, May 16, 1723.
     VIII. MEHITABLE,[3] m. ELKANAH SHAW, Plymouth, Jan. 11, 1726.

5.

JOHN[2] CHURCHILL (JOHN[1]).   Born in Plymouth   1657 and lived there. By his father's will he inherited land at "Mannonnett Ponds." He was admitted freeman in 1689; was chosen constable in 1686.

Died June 13, 1723, in 66th year of his age.

Married 1st, Dec. 28, 1686, REBECCA DELANO, daughter of Philip. She d. April 6, 1709, aged 52 years; 2d, March 4, 1715, MRS. HANNAH BARTLETT, who d. April 29, 1723, aged 61.

Children of First Wife, born in Plymouth.

I. ELIZABETH,[3] b. Oct. 7, 1687; m. JOEL ELLIS, of Plympton, April 6, 1710.

Children born in Plympton.

1. Joel Ellis, b. Feb. 12, 1712.
2. John Ellis, b. Sept. 18, 1714; m. Elizabeth Coomer.
3. Matthew Ellis.
4. Samuel Ellis.
5. Elizabeth Ellis, m. Gideon Southwick.
6. Rebecca Ellis, m. Samuel Lanman.
7. Charles Ellis, m. Bathsheba Fuller.
8. Thomas Ellis, b. in Middleboro, July 1, 1729; m. Ruth Thomas.

II. REBECCA,[3] b. Aug. 29, 1689; m. GEORGE MORTON, Feb. 4, 1713/4.

Children born in Plymouth.

1. Zephaniah Morton, b. Aug. 31, 1715.
2. William Morton, b. Oct. 2, 1717.
3. George Morton, b. Feb. 6, 1719/20.
4. Rebecca Morton, b. April 7, 1724; d. Sept. 23, 1759.

18 III. JOHN,[3] b. Dec. 20, 1691; m. BETHIAH SPOONER, dau. of Ebenezer, Feb. 16, 1720.
      IV. SARAH,[3] b. Feb. 10, 1695; m. JONATHAN SMITH, both of Middleboro, June 8, 1725, as his second wife. She died July 5, 1744.
       V. HANNAH,[3] b. April 27, 1697; m. SAMUEL BARTLETT, 1725.

Children.

1. Samuel Bartlett, m. Betsey Moore, in No. Carolina.
2. William Bartlett.
3. John Bartlett.
4. Judah Bartlett.

THIRD GENERATION.

6.

JOHN [3] CHURCHILL (JOSEPH,[2] JOHN [1]). Born at Plymouth, July 3, 1678. Married, Nov. 19, 1700, DESIRE HOLMES.

Children born in Plymouth.

I. PRISCILLA,[4] b. Nov. 27, 1701; m. THOMAS ROGERS, son of Eleazer, about 1721.

Children born at Plymouth.

1. Ruth Rogers, b. 1722; m. Samuel Morton.	6. Thomas Rogers, b. 1730.
2. Priscilla Rogers, b. 1723.	7. Hannah Rogers, b. 1734.
3. Desire Rogers, b. 1725.	8. Eleazer Rogers, b. 1736.
4. Willis Rogers, b. 1727.	9. Priscilla Rogers, b. 1739.
5. Samuel Rogers, b. 1728.	10. John Rogers, b. 1740.

19　II. SAMUEL,[4] b. March 8, 1703/4; m. HANNAH CURTIS, 1732.
　　III. SARAH,[4] b. April 25, 1706; m. ELKANAH TOTMAN, 1727.

Children.

1. Priscilla Totman, b. 1728.	3. Elkanah Totman, b. 1732.
2. Joshua Totman, b. 1730.	

IV　PHEBE,[4] b. Oct. 8, 1708; m. 1726, JOSEPH HOLMES, son of Joseph.

Children.

1. Jonathan Holmes, b. 1726.	5. Hannah Holmes, b. 1735
2. Phebe Holmes, b. 1727; m. William Benedick Pearson.	6. Mariah Holmes, b. 1737.
	7. Jane Holmes, b. 1738.
	8. Joseph Holmes, b. 1741.
3. Desire Holmes. b. 1731; m. John Swift.	9. Micah Holmes, b. 1743.
	10. Elkanah Holmes. b. 1745.
4. Samuel Holmes, b. 1733.	11. Susannah Holmes, b. 1747.

V　REBECCA, b. Dec. 11, 1713; m. 1st, 1731, ELNATHAN HOLMES, son of 1st, Elisha; m. 2d, AZARIAH WHITING.

Children by First Husband.

1. Sarah Holmes, b. 1732	3. Elnathan Holmes, b. 1735; m. 1761, Bathsheba Holmes, daughter of Abner.
2. Rebecca Holmes, b. 1734.	

7.

BARNABAS [3] CHURCHILL (JOSEPH,[2] JOHN [1]). Born in Plymouth, July 3, 1686, and lived there. Married, Feb. 5, 1714, LYDIA HARLOW, daughter of William Harlow and Lydia, daughter of Rev. Thomas Cushman, born 1688.

Children born in Plymouth.

20   I. BARNABAS,⁴ b. Oct. 19, 1714; m. LYDIA HOLMES, dau. of Eleazer, Nov. 13, 1744.
21   II. WILLIAM,⁴ b. Dec. 25, 1716; m. SUSANNAH CLARK, Nov. 13, 1746.
    III. ICHABOD,⁴ b. Jan. 12, 1718/9; d. Oct. 1. 1745; unmarried.
22   IV. JOSEPH,⁴ b. May 19, 1721; m. MARIAH RYDER, Sept. 23, 1745.
23   V. LEMUEL,⁴ b. July 12, 1723; m. 1st, LYDIA SYLVESTER, Oct. 13,
1747; m. 2d, ABIGAIL RYDER, Nov. 4, 1752.
24   VI. ISAAC,⁴ b. May 3, 1726; m. SARAH COBB, Oct. 2, 1756.
25   VII. THOMAS,⁴ b. April 30, 1730; m. MARY EWER, May 5, 1758.
26   VIII. EBENEZER,⁴ b. Nov. 9, 1732; m. JEAN FISHER, May 19, 1755.
    IX. LYDIA,⁴ b. March 9, 1734/5; m. 1st, June 1, 1754, NATHANIEL
HOLMES; m. 2d, Sept. 16, 1762, SETH EWER, as second wife.

Children by First Husband.

1. Nathaniel Holmes, b. 1754; d. in infancy.

Children by Second Husband.

2. Isaac Ewer, baptized 1763.
3. Lydia Ewer, b. Oct. 6, 1765.
4. Sylvanus Ewer, b. Oct. 4, 1768 (at Osterville); m. as second
wife, Margaret Folger, 1798.
5. Mary Ewer, b. Aug. 17, 1774.

27   X. JOHN,⁴ b. May 9, 1739; m. MOLLY BRADFORD, of Plympton, April
4, 1771.

8.

JOSEPH³ CHURCHILL (JOSEPH,² JOHN¹). Born in Ply
mouth, January, 1692; lived in Sandwich; married ABIAH BLACK-
WELL, of Sandwich, Dec. 13, 1716.

Children born in Sandwich.

I. ABIAH,⁴ b. Oct. 9, 1717; m. JAMES CORNISH. (He was the son of
Samuel and Susanna.)
II. MARGARET,⁴ b. Jan. 18, 1718/9; m. EZEKIEL RIDER, son of Samuel,
1737.

Children born in Plymouth.

1. Keziah Rider, b. Dec. 12, 1737.
2. Joseph Rider, b. March 22, 1739; m. Abigail Atwood, dau. of
John.
3. Deborah Rider, b. July 20, 1740.
4. Samuel Rider, b. Oct. 18, 1741; m. Jane Swift. about 1765.
5. Lemuel Rider, b. July 24, 1743; d. Aug. 4, 1743.
6. Patience Rider, b. July 7, 1744.
7. Lemuel Rider, b. July 7, 1745.
8. Ezekiel Rider, b. Dec. 21, 1746; d. Jan. 24, 1746/7.
9. Margaret Rider, b. March 15, 1749.
10. Ezekiel Rider, b. Jan. 14, 1751.
11. Sarah Rider, b. Nov. 14, 1752.
12. Joshua Rider, b. June 22, 1755.
13. Ezra Rider, b. March 6, 1757; m. Hannah Howland.

28   III. JOSEPH,⁴ b. July 14, 1722; m. AGNES FETTERS, in Boston.
29   IV. SAMUEL,⁴ b. June 24, 1724; m. HANNAH ELLIS, in Boston.
    V. JOSHUA,⁴ b. July 4, 1726. No further record.
    VI. SARAH,⁴ b. July 2, 1728; m. SETH BLOSSOM, Jan. 8, 1747.

Child.

Churchill[5] Blossom, b. Oct. 15, 1749.
   Mrs. Sarah (Churchill) Blossom died, and Seth Blossom married Abigail Crocker and had four children by her; viz.: (1) David b. Jan. 12, 1755; (2) Peter, b. Dec. 4, 1756; (3) Hannah, b. Aug. 15, 1766; (4) Lini, b. April 15, 1772.

VII. MERCY,[4] b. July 27, 1733; d. in infancy.
VIII. MERCY,[4] b. March 28, 1736.

9.

ELIEZER[3] CHURCHILL (ELIEZER,[2] JOHN[1]). Born in Plymouth in 1682, and lived there, a farmer. Died Sept 21, 1754, aged 72. From Mr. Davis's " Landmarks of Plymouth " we learn that

after the death of Eliezer the second, in 1754, the remainder of the original land was divided between his sons Jonathan and Eleazer. Jonathan taking what is now the Ichabod Morton estate and Eleazer what is now the Edwin Morton estate.

He married HANNAH BARTLETT, daughter of Robert, who was born 1691, and died Sept. 19, 1757.

Children born in Plymouth.

    I. ANSON,[4] b. May 12, 1712; d. July 21, 1712.
30 II. ELIEZER,[4] b. Feb. 26, 1714; m. SARAH HARLOW, Oct. 19, 1738.
31 III. JOSIAH,[4] b. July 20, 1716; m. PATIENCE HARLOW, Dec. 1, 1741.
32 IV. JONATHAN,[4] b. Oct. 19, 1720; m. HANNAH WORCESTER, Aug. 27, 1742.

10.

STEPHEN[3] CHURCHILL (ELIEZER[2] JOHN[1]). Born at Plymouth, February, 1684. Died 1750. Married 1708, EXPERIENCE ELLIS, daughter of Matthias, of Sandwich.

Children born in Plymouth.

33 I. EPHRAIM,[4] b. Oct. 15, 1709; m., March 27, 1730, PRISCILLA MANCHESTER.
34 II. NATHANIEL,[4] b. Dec. 19, 1712; m., Jan. 2, 1733, MARY CURTIS.
   III. MARY,[4] b. April 29, 1716; d. Dec. 13, 1716.
35 IV. STEPHEN,[4] b. Aug. 24, 1717; m., July 4, 1738, HANNAH BARNES, dau. of Jonathan.
   V. ZACHEUS,[4] b. Oct. 30, 1719; d. Nov. 18, 1732.
36 VI. BENJAMIN,[4] b. Aug. 19, 1725; m., Nov. 3, 1746, RUTH DELANO.

11.

ELKANAH[3] CHURCHILL (ELIEZER,[2] JOHN[1]). Born 1690. After his death, in 1764, the half of the original Churchill estate, which belonged to him, was divided between his sons Amaziah[4] and Elkanah,[4] the first taking the southerly half, the other the northerly. Died 1764. Married, Dec. 24, 1720, SUSANNAH MANCHESTER.

Children born in Plymouth.

37   I. AMAZIAH,[4] b. Nov. 29, 1721; m., Oct. 31, 1745, ELIZABETH SYL-
VESTER.

II. MARIAH,[4] b. Nov. 29, 1721; m. JABEZ MENDALL, of Plympton.

One Child.

1. Samuel Mendall, b. 1747.

38 III. ELKANAH,[4] b. April 10, 1726; m., March 8, 1747/8, SUSANNAH BART-
LETT.

12.

JOHN[3] CHURCHILL (ELIEZER,[2] JOHN[1]). Born in Plymouth, Sept. 12, 1698, but removed in youth to Portsmouth, N.H., and there spent his life, and died Oct. 7, 1769, aged 71 years 14 days. The inventory of his estate, taken Oct. 28, 1769, was £129.18.9. His widow, Elizabeth, sold her dower for £15, in 1770. A very interesting and precious letter, from his own hand, written some time in the year 1764, is still preserved in the hands of his descendants. It is the source of nearly all we know of his own family, and we regret that he did not tell more about himself. This letter was copied from a copy made from the original, by her grandfather Joseph, by Mrs. Mary W. (Churchill) Bailey, of Dysart, Iowa, in 1886.

LETTER WRITTEN BY JOHN[3] CHURCHILL OF PORTSMOUTH, N.H., 1764.

When my son John was born, I wanted four days of being twenty-one years old. I was born the 12th day of Sept. 1698. My son John was born the 8th day of Sept. Tuesday morn, 1719. Daniel was born Thursday Oct. 12, 1721. Mary, Born Wednesday March 4, 1724. Ebenezer Born Sabbath June 6, 1726. Arthur Born Monday Nov. 25, 1728. William born Tuesday March 14, 1732. Sanford, born Sabbath day May 20, 1733. Tobias born Sabbath, January 26, 1735. Martha born Saturday Oct. 15, 1737. Elizabeth born Tuesday April 10, 1740. Benjamin, born Tuesday Oct. 13, 1741. Joseph born Monday March 25, 1744. Mary died Sept. 21, 1743, aged 19 years 6 months 17 days. My wife died 27 of Dec. 1745. My son Daniel died in 1745. He sailed out of Boston, Master of a large ship in Nov. before bound for London, and the hands perished for the ship foundered. He was married in Boston and had one child that is dead also. Arthur left me the 26th of March 1744, and went to sea, he left me the next day after Joseph was born and I have not seen him for more than six years and God knows whenever I shall. My son John was married in New York to his second wife and sent for his son John that lived with me and I sent him to his father. My Sons John and Ebenezer both died sometime in 1751 with Small Pox at one time. As for John's children I know nothing about. Ebenezer never married. I pray the Lord to sanctify their death to me their father for the good of my soul, knowing that in a short time I shall go to them for they cannot return to me. My son Arthur after he first left me had the opportunity to come to Boston twice, and then sailed to England two voyages. The second voyage he was taken sick. I received a letter from him dated 3 of Oct. 1752, from London, then he wrote me word that he designed to go to the West Indies and from there to Piscataway to see me if God gave him opportunity but being led away by bad company he was tripanned by some means I can't give account of, that he was obliged to go to the East Indies as a soldier for two years, when I first heard of it I was greatly troubled to think one with so good sense and learning as he had and as good a sailor as need cross the sea, should take no more care of himself, but be led away in so unhappy condition.

It has been a great trouble to me and ever will be, for day nor night never passes but that I think of him, for I am out of all hope of ever seeing him again. I hope God will be with him and help him and give him a heart of grace to return from all his evil ways. My son Arthur left me the day after Joseph was born, and I have heard from one Brewster, that he had got mate of an Indiaman, and in the year 1763 he enquired after him and heard that he was dead.

Tobias died the 3 of August 1756 aged 21 years 3 mos and 17 days, and was buried in Thomas Cotton's orchard, his bearers were Samuel Hale, Benjamin Luce, Samuel Jackson, Joseph Jackson, Jonathan Long, and Edmund Loud, he was the first of my sons that died at home. My son William Sailed out of Newbury in the year 1755. I have heard one time about two years after that he was in Rhode Island and I have not heard whether he is living or not, he has been gone nine years. Sanford died July 3, 1733, aged 6 weeks 2 days.

Mrs. Bailey writes that the above John Churchill left valuable family records in the hands of his youngest son Joseph, her grandfather. These records she states went back to the time " our forefather left England," but her grandmother told her, about 1861, that the records had been taken from the old chest where they were kept, and were destroyed or lost. John Churchill, of Portsmouth, appears in many property transactions, and is then designated " cordwainer." His three sons, John, Benjamin, and Joseph only, of all his children, survived him, and evidently inherited his estate, as we find deeds from them disposing of their third parts of his property.

JOHN³ CHURCHILL, of Portsmouth, married 1st, in Portsmouth, MARY JACKSON, daughter of Daniel. She died Dec. 27, 1745, and he married 2d, MRS. ELIZABETH COTTON, widow of Thomas.

Children of the First Wife, born in Portsmouth.

39   I. JOHN,⁴ b. Sept. 8, 1719; m. MARY NOBLE, of Portsmouth,   1741.
     II. DANIEL,⁴ b. Oct. 21, 1721; m. SARAH ROGERS, Boston, April 2, 1744, by Rev. James Sewall.
        He died in 1745, leaving widow and one child who died young.
    III. MARY,⁴ b. March 4, 1724; d. Sept. 21, 1743, aged 19 years 6 months 17 days.
     IV. EBENEZER,⁴ b. June 6, 1726; d. unmarried, 1751.
      V. ARTHUR,⁴ b. Nov. 25, 1728; never married; d. abroad, probably at sea.
     VI. WILLIAM,⁴ b. March 14, 1732; never married.
    VII. SANFORD,⁴ b. May 20, 1733; d. July 3, 1733.
   VIII. TOBIAS,⁴ b. Jan. 26, 1735; d. Aug. 3, 1756, unmarried.
     IX. MARTHA,⁴ b. Oct. 15, 1737.
      X. ELIZABETH,⁴ b. April 10, 1740; d. Dec. 5, 1740, aged 7 months 20 days.
40   XI. BENJAMIN,⁴ b. Oct. 13, 1741; m. 1st, ABIGAIL DEVERSON, dau. of Thomas; m. 2d, ELIZABETH CLARK, dau. of Thomas.
41 XII. JOSEPH,⁴ b. March 25, 1744; m. ELIZABETH COTTON.

13.

WILLIAM³ CHURCHILL (WILLIAM,² JOHN¹). Born in Plympton, Aug. 2, 1685. Lived in Plympton at a place called " Rocky Gutter." Both himself and wife were members of the church in

Plympton. He was a man of character and influence, and several times a representative to the General Court. He died in Plympton, Feb. 3, 1760. Married, Jan. 4, 1704, RUTH BRYANT, daughter of John. She died in Plympton, May 17, 1757, aged 72.

Children born in Plympton.

42   EBENEZER,[4] b. Oct. 18, 1705; m. LEAH (———).

    II. HANNAH,[4] b. Oct. 23, 1707; m. HOPESTILL BISBEE, Nov. 25, 1731.

He was the son of John and Joanna (Brooks) Bisbee of Marshfield. They lived at Plympton.

Children born in Plympton.

1. Abner Bisbee, b. June 16, 1739; m. Bathsheba Palmer, of Halifax.
2. Hopestill Bisbee, b. May 28, 1741; m. Abigail Churchill, dau. of Nathaniel Churchill, of Plympton, Sept. 4, 1766, and had children, born in Plympton, (1) Abigail Bisbee, b. Oct. 21, 1768; (2) Hopestill Bisbee, b. Oct. 11, 1769. They removed to Rochester, Mass., and had there (3) Sylvanus Bisbee; (4) Josiah Bisbee; (5) Ansel Bisbee, who settled in Buckfield, Me., no children; (6) Levi Bisbee; (7) Susannah Bisbee; (8) Hannah Bisbee.
3. Issachar Bisbee, b. April 3, 1744; m. Mary Harlow, dau. of Thomas, April 28, 1768.
4. Sarah Bisbee, b. March 7, 1747.
5. Hannah Bisbee, b. Feb. 20, 1752.

43   III. DAVID,[4] b. Nov. 4, 1709; m. MARY MAGOON.

    IV. REBECCA,[4] b. Jan. 8, 1712; m. AMOS FORD, at Plympton, Nov. 25, 1731.

Children.

1. Noah Ford, b. Aug. 29, 1732.
2. Ruth Ford, b. Oct. 4, 1734.

    V. WILLIAM,[4] b. Dec. 15, 1714; d. unmarried, March 7, 1739.

    VI. RUTH,[4] b. Sept. 14, 1716; m. EBENEZER COLE, 1733, in Plympton.

They lived in Plympton for a while, but he died in Chesterfield, Mass., about 1790. They had one child born in Plympton.

1. Joanna[5] Cole, m. Nathl. Bryant of Plympton.

44   VII. NATHANIEL,[4] b. May 11, 1718; m. SUSANNAH McFARLAND, June 4, 1759.

    VIII. ABIGAIL,[4] b. July 11, 1720; m. JOHN BRYANT, of Plympton, Feb. 10, 1740. She died in 1820.

45   IX. ICHABOD,[4] b. Sept. 24, 1722; m. 1st, REBECCA CURTIS; m. 2d, SUSANNA GIBBS.

    X. SARAH,[4] b. Feb. 7, 1725; m. JOSIAH MARSHALL, Nov. 16, 1749.

    XI. JOANNA,[4] b. May 22, 1727; d. April 16, 1728.

14.

SAMUEL[3] CHURCHILL (WILLIAM,[2] JOHN[1]). Born in Plympton, April 15, 1688, and lived there in a house a few rods east of the house in which Micah Bryant lived in 1826. He was deacon of the church in Plympton. Was a farmer. Married 1st, JOANNA BRYANT, daughter of John. She died in Plympton, April 15, 1746; and he married 2d, MRS. MARCY ELLIS (widow).

Children of First Wife.

I. MARCY,[4] b. March 1, 1714.
II. MEHITABEL,[4] b. Nov. 5, 1717; m. JAMES MORTON, of Plymouth, 1736.
   He was the son of John Morton.
III. ALICE, [4] b. Jan. 18, 1719; m. JUPE LEACH, 1738.

15.

ISAAC[3] CHURCHILL (WILLIAM,[2] JOHN[1]). Born in Plympton, Oct. 4, 1693. Lived there, on the side of the brook, east of his father's house. He and his wife were members of the church in Plympton. He died in Plympton, April 8, 1778, aged 84 years 6 months 4 days. Married, Dec. 29, 1720, SUSANNAH LEACH. She died in Plympton, Jan. 11, 1790, in her 89th year.

Children born in Plympton.

I. ISAAC,[4] b. Oct. 1, 1722; d., aged 3 days.
II. AVERICK,[4] b. Sept. 15, 1723; m. by Thos. Croade, J.P., EBENEZER STANDISH, JR., a son of Zachariah, Dec. 27, 1739.

Children.

1. Mary Standish, b. 1740.
2. Ebenezer Standish, b. 1741.
3. Averick Standish, b..1744; m. Zadock Thomas.
4. Shadrach Standish, b. 1746; m. Mary Churchill, dau. of David.

III. SUSANNAH,[4] b. Dec. 3, 1726; m. DAVID WESTON.

Children.

1. Rebeckah Weston, b. June 7, 1746.
2. Mary Weston, b. Nov. 28, 1748.
3. Rufus Weston, b. April 25, 1751.
4. David Weston, b. Feb. 15, 1754.
5. Abner Weston, b. Dec. 10, 1756.
6. Jabez Weston, b. Feb. 26, 1759.

IV. ISAAC,[4] b. April 4, 1730; d. Dec. 11, 1734.
V. MARY,[4] b. 1733; d. Aug. 31, 1738.
VI. ELIZABETH,[4] b. June 4, 1737; m. LUKE PERKINS (son of Josiah), May 27, 1757.

Children.

1. Daniel Perkins.
2. John Perkins.

46   VII. ISAAC,[4] b. July 16, 1741; m. EUNICE RIPLEY, Jan. 21, 1764.

16.

BENJAMIN[3] CHURCHILL (WILLIAM,[2] JOHN[1]). Born in Plympton, 1695, and according to the gravestone in the burying-ground at Carver, died Dec. 6, 1771, in the 67th year of his age. While residing in Plympton, Benjamin and wife Mary occupied the house in which John Bonney lived in 1849, in the north part of the town. It is said that Benjamin removed from Plympton into

the border of Middleboro, near to "Pope's Point Furnace," in
Carver. A letter from Mr. Bradford, town clerk of Plympton, says
that the family lived much nearer to the meeting-house in Carver
than to that in Plympton, and attended church in the former place.
Married, Dec. 15, 1717, MARY SHAW.

Children.

    I. MARY,[4] b. April 17, 1720; m. JAMES DREW (it is said).
47 II. PEREZ,[4] b. Middleboro, Oct. 15, 1722; m. DEBORAH THAYER.
   III. ELIZABETH,[4] b. April 15, 1725; m. Dea. BENJAMIN THOMAS of Mid
      dleboro, Mass. She died Dec. 26, 1804. They had five children.
48 IV. JAMES,[4] b. Dec. 30, 1726; m. 1st, June 8, 1848, MARTHA BLACKWELL;
      m. 2d, MERCY COBB; 3d, Widow MARY GORHAM.
49   V. BENJAMIN,[4] b. Jan. 31, 1728; m. THANKFUL WOOD.
   VI. SUSANNAH,[4] b. April 2, 1733.

17.

JOSIAH[3] CHURCHILL (WILLIAM,[2] JOHN[1]). Born in Plympton, Aug. 21, 1702. Lived in Plympton in the house in which his
father had lived. Afterwards his brother Isaac bought the home
place, and he removed with his family to Easton, on the west of
Bridgewater, and was engaged in the work of the foundry there.
Married, May 16, 1723, JEMIMA HAMBLIN.

Four Children born in Plympton, the Rest in Easton.

50   I. JABEZ,[4] b. Jan. 21, 1724; m. ALICE BRIGGS.
    II. GERSHOM,[4] b. 1725. No further record, perhaps d. young.
51   III. ISRAEL,[4] b. 1727; m. HANNAH (———).
52   IV. JOSIAH,[4] b. March 6, 1730; m. BATHSHEBA CURTIS. Settled in
      Stockbridge. No issue.
53   V. WILLIAM,[4] b. 1733; m. MERIBAH GIBBS, Nov. 9, 1757.
54   VI. SAMUEL,[4] b. 1735. Enlisted in the army in 1757, in the expedition
      for the relief of Fort William Henry. No further record.
   VII. JEMIMA,[4] b. 1738; m. JOSEPH DAGGETT, of Attleboro; m. Jan. 26,
      1758.
55 VIII. JOSEPH,[4] b. Oct. 2, 1741; m. ANNE DAGGETT, of Attleboro.
56   IX. JACOB,[4] b. Nov. 3, 1744; m. LILLIS READ.

18.

SERGEANT JOHN[3] CHURCHILL (JOHN,[2] JOHN[1]). Born
in Plymouth, Nov. 29, 1691, and lived there. He died Feb. 25,
1730, aged 39 years. Married, Feb. 16, 1720, BETHIAH SPOONER,
daughter of Ebenezer. (After her first husband's death, in 1730,
she married, in 1732, JOSIAH CARVER, son of the third John, and as
his second wife.)

Children born in Plymouth.

57   I. EBENEZER,[4] b. Nov. 6, 1721; m. MERCY BRANCH, dau. of Thomas, of
      Marshfield.
    II. JOHN,[4] b. Oct. 24, 1723; d. Sept. 28, 1725.
58   III. JOHN,[4] b. April 15, 1727; m. SARAH COLE, 1750.

FOURTH GENERATION.

19.

SAMUEL[4] CHURCHILL (JOHN,[3] JOSEPH,[2] JOHN[1]). Born in Plymouth, March 8, 1703. Settled in Stockbridge. With his wife he joined the church in Stockbridge, June 5, 1763. Married, 1732, HANNAH CURTIS, who was born Sept. 15, 1710.

Children born in Stockbridge.

59   I. SAMUEL, Jr.,[5] b. 1733; m. ELIZABETH CURTIS, dau. of Elnathan and Rose (Weller).

    II. SARAH,[5] b. 1735; m. JOHN GAINES, and had a son,

    1. Daniel Gaines, killed while serving in the Revolutionary army in 1777, while on picket duty at Fort Edward.

60 III. DANIEL,[5] b. 1738. He was unmarried and lived with his mother at Stockbridge until October 1780, when he enlisted in the army and was killed at the battle in the Mohawk Valley.

  IV. WILLIAM,[5] b. 1740; unmarried. Killed at the battle in the Mohawk Valley.

20.

BARNABAS[4] CHURCHILL (BARNABAS,[3] JOSEPH,[2] JOHN[1]). Born in Plymouth, Oct. 19, 1714, and lived there. Married, Nov. 13, 1744, LYDIA HOLMES, daughter of Eleazer. She was born in 1716.

Children born in Plymouth

   I. ELIZABETH,[5] b. Jan. 16, 1746; m. ROBERT DAVIS, Nov. 13, 1766, son of 1st Thomas.

Children.

1. Samuel Davis, b. 1766.	4. Elizabeth Davis, m. Josiah Carver.
2. Robert Davis, b. 1768.	5. Lydia Davis, b. 1775; m. Ezra
3. Ichabod Davis, b. 1771.	Harlow.

61 II. BARNABAS,[5] b. Nov. 25, 1747; m. SARAH FAUNCE, dau. of Thomas, Oct. 11, 1780.

  III. JOB,[5] b. Jan. 15, 1751; d. Jan. 14, 1753.

62 IV. SAMUEL,[5] b. Jan. 9, 1753; m. 1st, SARAH ———, who died, 1791; m. 2d, ELIZABETH ———, who died, 1839. No further record.

63 V. SETH,[5] b. Oct. 1, 1754; m. ELIZABETH SYLVESTER, July 6, 1783.

64 VI. JOB,[5] b. Aug. 17, 1756; m. HANNAH HARLOW, Dec. 21, 1808.

  VII. LYDIA,[5] b. Dec. 16, 1758; m. WILLIAM RIDER, 1780.

21.

WILLIAM[4] CHURCHILL (BARNABAS,[3] JOSEPH,[2] JOHN[1]). Born Dec. 25, 1716, in Plymouth. Married, Nov. 13, 1746, SUSANNAH CLARK.

Children.

I. REBECCA,[5] b. Oct. 31, 1747: m. SYLVANUS HOLMES, Dec. 23, 1784.
II. MORDECAI,[5] b. April 24, 1749.
III. WILLIAM,[5] b. Jan. 24, 1751.
IV. SUSANNAH,[5] } twins, b. April 23, 1753.
V. MARY,[5]

22.

JOSEPH[4] CHURCHILL (BARNABAS,[3] JOSEPH,[2] JOHN[1]). Born in Plymouth, May 14, 1721. Married, Sept. 23, 1745, MARIAH RIDER, daughter of Samuel, of Plymouth. After the death of Joseph, the widow married Archippus Fuller, and removed with her children to Woodstock, Vt.

Children.

65   I. ICHABOD,[5] b. Aug. 9, 1746; m. SARAH TINKHAM, Nov. 7, 1771.
66   II. JOSEPH,[5] b. July 14, 1748; m. SARAH COBB, of Middleboro', dau. of Gershom, March 21, 1771.
     III. LUCY,[5] b. Aug. 22, 1750; unmarried.

23.

LEMUEL[4] CHURCHILL (BARNABAS,[3] JOSEPH,[2] JOHN[1]). Born in Plymouth, July 12, 1723, and lived there until 1764, when he removed to Chebeague, Nova Scotia. Married, 1st, Oct. 13, 1747, LYDIA SYLVESTER, daughter of Solomon. She was born 1726, and died Sept. 20, 1751; married 2d, Nov. 4, 1752, ABIGAIL RIDER, daughter of Joseph and Abigail (Warren) Rider, born 1726.

Benj K + Ma

Children of First Wife, born in Plymouth.

67   I. NATHANIEL,[5] b. March 29, 1749; m. 1st, ELIZABETH RIDER, Dec. 24, 1770; m. 2d, ELINOR METCALF, Nov. 20, 1800; m. 3d, ELIZABETH GREEN, Jan. 6, 1814.

Children of Second Wife.

     II. LEMUEL,[5] b. June 9, 1754; drowned near Causo, June 20, 1773, unmarried, aged 21.
     III. ABIGAIL,[5] b. Feb. 5, 1756; m. 1st, ABIJAH CROSBY, Dec. 13, 1775; m. 2d, MARCUS RING, Aug. 31, 1781.
68   IV. EZRA,[5] b. Oct. 11, 1758; m. MARY ROBERTS, of Argyle, Nova Scotia, May 6, 1779.
     V. LYDIA,[5] b. June 14, 1760; m. GEORGE RING, 2d, Dec. 16, and d. April 11, 1847.

24.

ISAAC[4] CHURCHILL (BARNABAS,[3] JOSEPH,[2] JOHN[1]). Born May 3, 1726. Followed the sea and became captain of a vessel. He removed to Boston in 1757, and died in 1761. Married in Plymouth, Oct. 14, 1756, SARAH COBB, daughter of Seth and Sarah (Nelson) Cobb, born May 17, 1739. After her husband, Isaac's, death she married Charles Churchill, son of Ephraim, *q. v.*

Children of Isaac[4] and Sarah Churchill, born in Boston.

I.   MARY BEEKMAN,[5] b. 1757, d. Aug. 1, 1765.
69 II. ISAAC,[5] b. July 19, 1758; m. SARAH MORTON.
70 III. SETH,[5] b. June 4, 1760; m. ELIZABETH SYLVESTER. No further record.

25.

THOMAS[4] CHURCHILL (BARNABAS,[3] JOSEPH,[2] JOHN[1]). Born April 30, 1730, and lived in Plymouth until after 1759, when he removed to Newmarket Plains, N.H. He settled upon a farm, and raised a large family of sons and daughters, worthy and respected in their day. Married, May 5, 1758, MARY EWER, daughter of Nathaniel and Mary (Stewart) Ewer, born Aug. 7, 1737, at Barnstable.

Children, the first born in Plymouth, the rest in Newmarket, N.H.

I.   GAMALIEL,[5] b. Aug. 30, 1759; d. unmarried, aged about 50.
II. POLLY,[5] b. Aug. 23, 1760; m. WIGGIN DOE; lived in Newmarket.

Children of Wiggin and Polly (Churchill) Doe.

1. Mary Doe, b. Feb. 20, 1783.
2. John Doe, b. Aug. 22, 1784.
3. Thomas Doe, b. July 29, 1786.
4. Andrew Doe, b. May, 1789; d. aged one year.
5. Andrew Doe, b. April, 1791.
6. Desire Doe, b. April 15, 1793.
7. Joseph R. Doe, b. Dec. 7, 1794.
8. Deborah Doe, b. Oct. 26, 1796.
9. Lydia Doe, b. Jan. 16, 1799.
10. Zebulon Doe, b. May 26, 1801.

71 III. THOMAS,[5] b. 1762; m. ALICE CREIGHTON, dau. James.
72 IV. ICHABOD,[5] b. June 24, 1764; m. 1st, ELIZABETH DOE; m. 2d, LEAH ALLEN.
V.   LYDIA,[5] b. Jan. 10, 1766; m. REUBEN FRENCH.

Children of Reuben and Lydia (Churchill) French.

1. Thomas French, b. July 17, 1786; m. Betsey Foss, and d. in 1864.
2. Lucy French, b. June 22, 1788; m. Ezekiel James, and d. 1866.
3. Mary French, b. Feb. 13, 1790; m. Timothy Joy, and d. 1869.
4. Lydia French.
5. Reuben French, b. June 3, 1792; m. Sally Badger.
6. Lydia French, b. Aug. 13, 1794; m. Ezra Shepard, and d. 1869.
7. Olive Wyman French, b. 1797; m. Eben Huckins, and d. 1868.
8. Sally French, } b. Feb. 27, 1800; m. Jonathan Langmaid, and d. 1862.
9. Betsey French, } b. Feb. 27, 1800; m. Daniel Murray, and d. 1825.

10. William French, b. April, 1802; d. 1834.
11. Edmund French, b. Sept. 20, 1805; m. Martha Brackett.
12. Bradstreet French, b. July 22, 1807; m. 1st, Olive Gilman; m. 2d, Mary J. Baker.

73   VI. JOSEPH,[5] b. May 7, 1768; m. SALLY TASH, in Newmarket.
    VII. SUSANNA,[5] b. Aug. 18, 1770; m. SAMUEL BADGER; lived in Deerfield, N.H.

Children.

1. Samuel Badger, b. Sept. 18, 1794; m. Alphia Fernald.
2. Mary Ewer Badger, b. 1796; m. David Marston.
3. Sally True Badger, b. 1797; m. Reuben French, her cousin.
4. Thomas Badger, b. 1799; m. Mary Goss.
5. Susan Churchill Badger, b. 1801; m. 1st, Simeon Goss; m. 2d, Michael Libby.
6. William Badger, b. 1804; m. Mary Joy.
7. Elizabeth Rice Badger, b. 1806; m. Abner Burbank.
8. Emily Badger, b. 1812; m. 1st, Rev. Mark Shepard; m. 2d, Rev. Mark Fernald; m. 3d, Robert Crosby.

74 VIII. NATHANIEL,[5] b. March 31, 1772; m. 1st, PATIENCE TASH; m. 2d, POLLY JACKSON.
    IX. JOHN,[5] b. 1774; d. soon.
75   X. JOHN,[5] b. May 11, 1776; m. SALLY TRUE.
    XI. DESIRE,[5] b. March 27, 1778; m. JOHN STEVENS.

Children.

1. Ann Stevens, b. Feb. 14, 1800; m. Moses Butler.
2. Mary Stevens, b. Sept. 4, 1801; m. Hiram Jones.
3. Joan Stevens, b. Jan. 29, 1803; m. Hiram Jones.
4. Hubbard Stevens, b. July 25, 1805; m. Harriet Brackett.
5. Thomas Stevens, b. Nov. 1, 1810; d. July 28, 1812.
6. John Stevens, b. May 13, 1812; d. June 8, 1812.

26.

EBENEZER[4] CHURCHILL (BARNABAS,[3] JOSEPH,[2] JOHN[1]). Born Nov. 9, 1732. Lived in Plymouth until about 1775, when he removed to Plympton, and thence about 1779 to Pittsfield, where he died. Married, May 5, 1755, JEAN FISHER, daughter of Archibald and Betsey (Bacon) Fisher.

Children born in Plymouth.

    I. EBENEZER,[5] b. Oct. 5, 1755; served in Revolution from Plympton, and died as prisoner, on British man-of-war, of small-pox.
   II. TIMOTHY,[5] b. Jan. 21, 1757; d. in New York of yellow fever contracted in the war of the Revolution.
  III. JOHN,[5] b. Feb. 4, 1759; d. Aug. 3, 1760.
  IV. JEAN,[5] b. Jan. 6, 1761; m. JOHN SNOW, of Pittsfield, and died Jan. 8, 1849.
      They lived in Pittsfield. He was a blacksmith. A daughter, Betsey Bacon Snow, married Dr. N. B. Mead in 1815.
76   V. JOHN,[5] b. June 23, 1763; m. MEHITABLE HUBBARD, of Pittsfield, 1788.
   VI. MARTHA,[5] b. Jan. 10, 1767; m. ALCOTT CHAPMAN, and d. Nov. 12, 1849.

27.

JOHN[4] CHURCHILL (BARNABAS,[3] JOSEPH,[2] JOHN[1]). Born in Plymouth, May 9, 1739, and lived there until about 1779, when he

removed to Pittsfield, Mass.   Married, in Plympton, March 9, 1771,
MOLLY BRADFORD, daughter of John, born 1746.

Children born in Plymouth and Pittsfield.

 I. SARAH,[5] b. Oct. 19, 1771; m. 1st TRUSTRUM LEFERONS, no children;
   m. 2d, AMOS SQUIRE; children by second husband, (1) Henry
   Squire, (2) Asabel Squire, (3) Frank Squire, (4) Almeda Squire,
   (5) Polly Squire, (6) Addie Squire.
77 II. LEMUEL,[5] b. Feb. 9, 1773; m. MINDWELL TILLOTSON, 1802.
 III. MOLLY,[5] b. June 17, 1775; m. ELIJAH BAGG, and had the following
   children: (1) Truman Bagg, (2) Elijah Bagg, (3) William Bagg,
   (4) John Bagg, (5) Polly Bagg, (6) Sarah Bagg, (7) Pauline
   Bagg, (8) Betsey Bagg.
 IV. LYDIA,[5] b. Jan. 11, 1777; m. HENRY BURHANS, son of Harry and
   Zerviah (Hall) Burhans, b. June 22, 1766; m. 1797.   She died
   March 2, 1847.   He died Sept. 18, 1848.

Children.

 1. Liertius Burhans, b. April 13, 1799; m. Eliza Ann Westcott,
   May 19, 1825; d. Sept. 14, 1875.
 2. Maria Burhans, b. Oct. 6, 1800; m. Zopher Wicks, April 7,
   1727; d. Dec. 5, 1859.
 3. Minerva Burhans, b. Sept. 11, 1802; m. Levant Sloan, Feb.
   27, 1822; d. July 21, 1855.
 4. Henry Burhans, b. April 22, 1804; d. unmarried July 12, 1828.
 5. Melancthon Burhans, b. Feb. 20, 1806; m. Patty Saxton; d.
   June 1, 1863.
 6. Abigail Burhans, b. Dec. 29, 1807; m. Eli D. Halbert; d. Sept.
   11, 1887.
 7. Lydia Burhans, b. July 14, 1809; m. Lucian Woodford, Sept.
   10, 1833; d. April 28, 1882.
 8. Tryphena Burhans, b. April 12, 1811; m. Asel Ingraham, Nov.
   19, 1829; d. about 1888.
 9. Spencer Churchill Burhans, b. July 11, 1813; m. Ruth Tibbetts,
   Jan. 4, 1838; d. Feb. 7, 1849.
 10. Daniel Burhans, b. Nov. 29, 1815; m. Nancy Carpenter, June
   7, 1838; d. June 22, 1887.
 11. Mary Burhans, b. Feb. 7, 1818; m. R. Tibbetts, M.D.

 V. ELIZABETH,[5] b. Dec. 8, 1778; m. DR. JOHN KENNEDY.
78 VI. JOHN,[5] b. in Pittsfield, Mass., March 27, 1780; m. HULDA BROWN, in
   Pittsfield, 1815.
 VII. OLIVE,[5] b. in Pittsfield, Mass., Dec. 16, 1781; m. —— BENTLEY.
 VIII. CYNTHIA,[5] b. Aug. 22. 1784; d. unmarried.
79 IX. BRADFORD,[5] b. Sept 13, 1786; m. SELINDA ROBBINS, of Pittsfield.
80 X. SPENCER,[5] b. June 10, 1789; m. CLARISSA MURPHY, Nov. 11, 1740.

28.

JOSEPH[4] CHURCHILL (JOSEPH,[3] JOSEPH,[2] JOHN[1]).   Born in
Plymouth, July 14, 1722.   He lived in Boston and Salem.   Died in
Boston, April 27, 1780, aged 58 years.   Married, in Boston, AGNES
FETTERS, who was born in Holland in 1722, and died in Boston,
Oct. 9, 1798, aged 76 years.

Children

81 I. JOSEPH,[5] b. in Boston, Sept. 19, 1745; m. ANNE NORTHY, dau. of
   David, 1768/9.
82 II. JOHN,[5] b. in Salem, 1748; m. SARAH STACEY, of Salem, 1773.

III. DOROTHY,[5] b. in Salem, 1751; d. unmarried.

There seems to be something of a romance connected with this Dorothy. In the town records of Salem, under "Intentions of Marriage," appears the following, under date of March 16, 1771:

"Samuel Chipman and Dorothy Churchill, both of Salem, intend marriage."

This marriage did not take place, and thirty years later Samue Chipman, still a bachelor, married, January, 1803, Elizabeth Obear, of Beverly, who died in 1807, and he married, as second wife, Feb. 7, 1809, Elizabeth Fowler, of Beverly, who died Aug. 29, 1852, leaving two children. This last from records at Essex Institute.

From the "Salem Gazette," at the Institute, is taken the following item:

"Whereas, there has been some disputes between Joseph Chipman and Dorothy Churchill, both of Salem, as to a marriage contract, made between them. And those disputes being amicably settled, Therefore, that the said Dorothy may not be in the least injured by any suspicions, mistakes, or rumors concerning the said disputes and settlement, I, the said Joseph Chipman do now sincerely and voluntarily declare that neither those disputes, nor the said settlement, nor any of my conduct in this matter, have been owing to any objections which I have or had to her moral character, and that I think that there hath not been any just foundation for any such objections by any one."

Dated Sept. 11, 1771, Signed, JOSEPH CHIPMAN

A true Copy of the Original.

IV. DEBORAH,[5] b. in Salem, Sept. 13, 1754; d. July 29, 1782, unmarried.

29.

SAMUEL[4] CHURCHILL (JOSEPH,[3] JOSEPH,[2] JOHN[1]). Born in Boston, June 24, 1724. Died Sept. 28, 1759. Married, in Boston, HANNAH ELLIS, daughter of Samuel. After the death of Samuel she married THOMAS GRANT, of Lancaster, Feb. 7, 1760.

Children of Samuel Churchill, born in Lancaster.

83 I. SAMUEL,[5] b. Oct. 31, 1749; m. REBECCA WILDER, of Sterling, March 6, 1781.

II. ABIAH,[5] b. Aug. 31, 1759; m. AMAZIAH CURRIER.

Children.

1. Samuel Churchill Currier, b. Jan. 1, 1791; m. Submittance Greenman.

Said to have had five sons and five daughters.

30.

ELIEZER[4] CHURCHILL (ELIEZER,[3] ELIEZER,[2] JOHN[1]). Born Feb. 26, 1713/14, in Plymouth, and lived there. He sold his share of estate, inherited from his father, in 1777, to Solomon Sylvester, whose heirs sold it, in 1786, to George Watson, and the old house was afterwards converted into the shop, subsequently used by L. and E. Morton.

Married, Oct. 19, 1738, SARAH HARLOW, daughter of William and Mercy, born 1715.

Children born in Plymouth.

  I. HANNAH,[5] b. July 14, 1739; d. Aug. 13, 1739.
  II. HANNAH,[5] b. June 5, 1740; m. JEREMIAH (——).
  III. SARAH,[5] b. Dec. 1, 1741; probably d. young.
  IV. MARCY,[5] b. April 27, 1743; m. ROBERT HOSEA.
84 V. ELIEZER,[5] b. Oct. 31, 1744; m. 1st, JANE RIDER, Sept. 27, 1764; m.
    2d, ABIGAIL BARTLETT.
85 VI. JAMES,[5] b. Jan. 9, 1747; m. 1st, LYDIA NICHOLS, April 9, 1774; m.
    2d, LYDIA SNOW, Nov. 8, 1778, in Bridgewater. No record.
  VII. ASA,[5] b. Dec. 20, 1748.
  VIII. SYLVANUS,[5] b. July 6, 1750; d. Jan. 29, 1754.
  IX. SARAH,[5] b. March 29, 1755; m. GEORGE BARTLETT, Jan. 16, 1776.
86 X. JOSIAH,[5] b. July 3, 1757; m. SARAH ROGERS, of Bridgewater, Feb. 1,
    1781. No further record.
  XI. PHEBE,[5] b. June 9, 1759; m. 1st, WILLIAM HUNT, Aug. 20, 1798; m.
    2d, ARNOLD HUNT.

31.

JOSIAH[4] CHURCHILL (ELIEZER,[3] ELIEZER,[2] JOHN[1]). Born
July 20, 1716; d. in N.S. abt. 1800. He lived in Plymouth until
about the time of the Revolution, when having lost his property he
removed to Nova Scotia and lived at "Ragged Islands," now Lockport. His wife did not go to Nova Scotia with him. Married,
1741, PATIENCE HARLOW, daughter of Eleazer and Hannah (Pratt)
Harlow, of Plympton.

Children born in Plymouth.

  I. JOSIAH,[5] b. Oct. 23, 1742; d. Oct. 25, 1742.
  II. JOSIAH,[5] b. Nov. 28, 1743; d. young.
87 III. THADDEUS,[5] b. Nov. 29, 1745; m. ASENATH DELANO, Dec. 3, 1774.
  IV. PATIENCE,[5] b. Nov. 23, 1747; m. ELLIS CHURCHILL, son of Ephraim
    1764.
  V. ELIPHAZ,[5] b. Feb. 10, 1750.
  VI. ALPHEUS,[5] b. June 30, 1753.
88 VII. SAMUEL,[5] b. July 10, 1754; m. ELIZABETH CHURCHILL, dau. of Ama-
    ziah, 1776.
89 VIII. ENOS,[5] b. March 10, 1759; m. MARY PAINE, R.I., 1780.
90 IX. SYLVANUS,[5] b. Jan. 23, 1766; m. LYDIA CHURCHILL, dau. of
    Wilson, 1798.

32.

JONATHAN[4] CHURCHILL (ELIEZER,[3] ELIEZER,[2] JOHN[1]). Born
Oct. 19, 1720. He lived for some years in Hingham, on Ship Street.
Married, Aug. 27, 1742, HANNAH FOSTER, daughter of Joseph and
Rachel (Bassett) Foster, of Sandwich, born June 17, 1718.

Children.

91 I. JONATHAN,[5] b. May 18, 1744–5; m. LYDIA GILBERT in Hingham,
    Nov. 26, 1767.
92 II. JESSE,[5] b. Oct. 30, 1746; m. ABIGAIL WORCESTER in Newburyport.
  III. SAMUEL,[5] b. Jan. 15, 1750; d. May 20, 1754.
  IV. JOSIAH,[5] b. March 18, 1753, in Hingham; d. June 8, 1754.
  V. SAMUEL,[5] b. March 9, 1755; d. May 25, 1755.
  VI. HANNAH,[5] b. Jan. 3, 1760; d. June 1, 1760.

93 VII. FRANCIS,[5] b. June 1, 1761; m. PHEBE LEATHERS, of Charlestown, June 17, 1786.
VIII. HANNAH,[5] b. March 8, 1763; d. young. A beautiful girl.
94 IX. REUBEN,[5] b. Aug. 1, 1765; m. HANNAH SAMPSON, Aug. 11, 1787. They lived in Hingham. No further record.

33.

EPHRAIM [4] CHURCHILL (STEPHEN,[3] ELIEZER,[2] JOHN[1]). Born in Plymouth, Oct. 3, 1709; died Dec. 14, 1749. Married, March 27 1730, PRISCILLA MANCHESTER. She died Dec. 17, 1749.

Children born in Plymouth:

I. MARY,[5] b. Aug. 14, 1730; m. JAMES DREW, 1750.
1. Hannah Drew, b. 1751.
2. James Drew, b. 1754.
3. William Drew, b. 1755.
4. Mary Drew, b. 1757.
5. William Drew, b. 1760.
6. Sarah Drew, b. 1762.
7. Priscilla Drew, b. 1765.
8. Lydia Drew, b. 1767; m. Matthew Cushing.
9. Betsey Drew, b. 1769.

95 II. CHARLES,[5] b. April 25, 1733; m. SARAH (COBB), widow of Isaac Churchill, son of 1st Barnabas, 1765.
96 III. ZACCHEUS,[5] b. Feb. 20, 1735; m. MARY TRASK, Sept. 16, 1754.
97 IV. EPHRAIM,[5] b. July 2, 1738; m. JEMIMA BRYANT, Nov. 28, 1751.
V. PRISCILLA,[5] b. Jan. 8, 1740; m. JOHN RIDER, April 25, 1758.
98 VI. ELLIS,[5] b. Nov. 25, 1742; m. PATIENCE CHURCHILL, dau. of Josiah,[5] 1764.
99 VII. ANSEL,[5] b. March 29, 1745; m. BETHIA HOLMES, July 17, 1765.
100 VIII. JOHN,[5] b. July 16, 1748; m. 1st, OLIVE COBB; m. 2d, Mrs. LUCY PRATT, Bridgewater, Dec. 27, 1776. No further record.

34.

NATHANIEL [4] CHURCHILL (STEPHEN,[3] ELIEZER,[2] JOHN[1]). Born in Plymouth, Dec. 19, 1712. Married, Jan. 2, 1734, MARY CURTIS, born 1714.

Children.

I. EXPERIENCE,[5] b. Aug. 27, 1735; m. JABEZ HARLOW.

Children born in Plymouth.

1. Jabez Harlow, b. Feb. 9, 1754.
2. Experience Harlow, b. April 3, 1756.
3. Nathaniel Harlow, b. Jan. 27, 1758; m. Mary Shaw.
4. Rebecca Harlow, b. Jan. 17, 1760; d. April 10, 1766.
5. John Harlow, b. April 14, 1762.

101 II. ELIEZER,[5] b. July 31, 1737. No further record.
III. MARY,[5] b. July 17, 1740.
102 IV. NATHANIEL,[5] b. Dec. 13, 174-. No further record.

35.

STEPHEN [4] CHURCHILL (STEPHEN,[3] ELIEZER,[2] JOHN[1]). Born in Plymouth, Aug. 24, 1717; died Sept. 5, 1751. Married, July 4, 1738, HANNAH BARNES, daughter of Jonathan and his wife, Widow

Mercy (Doten) Barnes. She was born 1718, and after the death of Stephen married JEREMIAH HOWES, and died 1793.

Children born in Plymouth.

 I. SARAH,[5] b. July 18, 1739; m. NATHANIEL CARVER, 1764.

Children born in Plymouth.

  1. Nathaniel Carver, b. 1766.
  2. John Carver.
  3. Josiah Carver.
  4. Mercy Carver, b. 1770; m. William Barnes.
  5. Lucy Carver, m. Rufus Sherman.
  6. Sally Carver, m. Barnabas Faunce.
  7. Betsey Carver, b. 1774; m. Barnabas Faunce.
  8. Polly Carver, m. David Bartlett.

 II. MERCY,[5] b. July 18, 1739.
 III. STEPHEN,[5] b. July 17, 1741; d. Sept. 14, 1742.
103 IV. STEPHEN,[5] b. June 7, 1743; m. LUCY BURBANK, dau. of Timothy, 1766.
 V. HANNAH,[5] b. Feb. 14, 1745; m. JOHN OTIS, of Barnstable, b. 1743.

Children born in Plymouth.

  1. Temperance Otis, b. 1766.
  2. Hannah A. Otis, b. 1768; m. Thomas Nicholson.
  3. Abigail Otis.
  4. Grace Hayman Otis, m. John Goddard.
  5. John Otis, b. 1774; d. in Plymouth, 1822.

104 VI. ZADOCK,[5] b. July 16, 1747; m. BATHSHEBA RIDER, dau. Joseph, Oct. 7, 1773.
 VII. PELEG,[5] b. July 9, 1749; d. Sept. 5, 1750.

36.

BENJAMIN[4] CHURCHILL (STEPHEN,[3] ELIEZER [2] JOHN [1]). Born in Plymouth, Aug. 19, 1725. Married, Nov. 3, 1746, RUTH DELANO. She died Aug. 22, 1798, aged 73. Lived in Plymouth.

Children.

105 I. WILSON,[5] b. April 23, 1747; m. LYDIA DARLING, dau. of Jonathan, Dec. 12, 1772.
106 II. BENJAMIN,[5] b. Nov. 17, 1748; m. PHEBE TINKHAM RANDALL, Jan. 13, 1782.
 III. ABNER,[5] b. April 8, 1750; said to have gone to New York. No further record.
 IV. ABIGAIL,[5] b. 1752; m. SAMUEL ROGERS (b. 1752), Feb. 8, 1776.

Children born in Plymouth.

  1. Betsey Rogers, m. Eleazer Holmes.
  2. Samuel Rogers, m. Betsey Babb.
  3. Ruth Rogers, m. ——— Simmons.
  4. Stephen Rogers.
  5. Abigail Rogers, m. John Chase.

 V. STEPHEN,[5] d. in West Indies.
 VI. NATHAN,[5] d. in West Indies.
 VII. BATHSHEBA,[5] m., Nov. 17, 1785, BENJAMIN WASHBURN, b. in 1761.

Child.

1. Joanna Washburn, m. Benjamin Weston.

VIII. JOANNA,[5] m. NATHANIEL CARVER, Oct. 4, 1789.

Children.

1. Stephen Carver.
2. Nathaniel Carver, b. 1791; m. Betsey Woodward, 1812.
3. Sally Carver, m. Seth F. Nye, of Sandwich.
4. Nancy Carver.
5. Mary Carver.

IX. RUTH,[5] b. 1760; m. THOMAS BARTLETT.

37.

AMAZIAH[4] CHURCHILL (ELKANAH,[3] ELIEZER [2] JOHN [1]). Born
Nov. 29, 1721. Married, Oct. 31, 1745, ELIZABETH SYLVESTER,
daughter of Solomon.

Children.

107   I. CALEB,[5] b. May 15, 1747; m. MRS. PATIENCE NELSON, March 4, 1775.
No further record.

  II. ELIZABETH,[5] b. Feb. 1, 1749; d. March 31, 1749.

108 III. AMAZIAH,[5] b. April 12, 1750; m. BETTY BARTLETT, dau. of Samuel
and Betsey (Moore) Bartlett, March 16, 1776.

  IV. FAITH,[5] b. March 13, 1753; m. EZEKIEL MORTON, JR., Dec. 16, 1776.

Children born in Plymouth.

1. Freeman Morton, m. Rebecca Harlow, 1806.
2. Caleb Morton, m. Hannah Leonard.
3. Mary Morton, m. Amasa Clark.
4. Lucy Morton, m. Elkanah Finney.
5. Hannah Morton, m. Ephraim Bradford.

  V. ELIZABETH,[5] b. March 21, 1755; m. SAMUEL[5] CHURCHILL, son of
Josiah.

  VI. LUCY,[5] b. Jan. 3, 1757; m. LEWIS WESTON, Dec. 1, 1782.

Children.

1. Benjamin Weston.
2. Hannah Weston.
3. Lewis Weston, m. Martha Bartlett Drew, dau. of Benjamin and
Sophia, 1818.
4. Lucy Weston, b. 1785.

  VII. MARY,[5] b. Oct. 3; 1758; m. WILLIAM WESTON, 1778.

Children.

1. Lewis Weston, b. 1778; m. Betsey Lanman, 1798.
2. Harvey Weston, m. 1st, Lucy Harlow,. 1816; 2d, Sarah Churchill, dau. of Daniel.
3. Almira Weston, m. 1st, Judson W. Rice; 2d, N. C. Lanman.
4. Polly Weston, m. Lazarus Symmes.
5. Betsey Weston, m. Lewis Finney.
6. William Weston.
7. George Weston, b. 1790; m. Polly Holmes, dau. of Joseph, 1813.

 VIII. MENDALL,[5] b. July 27, 1760; unmarried. Served in the Revolution
in Capt. Wm. Weston's Co., from July 1, 1776, to Nov. 19, 1776.
Company stationed at the Gurnet, for the defence of Plymouth
Harbor.

109   IX. SOLOMON,[5] b. July 27, 1762; m. BETSEY BARTLETT, dau. of Thomas,
Nov. 28, 1783.

X. SARAH,[5] b. Feb. 1, 1766; m. *ICHABOD MORTON, a fisherman and trader, Oct. 13, 1787.

Children.

1. Sarah Morton, b. 1788; m. Lemuel Stephens.
2. *Ichabod Morton, Jr., b. 1790; m. 1st, Patty Weston; m. 2d, Betsey Holbrook.
3. Hannah Morton, b. 1792.
4. Mary Morton, b. 1794; m. Elkanah Bartlett.
5. Abigail Morton, b. 1796; d. 1847.
6. Betsey Morton, b. 1802; m. 1st, Joseph Whiting; m. 2d, William Clark.
7. Edwin Morton, b. 1804; m. Betsey Towey Harlow.
8. Maria Morton, b. abt. 1806; m. William Churchill, *No. 253.*

38.

ELKANAH[4] CHURCHILL (ELKANAH,[3] ELIEZER,[2] JOHN[1]). Born in Plymouth, April 10, 1726. Lived upon that part of the original Churchill estate which he inherited from his father, including the old house. After his death his son Jabez[5] received the estate. He was drowned with his son Elkanah Sept. 6, 1775. Married at Plymouth, March 8, 1748, SUSANNAH BARTLETT.

Children born in Plymouth.

I. SUSANNA,[5] b. June 16, 1749; m. NICHOLAS SMITH, March 8, 1770.

Child born at Plymouth.

1. Nicholas Smith, m. Rebecca Sears.

II. MARIAH,[5] b. Oct. 17, 1751; m. WILLIAM HOLMES.
III. ELKANAH,[5] b. Aug. 8, 1754; never married. Was drowned with his father in 1775.
110 IV. JABEZ,[5] b. Oct. 2, 1756; m. MERCY (SYLVESTER) BARTLETT, widow of Judah.
V. ANDREW,[5] b. Jan. 20, 1758; died young.
VI. ABIGAIL,[5] b. July 14, 1760; m. CHARLES BARTLETT, Dec 4, 1785.
VII. ANDREW,[5] b. Jan. 7, 1763. Lost at sea; unmarried.
111 VIII. NATHANIEL,[5] b. 1768; m. SUSANNA HARLOW, Feb. 3, 1798.

39.

JOHN[4] CHURCHILL (JOHN,[3] ELIEZER,[2] JOHN[1]). Born in Portsmouth, Sept. 8, 1719. Settled first in Portsmouth, N.H., but removed soon to Boston, and thence, in company with his kinsman, Samuel Doty, to New York. He died in New York of small-pox, 1751. Married, 1st, MARY NOBLE, of Portsmouth, 1741; 2d, at New York (———).

Child of First Wife.

112 I. JOHN,[5] b. 1743; m. HANNAH SMITH.

* Ichabod Morton, Jr., b. in 1790; was a shipbuilder by trade, and was a sturdy Abolitionist and temperance reformer. By his first wife he had Abigail, who married a Diaz, our well-known Abby Morton Diaz.

40.

BENJAMIN[4] CHURCHILL (JOHN,[3] ELIEZER,[2] JOHN[1]). Born in Portsmouth, Oct. 13, 1741. Married, 1st, ABIGAIL DEVERSON, daughter of Thomas, who died October, 1795; and he married, 2d, ELIZABETH CLARK, daughter of Thomas.

Children.

    I. BETTY,[5] bapt. Jan. 8, 1769; d. in infancy.

113   II. SAMUEL CLARK,[5] b. Feb. 17, 1770; m. SUSANNAH COWEN.

41.

JOSEPH[4] CHURCHILL (JOHN,[3] ELIEZER,[2] JOHN[1]). Born in Portsmouth, March 25, 1744. He is called "Mariner" in a mortgage in which he gives one-third part of a lot of land on Pickering's Neck, "late belonging to John Churchill deceased on which his house now stands," etc. Date is Jan. 3, 1770, and Joseph is then of Portsmouth. Married ELIZABETH COTTON, of Portsmouth.

Children.

    I. MARY,[5] m. MOSES THOMPSON.

114   II. JOHN,[5] b. May 26, 1770; m. MERCY HUTCHINS.

115   III. WILLIAM,[5] b. July 9, 1776; m. MARY HUTCHINS, March, 1799.

116   IV. DANIEL,[5] m. LUCY FLETCHER.

117   V. TOBIAS,[5] b. June 12, 1780; m. JANE EVERETT, who was b. March 12, 1786.

117a VI. BENJAMIN,[5] b. 1782; m. CYNTHIA PARKER, of New Portland, Me.

    VII. BETSEY,[5] m. JAMES McFADDEN.

    VIII. MARTHA,[5] b. Oct. 19, 1788; m., April 1, 1809, BENJAMIN YORK, b. April 1, 1785, son of Robert.

        They first settled in New Portland, Me. In the spring of 1812, in company with his parents, his three brothers, and some fifteen other families, with his wife and one child, he migrated to New York State, and settled in Wayne County, that part which they occupied at that time being almost a wilderness, in what is now Huron, on the west side of Sodus Bay, Lake Ontario. After years of frugal fare and severe toil, they became a prosperous community, and the locality is known to this day as the " York Settlement." Benjamin died May 20, 1850, and his wife Martha died Jan. 14, 1878.

    Children born, the first at New Portland, Me., the rest in N. Y.

        1. John York, b. Aug. 23, 1810, in New Portland, Me.; m. Sarah Butler, March 13, 1832.

            They lived in " York Settlement " and had five children: (1) Martha York, (2) Mary York, (3) Samuel York, (4) John York, (5) Warren.

        2. Irena York, b. June 2, 1812, in N.Y. State; m. 1st, Asa Wilder; m. 2d, Henry Marquatt.

            Children: (1) Elizabeth Wilder; (2) Cyrus Marquatt.

        3. Lovilla York, b. Jan. 25, 1814; m., July 7, 1842, Warren Churchill, son of Daniel,[5] *q. v.*

        4. Lovina York, b. May 3, 1818; m. Aaron Wingate.

            Three children: (1) Benjamin Wingate, who became a Methodist minister of distinction, and Secretary of the Board of Foreign Missions, in Chicago; (2) Achsa Wingate; (3) Lovilla Wingate. These sisters lived (1901) at " York Settlement," Alton P.O.

5. Benjamin York, b. Nov. 23, 1825; m. Minerva Miller, Feb. 7, 1850.
   They lived (1901) in Alton, Wayne Co., N.Y., and have had four children : (1) Imogene York, m. Robert Kelley ; (2) Eliza York, m. Wm. A. Mitchell, 1894; (3) Josephine York; (4) Christiana York.
6. Emmeline York, b. June 6, 1829; m. Myron P. Lyndall, Sept. 1, 1851.
   They lived (1901) at Walcott, N.Y.

Children.

1. Caroline Lyndall, b. July 21, 1852; m. George C. Mitchell. They live in Wolcott, N.Y., and have one son, Charles H. Mitchell.
2. Rev. Henry M. Lyndall, b. July 21, 1855; m. Phebe A. Mitchell, Jan. 31, 1877. He became a minister of the Presbyterian fellowship, and served at Iron Mountain, Mich., five years, and then in 1892 became associate pastor in the Brown Street Tabernacle, N.Y. City, to inaugurate the missionary work known as the " People's Tabernacle in N.Y. City, in which work he is still (1901) engaged.

Children of Rev. Henry M. Lyndall.

(1) Mabel E. Lyndall, b. Sept. 29, 1878; (2) Carlton H. Lyndall, b. March 28, 1880; (3) Paul H. Lyndall, b. Aug. 10, 1887, d. June 18, 1888; (4) Ruth M. Lyndall, b. Aug. 16, 1890.
3. Rev. Charles H. Lyndall, b. July 31, 1857; m. Jessie Van Auken, 1885. He is a Presbyterian minister, served at Escanaba, Mich., '85–'89; pastor of the Browne Street Tabernacle, N.Y. City, '89–'95, and since 1897 pastor of the Reformed Church at Mt. Vernon, N. Y.
   His children are : (1) Gertrude Lyndall, b. 1888; (2) Helen Lyndall, b. 1892; (3) Dorothy Lyndall, b. 1895.

42.

EBENEZER[4] CHURCHILL (WILLIAM,[3] WILLIAM,[2] JOHN[1]). Born in Plymouth, Oct. 18, 1705; lived in Plympton. Married LEAH ———; she d. April 13, 1771. He died May 7, 1751.

Children born in Plympton.

     I. JOANNA,[5] b. April 28, 1730; d. May 14, 1730.
118   II. JOHN,[5] b. Nov. 14, 1731; m. JOANNA BISBEE, of Bridgewater, Feb. 12, 1756.
    III. EBENEZER,[5] b. April 26, 1734; d. April 10, 1738.
119   IV. ISAAC,[5] b. Feb. 11, 1735; m. MELETIAH BRADFORD, of Plympton, Aug. 1, 1765.
    V. REBECCA,[5] b. April 20, 1738; m. SYLVANUS HOLMES.
    VI. LEAH,[5] b. April 17, 1740; m. EBENEZER ATWOOD, Nov. 25, 1762.
120 VII. JOSHUA,[5] b. Feb. 23, 1742; m. ELIZABETH BONNEY, Feb. 4, 1768.
   VIII. RUTH,[5] b. Feb. 12, 1744; m. JONATHAN WHITMAN, of Bridgewater, Sept. 21, 1775.
    He was born 1751, and died in 1777. Child, (1) Leah Whitman, b. 1778; m. Sylvester Briggs.

    IX. HANNAH,[5] b. May 17, 1747.

43.

DAVID[4] CHURCHILL (WILLIAM,[3] WILLIAM,[2] JOHN[1]). Born in Plympton, Nov. 4, 1709. He is said to have built the house in Plympton where, in 1827, William Bradford lived. He died Sept. 27, 1785. They lived in Plympton. Married, 1729, MARY MAGOON. She died May 18, 1785.

Children born in Plympton.

121   I. DAVID,[5] b. Aug. 9, 1729; m. JANE ELLIS, Feb. 20, 1750.
     II. HANNAH,[5] b. June 17, 1733; d. March 17, 1744.
122   III. WILLIAM,[5] b. Nov. 28, 1739; m. SARAH RIDER, Nov. 29, 1759.
     IV. ELIAS,[5] b. Aug. 7, 1742; d. June 3, 1751.
123   V. JAMES,[5] b. May 29, 1746; m. PRISCILLA SOULE, Oct. 31, 1765.

44.

NATHANIEL[4] CHURCHILL (WILLIAM,[3] WILLIAM,[2] JOHN[1]). Born in Plympton, May 11, 1718. He served in the Revolution, in Capt. Thos. Loring's Company, Alarm of April 19, 1775, "Marched to Marshfield, 1. day." Married, 1st, June 4, 1741 SUSANNA McFARLAND, who died June 22, 1785; 2d, MRS. LYDIA (BRYANT) SAMPSON, widow of Thomas.

Children by First Wife, born in Plympton:

   I. ABIGAIL,[5] b. May 10, 1744; m. HOPESTILL BISBEE, JR., Sept. 4, 1766.
     They settled first in Plympton, but in 1771 removed to Rochester.

Children, the first two born in Plympton, the others in Rochester

1. Abigail Bisbee, b. Oct. 21, 1768; m. Jonathan Hall.
2. Hopestill Bisbee, b. Oct. 11, 1769; removed to Middleboro.
3. Sylvanus Bisbee.
4. Josiah Bisbee, never married.
5. Ansel Bisbee, removed to Buckfield, Me.; no children.
6. Levi Bisbee.
7. Susanna Bisbee.
8. Hannah Bisbee.

124   II. NATHANIEL,[5] b. May 10, 1746; m. DEBORAH WRIGHT, Dec. 27, 1770.
   III. LYDIA,[5] b. March 17, 1748; m., 1st, AMMITTAI EARLOW, of Rochester, June 6, 1781; m., 2d, NOAH HAMMOND, of Rochester, Nov. 9, 1786.

Children by Second Husband.

1. Noah Hammond, b. July 4, 1787; m. Martha Mayhew Dexter.
2. Ammittai Hammond, b. Aug. 30, 1789; m. Lucinda White, July 15, 1823.
3. Israel Hammond, b. Feb. 13, 1792; m. Joanna Burgess, July, 1830.

   IV. SAMUEL,[5] bapt. May 12, 1751; d. young.
    V. STEPHEN,[5] b. June 27, 1752; d. unmarried.
   VI. SYLVANUS,[5] b. May 10, 1755; d. unmarried.
  VII. SUSANNA,[5] b. June 18, 1757; m. THOMAS HARLOW.

45.

ICHABOD[4] CHURCHILL (WILLIAM,[3] WILLIAM,[2] JOHN[1]). Born
Sept. 24, 1722.   Died Aug. 24, 1808.   Lived in Plympton.   Married,
1st, REBECCA CURTIS.   She died Dec. 19, 1753.   2d, SUSANNA
GIBBS, Feb. 6, 1755.

Children by First Wife.

125   I. EBENEZER,[5] b. March 1, 1744; m. LUCY PALMER, July 17, 1764; d.
in 1824.

    II. JOANNA,[5] b. Jan. 27, 1747; m. SILAS TILLTON, Nov. 28, 1765.

    III. DEBORAH,[5] b. Jan. 7, 1749; m. ICHABOD PHINNEY, of Plympton.

126   IV. ICHABOD,[5] b. Sept. 7, 1751; m. ABIGAIL DOTEN, Oct. 12, 1775.

    V. REBECCA,[5] b. Dec. 9, 1753; m. EBENEZER CUSHMAN, Apri 14, 1771.

Children of Rebecca.

1. Hannah Cushman; d. unmarried.
2. Lydia Cushman, b. 1773; m., Oct. 20, 1797, Reuben Bisbee.
3. Zenas Cushman, d. at Demarara, Sept. 22, 1799.
4. Levi Cushman, d. unmarried.
5. Ebenezer Cushman, b. 1779; d. February, 1793.
6. Daniel Cushman, b. July 4, 1780; m. Priscilla Bassett, May 5, 1805.
7. Rebecca Cushman, b. Sept. 2, 1781.
8. Peleg Cushman, d. unmarried.
9. Valetta Brewster Cushman, b. May 27, 1786; d. 1842.

Children by Second Wife, Susanna.

127   VI. THOMAS,[5] b. March 7, 1756; m. MARY HOLMES, dau. of Zacheus, 1778.

    VII. SARAH,[5] b. March 9, 1758; d. July 27, 1848.

127a VIII. WILLIAM,[5] b. Feb. 18, 1761; m. CATHARINE TILTON, of Easton, (?) N.Y.; he d. Dec. 18, 1818.

    IX. EUNICE,[5] b. Jan. 20, 1765; m. JOSEPH CHURCHILL (No. 214), q. v.

46.

ISAAC[4] CHURCHILL, JR. (ISAAC,[3] WILLIAM,[2] JOHN[1]).   Born
July 16, 1741.   Died Oct. 23, 1826.   Lived in Plympton, and was a
large landholder and accounted rich.   Soldier in Revolution, private,
Capt. Thos. Loring's Company, at Lexington Alarm, April 19.
Married, Jan. 21, 1764, EUNICE RIPLEY, daughter Timothy and
Eunice (Coomer) Ripley.   She died April 6, 1821, aged 81 years 10
months.

Children born in Plympton.

    I. TIMOTHY,[5] b. Dec. 3, 1764; d. Sept. 19, 1794, at Martinique.

    II. JOSIAH,[5] b. July 23, 1766; d. Sept. 4, 1766.

128   III. DANIEL,[5] b. Aug. 4, 1767; m. LUCY CHURCHILL, dau. of Ebenezer.

129   IV. JOSIAH,[5] b. Jan. 19, 1770; m. DEBORAH PHINNEY.

    V. SIMEON,[5] b. Feb. 2, 1772; d. Sept. 22, 1777.

    VI. SUSANNA,[5] b. Oct. 1, 1774; d. May 4, 1785.

130   VII. SETH,[5] b. Sept. 29, 1777; m. REBECCA PHINNEY.

131 VIII. ISAAC, JR.,[5] b. April 26, 1782; m. MARY GROZIER, in Province-town, 1806.

47.

CAPT. PEREZ [4] CHURCHILL (BENJAMIN,[3] WILLIAM,[2] JOHN [1]).
Born in Middleboro', Oct. 15, 1722, died Oct. 2, 1797. He lived at
Pope's Point Furnace, in Middleboro'. He served in the war of the
Revolution, first as corporal in Capt. James Keith's Company, Col.
Paul Dudley Sargent's Regiment. Enlisted July 12, 1775. Service,
twenty days. Commissioned captain of 9th Company of Fourth
Plymouth County Regiment, May 9, 1776. Also captain in Col.
Ebenezer Sprout's Regiment. Served three days, May 6 to May 9,
1778, on an alarm at Dartmouth. Also in Colonel Daggett's Regi-
ment, Aug. 25 to Sept. 2, 1778, at Rhode Island. Again in Col.
Ebenezer White's Regiment, marched to Rhode Island on the alarm of
Aug. 1, 1780, and served nine days. He is buried in the Lakenham
burial-ground, with his two wives. His gravestone was standing in
1857. Married 1st, in Middleboro', 1741, DEBORAH THAYER, of
Carver. She died April 27' 1788, aged 64 years. He married 2d,
PERSIS RECORD, daughter of James Harlow, and widow, first of Isaac
Shaw, and second of Lemuel Record. No issue by this marriage
with second wife, who died Aug. 28, 1802.

Children of Perez [4] and Deborah, born in Middleboro'.

I. DELIVERANCE,[5] b. Dec. 29, 1742; m. as 2d wife, EBENEZER WRIGHT,
of Plympton, Feb. 1, 1776.

132   II. ZEBEDEE,[5] b. Aug. 19, 1745; m. SARAH CUSHMAN, dau. of Caleb,
May 24, 1764.

III. DEBORAH,[5] b. Dec. 29, 1747; m. TIMOTHY COBB, of Carver, April
16, 1765.

Children.

1. Deliverance Cobb, b. 1766.
2. Timothy Cobb, b. 1769; m. Rebecca Fuller.
3. Zabdiel Cobb, b. 1771.
4. Deborah Cobb, b. 1774.
5. Elizabeth Cobb, b. 1776.
6. Mary Cobb, b. 1778.
7. Nathaniel Cobb, b. 1780.
8. Thomas Cobb, b. 1782.
9. Elizabeth Cobb, b. 1785.
10. Alvan Cobb, b. 1787.

133   IV. PEREZ,[5] b. April 26, 1753; m. PATIENCE WOOD Oct. 1, 1778.

V. LYDIA,[5] b. June 20, 1756; m. HEMAN CROCKER, Oct. 13, 1774.
Heman died at sea, Sept. 5, 1801; Lydia, the mother, died in
Carver, Oct. 22, 1843.

Children.

1. Daniel Crocker, m. Mercy Pratt.
2. Perez Crocker, b. 1779; m. Freelove Thompson.
3. Eliezer Crocker, m. Lucy Nelson.
4. Heman Crocker, m. Rebecca Pratt.
5. Ebenezer Crocker, m. Abigail Edson.
6. Elizabeth Crocker, m. Israel Dunham.
7. Deborah Crocker, m. Ichabod Howland.
8. Lydia Crocker, m. Levi Sherman.
9. Rebecca Crocker.

134   VI. ISAAC,[5] b. Nov. 23, 1758; m. BETSEY RAYMOND, dau. of James.
135   VII. JOSEPH,[5] b. April 23, 1761; m. ALICE DRAKE, in Middleboro',
        March 8, 1785.

48.

LIEUT. JAMES [4] CHURCHILL (BENJAMIN,[3] WILLIAM,[2] JOHN [1]).
Born Dec. 30, 1726, in Middleboro'.   Removed to Barnstable.
Mentioned as lieutenant in Capt. Josiah Dunbar's Company, 1762
(Mass. Arch., Vol. 99, p. 217).   Married 1st, 1748, MARTHA BLACK-
WELL, of Sandwich, daughter of Samuel.   Married 2d, Jan. 10, 1751,
MARCY (BAKER) COBB.   She died Sept. 30, 1756.   No issue.
Married 3d, Feb. 30, 1757, MRS. MARY (COBB) GORHAM, widow of
Capt. Isaac, of Barnstable.   Mrs. Mary Churchill, the third wife, was
born June 14, 1721, and died at the age of 92 years in Yarmouth,
where she was living with her daughter, Mrs. Thacher.

Child by First Wife.
I.   SARAH,[5] b. Sept. 23, 1749.

Children by Third Wife.
II.   MARY,[5] b. Jan. 8, 1758; m. COL. THOMAS THACHER. ·

Children.
1. Armen Lewis Thacher, b. Dec. 3, 1788; d. unmarried.
2. Mary Thacher, b. April 28, 1791; d. unmarried.
3. Thomas Thacher, b. Dec. 29, 1793; d. young.
4. Thomas Thacher, b. July 25, 1795; d. March 3, 1863.
5. George Churchill Thacher, b. Dec. 30, 1796; d. in Dorchester,
     Oct. 21, 1856.
6. Sarah Thacher, b. May 13, 1800; d. young.

III.   EDWARD,[5] b. Oct. 25, 1761.
IV.   JAMES,[5] b. July 13, 1766.

49.

BENJAMIN [4] CHURCHILL (BENJAMIN,[3] WILLIAM,[2] JOHN [1]).
Born Jan. 3, 1728.   Lived in Middleboro' until 1801, when he moved
to the town of Hartford, Me.   He settled there with his son Jabez.
Married THANKFUL WOOD.

Children born in Middleboro'
136   I.   JABEZ,[5] m. LOUISA LUCAS.
        II.   JAMES,[5] d. unmarried in Livermore, Me., aged 80.
137   III.   WILLIAM,[5] m. LYDIA MAXIM, of Wayne, Me.
138   IV.   JOSEPH,[5] m. —— WILLIAMS, of Scituate, R.I.
139   V.   NELSON,[5] m. EUNICE SHAW, Jan. 12, 1786.
        VI.   DINAH.[5]

50.

JABEZ [4] CHURCHILL (JOSIAH,[3] WILLIAM,[2] JOHN [1]).   Born
Jan. 21, 1723/4.   Lived in North Bridgewater and died there in 1882.
After his death, the widow, with her family, moved to Hebron, Me.
Married, in North Bridgewater, ALICE BRIGGS.

Mrs. Murch, a granddaughter, says that in the spring of 1784 or 1785, the widow, Alice, sold her only remaining cow, and with the proceeds paid the passage of herself and family on a schooner to Yarmouth, Me., and thence made her way to the home of her eldest daughter, who had settled in Hebron some years before. She brought six children along with her. ·She died three years later and is buried on Greenwood Hill.

Children born in North Bridgewater.

139a *   I. ALICE,[5] b. Feb. 23, 1753; m. ELIAS MONK, of Bridgewater, Feb. 10, 1772.
139b   II. RACHEL,[5] b. Oct. 7, 1754; m. THADDEUS PRATT, of Bridgewater, July 23, 1772. Removed to Hebron, Me.
140   III. JABEZ,[5] b. 1759; m. MARIA BENSON.
140a   IV. SUSAN,[5] b. 1760; m. PHILIP MASON.
141   V. JOSIAH,[5] b. 1762; m. LYDIA ORR.
142   VI. BENJAMIN,[5] b. 1765; m. SALLY BENSON.
142a   VII. CHARLOTTE,[5] b. 1769; m. EPHRAIM BARROWS.
142b   VIII. CELESTIA,[5] b. 1772; m. 1st, —— BENSON; m. 2d, —— BESSE.
   IX. REBECCA,[5] b. April 20, 1774; m. DANIEL FAUNCE.

Children.

1. Sally Faunce, m. Joseph Swift.
2. Olive Faunce, m. Richard Hathaway.
3. Daniel Faunce, m. Hannah Graves.
4. Rebecca Faunce, m. Edmund Dean.
5. Ira Faunce, m. Sally Holmes.
6. Eliza Faunce, m. John Lewis.
7. Hannah Faunce, m. Joseph Murch.
8. Alden Faunce, m. Olive Atkins.
9. Polly Faunce, b. May 29, 1815; m. Benjamin Murch, Aug. 24, 1834.

   X. POLLY,[5] b. 1776; m. JOHN BIRD.

Children.

1. John Bird.	3. Lyman Bird.
2. Benjamin Bird.	4. Asaph Bird.

143   XI. ASAPH,[5] b. 1775; m. 1st, BETSEY DEAN; m. 2d, POLLY MERRILL.

51.

ISRAEL[4] CHURCHILL (JOSIAH,[3] WILLIAM,[2] JOHN[1]). Born in Plympton, 1727. He settled at Tribes Hill, in the Mohawk Valley, N.Y. (Tribes Hill was in Amsterdam Township.) In his old age he removed to Canada with his sons and daughters, and died there. It has seemed impossible to gain any more than this meagre information about this family. Married, at Tribes Hill, N.Y., HANNAH (——).

---

* The families of the first five daughters carried forward to numbers 139a, etc.

Children, all born in the Mohawk Valley.

       I. MARK,[5] never married.
      II. PATIENCE,[5] m. GEORGE BATES.
     III. DOLLY,[5] m. (———) O'REGAN.
     IV. THANKFUL,[5] m. (———) GILLET.
144   V. JOHN,[5] m. ANNA HEWITT.
145   VI. JOSEPH,[5] m. ABIGAIL HAWLEY.
146   VII. SOLOMON,[5] m. MRS. RACHEL BITTS.
   VIII. ELINOR,[5] m. (———) LILLIE.
     IX. ELIZABETH,[5] m. (———) HUBBARD.
147   X. CORNELIUS,[5] b. June 27, 1789; m. CHARLOTTE BARRY, April 29, 1810.
     XI. EZRA[5] married, it is said, but we have no record.

55.

JOSEPH[4] CHURCHILL (JOSIAH,[3] WILLIAM,[2] JOHN[1]). Born in Easton, Oct. 2, 1741. Married, in Attleboro, 1762, ANNE DAGGETT, of Attleboro', daughter of Nathaniel and Lydia (Tiffany) Daggett born Jan. 14, 1744.

Children.

148.   I. JACOB,[5] b. 1763; m. ABIGAIL TURNER, in Gloucester, R.I.
      II. SAMUEL,[5] b. 1764; d. unmarried in 1850.
    III. NATHANIEL,[5] b. 1769; d. at Comstock's Landing, Fort Anne, 1840.
149   IV. BENJAMIN,[5] b. 1778; m. TEMPERANCE PERRY, Putney, Vt., Oct. 6, 1799.

56.

JACOB[4] CHURCHILL (JOSIAH,[3] WILLIAM,[2] JOHN[1]). Born in Easton, Nov. 3, 1744. Settled in Stockbridge. Married LYLLIS REED, who joined the church in Stockbridge in 1783.

Children born in Stockbridge, exact order of birth not found.

    I. PHEBE,[5] m. 1st, MILES CURTIS, son of Jonathan, of Lenox, June 17, 1793. He died, and she married 2d, ELIAS HUBBARD, of Pompey, N.Y. By the first marriage she had two children.

     1. Miles Curtis. | 2. Nancy Curtis.

By second marriage.

     3. Elias Gilbert Hubbard.

150   II. ALVA,[5] m. 1st, ARVILLA ANDROS; m. 2d, ANNE MOTT.
     III. SYBIL,[5] m. 1st, COMFORT HART; m. 2d, ISAAC BALL.
    IV. ANNIS,[5] b. Sept. 20, 1782; m. 1st, ALANSON DEWEY, Nov. 29, 1802; m. 2d, (———) WARNER. Settled in Newark Valley, Tioga County, N.Y.
     V. NANCY,[5] b. Oct. 11, 1783; m. SAMUEL DRESSER, Dec. 14, 1809. He was born July 11, 1781, and died at Waterford, Ohio, Sept. 25, 1857. She died June 13, 1855. They lived at Stockbridge, and had nine children.

     1. Julia Dresser, b. March 23, 1811.
     2. Edwin J. Dresser, b. Dec. 12, 1813.
     3. Marshall Dresser, b. April 9, 1816.
     4. Samantha P. Dresser, b. Sept. 19, 1820.
     5. Emily A. Dresser, b. June 9, 1822.
     6. Sarah Dresser, b. June 7, 1824.

7. Jane Dresser, b. March 9, 1826; d. June, 1826.
8. Nancy Lovina Dresser, b. April 6, 1828.
9. Samuel Dresser, b. June 23, 1830.

VI. OLIVE,[5] m. ISAAC PERRY BALL.

Children.

1. Emmeline Ball. | 2. Lucy Ball. | 3. George Ball.

151 VII. SEYMORE,[5] m. REBECCA PALMER, Jan. 4, 1816.
152 VIII. DANIEL,[5] m. EXPERIENCE STAFFORD.
IX. AMANDA,[5] m. AARON BROWN.

Two Children.

1. Gilbert Brown. | 2. Henry Brown.

153 X. JACOB MILES,[5] b. May 10, 1799; m. LUCINDA THOMPSON.

57.

EBENEZER [4] CHURCHILL (JOHN,[3] JOHN,[2] JOHN [1]). Born in Plymouth, Nov. 6, 1721. Married 1st, Nov. 23, 1747, MERCY BRANCH, daughter of Thomas. Married 2d, Feb. 13, 1775, PATIENCE FAUNCE.

Children of First Wife.

I. EBENEZER,[5] b. June 20, 1749; m. JANE BARTLETT, Sept. 10, 1772.
She m. 2d, WM. DOTY, 1784. No further record.
154 II. BRANCH,[5] b. Dec. 17, 1751; m. MARY CHURCHILL, Sept. 28, 1778.
He served in the Revolution in Capt. Jesse Harlow's Company,
Minute-men, April, 1775; also in Captain Mayhew's Company
three months eight days. No record of children.
III. BETHIAH,[5] b. Sept. 13, 1753; d. Dec. 28, 1753.
IV. BETHIAH,[5] b. Nov. 24, 1754; m. ZEPHANIAH HOLMES, April 4, 1796.
One child, John Calderwood Holmes, b. 1797.
V. REBECCA,[5] b. Nov. 1, 1756; d. Aug. 12, 1760.
VI. MERCY,[5] b. April 19, 1759; d. Sept. 9, 1760.
155 VII. GEORGE,[5] b. April 18, 1761; m. ELIZABETH HARLOW, April 2, 1786.
VIII. MARY,[5] b. Nov. 10, 1763; m. JOHN WASHBURN, Nov. 25, 1784.

58.

JOHN [4] CHURCHILL (JOHN,[3] JOHN,[2] JOHN [1]). Born at Plymouth, April 15, 1727, died, 1759, aged 32. Married, at Plymouth, 1749, SARAH COLE.

Child born in Plymouth.

I. SARAH,[5] b. June 11, 1750; m. WILLIAM LEBARON.

Children.

1. William LeBaron, b. 1775.
2. Sarah LeBaron, b. 1776; m. Thomas Jackson.
3. Mary LeBaron, ⎱ b. 1778.
4. Lucy LeBaron, ⎰ b. 1778; m. Thomas Mayo.
5. Priscilla LeBaron, b. 1781; m. Gideon S. Alden, of New Bedford.
6. Eliza LeBaron, b. 1785.
7. William LeBaron, b. 1787.

FIFTH GENERATION.

59.

SAMUEL[5] CHURCHILL, JR. (SAMUEL,[4] JOHN[3] JOSEPH[2] JOHN[1]). Born in Stockbridge, 1733. With his wife he joined the church in Stockbridge, by profession, May 22, 1763. Married, at New Preston, Conn., 1761, ELIZABETH CURTIS, his cousin, daughter of Elnathan and Rose (Weller) Curtis, who was born March 23, 1738, at Woodbury, Conn., and died at Owego, N.Y., Aug. 17 1818.

Children.

    I. LUCY,[6] bapt. May 22, 1763; m. HENRY MOORE, Nov. 12, 1782. He was born Nov. 2, 1762.
    II. OLIVE,[6] bapt. April 8, 1764; m. 1st, ASA LEONARD; m. 2d, PERRY BALL, Nov. 28, 1799.

Child.

    1. Chester Leonard.

    III. ROSANNA,[6] bapt. Aug. 17, 1766; m. ABRAHAM PARKER, Feb. 24, 1785. He was born July 13, 1766.
156   IV. ASAHEL,[6] bapt. Aug. 6, 1769; m. POLLY HART, Feb. 4, 1785.
157   V. SAMUEL,[6] bapt. Jan. 19, 1772; m. PHEBE SEWARD, Feb. 25, 1796.
    VI. ELIZABETH,[6] bapt. Oct. 23, 1774; m. EBENEZER COOK, April 3, 1793. He was born Sept. 18, 1774.
    VII. SOLOMON,[6] bapt. Nov. 17, 1776; d. in infancy.
158   VIII. DANIEL,[6] bapt. June 7, 1778; m. JERUSHA WILLARD, May 25, 1795. She was born Jan. 31, 1778.

61.

BARNABAS[5] CHURCHILL (BARNABAS,[4] BARNABAS,[3] JOSEPH,[2] JOHN[1]). Born in Plymouth, Nov. 25, 1747. Lived in Plymouth and died Aug. 29, 1821. Married 1st, Oct. 8, 1780, SARAH FAUNCE, daughter of Thomas. She died Nov. 9, 1801, aged 48; 2d, 1803, LYDIA COLE, widow of Samuel H. She died Jan. 19, 1825.

Children born in Plymouth.

    I. BARNABAS,[6] b. Oct. 19, 1784; d. Sept. 14, 1785, aged 10 months.
159   II. JOB,[6] b. March 2, 1787; m. HANNAH T. HARLOW, Dec. 18, 1808.
    III. BARNABAS,[6] b. Feb. 5, 1789; d. Sept. 8, 1789, aged 7 months.

63.

SETH[5] CHURCHILL (BARNABAS,[4] BARNABAS,[3] JOSEPH,[2] JOHN[1]). Born in Plymouth, Oct. 1, 1754, and died Jan. 15, 1798. Married July 6, 1783, ELIZABETH SYLVESTER; she was born 1762, and died Sept. 5, 1814.

(38)

Children.

I. Lucy,[6] b. July 2, 1789; d. September, 1791.
II. David,[6] b. December, 1790; d. Sept. 30, 1791.
III. Seth,[6] b. May, 1794; d. Sept. 24, 1795.

65.

ICHABOD[5] CHURCHILL (Joseph,[4] Barnabas[3] Joseph[2] John[1]). Born in Middleboro', Aug. 9, 1746, and lived there till near the close of the Revolution. Removed from Middleboro' to Woodstock, Vt., about 1779/80, where he resided on what was known as "the road to Rutland." He served in the Revolutionary war as sergeant in Capt. Amos Wade's Third Middleboro' Company of Minutemen, on Alarm of April 19, 1775; marched to Marshfield, three days' service. Later same year, same company, served three months. Married, Nov. 7, 1771, Sarah Tinkham, of Halifax, Mass. · married by Rev. Ephraim Briggs.

Children born in Middleboro'.

160   I. Ichabod,[6] b. July 21, 1772; m. Priscilla Meacham, of Bridgwater, Vt.
161   II. Noah,[6] b. May 29, 1774; m. Polly Marshall, of Waterbury, Vt.,
May 29, 1798.
162   III. William,[6] b. Nov. 12, 1776; m. Eunice Badger, of Bridgwater,
Vt., June 1, 1802.
163   IV. Joseph,[6] b. Dec. 25, 1777; m. Dorothy Marshall, of Waterbury,
Vt., Dec. 25, 1803.
V. Eunice,[6] b. Oct. 10, 1779; m. Nathan Kelsey, of Stowe, Vt.
They lived in Stowe. She died Aug. 26, 1827. He died Aug. 1,
1861.

Children born in Stowe, Vt.

1. Mary Kelsey, m. John A. Upham.
2. Benjamin F. Kelsey, m. (———) Kimball, of Woodstock, Ohio.
3. Roxanna Kelsey, m. Luke Atwood, of Stowe, and moved to
Illinois.
4. Harrison Kelsey, m. (———) lived in Minonk, Ill., in 1870.
5. Elias Kelsey, m. (———) Spaulding, of Morristown.
6. Hiram Kelsey, m. (———) Town, of Cady's Falls, Morristown.

VI. Sarah,[6] b. Aug. 10, 1781; m. (———) Doubleday, of Pomfret,
Vt.
VII. Ruth,[6] b. March 24, 1783; m. Ebenezer Barrows, of Stowe, Vt.

Children.

1. Ebenezer Barrows, m. (———) Russell.
2. Ruth Barrows, m. Edwin Thomas, of Stowe, Vt.
3. Hannah Barrows, m. Adrian Thomas, of Stowe, Vt.
4. Thomas A. Barrows, d. unmarried. Lived in California.
5. Dr. Albert Barrows, m. (———) Daniels, of Woodstock, Vt.

VIII. Mary,[6] b. Dec. 1, 1784; m. Elijah Royce, of Woodstock, Vt.

Child.

1. Almira Royce, m. (———) Royce (a cousin), of Woodstock.

IX. Ellen,[6] b. Dec. 19, 1786; d. Jan. 17, 1787.
X. Salome,[6] b. March 28, 1788; m. Bartlett Elms, of Stowe, Vt.
They lived in Stowe, Vt., till about 1840, when they removed and
settled on the old Churchill homestead, in Woodstock.

Children born in Stowe.

1. Osro J. Elms, b. 1820; m. (———) Tracy, of Stowe, Vt.
2. Salome Elms.

XI. Asa,[6] b. March 14, 1790; m. Betsey Davenport, Oct. 26, 1815.
They lived in Dublin, N.Y. He was in the war of 1812. No
children.

164 XII. Jesse,[6] b. May 8, 1792; m. Mary Washburn, of Woodstock, at
Plymouth, Vt., March 1, 1819.

XIII. Nathan T.,[6] b. May 17, 1795; m. Elizabeth Raymond, of Bridg-
water, Vt., April 4, 1823.
He was a man of large influence, and held many high offices.
He left no children.

66.

JOSEPH[5] CHURCHILL (Joseph,[4] Barnabas,[3] Joseph,[2]
John [1]). He was born in Plymouth, July 14, 1748. After the
death of his father, and his mother's marriage to Archippus
Fuller, and removal to Woodstock, Vt., he was brought up by
Mr. Daggett, of Middleboro', and lived with him until he was
twenty-one years of age. He served in the war of the Revolution,
in Capt. Isaac Wood's Company, Minute-men; was then a corporal,
afterwards sergeant. He marched to Marshfield, April 19, 1775.
He served in other companies in 1777–1779, mostly in Rhode Island.
He lived in Middleboro' till the close of the war when he removed
to Woodstock, Vt., and settled there, on the north branch of the
Queechey River, two and a half miles west of "The Green." Married
March 21, 1771, in Middleboro', Sarah Cobb, daughter of Gershom.
She was born Sept. 20, 1747, and died in Stowe, Vt., in 1836.

Children.

165 I. Levi,[6] b. in Middleboro', April 24, 1772; m. 1st, Priscilla Simmons, at Woodstock, Vt., 1798; m. 2d, Keziah Fletcher,
March 24, 1800.

II. Miriam, b. in Middleboro', Aug. 16, 1774; m. 1st, Benjamin
Dimmock. He d. in 1797; m. 2d, Experience Raymond, 1806.

Child of First Husband.

1. Benjamin Churchill Dimmock; d. unmarried.

Children of Second Husband.

2. Joseph Churchill Raymond.
3. Sarah Raymond.

III. Sarah,[6] b. in Middleboro', April 13, 1777; m. Dea. Asa Raymond,
of Stowe, Vt. No children; d. Dec. 13, 1859.

IV. Lucy,[6] b. at Woodstock, Vt., March 24, 1779; m. Capt. Daniel
Lothrop, of Stowe, Vt.; d. at Williston, Vt., Feb. 5, 1853.

Children.

1. Nancy Hyde Lothrop, b. Dec. 11, 1793; m. Ellet Perkins,
Nov. 10, 1816.
2. Priscilla Lothrop, m. 1st, Daniel Robinson; m. 2d, Isaac Alger.

3. Sarah Lothrop, m. Noah Raymond.
4. Armenia Lothrop, m. Curtis (or Charles?) Cobb.
5. Daniel Lothrop, m. Philena Dow.

166   V. JOSEPH,[6] b. in Woodstock, July 7, 1781; m. MRS. CLARA EDDY MEECHAM, of Woodstock. February, 1813.
167   VI. SYLVESTER,[6] b. Aug. 2, 1783; m. at Windsor, LUCY HUNTER, Aug. 30, 1812.
168   VII. ISAAC,[6] b. Feb. 18, 1788; m. JULIA ARNOLD, Oct. 18, 1824.
    VIII. SUSAN W., b. July 19, 1793; m. HARPER D. SEARS, of Stowe, Vt. They lived in Stowe, Vt., and had children. She died Aug. 2, 1865.

Children.

1. Lucy H. Sears, b. Jan. 13, 1824; m. Wm. Morrison, Dec. 20, 1846.
2. Elizabeth R. Sears, b. June 16, 1825.
3. Nathan R. Sears, b. April 1, 1827.
4. Sylvester C. Sears, b. Feb. 5, 1829.
5. Julia C. Sears, b. Aug. 27, 1830.
6. Harper D. Sears, b. Feb. 20, 1832; d. July 3, 1834.
7. Fred M. Sears, b. Oct. 4, 1836, in Morristown, Vt.
8. Stephen D. Sears, b. May 3, 1838, in Morristown, Vt.

67.

NATHANIEL[5] CHURCHILL (LEMUEL,[4] BARNABAS,[3] JOSEPH,[2] JOHN). Born in Yarmouth, N.S., April 9, 1748. Lived in Yarmouth, N.S. Married 1st, Dec. 24' 1770, BETSEY RYDER. She died Jan. 7, 1794; 2d, Nov. 20, 1800, ELINOR METCALF (" Midkiff "); no children by second wife, who died July 25, 1813; 3d, Jan. 6, 1814, ELIZABETH GREEN. The father of this large family died Dec. 8, 1820.

Children by First Wife born in Yarmouth, N.S.

    I. BETSEY,[6] b. Nov. 1, 1771.
169   II. NATHANIEL,[6] b. Nov. 22, 1773; m. EUNICE KINNEY, 1797.
170   III. LEMUEL,[6] b. March 22, 1776. No further record.
    IV. LYDIA,[6] b. Sept. 7, 1778.
171   V. BARTLETT,[6] b. Jan. 7, 1781. No further record received.
    VI. HANNAH,[6] b. Feb. 14, 1783.
172   VII. STEPHEN,[6] b. Dec. 22, 1785. No further record.
    VIII. JERUSHA,[6] b. April 23, 1787.
173   IX. BENJAMIN,[6] b. Feb. 4, 1790; m. ELIZABETH EVERETT, July 15, 1813.
    X. MARY,[6] b. May 25, 1793.

Children of the Third Wife.

    XI. MATILDA,[6] b. Dec. 17, 1814; m. (————) ESTEY.
    XII. FANNY,[6] b. May 3, 1816; m. (————) KITCHEN.
    XIII. JOHN MULBURY,[6] b. Jan. 3, 1818; d. in infancy.
    XIV. WILLIAM,[6] b. July 4, 1819; d. in infancy.
    The above record is copied from the old family Bible of Nathaniel[5] Churchill, now owned by his descendant, Charles W. Whitfield of Langford, South Dakota.

68.

EZRA[5] CHURCHILL (LEMUEL,[4] BARNABAS,[3] JOSEPH,[2] JOHN [1]). Born in Plymouth, Mass., Oct. 11, 1758; died Nov. 24, 1843. Lived in Yarmouth, N.S. Married, May 6, 1779, MARY ROBERTS, of Argyle, N.S.

Children born in Yarmouth, N.S.

I. MARY,[6] b. Aug. 21, 1780; m. JONATHAN CROSBY, son of Ebenezer.

Children.

1. Eben Crosby.
2. John Crosby.
3. Margaret Crosby.
4. Mary Crosby.
5. Nehemiah Crosby.
6. Abiel Crosby.
7. Melinda Crosby.

   II. LEMUEL,[6] b. July 10, 1781; d. young.
174 III. EZRA,[6] b. May 17, 1782; m. ELIZABETH TREFRY.
175 IV. NEHEMIAH,[6] b. 1786; m. ELIZABETH CANN.
176 V. BENJAMIN,[9] b. 1788; m. 1st, LUCY RING; m. 2d, MRS. LYDIA (BUTLER) MOSES.
177 VI. LEMUEL,[6] b. Aug. 7, 1790; m. LYDIA GARDNER.
   VII. ABIGAIL,[6] b. Aug. 28, 1792.
178 VIII. JOHN,[6] b. Sept. 4, 1797; m. ABIGAIL ROGERS, 1818.
   IX. LYDIA,[6] b. Oct. 26, 1799; m. WILLIAM COFFRAN, son of William.

Children of Lydia and William Coffran.

1. Maria Coffran, m. William McKay, of Newburyport, Mass.
2. Lucy Coffran, m. John Parfitt.
3. Mary Coffran, m. Robert Weston.
4. Martha Coffran, m. Thomas Avery.
5. Whitman Coffran, m. 1st, Rosanna Hersey, Nov. 10, 1861; m. 2d, Mrs. Mary Crosby, widow.
6. Ezra Coffran, lost at sea.
7. Emily Coffran, m. James Riley.
8. Lydia A. Coffran, m. Zenas Eldridge, July 23, 1863.

X. NANCY,[6] b. June 4, 1806; m. 1st, SAMUEL HIBBARD; 2d, WATSON BAKER; 3d, PATRICK ROACH, Sept. 30, 1842; 4th, JOHN CRAWLEY, March 19, 1859.

Children of Nancy (Churchill) and Second Husband, Watson Baker

1. Ezra Baker, d. young.
2. Elmira Baker, m. Eben Scott.
3. Frederick Baker, m. Lucy Ann Weston, Feb. 14, 1856.
4. Ann Baker, m. Stephen Butler, Nov. 25, 1852.
5. Watson Baker, lost at sea; unmarried.

Children by Third Husband, Patrick Roach.

6. Ezra C. Roach, m. Mary A. Churchill, Jan. 16, 1868.
7. Matthew Roach, m. Phebe Whitman, Oct. 13, 1874.
8. Benjamin Roach, died unmarried.

XI. ELIZABETH,[6] m. NATHANIEL CURRIER; no issue.

69.

ISAAC[5] CHURCHILL (ISAAC,[4] BARNABAS,[3] JOSEPH[2] JOHN[1]). Born July 19, 1758, in Boston. He was a sea-faring man and was lost at sea with his son Isaac, aged 16 years. Married SARAH MORTON. She was born in 1757, and was descended from John[3] Churchill and Desire Holmes, through Priscilla,[4] who married Thomas Rogers, and had daughter Ruth, who married Samuel Morton, and had this Sarah.

Children born at Plymouth.

I. Isaac,⁶ b. 1781. Lost at sea with his father at the age of 16.
II. Sarah,⁶ b. Feb. 11, 1783; m. Jacob Curtis, of Duxbury, Oct. 15, 1805, and d. Oct. 13, 1837.

Children of Jacob and Sarah Churchill Curtis.

1. Sarah M. Curtis, b. Oct. 19, 1806; m. Perez (or Percy) Churchill, of E. Pembroke.
2. Rebecca Churchill Curtis, b. in Duxbury, March 20, 1808; m. James Ford, of Marshfield, and d. 1868.
3. Nancy Elizabeth Curtis, b. in Pembroke, July 27, 1809; m. Natl. Morse, of Duxbury, Feb. 12, 1835. He died in 1884, and she died in 1883.
4. Isaac C. Curtis, b. in Pembroke, May 28, 1811; m. Henrietta Churchill, Nov. 11, 1834.
5. William S. Curtis, b. in Pembroke, Jan. 31, 1813; m. Nancy S. Hunt, March 2, 1834, and d. 1872.
. Jacob Curtis, b. in Duxbury, Dec. 23, 1814. Lost at sea, 1833.
6. James Bird Curtis, b. March 25, 1817; m. 1st, Eliza T. White; m. 2d, Eveline T. Whiting, of Pembroke. James died in New Orleans, 1863.
8. Geo. R. Curtis, d. in infancy.
9. Meribah K. Curtis, b. in Duxbury, February, 1820; m. John T. Hunt, of Duxbury, November, 1838.
10. Hannah Curtis, b. Feb. 23, 1822; m. Briggs Paulding, of Duxbury, 1843.
11. Elizabeth R. Curtis, b. April 11, 1825; m. Daniel Delano, Aug. 31, 1847.

179 III. Timothy,⁶ b. 1785; m. Olive Curtis, of Marshfield; married in Duxbury, 1807.
IV. Rebecca,⁶ b. Oct. 17, 1787. Lived in Plymouth; d. unmarried, in Sandwich, Sept. 2, 1872.
180 V. Seth,⁶ b. 1790; m. Sarah S. Johnson, and d. 1816.
VI. Nancy,⁶ b. July 19, 1792; m. Samuel Chipman, of Barnstable, April 25, 1815. They were married in Plymouth and lived in Barnstable. She d. April 4, 1883.

Children born in Barnstable.

1. Nancy Chipman, d. in infancy.
2. Elizabeth Chipman, b. Oct. 10, 1817; m. Lemuel Nye, of Sandwich, Dec. 6, 1838; no issue.
3. Nancy Chipman, b. April 16, 1820; m. John S. Fiske, of Sandwich, Oct. 10, 1844.
4. William Churchill Chipman, b. Feb. 27, 1822; m. Love E. Nye, Jan. 4, 1849.
5. Samuel Chipman, b. Dec. 22, 1823; unmarried.
6. Isaac Kimball Chipman, b. March 9, 1826; m. Melinda N. Fiske, of Sandwich, Nov. 29, 1849.
7. James Chipman, b. Jan. 2, 1828; d. in Sandwich, April 20, 1850.

VII. William,⁶ b. 1794; d. unmarried about 1816.

71.

THOMAS⁵ CHURCHILL (Thomas,⁴ Barnabas,³ Joseph,² John¹). Born at Newmarket Plains, N.H., 1762, and lived there. He served in the war of the Revolution in the Company of Capt. Jacob Webster, Colonel Reynolds' Regiment of N.H. militia. He is credited with service in 1778 and again from Sept. 25 to Nov. 25, 1781. For the first term of service, he in common with other soldiers received from the New Hampshire authorities " twenty-five bushels of corn per month in full for three months' service." He died in 1807. Married, at Stratham, N.H., 1786, ALICE CREIGH-TON, daughter of James, born Oct. 13, 1767, and died April 10 1850.

Children born in Newmarket.

181   I. JAMES CREIGHTON,[6] b. April 24, 1787; m. ELIZA WALKER OS-BORNE."
      II. THOMAS,[6] b. April 4, 1791; d. unmarried in early manhood.
      III. ELIZABETH H.,[6] b. Sept. 2, 1799; m. SOLOMON PENDERGAST, Nov. 1, 1821.
      He was of Newmarket and they lived there.

Their Children born at Newmarket.

1. Nathaniel Pendergast, died, leaving no family.
2. Roswell H. Pendergast, b. Jan. 10, 1832; m. Helen L. Parker, April 16, 1858.
      They removed to the West, and settled at Newton, Iowa.
      Children, (1) Alice E. Pendergast, b. Feb. 10, 1860; d. Sept. 21, 1863; (2) Allan E. Pendergast, b. Jan. 3, 1862; d. Sept. 27, 1862; (3) Nettie M., b. April 6, 1863, d. Aug. 23, 1863; (4) Frederick N. Pendergast, b. July 8, 1864; (5) Charles Riley Pendergast, b. Sept. 4, 1865, d. Sept. 21, 1865; (6) Nellie B. Pendergast, b. Dec. 21, 1866; (7) Charles L. Pendergast b. May 12, 1873, d. Aug. 2, 1873; (8) Herbert L. Pendergast, b. April 11, 1878, d. Aug. 14, 1878; (9) Roy H. Pendergast, b. Feb. 10, 1880, d. Aug. 5, 1880.

72·

ICHABOD[5] CHURCHILL (THOMAS,[4] BARNABAS,[3] JOSEPH[2] JOHN[1]). Born at Newmarket Plains, N.H., June 24, 1764. He lived at Parsonsfield, Me., a farmer and shoemaker. " The Oxford County Record," published at Kezar Falls, Me., in the issue of Dec. 26, 1885, has a sketch of " Father Churchill," from which account it appears that he settled at Parsonsfield as early as 1798, and cleared and cultivated the farm, which his grandson Nathaniel Churchill owned and occupied in 1885. He is described as a push-ing, prosperous man, kind and benevolent, but withal somewhat eccentric. He was quite notable for his peculiar religious ideas and practices. He believed that he was under the special guidance of the Holy Spirit and, it is said, obeyed every impulse promptly, with-out consulting his reason. The sketch contains several amusing anecdotes illustrative of his peculiar traits. He died Sept. 15, 1855. First wife died Nov. 23, 1809. Second wife died Sept. 3, 1858. Married 1st, ELIZABETH DOE, born 1769. and 2d, LEAH ALLEN, Oct. 2, 1810. No children by last.

Children of the First Wife.

I. NICHOLAS,[6] b. June 3, 1790; d. unmarried, Aug. 10, 1845.
II. BETSEY,[6] b. March 27, 1793; d. unmarried, March 30, 1877.
III. JOHN,[6] b. Sept. 22, 1795; d. unmarried, Oct. 5, 1873.
182   IV. THOMAS,[6] b. Jan. 20, 1798; m. MARY BANKS, March 14, 1830; d. Oct. 16, 1878.
V. MARY,[6] b. Jan. 24, 1801; m. ROBINSON BLAISDELL, of Eaton, N.H. Dec. 29, 1830. Mary d. May 4, 1865. He d. Feb. 27, 1867.

They had three Children.

1. Nicholas Blaisdell, b. March 29, 1832; m. Martha C. Hood, of Somerville, Feb. 21, 1867.
2. Elizabeth Ann Blaisdell, b. Sept. 5, 1834. Lives in Boston, Mass.
3. Mary Melvina Blaisdell, b. Sept. 11, 1839; d. unmarried, Dec. 4, 1863.

VI. NANCY,[6] b. Oct. 9, 1803; m. GREENLEAF SMITH, of Cornish, Me. They lived at Cornish. He was a tanner. He d. 1867; she d. 1877.

Children born in Cornish.

1. Thomas Churchill Smith, b. Aug. 14, 1825; m. Mary Louisa Trafton, May 30, 1847.
2. John Franklin Smith, b. July 26, 1828; m. Mary Barker Chadbourne, March 4, 1852.
3. Henry Hyde Smith, b. Feb. 2, 1832; m. Mary Sherborn Dana, Dec. 24, 1861.
4. Roscoe Greenough Smith, b. April 4, 1836; m. Sarah Pingree Robinson, July 6, 1861.
5. Annie Clark Smith, b. Dec. 28, 1841; d July 19, 1846.

73.

JOSEPH[5] CHURCHILL (THOMAS,[4] BARNABAS,[3] JOSEPH,[2] JOHN[1]). Born in Newmarket, N.H., May 7, 1768; died in Brookfield, N.H., March 4, 1824. He was a farmer in Newmarket and Brookfield, N.H. Married, in Newmarket, 1794, SALLY TASH, of Lee, N.H.

Children, the first three born in Newmarket, the rest in Brookfield, N.H.

183   I. JOHN TASH,[6] b. Aug. 6, 1796; m. MEHITABLE GILMAN WILLEY, March 5, 1817.
184   II. JOSEPH TASH,[6] b. April 18, 1798; m. MARTHA M. WIGGIN, Sept. 1, 1824.
185   III. THOMAS TASH,[6] b. Aug. 26, 1800; m. 1st, ANN WENTWORTH; m. 2d, EUNICE KING.
186   IV. EBENEZER CHAPMAN,[6] b. Nov. 11, 1802; m. ANN E. GOVE, of Portsmouth.
V. SARAH TASH,[6] b. March 4, 1805; m. REV. SAMUEL NUTT.
187   VI. NATHANIEL,[6] b. April 2, 1807; m. SOPHIA K. KING.
VII. MARY A.,[6] b. March 26, 1809; unmarried.
188 VIII. DANIEL,[6] b. Dec. 3, 1811; m. ELEANOR LONGLEY, of Lee, N.H.
189   IX. CHARLES,[6] b. April 3, 1814; m. IRENE PURINGTON.
X. BETSEY TASH,[6] b. May 14, 1816; m. CYRUS C. PICKERING, Newmarket, N.H.

They lived at Manchester, N.H., and had Child.

1. James W. Churchill Pickering, b. Sept. 1, 1844; m. 1st, Julia T. Dow, at Woburn, Mass., and had children (1) Herbert Dow Pickering, b. April 23, 1870; (2) Josephine Belle Pick-

ering, b. June 24, 1872; (3) Harry Edward Pickering, b. Nov. 18, 1874; (4) Nellie Gertrude Pickering, b. March 28, 1876; (5) James William Churchill Pickering, Jr., b. May 21, 1878; d. Dec. 16, 1880. Mr. Pickering, Sr., m. 2d, Mary E. Bacon, of Waltham, but had no children by this marriage.

190   XI. JAMES MONROE,[6] b. Jan. 3, 1819; m. ELIZABETH PERKINS, of Exeter, N.H.

191   XII. WILLIAM,[6] b. Aug. 8, 1821; m. ELIZABETH KITTREDGE, of Lowell, Mass.

74.

NATHANIEL [5] CHURCHILL (THOMAS,[4] BARNABAS,[3] JOSEPH,[2] JOHN [1]). Born March 31, 1772. He lived in Brookfield and Eaton, N.H. He was a farmer and a deacon of the church. Married 1st, PATIENCE TASH (sister of Sally, his brother Joseph's wife); Patience died May 13, 1803; 2d, POLLY JACKSON.

Children of First Wife.

I. HOLLIS,[6] b. Aug. 20, 1801; m. MARY J. LATHERS; no children.
II. POLLY,[6] b. Feb. 24, 1803; d. in infancy, buried with her mother, in Brookfield.

Children of Second Wife.

III. JAMES, E.[6], b. Nov. 16, 1805; m. CAROLINE MARCH, 1829; both d. October, 1831.
   One daughter, Mary Emmeline, was reared by her grandparents.

192   IV. THOMAS C.,[6] b. Feb. 26, 1807; m. EMMELINE S. BAILEY, Bridg-ton, March 20, 1834.
    V. SALLY,[6] b. Oct. 9, 1809; m. 1st, J. LANGDON MARCH; m. 2d, AMOS TOWLE.

Children.

1. John L. March, b. June 12, 1831.
2. Abby March, d. young.
3. Edwin March, d. young.
4. Mary Ann March, d. young.

By the Second Husband.

5. Elizabeth Towle. | 6. Sarah Towle.

193   VI. JOHN,[6] b. June 17, 1811; m. MELISSA COLBY or CROSBY.
194   VII. NATHANIEL,[6] b. July 1, 1818; m. ELIZABETH GOLDTHWAIT, Nov. 4, 1841.
195   VIII. ICHABOD D.,[6] b. Sept. 29, 1845; m. 1st, CLARA QUINT; m. 2d, SARAH D. LORD.

75.

JOHN [5] CHURCHILL (THOMAS,[4] BARNABAS,[3] JOSEPH,[2] JOHN [1]). Born May 11, 1776. They lived in Deerfield, N.H. Married, Nov. 14, 1799, SALLY TRUE.

Children.

196   I. WILLIAM GRAVES,[6] b. July 29, 1809; m. SALLY MEAD PAGE.
    II. JOHN T. B.,[6] b. Sept. 23, 1816; d. unmarried in Washington, D.C., 1841.
   He died from the effects of a wound received in the war of the Rebellion.

76.

JOHN[5] CHURCHILL (EBENEZER,[4] BARNABAS,[3] JOSEPH,[2] JOHN[1]). Born in Plymouth, June 23, 1763.. His boyhood was passed at Plymouth, where he was engaged with his elders in fishing in the season. The year he was aged ten he earned $36.67 as his share of the catch of codfish. He was industrious and frugal, making the most of his chances of work and education. At fifteen years he went to Pittsfield and there worked on a farm by the month for three years, and then bought a farm of forty acres of Mr. James. He was strenuous, honest, and of good judgment, and these qualities made him a man of property and influence in the community, and he represented his town many times in the General Court of Boston. He died in Pittsfield, June 8, 1849. Married, 1788, in Pittsfield, MEHITABLE HUBBARD, of that town, born Dec. 17, 1767, and died Aug. 29, 1843.

Their Children born in Pittsfield.

I. MARTHA,[6] b. Aug. 20, 1789; m. CAPT. DANIEL MERRIMAN, of Pittsfield, Dec. 4, 1826. Captain Merriman was born in Dalton, Mass., June 23, 1777, and died in Pittsfield, June 3, 1850. They lived in Hinsdale for some years and their children were born there, viz.:

1. John Churchill Merriman, b. May 2, 1828; d. Dec. 21, 1849.
2. Clark Spencer Merriman, b. Sept. 26, 1829; m. Harriet Maria Mullen, of Binghamton, N.Y., b. March 22, 1832, and had, (1) Fannie Myra Merriman, b. at Osborn Hollow, N.Y., April 6, 1854; m. Lyman Chester Beebe, of Union, N.Y., May 6, 1873, and had two children born in Alton, Iowa: Clark Talmadge Beebe, b. Sept. 24, 1874, and Frank Chester Beebe, b. April 3, 1879.
3. Daniel Watson Merriman, b. Feb. 18, 1831; d. in Pittsfield, Nov. 4, 1849.
4. Wheelock Seymour Merriman, b. May 20, 1833; m. Mary E. Smith, of Pennsylvania, 1866.

II. JOHN,[6] b. July 5, 1791; d. Aug. 2, 1791.
III. SOPHIA,[6] b. July 25, 1792; m. LINUS PARKER, Oct. 12, 1815. Mr. Parker was born in Lenox, Oct. 30, 1790.' They lived in Pittsfield where he was a farmer and proprietor of a sawmill. He d. April 7, 1872, and Sophia d. March 14, 1872. Their children, born in Pittsfield, were:

1. Adelia Mehitable Parker, b. June 16, 1817; m. Buel B. Bull, of Kent, Conn., Sept. 14, 1833, and had at Pittsfield, (1) James Bull, b. May 10, 1838; (2) Mary Ellen Bull, b. March 28, 1842; d. in Lenox, Aug. 30, 1878; (3) Ulyssa Sophia Bull, b. April 22, 1850; m. Anthony Stewart, and had Wayne B. Stewart, Florence A., and Francis T. Stewart; (4) Jane Adelia Bull, b. July 19, 1853; m. Martin Sears, of Lenox, March 8, 1864, and had Frederick DeWitt Sears, Albert Eugene Sears, Robert L. Sears, James Buel Sears, and Clarence Luther Sears, all born between 1863 and 1874, in Lenox.
2. John Churchill Parker, m. 1st, Sarah Fulton, of Milan, N.Y., Sept. 4, 1848. She d. in Milan, Aug. 3, 1855, leaving three children, viz.: John Dwight Parker, b. April 9, 1850; Fulton Churchill Parker b. Aug. 31, 1851; and Sarah Fulton Parker,

b. June 26, 1855, who died nine days after the mother, Aug.
12, 1855. Mr. Parker m. 2d wife, Lydia Goodrich, of Pittsfield, Dec. 8, 1856, and had one child, Carrie Goodrich
Parker, b. March 13. 1861.

3. Jane Elizabeth Parker. b. May 26, 1823; m. Nathl. B. Williams,
of Lebanon, Conn., May 1, 1845, and had children born in
Lebanon, Conn., viz.: (1) Ellen Cornelia Williams, b. May
12, 1846, and (2) Mary Sophia, b. May 3. 1854.

4. Mary Sophia Parker, b. Sept. 30, 1824; m. Dr. John Manning,
of Lebanon, Conn., May 2. 1844. Their children were (1)
John Henry Manning, b. in Ellington. Conn., July 23, 1846;
m. Grace LeBaron Washburn, of Lenox. Mass., June 1, 1870,
and had Love LeBaron Manning, b. in Lenox, Nov. 11, 1871;
Franklin Washburn Manning, b. in Pittsfield, July 28, 1874;
Anna Parker Manning, b. in Pittsfield, Nov. 25, 1875, and
John Parker Manning, b. in Pittsfield, March 23, 1879; (2)
Mary Ellen Manning, b. in Ellington. Conn., July 30, 1848;
(3) Emily King Manning. b. in Pittsfield, Sept. 9, 1856; (4)
Jennie Augusta Manning, b. April 18, 1858.

5. Edwin Linus Parker, b. July 24, 1827: m. Jane Eliza Green, of
Pittsfield, Oct. 14, 1855. Lived in Pittsfield, and had children born there, viz.: (1) George Dwight Parker, b. June 11,
1857; (2) Lemuel Green Parker; and (3) Linus Root Parker,
twins, b. June 3, 1858 (the latter d. Sept. 27, 1858); (4)
Jennie Sophia Parker, b. Aug. 14, 1859; d. Sept. 27, 1859;
(5) Fannie Jane Parker, b. April 2, 1861; (6) Ella Gertrude
Parker. b. June, 1867; (7) Sarah Churchill Parker, b. July
15, 1873.

. James Dwight Parker, b. Aug. 31, 1829; d. Dec. 30, 1837.

6. Marilla Frances Parker, b. May 15, 1831; m. Henry Chapman,
of Pittsfield, Jan. 31, 1850. They had born in Pittsfield, (1)
Henry Temple Chapman, b. Jan. 21, 1852; m. Lucy Lapham,
of Adams, August, 1871. She d. in 1875, and he m. 2d, Mary
Overhalster, of Peach Grove, Tenn., in 1877.

8. Frederick Sereno Parker, b. May 29, 1833; m. Cynthia Bourne,
of Lenox, Jan. 1, 1856, and had children born in Pittsfield,
viz.: (1) Frederick Bourne Parker, b. May 10, 1860; d. Aug.
9, 1860; (2) Susan Cutting Parker, b. Oct. 3, 1861; (3)
Minnie Adelle Parker, b. April 19, 1864; (4) Frederick
Bourne Parker, b. June 24, 1865; d. Aug. 15, 1865; (5)
Dwight Bourne Parker, b. May 20, 1870; d. Aug. 2, 1871;
(6) Alice Bell Parker, b. March 20, 1873.

9. Ella Maria Parker, b. April 23, 1836; d. Dec. 31, 1837.

197 IV. Charles,[6] b. Feb. 25, 1796; m. Charlotte M. Francis, Dec. 4,
1826.

V. Laura,[6] b. July 5, 1797; m. Wells Fowler, of Fowlersville,
N.Y., 1839. No further record found.

VI. Lucy,[6] b. June 12, 1799; m. Almeron D. Francis, of Pittsfield,
April 29, 1829. They lived in Pittsfield and had children born
there.

1. Lucy Maria Francis, b. June 12, 1830; d. Jan. 29, 1838.

2. Henry Martin Francis, b. Aug. 3, 1835; d. June 20, 1845.

3. James Dwight Francis, b. Dec. 23, 1837; m. 1st, Martha J.
Tower, June 5, 1859; m. 2d, Annie M. Fabricius, Sept. 29, 1886.
They lived in Pittsfield and had children born there, viz.: (1)
Henry Almeron Francis, b. Oct. 6, 1861; (2) George Dwight
Francis, b. Jan. 22. 1866; d. March 27, 1886; (3) Frederick
Tower Francis, b. Nov. 21, 1869; (4) Clifford Francis, b.
March 3, 1872; (4) Robert Talcott Francis, b. Dec. 7, 1873.

VII. Jane,[6] b. Nov. 8, 1800; d. unmarried Sept. 22, 1822.

VIII. Frederick,[6] b. Aug. 15, 1802; d. September, 1802.

IX. Sarah Fowler,[6] b. Jan. 27, 1809; m. James Francis, of Pittsfield, June 14, 1832.

They lived in Pittsfield and their children were born there, viz.

1. Edward Stillman Francis, b. Dec. 20, 1835; m. 1st, Elinor H. Tucker, Jan. 13, 1857; m. 2d, Mrs. Delia Buell, of Utica, N.Y. Children, (1) Edward Norman Francis, b. in Shelburne Falls, Dec. 24, 1857; (2) Nellie Agnes Francis, b. in Shelburne Falls, April 14, 1861.
2. James Henry Francis, b. May 5, 1839; m. Francis Porter, of Coventry, Conn., May 8, 1873. They lived in Pittsfield and had (1) Thomas Porter, b. June 8, 1875; d. Aug. 14, 1875; (2) John Ernest Porter, b. Dec. 18, 1877.
3. Charles Churchill Francis, b. Dec. 11, 1841; m. Hattie A. Wood, of New York, March 11, 1868. They lived in Syracuse, N.Y., and had one daughter, (1) Daisy Wood Francis, b. Dec. 3, 1878.

198   X. SAMUEL ADAMS,[6] b. Sept. 28, 1810; m. ESTHER BROOKS, of Lenox, Sept. 23, 1870.

77.

LEMUEL [5] CHURCHILL (JOHN,[4] BARNABAS,[3] JOSEPH,[2] JOHN [1]). Born in Pittsfield, Mass., Feb. 9, 1773. Removed in 1803 to Truxton, N.Y. They moved in an ox-cart, when Sally, the first child, was about six months old, and located on a farm of one hundred acres about three miles north of what is now Truxton Village. He died March 3, 1813. Married, 1802, MINDWELL TILLOTSON, of Lanesboro', born 1773. She died March 6, 1828.

Children, all but first born in Truxton, N.Y.; first born in Massachusetts.
    I. SALLY,[6] b. Sept. 9, 1803; d. unmarried, Sept. 27, 1850.
    II. JOHN,[6] b. Aug. 26, 1805; d. Oct. 18, 1822.
    III. ELIZA,[6] b. Sept. 16, 1807; m. ERASTUS HOLLEY, Oct. 27, 1831.

Children born in Truxton, N.Y.
    1. Curtis D. Holley, b. Sept. 25, 1832.
    2. Arminda E. Holley, b. Feb. 24, 1836; m. Jason W. Crandall, of Truxton, Oct. 22, 1862. Lived in Homer, N.Y.
    3. Frances E. Holley, b. May 8, 1840; d. May 2, 1851.
    4. Marietta Holley, b. June 22, 1846; m. Michael Wiegand, Feb. 8, 1870. They lived at Truxton, N.Y. He was a farmer, son of Charles T. and Clara (Herbert) Wiegand.

Children born in Truxton.
    1. Hattie Arminda Wiegand, b. Dec. 19, 1870; d. Feb. 25, 1871.
    2. Charles Erastus Wiegand, b. Jan. 24, 1872; m. Grace Jones, April 20, 1898.
    3. Minnie Eliza Wiegand, b. July 8, 1874.
    4. Alena May Wiegand, b. Dec. 8, 1879; d. March 31, 1880.
    5. Elmer Jason Wiegand, b. Oct. 11, 1881.

199   IV. ORRIN,[6] b. Feb. 16, 1809; m. 1st, EMMELINE POPE, Feb. 1, 1832; m. 2d, JANE L. PORTER, Nov. 2, 1843. She died Nov. 16, 1854; m. 3d, FRANCES E. RICHARDSON, at Buchanan, Mich., Nov. 3, 1855.
    V. ANNA,[6] b. Sept. 4, 1811; d. unmarried in December, 1856.

78.

JOHN [5] CHURCHILL (JOHN,[4] BARNABAS,[3] JOSEPH,[2] JOHN [1]). Born in Pittsfield, Mass., March 27, 1780, and lived there. Married, 1815, in Pittsfield, HULDA BROWN.

Children born in Pittsfield.

200   I. LEMUEL B.,[6] b. Nov. 24, 1816; m. LYDIA BRADFORD, of Conway, Mass.
       II. THOMAS P.,[6] b. Feb. 18, 1818; unmarried, living in Pittsfield.
       III. JOHN B.,[6] b. March 2, 1819; unmarried, living in Pittsfield.
       IV. SARAH A.,[6] b. May 5, 1820; m. ELISHA JENKS; no children.
       V. MARY,[6] b. June 11, 1821; d. Jan. 19, 1835.
       VI. HULDA,[6] b. Aug. 29, 1822; d. October, 1879; m. 1st, OBADIAH KELLEY, of Pittsfield; m. 2d, RUFUS RICHMOND, of Adams, Mass.

Child by First Husband.
1. Huldah Kelley, died in a few hours.

Children by Second Husband.
2. Mary J. Richmond, b. 1877.
3. Clara K. Richmond, b. Oct. 25, 1879.

       VII. CLARISSA,[6] b. May 2, 1825; m. ALONZO GOODRICH.   No children.

79.

BRADFORD[5] CHURCHILL (JOHN,[4] BARNABAS,[3] JOSEPH,[2] JOHN[1]). Born in Pittsfield, Sept. 13, 1786. Removed to Truxton, N.Y., in 1804. Was a carpenter, and built the Baptist church in Truxton, from the steeple of which he fell and was killed. Married SELINDA ROBBINS, of Pittsfield.

Children.

201   I. ALANSON,[6] b. Sept. 4, 1812; m. ELIZA BURLINGAME, of Lanesboro'
       II. ALMIRA,[6] m. CALEB WARREN, of Dalton.

Child.
1. Caleb Warren, Jr.

       III. LEMUEL,[6] unmarried.

80.

SPENCER[5] CHURCHILL (JOHN,[4] BARNABAS,[3] JOSEPH,[2] JOHN[1]). Born in Pittsfield, Mass., June 10, 1789. Married, Nov. 11, 1820, CLARISSA MURPHY, of Pittsfield.

Child.
       I. HARRIET,[6] b. Feb. 9, 1822; m. ELI V. BEALS, Nov. 2, 1841.

Children.
1. Robert S. Beals, b. Aug. 12, 1842; d. Aug. 31, 1843.
2. Robert S. Beals, } b. Oct. 8, 1843.
3. Abbie C. Beals, }

81.

JOSEPH[5] CHURCHILL (JOSEPH,[4] JOSEPH,[3] JOSEPH,[2] JOHN[1]). Born in Boston, Sept. 19, 1745; died in Boston, Dec. 21, 1807. They settled first in Salem, about 1768, but before 1774 removed to Wells, Me. At Wells he raised a company, at his own expense, and joined Benedict Arnold in the expedition to Canada, but having some trouble with Arnold, he withdrew his company. He afterwards served as lieutenant in Capt. James Hubbard's Company, Col. Ephraim Doolittle's Regiment. Company's return dated at camp on Winter Hill, Oct. 10, 1775. In 1783 he removed to Boston, and kept a public house on Exchange street. He was a Freemason, and Master, for a time, of Columbia Lodge, of Boston. He married ANNE NORTHY, daughter of David, of Marblehead. She was born 1745, and died in Bristol, R.I., July, 1822.

Children.

I. JOSEPH,[6] b. in Salem, 1771/2. Went to sea and never returned.
II. NEHEMIAH, b. in Salem; died young.
202 III. BENJAMIN KING, b. in Wells, Me., July 13, 1774; m. 1st, CLARISSA EATON; m. 2d, ELIZABETH HOLMAN.
IV. DAVID NORTHY, b. in Boston. Probably lost at sea.

82.

JOHN[5] CHURCHILL (JOSEPH,[4] JOSEPH,[3] JOSEPH,[2] JOHN[1]). Born in 1748, in Salem, and lived there until 1775/6. Then settled in New Salem. Is said to have served in the war of the Revolution. Perhaps he was in Lieut. James Hubbard's Company, Aug. 17 to Aug. 23, 1777. In 1796 he removed to Benson, Vt., where he died Aug. 23, 1798. Married, 1773, SARAH STACY, of Salem. She was born in 1752, and after the death of her husband moved from Benson, Vt., to Mooers, N.Y., with her family, and there died, May 29, 1830.

Children born, the first in Salem, the rest in New Salem.

203 I. JOHN,[6] b. March 27, 1774; m. HANNAH SCHRIVER, dau. of Frederick, of Hemingford, Can.
204 II. JOSEPH,[6] b. Jan. 18, 1776; m. SUSANNAH BAILEY, in Chazy, N.Y.
III. MARY,[6] b. Dec. 21, 1777; m. DANIEL SOUTHWICK, of Benson, Vt., Oct. 5, 1797.
They removed to Mooers, N.Y., in 1802. She died there March 31, 1831. Mr. Southwick was born June 11, 1773, and died Jan. 15, 1839.

Children born at Mooers, N. Y.

1. Philetus E. Southwick, b. Nov. 7, 1802; m. Eliza Stacey, of Benson, Vt., 1827, and d. 1864.
2. Maria M. Southwick, b. Aug. 6, 1804; m. Abel Knapp, of Mooers, N.Y., Aug. 13, 1826; d. Aug. 25, 1874.
3. Almeda Southwick, b. July 4, 1810; m. Solon Knapp, 1838, and moved to Ottawa, Ill.
4. Royal Southwick, b. Feb. 7, 1813; m. Lydia R. Child, of Somerset, N.Y., June 13, 1841

IV. SARAH,[6] b. May 17, 1780; m. JOSHUA C. BOSWORTH, in Mooers, N.Y., 1806. She died in Mooers, March 3, 1853. He was born June 25, 1775, and died Feb. 14, 1860.

Children born at Mooers, N. Y.

1. Franklin C. Bosworth, b. 1809.
2. Chester Bosworth, b. Dec. 24, 1819.
   Two daughters died in infancy.

205   V. SAMUEL,[6] b. Aug. 8, 1782; m. MARTHA L. BOSWORTH, Feb. 8,
            1814; d. Feb. 23, 1865.
206   VI. JEREMIAH,[6] b. 1785; m. MARY FROST.
     VII. ELIZABETH,[6] b. 1787; m. (———) PYNCHON.
            She died leaving one daughter, but the father removed to the
          West with her, and all trace is lost in her mother's family.

   VIII. AGNES,[6] b. April 21, 1789; m. ISAAC FITCH, 1806. She died
          April 3, 1868. He was born Aug. 2, 1786, and died Oct. 1, 1851.

Children born at Mooers, N. Y.

1. James Fitch, b. 1807; m. Harriet Perry, of Champlain.

Children.

Marcellus, Emmett, Elmer, Katharine, Wilmer, Francis.

2. Jabez Fitch, b. Aug. 18, 1809; m. and settled in Ottawa, Ill.;
   d. 1851.
3. Jeremiah Fitch, b. July 7, 1811; d. 1811.
4. Julius Fitch, b. Aug. 21, 1812; settled in Rockford, Ill ; d.
   1879.
5. Joel Fitch, b. May 7, 1815; settled in Clinton, Ia.
6. Matilda C. Fitch, b. Aug. 20, 1817; m. Rev. Hiram Dunn.
7. Isaac Fitch, b. Jan. 20, 1820; d. February, 1843.
8. Maria Fitch, b. Jan. 21, 1822; m. (———) Brewster; lived in
   Ottawa, Ill.; d. 1890.
9. Pliny Fitch, b. Jan. 22, 1824; d. February, 1850.
10. Aurelia Fitch, b. April 9, 1826; d. June 9, 1832.
11. Alvah Fitch, b. Feb. 15, 1828; settled in Franklin Grove, Ill.
12. Susannah Fitch, b. Nov. 13, 1830; m. Dr. Joel Chandler; d. in
    1875, and left ten children.

   IX. DEBORAH,[6] b. Nov. 11, 1794; m. JONAS PARKER, Sept. 1, 1810;
          she d. Feb. 2, 1879.

Children born in Mooers, N. Y.

1. Sophia Parker, b. Dec. 11, 1812; m. John Henry, Feb. 15,
   1838. Lives in Keene, N.Y.
2. Eliza Parker, b. Feb. 7, 1815; m. Joseph Dumont, Sept. 10,
   1833.
3. Chauncy Parker, b. April 30, 1817; m. Melissa Eaton, 1840.
4. Isaac F. Parker, b. Nov. 4, 1818; m. Julia A. Tracy, Dec. 13,
   1842.
5. Edgar Alonzo Parker, b. Oct. 4, 1820; m. Mary E. Brewster,
   Oct. 5, 1845.
6. Jeremiah Churchill Parker, b. Aug. 4, 1823; d. unmarried, Nov.
   6, 1849.
7. Paschal Pevlah Parker, b. March 10, 1826; m. 1st, Miriam Mc-
   Ewer, Nov. 19, 1850; m. 2d, Martha McEwer, Jan. 7, 1852.

83.

SAMUEL [5] CHURCHILL (SAMUEL,[4] JOSEPH,[3] JOSEPH,[2] JOHN [1]).
Born in Lancaster, Oct. 20, 1749. He served in the Revolution, in
the Lancaster Company, Capt. Samuel Sawyer, Col. John Whitcomb's Regiment Minute-men, 1775. Corporal also under same

captain, marched to New York in Col. Jonathan Smith's Regiment, July to December, 1776. Married, March 6, 1781, REBECCA WILDER, of Sterling.

Children.

207   I. JOHN,[6] b. July 7, 1782; m. DOLLY MEARS, of Sterling, Dec. 12, 1813.
       II. REBECCA,[6] b. June 2, 1786; m. LEVI WELLINGTON, of Worcester, Aug. 16, 1819.

Child.

1. Samuel Torrey Wellington.

III. SAMUEL, JR.,[6] b. Oct. 24, 1788; d. unmarried, Jan. 31, 1827.
IV. SALLY,[6] b. Oct. 31, 1791; m. JOHN BURGESS, of Groton, Jan. 1, 1833. She died Jan. 12, 1862, leaving no issue.

84.

ELIEZER[5] CHURCHILL (ELIEZER,[4] ELIEZER,[3] ELIEZER,[2] JOHN[1]). Born in Plymouth, Oct. 31, 1744. Lived in Bridgewater and Abington; was a shoemaker. Married 1st, Sept. 27, 1764, MRS. JANE (SYLVESTER) RIDER; married 2d, Feb. 12, 1776, ABIGAIL BARTLETT.

Children by First Wife.

208   I. ELIEZER,[6] b. 1766; m. LUCY OTIS, of Scituate, Jan. 27, 1788.
       II. CHARLES,[6] m. JEDIDAH HAWES, May 24, 1794. No record.
      III. DEBORAH,[6] m. ELIEZER ALDEN, Jan. 1, 1797

Children.

1. Lewis Alden.   3. Rebecca Alden.
2. Isaac Alden.

Child by Second Wife.

IV. JANE,[6] b. 1777; m. 1st, ELISHA LINCOLN, Nov. 13, 1803; m. 2d, (———) HASKELL; lived in South Bridgewater.

87.

THADDEUS[5] CHURCHILL (ELIEZER,[4] ELIEZER,[3] ELIEZER,[2] JOHN[1]). Born Nov. 29, 1745. Lived in Plymouth, probably in the south part of the town. In 1803 he owned a half of old house known as the "Chandler House." Married, Dec. 3, 1774, ASENATH DELANO.

Children born in Plymouth.

209   I. THADDEUS,[6] b. March 23, 1776; m. MERCY FULLER, Nov. 11, 1798.
       II. PATIENCE,[6] m. SOLOMON FINNEY, Nov. 9, 1797. Moved to Chillicothe, O.
      III. WILLIAM,[6] m. MRS. MARTHA (ALBERTSON) HARLOW, May 24, 1807. She was the dau. of Jacob Albertson and the widow of Amaziah Harlow.
210   IV. JOSEPH,[6] b. 1782; m. 1st, MERCY LEBARON GOODWIN, July 28, 1804; m. 2d, LYDIA LEBARON GOODWIN, Oct. 19, 1823.
        V. ASENATH,[6] m. CAPT. JOHN PATY, March 25, 1802.

88

SAMUEL [5] CHURCHILL, (JOSIAH,[4] ELIEZER,[3] ELIEZER,[2] JOHN [1]). Born in Plymouth, July 10, 1754. Served in the war of the Revolution, probably in Capt. Jesse Harlow's Company of Minute-men on Alarm of April 19, 1775. Perhaps the pensioner of 1831. Married, Dec. 14, 1776, ELIZABETH CHURCHILL, daughter of Amaziah (No. 37).

Children.

211   I. SAMUEL,[6] b. May 3, 1779; m. NANCY COVINGTON, Nov. 8, 1801.
212   II. CALEB,[6] b. March 25, 1782; m. LYDIA GREENOLD.
      III. MENDALL,[6] b. April 13, 1786; m. MARY (———). Lost at sea.
      IV. LUCY,[6] b. June 24, 1788; m. ZECHARIAH RHODES, Nov. 6, 1804. They removed to and resided in Maryland.

Child.

1. Lucy Rea Rhodes, b. Oct. 28, 1822, at Joppa Mills, Md.; m. Wm. S. Thompson, M.D., at Catonville, Md.

     V. HENRY,[6] b. July 29, 1790; d. young; unmarried.
    VI. DEBORAH,[6] b. Aug. 12, 1793; m. JOSEPH VOSE, of Stoughton, Nov. 30, 1815.

Children.

1. Henry Clay Vose, b. Oct. 6, 1816; m. Rachel Wild Faxon, of Braintree, Nov. 6, 1839

Children of Henry C. and Rachel Vose.

1. Francis Henry Vose, b. at Taunton, Aug. 9, 1840; d. Sept. 27, 1840.
2. Clifton Henry Vose, b. at Rochester, April 1, 1842; d. in Rebel Prison, S.C., Oct. 27, 1864.
3. George Mendell Vose, b. Watertown, May 22, 1847; d. April 1, 1849
4. Thomas French Vose, b. Watertown, Jan. 24, 1849; d. Feb. 13, 1850.
5. Edwin Faxon Vose, b. Watertown, Oct. 17, 1850.
6. Albert Churchill Vose, b. Clinton, N.Y., April 26, 1853.
7. Frederick Parkhurst Vose, b. Marion, Mass., Jan 13, 1855; d. Feb. 23, 1880.
8. Agnes Allen Vose, b. Marion, Mass., Jan. 13, 1855; d. Feb. 23, 1880.

2. Almira Churchill Vose, b. May 5, 1818; m. Stephen A. Cornish of Taunton.

Children.

1. Henry A. Cornish.   4. Ellen Cornish.
2. Oscar W. Cornish.   5. Esther A. Cornish.
3. Emma Cornish.

3. Elizabeth Churchill Vose, b. Aug. 6, 1820; m. Samuel Bennett, of New Bedford.

Children.

1. Elizabeth Churchill Bennett.
2. Carrie Morton Bennett.

4. Jeremiah Mendall Vose, b. Oct. 9, 1822; m. Eliza Frances
Calder, of Providence, Aug. 5, 1856. They lived in Providence. He died in Providence, Nov. 6, 1896, and she died
there April 21, 1895.

Children.

. Annie Hill Vose, b. March 5, 1857; d. June 27, 1857.
. William Calder Vose, b. June 5, 1858; d. Jan. 22, 1865.
Joseph Mendall Vose, b. Oct. 5, 1860.
4: Alice Churchill Vose, b. Sept. 5, 1863; m. Frank Smith,
Jan. 25, 1899.
5. Eliza Spencer Vose, b. Nov. 18, 1865.
6. Eleanor Calder Vose, b. June 8, 1871; d. July 29, 1871.

5. Esther Collins Vose, b. Nov. 24, 1824; m. Albert Johnson, of
Stoughton.
One child only, who died in infancy.
6. Lydia Vose, d. young.
7. Lydia Churchill Vose, b. Feb. 4, 1829; m. Putnam D. Nichols,
of Taunton, and had Edwin Vose Nichols and Louisa Putnam
Nichols.
8. Seth Morton Vose, b. Aug. 5, 1831; m. Mary Branch, of Providence, Feb. 2, 1854. They lived in Seekonk, Providence,
and South Attleboro' and had

Children.

1. Mary Lee Vose, b. in Seekonk, May 9, 1855; m. Wilmot L.
Warren, of Springfield.
2. Lizzie Churchill Vose, b. in Providence, June 24, 1857; d.
June 20, 1863.
3. Carrie Morton Vose, b. in Providence, April 26, 1859; d.
June 30, 1863.
4. Mattie Edwards Vose, b. in Providence, July 6, 1864; m.
Horace Churchill Thompson, of Phœnix, Md., June 8,
1887.
5. Robert Churchill Vose, b. South Attleboro', Sept. 12, 1873.
6. Nathaniel Morton Vose, b. South Attleboro', May 5, 1879.

9. Joseph Alonzo Vose, b. May 13, 1833; m. Maria Allen, of
Providence.

Children.

1. Isabella Morton Vose.
2. Frederick Churchill Vose.
3. Philip Mendelsohn Vose.
4. Clifton Henry Vose.
5. Grace Vose.

VII. ESTHER,[6] b. March 17, 1795; m. SAMUEL AVERY COLLINS, Oct. 7,
1816. They lived in Easton, Randolph, and Taunton, Mass.

Children.

1. George Thacher Collins, b. in Easton, Jan. 13, 1819; m. Sophronia Tougee, of Warwick, R.I.
2. Lucy Rhodes Collins, b. in Randolph, Feb. 20, 1821; m. John
Tilton Carter, April 26, 1843.

Children.

1. Melinda Eliot Carter, b. May 18, 1845; d. March 11, 1847.
2. John Avery Carter, b. June 18, 1847; m. Elizabeth Frye Kilborn; no children.
3. Annie Weston Carter, b. Dec. 14, 1852; m. James Edgar
Cook, May 28, 1879.
4. George Tilton Carter, b. Feb. 18, 1855; m. Elizabeth Bertha
Matthews, Dec. 19, 1884.

3. Adelia Collins, b. April 15, 1823; d. young.
4. Samuel Avery Collins, b. Aug. 18, 1826; m. Mary Covington, of Middleboro'. He was a minister, and (May 16, 1877) lived in Cincinnati.
5. Adelia Relief Collins, b. July 22, 1829; m. James Powers Shipley, of Taunton, July 22, 1852.
6. Caleb Collins, b. March 13, 1831; m. Laura Augusta Walker, of Dighton, Dec. 5, 1855.
7. Mary Elizabeth Collins, b. in Taunton, Oct. 2, 1834; m. John S. Pinkerton, of Central Falls, R.I., May 29, 1860, and had

Children.

1. Henry William Pinkerton.
2. Elizabeth Esther Pinkerton.

8. Henry Erastus Collins, b. March 1, 1837; m. Mary Perry, July, 1860.

Children.

1. Clara Collins. | 3. Edward Collins.
2. Marion Collins. |

89.

ENOS [5] CHURCHILL (JOSIAH,[4] ELIEZER,[3] ELIEZER,[2] JOHN [1]). Born at Plymouth, Mass., March 10, 1759. Died 1834. Married, March 13, 1792, MARY PAINE, at Ragged Islands, Nova Scotia. She died in 1857.

Children.

213   I. ENOS,[6] b. at Ragged Islands, April 9, 1797; m. ABIGAIL LOCKE, of Ragged Islands.
      II. ELIZABETH.[6]
      III. MARY.[6]
      IV. PATIENCE.[6]

90.

SYLVANUS [5] CHURCHILL (JOSIAH,[4] ELIEZER,[3] ELIEZER,[2] JOHN [1]). Born in Plymouth, Jan. 23, 1766. Died April 25, 1847. Married, Sept. 22, 1797, LYDIA CHURCHILL, daughter of Wilson (No. 105). She died Aug. 13, 1854.

Children.

      I. SILVANUS,[6] b. Jan. 23, 1802; d. in infancy, Sept. 25, 1802.
214   II. SILVANUS,[6] b. Sept. 25, 1805; m. 1st, LYDIA RUSSELL, of New Bedford, 1836; m. 2d, ELIZA W. GIFFORD, of New Bedford, 1843.
      III. HIRAM,[6] b. Oct. 10, 1807; m. ELIZABETH ASHLEY, of New Bedford, no issue.
      IV. THOMAS GILMAN,[6] b. Dec. 30, 1809; m. 1st, MERCY J. WELLS, of Wells, Me.; m. 2d, MARGARET GREENWOOD; no issue.
      V. BENJAMIN,[6] b. April 23, 1812; unmarried.
      VI. JOSIAH W.,[6] b. March 23, 1815; d. unmarried, Jan. 18, 1885.
215   VII. JOHN D.,[6] b. Nov. 8, 1817; m. 1st, MARIA J. HOLMES, dau. of Thomas, April 1840; m. 2d, JULIA A. HAWLEY, December, 1883.

91.

JONATHAN [5] CHURCHILL (JONATHAN,[4] ELIEZER,[3] ELIEZER,[2] JOHN [1]). Born May 18, 1744, in Plymouth. He served in the Revolution in Captain Wadsworth's Company, May 2, 1775, to Aug. 1, 1775 three months, and again in Capt. Nathaniel Goodwin's Company, 1777 ; both companies in Colonel Cotton's Plymouth Regiment. In the United States pension files he is reported as having received a pension of $96 a year from April 16, 1818, to Dec. 6, 1830, when he died, aged 87 years. Married, Nov. 26, 1767, in Hingham, Mass., LYDIA GILBERT, and their home was in or near Hingham until after the war, when they removed to West Fairlee, Vt., where he spent the rest of his days.

Children born at or near Hingham.

  I. OLIVE,[6] b. Oct. 26, 1768.
  II. MERCY,[6] b. July 22, 1770.
  III. GILBERT.[6]
     He lived in later years at Burlington, Vt., unmarried, and is reported by an aged person of that town who knew him as having been a remarkable man.
  IV. HANNAH, m. JONATHAN WOODS.
  V. JOHN, died unmarried.
     No further account of this family has been obtained. — *Editor.*

92.

JESSE[5] CHURCHILL (JONATHAN,[4] ELIEZER,[3] ELIEZER,[2] JOHN[1]). Born in Plymouth, Oct. 30, 1746. He was a "master mariner." He served in the Revolution in Company of Capt. Nathaniel Goodwin, Colonel Cotton's Plymouth Regiment, Sept. 25, 1777, to Oct. 31, 1777. Service, one month six days, on a secret expedition to Newport, R.I. He lived at Plymouth till quite late in life, when he removed to Ohio, and there died, probably near Cincinnati, Dec. 16, 1831. Married, in Newburyport, Oct. 5, 1770, ABIGAIL WORCESTER, born July 12, 1750, and died Aug. 27, 1826.

Children born in Plymouth.

  I. JESSE,[6] b. Nov. 10, 1772; d. Nov. 12, 1772.
  II. JESSE,[6] b. Nov. 20, 1773; unmarried; a cabinet-maker.
216 III. LEMUEL,[6] b. Dec. 5, 1775; m. SARAH SUMNER, of Roxbury, Mass., March 21, 1803.
  IV. ABIGAIL WORCESTER,[6] b. June 25, 1778; d. Sept. 6, 1778.
  V. JOSEPH,[6] b. Oct. 10, 1779. Said to have settled in New Orleans, La. No further record.
  VI. ABIGAIL,[6] b. March 23, 1782; d. July 24, 1783.
  VII. DAVID,[6] b. July 30, 1784; d. Jan. 1, 1788.
217 VIII. SIMEON,[6] b. June 25, 1786; m. CAROLINE HUNT, of Baltimore.
  IX. HANNAH,[6] b. March 24, 1789; died unmarried, Nov. 6, 1811.
218 X. DAVID,[6] b. July 16, 1795; m. FRANCES ANN CLIFTON McKIN, Feb. 22, 1825.

93.

FRANCIS[5] CHURCHILL (JONATHAN,[4] ELIEZER,[3] ELIEZER,[2] JOHN[1]). Born in Plymouth, June 11, 1761. He served in Capt. Jesse Harlow's Company, coast guards, at Plymouth, as fifer, seven months in 1776. Settled in Charlestown, and was there a large landholder, but

disposed of his property there before 1790, and removed to West
Fairlee, Vt., where he lived thereafter. Died Oct. 27, 1841. He was a
carpenter and painter by trade. Was captain of a militia company
in Fairlee. Married, Sept. 24, 1786, PHEBE LEATHERS, daughter of
William, of Somerville. She was born Feb. 11, 1769, and died
May 8, 1852, at Nashua, N.H. at John E. Churchill's; buried at
Fairlee, Vt.

Children born, the two oldest in Charlestown, the rest in W. Fairlee, Vt.

219   I. WILLIAM LEATHERS,[6] b. March 22, 1787; m. ELIZA LAMPHIRE, of
          W. Fairlee.
220   II. FRANCIS WORCESTER,[6] b. Feb. 9, 1789; m. MILLICENT WHIT-
          COMB.
221 III. DAVID CARROLL,[6] b. Dec. 16, 1790; m. POLLY FRANKLIN, of Lynn.
     IV. ROBERT WALLACE,[6] b. Nov. 26, 1792; m. (———) STRETTON; d.
          without issue, in 1834, in Franconia, N.H.
222   V. SIMEON RICHARDSON,[6] b. Dec. 9, 1794; m. MARY ANN DOANE; d.
          in Syracuse, N.Y.
223   VI. SAMUEL STILLMAN,[6] b. May 26, 1796; m. SALLY COBURN, of Post
          Mills, Vt.
224 VII. JOSEPH WARREN,[6] b. Feb. 2, 1798; m. SARAH N. DOANE, Feb. 2,
          1825; d. Jan. 12, 1875.
225 VIII. REUBEN EDWARD,[6] b. Oct. 26, 1799. Lived in Paw Paw, Mich., and
          died there.
226   IX. THOMAS WORCESTER,[6] b. Sept. 20, 1802; m. POLLY BROWN, of
          Lowell, Mass.
      X. PHEBE LEATHERS,[6] b. June 19, 1804; m. NATHAN HASKELL, of
          Chelsea; no issue; d. April 21, 1863.
     XI. MARY FROTHINGHAM,[6] b. Feb. 14, 1808; m. WM. F. LAWRENCE,
          in Chelsea, and lived in Nashua, N.H., in 1832; she died Dec.
          3, 1858; he died March 22, 1856.

Children.

    1. Morgianna Lawrence, b. Nov. 1, 1833; d. Dec. 23, 1834.
    2. Georgianna Lawrence, b. Feb. 5, 1835.
    3. Mary L. Lawrence, b. April 7, 1836; m. Spencer C. Vose, Sept.
       4, 1862; lived in Providence, R.I.
    4. Sarah L. Lawrence, b. April 1, 1838; m. George E. Jaques, of
       Boston, in 1862.

227 XII. JOHN EMERY,[6] b. July 20, 1811; m. Eliza Ann Coburn; lived in
          Nashua, N.H.
228 XIII. GEORGE WASHINGTON,[6] b. Nov. 4, 1813; m. 1st, ELIZABETH MIL-
          LIKEN, in Troy, N.Y.; m. 2d, (———), in Port Mills, Vt.; m.
          3d, MRS. LYDIA ANN (WHARFF) SHAW.

95.

CHARLES [5] CHURCHILL (EPHRAIM,[4] STEPHEN,[3] ELIEZER,[2]
JOHN [1]). Born in Plymouth, April 25, 1733, and lived there.
Served in the war of the Revolution in Capt. Nathaniel Goodwin's
Company, Col. Theophilus Cotton's Regiment, service Sept. 25, 1777,
to Oct. 31, 1777, one month and six days, on a secret expedition
against Newport, R.I. He died Oct. 10, 1797. Married MRS. SARAH
(COBB) CHURCHILL, widow of Isaac (No. 24), *q. v.* She died Feb.
17, 1803.

Children of Charles and Sarah.

229   I. CHARLES,[6] b. Oct. 8, 1767; m. HANNAH NYE, of Wareham.
     II. JOSEPH,[6] b. Nov. 15, 1769; d. at sea, August, 1803, aged 33 years.
230   III. RUFUS,[6] b. April 12, 1772; m. EUNICE COVINGTON, March 10, 1797; d. April 26, 1826.
231   IV. SAMUEL,[6] b. Sept. 23, 1774; m. BATHSHEBA COLLINS, Nov. 11 1798.
     V. ELKANAH,[6] b. March 10, 1777; m. EUNICE FINNEY, Sept. 5, 1801. He d. at sea, Oct. 7, 1804. No further record.
     VI. SARAH,[6] b. Nov. 12, 1779; m. SETH FINNEY, Nov. 15, 1798. They lived at Plymouth, and had

Children.

1. Seth Finney, m. Betsey D. Whiting, 1821.
2. Elkanah Churchill Finney, m. Hannah Howland, 1829.
3. Hannah Finney, m. Ephraim Howard.
4. Mary Otis Finney, m. Augustus Burgess.

232   VII. EPHRAIM,[6] b. May 16, 1782; m. SALLY FINNEY, March 2, 1804.

96.

ZACCHEUS [5] CHURCHILL (EPHRAIM,[4] STEPHEN,[3] ELIEZER,[2] JOHN [1]). Born in Plymouth, Feb. 20, 1735. Married, in Plymouth, Sept. 6, 1754, MARY TRASK, daughter of Elias and Mary (Bolter) Trask.

Children.

     I. ELIZABETH,[6] b. Jan. 24, 1755/6; m. PAUL DOTEN, Nov. 6, 1774.
     II. ZACCHEUS,[6] b. Dec. 1, 1757.
     III. MARY,[6] b. Nov. 24, 1758; m. WILLIAM HUESTON (or HUSTON), Aug. 8, 1777.

Children.

1. William Hueston.
2. Hannah Hueston, m. Henry McCartey.
3. Nathaniel Hueston, b. 1786.
4. Elizabeth Hueston, m. Thomas Covington.
5. Priscilla Hueston, m. Edward Morton, 1810.

233   IV. EPHRAIM,[6] b. September, 1759; m. ASENATH HIBBARD, in Yarmouth, Nova Scotia.
234   V. THOMAS,[6] m. MARY KIEF, of Boston, May 23, 1777.
235   VI. RUFUS.[6] No further record.
236   VII. NATHANIEL.[6] No further record.
     VIII. PRISCILLA.[6] No further record.

97.

EPHRAIM [5] CHURCHILL (EPHRAIM,[4] STEPHEN [3] ELIEZER,[2] JOHN [1]). Born in Plymouth, July 2, 1738. They lived in Bridge water, Mass. Perhaps he served in the Revolution in Captain Dean's Company, Bridgewater, instead of his son Ephraim, or perhaps both served in same company, April 19, 1775. Married, in Halifax, Mass., Nov. 28, 1752, JEMIMA BRYANT, of Halifax. Died Dec. 13, 1817.

Children born in Bridgewater.

I. EPHRAIM,[6] b. Jan. 7, 1753; m. SILENCE FRENCH, dau. of Depend-
ence, of Stoughton, 1787; no children. Probably served in the
Revolution in Capt. Josiah Hayden's Company, May 1, 1775, to
Aug. 1, 1775.
II. HANNAH,[6] b. Feb. 5, 1755; m. CALVIN SNOW, 1784.
III. DORCAS,[6] b. May 21, 1759; m. ELIAB SNOW, 1787.

Children.

1. Anson Snow, m. Sally Trask.
2. Olive Snow, m. Apollo Dodge.
3. Lydia Snow, m. Dennis Libby.
4. Churchill Snow, b. Aug. 11, 1794; m. Eunice Bolton, Sept. 9,
1820.

IV. JEMIMA,[6] b. Oct. 14, 1761; m. JAMES PACKARD, 1778.
V. JAMES,[6] b. Aug. 17, 1764; m. 1st, LYDIA SNOW, 1788. She died
April 4, 1790; no issue; m. 2d, MARY GURNEY, dau. of Zech-
ariah, 1794. He died Jan. 12, 1846; no children.
VI. SARAH,[6] b. June 13, 1767; d. unmarried, April 12, 1801.
VII. SUSANNA,[6] b. Aug. 7, 1770; m. ELIJAH DRAKE, 2D, 1800

Children.

1. Jabez Drake.
2. Hannah Drake.
3. Emily Drake.
4. Charles Drake.
5. Jonathan Drake, b. Nov. 9, 1814.
6. James Drake.

98.

ELLIS [5] CHURCHILL (EPHRAIM,[4] STEPHEN,[3] ELIEZER,[2] JOHN[1]).
Born at Plymouth, Nov. 25, 1742. Served in the Revolution several
terms. First in Sergt. Enos Dean's Guards over the British prisoners in Taunton jail, December, 1776, nineteen days. Also enlisted in
regular army First Company, Third Regiment, for three years, March
21, 1781. Description at this latter date: " Age, 39 years; residence, Taunton; stature, 5 feet 6 inches; complexion, dark; hair,
brown; eyes, gray; occupation, cordwainer." Another term, July
27 to Oct. 31, 1780, may have been his or that of his son Ellis.
Married 1st, Oct. 18, 1764, PATIENCE CHURCHILL, daughter of
Josiah [4] (No. 31). She died Sept. 11, 1772; married 2d, SARAH
BALL.

Children.

I. ELLIS,[6] b. June 24, 1765; d. unmarried.
Probably in the Revolution, private, Captain Gifford's Company,
July 12 to Nov. 27, 1781. Service at R.I.
237　II. LEWIS,[6] m. NANCY MITCHELL, March 24, 1792.
238　III. CHARLES,[6] m. JEDIDAH HAWES, May 24, 1794.
No further record.

By Second Wife.

239　IV. WILLIAM,[6] b. Dec. 12, 1780; m. SALLY ROUNDS, 1805.

99.

ANSEL [5] CHURCHILL (EPHRAIM,[4] STEPHEN,[3] ELIEZER,[2]
JOHN[1]). Born in Plymouth, March 29, 1745. Married, July 17,
1765, BETHIA HOLMES.

MARIA (CHURCHILL) SHAW.
(Under No. 103, page 61.)

Children.

I. ANSEL.[6] Removed to Rhode Island; no further record.
II. PRISCILLA,[6] m. BENJAMIN SAMPSON, Aug. 29, 1786.
III. PATIENCE,[6] m. JOHN CALDERWOOD. Oct. 4, 1792
240   IV. JOHN,[6] b. 1775; m. NANCY JACKSON, dau. of Isaac, June 6, 1801.
V. BETHIA,[6] m. ZEPHANIAH HOLMES, April 4, 1796.

103.

STEPHEN[5] CHURCHILL (STEPHEN,[4] STEPHEN,[3] ELIEZER[2] JOHN[1]). Born in Plymouth, June 7, 1743, and lived there. Served in Revolution. Lieutenant in command of Plymouth Company at Lexington Alarm; first lieutenant Fifth Company, First Plymouth Regiment, June 6, 1776; captain of Seacoast Company, April 8, 1778, stationed at "the Gurnet"; captain in Colonel Cotton's regiment, Newport, R.I., March, 1781. Married, July 10, 1766, LUCY BURBANK, daughter of Timothy, born 1745.

Children.

I. LUCY,[6] b. Jan. 12, 1767; m. SAMUEL BRADFORD, Nov. 24, 1785.

Children.

1. Samuel Bradford, m. Lucy Gibbs.
2. Stephen Bradford, m. Hannah Wadsworth.
3. Hannah Bradford, m. Stephen Mason Burbank.
4. Lucy Bradford, m. Bartlett Bradford.
5. Ellen Bradford, m. Charles Brewster.
6. Harvey Bradford, m. Wealthy Hathaway, of Rochester.

241   II. STEPHEN;[6] b. May 7, 1768; m. 1st, ELIZABETH GRAY, June 4, 1791; m. 2d, NANCY (JACKSON) CHURCHILL, widow of John (No. 240).
242   III. PELEG,[6] b. Aug. 11, 1769; m. 1st, (———) BRADFORD; m. 2d, HANNAH HOSEA, April 14, 1791.
243   IV. HEMAN,[6] b. March 10, 1771; m. JANE CHURCHILL, Jan. 1, 1795.
244   V. DANIEL,[6] b. Feb. 5, 1773; m. 1st, SALLY COLLINS, Nov. 12, 1797; m. 2d, MRS. NANCY BREWSTER, widow, Oct. 8, 1837.
VI. OTIS,[6] b. Sept. 6, 1774; d. unmarried.
VII. HANNAH,[6] b. June 30, 1776; m. LEWIS HARLOW, April 15, 1796.

Children.

1. Lewis Harlow, m. Betsey Holmes, 1821, dau. Barnabas.
2. Lucy C. Harlow, m. Isaac Barnes.
3. Hannah Harlow, m. Charles Goodwin.
4. Betsey Harlow, m. Jabez Harlow.
5. John Harlow, m. Jane C. Bradford.
VIII. MARIAH,[6] b. March 20, 1778; m. SOUTHWORTH SHAW, Oct. 14, 1798.

Children.

1. Betsey Shaw, b. 1799.
2. Southworth Shaw, b. 1801; m. Abby Atwood Shurtleff, of Boston, dau. of Benjamin, 1826.
3. Ichabod Shaw, b. 1803.
4. Betsey Shaw, b. 1805; m. William Bramhall.
5. Samuel Shaw, b. 1808; m. Mary Gibbs Dike, dau. of Simeon.
6. Maria Shaw, b. 1811.
7. George Atwood Shaw, b. 1813.
8. George Atwood Shaw, b. 1816.
9. James R. Shaw, b. 1820; m. Susan Finney, dau. Ephraim.
IX. NANCY,[6] b. July 10, 1780; m. JOHN ATWOOD, Nov. 3, 1799.

Children born in Plymouth.

1. John Atwood, m. Hannah Wiswall, 1828.
2. William Atwood.
3. Maria Shaw Atwood, m. Ignatius Pierce.
4. Mary Ann Atwood, m. Ephraim Holmes.
5. Nancy Atwood.

X. SALLY,[6] b. May 8, 1782; m. DAVID DREW, 1803.

Children born in Plymouth.

1. Ellis Drew, m. Sarah Dickson.
2. David Drew, m. Ann D. Burgess.
3. Lucinda Drew, m. William T. Drew.
4. Sarah Drew, m. Lewis Perry

XI. ELKANAH,[6] b. May 23, 1783; d. young.
XII. POLLY,[6] b. Jan. 21, 1786; m. SAMUEL DICKSON, 1803

Children.

1. Samuel Dickson.
2. David Dickson.
3. Mary Dickson, m. Benjamin Bullard.
4. James Dickson.

XIII. ELIZABETH,[6] b. May 5, 1788; m. JESSE ROBBINS, 1804.

Children born in Plymouth.

1. Heman C. Robbins, m. Mary Ann Spear, 1832.
2. Betsey Otis Robbins, m. James Burgess.
3. Augustus Robbins, m. Mary C. Turner, dau. of Ezekiel C.

104.

ZADOCK[5] CHURCHILL (STEPHEN,[4] STEPHEN,[3] ELIEZER,[2] JOHN[1]). Born in Plymouth, July 16, 1747. He served in the war of the Revolution as sergeant in Capt. Jesse Harlow's Company upon Alarm of April 19, 1775; service, seven days. He is credited with several later terms of service in 1777 and 1778. Married, Oct. 7, 1773, BATHSHEBA RIDER, daughter of Joseph.

Child.

I. BATHSHEBA,[6] b. March 26, 1776; m., March 21, 1795, THOMAS LONG, the son of Miles Long and Thankful (Clark) Long, his wife. Bathsheba Churchill is said to have been beautiful both in mind and person. Her parents both died when she was a child.

Children born in Middleboro', Mass.

1. Betsey Long, b. Aug. 31, 1796; m. Isaac Ellis.
2. Thomas Long, b. July 25, 1798; m. Mary Ann Dunham, of Plymouth, 1822.
*3. Zadock R. Long, b. July 28, 1800; m. Aug. 31, 1824, at New Gloucester, Me., Julia Temple Davis, b. at Falmouth, Me., Feb. 17, 1807.

* This couple lived in Buckfield, Me., and there, Oct. 27, 1838, the youngest of their four children, JOHN DAVIS LONG, the eminent scholar, jurist, and statesman was born. As member of Congress, governor of Massachusetts, and Secretary of the Navy in the cabinet of President McKinley, in the trying period of the Spanish and Philippine Wars, he has won and will ever hold a place of high honor among the most illustrious sons of the American Republic.— *Editor.*

4. Sally Long, b. April 7, 1802; m. Lucius Loring.
5. Miles Long, b. June 8, 1804; m. Ann Bridgham.
6. Harriet Long, } b. in Buckfield, Me., April 6, 1811; d. young.
7. Washington Long, } b. in Buckfield, Me., April 6, 1811.
8. Bathsheba Churchill Long, b. Jan. 21, 1813; m. Isaac Bearse.
9. Thankful Clark Long, b. Sept. 15, 1818; m. William Bacon.

105.

WILSON[5] CHURCHILL (BENJAMIN,[4] STEPHEN,[3] ELIEZER,[2] JOHN[1]). Born in Plymouth, April 23, 1747. Served in Revolution in Lieut. Stephen Churchill's Company, April 19, 1775. Marched to Marshfield April 20. Service seven days. Also in regular army, Aug. 9, 1780. Age, 34; height, 5 feet 8 inches; complexion, ruddy; residence, Plymouth. Marched from Springfield under Captain Lunt. Also other service in 1777, with Captain Goodwin. Married, Dec. 12, 1772, LYDIA DARLING. She was the daughter of Jonathan and Martha (Bramhall) Darling, and born 1750.

Children.

I. LYDIA,[6] b. Aug. 6, 1775; m. SYLVANUS CHURCHILL (No. 90), Sept. 22. 1797. q.v.
245   II. WILSON,[6] b. 1778; m. 1st, RUTH HINCKLEY, Dec. 9, 1804; m. 2d, SUSAN LUCAS, May 25, 1816.
III. HANNAH,[6] b. Dec. 2, 1780; m. JAMES HOWARD, 1800. He was born Oct. 14, 1777.

Children.

1. Hannah Howard, b. April 22, 1805; m. William D. Winsor, of Kingston.
2. James H. Howard, b. Nov. 9, 1807.
3. Cordelia Howard, b. Oct. 10, 1809; m. Thomas May.
4. Ellen Howard, b. Dec. 11, 1812; m. William Congdon.
5. John Wilson Howard, b. March 20, 1815; d. in two weeks.
6. Curtis Cushman Howard, b. April 16, 1816; m. Roxanna Hatch.

106.

BENJAMIN[5] CHURCHILL (BENJAMIN,[4] STEPHEN,[3] ELIEZER,[2] JOHN[1]). Born in Plymouth, Nov. 17, 1748. Served in the Revolution, Captain Goodwin's Company, September and October, 1777, one month six days; on secret expedition against Newport, R.I. Married, Jan. 13, 1782, MRS. PHEBE (TINKHAM) RANDALL, widow of Enoch and daughter of Ebenezer Tinkham.

Children.

246   I. NATHAN,[6] } b. Dec. 16, 1785; m. ELIZABETH SYLVESTER, Aug. 29, 1804.
II. BENJAMIN,[6] } b. Dec. 16, 1785. Lost at sea, unmarried.

108.

AMAZIAH[5] CHURCHILL (AMAZIAH,[4] ELKANAH,[3] ELIEZER,[2] JOHN[1]). Born in Plymouth, April 12, 1750. Served in the Revolution, as a private in Lieut. Stephen Churchill's Company, Minute

men, April 19, 1777.   Marched to Marshfield, April 20, seven days.
Married, March 16, 1776, BETTY BARTLETT, daughter of Samuel and
Betsey (Moore) Barlett.

Children.

247   I. AMAZIAH,[6] m. 1st, MARTHA DOTEN, June 26, 1799; m. 2d, MAR-
         GARET WALLACE, of Newbern, N.C.; m. 3d, MARY HARLOW,
         April 8, 1805.
248   II. EDMOND,[6] m. MARY HOUSTON, Oct. 10, 1801.
    III. BETSEY,[6] m. 1st, GEORGE H. ROBBINS, Sept. 12, 1806; m. 2d,
         HENRY ROBBINS (as his 2d wife), 1831.

Children by First Husband.

1. George Edwin Robbins, b. 1809; d. young.
2. Elizabeth Robbins, b. 1812; m. Isaac L. Wood, 1838.
3. Harriet N. Robbins, b. 1814; m. Levi Robbins.
4. Thomas Robbins.
5. Samuel B. Franklin Robbins, b. 1818.
6. George Edwin Robbins, b. 1820; m. Sarah Byron, of Taunton.
7. Amasa Robbins, b. 1822; m. Susan Bates, of Braintree.

    IV. HARRIET,[6] m. GEORGE BRADFORD, Oct. 27, 1807.

Children.

1. George Bradford.
2. Edmond Bradford.
3. Lemuel Bradford.
4. Harriet Bradford.

    V. ELLEN,[6] unmarried.

109.

SOLOMON[5] CHURCHILL (AMAZIAH,[4] ELKANAH,[3] ELIEZER,[2]
JOHN[1]). Born in Plymouth, July 27, 1762, and lived there. He
received a pension in 1831 of $40 per year for services as a private
in the war of the Revolution. This is recorded in the U. S. Senate
Documents for 1835, and a pension certificate is still preserved by
one of his descendants. His name does not appear on the printed
Rolls of Massachusetts soldiers and sailors. On one old document,
an annuity bond of 1835 from his son William, he is described as
" formerly mariner," and this may indicate that his service was at sea.
He died April 10, 1835, at Perry Township, Ohio, while on a visit
to his son Solomon and his family. Married, at Plymouth, Nov. 28,
1783, ELIZABETH BARTLETT, born Nov. 3, 1766, and died Oct. 26,
1811.

Children born in Plymouth.

249   I. SOLOMON,[6] b. Aug. 26, 1788; m. MARY PRITCHARD, March 16,
         1818.
    II. MENDALL,[6] b. Nov. 8, 1789. No record of any marriage.
         He served in the war of 1812. Probably on the sea. Died in
         New York Jan. 22, 1832.
    III. ELIZABETH,[6] b. July 4, 1792; died in 1793.
    IV. SYLVANUS,[6] b. Aug. 30, 1795; died in 1796.
    V. WILLIAM,[6] b. July 13, 1798; m. MARY MYRICK, of Nantucket.
    VI. ELIZABETH,[6] b. March 10, 1800; d. 1802.
    VII. MARIAH,[6] b. Oct. 26, 1801; d. 1802.

110.

JABEZ[5] CHURCHILL (ELKANAH,[4] ELKANAH,[3] ELIEZER,[2] JOHN[1]). Born in Plymouth, Oct. 2, 1756. He inherited from his father that part of the original Churchill homestead upon which the first house stood. Here he lived, and his shop standing on the lot gave the name "Jabez Corner" to the location. He died in 1843. His grandson Jabez, Jr., sold the site to the town in 1871 for the present schoolhouse. Married, April 23, 1803, MERCY (SYLVESTER) BARTLETT, widow of Judah.

Children.

I. MERCY,[6] m. WILLIAM SEARS, son of Eleazer.

Children born in Plymouth.
1. William Henry Sears, b. 1833.
2. Andrew Churchill Sears, b. 1836.
3. Everett H. Sears, m. Angelina R. Tripp.
4. Herbert Sears, b. 1841.

251   II. JABEZ, JR.,[6] b. June 30, 1806; m. CHARLOTTE W. KEENE, Sept. 25, 1832.

III. LYDIA,[6] m. GILBERT HAYNES, of Lowell, 1831.

111.

NATHANIEL[5] CHURCHILL (ELKANAH,[4] ELKANAH,[3] ELIE-ZER,[2] JOHN[1]). Born at Plymouth, 1767. Lived and died there. He died August, 1834. Married, Feb. 3, 1798, SUSANNAH HARLOW, of Plymouth.

Children born in Plymouth.

        I. SUSANNAH,[6] b. 1800; m. ICHABOD W. THOMPSON, of Plympton.

252   II. NATHANIEL,[6] m. 1st, LUCY MORTON; m. 2d, ALMIRA BARTLETT, of Plymouth.

      III. REBECCA,[6] d. unmarried, aged 22 years.

      IV. ABIGAIL W.,[6] b. Jan. 28, 1808; m. SIMEON THOMPSON, Sept. 27, 1833. She died in Abington, Aug. 31, 1853. He died in Abington May 1, 1858, aged 51 years.

Children.
1. William Austin Thompson, b. in Plympton, July 13, 1834.
2. Abby Washburn Thompson, b. in Plympton, June 24, 1835.
3. Sarah Burgess Thompson, b. in Abington, Nov. 21, 1849.

253   V. WILLIAM,[6] m. MARIA MORTON, June 30, 1833.

      VI. SARAH,[6] b. Dec. 5, 1813; m. CAPT. LEWIS BURGESS, Aug. 9, 1838.

Children born in Plymouth.
1. Lewis Warren Burgess, b. May 17, 1841; d. in Plympton, Aug. 16, 1841.
2. Susan Harlow Burgess, b. Oct. 8, 1842.
3. Charles Lewis Burgess, b. Jan. 20, 1845; d. at sea, April 29, 1871. He became captain of a ship, and died on his first voyage as captain, aged 26 years.

      VII. SIMEON,[6] b. 1815. Went to Alabama in 1837, and died there, unmarried, soon after.

112.

JOHN[5] CHURCHILL (JOHN,[4] JOHN,[3] ELIEZER,[2] JOHN [1]). Born in Portsmouth, 1743. After his mother's death he lived in the family of his grandfather Churchill until his father married a second wife, in New York, and there sent for him. Of his subsequent history we know nothing save the record below. He lived in New Hackensack, N.Y. He was killed by falling from a barnframe. Married HANNAH SMITH, born July 22, 1745.

Children born in New Hackensack, N.Y.

254 I. JOHN,[6] b. May 26, 1769; m. ANNA LEYSTER.
255 II. BENJAMIN,[6] b. Dec. 4, 1770; m. MARY BLOOM.
  III. MARY,[6] b. Sept. 28, 1772; m. THOMAS WOOD.

Child.

1. John Wood, b. July 3, 1794.

  IV. SAMUEL,[6] b. Sept. 9, 1774; d. in infancy.
  V. ELIZABETH,[6] b. Oct. 17, 1776; m. LEVI SIMMONS, of Seneca County, N.Y.
256 VI. WILLIAM,[6] b. Sept. 20, 1779; m. CORNELIA VAN NOSTRAND, Nov. 19, 1790.
 VII. REBECCA,[6] b. Aug. 18, 1781.
 VIII. AMELIA,[6] b. May 10, 1783; m. DR. ISAAC WARD.

Children.

1. John Churchill Ward, b. Oct. 2, 1804; m. Hannah Shuguland, 1825.

Children.

1. Aaron S. Ward, b. Jan. 13, 1826; m. 1st, Maria Shufelt; m. 2d, Rebecca Shufelt; and d. August, 1855.
2. Amelia Ward, b. Jan. 18, 1829; d. April 24, 1849.
3. John Ward, b. Dec. 24, 1830; m. Harriet Pearse.
4. Rachel Ward, b. Sept. 22, 1832; d. Sept. 12, 1832.
5. Hannah M. Ward, b. March 5, 1834; m. Marshall Williamson; d. March 27, 1873.
6. Gerrett D. Ward, b. Nov. 4, 1837; d. in infancy.

2. Mary Ward, b. December, 1805; m. John Shutter, and d. April, 1891.
3. Hannah Ward, b. Feb. 2, 1810; m. Jacob Baidaux; d. 1863.
4. Sarah Ward, b. April 11, 1818; m. Jacob Van Duza.
5. Isaac Ward, b. May 22, 1820; d. unmarried, May 22, 1845.
6. Amelia Ward, b. Nov. 14, 1825; m. W. N. McHench.

257 IX. SAMUEL,[6] b. May 10, 1785; m. SALLIE (———), of New Hackensack.
  X. HANNAH,[6] b. May 7, 1787; m. WILLIAM POLLOCK.

Children.

1. John Pollock. 5. Benjamin Pollock.
2. Joseph Pollock. 6. James Pollock.
3. Phebe Pollock. 7. Anne Pollock.
4. Isaac Pollock. 8. Jane Pollock.

 XI. JOSEPH,[6] m. REBECCA (———).

113.

SAMUEL CLARK [5] CHURCHILL (Benjamin,[4] John,[3] Eliezer [2] John[1]). Born in Portsmouth, N.H., Feb. 17, 1770. They lived in Augusta, Me. Married, October, 1795, Susannah Cowen, born Oct. 20, 1772.

Children born in Augusta, Me.

       I. Abisha,[6] b. April 10, 1797.
258   II. Samuel Clark,[6] b. Feb. 14, 1799; m. Lucy Savage, May 8, 1823.
259   III. Alfred Delura,[6] b. June 23, 1801; m. Jane Chambers, Dec. 28, 1828.
260   IV. Edgar M.,[6] b. Feb. 19, 1804; m. (———), and had William, who changed his name from Churchill to Lewis. No further record.
      V. Paulina,[6] b. July 9, 1806; m. Jeremiah Bean, Oct. 25, 1832.

Children.

1. Homer S. Bean, b. Dec. 2, 1833.
2. George M. Bean.
3. Orland Bean.
4. Eunice Bean.

114.

JOHN [5] CHURCHILL (Joseph,[4] John,[3] Eliezer [2] John[1]). Born in Portsmouth, N.H., May 26, 1774. He settled in New Portland, Me. A farmer. Married Mercy Hutchins, who was born July 9, 1774.

Children born in New Portland, Me.

261   I. John,[6] b. June 10, 1793; m. Mary Dennis, May, 1818, in Sodus, N.Y.
262   II. Joseph,[6] b. June, 1795; m. Hannah B. Sisson.
      III. Polly,[6] b. May 18, 1797; m. Daniel Fling, August, 1818.

Children.

1. Daniel Fling, b. May 11, 1819.
2. Lydia Fling, b. May 13, 1821.

263   IV. James,[6] b. July 4, 1799; m. Clarissa Thompson.
264   V. Sanford,[6] b. July, 1801; m. Thankful Eames.
      VI. Lavinia,[6] b. April 30, 1803; m. Joseph L. Boynton, April 13, 1838.

Children.

1. George R. Boynton, b. Jan. 17, 1840; m. 1st, Eliza A. Goodwin. She died without children, July 21, 1872; m. 2d, Abbie R. Lansing, of Lewiston, Me.

Children of Second Wife.

1. Cora Boynton, d. soon.
2. Herbert C. Boynton.
3. Walter A. Boynton.
4. John L. Boynton.

2. Amanda M. Boynton, b. March 21, 1841.
3. Lydia F. Boynton, b. Oct. 9, 1842.
4. Sarah L. Boynton, b. July 16, 1843; m. Amos Norton.

Child.

Delmont Norton, m. Florence Berry, of Lexington, Me.

      VII. Olive,[6] b. September, 1806; m. Nathaniel Page.

Children.

1. Cyrus Page.	4. Charles Page.
2. Llewellyn Page.	5. Sylvia Page.
3. Sewall Page.	6. Olive F. Page.

VIII. ELVIRA,[6] b. Jan. 4, 1809; m. JOHN KNAPP, May 6, 1835.

Children.

1. James Knapp, b April 3, 1836.
2. Owen Knapp, b. July 4, 1837.
3. John Knapp, b. Dec. 6, 1838.

265 IX. EMERY,[6] b. Oct. 12, 1812; m. LYDIA K. (CARLTON) BRAZER, widow of John S. No issue.
He died Jan. 4, 1872. No further record.

266 X. SAMUEL,[6] b. March 19, 1816; m. LYDIA SMALL.

XI. MERCY,[6] b. August, 1818; m. THOMAS HUTCHINS, March 11, 1838

Children.

1. Harriet B. L. Hutchins, b. April 8, 1839.
2. Frances H. Hutchins, b. April 15, 1841.
3. Augustus Mellen Hutchins, b. Sept. 7, 1842.
4. Cornelia A. Hutchins, b. Sept. 3, 1844.
5. Frederick W. Hutchins, b. June 9, 1846.
6. Frank D. Hutchins, b. Feb. 29, 1848.
7. George A. Hutchins, b. June 28, 1850.

XII. CYRUS,[6] b. 1820; drowned in 1832.

115.

WILLIAM[5] CHURCHILL (JOSEPH,[4] JOHN,[3] ELIEZER,[2] JOHN[1]).
Born in Portsmouth, N.H., July 9, 1776. Lived in New Portland, Me. Married, March, 1799, MARY HUTCHINS, who was born July 11, 1779, and died April 19, 1869.

Children born in New Portland, Me.

I. ELIZABETH.[6] b. March 1, 1800; m. LEVI ANDREWS. No children.
II. LUCY,[6] b. Feb. 2, 1801; m. JOSIAH EVERETT.

Children.

1. Orra Everett, b. 1822; m. Hosea Pease, 1842.
2. Josiah Everett, Jr., b. 1825; m. Arvilla Carlton.
3. Andrew Everett, b. 1828; m. Sarah Peck.
4. Franklin Everett, b. 1831; m. Clara Spencer.
5. Lucy J. Everett, b. 1834; m. C. W. Harvey, 1855.
6. Benaiah W. Everett, b. 1836; m. Eliza Grout.
7. Seth Everett, b. 1840; m. Patty Denison, 1868.

267 III. WILLIAM,[6] b. Feb. 13, 1803; m. NANCY WALKER.

IV. MARTHA,[6] b. Jan. 9, 1805; m. SETH SOULE. She died May 1, 1881.

V. SAMUEL,[6] b. March 27, 1807; d. April, 1815.

268 VI. TILSON,[6] b. Jan. 29, 1810; m. SALLY ELLIOTT.

VII. EBEN,[6] b. Feb. 23, 1812; d. unmarried, April, 1868.

VIII. LYDIA,[6] b. Feb. 16, 1815; m. E. LOVEJOY.

IX. SARAH,[6] b. June 22, 1817; d. Oct. 1, 1843.

X. MARY W.,[6] b. Dec. 10, 1819; m. 1st, B. T. WETHERN, June 28, 1840. He died April 22, 1844; m. 2d, WILLIAM BAILEY, January, 1847.

Children of First Husband.

1. Micah Delmont Wethern, b. May 14, 1841; d. May 28, 1877.
2. William Corydon Wethern, b. Nov. 28, 1842.

Children of Second Husband.

3. Sarah R. C. Bailey, b. Oct. 25, 1847; m. Samuel Hansell.
4. Melburn C. Bailey, b. Sept. 25, 1849; d. Sept. 13, 1868.
5. Clement Perham Bailey, b. March 10, 1853; d. March 21, 1853.

279 XI. SAMUEL,⁶ b. March 28, 1822; m. ELIZABETH YEATON. He died
Feb. 5, 1845. No further record.

116.

DANIEL⁵ CHURCHILL (JOSEPH,⁴ JOHN,³ ELIEZER,² JOHN¹).
Born in Portsmouth, N.H. Settled in Maine; lived in Litchfield,
Bingham, and Madison, Me. Married LUCY FLETCHER.

Children.

269 I. DANIEL,⁶ b. April 20, 1800; m. CAROLINE BAKER, b. Oct. 18, 1811.
270 II. ASA,⁶ b. 1802; m. MARY HOLDEN, of Moose River, Me.
III. DORCAS,⁶ m. SHURTLEFF SMITH (no children).
271 IV. AMOS,⁶ b. March 27, 1805; m. ELLEN CHASE.
272 V. ELI,⁶ m. RACHEL STEWARD.
VI. BELINDA.⁶
273 VII. WARREN,⁶ m. LOVILLA YORK, July 7, 1842.
274 VIII. WILLIAM FLETCHER,⁶ b. Feb. 1, 1814; m. 1st, SARAH CHASE, of
Bingham, Me.; m. 2d, EUNICE YORK, of Brighton, Me.; m. 3d,
EMMA BOISE, of Skowhegan, Me.
IX. LUCINDA,⁶ b. Oct. 30, 1818: m. LOVELL FELKER, April 17, 1842.
They lived in Omro, Wis., where she died May 14, 1895. No
children.
X. HANNAH,⁶ m. DAVID MCINTIRE.

Children.

1. Danville McIntire.
2. Byron McIntire.
3. Lucy McIntire, m. Isaac Curtis.
4. Alfreda D. McIntire.
5. Maynard McIntire, m. Etta Bates.
6. Cora E. McIntire.

117.

TOBIAS⁵ CHURCHILL (JOSEPH,⁴ JOHN,³ ELIEZER,² JOHN¹).
Born probably in Portsmouth, June 12, 1780. Removed to Somer-
set County, Me., and settled at New Portland. Married, 1806
JANE EVERETT, who was born March 12, 1786.

Children born at New Portland, Me.

275 I. TOBIAS,⁶ b. Jan. 23, 1807; m. IRENE WALTON.
II. MINDWELL,⁶ b. July 13, 1808; m. JOHN WALTON.
III. JOHN,⁶ b. March 25, 1810; d. in infancy.
IV. CLIMENA,⁶ b. Feb. 23, 1811; m. SAMUEL WALTON.
V. JANE,⁶ b. April 27, 1813; m. ALEXANDER HILMAN.
VI. MARY,⁶ b. March 16, 1815; m. HIRAM KNOWLTON.

VII. CAROLINE,[6] b. June 17, 1817; m. JOHN KNOWLTON
VIII. EMILY,[6] b. May 6, 1819; m. WILLIAM SAWYER.
 IX. JOANNA,[6] b. July 22, 1821; m. ISAAC WEBBER.
  X. LUCY,[6] b. Oct. 6, 1823; m. 1st, TRISTRAM NORTON DAGGETT, June
        9, 1846; m. 2d, PHINEAS HOUGHTON.
      They lived at New Vineyard, Me.

Children born at New Vineyard, Me.

1. Oraville Daggett, } b. June 19, 1847; d. Aug. 8, 1863.
2. Orrington Daggett, } b. June 19, 1847; d. July 1, 1863.
3. Isaac W. Daggett, b. Jan. 2, 1851.
4. Sarah E. Daggett, b. Feb. 28, 1853; d. June 16, 1863.
5. Russell E. Daggett, b. Sept. 28, 1855; d. July 12, 1863.
6. Warren Tristram Daggett, b. July 21, 1858; d. June 25, 1863.
7. Lucy Anna Daggett, b. Aug. 11, 1860; d. Sept. 4, 1863.

 XI. WARREN,[6] b. Sept. 28, 1826; d. in infancy.
XII. ELIZABETH,[6] b. March 28, 1828; d. in infancy.

117A.

BENJAMIN [5] CHURCHILL (JOSEPH,[4] JOHN,[3] ELIEZER,[2] JOHN[1]).
Born, 1782; married CYNTHIA PARKER, of New Portland, Me.

Children.

276   I. JOSIAH,[6] b. 1807; m. LYDIA WALKER.
277   II. JESSE,[6] b. 1809; m. CLYMENA WALTON.
     III. CYNTHIA,[6] b. 1811; m. DANIEL G. METCALF.
278   IV. BENJAMIN,[6] b. 1813; m. RACHEL MITCHELL.

118.

JOHN [5] CHURCHILL (EBENEZER,[4] WILLIAM[3] WILLIAM,[2]
JOHN[1]). Born in Plympton, Nov. 14, 1731. They lived in Plymp-
ton until about 1785, when they removed to Chittenden, Vt. He
was a soldier in the Revolutionary War, Capt. Thomas Loring's
Company. Marched on Alarm of April 19 to Marshfield, and in
Capt. Thomas Lamson's Company at Bristol, R.I., December, 1776.
He died in Chittenden, Feb. 24, 1826. Married, Feb. 12, 1756,
JOANNA BISBEE, of Bridgewater.

Children born in Plympton.

280   I. CALEB,[6] b. April 4, 1757; m. SARAH HAWLEY, Nov. 14, 1788.
      II. MIRIAM,[6] b. Sept. 20, 1759; d. July 21, 1825.
     III. JOANNA,[6] b. 1762; m. (———) HOLMES.
             Said to have had a family, but no further record has been found
             even after a diligent search.
      IV. ABIGAIL,[6] b. Aug. 28, 1765; m. NATHAN HAWLEY, of Pittsford, Vt.
             They lived in Pittsford. She died at Brandon, Vt., April 23,
             1851, and he died at Pittsford, Vt., June 7, 1849.

Children born in Pittsford.

1. Joanna Hawley, m. Jacob Sheldon, of Pittsford.
2. Sarah Hawley, b. May 28, 1794; m. Anson Manley, of Brandon,
     Vt., Sept. 25, 1849. She died in Brandon, Nov. 29, 1852,
     and he died there Jan. 30, 1854.

3. John Hawley. Said to have followed the sea for many years, and then to have settled near Philadelphia, where he died unmarried.

V. LEAH,[6] b. Jan. 18, 1768; m. ZENAS SMITH, in Middleboro', and lived there until May, 1809, when they moved to Pittsford, Vt., and settled on a farm, where they spent the remainder of their lives. She died July 15, 1835, and he died Aug. 15, 1833.

Children born, four in Middleboro', Mass., and one in Pittsford, Vt.

1. Sarah Smith, b. Middleboro', May 5, 1803; m. Lebbeus Goodrich, of Brandon, Vt. They removed to Rome, Mich., where she died March 7, 1885, and he died Sept. 13, 1901.
2. George Smith, b. probably at Middleboro', Dec. 3, 1805; m. Sylvia Churchill, dau. of Caleb.
3. Lydia Smith, m. Elijah Heeler, of Brandon Vt.
4. Joseph Smith, d. at Pittsford, Vt., Sept. 20, 1817, aged 13 years.
5. James Smith, d. Nov. 24, 1829, aged 22 years.

119.

ISAAC[5] CHURCHILL (EBENEZER,[4] WILLIAM,[3] WILLIAM,[2] JOHN[1]). Born in Plympton, Feb. 22, 1736. He lived there until 1785, when he removed with his family to Chittenden, Vt. He was called "Isaac, the Good," to distinguish him from another of the same name. I find no reference to Revolutionary service in the quite full information received from his descendants, while the published rolls, having several Isaac Churchills, do not sufficiently identify him to justify a claim of such service. He died in Chittenden, Feb. 25, 1826. Married, Aug. 1, 1765, MELATIAH BRADFORD, of Plympton, daughter of Joshua and Hannah (Bradford) Bradford. It is said that her parents were killed by Indians, and herself, struck by a tomahawk, bore the scar through life. She died in Chittenden, Aug. 15, 1826, aged 82 years.

Children born in Plympton, except two last.

281   I. MICHAEL,[6] b. Jan. 26, 1766; m. LUCY DODGE, of Brandon, Vt.
      II. ZERUIAH,[6] b. March 16, 1767; m. JOHN BULLEN.
      III. RACHEL,[6] b. Jan. 4, 1769; m. FREEMAN EGGLESTON.
282   IV. WINSLOW,[6] b. Dec. 30, 1770; m. MERCY DODGE, November (Thanksgiving Day), 1796.
283   V. SETH,[6] b. June 28, 1773; m. EUNICE DURKEE, Feb. 14, 1793.
      VI. ISRAEL,[6] b. May 5, 1775; died young.
      VII. HANNAH,[6] b. March 28, 1777; m. FREEMAN EGGLESTON.
      VIII. ISRAEL,[6] b. Oct. 30, 1779; m. WIDOW (HASKINS) BLAKESLEY.
         He settled in Lyons, N.Y., where he owned a small place and lived alone unmarried many years and worked at the carpenter's trade. In 1854 he moved to Rose, N.Y., where he married as above. He was then about 75 years old. His wife had a daughter then about 12 years old who afterwards married Walter Winchell. Mr. Churchill died in 1884, and is buried at Rose. After his death, his widow, with her daughter and Mr. Winchell, removed to Deerfield, Mich.
284   IX. ELISHA,[6] b. Aug. 16, 1781; m. LYDIA LACKEY.
      X. DRUSILLA,[6] b. Aug. 16, 1783; m. JACOB ATWOOD.
      XI. CHRISTIANA,[6] b. Sept. 14, 1789; m. ASA HUTCHINSON.

120.

JOSHUA[5] CHURCHILL (EBENEZER,[4] WILLIAM,[3] WILLIAM,[2] JOHN[1]). Born Feb. 23, 1742, and died Oct. 17, 1831. Served in Capt. Thomas Loring's Company, Alarm of April 19, 1775, to Marshfield. Also Capt. John Bradford's Company. Enlisted May 3, 1775. Served three months six days. Also Capt. Thomas Turner's Company, Col. Gamaliel Bradford's Regiment. Enlisted May, 1778. Service eight months. Also enlisted for town of Plympton in Capt. James Harlow's Company, Colonel Gates' Regiment. Service nine months to Jan. 1, 1779. Lived in Plympton till 1800, when he moved his family to Hartford, Me. He drew a pension from 1818. Married, Feb. 4, 1768, ELIZABETH BONNEY, in Plympton. She was born April 21, 1746, and died July 18, 1820.

Children born in Plympton.

285   I. JOSHUA,[6]   } b. Feb. 1, 1769; m. SYLVIA CHURCHILL, dau. of David,
                     Jr. (No. 121), *q. v.*, and Jennie (Ellis) Churchill.
    II. ELIZABETH,[6] } b. Feb. 1, 1769; m. LEMUEL KEENE, Jan. 16, 1800.
    III. ALEXANDER,[6] b. Nov. 22, 1770; d. young; unmarried.
286   IV. ANDREW,[6] b. Nov. 18, 1772; m. POLLY OLDHAM.
    V. OLIVE,[6] b. Feb. 22, 1774/5; m. SAMUEL CHURCHILL.
    VI. PHEBE,[6] b. Jan. 18, 1779; m. OLIVER CUMMINGS.

Children.

1. Betsey Bailey Cummings, b. Dec. 3, 1804; d. at the age of 12.
2. Larned Cummings, b. Aug. 13, 1806; m. Nancy White, May 27, 1837.

Children.

    1. Julia Ann Cummings, b. July 4, 1838, m. Caleb Thomas.
    2. Whitney Cummings, b. Feb. 14, 1841; d. at the age of 14 years.
    3. Marilla J. Cummings, b. May 16, 1849; never married.
    4. James Lamond Cummings, b. June 1, 1854; m. Clara Washburn.

3. Whitney Cummings, b. Dec. 18, 1808; m. Mary Hart Prentiss, March 27, 1833.

Children.

    1. Isabella Cummings, b. April 15, 1834; m. Joseph S. Ingraham, Nov. 10, 1852.
    2. Prentiss Cummings, b. Sept. 10, 1840; m. Anna D. Snow, Feb. 25, 1880.
    3. Mellen Cummings, b. Sept. 27, 1847; d. March 23, 1855.

287   VII. EZRA,[6] b. Sept. 25, 1780; m. BETHIA MEHURIN, b. in Jay, Me., May 25, 1783.
    VIII. POLLY,[6] b. Sept. 30, 1784; m. OLIVER CUMMINGS, JR.
    IX. BETHANY,[6] b. Jan. 1, 1789; never married.
    X. LUCINDA,[6] b. July 31, 1793; m. CALVIN HARDING.

Children.

1. Luther Harding, b. April 4, 1816; d. March 6, 1844.
2. Calvin Harding, b. Feb. 24, 1818; m. 1st, Lydia O. Keene; m. 2d, Ruby White.
3. Lizzie, b. Aug. 29, 1820; m. Washington Bates.
4. Mary, b. Jan. 1, 1823; d. May 24, 1847.
5. Lydia, m. Samuel Crockett.

121.

DAVID[5] CHURCHILL, JR. (DAVID,[4] WILLIAM,[3] WILLIAM,[2] JOHN[1]). Born in Plympton, Aug. 4, 1729. Lived in Plympton, and late in life in Hingham. ' He served in the Revolution, Capt. Thomas Loring's Company, Alarm of April 19, 1775, marched to Marshfield. Married 1st, Feb. 20, 1750, JANE ELLIS. She died Aug. 21, 1775. Married 2d, LURANA MCFARLAND. He died Feb. 23, 1812, aged 82 years.

Children born in Plympton.

  I. HANNAH,[6] b. June 14. 1752; m. ELKANAH CUSHMAN. May 17, 1770. She died at Kingston, Feb. 4, 1825. He died at Plympton, 1787.

Child.

    1. Ezra Cushman, b. July 29, 1771; drowned at Kingston, July 24, 1797; unmarried.

  II. MOLLY,[6] b. July 21, 1754; m. SHADRACH STANDISH, of Plympton.

Children born in Plympton.

    1. Averick Standish, b. 1772; m. John Avery Parker, of New Bedford.
    2. Ellis Standish, b. 1774; m. Polly Bradford, settled in Sumner, Me.
    3. Jane Standish, b. 1777.
    4. Shadrach Standish, } b. 1779; m. Mehitable Clark.
    5. Levi Standish,   } b. 1779; m. Lucy Randall.
    6. Abigail Standish, b. 1781.
    7. Mary Standish, b. 1783.
    8. Sarah Standish, b. 1788.

      III. JANE,[6] b. Aug. 30, 1756; m. DANIEL RIPLEY.
288 IV. ELIAS,[6] b. Jan. 26, 1759; m. HANNAH CUSHMAN.
      V. LEVI,[6] b. July 4, 1761; d. Aug. 18, 1775.
      VI. PATTE,[6] b. March 12, 1764; d. Sept. 25, 1775.
      VII. SYLVIA,[6] b. Feb. 21, 1767; m. JOSHUA CHURCHILL (No. 285), *q. v.*
      VIII. DAVID,[6] b. May 18, 1771; d. Sept. 18, 1775.

Children of Second Wife, Lurana McFarland.

289 IX. DAVID,[6] b, June 11, 1778; m. MARY HERSEY, of Boston.
290 X. LEVI,[6] b. Feb. 20, 1780; m. CYNTHIA PACKARD, of East Bridgewater.
      XI. THADDEUS,[6] b. March 18, 1782. He was a seaman, lived in Hingham.
291 XII. JESSE,[6] b. Aug. 28, 1784; m. ANNA BARRELL, of Scituate.
      XIII. ASABA,[6] b. Feb. 19, 1787.
292 XIV. RUFUS,[6] b. Oct. 10, 1789; m. EUNICE LEWIS, of Hingham, Jan. 4, 1818.
      XV. LYDIA,[6] m. (———) MOTT, of Hingham.
      XVI. OTIS,[6] d. young. No record.

122.

WILLIAM[5] CHURCHILL (DAVID,[4] WILLIAM,[3] WILLIAM,[2] JOHN[1]). Born in Plympton, Nov. 25, 1739, and lived there. He probably served in the war of the' Revolution, from Plympton. Several of the names are on the published rolls, either one of proper

age, and no document or information to identify them.   Died
March 7, 1824.   Married, Nov. 29, 1759, SARAH RIDER.   She died
June 16, 1826.

Children born in Plympton.

293   I. SAMUEL,⁶ b. June 29, 1760; m. DEBORAH WRIGHT.
294   II. JOSEPH, b. Oct. 24, 1761; m. EUNICE CHURCHILL, dau. of Ichabod⁴
         (No. 45), *q.v.*
     III. ELIZABETH,⁶ b. March 24, 1763; d. Dec. 4, 1785, unmarried.
     IV. SARAH,⁶ b. Feb. 15, 1765; d. Oct. 29, 1785, unmarried.
295   V. WILLIAM,⁶ b. March 8, 1767; m. MARGARET TILTON, of Easton,
         N.Y.
     VI. MARCY,⁶ b. Feb. 2, 1769; m. JONATHAN HOLMES.

Children.

1. Caleb Holmes.   7. Esther Holmes.
2. Eliezer Holmes.   8. Lydia Holmes.
3. Mercy Holmes.   9. Zenas Holmes.
4. Sally Holmes.   10. William Holmes.
5. Jonathan Holmes.   11. Harriet Holmes.
6. Gamaliel Holmes.

    VII. ZENAS,⁶ b. May 28, 1771; m. ABIGAIL WASHBURN, dau. of Seth,
         of Kingston, said to have been lost at sea.   No further record.
    VIII. HANNAH, b. Sept. 8, 1773; m. ISAAC CUSHING, 1795.
     IX. MOLLY,⁶ b. July 26, 1777; m. BARNABAS PHINNEY, 1797.

123.

CAPT. JAMES⁵ CHURCHILL (DAVID,⁴ WILLIAM,³ WILLIAM,²
JOHN¹).   Born May 29, 1746.   Lived in Plympton.   He served in
the Revolutionary War as sergeant in Capt. Thomas Loring's Company, April 19, 1775, also ensign and lieutenant in Capt. Jesse
Harlow's Company.   Commissioned as lieutenant Jan. 16, 1776.
Service at Plymouth, seacoast defence, Feb. 29, to May 31, 1776.
Died March 12, 1803.   Married 1st, Oct. 31, 1765, PRISCILLA SOULE
daughter of Benjamin, b. April 1, 1745; died in Plympton, Oct. 9
1837, aged 92 years 5 months 27 days.   Her grandfather, Benjamin Soule, married Sarah, the daughter of Alexander, son of Capt.
Miles Standish.   George Soule, the Pilgrim, was also her ancestor.
He married 2d, REBECCA CROCKER.

Children of First Wife born in Plympton.

296   I. OLIVER,⁶ b. April 21, 1766; m. SABA SOULE, 1793.
     II. PRISCILLA,⁶ b. April 30, 1768; m. LIEUT. JOSEPH WRIGHT, son of
         Jacob, of Plympton.   She died Nov. 7, 1863.
         Said to have had five children; names not found.
297   III. JAMES,⁶ b. Feb. 26, 1771; m. SARAH SOULE, dau. Ebenezer, Feb.
         16, 1794.   He d. Nov. 1, 1803.
     IV. ISAIAH,⁶ b. Oct. 5, 1773; d. in Demerara, Sept. 23, 1799.
     V. JANE,⁶ b. March 21, 1776; m. FRANCIS WOODS, Sept. 22, 1799.
     VI. CHRISTIANA,⁶ b. Sept. 10, 1788.
     VII. CLARA,⁶ b. June 15, 1782; m. 1st, JOEL ELLIS, April, 1802; m. 2d,
         PELEG CHANDLER, of Duxbury, April 28, 1817.

VIII. HARRIET,[6] b. March 25, 1785; died young.
IX. SOPHIA,[6] b. Nov. 3, 1787; m. MARWICK ELLIS, of Plympton, 1807.
X. HARRIET,[6] b. June 18, 1791; m. PRINCE BRADFORD, b. Dec. 19, 1783, a direct descendant of Governor William Bradford in the seventh generation.

Children.

1. Gershom Bradford, b. 1816.
2. Perez Bradford, b. 1818.
3. Harriet Bradford, b. 1821.
4. Otis Bradford, b. 1823.
5. Hannah Bradford, b. 1825.
6. Lydia Bradford, b. 1827.
7. Susan Bradford, b. 1832.

Children of James Churchill and Second Wife.

XI. EDWIN.[6]
XII. ALICE,[6] m. LUTHER W. SAVERY..

124.

NATHANIEL[5] CHURCHILL (NATHANIEL,[4] WILLIAM,[3] WILLIAM,[2] JOHN [1]). Born in Plympton, May 10, 1746. Served in the Revolution. On the alarm of April 19, 1775, marched to Marshfield, and again, July 25, 1776, was drafted into the service, on the day on which his son Levi was born. He lived in Plympton, and died Nov. 18, 1784. Married, Dec. 27, 1770, DEBORAH WRIGHT, daughter of Joseph and Sarah (Brewster) Wright.

Children born in Plympton.

298 I. LEWIS,[6] b. Dec. 12, 1771; m. 1st, DESIRE BARKER BREWSTER, in Corinth, N.H.; m. 2d, PATTY THURSTON; m. 3d, RUTH QUIMBY, 1826.
299 II. HOSEA,[6] b. Feb. 21, 1774. No further record.
300 III. LEVI,[6] b. July 25, 1776; m. LYDIA RIPLEY, Nov. 3, 1799.
301 IV. STEPHEN,[6] b. April 19, 1779. He is said to have married and lived in Taunton, and to have had four children. The name of one of the children only has come to us, and this information is from Mrs. Deborah (Churchill) Hyde, of Glenmore, N.Y., aged 95 in 1901, a daughter of Joseph [6]. The name was Deborah.
302 V. JOSEPH,[6] b. Dec. 13, 1781; m. HANNAH WOODWARD, of Thompson, Conn.
303 VI. NATHANIEL,[6] b. May 13, 1784, married and lived in Grantham, N.H.

125.

EBENEZER [5] CHURCHILL (ICHABOD,[4] WILLIAM [3] WILLIAM,[2] JOHN [1]). Born in Plympton, March 1' 1744. Lived in Plympton. Served in the Revolution from Plympton in Capt. Thomas Loring's Company, April 19, 1775. Marched to Marshfield. Also several other longer terms of enlistment in other commands during 1775 to 1777. Died in 1824. Married, July 17, 1764, LUCY PALMER.

Children born in Plympton.

304   I. PRINCE,[6] b. Aug. 23, 1765; m. MRS. (——) RANDALL, widow.
            No further record.
305   II. JACOB,[6] b. Dec. 21, 1766; m. 1st, EUNICE STURTEVANT; m. 2d,
            JOANNA STURTEVANT.
306   III. EBENEZER,[6] b. July 3, 1768. No further record.
       IV. SAMUEL,[6] b. Aug. 29, 1770. No further record.
307   V. ALFORD,[6] b. Feb. 19, 1773; m. LYDIA CUSHMAN.
       VI. LUCY,[6] b. Feb. 20, 1776; m. DANIEL CHURCHILL (No. 128), *q. v.*
      VII. REBECCA,[6] b. September, 1778.
308   VIII. CORNELIUS,[6] b. Nov. 4, 1780; m. DESIRE LITCHFIELD.
       IX. BATHSHEBA,[6] b. Aug. 29, 1784; m. ELIJAH VICKERY.
309   X. ANSEL,[6] b. Aug. 22, 1787; m. LOIS CASWELL, of New Bedford.

126.

ICHABOD[5] CHURCHILL (ICHABOD,[4] WILLIAM,[3] WILLIAM[2] JOHN[1]). Born Sept. 7, 1751. He lived at Plympton until after 1784, when he removed to Middleboro', and thence to Pomfret, Vt., where he died May 7, 1813. He was a farmer. He served in the Revolution as private in Capt. James Harlow's Company, Colonel Cary's Regiment, January, 1776. Also Capt. Nathaniel Goodwin's Company in September and October, 1777. Died May 7, 1813. Married, Oct. 12, 1775, ABIGAIL DOTEN, daughter of Edward and Joanna (Whiting), b. Plympton, Jan. 28, 1755, O.S. She married 2d, JOSIAH BABCOCK, who died soon after. She died in Woodstock, Vt.

Children, first three born in Plympton.

   I. EDWARD.[6] b. Sept. 1, 1776. No further record.
  II. JOANNA,[6] b. Oct. 20, 1779; m. JOSIAH CROCKER, Jan. 11, 1798.
      Moved to Canada.

Child.

   1. Heman Crocker, and perhaps others.

 III. SERVIAH,[6] b. Sept. 20, 1781; m. 1st, SAMUEL COLWELL, Dec. 10,
      1801; m. 2d, SIMEON DUNHAM, Sept. 7, 1814. She d. Jan. 25,
      1840.

Children of Serviah by First Husband.

   1. Seth Colwell. | 3. Harriet Colwell.
   2. Mary Colwell. |

By Second Husband.

   4. Pattie Dunham. | 6. Horace Dunham.
   5. Simeon Dunham. |

310   IV. ZEBEDEE.[6] b. May 15, 1784; m. SARAH B. COLWELL, about 1809;
           d. 1827.
       V. ABIGAIL,[6] b. about 1790; m. ABEL SANDERS; no children.
311   VI. SETH WASHBURN,[6] b. 1797; m. PHEBE DARLING, of Woodstock,
           Vt.

127.

THOMAS [5] CHURCHILL (ICHABOD,[4] WILLIAM,[3] WILLIAM,[2] JOHN[1]). Born in Plymouth, March 7, 1756; died Feb. 26, 1826. Lived in Plympton and Plymouth. Served in the Revolution, Capt. Seth Stower's Company, July 1, 1777, six months at Rhode Island. Married MARY HOLMES, daughter of Zaccheus. She died July 12, 1835.

Children, the four oldest born in Plympton, the rest in Plymouth.

312   I. ZACCHEUS,[6] b. 1779; m. ALICE DUNCKLER, of Danvers.
      II. NANCY,[6] b. 1781; m. JOHN ATWOOD, 1799.

Children.

      1. John Atwood, m. Hannah Wiswall, 1828.
      2. William Atwood, m. Lydia (Holmes) Savary, dau. George Holmes.
      3. Maria Shaw Atwood, m. Ignatius Pierce.
      4. Mary Ann Atwood, m. Ephraim Holmes.
      5. Nancy Atwood.

      III. TEMPERANCE,[6] b. June 30, 1783; m. WILLIAM ATWOOD, 1804.

Children.

      1. William Atwood.
      2. Nancy Atwood, m. 1st, Branch Johnson; m. 2d, Anthony Morse.
      3. Thomas C. Atwood.
      4. Henry Atwood.
      5. Isaac Atwood, m. Ann Brown.
      6. Eunice Atwood, m. Charles Raymond.

      IV. POLLY,[6] b. Dec. 18, 1786.
313   V. CHARLES,[6] b. Sept. 10, 1792; m. ABIGAIL RUSSELL.
      VI. THOMAS,[6] b. Aug. 4, 1796. Drowned at sea, June 8, 1816.

128.

DANIEL [5] CHURCHILL (ISAAC,[4] WILLIAM,[3] WILLIAM,[2] JOHN[1]). Born Aug. 4, 1767, in Plympton, and lived there. Died June 7, 1858. Married LUCY CHURCHILL, daughter of Ebenezer [5] (No. 125). She died December, 1858.

Children born in Plympton.

      I. EUNICE,[6] b. April 1, 1798; d. March 7, 1799.
314   II. DANIEL,[6] b. June 19, 1800; m. REBECCA W. SOULE.
315 III. HARVEY,[6] b. April 11, 1805; m. ELIZA VOSE, June, 1843.

129.

JOSIAH [5] CHURCHILL (ISAAC,[4] ISAAC,[3] WILLIAM,[2] JOHN[1]). Born in Plympton, Jan. 19, 1770, and lived there. Died Dec. 14, 1844. Married DEBORAH PHINNEY (daughter of Ichabod, of Plympton, and his wife Deborah Churchill, daughter of Ichabod), b. Sept. 21, 1776. She died March 5, 1853.

Children born in Plympton.

      I. SUSANNA,[6] b. Aug. 20, 1795; m. 1st, JOSEPH NYE; m. 2d, JOHN
          DELANO. She d. March 31, 1861.

316   II. TIMOTHY,[6] b. Aug. 7, 1797; m. RUTH SOULE, of Plympton.

317   III. PELHAM,[6] b. March 14, 1800; m. EUNICE T. SIMMONS, of Ply-
          mouth.

318   IV. SIMEON,[6] b. May 25, 1802; m. MRS. SALLY (BISBEE) CUSHMAN,
          March, 1830.

      V. SYLVANUS,[6] b. Dec. 15, 1804; m. ABBIE BILLINGS, of Vermont.
         . No children.

319   VI. ALEXANDER,[6] b. April 3, 1807; m. LYDIA BOSWORTH, of Halifax,
          Mass.

   VII. JOANNA,[6] b. May 27, 1812; unmarried.

320 VIII. ALBERT SMITH,[6] b. April 19, 1815; m. PRISCILLA S. SIMMONS, at
          Plymouth, 1841.

130.

SETH[5] CHURCHILL (ISAAC,[4] ISAAC,[3] WILLIAM,[2] JOHN[1]).
Born Sept 29, 1777, in Plympton. Died June 4, 1849. Married
REBECCA PHINNEY, daughter of Ichabod. She died Sept. 16, 1854.

Children.

      I. EUNICE,[6] b. March 22, 1808.
     II. DEBORAH,[6] b. Feb. 3, 1810; m. (———) STURTEVANT.
    III. SALLY,[6] b. Feb. 13, 1813.
    IV. REBECCA.[6] b. Nov. 23, 1816; d. July 22, 1820.

131.

ISAAC[5] CHURCHILL (ISAAC,[4] ISAAC,[3] WILLIAM,[2] JOHN[1]).
Born in Plympton, April 26, 1782. Lived in Plympton and Abington, to which latter place he removed about 1820. Died in Abington, Aug. 7, 1842. Married, in Provincetown, 1806, MARY
GROZIER.

Children born in Plympton and Abington.

      I. ISAAC,[6] b. Oct. 14, 1807.
     II. MARY GROZIER,[6] b. June 9, 1809; m. HECTOR FOSTER, Nov. 30,
         1828. She was living in So. Abington in 1896.

Children born in Abington.

     1. Mary M. Foster, b. Oct. 25, 1829; m. 1st, B. Frank Hutchinson,
        March 2, 1848; m. 2d, James A. Bates, Nov. 26, 1865.
     2. Rolinda Holmes Foster, b. Oct. 31, 1831; d. April 2, 1834.
     3. Thomas Foster. b. June 9, 1833; m. Mary Hutchinson, May 27,
        1853, and d. Jan. 12, 1860.
     4. Samuel Foster, b. July 22, 1835; m. Abigail P. Porter, Oct. 15
        1857.
     5. Rolinda Holmes Foster, b. March 14, 1837; m. Henry West,
        July 17, 1853.
     6. Sophia Wade Foster, b. Dec. 30, 1839; d. Jan. 8, 1844.
     7. John Albert Foster, b. Sept. 13, 1845; d. as soldier in First Regi-
        ment Artillery, Mass. Vols., May 19, 1864.
     8. Arthur Waldo Foster, b. May 12, 1850; d. Sept. 14, 1861.

    III. SOPHIA.[6] b. April 29, 1810; m. ORRIN WADE, at Plympton, Aug.
      24, 1834.

Children.

1. Allen Wade, b. June 14, 1835; m. Sarah Smith, Nov. 22, 1862.
2. Isaac E. Wade, b. Aug. 12, 1839; m. Martha A. Hunt, Nov. 26 1862.

IV. WILLIAM GROZIER,[6] b. Nov. 17, 1811.

321 V. REUBEN,[6] b. May 30. 1813; m. MARIA CROCKETT, Oct. 27, 1847.
322 VI. FREEMAN GROZIER,[6] b. Jan. 2, 1815; m. ELIZABETH WINSLOW, June 2, 1836.

VII. JANE,[6] b. July 6, 1816; m. THOMAS DRAYTON, of Bridgewater, May 3, 1840.

Children born at Bridgewater.

1. Charles Drayton, b. July 2, 1843; m. 1st, Georgianna Osgood, Nov. 21, 1866; m. 2d, Mary Jane Latuck, June 3, 1882.
2. Frank Otis Drayton, b. Dec. 29, 1846; m. Jane E. Taggart, May 22, 1878.

VIII. EMILY,[6] b. Aug. 10, 1818; m. JARED VINING, of Weymouth, Dec. 8, 1837.

Children born in Weymouth.

1. Jefferson Vining, b. Aug. 29, 1839; m. a Brazilian woman in 1867.
2. Geo. Henry Vining, b. March 16, 1847; m. a Texan woman.
3. James Vining, b. June 19, 1850; m. Jennie Vogel, in 1850.
4. Emma C. Vining, b. April 3, 1854; m. Reuben D. Burrell in 1870; d. 1877.
5. Laura Vining, b. July 19, 1856; m. Edward Paine, May, 1876.

IX. RUTH DYER,[6] b. May 12, 1820, at Abington; m. SPENCER GLOYD, May 22, 1844. She d. April 3, 1862.

Children born in Abington.

1. Sophia Wade Gloyd, b. Oct. 13, 1845; m. Silas Warren Hall, Nov. 28, 1867.
2. Henry Gloyd, b. Oct. 25, 1846; m. Ruth A. Orcutt, July 20, 1871; d. Feb. 4, 1872.
3. Geo. Spencer Gloyd, b. Sept. 30, 1848.
4. Andrew Gloyd, b. Aug. 31, 1850.
5. Betsey Jane Gloyd, b. Nov. 30, 1852.
6. Ruth Alice Gloyd, b. Jan. 14, 1854.

X. EZRA,[6] b. May 21, 1821; d. Jan. 17, 1827.
XI. EUNICE RIPLEY,[6] b. April 15, 1823; d. June 11, 1823.
XII. ALMIRA,[6] b. Feb. 21, 1825; m. WILLIAM BELCHER, of Randolph, June 21, 1840.

Children born in Randolph.

1. Almira Jane Belcher, b. Nov. 27, 1842; d. Dec. 1, 1842.
2. Jane Belcher, b. Oct. 29, 1843; m. Jonathan Hopkins, March 24, 1862.
3. William B. Belcher, b. Oct. 1, 1847; m. Laura E. Blanchard, Nov. 13, 1867.
4. Allen W. Belcher, b. Nov. 27, 1849; d. March 4, 1850.
5. Caroline Belcher, b. Oct. 31, 1852; m. Calvin Orcutt, May 13, 1869.
6. Almira Anna Belcher, b. April 10, 1855; m. Roscoe Childs, May 17, 1872.
7. Laura Etta Belcher, b. March 11, 1857; d. March 26, 1857.
8. Lillian Belcher, b. Dec. 24, 1859; m. C. U. Turner, Dec. 24, 1876.
9. Emily Louisa Belcher, b. Nov. 25, 1861; m. N. H. Small, July 16, 1879.
10. Irene Estella Belcher, b. Aug. 27, 1866; d. March 23, 1869.

323 XIII. Ezra,[6] b. Jan. 18, 1827; m. Myra Jane Bosworth, of Belling-
　　　ham, Oct. 20, 1856.
324 XIV. Otis,[6] b. Oct. 6, 1828; m. Mary A. Temple, of Marlboro'.

132.

ZEBEDEE[5] CHURCHILL (Perez,[4] Benjamin,[3] William,[2]
John[1]). Born Aug. 19, 1745, in Middleboro'. Lived in Middleboro', probably at Pope's Point Furnace. Married at the age of
19, he died at 22, Dec. 13, 1767. Married, May 24, 1764, Sarah
Cushman, daughter of Caleb. She was born Nov. 12, 1743, and
after the death of her first husband, Zebedee, she married Samuel
Cobb, of Middleboro', Sept. 24, 1772. She was then of Wareham. She died in ·Middleboro', March 14, 1834, aged about 91
years.

Children born in Middleboro'

325 I. Asaph,[6] b. May 5, 1765; m. Mary Gardner, dau. of Edward.
　　　II. Zebedee,[6] d. young.

133.

PEREZ[5] CHURCHILL (Perez,[4] Benjamin,[3] William[2]
John[1]). Born April 26, 1753. Lived in Middleboro'. Served in
Revolution, in his father's company, Colonel Sprout's Regiment,
first as private and later as a sergeant, in 1778 and 1780. Married
Oct. 1, 1778, Patience Wood.

Children born in Middleboro'.

326 I. Asaph,[6] b. March 7, 1789; m. Rhoda J. Atwood, 1819.
　　　II. Lydia,[6] m. (———) Tubbs.
　　　III. Patience,[6] m. (———) Jackson
　　　IV. Deborah,[6] m. (———) Markham.
　　　V. Benjamin,[6] d. unmarried; drowned at sea.
　　　VI. Edmund,[6] d. unmarried.

134.

ISAAC[5] CHURCHILL (Perez,[4] Benjamin,[3] William,[2]
John[1]). Born in Middleboro', Nov. 23, 1758. Lived in Middleboro' until about 1795–8, when they removed to Pomfret, Vt. He
probably served in the Revolution, but I cannot identify him in the
rolls. Perhaps in Capt. John Gibb's Company, 1778. He died in
Pomfret, Jan. 5, 1803. Married, Jan. 21, 1777, Betsey Raymond,
daughter of James, of Middleboro'

Children born in Middleboro'

327 I. Joseph,[6] b. June 6, 1778; m. Margaret Gardner, Nov. 6, 1817.
328 II. Zebedee,[6] b. Feb. 19, 1779; m. Azubah Cheedle, Nov. 4, 1809.
　　　III. Martha,[6] b. Feb. 9, 1782; m. Zebulon Thomas, March, 1804.
　　　Lived in Montgomery, Vt., in 1857.

IV. BETSEY,[6] b. Dec. 26, 1784; m. JOHN THOMPSON, of Bridgewater, Vt., Dec. 21, 1803.

329   V. ISAAC,[6] b. June 30, 1786; m. LYDIA ROGERS, December, 1804, and lived in Urbana, Ill., 1859.

VI. RUTH,[6] b. March 8, 1789; m. ELISHA WATKINS, July, 1818.

Children born in Pomfret, Vt.

1. Charles C. Watkins.
2. Frank W. Watkins.
3. Chauncy Watkins.
4. Mary Watkins, m. Boynton.
5. Harriet Watkins.
6. Henry Watkins.
7. Jane Watkins.
8. Betsey Watkins.

330   VII. PHINEAS,[6] b. April 28, 1793; m. ARVILLA GROW, 1815.
331   VIII. JACOB,[6] b. April 5, 1795; m. BETSEY HOWARD, April 4, 1821.

135.

JOSEPH [5] CHURCHILL (PEREZ,[4] BENJAMIN,[3] WILLIAM,[2] JOHN [1]). Born April 23, 1761. Lived first in Middleboro'. Moved later to Hebron, Me., but soon after to Paris, Me., and settled in the Swift neighborhood. Joseph, about 1809, went on a visit to Dunstable, Mass., and died there. The mother, Alice, died in Paris, Me. Married, March 8, 1785, ALICE DRAKE, in Middleboro'.

Children.

332   I. SPRAGUE,[6] b. April 28, 1787; m. HARRIET HOLMES.

II. POLLY,[6] b. April 3, 1790; m. DANIEL DUDLEY, June 9, 1835. She was his second wife.

333   III. WILLIAM,[6] b. May 21, 1792; m. 1st, POLLY BIRD; m. 2d, REBECCA CHURCHILL, of Buckfield, Me., dau. of No. 142.

IV. SALLY,[6] b. 1795; m. SHADRACH KEEN, of Sumner, Me.

334   V. SULLIVAN,[6] b. 1798; m. MARTHA SMITH.

VI. SOPHIA,[6] b. April 12, 1801; m. NATHANIEL LIBBY, Dec. 2, 1819.

Children born in Greenwood, Me.

1. Alice Jane Libby, b. Feb. 15, 1823; m. Albert Winslow, July 3, 1841.
2. Joseph Lamoine Libby, b. April 30, 1827; m. Evelyn J. Stuart, Harrison, Me., Nov. 4, 1857. Live in So. Paris, Me.
3. Sarah Sophia Libby, b. Sept. 20, 1832; m. Stetson L. Gordon, Sept. 2, 1853.
4. Nathaniel William Libby, b. June 24, 1834; m. Effie A. Nelson, of Cynthiana, Ky.

VII. BURUDEL,[6] b. April 17, 1805; m. JASON HAMMOND.

VIII. MILLICENT,[6] b. April 25, 1808; m. 1st, LEVI FRANK; m. 2d, BENJAMIN BACON.

136.

JABEZ [5] CHURCHILL (BENJAMIN,[4] BENJAMIN,[3] WILLIAM,[2] JOHN [1]). Born in Middleboro', 1754. Served in the Revolutionary War, in Capt. Perez Churchill's Company, Colonel Sproutt's Regiment. Credited as company clerk. Company marched to Dartmouth on two different alarms. His youngest daughter, Lucinda, was living in Augusta, Me., in 1889, and our senior compiler, Mr. N. W. Churchill, visited her. She was nearly ninety years old, but still clear and bright of mind and memory.   Several letters from her are before me.   In one she says that her father served in the war four years and while the records do not substantiate the statement, it is probable that she had good foundation for it.   She says in the same letter that her parents " were married in Mass. before the Dark Day," and their children were born in Middleboro', Mass. Her father was paid off for his services in the war in "bad money " He removed, in 1801, to Hartford, Me., bringing his father and mother along with him.   He died Dec. 20, 1840.   Married, before May 19, 1780, Louisa Lucas.

Children born in Middleboro'.

	I.	Mary,[6] b. February, 1782; d. aged 2 years.
335	II.	Joab,[6] b. March 2. 1784; m. Philena Hayford, Feb. 26, 1789.
	III.	Louisa,[6] b. Feb. 20, 1786; m. James Keene. One of their children was Zilpah Keene, who married Nathan [6] Churchill (No. 338).
	IV.	Rizpah,[6] b. Jan. 20, 1789; m. Reuben Bartlett. Had seven children.
	V.	Hannah,[6] b. March 13. 1792; d. unmarried.
	VI.	Zilpah.[6] b. May 2, 1794; d. aged 16 years.
	VII.	Polly,[6] b. 1796; m. James Keene.
336	VIII.	Jabez,[6] b. March 14. 1797; m. Phebe Hazleton.
	IX.	Lucinda,[6] b. April 25, 1800; m. John Savage; no children. They lived at Augusta, Me. She died there in 1889, aged 89 years 10 months.

137.

WILLIAM [5] CHURCHILL (Benjamin,[4] Benjamin,[3] William,[2] John [1]).   Born in Middleboro' in 1755, and lived there until after the war of the Revolution, in which he served, in the Company of Capt. Calvin Partridge, Lieut.-Col. Samuel Pierce's Regiment. Marched May 21, 1779, and was stationed at Little Compton, R.I. Some time before 1784 he settled in Buckfield, Me.   About 1796 or 1797 he removed to Wayne, Me.   He drew a pension for his service in the Revolution, according to the account of one of his grandsons.   Married, in Middleboro', Mass., Lydia Maxim.

Children, four born in Buckfield, two in Wayne, Me.

	I.	Lydia,[6] b. Dec. 13, 1784; m. Samuel Dinsmore; both of Wayne. Intentions, July 15, 1809. They removed to Ohio.
	II.	Mary,[6] b. June 1, 1788; m. James Decker, of Temple, Me.

Children.

1. Benjamin Decker.	3. Lucy Decker.
2. Rosella Decker.	4. Hannah Decker.

	III.	Benjamin,[6] b. July 22, 1791; d. unmarried in the " Florida War."
337	IV.	William,[6] b. Aug. 5, 1796; m. Phebe Maxim, both of Wayne. Intentions May 24, 1817.
	V.	Hepsibah,[6] d. unmarried.
338	VI.	Nathan,[6] b. March 23, 1807; m. Zilpah Keene, Oct. 19, 1834.

138.

JOSEPH[5] CHURCHILL (BENJAMIN,[4] BENJAMIN,[3] WILLIAM,[2] JOHN[1]). Born in Middleboro'. He served in the war of the Revo lution, three brief terms of enlistment in the year 1779, viz., March 14, for thirty days, under Captain Wilmarth at Howland's Ferry; from May 20 to July 1, at Tiverton, R.I., and from Aug. 13 to Sept. 13, 1779. It is supposed that after the war he settled in Rhode Island at either Gloucester or Scituate. In 1792 he had a deed of land from Jabez Williams, of Gloucester, and was himself of Gloucester. One of his grandsons, writing of him in 1900, says he was a poor man and did not keep his family together. So it seems that they scattered early, and settled later, in different localities. Three of the sons removed to Pennsylvania, as will be seen, while the daughters, it is said, married and lived in central Massachusetts. He married in Rhode Island (———) WILLIAMS, a descendant of Roger.

Children.

339   I. ABRAHAM,[6] m. and settled in Rhode Island, it is said. No record found.
340   II. PARDON,[6] b. about 1793; m. ABIGAIL WILLIAMS.
341   III. WILLIAMS,[6] b. March 21, 1795; m. BATHSHEBA WILLIAMS.
342   IV. CYRIL,[6] m. and settled at Susquehanna, Pa. Lived and died there.
343a   V. ASA.[6] No further record found.
     VI. ASHA,[6] b. July 11, 1799; m. WILLIAM JEPHERSON. He was a farmer and lived near Webster, and had a family.

Children.

1. Abel Jepherson, b. Oct. 1, 1819; m. Eunice Bown.
2. Elizabeth Jepherson, b. Aug. 3, 1821; m. Amos Morse.
3. George Jepherson, b. Aug. 30, 182–; m. Mary D. Scarborough.
4. Willis Jepherson, died at the age of 15 years.
5. Amos Jepherson, died at the age of 17 years.
6. William Jepherson, died at the age of 2 weeks.
7. William Jepherson, m. Sarah (———).
8. Esther Jepherson, died at the age of 6 years.
9. A daughter died in infancy.
10. Sabia Jepherson, died at 17 years.
11. Melvin Jepherson, died at 17 years.

   VII. PHEBE,[6] b. 1802; m. SIMON FAIRFIELD.

Children.

1. Bathsheba Fairfield.
2. James Marshall Fairfield, b. Nov. 16, 1823.
3. Charles Fairfield.
4. Enos W. Fairfield.
5. John Nelson Fairfield.
6. Clark Fairfield.
7. Albert Fairfield.
8. Asa Churchill Fairfield.
9. Maria Fairfield, died in infancy.

139.

NELSON[5] CHURCHILL (BENJAMIN,[4] BENJAMIN,[3] WILLIAM,[2] JOHN[1]). Lived in Middleboro' and Carver, until 1802, when they removed to Colerain, Mass. Settled on a farm on "Catamount

Hill." He was a farmer and a fine scholar. In his youth he was a molder. He died in Rowe, Mass. Married, Jan. 12, 1786 EUNICE SHAW.

Children born in Middleboro'.

343   I. ARTEMAS,[6] b. July 5, 1786; m. RUTH MAXIM, March 6, 1812.
344   II. NELSON,[6] b. March 2, 1788; m. 1st, NANCY LAKE; m. 2d, LUCY WILLIS MAXIM, of Charlemont.
     III. RUTH,[6] b. Nov. 29, 1790; m. JAMES BELL, of Colerain.

Children.

1. Thomas Bell.
2. Edward Bell.
3. Emily Bell.

     IV. LOVINA,[6] b. May 12, 1797; m. ALDEN WILLIS.
345   V. ALVIN,[6] b. September, 1799; m. EMILY WILLIS, of Charlemont, Dec. 2, 1825.

139a.

ALICE[5] (CHURCHILL) MONK (JABEZ,[4] JOSIAH,[3] WILLIAM,[2] JOHN[1]). Born in North Bridgewater, Feb. 23, 1753. Married ELIAS MONK, of Bridgewater, Feb. 10, 1772. Mr. Monk served in the Revolution, first on the Lexington Alarm, April 19, 1775, in Capt. Peter Talbot's Company, Col. Lemuel Robinson's Regiment, seven days; and in various enlistments under different officers, covering almost the entire period of the war. He is said to have been of Stoughton. They removed, about 1781 or 1782, to Hebron, Me., and settled on a farm. Mrs. Alice Monk died Aug. 15, 1806, and Elias Monk died Dec. 17, 1842.

Children, the first born in Bridgewater, the rest in Hebron.

     I. LEWIS[6] MONK, b. Sept. 14, 1779.
     II. JAMES[6] MONK, b. Dec. 12, 1782; m. POLLY JORDAN, of Hebron, May 9, 1802.
     III. MARTHA[6] MONK, b. Aug. 24, 1784; m. JAMES FARRIS, JR., of Hebron, Aug. 2, 1806.
     IV. ALFRED[6] MONK, b. Sept. 8, 1786; m. RELIEF IRISH
     V. REBECKAH[6] MONK, b. Sept. 7, 1788; m. MOSES TWITCHELL. Lived in Paris, Me.
     VI. BETTY[6] MONK, b. April 4, 1791.
     VII. LOVINA[6] BISBEE MONK, b. Oct. 17, 1792; m. JOSEPH PENLEY.
     VIII. MELATIAH[6] MONK, b. Oct. 28, 1794.

139b.

RACHEL[5] (CHURCHILL) PRATT (JABEZ,[4] JOSIAH,[3] WILLIAM,[2] JOHN[1]). Born in North Bridgewater, Oct. 17, 1754. Married there, July 23, 1777, THADDEUS PRATT, son of Barnabas and Isabella (Downey) Pratt, of Bridgewater, born in 1755. Mr. Pratt served in the Revolution, first on the Lexington Alarm, April 19, 1775; marched from Bridgewater; served twelve days in the company of Capt. Josiah Hayden, Colonel Bailey's Regiment of Minutemeń. He was in other companies in various service later, and in a "Descriptive list of the men raised in Plymouth County to serve in the Continental Army" he is described as, "Age, 24 years; stature, 5 feet 7 inches; complexion, dark; residence, Bridgewater; delivered to Capt. L. Bailey." This last enlistment was on July 23, 1779, for nine months, and he was discharged April 23, 1780. He removed to Hebron, Me., in 1782, where he is said to have been the tenth settler of the new town.

Children of Thaddeus and Rachel (Churchill) Pratt.

I. WILLIAM.[6] PRATT, b. March 12, 1779; m. MARTHA GURNEY, July 1, 1804.
II. JOSIAH[6] PRATT, b. May 3, 1783; m. SIBYL GURNEY, 1807.
III. BARNABAS[6] PRATT, b. July 13, 1785; d. March 12, 1790.
IV. RACHEL[6] PRATT, b. Feb. 9, 1788; m. ELIPHALET STURTEVANT, March, 1807. She died March 11, 1817, at Hebron.
V. BARNABAS[6] PRATT, b. March 18, 1790. Never married.
VI. SUSANNA[6] PRATT, b. June 1, 1793.
VII. POLLY[6] PRATT, b. July 5, 1795; m. ELIPHALET STURTEVANT, April 23, 1818. She died Nov. 16, 1833.
VIII. CYPRIAN[6] PRATT, b. Aug. 8, 1797; m. BETSEY DUNHAM, June 24, 1819.
IX. RUBY[6] PRATT, b. Feb. 14, 1801.

140.

JABEZ[5] CHURCHILL (JABEZ,[4] JOSIAH,[3] WILLIAM,[2] JOHN[1]). Born in Bridgewater, Mass., 1759. He enlisted in the Revolutionary service, as private in Capt. Henry Prentiss's Company, Col. Thomas Marshall's Regiment, June 8, 1876; discharged Dec. 1, 1776. Service five months twenty-four days. Again enlisted March 27, 1777, in Capt. John Porter's Company, Col. Michael Jackson's Regiment; age, 18 years; residence, Bridgewater; term of enlistment three years. One of his descendants claims that he served four years and nine days. About 1782 he went to Hebron, Me., and resided there afterwards. Married, 1785, MARIA BENSON.

Children born in Hebron, Me.

346   I. SHEPARD,[6] ⎫ b. 1786/7; m. POLLY DUDLEY, Oct. 6, 1808. She was
                   ⎬   of Hebron.
347   II. JOSIAH,[6] ⎭ b. 1786/7; m. RACHEL CURTIS, of Woodstock, Me.
348   III. BELA,[6] m. SARAH DUDLEY.
349   IV. MATTHEW,[6] b. March 20, 1792; m. DOROTHY HALL, of Falmouth.
      V. RUHAMAH,[6] b. Feb. 1, 1794; m. AMOS WINSLOW, Sept. 11, 1813. She d. in Buckfield, Dec. 16, 1877. He d. in Buckfield, Jan. 6, 1855.

Children born in Buckfield.

1. Amos Winslow, d. young.
2. Hannah Winslow, d. young.
3. Solomon Winslow, b. Aug. 21, 1820.
4. Hiram Winslow, b. March 12, 1822.
5. Stephen Winslow, b. Feb. 19, 1824.

6. Maria Winslow, b. Dec. 22, 1826.
7. Miranda Winslow, b. Aug. 17, 1829.
8. George Clinton Winslow, b. July 12, 1832.
9. Amos Kendall Winslow, b. July 28, 1834.

350 VI. JABEZ,[6] m. TIRZAH DUDLEY.
   VII. MARCENA,[6] m. JOHN BICKNELL.

141.

JOSIAH[5] CHURCHILL (JABEZ,[4] JOSIAH,[3] WILLIAM,[2] JOHN[1]). Born, 1762, in Bridgewater, Mass. It is probable that he served in the Revolution in 1779 among the nine months' men. It is a tradition in the family that he went to Hebron before the others, but after a few years removed to Yarmouth or Falmouth, Me. Married LYDIA ORR. She died April 11, 1790, aged 25 years.

Child.

351 I. JOSIAH.[6] No record.

142.

BENJAMIN[5] CHURCHILL (JABEZ,[4] JOSIAH,[3] WILLIAM,[2] JOHN[1]). Born in Bridgewater about 1765, and removed with his mother and her family to Hebron in the spring of 1783 or '84 · married 1st, SALLY BENSON.

*Children born in Hebron, some, perhaps, elsewhere.

 I. SALLY,[6] m. NATHAN DUDLEY.

They lived at Oxford, Me., and had children.

1. Benjamin Dudley.
2. Caleb Dudley.
3. Nathan Dudley.
4. Samuel Dudley.
5. Simon Dudley.
6. William Dudley, d. in 1854.

 II. RUTH,[6] m. EBENEZER DUDLEY, May 18, 1824, of Hebron, Me., in Hebron.

Children.

1. Seth B. Dudley, b. 1825.
2. Sarah Dudley, b. 1829.
3. Jane Dudley, b. 1831.
4. Daniel Dudley, b. 1834.
5. Harrison Dudley

 III. CELIA,[6] m. BENJAMIN WITT, of Norway.

Children.

1. Daniel Witt.
2. George Witt.
3. Cyrus Witt, m. Angie Bird.
4. Betsey Witt.

 IV. POLLY,[6] m. (———) BIGELOW, of Worcester.

One child.

1. Harriet Bigelow.

 V. REBECCA,[6] m. WILLIAM[6] CHURCHILL (No. 333), *q. v.*
 VI. MIRANDA,[6] b. 1813; d. 1886, aged 73; m. JOHN WITT, of Norway.
 VII. OLIVE,[6] m. RUFUS BRIGGS, of Norway.

* NOTE —I am not sure that the above is the proper order of births. — *Editor.*

Children.

1. Sarah Briggs, m. Albert Moss.
2. Emmeline Briggs, unmarried.
3. Ellen Briggs, m. Hiram Moore.
4. Charles Briggs, lives in Indianapolis.
5. Ada Briggs, married in Dallas, Texas.

142a.

CHARLOTTE [5] (CHURCHILL) BARROWS (JABEZ,[4] JO
SIAH,[3] WILLIAM,[2] JOHN [1]). Born in North Bridgewater, Mass.,
Nov. 1, 1767. Married EPHRAIM BARROWS, of Hebron, born
Aug. 14, 1762. Served in the Revolution, from Plympton, Mass.,
June, 1778; age, 16. Died May 2, 1838

Children.

I. JABEZ [6] BARROWS, b. Jan. 16, 1786; d. in Foxcroft, Me.
II. ABIGAIL [6] BARROWS, b. July 15, 1787; m. REUBEN CHANDLER.
III. EPHRAIM [6] BARROWS, JR., b. Nov. 9, 1789; d. in Bangor, Me.
IV. BENJAMIN [6] BARROWS, b. Sept. 2, 1792; d. in Norway, Me.
V. MARY [6] BARROWS, b. June 25, 1794.
VI. JOEL [6] BARROWS, b. May 17, 1796; d. in Sumner, Me.
VII. CHARLOTTE [6] BARROWS, b. Oct. 2, 1798; never married.
VIII. KEZIAH [6] BARROWS, b. April 27, 1801; never married.
IX. LUCINDA [6] BARROWS, b. Sept. 25, 1803; m. RICHARD HOUGHTON.
X. HIRAM [6] BARROWS, b. May 7, 1805; d. in Otisfield, Me.
XI. MIRANDA [6] BARROWS, b. Dec. 8, 1808; d. April 26, 1815.

142b.

* SILENCE [5] (CHURCHILL) BESSEY (JABEZ,[4] JOSIAH,[3]
WILLIAM,[2] JOHN[1]).* Born in North Bridgewater, Mass., in 1772.
Moved to Hebron, Me., with her mother in 1784-5. Married 1st,
JEPTHAH BENSON, who was born Sept. 4, 1763. Married 2d,
JOHN BESSEY, as his second wife. We have found no record of
children of first husband, but by second husband she had three
children born in Paris, Me.

Children by Second Husband.

I. JOSHUA [6] BESSEY, b. May, 1802.
II. CHARITY [6] BESSEY, b. March, 1804; m. JOHN THURLOW, of Wood-
stock.
III. MAHALA [6] BESSEY, b. May, 1806; m. SUMNER STEARNS, of Bethel.

143.

ASAPH [5] CHURCHILL (JABEZ,[4] JOSIAH,[3] WILLIAM,[2] JOHN[1]).
Born in 1775 in Bridgewater, and lived in Hebron and Paris, Me.
Married 1st, BETSEY DEAN; married 2d, 1806, POLLY MERRILL.

---

* The name referred to this number was given incorrectly CELESTIA, and
printed so before the error was discovered. One informant wrote the name in
that way. No record of the family of Susan (140a) has been found. — *Editor.*

Child of First Wife, born in Buckfield

352   I. ASAPH,[6] b. July 31, 1803; m.-1st, SALLY PETERSON, 1825; m. 2d,
          LOVINA MOODY, 1842.

Children of Second Wife, born in Buckfield.

353   II. HIRAM,[6] b. Aug. 20, 1808; m. 1st, MARGARET TARBOX; m. 2d,
          MELINDA S. ROCKWELL.
354 III. NATHANIEL,[6] b. May 28, 1810; m. ABBY W. STEVENS, of Shap-
          leigh, Me.
355   IV. ELBRIDGE,[6] b. Jan. 28, 1812; m. 1st, MARY PETERSON; m. 2d,
          ABBIE COLE.
       V. BETSEY,[6] b. Jan. 22, 1814; m. MARTIN CHURCHILL (No. 732), *q. v.*
356   VI. ALBERT,[6] b. May 21, 1816; m. MERCY FREEMAN.
     VII. POLLY,[6] b. May 26, 1818; m. HANSON HAM, of Saco. She had two
          children who died in infancy. She died at the age of 48 years.

Children born, probably, in Paris, Me.

    VIII. LUCY,[6] b. March 4, 1822; m. 1st, (———) (———); m. 2d, ISAAC
          SCAMMAN.

Child.

    1. Child by first husband died in infancy.

Children by Second Husband.

    2. Lizzie P. Scamman, b. in Portland, Sept. 14, 1852; m. Fred C.
       Merrill.
    3. Mary E. Scamman, b. in Portland, Sept. 2, 1854; m. John Γ.
       Smith.
    4. Charles L. Scamman, b. in Presque Isle, June 28, 1858; m. Vira
       Packard.
    5. Helen Amanda Scamman, b. in Presque Isle March 12, 1860;
       d. Dec. 18, 1860.

      IX. NANCY,[6] b. Feb. 8, 1824; m. JOHN F. EMERY, Dec. 10, 184

Children.

    1. Lyman C. Emery, b. April 6, 1846, in Alfred, Me.; d. Sept. 2,
       1847, in Portland, Me.
    2. Infant son, b. July 10, 1848, in Portland, Me; d. July 18, 1848.
    3. John C., b. Sept. 16, 1850, in Saco, Me.; d. Oct. 17, 1851.
    4. Howard, b. Oct. 3, 1853; m. Elizabeth A. Sanborn, June 15,
       1885.
    5. Herbert, b. Oct. 10, 1856, in Saco, Me.; d. Dec. 17, 1863.

144.

JOHN[5] CHURCHILL (ISRAEL,[4] JOSIAH,[3] WILLIAM,[2] JOHN[1]).
Born (probably) at Tribes' Hill, in the Mohawk Valley, and settled
at Yonge, Leeds County, Ont. Married ANNA HEWITT.

Children born in Yonge, Ont.

       I. NANCY,[6] b. 1802; m. JAMES NICHOLSON.
      II. JANE,[6] b. 1805; m. JOHN CHAPMAN.
357 III. DAVID RUSSELL,[6] b. 1808; m. JANE McVEIGH.
      IV. MARY ANN,[6] b. 1810; m. JOHN BURNES.
       V. WILLIAM,[6] b. 1812; never married.
      VI. RUHAMA,[6] b. 1814; m. JOHN COWAN.

358   VII.   JOHN,[6] b. 1816; m. 1st, (——)(——); m. 2d, SOPHIA TOMPKINS.
         VIII.   EDWARD SYDNEY,[6] b. 1818; never married.
         IX.   ELIZABETH,[6] b. 1820; never married.
         X.   ELEANOR,[6] b. Sept. 15, 1822; m. PETER KELLEY.
         XI.   MARIA.[6] b. 1824; m. OMAR COOK.
359   XII.   JONES,[6] b. 1829; m. ELIZABETH FORRESTER.
         XIII.   CHARLES STUART,[6] never married.

145.

JOSEPH [5] CHURCHILL (ISRAEL,[4] JOSIAH,[3] WILLIAM,[2] JOHN [1]).
Born at Tribes Hill, probably. Settled at Yonge near Farmers-
ville, Ont. Married ABIGAIL HANLEY.

Children born at Yonge.

       I.   EZRA,[6] b. 1800. No further record.
      II.   HANNAH.[6]
     III.   EZEKIEL.[6] No further record.
360   IV.   JEHIEL,[6] b. Feb. 9, 1807; m. SARAH SHANARD. No record.
      V.   LUCY ANN,[6] m. (——) BEEBE.
     VI.   LEWIS.[6] No further record.
    VII.   ALBERT.[6] No further record.
   VIII.   DORCAS,[6] m. (——) BEEBE.

147.

CORNELIUS PHILLIPS [5] CHURCHILL (ISRAEL,[4] JOSIAH,[3]
WILLIAM,[2] JOHN [1]). Born in the Mohawk Valley, June 27, 1789.
Settled at Pickering, Canada. Married, April 29, 1810, CHARLOTTE
BARRY. He died at Pickering, Ontario County. When married
they were both of the Township of Yonge, County Leeds, District
of Johnstown, Canada West.

Children born in Yonge.

361   I.   LEVIUS,[6] b. Jan. 29, 1812; m. DELILAH BETTS, Nov. 6, 1836.
     II.   ALMIRA,[6] b. Nov. 12, 1814; m. DAVID HOGLE. April 21, 1842.
    III.   ELEANOR,[6] b. Dec. 23, 1818; m. WILLIAM MARR, of Pickering,
            Nov. 31, 1839.
    IV.   HARRIET,[6] b. Feb. 20, 1826; m. THOMAS HUBBERT, Oct. 21, 1843.
362   V.   CHARLES,[6] b. Oct. 8, 1828; m. JANE MAJOR, May 10, 1848.

148.

JACOB [5] CHURCHILL (JOSEPH,[4] JOSIAH,[3] WILLIAM,[2] JOHN [1]).
Born in Gloucester or Scituate, R.I. Lived in Gloucester till after
1790, then near Providence, and thence moved to Williamstown, Vt.
He was a nail maker. He died in Sterling, N.Y., in 1847. Mar-
ried, 1788, at or near Bellows Falls, Vt., ABIGAIL TURNER, of
Gloucester, R.I. Abigail died in Vermont about 1830.

Children.

363   I.   WILLIAM T.,[6] b. June 21, 1790; m. ISABEL GILBERT.
     II.   SUSAN,[6] b. 1794; m. TIMOTHY CLAFLIN.

Child.

    1. Maria Claflin, m. Van Allen.
364   III. Artemas,[6] b. Aug. 4, 1797; m. Annie Mattison, Dec. 31, 1820.
      IV. Lydia,[6] unmarried.
      V. Olive,[6] b. 1799; m. Eli Boutelle.
      VI. Gardner,[6] never married.
365   VII. Palmer,[6] b. 1805; m. Susan Henry.
366 VIII. Otis,[6] b. Oct. 10, 1808; m. Maria Vaughn.
367   IX. Jacob,[6] b. July 13, 1810; m. Clarissa Vaughn, 1830.
      X. Abigail,[6] m. David Fish.
      XI. Sophia,[6] m. George Vanderwater.

149.

BENJAMIN[5] CHURCHILL (Joseph,[4] Josiah[3] William[2] John[1]). Born in Bristol County, Mass., 1778. Settled with his brothers, Samuel, Nathaniel, and William, in Westminster, Vt., some time before October, 1799. Lived for a time at Putney, and then in Westminster. He may have removed to Washington County, N.Y., where his oldest brother Jacob lived at Fort Edward, and Nathaniel at Fort Ann. Married, at Putney, Oct. 6, 1799, Temperance Perry, of Putney, Vt., by Asa Washburn, Justice of the Peace.

Children born in Putney, Vt.

368   I. Sylvester,[6] b. March 6, 1801; m. Fanny Davenport.
     II. Temperance.[6]
     III. Araminta.[6]
369   IV. Erastus,[6] b. Dec. 13, 1809; m. Almira Churchill.
370   V. Charles Perry,[6] b. March 29. 1812; m. 1st, Amelia Ann Davenport, March 20, 1834; m. 2d, Elizabeth Van Sheick, Sept. 12, 1856.
     VI. Irena.[6]
371   VII. James,[6] m. 1st, Charlotte (———); m. 2d, (——— ———).

150.

ALVA[5] CHURCHILL (Jacob,[4] Josiah,[3] William,[2] John[1]). Born in Stockbridge. Joined the church there in 1803. Settled at first in Stockbridge, but after the first wife's death removed to Lenox, thence to New Marlborough, and lived there till 1817, when the family removed to Pennsylvania. Married 1st, Arvilla Andrus, daughter of Elisha, of Great Barrington; 2d, Ann Mott.

Children of First Wife, first three born in Stockbridge.

     I. Achsah,[6] m. Dunham Ross. He died during the Civil War. She died in 1852, leaving a family of six children, viz.: (1) Dunham Ross, (2) Develon Ross, (3) Dennis Ross, (4) Lillis Ross, (5) Phebe Ross, (6) Amanda Ross.
372   II. Calvin W.,[6] b. July 23, 1809; m. 1st, Luna Holcomb, Nov. 8, 1832; m. 2d, Mehitable Gee.

III. AMANDA,⁶ m. HARRY BAILEY. Five children, viz.: (1) Festus
Bailey, (2) Sybil Bailey, (3) Persons Bailey, (4) Lution Bailey,
(5) Arvilla Bailey.
373 IV. LA FAYETTE,⁶ b. June 22, 1828; m. SUSANNA VROOMAN, Dec. 21,
1847.

151.

SEYMOUR⁵ CHURCHILL (JACOB⁴ JOSIAH,³ WILLIAM²
JOHN¹). Born in Stockbridge, and lived and died there. Married
REBECCA PALMER.

Children born in Stockbridge.

374 I. ROSWELL PALMER,⁶ b. Sept. 14, 1818; m. MARIA KNAPP.
II. WILLIAM PITT,⁶ d. young; unmarried.
III. CHARLES SEYMOUR,⁶ d. at the age of 18.

152.

DANIEL⁵ CHURCHILL (JACOB,⁴ JOSIAH,³ WILLIAM,² JOHN¹).
Born in Stockbridge. Lived at Newark Valley, N.Y. We have not
been able to find anything further about this family. Married
EXPERIENCE STAFFORD.

Children.

I. MARY.⁶
II. SEYMOUR.⁶
Said to have been a physician in Oswego, N.Y.

153.

JACOB⁵ MILES CHURCHILL (JACOB,⁴ JOSIAH,³ WILLIAM,²
JOHN¹). Born in Stockbridge, May 10, 1799. Lived in Delhi,
N.Y. He died Jan. 14, 1876. Married LUCINDA THOMPSON, at
Stockbridge, Mass., where she was born May 30, 1800. She died
Oct. 5, 1880.

Children.

I. PAMELIA,⁶ b. Feb. 18, 1826; m. 1st, ALFRED FITCH, at Delhi, May
22, 1849. Mr. Fitch died Sept. 23, 1854; m. 2d, JOSEPH H.
FOOTE, May 21, 1856. He was a physician, at Franklin, N.Y.

Child by First Husband.

1. Helen B. Fitch, b. April 3, 1850; d. Nov. 8, 1865.

Children by Second Husband.

2. Julia Foote, b. April 8, 1858; d. April 26, 1858.
3. Stella Foote, b. July 1, 1859.
375 II. CHARLES F.,⁶ b. in Delhi, N.Y., May 20, 1837; m. HARRIET F.
ARMSTRONG, June 14, 1876.
III. HELEN,⁶ b. Oct. 1, 1844; d. May 15, 1845.

155.

GEORGE[5] CHURCHILL (EBENEZER[4] JOHN,[3] JOHN,[2] JOHN[1]).
Born in Plymouth, April 18, 1761.   Served in Revolution in Capt.
Ebenezer Washburn's Company, Col. Eleazer Brook's Regiment.
Enlisted Nov. 7, 1777; served to Feb. 3, 1778; in regular army,
1779. Descriptive list says 18 years old, stature, five feet eleven
inches; complexion, dark; residence, Plymouth.   He died at
Martha's Vineyard, Sept. 14, 1796.   Married, April 2, 1786, ELIZA-
BETH HARLOW.

Children.

376   I. EBENEZER,[6] b. March 19, 1787; m. ELIZABETH PEABODY.
        II. ELIZABETH,[6] b. July 25, 1789.
       III. BRANCH,[6] b. Aug. 23, 1792.
        IV. SARAH WARREN,[6] b. July 15, 1795.

SIXTH GENERATION.

156.

ASAHEL⁶ CHURCHILL (SAMUEL,⁵ SAMUEL,⁴ JOHN,³ JOSEPH² JOHN¹). Born in Stockbridge, Mass., July 3, 1769; baptized Aug. 6, 1769. After marriage removed to New York State and settled on the Susquehanna River, about nine miles above Oswego, now Apalachin. The family removed from that place about 1809, came down the river into Pennsylvania, across the country to the Ohio River, and then down that stream to Cincinnati, at that time a small village. The party consisted of Asahel's family, including his daughter Sarah and her husband, Mary, Daniel, Olive, and Samuel. From Cincinnati they went into Indiana and settled at Brookville in Franklin County, then scarcely more than a wilderness. The Indians were not friendly, and the families, for security, gathered into block-houses at night. About two years after the settlement there, Asahel, the father, died, leaving the family in destitute circumstances. The mother lived to be 95 years old, and died in 1864. Married, Feb. 4, 1785, POLLY HART, who was born July 3, 1769.

Children.

I. SARAH,⁷ m. GEORGE GILTNER.

Children.

1. Asahel Giltner, b. July 16, 1809.
2. Milton Giltner, } twins.
3. Amanda Giltner, }
4. Pamelia Giltner.
5. Hamilton Giltner.
6. William Giltner.
7. John Giltner.

II. MARY,⁷ m. (———) MOUNT.
III. OLIVE.⁷
IV. ASAHEL⁷ JR., d., aged 9 years.
377 V. WILLIAM,⁷ b. 1795; m. HANNAH FREELAND.
377a VI. SAMUEL,⁷ m. 1st, (———) ABERNATH; m. 2d, MRS. SNOWDON.
378 VII. DANIEL,⁷ b. 1800; m. 1st, NANCY STREET; m. 2d, JULIA STREET.

157.

SAMUEL⁶ CHURCHILL (SAMUEL,⁵ SAMUEL,⁴ JOHN,³ JOSEPH² JOHN¹). Born in Stockbridge, Jan. 9, 1772. Married, Feb. 25, 1796, PHEBE SEWARD, who was born Dec. 10, 1771.

Children.

    I. FREDERICK SEWARD,[7] b. Sept. 9, 1797; d. at 20 years.

379   II. LYMAN,[7] b. Sept. 17, 1799; m. CHARLOTTE DEWEY, Sept. 20, 1826.

    III. PHEBE,[7] b. Jan. 14, 1803; m. HENRY CURTIS, Dec. 14, 1824.

    IV. CAROLINE,[7] b. April 30, 1805; m. FEDERAL WHITTLESEY, Dec. 15, 1824.

    V. JERUSHA,[7] b. Jan. 3, 1808; m. ALBERT BROWN, Oct. 10, 1827.

Children born in Stockbridge, Mass., and Schenectady, N. Y.

    1. Theodore Backus Brown, b. July 20, 1828; m. Julia E. Strong.

    2. Emily Brown, b. May 30, 1830; d. in infancy.

    3. Henrietta Brown, b. July 17, 1832; d. young.

    4. Clinton C. Brown, b. Jan. 16, 1835; m. Anna Ramsay, Oct. 20, 1869.

    5. Emily W. Brown, b. Nov. 22, 1836.

    6. Mary G. Brown, b. Nov. 30, 1841; m. Clark Brooks.

    7. Alice Seward Brown, b. April 7, 1844.

380   VI. HENRY,[7] b. July 7, 1812; m. SARAH DEWEY, May 20, 1835.

158.

DANIEL[6] CHURCHILL (SAMUEL,[5] SAMUEL[4] JOHN,[3] JOSEPH,[2] JOHN[1]). Born in Stockbridge, June 7, 1778, and lived there or in the vicinity. Married, May 25, 1799, JERUSHA WILLARD, who was born Jan. 31, 1778.

Children born in Stockbridge or Vicinity.

    I. MARY,[7] b. 1800.

    II. ABBIE,[7] b. 1803; m. (———) COOPER.

381   III. WILLIAM C.,[7] b. July 7, 1810; m. 1st, ELIZA S. ARIEL; m. 2d, JANE W. LEONARD; m. 3d, CAROLINE SHERRILL.

382   IV. SAMUEL,[7] b. 1811; m. MARY TAYLOR, of Lee, Mass., Oct. 14, 1835.

159.

JOB[6] CHURCHILL (BARNABAS,[5] BARNABAS,[4] BARNABAS[3] JOSEPH,[2] JOHN[1]). Born at Plymouth, March 2, 1787, and lived there. Married, Dec. 18, 1808, HANNAH T. HARLOW, daughter of Jesse, of Plymouth.

Children born in Plymouth.

383   I. BARNABAS,[7] b. Sept. 30, 1809; m. ELIZA EDDY, March 10, 1833.

    II. JOB,[7] b. Jan. 17, 1812; m. 1st, JANE D. REED, Oct. 27, 1833; m 2d, WIDOW SUSAN ROGERS, September, 1853; m. 3d, WIDOW NANCY J. STETSON, Oct. 10, 1863; no children.

384   III. SYLVANUS H.,[7] b. Feb. 23, 1815; m. LUCRETIA ANN BACON, Oct. 10, 1837, dau. of Captain George.

    IV. HANNAH FAUNCE,[7] b. Jan. 1, 1817; m. ALLEN HOLMES, March 17, 1840. She d. Feb. 12, 1884.

Children born at Plymouth.

    1. Susan Augusta Holmes, b. May 16, 1841

    2. Allen Turner Holmes, b. Dec. 18, 1844.

    3. Frank Holmes, b. September, 1846.

    4. Esther Holmes, died in infancy.

V. SALLY,[7] b. Dec. 14, 1819; d. Feb. 16, 1821.
VI. SALLY,[7] b. Nov. 23, 1821; d. April 20, 1823.
385 VII. CORNELIUS BRADFORD,[7] b. March 26, 1824; m. 1st, SARAH F. CUSHING, Nov. 15, 1846; m. 2d, CARRIE R. TAYLOR, of Natchez, La., Dec. 6, 1856. He d. at New Orleans, Nov. 6, 1879.

160.

ICHABOD[6] CHURCHILL (ICHABOD,[5] JOSEPH,[4] BARNABAS,[3] JOSEPH,[2] JOHN[1]). Born in Middleboro', Mass., July 21, 1772. Lived in Bridgewater, Vt., was a farmer, and died in Stowe, Vt., 1834. Married PRISCILLA MEACHAM. She was born April 30, 1780, and died in Stowe about 1840.

Children born in Bridgewater, Vt.

I. SALOME,[7] b. April 3, 1807; m. JONATHAN BARROWS, of Stowe, Vt.
386 II. JOSEPH,[7] b. Aug. 26, 1811; m. ELIZA ANN RUSSELL, of Stowe, Vt., Feb. 28, 1833.
III. ABIGAIL.[7]

161.

NOAH[6] CHURCHILL (ICHABOD,[5] JOSEPH,[4] BARNABAS,[3] JOSEPH,[2] JOHN[1]). He was born in Middleboro', Mass. May 29, 1774. but went to Woodstock, Vt., in his father's family, at an early age, He lived in Stowe, and was one of the leading men of that town, first selectman of the town, and representative to the Legislature. He was the first man married in town, — the "Intentions of Marriage" being published by the town-clerk, Josiah Hurlburt, at the "raising" of James Town's barn. "The clerk stood on one of the plates of the frame and cried aloud, ' Hear ye! Hear ye! marriage is intended between Noah Churchill and Polly Marshall,' " giving the date and adding the usual ascription, "God save the people!" He died Nov. 4, 1843. Married, May 29, 1798, POLLY MARSHALL, of Waterbury, Vt. She was born in Dudley, Mass., August, 1782, and died in Stowe, Jan. 5, 1849. She was the daughter of Amasa and Tamar Marshall.

Children born in Stowe, Vt.

I. HIRAM,[7] b. June 4, 1799; d. Sept. 4, 1803.
II. SARAH,[7] b. March 23, 1801; d. Sept. 30, 1803.
III. MINERVA,[7] b. Oct. 23, 1802; d. June 1, 1815.
IV. ALMIRA,[7] b. Feb. 7, 1805; m. KENDRICK JENNEY, Dec. 4, 1830. She d. 1843.

Children.

1. Harriet Jenney.   3. Ann Jenney.
2. Edwin C. Jenney, d.   4. Lucia Jenney.
   at 20 years.   5. George Jenney.

V. NOAH,[7] b. June 8, 1806; d. May 23, 1809.
VI. HIRAM NOAH,[7] b. Aug. 27, 1807; d. Aug. 11, 1810.
VII. MILAN,[7] b. Jan. 5, 1811; d. Sept. 26, 1811.

387   VIII. Stillman,[7] b. Sept. 13, 1812; m. Roxa Ann Marsh, of Mont-
           pelia, Vt., May 20,*1841.
388   IX. Edwin,[7] b. Jan. 4, 1815; m. Mary M. Robinson, of Stowe, March
           5, 1837.
389   X. Heman Allen,[7] b. July 27, 1816; m. Mariette L. Benson,
           of Stowe, May 1, 1844.
        XI. Harriet E.,[7] b. March 30, 1823; d. Sept. 4, 1824.

162.

WILLIAM [6] CHURCHILL (Ichabod,[5] Joseph,[4] Barnabas,[3]
Joseph,[2] John [1]).   Born in Middleboro', Mass., Nov. 12, 1776. He
lived in Stowe, Vt., a farmer, and died about 1830.   Married 1st,
Jan. 1, 1802, Eunice Badger, of Bridgewater, Vt.; married 2d,
Orinda Badger.

Children born in Stowe, Vt.

390   I. John,[7] b. Oct. 2, 1802; m. Experience Hale.
        II. Lyman,[7] b. Feb. 12, 1804; died young.
391   III. William,[7] b. Aug. 16, 1805; m. Adaline H. Darling, of Water-
           bury, Vt., Aug. 15, 1830.
        IV. Lucy,[7] b. Sept. 3, 1807; m. William Small, of Morristown, Vt.
392   V. Norman,[7] b. Jan. 15, 1811; m. Eliza Spaulding.
        VI. Jefferson,[7] b. Sept. 12, 1815.

Children of Second Wife.

       VII. Eunice,[7] m. William Jenkins.
      VIII. Orinda.[7]

163.

JOSEPH [6] CHURCHILL (Ichabod,[5] Joseph,[4] Barnabas,[3]
Joseph,[2] John [1]).   Born in Middleboro', Mass., Dec. 25, 1777.
Was taken with his father's family to Woodstock, Vt., in 1780, and
there grew to manhood, working on the farm and attending the
public school.   He was five feet ten inches in stature, light complexion, gray eyes, dark hair.   He was a farmer and lived in
Stowe, Vt., until after 1830, when he removed to the West and
settled for a time in Illinois.   He died in Benton City, Iowa, March
21, 1857.   Married 1st, in Stowe, Vt., Dec. 25, 1803, Dorothy
Marshall.   She died in Stowe, Vt., May 2, 1829.   Married 2d, in
Champaign, Ill., May 2, 1832, Betsey Parker.

Children born in Stowe, Vt.

         I. Emily,[7] b. June 18, 1805; d. March 12, 1820.
393   II. Almond M.,[7] b. April 24, 1808; m. Anna Lovejoy, March 24,
           1834.
       III. Adaline,[7] b. July 27, 1812; m. John W. Sessions, in Stowe, Jan.
           22, 1832.
           Mr. Sessions was a cabinet-maker, but they removed to Wood-
           stock, Ohio, and he was there settled as a minister. After his death
           she lived in North Lewisburg, Ohio, and died there in 1897–8.
        IV. Sophronia,[7] b. Jan. 27, 1817; d. Aug. 22, 1817, in Stowe, Vt.
         V. Susan,[7] b. Jan. 16, 1823; d. March 6, 1823, in Stowe, Vt.

164.

JESSE[6] CHURCHILL (ICHABOD,[5] JOSEPH,[4] BARNABAS,[3] JOSEPH,[2] JOHN[1]). Born in Woodstock, Vt., May 8, 1792, and was brought up there on his father's farm, attended the district school, and learned the trade of wheelwright. He served in the war of 1812. He lived in Woodstock, Vt., where he was a farmer as well as a wheelwright. Married, at Plymouth, Vt., March 1, 1819, MARY WASHBURN, of Woodstock. She died March 14, 1859.

Children born in Woodstock.

394   I. ALDEN P.,[7] b. July 8, 1822; m. ELIZABETH M. GILMAN.
395   II. HORACE M.,[7] b. Aug. 8, 1824; m. MARY ANN FLYNN, in Fitchburg, Mass., Nov. 1, 1860.

         Enlisted in the 53d Regiment Massachusetts Volunteers in Civil War. Served with the army in Louisiana, and died in the service from exposure. No record of children.

396 III. JESSE F.,[7] b. Dec. 16, 1826; m. SABRA CARTER, at Bellows Falls, Vt., Aug. 2, 1854.

165.

LEVI[6] CHURCHILL (JOSEPH,[5] JOSEPH,[4] BARNABAS,[3] JOSEPH,[2] JOHN[1]). Born in Middleboro', Mass., April 24, 1772. Lived in Woodstock, Vt., and died there, May 4, 1845. He was a farmer. Married 1st, at Woodstock, Vt., 1798, PRISCILLA SIMMONS. She died 1799, without issue; 2d, 180– KEZIAH FLETCHER; she died June 4, 1849.

Children of Second Wife, born at Woodstock, Vt.

     I. PRISCILLA E.,[7] b. 1807; d. unmarried in 1876.
    II. ORAMEL W.,[7] b. 1809; d. unmarried in 1878.
397 III. EDMUND FLETCHER,[7] b. 1811; m. MARIA MARBLE, at Hartland, Vt., Sept. 25, 1844.
398 IV. LEVI,[7] b. Sept. 16, 1813; m. ELIZABETH M. PROCTOR, Oct. 2, 1844.
     V. HARRIET,[7] b. 1815; m. GEORGE MERRIFIELD. No children.

166.

JOSEPH[6] CHURCHILL (JOSEPH,[5] JOSEPH,[4] BARNABAS,[3] JOSEPH,[2] JOHN[1]). Born in Woodstock, Vt., July 7, 1781. Lived in Woodstock, Vt.; was a painter by trade, and died Aug. 25, 1873. Married, Feb. 24, 1813, MRS. CLARA (MEECHAM) EDDY, widow of Stafford Eddy. She died in 1870.

Children born at Woodstock, Vt.

     I. LAURA MEECHAM,[7] b. Oct. 18, 1814; d. unmarried, Oct. 27, 1885.
    II. MARY EDDY,[7] b. Jan. 18, 1816. Living unmarried in Elizabethtown, N.Y., 1896.

III. ELIZABETH PALMER,[7] b. March 17, 1818; m. STAFFORD EDDY HALE, Sept. 23, 1843. She d. March 8, 1871.

Children.

1. Frederick Churchill Hale, b. June 24, 1844; m. Mary Louise Kenicutt, June, 1878, at Wheeling, Ill.
2. Clara Lucinda Hale, b. Jan. 12, 1851. Lives at Elizabethtown, N.Y.
3. Joseph Churchill Hale, b. Sept. 6, 1855. Lives at Leadville, Col.

IV. FREDERICK MEECHAM,[7] b. 1820; d. at Woodstock, Oct. 3, 1835.
V. SARAH,[7] b. Jan. 20, 1822. Lived at Elizabethtown, N.Y.
VI. JOSEPH,[7] b. June, 1828; d. unmarried at Woodstock, Oct. 15, 1882.

167.

GEN. SYLVESTER[6] CHURCHILL (JOSEPH,[5] JOSEPH,[4] BARNABAS,[3] JOSEPH,[2] JOHN[1]). Born at Woodstock, Vt., Aug. 2, 1783. He was reared in that town and received his education in the public schools there. He early showed somewhat of the fibre and calibre of his mind and ambition. He found time and means of training for leadership of men. At the age of twenty-five we find him publishing a weekly newspaper at Windsor, Vt., called the "Vermont Republican," which he continued until 1812, during which time he was largely instrumental in changing the politics of his State from Federal to Democratic. He was active in military affairs, and upon the outbreak of the War of 1812 he was appointed captain of infantry, but declined, and, having recruited a company of light artillery, received a commission as first lieutenant of artillery in the army. Under General Dearborn, and later, he rendered distinguished service with this company, which under his drill became very efficient. It was his company which constructed the battery at Burlington, Vt., under whose protecting guns Commodore McDonough's storm-crippled and weakened fleet took shelter from the furious attacks of the British, till the necessary repairs were made. He was promoted to captain and served in the Chateaugay campaign under General Wade Hampton, and soon after was appointed inspector general with rank of major, which position he held till the close of the war, serving on the staffs of General Wilkinson, General Izard, and General McComb, successively. He still retained his office as inspector-general, and was stationed at different points on the Northern frontier and Atlantic coast. He was called to active service in the Creek Indian war of 1836, where he won distinguished honor by his administration, and was promoted to a colonelcy, to succeed General Wool, promoted in 1841. In 1845, by President Polk's clumsy attempt to reduce the army roster, Colonel Churchill was retired with honor, but upon the reassembling of Congress he was at once restored to his rank and position. In 1846, by General Wool's special request, Colonel Churchill went with him to Mexico, and, as most of the forces were raw recruits, his work of directing the training and drilling, and rigidly holding officers and men up to a proper military standard of efficiency, was very arduous, and at first made him unpopular, but soon afterwards resulted in his becoming one of the most honored and beloved officers in the army. At the battle of Buena Vista his heroism and wise posting of troops in the temporary absence of the general officers undoubtedly saved the whole army from disaster, and resulted in a victory. His horse was shot under him, but he escaped without wounds. For his gallant services in this battle he was promoted to brigadier-general by brevet. After the Mexican war he retained his position, being engaged for many months mustering out the returning troops. Then up to 1856 he was engaged in the duty of inspecting the army posts, travelling at least 10,000 miles a year to all the frontier outposts. In 1856 a long-continued and confirmed lameness demanded his release from his arduous duties, and he was retired with high honor from his post. He died in Washington, D.C., Dec. 7, 1862, in his 80th year. General Churchill married, at Windsor, Vt., Aug. 30, 1812, LUCY HUNTER, daughter of William and Mary (Newell) Hunter, born at Windsor, Vt., July 17, 1786, and died at Carlisle, Pa., Sept. 6, 1862.

Children.

    I. HELEN SUSAN,[7] b. at Governor's Island, N.Y., May 29, 1817; d. Sept. 27, 1818.

399 II. WILLIAM HUNTER,[7] b. at Fort Wood, Bedloe's Island, July 8, 1819; m. ELIZABETH M. CUYLER, of Savannah, Ga., 1844.

    III. MARY HELEN,[7] b. at Windsor, Vt., Aug. 30, 1821; m. SPENCER F. BAIRD, at Carlisle, Pa., Aug. 8, 1846. He was born Feb. 3, 1823, and died at Wood's Holl, Mass., Aug. 19, 1887. Mrs. M. H. Baird died at Washington, D.C., Dec. 22, 1891.

Child.

    1. Lucy Hunter Baird, b. at Carlisle, Pa., Feb. 8, 1848. Resides in Philadelphia, Pa.

    IV. FRANKLIN HUNTER,[7] b. at FORT HAMILTON, April 22, 1823; d. unmarried at Newport, R.I., May 24, 1889. He was educated as a lawyer and practised for years in Brooklyn, N.Y. He prepared and published a sketch of his father's life in the later years of his own life.

    V. CAPT. CHARLES COURCELLE,[7] b. at Allegheny Arsenal, Pittsburgh, Pa., July 18, 1825. He received a thorough military education, and was appointed captain of Third Artillery, U.S.A.; m. at Portland, Me., April 22, 1868, ALICE DOW, dau. of William H. and Delia L. He resides, in 1903, at Newport R.I.

168.

ISAAC[6] CHURCHILL (JOSEPH,[5] JOSEPH,[4] BARNABAS,[3] JOSEPH, JOHN[1]). Born in Woodstock, Vt., Feb. 19, 1787. Lived there, a merchant, and died Dec. 7, 1870, in the 84th year of his age. Married, at Woodstock, Oct. 18, 1824, JULIA ARNOLD, daughter of Isaac and Sarah (Howe) Arnold, born in Mansfield, Conn., Nov. 12, 1797, and died at Woodstock, Vt., Sept. 18, 1879.

Children of Isaac and Julia Churchill, born at Woodstock.

I. MARIA FRANCES,[7] b. Sept. 21, 1825; m. EDWARD JOHNSON, son of Eliakim and Mary (Hall) Johnson, b. Sept. 18, 1823, at Wallingford, Vt., and died at Port au Prince, Hayti, Sept. 15, 1864.

Children of Edward and Maria F. (Churchill) Johnson.

    1. Julia Churchill Johnson, b. at Woodstock, Jan. 19, 1855, m. Edwin A. Vaughan. They settled at Princeton, Ill., and had one child, Marjorie Vaughan, b. Sept. 25, 1885.

    2. Frederick Churchill Johnson, b. at Montgomery, Ala., Nov. 3, 1858, and died there April 10, 1860.

    3. Philip Edward Johnson, b. at Woodstock, June 7, 1861.

II. DELIA ARNOLD,[7] b. Sept. 4, 1833; m. WARD A. THOMPSON, who was born at Bridgewater, Vt., April 24, 1835, son of Ovid and Waitstill (Shurtleff) Thompson.

Children of Ward A. and Delia A. (Churchill) Thompson.

    1. Arthur Churchill Thompson, b. at Woodstock, July 8, 1864, and died there Sept. 30, 1883.

    2. Mary Thompson, b. at Woodstock, May 8, 1866.

169.

NATHANIEL[6] CHURCHILL (NATHANIEL,[5] LEMUEL[4] BARNABAS,[3] JOSEPH,[2] JOHN[1]). Born in Yarmouth, N.S., Nov. 22, 1773, and lived there until 1831. They, with most of their sons and daughters, in 1831 removed to Ontario and settled in the vicinity of what is now Bealton. He died at Townsend, Ont., 1850 Married, at Mangersville, 1797, EUNICE KINNEY, born April 19, 1782; married by Parson Basley. She died in Buford, Ont., in 1859.

Children.

400   I. NATHANIEL,[7] b. May 9, 1799; m. JERUSHA FREEMAN, July 30, 1822.

401   II. JESSE,[7] b. Jan. 7, 1801; m. 1st, PHEBE BARLOW; m. 2d, MARY HART.

402   III. CHARLES,[7] b. Jan. 1, 1803; m. MARY J. DUMPHY.

    IV. ELIZA,[7] b. March 19, 1805; m. DANIEL KINNEY

Children.

1. Daniel Kinney.	5. Jesse Kinney.
2. Rhoda Kinney.	6. Stephen Kinney.
3. Cyrus Kinney.	7. Israel Kinney.
4. Eunice Kinney.	8. Susan Kinney.

Said to have been three more children, names not received.

403   V. ISAIAH,[7] b. Feb. 6, 1807; m. MARY FREEL.
          VI. RHODA,[7] b. Dec. 22, 1809; m. JOHN SCHNEIDER.

Children.

1. John Schneider, Jr. | 3. Rhoda Schneider.
2. Winslow Schneider. | 4. Nathaniel Schneider.

VII. SUSANNAH,[7] b. Dec. 23, 1811; m. FREDERICK JOHN WHITFIELD,
Dec. 24, 1828. He was born in Woolwich, England, May 9,
1800; m., as above, in Wakefield, N.B. They lived in various
towns of Canada, as the births of the children show. Died in
Paris, C.W., Oct. 21, 1865. She died in Keen, Mich., July 21,
1862. This family moved from New Brunswick to Ontario in
1831.

Children.

1. Mariah Whitfield, b. Wakefield, N.B., March 19, 1830; d. in
   Upper Canada, Oct. 13, 1831.
2. Dr. George Frederick Whitfield, b. in Hamilton, C.W., Nov.
   30, 1832; m. Phebe Brant.
   Dr. Whitfield was a prominent physician in Grand Rapids,
   Mich., and furnished valuable help upon this line of the
   family.
3. John Isaiah Whitfield, b. in Selfleet, C.W., Feb. 23, 1835; m.
   Kate Knapp.
4. Charles Watts Whitfield, b. in Selfleet, C.W., April 17, 1837;
   m. 1st, Orphia White; m. 2d, Phebe Fletcher.
5. Thomas Nice Whitfield, b. in Burford, C.W., Oct. 29, 1839;
   d., Baltimore, Md., Dec. 6, 1863, in Marine Hospital.
6. Nathaniel Churchill Whitfield, b. in Norwich, C.W., May 7,
   1843; m. 1st, Julia Wood; m. 2d, Amelia M. Atkins.
7. Henry Allen Whitfield, b. in Burford, C.W., May 14, 1845; m.
   Minnie Wead.
8. Rebecca Carr Whitfield, b. in Burford, C.W., July 23, 1847;
   m. Orrin T. Fuller.
9. James Carr Whitfield, b. in Burford, C.W., June 11, 1849; d.
   June 25, 1849.
10. Zenas Elliot Bliss Whitfield, b. July 1, 1854.

404 VIII. ISRAEL,[7] b. March 13, 1813; m. ELIZA DUMPHY.
405   IX. ELIAS WINSLOW,[7] b. Jan. 26, 1817. No further record.
          X. EUNICE,[7] b. Sept. 26, 1818.
          XI. MARIA,[7] b. July 20, 1823; m. THOMAS GARDNER.

Children.

1. Eliza J. Gardner, b. Norwich, Can., Feb. 17, 1843.
2. John W. Gardner, b. Brantford, Oct. 19, 1844.
3. Martha M. Gardner, b. Brantford, Oct. 26, 1846.
4. Ethelyn Gardner, b. Keen, Mich., Oct. 18, 1848.
5. Julia Gardner, b. Keen, Mich., Feb. 6, 1851.
6. Wellington Gardner, b. Keen, Mich., May 1, 1853.
7. Annie May Gardner, b. Keen, Mich., Feb. 25, 1856.
8. Charles Gardner, b. Keen, Mich., Aug. 17, 1858.
9. Thomas W. Gardner, b. Keen, Mich., Dec. 3, 1860.
10. Neadora Gardner, b. Keen, Mich., Dec. 16, 1862.

406 XII. RICHARD WATTS,[7] b. July 19, 1826; m. 1st, MARY C. TAYLOR; m.
          2d, MAHALA BEAL.

170.

LEMUEL [6] CHURCHILL (NATHANIEL,[5] LEMUEL,[4] BARNABAS,[3]
JOSEPH,[2] JOHN [1]). Born in Yarmouth, N.S., Feb. 20, 1777. The
information relating to this family is meagre and very late in com-

ing, so that in the first mention we had to report "no further record," but since that have received the few items below. He lived in New Brunswick, Carlton County, removed to Niagara Township, Upper Canada. My informant, Mr. George W. Boyer, of Hartland, N.B., is able to give but little account of his after life. He died Dec. 14 1859. Married 1st, LOIS FOSTER, who was born April 21, 1783; married 2d, MARY BROWN.

Children by First Wife, born in New Brunswick.

406a   I.   JAMES C.,[7] b. Feb. 18, 1805. He had three wives, as will appear.
406b   II.   AMOS,[7] m. ELEANOR SINCLAIR.
        III.   STEPHEN.[7] Drowned while crossing St. John's river.
406c   IV.   CHLOE ANN,[7] m. GEORGE R. BOYER.

Children by Second Wife, born in New Brunswick.

406d   V.   DANIEL.[7]
406e   VI.   EDWARD.[7]
406f   VII.   REBECCA,[7] m. DAVID PHILLIPS, of Ontario, 1836.
406g VIII.   BETSEY.[7]

173.

BENJAMIN[6] CHURCHILL (NATHANIEL,[5] LEMUEL,[4] BARNA-BAS,[3] JOSEPH,[2] JOHN[1]). Born at Kingston, N.S, Feb. 4, 1790, and died Dec. 29, 1871. The record of births of this family is from Mr. Calvin Churchill, of Lakeville, N.B., and he furnishes mostly the other items. No returns have been received from the families of the daughters. Married, July 15, 1813, ELIZABETH EVERETT, who was born Feb. 16, 1793, and died Aug. 2, 1879.

Children.

I. HANNAH,[7] b. May 28, 1814; m. W. B. ESTEY, b. Nov. 10, 1804.

Children.

1. William E. Estey, b. July 30, 1833.
2. Joseph E. Estey, b. Dec. 11, 1835; died.
3. Charles L. Estey, b. Oct. 17, 1837.
4. Benjamin F. Estey, b. Oct. 19, 1839.
5. Hannah E. Estey, b. Aug. 4, 1841.
6. George H. Estey, b. Sept. 12, 1843.
7. Mary H. Estey, b. Dec. 22, 1845.
8. Aaron S. Estey, b. Dec. 28, 1847.
9. Henrietta A. Estey, b. March 1, 1850.
10. Frederick M. Estey, b. March 28, 1852.
11. Alice M. Estey, b. Sept. 9, 1854.
12. Jane H. Estey, b. Nov. 10, 1857.

II   MARY ANN,[7] b. Oct. 15, 1815, at Wakefield, N.B.; m. MICHAEL CAMPBELL, Oct. 24, 1833.
They lived at Wakefield, N.B., until 1895, when they removed to Washburn, Me., to live with their son Benjamin, and she died there Sept. 3, 1895. He was born at Queensbury, N.B., Aug. 28, 1808, and died at Washburn, Me., Nov. 15, 1901.

Children born in Wakefield, N.B.

1. Benjamin Campbell, b. Dec. 15, 1834; m. Frances Jane Estey, Feb. 7, 1857.
2. George Campbell, b. July 10, 1837; m. Sophronia Tracy, Aug. 28, 1858.
3. Elizabeth Campbell, b. Nov. 6, 1838; m. Hiram Smith, Aug. 23, 1859.
4. Thomas Campbell, b. March 26, 1840; m. Sarah Beardsley, March 15, 1862.
5. Mary Hester Campbell, b. July 14, 1843; d. April 23, 1846.
6. William Harrison Campbell, b. March 12, 1845; d. Jan. 25, 1866.
7. Sarah J. Campbell, b. March 18, 1848; m. Charles W. Plummer, March 5, 1873.
8. Hannah Ann Campbell, b. May 8, 1850; m. J. H. Seely, Nov. 3, 1867.
9. James Todd Campbell, b. May 3, 1852; m. Mary H. Corson, April 11, 1878.
10. John Calvin Campbell, b. March 3, 1856; m. Adelia A. Little.
11. Jarvis Campbell, b. July 10, 1858; d. same day.

407   III. John Russell,[7] b. Aug. 22,.1817; m. Margaret B. McIntosh.
   IV. George Lathrop,[7] b. Oct. 25, 1819; m. Mary Watson.
           They had no children. They lived in Portland. He died there Jan. 2, 1889.
   V. Elizabeth,[7] b. Dec. 19, 1821; m. Alexander Sharp.
           They had three children, viz.: (1) Joel Sharp; (2) Alonzo Sharp; (3) Melissa Sharp. The mother died many years ago.
   VI. Calvin,[7] b. Jan. 3, 1824; m. 1st, Ann Loomer, September, 1846, and she d. April 22, 1854; m. 2d, Elizabeth A. Corbette, Oct. 2, 1856.
408   VII. Benjamin,[7] b. Jan. 11, 1826; m. Rachel Howard, "in the States." He died in Ohio, leaving one daughter, Ella. No further known.
   VIII. Thomas,[7] b. April 26, 1828; m. 1st, Nancy Watson, who died without children. He removed to Texas and m. 2d, name unknown, and had several children. No more heard from the family.
409   IX. William,[7] b. March 21, 1830; m. Jane Good. He died before 1889.
           In 1889 his family lived in Jacksontown, N.B., his son George Churchill being one.
   X. Jarvis,[7] b. Oct. 5, 1832. Went to California and died there unmarried.
   XI. Sarah Estey,[7] b. March 11, 1835; m. Leonard Watson.
         They lived in Jacksontown, Carlton County, N.B., and had children, of whom George Watson, a son, was living there in 1889.

174.

EZRA [6] CHURCHILL (Ezra,[5] Lemuel,[4] Barnabas,[3] Joseph,[2] John [1]). Born at Yarmouth, N.S., May 17, 1784. He was a sailor, and was lost on the brig " Hibernia," wrecked on the "Mud Islands," on a voyage from New York to Yarmouth, Oct. 16, 1807. Married, 1802, Elizabeth Trefry, of Hantsport, N.S., daughter of Joshua P. After the death of Mr. Churchill the widow removed to Hantsport, and married Mr. Faulkner.

Children.

410   I. EZRA,[7] b. Nov. 1, 1804; m. 1st, ANNE DAVIDSON, of Falmouth,
        N.S.; m. 2d, RACHELL BURGESS, of Billtown, N.S.; d. April 14,
        1879.
        II. ELIZABETH,[7] b. July 2, 1806; m. BENJAMIN DAVIDSON, Sept. 21,
        1825.
        Their home was in Halifax. He died at "West River," Neb.,
        1870, and she died at Halifax, June 8, 1874.

Children born in Halifax, N.S.

1. Edgar Davidson, b. July 13, 1826; d., at Halifax, Nov. 8, 1846.
2. Churchill Davidson, b. Sept. 18, 1827; m. Martha M. Gruber,
   June 24, 1852.
3. Cyrena Davidson, b. May 22, 1829; m. Joshua E. Hall, of
   Cleveland, Ohio, June 17, 1851. Live in Australia.
4. Leander Davidson, b. Aug. 16, 1831; d. Aug. 26, 1873; m.
   Tibbie Burton, of Hantsport, Nov. 16, 1858. Moved to
   California.
5. Learchus Davidson, b. Dec. 24, 1833; d. June 30, 1886; m.
   Sophia A. McIlreath, Halifax, Oct. 11, 1858.
6. Ezra Davidson, b. Sept. 4, 1836; m. Mary F. McPherson, June
   6, 1867. Lives at Halifax.
7. Almira Davidson, b. Nov. 21, 1838; m. Francis A. Beamish
   of Halifax, Nov. 20, 1861.
8. Louisa Davidson, b. April 10, 1841; d. March 16, 1880; m.
   George A. Tupper, of Halifax, June 25, 1872
9. Andrew Davidson, b. Aug. 3 1842; m. Abbie Murphy, Dec. 22,
   1877.
10. Lewis Davidson, b. Sept. 11, 1845; unmarried, lived in Cali-
    fornia. Lost at sea.

175.

NEHEMIAH[6] CHURCHILL (EZRA,[5] LEMUEL,[4] BARNABAS,[3]
JOSEPH,[2] JOHN[1]). Born in Yarmouth, N.S., 1786, and lived there.
Married ELIZABETH CANN, daughter of Hugh.

Children.

   I. MARY,[7] m. 1st, EDMUND R. WYMAN; m. 2d, THOMAS O'BRIEN.

Children.

1. Nehemiah C. Wyman, lost at sea, 1855.
2. William Jesse Wyman, m. Elizabeth Crosby.
3. Hannah Alice Wyman, m. James W. Shaw, Dec. 30, 1862.
4. Elizabeth Wyman, d. unmarried, Oct. 8, 1895.
5. Edmund R. Wyman, m. 1st, Drusilla Shaw, Dec. 30, 1862; m.
   2d, Harriet Strickland.
6. George Wyman, m. Letitia Mayer, of St. John's, N.B.
7. Jacob Wyman, d. unmarried, aged 20 years.
8. James Wyman, settled in the United States.

   II. ELIZABETH,[7] b. 1813; m. LEVI ELDRIDGE.

Children.

1. Nathaniel Eldridge, m. Victoria Crosby.
2. Harvey Eldridge; b. 1842; d. March 22, 1854, aged 12 years.
3. Wallace N. Eldridge, m. Thankful Crosby, July 10, 1875.
4. Levi Eldridge, m. in England.

5. Laura Ann Elizabeth Eldridge, b. March, 1855; d. Jan. 1, 1856,
   aged 10 months.

III. CYNTHIA,[7] b. 1815; m. WILLIAM DOANE.

Children.

1. Augustus Doane, d. unmarried.
2. William Doane. Lost at sea, April 21, 1856; unmarried.
3. James Doane.
4. Harvey Doane, m. Elizabeth Crowell, dau. of Enoch.
5. Elizabeth Doane, m. 1st, Samuel Winter, Nov. 20, 1859; m.
   2d, Simeon Ryerson.
6. Sabra Doane, m. Edward Fletcher, Nov. 7, 1866.
7. Martha Doane, m. 1st, Thomas Crowell; m. 2d, James Killam.
8. Mary Doane, m. Isaiah Crosby, son of John.
9. Ellen Doane, m. George Buchanan, of Boston.

411   IV. JAMES,[7] m. ELIZABETH BYRNE, Jan. 31, 1839. He d. Dec. 28,
             1892.
       V. EDITH,[7] m. 1st, CAPT. JAMES DURKEE, son of Amasa, Sept. 12,
             1842; m. 2d, JOSEPH HURLBURT, Jan. 21, 1856.

Children.

1. Anna Durkee, m. (————) Ray, of Weymouth.
2. Maria Durkee, unmarried. Lives in Boston.

VI. SOPHRONIA,[7] m. 1st, CYRUS MOSES, Nov. 5, 1844; m. 2d, GEORGE
    MCCONNELL.

Children.

1. Cyrus Moses, m. Adelaide Landers

VII. JANE,[7] m. RICHARD TEDFORD, March 9, 1847.

Children.

1. Henry Ashlon Tedford, b. November, 1854; d. April 25, 1855,
   aged 5 months.
2. Richard B., b. May, 1856; d. Sept. 19, 1856, aged 4 months.

      VIII. ANN.[7]
412   IX. NEHEMIAH,[7] m. 1st, SARAH H. KINNEY; m. 2d, AMANDA KINNEY.
413   X. WILLIAM,[7] m. MATILDA ALLEN.
        XI. ASENATH.[7]

176.

BENJAMIN[6] CHURCHILL (EZRA,[5] LEMUEL,[4] BARNABAS[3]
JOSEPH,[2] JOHN[1]). Born in Yarmouth, July 26, 1788, and died
Dec. 18, 1849. Married 1st, LUCY RING, who was born Dec. 18,
1788, and died Sept. 25, 1825; married 2d, MRS. LYDIA ANN
(BUTLER) MOSES.

Children by First Wife.

I. COLEMAN,[7] b. Aug. 5, 1812; d. at sea, unmarried, May 16, 1840.
II. EMILY,[7] b. Sept. 26, 1814; m. WILLIAM FLETCHER.

Children.

1. George Fletcher, b. 1840; lost at sea, March 2, 1867.
2. Edward Fletcher, m. Sabra Doane, Nov. 7, 1866.
3. Coleman Fletcher, m. Mary Pitman, dau. of Nelson.

4. Emily Fletcher, m. Ebenezer Clark, March 8, 1867.
5. Elizabeth Fletcher, m. Ammiel R. Brownson, son of Charles.
6. Lalia Fletcher, m. William Lamont.
7. Rachel Fletcher, m. John Gowdy.
8. Mary Fletcher, unmarried.

III. GEORGE,[7] b. Aug. 3, 1816; d. single, Nov. 6, 1842.
414 IV. EZRA,[7] b. Dec. 30, 1817; m. MARY CROSBY, Feb. 1, 1842.
415 V. BENJAMIN,[7] b. July 7, 1819; m. ABBY DUNHAM.
VI. LUCY,[7] b. May 29, 1821; m. ELIAS CROSMAN, Jan. 8, 1846.

Children.

1. George N. Crosman.
2. Sarah J. Crosman, b. Jan. 5, 1854; m. Isaiah Crosby, Feb. 2, 1879; she d. Sept. 2, 1881.

VII. LYDIA,[7] b. Jan. 2, 1823; m. JOHN WINTER, April 17, 1850.

Children.

1. (——) Winter, m. James Clements.

VIII. MARY,[7] b. Feb. 26, 1824; m. JAMES CLELAND.

Children.

1. James Cleland, m. 1st, Emmeline Saunders; m. 2d, Margery L. Cann.
2. Jane Cleland, m. Henry W. Crowell.
3. Jacob Cleland.
4. Margaret Cleland, m. Clifford Locke, of Lockport.
5. George Cleland, m. Margaret A. Moses.
6. William Cleland, m. Alice L. Moses.

416 IX. EDSON,[7] b. July 29, 1825; m. SARAH JANE CARVER.

Children by Second Wife.

417 X. JOHN,[7] b. Aug. 21, 1833; m. ELIZA REDDING, dau. of Joseph.
418 XI. LEWIS,[7] b. March 16, 1835; m. SARAH DURKEE.
XII. NATHANIEL,[7] b. Nov. 1, 1837; m. WEALTHY PORTER. No children.

177.

LEMUEL[6] CHURCHILL (EZRA,[5] LEMUEL,[4] BARNABAS,[3] JOSEPH,[2] JOHN[1]). Born in Yarmouth, N.S., Aug. 7, 1790, and lived there. Married, Dec. 25, 1809, LYDIA GARDNER, who was born August, 1788.

Children.

I. ABIGAIL,[7] b. Jan. 27, 1811; m. CHARLES BROWN, Jan. 10, 1828.

Children.

1. Mary Brown, b. Nov. 28, 1828; m. Gabriel Trefry, Dec. 8, 1846.
2. Agnes Brown, b. July 7, 1833; m. Nathaniel Ward, Dec. 16, 1849.
3. William Brown, b. July 7, 1833; m. 1st, Sarah Murray, Aug. 2, 1856; m. 2d, Emma Wyman, April 3, 1865.
4. Ammiel R. Brown, b. Oct. 1, 1849; m. Elizabeth Fletcher.
5. Lydia C. Brown, b. June 25, 1851; m. James T. Currier.

II. MARY,[7] b. Aug. 7, 1812; m. THOMAS NICKERSON.

Children.

1. Maria Nickerson, m. Edward R. Perry, son of Capt. Joseph.
2. Lemuel C. Nickerson, m. Elbertine (——).
3. Charles Nickerson, unmarried; lost at sea.
4. Rufus S. Nickerson, m. Mary Whitman, dau. of Rev. Jacob; lost at sea.
5. Theodore Nickerson.
6. Thomas Nickerson, m. Lydia Perry, dau. of Capt. Joseph.
7. Stephen Nickerson, m. (——) Goodnow.

419 III. THEODORE,[7] b. Aug. 14, 1814; m. MARTHA JEFFREY, dau. of Matthew, 2d.
IV. ELIZABETH,[7] b. June 1, 1816; m. HEMAN ROGERS.
V. LEMUEL,[7] b. May 9, 1819; d. July 18, 1831.
VI. LYDIA ANN,[7] b. Feb. 19, 1823; m. THOMAS C. TREFREY.
VII. BETHIAH,[7] b. Dec. 20, 1826; m. BENJAMIN RICHARDS.

Children.

1. Margaret A. Richards, b. March 30, 1846; m. Thomas B. Crosby, Sept. 6, 1864.
2. Ammiel Rogers Richards, b. 1847; d. May 16, 1848.
3. Thomas Barnard Richards, b. 1849; m. Jessie Brown Kirby.
4. Edson Churchill Richards, b. 1852; d. May 3, 1854.
5. Benjamin Franklin Richards, b. 1857; d. Sept. 13, 1866.
6. Martha Ellen Churchill Richards, b. 1863; d. April 8, 1863.

178.

JOHN[6] CHURCHILL (EZRA,[5] LEMUEL,[4] BARNABAS,[3] JOSEPH,[2] JOHN[1]). Born in Yarmouth, Sept. 4, 1797. They lived in Yarmouth, N.S. Married, 1817, ABIGAIL ROGERS, daughter of John.

Children.

I. DORCAS,[7] b. March 19, 1818; m. NATHAN WESTON, son of Zadoc.

Children born in Yarmouth.

1. Matilda Weston, m. 1st, William F. Brown; m. 2d, W. T. Lent.
2. Frederick Weston, m. Martha Jenkins.
3. Robert Weston.
4. Elinor Weston, b. February, 1841; d. Sept. 13, 1841.
5. Lydia E. Weston, b. 1844; m. Josiah Ross.
6. Jacob Weston, m. (——) Eldredge.
7. Lemuel Weston, m. Elizabeth Hatfield.
8. Norman J. Weston, m. Sophie Jenkins, dau. of George.
9. George Weston, m. Leoni Kelley.

II. ALMIRA,[7] b. June 19, 1819; m. ANDREW McGRAY, April 5, 1838.

Children.

1. Fanny McGray, m. William Morrill, of Westport.
2. Mary McGray, m. Joseph Durkee.
3. Albert McGray, lost at sea.
4. Andrew McGray, Jr., m. Julia Perry.
5. Benjamin McGray.
6. Frederick McGray, m. Elvira Devilla.
7. Almira McGray, m. Nathan Thurber, of Westport.

420 III. JOHN,[7] b. March 6, 1821; m. MARY A. TAYLOR, Dec. 29, 1844.
IV. CHLOE,[7] b. Feb. 16, 1823.
421 V. JOSEPH,[7] b. Sept. 15, 1824; m. CAROLINE ARCHER, Nov. 15, 1843.

422   VI. FREEMAN,[7] b. April 4, 1826; m. MARTHA PURDY.
423   VII. JACOB,[7] b. Jan. 29, 1828; m. 1st, MARTHA PITMAN; m. 2d, ADA
          EARLE.
424   VIII. SAMUEL,[7] b. Jan. 27, 1831; m. HANNAH CHURCHILL, July 8, 1858.
425   IX. LEMUEL,[7] b. September, 1832; m. ADALINE HEMEON, Oct. 28, 1861.
        X. ELIZA,[7] b. Jan. 29, 1835; m. THOMAS PERRY.

Children.

1. Martha Perry, m. T. R. Hogan.
2. Ida May Perry, m. Wellington W. Perry.
3. George Perry, m. Alice Cook.
4. William E. Perry, unmarried.
5. Ellen H. Perry, m. Henry R. Moody.
6. Alvin Perry, unmarried.

XI. ISRAEL,[7] b. Feb. 12, 1837; unmarried.

179.

TIMOTHY[6] CHURCHILL (ISAAC,[5] ISAAC,[4] BARNABAS,[3] JOSEPH,[2] JOHN[1]). Born at Plymouth in 1785. Married in Duxbury, 1804, OLIVE CURTIS, of Marshfield.

Children.

 I. NANCY,[7] b. in Plymouth; d. in infancy.
 II. HENRIETTA,[7] b. May 2, 1812; m. ISAAC CURTIS, of Pembroke,
       Nov. 11, 1834.

One Child born in Pembroke.

1. Albert W. Curtis, b. Nov. 9, 1840; m. Hannah M. Taylor, of
       Duxbury, March 18, 1864.
III. HANNAH W.,[7] b. in Duxbury, April 26, 1816; m. WARREN T.
       WHITING, Nov. 5, 1834. She died 1862. He died in 1882.

Children born in Pembroke, Mass.

1. Sarah M. Whiting, b. November, 1835; m. Hiram Delano, of
       Pembroke, May, 1859; d. 1867.
2. Olive F. Whiting, b. December, 1837; m. Peleg B. Ford,
       of Pembroke, 1868.
3. George W. Whiting, b. January, 1840; m. Louisa Glover,
       of Duxbury, April, 1864.
4. Franklin T. Whiting, b. March, 1842; m. Ida Sprague, of
       Marshfield, June, 1866.
5. William H. Whiting, b. October, 1843; m. Martha Pratt, of
       Weymouth, 1865 -
6. Ida J. Whiting, b. August, 1847; d. November, 1862.
7. Rosilla E. Whiting, b. November, 1849; d. 1865.

180.

SETH[6] CHURCHILL (ISAAC,[5] ISAAC,[4] BARNABAS,[3] JOSEPH,[2] JOHN[1]). Born in Plymouth, 1790. He was a seaman, a privateer, in the War of 1812. and died in 1816. Married SARAH S. JOHNSON.

Children.

 I. ELIZA,[7] b. in Plymouth, 1812; m. ALFRED CHUBBUCK, of Valley
       Falls, R.I., where she died Sept. 4, 1889.

HON. JAMES CREIGHTON CHURCHILL.

(No. 181, page 109.)

Child.

1. William Chubbuck, lived in Valley Falls in 1890.

426 II. BENJAMIN,[7] b. Jan. 6, 1814; m. BETSEY BUMPUS, Nov. 12, 1835.
427 III. JAMES W.,[7] m. SARAH ANN CARR.

Said to have lived in Atlanta, Ga., and to have died there, leaving one son, Augustus R. Churchill, who was living in Atlanta in 1890.

181.

JAMES CREIGHTON[6] CHURCHILL (THOMAS,[5] THOMAS,[4] BARNABAS,[3] JOSEPH,[2] JOHN[1]). Born in Newmarket, N.H., April 24, 1787. Died in Portland, Me., Nov. 20, 1865. His early life was passed in his native town where he received the usual common-school education of that day. He evidently had experience also on ship-board, as he was in command of a vessel in his early manhood. He learned the trade of ship-carpenter and later engaged in ship-building at Portland, Me. In the War of 1812 he served as a sergeant, in the 34th U.S. Infantry, Capt. David Sherman's Company. Was later appointed quartermaster, serving two enlistments consecutively, from May 13, 1814, to June 15, 1815, when he was honorably discharged at Portland, Me. After engaging in ship-building for a few years he became interested in the trade with the West Indies, then just beginning to attract the attention of Northern merchants. After a few voyages of investigation he combined with several associates and bought some sugar plantations near Cardenas, Cuba, which was soon made a port of entry, and established there the beginning of the large and prosperous business which later made Portland one of the most important seaports on the coast. He was thus a pioneer and leading spirit among the notable old-time Portland merchants. He was public-spirited and influential in many directions. In 1828 he was elected one of the presidential electors, in the bitter contest waged between the parties, and he was known long after as " the star of the East," because of his solitary persistent vote for Andrew Jackson. In the political upheaval of 1834 he was Whig candidate for Congress, but the party was in the minority and he failed of election. In 1844 he was elected mayor of Portland, and is remembered as one of the ablest and most popular of the city's old-time rulers. He was a natural organizer of commercial enterprises, and in the agitation of the plan to connect Portland and Montreal by a railroad he was chief actor, and became treasurer of the old " Portland Company," organized for the manufacture of locomotives, cars, and railroad machinery, furnishing much of the rolling stock and running material of the old " Atlantic and St. Lawrence Railroad," now a part of the " Grand

Trunk" system. He held the position of treasurer of the railroad
till a short time before his death. He was also chiefly instrumental
in organizing the "Casco Iron Works," of which he was treasurer,
while for many years he conducted an extensive insurance business,
and to his last days attended promptly and faithfully to all his
official duties. He was a prominent Mason, a member of "Ancient
Landmark Lodge No. 17, of Free and Accepted Masons." Was a
Past Grand High Priest of the Grand Chapter of Maine. He is
remembered in all his public relations and in his personal life as
one of Portland's most useful and honored citizens. His funeral
service was held in the Pearl Street Universalist Church, of which
society he was an honored member, and was attended by a great
concourse of his fellow-citizens, Masonic brethren, and members of
city, State, and national governments. Three of his personal friends,
and prominent clergymen, officiated at the service : Revs. Dr. Bolles,
George W. Quimby, and I. M. Atwood. He married, in Portland,
at her father's house, Jan. 8, 1809, Eliza Walker Osborne,
daughter of Rev. John Osborne, a Baptist minister, who officiated
at the marriage ceremony. They lived for some time after marriage at Lee, and New Market, N.H., where their eldest child was
born, and, after 1815. at Portland, Me.

Children of James Creighton and Eliza W. Churchill.

I. Jane Alice,[7] b. March 30, 1810; m. Caleb S. Carter, of Portland,
   Aug. 23, 1865.
      They lived in Portland, where he died Dec. 18, 1855, and she
   died Aug. 20, 1865.

They had Children born in Portland.

1. Alice Eliza Carter, b. April 19, 1831; m. William Henry Stephenson, May 3, 1853. He was born Jan. 12, 1824, and died
   Aug. 21, 1882. Mrs. Stephenson was greatly interested in
   the compilation of this volume of Churchill history and has
   been a ready and able helper in this Portland line. She died
   March 3, 1903, at Portland. Children: (1) William Stephenson, b. March 3, 1855. He served as brigade-surgeon, with
   rank of major, in the Spanish war, on the staff of Gen. Fred.
   D. Grant; (2) Marian Stephenson, b. Jan. 15, 1857; (3)
   Marion Alice Maud Stephenson, b. May 4, 1858; (4) Henry
   Stephenson, b. March 30, 1865; (5) Mabel Stephenson, b.
   May 17, 1868; d. in Portland, Dec. 5, 1897.
2. James E. Carter, b. June 14, 1833, unmarried.
3. Mary Georgianna Carter, b. Aug. 18, 1834; m. William O. Fox,
   Portland, June 12, 1862. She d. March 25, 1895. He d.
   June 4, 1899. They had children: (1) James Fox, b. April 1,
   1864; (2) Selden Connor Fox, b. Feb. 16, 1866; (3) William
   L. Fox, b. April 27, 1867; d. Dec. 3, 1887; (4) Arthur
   Churchill Fox, Sept. 29, 1868; d. Feb. 2, 1869; (5) Sidney
   Fox, b. July 10, 1870; d. July 4, 1887.

4. Jane Adelaide Carter, b. Aug. 9, 1836; m. Henry Evans, Nov. 24' 1859. She d. Oct. 6, 1875. They had children: (1) Mildred Evans, b. Dec. 18, 1860; (2) Jane Evans, b. Aug. 13, 1862; (3) George Evans, b. February, 1864; d. young; (4) Edwin, d. young; (5) Adelaide May Evans, b. May 2, 1868; m. Dr. Joseph L. Goodale, Aug. 30, 1893, and has three children.

5. Caleb Thomas Carter, b. May 7, 1841; d. June 20, 1842.

6. Ada Celestine Carter, b. Sept. 13, 1842; d. Oct. 7, 1876.

7. Caleb Stoddart Carter, b. Feb. 23, 1844; d. Jan. 1, 1846.

8. Henry Theophilus Carter, b. June 4, 1845; m. Hannah J. True, of Portland, Dec. 17, 1868. He d. Jan. 14, 1878. They had children: (1) Clara C. Carter, b. Dec. 13, 1869; d. Dec. 11, 1875; (2) Philip Greenleaf Carter, b. Oct. 29, 1871.

428   II. Edwin,[7] b. March 15, 1812; m. 1st, Mary P. Carter, Sept. 29, 1834; m. 2d, Anna Hoole, June, 1865.

    III. Thomas,[7] b. Oct. 2, 1814; m. Eunice Dyer. They had no children. He died at sea, June 15, 1838, and she died in Portland Nov. 17, 1838.

429   IV. James Morrill,[7] b. in Portland, June 11, 1816; m. Harriet E. Hoole, Dec. 30, 1838.

    V. John Osborne,[7] b. April 26, 1818; d. in infancy.

430   VI. George Albert,[7] b. Dec. 25, 1820; m. Sarah Allen Lunt, Aug. 26, 1856.

   VII. Henry Hill Boody[7], b. June 15, 1823; died unmarried.

  VIII. Eliza Clara,[7] b. July 15, 1826; m. Marshall P. Wilder, Jr., of Boston. No children.

   IX. William Creighton,[7] died young.

431   X. Frederick Augustus,[7] b. May 5, 1834; m. Annie L. Levering, of St. Louis, June 20, 1860.

182.

THOMAS[6] CHURCHILL (Ichabod,[5] Thomas,[4] Barnabas, Joseph,[2] John[1]). Born in Parsonsfield, Me., Jan. 20, 1798, and lived there. A farmer. Married 1st, at Parsonsfield, Me., March 14, 1830, Mary Banks, born July 9, 1806; married by Rev. John Buzzell. Married 2d, Mrs. Olive B. Roberts, of Whitestown, N.Y.

Children born in Parsonsfield.

432   I. Thomas S.,[7] b. May 6, 1831; m. Mary A. Dixon, Jan. 1, 1855. She was born Oct. 2, 1833.

433   II. Otis B.,[7] b. Nov. 5, 1832; m. Susan E. Ferrin, Jan. 2, 1861; b. Jan. 14, 1839.

434   III. John C.,[7] b. Dec. 11, 1834; m. Annie Burk, Oct 18, 1869.

    IV. Mary Reliance,[7] b. Feb. 12, 1837; m. Nehemiah T. Libby, Feb. 23, 1860.

Children.

1. Emma A. Libby, b. Nov. 2, 1862.
2. Walter D. Libby, b. Nov. 8, 1864.

    V. Nathaniel,[7] b. May 8, 1839; unmarried.

   VI. Elizabeth A.,[7] b. March 15, 1841; d. March 17, 1844.

  VII. Joseph,[7] b. 1843; d. Oct. 18, 1844.

  VIII. Lydia F.,[7] b. March 15, 1851; m. John Colcord, of Cornish, Me., May 5, 1880.

Child.

1. Lura M. Colcord, b. Aug. 31, 1882.

183.

COL. JOHN TASH[6] CHURCHILL (JOSEPH,[5] THOMAS,[4] BAR-
NABAS,[3] JOSEPH,[2] JOHN[1]). Born in Newmarket, N.H., Aug. 6,
1796, and lived there and at Brookfield. He was a farmer, drover,
merchant, and hotel keeper. He was colonel of a regiment of New
Hampshire militia. He died at Brookfield, N.H., Dec. 6, 1873.
Married, March 5, 1817, MEHITABLE GILMAN WILLEY, of Brookfield, N.H. She was born Dec. 15, 1795, and died July 15, 1869.

Children born at Newmarket.

435   I. JOHN,[7] b. May 19, 1818; m. ELIZA LANG.
436   II. GEORGE HARRIS,[7] b. Nov. 7, 1819; m. MARY EMILY DANIELS, of
            Durham, May 10, 1849.
437   III. THOMAS LINDSAY,[7] b. April 16, 1822; m. 1st, SARAH STACKPOLE,
            March 2, 1847; m. 2d, NANCY SEWARD.
438   IV. ALFRED,[7] b. Nov. 24, 1823; m. LOUISA W. GILES.
439   V. JOSEPH,[7] b. Sept. 10, 1825; m. MERCY ANNE BAILEY.
440   VI. NATHANIEL WILEY,[7] b. Oct. 12, 1827; m. MARTHA J. WIGGIN,
            March 10, 1852.
       VII. HENRY,[7] b. Nov. 21, 1829; d. Jan. 21, 1831.
      VIII. HARRIET EMMELINE,[7] b. March 25, 1831; m. W. K. LINDSAY.
       IX. HENRY,[7] b. June 26, 1834; m. ANNIE E. NOYES. No children.
            He was a lieutenant in the Thirteenth New Hampshire Regiment,
            in the War of the Rebellion.
        X. CHARLES EDWIN,[7] b. June 30, 1836; d. April 1, 1837.

184.

JOSEPH TASH[6] CHURCHILL (JOSEPH,[5] THOMAS,[4] BARNA-
BAS,[3] JOSEPH,[2] JOHN[1]). Born April 18, 1798; died Oct. 17, 1875.
Born in Newmarket; lived in Cornish, Me., a farmer and drover, a
man of influence, selectman, and representative to Legislature.
Married, Sept. 1, 1824, MARTHA M. WIGGIN. She was born May
7, 1803, and died Feb. 19, 1881.

Children born at Brookfield, N.H.

       I. NOAH WIGGIN,[7] b. March 26, 1826; d. Jan. 27, 1852.
      II. LUTHER,[7] b. April 1, 1828; d. Sept. 16, 1833.
     III. ALEXANDER,[7] b. Aug. 15, 1830; d. Sept. 15, 1833.
      IV. SUSAN,[7] b. July 16, 1832; d. Sept. 16, 1833.
       V. SUSAN A.,[7] b. July 5, 1834; d. Aug. 23, 1839.
      VI. MARY A.,[7] b. April 3, 1837; d. Aug. 16, 1839.
     VII. MARTHA,[7] b. Sept. 16, 1840; m. HENRY H. GILMAN, June 3, 1877.
    VIII. JOSEPH,[7] b. June 30, 1843; unmarried; living.
      IX. CHARLES,[7] b. Dec. 30, 1845; unmarried; living.
       X. GEORGE A.,[7] b. April 13, 1852; unmarried; living.

185.

THOMAS TASH[6] CHURCHILL (JOSEPH,[5] THOMAS,[4] BAR-
NABAS,[3] JOSEPH,[2] JOHN[1]). Born in Newmarket, N.H., Aug. 6,
1800. Married 1st, ANN WENTWORTH, daughter of Thomas, of
Wakefield, N.H.; m. 2d, MRS. EUNICE (KING) HOYT, widow.

Children of First Wife.

I. JULIA ANN,[7] b. March 29, 1823; d. unmarried.
II. SARAH,[7] b. March 27, 1824; m. JOHN H. CHAPMAN, May 13, 1846.

Children.

1. George Elbridge Chapman, b. July 1, 1847.
2. Nellie Ann Chapman, b. July 27, 1851.
3. Frank Dudley Chapman, b. July 4, 1853.
4. Susan Maria Chapman, b. April 4, 1859.
5. Henry Jay Chapman, b. March 10, 1863.
III. THOMAS CHARLES,[7] b. 1827; d. in infancy.
IV. ABBY STONE,[7] b. 1829; d. in infancy.
V. SUSAN MARIA,[7] b. 1832; m. GEORGE ROBINSON, of Newmarket. No issue.
VI. JAY,[7] b. 1834; d. unmarried, 1861.

Children of Second Wife.

VII. EUNICE ELLEN,[7] b. Oct. 25, 1843; m. WILLIS K. PLUMMER, b. in Mason, N.H., July 5, 1838.
They lived at Newmarket, N.H.

Children.

1. Frederick C. Plummer, b. in South Lawrence, Mass., Feb. 6, 1867.
2. Harry Churchill Plummer, b. in South Lawrence, Mass., Jan. 29, 1883.
VIII. ARABELLA,[7] b. June 15, 1846; m. ALFRED S. HORNE, of Lowell.

Children born in Lowell.

1. Edward Alfred Horne, b. Aug. 7, 1872; d. June 20, 1890.
2. Samuel Churchill Horne, b. Aug. 17, 1878; m. Grace Varnum, June 28, 1900.
IX. LUELLA FRANCES,[7] b. Oct. 2, 1848; m. EDGAR L. LOWELL.

Child.

1. George Elbridge Lowell; drowned.

186.

EBENEZER CHAPMAN [6] CHURCHILL (JOSEPH [5] THOMAS,[4] BARNABAS,[3] JOSEPH,[2] JOHN [1]). Born in Brookfield, N.H., Nov. 11, 1802. Married, 1827, ANN LANGDON GOVE, of Portsmouth, N.H.

Children.

I. HANNAH LANGDON,[7] b. Sept. 30, 1828; m. ISAAC TOWNSEND CLARK, of Wakefield, N.H., March 4, 1850.

Children.

1. Mayhew Clark, b. Jan. 3, 1853.
2. Ellen I. Clark, b. Nov. 25, 1855.
441 II. ALBERT,[7] b. April 13, 1830; m. 1st, BELINDA COLBATH, 1863; m. 2d, HANNAH J. BAILEY, of Plymouth, N.H., 1870.
III. MARY JANE,[7] b. May 15, 1832; m. WILLIAM COLBATH, Nov. 19, 1855.

Children.

1. Charles William Colbath, b. Aug. 13, 1857.
2. Emily Jane Colbath, b. July 13, 1859; d. Oct. 13, 1859.
3. Edwin Churchill Colbath, b. Oct. 8, 1862.
4. Annie Laura Colbath, b. March 21, 1864.
5. George Colbath, b. May 1, 1869.
6. Albert Payson Colbath, b. Nov. 26, 1874.
7. Irving Colbath, b. Jan. 16, 1877.

442   IV. EBEN,[7] b. March 2, 1834; m. EMMA BOWEN, dau. of William.
         V. LYDIA ANN,[7] b. Jan. 2, 1836; m. CHARLES BREWSTER. Nó children.
        VI. SARAH ELIZABETH,[7] b. Sept. 7, 1837; m. WILLIAM SIMS.

Children.

1. Frank Sims. | 2. William Sims.

     VII. HELEN,[7] ⎫ b. March 23, 1839; d. in infancy.
    VIII. ELLEN,[7] ⎭ b. March 23, 1839; d. in infancy.
      IX. ROENA A.,[7] b. Nov. 8, 1840; d. unmarried, aged about eighteen years. A lovely girl both in person and character.
443   X. JOSEPH EDWARD,[7] b. Aug. 1, 1842; m. ANNA HARMUS, Sept. 20, 1871.
       XI. ROCKWELL PLUMMER,[7] b. May 14, 1844; m. LUCY JENNESS, of Wolfborough, March 7, 1872. No children.
444   XII. WOODBURY LANGDON,[7] b. Aug. 9, 1847; m. MARY A. NASON. No children.

187.

NATHANIEL [6] CHURCHILL (JOSEPH,[5] THOMAS,[4] BARNABAS,[3] JOSEPH,[2] JOHN [1]). Born in Brookfield, N.H., April 7, 1807. Lived in Exeter. Married, May 20, 1830, SOPHIA KING. She was born Jan. 6, 1808; died Aug. 18, 1885.

Children born in Exeter.

445   I. ADDISON,[7] b. May 27, 1831; m. JENNIE ISABELLA GREEN.
         II. ROSINA,[7] b. Oct. 6, 1832; d. Aug. 18, 1834.
446   III. ALMANDER,[7] b. July 14, 1834; m. 1st, CLARA F. TAYLOR; m. 2d, CATHARINE C. PARKHURST.
447   IV. NATHANIEL,[7] b. Aug. 17, 1836; m. ELIZABETH A. JAMES, Dec. 21, 1858.
          V. JASPER HAZEN,[7] b. Sept. 17, 1838; d. June 12, 1841.
         VI. SYLVESTER EDWIN,[7] b. March 25, 1841; d. Sept. 6, 1846.
        VII. SOPHIA HELEN,[7] b. Aug. 14, 1842; d. Aug. 14, 1843.
448   VIII. JASPER HAZEN,[7] ⎫ b. Nov. 25, 1844; m. ELLA A. PORTER, May 31, 1877, at Exeter, N.H.; d. Oct. 6, 1879.
         IX. SOPHIA HELEN,[7] ⎭ b. Nov. 25, 1844; d. July 1, 1845.
          X. SYLVESTER EDWIN,[7] b. March 19, 1847; d. unmarried, May 15, 1870.

188.

DANIEL [6] CHURCHILL (JOSEPH,[5] THOMAS,[4] BARNABAS,[3] JOSEPH,[2] JOHN [1]). Born in Brookfield, N.H., Dec. 3, 1811; died March 23, 1884.' Married, May 5, 1834, ELEANOR LONGLEY, who died Feb. 18, 1880.

Children.

449   I. SHELDON W.,[7] b. Feb. 14, 1835; m. 1st, OLIVE A. WIGGIN, May 14. 1861; m. 2d, CLARA B. DOUGLAS.
II. ORISSA JANE,[7] b. Jan. 29, 1838; m. ORRIN MURRAY, of Newmarket, N.H., Feb. 25, 1862.

Children.

1. Fred H. Murray, b. July 15, 1864.
2. Frank C. Murray, b. April 11, 1868.
3. Harry E. Murray, b. March 12, 1870.
III. SAREPTA,[7] b. July 7, 1840; m. CHARLES E. WIGGIN, Nov. 25, 1870.

Children.

1. Rissa May, b. March 16, 1872.
2. Alice C., b. April 7, 1874.
IV. MARY A.,[7] b. Dec. 16, 1850; m. CHARLES JAY, Nov. 15, 1883.

189.

CHARLES[6] CHURCHILL (JOSEPH,[5] THOMAS,[4] BARNABAS,[3] JOSEPH,[2] JOHN[1]). Born in Brookfield, N.H., April 3, 1814, died Nov. 2, 1866. Married, July 6, 1837, HYRONA FOLSOM PURINTON, born June 26, 1816.

Children.

I. ALMENA AUGUSTA,[7] b. March 17, 1839; m. JAMES DANA HARTWELL, May 5, 1857.

Children.

1. Emma Belinda Hartwell, b. March 14, 1859; m. James B. Ruddick, June 21, 1880.
2. Charles Churchill Hartwell, b. Sept. 18, 1860; m. Rosa A. Ryder, Sept. 21, 1884.
3. George Washington Hartwell, b. June 29, 1862; m. Ida Lennox Harriman, June 29, 1887.
4. Jennie Louise Hartwell, b. Aug. 7, 1864; d. Feb. 7, 1887.
II. IRENA,[7] b. Sept. 17, 1841; d. Sept. 19, 1841.
III. JENNIE ADELAIDE,[7] b. March 10, 1844; m. SOLOMON AUGUSTUS LENFEST, Dec. 7, 1865.
IV. ELLA FRANCES,[7] b. Nov. 5, 1848; m. WILLIAM PITT CANNING, Feb. 8, 1871.

Children.

1. Edith Almena Canning, b. May 24, 1875.
2. Alice Churchill Canning, b. Feb. 13, 1878.
3. Edward Weeks Canning, b. Sept. 30, 1880.
V. EMMA IRENE,[7] b. Oct. 3, 1850; d. unmarried, Sept 22, 1873.

190.

JAMES MONROE[6] CHURCHILL (JOSEPH,[5] THOMAS,[4] BARNABAS,[3] JOSEPH,[2] JOHN[1]). Born in Brookfield, N.H., Jan. 3, 1819. Married, March 3, 1852, ELIZABETH PERKINS, of Exeter.

Child.

I. ELIZABETH,[7] b. Sept. 30, 1865; unmarried.

191.

WILLIAM[6] CHURCHILL (JOSEPH,[5] THOMAS,[4] BARNABAS,[3] JOSEPH,[2] JOHN[1]). Born Aug. 8, 1821. Married ELIZABETH KITTREDGE, of Lowell, Mass.

Children.

I. HERBERT,[7] b. June 10, 1849; d. unmarried, April 10, 1870.
II. ERNEST,[7] b. May 11, 1855; m. ADA UPHAM; no issue
III. FRANK,[7] d. in infancy.

192.

THOMAS C.[6] CHURCHILL (NATHANIEL,[5] THOMAS,[4] BARNABAS,[3] JOSEPH,[2] JOHN[1]). Born Feb. 26, 1807, at Eaton, N.H. He was living, in 1895, at Murphy, Calaveras County, California. Married, March 20, 1834, EMMELINE STEVENS BAILEY, daughter of Richard G. and Emma Bailey, of North Bridgton, Me. She died at North Bridgton, Dec. 20, 1873.

Children.

I. ELLEN MARIA,[7] b. at Waterford, Me., March 19, 1835; d. at Sanbornton Bridge, N.H., Sept. 3, 1849.
450   II. ALGERNON HOWE,[7] b. at Wilton, Me., June 16, 1837; m. MARTHA HELEN STINCHFIELD Nov. 9, 1861, at Lewiston, Me.
III. MARGARET ANN,[7] b. Sept. 13, 1839, in Wilton, Me., and died there June 27, 1841.
IV. ESTELLE MARIA,[7] b. at Sanbornton Bridge, N.H., Dec. 23, 1851; d. at No. Bridgton, Aug. 16, 1872.
V. FRANCES ILSLEY,[7] b. at No. Bridgton, Aug. 6, 1856; d. there Aug. 12, 1858.

193.

JOHN[6] CHURCHILL (NATHANIEL,[5] THOMAS,[4] BARNABAS,[3] JOSEPH,[2] JOHN[1]). Born June 17, 1811. Married, October, 1834, MELISSA COLBY. She was born June 27, 1813.

Children.

I. MARY ANN,[7] b. Jan. 20, 1837; d. Oct. 13, 1864.
II. NANCY C.,[7] b. March 31, 1839; d. Nov. 30, 1852.
451   III. JOHN HENRY,[7] b. July 1, 1844; m. IRENE GERTRUDE CANFIELD.
IV. CHARLES FREDERICK,[7] b. April 22, 1847; d. Dec. 2, 1852.

194.

NATHANIEL[6] CHURCHILL (NATHANIEL,[5] THOMAS,[4] BARNABAS,[3] JOSEPH,[2] JOHN[1]). Born July 1, 1818. Lived in Madison, N.H. Married, Nov. 4, 1841, ELIZABETH GOLDTHWAIT.

Children.

452   I. NAHUM B.,[7] b. Jan. 8, 1843; m. LYDIA A. MOORE, June 8, 1867.
II. SARAH E.,[7] b. May 24, 1847; unmarried.
III. EDWIN N.,[7] b. April 6, 1848; deceased.
IV. MARY ELLEN,[7] b. July 6, 1852; unmarried.

195.

ICHABOD D.⁶ CHURCHILL (NATHANIEL,⁵ THOMAS,⁴ BARNABAS,³ JOSEPH,² JOHN¹). Born Sept. 29, 1845. Lived in Madison, N.H. Married 1st, Dec. 30, 1847, CLARA QUINT. She died March 24, 1865. Married 2d, Sept. 8, 1866, MRS. SARAH D. LORD.

Children by First Wife.
- I. MIRANDA C.,⁷ b. May 21, 1851; m. FREEMAN JOHNSON, March 3, 1872.
- II. SARAH A.,⁷ b. April 14, 1856; m. FRANK WENTWORTH, June, 1878, and died 1883.
- 453 III. NATHANIEL I.,⁷ b. Dec. 28, 1857; m. CARRIE LOUD, Dec. 7, 1880. No further record.
- IV. ICHABOD F.,⁷ b. Aug. 6, 1859; d. March, 1865.
- V. LYDIA,⁷ b. Dec. 23, 1863.

By Second Wife.
- 454 VI. HERBERT C.,⁷ b. May 12, 1878. No further record.

196.

WILLIAM GRAVES⁶ CHURCHILL (JOHN,⁵ THOMAS⁴ BARNABAS,³ JOSEPH,² JOHN¹). Born July 29, 1809. Married, June 20, 1831, SALLY MEAD PAGE. She was born May 12, 1809, and died Aug. 6, 1868.

Children.
- 455 I. WILLIAM ALVAH,⁷ b. June 4, 1832; m. MARTHA FOLSOM ROBINSON, of Greenland, b. Jan. 30, 1831.
- II. MARY MEAD,⁷ b. Aug. 28, 1834.

197.

CHARLES⁶ CHURCHILL (JOHN,⁵ EBENEZER,⁴ BARNABAS,³ JOSEPH,² JOHN¹). Born in Pittsfield Feb. 25, 1796. Lived in Pittsfield; representative in Legislature, 1855. Died Dec. 23, 1881. Married, Dec. 4, 1826, CHARLOTTE M. FRANCIS, of Pittsfield.

Children born in Pittsfield.
- I. JANE CHARLOTTE,⁷ b. Jan. 7, 1828; m. WILLIAM WATT, May 27, 1857.

  Their Children born in Pittsfield.
  1. Charles Adams Watt, b. May 28, 1858; m. Mollie O'Donald, June 3, 1885.
  2. William Edward Watt, b. July 8, 1859.
  3. Clara Maria Watt, b. March 5, 1861.
  4. Mary Kate Watt, b. Oct. 7, 1863; m. George E. Ferguson, Oct. 6, 1880. Had John C., b. 1882.
- II. FREDERICK AUGUSTUS,⁷ b. Oct. 20, 1829; d. June 30, 1830.
- 456 III. FREDERICK AUGUSTUS,⁷ b. Sept. 6, 1831; m. CLARA P. BUTLER, Sept. 11, 1861. Lives in Pittsfield.
- 457 IV. EDWARD PAYSON,⁷ b. Aug. 6, 1834; m. DORA KETTELL, of Pittsfield, Jan. 3, 1870. Died Sept. 28, 1874.
- V. MARIA FRANCIS,⁷ b. April 28, 1840; d. Aug. 3, 1863.

198.

SAMUEL ADAMS [6] CHURCHILL (JOHN,[5] EBENEZER [4] BAR-
NABAS,[3] JOSEPH,[2] JOHN [1]). Born in Pittsfield, Sept. 28, 1810.
Lived in Pittsfield. Married, Sept. 22, 1840, ESTHER BROOK, of
Lenox, Mass.

Children born in Pittsfield.

 I. JANE C.,[7] b. Feb. 18, 1842; m. WILLIAM HENRY THOMPSON, Nov.
  13, 1867, of Chatham, N.Y.

Children.

  1. Mary Churchill Thompson, b. in Greenbush, N.Y., Jan. 19,
   1869.
  2. Emily Churchill Thompson, b. in Chicago, Sept. 4, 1875.

458 II. JOHN B.,[7] b. Dec. 12, 1844; m. MARY BELDEN, April 8, 1868, of
   Lenox.

199.

ORRIN [6] CHURCHILL (LEMUEL,[5] JOHN,[4] BARNABAS,[3] JOSEPH,[2]
JOHN [1]). Born in Truxton N.Y., Feb. 16, 1809. In 1833 he went
to Buffalo by the Erie canal, thence by boat to Detroit, and walked
across Michigan to Berrien County, where he took up a government
grant of land in the heavily wooded section, where deer, wolves, and
bears were very abundant. Making such improvements for occu-
pancy as he was able, he returned in the fall to his home in New
York, and the following spring, taking his family and effects in an
ox-cart, he made the journey to his new home, opening up a large
farm, but later settled in what is now Buchanan, Mich., in the hardware business, the farm being in the same town, but some distance
from his store. He died Sept. 13, 1881, at Buchanan, Mich.
Married 1st, in Truxton, N.Y., Feb. 1, 1832, EMMELINE POPE
who died in 1842 ; married 2d, in Buchanan, Mich., Nov. 2, 1843,
JANE L. PORTER, died Nov. 16, 1854; married 3d, in Buchanan,
Mich., Nov. 3, 1855, FRANCES E. RICHARDSON.

Children of First Wife, born in Truxton, N.Y.

  I. LEMUEL,[7] b. Oct. 27, 1832; d. Oct. 14, 1842.
459 II. GEORGE,[7] b. April 12, 1834; m. ELIZABETH HALSTED, July 15, 1856;
   d. 1900.
  III. CAROLINE,[7] b. March 24, 1837; d. Dec. 6, 1855.
460 IV. OWEN,[7] b. April 24, 1840; m. FLORA ADAMS, Dec. 20, 1869.

Children of Second Wife, born at Buchanan, on the farm.

461 V. JOHN PORTER,[7] b. Dec. 2, 1846; m. HARRIET MOORE, Oct. 12,
   1873.
  VI. ALMIRA LOUISA,[7] b. Feb. 12, 1848; m. 1st, DAVID CASSLER, April
   29, 1866 (divorced) ; m. 2d, MICHAEL HARNER.

CAPT. BENJ. K NG CHURCHILL.
(No. 202, page 1 9.)

THE CAPT. CHURCHILL HOUSE.
BRISTOL, R.I.
(Page 119.)

Child by First Husband.

1. George B. Cassler, b. Feb. 4, 1867

Children by Second Husband.

2. Willard A. Harner, b. 1878.
3. Orrin C. Harner, b. 1879.
4. Murray P. Harner, b. 1880.
5. Alfred L. Harner, b. 1882.
6. Orne C. Harner, b. 1884.
7. Alma Bessie Harner, b. 1885.
8. Roy Harner, b. 1886.

VII. LENORA,[7] b. Aug. 18, 1850; m. FRANK MUNSON, Dec. 25, 1867; d. June 10, 1868.

VIII. ORRIN L ,[7] b. Dec. 10, 1852; unmarried.
He is a merchant, firm of Churchill, Webster & Bolinger, Jamestown, North Dakota.

200.

LEMUEL [6] CHURCHILL (JOHN,[5] JOHN,[4] BARNABAS,[3] JOSEPH,[2] JOHN [1]). Born in Pittsfield, Nov. 24, 1816, and lived there. Married LYDIA BRADFORD, of Conway, Mass.

Children.

I. SUSAN ANNE,[7] b. June 7, 1855; unmarried, in Pittsfield.
II. JOHN B.,[7] b. Aug. 11, 1858; unmarried, in Pittsfield.

201.

ALANSON [6] CHURCHILL (BRADFORD,[5] JOHN,[4] BARNABAS,[3] JOSEPH,[2] JOHN [1]). Born in Truxton, N.Y., Sept. 4, 1812. Married ELIZA BURLINGAME, of Lanesboro', N.Y.

Children.

I. HARRIET,[7] b. Oct. 18, 1835; m. GEORGE MURDOCK.
II. MARIETTA,[7] b. March 4, 1837
III. ELLEN,[7] b. Jan. 25, 1839.
IV. BRADFORD,[7] b. Feb. 1, 1840; never married.
V. HELEN.[7]
VI. ROBERT,[7] d. young.
462 VII. GEORGE CLINTON,[7] b. Dec. 27, 1847; m. EUNICE FOLLANSBEE.

202.

BENJAMIN KING [6] CHURCHILL (JOSEPH,[5] JOSEPH,[4] JOSEPH,[3] JOSEPH,[2] JOHN [1]). Born July 13, 1774, in Wells (or Kennebunk), Me. He went to sea young, and, it is related, was captured by an English press-gang, and made to serve for two years on a British man-of-war. With another sailor, while the ship was near the coast of Cuba, he jumped overboard and swam to the shore. From Cuba he returned in an American ship to his home, resumed his sea-faring life, and became captain of a ship as early as 1800. He commanded the privateer "Yankee Lass," in the War of 1812, and was second in command of the privateer "Yankee," which took five valuable prizes. Captain Churchill's share of the prize-money was quite large. In one of the battles at sea he was wounded and lost a leg. He settled in Boston at the time of his marriage, then lived at Salem a while, but removed to Bristol, R.I., as early as 1813. He is mentioned as living in the "Capt. Jonathan Mason House" in Salem, on the road from North Street to near "Mack's Hill." (Coll. Essex Inst., Vol. 31, p. 122.) He died in 1858. Married 1st, CLARISSA EATON, of Boston; married 2d, March, 1822, MRS. ELIZA (HOLMAN) NORRIS, widow of Capt. H. L.

Children born in Boston.

I. ANN NORTHY,[7] b. June 28, 1798; m. REV. ALEXANDER JONES, of Providence, R.I., Nov. 3, 1819.

Children born in Providence, R.I.

1. Clara Churchill Jones, b. May 31, 1821; m. Alexander P. Crittenden, April 24, 1838.
   . Alexander Jones, b. Aug. 5, 1822; m. Mary Lee.
3. Benjamin Churchill Jones, b. Aug. 23, 1824; m. Josephine McGreal.
4. Mary Farquhar Jones, b. July 26, 1826; m. Amos Joliffe, Nov. 16, 1848.
5. George Wardwell Jones, ⎫ b. June 11, 1828; m. 1st, Louisa Adams Carrington; m. 2d, (————) (————).
6. Joseph Jones, ⎬ b. June 11, 1828; m. Courtney Bowdoin.
7. Charles Christian Jones, b. Jan. 23, 1830; d. unmarried.
8. William Marlborough Jones, b. Jan. 28, 1832; m. Mary Lambert McMurdo.
9. Rebecca Churchill Jones, b. Dec. 11, 1833; m. Col. William P. Craighill.
10. Anne Northy Jones. b. Sept. 26, 1835; m. Dr. Johnson Price, of Kentucky.
11. Larran Farquhar Jones, b. Nov. 9, 1837; m. Matilda Fontain Berkeley.
12. Henry Holman Jones, b. Feb. 26, 1839; d. aged 20 years.
13. Margaretta Brown Jones, b. Dec. 22, 1840; d. Jan. 10, 1841.

II. REBECCA JENKS,[7] b. November, 1800; m. GEORGE WARDWELL, of Providence, April, 1819.

Children.

1. Caroline Churchill Wardwell, b. June 23, 1824; m. Samuel D. Wyeth, Sept. 11, 1844.
2. Edward Wilkinson Wardwell, b. 1826; d. in infancy.
3. Annie Jones Wardwell, b. Jan. 28, 1828; d. April, 1851.
4. George Marlborough Wardwell, b. 1832; d. in infancy.

III. HARRIET,[7] b. 1802; d. unmarried.
IV. BENJAMIN KING, JR.,[7] b. Nov. 14, 1805; d. unmarried in 1832.
V. CLARA EATON,[7] b. 1808; m. GEORGE W. LITTLE, of Charlestown, Va., Oct. 11, 1831.

Children.

1. Ann Churchill Little, b. July 31, 1832; d. unmarried.
2. Jane Craighill Little, b. April 25, 1834; d. Oct. 15, 1835.

Children born in Bristol, R.I.

VI. SARAH KING,[7] b. 1813; m. CAPT. H. L. NORRIS, Nov. 2, 1837. She d. Oct. 9, 1840, leaving no children.
463 VII. MARLBOROUGH,[7] b. February, 1816; m. ELIZABETH LOUISE VORIS, 1837.
VIII. WILLIAM EZRA,[7] b. 1818; d. unmarried.
IX. CAROLINE ELECTRA,[7] b. 1820; d. in infancy.

Children by Second Wife.

X. AGNES FETTERS,[7] b. Dec. 25, 1822. Living. unmarried, in 1895.
464 XI. SAMUEL HOLMAN,[7] b. July 13, 1826; m. ADELAIDE M. NORRIS, Sept. 17, 1853. He d. in 1856. No further record.

203.

JOHN [6] CHURCHILL (JOSEPH,[5] JOSEPH,[4] JOSEPH,[3] JOSEPH [2] JOHN [1]). Born in Salem, March 27, 1774, and died in Mooers N.Y., May 2, 1858. Removed to the west side of Lake Champlain, where the Southwick Brothers, of Benson, Vt., had purchased a large tract of land, and settled what was then Champlain, but in 1804 became the town of Mooers. All of his brothers and sisters settled, lived, and are buried there. Married HANNAH SCHRIVER, daughter of Frederick, Esq., of Hemmingford, Can. She was sister of Col. John Schriver, M.P.

Children born in Mooers, N.Y.

I. CLARISSA,[7] b. March 19, 1803; m. ALBERT BELDEN, and d. 1837. No children.
465 II. WARNER,[7] b. July 16, 1808; m. ALMIRA SCHRIVER, Feb. 13, 1835.
466 III. GILBERT,[7] b. May 18, 1810; m ELIZABETH (———)
IV. JULIA ANN,[7] b. Aug. 20, 1811; m. 1st, JABIN FITCH; m. 2d, ALEXANDER FERRY, of Albaugh, Vt.

Children of First Husband.

1. Susan Fitch, d. early.
2. Harlow Fitch, d. early.
3. George Fitch, d. early.
4. Harrison Fitch, m. Addie Twombly, of Chazy, N.Y.
5. Martha Fitch, m. Daniel McLaughlin, of Anoka, Minn.
6. Henderson Fitch, d. young.

V. POLLY,[7] b. Oct. 10, 1813; d. at Mooers, in 1814.
VI. HARRIET,[7] b. June 26, 1815; m. ALONZO STACY, Sept. 7, 1836, at Mooers.

Children.

1. Hiram Stacy, d. April 30, 1840.
2. Mary Stacy, m. George Dixon, July 9, 1859.
3. Eleanor Stacy.
4. Frederic Stacy.
5. Emily Stacy.

VII. VIOLETTA,[7] b. July 9, 1817; d. March, 1833.

467   VIII. JOHN,[7] b. Jan. 30, 1820; m. HARRIET (———). Said to have had
             a family and to have lived in Greenville, Mich., but we have no
             record.
468   IX. THEODORE,[7] b. May 25, 1822; m. LUCY FROST.
        X. SARAH,[7] b. July 25, 1824; m. DAVID WATERMAN. Live in Bath,
             N.H.

Children.

1. Frederic Waterman.   5. Nellie Waterman.
2. Julia Waterman.   6. Stella Waterman.
3. Emma Waterman.   7. George Waterman.
4. Charles Waterman.

       XI. FREDERICK,[7] b. Aug. 30, 1826; d. Sept. 2, 1850.
      XII. HANNAH M.,[7] b. Feb. 16, 1829; d. January, 1837.

204.

JOSEPH[6] CHURCHILL (JOHN,[5] JOSEPH,[4] JOSEPH[3] JOSEPH[2]
JOHN[1]). Born in New Salem, Mass., Jan. 18, 1776, and died in
Mooers, N.Y., Jan. 25, 1848. He also settled in Mooers, and lived
there near his brothers and sisters, whose farms, it is said, extended
in an almost unbroken line, for five miles, through the centre of the
town, from the Canada border. Married SUSANNA BAILEY, in
Chazy, N.Y. She was born in Windsor, Vt., Nov. 1, 1792, and died
in Morrison, Ill., Nov. 25, 1884.

Children born in Mooers, N.Y.

        I. ELIZA,[7] b. Oct. 24, 1810; d. Oct. 29, 1829.
       II. CALISTA,[7] b. Sept. 28, 1812; d. Nov. 8, 1833.
      III. JOSHUA B.,[7] b. Nov. 11, 1814; d. March 5, 1815.
469   IV. BENJAMIN LEVERY,[7] b. Feb. 7, 1816; m. MARIA FASSETT, Dec. 7,
             1844; d. in army, March 14, 1865.
        V. JEREMIAH,[7] b. May 4, 1818; m. ELIZA VASBURGH, Nov. 23, 1840.
             They were drowned in Lake Michigan, April 1, 1849.
470   VI. JOSEPH B.,[7] b. June 23, 1820; m. ELIZA TURNBULL, Dec. 11, 1841.
471   VII. GEORGE,W.,[7] b. April 10, 1825; m. 1st, ABIGAIL HITCHCOCK, Sept.
             26, 1852; m. 2d, ELLEN F. STRONG.
472 VIII. SYLVESTER S.,[7] b. Nov. 6, 1827; m. JANE R. RANSOM, Oct. 19,
             1853.
       IX   SUSANNA E.,[7] b. Oct. 9, 1830; m. M. S. HEATON, Feb. 27, 1861.
             They live in Morrison, Ill., and have one child.

Child.

1. Nellie Churchill Heaton, b. Sept. 6, 1868.

473   X. CHARLES C.,[7] b. June 15, 1836; m. HARRIET A. MCKIBBEN, April
             7, 1866.

205.

SAMUEL[6] CHURCHILL (JOHN,[5] JOSEPH,[4] JOSEPH,[3] JOSEPH,[2]
JOHN[1]). Born in New Salem, Aug. 8, 1782. Settled in Mooers,
N.Y., in 1806. He was there prominent and respected, and always
active in all matters of public interest and welfare for more than
a half century. His wife was a woman of rare intelligence and of
lovely character. He died Feb. 23, 1865. Married, Feb. 8, 1814,

MARTHA LOUISA BOSWORTH, daughter of John, Esq., of Sandisfield, Mass., where she was born Jan. 25, 1796. She died May 15, 1844.

Children born at Mooers, N.Y.

I. LOUISA HANNAH,[7] b. May 10, 1815; m. REV. STEPHEN HOUSE WILLIAMS, Aug. 6, 1844.

Children.

1. John Charles Williams, b. May 15, 1845.
2. Sidney Phœnix Williams, b. Aug. 16, 1847.
3. Mary Louisa Williams, b. Feb. 26, 1850.
4. Samuel Harvey Williams, b. July 28, 1851.
5. James E. Williams, b. Feb. 10, 1856.

II. EMMELINE AMELIA,[7] b. Feb. 20, 1817; m. JOHN SHEDDEN, 1860. Live in Mooers; no children.

474 III. SAMUEL HARVEY,[7] b. Jan. 24, 1819; m. EMELINE H. KNAPP, of Berlin, Vt., Feb. 19, 1851.

475 IV. JOHN CHARLES,[7] b. Jan. 17, 1821; m. KATHARINE T. SPRAGUE, Sept. 11, 1849.

V. MARY ELIOTT,[7] b. Oct. 16, 1822; lives unmarried in Mooers, N.Y.

476 VI. JAMES GUILFORD,[7] b. Jan. 4, 1825; d. at Alma, Parke County, Colo., Sept. 18, 1879. No further record.

VII. PLINY FISK,[7] b. April 15, 1830; d. unmarried, Oct. 1, 1857.

VIII. CAROLINE MARTHA,[7] b. Dec. 10, 1833; m. HON. SAMUEL C. WINGARD. Live at Walla Walla, Wash.

206.

JEREMIAH[6] CHURCHILL (JOHN,[5] JOSEPH,[4] JOSEPH,[3] JOSEPH[2] JOHN[1]). Born in New Salem, 1785. Settled in Mooers, N.Y., 1802. He was a lieutenant in the War of 1812. He died Aug. 8 1817, in Mooers, N.Y.; married MARY FROST.

Child.

I. SARAH SOPHRONIA,[7] b. Nov. 11, 1815; m. CHARLES R. ROOD, of Mooers, Oct. 27, 1842. They live at Gardner Plain, Whiteside County, Ill. He was born July 20, 1813.

Their Children.

1. Almira A. Rood, b. Aug. 12, 1845.
2. Albert Lawrence Rood, b. Oct. 11. 1847; d. Jan. 3, 1848.
3. Helen Electa Rood, b. Nov. 12, 1848.
4. Julia Elva Rood, b. March 11, 1856.

207.

JOHN[6] CHURCHILL (SAMUEL,[5] SAMUEL,[4] JOSEPH,[3] JOSEPH,[2] JOHN[1]). Born in Sterling, July 7, 1782. Lived in Boston, and later in Chelmsford, Mass. Died in Chelmsford early in 1825, and his estate there was administered upon July 13, 1825. Married, in Sterling, Dec. 12, 1813, DOLLY MEARS. She was born Jan. 14, 1777, and died in Clinton, Aug. 30, 1864.

Child born in Boston.

I. JANE,[7] b. Nov. 20, 1815; m. HORACE JEWETT, in Lowell, Dec. 17, 1832. Mr. Jewett was born April 10, 1809.

Children.

1. Mary Jane Jewett, b. in Lowell, Sept. 28, 1834; m. William Lawrence.
2. George Horace Jewett, b. in Sterling, May 1, 1837; m. Eliza J. Taylor.
3. John Stewart Jewett, b. in Lancaster, Sept. 12, 1839; single.
4. Sarah Churchill Jewett, b. in Lancaster, Sept. 25, 1842; m. William Mirick.
5. Emily Louisa Jewett, b. in Lancaster, Dec. 11, 1844; m. Palmer Fitts.
6. Erastus Jewett, b. in Lancaster, Jan. 26, 1847; m. Annette Holland.
7. Ella Josephine Jewett, b. in Sterling, Feb. 14, 1850; m. George Hall.
8. Annie Maria Jewett, b. in Sterling, April 26, 1852; m. Levi H. Wiggin.
9. Wilfred Emery Jewett, b. in Sterling, Nov. 13, 1854; single.
10. Eugenia Olive Rebecca Jewett, b. in Sterling, Dec. 27, 1856; m. Edward S. Crocker.
11. Flora Mabel Jewett, b. in Clinton, March 28, 1865; d. Jan. 20, 1866.

208.

ELIEZER [6] CHURCHILL (ELIEZER,[5] ELIEZER,[4] ELIEZER,[3] ELIEZER,[2] JOHN [1]). Born in 1765. They lived in West Bridgewater. Died suddenly in 1818. Married, Jan. 27, 1788, LUCY OTIS, of Scituate, born Jan. 27, 1769.

Children born in West Bridgewater.

I. SOPHIA,[7] b. July 1, 1789; m. BETHUEL PENNYMAN, of Abington, Feb. 16, 1814. He was born May 8, 1787.

Children.

1. Sophia Pennyman, b. Aug. 18, 1810.
2. Lucy Ann Pennyman, b. March 2, 1813.
3. Mary Pennyman, b. Dec. 11, 1814.
4. Eliza Pennyman, b. Jan. 9, 1817.
5. Bethuel Pennyman, Jr., b. Feb. 11, 1819.
6. William Pennyman, b. March 5, 1822.
7. Addison Pennyman, b. April 29, 1827.
8. Samuel Pennyman, b. Sept. 27, 1829.

477   II. CHARLES,[7] b. Aug. 17, 1791; m. DORCAS PRATT HAWES, July 28, 1814.

III. MARY OTIS,[7] b. March 26, 1794; m. JAMES NASH, of Abington, Oct. 29, 1812.
   She died Oct. 27, 1864, and he died March 18, 1858.

Children.

1. James Otis Nash, b. Feb. 2, 1814; d. Dec. 27, 1880.
2. Merit Nash, b. Oct. 10, 1815.
3. Mary Ann Nash, b. Nov. 4, 1817; d. June 18, 1864.
4. Sylvanus Nash, b. Sept. 14, 1819; d. Feb. 5, 1882.
5. Eleazer Dexter Nash, b. Jan. 23, 1821.

IV. DEBORAH,[7] b. May 26, 1796; d. in infancy.
V. LUCY,[7] b. May 21, 1798; m. DAVID JENKINS, Aug. 31, 1817; he
was born Jan. 15, 1790. She died Oct. 13, 1834. He died Jan.
7, 1881.

Children.

1. Spooner Jenkins. b. in Southbridge, Sept. 11, 1819.
2. David Jenkins, Jr., b. in Southbridge, June 5, 1822; d. June
17, 1848.
3. Lucy Otis Jenkins, b. in New Bedford, July 22, 1829.

VI. JOSHUA,[7] b. 1800; d. in infancy.
VII. HARRIET,[7] b. Sept. 18, 1802; m. JOHN REED, JR., Jan. 28, 1819.
VIII. DEBORAH,[7] b. June 29, 1804; m. COMFORT WHITING, of New
Bedford.
IX. HANNAH OTIS,[7] b. May 15, 1806; m. GEORGE DOUGLAS.
X. RHODA,[7] b. July 16, 1808; m. SAMUEL KEENE, of East Bridge-
water.
XI. JANE,[7] b. Sept. 11, 1811; m. VALENTINE ERSKINE, of Abington.

209.

THADDEUS[6] CHURCHILL (THADDEUS,[5] ELIEZER,[4] ELIEZER,[3]
ELIEZER,[2] JOHN[1]). Born March 23, 1776, in Plymouth, and died
Sept. 10, 1832. Married, Oct. 11, 1798, MERCY FULLER, daughter
of Captain John, of Kingston. She was born Oct. 16, 1776, and
died April 8, 1861.

Children.

I. WILLIAM,[7] b. July 22, 1799; d. Sept. 22, 1799.
478 II. WILLIAM,[7] b. Nov. 25, 1800; m. 1st, MARY C. FULLER, Sept. 27,
1828. She d. June 22, 1829; m. 2d, BEULAH ORTON, Aug. 28,
1830. She d. Dec. 18, 1851; m. 3d, JANE R. SQUIRES, Aug. 28,
1852.
479 III. HENRY,[7] b. Nov. 18, 1802; m. MARIA B. SWIFT, Aug. 2, 1832.
IV. ASENATH D.,[7] b. Aug. 5, 1805; m. JAMES FULLER, May 11, 1830.

Children.

1. Mary Fuller, m. George Collingwood.
2. James A. Fuller, unmarried.
3. William H. Fuller, m. Clarissa Burns. Lives in Cambridgeport.
4. Lucia C. Fuller, m. John Brown. Lives in Haverhill.
5. Arabella J. Fuller, m. Horace Page. Lives in Haverhill.
6. Chester H. Fuller, unmarried. Lives in Kingston.

V. MARIA,[7] b. Oct. 14, 1807; m. EDWIN POWERS, December, 1839.
Lived in Kingston.

Children.

1. Maria E. Powers, m. Asa U. Bray.
2. Charles T. Powers, unmarried.

VI. ELIZABETH F.,[7] b. May 12, 1811; m. DR. FRANCIS BARKER, August,
1839. She d. August, 1883.
Immediately after marriage they went as missionaries to the
Shoshone Indians for thirteen years, when they settled in Lawrence,
Kansas, and spent the remainder of life there.

Children.

1. William Barker, m. in Kansas.
2. Sophronia Barker, m. in Kansas.
3. Mary F. Barker, m. William H. Miles, of So. Hanson.

VII. MARCIA,[7] b. Dec. 1, 1813; m., Jan. 16, 1868, DEA. THOMAS POTTER, of New London, Conn. No children.
VIII. LUCIA R.,[7] b. Aug. 26, 1816; d. Jan. 3, 1835.
IX. LEWIS,[7] b. Feb. 18, 1819; d. Sept. 21, 1835.

210.

JOSEPH[6] CHURCHILL (THADDEUS,[5] ELIEZER,[4] ELIEZER,[3] ELIEZER,[2] JOHN[1]). Born about 1782. He sailed out from Boston in 1836, aged fifty-four years, and was never heard from afterwards. Married 1st, July 28, 1804, MERCY LeBARON GOODWIN, daughter of Thomas. She died Oct. 2, 1822. Married 2d, LYDIA LeBARON GOODWIN, sister of Mercy.

Children born in Plymouth.

480   I. JOSEPH LEWIS,[7] b. Aug. 21, 1805; m. ABIGAIL MERRILL GOODWIN, of Falmouth, May 27, 1830.
He died at sea, August, 1842.
II. AMELIA,[7] b. Feb. 7, 1807; d. Sept. 12, 1807.
III. EDWARD,[7] b. Dec. 13, 1808; d. Jan. 3, 1809.
IV. GEORGE,[7] b. Aug. 2, 1811; d. Oct. 2, 1811.
V. GUSTAVUS,[7] b. Dec. 27, 1814; unmarried; lost at sea between Boston and Bangor.
VI. MARCIA,[7] b. June 15, 1817; d. unmarried in 1839.
VII. CHARLES THOMAS,[7] b. April 21, 1820; d. Feb. 13, 1825.

211.

SAMUEL[6] CHURCHILL (SAMUEL,[5] JOSIAH,[4] ELIEZER,[3] ELIEZER,[2] JOHN[1]). Born in Plymouth, May 3, 1779, and lived there. Married, Nov. 8, 1801, NANCY COVINGTON. After the death of Samuel, the widow married Benjamin Dillard, as his third wife.

Children born in Plymouth.

481   I. SAMUEL,[7] b. Aug. 31, 1802; m. RACHEL CAPEN, Jan. 1, 1827.
482   II. EZRA,[7] b. March 10, 1805; m. MEHITABLE PORTER, June 29, 1830.
III. FRANCIS,[7] died at sea.
IV. POLLY,[7] m. WILLIAM RAYMOND, of No. Bridgewater.
V. NANCY,[7] b. Feb. 6, 1814; m. AVERY CAPEN, of Stoughton.

Children born in Stoughton.

1. Arabella Capen, b. Dec. 22, 1836; d. Dec. 20, 1841.
2. Nancy Arabella Capen, b. May 11, 1843; m. Charles Tucker, June 29, 1865; d. Sept. 18, 1867.
3. Avery Augustus Capen, b. May 9, 1844; killed at Fredericksburg, Dec. 13, 1862.
4. Elizabeth Churchill Capen, b. Aug. 15, 1853; m. William E. Hayward, of Uxbridge.

483   VI. JACOB,[7] m. MARIA MOSIER, of New Bedford.
484   VII. JOHN E.,[7] m. ELEANOR SHUMAN.

212.

CALEB[6] CHURCHILL (SAMUEL,[5] JOSIAH,[4] ELIEZER,[3] ELIEZER,[2] JOHN[1]). Born in Plymouth, March 25, 1782. Married, Nov. 21, 1801, LYDIA GREENOLD.

One Child.

I. ELIZA,[7] m. JOHN BRIGGS, of Berkeley, Mass.

Children.

1. John C. Briggs.
2. Eliza Ann Briggs, m. Reuben Richmond, of Taunton.
3. Lydia Southworth Briggs, m. 1st, Dr. (———) Larkin, of Wrentham; m. 2d, Rev. (———) Sheff, of Wrentham.

213.

ENOS[6] CHURCHILL (ENOS,[5] JOSIAH,[4] ELIEZER,[3] ELIEZER,[2] JOHN[1]). Born at Ragged Island, Nova Scotia, April 9, 1797. Married, Dec. 19, 1822, ABIGAIL LOCKE.

Children.

485   I. LEWIS P.,[7] b. Nov. 8, 1826; m. ANN LOCKE.
       II. ELIZABETH,[7] m. JOHN LOCKE.
      III. TRYPHENIA,[7] m. ANDREW C. CONGDON.
      IV. PRISCILLA.[7]
       V. LOUISA.[7]
      VI. EMILY,[7] m. HENRY STUDLEY, M.D.
     VII CECILIA.[7]
    VIII. AUGUSTA.[7]

214.

SILVANUS[6] CHURCHILL (SILVANUS,[5] JOSIAH,[4] ELIEZER[3] ELIEZER,[2] JOHN[1]). Born Sept. 25, 1805. He died July 26, 1879. Married 1st, 1836, LYDIA RUSSELL, of New Bedford; 2d, 1843, ELIZA W. GIFFORD, of New Bedford.

One Child by Second Wife.

486   I. ROBERT, b. in New Bedford, Dec. 13, 1848. No further record.

215.

JOHN DARLING[6] CHURCHILL (SILVANUS[5] JOSIAH,[4] ELIEZER,[3] ELIEZER,[2] JOHN[1]). Born in Plymouth, Nov. 8, 1817, and lived there. Married 1st, April 11, 1840, MARCIA J. HOLMES. She died May 22, 1882. 2d, Dec. 30, 1883, JULIA A. HAWLEY

Children.

487   I. JOHN FRANKLIN,[7] b. Jan. 11, 1841; m. CLARA FINNEY, Dec. 30, 1866.

Born in Plymouth and lived there till the close of his school-days, when he received the appointment of cadet at the Annapolis Naval Academy, by the suggestion of Congressman Robert B. Hall. Upon graduation he entered the merchant service until the opening of the Civil War, when he was appointed ensign in the navy, and served on the U.S. man-of-war "Yantic." He was attached to Admiral Porter's fleet with Dewey and Schley, and was engaged in both battles at Fort Fisher. At the close of the war he returned to Plymouth and entered the store of his uncle, and continued in the business until he became secretary of the "Mixter

Saw Gummer Company," of whose Eastern interests he had charge
until his death, March 29, 1903, at his home in Plymouth.   He was
a member of the Masonic order.   No children.

488   II. FRED LEE,⁷ b. Feb. 8, 1846; m. MARY N. DIMON, June 7, 1874.
489   III. JOSIAH DARLING,⁷ b. Oct. 24, 1853; m. MARTHA TILLSON, Oct. 6,
                1876.

216.

LEMUEL⁶ CHURCHILL (JESSE,⁵ JONATHAN,⁴ ELIEZER,³
ELIEZER,² JOHN¹).   Born Dec. 5, 1775.   He settled, after marriage,
at Richmond, Va.   Married, March 21, 1803, SARAH SUMNER, of
Roxbury, daughter of Deacon Samuel.

Children born, some at Roxbury and the younger at Richmond, Va.

          I. ELIZABETH,⁷ b. 1804; d. unmarried.
         II. ELIPHALET PORTER,⁷ d. unmarried.
        III. HANNAH,⁷ d. in infancy.
490   IV. GUSTAVUS VASA,⁷ b. 1809; m. SOPHIA PRESCOTT. Had one son
                Harry; d. in infancy. No further record.
          V. ABIGAIL,⁷ d. young.
         VI. MARY ANN,⁷ b. 1813; m. JONATHAN BUFFINTON.
491   VII. WILLIAM WORCESTER,⁷ m. 1st, CAROLINE GORE WOODMAN; m. 2d,
                MRS. HURLL.

217.

SIMEON⁶ CHURCHILL (JESSE,⁵ JOHNATHAN,⁴ ELIEZER,³
ELIEZER,² JOHN¹).   Born June 25, 1786.   Lived in Cincinnati, a
cabinet-maker.   Married CAROLINE HUNT, of Baltimore.

Children.

492   I. FREDERICK AUGUSTUS,⁷ b. in Baltimore, Aug. 13, 1811; m. (——)
                (——).
                They had four children, viz.
                1, William ; 2, Frederick A.; 3, Elizabeth; 4, Caroline.
                All of these died without issue, and we have no record.
         II. HANNAH HUNT,⁷ b. in Cincinnati, Jan. 29, 1813.
        III. ALONZO WOOSTER,⁷ b. in Cincinnati, Jan. 9, 1816; m. ELLEN
                SAND; no children.
         IV. LAURA SPENCER,⁷ b. in Cincinnati, March 23, 1819, d. in infancy.

218.

DAVID⁶ CHURCHILL (JESSE,⁵ JONATHAN,⁴ ELIEZER,³ ELIEZER,²
JOHN¹).   Born July 16, 1795.   He lived in Cincinnati ; was a cabinet-maker.   He was a very large man, six feet two inches in height,
and weighed three hundred pounds.   Died May 17, 1853.   Married,
Feb. 22, 1825, FRANCES ANN CLIFTON MCKIN.

Children born in Cincinnati.

          I. ABIGAIL WOOSTER,⁷ b. 1826; unmarried.
         II. GEORGE WASHINGTON,⁷ b. 1828; never married.
        III. FRANKLIN,⁷ b. 1830; never married.

219.

WILLIAM LEATHERS [6] CHURCHILL (FRANCIS,[5] JONA-THAN,[4] ELIEZER,[3] ELIEZER,[2] JOHN [1]). Born March 22, 1787. Lived at West Fairlee, Vt. Held a captain's commission in War of 1812. Married ELIZA LAMPHIRE, of West Fairlee, Vt.

Children born in West Fairlee.

493   I. WILLIAM LEATHERS, JR.,[7] b. Sept. 5, 1811; m. MINERVA NICHOLS, of Corinth, Vt.
    II. AUSTIN FINLEY,[7] b. Oct. 6, 1813; d. unmarried Jan. 26, 1823.
494   III. CHAUNCY CARROLL,[7] b. Sept. 26, 1815; m. PAMELIA SABIN, of Amesbury, Mass.
    IV. ELIZA JANE,[7] b. June, 1818; m. ASA SOUTHWORTH, of West Fairlee. She d. in Boston.
495   V. BENJAMIN PIXLEY,[7] b. Sept. 2, 1822; m. SUSAN THOMPSON. He d. in Fairlee, Aug. 14, 1864.
496   VI. FRANCIS VENNELL,[7] b. Dec. 6, 1827; m. MARINDA E. MUNN, Jan. 31, 1854.

220.

CAPT. FRANCIS WORCESTER [6] CHURCHILL (FRANCIS,[5] JONATHAN,[4] ELIEZER,[3] ELIEZER,[2] JOHN [1]). Born Feb. 9, 1789. Lived in East Fairlee, Vt. He was a carpenter and architect, and was captain of a cavalry company in the War of 1812. Married MILLICENT WHITCOMB.

Children.

    I. LAUNCELOT,[7] no record.
497   II. JAMES MONROE,[7] b. April 3, 1813; m. RUTH E. TILDEN, of Thetford, Vt., 1844. No further record.
    III. ORLANZO,[7] d. at 10 years.
    IV. SARAH ADELINE,[7] b. July 29, 1815; m. MOODY COFFIN, of Haverhill, Mass.
    V. CAROLINE HOUGHTON,[7] b. July 29, 1817; m. PHINEAS E. DAVIS, Sept. 3, 1839.
    VI. MARY MARION.[7]
    VII. HELEN MAR,[7] b. in Lowell about 1830; d. in East Fairlee, Vt.

221.

DAVID CARROLL [6] CHURCHILL (FRANCIS,[5] JONATHAN,[4] ELIEZER,[3] ELIEZER,[2] JOHN[1]). Born in East Fairlee, Vt., Dec. 16, 1790. Lived in Fairlee, Vt.; a man of ability and influence. He was for years sheriff of Grafton County, N.H. He was judge of the county, and several times representative from his town to the Legislature. Married, Jan. 3, 1816, POLLY FRANKLIN, of Lyme, N.H.

Children.

    I. MARIA,[7] b. April 11, 1817; d. May 29, 1838.
    II. JONATHAN FRANKLIN,[7] b. Feb. 8, 1819; d. Sept. 28, 1827.
498   III. DAVID CARROLL, JR.,[7] b. April 12, 1821; m. LYDIA ANN PERRY, Oct. 20, 1847.

499   IV. CHARLES HENRY,[7] b. Aug. 21, 1824; m. 1st, MARY JANE TURNER, of Oberlin, O., Nov. 26, 1846; m. 2d, HENRIETTA VANCE, of Lima, Ind., Oct. 10, 1859.

500   V. LEWIS FRANKLIN,[7] b. June 1, 1826; m. HARRIET AUGUSTA DREW, Dec. 31, 1849.

   VI. LUCRETIA,[7] b. Aug. 9, 1828; m. THOMAS L. NELSON, of Elyria, O. She d. in childbirth.

Child.

1. Lucretia Nelson, m. Rev. (———) Butler, of Sunderland, Mass.

501   VII. JONATHAN FRANKLIN,[7] b. June 26, 1833; m. LAURA A. CHANDLER, of Oxford, N.H.

   VIII. MARY,[7] b. July 3, 1839; m. A. W. DIMMICK, of Watertown, Mass. One child, which, with the mother, died at the birth.

222.

SIMEON RICHARDSON[6] CHURCHILL (FRANCIS,[5] JONATHAN,[4] ELIEZER,[3] ELIEZER,[2] JOHN[1]). Born in East Fairlee, Vt., Dec. 9, 1794. Died in Syracuse, N.Y. Married, 1821, MARY ANN DOANE, of Troy, N.Y.

Children.

   I. MARY ANN,[7] d. in infancy.
   II. CHARLES,[7] b. March 11, 1823; d. unmarried.
   III. CLEOPATRA,[7] b. April 17, 1825; d. young.
   IV. MARY ANN,[7] b. May 1, 1827; m. EDWARD SEABURY, of Troy.

502   V. FRANCIS,[7] b. March 20, 1829; m. 1st CHARLOTTE STAATS; m. 2d MARY KIBBE, March 16, 1854. Lived in Batavia, N.Y.

   VI. CLEOPATRA,[7] b. April 3, 1831; m. JOHN M. KIRK, April 16, 1851. Lived in Rochester, N.Y.

Children born in Rochester, N.Y.

1. Lilian Kirk, b. Feb. 11, 1852.
2. Ida M. Kirk, b. Nov. 30, 1853.
3. Charles LeGrande Kirk, b. Aug. 1, 1856.
4. Ella Kirk, b. Nov. 6, 1858.
5. Henry Richardson Kirk, b. Aug. 31, 1860.
6. Gertrude Kirk, b. April 26, 1868; d. in infancy.

   VII. LOVINA,[7] b. Aug. 10, 1833; m. AMOS GOULD, Sept. 4, 1850. Lived in Buffalo.

Children.

1. Cynthia Gould, b. July 9, 1858.
2. Grace Gould, b. Jan. 22, 1871; d. at the age of 4 years 10 months.
3. George C. Gould, b. Oct. 27, 1875.
4. Mortimer Gould, b. Feb. 29, 1879.

   VIII. ELIZABETH,[7] b. June 26, 1836; m. JAMES GIRARD. Lived in Michigan. No children.

   IX. CYNTHIA,[7] b. May 24, 1841; m. HENRY H. WARNER, Jan. 12, 1860. Lived at Rochester, N.Y.

Children.

1. Jennie Elizabeth Warner, b. Jan. 10, 1861.
2. Charles Shattuck Warner, b. May 18, 1863.
3. Henry Plato Warner, b. Aug. 24, 1864.
4. William Thomas Warner, b. Aug. 14, 1876.

   X. SARAH,[7] b. May, 1844; m. WASHINGTON PERKINS.

Children.

1. Arthur Perkins.
2. Maude Perkins.
3. Carl Perkins.

4. Blanche Perkins.
5. Harry Simeon Perkins.

223.

SAMUEL STILLMAN[6] CHURCHILL (FRANCIS,[5] JONATHAN,[4] ELIEZER,[3] ELIEZER,[2] JOHN[1]). Born at East Fairlee, Vt., May 26, 1796. Lived in Thetford, Vt., Lowell, Mass., and Fairlee, Vt. Married SARAH C. COBURN, of Fairlee, Vt. Born Aug. 3, 1797.

Children.

    I. RODNEY,[7] b. in Thetford, Vt., Sept. 20, 1820.

503   II. STILLMAN,[7] b. in Lowell, Mass., July 28, 1823; m. LUCINDA HATHORN, Oct. 13, 1848.

    III. JOSEPHINE,[7] b. in Thetford, Vt., Aug. 22, 1825.

504   IV. SAMUEL,[7] b. June 19, 1829, in Lowell, Mass. No further record obtained.

505   V. HENRY,[7] b. Sept. 15, 1831, in Lowell, Mass. No further record obtained.

    VI. ROBERT WALLACE,[7] b. Jan. 7, 1834, in Fairlee, Vt. No further record obtained.

506   VII. GEORGE WEBSTER,[7] b. June 5, 1836, in Fairlee, Vt. No further record obtained.

507   VIII. MARY LAWRENCE,[7] b. July 20, 1840, in Fairlee, Vt. No further record obtained.

224.

JOSEPH WARREN[6] CHURCHILL (FRANCIS,[5] JONATHAN,[4] ELIEZER,[3] ELIEZER,[2] JOHN[1]). Born at Fairlee, Vt., Feb. 2, 1798. He was a merchant and lived in Troy from the age of twenty-one years to his death. He died Jan. 12, 1875. Married, Feb. 2, 1825, SARAH N. DOANE.

Children born in Troy.

    I. JANE,[7] b. Dec. 23, 1825; m. NELSON PENFIELD, Jan. 18, 1842.

508   II. GEORGE,[7] b. Aug. 18, 1827; m. ANNA L. SULLIVAN, Feb. 14, 1859. Said to have had one child, but no record found.

    III. WATTS,[7] b. Feb. 13, 1831; d. Aug. 8, 1831.

509   IV. LEE,[7] b. April 20, 1836; m. ELLA HIGGINS, Sept. 20, 1871.

510   V. DEWITT,[7] b. June 10, 1838. No further record.

    VI. JAY,[7] b. May 20, 1840; d. June 26, 1842.

225.

REUBEN EDWARD[6] CHURCHILL (FRANCIS,[5] JONATHAN,[4] ELIEZER,[3] ELIEZER,[2] JOHN[1]). Born at Fairlee, Vt., Oct. 26, 1799. Settled in Paw Paw, Mich. He died Dec. 29, 1856. Married, Dec. 1, 1823, MARY GOODIN, born April 6, 1803; died Dec. 4, 1884.

Children.

    I. LORENZO GOODIN,[7] b. Aug. 29, 1824: d. Oct. 16, 1868. No further record.

    II. ALONZO PERRY,[7] b. March 1, 1826; d. Feb. 18, 1847. No further record.

III. MARY MELISSA,[7] b. Aug. 19, 1828; d. Sept. 10, 1830. No further
record.
IV. SALLY MELISSA,[7] b. Nov. 28, 1832; d. Jan. 20, 1880. No further
record.
V. MARY LOUISA,[7] b. May 1, 1837; d. Jan. 5, 1874.
VI. GEORGE WASHINGTON,[7] b. Nov. 9, 1840; d. in Andersonville prison,
September, 1864.
VII. HANNAH MALINDA,[7] b. Sept. 15, 1844; m. JAMES FREDERICK BUL-
LARD, June 30, 1866.

Children.

1. Edwin Leroy Bullard, b. July 14, 1868.
2. Frederick Irwing Bullard, b. Feb. 14, 1881; d. June 20, 1881.

226.

THOMAS WORCESTER[6] CHURCHILL (FRANCIS,[5] JONA-
THAN,[4] ELIEZER,[3] ELIEZER,[2] JOHN[1]). Born in East Fairlee, Vt.,
Sept. 20, 1802. Lived in Utica, N.Y. Married, in Exeter, N.H.,
Sept. 8, 1827, POLLY BROWN, of Lowell, Mass.

Children born in Utica.

511   I. FRANKLIN GREEN,[7] m. 1st, AMELIA LAYMAN; m. 2d, IDA HALL.
We have the name of one child.

Child.

1. Frank Albert, b. in Dundee, N.Y. No further record.
II. SARAH E.,[7] m. JOSEPH W. CUSHING, March 8, 1843.

227.

JOHN EMERY[6] CHURCHILL (FRANCIS,[5] JONATHAN,[4]
ELIEZER,[3] ELIEZER,[2] JOHN[1]). Born in East Fairlee, Vt., July 20,
1811. Lived in Nashua, N.H. Married ELIZA ANN COBURN.

Children born in Nashua, N.H.

512   I. JOHN WESLEY,[7] b. May 26, 1839; m. MARY J. DONALD, of Fairlee,
Vt.
II. ELIZA JANE,[7] b. June 14, 1840; m. STEPHEN COOK, Oct. 17, 1871.
No children.
III. PHEBE E.,[7] b. Aug. 30, 1842; unmarried.
IV. MARY ESTHER,[7] b. Nov. 14, 1845/6; m. REUBEN WEBBER SWIFT,
of Provincetown, Dec. 26, 1871. They were married in Nashua,
N.H., but lived in Provincetown, where were born their chil-
dren.

Children.

1. Jennie C. Swift, b. Jan. 16, 1873; m. Frank G. Westwood, of
Newton, Sept. 18, 1895.
2. George W. Swift, b. May 31, 1875.
3. Edith T. Swift, b. May 29, 1879.
4. Helen M. Swift, b. July 24, 1882; d. Sept. 26, 1882.
513   V. GEORGE FRANCIS,[7] b. Oct. 6, 1846; m. ELLA G. HOLBROOK.
VI. MORGIANA FRANCELIA,[7] b. Oct. 25, 1848; unmarried; d. in Boston,
Dec. 12, 1887.
VII. WILLIAM H.,[7] Aug. 11, 1851; d. July 18, 1852.
514 VIII. ELBERT LAWRENCE,[7] b. at East Cambridge, April 13, 1857; m.
GERTRUDE A. TAYLOR, April 9, 1884.

228.

DR. GEORGE WASHINGTON[6] CHURCHILL (FRANCIS,[5] JONATHAN,[4] ELIEZER,[3] ELIEZER,[2] JOHN[1]). Born in Fairlee, Vt., Nov. 4, 1814. He was a physician. Married 1st, in Troy, N.Y., ELIZABETH MILLIKEN; 2d, in Post Mills, name not obtained; 3d, MRS. LYDIA ANN (WHARF) SHAW.

One Child by First Wife.

I. MARY JANE.[7] No record.

229.

CHARLES[6] CHURCHILL (CHARLES,[5] EPHRAIM,[4] STEPHEN,[3] ELIEZER,[2] JOHN[1]). Born at Plymouth, Oct. 8, 1767. Married HANNAH NYE, of Wareham, Mass.

Children.

515   I. CHARLES,[7] b. Aug. 26, 1797. No further record.
        II. BETSEY,[7] b. Dec. 9, 1799.
516   III. NELSON.[7] No record.
517   IV. JOSEPH,[7] b. Jan. 1, 1805; m. BETSEY ELLIS.
518   V. ELKANAH,[7] b. 1809; m. LYDIA SHERMAN, of Carver, dau. of John.

230.

RUFUS[6] CHURCHILL (CHARLES,[5] EPHRAIM,[4] STEPHEN,[3] ELIEZER,[2] JOHN[1]). Born in Plymouth, April 12, 1772. He died April 26, 1826. Married, March 10, 1797, EUNICE COVINGTON.

Children.

519   I. ISAAC COVINGTON,[7] b. Nov. 28, 1797; m. MARY T. JENNEY, Dec. 16, 1820.
        II. RUFUS,[7] b. May 25, 1799; d. Nov. 1, 1799.
        III. EUNICE,[7] b. March 14, 1803; m. RICHARD POPE.

Children.

1. Richard Pope, unmarried; settled in California.	4. Joseph Pope.
	5. Lydia Pope.
	6. Eunice Pope.
2. William Pope, settled in California.	7. Lucy Ann Pope.
	8. Adrianna Pope.
3. Rufus Pope.	

520   IV. RUFUS,[7] b. March 9, 1806; m. LUCY W. NYE, dau. of William, and d. April 14, 1828.
521   V. WILLIAM,[7] b. Nov. 25, 1816; m. EMILY TRIBBLE, Jan. 3, 1841. Lived in Plymouth.

231.

SAMUEL[6] CHURCHILL (CHARLES,[5] EPHRAIM,[4] STEPHEN,[3] ELIEZER,[2] JOHN[1]). Born at Plymouth, Sept. 23, 1774. Died March 1, 1803. Married, Nov. 11, 1798, BATHSHEBA COLLINS. She died Aug. 30, 1803.

One Child.

522   I. SAMUEL,[7] m. CALISTA POOL, dau. of Perez. No record.

232.

EPHRAIM[6] CHURCHILL (CHARLES,[5] EPHRAIM,[4] STEPHEN,[3] ELIEZER,[2] JOHN[1]). Born May 16, 1782. He left his family many years ago and went to Ohio, and never returned. Married, March 2, 1804, SALLY FINNEY, daughter of William.

One Child.

523   I. EPHRAIM FINNEY,[7] m. MARTHA H. WHITING.
             They lived in Chiltonville. No further record.

233.

EPHRAIM[6] CHURCHILL (ZACCHEUS,[5] EPHRAIM,[4] STEPHEN,[3] ELIEZER,[2] JOHN[1]). Born September, 1759. Perhaps served in Revolution, Captain Packard's Company, Colonel Cary's Regiment, alarm on July, 1780, eleven days in R.I. Settled, about the close of the Revolution, in Yarmouth, N.S., and there died March 22, 1826. They lived just south of the village. Married, in Yarmouth, N.S., ASENATH HIBBARD. She was born 1768, and died February, 1830.

Children born in Yarmouth, N.S.

524   I. ZACCHEUS,[7] b. Feb. 23, 1786; m. SUSANNAH (ROSE) KILLAM; d. Yarmouth, May 23, 1861.
            II. STEPHEN,[7] b. April 15, 1789. Lost at sea.
525   III. THOMAS,[7] b. June 6, 1791; m. MARY HARRIS; d. Yarmouth, Nov. 7, 1847.
526   IV. RUFUS;[7] b. May 19, 1793; m. GERTRUDE FLINT, Dec. 10, 1816; d. Yarmouth, Aug. 25, 1865.
527   V. NATHANIEL,[7] b. July 1, 1795; m. ABIGAIL VALPEY.
            VI. MARY,[7] b. Sept. 1, 1798; m. DAVID FLINT, Jan. 26, 1819. She died in Yarmouth, Oct. 4, 1891.

Children.

1. William Flint, b. Jan. 12, 1820; m. Emmeline Vickery, dau. of Moses.
2. Samuel S. Flint, b. March 18, 1822; m. Elizabeth Walker, December, 1844.
3. Mary Ellen Flint, b. Aug. 19, 1823; m. 1st, Alfred Morrill, son of Capt. Moses; m. 2d, Robert Spiers.
4. Catharine Flint, b. May 24, 1825; m. Robert Spiers.
5. Asenath Flint, b. April 10, 1827; d. June 28, 1828.
6. David Flint, b. Oct. 8, 1828; m. Emma Rusco, of Cornwallis.
7. Jacob Flint, b. Sept. 28, 1832; m. 1st, Margaret Harding, May 21, 1886; m. 2d, Anne H. Haley.
8. John E. Flint, b. July 27, 1836; d. unmarried.

           VII. WILLIAM,[7] b. Dec. 17, 1800; m. 1st, MARY CORNING, Dec. 28, 1828; no issue; m. 2d, LETITIA DURKEE, April 21, 1855; no issue.
          VIII. ELIZABETH.[7] b. May 10, 1803; m. 1st, EBENEZER CORNING; no issue; m. 2d, ABRAHAM KILLAM.

Children.

1. Harriet N. Killam, b. 1831; m. Capt. George R. Doty.
2. Ebenezer C. Killam, } b. 1833; m. Lois R. Moses, Nov. 25,
   1863.
3. Abram Killam, } b. 1833; d. Feb. 21, 1843.
4. William Killam, b. 1834; d. May 5, 1835.
5. Elizabeth Killam, b. 1837; m. William G. Sims, Nov. 20, 1862.
6. Martha Killam, b. 1838; m. James McConnell.
7. William A. Killam, b. 1844; m. Sarah J. Moses, dau. of Capt.
   Nathan.

528   IX. WALTER,[7] b. June 3, 1805; m. 1st, SARAH FLINT; m. 2d, ELSIE
           MURPHY.
        X. HANNAH,[7] b. Sept. 9, 1807; m. THOMAS BYRNES, Oct. 29, 1826.

Children.

1. William Byrnes, b. Dec. 24, 1827; d. unmarried March 1,
   1858.
2. Eben Corning Byrnes, b. Jan. 18, 1829; m. 1st, Lois E. Perry,
   Nov. 27, 1856; m. 2d, Marie Curry.
3. Ann Byrnes, b. March 30, 1831; m. Capt. Thomas Perry.
4. Martha Greenough Byrnes, b. Aug. 18, 1833; d. young.

   XI. EPHRAIM,[7] b. July 29, 1809; d. young.
  XII. ASENATH,[7] b. March 30, 1812; m. JOHN W. SCOTT.

Children.

1. Hugh Scott, b. Sept. 3, 1840; m. Lovina Barker, of Clinton,
   Me., Sept. 2, 1879.
2. Mary Scott, b. Sept. 2, 1842; m. William Harris, of Dixmont,
   Me., 1865.
3. Amelia Scott, b. May 5, 1844; m. Norman Brown, March,
   1870.
4. William Scott, b. Sept. 17, 1846; d. unmarried, 1880.

529 XIII. JOHN,[7] b. Sept. 23, 1814; m. 1st, BETSEY FLINT, Feb. 4, 1832; m.
           2d, MARIA ANNE HASKELL; m. 3d, ALMIRA (GOUDAY) SANDERS;
           no issue.

237.

LEWIS[6] CHURCHILL (ELLIS,[5] EPHRAIM,[4] STEPHEN,[3] ELIEZER,[2]
JOHN[1]). Place and date of birth not found. Married, Oct. 21,
1792, NANCY MITCHELL.

Children.

530   I. LEWIS,[7] b. Feb. 12, 1794; m. HANNAH COVINGTON, at Plymouth,
          July 28, 1817. No record obtained.
531   II. SYLVANUS,[7] b. July 25, 1796; m. BETSEY CARVER. No further
          record.
     III. MARY,[7] b. July 1, 1798; m. ZACCHEUS BARNES, August, 1821, in
          Plymouth.

One Child.

1. Nancy Paty Barnes; m. Ozen Bates.

532   IV. JOSEPH,[7] b. June 8, 1804. No further record.

239.

WILLIAM [6] CHURCHILL (ELLIS,[5] EPHRAIM,[4] STEPHEN,[3] ELIEZER,[2] JOHN [1]). Born in Plymouth, Dec. 12, 1780. Lived in Plymouth, and died May 15, 1870. Married 1st, 1805, SALLY ROUNDS. She died May 16, 1823; married 2d, ABIGAIL KNOPP. She died in 1867.

Children of First Wife.

I. ELLIS,[7] b. 1806; d. March 29, 1835; unmarried
II. WILLIAM,[7] b. 1808; d. 1850; unmarried.
III. SARAH,[7] b. Nov. 11, 1810; m. DEXTER PACKARD, 1835. Mrs. Packard d. April 13, 1885.

Children.

1. William D. Packard.
2. Hiram R. Packard.
3. Amelia Packard.

IV NANCY E.,[7] b. April 10, 1813; m. 1st, JOHN ADAMS, Oct. 5, 1831· m. 2d, LEONARD BURT, Dec. 30, 1863.

Children.

1. John S. Adams, b. April 15, 1834; d. in California.
2. Oscar C. Adams, b. March 20, 1847; d. April 25, 1894. Two other children died young.

V. AMANDA,[7] b. March. 1816; d. unmarried, July 18, 1848.
533 VI. SIMEON R.,[7] b. Feb. 23, 1819; m. ABIGAIL EDDY, and d. July, 1865. A daughter, it is said, married Alden Lee. No further record.

240.

JOHN [6] CHURCHILL (ANSEL,[5] EPHRAIM,[4] STEPHEN,[3] ELIEZER,[2] JOHN [1]). Born in Plymouth, 1775, and there lived, and died Oct. 14, 1841. Married, June 6, 1801, NANCY JACKSON, of Carver.

Children born in Plymouth.

I. HANNAH,[7] b. 1802; m. BARTLETT ELLIS, of Plymouth, 1821.

Children.

1. Nancy Ellis, m. Willard Wood.
2. Nathaniel Ellis.
3. Hannah E. Ellis, m. Charles Ryder.
4. George Ellis.
5. Charles Ellis.

534 II. GEORGE,[7] b. 1803; m. MARTHA C. HOLMES, March 5, 1826.
III. JOHN,[7] b. June, 1805; d. May 15, 1806.
IV. BETHIA,[7] b. April 12, 1807; m. THOMAS B. BARTLETT, Nov. 26, 1829.

Children.

1. Charles Bartlett, b. July 3, 1831; m. Lucy A. Pratt.
2. Mary A. Bartlett, b. May 10, 1836; m. Capt. Charles C. Doten.
3. Thomas Bartlett, b. Jan. 6, 1840; m. 1st, Emmeline Savery; m. 2d, Ruhamah D. Raymond.
4. Priscilla Sampson Bartlett, b. Dec. 7, 1845.

V. NANCY,[7] b. 1808; d. in 1822, aged 14.
VI. SALLY ANN,[7] b. Aug. 26, 1811; m. ALDEN WINSOR, of Duxbury, February, 1835. They lived in Lynn. She d. May 12, 1892. Alden d. Aug. 15, 1868.

Children born in Lynn.

1. Henry A. Winsor, b. April 25, 1837.
2. Maria E. Winsor, b. Nov. 17, 1839.
3. Harriet G. Winsor, b. October, 1841; d. Nov. 30, 1863.
4. Sarah A. Winsor, b. Sept. 8, 1845.
5. Charles E. Winsor, b. April 18, 1852.

VII. LILLIS BARTON,[7] b. Nov. 22, 1813; m. JOSHUA B. LOUD, of Abington, Nov. 2, 1837. She d. Sept. 16, 1871. He d. Feb. 13, 1873.

Children.

1. Isabel F. Loud, b. April 6, 1839.
2. John M. Loud, b. Feb. 3, 1841.
3. Millard E. Loud, b. July 25, 1851.
4. George Churchill Loud, b. Dec. 31, 1854.

241.

STEPHEN [6] CHURCHILL (STEPHEN,[5] STEPHEN,[4] STEPHEN,[3] ELIEZER,[2] JOHN [1]). Born in Plymouth, May 7, 1768. Lived in Duxbury. Married 1st, June 4, 1791, ELIZABETH GRAY. Married 2d, MRS. NANCY (JACKSON) CHURCHILL, widow of John (No. 240).

One Child.

I. JOHN STEPHEN,[7] b. in Duxbury, April 24, 1826.

242.

PELEG [6] CHURCHILL (STEPHEN,[5] STEPHEN,[4] STEPHEN,[3] ELIEZER,[2] JOHN [1]). Born in Plymouth, Aug. 11, 1769. Lived in Duxbury. He died in 1810 and his widow married Studley Sampson, of Duxbury, and died Nov. 24, 1848, aged 76 years. Married 1st, (———) BRADFORD. Married 2d, April 14, 1791, HANNAH HOSEA.

Children born in Duxbury.

I. HARRIET,[7] b. Oct. 4, 1791; m. PRINCE BRADFORD, son of Samuel,[6] b. Dec. 19, 1783.

Children born in Duxbury.

1. Gershom Bradford, b. 1816.
2. Perez Bradford, b. 1818.
3. Harriet Bradford, b. 1821.
4. Otis Bradford, b. 1823.
5. Hannah Bradford, b. 1825.
6. Lydia Bradford, b. 1827.
7. Susan Bradford, b. 1832.

535 II. PELEG,[7] m. 1st, LUCY SPRAGUE; m. 2d, JANE PEASE.
III. ELIZA,[7] b. 1795; m. JOSEPH CHANDLER.

Children.

1. James Chandler.
2. Joseph Chandler.
3. Albert H. Chandler.
4. Peleg C. Chandler.
5. Ezra Chandler.

536   IV. WILLIAM,[7] b. May 18, 1798; m. MARY HOLMES, Oct. 5, 1823.
537   V. OTIS,[7] m. ESTHER HARLOW.
538   VI. EZRA,[7] m. SUSAN ALLEN.

243.

HEMAN[6] CHURCHILL (STEPHEN,[5] STEPHEN,[4] STEPHEN[3] ELIEZER,[2] JOHN[1]). Born in Plymouth, March 10, 1771. Lived in Plymouth. Died Nov. 22, 1840. Married, Jan. 1, 1795, JANE CHURCHILL; she died April 2, 1848.

Children born in Plymouth.

   I. MARY ANNE,[7] b. 1795. She was living in Plymouth in 1888.
  II. LEMUEL,[7] b. 1797; d. Oct. 1, 1802.
 III. PATIENCE,[7] b. 1799; m. CAPT. WILLIAM RANDALL, in 1819.

Children.

   1. William Randall, b. 1820.
   2. George Randall, b. 1822.
   3. Charles Randall, b. 1824.
   4. James Randall, b. 1826.

  IV. HEMAN,[7] d. Oct. 1, 1802.
   V. JANE,[7] d. June 11, 1808.
  VI. HEMAN,[7] b. 1805; d. April 6, 1808.
 VII. JANE,[7] b. 1809/10; d. April 26, 1812.

244.

DANIEL[6] CHURCHILL (STEPHEN,[5] STEPHEN[4] STEPHEN,[3] ELIEZER,[2] JOHN[1]). Born at Plymouth, Feb. 5, 1773. He died March 5, 1855. Married 1st, 1796, SARAH COLLINS; she died Nov. 3, 1836. Married 2d, NANCY (HOLMES) BREWSTER.

Children.

        I. SALLY,[7] b. Nov. 17, 1799; d. Aug. 16, 1801.
       II. SALLY,[7] b. Aug. 1, 1801; m. HARVEY WESTON.
539 III. DANIEL,[7] b. Sept. 9, 1803; m. MARY BRIGGS BROWN, 1826.
       IV. LOIS COLLINS,[7] b. Oct. 22, 1805; d. Aug. 14, 1806.
        V. LOIS COLLINS,[7] b. June 19, 1807; m. WILLIAM F. SOULE.
       VI. JANE,[7] b. July 27, 1809; m. GEORGE RYDER, Aug. 14, 1831.

Children.

   1. Sarah Jane Ryder, b. May 17, 1832.
   2. Helen M. Ryder, b. Sept. 10, 1833; d. Feb. 6, 1866. She married William H. Winsor, and had four children.
   3. George S. Ryder, b. April 27, 1835; d. Dec. 13, 1877.
   4. Julia Ryder, b. Feb. 17, 1837; d. Feb. 23, 1837.
   5. William E. B. Ryder, b. March 10, 1838.
   6. Charles E. Ryder, b. Feb. 11, 1841.
   7. Harriet J. Ryder, b. Oct. 27, 1843.
   8. Alfred H. Ryder, b. Sept. 29, 1848; d. Feb. 11, 1872.

      VII. ELEANOR,[7] b. Jan. 15, 1811; m. ALBERT LEACH, 1830.
540 VIII. HEMAN,[7] b. May 1, 1816; m. ALMIRA HOLMES. No further record.
       IX. WINSLOW BRADFORD,[7] b. June 26, 1819; d. April 12, 1820.

245.

WILSON [6] CHURCHILL (WILSON,[5] BENJAMIN,[4] STEPHEN,[3] ELIEZER,[2] JOHN [1]). Born in Plymouth, December, 1778. Married 1st, Dec. 9, 1804, RUTH HINCKLEY, daughter of Jabez, of Barnstable; 2d, May 25, 1816, SUSAN LUCAS.

Children of First Wife.

I. RUTH HINCKLEY,[7] b. 1812; m. WILLIAM L. FINNEY, 1834.

Children.

1. William Finney.
2. Ruth H. Finney, m. M. F. Holmes.

II. DEBORAH HINCKLEY,[7] m. EPHRAIM FINNEY.

Children of Second Wife.

541 III. ANSEL R.[7] No record.
542 IV. WILSON.[7] No record.
     V. SUSAN,[7] b. 1820; m. EPHRAIM FINNEY.

246.

NATHAN [6] CHURCHILL (BENJAMIN,[5] BENJAMIN,[4] STEPHEN,[3] ELIEZER,[2] JOHN [1]). Born in Plymouth, Dec. 16, 1785, and lived there; was alive in 1884, it is said. Married, Aug. 29, 1804, ELIZABETH (SYLVESTER) TINKHAM, widow of Enoch Tinkham.

Children born in Plymouth.

I. BETSEY,[7] m. ABBOT DREW, 1823.

Children.

1. Mary Drew, b. 1827; m. Benjamin F. Pierce.
2. Ann Russell Drew, b. 1830; m. Robert D. Fuller.
3. Francis Abbot Drew, b. 1832; m. Margaret Coates, of Morristown, Pa.
4. George Franklin Drew, b. 1835; m. Lucy Pettingill, of Lynn.
5. Josiah Russell Drew, b. 1839; m. Hatty Whitten.
6. Adaline Drew, b. 1841.
7. Helen Augusta Drew, b. 1844; m. Gideon F. Holmes.

     II. MARY SYLVESTER,[7] m. JOHN PARSONS.
543 III. NATHAN.[7] No record.
544 IV. SOLOMON SYLVESTER,[7] b. April 4, 1817; m. RUTH NELSON COBB, April 23, 1840.
     V. CHARLOTTE SYLVESTER,[7] m. JAMES A. SYLVESTER.

Children born in Plymouth.

1. Catharine Sylvester.
2. Charles Sylvester.

247.

AMAZIAH [6] CHURCHILL (AMAZIAH,[5] AMAZIAH,[4] ELKANAH,[3] ELIEZER,[2] JOHN [1]). Born in 1772. Lived in Plymouth. Married 1st, Jan. 26, 1799, MARTHA DOTEN; married 2d, MARGARET WALLACE, of Newbern, N.C.; married 3d, April 8, 1805, MARY HARLOW.

Children of First Wife.

I. MARTHA,[7] b. Oct. 12, 1799; unmarried.
II. BETSEY,[7] b. July 17, 1802; m. HENRY ROBBINS.

Children.

1. Edward L. Robbins, b. 1836.
2. Martha Robbins, b. 1839.
3. Harry H. Robbins, b. 1840.
4. Margaret H. Robbins, b. 1843.

Child of Second Wife.

III. A SON; died soon.

Children of Third Wife.

IV. LOUISA,[7] b. Feb. 18, 1809; m. THOMAS BARTLETT SEARS.

Children born in Plymouth.

1. Louisa Frances Sears, b. Dec. 25, 1831.
2. Thomas Bartlett Sears, b. July 2, 1834.
3. Amasa Churchill Sears, b. July 22, 1836.
4. Walter Herbert Sears, b. Dec. 8, 1847.
5. Francis Dana Sears, b. Aug. 30, 1851.

545   V. AMASA,[7] b. June 12, 1811; m. LEONICE HARLOW. No further record.

248.

EDMOND [6] CHURCHILL (AMAZIAH,[5] AMAZIAH,[4] ELKANAH,[3] ELIEZER,[2] JOHN [1]). No dates or other particulars about this family have been found. Married, Oct. 10, 1801, MARY HUESTON.

Children.

I. MARY,[7] m. ALBERT THOMAS, of Middleboro, June 22, 1831.
II. HARRIET B.,[7] m. JOSEPH BARDEN, of Middleboro, Oct. 9, 1833.
III. ELIZA W.,[7] m. CEPHAS SIMMONS, Oct. 18, 1832.

249.

SOLOMON [6] CHURCHILL (SOLOMON,[5] AMAZIAH,[4] ELKANAH,[3] ELIEZER,[2] JOHN [1]). Born in Plymouth, Aug. 26, 1788. He followed the sea in early life, and became captain of a vessel. Later he settled in Union Township, Lawrence County, O., and died March 14, 1835, at Portsmouth, O. Married, at Union Township, March 16, 1818, MARY PRITCHARD, daughter of Nathaniel and Comfort, born at Milton, N.Y., Sept. 16, 1800, and died at Portsmouth, O., March 20, 1873.

Children.

I. ELIZABETH BARTLET,[7] b. Sept. 20, 1820; m. ELISHA B. GREENE, Dec. 27, 1838, at South Point, O.

Children.

1. Charles William Greene, b. March 20, 1841; m. Isabel Blocksom, of Zanesville, O., Jan. 20, 1876.
2. Albert Edward Greene, b. Sept. 20, 1843; d. May 26, 1844.

3. Mary Ellen Greene, b. June 20, 1845; m. J. J. Gist; and died Jan. 16, 1881.
4. Elisha Barton Greene, b. May 12, 1849; m. Virginia S. Moore, March 11, 1895.
5. Albert Edward Greene, b. Jan. 24, 1851; d. Nov. 3, 1854.
6. Cyrus Dwight Greene, b. July 14, 1854; living in Zanesville.
7. Elizabeth B. Greene, b. Feb. 1, 1858; d. Nov. 10, 1860.
8. Fred Churchill Greene, b. March 2, 1862.

II. CHARLES WILLIAM,[7] b. Nov. 22, 1822; d. unmarried at Quartzburg, Cal., July 13, 1855.
III. MELISSA,[7] b. Sept. 18, 1827; m. 1st, JOSEPH F. WHEELER, Sept. 15, 1844; b. at Burlington, O., Dec. 24, 1823; d. there Oct. 18, 1851; m. 2d, DR. C. C. BRONSON, at Ironton, O., March 31, 1856.

Children born at Burlington.

1. Edward Churchill Wheeler, b. Aug. 26, 1846; d. Aug. 12, 1851.
2. James Snow Wheeler, b. Oct. 26, 1848.
3. Joseph Franklin Wheeler, b. May 27, 1851

545   IV   MENDALL,[7] b. July 23, 1829; m. MARY CARLISLE LOUGHRY, Nov. 28, 1861. No children.
Born in Union Township, Lawrence County, O. His father dying in middle life he was early thrown upon his own resources, with limited opportunity for school, but he made the most of his chances at the common school, and attended two terms at the County-seat Academy. He worked in a country store during his boyhood and youth, and at twenty-one gained the position of store-keeper and book-keeper at the Keystone, O., iron works, which he held until the breaking out of the Civil War, when he enlisted as a private, but was soon chosen captain of Company E, 27th Regiment, Ohio Volunteer Infantry. In December, 1862, he was appointed major and afterward rose to be lieutenant-colonel and colonel of the regiment, and then was commissioned as brigadier-general by brevet for meritorious service. The 27th Ohio was a fighting regiment, and was engaged in many battles, first in the Army of Missouri, then in the Army of the Mississippi, and last in the Army of the Tennessee. In the battle of Atlanta, July 22, 1864, his regiment had one hundred and fifty men killed or wounded, Colonel Churchill himself being wounded. September, 1864, with his health much impaired, he resigned. Later he engaged in the iron business at Zanesville, O., and became one of the leading iron men of that section, until 1891, when he retired, and enjoyed his well-earned competency in extensive travel. He held many positions of honor and trust, was an ardent Republican in politics, a presidential elector in 1880, and a member of the national convention in 1888. He was a warm personal friend of Mr. McKinley. His wife died in 1886. He spent his last years in Coronado, Cal., where he died Oct. 28, 1902.

V. JULIA,[7] b. Feb. 25, 1832; m. DR. EDWIN H. GRISWOLD, June 6, 1853, at Gallipolis, O. They had one child who died in infancy. Dr. Griswold died in Portsmouth, O., June, 1859, and she died there March 15, 1871.
546   VI. SOLOMON,[7] b. July 19, 1834; m. MRS. E. L. KEYS, at Logan, O., Feb. 20, 1878, and died April 21, 1886. No further record.

250.

WILLIAM[6] CHURCHILL (SOLOMON,[5] AMAZIAH,[4] ELKANAH[3] ELIEZER,[2] JOHN[1]). Born in Plymouth, July 13, 1798. He became a merchant in New York, of the firm of Churchill & Collamore,

dealers in chinaware, a very prominent and prosperous firm.   He
died in Brooklyn, N.Y., Jan. 13, 1861.   Married MARY MYRICK
HADEN, who was born in Nantucket, Sept. 21, 1803, and died in
Smithson, L.I., February, 1850.

Children.

547   I. WILLIAM,[7] b. in Boston, Feb. 4, 1825; m. 1st, LUCY C. AVERILL,
            July 28, 1847; m. 2d, SARAH J. STARKWEATHER, Oct. 6, 1858.
        II. MARY ELIZABETH,[7] b. in Staffordshire, Eng., Jan. 23, 1831; m.,
            March 6, 1856, HENRY HUNGERFORD, b. in Seymour, Conn., June
            21, 1825.

Children.

        1. Harry Hungerford, b. in Brooklyn, Feb. 9, 1857.
        2. Hattie Churchill Hungerford, b. in Brooklyn, Oct. 5, 1858.
        3. Churchill Hungerford, b. in New Haven, Nov. 25, 1867.
        4. Mai Hungerford, b. in New Haven.

251.

JABEZ[6] CHURCHILL (JABEZ,[5] ELKANAH,[4] ELKANAH,[3]
ELIEZER,[2] JOHN[1]).   Born in Plymouth, June 30, 1806.   Died Oct.
19, 1841, of yellow fever, on voyage from West Indies.   Married,
Sept. 25, 1832, CHARLOTTE W. KEEN.

Children.

548   I. JABEZ,[7] b. June 26, 1835; m. ABBY A. BARNES, of Stockton, Cal.,
            and lived there.   No further record.
        II. SYLVESTER,[7] b. April 24, 1838; d. unmarried in 1858.
       III. CHARLOTTE,[7] b. Feb. 3, 1840; d. Aug. 21, 1844.
549   IV. WILLIAM KEEN,[7] b. Feb. 21, 1842; m. SARAH E. NELSON, of
            Plymouth.
            In 1888 they were living in Walpole, Mass.   No further record.

252.

NATHANIEL[6] CHURCHILL (NATHANIEL,[5] ELKANAH,[4] EL-
KANAH,[3] ELIEZER,[2] JOHN[1]).   Born in Plymouth.   Married 1st,
LUCY MORTON ; married 2d, ALMIRA BARTLETT.

Child of First Wife.

        I. A DAUGHTER; d. in infancy.

Children of Second Wife.

        II. NATHANIEL,[7] b. July 5, 1832; unmarried.
       III. ALMIRA B.,[7] b. in Plymouth, Oct. 25, 1834; m. STEPHEN PEMBER,
            June 20, 1851.   They lived at Plymouth and Walpole.   He was
            b. in Randolph, Vt., Aug. 28, 1827; d. Feb. 7, 1881.

Children, first nine born in Plymouth.

        1. Henry S. Pember, b. Jan. 1, 1853; d. Jan. 1, 1877.
        2. Howard Pember, b. June 17, 1855.
        3. Mabel Pember, b. Oct. 17, 1856.
        4. Florena Pember, b. Nov. 22, 1860.
        5. John Pember, b. Nov. 24, 1862.
        6. Charles Pember, b. Aug. 10, 1863.

7. Walter Stephen Pember, b. July 16, 1865; d. Dec. 22, 1883.
8. Myra Pember, b. Nov. 28, 1866.
9. Nathaniel Churchill Pember, b. Dec. 10, 1873.
10. Harry Edgarton Pember, b. Dec. 10, 1842.

253.

WILLIAM [6] CHURCHILL (NATHANIEL,[5] ELKANAH,[4] ELKANAH,[3] ELIEZER,[2] JOHN[1]). Born in Plymouth, 1811. He died Sept. 8, 1839. Married, June 3, 1833, MARIA MORTON, daughter of Ichabod, Jr. She died Oct. 9, 1841.

Children born in Plymouth.

550   I. WILLIAM,[7] b. Feb. 19, 1835; m. MARY ASH, March 2, 1864.
     II. HANNAH,[7] b. June 7, 1838; d. Feb. 11, 1839.

254.

JOHN [6] CHURCHILL (JOHN,[5] JOHN,[4] JOHN,[3] ELIEZER,[2] JOHN[1]). Born in New Hackensack, N.Y., May 26, 1769. Married ANNA LEYSTER.

Children.

     I. MARIA,[7] b. July 17, 1789.
551 II. JOHN.[7] No record.
552 III. BENJAMIN.[7] No record.
     IV. CATHERINE LEYSTER,[7] b. Aug. 4, 1799.
     V. HETTY,[7] b. Jan. 10, 1801.

255.

BENJAMIN [6] CHURCHILL (JOHN,[5] JOHN,[4] JOHN,[3] ELIEZER,[2] JOHN[1]). Born Dec. 4, 1770, in New Hackensack, N.Y. He died Feb. 21, 1848, aged 77 years 2 months 17 days. Married, June 21, 1795, MARY BLOOM, who was the daughter of Sylvester Bloom, and born Aug. 18, 1778.

Children.

     I. MARY,[7] b. Nov. 7, 1796.
     II. SUSANNAH,[7] b. Jan. 24, 1799.
     III. HANNAH,[7] b. Jan. 29, 1801.
     IV. PHEBE,[7] b. Feb. 12, 1803.
554 V. JOHN B.,[7] b. March 26, 1805; m. JANE GREEN.
     VI. SARAH,[7] b. April 15, 1807.
     VII. JEMIMA,[7] b. July 17, 1809.
     VIII. LAURA,[7] b. March 13, 1812.
555 IX. BENJAMIN,[7] b. April 8, 1814. No further record.
     X. ELENOR ANN,[7] b. March 9, 1817.
     XI. RUTH,[7] b. Feb. 28, 1819; m. JOHN OAKLEY, Nov. 19, 1840.
556 XII. SYLVESTER,[7] b. Jan. 1, 1822; m. JANE DEPNEY, of Middleport, N.Y., in 1844. No further record obtained.

256.

WILLIAM [6] CHURCHILL (JOHN,[5] JOHN,[4] JOHN,[3] ELIEZER,[2] JOHN[1]). Born Sept. 26, 1779, in New Hackensack, N.Y., and lived there. Married CORNELIA VAN NOSTRAND, born Nov. 19, 1793.

Children born in New Hackensack, N. Y.

I. JOHN,[7] b. Dec. 8, 1810.
II. CAROLINE,[7] b. Aug. 10, 1812; unmarried.
III. SARAH ANN,[7] b. Nov. 5, 1814; unmarried.
IV. HANNAH ELIZA,[7] b. Nov. 22, 1816; unmarried.
V. CATHERINE,[7] b. Feb. 6, 1819; m. JOHN W. LEAVITT.

Children.

1. John Leavitt. | 2. Grace Leavitt, and several more.

VI. JANE DOTY,[7] b. June 18, 1821; m. 1st, SAMUEL H. SMITH; m. 2d, SAMUEL STEWART.

Children.

1. Jane Emily Stewart, b. Oct. 22, 1839.
2. Frederick Stewart, b. Dec. 19, 1841.
3. William Stewart, b. March 25, 1844.
4. Cornelia Stewart, b. Jan. 2, 1847; died in infancy.
5. Harry Stewart, died in infancy.

557   VII. CORNELIUS,[7] b. Oct. 30, 1823; m. ELIZABETH KNAPP.
       VIII. HARRY,[7] d. in infancy.

257.

SAMUEL [6] CHURCHILL (JOHN,[5] JOHN,[4] JOHN,[3] ELIEZER,[2] JOHN [1]). Born April 7, 1785, in New Hackensack, N.Y. Married, in New Hackensack, SALLIE (——), of New Hackensack.

Children.

558   I. WILLIAM.[7] No record.
559   II. ISAAC.[7] No record.
560   III. HENRY.[7] No record.
561   IV. CHARLES.[7] No record.
       Said to be two daughters whose names are not received.

258.

SAMUEL [6] CLARK CHURCHILL (SAMUEL,[6] CLARK,[5] BENJAMIN,[4] JOHN,[3] ELIEZER,[2] JOHN [1]). Born in Augusta, Me., Feb. 14, 1749, and lived there. Married, in Augusta, Me., May 8, 1823, LUCY SAVAGE, born Aug. 5, 1799.

Children born in Augusta, Me.

I. LUCY ANN,[7] b. May 17, 1825; m. DANIEL MOORE.
   They lived in Augusta, Me., and had

Children.

1. Esther Moore, b. July 4, 1844; m. Henry Potter.
2. Sylvester Moore, b. Jan. 21, 1846; d. April 2, 1847.
3. Silas Moore, b. April 16, 1848; d. July 4, 1850.
4. Paulina M. Moore, b. Sept. 5, 1849; m. Humphry P. Webber.
5. Daniel F. Moore, b. Feb. 15, 1853.
6. Nellie R. Moore, b. Sept. 7, 1861.
7. Ida M. F. Moore, b. Dec. 26, 1864.

562   II. SAMUEL CLARK,[7] b. July 11, 1827; m. 1st, ELIZA J. MORRILL, July 8, 1861; m. 2d, ANNA J. McCLURE.
563   III. COLUMBUS,[7] b. Nov. 12, 1829; m. ELSIE JANE WHITE.
       IV. SUSANNAH ELIZABETH,[7] b. May 6, 1833; unmarried.
       V. HELEN MARR,[7] b. April 28, 1836; d. Nov. 5, 1854.
      VI. LORENZO WESLEY,[7] b. Oct. 21, 1846; unmarried.

259.

ALFRED DELURA[6] CHURCHILL (SAMUEL CLARK,[5] BEN-JAMIN,[4] JOHN,[3] ELIEZER,[2] JOHN[1]). Born in Augusta, Me., June 23, 1801, and lived there. Married, Dec. 28, 1828, JANE CHAMBERS of St. John, N.B.

Children born in Augusta, Me.

       I. PAULINA,[7] b. Sept. 23, 1829; m. LEWIS WARD.
      II. ANGELINE,[7] b. Aug. 13, 1833; d. Dec. 23, 1848.
    III. ROSELLE,[7] d. in infancy.

261.

JOHN[6] CHURCHILL (JOHN,[5] JOSEPH,[4] JOHN,[3] ELIEZER,[2] JOHN[1]). Born in New Portland, Me., June 10, 1793. Married, May, 1818, MARY DENNIS.

Children.

564   I. GEORGE W. D.,[7] b. May 24, 1819; m. 1st, CYNTHIA CARTER; m. 2d, ELMIRA CALISS.
      II. SANFORD,[7] b. July 29, 1821; d. in 1842.
565   III. CYRUS,[7] b. May 21, 1823; m. ELIZA MELLEN.
      IV. CHARLES W.,[7] b. Aug. 25, 1825; m. TALISTA CLEVELAND. No children.
      V. LAVINA,[7] b. January, 1830; m. GEORGE W. STEWART.
     VI. ROCILDA,[7] b. 1832; d. 1836.
    VII. ELIZA,[7] b. 1834; d. in infancy.

262.

JOSEPH[6] CHURCHILL (JOHN,[5] JOSEPH,[4] JOHN,[3] ELIEZER,[2] JOHN[1]). Born June, 1795, in New Portland, Me. Married HANNAH B. SISSONS.

Children.

566   I. JASON,[7] b. April 24, 1819; m. JANE GUNN.
567   II. JOSEPH,[7] b. Oct. 20, 1821.
568   III. BURDECK,[7] b. 1824.
      IV. ELIZABETH,[7] b. Dec. 15, 1831; m. WASHBURN CAMPBELL.

263.

JAMES[6] CHURCHILL (JOHN,[5] JOSEPH,[4] JOHN,[8] ELIEZER[2] JOHN[1]). Born in New Portland, Me., July 4, 1799. Married, Nov. 25, 1816, CLARISSA THOMPSON.

Child.

264.

SANFORD [6] CHURCHILL (JOHN,[5] JOSEPH,[4] JOHN,[3] ELIEZER,[2] JOHN[1]). Born in New Portland, Me, July, 1801. Settled in Stark, Me. Married THANKFUL EAMES, of Madison, Me.

Children born in Stark, Me.

568a	I.	DIADEMA.[7]
568b	II.	IRENE.[7]
569	III.	CYRUS.[7]
570	IV.	HOLLIS HUTCHINS.[7]
570a	V.	CYRENA EAMES,[7] m. (——) PERKINS.
570b	VI.	LUCINDA.[7]
571	VII.	JOHN.[7]
572	VIII.	ELIAS HUTCHINS,[7] b. July 25, 1833; m. NANCY GREENLEAF, Sept. 21, 1858.
572a	IX.	MARCIA ANN.[7]

266.

SAMUEL [6] CHURCHILL (JOHN,[5] JOSEPH,[4] JOHN,[3] ELIEZER,[2] JOHN[1]). Born in New Portland, Me., March 19, 1816. Married LYDIA SMALL.

Children.

573	I.	JOHN.[7]
574	II.	GEORGE M.,[7] b. Dec. 22, 1845.
575	III.	EMERY S.,[7] b. July 21, 1847.
576	IV.	ISAAC,[7] b. 1849.
577	V.	JOEL,[7] b. Dec. 20, 1851.
578	VI.	EDSIE,[7] b. April 2, 1853.

267.

WILLIAM [6] CHURCHILL (WILLIAM,[5] JOSEPH,[4] JOHN,[3] ELIEZER,[2] JOHN[1]). Born in New Portland, Me., Feb. 13; 1803, and lived there. Married 1st, 1826, NANCY WALKER, who died Dec. 24, 1841. Married 2d, Jan. 12, 1843, ASEÑATH S. NEWELL.

Children of First Wife born in New Portland, Me.

I. TABITHA,[7] b. July 22, 1827; d. Nov. 6, 1833.
II. MARY,[7] b. Oct. 26, 1829; d. April 29, 1849.
III. NANCY,[7] b. April 29, 1832; d. Nov. 30, 1855.
579   IV. JOHN WILLIAM,[7] b. Sept. 13, 1835; m. HANNAH BAILEY.
V. JOSEPH,[7] b. March 13, 1838; d. Jan. 18, 1839.
VI. ELIZABETH,[7] b. March 15, 1841; m. JAMES DOBBINS.
They lived at Farmington, Me., and had six children.

Children.

1. Maria.	4. Katharine.
2. Elvira.	5. Daniel.
3. Harriet.	6. John.

Children of Second Wife.

VII. SARAH,[7] b. Nov. 7, 1843; m. ABEL THOMPSON, of New Portland, Oct. 22, 1860.

Children born in New Portland.

1. Ida M. Thompson, b. April 25, 1861; m. Alvarus Churchill, son of No. 580.
2. Charles L. Thompson, b. April 18, 1870; m. Jennie Greenwood, June 16, 1891.
    Children: (1) Hazel Thompson, b. March 31, 1894; (2) Evan G. Thompson, b. May 19, 1896; (3) Melvina Thompson, b. May 2, 1898.

VIII. MARTHA S.,[7] b. July 26, 1845; m. HENRY J. WHITMAN, of Turner, Me.

IX. DELPHINA,[7] b. March 1, 1849; m. ASBURY SOULE, of Lewiston, Me., Nov. 29, 1873.
    One child, Elmer Linwood Soule, b. June 1, 1882.

X. ELLA,[7] b. May 8, 1852; m. 1st, WILLIAM PARLIN; m. 2d, EDWIN MARTIN, of Lewiston, Me.

268.

TILSON [6] CHURCHILL (WILLIAM,[5] JOSEPH,[4] JOHN,[3] ELIEZER,[2] JOHN [1]). Born in New Portland, Me., Jan. 29, 1810, and lived there. Married SALLY ELLIOTT. He died Sept. 5, 1833.

Child born in New Portland.

580   I. WILLIAM TILSON,[7] b. Sept. 30, 1833; m. ABIGAIL LUCE.

269.

DANIEL [6] CHURCHILL (DANIEL,[5] JOSEPH,[4] JOHN,[3] ELIEZER [2] JOHN [1]). Born in Bingham, Me., April 20, 1800. Brought up on his father's farm, his school advantages were very limited, yet in the practical hard work which was his "school," he gained the knowledge which made a self-reliant and successful business man. At twenty-seven years he settled on a farm at the forks of the Kennebec. He afterwards became extensively engaged in the lumber trade in Maine and somewhat in Canada. He removed to Solon, Me., in 1837, and then in 1856 he was one of the many who removed to the attractive farm and timber lands of the Great West. He settled at Symco, Wis., where he kept up his business of farming and lumbering. He lived to a good old age, and died at Symco, Nov. 24, 1887. Married CAROLINE BAKER, who was born Oct. 8, 1811.

Children born, the first seven at the Forks, the others at Solon.

     I. MARY,[7] b. Feb. 22, 1828; died in six days.
581   II. ALBERT,[7] b. Oct. 29, 1829; m. IRENA BERRY, 1854.
     III. OCTAVIA,[7] b. July 2, 1831; d. March 22, 1834.
582   IV. ABEL,[7] b. May 3, 1833; m. LYDIA M. BERRY.
     V. JULIA ANN,[7] b. May 14, 1835; m. 1st, JAMES RICKER, 1854. No children; m. 2d, A. T. STEVENS.
     There were eight children by the second marriage, names not received.

VI. LEWIS,[7] b. April 19, 1837; d. June 20, 1855.
VII. DORCAS FOSTER,[7] b. May 25, 1839; m. 1st, H. C. EASTMAN, 1860;
m. 2d, J. H. BAKER, 1888.

One Child by First Husband.

1. Julia Ellen Eastman, b. 1861; m. Herbert H. Jenkins, 1881.
They had two daughters, Cora and Cleora.

584   VII. DANIEL FOSTER,[7] Jan. 6, 1842; m. LUCENA I. DAME.
    IX. WARREN,[7] b. Feb. 17, 1844; d. Aug. 6, 1846.
585   X. WARREN,[7] b. Sept. 6, 1846; m. 1st, CLARA E. WOODBURY; m. 2d,
        ADA HILL.
    XI. MARY CAROLINE,[7] b. Jan. 6, 1849; m. 1st. Amos CHURCHILL (No.
        591); m. 2d, CHARLES JENKINS. Children by 2d husband,
        William, Leslie, Floyd, and Ray H., Jenkins.
   XII. MELVIN,[7] b. Dec. 20, 1851; unmarried.
  XIII. HANNAH E.,[7] b. April 26, 1854; m. 1st, HOMER W. CARPENTER,
        Dec. 25, 1873; m. 2d, WILLIAM H. POTTS, June 3, 1899, of
        Plainfield, Wis.

Children by First Husband.

1. Avril C. Carpenter, b. in Union, Wis., Oct. 6, 1874; m. Charles
Lawson, April 30, 1899.
2. Lewis Lester Carpenter, b. in Lanark, Wis., Feb. 21, 1876.

270.

ASA[6] CHURCHILL (DANIEL,[5] JOSEPH,[4] JOHN,[3] ELIEZER,[2]
JOHN[1]). Born in Litchfield, probably, 1802. Lived at Moose
River, Me., where he died Aug. 7, 1847. Married MARY HOLDEN,
of Moose River, Me. After Mr. Churchill's death the widow mar-
ried John Doyle, of Moose River. She died at Manton, Mich.,
March 4, 1878.

Children born at Moose River.

I. JOSEPHINE,[7] b. March 8, 1832; m. SPENCER COLBY, April 7, 1855.
Mr. Colby was born at Embden, Somerset County, Me., April 12;
1835; son of Ambrose. This family removed to Kent City, Mich.,
in 1867. Mrs. Josephine Colby was living in Marquetta, Neb., in
1901.

The First Six Children born at Moose River, Me.

1. Sumner E. Colby, b. Feb. 26, 1856. Killed by a falling tree,
Feb. 8, 1875.
2. Laura Colby, b. Jan. 16, 1858.
3. Ansel S. Colby, b. May 31, 1859.
4. Webster W. Colby, b. April 28, 1861.
5. Mary J. Colby, b. Sept. 17, 1862.
6. Asa W. Colby, b. Sept. 15, 1864.
7. Alice J. Colby, b. Jan. 13, 1867, at Pleasant Ridge, Me.
8. Myra T. Colby, b. Sept. 9, 1868, at Kent City, Mich.
9. Hartwell C. Colby, b. Jan. 15, 1871, at Kent City, Mich.; d.
in infancy.
10. Willard D. Colby, b. Aug. 21, 1872.

II. CLARISSA,[7] b. March 28, 1834; m. JONAS HOLDEN COLBY, of Embden, Me., Dec. 4, 1854. Mr. Jonas H. Colby was born May
5, 1833. Mrs. Clarissa Colby was living at Moose River, 1901.

Children.

1. Emily Adelia Colby, b. June 19, 1856.
2. Elmer Enrique Colby, b. June 13, 1859.
3. Viola May Colby, b. Sept. 20, 1861.
4. George Boomer Colby, b. March 25, 1864.
5. Calvin Herbert Colby, b. July 26, 1868.

586   III. JOHN,[7] b. June 6, 1836; m. HARRIET L. PARKER, Sept. 27, 1870.
587   IV. HARRISON,[7] b. May 2, 1841; m. DORA OLIVER, March 12, 1886.
588   V. HORATIO,[7] b. April 1, 1843; m. 1st, MELINDA H. KELIHER, Dec. 10,
         1874; m. 2d, MARY H. HODGETTS, Sept. 12, 1881.
589   VI. HARTWELL,[7] b. Feb. 2, 1845; m. LYDIA E. PRATT, Jan. 13, 1870.

271.

AMOS [6] CHURCHILL (DANIEL,[5] JOSEPH,[4] JOHN,[3] ELIEZER [2] JOHN [1]). Born in Bingham, Me., March 27, 1805. They lived on a farm in Madison, Me. Married ELLEN CHASE.

590   I. LUTHER,[7] m. ELIZABETH PALMER.
         One daughter Francelia.
     II. EUNICE,[7] m. DAVID HUNNEWELL.
    III. ELLEN,[7] m. CHARLES BEAN.
         They had five children, names not obtained.
    IV. FLORA,[7] m. MR. SCRIBNER.
     V. MARY.[7] No record.
591   VI. AMOS,[7] b. Sept. 5, 1845; m. MARY CAROLINE CHURCHILL.
592   VII. JOEL.[7] No record.
   VIII. ALMEDA,[7] m. MR. DAVENPORT.
    IX. SARAH,[7] m. WALTER PEARSON.
         They had one daughter, name not obtained.
     X. EMMA,[7] no record.
    XI. LILIE,[7] m. MR. SITER.

272.

ELI [6] CHURCHILL (DANIEL,[5] JOSEPH,[4] JOHN,[3] ELIEZER,[2] JOHN [1]). Born in Bingham, Me. Married RACHEL STEWARD.

Children.

   I. DANIEL.[7]
  II. EBER.[7]

273.

WARREN [6] CHURCHILL (DANIEL,[5] JOSEPH [4] JOHN,[3] ELIEZER,[2] JOHN [1]). Born in Bingham, Me. Removed to the "York Settlement," N.Y., and settled among his kindred. He was killed by an explosion in a sawmill about 1860. Married, at Huron, N.Y., July 7, 1842, LOVILLA YORK (his cousin), who was born Jan. 25, 1814, and died December, 1846.

Child.

597   I. CYRUS,[7] b. Nov. 8, 1846; m. 1st, EMMA A. WOOLEY, Feb. 7, 1867; m.
         2d, Sarah Allen, July, 1880. He was taken by his grandmother
         York after his mother's death, and brought up. Removed in early
         manhood to Wisconsin, near his uncle Daniel Churchill's, and
         settled on a farm in Helvetia, Wis. He d. May 5, 1889, at his
         home, Ogdensburg, Waupaca County, Wis.

Children born in Helvetia, Wis., of First Wife.

1. Louis L. Churchill, b. Jan. 26, 1869; m. Arvilla B. Mowry,
May 31, 1896, and has one son Lawrence E. Churchill, b.
March 5, 1901.

Child of Second Wife.

2. Clyde Churchill, b. February, 1885.

274.

WILLIAM FLETCHER[6] CHURCHILL (DANIEL,[5] JOSEPH,[4]
JOHN,[3] ELIEZER,[2] JOHN[1]). Born in Bingham, Me., Feb. 1, 1814.
He died Feb. 9, 1869. Married 1st, at Bingham, Me., SARAH
CHASE, of Bingham, who died Jan. 3, 1849; married 2d, EUNICE
YORK, of Brighton, Me.; married 3d, EMMA BOISE, of Skowhegan,
Me.

Children of First Wife.

I. CHARLES,[7] d. in infancy.
II. CLIMENA,[7] m. 1st, AUGUSTUS HUNNEWELL, d. in 1889; m. 2d,
    OLIVER MOULTON.
III. MARDEN,[7] d. in infancy.
IV. CORDELIA,[7] b. Jan. 31, 1844; m. JOHN B. TAYLOR, April 7, 1892.

Children of Second Wife.

V. SARAH,[7] m. DANIEL DENMON.
VI. WILLIAM,[7] d. young.

Child of Third Wife.

VII. LILLIAN,[7] m. FREMONT DRESSER.

275.

TOBIAS[6] CHURCHILL (TOBIAS,[5] JOSEPH,[4] JOHN,[3] ELIEZER[2]
JOHN[1]). Born at New Portland, Me., Jan. 23, 1807. Married
IRENE WALTON, who was born Dec. 16, 1809.

Children.

598   I. BYRON,[7] b. March 11, 1828.
       II. ROSEA,[7] b. July 14, 1829.
       III. TOBIAS,[7] b. November, 1830; d. at 2 years.
       IV. IRENE,[7] b. Jan. 23, 1838.
599   V. TOBIAS BERTRAM,[7] b. March 14, 1840.
       VI. PARTHENIA,[7] b. Nov. 9, 1842.

277.

JESSE[6] CHURCHILL (BENJAMIN,[5] JOSEPH,[4] JOHN,[3] ELIEZER,[2]
JOHN[1]). Born in New Portland, Me. (probably), in 1809. No
further records relating to this family have been obtained. Married
CLYMENA WALTON, of New Portland, Me.

CALEB CHURCHILL.

(No. 280, page 151.)

Children.

600 I. MARCELLUS,[7] b. 1834; m. ZELINDA DITSON.
601 II. JOEL,[7] b. Sept. 20, 1836; m. LORINDA CHASE.
III. RUTH,[7] b. 1839; m. JOSIAH CHASE.
602 IV. MYRON,[7] b. 1841; m. ELIZABETH TAYLOR.
603 V. CHARLES,[7] b. 1844; m. VILLA A. BOYNTON.
604 VI. BENJAMIN,[7] b. 1851; m. EDITH W. HUTCHINS.
605 VII. FOREST F.,[7] b. 1858; m. MARY STALKER.

280.

CALEB [6] CHURCHILL (JOHN,[5] EBENEZER,[4] WILLIAM,[3] WILLIAM,[2] JOHN [1]). Born in Plympton, April 4, 1757, and lived there until the age of twenty-five years, when, with his father, he removed to Chittenden, Vt. He served in the war of the Revolution, Capt. Thomas Sampson's Company, from Plympton; Col. Theophilus Cotton's Regiment; General Palmer's Brigade, September and October, 1777; thirty-two days on a secret expedition to Newport, R.I. Also in Captain Curtis's Company Oct. 13 to Dec. 1, 1779, at Rhode Island. Enlisted March 14, 1781, and served in Rhode Island, three days; discharged March 17, 1781; roll dated at Plympton. His father's family was the third settling in the town, which was then called Philadelphia, Vt. He purchased or "took up" a farm and lived upon it until his death. He was a respected citizen, with large influence for good in the town and community; a member of the Congregational Church in Pittsford, Vt., from 1817 to the close of his life. His mind remained clear and his memory good to the last. He died Sept. 15, 1856, aged 99 years 5 months and 11 days. He married at Chittenden (then Philadelphia, Vt.), Nov. 14, 1788, SARAH HAWLEY, of Pittsford, Vt., whose father, Nathan Hawley, was one of the first settlers of Pittsford about 1780. She was born in New Milford, Conn., Nov. 3, 1768, and died in Chittenden, Nov. 12, 1842.

Children born in Chittenden.

I. BETSEY,[7] b. April, 24, 1789; m. ANSON MANLEY, Nov. 8, 1807. He was of Brandon and they lived there and had

Children.

1. Abigail Manley, b. July 10, 1809; m. Samuel Lackman, Feb. 6, 1834.
2. Dan P. Manley, b. May 10, 1811; m. Mrs. Martha Parmenter, April 13, 1834.
3. Laura Manley, b. Feb. 25, 1813; m. Harry Sessions, Dec. 23, 1830.
4. Betsey M. Manley, b. March 29, 1822; m. Joseph Bushey.

606 II. JOHN,[7] b. Dec. 12, 1790; m. LOIS LATHAM, Nov. 26, 1818. Lived in Brandon.
III. LEAH,[7] b. Dec. 9, 1792; m. THOMAS ROGERS, of Brandon, Vt., March 6, 1821. She died at Leicester Vt., Feb. 1, 1864, and he died there April 1, 1859. They lived in Brandon, and had there seven children, viz.:

Children.

1. Sarah M. Rogers, b. March 13, 1822; m. William Wood.
2. Thomas S. Rogers, b. Sept. 14, 1823; d Sept. 24, 1833.
3. Hannah M. Rogers, b. July 24, 1825; m. 1st, Reuben Martin, April 22, 1846; m. 2d, Joel Baird, Nov. 29, 1849.
4. Caleb A. Rogers, b. July 3, 1827; m. Martha C. Simons, Jan. 1, 1857.
5. George T. Rogers, b. Jan. 12, 1830; m. Mary A. Handy, Feb. 1, 1853, at Fairhaven, Mass.
6. Mary E. Rogers, b. May 24, 1832; m. Thomas Hendry, Aug. 1, 1850.
7. Alonzo M. Rogers, b. Oct. 31, 1834; m. Delia Bump, Oct. 7, 1860. Lived in Chittenden.

607 IV. CALEB,[7] b. Dec. 15, 1794; m. MIRIAM PARMELEE, Dec. 19, 1832.
  V. SARAH,[7] b. March 10, 1797; m. EBENEZER NUTTING, Nov. 23, 1817, of Brandon, Vt. She died in Pittsford, Vt., July 12, 1876; and he died April 14, 1876. They lived at first in Chittenden and later in Brandon. Late in life they went West and settled for a few years at Fond du Lac, Wis., but returned to Pittsford, Vt., and lived with their son William.

Children born in Chittenden or Brandon, Vt.

1. William J. Nutting, b. Sept. 7, 1818; m. Esther L. Manley, Aug. 7, 1856.
2. Willard Nutting, b. Sept. 2, 1822; d. April 28, 1823.
3. Albert Nutting, b. July 2, 1824; m. Helen C. Stewart.
4. Edmond D. Nutting, b. June 19, 1826; m. Caroline H. Parmelee, Feb. 22, 1842.
5. John A. Nutting, b. July 22, 1829; d. June 1, 1845.

608 VI. ZACCHEUS H.,[7] b. March 29, 1799; m. HANNAH M. BACON, Dec 4, 1827. He settled near Erie, Penn. No further record obtained.
609 VII. NATHAN H.,[7] b. June 11, 1803; m. 1st, DOROTHY SHELDON, Oct. 4, 1825. She d. March 10, 1838; m. 2d, NANCY LYON, March 10, 1839. Lived in Chittenden.
610 VIII. AZEM,[7] b. Nov. 13, 1805; m. MERCY M. MANLEY, of Chittenden, Aug. 29, 1831.
  IX. JOANNA,[7] b. March 26, 1808; d. March 31, 1814.
  X. MARIAH,[7] b. May 29, 1810; m. 1st STEPHEN H. SPARKS, Jan. 27, 1831; m. 2d, (———) (———); m. 3d, GRAHAM ROGERS, April 25, 1833. Lived near Buffalo, N.Y., and later in Pennsylvania. No record of children.
  XI. SYLVIA,[7] b. Aug. 1, 1814; m. GEORGE SMITH, son of Zenas and Leah (Churchill) Smith, April 25, 1833, at Chittenden. She died at Brandon, Vt., June 8, 1895. He died at Brandon, Dec. 31, 1876. He was a farmer, lived in Pittsford and Chittenden, and last in Brandon.

Children born, three in Chittenden, two in Pittsford.

1. Jane D. Smith, b. November, 1834; d. April 8, 1835.
2. George W. Smith, d. June 26, 1862, at New Orleans, La., in the army, Company D, Seventh Regiment, Vermont Volunteers; date of his birth not received.
3. Otis E. Smith, b. April 7, 1837; d. unmarried at Brandon, Jan. 19, 1897.
4. Julia N. Smith, b. Dec. 25, 1839; m. Willard S. Johnson, Dec. 1, 1858.
5. William H. Smith, b. Jan. 17, 1842; m. 1st, Mrs. Martha A. Sprague, Feb. 13, 1867; m. 2d, Mrs. Cynthia A. Clark, Jan. 1, 1896.

DEACON WINSLOW CHURCHILL.

(No. 282, page 153.)

281.

MICHAEL [6] CHURCHILL (ISAAC,[5] EBENEZER,[4] WILLIAM [3] WILLIAM,[2] JOHN [1]). Born in Chittenden, Vt., 1767. Settled in St. Lawrence County, N.Y. After much research I have just found a probable descendant of the eldest son of this family at Brasher Falls, N.Y. (May 29, 1903). Married LUCY DODGE, of Brandon, Vt.

Children, probably not in proper order of birth.

611   I. ISAAC.[7]
      II. LUCY.[7]
     III. SARAH.[7]
     IV. MOLLY.[7]
      V. ANNA.[7]
     VI. DIANA.[7]
   VII. RACHEL.[7]
  VIII. MERCY.[7]
612   IX. WILLIAM.[7]

282.

DEACON WINSLOW [6] CHURCHILL (ISAAC,[5] EBENEZER [4] WILLIAM,[3] WILLIAM,[2] JOHN [1]). Born in Plympton, Mass., Dec. 30, 1770, and removed with his father to Chittenden, Vt., in 1785. He became a farmer and also exercised the mason's vocation. In 1804 he removed with his young family to Camillus, Onondaga County, N.Y., where he purchased a farm, which he cultivated for thirty years. The Erie canal was afterwards cut through his farm, and he built and "ran" a boat called "The Growler" on the canal. As a member of the New York militia he was called into service for a time in the War of 1812. May 6, 1834, he removed West with his family, going by the canal as far as Buffalo, thence by sail-boat on the lake to Chicago, where he arrived June 4, 1834, and bought an ox-team, and started out to locate a new home. With him on his journey were his children, viz., Lurana, Seth, Betsey, Winslow, Jr., Amanda, Isaac, Bradford, and Hiram. William and Christiana joined him some four years later. After a somewhat prolonged search for a location, he finally chose a claim in the north-east corner of Milton township (as it was then called), Du Page County, Ill. The log-house which he built at the time of his settlement is (1900) still standing. He cultivated and improved this farm during the remainder of his active life. He became a member of the Presbyterian church in early life, and in that communion was deacon and chorister for many years. Upon his settlement in the West he joined the Congregational church, and when the Methodists came and established religious services in a school-house in the town Deacon Churchill often

officiated, in the absence of the regular minister, his son, Isaac B
reading a sermon selected from some authorized book. In politics
Mr. Churchill was an ardent Whig, though never seeking office.
He was public-spirited and patriotic, diligent and earnest in what-
ever he undertook. He won the respect and confidence of all, and
holds an honored place among the pioneers of Du Page County.
He died Sept. 18, 1847. "Milton Township" became Babcock
Grove, and, the name was later changed to Danby, then Prospect
Park, and later, still to Glen Ellyn, the present name. Married,
Thanksgiving Day, November, 1796, MERCY DODGE, who was the
daughter of William and Mercy, of Rutland, Vt., and was born
June 15, 1774, and died Feb. 21, 1863.

Children, the first four born in Chittenden, the rest in Camillus, N. Y.

612   I. WILLIAM,[7] b. Aug. 16, 1797; m. MRS. POLLY HAND, widow, at
            Camillus.
       II. MELINDA,[7] b. July 24, 1799; m. SYLVESTER KETCHUM, d. Nov. 8,
            1877; no issue.
      III. *LURANA,[7] b. Feb. 15, 1802; m. JOHN D. AKERMAN, at Camillus,
            N.Y.

Children born, four at Camillus, the last at Glen Ellyn.

       1. Winslow Akerman, m. Pamelia Holmes.
       2. Elbyron Akerman, m. (———) Russell.
       3. Miles Akerman, m. Mary J. Cox.
       4. Erastus Akerman.
       5. Alonzo Akerman.

      IV. *CHRISTIANA,[7] b. Feb. 15, 1802; m. 1st, ERASTUS KETCHUM; m. 2d,
            DAVID CHRISTIAN. Settled at first at Camillus, later at Glen
            Ellyn.

Child of First Husband.

       1. Erastus Ketchum, b. Feb. 15, 1826, m. Mary J. Churchill,
            dau. of No. 613.

---

* These names deserve more than the above brief record. They were still
living in the town of Glen Ellyn, Feb. 15, 1893, at the age of 91 years, and
said to be then "the oldest twins in the world." Born in Chittenden, Vt.,
as above noted, they spent their girlhood and young womanhood in Camillus,
N.Y. A Chicago paper of February, 1893, commenting upon the celebration
of their ninety-first birthday at Glen Ellyn, on the 15th of the month, mentions
several interesting points. There has never been more than a mere family resemblance between them, their tastes have never been similar, they have never
dressed alike. They were born in a log-house, common to pioneers of the then
wild country, and have preserved some rare bits of household ware and kitchen
furnishings of those early days. The correspondent of 1893 says: "They are
now two quaint little old women, slight and frail, with placid, kindly faces and
snow-white hair drawn smoothly down under black lace caps." Mrs. Ackerman
dresses in black, Mrs. Christian in gray, but the soft old-fashioned silk kerchief,
folded around the neck and crossing upon the breast, is worn by both. They
delight to tell over the reminiscences of their early days and the labors and en-
joyments of those primitive times. Their younger brother, Isaac Bradford
Churchill, lives near them at Glen Ellyn, and in September, 1891, celebrated,
with his wife, his own golden wedding.

MRS. CHRIST ANA (CHURCHILL) CHRISTIAN.
MRS. LURANA (CHURCHILL) AKERMAN.
(See Note under No. 282, page 154.)

Children of Second Husband.
2. Wesley Christian, b. 1835.
3. William Christian.

613   V. SETH,[7] b. May 25, 1805; m. ROXANA WARD.
614   VI. MAJOR,[7] b. July 8, 1807; m. MARY A. DELANO, Dec. 31, 1835.
       VII. BETSEY,[7] b. Aug. 4, 1809; m. SAMUEL MAHAFFY, at Babcock's Grove. They live at Palos, Cork County, Ill. He is a farmer.

Children born at Palos.
1. Samuel Mahaffy, d. in infancy.
2. William Mahaffy, d. in the army in the Civil War.
3. Winslow Mahaffy.

615   VIII. WINSLOW, JR.,[7] b. June 13, 1812; m. 1st, JULIETTE MORTON, of Babcock's Grove; m. 2d, SARAH A. NICHOLS; m. 3d, MARGARET WILLARD; m. 4th, ELIZABETH EVANS.
       IX. AMANDA,[7] b. May 6, 1814; d. unmarried, June 12, 1835, in Illinois.
616   X. ISAAC BRADFORD,[7] b. April 22, 1818; m. ANGELINE BARKER, Sept. 15, 1844.
617   XI. HIRAM,[7] b. April 7, 1820; m. DRUSILLA MILLER.
       He was killed near Fort Carney on his way to California in 1849.

283.

SETH[6] CHURCHILL (ISAAC,[5] EBENEZER,[4] WILLIAM,[3] WILL-
IAM,[2] JOHN[1]). Born in Plympton, June 28, 1773; reared in Chitten-
don, Vt. Settled with his brother Winslow in Milton Township,
now Glen Ellyn, Ill. Married, Feb. 14, 1793, EUNICE DURKEE, who
was born April 28, 1772.

Children born at Chittenden, Vt.
       I. STEPHEN,[7] b. Sept. 27, 1793; d. young.
       II. JERUSHA,[7] b. March 16, 1796; m. SETH WARREN, about 1818, in N.Y. State.
618   III. BRADFORD,[7] b. Aug. 23, 1800; m. MARY ADAMS.
       IV. ALZINA,[7] b. Jan. 10, 1805; m. IRA BALCH, and d. in Wisconsin, June, 1881.
619   V. ENOS,[7] b. March 13, 1807; m. NANCY SEARLES.

284.

ELISHA[6] CHURCHILL (ISAAC,[5] EBENEZER,[4] WILLIAM,[3] WILL-
IAM,[2] JOHN[1]). Born in Plympton, Mass., Aug. 4, 1781. He was
reared in Chittenden, Vt.; settled in East Swanton, Vt. He was a
farmer and carpenter, and lived an industrious, upright, and honorable life. In stature he was six feet four inches. He was strictly
temperate in habits and language, and was highly respected in his
community. He died Sept. 1, 1831. Married, 1806, LYDIA
LACKEY, b. 1784; d. April 9, 1827.

Children born in Swanton, Vt.
620   I. ELISHA BRADFORD,[7] b. June 14, 1807; m. MIRANDA BARBER, 1833.
       II. AUGUSTUS,[7] b. Aug. 10, 1808; m. WIDOW BETSEY (CHAPMAN) CASWELL, Aug. 28, 1831. No issue.
       III. AVALINA,[7] b. Oct. 3, 1809; d. unmarried, Sept. 22, 1846.
       IV. SARAH,[7] b. July 23, 1811; d. unmarried, Aug. 17, 1839.

621   V. LUTHER,[7] b. Aug. 6, 1812; m. CHLOE BARBER, 1833. She died
           July 1, 1842. They lived first at St. Albans, Vt., but moved to
           Milwaukee, Wis., in 1837. He was a merchant. They had a
           family, but all died young; no record found.
622   VI. HORACE,[7] b. Dec. 14, 1814; m. ALSISTA ITALY BOWEN.
      VII. LUCRETIA,[7] b. Aug. 25, 1817; m. H. O. GREEN, at St. Albans, Vt.,
           1834. They lived first at Highgate, Vt., but moved to Milwau
           kee, Wis. She died Dec. 21, 1878.

                    Children born in Highgate, Vt.

      1. Willard Owen Green, b. June *i*, 1837; m. Imogene Bates, Ken-
         ellville, Ind., May, 1862.
      2. Charles Fay Green, b. July 27, 1839; m. Ursula Adams, of Mil
         waukee, Wis., 1875.
      3. Sarah L. Green, b. Jan. 28, 1841; m. Edgar Martin, of Milwau
         kee, Wis., 1861.

623 VIII. SETH WARREN,[7] b. May 17, 1821; m. SOPHIA MAY, Dec. 31, 1854.
624   IX. HENRY,[7] b. Sept. 23, 1823; m. MIRANDA GATES, Sept. 28, 1847.
      X. PHILANDER,[7] b. June 29, 1825. We have no record of marriage;
         d. at North Hammond, N.Y., May 14, 1899.

285.

JOSHUA [6] CHURCHILL (JOSHUA,[5] EBENEZER,[4] WILLIAM,[3]
WILLIAM,[2] JOHN [1]). Born in Plympton, Feb. 1, 1769. Moved with
his father to Hartford, Me., in 1800. Lived in Salem Mass. He
died in Sumner, Me., in 1870, aged 101 years. Married SYLVIA
CHURCHILL, daughter of David, Jr. She was born Feb. 21, 1767.

              Children born in Salem, except the first.
      I. INFANT, b. Jan. 31, 1795; d. in Buckfield, Me., Feb. 8, 1795.
      II. ELLIS,[7] b. Sept. 10, 1796. Never married.
      III. HARVEY,[7] b. Feb. 23, 1801; died young.
      IV. MARIA,[7] b. March 31, 1803; d. Jan. 31, 1836.
      V. LEBBEUS,[7] b. Aug. 23, 1805; m. MRS. (———) STURTEVANT. No
         record.
      VI. ACHSAH,[7] b. Sept. 2, 1808; m. SAMUEL CHURCHILL, April, 1834.
         Son of Ezra (287).

286.

ANDREW [6] CHURCHILL (JOSHUA,[5] EBENEZER,[4] WILLIAM,[3]
WILLIAM,[2] JOHN [1]). Born in Plympton, Nov. 18, 1772. Removed
with his father's family to Hartford, Me., and was there brought up,
and lived there and at Sumner, Me., where he died, Oct. 22, 1821.
Married, April 15, 1831, in Sumner, POLLY OLDHAM, who died May
7, 1863.

                          One child.
625   I. ANDREW JACKSON,[7] b. June 12, 1821; m. NANCY WYMAN.

287.

EZRA [6] CHURCHILL (JOSHUA,[5] EBENEZER,[4] WILLIAM,[3] WILL-
IAM,[2] JOHN [1]). Born in Plympton, Sept. 25, 1780. Moved with
his father to Hartford, Me., in 1803, and settled, after marriage,

in Sumner, Me. Moved afterward to Montville Centre, Me. Married BETHIA MEHURIN, born in Jay, Me., May 25, 1783.

Children born in Sumner, Me.

I. DEBORAH,[7] b. April 28, 1800; m. JOSEPH PALMER, Nov. 6, 1825.

Children.

1. Adeline Palmer, b. Nov. 4, 1826.
2. Ira Palmer, b. Oct. 17, 1829.
3. Deborah Palmer, b. Sept. 15, 1831.
4. Joseph Palmer, Jr., b. Jan. 31, 1835.
5. Emily Palmer, } twins.
6. Daniel Palmer, }
7. Ezra Palmer, b. Nov. 23, 1843.

626   II. ALEXANDER,[7] b. April 11, 1802; m. MARGARET DAVIS. No further record.
III. BETHANY,[7] b. Oct. 17, 1804; m. SEWALL CURTIS. No children.
IV. OLIVE,[7] b. Dec. 6, 1807; m. DANIEL PHILLIPS. One son, Augustus Phillips.
627   V. SAMUEL,[7] b. Aug. 15, 1810; m. 1st, ACHSAH CHURCHILL; m. 2d, NANCY PENNEY, March 15, 1868.
628   VI. JAMES A.,[7] b. Sept. 13, 1812; m. POLLY THOMPSON.
629   VII. EZRA, JR.,[7] b. Sept. 18, 1814; m. KEZIAH MITCHELL. No further record.
VIII. PHEBE C.,[7] b. Aug. 17, 1817; m. 1st, DANIEL DAVIS; m. 2d. ASA THOMPSON. No children by second husband.

Children by First Husband.

1. Elbridge Davis. | 2. Otis Davis

IX. BETHIA,[7] b. Nov. 1, 1819; m. ASA MEHURIN, March 28, 1837. He died April 1, 1871.

Children.

1. Achsa J. Mehurin, b. May 7, 1843.
2. Alvarado F. Mehurin, b. Nov. 30, 1847.
3. Ellen E. Mehurin, b. Jan. 16, 1853.
4. Winfield S. Mehurin, b. Feb. 22, 1861.

630   X. BARNARD,[7] b. April 17, 1822; m. CHARLOTTE THOMAS.
63   XI. OTIS M.,[7] b. Nov. 3, 1824; m. ELIZA J. PHILLIPS.
XII. NARCISSA,[7] b. Feb. 3, 1828; m. WILLIAM BRACKET.

Children of William and Narcissa Churchill Bracket.

1. Phebe C. Bracket, b. March 15, 1852.
2. Narcissa S. Bracket, b. Nov. 30, 1853.
3. Joseph W. Bracket, b. Feb. 2, 1856.
4. Emma F. Bracket, b. March 19, 1858.
5. Orrington A. Bracket, b. Jan. 26, 1860.
6. Ida B. Bracket, b. Aug. 13, 1863.
7. Loring E. Bracket, b. May 4, 1865; d. April 12, 1872.
8. Lottie J. Bracket, b. April 2, 1867.
9. Oscar M. Bracket, b. Dec. 25, 1870; d. April 25, 1872.
10. Oscar L. Bracket, b. Aug. 29, 1874; d. Jan. 21, 1876.

288.

CAPTAIN ELIAS[6] CHURCHILL (DAVID,[5] DAVID,[4] WILLIAM,[3] WILLIAM,[2] JOHN[1]). Born in Plympton, Jan. 26, 1759, and lived there until about 1800, when he removed to Duxbury and there died May 3, 1829. Married HANNAH CUSHMAN, daughter of Elkanah, b. July 2, 1759, and died at Duxbury, Feb. 12, 1828.

Children born at Plympton.

I. LEVI,[7] b. Aug. 14, 1779; d. Aug. 28, 1779.
II. PATTY,[7] b. May 10, 1782; m. LUTHER STURTEVANT.
III. ELIAS, JR.,[7] b. Nov. 4, 1785; d. May 28, 1786.
IV. JANE,[7] b. Aug. 19, 1787; m. JOHN STANDISH.
They lived in Plympton, Halifax, and later (in 1857) in Stoughton, Mass.

Children.

1. Elias Ellis Standish, b. June 29, 1806; m. Rachel Rickard.
2. John Ellis Standish, b. 1808; d. young.
3. Alexander Standish, b. Oct. 29, 1809; m. 1st, Sarah W. Dean; m. 2d, Elizabeth S. Wright.
4. Erastus Warren Standish, b. 1812; died young.
5. Jane Ellis Standish, b. in Plympton, Jan. 25, 1816; m. Ellis Delano.
6. William Henry Standish, b. 1818; d. young.
7. Joseph Warren Standish, b. 1820; d. young.
8. Benjamin William Standish, d. young.
9. Lewis Weston Standish, b. 1822; d. young.
10. Laura A. Standish, b. in Middleboro', May 5, 1823; m. Isaac Thayer. Sept. 20, 1847.
11. George Washington Standish, b. in Middleboro', April 27, 1826; m. Mary J. Thompson, 1847.

V. HANNAH,[7] b. Feb. 20, 1790; m. LEWIS WESTON.
VI. ESTHER,[7] b. Oct. 2, 1792; m. 1st, NATHAN MORTON; m. 2d, SAMUEL WESTON.
VII. CLARISSA,[7] b. July 30, 1796; m. OTIS WESTON, of Marshfield. Lived in Charlestown in 1857.
632 VIII. IVORY,[7] b March 18, 1799; m. MARY ELEANOR CLARK, of Boston, 1823.
IX. EARL,[7] b. May 14, 1801; d. July 15, 1801.
X. ELIZA ELLIS,[7] b. March 17, 1803; m. RUFUS WESTON; d. in Duxbury.

289.

DAVID[6] CHURCHILL (DAVID,[5] DAVID,[4] WILLIAM,[3] WILLIAM,[2] JOHN[1]). Born in Plympton, June 11, 1778. Lived in Boston after marriage. He was a brickmaker by trade. He died in Plympton, September, 1806. Married MARY HERSEY, of Boston.

Children born in Boston.

633 I. SOLOMON,[7] b. 1799; m. ESTHER SHEPARD. No further record.
634 II. DAVID, JR.,[7] b. 1801; m. ARABELLA COOPER. Had a family, it is said, but we have no record of them. He died aged 80.
III. MARY SALOME,[7] b. 1803; d. young.
635 IV. OTIS,[7] b. in Plympton, Jan. 12, 1805; m. 1st, MARY RUSSELL, May 30, 1831; m. 2d, BELINDA RUSSELL. Dec. 14, 1842; m. 3d, MARY L. (CALKINS) POMEROY, widow of Charles B. Pomeroy, Dec. 17, 1862; d. at Watertown, Wis.

290.

LEVI [6] CHURCHILL (DAVID,[5] DAVID,[4] WILLIAM,[3] WILLIAM,[2] JOHN [1]). Born in Plympton, Feb. 20, 1780. Lived in Hingham. He died 1843. Married 1st, Sept. 19, 1799, CYNTHIA PACKARD, of East Bridgewater. She died 1832. Married 2d, Oct. 20, 1833, ADALINE C. WRIGHT, of Plympton.

Children of First Wife.

I. ASABA,[7] b. Aug. 9, 1801; m. LEWIS KEITH. 1819. He was born April 12, 1799.

Children.

1. Harriet L. Keith, b. Feb. 24, 1820.
2. Eliza A. Keith, b. July 2, 1822; d. Jan. 12, 1823.
3. Eliza A. Keith, b. July 18, 1823; d. Feb. 17, 1851.
4. Lurana Keith, b. March 11, 1825; d. April 4, 1844.
5. Marcus M. Keith, b. March 20, 1827; m. Mary A. Bailey, June 18, 1857.
6. Adaline C. Keith, b. March 22, 1829; d. July 31, 1845.
7. Lewis Keith, b. July 4, 1831; d. April 3, 1859.
8. Nahum Keith, b. May 29, 1833.
9. Maria B. Keith, b. June 26, 1835; d. April 12, 1846.
10. Joshua S. Keith, b. April 25, 1837; d. Dec. 29, 1879.
11. Elizabeth C. Keith, b. Feb. 8, 1839; d. Sept. 20, 1839.
12. William H. H. Keith, b. April 1, 1840; d. May 5, 1870.

636   II. LEVI,[7] b. March 5, 1803; m. LUCRETIA KEEN, of E. Bridgewater, Sept. 10, 1828.

III. LURANA,[7] b. April 17, 1804; unmarried.

637   IV. LUTHER,[7] b. April, 1805; m. EVELINE BLANCHARD.

638   V. ABISHA S.,[7] b. Oct. 13, 1807; m. MERCY L. WHITMAN.

VI. CYNTHIA,[7] b. Jan. 27, 1809; m. JOSHUA BENNETT, 1825.

Children.

1. Maria Miles Bennett, b. 1826; d. at age of 5 years.
2. Edwin Scott Bennett, b. Sept. 15, 1828.
3. Andrew J. Bennett, b. Dec. 15, 1832.
4. James H. Bennett, b. January, 1834.
5. George W. Bennett, b. January, 1837; d. aged 8 years.

VII. SARAH C.,[7] b. in Boston, March 9, 1811; m. ELIJAH SCOTT, of Ludlow, Vt.

Children.

1. Elizabeth A. Scott, b. Sept. 29, 1839; m. Charles H. Merrill.
2. Henry L. Scott, b. Jan. 16, 1841; unmarried.
3. Annie C. Scott, b. Oct. 17, 1843; m. Frank Libby.
4. Josephine F. Scott, b. Jan. 8, 1845; m. Montville Graves, June 20, 1877.
. Clémentine Scott, b. Dec. 12, 1847; d. Nov. 20, 1855.
5. Walter W. Scott, b. Jan. 23, 1854; m. Hattie Perham.

VIII. DAVID,[7] b. June, 1812; d. unmarried, aged 36 years.

639   IX. WILLIAM MORTON,[7] b. Aug. 24, 1814; m. MARY R. TRIBEAU. No further record.

X. BETHIA,[7] b. May 11, 1816; m. NICHOLAS VELLA, who was b. May 25, 1812.

Children.

1. Joseph F. Vella, b. July 30, 1835.
2. William Wallace Vella, b. March 19, 1837.
3. Valanca Vella, b. Nov. 8, 1840.
4. Henry Washington Vella, b. May 10, 1842.
5. Levi Churchill Vella, b. July 10, 1845.
6. Samuel Vella, b. Nov. 17, 1847.

XI.   ELIZABETH,[7] b. Jan. 6, 1818.
XII. BENJAMIN PIERSON,[7] b. February, 1820; m. AMANDA N. BANCROFT, 1845. No children.
XIII. GEORGE,[7] b. May 5, 1821; m. JULIA SOULE, of Lynn, Mass., February, 1846. No children.

By Second Wife.

640 XIV. ETHAN S.,[7] b. Jan. 11, 1835; m. ADALINE WRIGHT. No further record.

291.

JESSE[6] CHURCHILL (DAVID,[5] DAVID,[4] WILLIAM,[3] WILLIAM,[2] JOHN[1]). Born in Plympton, Aug. 28, 1784. Lived at West Hingham. He was a soldier in the War of 1812. He was a stonemason by occupation. He died Sept. 20, 1853. Married, 1805 ANNA BARREL, of Scituate. She died July, 1861, aged 76 years.

Children born in Hingham.

641 I.   JESSE,[7] b. Jan. 30, 1806; m. CHRISTIANA CUSHING, Oct. 20, 1833.
642 II.   JAMES,[7] } b. Feb. 5, 1808; m. CYNTHIA HUMPHREY, of Hingham, November, 1834. He died in Hingham in 1870.
643 III. THOMAS,[7] } b. Feb. 5, 1808; m. SALLY SPRAGUE.
644 IV.   CHARLES,[7] b. July 10, 1810; m. 1st, MORGIANA GILL, 1833; m. 2d, SARAH NICHOLS, of Boston.
        V.   MARTHA ANN,[7] b. Dec. 12, 1812; m. LORING HERSEY, April 10, 1831.

        Children.

        1. George Loring Hersey, b. July 18, 1832; m. Mary A. Bates, Dec. 21, 1851.
        2. Charles Churchill Hersey, b. May 3, 1836; m. Lucy J. Haskell, of Hallowell, Me., May 10, 1857.
        3. Francis Henry Hersey, b. Feb. 16, 1840; d. Nov. 3, 1842.

645 VI.   RUFUS,[7] b. April 23, 1815; m. LUCY BURR.
        VII. POLLY BARNES,[7] b. Jan. 1, 1818; d. May 4, 1819
        VIII. DAVID,[7] b. June 8, 1820; m. MARY ELIZA PITTS, of Boston, March 1, 1851; d. in Boston, 1869. No children.
646 IX.   THADDEUS,[7] b. Feb. 27, 1823; m. 1st, MARGARET M. F. GREEN, 1844; m. 2d, MARY JANE HERSEY, b. Jan. 7, 1837.

292.

RUFUS[6] CHURCHILL (DAVID,[5] DAVID,[4] WILLIAM,[3] WILLIAM[2] JOHN[1]). Born in Plympton, Oct. 10, 1789. Lived in Hingham, on Main street; was a master mariner. Married, 1818, EUNICE LEWIS, of Hingham. She died 1871.

Children born in Hingham.

I. SUSAN,[7] b. 1821; m. SAMUEL B. LINCOLN, March 29, 1841. She
   d. 1841.
II. ELIZABETH L.[7] m. BLOSSOM SPRAGUE, Nov. 29, 1843.
III. WILLIAM,[7] b. 1825; d. at Calcutta, 1855.
IV. MARIA,[7] b. 1830; m. EDWIN TOWER, Jan. 1, 1851. No issue.

293.

SAMUEL[6] CHURCHILL (WILLIAM,[5] DAVID,[4] WILLIAM,[3] WILL-
IAM,[2] JOHN[1]). Born in Plympton, June 29, 1760. Married DEBO-
RAH WRIGHT, daughter of Jacob.

Children.

647   I. ZADOCK,[7] b. July 13, 1780; m. BETSEY PALMER.
      II. DESIRE,[7] b. Sept. 21, 1782; d. in childhood.
      III. DEBORAH,[7] b. April 12, 1785; m. SETH BOSWORTH.

Children.

1. Martin Bosworth. | 2. Sarah Bosworth.

      IV. ELIZABETH,[7] b. Oct. 14, 1788; d. in childhood.
      V. MERCY,[7] b. Oct. 4, 1791; m. STILLMAN PRATT.

Child.

1. Harriet Pratt.

      VI. RUTH,[7] b. Sept. 27, 1795; never married.
648   VII. SAMUEL,[7] b. May 24, 1804, m. 1st, SABA CHURCHILL, dau. of
           Oliver, No. 296; m. 2d, SARAH STURTEVANT, April 30, 1837.

294.

JOSEPH[6] CHURCHILL (WILLIAM,[5] DAVID,[4] WILLIAM,[3]
WILLIAM,[2] JOHN[1]). Born in Plympton, Oct. 24, 1761, and
lived there. Married EUNICE CHURCHILL, daughter of Ichabod,
No. 45.

Children born at Plympton.

I. SUSANNAH,[7] b. April 11, 1784; m. PETER TOWER; b. April 14,
   1787, died in Belmont, Me., Sept. 30, 1865.

Children of Peter and Susannah Tower.

1. Martin Windsor Tower, b. Nov. 10, 1806, in Plympton; m.
   Elenor Spencer.
2. Malachi Tower, b. June 30, 1808; m. Ruth Hunt.
3. Eunice Churchill Tower, b. May 12, 1810; m. Nathaniel
   Elmes.
4. Sarah A. Tower, b. Nov. 12, 1812; unmarried.
5. Warner C. Tower, b. Jan. 2, 1814; m. Mary Jones.
6. Peter Tower, b. April 24, 1816; m. Hulda Frohock.
7. Elbridge Gerry Tower, b. March 29, 1818; m. Mary Edge-
   .comb.
8. Susan Gibbs Tower, b. Dec. 16, 1819; m. Nathaniel Warren.
9. Nehemiah Hayward Tower, b. July 31, 1822; m. Mary (——).
10. Jerome A. Tower, b. Nov. 7, 1823; d. unmarried in Belmont
    Me., Aug. 10, 1872.
11. John Crosby Tower, b. April 24, 1825; m. (——) Clark.

II. SALLY,[7] b. June 13, 1786.

649   III. Joseph,[7] b. Aug. 10, 1788; m. Rebecca Dunham Morey, of
            Plymouth.
       IV. Sylvanus,[7] b. March 9, 1790.
650   V. Hosea,[7] b. Aug. 24, 1792; m. Eunice Morey, of Plymouth.
       VI. Mary,[7] b. Aug. 20, 1794; m. Ichabod Morey; he died in 1816;
            she died Dec. 25, 1895.
            They had two sons, names not obtained.

651   VII. Zenas,[7] b. June 28, 1797. No further record.
652   VIII. Hiram,[7] b. Sept. 1, 1800. No further record.
653   IX. George,[7] b. Oct. 29, 1802; m. Lydia Morton.
654   X. John,[7] b. Aug. 15, 1804; m. Margaret Tilden.

295.

WILLIAM[6] CHURCHILL (William,[5] David,[4] William[3]
William,[2] John[1]). Born in Plympton, March 8, 1767; followed
the sea and rose to command a vessel. Afterwards was a stonemason and bricklayer. He died in Bainbridge, N.Y., where they
lived after marriage. Married Joanna Tilton, of Easton, N.Y.

Children born at Easton, N.Y.

655   I. William,[7] b. May 22, 1790; m. Minerva Luther, who was born
            March 1, 1800.
       II. Catherine.[7]
       III. Margaret.[7]
       IV. Zenas.[7]

296.

OLIVER[6] CHURCHILL (James[5] David,[4] William,[3] William,[2] John[1]). Born in Plympton, April 21, 1766. Died Nov. 24,
1851. Lived in Plympton. Married Saba Soule, who was born
Jan. 16, 1773, and died Jan. 31, 1839.

Children born in Plympton.

656   I. Oliver,[7] b. Nov. 19, 1794; m. 1st, Sally Bradford, in 1826; m. 2d
            Mary Ann Loring, of Plympton. She d. 1873.
       II. Frances,[7] b. Aug. 28, 1797; m. Stephen Bonney, Nov. 17, 1822.

Children.

       1. James S. Bonney.
       2. Thomas Bonney, d. September, 1861.

       III. Saba,[7] b. July 5, 1800; m. James Churchill, of Halifax. He
            d. 1884. She d. 1836. No children.
657   IV. Isaiah,[7] b. Oct. 10, 1806. He d. May 19, 1877; m. 1st, Polly
            Stevens Parker; m. 2d, Jane Bradford Hayward; m. 3d,
            Angeline Standish, dau. of John.
       V. Mary Magoon,[7] b. June 16, 1811; m. Martin Bosworth, of
            Halifax. She d. 1838.

Children.

       1. Seth Bosworth, b. Feb. 15, 1830; d. March 26, 1831.
       2. Mary Elizabeth Bosworth, b. March 15, 1835.
       3. Saba Soule Bosworth, b. Jan. 24, 1837; m. Bradley F. Durphy,
            of Sharon, Mass.

VI. JANE HUDSON,[7] b. June 22, 1817; m. CHARLES W. ENGLESLID, Sept. 9, 1850. He was born in Sweden. They had three children.

1. Norman Engleslid, b. July 7, 1852.
2. Jane Engleslid, b. May 5, 1855.
3. Charles A. Engleslid, b. May 28, 1857.

297.

JAMES [6] CHURCHILL (JAMES,[5] DAVID,[4] WILLIAM,[3] WILLIAM,[2] JOHN [1]). Born Feb. 26, 1771, in Plympton, Mass., and lived there. Died March, 1803. Married, Feb. 16, 1794, SARAH SOULE, daughter of Ebenezer. After the death of first husband she married JEPTHA DELANO, of Duxbury.

Children born in Plympton.

I. OLIVE SOULE,[7] b. Feb. 11, 1795; m. LEMUEL STURTEVANT, Aug. 17, 1817.
II. SARAH HUDSON, b. May 6, 1797; m. JABEZ FULLER, of Bridgewater, 1815.

298.

LEWIS [6] CHURCHILL (NATHANIEL [5] NATHANIEL,[4] WILLIAM,[3] WILLIAM,[2] JOHN [1]). Born Dec. 12, 1771, in Plympton, Mass. Lived in Plymouth until after January, 1797, when he moved to Cornish, N.H. He was a farmer, very active and agile even to old age. When 83 years of age he used to mount his horse and ride a distance of ten miles, as well as a young man. He died in Cornish, July 15, 1855, aged 83 years 7 months 3 days, and there lies buried with his three wives. He married 1st, DESIRE BARKER BREWSTER; 2d, PATTY THURSTON, daughter of Stephen and Keziah (Cheney) Thurston, born in Rowley, April, 1784; 3d, 1826, RUTH QUIMBY.

Children of First Wife.

I. DEBORAH,[7] b. Oct. 22, 1794, at Plymouth, and died May 3, 1803.
II. HOSEA,[7] b. Jan. 18, 1797, at Plymouth; m. POLLY HARDY. Lived in Sempronius, N.Y. Had no children.
658 III. NATHAN,[7] b. April 17, 1799, at Cornish, N.H. Lived in Iowa. No record.
659 IV. LOUIS,[7] b. Jan. 15, 1802, at Cornish, N H.; m. ROSAMOND RECORD.
V. EDNA,[7] b. Aug. 14, 1804, at Cornish, N.H.
VI. DEBORAH,[7] b. March 24, 1807; m. ANSEL BARNES, June, 1832, in Millbury, Mass. Mr. Barnes was born in Hardwick, Mass., and soon after marriage settled in his native town, and lived there until after their four eldest children were born, when they moved to Pelham, Mass., and spent the rest of their lives there, and there died, — Mrs. Barnes Feb. 14, 1868, and Mr. Barnes Aug. 12, 1878.

Children.

1. Susan E. Barnes, b. March 6, 1833; m. Ziza Hanks, Nov. 26, 1850.
2. Lewis Churchill Barnes, b. April 9, 1835; m. Jane Boynton, May 26, 1857. He died Oct. 14, 1857.
3. Lucretia Barnes, b. Sept. 27, 1837; d. June 29, 1840.
4. Martha Ann Barnes, b. Feb. 26, 1840; d. Nov. 6, 1848.
5. Dexter Randall Barnes, b. Oct. 8, 1842; m. Jennie Kellogg, Oct. 17, 1868. Lives in Granby.
6. Harriet Louise Barnes, b. Oct. 29, 1845; m. Albert Avery, Oct. 27, 1869.
7. Lois Maria Barnes, b. Aug. 23, 1848; m. Levi Gold, Jan. 26, 1870. Lives in Barkhamstead.
8. Hosea Ansel Barnes, b. Jan. 29, 1854. Unmarried.

660 VII. NATHANIEL,[7] b. April 12, 1809; m. MARIA (———). Lived in California and Pennsylvania. Had a daughter married a Mr. Dick. No records received.

Children of Second Wife, born at Cornish.

661 VIII. BARKER BREWSTER,[7] b. Feb. 4, 1815; m. 1st, MARY A. ANGIER; m. 2d, MRS. MARY J. (WESTGATE) BRITTON, Jan. 31, 1867.
IX. LYDIA,[7] b. June 1, 1819; m. EPHRAIM NELSON, March 26, 1844. They settled in Croyden, and their children were there born; Lydia, the mother, d. Oct. 9, 1881.

Children.

1. Mira A. Nelson, b. Feb. 11, 1845; m. John Lear, March 4, 1867.
2. Marietta Nelson, b. Sept. 4, 1846; m. Charles Upton, Feb. 22, 1898.
3. Hial Flanders Nelson, b. Feb. 4, 1848; m. Ida L. Farr, Oct. 11, 1876.
4. John Lewis Nelson, b. April 6, 1850; m. Sarah E. Farr, Oct. 11, 1876.
5. Jane Patty Nelson, b. Sept. 8, 1853; m. 1st, Brooks Burns, of Hollis, July 5, 1887; m. 2d, John Trow, of Sunapee, April 11, 1896.
6. Sylvia Hardy Nelson, b. April 8, 1855; d. June 5, 1865.

X. EMILY,[7] b 1821; d. at the age of twelve years.

Child of Third Wife.

XI. SARAH,[7] b. 1830; d. May 12, 1874; m. LEMUEL BENWAY, of Cornish, N.H.

Child.

1. Arthur L. Benway, b. May 18, 1860; m. Sarah J. Tandy, Nov. 16, 1880. Have one child, Lucy E. Benway, b. Sept. 21, 1881.

300.

LEVI[6] CHURCHILL (NATHANIEL,[5] NATHANIEL,[4] WILLIAM[3] WILLIAM,[2] JOHN[1]). Born July 25, 1776, in Plympton. He was a farmer. Removed from Massachusetts to Croydon, N.H., and later settled in Stowe, Vt. About 1816/17 he removed to Union County, Ohio, and later to Missouri, and died there in 1845. Married, Nov. 3, 1799, LYDIA RIPLEY. She died in 1847.

Children.

662 I. PHILANDER,[7] b. Sept. 20, 1800; m. DOROTHY FEREBOUT. No further record.
663 II. LEVI,[7] b. Oct. 17, 1802, in Croydon County, N.H.; m. NANCY A. SPRAGUE, March 28, 1827.
664 III. DAVID RIPLEY,[7] b. 1805, in Stowe, Vt.; m. MARY A. PEREW, April 24, 1829, in Ohio.
    IV. JANE,[7] b. Oct. 13, 1807, in Stowe, Vt.; m. 1st, JOSEPH GEER, April 6, 1823, in Ohio; m. 2d, GARET TEASE. One child of first husband, died young.
    V. LYDIA DEBORAH,[7] b. Jan. 25, 1811; m. JOHN GEORGE.
    VI. HANNAH,[7] b. April 14, 1817, in Union County, Ohio; d. unmarried.

301.

STEPHEN [6] CHURCHILL (NATHANIEL,[5] NATHANIEL,[4] WILLIAM,[3] WILLIAM,[2] JOHN [1]). Born in Plympton, April 19, 1779. Lived in Taunton, Mass. Since passing this number, 301, we have received the name of another of the children of Stephen, but we have not learned the name of his wife. Of their four children, born in Taunton, we have only two names.

Children.

    I. DEBORAH.[7] No further record.
665 II. NATHANIEL.[7] No further record.

302.

JOSEPH [6] CHURCHILL (NATHANIEL,[5] NATHANIEL,[4] WILLIAM,[3] WILLIAM,[2] JOHN [1]). Born in Plympton, about 1784. He removed to Thompson, Conn., where four of his children were born. Between 1815 and 1825 he removed to Annsville, N.Y., where his wife died about 1855, and he died about 1862. Married at Thompson, Conn., 1804/5, HANNAH WOODWARD, of Thompson, Conn.

Children.

    I. DEBORAH,[7] b. May 4, 1806; m. WATERMAN HYDE, of Annsville, N.Y., 1830.

Children, dates of birth not received.

    1. Mary Hyde.
    2. Ezra Hyde. Killed at Gettysburg.
    3. Harriet Hyde.
    4. Niles Hyde. Mortally wounded at Gettysburg.
    5. Joseph Hyde.

666 II. NATHANIEL,[7] b. April 23, 1810; m. NANCY MOWERS.
667 III. ORRIN,[7] b. Dec. 18, 1812; m. SARAH E. SPRAGUE.
668 IV. GEORGE,[7] b. June 7, 1815; m. 1st, SARAH POWERS CLARK, April, 1842; m. 2d, Mrs. LUCINDA MONELL, 1846.
669 V. EDWIN LEWIS,[7] b. in Annsville, N.Y.; m., 1825, CHARITY COLLINS, of Annsville.

303.

NATHANIEL⁶ CHURCHILL (NATHANIEL,⁵ NATHANIEL,⁴ WILLIAM,³ WILLIAM,² JOHN¹). Born in Plympton, May 13, 1784. Settled in Grantham, N.H., a farmer. He was killed by being thrown from his horse while riding across a brook, Jan. 4, 1808, aged about 24 years. Married (———) HARDY. After his death his widow married Mr. Clifford.

One Child.

I. ALICE,⁷ b. in Cornish, N.H., Aug. 5, 1808; m. VARNUM STONE, March 24, 1830, and lived for a time in Grantham, but in September, 1833, removed to Palermo, Me., where they lived thirty-five years, and then, April 1, 1868, moved to Fairfield, Me., where Mr. Stone, who was born in Grantham, June 9, 1806, died May 14, 1883. The widow, Alice Churchill Stone, died in Fairfield, April 7, 1888.

Children.

1. Vesta A. Stone, b. in Grantham, Feb. 7, 1832; m. Josiah Foye, and had one son, Dana W. Foye, who lives at Fairfield, Me., where Vesta, the mother, died Nov. 29, 1890.
2. Willard Rawson Stone, b. in Palermo, Me., June 1, 1834. He was living in Augusta, Me., in December, 1899.

305.

JACOB⁶ CHURCHILL (EBENEZER,⁵ ICHABOD,⁴ WILLIAM,³ WILLIAM,² JOHN¹). Born in Plympton, Dec. 21, 1766. Was of Plympton, Oct. 15, 1787, when his marriage intentions were published. We have not been able to get any further information about this family. He died at sea. Married 1st, EUNICE STURTEVANT, of Halifax, Mass.; d. March 7, 1789. Married 2d, JOANNA STURTEVANT; d. March 28, 1843.

Child of First Wife.

670   I. JACOB,⁷ b. March 14, 1788. No further record received.

Children of Second Wife.

671   II. CYRUS,⁷ b. May 3, 1793. No further record received.
      III. REBECCA,⁷ b. Sept. 9, 1797.
      IV. JOANNA,⁷ b. March 14, 1801.

307.

ALFORD⁶ CHURCHILL (EBENEZER,⁵ ICHABOD,⁴ WILLIAM,³ WILLIAM,² JOHN¹). Born in Plympton, Feb. 19, 1773. Married LYDIA CUSHMAN. She died Jan. 27, 1840.

Children.

  I. LYDIA,⁷ b. Nov. 18, 1793.
  II. NANCY,⁷ b. Aug. 25, 1798.
  III. LUCY,⁷ b. Nov. 8, 1805.
  IV. ABIGAIL,⁷ b. Nov. 6, 1809; d. Feb. 26, 1821.

308.

CORNELIUS [6] CHURCHILL (EBENEZER,[5] ICHABOD,[4] WILLIAM,[3] WILLIAM,[2] JOHN [1]). Born in Plympton, Nov. 4, 1780, and died Dec. 10, 1833. Married DESIRE LITCHFIELD. She died March 18 1813.

Children.

      I. OLIVE,[7] b. Feb. 21, 1801.
672   II. CORNELIUS,[7] b. Nov. 22, 1802.
673 III. EPHRAIM,[7] b. Nov. 3, 1804.
674 IV. CHARLES,[7] b. July 16. 1807; m. MARY B. WALES.
675   V. JOHN,[7] b. July 9, 1809.
     VI. BETHANY,[7] b. April 21, 1812.

309.

ANSEL [6] CHURCHILL (EBENEZER,[5] ICHABOD,[4] WILLIAM,[3] WILLIAM,[2] JOHN [1]). Born in Plympton, Aug. 27, 1787. Married LOIS CASWELL, of New Bedford.

Children.

676   I. ANSEL,[7] b. Dec. 23, 1809; m. SARAH P. DELANO.
     II. ELIZA,[7] b. May 10, 1811; m. SMITH FULLER.

Children.

1. Ansel Fuller.	4. Hannah Fuller.
2. Eliza Fuller.	5. Ann Fuller.
3. Nathan Fuller.	

677 III. HENRY,[7] b. Jan. 13, 1813; m. ESTHER SHAW.
678 IV. JAMES,[7] b. July 5, 1815; m REBECCA CROCKER.
679   V. GEORGE LEWIS,[7] b. Sept. 15, 1817; m. LOUISE BONNEY.
    VI. MARCIA,[7] b. Aug. 18, 1819; m. SAMUEL FULLER.

Children.

1. Maria T. Fuller.	3. Waldo Fuller.
2. Lois F. Fuller.	

   VII. MERCY SEEKINS,[7] b. Jan. 25, 1823; m. ROBERT WESTON.

Children.

1. Robert Weston.	4. William Weston.
2. Charles Weston.	5. Lucy Weston.
3. Merey M. Weston.	

310.

ZEBEDEE [6] CHURCHILL (ICHABOD,[5] ICHABOD,[4] WILLIAM,[3] WILLIAM,[2] JOHN [1]). Born at Plympton, May 15, 1784. Soon after marriage he moved to Pomfret, Vt. He was a builder by trade. He died about 1827. Married SARAH B. CASWELL, of Middleboro'; she died in Taunton, July 6, 1814.

Children.

   I. LEBBEUS C.,[7] b. in Woodstock, Vt., April 25, 1811; m. MALANEY J. HART, of Taunton; no children. They lived in Middleboro'.

II. Lydia,[7] b. in Pomfret, Vt., June 13, 1813; m. Roswell Hill. They live at Milton Junction, Wis.
III. George W. C.,[7] b. at Pomfret, Vt., July 14, 1816; m. 1st, Chloe Jones, June 3, 1837; she d. without children, May 17, 1877; m. 2d, Jane Moore, Oct. 10, 1880; no issue.
IV. Susan B.,[7] b. at Woodstock, Vt., 1820; m. George Wilbur, of Dighton, Mass. They lived in Taunton.

Children.

1. George E. Wilbur. | 2. Francis M. Wilbur.

680	V. Oramel H.,[7] b. at Woodstock, May 20, 1825; m. Sarah C. Smith, of Middleboro', Sept. 16, 1848.

311.

SETH WASHBURN [6] CHURCHILL (Ichabod,[5] Ichabod, William,[3] William,[2] John [1]). Born in Plympton, 1797. Lived in Woodstock, Vt., a farmer. Married 1st, Phebe Darling, in Woodstock, Vt. She died there Dec. 2, 1833.

Children born in Woodstock, Vt.

I. Maria,[7] b. July 13, 1815; m. 1st, John Wait; m. 2d, Volney Bradley, of Woodstock.
681	II. Ichabod Sylvester,[7] b. 1817; m. Adeline Dickerman, of Chicopee, Mass.
682	III. Joseph Henry,[7] b. Sept. 28, 1820; m. Caroline Sikes, of Agawam, Jan. 29, 1843.
683	IV. Seth Doten,[7] b. May 5, 1823; m. Eliza Tinkham, of Westfield.
	V. Hannah Crawford,[7] b. 1826; m. John G. Daniels, of Springfield, 1850.

Children.

1. Clara Daniels, m. (———) Wait; lives in Springfield.
2. William Daniels.
3. George Daniels.

VI. Nancy Eveline,[7] b. November, 1831; m. Lyman C. Frost; lives in Springfield, Mass.

Children.

1. Frank P. Frost, b. July 5, 1854.
. Edgar Lyman Frost, b. Sept. 9, 1856.
Henry Lyman Frost, b. March 9, 1860.
. Lizzie Amelia Frost, b. Sept. 2, 1862.
. Ella Jean Frost, b. Jan. 29, 1865.
6. Charles Lyman Frost, b. Oct. 6, 1868.
7. Arthur B. Frost, b. Aug. 2, 1871.
8. Harold Lewis Frost, b. May 13, 1881.

Of Second Wife.

684	VII. Daniel Brainard,[7] b. Dec. 20, 1838; m. Lydia Gray, of Providence, R.I., July 11, 1858. He was captain of a company in the War of 1861. Lives in Brooklyn, N.Y.

312.

ZACCHEUS [6] CHURCHILL (Thomas,[5] Ichabod,[4] William,[3] William,[2] John [1]). Born in Plympton, April 20, 1779. He was a house and ship joiner, and lived in Salem. Married Alice Dunkler, of Danvers.

Children born in Salem.

685   I. ZACCHEUS,[7] b. 1799; m. ELIZABETH GILBERT, of Magnolia, 1819.
     II. NANCY,[7] b. Nov. 12, 1805; m. WILLIAM McLEAN, April 29, 1829,
       of Salem.
686   III. WILLIAM,[7] b. June 16, 1807; m. SARAH L. CURTIS, Jan. 13, 1828.
     IV. MARY,[7] m. JONATHAN HORTON, in Salem, Aug. 21, 1825.
     V. ABIGAIL M.,[7] b. Nov. 11, 1813; m. FRANCIS PHELPS.

Children.

1. Abby Churchill Phelps, b. March 2, 1834; m. Moses Wingate,
   Oct. 4, 1837.
2. Alice Hunt Phelps, b. Nov. 10, 1841.

313.

CHARLES [6] CHURCHILL (THOMAS,[5] ICHABOD,[4] WILLIAM,[3] WILLIAM,[2] JOHN [1]). Born in Plymouth, Sept. 10, 1792, and prob-ably lived there. Married ABIGAIL RUSSELL.

Children.

     I. MARY E.,[7] d. in infancy.
687   II. CHARLES OTIS,[7] b. Feb. 25, 1821.
   III. BETSEY RUSSELL,[7] m. NATHANIEL WOOD.
   IV. CATHARINE BRIDGHAM,[7] d. at 12 years.
   V. REBECCA TWINER,[7] d. in infancy.

314.

DANIEL [6] CHURCHILL (DANIEL,[5] ISAAC,[4] WILLIAM,[3] WILL-IAM,[2] JOHN [1]). Born in Plymouth, June 19, 1800. Married 1st, REBECCA SOULE.

Children.

     I. RUTH H.,[7] b. Aug. 17, 1821; m. NELSON WRIGHT, March 3, 1837.
       No children.
     II. REBECCA S.,[7] b. May 8, 1825; m. 1st, IRA SUMNER, February, 1841;
       m. 2d, ORRIN CLARKE, 1865.
   III. LUCY A.,[7] b. Aug. 22, 1827; m. OTIS W. PHINNEY, October, 1842.
   IV. EUNICE R.,[7] b. Nov. 1, 1832; m. CALVIN H. BRYANT, Oct. 8, 1850.

315.

HARVEY [6] CHURCHILL (DANIEL,[5] ISAAC,[4] WILLIAM,[3] WILL-IAM,[2] JOHN [1]). Born in Plympton, April 11, 1805. Married ELIZA VOSE, June, 1843.

Children.

     I. ELIZA J.,[7] m. JOSHUA CHURCHILL, of Abington. No children.
     II. EUNICE R.,[7] m. LAWRENCE FELCH, of Boston, 1872.

316.

TIMOTHY [6] CHURCHILL (JOSIAH,[5] ISAAC,[4] ISAAC,[3] WILLIAM,[2] JOHN [1]). Born in Plympton, Aug. 7, 1797. Died Nov. 23, 1869. Married RUTH SOULE, of Plympton.

Children.

     I. SARAH,[7] b. Dec. 20, 1826; m. WILLIAM ROUNDS.
    II. DELIA,[7] b. Oct. 3, 1829; m. GEORGE H. SHERMAN.
688   III. JOSIAH,[7] b. Sept. 19, 1833; m. ANNA ASHLEY.
   IV. MARIA,[7] b. June 24, 1837; m. JOHN MATTHEWS.

317.

PELHAM [6] CHURCHILL (JOSIAH,[5] ISAAC,[4] ISAAC,[3] WILLIAM [2] JOHN [1]). Born in Plympton, March 14, 1800. Lived in Newport, R.I., and Plympton. He was an invalid for many years. Died Feb. 1, 1861. Married EUNICE T. SIMMONS, of Plymouth.

Children born at Newport.

689   I. PELHAM F. R.,[7] b. Dec. 11, 1828; m. CHARLOTTE M. (KING) BEN-
           SON, Jan. 8, 1863.
690   II. LEMUEL P.,[7] b. April 2, 1831; m. PRISCILLA F. PERKINS.

318.

SIMEON [6] CHURCHILL (JOSIAH,[5] ISAAC,[4] ISAAC,[3] WILLIAM,[2] JOHN [1]). Born in Plympton, May 25, 1802. Married, March 7, 1830, MRS. SALLY (BISBEE) CUSHMAN. She was the daughter of John Bisbee and Priscilla (Ripley) Bisbee, his wife, and was born Oct. 9, 1805.

Children.

     I. ANN JANET,[7] b. May 13, 1831; m. WILLIAM PERKINS, of Plympton,
          June 6, 1850.
691   II. LEANDER SCOTT,[7] b. Dec. 19, 1832; unmarried.
   III. PRISCILLA RIPLEY,[7] b. Oct. 24, 1835; m. MARTIN RICARD.
   IV. BARTHOLOMEW CUSHMAN,[7] b. Nov. 23, 1837; unmarried.
    V. CHARLOTTE,[7] b. July 20, 1840; d. July 10, 1842.

319.

ALEXANDER [6] CHURCHILL (JOSIAH,[5] ISAAC,[4] ISAAC [3] WILLIAM,[2] JOHN [1]). Born in Plympton, April 3, 1807. Married LYDIA BOSWORTH, of Halifax, Mass.

Children.

692   I. ASA LYMAN.[7]
   II. SUSAN L.[7]

320.

ALBERT SMITH [6] CHURCHILL (JOSIAH,[5] ISAAC [4] ISAAC,[3] WILLIAM,[2] JOHN [1]). Born in Plympton, April 19, 1815. Lived in Halifax, Mass. He died Sept. 18, 1882. Married, 1841, PRISCILLA S. SIMMONS.

Children born at Halifax.

     I. HELEN,[7] b. March 30, 1843; m. ELMER JOSCELYN.
693   II. JOSIAH,[7] b. Feb. 14, 1845; m. MARY H. WILLIS, October, 1867.

321.

REUBEN[6] CHURCHILL (ISAAC,[5] ISAAC[4] ISAAC,[3] WILLIAM[2] JOHN[1]). Born in Plympton, May 30, 1813. Married, Oct. 27 1847, MARIA CROCKETT, at Abington.

Children.

      I. MARY,[7] b. Sept. 14, 1848; m. HARRISON A. WADE, July 2. 1866.
      II. CHASTINA,[7] b. Sept. 24, 1850; m. GEORGE H. MERRILL, Dec. 15, 1875.
      III. ELLA,[7] b. May 26, 1854; d. Oct. 2, 1854.
694   IV. NELSON,[7] b. May 12, 1856; m. AMY REED, Aug. 11, 1877.
695   V. EDWARD CLINTON,[7] b. Aug. 16, 1864; d. Oct. 22, 1864.

322.

FREEMAN GROZIER[6] CHURCHILL (ISAAC,[5] ISAAC,[4] ISAAC,[3] WILLIAM,[2] JOHN[1]). Born at Abington, Jan. 2, 1815. Married June 2, 1836, ELIZABETH WINSLOW, daughter of Thomas, of Hanover.

Children.

696   I. JOSHUA FREEMAN,[7] b. Jan. 13, 1837; m. JOSEPHINE CHURCHILL, July 6, 1864.
      II. ISAIAH JENKINS.[7] b. April 23, 1843; d. Aug. 31, 1843.
697   III. ISAIAH THOMAS,[7] b. April 19, 1844; m. JANE FRENCH, Nov. 29, 1865.
698   IV. GEORGE QUINCY,[7] b. May 25, 1852; m. AGNES HOWARD, Sept. 27, 1876.
699   V. FRANKLIN NEWTON,[7] b. Nov. 24, 1853; d. Sept. 13, 1854.
      VI. LOUISE FLEEDA,[7] b. Nov. 3, 1857; d. Sept. 9, 1858.

323.

EZRA[6] CHURCHILL (ISAAC,[5] ISAAC,[4] ISAAC,[3] WILLIAM,[2] JOHN[1]). Born in Plympton, Jan. 18, 1827. Lived in Worcester. Married, Oct. 20, 1855, MYRA JANE BOSWORTH, of Bellingham.

Children born in Worcester.

      I. LILLIE ELIZA,[7] b. Feb. 26, 1859; d. Sept. 11, 1859.
      II. NELLIE EVELYN,[7] b. Jan. 11, 1861; m. SIDNEY P. HARDING, of Worcester, July 28, 1880.
      III. FANNIE HART,[7] b. Sept. 20, 1863.
700   IV. GEORGE BOSWORTH,[7] b. Oct. 24, 1866.
      V. FLORENCE ALINE,[7] b. Dec. 30, 1871.

324.

OTIS[6] CHURCHILL (ISAAC,[5] ISAAC,[4] ISAAC,[3] WILLIAM,[2] JOHN[1]). Born in Plympton, Oct. 6 1828. Lived in Abington. Married MARY A. TEMPLE, of Marlboro'.

Children.

    I. ELLEN SOPHIA,[7] b. Dec. 18, 1851; d. Dec. 2, 1870.
   II. ALICE LOUISE,[7] b. Oct. 15, 1854; m. EDGAR S. DODGE, of Natick
       April 15, 1880.
  III. IDELLA FRANCIS,[7] b. June 22, 1856.
  IV. ABBEY PIERCE,[7] b. June 9, 1859.
701   V. CHARLES OTIS,[7] b. May 31, 1861.

325.

ASAPH[6] CHURCHILL (ZEBEDEE[5] PEREZ,[4] BENJAMIN,[3] WILLIAM,[2] JOHN[1]). Born in Middleboro', May 5, 1765. His father died when he was about two years old, and his mother soon married again. Nothing is known of his childhood, until in his early youth he told of working in an iron-foundry, at six and one-quarter cents a day, and living on corn-bread and milk and fish, the latter then very plentiful. The facts of those early years are not known, but it is certain that he had an ambition to break away from his narrow surroundings, and conceived the idea that the way out was by means of an education. From some one he learned about Harvard College, and that to be admitted there one must have at least the rudiments of Greek and Latin. From some source he secured the books and the instruction, and one day, in the summer of 1785, he took his little bundle of earthly belongings, including his only pair of shoes, and started out into the world alone to "try his fortune." He walked from Middleboro' to Cambridge, barefoot, to save the wear of the shoes. He presented himself, was examined and admitted, and was graduated, well up in his class, in 1789. By teaching, and, it is said, preaching, as was the custom of graduates of that day, he gained the means of pursuing the study of the law. He studied for a time with the Hon. John Davis, and was admitted to the Plymouth County bar, Aug. 13, 1793, at the age of 28 years. He soon after settled in Boston, and about 1805 began practice in Milton, where he continued until his death. He was one of the ablest lawyers in Norfolk County. Mr. Churchill was a very industrious student, a diligent reader of the French classics, reading and speaking the language with fluency. He had almost a passion for the acquisition of land, and became an extensive owner in Milton and vicinity. He served a brief enlistment in the War of 1812. He represented the town of Milton in the General Court for the years 1810 and 1812. Mr. Churchill was a man of public spirit and enterprise, but of independent disposition and strong individuality. He took great pains in the training of his children, seeking to shield them from the hardships which he had endured. He sought to leave them a competency, as well as an education fitting them for

ASAPH CHURCHILL.
(No. 702, page 296.)

ASAPH CHURCHILL.
(Page 298, under No. 1165.)

NERATIONS.

useful and happy lives. He was a member of the Third Church in Dorchester. In 1810 he purchased the fine estate, on Milton Hill, known as " the Governor Robbins place," and there established his home with a lady of distinguished beauty and lovely character as his wife. Married, in Charlestown, May 5, 1810, MARY GARDNER, daughter of Dr. Edward, of Charlestown. She died in Milton, Jan. 21, 1859. Mr. Churchill died in 1841.

Children born in Milton.

I. MARY,[7] b. April 12, 1811; d. Feb. 14, 1828.
II. JULIET,[7] b. Dec. 12, 1812; d. unmarried, May 30, 1862.
702 III. ASAPH,[7] b. April 20, 1814; m. 1st, MARY BUCKMINSTER BREWER, May 1, 1838; m. 2d, MARY ANN WARE, of Milton, 1862.
IV. SARAH,[7] b. Feb. 1, 1816; d. unmarried, June 28, 1886.
V. CHARLES MARSHALL SPRING,[7] b. April 25, 1819; d. Oct. 9, 1822.
703 VI. JOSEPH McKEEN,[7] b. April 29, 1821; m. AUGUSTA PHILLIPS GARD-NER, of Richmond, Va., June 6, 1861.
704 VII. CHARLES MARSHALL SPRING,[7] b. May 1, 1825; m. SUSAN E. SPOONER, dau. of Dr. John P. Spooner, of Dorchester, April 6 1853.

326.

ASAPH[6] CHURCHILL (PEREZ,[5] PEREZ,[4] BENJAMIN,[3] WILLIAM,[2] JOHN[1]). Born in Middleboro', March 7, 1789, and lived there until his death in 1861. Mr. Churchill learned and followed the dyers' trade for some years, but settled down to farming later. Married, at Middleboro', Jan. 6, 1819, RHODA JOHNSON ATWOOD, daughter of John and Rhoda Atwood, born in Bridgewater, Aug. 30, 1798. When she was four years old her parents removed to Middleboro', and she always lived there afterwards. On the occasion of her one hundred and first birthday, sketches appeared in Massachusetts papers, telling something of her life. She lived in her later years with her daughter, Mrs. J. H. Waterman, on Spring street, Middleboro'. Aug. 30, 1899, she was still bright and active, retaining her faculties remarkably, especially her memory. She was very fond of recalling the incidents of her girlhood, remembering distinctly the marching of the soldiers in the War of 1812, as they marched through Middleboro' to Plymouth for the protection of that port. Neither of her parents lived to old age, her mother dying of consumption at the age of thirty-nine years, and her father at sixty-three years. She has lived a simple, hard-working, cheerful, and healthy life. She died Sept. 7, 1902, aged 104 years and 8 days, retaining her mental faculties to the end.

Children born in Middleboro'.

705 I. GEORGE ATWOOD,[7] b. Sept. 26, 1819; m. AMARANTHA J. BURGESS, March 2, 1842.
II. CHARLOTTE AUGUSTA,[7] b. May 26, 1821; m. EDMOND POPE.

174 THE CHURCHILL FAMILY.

One child.

1. Henry Freeman Pope, b. July 5, 1843; d. June 11, 1895.

III. RHODA JOHNSON,[7] b. Sept. 16, 1823; m. GEORGE S. SAVORY. She died in Middleboro', Jan. 7, 1899. No children.

IV. JULIA ALLEN,[7] b. Oct. 11, 1827; m. JAMES H. WATERMAN, Nov. 28, 1855.

They lived in Middleboro' and had three children

Children.

1. Mary Isabella Waterman, b. Sept. 17, 1856; m. Edward S. Gay.
2. Julia Ann Waterman, b. June 14, 1858; d. Jan. 8, 1864.
3. Rhoda Savory Waterman, b. June 17, 1869; m. Harrison B. Ellis, June 9, 1892.

706   V. CHARLES ASAPH,[7] b. Nov. 6, 1835; m. HANNAH D. DRINKWATER.

327.

JOSEPH[6] CHURCHILL (ISAAC,[5] PEREZ,[4] BENJAMIN,[3] WILLIAM,[2] JOHN[1]). Born in Middleboro', June 6, 1778. Lived there, and later in Pomfret, Vt. Married, Nov. 6, 1817, MARGARET GARDNER. She died Nov. 11, 1830.

Children.

I. MATILDA,[7] b. 1818.
707   II. DANIEL,[7] b. 1820. No further record.
III. CLARINDA,[7] b. 1830.

Four other children, whose names are not received, died young.

328.

ZEBEDEE[6] CHURCHILL (ISAAC,[5] PEREZ,[4] BENJAMIN,[3] WILLIAM,[2] JOHN[1]). Born in Middleboro', Feb. 19, 1779. Settled in Pomfret, Vt. Married, at Pomfret, Vt., Nov. 4, 1809, AZUBAH CHEEDLE, of Pomfret, Vt.

Children born in Pomfret.

I. RACHEL,[7] b. Aug. 21, 1810; m. EDWARD BROWN, April 22, 1832.
They lived in Bridgewater, Vt., where she died Dec. 20, 1857. A son, James Brown, was living in Plymouth, Vt., in 1887.

II. ISAAC O.,[7] b. March 27, 1812; never married; d. Oct. 1, 1886.

III. ASAPH W.,[7] b. March 16, 1814; m. MRS. OLIVIA M. JACKMAN, March 20, 1844. No children.
They were living in Pomfret, Vt., in 1887

IV. MARY ANN, b. Feb. 11, 1816; m. ZENAS ADAMS, at Pomfret, Vt., Nov. 25, 1837.
They were living in Florida in 1888.

Children.

1. Martha L. Adams, b. Nov. 27, 1839.
2. Milo P. Adams, b. Oct. 8, 1841.
3. Wealthy B. Adams, b. Nov. 13, 1843.
4. Zenas Adams, b. Feb. 22, 1849.
5. Frank Adams, b. Jan. 19, 1855

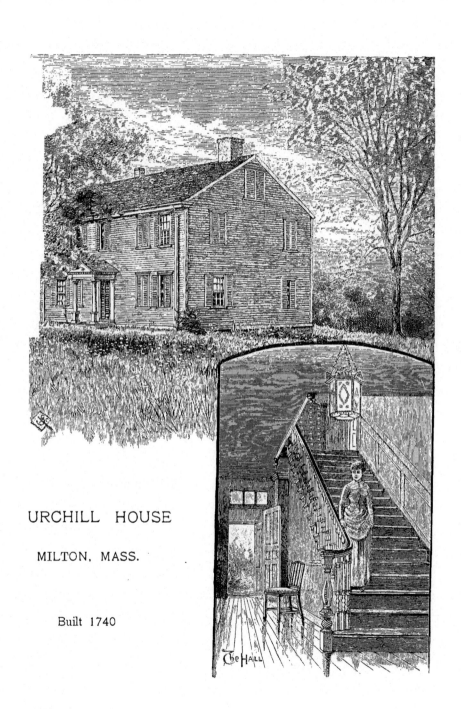

URCHILL HOUSE

MILTON, MASS.

Built 1740

The HALL

708   V. ZEBEDEE P.,[7] b. May 15, 1818; m. 1st, ORLEANA BOUTWELL, June 1, 1846; m. 2d, EMILY ORDWAY.

    VI. FRANCES MARIA,[7] b. May 22, 1820; m. ALVIN PERHAM, May 14, 1849.

        They lived, in 1857, at Barnard, Vt. She died May 3, 1867.

    VII. FIDELIA,[7] b. March 3, 1822; m. LYMAN PERKINS, May 1, 1849.

        They lived, in 1857, in Bridgewater, Vt. A son, Lyman Perkins, was living in Taftsville, Vt., in 1887.

329.

ISAAC[6] CHURCHILL (ISAAC,[5] PEREZ,[4] BENJAMIN,[3] WILLIAM,[2] JOHN[1]). Born at Middleboro', June 30, 1786, and moved to Pomfret, Vt., with his father's family. He served in the War of 1812, and his wife was with him at Plattsburgh, and one of their children was born in camp during the battle. In 1857 they lived at Mt. Anna, Ill., and he died about 1869. Married, December, 1809, in Vermont, LYDIA ROGERS, who was born in Lynn, Conn.

Children.

    I. ARETHUSA,[7] b. July 10, 1811.
709   II. LIBERTY,[7] b. at battle of Plattsburgh, Sept. 11, 1814.
710   III. DANIEL H.,[7] b. March 1, 1818.
711   IV. LORENZO DOW,[7] b. May 3, 1820; m. LOVISA JANE HACKETT.
        This man was living at Mellette, S. Dak., in 1887, and wrote t. o letters, but made no mention of having any children.
    V. MALENTHA,[7] b. Aug. 22, 1823.

330.

PHINEAS[6] CHURCHILL (ISAAC,[5] PEREZ,[4] BENJAMIN,[3] WILLIAM,[2] JOHN[1]). Born in Middleboro', April 28, 1793. Lived in Pomfret, Vt., and later in Barnard, Vt. He died August, 1886. Married, 1814, ARVILLA (GROW) WATKINS.

Children born in Pomfret.

    I. ARABELLA E.,[7] b. Aug. 19, 1815; m. OBED ADAMS, in Woodstock, Vt., Nov. 23, 1834.

Children.

1. Martin V. Adams, b. Aug. 29, 1835; unmarried.
2. Austin V. Adams, b. May 26, 1837.
3. Edgar A. Adams, b. July 26, 1840; d. Jan. 3, 1863; unmarried.
4. Owen O. Adams, b. Sept. 30, 1841; m. 1st, Sarah Gibbs, Sept. 17, 1867; m. 2d, Alice Perry, Nov. 13, 1873.
5. Celestia Adams, b. April 22, 1843; m. Morillo M. Whipple, Feb. 16, 1871.
6. Willis C. Adams, b. May 18, 1845; m. Ollie Norcross, July 10, 1883.
7. James D. Adams, b. May 28, 1846; m. Effie Dana, Sept. 7, 1873.
8. Annette Adams, b. Feb. 18, 1848; m. Henry L. Stevens, Sept. 5, 1867.
9. Millard O. Adams, b. July 6, 1850; d. March 22, 1852.
10. Martha A. Adams, b. Sept. 11, 1851; d. March 27, 1852.

    II. Adeline,[7] b. June 27, 1817; m. Maverick Adams.
   III. James,[7] b. Oct. 15, 1819; d. unmarried at the age of 64 years.
   IV. Elvira,[7] b. July 22, 1822; m. Charles Howard, of Bethel, Vt.
712   V. Orlando,[7] b. Oct. 23, 1825; m. Temperance Holmes, at Little Falls, Minn.
   VI. Arvilla,[7] b. June 15, 1829; m. Horace Dewey.
  VII. Henry,[7] b. July 30, 1832; d. aged 11 years.
 VIII. Martha,[7] b. Aug. 17, 1834; m. Allen Kendall.

331.

JACOB[6] CHURCHILL (Isaac,[5] Perez,[4] Benjamin,[3] William,[2] John[1]). Born in Middleboro', April 5, 179–. Lived in Pomfret, Vt. Married at Pomfret, April 4, 1821, Betsey Howard.

They had one Child.

   I. Emily,[7] no record received.

332.

SPRAGUE[6] CHURCHILL (Joseph[5] Perez,[4] Benjamin,[3] William,[2] John[1]). Born in Middleboro', April 28, 1787. Moved with his father's family to Paris, Me., and settled on the lot, now the homestead of his son, Kingman Churchill. Married Harriet Holmes, daughter of Captain Lemuel.

Children born in Paris, Me.

713   I. William,[7] b. Sept. 5, 1814; m. Mary Libby, Nov. 30, 1841.
   II. Harriet,[7] b. Sept. 28, 1816; m. 1st, Wright Barrett; m. 2d, Soloman Chase.
  III. Polly,[7] b. April 26, 1819; d. Oct. 12, 1838; unmarried.
  IV. Clara,[7] b. June 24, 1821; m. 1st, Joseph C. Tuttle, Feb. 19, 1851, in Paris, Me.; m. 2d, America Bisbee.

Children.

   1. Walter H. Tuttle, b. April 22, 1856; d. March 2, 1859.
   2. Clara F. Tuttle, b. Feb. 6, 1858; m. George P. Downing, of Norway, Me., Dec. 24, 1887.
714   V. Kingman,[7] b. June 18, 1823; m. Loretta Andrews, dau. of David.

333.

WILLIAM[6] CHURCHILL (Joseph,[5] Perez,[4] Benjamin,[3] William,[2] John[1]). Born in Oxford County, Me., May 21, 1792. He was a soldier in the War of 1812. He lived in Buckfield. Married 1st, Polly Bird. No children. Married 2d, Rebecca Churchill, of Buckfield. She was born Oct. 9, 1802, and died in Norway, July 9, 1880.

Children of Second Wife.

716   I. Joseph,[7] b. Feb. 2, 1828; m. 1st, Betsey Moody, of New Gloucester; m. 2d, Viana Perham, of Woodstock.
   II. Calista,[7] b. March 22, 1833; m. Calvin Richardson, of Greenwood, Oct. 13, 1856.

Children born in Norway.

1. Herbert Richardson, b. Nov. 27, 1857.
2. Emma Richardson, b. Aug. 14, 1861.
3. Hattie Richardson, b. April 21. 1864.
4. Levi Richardson, b. Feb. 26, 1868.

717   III. WILLIAM,[7] b. Jan. 22, 1837; m. MARY PERLEY, of Norway. Dead.
     IV. ELLEN,[7] b. Jan. 1, 1839; m. JOHN GERRY, of Norway, Me., March 13, 1860. Mr. Gerry was born in Fermoy, Munster County, Ireland, Aug. 3, 1826, and died in Norway, Me., May 12, 1877. Lived in Greenwood and Norway, Me.

Children.

1. Cora Gerry, b. in Greenwood, Feb. 18, 1864; d. in Norway, May 1, 1879.
2. Ina Gerry, b. in Norway, Nov. 12, 1867.
3. William Gerry, b. in Norway, Oct. 29, 1875.

334.

SULLIVAN[6] CHURCHILL (JOSEPH,[5] PEREZ,[4] BENJAMIN,[3] WILLIAM,[2] JOHN[1]). Born in 1798. Lived in Oxford County, Me. Married MARTHA SMITH.

One son.

I   HORACE P.,[7] said to have lived in Gorham, N.H., in 1900. No further record obtained.

335.

JOAB[6] CHURCHILL (JABEZ,[5] BENJAMIN,[4] BENJAMIN,[3] WILLIAM,[2] JOHN[1]). Born in Middleboro', Mass., March 2, 1784. Went with his father's family to Hartford, Me., about 1800. Died April 12, 1857. He lived in Hartford, Me. Married, Feb. 26, 1809, PHILENA HAYFORD.

Children born in Hartford, Me.

I. JULIA FRENCH,[7] b. June 7, 1810; m. DANIEL THURSTON STEVENS, Dec. 3, 1834. She d. Nov. 16, 1860.
II. PHILENA HAYFORD,[7] b. June 12, 1812; m. BROWNELL M. BICKNELL, Dec. 7, 1834. She d. Feb. 19, 1841.
III. MARIA,[7] b. May 19, 1814; d. Aug. 23, 1814.
IV. NANCY HARMON,[7] b. May 9, 1816; m. REV. CHARLES P. BARTLETT, May 6, 1840.

336.

JABEZ[6] CHURCHILL (JABEZ,[5] BENJAMIN,[4] BENJAMIN,[3] WILLIAM,[2] JOHN[1]). Born in Middleboro', March 14, 1797. Removed with his father's family to Hartford, Me. He settled first in Parkman, Me., later in Portland and Hallowell. Died in Stockton Minn., 1876. Married PHEBE HAZELTON.

Children.

I. MARY D.,[7] b. Aug. 18, 1828; m. ALBERT THOMAS.

Children.

1. Fred A. Thomas, b. in Hallowell, Me., June 2, 1854.
2. Charles F. Thomas, b. in Hallowell, Me., Aug. 2, 1856.
3. Walter U. Thomas, b. in Stockton, Minn., Nov. 20, 1859.
4. Alberta Thomas, b. in Winona, Minn., July 30, 1869.

718   II. CHAUNCEY,[7] b. March 28, 1830, in Parkman, Me.
      III. LUCY ELLEN,[7] b. Jan. 2, 1834, in Portland; m. JESSE TUCK.

Child.

1. William A. Tuck, b. in Hallowell, Me., Dec. 26, 1864.

719   IV. CHARLES E.,[7] b. May 22, 1836, in Portland, Me.
      V. SARAH F.,[7] b. May 16, 1839, in Hallowell, Me.
720   VI. WILLIAM H.,[7] b. Oct. 10, 1841, in Hallowell, Me.

337.

WILLIAM [6] CHURCHILL (WILLIAM,[5] BENJAMIN,[4] BENJAMIN,[3] WILLIAM,[2] JOHN [1]). Born in Buckfield, Me., Aug. 5, 1796, but removed soon with his father's family to Wayne. He was of a roving and adventurous nature and followed the sea for many years, returning to his family in Wayne after his voyages. He related many wonderful adventures at sea. He was once wrecked and with one companion swam to a wild shore where they were captured by the natives and made slaves, but escaped to a passing vessel and so got home. On another voyage he was captured by pirates, and on their capture of a prize they paid him five hundred dollars, and he soon after made his escape while the ship was in a West Indian port taking fuel and water. He lived on his farm in Wayne later. He was a large and powerful man, active in hunting and fishing. He was drowned in Wayne Pond, Dec. 3, 1832, while skating across in pursuit of some wild ducks which had lighted in an open place. He skated into a hole, while his three eldest children stood on the shore watching, but unable to help. They ran to call a neighbor, but their father crawled out and came nearly to the shore when the ice again gave way, and he was so exhausted and chilled that he sank down before help could reach him. Married in Wayne (intentions published May 24, 1809), PHEBE MAXIM, of Wayne, who was born Aug. 5, 1795.

Children born in Wayne, Me.

I. FLORINDA W.,[7] b. Oct. 8, 1817; m. CHARLES GORDON, at Monmouth, May 20, 1838.
    He was the son of Jonathan and Sarah (Pettingill) Gordon, died July 1882. She died May 21, 1886.

Children born in Leeds, Me.

1. Phebe J. Gordon, b. July 21, 1845; m. Hezekiah Gordon, Jan. 1. 1868.
2. Charles W. Gordon, b. Jan. 15, 1849; m. Annie Burrell, of Milford, Mass., Jan. 1, 1868.
3. Lydia A. Gordon, b. Nov. 10, 1850; m. Herbert Millett, of Leeds, 1871.

721   II. Thomas Wilson,[7] b. June 28, 1821; m. Sarah Ireland.
722   III. Lewis,[7] b. March 2, 1823; m. Ruth Pettingill, of Presque Isle, Me., Feb. 19, 1850.
     IV. William,[7] b. May 1, 1825; m. Mary J. Gordon, of Leeds, Me., 1852.
     V. Jemima,[7] b. July 6, 1827; m. Lyman Sea'bury.

Child.

1. Mary Seabury; m. Frederick Flanders, of Monmouth.

     VI. Lydia,[7] b. April 16, 1829; d. unmarried, June 30, 1845; aged 16 years.
   VII. Emily,[7] b. April 27, 1831; d. March, 1833.
  VIII. Emily A.,[7] b. March 19, 1833; m. Daniel H. Peaslee, at Lewiston, Feb. 13, 1849.
     He was the son of Jonathan and Sally (Hook) Peaslee, and was born in Weare, N.H., March 15, 1818. He acquired a good business education; he was a farmer in Springfield, N.H., a respected and influential citizen, and died Jan. 1, 1877.

Children of Daniel H. and Emily (Churchill) Peaslee.
The first born in Monmouth, Me., the rest in Springfield, N.H.

1. Emily Amanda Peaslee. b. Dec. 13, 1849; m. William Severance, of Grafton, N.H., Oct. 20, 1869.
2. Alice Alta Peaslee, b. Nov. 24, 1852; d. unmarried, Oct. 31, 1869.
3. Ida Irene Peaslee, b. Aug. 3, 1854; m. Frank Sargent, of Grafton, N.H., Nov. 29, 1876.
4. Lewis Churchill Peaslee, b. Sept. 30, 1856; m. Minnie Truell, of Cornish, N.H.
5. Phebe Ellen Peaslee, b. Nov. 3. 1857; m. George H. Cross, Nov. 22, 1885, of Springfield, N.H.
6. Daniel Hook Peaslee, Jr., b. Aug. 13, 1859; m. Abbie M. Hardie, of Springfield, Nov. 10, 1882.
7. Carrie Peaslee, b. June 8, 1861; m. Henry G. Gordon, of Wayne, Me., Nov. 11, 1884.
8. Ernest Peaslee, b. March 13, 1866.
9. George Wilson Peaslee, b. Feb. 18, 1870; m. Kate Eastman, of Danbury, N.H.
10. Alice Alta Peaslee, b. Dec. 29, 1871; m. John F. Richmond, of Farmington, Me., March 25, 1891.
11. Stephen Bailey Peaslee, b. March 14, 1874.
     Mrs. Emily A. Peaslee, the mother and widow, lives with Stephen B., her youngest son, on his farm at North Wilmot, N.H.

338.

NATHAN[6] CHURCHILL (William,[5] Benjamin,[4] Benjamin,[3] William,[2] John[1]). Born in Wayne, Me., March 23, 1807. He was a farmer, and lived in Avon, Me. Married, Oct. 19, 1834, Zilpah Keene, of Salem, Me.

Children born in Avon, Me.

724   I. Addison H.,[7] b. April 23, 1836; m. Mary Tebbetts, of Avon, September, 1867.
     II. Lydia D.,[7] b. July 12, 1838; m. 1st, Anson Lombard, of Carthage, Me., 1857; no issue; m. 2d, S. Littlefield, of Dixfield, June 1, 1877; no children.
     III. Louisa,[7] b. June 1, 1840; unmarried; lived at Augusta, Me.

725   IV. WILLIAM W.,[7] b. Oct. 1, 1846; m. CORA M. RANGER, Jan. 1, 1878.
     V. MARY A.,[7] b. Jan. 5, 1850; m. E. H. VAUGHN, September, 1869.
        Mr. Vaughn was a shoemaker and lived in Strong, Me. ; d. February, 1881.

Child.

    1. Frank Vaughn.

    VI. FLORINDA[7], b. Jan. 30, 1855; d. May 16, 1860.

340.

PARDON[6] CHURCHILL (JOSEPH,[5] BENJAMIN,[4] BENJAMIN,[3] WILLIAM,[2] JOHN[1]). Born in Mansfield, Mass., or near there. In the year 1816 he made a journey into the forest lands of the Susquehanna County, Pa., purchased a tract of woodland, made a small clearing, and built a house. Returning home, he made preparations for removal, and in the winter of 1817–18, having constructed a cloth-covered house or tent upon an ox-sled, and packing their supplies and necessary furnishings, and accompanied by his young wife and infant son, Asa, with John and Bathsheba Williams, his wife's mother and sister, he set out for the new home. They were fourteen days on the journey to the wilderness, in the town of Herrick, where his farm was located. He died about 1825, leaving a widow and one son. He married in Scituate, R.I, ABIGAIL WILLIAMS, daughter of Squire and Anna Williams, the father being a descendant of Roger Williams, the pioneer settler of Providence, R.I. Squire Williams was in the fifth generation from Roger, and was born in Scituate, R.I., May 20, 1753, son of Benoni and Abigail (Smith) Williams.

Children of Pardon and Abigail (Willliams) Churchill.

    I. ASA,[7] b. 1817; died early.
725a   II. ASA.[7]
        He is said to have settled in Toronto, Can., but no record has been received.

341.

WILLIAMS[6] CHURCHILL (JOSEPH,[5] BENJAMIN,[4] BENJAMIN[3] WILLIAM,[2] JOHN[1]). Born in Mansfield, Mass., March 21, 1795. He obtained a fairly good education by his industrious and studious habits, and learned the fuller's trade. In the spring of 1818 he followed his brother, Pardon, to Herrick, Pa., built a small house near by, and lived by himself for some two years, while working at his trade at Mount Pleasant, five miles away. Upon his marriage to his brother's wife's sister he took a farm a mile away at a clearing where there was a saw mill, built a log house, and lived there five years, until the death of his brother Pardon, when he removed to that farm, and there spent the rest of his strong, useful, and upright life. He became a member of the Methodist Church in early life, and was a preacher in many pulpits of that denomination from the age of 27, until his death, April 28, 1877. He married, in Herrick, Pa., May 18, 1820, BATHSHEBA WILLIAMS, daughter of Squire and Anna Williams, of Scituate, R.I. Her father was a descendant in the fourth generation of Roger Williams, of Providence R.I. She was born May 9, 1800, and died Sept. 29, 1875:

Children born in Herrick, Pa.

725b I. ABRAHAM,[7] b. Jan. 16, 1821; m. MARGARET CLARKSON, Feb. 26, 1845.
  II. MARY,[7] b. June 30, 1822; m. JOHN C. HIGGINS.
  III. SUSAN,[7] b. Feb. 5, 1824; m. HOMER DAVISON, Oct. 2, 1845.

Children born in Susquehanna County. In 1900 they lived in No. Jackson.

  1. Pauline E. Davison, b. in Greenfield, Pa., Oct. 11, 1846; m. John M. Prime, No. Jackson, Pa., Aug. 7, 1876. She died in Brooklyn, N.Y., Aug. 3, 1895.
  2. Daniel D. Davison, b. in Greenfield, Pa., Feb. 3, 1850; m. Jennie Lind Butterfield, of No. Jackson, Pa., Nov. 12, 1872.
  3. Mary L. Davison, m. Chas. Elmer Curtis, and had one child, Edith May Curtis.
  4. Annie E. Davison, m. Mr. Pope, and had two children.

Children.

  (1) William Pope, and (2) Gertrude Pope.

725c IV. JOSHUA WILLIAMS,[7] b. Dec. 31, 1825; m. 1st, SARAH GILL, in 1850; m. 2d, LOUISA R. TREAT, in 1859.
725d V. ELISHA W.,[7] b. Dec. 28, 1827; m. SARAH BAKER, Oct. 7, 1831.
725e VI. JAMES,[7] b. June 17, 1829; m. CORNELIA KING. No children.
  VII. EMMELINE,[7] b. Dec. 26, 1831; m. ISRAEL ROUNDS, in Dundaff, Pa., March 20, 1850.

Children.

  1. Maurice Olin Rounds, b. July 28, 1851; m. Hannah Adelia Capewell, Dec. 9, 1874.
  2. Orilla Rounds, b. March 21, 1853; d. April 7, 1853.
  3. Emma Sophronia Rounds, b. Jan. 15, 1855; m. A. E. Tiffany, Jan. 25, 1882. She d. July 16, 1884.
  4. Frank Wilmot Rounds, b. Dec. 2, 1862; d. Oct. 6, 1872.
  5. Henry H. Rounds, b. May 8, 1869; m. Lou H. Brown, Aug. 29, 1894.
  6. Wellington Rounds, b. June 5, 1872; m. Edna Taylor, Aug. 1, 1895.
  7. Rufus Williams Rounds, b. Aug. 23, 1877; d. June 19, 1881.

725f VIII. CHARLES,[7] b. June 12, 1834; m. ESTHER JANE ROGERS.
  IX. ABBA MARIA,[7] b. June 23, 1836; m. ALVIN CHANDLER.
  They both died, leaving one

Child.

  1. Oliver W. Chandler, who lives at Elkdale, Pa.

725g X. SILAS OWEN,[7] b. July 15, 1844; m. HELEN E. CARPENTER, b. Nov. 21, 1849.

342.

CYRIL[6] CHURCHILL (Joseph,[5] Benjamin,[4] Benjamin,[3] William,[2] John[1]). Born probably at or near what is now Mansfield, Mass., about 1797. He settled in Herrick, Pa., near his brothers, but afterwards removed to Susquehanna, Pa. Married, but we have not the name of his wife.

One Son.

I. William.[7] No record.

343.

ARTEMAS[6] CHURCHILL (Nelson,[5] Benjamin[4] Benjamin,[3] William,[2] John[1]). Born in Middleboro', Mass., July 5, 1786. Lived in Coleraine, Màss. He served three years in the War of 1812. He lived a while at New Salem, Mass., and at Readsboro', Vt., and died June 9, 1864, aged 78 years. Married, March 19, 1812, Ruth Maxim, in Coleraine, Mass., on "Catamount Hill." She died at Hàverhill, Minn., Sept. 5, 1883, aged 95 years.

Children born in Coleraine, except first and seventh.

I. Cynthia,[7] b. in Heath, July 30, 1813; m. Russell Stone, Sept. 17, 1832. She d. at Shelburne Falls, Aug. 1, 1867.
II. Lovina,[7] b. May 27, 1815; m. Francis Cressey, July 14, 1839.
III. Hervey Shaw,[7] b. Oct. 22, 1817; m. 1st, Mary Walker, of Williamstown, Nov. 5, 1844; d. Sept. 14, 1870; no children; m. 2d, Mrs. Lucretia Holbrook. May 27, 1871; no children.
IV. Emily,[7] b. May 21, 1820; m. Enos Clemens, in Heath, Mass., Nov. 30, 1838.
V. Laura,[7] b. March 21, 1822; m. Nathan Chaffin, Feb. 17, 1842.
VI. John Maxim,[7] b. March 7, 1824; m. 1st, Julia A. Thomas, in Heath, Mass., Nov. 27, 1848; m. 2d, Almeda Culver, of Halifax, Vt., 1878; no children.
VII. Saloma Ann,[7] b. in Readsboro', Vt., Sept. 3, 1826; m. Robert Clemens; no children.
VIII. Huldah Jane,[7] b. July 17, 1828; m. 1st, Joseph F. Vincent; m. 2d, Francis Henshaw.

344.

NELSON[6] CHURCHILL (Nelson,[5] Benjamin,[4] Benjamin,[3] William,[2] John[1]). Born in Middleboro', March 2, 1788. Lived in Coleraine, Mass., and died October, 1865. Married 1st, Nancy Lake; married 2d, Lucy Willis Maxim, of Charlemont, N.H.

Children born in Coleraine.

726   I. William,[7] m. Julia Mosher.
II. Electa.[7]
III. Erastus.[7]
IV. Elvira.[7]
V. Nancy.[7]

Children by Second Wife, born in Heath and Coleraine.

727   VI. CHANDLER,[7] b. July 23, 1826; m. LUCY FLAGG, in Charlemont, Nov. 8, 1849.

     VII. LOUISA,[7] b. in Coleraine; d. young.

     VIII. BETSEY,[7] b. in Heath; d. young.

345.

ALVIN[6] CHURCHILL (NELSON,[5] BENJAMIN,[4] BENJAMIN[3] WILLIAM,[2] JOHN[1]). Born in Middleboro', September 1799, lived in Coleraine and Charlemont; died Oct. 31, 1876, in Heath. Married, December, 1825, EMILY WILLIS, of Charlemont.

Children born in Coleraine and Charlemont.

     I. LOUISA,[7] b. Dec. 30, 1826; d. July 1, 1829.

     II. ROSINA,[7] b. May 30, 1828; d. July 9, 1829.

     III. HOLLIS,[7] b. Sept. 12, 1829; d. Nov. 9, 1836.

     IV. IZANA,[7] b. Oct. 26, 1832; m. JOSIAH AMES HATHAWAY, of Buckland. She d. Sept. 30, 1859.

728   V. HORACE,[7] b. Jan. 1, 1833; m. CYNTHIA J. CHAFFIN, of Heath, Mass., Sept. 18, 1862.

729   VI. FREDERICK,[7] b. Nov. 8, 1839, at Charlemont; m. JOSEPHINE WILLIS, of Charlemont, Dec. 30, 1870.

730   VII. ANSON IRVING,[7] b. Nov. 1, 1849; m. ANNA CILLEY, of Heath, Nov. 28, 1874.

346.

SHEPARD[6] CHURCHILL (JABEZ,[5] JABEZ,[4] JOSIAH,[3] WILLIAM,[2] JOHN[1]). Born in Hebron, Me., 1780. Lived in Buckfield, Me. Married, Oct. 6, 1808, POLLY DUDLEY.

Children born in Buckfield.

731   I. SAMUEL.[7] b. April 1, 1809; m. LOVINA PACKARD.

732   II. MARTIN,[7] b. April 12, 1811; m. BETSEY CHURCHILL.

     III. MARY ANN,[7] b. Oct. 8, 1817; m. LEBBEUS ROBBINS, in Buckfield, Sept. 22, 1835.

         They lived in Buckfield, and had one child. Mr. Robbins was a farmer.

Child.

     1. Emily Ellen Robbins, b. Sept. 6, 1838; m. John T. Berry, July 4, 1860.

733   IV. NATHAN,[7] b. 1819; m. HARRIET THOMAS.

     V. SARAH,[7] b. 1822; m. HANSON BROWN.

Children.

     1. Henry Brown. | 3. Helen Brown, m. Harrison Dudley.

     2. George Brown. | 4. Eliab Brown.

734   VI. JOSIAH,[7] b. Dec. 4, 1825; m. MARY HOLT.

     VII. SHEPARD,[7] b. May 15, 1830; unmarried.

     VIII. LUCY ANN,[7] b. 1834; m. AUGUSTUS WASHBURN.

         They lived in White Haven, Pa. He was employed in a mill.

Children born, first two in Buckfield.

     1. Edith Washburn.

     2. Shepard Washburn.

     3. —— Washburn, b. in White Haven, Pa.

347.

JOSIAH [6] CHURCHILL (JABEZ,[5] JABEZ,[4] JOSIAH,[3] WILLIAM,[2] JOHN [1]). Born in Hebron, Me., May 13, 1786. He settled in Wood stock, Me., about 1812, from Buckfield. He lived on the old road between Stephen Chase's and Asa Thurlow's. Mr. Churchill was a supporter of the Universalist Society at Bryant's Pond. Married, June 18, 1784, RACHEL CURTIS, of Woodstock, Me.

Children.

I. NANCY,[7] b. 1814; m. DEMERIC SWAN.

Child.

1. Nancy Swan, b. 1837; m. William Balch, of Minot.

735   II. EZRA,[7] m. LYDIA BRIGGS.
       III. NOAH,[7]   } twins. Noah d. in infancy.
       IV. HANNAH,[7] }
       V. LEVI,[7] m. LUCY (SWAN) BILLINGS, of Woodstock.
736   VI. DANIEL C.,[7] m. ELIZABETH D. CURTIS, of Woodstock.

348.

BELA [6] CHURCHILL (JABEZ,[5] JABEZ,[4] JOSIAH,[3] WILLIAM [2] JOHN [1]). Born in Hebron, Me. Lived in Buckfield, Me. Married SARAH DUDLEY.

Children born in Buckfield.

I. JANE,[7] b. Jan. 8, 1814; m. DANIEL DUDLEY.
II. MARIA,[7] b. May 9, 1817; m. DEMERIC SWAN (his second wife).

Children.

1. Sarah Swan, b. 1840; m. Ethiel Bumpus.
2. Catharine Swan, b. 1842; m. Charles Wight, of Oxford.
3. Ambrose Swan, b. 1845; m. Frances Taylor.
4. Lorinda Swan, b. 1847; m. Adelbert Jordan, of Buckfield.
5. Orphia Swan, b. 1849; m. Greenleaf Furness, of Buckfield.
6. Henry Swan, b. 1855.

III. ORPHIA,[7] b. 1818; m. JAMES N. D. CHURCHILL, son of Matthew, April 7, 1836. See No. 737.

349.

MATTHEW [6] CHURCHILL (JABEZ,[5] JABEZ,[4] JOSIAH,[3] WILLIAM,[2] JOHN [1]). Born in Hebron, March 20, 1791. Lived in North Raymond, Me. He was a farmer, a leading citizen of the town, a man of wide and good influence in the community, a justice of the peace. Married DOROTHY HALL, of Falmouth, born Feb. 11, 1788.

Children.

737   I. JAMES N. D.,[7] b. in Falmouth. Me., March 25, 1815; m. 1st, ORPHIA CHURCHILL, dau. of Bela, April 7, 1836. She d. April 14, 1854. He m. 2d, HANNAH WHITE.
       II. MARIA BENSON,[7] b. in Falmouth, Jan. 14, 1817; m. WILLIAM MORRILL, JR., of Raymond, Nov. 30, 1837.

Children born in Raymond.

1. Margaret E. Morrill, b. July 9, 1838; m. Stephen R. Small.
2. Mary A. Morrill, b. July 13, 1840; d. March 22, 1843.
3. Matthew C. Morrill, b. Nov. 5, 1842; m. 1st, Mary Brown, Jan. 12, 1867; m. 2d, Mary J. McConkey, Jan. 17, 1874.
   They lived in Gray, Me. Mr. Morrill was a soldier of the Civil War, Second Maine Cavalry. Has served in the Maine Legislature, two years in the House and four years in the Senate. The children of first wife were all born in Gray, Me. Hugh P., b. Dec. 3, 1868; m. Dora S. Brown, Feb. 8, 1893; d. June 7, 1896; (2) John, b. June 8, 1870; d. Aug. 7, 1872; (3) Mary B., b. Oct. 9, 1872; m. Isaiah Hawkes, March 19, 1894, and d. Nov. 26, 1895. The children of second wife were (4) Ada E., b. Feb. 27, 1876; d Jan. 27, 1880; (5) John W., b. July 7, 1878; m. Bessie W. Anderson, Sept. 20, 1899; (6) George A., b. June 7, 1880; (7) True C., b. July 23, 1881; d. Aug. 3, 1884; (8) True C., b. May 3, 1885; (9) Margaret E., b. May 29, 1895; d. Jan. 7, 1896.
4. Mary A. Morrill, b. Feb. 16, 1845; d. Aug. 10, 1848.
5. Asa P. Morrill, b. Jan. 26, 1847; m. 1st, Lydia A. Morrill; m. 2d, Eunice H. Powers.
6. William Morrill, b. Nov. 29, 1848; m. Alice Doughty.
7. Mary A. Morrill, b. Dec. 6, 1850; d. March 2, 1869.
8. Maria Morrill, b. July 8, 1852; m. Benjamin Haskell, of Gorham, May 12, 1877.
9. Anna F. Morrill, b. Feb. 15, 1855; m. Nelker D. Haskell, Aug. 17, 1873.

738   III. SILAS H.,[7] b. in Falmouth, Jan. 19, 1819; m. ARDELLA H. TOBIE, of New Gloucester, April 10, 1853.
739   IV. MATTHEW,[7] b. in Raymond, Jan. 11, 1821; m. SARAH ABIGAIL ADAMS, in Boston, Nov. 13, 1851.
         V. HANNAH N.,[7] b. in Raymond, Oct. 27, 1823; m. BELA LATHAM, of Raymond, Oct. 19, 1841. He was born Feb. 15, 1819

Children born in Raymond.

1. Lucy A. Latham, b. Aug. 9, 1841; d. March 16, 1842.
2. Bela E. Latham, b. March 16, 1845; d. in U.S. Army, Aug. 23, 1864.
3. Charles H. Latham, b. April 19, 1847; m. Adeline E. Hutchins, Aug. 11, 1870.
4. Pheba J. Latham, b. Aug. 13, 1850; m. James H. Leach, Sept. 24, 1868.

         VI. SARAH ANN,[7] b. in Raymond, April 25, 1825; m. WILLIAM SMALL, of Gray, March 26, 1845.
        VII. PERSIS M.,[7] b. in Raymond, Sept. 17, 1827; m. SAMUEL HODGDON, Dec. 27, 1850.

Children.

1. Lucy Hodgdon, d. in infancy.
2. Elizabeth Hodgdon, b. Sept. 30, 1856; m. Horace Strout.
3. Samuel Hodgdon, b. Sept. 9, 1859; m. Fannie McNally.
4. Ellen Hodgdon, b. Sept. 5, 1861; m. Hadley Hunt.
5. Mabel Hodgdon, b. May 23, 1863; m. Zenas Haines.
6. Alfred Lyman Hodgdon, b. June 6, 1865.

740 VIII. JOSEPH WARREN,[7] b. in Raymond, Aug. 9, 1829; m. MARY J. DOANE, of Durham, Me., July 8, 1849.
         IX. LOUISA S.,[7] b. in Raymond, June 17, 1831; m. LUTHER EDWARDS, of Casco.

350.

JABEZ[6] CHURCHILL (JABEZ,[5] JABEZ,[4] JOSIAH,[3] WILLIAM[2] JOHN[1]). Born in Hebron, Me.; m. TIRZAH DUDLEY.

Child.

741   I. OSGOOD B.[7] No record.

351.

JOSIAH[6] CHURCHILL (JOSIAH,[5] JABEZ,[4] JOSIAH[3] WILLIAM[2] JOHN[1]). The place and date of his birth have not been found. By a mistake of an informant, the name of his wife was given as his father's wife. We do not know the name of his father's wife. He settled in New Gloucester and married LYDIA ORR. Intentions published in New Gloucester, Me., Dec. 17, 1808.

Children born in New Gloucester and Raymond.

741a   I. JOSIAH,[7] b. May 22, 1809; m. KATHARINE HILTON.
      II. JERATHMEEL,[7] b. April 26, 1811; d. soon.
     III. JERATHMEEL,[7] b. May 4, 1813; d. soon.
      IV. JOSEPH FESSENDEN,[7] b. June 4, 1815.
       V. SALLY ROGERS,[7] b. July 31, 1817.
      VI. OLIVE,[7] b. March 19, 1819.
     VII. ASAPH,[7] b. Nov. 28, 1821; d. April 9, 1822.
    VIII. LYDIA R.,[7] b. Dec. 13, 1825; d. March 7, 1826.

352.

ASAPH[6] CHURCHILL (ASAPH,[5] JABEZ,[4] JOSIAH,[3] WILLIAM,[2] JOHN[1]). Born in Buckfield, July 31, 1803, and lived there. Died 1876. Married, 1st, in 1825, SALLY PETERSON. She died in 1840. Married 2d, LOVINA MOODY, in 1842.

Children of First Wife.

742   I. RICHARD,[7] b. Jan. 28, 1828; m. SARAH DANIELS, April 19, 1854.
      II. FRANCIS,[7] d. young.
     III. EDWIN,[7] d. young.
743   IV. GEORGE,[7] b. Sept. 4, 1837; m. ANNIE H. DWYER, Dec. 12, 1866.

Children of Second Wife.

744   V. ALLEN MOODY,[7] b. July 21, 1842; m. MARY S. NEWBEGIN, Oct. 4, 1866.
      VI. FABYAN,[7] b. March 17, 1844; killed in battle during the Civil War.
     VII. CELESTE,[7] b. Nov. 11, 1845; m. METCALF ANDREWS.
    VIII. ADELBERT,[7] b. September, 1847; killed in battle during the Civil War.
      IX. ELLA,[7] b. May 6, 1849; m. HUMPHREY HERRICK.
       X. EDGAR ENSIGN,[7] b. March, 1851; d. in infancy.
      XI. A SON, not named, b. April, 1852; d. in infancy.
     XII. HANNAH,[7] b. March 16, 1853; m. EDMUND L. BAILEY.
745   XIII. AUGUSTUS EUGENE.[7] b. April 28, 1856.
746   XIV. SHERMAN,[7] b. April 21, 1861.

353.

HIRAM [6] CHURCHILL (ASAPH,[5] JABEZ,[4] JOSIAH,[3] WILLIAM,[2] JOHN [1]). Born in Paris, Me., 1808. Died Jan. 5, 1882. Married 1st, MARGARET TARBOX. Married 2d, July 14, 1861, MELINDA S. ROCKWELL. She was born Jan. 13, 1842.

Children of First Wife.

    I. ELLEN,[7] d. unmarried.

Children of Second Wife.

747   II. GEORGE HIRAM,[7] b. Oct. 4, 1864, at Charlestown, Mass.
748 III. FREDERICK AUGUSTUS,[7] b. Dec. 21, 1867, at Charlestown, Mass.
    IV. NETTIE AUGUSTA,[7] b. April 3, 1870, at Charlestown, Mass.
749   V. EDWARD EVERETT,[7] b. Feb. 3, 1873, at Charlestown, Mass.

354.

NATHANIEL [6] CHURCHILL (ASAPH,[5] JABEZ,[4] JOSIAH [3] WILLIAM,[2] JOHN [1]). Born in Paris, Me., May 28, 1810. Lived at Emory's Mill, Me. He died May 18, 1866. Married, Nov. 6, 1843, ABBY W. STEVENS, of Shapleigh, Me., born Sept. 3, 1819.

Children.

    I. BELLE G.,[7] b. Aug. 23, 1845; m. GEORGE L. PRESCOTT, Nov. 5, 1870.
750   II. ROGER WILLIAMS,[7] b. Aug. 30, 1847; m. MAGGIE A. ARCHIBALD, Dec. 13, 1883.
   III. RUFUS S.,[7] b. Dec. 6, 1856; d. March 9. 1857.
751   IV. EDGAR W.,[7] b. Dec. 15, 1858; unmarried in March, 1889.

355.

ELBRIDGE [6] CHURCHILL (ASAPH,[5] JABEZ,[4] JOSIAH,[3] WILLIAM,[2] JOHN [1]). Born in Paris, Me., 1812. Married 1st, MARY SOPHIA PETERSON. She was born Sept. 27, 1824; married 2d, ABBIE COLE. She was born Sept. 22, 1824.

One Child by First Wife.

    I. NANCY,[7] d. aged 2 years 6 months.

Children by Second Wife.

    II. NANCY,[7] b. Nov. 8, 1844.
   III. MARY SOPHIA,[7] b. Sept. 22, 1846.
   IV. ASAPH,[7] d. in infancy.
    V. MARILDA,[7] d. in infancy.
   VI. ANNETTE,[7] d. in infancy.
  VII. AMERICUS,[7] d. at the age of 15 years.
752 VIII. FERGUSON,[7] b. April 1, 1859.
   IX. MARIA,[7] d. in childhood.
753   X. ALBERT,[7] b. Oct. 7, 1866.

356.

ALBERT [6] CHURCHILL (ASAPH,[5] JABEZ,[4] JOSIAH,[3] WILLIAM [2] JOHN [1]). Born in Paris, Me., May 21, 1816. Married, 1842, MERCY FREEMAN.

Children.

I. ANGERONE,[7] b. 1843; d. unmarried, 1882.
II. ELLEN A.,[7] b. Dec. 25, 1846; m. JASON McLEOD, July 8, 1871.

Children.

1. Malcolm McLeod, b. June 23, 1872; d. Feb. 4, 1885.
2. Albert Churchill McLeod, b. March 22, 1874.
3. Arthur James McLeod, b. Aug. 16. 1878.
4. Nettie Winfred McLeod, b. June 23, 1880.
5. Mabel Angie McLeod, b. March 12, 1883
6. Ethel McLeod, b. Aug. 5, 1888.

III. ALBERT F.,[7] b. 1850; d. March, 1852.
IV. WINNIE,[7] b. 1856.
V. ADA F.,[7] b. 1861.
754		VI. EDWIN P.,[7] b. 1865.

357.

DAVID RUSSELL[6] CHURCHILL (JOHN[5] ISRAEL[4] JOSIAH,[3] WILLIAM,[2] JOHN[1]). Born at Yonge, Ont., January, 1813. Married, at Yonge, JANE McVEIGH.

Children born at Yonge, Leeds County, C. W.

755		I. ARZA,[7] b. March 8, 1835; d. in Detroit.
756		II. MALCOLM,[7] m. HARRIET HAMBLEN, settled in North Dakota.
		III. ADELINE ADELLA,[7] m. WILLIAM BRADLEY.
757		IV. WILLIAM MURRAY,[7] m. LUCY SCOTT, at Elizabeth, Ont.
		V. LAVINIA,[7] no record.
		VI. ANN ELIZA,[7] m. WILLIAM H. MOULTON.
			They had a son, J. H. Moulton, who lived at Westport, Ont., April, 1901.
		VII. DIANTHA JANE,[7] died young.
		VIII. SARAH DIANTHA,[7] died young.
758		IX. BENJAMIN McVEIGH,[7] m. 1st, MARY WHALEN, in Westport, Ont.; m. 2d, (——) (——), in East Saginaw; m. 3d, (——) (——), in East Saginaw.

358.

JOHN[6] CHURCHILL (JOHN,[5] ISRAEL,[4] JOSIAH,[3] WILLIAM,[2] JOHN[1]). Born in Yonge, Ont., in 1816, and died in 1860. Married 1st, (——) (——); married 2d, in Oshawa, Whitly County, C.W., SOPHIA TOMPKINS, July 28, 1847.

Children by First Wife.

759		I. WILLIAM HENRY,[7] b. April 11, 1844; m. ALICE TITUS, who was b. Jan. 30, 1848.

Children by Second Wife.

		II. SARAH ANN,[7] b. in Oshawa, May 24, 1848; m. WILLIAM LAMB, of Oshawa, 1868.
			They had three children, names not received by us.
		III. MINERVA,[7] b. in Oshawa, Feb. 29, 1852; m., in 1870, CHARLES ROBINSON, of Highland Creek, Ont.
			They had five children, names not received by us.
760		IV. GEORGE FREDERICK,[7] b. Dec. 19, 1854; m. LIZZIE M. ADDY, of Chicago.
		V. MINNIE,[7] b. Aug. 17, 1857; unmarried, living, in 1901, in Chicago.

359.

JONAS[6] CHURCHILL (JOHN,[5] ISRAEL,[4] JOSIAH,[3] WILLIAM[2] JOHN[1]). Born at Yonge, Ont., 1827. He was a farmer and lived at Yonge. Married, in Westport, Can., April 18, 1859, ELIZABETH FORRESTER, b. April 18, 1833.

Children.

I. JANE,[7] b. Feb. 11, 1861; m. JOSEPH MOULTON, July 9, 1883.
They live at Farrensville, Ont., and have two children.

Child.

1. William John Moulton, b. April 11, 1885.

761   II. JOHN,[7] } b. June 12, 1863;
     III. ANN,[7] } b. June 12, 1863; m. CHRISTOPHER JOHNSTON, March 9, 1882.
     IV. JONES,[7]   } b. May 10, 1868; died at 3 months.
     V. ELIZABETH,[7] } b. May 10, 1868; m. (as his second wife) CHRISTO-PHER JOHNSTON.

361.

LEVIUS[6] CHURCHILL (CORNELIUS,[5] ISRAEL,[4] JOSIAH,[3] WILL-IAM,[2] JOHN[1]). Born Jan. 29, 1812, in Yonge, Ont. Married, Nov. 6, 1836, DELILA BETTS.

Children.

I. LYDIA,[7] b. December, 1837; m. DR. STANLEY SCOTT
II. CHARLOTTE,[7] m. WILLIAM PAXTON.
III. CAROLINE,[7] m. JARVIS CORNELL.
IV. DELILA,[7] m. (———) BOGART.

362.

CHARLES[6] CHURCHILL (CORNELIUS,[5] ISRAEL[4] JOSIAH,[3] WILLIAM,[2] JOHN[1]). Born Oct. 8, 1828, at Yonge, Ont. Married, May 10, 1848, JANE MAJOR.

Children.

     I. ADELIA.[7]
     II. HARRIET.[7]
762   III. LEVIUS.[7]
763   IV. FREDERICK.[7]
764   V. BENJAMIN.[7]

363.

WILLIAM TURNER[6] CHURCHILL (JACOB,[5] JOSEPH,[4] JOSIAH,[3] WILLIAM,[2] JOHN[1]). Born in Gloucester, R.I, June 21, 1790. Removed with his father's family to Williamstown, Vt., and lived there until 1838, when with his father he removed first to Kingsbury and then to Sterling, N.Y., where he kept a tavern. Died July 21, 1866, at Sterling. Married, 1811, ISABEL GILBERT.

Children born in Williamstown, Vt.

    I. ANNA,[7] b. 1813; d. 1822.

764   II. CURTIS M.,[7] b. 1815; m. 1st, JANE ANN GILCHRIST; m. 2d, MARY L. BUNNELL.

    III. CHARLES,[7] b. May 3, 1817; d. 1822.

765   IV. JOEL GILBERT,[7] b. July 26, 1819; m. MARGARET HEWETT, August 1842.

    V. LYDIA ANN,[7] b. 1821; m. ISAAC PARCEL.

One Child.

    1. William Turner Parcel, b. at Sterling, N.Y., 1844.

364.

ARTEMAS [6] CHURCHILL (JACOB,[5] JOSEPH,[4] JOSIAH,[3] WILLIAM,[2] JOHN[1]). Born in Williamstown, Vt., Aug. 4, 1797. He went to Kingsbury, N.Y., Sept. 8, 1820, and engaged to "carry on" the farm of Mr. Mattison of that town. He became engaged to the eldest of his employer's daughters and married, Dec. 31, 1820, ANNA MATTISON, who was born in Kingsbury, N.Y., Sept. 15, 1800. They lived in Kingsbury till near 1840, when they removed to Sterling, and afterwards lived at Scriba and Hannibal. He died at Cicero, Sept. 5, 1873. Mrs. Anna Mattison Churchill, in 1884, at the age of 84, wrote two clear and very full letters about her husband's father's family and her own, these letters being the basis of most of what is known about the origin and connections of the family. She was still living in Fairhaven, N.Y., with her daughter, Mrs. Pettitt on July 17, 1887. She died September, 1892.

Children born, the first six in Kingsbury, the rest in Sterling.

766   I. CARMI D.,[7] b. Dec. 7, 1821; m. SILDA KIMBALL, Feb. 10, 1850.

767   II. CHARLES R.,[7] b. Nov. 24, 1824; m. MARY J. ASSELTINE, May 10, 1854.

    III. SARAH E.,[7] b. Sept. 30, 1826; m. DORASTUS PETTITT, Sept. 30, 1854, in Sterling.
They lived in Sterling and Fairhaven, N.Y. He is a farmer.

768   IV. MATTISON A.,[7] b. Dec. 20, 1830; d. unmarried July 4, 1865.

769   V. JULIUS B.,[7] b. March 5, 1832; m. ELIZA KNIGHT, June 18, 1859, in Scriba, N.Y.

    VI. MARY J.,[7] b. Oct. 8, 1834; m. EMERY MOULTON, June 6, 1860, in New Haven.
They lived in Cicero, Onondaga County, N.Y. He is a farmer.

770   VII. WILLIAM T.,[7] b. April 21, 1841; m. 1st, SARAH LONG, in Scriba, March 27, 1864; m. 2d, ELLEN BENSON.
He served in the Civil War of 1861-1865. Afterwards a farmer in Scriba and Lansing.

    VIII. MARTHA A.,[7] b. Dec. 21, 1843; m. COL. L. V. S. MATTISON, March 26, 1864. She d. June 30, 1865.

365.

PALMER [6] CHURCHILL (JACOB,[5] JOSEPH,[4] JOSIAH,[3] WILLIAM,[2] JOHN[1]). Born in Williamstown, Vt., 1805, and probably lived there. He died in Williamstown, Vt. Married SUSAN HENRY.

Child.

771   I. HENRY PALMER,[7] b. Aug. 11, 1830; m. 1st, MARIAH BROWN, June, 1853; m. 2d, CLARISSA MEADE, Dec. 18, 1879.

366.

OTIS[6] CHURCHILL (JACOB,[5] JOSEPH,[4] JOSIAH,[3] WILLIAM,[2] JOHN[1]). Born in Williamstown, Vt., Oct. 10, 1808. Lived at Amsterdam, N.Y. Married, Sept. 18, 1829, MARIAH L. VAUGHN.

Children born in Amsterdam, N. Y.

    I. LODUSKY,[7] b. June 4, 1834; m. AUGUSTUS V. WILDER, Sept. 15, 1857.

772   II. FRANK ALANSON,[7] b. Aug. 9, 1838; m. MARY L. SHAFFER, Oct. 4, 1864.

367.

JACOB[6] CHURCHILL (JACOB,[5] JOSEPH,[4] JOSIAH,[3] WILLIAM,[2] JOHN[1]). Born near Providence, R.I., July 13, 1810. Moved with his father's family to Vermont at the age of 4 years. He was a house-joiner. Lived first at Kingsbury and Sterling, N.Y., but in 1833 removed to Fort Edward. Married, in 1830, CLARISSA VAUGHN.

Two Children, the Son born at Kingsbury, the Daughter at Fort Edward, N. Y.

773   I. CHARLES PALMER,[7] b. July 26, 1832; m. EMELINE BEEBE, July 3, 1854.

    II. ADELIA,[7] b. June 11, 1837; m. DANIEL WHITFORD, of Saratoga, N.Y., 1857.
They lived at Saratoga. She died in May, 1885. They had six children, names not obtained.

368.

SYLVESTER[6] CHURCHILL (BENJAMIN,[5] JOSEPH,[4] JOSIAH,[3] WILLIAM,[2] JOHN[1]). Born at Putney, Vt., March 6, 1801. Re moved to Waukesha and thence to Manston, Wis., where he died about 1862. He was a farmer. Married FANNY DAVENPORT.

Child.

    I. FANNY,[7] m. HARRY SMITH.

Child.

    1. Christopher Smith, m. Eliza Howard. One son, Benj. Smith, lives at Salesville, Wis.

369.

ERASTUS[6] CHURCHILL (BENJAMIN,[5] JOSEPH,[4] JOSIAH,[3] WILLIAM,[2] JOHN[1]). Born at Putney or Westminster, Vt., Dec. 13, 1809. Removed to New York State, and lived at Manlius, N.Y.

Removed to Waukesha, Wis. He has been a farmer. He was living in March, 1900, with his daughters, Mary and Emily, at Eagle, Wis. Married, at Manlius, N.Y., ALMIRA CHURCHILL, daughter of Joseph.

Children.

774a   I. CHARLES HAMILTON,[7] b. at Manlius, N.Y.; m. ELIZABETH REG-
          ULAR.
      II. AUSTIN,[7] b. at Manlius, N.Y., and d. May 15, 1863.
774b   III. HIRAM DEFORREST,[7] b. at Manlius, N.Y.; m. MARY ANN HOWARD,
          1861.
774c   IV. WILLIAM NELSON.[7] b. at Manlius, N.Y.; m. ELIZABETH S. TAYLOR,
          at Waukesha. May 14, 1862.
      V. MARY,[7] b. at Waukesha; m. MARCELLIUS WHITE, March 26, 1862.
          Mr. White died April 8, 1885.

One Child.

     1. Ida Mae White, b. June 10, 1864; m. George Weston, Feb. 4,
        1883. (Divorced.) One child, Florence White.

   VI. IRENE SOPHRONIA,[7] d. March 25, 1878.
  VII. EMILY AMANDA,[7] m. SILAS STICKLES, 1877.

Children.

     1. Maude Stickles, b. September, 1879.
     2. Roland Stickles, b. Sept 17, 1880.
     3. Harry Stickles, b. Oct. 15, 1883.
     4. Fred Stickles.

370.

CHARLES PERRY[6] CHURCHILL (BENJAMIN,[5] JOSEPH,[4] JOSIAH,[3] WILLIAM,[2] JOHN[1]). Born March 29, 1812, at Putney, or Westminster, Vt. Married 1st, March 20, 1834, at Manlius, N.Y., AMELIA ANN DAVENPORT. She was born Aug. 1, 1815, and died March 3, 1852; married 2d, Sept. 12, 1856, ELIZABETH VAN SHEICK.

Children.

774d   I. CHARLES HAWLEY,[7] b. Feb. 20, 1835; m. SARAH VAN SHEICK,
          March 1, 1857.
     II. FRANCIS HENRY.[7] b. Jan. 26, 1837; d. in the Union Army, Sept. 11,
          1863; unmarried.
   III. ALMERON PERRY,[7] b. July 20, 1839; unmarried.
774e   IV. JOHN IRA,[7] b. March 18, 1842; m. (———) McVICCAR.
     V. FANNY,[7] b. July 20, 1845; d. Oct. 10, 1854.
   VI. AMELIA ANN,[7] b. Aug. 11, 1848; m. CHARLES P. PEABODY, April
          7, 1866. Said to have had a family of seven children, names not
          received.

Children of Second Wife.

774f   VII. ALPHONZO THEODORE,[7] b. March 13, 1858.
  VIII. MARY ALICE,[7] b. Jan. 29, 1860; m. SEYMORE E. COURTWRIGHT,
          Feb. 21, 1880.
   IX. FRANK H.,[7] b. July 18, 1864; d. Sept. 4, 1873.
    X. ELLA EVELYN,[7] b. March 8, 1866.

371.

JAMES [6] CHURCHILL (BENJAMIN,[5] JOSEPH,[4] JOSIAH [3] WILL-
IAM,[2] JOHN [1]). Born at Putney, Vt. We have been able to get very
little information about him, and this from Miss Alice Churchill, of
Waukesha, Wis., a grand-niece. He was a stage driver, and later
a railroad man. He was twice married ; the first wife's name was
CHARLOTTE, to whom no children were born ; but by the second wife,
whose name is not known to us, he had two children.

Children.

I. PAMELIA,[7] who married and lived in California.
II. GEORGE,[7] of whom nothing is known.

372.

CALVIN W.[6] CHURCHILL (ALVA,[5] JACOB,[4] JOSIAH,[3] WILL-
IAM,[2] JOHN [1]). Born July 23, 1809, in Stockbridge, Mass. Married
1st, Nov. 8, 1832, LUNA HOLCOMB ; she died March 23, 1876 ; married 2d, Oct. 8, 1876, MEHITABLE GEE.

Children.

I. CHILD not named, died soon.
II. OLNEY.[7] b. May 18, 1836 ; unmarried.
   He practised dentistry and was interested in the rubber type
   business in Philadelphia. Died of consumption, July 1, 1874.
III. LUTILDA,[7] b. Nov. 7, 1839 ; m. HOLLIS HOLCOMB, October, 1866.

Children.

1. Charles S. Holcomb, b. May 24, 1868 ; m. Sadie Mott, July 3,
   1889.
2. Dean Holcomb, b. Oct. 9, 1877.
3. Lura M. Holcomb, b. June 19, 1880.

IV. MARTHA,[7] b. April 11, 1849 ; m. DUDLEY S. SHERMAN, Aug. 30,
   1888.
   They lived in Leroy, Penn.

373.

LAFAYETTE [6] CHURCHILL (ALVA [5] JACOB [4] JOSIAH,[3] WILL-
IAM,[2] JOHN [1]). Born in Stockbridge, June 22, 1828. Removed
with his father to Pennsylvania. Married, Dec. 31, 1847, SUSANNA
VROOMAN, b. Feb. 26, 1830.

Children.

I. SARAH MELLISSA,[7] b. Dec. 26, 1848 ; m. SIDNEY W. CLARK, July
   4, 1865.

Children.

1. Mina A. Clark, b. April 28, 1866 ; m. Kimberly Wilcox, June
   19, 1892.
2. Julia Clark, b. March 21, 1868 ; d. June 31, 1871.
3. Rosa Bell Clark, b. April 21, 1870 ; d. Aug. 25, 1879.

    4. Ruby May Clark, b. Jan. 4, 1874; d. Aug. 19, 1879.
    5. Jennie Clark, b. April 16, 1876; d. Aug. 27, 1879.
    6. Sadie Clark, b. May 8–15, 1878; d. Aug. 25, 1879.
    7. Encil Ernest Clark, b. May 6, 1881; m. Tyra Holcomb, Dec. 26, 1900.

  II. POLLY DIANA,[7] b. Feb. 19, 1850.
  III. CALVIN MALLORY,[7] b. May 16, 1852.
  IV. MARAH MINA,[7] b. Oct. 22, 1854.
  V. MELBOURNE,[7] b. Sept. 12, 1856; m. BRIDGET CUSTY, Feb. 25, 1879.
  VI. DORA ANN,[7] b. Sept. 9, 1863.
  VII. ELMER,[7] b. July 31, 1868; m., April 15, 1890, IGNATIA STORRS, who was b. Feb. 26, 1872.

374.

ROSWELL PALMER [6] CHURCHILL (SEYMORE,[5] JACOB,[4] JOSIAH,[3] WILLIAM,[2] JOHN [1]). Born in Stockbridge, Mass., Sept. 24, 1818. Married MARIA KNAPP, who was born Oct. 29, 1830.

Children.

  I. CHARLES SEYMORE,[7] b. July 16, 1850; m. MRS. ALICE (ROTE) AYER; no issue.
  II. ALIDA JANE,[7] b. Nov. 14, 1852; d. Aug. 8, 1854.
774 III. JOHN PITT,[7] b. Dec. 13, 1858; m. ELIZABETH PHREUN.
  IV. CLARK,[7] b. Feb. 9, 1862; d. at 9 days of age.

375.

CHARLES FREDERICK [6] CHURCHILL (JACOB,[5] JACOB,[4] JOSIAH,[3] WILLIAM,[2] JOHN [1]). Born in Delhi, N.Y., May 20, 1837, and lived there in 1890 when we received letters from him. Married, June 14, 1870, HARRIET FRANCES ARMSTRONG, b. in Walton, April 25, 1844.

Children.

  I. NELLIE,[7] b. July 29, 1871; d. Jan. 3, 1873.
  II. LOUISE,[7] b. July 25, 1879.
775 III. WILLIAM WHEELER,[7] b. July 3, 1882.

376.

REV. EBENEZER [6] CHURCHILL (GEORGE,[5] EBENEZER,[4] JOHN,[3] JOHN,[2] JOHN [1]). Born at Plymouth, May 19, 1787. He removed to Ohio, where he became a Presbyterian minister. Married ELIZABETH PEABODY. Died in Liverpool, Ohio, 1853.

Children born in Middletown, Ohio.

  I. ELIZABETH A.,[7] b. Feb. 10, 1825; m. WILLIAM MARLNEE, July 6, 1843.

Children.

  1. Andrew Marlnee, b. May 3, 1844; m. (———) Coffee.
  2. Ebenezer Marlnee, b. April 24, 1846.
  3. J. B. Marlnee, b. April 15, 1848; m. Mary E. Galbraith.
  4. George Marlnee, b. May 21, 1852; d. unmarried.
  5. Sarah J. Marlnee, b. March 12, 1854; m. S. A. McLane.
  6. Mary E. Marlnee, b. September, 1856; m. (———) Ford, of Iowa.

II. SARAH B.,[7] b. Sept. 5, 1827; m. GEORGE BURSON, March 8, 1847. He was born July 1, 1825.   They lived in Middletown, Ohio.

Children born in Middletown.

1. Elizabeth Ann Burson, b. Sept. 17, 1849.
2. Benjamin P. Burson, b. Jan. 18, 1852; m. Emma J. Huston.
3. Phebe Burson, b. Nov. 8, 1856; m. Alvin C. Huston.
4. Nancy Emma Burson, b. March 1, 1861; m. Thomas F. Shaffer.
5. George Churchill Burson, b. July 24, 1867.

776   III. GEORGE W.,[7] b. June 27, 1830; m. ELIZABETH GEORGE, Sept. 28, 1850.

777   IV. BENJAMIN PEABODY,[7] b. Aug. 4, 1832; m. EVELINE E. BRADFIELD, of E. Fairfield, Ohio, 1854.

SEVENTH GENERATION.

377.

WILLIAM[7] CHURCHILL (ASAHEL,[6] SAMUEL,[5] SAMUEL,[4] JOHN,[3] JOSEPH,[2] JOHN[1]). Born at Apalachin, N.Y., April, 1795. Lived in Caroline, N.Y., and died in Bingham, Pa., April 9, 1850. The account of this line was compiled for us by Mrs. Annie J., wife of Frank Churchill Scoville, of Greenwich, N.Y. WILLIAM[7] married in Berkshire, N.Y., August, 1818, HANNAH FREELAND, who was born Aug. 12, 1795, and died at Spring Mills, N.Y., Oct. 2, 1875.

Children born at Caroline, N.Y.

I. ELIZA LAVINA,[8] b. May 16, 1819; m. WILLIAM COBB, at Bingham, Pa., Nov. 20, 1838.
They lived for fifty-seven years at Spring Mills, N.Y. She died Nov. 9, 1895.

Children.

1. Emmaline Cobb, b. Nov. 27, 1839; m. 1st, Ebenezer L. Nelson, Oct. 28, 1858; m. 2d, Delancey Freeborn, June 30, 1860.
They lived at Spring Mills and had four children; viz., Gertrude, Angelo, Fairman, and Fawn W.
2. Angeline Cobb, b. March 22, 1841; m. Eugene B. Fullar, June 1, 1874.
They live at Wellsville, N.Y., and have one child, Bayard C., b. Aug. 26, 1875.
3. Theodore Cobb, b. Feb. 8, 1843; m. Margaret P. Metzger, July 13, 1864.
They live at Spring Mills and have six children; viz. (1) William M.; (2) Howard; (3) Arling; (4) Mary A.; (5) Churchill; (6) Claire.
4. William Cobb, Jr., b. Aug. 23, 1848; m. Delia Lawrence, Aug. 9, 1870.
They live in Spring Mills and have five children: (1) Fordyce A.; (2) Eunice E.; (3) Lera Lawrence; (4) Herbert L.; (5) Camilla Angie.

II. HARRIET AMANDA,[8] b. Oct. 8, 1821; m. LUMAN H. SCOVILLE, Oct. 22, 1845 in Bingham, Pa., and had

Children.

1. Fayette L. Scoville, b. in Harrison, Pa., Oct. 31, 1846; m. Alice O. Johnson in Knoxville, Pa., Oct. 31, 1875. They live in Wellsville, N.Y., and have two children: (1) Lewis Luman; (2) Harriet Caroline.
2. Frank Churchill Scoville, b. in Bingham, Pa., June 4, 1850; m. Annie Judson Dobbins, of Wellsville, N.Y., July 18, 1878. No children.

III. THEODORE,[8] b. in Carolina, N.Y., June 10, 1826; d. in Bingham, Pa., Feb. 24, 1838.
IV. DORCAS MARIA,[8] b. March 23, 1829; m., in Bingham, Pa., WALTER LEONARD, Dec. 25, 1853.
They lived in Spring Mills and had (1) Fred Churchill Leonard, b. Feb. 16, 1856; m. Estella G. Cook, and had Louise, Shirley, Walter C., and Marjorie. (2) Arthur George Leonard, b. June 26, 1859; d. April 14, 1872. (3) Luman W. Leonard, b. Jan. 22, 1866; m. Mary Wood Horton, and had Ruth Leonard, b. Jan. 26, 1890. (4) Myra Leonard, b. Sept. 25, 1872; m. Willet Lyon Ward, Nov. 17, 1897.

778 V GEORGE WILLIAM,[8] b. Feb. 24, 1834; m. 1st, MARY A. YOUNGMAN, of Bingham, Pa., 1854; m. 2d, SUSAN CHEESBRO, of Huntington, Ind., Dec. 30, 1860.

Children.

1. Charles D., b. May 7, 1862, who lived (1899) at East View, New Mexico.
We have not been able to get any further account of him except that in 1899 he lived at East View, New Mexico. If without issue, he is the only living descendant of William[7] Churchill who bears the Churchill name.
2. Fred H., b. Feb. 27, 1867; d. Aug. 6, 1889.

377a.

SAMUEL[7] CHURCHILL (ASAHEL,[6] SAMUEL,[5] SAMUEL,[4] JOHN,[3] JOSEPH,[2] JOHN[1]). Born at Apalachin, N.Y. Very little has been learned of his subsequent history. Mr. Frank Churchill Scoville, of Greenwich, N.Y., a grand-nephew, says that in 1862, as a small boy, he visited the family then living at Antioch, Ind. He was then living with his second wife. We have no dates at all and our only information comes from Mr. Scoville. Mr. Churchill is said to have died at Huntington, Ind. Married 1st, MISS ABERNATH, and married 2d, MRS. SNOWDON.

Children, of which wife not known, nor order of birth.
NELSON.[8]
AMANDA.[8]
OLIVE.[8]
FRANK.[8]

378.

DANIEL[7] CHURCHILL (ASAHEL[6] SAMUEL,[5] SAMUEL,[4] JOHN,[3] JOSEPH,[2] JOHN[1]). Born in Apalachin, N.Y., July 31, 1800. Went, when 9 years old, with his father's family to the new Western home at Brookville, Ind. He died in 1858. Married 1st, 1825, NANCY STREET. Married 2d, 1851, JULIA STREET.

Children, all of First Wife.
779 I. JAMES MORTIMER,[8] b. Jan. 11, 1827; m. ELIZABETH MCKAY, Dec. 31, 1856.
780 II. WILLIAM,[8] b. Aug. 4, 1828; m. ANNA R. BUSH, Oct. 29, 1872. Lives at Rushville, Ind. A lumber dealer.

Children.

1. Jane B.. b. July 5, 1875; m. Ned Abercrombie, Dec. 28, 1899.
2. Kate Wilma, b. April 25, 1881.

III. JEFFERSON,[8] b. March 13, 1830; m. MATILDA REEVES.

Children.

1. Lena M., b. May 21, 1857; d. aged 4 years.
2. Ernest M., b. Oct. 1, 1860; d. at 2 years 6 months.
3. Anna Bruce, b. June 20, 1865; died young.
4. Earl Reeves, b. Aug. 27, 1874.

IV. SARAH ANN,[8] b. March 14, 1832; m. JOHN S. LEWIS.
781   V. JOHN WESLEY,[8] b. May 23, 1834; m. ANNIE MINTNER.
782   VI. GEORGE TEYLOR,[8] b. Oct. 28, 1837; m. ANNA GUNIT, October, 1868.
VII. MARY ELIZABETH,[8] b. Sept. 10, 1840; d. young.
VIII. MALINDA,[8] b. July 19, 1842; d. young.
783   IX. MILTON,[8] b. Nov. 11, 1843; m. CLARA MATILDA ALESWORTH, Aug. 8, 1867.
        Lived in Toledo, Ohio.

379.

LYMAN [7] CHURCHILL (SAMUEL,[6] SAMUEL,[5] SAMUEL,[4] JOHN [3] JOSEPH,[2] JOHN [1]). Born Sept. 17, 1799. Place of birth and residence not obtained. Married, Sept. 20, 1826, CHARLOTTE DEWEY.

Children.

I. HELEN DEWEY.[8]
784   II. FREDERICK.[8] No further record.
III. CHESTER,[8] d. in infancy.
785   IV. HERBERT,[8] m. CAROLINE J. SCRIBNER.
V. HENRY,[8] d. in infancy.
VI. CATHARINE A.,[8] m. ALONZO P. STRONG.

380.

HENRY [7] CHURCHILL (SAMUEL,[6] SAMUEL [5] SAMUEL,[4] JOHN,[3] JOSEPH,[2] JOHN [1]). Born July 7, 1812. Lived in Rochester, N.Y. He was still living in Rochester, Aug. 15, 1887, but no answers were received to applications. These meagre notes were from a personal interview of Mr. N. W. Churchill, at Rochester, and a letter from Edward S., of Napa City, Cal. Married, May 20, 1835, SARAH DEWEY, who was born April 7, 1814.

Children.

786   I. ARTHUR,[8] b. March 1, 1836.
II. FRANCES V.,[8] b. Aug. 7 1837; m. JOHN HUMPHREY.
787   III. HENRY L.,[8] b. Sept. 29, 1839.
788   IV. EDWARD S.,[8] b. April 6, 1842; m. at Rochester, N.Y., April 28, 1868, MARY CORNELIA WILDER, who was born in Memphis, Tenn., Nov. 3, 1844, dau. of Daniel and Eliza (Goodman) Wilder. Mr. Churchill is a graduate of the University of Rochester, N.Y., in 1862. He settled in California in 1875, and since that time has been in the banking business; member of the firm of James H. Goodman & Co., Napa City, Cal. They lived at Napa City, Cal., in 1887.

Children born at Rochester, N.Y.

1. Edward Wilder, b. July 1, 1870.
2. Mary Louise, b. Sept. 3, 1872.

V. MARY,[8] b. April 6, 1842; d. Oct. 9, 1867.

381.

WILLIAM CURTIS[7] CHURCHILL (DANIEL,[6] SAMUEL,[5] SAMUEL,[4] JOHN,[3] JOSEPH,[2] JOHN[1]). Born in Stockbridge, July 6 1809. Lived there until about 1852, when he removed to Utica, N.Y. Married 1st, ELIZA S. ARIEL, who was born 1813; d. 1837 · married 2d, July 23, 1839, JANE WALDO LEONARD, daughter of Solomon, born Nov. 1, 1813; married 3d, December, 1851, CAROLINE SHERRILL, at New Hartfort, N.Y. Caroline died May 10, 1890.

Children of First Wife.

I. HORACE,[8] b. May, 1833; d. Aug. 5, 1833.
II. ISABEL,[8] b. March, 1835; d. Aug. 25, 1835.

Children of Second Wife.

III. ELIZA,[8] b. July 16, 1840.
IV. WILLIAM,[8] born in the spring of 1851; died in infancy.

Children of Third Wife, born in Utica, N.Y.

V. FRANCES CAROLINE,[8] b. July 5, 1854; m. H. B. RIGGS, 1871.
789   VI. WILLIAM HUNTINGTON,[8] b. March 10, 1855.
VII. CORNELIA SHERRILL,[8] b. March 4, 1858; m. GEORGE WOLLCOTT HUBBELL, of Newark, N.J.. Jan. 26, 1876.
VIII. JAMES SHERRILL,[8] b. Aug. 20, 1861; unmarried.
IX. A CHILD, died in infancy.
X. GRACE HUNTINGTON,[8] b. Sept. 25, 1863; m. HENRY LORILLARD CAMMANN, June 5, 1898. No children

382.

SAMUEL[7] CHURCHILL (DANIEL,[6] SAMUEL,[5] SAMUEL,[4] JOHN,[3] JOSEPH,[2] JOHN[1]). Born 1811. Married, Oct. 4, 1835, MARY TAYLOR, of Lee, Mass.

Children.

790   I. CHARLES TAYLOR,[8] b. August, 1845; m. MINNIE BUTLER, of New York, 1869.
791   II. EVERETT,[8] b. December, 1852; m. AGNES S. GOODNOW, 1883.

383.

BARNABAS[7] CHURCHILL (JOB,[6] BARNABAS,[5] BARNABAS,[4] BARNABAS,[3] JOSEPH,[2] JOHN[1]). Born at Plymouth, Sept. 30, 1809, and lived there. Married, March 10, 1833, ELIZA EDDY, the daughter of John.

Children.

I. BARNABAS LOTHROP,[8] b. April 1, 1834; drowned at the age of 17 years.
II. ROBERT ROBERTS,[8] b. Jan. 1, 1836; d. aged 1 year 5 months.
III. ELIZABETH EDDY,[8] b. Oct. 16, 1837; m. LOTHROP KIMBALL.

Children.

1. Mary Elizabeth Kimball, b. 1863.
2. Carrie Gibson Kimball, b. 1865.
3. Barnabas Lothrop Kimball, b. 1868.
4. Emma Frances Kimball, b. 1870.

793   IV. ROBERT BRUCE,[8] b. June 8, 1841.
V. FRANCES MARION,[8] b. Nov. 5, 1844; d. at the age of 2 years.
VI. EMMA FRANCES,[8] b. February, 1846; m. HENRY L. LARNED, of Buffalo, N.Y.
VII. MARY LOUISE,[8] b. Aug. 1, 1847; m. CHARLES COBB.
VIII. ANNIE,[8] b. May 6, 1849; m. ARTHUR E. LEWIS.

384.

SYLVANUS[7] CHURCHILL (JOB,[6] BARNABAS,[5] BARNABAS,[4] BARNABAS,[3] JOSEPH,[2] JOHN[1]). Born in Plymouth, Feb. 23, 1815, and lived there. Married, Oct. 10, 1837, LUCRETIA ANN BACON, daughter of Captain George and Hannah.

Children born in Plymouth.

I. LUCRETIA L.,[9] b. July 27, 1839; m. ISAAC W. JACKSON, Dec. 25, 1864.
794   II. GEORGE BACON,[8] b. July 28, 1841; m. WIDOW MARY RAMSAY, of Nevada, March 12, 1871.
III. JOB,[8] b. Dec. 10, 1843; unmarried.
IV. TIMOTHY G.,[8] b. Aug. 6, 1846; d. May 8, 1848.
V. ALICE G.,[8] b. Oct. 17, 1848; d. April 26, 1866, at Manchester, N.H.
VI. JENNIE E.,[8] b. Dec. 23, 1851; d. at Columbiana, Feb. 12, 1864.
VII. REBECCA J.,[8] b. Aug. 27, 1856; m. LUCIUS P. NELSON, of Arlington, Feb. 10, 1881.

385.

CORNELIUS BRADFORD[7] CHURCHILL (JOB,[6] BARNABAS,[5] BARNABAS,[4] BARNABAS,[3] JOSEPH,[2] JOHN[1]). Born in Plymouth March 26, 1824. In 1852 removed from Plymouth to the South, and settled in Natchez, Miss. In 1873 moved to New Orleans, La., where he died Nov. 6, 1879. He was in the foundry business, a noted mechanic, and invented the cotton-tie and a cotton-press. Married 1st, Nov. 15, 1846, SARAH F. CUSHING, daughter of Ezra. She died in Natchez, in 1853. Married 2d, 1856, CARRIE R. TAYLOR, of Natchez, La., Dec. 6, 1856.

Child by First Wife.

I. SARAH C.,[8] b. Oct. 10, 1852.

Children by Second Wife.

795   II. JOHN HARRY,[8] b. May 31, 1858.
796   III. ERNEST T.,[8] b. Aug. 27, 1860; m. MRS. WATKINS, of Brooklyn, N.Y.

Children.

1. Cornelius Ward Churchill, b. 1887.
2. Catherine C. Churchill, b. 1889.
3. Effie Hepsibah Churchill, b. 1894.

797 IV. WILLIAM HOLMES,[8] b. Oct. 12, 1863; m. KATHERINE HIGGINBOTHAM, of New Orleans.

Child.

1. Harold Earle Churchill, d. in infancy.

798 V. CORNELIUS BRADFORD, JR.,[8] b. Sept. 1, 1866. ⎤ In 1899 these four
799 VI. ALBERT CUMMINGS,[8] b. Jan. 19, 1873. ⎟ were still unmar-
800 VII. FRANCIS GORTON,[8] b. Feb. 12, 1876. ⎟ ried and lived with
  VIII. CARRIE ELIZABETH,[8] b. Nov. 12, 1878. ⎦ the mother in N.O

386.

JOSEPH[7] CHURCHILL (ICHABOD,[6] ICHABOD,[5] JOSEPH,[4] BARNABAS,[3] JOSEPH,[2] JOHN[1]). Born in Bridgewater, Vt., Aug. 26, 1811. Lived in Stowe, Vt. Married, in Stowe, Feb. 8, 1833, ELIZA ANN RUSSELL, who was born Oct. 8, 1813.

Children.

  I. MARY JANE,[8] b. Oct. 10, 1839; m. RODNEY CORSE, Nov. 8, 1857
801 II. LYMAN ALONZO,[8] b. Nov. 15, 1841; m. FRANCES MARSHALL, July 16, 1865.
  III. ABIGAIL,[8] d. in infancy.

387.

STILLMAN[7] CHURCHILL (NOAH,[6] ICHABOD,[5] JOSEPH,[4] BARNABAS,[3] JOSEPH,[2] JOHN[1]). Born in Stowe, Vt., Sept. 13, 1812. Worked on the farm and attended the district school until eighteen years of age, when he went to Montpelier, and attended the academy, and taught school until, at the age of twenty-three, he entered upon the study of the law in the office of Lucius B. Peck, afterward U.S. Senator from Vermont. Young Churchill was admitted to the bar at twenty-six and two years later was elected Clerk of Courts in Montpelier, which office he held for six years. He resigned the office and purchased the home-farm and lived there until 1850, when he moved to Stowe village and built a hotel for summer tourists, and was largely instrumental in building a road to the top of Mount Mansfield, where he placed a tent for public use of travellers, and was the first to advertise Stowe as a summer resort. Like many pioneers of such enterprises he did not receive the coöperation needed to assure prosperity, and later on others profited by his sacrifices and efforts. He removed to Montpelier in 1857, and to the West in 1862, and settled first in Woodford County, Ill., and later in Bloomington, Ill. He was engaged in Fire and Life Insurance, until 1875, when he removed his office to Chicago and there continued until 1890, when he moved to Allerton, Iowa, where he died Nov. 6, 1892. (The account of this family has been collected by Mrs. Effie J. (Churchill) Clarke, of Allerton, Iowa.) Married, at Montpelier, Vt., May 20, 1841, ROXY ANN MARSH, daughter of Perry and Fannie (Wheelock) Marsh.

Children.

I. ISABEL,[8] b. at Montpelier, Vt., Nov. 19, 1842; d. at Calais, Vt., Sept. 29, 1844.

II. RICHARD HENRY,[8] b. at Stowe, Vt., Sept. 2, 1845; d. at Stowe, Aug. 23, 1847.

III. ALICE CARY,[8] b. at Stowe, Vt., July 29, 1847; m. ALPHEUS H. PIKE, at Bloomington, Ill., Oct. 27, 1870, and died in Chicago Ill., April 1, 1889, without children.

IV. EFFIE JANE,[8] b. Jan. 29, 1850; m. CHARLES W. CLARK, of Bloomington, Ill., April 20, 1871. At six years she removed with her parents to Montpelier, where she attended school and passed her girlhood until twelve years, when she removed with her parents to Woodford County, Ill. She entered the State Normal University at Bloomington, Ill., at seventeen years of age, taught school for a few years before her marriage with Mr. Clark, who was born at East Concord, N.Y., Aug. 27, 1843, son of David and Eunice (Beach) Clark. He was a mechanic. They have lived at Bloomington and Chicago, Ill., and Allerton, Iowa.

Children.

1. Ellery Channing Clark, b. at Bloomington, Ill., April 24, 1872; d. July 31, 1872.

2. Richard Churchill Clark, b. in Chicago, Ill., Sept., 1876; d. Jan. 12, 1881.

802   V   EDWARD PAYSON,[8] b. at Montpelier, Vt., Nov. 21, 1857; m. FLAVILLA V. KELLOGG, dau. of Alvaro V. and F. Jane (Marsh) Kellogg, Oct. 9, 1881. He removed with his parents to Illinois in 1862, and to Bloomington in 1866, where he attended the public schools, then to Chicago in 1875, where he lived until his marriage as above, since which he has been a farmer in Harvard, Iowa, where their children were born.

Children.

1. Edward P., b. July 19, 1882.
2. Francis Gerald, b. Oct. 1, 1884.
3. Howard Kellogg, b. Jan. 15, 1887; d. Aug. 31, 1888.
4. Garth, b. June 12, 1895.

388.

EDWIN[7] CHURCHILL (NOAH,[6] ICHABOD,[5] JOSEPH,[4] BARNABAS,[3] JOSEPH,[2] JOHN[1]). Born in Stowe, Vt., Jan. 4, 1815. Married, in Stowe, March 5, 1837, MARY M. ROBINSON, of Stowe. Died Sept. 26, 1883, at Vermont.

Children born in Stowe.

I. SUSAN R.,[8] b. Jan 17, 1838; m. HAMLET W. BARROWS.

803   II. CHARLES REED,[8] b. June 1, 1840; m. JANE M. WILKINS.

III. CELIA L.,[8] b. Aug. 13, 1845; m. LOUIS W. RAYMOND.

803a   IV. ARUNAH,[8] b. Aug. 7, 1847; m. IDA C. MATTHEWS.

389.

HEMAN ALLEN[7] CHURCHILL (NOAH,[6] ICHABOD[5] JOSEPH,[4] BARNABAS,[3] JOSEPH,[2] JOHN[1]). Born in Stowe, Vt., July 27, 1816 · lived at Barton Landing, Vt.; died at Irasburg, Vt., Sept. 3, 1883. Married, May, 1844, MARGETTE L. BENSON, of Stowe.

Children born in Stowe, Vt.

804 I. GEORGE E.,[8] b. July 29, 1847; m. EMMELINE E. DODGE, of Barton Landing, Vt.
805 II. FRANK H.,[8] b. June 12, 1857; m. HATTIE E. HAMBLET.
806 III. HOPE E.,[8] b. Oct. 22, 1862, m. WILLIAM W. BREENAN, of Barton Landing, Sept. 16, 1885.

390.

JOHN[7] CHURCHILL (WILLIAM,[6] ICHABOD,[5] JOSEPH,[4] BARNABAS,[3] JOSEPH,[2] JOHN[1]). Born in Stowe, Oct. 2, 1802; lived at Georgia, Vt., till about 1845, then moved to Freeport, Ill., and later to Lansing, Iowa; served as private in the Twenty-seventh Regiment Iowa Volunteers, and died in the hospital at Memphis, Tenn., while in the army. Married EXPERIENCE HALE, of Georgia, Vt.

Children born at Georgia, Vt.

I. LUCY H.,[8] b. Dec. 16, 1828; m. A. G. HEMENWAY, of Franklin.
II. HARRIET E.,[8] b. July 12, 1830; m. D. C. SHOEMAKER.
807 III. LUTHER B.,[8] b. Dec. 12, 1831; m. MARY JANE HAWKINS, in Illinois, February, 1853.
IV. JANE H.,[8] b. Nov. 21, 1833; m. ALBERT D. HANAN.
V. EMILY J.,[8] b. July 23, 1835; m. E. L. STONE.
VI. SOPHRONIA,[8] b. Dec. 20, 1837; m. GEORGE F. NYE.
809 VII. JOHN FRANKLIN,[8] d. Sept. 19, 1856.
VIII. ABIGAIL W.,[8] b. at Brandon, Vt., Nov. 30, 1843; m. CHARLES ALLISON, at Canton, Iowa, Oct. 18, 1861.
810 IX. EDWIN,[8] b. at Brandon, Vt.; m. ELIZABETH PHILLIPS.

391.

WILLIAM[7] CHURCHILL (WILLIAM,[6] ICHABOD,[5] JOSEPH,[4] BARNABAS,[3] JOSEPH,[2] JOHN[1]). Born in Stowe, Vt., Aug. 16, 1805; lived in Elmore, Vt., a farmer. Married, 1830, ADELINE H. DARLING, of Waterbury, Vt.

Children.

I. ELIZABETH J.,[8] b. Feb. 14, 1832; m. FRANCIS E. WOLSTENHOLM, of Lowell, Mass
811 II. WILLIAM JEFFERSON,[8] b. Feb. 2, 1835; m. ELLEN L. HATCH.
812 III. HENRY HARRISON,[8] b. July 31, 1836; m. WEALTHY P. HATCH.
813 IV. NATHAN T.,[8] b. July 17, 1844; m. RHODA GOBAR, May 30, 1878.

392.

NORMAN [7] CHURCHILL, (WILLIAM,[6] ICHABOD,[5] JOSEPH,[4] BARNABAS,[3] JOSEPH,[2] JOHN [1]). Born in Stowe, Vt., Jan. 15, 1811. We have nothing further relating to this family. Married ELIZA SPAULDING.

Children.

814   I. LYMAN.[8]
      II. CHARLES.[8]

393.

ALMON [7] CHURCHILL (JOSEPH,[6] ICHABOD,[5] JOSEPH,[4] BARNABAS,[3] JOSEPH,[2] JOHN [1]). Born in Stowe, Vt., April 23, 1808, where he was reared, on the farm, and educated in the district school. He lived in Stowe until 1850, when he went to California, but returned in 1852. In 1854 he went West and settled in Benton County for eight years, and then removed to Cedar Rapids, Lime County, Iowa. He was a farmer. He died at Cedar Rapids, March 21, 1868. Married in Stowe, Vt., March 24, 1834, ANNA LOVEJOY, of Mansfield, Vt., where she was born Sept. 12, 1812.

Children born in Stowe, except last two born in Shellsburg, Iowa.

815   I. GEORGE ROLLIN,[8] b. Feb. 17, 1835; m. ELIZABETH ANN (ARTHUR) NILES, at Cedar Rapids, Sept. 30, 1869.
        He received a common school education in Stowe, and worked on the farm until the removal of the family to Cedar Rapids, Iowa, where he still lives (1902), a farmer. His wife Elizabeth died March 21, 1901.

Children born in Cedar Rapids.

1. Edith M., b. Sept. 14, 1870.
2. Myra J., b. July 27, 1872.
3. Howard R., b. 1874.
4. Albert M., } twins, b. July 4, 1877.
5. Alice M.,
6. Earl A., b. Aug. 4, 1885.

   II. CAROLINE K.,[8] b. June 29, 1839; m. JOHN C. HAMMETT, Aug. 26, 1877.
        They had no children. She died at Sheridan, Kan., Aug. 26, 1881.

816   III. HENRY CLAY,[8] b. Aug. 10, 1840; m. SARAH J. POOL.
        They lived in Ceresco, Neb., in 1902.

Children.

1. William H.   3. Roy.
2. Mark.   4. Carl.
And perhaps others.

   IV MAY,[8] b. May 13, 1842; m. S. B. OBERLENDER, of Howard, Kan.
        She d. March 29, 1882.

Children.

1. Viola M. Oberlender,   3. Jennie L. Oberlender.
   m. Curtis Errid,   4. Fred Oberlender.
   of Oklahoma.   5. Mildred Oberlender.
2. Myrtle Oberlender.   6. Jeannette Oberlender.

817   V. PETER LOVEJOY,[8] b. Nov. 29, 1846; d. unmarried, Feb. 25, 1872.

818   VI. FRANK M.,[8] b. Aug. 29, 1850; m. LAURA LINDERMAN, Oct. 25, 1876.

> They lived at Bannister, Mich., and had, it is said, nine children, but we have not been able to get the names.

819 VII. OMAR A.,[8] b. May 17, 1853; m. SALLIE E. DUTTON, Feb. 6, 1876.

> They are said to have had four children; names not received. He died Dec. 15, 1887.

      VIII. LILLIS NEVADA,[8] b. at Shellsburg, Iowa, June 18, 1855; m. SAMUEL F. NEGLEY, Jan. 1, 1880, at Wahoo, Neb.

> He was the son of James S. and Jane Negley. He was a farmer and mechanic, and lived at Wahoo, Neb., where they had seven children, viz.:

Children.

1. Ferne Anna Negley, b. Jan. 1, 1881.
2. Floyd Carroll Negley, b. Aug. 8, 1884.
3. Grace Marshall Negley. Oct. 20, 1887.
4. Noel Ardis Negley, b. Feb. 27, 1889.
5. Doris Opal Negley, b. Sept. 7, 1892.
6. Marjorie Thankful Negley, b. July 2, 1895.
7. Bernice Winifred Negley, b. Sept. 26, 1899.

      IX. HARRY E.,[8] b. July 16, 1861; m. ISABELLA VAN OSDALL, at Genesee, Ill., June 6, 1882.

> Born at Shellsburg, Iowa. Educated at Coe Institute, Cedar Rapids, Iowa, and Western College. Lived at Toledo, Iowa. Practised law, and was deputy auditor and treasurer of Tama County, Iowa; removed before 1889 to Greeley, Col., where he is an eminent member of the bar.

Children.

1. Flossie Estelle, b. May 26, 1883, in Toledo, Iowa.
2. Harry Van Osdall, b. May 10, 1886, in Toledo, Iowa.
3. Isabel Lovejoy, b. Feb. 4, 1889, in Greeley, Col.

394.

ALDEN P.[7] CHURCHILL (JESSE,[6] ICHABOD,[5] JOSEPH,[4] BARNABAS,[3] JOSEPH,[2] JOHN[1]). Born in Woodstock, Vt., July 8, 1822, and lived with his uncle, Nathan T., until manhood. Married ELIZABETH M. GILMAN.

Children.

    I. HORACE H.,[8] b. May 3, 1847; d. Sept. 2, 1848.
   II. JULIA E.,[8] b. May 11, 1850; d. Jan. 8, 1860.
  III. EDWIN A.,[8] b. July 10, 1854; d. Aug. 12, 1854.

396.

JESSE F.[7] CHURCHILL (JESSE,[6] ICHABOD,[5] JOSEPH,[4] BARNABAS,[3] JOSEPH,[2] JOHN[1]). Born in Woodstock, Vt., Dec. 16, 1826. Lived at Fitchburg, Mass. Married at Bellows Falls, Aug. 2, 1854, SABRA CARTER.

Children.

I. Charles F.,[8] b. May 2, 1854; d. March 5, 1874.
II. Lillian,[8] b. Oct. 13, 1860.
III. Julia E.,[8] b. Dec. 24, 1862.
IV. Sarah G.,[8] b. May 5, 1866; d. Sept. 4, 1866.
V. Ada W.,[8] b. Dec. 5, 1867; d. Aug. 9, 1868.

397.

EDMUND FLETCHER[7] CHURCHILL (Levi,[6] Joseph[5] Joseph,[4] Barnabas,[3] Joseph,[2] John[1]). Born at Woodstock, Vt., 1811. He died at Proctorsville, Vt., Aug. 13, 1846. Married at Hartland Vt., Sept. 25, 1844, Maria Marble, who was born in Charlestown, Mass., Jan. 14, 1814.

Child born at Proctorsville, Vt.

I. Elizabeth Keziah,[8] b. Sept. 29, 1845; m. Edwin Ellis Woodman, at Munroe, Wis., May 10, 1871.
They resided in St. Paul, Minn. He was born in St. Louis, and was captain of the Thirteenth Wisconsin Volunteers in the Civil War.

398.

LEVI[7] CHURCHILL (Levi,[6] Joseph,[5] Joseph,[4] Barnabas.[3] Joseph,[2] John[1]). Born Sept. 16, 1813, at Woodstock, Vt. He moved to the West, and lived a while in Minnesota and then in St. Louis, where he died in 1857. His widow lived there in 1895. Married, Oct. 2, 1844, Elizabeth M. Proctor, at Proctorsville, Vt.

One Child born in Proctorsville, Vt.

I. Nelly,[8] b. June 7, 1849; d. at Stillwater, Minn., Aug. 22, 1850.

399.

CAPT. WILLIAM HUNTER[7] CHURCHILL (Sylvester,[6] Joseph,[5] Joseph,[4] Barnabas,[3] Joseph,[2] John[1]). Born at Bedloe's Island, July 8, 1819. Graduated at West Point, 1840; died in 1847, at Point Isabel, Tex. Married, at Savannah, Ga., 1844, Elizabeth Margaret Cuyler.

Child born in Savannah, Ga.

821   I. Richard Cuyler,[8] b. Dec. 12, 1845; m. Josephine Young, of Brooklyn, N.Y., 1866.
They lived at Fort Delaware, West Point, and Assining, N.Y.

Children.

1. William Hunter, b. at Fort Delaware, Sept. 12, 1867; unmarried.
2. Annie Mason, b. at Fort Delaware, March 15, 1869; m. Bertram Dawson Coleman, of Lebanon, Penn.

3. Maud, b. at West Point, July 12, 1872; m. DeLancy Nicoll, Dec. 11, 1890. Mr. Nicoll was district attorney of New York City from fall of 1890 to 1893.
4. Elizabeth Margaret, b. at Assining, N.Y., May 22, 1874; d. in infancy.
5. Richard Randolph Cuyler, b. Nov. 2, 1877, at Assining, N.Y.

400.

NATHANIEL[7] CHURCHILL (NATHANIEL,[6] NATHANIEL,[5] LEMUEL,[4] BARNABAS,[3] JOSEPH,[2] JOHN[1]). Born in Wakefield, N.B., May 9, 1799. Lived first at Andover, N.B., and then settled in Washburn, Me., about 1824, and lived there. Married 1st, July 30, 1822, at Andover, N.B., JERUSHA FREEMAN, born July 24, 1803, and 2d, MELINDA HOYT, at St. John, N.B.

Children.

822 I. JOB,[8] b. at Andover, N.B., May 20, 1823; m. ANN CROUSE, at Maysville, Me., March 18, 1855.

Children.

1. J. Allen, b. Feb. 20, 1857.
2. Mary A., b. Dec. 11, 1858.
3. Jesse P., b. Dec. 31, 1859.
4. Amos F., b. Sept. 4, 1861.
5. Lucinda J., b. July 1, 1863.
6. Nathaniel G., b. Aug. 31, 1864.
7. William C., b. Nov. 16, 1866.
8. Minna A., b. Sept. 29, 1868.
9. Samuel J., b. March 13, 1870.
10. Abbie C., b. March 25, 1872.
11. Frank E., b. Feb. 14, 1874.
12. Miles G., b. July 1, 1876; d. in infancy.
13. Miles G. (2d), b. June 10, 1877.
14. Marshall E., b. July 22, 1878.

823 II. NATHANIEL W.,[8] b. in Washburn, Me., March 23, 1825; m. IRENE GRANT, of Southampton, N.B.

Children. Dates and Places of Birth not Received.

1. Charles W.	6. Allen, 2d.
2. Eva.	7. Almira.
3. Isadore.	8. Esther.
4. Allen.	9. Jane.
5. Theodore.	10. Mary J.

III. MARY JANE,[8] b. Oct. 6, 1827, in Washburn, Me.; m. 1st, JOHN L. GRANT, in Fredericton, N.B.; m. 2d, in Southampton, SAMUEL FOX.
The names of her children not received.

IV. ELIZABETH A.,[8] b. March 10, 1829, at Washburn, Me.; m. AMOS FOX, in Southampton. No further data of this family furnished.

V. EUNICE J.,[8] b. March 23, 1831, at Washburn, Me.; m. WILLIAM MILLER.
They were living in 1887 in Providence, R.I., but no further record has been received.

VI. SAMUEL J.,[8] b. in Washburn, Me., April 6, 1833; unmarried in 1887.

Children of Second Wife.

VII. C. F.,⁸ b. at Bear Island, N.B., April 29, 1837; m. ANNIE EVANS, April 30, 1862, at Washburn, Me.

VIII. PRUDENCE H.,⁸ b. in Washburn, Me., June, 1839; m. WILLIAM CROUSE.

IX. ASENATH,⁸ b. in Washburn, Me., October, 1841; m. ISAIAH SHARPE.

X. JOSEPH A.,⁸ b. in Washburn, Me., Dec. 24, 1847; m. 1st, CASSIE IRVING; m. 2d, VELINA NORTON; m. 3d, JANE TAYLOR.

401.

JESSE⁷ CHURCHILL (NATHANIEL,⁶ NATHANIEL,⁵ LEMUEL,⁴ BARNABAS³ JOSEPH,² JOHN¹). Born in Yarmouth, N.S., Jan. 7 1801. Removed to Ontario in 1831. Married 1st, PHEBE BARLOW who died in New Brunswick; married 2d, MARY HART. We have been disappointed that we cannot get any further record of this family. We learned that Jesse's eldest son, Elias, lived at Paris, Brant County, Ont., in 1890, but we could get no answer to our inquiries. Later we learn that Mr. Elias Churchill died soon after receiving our inquiries. He has a grandson, W. F. Churchill, at Paris, Ont.

402.

CHARLES L.⁷ CHURCHILL (NATHANIEL,⁶ NATHANIEL,⁵ LEMUEL,⁴ BARNABAS,³ JOSEPH,² JOHN¹). Born in Yarmouth, Jan. 7, 1803. Married, at Kingston, N.B., MARY J. DUNPHY.

Children.

826   I. NATHANIEL,⁸ b. September, 1830; m. MARY EBBETT.
827   II. SAMUEL LOTHROP,⁸ b. in Wakefield, N.B., Oct. 1, 1832; m. MARY E. VAN WART, Oct. 1, 1857.
       III. EMMA LOUISE,⁸ b. July 22, 1834.
       IV. MARY ANN,⁸ b. Sept. 22, 1836; m. ABNER VESEY.
828   V. GEORGE MILFORD,⁸ b. Sept. 18, 1839; m. SADIE BAKER.
829   VI. CHARLES RICE,⁸ b. Sept. 1, 1845; m. JULIA ANN MARRA, March 3, 1878.
       VII. MARIA ELIZA,⁸ b. Dec. 16, 1848; m. MATTHEW STEPHENSON.

403.

ISAIAH⁷ CHURCHILL (NATHANIEL,⁶ NATHANIEL,⁵ LEMUEL,⁴ BARNABAS,³ JOSEPH,² JOHN¹). Born in Yarmouth, N.S., Feb. 6, 1807. Removed in 1831, with the larger part of his father's family to Ontario. The information about this family came from Amos Churchill, the eldest son, in 1890, and from Richard Watts Churchill, of Bealton, Ontario, in 1889. He died June 1, 1874. Married, in Yarmouth, July 9, 1838, MARY FREEL, born Oct. 31, 1807. She died July 21, 1856.

Children born in Ontario.

I. Amos,[8] b. Nov. 28, 1839; m. Maria Vyse, April 7, 1868.
They lived in Ridgetown, Ont. They have no children.
II. Isaiah,[8] b. Feb. 9, 1841; m. Eliza Collison, Dec. 8, 1870.
Family lived, 1899, at Highgate, Ont.

Children.

1. Samuel Jones, b. Sept. 29, 1871.
2. Jedediah Nathaniel, b. Sept. 13, 1873.
3. Mary Ann. b. Nov. 18, 1875.
4. John Wesley, b. Aug. 29, 1881.

III. Mary Alemath,[8] b. Sept. 12, 1842; m. Abisha Dunning, Feb. 14, 1859.
IV. Eunice,[8] b. May 16, 1844; m. John H. DeWitt, April, 1865.
They lived, in 1890, in Nepawail, Manitoba.
V. Samuel J.,[8] b. Feb. 13, 1846; m. Mary Jane Bothwell, October, 1868.
VI. Mahaleth Ann,[8] b. Sept. 2, 1848; m. Jesse Harrison, March, 1868.
The mother died March 1, 1875.

Two Children.

1. Mary Ellen Harrison. | 2. John Harrison.

VII. Nathaniel,[8] b. Jan. 7, 1851; m. Hannah Holmes, Dec. 6, 1834.
They lived in Nepawa, Manitoba.
VIII. Richard Franklin,[8] b. June 12, 1853; d. Aug. 15, 1854.

404.

ISRAEL[7] CHURCHILL (Nathaniel,[6] Nathaniel,[5] Lemuel[4] Barnabas,[8] Joseph,[2] John[1]). Born at Wakefield, N.B., March 13, 1813. Settled at Woodstock, where he was a deacon of the Baptist church for many years. He was a painter by trade. Married, at Douglas, N.B., Eliza Dunphy, born in Douglas, N.B., daughter of Andrew and Annie (Foster) Dunphy.

Children born, the first two at Victoria Corner, the rest in Woodstock, N.B.

I. Elethea,[8] b. March 9, 1834; m. Rev. J. C. Bleakney, at Woodstock, Dec. 17, 1860. She died at Woodstock, Jan. 19, 1900.
They lived in Woodstock, and had one child.

Child.

1. Leila Blanche Bleakney, b. in St. John, July 7, 1863; m. Dr. J. W. N. Baker, August, 1884.

II. Sarah Eliza,[8] b. May 16, 1835; m. Rev. Peter R. Knight, Oct. 10, 1856.
They lived at Woodstock, and later at Lower French Village, N.B. He was a clergyman.

They had Three Children born in Woodstock.

1. Clara Blanche Knight, b. July 15, 1860; m. Manasseh Dunphy, October, 1892.
2. Eliza Knight, b. June 28, 1865; m. Judson H. Dunphy, November, 1889.
3. Herbert Knight, b. July 27, 1875; m. A. Dunphy, of Winnipeg.

III. ISRAEL GEROW,[8] b. Feb. 22. 1837; m. ELMIRA WILLIAMS, Feb. 14; 1859; d. in Woodstock, Jan. 22, 1900. T'ey had seven children, viz., (1) Anna Maria, (2) Mary Eliza, (3) Winnie J., (4) Ella, (5) Rhoda Alma, (6) Charles Israel, (7) Joseph E.

IV. CHARLES BARTLETT,[8] b. Dec. 25, 1838; m. 1st, LAVINIA SMITH; m. 2d, MRS. JANE (REID) CORRON. They had four children, viz., (1) Eliza, m. 1st, Mr. Baker and 2d, Thomas Reid; (2) Alma, m. Frank C. Foster; (3) Madeline, m. Freeland McKenzie; (4) Nellie, m. George Doherty.

V. DR. ESBON,[8] b. April 17, 1841; m. SUSAN MILLS, Feb. 17, 1866, at Woodstock.

He is a physician at Woodstock, N.B. They had four children, viz., (1) Lillie Maud, m. William Kendall; (2) Walbergia, m. John Orchard; (3) Bruce, b. June, 1882; (4) Carey, b. 1884.

VI. JAMES EDWARD,[8] b. Feb. 1, 1843; d. at Woodstock, Aug 17, 1854.

VII. LOUISA JANE,[8] b. Nov. 30. 1845; m. 1st, ABIATHAR JOHNSTON, who died; m. 2d, STEPHEN TAYLOR; m. 3d, JOSEPH CHURCHILL.

They lived in Washburn and Jacksonville, Me.

Children of First Husband, born at Jacksonville.

1. Horace Johnston, b. Aug. 9, 1865; m. Ada Dickinson, of Houlton, Me.
2. Wilmot Johnston, b. Dec. 1, 1867; m. Jennie Davis, Sept. 23, 1899.
3. Ella May Johnston, b. Nov. 30, 1870; m. William Ernest Puddington, Feb. 27, 1890.

VIII. FRANCES MARY,[8] b. March 1, 1847; m. C. N. SCOTT, at Woodstock, Jan. 4, 1869.

Mr. Scott was the son of Murray and Mehitable Jane (Merrithew) Scott. He graduated at the Normal School at St. John's, and at Collegiate School, Fredericton, N.B. He has been a teacher, and later an accountant. They live at Woodstock, N.B.

Children born, the first at Campbellton, the rest at Woodstock.

1. Charles George Coster Scott, b. Oct 23, 1870; d. Nov. 25, 1875.
2. Frances Mary Scott, b. July 21, 1872; d. Oct. 7, 1872
3. Walter Scott, b. Aug. 6, 1873; d. Feb. 18, 1881.
4. Clara Meta Scott, b. Nov. 17, 1877.
5. Lina Mae Scott, b. Sept. 11, 1882.
6. Bertha Scott, b. Sept. 5, 1884; d. Aug. 23, 1900.

IX. JOSHUA TODD,[8] b. Feb. 22, 1849; m. HENRIETTA ESTEY, Jan. 5, 1868. He died at Newburgh, Oct. 18, 1883, from an accident. They had two children, viz., (1) Ada, m. William Austin; (2) Havelock.

X. ANNA MARIA,[8] b. March 3, 1853; m. 1st, E. B. JEWETT, at Woodstock. Nov. 26, 1868; m. 2d, E. M. SMITH, July 8, 1902.

The family resides, in 1903, at Houlton, Me.

Children of First Husband born, three at Woodstock, and Ella at Prince William.

1. James Edward Jewett, b. Feb. 26, 1873; m. Mary Lois Goodspeed, June 22, 1898.
2. Ella Blanche Jewett, b. July 15, 1875; m. Rev. Miles S. Trafton, Sept. 21, 1897.
3. Grace Jewett, b. June 26, 1877; m. Herbert Story, of St. John, June 26, 1902.
4. Lulu May Jewett, b. Aug. 15, 1881; d. Dec. 25, 1883.

406.

RICHARD WATTS [7] CHURCHILL (NATHANIEL,[6] NATHANIEL,[5] LEMUEL,[4] BARNABAS,[3] JOSEPH,[2] JOHN [1]). Born in Yarmouth, N.S., July 19, 1826. Removed in early manhood to New York State, and lived, in later years, at Bealton, Ont., where he was living Nov. 23, 1899. He has given much of the information we have of his father's family. Married 1st, in Cambour County, N.Y., May 27 1847, CATHARINE TAYLOR; she died leaving three children, and he married 2d, May 29, 1855, MAHALA BEAL, of Bealton, N.Y.

Children of First Wife, Catharine.

I. ARTHUR W.,[8] b. June 26. 1848; d. in infancy.
II. RHODA C.,[8] b. June, 1850; m. 1st, CHARLES McGREAGOR, of Michigan; m. 2d, JOHN ANDERSON.
There were children, one daughter by the first husband, and three sons and two daughters by the second. The Andersons live in Bealton.

III. OLIVE C.,[8] b. March 29, 1852; m. LYMAN SLEIGHT.
They live in Brantford and have three children.

Children of Second Wife, Mahala.

IV. MARY E.,[8] b. July 13, 1856; m. LEMUEL KITCHEN. She died leaving one child.

Child.

1. Mary E. Kitchen, b. April 4, 1873, who was adopted by her grandparents, R. W. and Mahala Churchill.

V. REUBEN W. S.,[8] b. May 31, 1858.
VI. WILLIAM W. C.,[8] b. Dec. 28, 1860.
VII. CHARLES H. V.,[8] b. June 16, 1862.

406a. ℭ

CHLOE ANN [7] (CHURCHILL) BOYER (LEMUEL [6] NATHANIEL,[5] LEMUEL,[4] BARNABAS,[3] JOSEPH,[2] JOHN [1]). Born at Lincoln, Sunbury County, N.B., 1801. Lived in Wakefield. When a young child she removed with her parents to what is now Lower Brighton, Carlton County, where her mother died, and she went to live for some ten years in the family of her aunt, wife of Mr. Elias Haney, thence she went to Wakefield where she was married. She was a devout and consistent Christian woman, wife, and mother, and a beloved member of the First F. C. Baptist Church in Wakefield, N.B. She died Nov. 22, 1882. Married GEORGE R. BOYER, of Wakefield, N.B. Mr. Boyer was a manufacturer of leather and shoes. He was deacon of the F. C. Baptist Church for a long series of years, and in every way was an upright and much respected man. He died at Wakefield (Victoria Corner), June 10, 1886, aged 86 years.

Children born at Wakefield, now Victoria Corner.

I. GEORGE GREENLEAF [8] BOYER, died young.
II. GEORGE W. [8] BOYER, b. Jan. 22, 1834; m. ANNA M. KIMBALL, Sept.
2, 1856, who died Aug. 14, 1886.
They adopted a daughter, Josie, who married George M. Davis,
of Hartland.
III. JAMES WILLIAM [8] BOYER, b. 1836; m. SARAH LOVELY, who died
Feb. 18, 1902.
Mr. Boyer was a manufacturer of harnesses and boots; a man
of large influence and excellent character. Lived at Victoria Cor-
ner; and died Feb. 18, 1892.

Children born at Victoria Corner.

1. George R. Boyer, d. in infancy.
2. Samuel R. Boyer, m. Miss Dewett.
3. Frederick J. Boyer, m. Miss McLoud.
4. Ann J. Boyer. m. J. B. Bowser, of British Columbia.
5. Ada Boyer, m. McAnn Barrester
6. Ella Boyer.

IV Amos L. [8] BOYER, m., about 1859, HANNAH MILLS, of Victoria Cor-
ner.
They removed to Denver, Col., where he was engaged in mining.
They had one son.

Child.

1. Burzil Boyer, who married in Denver.

V. ELIZABETH [7] BOYER, m. DUNCAN DICKINSON.
VI. LOIS [8] BOYER.
VII. PAMELIA F. [8] BOYER, m. WILLIAM TAYLOR. No children.
VIII. CAROLINE [8] BOYER, m. MOSES P. ORSEN. Had three daughters.

Children.

1. Lois. | 2. Minnie. | 3. Chloe.

IX. SUSANNA [8] BOYER, d. young.

406b.

JAMES C. [7] CHURCHILL (LEMUEL,[6] NATHANIEL,[5] LEMUEL,[4]
BARNABAS,[3] JOSEPH,[2] JOHN [1]). Born in Fredericton, N.B., Feb. 18,
1805. Removed with his father's family later to Lower Brighton
N.B. He lived in Bangor, Me. He appears in Boston Directory
at 256 Hanover street, in 1845, and from 1846 to 1850 kept a
restaurant at Traverse, corner Haverhill street. His name does not
appear in 1851–1853, but from 1854 to 1860 he kept a grocery store
at 84 Charlestown street, and lived at No. 82, next door. In 1861
his name is not in Directory, but from 1862 to 1867 he kept a
liquor store on Traverse, corner Charlestown street, and lived at
Cambridgeport. From 1870–1874 he had a grocery store in Charlestown at 38 Medford street, and lived there. On May 19, 1858, he
sailed from Boston to Liverpool on the steamer "Europe," Captain
Leach, commander, the passage being made in eleven days five
hours. His passport was signed by Lewis Cass, United States

Secretary of State. Mr. Churchill travelled on the continent, through France, Germany, and back through England, Scotland, and Ireland and Wales, and from Liverpool home to Boston, where he arrived Oct. 14, 1858. On the back of his passport he wrote out a full list of the chief places he visited, and this document has been loaned me by his nephew, George W. Boyer, of Hartland, N.B. In this paper he is described at five feet nine and three-quarter inches in height, light complexion, blue eyes, dark hair, etc., age 53 years. Married 1st,* in Bangor, Me. (——) ROSE, from whom he separated. Married 2d, in Millstream, King's County, N.B., ELIZABETH HANEY, his cousin, daughter of Elias. Married 3d, in Wakefield, N.B., RUTH SHAW.

One Child by First Wife.

I. ARMINE.[8]

Two Children by Second Wife.

II. JOSEPHINE A.,[8] b. in Boston, Aug. 24, 1845; m. (——) MANSFIELD.
   Two children were born of this marriage, names not known.
III. JAMES L.[8]

One Child by Third Wife.

IV. BYRON,[8] b. in Boston. No further record.

406ę. ƀ

AMOS[7] CHURCHILL (LEMUEL,[6] NATHANIEL[5] LEMUEL[4] BARNABAS,[3] JOSEPH,[2] JOHN[1]). Born in 1809 in Fredericton, N.B., but later removed with his father's family to what is now Lower Brighton. Here his mother died while he was a child. He lived in Bangor in 1843 on Boyd street, and in 1846 on Grove street. A shoemaker. He died at Brewer, Me., Feb. 22, 1846, aged 37 years. Married ELEANOR SINCLAIR. She died in Brewer, Oct. 13, 1847, aged 33 years.

Children.

I. GEORGE BOYER.[8] m. 1st, (——) KENNEY; m. 2d, SARAH EMILY HOWARD.
   He was a music-teacher and millwright, and lived at Brewer, Me., where he died Sept. 12, 1867, aged 30 years.

One Child by First Wife.

1. William, d. aged 3 months.

One Child by Second Wife.

2. Frances Lenore, b. in Brewer, Me., Nov. 30, 1867; m. Samuel Hart Furber, at Snohomish, Wash., April 8, 1897. Mrs. Furber graduated from the University of Washington at Seattle in 1889. Samuel H. Furber is a lawyer and court reporter at Seattle. They live at Seattle, No. 312 1st avenue N.

They have one Child.

1. George Churchill Furber, b. in Seattle, Feb. 21, 1898.

II. WILLIAM,³ d. Oct. 13, 1854, in Brewer, Me., aged 16 years.
III. CHARLES ISRAEL,⁸ b. in Bangor, Me., Dec. 7, 1844; m. ELVIRA D.
HOWARD, at Brewer, Me., Sept. 1, 1872. She was the dau. of
Willard and Sarah T. (Johnson) Howard, and a sister of his
brother's, George B.'s, wife. They lived at Merrimac, Mass.,
where he is a wheelwright. He was a soldier of the Civil War,
in Company A, 31st Regiment Maine Volunteers.

They have one Son.

1. William H., b. in Merrimac, March 29, 1880.

NOTE. Of LEMUEL⁶ CHURCHILL (No. 170) and his family by the second wife,
Mary Brown, much new information has been received since the family sketch
was passed in the regular course, and printed. The second family is therefore
here revised with corrections and additions.

After the death of his first wife, Mr. Churchill continued to live in Carlton
County, N.B., where he married a second wife, Mary Brown, and by her had
nine children. About 1833 he removed with his family to Upper Canada, and
settled for a while at Niagara and Saltfeet townships, but removed later to
Sweaburg, Oxford County.

Children of MARY BROWN, *the Second Wife, born in N.B.*

406d   V.   BENJAMIN,⁷ m. ANNE SECORD, of Walsingham, Ont. No children.
406e   VI. BETSEY,⁷ m. PALMER CHAMBERLAIN, in Oxford County.
406f VII.   REBECCA,⁷ b. in 1818; m. DAVID PHILLIPS, at Sweaburg, Ont.,
             1836.
406g VIII.   LEMUEL,⁷ m. EMILY BENNETT, of Brantford.
        IX. CHARLES,⁷ died unmarried, at Galt, Ont., aged 22 years.
406h   X.   EDWARD,⁷ m CHARITY COOK, of Houghton, Ont. No children.
406i   XI.   SUSAN,⁷ m. THOMAS PHILLIPS, of Houghton, Ont.; died in Hough-
             ton, aged 40.
406j XII.   DANIEL,⁷ b. April 9, 1830; m. MARY ANN KELLY, of Tilsonburg,
             Ont.
406k XIII.   GEORGE,⁷ m. SARAH GOODLIN, of Simcoe, Ont. No children.

406e.

BETSEY⁷ CHURCHILL (LEMUEL,⁶ NATHANIEL,⁵ LEMUEL⁴
BARNABAS,³ JOSEPH,² JOHN¹). Born in Carlton County, N.B. Married PALMER CHAMBERLAIN, in Oxford County, Ont., and lived
there. He was a farmer.

Children.

I. OLIVER⁸ CHAMBERLAIN, m. MISS KELLY. They live in Petrolia.
II. HESTER⁸ CHAMBERLAIN, m. EDWARD BECKER.
III. AMOS⁸ CHAMBERLAIN, died unmarried.
IV. THEODORE⁸ CHAMBERLAIN, m. MARY FENTON. They live in Toronto.
V. HANNAH⁸ CHAMBERLAIN.
VI. HARVEY⁸ CHAMBERLAIN.
VII. ADELINE⁸ CHAMBERLAIN.

406f.

REBECCA⁷ CHURCHILL (LEMUEL⁶ NATHANIEL,⁵ LEMUEL⁴
BARNABAS,³ JOSEPH,² JOHN¹). Born in Woodstock, N.B., and
lived there until fifteen years old, when she removed with her father's
family to Upper Canada. Married, Sept. 27, 1836, at E. Oxford, Ont.,
DAVID PHILLIPS, of the same town. In 1846 they removed with their

family to Dereham, then an almost unbroken forest, and settled near the then small hamlet of Ingersoll. Here they spent the remainder of their long and useful lives. She died March 31, 1900, aged 82 years. Mr. Phillips died Oct. 7, 1896. Their home was on the fourth line in the fine district between what are now the villages of Verschoyle and Mount Elgin. Mr. Phillips was a farmer.

They had Eleven Children, born in Oxford County, Ont.

I. RUTH[8] PHILLIPS, b. July 27, 1837; m. SIMEON MABEE, Sept. 28, 1863. They had children, viz.: (1) Alice Mabee, (2) Julia Mabee, (3) Carrie Mabee.

II. CHARLES W.[8] PHILLIPS, b. Jan. 8, 1839; m. EMILY VANCE, at Houghton, Ont., Sept. 26, 1861. They had children, viz.: (1) Minnie Phillips, (2) Charles Phillips, (3) Emily Phillips, d. 1882.

III. DAVID L.[8] PHILLIPS, b. Feb. 2. 1841; m. MARIA FRANCIS, at Houghton, Ont., Dec. 22, 1870. They lived at Mt. Elgin, and had children: (1) Edith Phillips, b. May 14, 1872; m. Ambrose Hobson; (2) Ella Phillips, b. Feb. 14, 1877; m. Harman Moulton, 1900; (3) Clare E. Frances Phillips, b. Oct. 18, 1880; (4) Charles Cecil Phillips, b. Jan. 9, 1886.

IV. ALMIRA[8] PHILLIPS, b. Sept. 3. 1843; m. D. A. MITCHELL, at Verschoyle, May 5, 1864. Children: (1) Elizabeth Churchill Mitchell; m. Charles Tague; (2) Levange; m. Dr. S. D. Barnes, of Bridgeport, Tenn. Mrs. Almira Phillips died at Ingersoll, Aug. 16, 1869.

V. MARY ELIZABETH[8] PHILLIPS, b. Nov. 29, 1845; m. D. A. MITCHELL, as his second wife, Sept. 11, 1872.

VI. SUSAN[8] PHILLIPS, b. July 26, 1848; d. May 21, 1883.

VII. ANNA M.[8] PHILLIPS, b. Feb. 24, 1851; d. May 17, 1879.

VIII. SARAH ELLA[8] PHILLIPS, b. Aug. 6, 1853; d. Feb. 1. 1883.

IX. ALEXANDER S.[8] PHILLIPS, b. Feb. 27, 1856; m. MARY WHALEY, at Cadillac, Mich., November, 1877. He died Oct. 12, 1882. They had children: (1) Archie, (2) Alexander.

X. GEORGE WHITFIELD[8] PHILLIPS, b. Jan. 2, 1859; m. 1st, 1884, DENSIE SNIVELY, and 2d, ANNA BRIGGS, at Minneapolis, in 1890.

XI. MANSHMAN HAVELOCK[8] PHILLIPS, b. June 9, 1861; m. HARRIET SMITH, at London, Ont., Sept. 28, 1887. Children: (1) Mabel Phillips, (2) George Phillips, (3) Cecil Phillips.

406g.

LEMUEL[7] CHURCHILL (LEMUEL,[6] NATHANIEL,[5] LEMUEL,[4] BARNABAS,[3] JOSEPH,[2] JOHN[1]). Born in N.B. Married EMILY BENNETT, at Oxford, Ont.

Children.

I. WILLIAM.[8] No record.

II. MIRIAM.[8] Nothing further received.

406i.

SUSAN[7] CHURCHILL (LEMUEL,[6] NATHANIEL,[5] LEMUEL,[4] BARNABAS,[3] JOSEPH,[2] JOHN[1]). Born in N.B. Married THOMAS PHILLIPS, of Houghton, Ont.

Children.

I. GALUSHA⁸ PHILLIPS.
II. EDWARD⁸ PHILLIPS.
III. GEORGE⁸ PHILLIPS.
IV. MELISSA⁸ PHILLIPS.
V. SUSAN⁸ PHILLIPS.
VI. VICTORIA⁸ PHILLIPS.
VII. DANIEL⁸ PHILLIPS.

406j.

DANIEL⁷ CHURCHILL (LEMUEL,⁶ NATHANIEL⁵ LEMUEL,⁴ BARNABAS,³ JOSEPH,² JOHN¹). Born in New Brunswick, April 9, 1830. Removed with his father's family to Upper Canada about 1833. Attended school in West Oxford. Lived at South Norwich, and Springford, Ont., a farmer. Married, April 25, 1856, at Tilsonburg, MARY ANN KELLY, daughter of Michael and Ann (Tomlinson) Kelly.

Children born at South Norwich.

I. CHARLES H.,⁸ b. Jan. 12, 1857; m. KATE KELLEY, 1889.
II. MARIETTA,⁸ b. May, 1859. She was killed by a horse at the age of 3 years 6 months.
III. CECILIA A.,⁸ b. July 23, 1860; m. NORMAN WATSON, of Cornell, 1881.
IV. JAMES R.,⁸ b. Oct. 5, 1862; m. ANNA SEN, 1900.
V. EDWARD,⁸ b. Jan. 1, 1866; m. FLORENCE HARRIS, of South Norwich, June, 1892.
VI. KATHERINE,⁸ b. Aug. 1, 1868; m. MARTIN SIMONSON, of Portland, Ore., Feb. 14, 1891.
      They live in Brooklyn, N.Y., where Mr. Simonson is, staff-captain in the Salvation Army.
VIII. GERTRUDE,⁸ b. Nov. 11, 1870.

407.

JOHN RUSSELL⁷ CHURCHILL (BENJAMIN,⁶ NATHANIEL,⁵ LEMUEL,⁴ BARNABAS,³ JOSEPH,² JOHN¹). Born at Kingston, N.S., Aug. 22, 1817. Married, Dec. 24, 1840, MARGARET BURNS MCINTOSH, b. Aug. 6, 1824, and died in 1866.

Children.

I. GEORGE FREDERICK,⁸ b. April 15, 1842.
II. HANNAH JANE,⁸ b. Oct. 10, 1843; d. Oct. 24, 1847.
III. LUDLOW,⁸ b. July 28, 1845; d. Aug. 18, 1901.
IV. FRANCES MARIA,⁸ b. June 10, 1847; d. Aug. 31, 1848.
V. MARY ELIZABETH,⁸ b. Aug. 25, 1849; m. A. L. MANNING.
VI. EMMA OLIVIA,⁸ b. March 25, 1851; m. E. R. JOHNSON.
VII. LUELLA ANN,⁸ b. Jan. 12, 1853; d. March 22, 1853.
VIII. BENJAMIN FRANKLIN,⁸ b. Aug. 16, 1854.

410.

EZRA⁷ CHURCHILL, 3D (EZRA,⁶ EZRA,⁵ LEMUEL,⁴ BARNABAS,³ JOSEPH,² JOHN¹). Born May, 1804. Lived at Hantsport, N.S. He was the largest shipowner in Nova Scotia. He represented

Hants County in the House of Assembly. After the confederation he was appointed senator. He was thrown from a carriage and killed Aug. 20, 1869. Married 1st, ANNE DAVIDSON, of Falmouth, N.S.; married 2d, RACHEL BURGESS, of Billtown, N.S.; died April 14, 1879.

Children of First Wife.

    I. ANN ELIZA,[8] b. April 27, 1827; m. DENNIS SHERIFF, of Ontario, 1863.
    II. JOANNA,[8] b. May 20, 1830; m. GIDEON REID, of Horton, N.S., 1850.
    III. MARY JANE,[8] b. July 18, 1832; m. 1st, E. McKINNON; m. 2d, CAPT. ARTHUR CAMPBELL, of New York; m. 3d, THOMAS WOODWORTH.
835   IV. GEORGE WASHINGTON,[8] b. March 3, 1835; m. SUSANNAH DAVIDSON, of Hantsport, July 1, 1856.
    V. RHODA,[8] b. Falmouth, N.S., Aug. 1, 1837; m. JEDIDIAH E. NEWCOMB. of Cornwallis, N.S.
836   VI. JOHN WILEY,[8] b. Falmouth, May 29, 1840; m. 1st, EMMELINE BURGESS, 1864; m. 2d, MARY MESSENGER, of Kingston, N.S.
    VII. ELIZABETH,[8] b. at Falmouth, Aug. 22, 1842; m. DOUGLAS B. WOODWORTH, of Canning, Me.; live at Ottawa.
    VIII. REBECCA,[8] b. at Falmouth. July 4, 1845; m. DR. J. B. BLACK, of St. Stephens; live at Winsor.
837   IX. CYRUS WARREN,[8] b. at Falmouth, April 15. 1848; d. in 1853.
    X. REGINA,[8] b. Dec. 21, 1852; m. JOHN W. WOLAVER, May 25, 1872.

Children by Second Wife.

838   XI. WILLIAM BURPEE,[8] b. Sept. 17, 1863.
839   XII. JOSEPH REGINALD EARLE,[8] b. Oct. 5, 1865.
840 XIII. EZRA.[8]
841 XIV. THOMAS.[8]

411.

JAMES[7] CHURCHILL (NEHEMIAH,[6] EZRA,[5] LEMUEL,[4] BARNABAS,[3] JOSEPH,[2] JOHN[1]). He died Dec. 28, 1892. Married, Jan. 31, 1839, ELIZABETH BYRNE, daughter of Thomas.

Children.

842   I. HENRY,[8] drowned while skating, Dec. 16, 1857.
    II. ELEANOR T.,[8] m. CAPT. THOMAS K. S. DOANE, Sept. 11, 1862. She died Oct. 22, 1891.

Children.

    1. Annie Starr Doane, b. June 9, 1863; m. Dr. Henry Churchill, November, 1887.
    2. George H. Doane, b. Jan. 11, 1865.
    3. Miriam Churchill Doane, b. April 28, 1866.
    4. Harriet Guest Doane, b. April 6, 1868; m. Arthur S. Everett, Dec. 12, 1892.
    5. Thomas K. S. Doane, b. Dec. 9, 1870.
    6. Frank Edmund Doane, b. July 22, 1875.

843   III. REV. GEORGE,[8] m. MATILDA FALKNER, dau. of William.
844   IV. WILLIAM.[8]
    V. LYDIA.[8]
    VI. ALICE.[8]
    VII. ELIZABETH.[8]

413.

WILLIAM [7] CHURCHILL (Nehemiah,[6] Ezra,[5] Lemuel,[4] Barnabas,[3] Joseph,[2] John [1]). Married Matilda Allen, daughter of Thomas.

Children.

    I. Benjamin Hanley,[8] b. 1841; d. May 10, 1860, aged 19 years.
846 II. Frederick.[8] No further record.

414.

EZRA [7] CHURCHILL (Benjamin,[6] Ezra,[5] Lemuel,[4] Barnabas,[3] Joseph,[2] John [1]). Born in Yarmouth, N.S., Dec. 30, 1817. Died June 14, 1881. Married, Feb. 1, 1842, Mary Crosby, born Aug. 28, 1818.

Children.

    I. Benjamin,[8] b. Jan. 26, 1844; m. Mary J. Churchill, b. May 20, 1850.

      Children of Benjamin and Mary J. Churchill.

    1. Harry W., b. Nov. 10, 1872.
    2. Luella M., b. June 30, 1875.
    3. Arthur R., b. June 24, 1880.
    4. Jennie F., b. Aug. 28, 1882.
    5. Effie, b. May 19, 1886.

    II. Lydia,[8] b. Jan. 19, 1847; m. George Bell Porter.
    III. William H.,[8] b. Feb. 1, 1849.
    IV. Lucy A.,[8] b. Oct. 17, 1851.
    V. Harriet A.,[8] b. Sept. 14, 1855; m. Walter W. Harris.
    VI. Altha E.,[8] b. Sept. 6, 1856.
    VII. Mary Z.,[8] b. April 19, 1862.
    VIII. Georgia,[8] b. March 6, 1864.

415.

BENJAMIN [7] CHURCHILL (Benjamin,[6] Ezra,[5] Lemuel,[4] Barnabas,[3] Joseph,[2] John [1]). Born in Yarmouth, July 7, 1819. Married, Nov. 23, 1850, Abby Dunham, of Digby County, daughter of Captain Jonathan.

Children.

    I. Lucy,[8] m. Thomas Wyman, son of Henry, 1874.
847 II. George,[8] m. Lydia Jenkins. 1887.
848 III. Edward,[8] m. Florence Hubbard, 1895.
    IV. Sarah,[8] m. Capt. Edmund Ritchie. 1885.
849 V. Benjamin,[8] m. Mary Murray. of New York, 1887.
850 VI. Adelbert,[8] m. Lizzie Murray, of New York, 1896.
    VII. Eva C.,[8] m. Enos Cook Ryder, Oct. 4, 1896.

416.

EDSON [7] CHURCHILL (Benjamin,[6] Ezra,[5] Lemuel,[4] Barnabas,[3] Joseph,[2] John [1]). Born in Yarmouth, July 29, 1825. He died July 24, 1897. Married, Dec. 31, 1853, Sarah Jane Cann, daughter of Lyman.

Children.

I. JOANNA H.,[8] m. FITZ HOMER, son of Andrew W.
II. SARAH ELIZABETH,[8] m. M. PICKLES COOK, son of George.
III. NELLIE G.,[8] unmarried.

417.

JOHN [7] CHURCHILL (BENJAMIN,[6] EZRA,[5] LEMUEL,[4] BARNA-
BAS,[3] JOSEPH,[2] JOHN [1]). Born in Yarmouth, Aug 21, 1833. Married,
Nov. 15, 1855, ELIZA REDDING, daughter of Joseph.

Children.

I. LYDIA,[8] m. EBENEZER CHURCHILL, son of John, of Chegoggin.
II. ARABELLA,[8] unmarried.
III. GEORGIANNA,[8] m. HIRAM GOUDY, son of Zebina.
851 IV. HARVEY G.,[8] m. EMILY CROSBY, Jan. 2, 1895.
852 V. CHARLES,[8] m. and lived in New Hampshire.
VI. LOIS,[8] m. BLAND COUSINS, of Digby
VII. JOSEPHINE S.,[8] m. SAMUEL N. PATTEN, March 15, 1886.
VIII. GEORGE,[8] unmarried, a professor of music.
IX. WATSON,[8] unmarried.

418.

LEWIS C.[7] CHURCHILL (BENJAMIN,[6] EZRA,[5] LEMUEL [4]
BARNABAS,[3] JOSEPH,[2] JOHN [1]). Born March 16, 1835. Married,
Dec. 30, 1857, SARAH DURKEE, daughter of Robert.

Children.

853 I. OSBORNE,[8] m. JULIA IDA PATTEN, Nov. 11, 1885.
II. FRANCES,[8] m. MELZAR SPINNEY.
III. JANE,[8] m. HOWARD TINKHAM.
IV. MARTHA,[8] m. JOSEPH D. SHAW, 1889.
V. GEORGE,[8] unmarried.

419.

THEODORE [7] CHURCHILL (LEMUEL,[6] EZRA,[5] LEMUEL,[4] BAR-
NABAS,[3] JOSEPH,[2] JOHN [1]). Born Aug. 14, 1814, in Yarmouth, N.S.
Married MARTHA JEFFERY, daughter of Matthew.

Children.

I. HANNAH,[8] b. Nov. 12, 1837; m. CAPT. SAMUEL CHURCHILL (No.
424) July 8, 1858.
II. LEMUEL,[8] b. Dec. 6, 1840; m. ADDIE NICKERSON, of Liverpool,
N.S.
III. ELLEN,[8] b. Nov. 16, 1842; unmarried.
IV. MARGERY A.,[8] b. Feb. 1, 1844; m. JONATHAN HORTON, July 24
1862.

Children.

1. Arthur W. Horton, b. June 18, 1863.
2. Grace E. Horton, b. July 15, 1866.

V. GEORGE,[8] b. April 6, 1847; d. unmarried, June 9, 1874.
VI. THEODORE,[8] died in infancy.

VII. ANNIE L.,[8] b. May 23, 1849; m. WILLIAM H. STERRITT, son of James A.

Children.

1. George W. Sterritt, b. Feb. 4, 1878.
2. Donald B. Sterritt, b. Oct. 5, 1879.
3. Mary E. Sterritt, b. Jan. 8, 1882.
4. Grace Evelyn Sterritt, b. Oct. 16, 1884.
5. James Percy Sterritt, b. Dec. 1, 1885.

VIII. ELIZABETH,[8] b. April, 1854; d., aged 17 years, Feb. 8, 1879.

420.

JOHN[7] CHURCHILL (JOHN,[6] EZRA,[5] LEMUEL,[4] BARNABAS,[3] JOSEPH,[2] JOHN[1]). Born in Yarmouth March 6, 1821. Died Dec. 30, 1896. Married, Dec. 29, 1844, MARY ANN TAYLOR.

Children.

	I.	ALVINIA A.,[8] m. ANSEL KINNEY, Sept. 4, 1865.
854	II.	JOHN.[8] No further record.
855	III.	WILLIAM,[8] m. CAROLINE B. CROWELL.
856	IV.	HENRY.[8] No record.
	V.	ANN,[8] m. GEORGE HATFIELD.
	VI.	LYDIA,[8] m. CHARLES CAREY.
	VII.	CLARA,[8] m. ARTHUR BINGHAM, of Boston, Mass.
	VIII.	HARRIET,[8] m. HARTLEY HURLBURT.
	IX.	EMMA,[8] m. ARTHUR FADER, of Boston, Mass.

421.

JOSEPH[7] CHURCHILL (JOHN,[6] EZRA,[5] LEMUEL,[4] BARNABAS,[3] JOSEPH,[2] JOHN[1]). Born Sept. 15, 1824. Lived at Chebogue, N.S. Married CAROLINE ARCHER, daughter of Joseph T., of Chebogue, Nov. 15, 1843.

Children.

	I.	ALMIRA,[8] b. 1845; m. GILBERT BENNETT, of Digby.
857	II.	CHARLES,[8] b. 1847; m. ANNA HORTON, of Cumberland.
858	III.	JAMES EDWARD,[8] b. 1848; m. ADELAIDE LEPORD.
859	IV.	JOSEPH,[8] died young.
	V.	MARGERY A.,[8] b. 1850; m. CAPT. BRADFORD R. HILTON, July 21, 1871.
	VI.	DELIA,[8] m. JAMES GRIFFITH, of England.
870	VII.	ALFRED,[8] b. 1855; died young.
	VIII.	FLORENCE.[8]
871	IX.	ARTHUR.[8]
872	X.	FRANK.[8]

422.

FREEMAN[7] CHURCHILL (JOHN,[6] EZRA,[5] LEMUEL,[4] BARNABAS,[3] JOSEPH,[2] JOHN[1]). Born April 4, 1826. Married MARTH PURDY, daughter of Samuel.

Children.

I. ELLA.[8]
II. IDA.[8]
873 III. WILLARD.[8]

423.

JACOB[7] CHURCHILL (JOHN,[6] EZRA[5] LEMUEL,[4] BARNABAS,[3] JOSEPH,[2] JOHN[1]). Born Jan. 29, 1828. Married 1st, MARTHA PITMAN, daughter of William; married 2d, ADA EARL, daughter of Abram.

Child by First Wife.

874 I. JACOB,[8] m. MARY HALEY, dau. of Captain Joseph.

Children.

1. Charles.
2. Henry.
3. Benjamin.
4. George.
5. Sarah.

By Second Wife.

875 II. GEORGE L.[8]

424.

SAMUEL[7] CHURCHILL (JOHN,[6] EZRA,[5] LEMUEL,[4] BARNABAS,[3] JOSEPH,[2] JOHN[1]). Born Jan. 27, 1831. Married, July 8, 1858 HANNAH CHURCHILL, daughter of Theodore (No. 419).

Children.

876 I. OSCAR D.,[8] b. April 25, 1859; killed on board ship at age of 17.
877 II. FRANK R.,[8] b. July 31, 1867.
878 III. GEORGE ERNST,[8] b. July 1, 1876.

425.

LEMUEL[7] CHURCHILL (JOHN,[6] EZRA,[5] LEMUEL,[4] BARNABAS,[3] JOSEPH,[2] JOHN[1]). Born in Yarmouth, September, 1832. Married, Oct. 28, 1860, ADALINE JANE HEMEON, daughter of Captain Eleazer.

Children.

879 I. ERNST.[8]
880 II. MURRAY.[8]
881 III. ROBERT.[8]
IV. ADA.[8]
V. LUELLA.[8]
882 VI. GEORGE.[8]
883 VII. ADOLPHUS.[8]
VIII. JANE.[8]
IX. ISABELLA[8]

426.

BENJAMIN[7] CHURCHILL (SETH,[6] ISAAC,[5] ISAAC,[4] BARNABAS,[3] JOSEPH,[2] JOHN[1]). Born in Plymouth, Jan. 6, 1814. Lived in Wareham, Mass. Married, Nov. 12, 1835, BETSEY BUMPUS.

Children.

I. ANN CARR,[8] b. July 4, 1836. She was living, unmarried, in Wareham, in 1890.
II. BETSEY LOUISA,[8] b. Nov. 1, 1838; d. March 26, 1839.
III. BENJAMIN, JR.,[8] b. March 23, 1840; d. April 2, 1840.

428.

EDWIN[7] CHURCHILL (JAMES,[6] THOMAS,[5] THOMAS,[4] BARNABAS,[3] JOSEPH,[2] JOHN[1]). Born in Newmarket, N.H., March 15, 1812. He was concerned with his father in business, and lived in Portland, and for a time in Cuba, where he established a branch of the Portland firm of Churchill & Carter. Later he turned over this business to his brother, James, Jr., and returned to Portland, where he became the head of the new firm of E. Churchill & Co. He was a member of Ancient Landmark Lodge of Free Masons, Portland, from Sept. 1, 1845. He died in Portland, March 19, 1875. Married 1st, in Portland, Sept. 29, 1834, MARY PHIPPS CARTER, born May 16, 1812, and died May 3, 1863. Married 2d, WELTHA A. JENKINS HOOLE, June, 1865.

Children of First Wife born, the Second and Third in Cuba, the rest in Portland.

I. HENRIETTA JANE,[8] b. Aug. 30, 1836; m. THEODORE KINSEY, Dec. 27, 1865.
They live in Savannah, and have six children whose names we have not obtained.
II. MARY MATILDA,[8] b. in Cardenas, Cuba, 1839, and died in 1842.
884   III. JAMES EDWIN PLACIDO,[8] b. in Regla, Cuba, 1841; d. 1844.
IV. MARY STUART,[8] b. April 3, 1844; m. WILLARD LIBBY, June 13 1866.
He died in 1887. They had no children.
885   V. EDWARD SPAULDING,[8] b. April 2, 1846; m. 1st, EMMA BLAINE, Jan. 30, 1871. They were married in St. Louis, and lived there. She died in 1872.

One Child.

1. Winston Churchill.
Born in St. Louis, Nov. 10, 1871, who, upon the death of his mother, was taken by her sister, Mrs. James Brading Gazzam, and brought up by her. He was educated at the Smith Academy in St. Louis, and at the age of seventeen was appointed from one of the St. Louis districts to the United States Naval Academy at Annapolis, where he was graduated in 1894, and was assigned to the cruiser "San Francisco." In February of that year he resigned that office to take an editorial position on the "Army and Navy Journal" of New York. In February, 1895, he was appointed assistant editor of the "Cosmopolitan" magazine,

Winston Churchill

(Under No. 428, page 222.)

and in June following became managing editor. Later the same year he resigned that position, in order to devote himself exclusively to the writing of books. He published "The Celebrity," February, 1898, and "Richard Carvel" in June, 1899. The latter work at once won a place for the author in the front rank of American novelists, and was one of the most notable books of the year. "The Crisis," Mr. Churchill's latest novel, has added greatly to his high standing among American authors.

Mr. Churchill, in 1899, purchased a tract of land in Cornish, N.H., and built a fine house overlooking the Connecticut river, and resides there. Married, in St. Louis, Oct. 27, 1895, Mabel Harlakenden Hall, a lineal descendant of Mabel Harlakenden, sister of Roger, who came from Earles Colne, Essex, England, in the "Defence" in 1635, and settled at Cambridge, Mass. She married Gov. John Haynes, of Hartford, Conn., as his second wife. Winston and Mabel H. Churchill have one child, Mabel Harlakenden Churchill, b. July 9, 1897.

VI. ISABELLA,[8] b. Dec. 1, 1853; unmarried, resides in Portland, Me.

Children of Second Wife.

886 VII. HEBER BISHOP,[3] b. Dec. 1, 1866.
VIII. LAURA,[8] b. May 21, 1868.

429.

JAMES MORRILL[7] CHURCHILL (JAMES C.[6] THOMAS[5] THOMAS,[4] BARNABAS,[3] JOSEPH,[2] JOHN[1]). Born in Portland, June 11, 1816. He was brought up in his native town, and educated in the schools there. In 1825–27 he was attending the school of Master Albert Winslow, kept then on the corner of Newmarket and Newbury streets, afterwards removed to Free street, where Kilborn's carpet store now stands. He went to sea early, and was master of one of the fine ships of his father's firm at twenty-one, and afterwards had charge of the West India branch of the business, in Cuba, where he spent the winters for many years. He was senior partner of the firm of Churchill, Brown & Manson, in Portland, in 1866, at the time of the great fire. After this he went to Cuba and remained there, residing at Cardenas. Under President Cleveland he received the appointment of United States commercial agent. He died at Cardenas, April 4, 1890, and was buried in the tomb of his granddaughter, on their estate at Navajas, Cuba. He was a member of Ancient Landmark Lodge of Free Masons, at Portland, from Oct. 6, 1847, to his death. Married, in Portland, Dec. 20, 1838, HARRIET E. HOOLE, daughter of Joseph and Huldah (Fisher) Hoole, born in Portland, Sept. 21, 1818; died Jan. 5, 1894, in Cambridgeport, Mass., and buried in Evergreen Cemetery, Deering, Me.

Children of James M. and Harriet E. (Hoole) Churchill.

I. MARY LOUISA,[8] b. Oct. 22, 1839; m. MIGUEL DE SATRUSTEGUI, Oct. 4, 1858. She died at Portland, March 12, 1886. He died at Matamoras, Mexico, Jan. 5, 1882.

Children.

1. Enriqueta Satrustequi, b. Sept. 14, 1864, in Cadiz, Spain; m.
   William Santa Maria, in Boston, Sept. 14, 1885. They lived
   at Cardenas and Navajas, Cuba. Children: (1) Luis Adolfo
   Santa Maria, b. May 13, 1888; (2) Maria Alicia Santa Maria,
   b. June 24, 1889; (3) Enrique Miguel Santa Maria, b. at
   Navajas, Dec. 30, 1892. William Santa Maria died Jan. 3,
   1895. The widow, Enriqueta, came with her family to the
   States, and lived for a time in Cambridge, and later in Philadelphia, where she married Leonardo de Barros. May 1, 1897.
   Of this second marriage were born (4) Leonardo Satrustequi
   de Barros, April 18, 1898. Family lives in New York, 1902.
2. Eugenia Ynez de Satrustequi, b. Nov. 13, 1869; d. June 23,
   1870.

II. HARRIET ELIZA,[8] b. Jan. 30, 1842; m. SAMUEL S. BOYD, Oct. 5,
    1863. He was born in Portland, May 16, 1837, and died in St.
    Louis, March 5, 1883. .

Children born in St. Louis.

1. Louie Churchill Boyd, b. May 12, 1865; m. Edward Ward Corey,
   in Cambridge, Oct. 22, 1884.
2. Margaret Churchill Boyd, b. Feb. 13, 1868; m. Edwin L.
   Stanwood, Jr., Oct. 3, 1894.
3. James Churchill Boyd, b. Aug. 19, 1871; m. Ada Yerxa, of
   Smyrna, Me.
4. Samuel S Boyd, b. Feb. 12, 1874; m. Gertrude A. Peckham,
   Nov. 2, 1897.
5. Alice Churchill Boyd, b. Sept. 9, 1875.
6. Robert Southgate Boyd, b. May 6, 1877.

III. ALICE CREIGHTON,[8] b. May 6, 1844, in Portland.
IV. JULIA EDITH,[8] b. in Cardenas, Cuba, May 22, 1854; m. ARTHUR S.
    BIRD, M.D., May 22, 1877, in Portland.
    She died in Stockton, Me., July 31, 1883.

Child.

1. George Emerson Bird, Jr., b. June 9, 1878; d. Oct. 25, 1878.

V. GRACE CORA,[8] b. in Portland, Sept. 13, 1856; m. JAMES H.
   O'DONNELL, Sept. 4, 1879, and had two children.

Children.

1. Churchill O'Donnell, b. June 8, 1880.
2. Arthur Bird O'Donnell, b. July 11, 1881.

VI. MABEL,[8] b. March 8, 1859; m. PHILIP INGRAHAM JONES, in St.
    Louis, April 13, 1882.
    They lived in Portland.

Children.

1. Lawrence Churchill Jones, b. Feb. 7, 1885.
2. Helen Creighton Jones, b. Feb. 5, 1888.
3. Harold Jones, b. Feb. 7, 1891, Saturday, and died the following Monday.

430.

GEORGE ALBERT[7] CHURCHILL (JAMES C.,[6] THOMAS,[5]
THOMAS,[4] BARNABAS,[3] JOSEPH,[2] JOHN[1]). Born in Portland, Me.,
Dec. 25, 1820. Died in Washington, D.C., Jan. 30, 1890. They

JAMES MORRILL CHURCHILL.

(No. 429, page 223.)

lived in Portland until after 1861, when they removed to Washington, D.C. Married, in Portland, Aug. 26, 1856, SARAH ELLEN LUNT.

Children.

887   I. JAMES CREIGHTON,[8] b. Sept. 17, 1857; m. VIRGINIA REED MADISON, in St. Louis, Dec. 17, 1879. They lived in New Mexico, Washington, D.C., and Portland, Me.

Children.

1. James Madison, b. at Las Vegas, N.M., Oct. 3, 1880.
2. Creighton, b. at Mineral City. N.M.. Dec. 28. 1881.
3. Sarah Eleanor, b. at Washington. D.C., April 28, 1884.
4. Henry, b. April 8, 1861, at Portland, Me.; d. in Washington, July 21, 1862.
5. William Pitt Fessenden, b. Jan. 3, 1868, in Washington.

431.

FREDERICK AUGUSTUS[7] CHURCHILL (JAMES C.,[6] THOMAS,[5] THOMAS,[4] BARNABAS,[3] JOSEPH,[2] JOHN[1]). Born in Portland, Me., May 5, 1834. Lived in St. Louis, Mo. He attended the public schools of Portland, and studied law, and began practice in St. Louis. In March, 1862, he joined the army of the Potomac at Washington, as a topographical engineer, with the rank of captain on the staff of General McLellan, and served until he was superseded by General Burnside, when he was transferred to the new command and served until General Hooker succeeded to Burnside's place, when he resigned, and went to St. Louis, when the governor of Missouri appointed him to a colonelcy, with power to raise a regiment of cavalry, but he declined the appointment, and resumed his business. He has been a lawyer, eminent and prosperous, for many years. Married, at St. Louis, June 19, 1860, ANNIE LAURASON LEVERING, who was born in St. Louis, July 16, 1839, and died Jan. 25, 1882, at St. Louis.

Children born in St. Louis.

I. ALICE LAURASON,[8] b. Feb. 15, 1863; m. Arthur F. Garesché, of St. Louis, Nov. 18, 1885.

Children.

1. Frederick Churchill Garesché, b. Nov. 2, 1886; d. July, 1890.
2. Francis Van Zant Garesché, b. July 10, 1888.
3. Albert Levering Garesché, b. November, 1891.

II. KATIE,[8] b. May 8, 1865; d. Feb. 16, 1871.
888   III. CREIGHTON,[8] b. Sept. 9, 1866; m. SARAH STEVENS NEWTON, April 2, 1902.
IV. BRIANNA,[8] b. May 21, 1868; m. HERBERT MCNAMARA DIX, of St. Louis, May 20, 1891. They have no children.
889   V. FREDERICK A., JR.,[8] b. Oct. 26, 1870. He served in the Spanish-American war, in 1898; stationed at Guayamo, Porto Rico, under Colonel Sharpe.

432.

THOMAS SMITH[7] CHURCHILL (THOMAS,[6] ICHABOD,[5] THOMAS,[4] BARNABAS,[3] JOSEPH,[2] JOHN[1]). Born at Parsonsfield, Me., May 6, 1837. Lived there. Educated at Parsonsfield Acad emy. He purchased the farm of his father-in-law. He was a man of sound judgment and strict integrity, a worthy citizen, a true friend. Married 1st, at Parsonsfield, Jan. 1, 1855, MARY A. DIXON, daughter of William D. Dixon, born Oct. 2, 1833; married 2d, at Whitestown, N.Y., MRS. OLIVE B. ROBERTS.

Children.

    I. EVA,[8] b. Dec. 19, 1856; m. 1st, JOSEPH BOOTHBY, of Parsonsfield, June, 1876; m. 2d, REV. JEREMIAH BULLOCK, Dec. 22, 1880. She d. Sept. 12, 1883.

Child.

    1. Lillian R. Boothby, b. Sept. 15, 1878.

890   II. WILLIAM, D.D.,[8] b. Oct. 6, 1858; m. MABEL SWEAT, dau. of Dr. Moses E. Sweat, Dec. 2, 1880. They live in Cornish, Me. Mr. Churchill is of the Rural Telephone Company, Lord & Churchill.

One Child.

    1. Henry W., b. Dec. 29, 1884.

    III. THOMAS G.,[8] b. Nov. 20, 1863; died unmarried, Nov. 13, 1878.

433.

OTIS BANKS[7] CHURCHILL (THOMAS,[6] ICHABOD[5] THOMAS,[4] BARNABAS,[3] JOSEPH,[2] JOHN[1]). Born at Parsonsfield, Nov. 5, 1832. Married, Jan. 2, 1861, SUSAN E. FERREN, of Freedom, N.H., born Jan. 14, 1839.

Children.

891   I. CHARLES C.,[8] b. June 2, 1863.
    II. SARAH MAY,[8] b. June 8, 1865.

434.

JOHN C.[7] CHURCHILL (THOMAS,[6] ICHABOD,[5] THOMAS,[4] BARNABAS,[3] JOSEPH,[2] JOHN[1]). Born Dec. 11, 1834; married, Oct. 18, 1869, ANNIE BURK.

Children.

892   I. FRANK P.,[8] b. Nov. 24, 1872.
893   II. PRESTON,[8] b. April 21, 1876.
894   III. LINDSEY,[8] b. Dec. 18, 1881.
    IV. EULALA,[8] b. April 5, 1883.

435.

JOHN [7] CHURCHILL (JOHN T.,[6] JOSEPH,[5] THOMAS,[4] BARNA-BAS,[2] JOSEPH,[2] JOHN [1]). Born in Newmarket, N.H., May 19, 1818. Lived at Brookfield, N.H. Married, Feb. 23, 1840, ELIZA LANG, daughter of Samuel Lang, Esq.

Children born at Brookfield, N.H.

895   I. EDWIN,[8] b. April 30, 1843; m. VESTA A. CROWELL, Jan. 20, 1865, at Lawrence.

Children born in Lawrence, Mass.

1. Helen C., b. Nov. 13, 1867; d. in infancy.
2. Helen E., b. Aug. 14, 1869.
3. Edwin, Jr., b. April 10, 1881.

II. HELEN E.,[8] b. June 14, 1846; m. 1st, ALBERT D. SWAN, May 10, 1866; d. 1885; m. 2d, EDWIN W. BARTON, Jan. 10, 1887. No children.

III. JOHN,[8] b. June 14, 1858; d. in infancy.

436.

GEORGE HARRIS [7] CHURCHILL (JOHN T.,[6] JOSEPH,[5] THOMAS,[4] BARNABAS,[3] JOSEPH,[2] JOHN [1]). Born in Newmarket N.H., Nov. 7, 1819. Lived at Lawrence, Mass. Married, May 10, 1849, MARY EMILY DANIELS, daughter of Joseph, of Newmarket.

Children born in Newmarket

I. GEORGIA E.,[8] b. Aug. 19, 1851; m. CHARLES W. BRIDGE, Nov. 21, 1877.

Children.

1. William D. I. Bridge, b. in Lawrence, Nov. 26, 1878.
2. Ethel May Bridge, b. in Fall River, Feb. 10, 1883.
3. Carl Churchill Bridge, b. in Haverhill, Aug. 26, 1891

II. EVA M.,[8] b. Jan. 13, 1853; m. CHARLES HENRY EVERETT, Nov. 5, 1873.

Child.

1. Grace Everett, b. in Lawrence, Jan. 26, 1875; d. Dec. 19, 1895.

III. CORA G.,[8] b. Sept. 13, 1854; d. June 5, 1857.
IV. LUCIUS I.,[8] b. Jan. 6, 1858; d. April 7, 1859.
V. JOHN L.,[8] b. June 2, 1860; d. Oct. 4, 1864.

437.

THOMAS LINDSAY [7] CHURCHILL (JOHN T. [6] JOSEPH,[5] THOMAS,[4] BARNABAS,[3] JOSEPH,[2] JOHN [1]). Born at Newmarket, N.H., April 16, 1822. Lived at Brookfield, N.H. Married 1st, March 2, 1847, SARAH A. STACKPOLE, of Rollinsford, N.H. Married 2d, Nov. 27, 1867, NANCY M. W. SEWARD, of Boston, Mass.

Children of First Wife.

I. AZELIA C.,⁸ b. June 2, 1848; m. GEORGE H. LUCAS, of Farmington, N.H.

Child.

1. Ethel Churchill Lucas, b. May 15, 1879.

896   II. CLARENCE EDGAR,⁸ b. Sept. 5, 1849; m. ELLEN WEBSTER, in Lawrence.

Child.

1. Lotta Belle, b. March 9, 1883.

897   III. HERBERT H.,⁸ b. Sept. 2, 1853; m. FLORA G. JACK, of Gardiner, Me., June 3, 1880. They live in Lawrence, Mass.

Children.

1. Amy Phebe, b. April 29, 1881.
2. Herbert Leon, b. Aug. 29, 1884.
3. Chester Lindsay, b. Oct. 21, 1891.

IV. ESTHER ANNETTE,⁸ b. Dec. 22, 1854; m. 1st, DR. GEORGE W. PEAVEY, Aug. 6, 1878; m. 2d, CHARLES HOVEY; m. 3d, CALEB SAUNDERS. No children.

898   V. LESTER LINCOLN,⁸ b. Nov. 2, 1859; m. HATTIE BURLEY FERGUSON, Nov. 1, 1882·
They were married at Portsmouth, and lived in Brookfield, N.H., and had there

Children.

1. Guy Lester, b. June 5, 1885.
2. Gladys Ferguson, b. Jan. 24, 1890.

VI. SARAH,⁸ b. Nov. 1, 1863

Children of Second Wife.

899   VII. CHARLES I.,⁸ b. Oct. 31, 1868; m. MANDA ELLEN PLACE.
They lived in Brookfield, and had

Children.

1. Agnes Marilla, b. Oct. 21, 1893.
2. Catharine Marjorie, b. Aug. 18, 1896.

438.

ALFRED⁷ CHURCHILL (JOHN T.,⁶ JOSEPH,⁵ THOMAS,⁴ BARNABAS,³ JOSEPH,² JOHN¹). Born in Brookfield, N.H., Nov. 24, 1823. Married, May 12, 1844, LOUISA WENTWORTH GILES.

Children.

I. ELLEN ANNETTE,⁸ b. Nov. 6, 1845; m. JAMES A. MORSE.
They had one child, a daughter, name not received.

900   II. FRANK GILES,⁸ b. June 18, 1852; m. LILLIAN A. AUSTIN, of Lawrence. Lived in Lawrence.

Children.

1. Ethel Austin, b. Dec. 13, 1884.
2. Kenneth, b. Aug. 2, 1901.

439.

JOSEPH[7] CHURCHILL (JOHN T.,[6] JOSEPH,[5] THOMAS,[4] BARNABAS,[3] JOSEPH,[2] JOHN[1]). Born in Brookfield, N.H., Sept. 10, 1825. Married, Dec. 29, 1846, MERCY ANN BAILEY, of Plymouth, N.H.

Children.

I. HARRIET ANNA,[8] b. April 24, 1848; m. ARTHUR WARREN KNOWLTON, of Newburgh, Me. No children.

901 II. ORLANDO FITZLAND,[8] b. May 24, 1850; m. MARY BARBARA WEST, of Lawrence, May 3, 1873.

Child.

1. Estelle, b. July 2, 1876.

902 III. FREDERICK ARTHUR,[8] b. Aug. 12, 1861; m. ELLA M. ALLEN, of Warren, Me., Oct. 17, 1880.

Child.

1. Arthur Warren, b. Aug. 14, 1881, in Lawrence.

440.

NATHANIEL WILEY[7] CHURCHILL (COL. JOHN T.,[6] JOSEPH,[5] THOMAS,[4] BARNABAS,[3] JOSEPH,[2] JOHN[1]). Born at Brookfield, N.H., Oct. 12 1827. Died in Dorchester, Mass., May 8, 1903. Mr. Churchill was a chief compiler of " Churchills in America," and will receive a more complete notice in the introductory section of this volume. His childhood and boyhood were spent in his native town, where he attended the public schools, and passed through the common experiences of boys on New England farms. A term at South Berwick Academy, Maine, and another at Wakefield Academy, New Hampshire, completed his education. He taught a winter term in a district school, and then entered business life as a clerk in a dry-goods store in Dover, N.H. Later he succeeded to the business as principal. He later engaged in the same business at Lawrence, Mass., and Concord, N.H., for about eight years, when he sold out, and removed to Boston, forming a partnership, which, after a time, proved so unsatisfactory that he withdrew and entered upon a career as a travelling salesman, in which business he achieved great success. He entered the employment, largely, of New York firms, and his territory covered nearly the whole of the northern part of the United States, including also Delaware, Maryland, Virginia, Kentucky, Missouri, and the District of Columbia. After many years of this constant travelling, he settled down to business in Boston, in the line of manufacturing knit shawls and worsted goods, for some eighteen years, and up to his retirement in May, 1902, he continued in this business. I have been carefully through his note-books and correspondence, and while I find little previous to 1883 and 1884, I judge that his tastes had always inclined him to genealogical investigation. In his travels I find his note-books, from 1884 on, filled at one end with his business orders, and at the other with his genealogical notes. In nearly all the cities and towns he visited he evidently copied the names and addresses of Churchills in the directories, or obtained the names from the post-offices, and then, if possible, called upon such as he found to represent different families. Indeed, he has told me of this method of collecting material. In this way he collected a vast amount of data and became personally acquainted with a great number of the Churchill kindred, and his memory of them and their conditions and characteristics was marvellous. It is a matter of regret that he did not put any of this valuable information into written form. He was eager to get the *facts* of *births*, *marriages*, and *deaths*, which he deemed the most important part, and often spoke to me of going over the names in review, " sometime," when he could give me, from his memory, a biography, or some facts about each one. The " sometime " never came. We were so busy getting the vital facts that we never found time to make any attempt to formulate any of these sketches. It was only by earnest and continued urging that I was able, sometime after his retirement, to secure from him a brief statement of his own business career, just the bare facts. Mr. Churchill was of fine presence and genial manners, warmly attached to his home and family, and devoted in his friendships. Of his association with Mr. Gardner A. Churchill, of Dorchester, and their co-operation in this work until the death of the latter, the story will be given elsewhere, as well as my own connection with him, as editor and assistant compiler. For many years much of his energy, time, and interest have been devoted to the gathering and recording of material for this volume, and his loss has been a great calamity to its completion. From scores of the kindred scattered over the country who have known him, either by personal interview or correspondence, we have received letters of regret and tribute. Mr. Churchill was a member of the Massachusetts Society of Colonial Wars, in the eighth generation from Capt. John Gilman, and also in the sixth degree from Isaac Allerton. He married, March 10, 1852, MARTHA J. WIGGIN, of Dover, N.H., daughter of Capt. Benjamin and Mary (Dow) Wiggin. Mrs. Martha J. Churchill died Jan. 28, 1895.

Children.

I. ISABELLA.[8] b. at Dover, Dec. 28, 1852; died, aged fourteen months.
II. JENNIE RUSSELL,[8] b. Aug. 31, 1855; m. JOHN WOODBURY, Feb 18, 1885.

Mr. Woodbury is the son of John P. Woodbury, of Boston. He graduated at Harvard in 1880 in the class with President Roosevelt. Graduate also of Harvard Law School. Practised law until 1896, when he was appointed secretary of the Metropolitan Park Commission of Massachusetts, which position he still holds (1903) They live in Lynn. They have no children.

III. JOSEPHINE HILL,[8] b. Oct. 23, 1865. Unmarried, lived with her father until his death.

441.

ALBERT[7] CHURCHILL (EBENEZER CHAPMAN,[6] JOSEPH,[5] THOMAS,[4] BARNABAS,[3] JOSEPH,[2] JOHN[1]). Born April 13, 1813, probably in Portsmouth, N.H. Married 1st, 1863, BELINDA COLBATH, of Dover, N.H. She died 1869, aged 35. Married 2d, 1870, HANNAH J. BAILEY, of Plymouth, N.H., daughter of Joseph and Hannah.

Children of First Wife.

903   I. ALBERT ROCKWELL,[8] b. April 7, 1866.

Children of Second Wife.

II. LOTTIE MAY,[8] b. Sept. 22, 1872; d. Aug 12, 1873.
III. JENNIE LULU,[8] b. March 7, 1875.

442.

EBEN[7] CHURCHILL (EBENEZER CHAPMAN,[6] JOSEPH,[5] THOMAS[4] BARNABAS,[3] JOSEPH,[2] JOHN[1]). Born March 2, 1834, at Portsmouth, probably. Married EMMA BOWEN, daughter of William.

Children.

904   I. EDWIN,[8] b. 1861.
     II. ROENA A.,[8] b. March 28, 1862; m. CYRUS E. UDELL.
     III. DORA E.,[8] b. 1865.
905   IV. FRANK,[8] b. 1867.
906   V. JOSEPH,[8] b. 1874.

443.

JOSEPH EDWARD[7] CHURCHILL (EBENEZER CHAPMAN,[6] JOSEPH,[5] THOMAS,[4] BARNABAS,[3] JOSEPH,[2] JOHN[1]). Born at Portsmouth or Dover, Aug. 1, 1842. Married, Sept. 20, 1871, ANNIE HARMUS, of Wakefield, Mass.

Children.

907   I. CHARLES LEWIS,[8] b. Oct. 23, 1874.
908   II. WILLIAM EDWARD,[8] b. Dec. 1, 1876.
909   III. WALTER ERVING,[8] b. July 18, 1878.
     IV. LAURA MABEL,[8] b. Sept. 3, 1883.

444.

WOODBURY LANGDON[7] CHURCHILL (EBENEZER[6] JOSEPH[5] THOMAS,[4] BARNABAS,[3] JOSEPH,[2] JOHN[1]). Born in New Hampshire, Aug. 9, 1847.

The names of children were found after the name was passed on
page 115.
Married MARY A. NASON.

Children.

I. ELLA M.,[8] b. Aug..26, 1878.
II. EMMA T.,[8] b. Nov. 3, 1880.

445.

ADDISON[7] CHURCHILL (NATHANIEL[6] JOSEPH[5] THOMAS[4]
BARNABAS,[3] JOSEPH,[2] JOHN[1]).   Born in Exeter, N.H., May 27,
1831.   Married JENNIE ISABELLA GREEN, born May 17, 1833.

Children.

    I. MINNIE.[8] b. May 28, 1856; d. May 31, 1856.
    II. CHARLES SIDNEY,[8] b. July 4, 1857; d. June 18, 1866.
910   III. ADDISON,[8] b. Oct. 4, 1860.
    IV. LeFOREST E.,[8] b. Nov. 9, 1862; d. May 4, 1863.

446.

ALMANDER[7] CHURCHILL (NATHANIEL,[6] JOSEPH,[5] THOMAS,[4]
BARNABAS,[3] JOSEPH,[2] JOHN[1]).   Born at Exeter, N.H., July 14,
1834.   Married 1st, CLARA F. TAYLOR; married 2d, CATHARINE C.
PARKHURST.

Child of First Wife.

    I. CLARA S.,[8] b. March, 1856.

Children of Second Wife.

    II. CARRIE H.,[8] b. March 31, 1858.
911 III. FRANK A.[8]
912 IV. FRED S.[8]
    V. JAMES LOUIS,[8] d. in infancy.
    VI. BLANCHE C.,[8] d. in infancy.
    VII. JAMES LOUIS, 2D,[8] d. in infancy.

447.

NATHANIEL[7] CHURCHILL (NATHANIEL,[6] JOSEPH,[5] THOMAS,[4]
BARNABAS,[3] JOSEPH,[2] JOHN[1]).   Born at Exeter, N.H., Aug. 17,
1836.   Married, Dec. 21, 1858, ELIZABETH A. JAMES, who was born
in Hampton, N.H., Nov. 9, 1837.

Children.

    I. ALICE,[8] b. May 26, 1860; m. WILLIAM T. WILDER, April 30, 1884.
    II. WALTER J.,[8] b. Aug. 18, 1862; d. Sept. 27, 1863.

448.

JASPER HAZEN[7] CHURCHILL (NATHANIEL,[6] JOSEPH,[5]
THOMAS,[4] BARNABAS,[3] JOSEPH,[2] JOHN[1]).   Born at Exeter, N.H.,
Nov. 25, 1844; died Oct. 6, 1879.   Married at Exeter, N.H., May
31, 1877, ELLA A. PORTER.

Child.

913   I. JOSEPH PORTER,s b. March 17, 1878.

449.

SHELDON W.[7] CHURCHILL (DANIEL,[6] JOSEPH,[5] THOMAS,[4] BARNABAS,[3] JOSEPH,[2] JOHN [1]). Born in New Hampshire, Feb. 14, 1835. Married 1st, May 14, 1861, OLIVE A. WIGGIN; she died Oct. 31, 1873; married 2d, Nov. 10, 1875, CLARA B. DOUGLAS.

Children of First Wife.

   I. ELLINOR G.,[8] b. June, 1862; d. Jan. 7, 1864.
  II. ISABELLE,[8] b. February, 1865; d. June 13, 1879.
 III. FRANK S.,[8] b. August, 1869; d. May 14, 1873.
 IV. OLIVE A.,[8] b. October, 1873; d. April 27, 1874.

Children of Second Wife.

   V. ELLINOR M.,[8] b. August. 1876.
  VI. CLARA L.,[8] b. July. 1878.
914 VII. DANIEL,[8] b. January, 1881.

450.

ALGERNON HOWE[7] CHURCHILL (THOMAS C.,[6] NATHANIEL,[5] THOMAS,[4] BARNABAS,[3] JOSEPH,[2] JOHN [1]). Born at Wilton, Me., June 16, 1837. He served in the Civil War, in Company K, First Maine Regiment. Married, Nov. 9, 1861, MARTHA HELEN STINCH-FIELD, of Clinton, Me.

Children born, first in Lewiston, Me., second in Salem, Mass.

  I. ADELLA ASHLEY,s b. Sept 9, 1862, d. Jan. 30, 1865.
 II. MABEL GERTRUDE,[8] b. Oct. 7, 1867, m. CHARLES O. FARRAR, Sept. 30, 1889.

451.

JOHN HENRY[7] CHURCHILL (JOHN,[6] NATHANIEL,[5] THOMAS,[4] BARNABAS,[3] JOSEPH,[2] JOHN [1]). Born July 1, 1844. He was a physician at Cross Rivers, N.Y. They lived at Middleton, Conn., and Cross Rivers, N.Y. Married, Feb. 9, 1868, IRENE G. CANFIELD, of Middleton, Conn.

Children.

  I. IRENE,s b. at Middleton, Conn., Oct. 19, 1869.
915 II. PAUL,[8] b. at Cross Rivers, N.Y., Aug. 25, 1871.

452.

NAHUM B.[7] CHURCHILL (NATHANIEL,[6] NATHANIEL,[5] THOMAS,[4] BARNABAS,[3] JOSEPH,[2] JOHN [1]). Born Jan. 8, 1843. Lived in Lynn, Mass. Married, June 8, 1867, LYDIA A. MOORE.

One child.

  I. ALBERTA S.,[8] b. Oct. 16, 1876.

455.

WILLIAM ALVAH[7] CHURCHILL (WILLIAM G.,[6] NATHANIEL,[5] THOMAS,[4] BARNABAS,[3] JOSEPH,[2] JOHN[1]). Born June 4, 1832, probably in New Hampshire. Married MARTHA FOLSOM ROBINSON, of Greenland, who was born Jan. 30, 1831.

Children.

	I.	CHARLOTTE ANN,[8] b. Dec. 23. 1853.
916	II.	HORACE MANN,[8] b. Aug. 21, 1855.
	III.	HARRIET BEECHER,[8] b. April 18, 1857.
	IV.	ALICE BELL,[8] b. Oct. 6, 1859.
917	V.	WINFIELD SCOTT,[8] b. Oct. 28, 1861.
	VI.	ETTA MYRTILLA,[8] b. Sept. 14, 1864.
	VII.	FLORENCE MAY.[8] b. June 24, 1867.
918	VIII.	ARTHUR LESLIE,[8] b. Oct. 21, 1871.
	IX.	GRACE EDNA,[8] b. Aug. 31, 1874.

456.

FREDERICK AUGUSTUS[7] CHURCHILL (CHARLES,[6] JOHN,[5] EBENEZER,[4] BARNABAS,[3] JOSEPH,[2] JOHN[1]). Born in Pittsfield, Sept. 6, 1831. Married, Sept. 11, 1861, CLARA BUTLER, of Pittsfield.

Children.

	I.	CHARLOTTE MARIA,[8] b. Dec. 8, 1863; m. WILLIAM BARROWS, of Pittsfield, March 13, 1884.
919	II.	CHARLES EDWARD,[8] b. Dec. 5, 1865.

457.

EDWARD PAYSON[7] CHURCHILL (CHARLES,[6] JOHN,[5] EBENEZER,[4] BARNABAS,[3] JOSEPH,[2] JOHN[1]). Born in Pittsfield, Aug. 6, 1834. They lived in Pittsfield. He died Sept. 28, 1874. Married, at Pittsfield, Jan. 3, 1870, DORA KETTELL. They had one son.

Child.

I. GEORGE,[8] b. Nov. 7, 1870; d. July 22, 1871.

458.

JOHN B.[7] CHURCHILL (SAMUEL A.,[6] JOHN,[5] EBENEZER[4] BARNABAS,[3] JOSEPH,[2] JOHN[1]). Born in Pittsfield, Dec. 12, 1844. Married, April 8, 1868, MARY BELDEN, of Lenox.

Children born in Pittsfield

920	I.	SAMUEL BELDEN,[8] b. May 22, 1872.
	II.	JENNIE ESTHER,[8] b. Nov. 13, 1876; d. April 11, 1880.
	III.	EVA BELDEN,[8] b. Jan. 15, 1884.

459.

GEORGE⁷ CHURCHILL (Orrin,⁶ Lemuel,⁵ John,⁴ Barnabas ³ Joseph,² John¹). Born April 12, 1834. Lives at Buchanan, Mich. Married, July 16, 1856, Elizabeth Halsted.

Children.

921   I. William,⁸ b. Dec. 25, 1858.
922   II. Harry,⁸ b. Feb. 21, 1862.

460.

OWEN⁷ CHURCHILL (Orrin,⁶ Lemuel,⁵ John,⁴ Barnabas,³ Joseph,² John¹). Born in Truxton, N.Y., April 24, 1840. Lived at Three Oaks, Mich. Married, Dec. 20, 1869, Flora Adams.

Children.

923   I. Lemuel.⁸
     II. Emma.⁸
924   III. John.⁸

461.

JOHN PORTER⁷ CHURCHILL (Orrin,⁶ Lemuel,⁵ John,⁴ Barnabas,³ Joseph,² John¹). Born at Buchanan, Mich., Dec. 2, 1846, and lived there. Married, Oct. 12, 1873, Harriet Moore.

Children.

     I. Mertie,⁸ b. July 25, 1874; d. Aug. 26, 1878.
925   II. Clyde,⁸ b. July 30, 1879.
     III. Leonora,⁸ b. May 18, 1881.
926   IV. Guy.⁸ No record.

462.

GEORGE CLINTON⁷ CHURCHILL (Alanson ⁶ Bradford,⁵ John,⁴ Barnabas,³ Joseph,² John¹). Born Dec. 27, 1847. Lived in Pittsfield. Married Eunice Follansbee.

Children.

927   I. George.⁸
928   II. Robert.⁸
929   III. Raymond.⁸
930   IV. Bradford.⁸

463.

MARLBOROUGH⁷ CHURCHILL (Benjamin K.,⁶ Joseph,⁵ Joseph,⁴ Joseph,³ Joseph,² John¹). Born in Bristol, R.I., February, 1816. Graduated at West Point in 1836. Appointed assistant inspector of artillery, under General Anderson. Resigning, he was made engineer of Croton Water Works in 1842. Afterwards he was appointed superintendent of a military school at Sing Sing. Married, Sept. 2, 1837, Elizabeth Louise Voris.

Children.

    I. MARY,[8] b. September, 1848; unmarried.
   II. MARLBOROUGH, JR.,[8] b. January, 1856; unmarried.

, 465.

WARNER[7] CHURCHILL (JOHN,[6] JOSEPH,[5] JOSEPH,[4] JOSEPH,[3] JOSEPH,[2] JOHN[1]). Born in Mooers, N.Y., July 16, 1808. Settled for a time in Hemmingford, Canada. He removed to Michigan in 1843, and lived at Onion, in that State, where he was a merchant, and where he died, Dec. 24, 1858. Married at Hemmingford, Canada, Feb. 18, 1835, ALMIRA SCHRIVER, who was born Nov. 12, 1812, and died June 21, 1886.

Children born, except the youngest, in Michigan.

     I. WILLIAM ASHER,[8] b. Nov. 26, 1835; unmarried. He served in the Civil War, and was killed in the battle of Antietam, Sept. 17, 1862.
    II. CHARLES,[8] b. Oct. 14, 1837; d. Feb. 27, 1867.
   III. JOHN,[8] b. June 15, 1839; d. unmarried Jan. 29, 1870.
931   IV. WARNER, JR.,[8] b. Jan. 11, 1841; m. SARAH HARRIS, Feb. 25, 1864. They lived in Mt. Pleasant, Mich. He served in the Civil War four and one-half years. Then "farmed" for eight years, and for twenty-four years has been engaged in a flourishing flour business.
932   V. JAMES H.,[8] b. April 5, 1844; m. CATHERINE SIMPSON, April 14, 1875.
        They lived in Pontiac, Mich., and had

Children.

    1. Edward H., b. Feb. 19, 1876.
    2. Charles, b. Feb. 14, 1878; d. Aug. 30, 1893.
    3. Jennie, b. April 15, 1880.
    4. Fannie, b. Nov. 2, 1882.
    5. Warner A., b. June 1, 1886.
    6. Sarah E., b. Nov. 29, 1891.

466.

GILBERT[7] CHURCHILL (JOHN,[6] JOSEPH,[5] JOSEPH,[4] JOSEPH[3] JOSEPH,[2] JOHN[1]). Born in Mooers, N.Y., May 18, 1810. Died in Wallace, Ont., Sept. 6, 1858. Married ELIZABETH (———).

Children.

     I. LAVINA.[8]
    II. HARRIET.[8]
   III. ALMIRA.[8]
   IV. MARY ANN.[8]
    V. JENNIE.[8]
   VI. LIZZIE.[8]

468.

THEODORE[7] CHURCHILL (JOHN,[6] JOSEPH,[5] JOSEPH,[4] JOSEPH,[3] JOSEPH,[2] JOHN[1]). Born in Mooers, N.Y., May 25, 1822, and lived there. Married LUCY FROST.

Children.

I. JESSIE.[8]
933   II. LUCIUS.[8]

469.

BENJAMIN LEVERY[7] CHURCHILL (JOSEPH,[6] JOHN,[5] JOSEPH,[4] JOSEPH,[3] JOSEPH,[2] JOHN[1]). Born in Mooers, N.Y., Feb. 7, 1816. Served in Civil War. Died at Point of Rocks, Va., March 14, 1865. Married MARIA FASSETT.

Children born in Mooers, N. Y.

934   I. MALCOLM S.,[8] b. Jan. 9, 1845; m. CARRIE HENDERSON, April 23, 1879.
II. BENJAMIN M.,[8] b. Aug. 22, 1847.
III. CALISTA M.,[8] b. Sept. 21, 1849; d. March 29, 1867.
935   IV. ALANSON B.,[8] b. June 27, 1853; m. EMMA LAKE, June 17, 1884.
V. LUCY M.,[8] b. May 18, 1856; m. ROBERT E. MARKEE, July 4, 1871.
VI. NELLIE M.,[8] b. Sept. 6, 1858; d. June 23, 1864.[1]
VII. HARRIET S.,[8] b. Feb. 9, 1862.
VIII. LILLIE F.,[8] b. April 13, 1864; m. PLINY A. CONKEY, of Windom, Minn., Dec. 27, 1883.

470.

JOSEPH B.[7] CHURCHILL (JOSEPH,[6] JOHN,[5] JOSEPH,[4] JOSEPH,[3] JOSEPH,[2] JOHN[1]). Born in Mooers, N.Y., June 23, 1820. Lived in Clintonville and Mooers, N Y., and St. Croix Falls, Wis. Married, Dec. 11, 1841, ELIZA TURNBALL.

Children.

I. CHARLES HENRY,[8] b. at Clintonville, N Y., May 19, 1843; d. at Petersburg, Va., Dec. 17, 1866.
II. MARCIA MARIA,[8] b. at Clintonville, N.Y., June 7, 1844; m. PHINEAS B. LACY, Oct. 7, 1861.
III. LEMUEL THOMAS.[8] b. at Clintonville, N.Y., Oct. 11, 1845; drowned at St. Croix Falls, Wis., in 1857.
IV. AMANDA A.,[8] b. at Mooers, N.Y., July 8, 1847; m. JOSEPH ROGERS, May 11, 1865.
V. OLIVE L.,[8] b. at Mooers, N.Y., Dec. 9, 1850; d. at Hadran, Mich., Jan. 25, 1883.
936   VI. GEORGE W.,[8] b. at Mooers, N.Y., May 5, 1852; m. REBECCA ORR, July 3, 1878.
VII. JEROME B.,[8] b. at St. Croix Falls, Wis., May 28, 1855; d. Oct. 25 1855.
VIII. ELEANOR S.,[8] b. at St. Croix Falls, Wis., Nov. 12, 1856; d. Aug. 31, 1858.
937   IX. WILLIAM A.,[8] b. at St. Croix Falls, Wis., Sept. 26, 1859; m. ANNA A. PAYNE, of Taylor's Falls, Minn., in 1882.
X. MARTHA S.,[8] b. at St. Croix Falls, Oct. 12, 1862.

471.

GEORGE W.[7] CHURCHILL (JOSEPH,[6] JOHN,[5] JOSEPH,[4] JOSEPH,[3] JOSEPH,[2] JOHN[1]). Born at Mooers, N.Y., April 10, 1825. Married 1st, Sept 26, 1852, ABIGAIL J. HITCHCOCK. She died without issue in 1854. Married 2d, ELLEN F. STRONG, of Downer's Grove, Ill.

Children by Second Wife.

938 I. GEORGE W.,[8] b. Dec. 11, 1862.
 II. MINNIE B.,[8] b. March 16, 1864.
 III. KATE F.,[8] b. Aug. 5, 1868.

472.

SYLVESTER S.[7] CHURCHILL (JOSEPH,[6] JOHN[5] JOSEPH[4] JOSEPH,[3] JOSEPH[2] JOHN[1]). Born in Mooers, N.Y., Nov. 6, 1827. He died in Mooers, N.Y., in 1884. Married, in Chazy, N.Y., Oct. 19, 1853, JANE R. RANSOM.

Children

 I. DORA M.,[8] b. at Mooers, N.Y., May 17, 1857; m. JOHN W. HAVEN, April 29, 1883.
 II. WILLIS PHILLIPS,[8] b. at Burlington, Vt., Nov. 6, 1861; d. April 26, 1868.
 III. ESTELLA M.,[8] b. at Mooers, N.Y., Feb. 13, 1866.
 IV. JANE RANSOM,[8] b. at Mooers, N.Y., Feb. 14, 1871.

473.

CHARLES C.[7] CHURCHILL (JOSEPH,[6] JOHN,[5] JOSEPH[4] JOSEPH,[8] JOSEPH,[2] JOHN[1]). Born at Mooers, N.Y., June 15, 1836. Lived in Georgetown, Col. Married, at Taylorsville, Iowa, April 7, 1866, HARRIET A. MCKIBBEN.

Children.

 I. KATE E.,[8] b. at Taylorsville, May 7, 1868.
939 II. CHARLES FREDERICK,[8] b. May 16, 1871; d. Oct. 7, 1877.
 III. FANNIE G.,[8] b. June 2, 1873; d. July 17, 1874.
 IV. LE ROY,[8] b. March 2, 1875; d. April 20, 1880.
 V. LA RUE,[8] b. Nov. 13, 1878; d. April 14, 1880.
940 VI. HENRY C.,[8] b. at Georgetown, Col., April 1, 1881.

474.

SAMUEL HARVEY[7] CHURCHILL (SAMUEL,[6] JOHN,[5] JOSEPH,[4] JOSEPH,[8] JOSEPH,[2] JOHN[1]). Born Jan. 24, 1819, at Mooers, N.Y. Married, Feb. 19, 1851, EVELINE H. KNAPP.

Children.

 I. ELLA.[8]
 II. KATHARINE SPRAGUE.[8]
 III. FRANCES,[8] d. in infancy.
 IV. CAROLINE,[8] d. in infancy.
941 V. PLINY FISK.[8]
942 VI. JOHN CHARLES.[8]

HON. JOHN CHARLES CHURCHILL,
OSWEGO, N.Y.
(No. 475, page 239.)

475.

HON. ,JOHN CHARLES[7] CHURCHILL (SAMUEL,[6] JOHN,[5] JOSEPH,[4] JOSEPH,[3] JOSEPH,[2] JOHN[1]). Born in Mooers, N.Y., Jan. 17, 1821. Attended the common schools of his native town, and completed his college preparation at Burr Seminary, Manchester, Vt. He graduated at Middlebury College in 1843. He became a teacher, first at Castleton Seminary and later in Middlebury College, attended a course in the Harvard Law School, and entered the office of Joshua A. Spencer, of Utica, where he was associated with the late Roscoe Conklin and Hon. Albertus Perry, formerly of Oswego. Mr. Churchill was admitted to the bar in July, 1847, and commenced the practice of his profession. In 1848 Mr. Churchill opened an office in Oswego, where he has since resided. He has been called repeatedly·by his townsmen to fill places of public honor and trust. He was elected in 1857 county attorney of Oswego, and 1860, county judge. In 1866, and again in 1868, he was elected representative to Congress from his district, where he served with distinguished ability and honor. He has been a trusted leader in politics, influential as a member of the Cincinnati convention of 1876, and presidential elector-at-large in 1880 of the convention which nominated Mr. Garfield. In 1881 Mr. Churchill received the high honor of being appointed judge of the Supreme Court, which place he filled until 1892, the end of the constitutional age limit. He was on the faculty of the College of Law, in Syracuse, many years, up to February, 1897, when ill-health forced him to resign. After his retirement from the bench he resumed the practice of the law in company with his son, Lawrence W. Churchill, under the firm name of J. C. & L. W. Churchill. The degree of LL.D was conferred upon him by Middlebury College in 1874, and the same honor was received· from Hamilton College in 1882. Judge Churchill married, at Oswego, N.Y., Sept. 11, 1849, KATHARINE THOMAS SPRAGUE, daughter of Dr. Lawrence Sprague and his wife Katharine, and born at Wiscasset, Me., May 21, 1821.

Children of Hon. John C. and Katharine T. Churchill.

I. LAWRENCE SPRAGUE,[8] b. June 21, 1850; d. at Oswego, April 6, 1862.

II. KATHARINE SPRAGUE,[8] b. Sept. 6, 1853; d. Aug. 2, 1899, at Oswego, N.Y.

943 III. JOHN CHARLES,[8] b. Sept. 10, 1856; m. MARY B. WESTBROOK, of Ogdensburg, N.Y., Dec. 10, 1887. He graduated at La Fayette College, 1878. Lives in Oswego, a civil engineer. They have three children: (1) John Westbrook, b Feb. 5, 1889; (2) Lawrence S., b. June 10, 1890; (3) Walter Allen, b. May 10, 1893; (4) a daughter, d. in infancy.

IV. MARTHA ELIOT,[8] b'. Nov. 3, 1858; m. DR. WALTER R. FISHER,
Oct. 7, 1886. Dr. Fisher was a surgeon in the United States
army, and died at Fort Mead, South Dakota, June, 1896. Mrs.
Fisher lives with her father in Oswego.

V. ALICE,[8] b. Sept. 26, 1860; d. Sept. 25, 1895, at Oswego, N.Y.

944   VI. LAWRENCE WILLIAM,[8] b. Sept. 7, 1862; m. IDA C. LILLEY, of New
York, June 7, 1899. He graduated at Yale College in 1886, and
is now in the practice of the law, with his office at No. 2 Wall
street, New York.

477.

CHARLES[7] CHURCHILL (ELIEZER,[6] ELIEZER,[5] ELIEZER,[4]
ELIEZER,[3] ELIEZER,[2] JOHN[1]). Born in West Bridgewater, Aug. 17,
1791. Lived in Weymouth and West Bridgewater. Married, July,
28, 1814, DORCAS PRATT HAWES. She was born Dec. 12, 1795.

Children.

I. LUCY,[8] b. in Weymouth, April 19, 1816. .
II. LYDIA,[8] b. in Weymouth, Dec. 13, 1818.
III. HARRIET,[8] b. in West Bridgewater, Nov. 14, 1820.
IV. CHARLES,[8] b. in West Bridgewater, Jan. 23, 1823; d. aged 3 months.
945   V. CHARLES EDWARD,[8] b. in West Bridgewater, June 1, 1824.
   VI. ELIZABETH,[8] b. in West Bridgewater, June 2, 1827.
VII. MARY PORTER,[8] b in West Bridgewater, June 9, 1831.
VIII. DORCAS ANN,[8] b. in West Bridgewater, Feb. 11, 1834.
946   IX. RODNEY,[8] b. in West Bridgewater, May 12, 1837.
947   X. NEWTON,[8] b. in West Bridgewater, April 13, 1839.
948   XI. GEORGE,[8] b. in West Bridgewater, March 9, 1844.

478.

WILLIAM[7] CHURCHILL (THADDEUS,[6] THADDEUS,[5] ELIEZER,[4]
ELIEZER,[3] ELIEZER,[2] JOHN[1]). Born, probably, in Kingston, Nov.
25, 1800. Died Jan. 16, 1862. Married 1st, Sept. 7, 1828, MARY C.
FULLER. She died June 22, 1829; no children. Married 2d, Aug.
28, 1830, BEULAH ORTON. She died Dec. 18, 1851; no children.
Married 3d, Aug. 28, 1852, JANE R. SQUIRES. Died Feb. 24,
1887. She was born in New London, Conn.

One Child by Third Wife.

I. CHARLES W.[8] Unmarried. In 1900 was living in New London.

479.

HENRY[7] CHURCHILL (THADDEUS,[6] THADDEUS,[5] ELIEZER,[4]
ELIEZER,[3] ELIEZER,[2] JOHN[1]). Born, probably, in Kingston, Nov.
18, 1802. They lived in Kingston, Mass. Married, Aug. 2, 1832,
MARIA B. SWIFT.

Children born in Kingston.

949   I. HENRY L.[8] Lived in North Cambridge.
II. LUCIA M.[8] Lived in New Hampshire.

480.

CAPT. JOSEPH LEWIS[7] CHURCHILL (JOSEPH,[6] THAD-DEUS,[5] ELIEZER,[4] ELIEZER,[3] ELIEZER,[2] JOHN[1]). Born in Plymouth, Aug. 1, 1805. He was a sailor, and died at sea, Aug. 18, 1842, on board the brig "Androscoggin," of Portland, on the passage from Wilmington, N.C., to Jamaica. Married, May 27, 1830, ABIGAIL MERRILL GOODWIN, of Falmouth, Me. She died August, 1846.

Children.

950   I. CHARLES THOMAS,[8] b. June 16, 1833.
     II. LOUISA LE BARON,[8] b. June 22, 1835; m. BENJAMIN F. DYER, Feb. 22, 1854.
     III. SARAH ANN,[8] b. Nov. 2, 1837; m. GEORGE F. MERRILL, Jan. 3, 1856.
     IV. ABBY LEWIS,[8] b. Sept. 12, 1839; m. DAVID HALL, Aug. 4, 1856.
     V. HELEN HARVEY,[8] b. Oct. 15, 1841; d. Aug. 30, 1842.

481.

SAMUEL[7] CHURCHILL (SAMUEL,[6] SAMUEL,[5] JOSIAH,[4] ELIE-ZER,[3] ELIEZER,[2] JOHN[1]). Born in Plymouth, Aug. 31, 1802. Married, Jan. 1, 1827, RACHEL CAPEN, who was born July 25, 1804.

Children.

     I. ELIZABETH CAPEN,[8] b. Sept. 2, 1827; d. June 27, 1847.
     II. SARAH FRANCES,[8] b. April 29, 1829; m. HENRY B. CRANE, Dec. 12, 1848.
     III. MARTHA ANN,[8] b. March 10, 1831; m. MASSENA BALLOU, Nov. 4, 1849.
     IV. LAURA AURELIA,[8] b. March 18, 1833; m. CHARLES UPHAM, Nov. 12, 1852.
     V. INFANT, not named, died soon.
     VI. ELLEN COVINGTON,[8] b. May 19, 1837; m. GEORGE P. REYNOLDS, April 18, 1868.
     VII. SAMUEL HENRY,[8] d. in infancy.
     VIII. MARY ELMIRA,[8] b. Dec. 24, 1842; m. ALFRED UPHAM, Dec. 25 1861.
     IX. ALICE ISABEL,[8] b. Jan. 26, 1846; m. NATHANIEL F. FOSTER, Jan. 25, 1865.

482.

EZRA[7] CHURCHILL (SAMUEL,[6] SAMUEL,[5] JOSIAH,[4] ELIEZER,[3] ELIEZER,[2] JOHN[1]). Born in Plymouth, March 10, 1805. He died April 17, 1850. Married, June 29, 1830, MEHITABLE PORTER, who was born in Stoughton, Dec. 3, 1808, and died Dec. 28, 1863.

Children.

     I. MARY ELIZA,[8] b. Oct. 11, 1832; d. Sept. 28, 1853; unmarried.
     II. FREDERICK,[8] b. Jan. 5, 1839; d. unmarried (lost at sea), 1860/61.
     III. CATHERINE PORTER,[8] b. Oct. 21, 1843; d. Oct. 29, 1845.
951   IV. EZRA RHODES,[8] b. April 4, 1847, at North Bridgewater; m. ELLA JANE THAYER, April 2, 1870; b. March 4, 1850.

484·

JOHN E.[7] CHURCHILL (SAMUEL,[6] SAMUEL,[5] JOSIAH,[4] ELIEZER,[3] ELIEZER,[2] JOHN [1]). Born in Stoughton, 1814. Married ELEANOR SHUMAN.

Children born in Plymouth.

952   I. FRANCIS H.,[8] b. July 6, 1840.
953   II. SAMUEL E.,[8] b. Aug. 31, 1842.
       III. A DAUGHTER, d. in infancy.
       IV. A DAUGHTER, d. in infancy.

485.

LEWIS P.[7] CHURCHILL (ENOS,[6] ENOS,[5] JOSIAH,[4] ELIEZER,[3] ELIEZER,[2] JOHN [1]). Born Nov. 8, 1826. Married ANN LOCKE, in Lockport, N.S.

Children.

954   I. ENOS,[8] b. Sept. 6, 1852.
       II. TRYPHENIA,[8] b. Oct. 5, 1854.
955   III. EDMUND,[8] b. Aug. 7, 1856.
       IV. FLORENCE,[8] b. Sept. 11, 1858
956   V. ARCHIBALD,[8] b. Dec. 9, 1860.
957   VI. LEWIS,[8] b. March 2, 1863.
958   VII. HENRY,[8] b. April 7, 1865.
959   VIII. FRANK,[8] b. Jan. 14, 1867.
960   IX. JOHN,[8] b. Jan. 1, 1869.
       X. JOSEPHINE,[8] b. Sept. 15, 1871.

488.

FRED LEE [7] CHURCHILL (JOHN D.,[6] SILVANUS,[5] JOSIAH,[4] ELIEZER,[3] ELIEZER,[2] JOHN [1]). Born at Plymouth, Feb. 8, 1846. Married, June 7, 1874, MARY N. DAMON.

Children.

961   I. JOHN DARLING,[8] b. June 4, 1875.
962   II. FREDERICK,[8] b. June 11, 1884.
963   III. THOMAS GILMAN,[8] b. Sept. 30, 1886.

489.

JOSIAH DARLING [7] CHURCHILL (JOHN D.,[6] SILVANUS [5] JOSIAH,[4] ELIEZER,[3] ELIEZER,[2] JOHN [1]). Born at Plymouth, Oct. 24, 1853. Married, Oct. 6, 1876, MARTHA TILLSON.

Child.

       I. MARCIA J.,[8] b. Aug. 26, 1877.

491.

WILLIAM WORCESTER [7] CHURCHILL (LEMUEL,[6] JESSE,[5] JONATHAN,[4] ELIEZER,[3] ELIEZER,[2] JOHN [1]). Born at Richmond, Va., 1819. Married 1st, Feb. 13, 1850, CAROLINE GORE WOODMAN, who died Dec. 31, 1860. Married 2d, MRS. (———) HURLL.

Children of First Wife.

       I. CAROLINE.[8] b. Jan. 6, 1851; m. FRANK BANCROFT, May 7, 1872.
       II. WILLIAM WORCESTER, JR.,[8] b. Aug. 29, 1858; unmarried.

493.

WILLIAM LEATHERS[7] CHURCHILL, JR. (WILLIAM L.[6] FRANCIS,[5] JONATHAN,[4] ELIEZER,[3] ELIEZER,[2] JOHN[1]). Born in West Fairlee, Vt., Sept. 5, 1811. Married MINERVA NICHOLS, of Corinth, Vt.

Children.

I. SOPHIA.[8]
II. EMILY HOWARD.[8]
III. PAMELIA.

494.

CHAUNCEY CARROLL[7] CHURCHILL (WILLIAM L.,[6] FRANCIS,[5] JONATHAN,[4] ELIEZER,[3] ELIEZER,[2] JOHN[1]). Born at West Fairlee, Sept. 26, 1815. He was treasurer of Norfolk County for thirty-four years, and died April 18, 1889. Married PERMELIA SABIN, of Amesbury, Mass.

Children born in Dedham.

I. ISADORA M.,[8] b. Nov. 9, 1846; m. CHARLES H. LELAND.
963a   II. CHAUNCEY SABIN,[8] b. Aug. 7, 1854; m. GRACE A. CHURCHILL at Hyde Park, April 17, 1879. She was the daughter of Ethan Stetson Churchill and Annie M., his wife.

Children born in Dedham.

1. Grace Ethel, b. April 25, 1881.
2. Marion Sabin, b. Aug. 9, 1882.
3. Chauncey Carroll, b. June 23, 1887.

495.

BENJAMIN PIXLEY[7] CHURCHILL (WILLIAM L.,[6] FRANCIS,[5] JONATHAN,[4] ELIEZER,[3] ELIEZER,[2] JOHN[1]). Born at West Fairlee, Vt., Sept. 2, 1822. He died in Fairlee, Aug. 14, 1864. Married SUSAN THOMPSON, of West Fairlee, Vt.

Children.

964   I. FRANCIS C.[8]
965   II. WILLIAM A.[8]

496.

FRANCIS VENNELL[7] CHURCHILL (WILLIAM L.[6] FRANCIS,[5] JONATHAN,[4] ELIEZER,[3] ELIEZER,[2] JOHN[1]). Born at West Fairlee, Dec. 6, 1827. Lives at Bradford, Vt. Married MARINDA E. MUNN, Jan. 31, 1854.

Child.

I. JOHN FRANK,[8] b. Sept. 7, 1868; d. July 22, 1873.

498.

DAVID CARROLL[7] CHURCHILL, JR. (DAVID C.,[6] FRANCIS,[5] JONATHAN,[4] ELIEZER,[3] ELIEZER,[2] JOHN[1]). Born in Lyme, N.H., April 13, 1821. Married, Oct. 20, 1847, LYDIA ANN PERRY, who was born July 17, 1823.

Children.

I. CAROLINE PERRY,[8] b. Nov. 6, 1852; m. PEYSON E. FAIRFIELD, Nov. 6, 1875.

II. HARRIET MARIA,[8] b. Aug. 19, 1854; d. July 5, 1863.

III. JULIA GRAY,[8] b. Jan. 13, 1857; d. May 10, 1865.

IV. EMMA FRANKLIN,[8] b. May 8, 1861; m. EDWIN D. CHASE, Oct. 10, 1884.

V. ALICE GRAY,[8] b. April 29, 1865; m. HORACE W. OTIS, April 8, 1898.

499.

CHARLES HENRY[7] CHURCHILL (DAVID C.,[6] FRANCIS,[5] JONATHAN,[4] ELIEZER,[3] ELIEZER,[2] JOHN[1]). Born in Lyme, N.H. Aug. 24, 1824. Lives in Oberlin, O., and is a professor in Oberlin College. Married 1st, Nov. 26, 1846, MARY JANE TURNER, of Oberlin, O.; married 2d, Oct. 10, 1859, HENRIETTA BEACH VANCE, of Lima, Ind.

Children born in Oberlin, O.

966   I. CHARLES CARROLL,[8] b. December, 1847.
967   II. HENRY FRANKLIN,[8] b. September, 1852.
968   III. FREDERICK ARTHUR,[8] b. December, 1856.
        IV. MARY LUCRETIA,[8] b. May, 1858.

Children of Second Wife.

969   V. EDWARD PAYSON,[8] b. September, 1860.
970   VI. ALFRED VANCE,[8] b. August, 1864.
        VII. LEWIS NELSON,[8] b. May, 1869; d. May, 1869.
        VIII. MARY,[8] b. June, 1871.
971   IX. DAVID CARROLL,[8] b. March, 1873.

500.

LEWIS FRANKLIN[7] CHURCHILL (DAVID C.,[6] FRANCIS,[5] JONATHAN,[4] ELIEZER,[3] ELIEZER,[2] JOHN[1]). Born in Lyme, N.H., June 1, 1826. Died in 1899. He lived in Rutherford, N.C., and was a lawyer of good standing. Married, in Washington, D.C., Dec. 31, 1849, HARRIET AUGUSTA DREW, who was born July 10, 1830, in Charleston, S.C.

Child.

972   I. HARRY AUGUSTUS,[8] b. Aug. 15, 1853.

502.

FRANCIS[7] CHURCHILL (SIMEON R.,[6] FRANCIS,[5] JONATHAN,[4] ELIEZER,[3] ELIEZER,[2] JOHN[1]). Born March 20, 1829. Lived in Batavia, N.Y. Married 1st, March 16, 1854, CHARLOTTE STAATS. She died Feb. 19, 1881. Married 2d, July 10, 1883, MRS. MARY (ATWOOD) KIBBE.

Children.

I. GEORGIA,[8] b. Jan. 30, 1855.
II. JENNIE FRANCES,[8] b. 1859.
973   III. FRANK,[8] b. July 30, 1861.

503.

STILLMAN [7] CHURCHiLL (Samuel Stillman,[6] Francis [5] Jonathan,[4] Eliezer,[3] Eliezer,[2] John [1]). Born in Lowell, Mass., July 28, 1823. Married, Oct. 13, 1848, Lucinda Hathorn, of West Henniker, N.H.

Children.

974   I. Clarence Elmore,[8] b. Aug. 20, 1851.

II. George Sumner,[8] b. April 9, 1856; m. Harriet J. Stowell.

975   III. Edward Everett,[8] b. Dec. 9, 1864; m. Lena M. Bradford.

509.

LEE [7] CHURCHILL (Joseph W.,[6] Francis,[5] Jonathan,[4] Eliezer,[3] Eliezer,[2] John [1]). Born at Troy, April 20, 1836. Married, Sept. 20, 1871, Ella Higgins.

Children.

976   I. Le Grand,[8] b. Sept. 9, 1872.

II. Warren,[8] b. Jan. 20, 1875; d. Jan. 9, 1880.

III. Nellie,[8] b. July 10, 1881.

IV. Arthur,[8] b. Sept. 11, 1884; d. Oct. 12, 1892.

512.

PROF. JOHN WESLEY [7] CHURCHILL (John E.,[6] Francis,[5] Jonathan,[4] Eliezer,[3] Eliezer,[2] John [1]). Born in Fairlee, Vt., May 26, 1839. He removed in boyhood to Nashua, N.H., where he received his early schooling, which was closed with a course at Appleton Academy. He planned to follow the profession of civil engineer, and obtained an engagement as a mechanical draughtsman on the bridge across the Mississippi river at Davenport, Iowa. Friends in Davenport discovered that he was destined for a different career, and he soon returned East and took a preparatory course at Phillips Andover Academy, and then took a four years' course at Harvard College where he graduated in 1865. He then returned to Andover for a final course at the Theological Seminary, where he graduated in 1867. He immediately received the appointment of Jones Professor of Pulpit Oratory, in Andover, which position he held until his death. In 1896 he was appointed Bartlett Professor of Homiletics, and proved a worthy successor to illustrious predecessors. The special work of Professor Churchill at the seminary was to teach the young men who were preparing for the ministry to preach to the people so that the people would be glad to listen to them. In this he was peculiarly successful. But he grew to be more than the teacher of elocution. He became the wise counsellor, the sympathetic friend, the inspirer of new hopes in cases of discouragement and doubt. Hundreds of graduates, scattered over the whole country, attest his wonderful influence as teacher, adviser, and friend. He became ·a preacher of high ability and power, as well as a writer of note, in the line of religious thought and culture. Many other institutions besides Andover enjoyed his instruction, at different times; among these, Dartmouth, Amherst, Brown University and Wellesley, Smith and Mt. Holyoke; while, since 1890, he had been instructor of elocution in Harvard Divinity School. He was best known to the great public by his marvellous power as a public reader. In this field, in the great lecture courses, some twenty-five years ago, Professor Churchill's evening was the popular feature of the course. In his power of expression, and range of voice and tone, his taste and adaptation, he stands unrivalled. He was a public-spirited and popular citizen in his own town. Professor Churchill died at Andover, Mass., April 13, 1900. His funeral services at Andover were attended by a great congregation of his towns-people and his friends from far and near, and a notable procession of professors and students and distinguished educators of many different institutions of New England followed him to his grave. The clergymen officiating were Dr. Donald, his brother-in-law, Dr. McKenzie, Cambridge, and Dr. Bancroft. He married, at Andover, July 27, 1859, MARY JANE DONALD, daughter of William C. Donald, who survived him.

Their Children born at Andover.

977   I. DONALD,[8] b. May 20, 1870.
         He is a resident physician at the Rhode Island General Hospital
978   II. MARLBOROUGH,[8] b. Aug. 11, 1878.
         Graduated at Harvard College, 1900.

513.

GEORGE FRANCIS[7] CHURCHILL (JOHN E.,[6] FRANCIS,[5] JONATHAN,[4] ELIEZER,[3] ELIEZER,[2] JOHN[1]). Born in Nashua, N.H., Oct. 6, 1846. Married, Oct. 16, 1873, ELLA GERTRUDE HOLBROOK

One Child.

   I. GERTRUDE,[8] b. Oct. 28, 1876.

514.

· ELBERT LAWRENCE[7] CHURCHILL (JOHN E.,[6] FRANCIS,[5] JONATHAN,[4] ELIEZER,[3] ELIEZER,[2] JOHN[1]). Born in Nashua, April 13, 1857. Married, April 9, 1884, GERTRUDE ABBY TAYLOR, daughter of Mrs. Abby Smith (Stewart) Taylor.

Children born in Abington.

   I. MARION,[8] b. Feb. 2, 1885.
979   II. KENNETH,[8] b. Feb. 15, 1890.

517.

JOSEPH[7] CHURCHILL (CHARLES,[6] CHARLES,[5] EPHRAIM,[4] STEPHEN,[3] ELIEZER,[2] JOHN[1]). Born Jan. 1, 1805. Married BETSEY ELLIS, daughter of William.

Children.

   I. REENETTE ELIZABETH,[8] b. Dec. 27. 1830; m. CHARLES F. HARLOW.
   II. HANNAH NELSON,[8] b. Sept. 10, 1834.
980 III. FREDERICK ELLIS,[8] b. July 23, 1837.
   IV. ANN MARIA,[8] b. Sept. 2, 1838; m. NATHANIEL BARNES, of Plymouth; no issue.
   V. BETSEY HARLOW,[8] m. BENJAMIN WESTON, of Plymouth.
981 VI. JOSEPH LOTHROP,[8] b. June 12, 1842.
   VII. ANN.[8]
   VIII. MARY.[8]

518.

ELKANAH[7] CHURCHILL (CHARLES,[6] CHARLES,[5] EPHRAIM,[4] STEPHEN,[3] ELIEZER,[2] JOHN[1]). Born in 1809. Married, Jan. 29 1835, LYDIA SHERMAN, of Carver, daughter of John.

Children.

   I. CHARLES HENRY,[8] b. Dec. 21, 1835; d. unmarried.
   II. LYDIA ANN,[8] b. Sept. 22, 1837; d. unmarried, 1853.
   III. ELLEN BARNES,[8] unmarried.

519.

ISAAC COVINGTON[7] CHURCHILL (RUFUS,[6] CHARLES,[5] EPHRAIM,[4] STEPHEN,[3] ELIEZER,[2] JOHN[1]). Born Nov. 28, 1797. Married, Dec. 16, 1820, MARY T. JENNEY.

Children.

982 I. ISAAC,[8] b. Oct. 18, 1822; m. SARAH E. RYDER, Sept. 29, 1859.
   II. FRANKLIN,[8] b. Sept. 24, 1824; d. Oct. 3, 1825.
   III. MARY ANN,[8] b. Feb. 2, 1831; m. JOHN SPAULDING, May 2, 1852.
   IV. ELIZABETH T.,[8] b. Aug. 6, 1834; d. September, 1834.
   V. ELIZABETH T.,[8] b. Aug. 10, 1836; d. Jan. 25, 1839.
   VI. RUFUS,[8] b. 1838; d. September, 1838.
   VII. BENJAMIN F.,[8] b. Nov. 2, 1840; d. Aug. 29, 1841.

520.

RUFUS[7] CHURCHILL (RUFUS,[6] CHARLES,[5] EPHRAIM[4] STEPHEN,[3] ELIEZER,[2] JOHN[1]). Born March 9, 1806. He died April 14, 1828. Married LUCY W. NYE, daughter of William.

Children.

   I. WILLIAM CROCKER,[8] m. (———) HOLMES; no children.
984 II. RUFUS HINKLEY,[8] no record. Lived, it is said, in Los Angeles, Cal.

521.

WILLIAM[7] CHURCHILL (RUFUS,[6] CHARLES,[5] EPHRAIM,[4] STEPHEN,[3] ELIEZER,[2] JOHN[1]). Born Nov. 21, 1816. Lived in Plymouth. Married, Jan. 3, 1841, EMILY TRIBBLE.

Children.

985   I. WILLIAM E.,[8] b. April 28, 1843.
       II. EMILY F.,[8] Aug. 4, 1845.
       III. MARY H.,[8] b. Dec. 6, 1848.
986   IV. HERBERT,[8] b. Sept. 27, 1857.
987   V. ALFRED G.,[8] b. Jan. 22, 1861; m. ADA PHILLIPS.

523.

EPHRAIM FINNEY[7] CHURCHILL (EPHRAIM,[6] CHARLES,[5] EPHRAIM,[4] STEPHEN,[3] ELIEZER,[2] JOHN[1]). Born in Plymouth Married MARTHA H. WHITING, Oct. 17, 1827. They lived in Chiltonville, Mass..

Children.

       I. EPHRAIM F.[8]
       II. MARTHA A.[8]
       III. ALMIRA C.[8]
       IV. WINSLOW W.,[8] m. MARY A. BURGESS, May 20, 1863.

Children.

1. Carrie R.   4. Mary A.
2. Josephine W.   5. Evelyn B.
3. Rebecca F   6. Almira H.

524.

ZACCHEUS[7] CHURCHILL (EPHRAIM,[6] ZACCHEUS,[5] EPHRAIM[4] STEPHEN,[3] ELIEZER,[2] JOHN[1]). Born in Yarmouth, N.S., Feb. 23, 1788, and lived there. In early life he taught school, and later was appointed government surveyor of land. Married 1st, MRS. SUSANNAH (ROSE) KILLAM, widow of Abraham. She died November, 1831, aged 52 years. Married 2d, MIRIAM DOANE. She died May 9, 1882, aged 86.

Children born in Yarmouth.

       I. DRUSILLA,[8] b. Jan. 3, 1810; m. BENJAMIN REDDING, 1832.
          They lived in Yarmouth and had children born there.

Children.

1. Susan Redding, b. Oct. 18, 1834; m. Calvin Frost, of Yarmouth.
2. Zaccheus Redding, b. March 18, 1827. He was drowned Jan. 26, 1848.
3. John Redding, b. Oct. 10, 1838; m. Asenath S. Gallie, March 28, 1862.

988   II. STEPHEN,[8] b. Oct. 11, 1811; m. 1st, ELIZABETH BLANEY, of Yarmouth, Dec. 22, 1835; m. 2d, MRS. JULIA (PHILLIPS) PORTER, widow of Capt. Horace.
           They lived in Yarmouth. He was a farmer.

Children of First Wife.

1. Elizabeth A., b. Oct. 1, 1836; m. Harvey Cann, of Yarmouth, May 24, 1860.
2. Amos B., b. Sept. 12, 1838; d. July 3, 1860.

3. Annie R., b. Oct. 5, 1841; m. Capt. Samuel F. Stanwood, Feb. 5, 1868.
4. Nathan, b. March 22, 1843; d. June 2, 1865.
5. Stephen B., b. Nov. 29, 1844; m. Annie Brown, Nov. 1, 1866.
6. George W., b. Feb. 10, 1847; m. Martha W. Huntington, April 21, 1875.
7. Susan E., b. July 27, 1849; m. Edward Knight, Nov. 22, 1882.
8. Sarah J., b. July 17, 1853; m. Capt. C. Hemeon, Oct. 25, 1886.

III. HANNAH,[8] b. Oct. 14, 1813; m. WILLIAM MURPHY, of Yarmouth, 1833.
They lived in Yarmouth and had children.

Children.

1. William Murphy, b. Sept. 11, 1834.
2. Emily H. Murphy, b. Sept. 10, 1837. Drowned in Yarmouth, Sept. 10, 1841.

989 IV ZACCHEUS,[8] b. July 1, 1815; m. 1st, SUSAN P. SAUNDERS, April 23, 1840; m. 2d, DRUSILLA (EARLE) SHAW, July 13, 1859.
They lived at Yarmouth, where he was a school-teacher.

Children of First Wife, born in Yarmouth.

1. Caroline C., b. May 6, 1841; m. 1st, John Bain, July 14, 1861· m. 2d, Thomas Dane, Sept. 10, 1886.
2. Sarah C., b. June 3, 1843; m. Robert Thurston, Nov. 19, 1864.
3. John S., b. Feb. 22, 1847; m. Sarah R. Wyman, July 19, 1874.

Children of Second Wife.

4. Augusta, b. May 1, 1861.
5. Elizabeth, b. July 12, 1863; m. Arthur W. McKinnon, May 1, 1889.

990 V. RICHARD,[8] b. Feb. 19, 1818; m. DEBORAH CROSBY, Dec. 28, 1841.
They lived at Yarmouth and had children.

Children.

1. Charles, b. Oct. 26, 1842; m. Lucy J. Rodney.
2. William M., b. March 8, 1846; m. Isabel Rodney, Nov. 10, 1870.
3. Lewis, b. June 17, 1848; m. Matilda Thurston, March 31, 1872.
4. Eliza A., b. Aug. 11, 1851.
5. Albert, b. May 20, 1853. Lost at sea, September, 1874.
6. Amanda, b. June 1, 1856; m. Augustus Williams, Feb. 5, 1878· d. Lynn, March 25, 1882.
7. Matilda, b. July 26, 1858.
8. Amos B., b. Dec. 14, 1860; m. Laura Eldridge, Nov. 15, 1886.
9. Henry D., b. Dec. 14, 1860; m. Annie Doane, Nov. 1, 1887.

991 VI. NATHAN,[8] b. Aug. 14, 1820; m. MARTHA DOANE; b. Nov. 25, 1845.
They lived in Yarmouth. He was a farmer. They had children.

Children.

1. Elmira, b. May 7, 1846; m. John Saunders, May 7, 1863.
2. Lydia Ann, b. Sept. 22, 1848; m. Joseph Eldridge, April 29, 1871.
3. Miriam, b. June 29, 1850; m. Howard Thurston, Dec. 14, 1864.
4. Calvin E., b. Sept. 30, 1857; m. Anna C. Churchill, March 9, 1881.
5. Charles E., b. Aug. 1, 1865; m. 1st, Sadie R. Ellis; m. 2d, Mary R. Wyman, July 17, 1891.
6. Ada A., b. Jan. 14, 1864; d. July 19, 1864.

525.

CAPT. THOMAS[7] CHURCHILL (EPHRAIM,[6] ZACCHEUS,[5] EPHRAIM,[4] STEPHEN,[3] ELIEZER,[2] JOHN[1]).　Born in Yarmouth, N.S., June 6, 1791, and lived there.　Married, at Yarmouth, Nov. 22, 1815, MARY HARRIS, daughter of William.　She died June 2, 1890, aged 96 years.

Children born in Yarmouth.

992　　I. ELEAZER,[8] b. April 6, 1817, m. LOIS ANNIE TRASK, of Yarmouth, Jan. 6, 1841.　She was b. April 18, 1820, and d. in Yarmouth, June 29, 1896

Children born in Yarmouth.

1. Jonathan, b. June 2, 1843; d. Sept. 15, 1850.
2. Mary A., b. Feb. 6, 1845; m. Ezra Roach, Jan. 16, 1863.
3. Eleazer, b. July 26, 1846; m. Catherine Crowell, Sept. 10, 1870.
4. Sophia, b. July 26, 1846; d. Sept. 15, 1850.
5. Edna, b. Aug. 15, 1849; m. Joseph Cook, Nov. 24, 1870.
6. Henry, b. Oct. 3, 1852; m. Susan Clark, March 31, 1877.
7. Clement, b. May 15, 1855; m. Carrie Trask, May 29, 1877.
8. Harvey, b. Oct. 3, 1857; m. Annie Vickery, March 12, 1882.
9. Fannie, b. July 11, 1860; m. Edgar Rundlett, May 15, 1881.

993　　II. DAVID,[8] b. Sept. 14, 1818; m. 1st, SARAH STRICKLAND, Jan. 19, 1845; m. 2d, MRS. ELIZABETH (SHAW) DUROND.

Child born in Yarmouth.

1. Joseph M., b. March 27, 1850; m. Sarah B. Symonds, of Yarmouth, Sept. 9, 1873.

994　　III. THOMAS,[8] b. Aug. 20, 1820; m. PHEBE SHAW, March 31, 1842. She was the dau. of Capt. Moses Shaw, and d. in Yarmouth Dec. 11, 1879.

Children.

1. Thomas W., m. Ruby Crocker.
2. Annie B., m. George W. Raymond.
3. Ephraim E., m. Inez Lent.
4. George W., m. Annie Goudey.
5. Ralph O., m. Emma Rose, Dec. 1, 1876.
6. Gilbert F., m. Alice Collins.

995　　IV WILLIAM,[8] b. May 29, 1822; m. SARAH CROSBY, of Yarmouth, dau. of William Crosby.
They lived in Yarmouth.　He was a sea captain.

Children born in Yarmouth.

1. Lois, b. Sept. 27, 1849; m. Aaron Churchill, July 4, 1874.
2. Norman B., b. Aug. 9, 1854; m. Annie Tedford, Dec. 19, 1882.
3. Mary A., b. July 30, 1866.

　　　V EDITH,[8] b. June 29, 1824; m. 1st, AMASA G. RODNEY, Oct. 5' 1845; m. 2d, ISAAC R. CHUTE, Feb. 5, 1858; m. 3d, CHAPMAN P. DOTY, April 9, 1898.

Child by First Husband.

1. Alma G. Rodney, m. Capt. George R. Vickery.

Child by Second Husband.

2. May Edith Chute, b. March 18, 1869; m. Edward F. Cann, of Yarmouth.

996   VI. JESSE,[8] b. Nov. 28, 1826; m. JOANNA JEFFREY, at Yarmouth, Dec. 30, 1851.

She was the dau. of David Jeffrey. They lived at Yarmouth. He was a sea captain.

Children.

1. David Jeffrey, b. Jan. 4, 1854; m. Elizabeth Clark, June, 1875.
2. Letitia, b. July 18, 1856; d. July 3, 1863.
3. Annie A., b. Dec. 12, 1858; m. Calvin Churchill.
4. Irving F., b. June 3, 1868; m. Jessie F. Shaw, June 30, 1894.

VII. ASENATH,[8] b. July 2, 1829; m. JOHN S. ROSE, May 16, 1848.

Children.

1. Caroline Rose, b. July 19, 1850; m. William Ritchie, July 27, 1869. She d. Nov. 1, 1872.
2. Asenath Rose, b. June 26, 1852; m. William Ritchie, as second wife, Sept. 25, 1874.
3. Emma Rose, b. July 5, 1854; m. Ralph Churchill, Dec. 1, 1876.
4. Ella Rose, b. Aug. 19, 1859; m. John Thorne, Nov. 22, 1887.

997   VIII. NATHAN,[8] b. Oct. 12, 1832; m. RUTH ANN WYMAN, December, 1857.

They lived in Yarmouth. He was a farmer, and their children were born in Yarmouth.

Children.

1. Nelson, b. Oct. 6, 1858; m. Margaret Lamont, Dec. 20, 1891.
2. George E., b. April 12, 1860.

526.

RUFUS[7] CHURCHILL (EPHRAIM,[6] ZACCHEUS,[5] EPHRAIM,[4] STEPHEN,[3] ELIEZER,[2] JOHN[1]). Born in Yarmouth, N.S., May 19, 1793. Millwright, shipbuilder, and farmer. Married, at Yarmouth, Dec. 10, 1816, GERTRUDE FLINT, daughter of Captain David. She died July 30, 1881, aged 85 years 11 months.

Children.

I. MARTHA,[8] b. Dec. 17, 1817; m. MOSES S. CROSBY, Nov. 26, 1839. She d. in Denver, Col., July 13, 1887.

Children born in Yarmouth, N.S.

1. Annie Flint Crosby, b. June 21, 1841; m. Fred Jones, Dec. 24, 1864.
2. May Corning Crosby, b. March 21, 1844; m. James A. Bell, Sept. 30, 1862.
3. Herbert H. Crosby, b. March 15, 1846; m. M. Jane Kimball, June 22, 1866.
4. David O. Crosby, b. Jan. 30, 1850; m. 1st, Annie Goudey, Dec. 5, 1871; m. 2d, Elizabeth L. Crosby, Dec. 29, 1891.
5. Emma J. Crosby, b. April 10, 1853; m. Josiah S. Karney, July 31, 1870.

998   II. RUFUS,[8] b. Aug. 2, 1819; m. EMILY KENDRICK, Dec. 23, 1845. They lived in Yarmouth, N.S. He was a contractor.

Children born in Yarmouth.

1. Delilah, b. Sept. 22, 1846; m. Samuel Corning, March 18, 1868. She d. Jan. 22, 1879.
2. Norman, b. June 17, 1848; m. Sadie G. Gillis, of Montreal, July 17, 1879.
3. Aaron, b. May 19, 1850; m. Lois Churchill, July 4, 1874.
4. Maria P., b. July 18, 1852; d. in Yarmouth, Feb. 20, 1877.
5. Major W., b. Nov. 1, 1855; m. Frances Dervan, of Boston, May 15, 1874.
6. Margery F., b. April 3, 1858.
7. Emeline R., b. June 9, 1860.
8. Annie F., b. April 17, 1862.

III. MARY,[8] b. June 14, 1821; m. ZECHARIAH CORNING, March 14, 1841. They lived in Yarmouth. He was a farmer.

Children born in Yarmouth.

1. Mary E. Corning, b. Dec. 19, 1841; m. Thomas Sullivan, Feb. 21, 1865.
2. Hannah Corning, b. Sept. 21, 1843; m. Augustus Goudey, June 7, 1871.
3. Harriet G. Corning, b. May 4, 1846; m. Samuel Burrill, May 4, 1882.
4. Letitia Ann Corning, b. March 10, 1850.
5. Rufus C. Corning, b. March 11, 1857; m. Ada Corning, Oct. 31, 1880.

999 IV DAVID,[8] b. Feb. 20, 1823; m. MARTHA WILLIAMS, Jan. 30, 1849. They lived in Yarmouth, and St. John's, N.B. He was a sea captain.

Children born in Yarmouth.

1. Henry D., b. October 1856; d. at sea.
2. John, b. 1858; d. at St. John's.
3. David.
4. Robbins.
5. Adena.

V SARAH,[8] b. Dec. 31, 1824; m. SAMUEL M. KILLAM, Nov. 26, 1848. They lived in Yarmouth, N.S.

Children born in Yarmouth.

1. Catharine Killam, b. Sept 27, 1849; m. John Cann, Sept. 10, 1875.
2. Gertrude Killam, b. Feb. 10, 1851; d. July 18, 1874.
3. Evangeline Killam, b. May 14, 1853; m. Amos Gray, November 1873.
4. Samuel F. Killam, b. Oct. 7, 1855; m. Mary Cavanagh, July 6, 1882.
5. Melvaretta Killam, b. Jan. 19, 1858; d. in Yarmouth, Jan. 19, 1879.
6. Marietta Killam, b. Oct. 9, 1860; m. Frank Farnham, of Mass., August, 1886.
7. Rufus C. Killam, b. May 19, 1864; d. in Yarmouth, Feb. 10, 1895.
8. George Killam, b. April 26, 1866.

VI. HARRIET,[8] b. Oct. 15, 1826; m. BENJAMIN PITMAN, Jan. 7, 1851 Lived in Yarmouth, N.S. He was a farmer.

Children born in Yarmouth.

1. Israel Pitman, b. Oct. 12, 1851; m. Annie C. Hatfield, of Yarmouth, Sept. 23, 1884.
2. Harriet R. Pitman, b. June 14, 1853.
3. Warren Pitman, b. April 21, 1855; m Sarah A. Perry, of Yarmouth, July 7, 1879.

4. Elizabeth M. Pitman, b. Dec. 17, 1857; d. April 21, 1873.
5. George W. Pitman, b. Nov. 26, 1859; d. April 15, 1873.
6. Jane C. Pitman, b. Oct. 13, 1861; d. Dec. 6, 1888.
7. Amos C. Pitman, b. Sept. 30, 1864.
8. Henry D. Pitman, b. Oct. 28, 1866.
9. Emily H. Pitman, b. Oct. 1, 1870.

VII. NANCY,[8] b. Aug. 30, 1828; m. CHARLES WALKER, of Yarmouth,
Oct. 3, 1850. They lived in Calais, Me.

Children.

1. Fanny Walker, b. Yarmouth, Feb. 1, 1852; m. Nathaniel S.
Jordan, of Maine, April, 1874.
2. J. Ernest Walker, b. Calais, Me., July 16, 1859; m. Frances E.
Jones, of New York, Oct. 7, 1890.
3. George Walker, b. Calais, Me., May 3, 1861; m. Ella Hardista,
Portland, Ore., June, 1885.
4. Harry Walker, b. Calais, Me., Aug. 1, 1863; d. young.

1000 VIII. ALVIN,[8] b. May 1, 1830; m. JANE CAREY, Dec. 16, 1852. They
lived in Yarmouth. He was a farmer.

Children born in Yarmouth.

1. Letitia, b. Feb. 18, 1855; m. Pasco Allen, Yarmouth, May 4,
1877.
2. Elizabeth, b. Nov. 22, 1857; m. Frank Foote, in Yarmouth,
June 9, 1880.
3. Alvin, b. Nov. 10, 1859; m. Ella Arthuro, Colorado, July, 1891.
4. Israel L., b. July 4, 1862.
5. Charles L., b. Sept. 17, 1865; d. Oct. 21, 1865.

IX. HANNAH,[8] b. Oct. 4, 1832; m. LUDOVIC CHIPMAN, Yarmouth, Dec.
19, 1850. They lived in Yarmouth.

Children born in Yarmouth.

1. Lois Chipman, b. Sept. 26, 1851; m. Benjamin W. Gillis, Yarmouth, 1874.
2. Charles W. Chipman, b. July 18, 1853; m. Ada F. Perkins,
Essex, Mass., Aug. 5, 1875.

1001 X. GEORGE W.,[8] b. Dec. 18, 1835; m. LOUISA SMITH, Portland, Me.
June 16, 1866. They lived at Yarmouth. He was a sea captain.

Children born in Yarmouth.

1. Louisa, b. April 13, 1867; m. Joseph Kinney, Yarmouth, Nov.
16, 1888.
2. Hannah E., b. May 7, 1869; m. James Frost, Yarmouth, Oct.
31. 1890.
3. M. Gulielma, b. March 2, 1873; m. Edward Porter, Yarmouth,
June 26, 1894.

1002 XI. WILLIAM P.,[8] b. June 11, 1839; m. CATHARINE DOUCETTE, Feb. 18,
1860. She was the daughter of Mark and Helen (Melanson)
Doucette. They lived in Yarmouth, N.S. His business was
lumbering.

Children born in Yarmouth.

1. Rupert G., b. March 12, 1862; m. 1st, Rachel Doane, March 12,
1885; m. 2d, Annie Thomes.
2. Laleah J., b. Feb. 27. 1864; m. Clarence Phalen, Boston, April
29, 1891.
3. Byron L., b. Nov. 22, 1865; m. Emily King, Yarmouth, Feb. 18,
1888.
4. Catharine, b. Dec. 3, 1867; m. Attilia Amorosa, April 2, 1894,
Boston.

5. Walter, b. Dec. 13, 1869; m. Sarah W. Pitman, Yarmouth,
   May 1, 1889.
6. Rufus, b. Sept. 5, 1872; d. Sept. 13, 1872.
7. Fannie, b. Dec. 5, 1873; d. Dec. 16, 1873.
8. Charles H., b. Dec. 10, 1875
9. Grace D., b. Sept. 6, 1879.

527.

NATHANIEL[7] CHURCHILL (EPHRAIM,[6] ZACCHEUS,[5] EPH-
RAIM,[4] STEPHEN,[3] ELIEZER,[2] JOHN[1]).   Born in Yarmouth N.S.,
July 1, 1795. Lived in Yarmouth, a farmer. Married ABIGAIL
VALPEY, of Yarmouth, daughter of Capt. John Valpey.

Children born in Yarmouth.

I. ELEANOR,[8] b. Feb. 19, 1819; m. NATHANIEL TRAVIS, Yarmouth,
   March 9, 1840. She died June 3, 1896.

Children born in Yarmouth.

1. Nathaniel Travis, b. Dec. 22, 1841; d. Jan. 6, 1842.
2. Nathaniel Travis, b. April 18, 1843; m. Harriet Ring, Yarmouth, Aug. 11, 1863.
3. Abner A. Travis, b. Nov. 23, 1844.
4. Elkanah Travis,   ⎫ b. Oct. 19, 1846; m. Elizabeth Randall,
                      ⎪   Yarmouth, Dec. 31, 1868.
5. Daniel R. Travis, ⎬ b. Oct. 19, 1846. He was killed in a mine
                      ⎭   in Nevada, June 26, 1880.
6. James H. Travis, ⎫ b. Oct. 23, 1849.
7. Alice A. Travis, ⎬ b. Oct. 23, 1849; m. William Reid, Yar-
                      ⎭   mouth, Dec. 9, 1872.
8. Abigail C. H. Travis, b. Oct. 21, 1851; m. Fred. R. S. Mildon,
   Yarmouth, Sept. 9, 1873.
9. Delight C. Travis, b. June 12, 1854; m. David Greenlaw, East
   Boston, June 27, 1880.
10. Sabina J. Travis, b. Feb. 16, 1859; m. William S. Mildon,
    Eastport, April 2, 1884.
11. Sarah A. Travis, ⎫ b. April 21, 1861; m. Edgar E. Patten,
                       ⎬   Great Falls, N.H., Jan. 5, 1893.
12. Letitia W. Travis, ⎭ b. April 21, 1861

1003   II. NATHANIEL,[8] b. Dec. 1, 1821; m. 1st, LYDIA ANN CROSBY, Dec. 1,
       1846; m. 2d, SARAH C. HATFIELD, Oct. 17, 1850; m. 3d, MRS.
       REBECCA (———) CUSHING, Nov. 22, 1884. They lived in Yar-
       mouth, N.S.

Children of Second Wife, all born in Yarmouth.

1. Emmeline V., b. April 7, 1852; m. Dr. C. M. Tolles, Clare-
   mont, N.H.
2. William A., b. Nov. 10, 1859; d. June 5, 1863.
3. Alice, b. Dec. 27, 1860; d. Feb. 18, 1861.
4. William Edgar, b. July 27, 1864; m. Sadie Caskey.

III. SARAH,[8] b. Jan. 13, 1823; m. JOHN HARDING, Jan. 4, 1844.

Children.

1. Sarah Harding, m. Nathaniel Simmes.
2. Albert Harding, m. Capt. Robert Crowell.
3. John Harding, m. Alma Tedford.
4. Lillian Harding.
5. Robert Harding.
6. Elizabeth Harding

IV. ELIZABETH,[8] b. Sept. 30, 1825; m. WILLIAM J. HATFIELD, Dec. 25, 1854. She died Nov. 12, 1895.

Children born in Yarmouth.

1. Fred S. Hatfield, b. March 26, 1850; m. Annie S. Wyman, Nov. 25, 1885.
2. Fannie C. Hatfield, b. in Plymouth, Sept. 23, 1861; m. Charles J. Cragg, Sept. 25, 1885.

V. DELIGHT,[8] b. June 12, 1827; m. 1st, DOUGLAS THORPE, Sept. 12, 1857; m. 2d, JAMES CUSHING.
VI. ABNER,[8] b. Aug. 30, 1829; d. in Liverpool, Eng., Feb. 28, 1848.
VII. BENJAMIN,[8] b. Aug. 1, 1831; d. April 3, 1889.
VIII. ABBIE,[8] b. Nov. 11, 1833; m. E. W. DARLING, Mass., 1862.
IX. FANNIE,[8] b. Feb. 29, 1835; unmarried; d. Jan. 5, 1890, at Portland, Ore.

528.

WALTER[7] CHURCHILL (EPHRAIM,[6] ZACCHEUS,[5] EPHRAIM,[4] STEPHEN,[3] ELIEZER,[2] JOHN[1]). Born June 3, 1805, in Yarmouth, N.S. Married 1st, 1828, SARAH FLINT. Married 2d,- ELSIE MURPHY.

Children of First Wife.

I. JOHN,[8] b. 1827; d. unmarried, in California in 1854.
II. ISRAEL HARDING,[8] b. 1829; d. unmarried, April, 1850.
III. MARY,[8] b. 1831; m. HENRY PITMAN, no issue.
IV. ELIZABETH,[8] b. 1833; m. JOHN TRASK.
V. HANNAH,[8] b. 1835; m. GEORGE W. WARE. Moved to the States.
VI. SARAH,[8] b. 1837; d. in infancy.

Children of Second Wife.

VII. SARAH,[8] b. Aug. 3, 1841; m. JEFFERSON CORNING, March 28, 1865.
VIII. ALICE,[8] b. March 26, 1843; m. ALEXANDER McKINNON, son of Randall.
IX. LYDIA,[8] b. May 3, 1844; m. CAPT. HERBERT H. CANN, son of Samuel.
X. ASENATH,[8] b. May 12, 1848; m. JAMES PORTER, son of Enoch.

529.

JOHN[7] CHURCHILL (EPHRAIM,[6] ZACCHEUS,[5] EPHRAIM,[4] STEPHEN,[3] ELIEZER,[2] JOHN[1]). Born in Yarmouth, N.S., Sept. 23 1814. Married 1st, Feb. 4, 1832, BETSEY FLINT. Married 2d, MARIA ANNE HASKELL. Married 3d, MRS. ALMIRA (GOODAY) SANDERS.

Children of First Wife.

1004   I. WARREN FLINT,[8] b. Nov. 22, 1838; m. FANNIE TINKHAM.

Children.

1. Charles, m. Bertha B. Killian.
2. Thomas, m. Grace M. Allen.
3. Belle, m. Abner Porter.
4. Norman, died.
5. Cora, died.

1005   II. WILLIAM,[8] b. Oct. 7, 1840; m. MARY HASKELL.
     III. CHARLES,[8] b. July 2, 1843; d. June 1, 1859.

Children of Second Wife.

IV. MERCY JANE,[8] b. July 31, 1847; m. JAMES K. ROSE.
V. ANNA ARABELLA,[8] b. Oct. 17, 1848; m. CHARLES BLAKE, Amesbury, Mass.
1006   VI. EBENEZER,[8] b. Oct. 11, 1850; m. LYDIA CHURCHILL, daughter of John.
VII. JOHN,[8] b. May 16, 1855; unmarried.

534.

GEORGE [7] CHURCHILL (JOHN,[6] ANSEL,[5] EPHRAIM,[4] STEPHEN,[3] ELIEZER,[2] JOHN [1]). Born at Plymouth and was a baker by trade. He died June 16, 1871. Married, March 5, 1826, MARTHA C. HOLMES, daughter of Joseph. She died Sept. 26, 1868.

Children.

I. MARTHA,[8] b. Jan. 21, 1827; d. Sept. 26, 1827.
1007   II. JOHN,[8] b. July 6, 1828; m. MARTHA J. BAGNELL.
III. MARTHA,[8] b. Oct. 10, 1835; m. 1st, GEORGE SAMPSON; m. 2d, JOHN MCADAMS.
IV. GEORGE,[8]
V. JAMES,[8] } b. Feb. 28, 1846, and d. March 1, 1846.

535.

PELEG [7] CHURCHILL (PELEG,[6] STEPHEN,[5] STEPHEN,[4] STEPHEN,[3] ELIEZER,[2] JOHN [1]). Born in Duxbury. Married 1st, LUCY SPRAGUE; married 2d, JANE PEASE.

Children of First Wife.

I. EUNICE,[8] m. (———) TUFTS.
II. LUCY,[8] m. FREDERICK BENSON.
1008   III. PELEG,[8] m. AMELIA KENT, of Boston.
1009   IV. WILLIAM,[8] m. SARAH CLARK, of Amherst.
V. ELIZA BIGELOW,[8] m. GEORGE M. BACON, of Newton.
1010   VI. HENRY PERKET,[8] b. April 12, 1833; m. ANNIE JEFFREYS WASHBURN, May 28, 1857.
VII. HARRIET NEWELL,[8] d. in infancy.

Child of Second Wife.

VIII. HARRIET NEWELL,[8] m. (———) MASON.

536.

WILLIAM [7] CHURCHILL (PELEG,[6] STEPHEN,[5] STEPHEN,[4] STEPHEN,[3] ELIEZER,[2] JOHN [1]). Born in Duxbury, May 18, 1798. Married, Oct. 5, 1823, MARY HOLMES, born in Plymouth, May 13, 1804, died June 26, 1883.

Children.

I. HANNAH HOSEA,[8] b. Aug. 1, 1824; m. 1st, MARTIN WILDER, May 20, 1847. He died May 9, 1863; m. 2d, JAMES S. BEAL, of Hingham, Jan. 10, 1867. No issue. He died October, 1883.

Children.

1. Daughter, b. Feb. 19, 1848; d. soon.
2. Martin Wilder, Jr., b. July 9, 1849; d. young.

MARY HOLMES,[8] b. Feb. 3, 1826; m. GEORGE W. HAVEN, May 25, 1849.

Children.

1. Albert C. Haven, b. May 16, 1850.
2. Mary L. Haven, b. June 20, 1852.
3. Carrie A. Haven, b. Nov. 13, 1855.

JANE HEMAN,[8] b. July 28, 1828; m. T. HENRY PERKINS, Feb. 1, 1849.
She died, and he married her sister, LUCY S. CHURCHILL.

Children.

1. Infant daughter, b. November, 1849; d. soon.
2. Ella J. Perkins, b. June 16, 1851.

WILLIAM OTIS,[8] b. June 26, 1830; m. SARAH C. GERRY, June 24, 1852.

Children.

1. Adrianna, b. Oct. 3, 1853; d. April 8, 1881; m. Charles A. Sawtelle, May 17, 1874.
2. Sarah Alice, b. Dec. 31, 1854; m. A. D. Rutherford, July 7, 1878.
3. William Herbert, b. Sept. 5, 1858; m. Laura Conners, Jan. 19, 1884. They were divorced and he m. 2d, Eva Upton.
4. Charles Wilder, b. Aug. 4, 1860; m. Annette Chamneys, Dec. 25, 1885.
5. Charlotte Belle, b. Jan. 14, 1867; m. J. Weller Reed, Oct. 1, 1887.
6. Miriam Wilder, b. Nov. 5, 1868.
7. George Knox, b. Nov. 21, 1872; d. Oct. 9, 1873.

ADRIANNA,[8] b. Feb. 4. 1832; d. May 15, 1837.
INFANT DAUGHTER, unnamed, b Nov. 23, 1834; d. Dec. 12, 1834.
LUCY S.,[8] b. Nov. 25, 1835; m. T. HENRY PERKINS, as his second wife.
ADRIANNA,[8] b. Aug. 16, 1838; d. Sept. 9, 1838.
ELIZA A.,[8] b. Jan. 30, 1841; m. ALBERT H. BIRD, Nov. 10, 1864.
ALGERNON B.,[8] b. Sept. 15, 1844; m. MARY BEAL, June 5, 1867.

Children.

1. James B., b. March 27, 1869.
2. Frank M., b. Sept. 5, 1872.
3. Harry B., b. June 5, 1878.

537.

CHURCHILL (PELEG,[6] STEPHEN,[5] STEPHEN,[4] STEPHEN,[3] JOHN[1]). Born in Duxbury. Married 1st, SARAH COBB. Married 2d, ESTHER HARLOW. Married 3d, MARION E. No issue.

Children by Second Wife.

SARAH OTIS,[8] b. May 17, 1831.
HOWARD MALCOLM,[8] b. May 15, 1833.

538.

EZRA⁷ CHURCHILL (PELEG,⁶ STEPHEN,⁵ STEPHEN,⁴ STEPHEN,³ ELIEZER,² JOHN¹). Born in Duxbury. Married SUSAN ALLEN.

One Child.

I. SUSAN,⁸ m. DANIEL CURRIER.

539.

DANIEL⁷ CHURCHILL (DANIEL,⁶ STEPHEN,⁵ STEPHEN,⁴ STEPHEN,³ ELIEZER,² JOHN¹). Born in Plymouth, Sept. 9, 1803. Married, 1826, MARY BRIGGS BROWN.

Child:

1014   I. DANIEL,⁸ b. March 20, 1828; m. ELIZA HUDSON.

544.

SOLOMON SYLVESTER⁷ CHURCHILL (NATHAN,⁶ BENJA-MIN,⁵ BENJAMIN,⁴ STEPHEN,³ ELIEZER,² JOHN¹). Born in Plymouth, April 4, 1817. Lived at Plymouth till 1856. They removed and lived at North Bridgewater and Brockton from 1857 on. He was a wood-turner by occupation. Married, April 23, 1840, RUTH NELSON COBB, daughter of John Kempton Cobb and Polly (Nelson).

Children born in Plymouth.

1015   I. SOLOMON SYLVESTER,⁸ b. March 31, 1841; m. OLIVE AUGUSTA HAYWARD, at Boston, Aug. 6, 1866. She was the daughter of Bela Baylies Hayward and Olive Porter (Copeland) Hayward. They lived in Brockton. He was foreman in a shoe manu-factory. He was educated in the public schools, and served one year in the U. S. Navy during the Civil War. He died Oct. 13, 1889.

Children born in Brockton.

    1. Fred Sylvester, b. Sept. 26, 1867; m. Lillie C. White, of Hol-brook, May 29, 1892. She was the daughter of Cornelius L. and Elizabeth (Hodge) White. They lived at Brockton. Children: Fred Loring, b. Dec. 13, 1893, and Forest White, b. Aug. 13, 1895.

    2. Amy Hayward, b. Feb. 24, 1873; d. at Brockton, June 6, 1891.

  II. MARIA ISABELLA,⁸ b. at Plymouth, May 19, 1843; d. June 14, 1846.

  III. ELIZABETH,⁸ b. at Plymouth, Feb. 14, 1845. Married HENRY H. BILLINGS, March 15, 1870, son of Jesse.

Children.

    1. Grace Holmes Billings, b. at No. Bridgewater, May 23, 1871; m. Fred G. Doyle, April, 1891.

    2. Mary Ellen Billings, b. at Brockton, Sept. 14, 1873; m. George H. Wade, May 30, 1896.

    3. Bertha Billings, b. at Brockton, Jan. 2, 1876; m. Lester Green, Dec. 31, 1897.

1016   IV. CHARLES AUGUSTUS,⁸ b. at Plymouth, April 27, 1847; m. LUTHERA E. PACKARD, Jan. 19, 1867.

  V. HENRY MELVILLE,⁸ b. at Plymouth, Feb. 14, 1853; d. Feb. 6, 1854.

  VI. ANNA ISABELLE,⁸ b. at North Bridgewater, Nov. 16, 1857; m. ARTHUR E. KENDRICK.

547.

WILLIAM[7] CHURCHILL (WILLIAM,[6] SOLOMON,[5] AMAZIAH[4] ELKANAH,[3] ELIEZER,[2] JOHN[1]). Born in Boston, Feb. 4, 1825. He died at Montclair, N.Y., June 7, 1873. Married 1st, at Woodbury, Conn., July 28, 1847, LUCY CAROLINE AVERILL, daughter of Augustine. She was born at New Utrecht, N.Y., June 17, 1826, and died at West Point, July 13, 1856. Married 2d, Oct. 6, 1858, at Middletown, Conn., SARAH JANE STARKWEATHER.

Children by First Wife.

    I. MARY CAROLINE,[8] b. New York City, July 16, 1849; m. GEORGE H. RIPLEY, Nov. 9, 1870.
   II. FLORENCE,[8] b. at Brooklyn, April 21, 1851; m. WILLIAM L. GERRISH, JR., Oct. 19, 1875.
 III. WILLIAM,[8] ⎱ b. at Peekskill, Aug. 9, 1853; d. Aug. 9, 1853.
 IV. LUCY,[8]   ⎰ b. at Peekskill, Aug. 9, 1853; d. Sept. 30, 1853.

By Second Wife.

1017   V. WILLIAM,[8] born in Brooklyn, N.Y., Oct. 5, 1859.
1018   VI. ARTHUR HOWARD,[8] b. in Brooklyn, N.Y., April 14, 1862.
1019 VII. CLARENCE,[8] b. in Smithtown, May 21, 1865.
      VIII. PERCY,[8] b. in Brooklyn, Dec. 1, 1868; d. Aug. 9, 1869.
     IX. ETHEL,[8] b. in Brooklyn, June 1, 1870; d. Feb. 19, 1871

550.

WILLIAM[7] CHURCHILL (WILLIAM,[6] NATHANIEL,[5] ELKANAH[4] ELKANAH,[3] ELIEZER,[2] JOHN[1]). Born in Plymouth, Feb. 19, 1835. Married, in DePau, Ind., March 2, 1864, MARY ASH.

Children.

       I. MARTHA J.,[8] b. Aug. 19, 1866.
1020   II. GEORGE W.,[8] b. Nov. 20, 1868.
    III. NANCY M.,[8] b. Dec. 1, 1871.
    IV. LAURA B.,[8] b. Feb. 17, 1874.
     V. ABBY A.,[8] b. June 27, 1877.
    VI. MARY G.,[8] b. Feb. 25, 1880.
1021 VII. ROBERT E.,[8] b. Dec. 24, 1882.
1022 VIII. RAYMOND,[8] b. July 26, 1885.

554.

JOHN B.[7] CHURCHILL (BENJAMIN,[6] JOHN[5] JOHN[4] JOHN,[3] ELIEZER,[2] JOHN[1]). Born in Pataukunk, March 26, 1805, and lived there on the old homestead, a farmer. He died April 27, 1900. Married, at Pine Bush, N.Y., June 28, 1838, JANE GREEN, daughter of William, of Pine Bush, N.Y. She died June 3, 1847.

Children born at Pataukunk.

    I. EDGAR,[8] b. May 27, 1839; d Oct. 4, 1843.
   II. AMELIA,[8] b. Aug. 29, 1841; d. uumarried, April 6, 1896.
1023 III. BENJAMIN B.,[8] b. Nov. 14, 1844; m. ARVILLA DUNN, dau. of Anthony and Sarah (Terwiliger) Dunn.
        Lived on the old homestead, Pataukunk, N.Y.; a farmer.

Children.

1. Ralph J., b. Jan. 11, 1889.
2. Maud E., b. Aug. 26, 1890.
3. Leroy E., b. July 18, 1893.
4. Elson, b. July 19, 1897.
5. Lloyd, b. July 13, 1898.
6. Howard D., b. March 13, 1900.
7. Ruth, b. March 21, 1901.

IV. HARRIET M.,[8] b. April 30, 1847; m. ISAIAH DAVENPORT, of Accord, N.Y., Dec. 26, 1888; d. Nov. 28, 1894, at Pataukunk.

556.

JOHN[7] CHURCHILL (WILLIAM,[6] JOHN,[5] JOHN,[4] JOHN,[3] ELIEZER,[2] JOHN[1]). Born in New Hackensack, N.Y., Dec. 8, 1810. Married a wife whose name has not been ascertained.

Children, names not in proper order probably.

1024   I. WILLIAM.[8] He was engaged with P. T. Barnum for years.
II. ISAAC.[8] He was in the army in the Rebellion and died there.
III. CHARLES.[8] He was in the army also and died from wounds received in battle.
IV. SARAH,[8] m. JOSEPH KRAMER.
V. CORNELIUS.[8] He was in the army in the Civil War and was killed in battle.
VI. MARY,[8] m. a MR. HACKET.
1025 VII. CLARENCE,[8] m. (———) STBTSON.

557.

CORNELIUS[7] CHURCHILL (WILLIAM[6] JOHN,[5] JOHN,[4] JOHN,[3] ELIEZER,[2] JOHN[1]). Born Oct. 30, 1823, in New Hackensack, N.Y. Married ELIZABETH KNAPP, born in Yorktown, N.Y., 1837.

Children.

I. EMMA ADELIA,[8] b. Oct. 6, 1849; m. WILLIAM McDONOUGH.
1026 II. HERBERT REMSON,[8] b. Feb. 23, 1851; m. NELLIE BRUSH. Live in Brooklyn, N.Y.

Children.

1. Clara Nellie, b. Oct. 23, 1873.
2. Herbert R., Jr., b. Dec. 24, 1875.
3. Juliette, b. Sept. 13, 1878.
4. Frank Homer, b. 1881.
5. Ethel May, b. March 15, 1884.
6. Elbert Knapp, b. Aug. 15, 1886.
7. Cornelius Irving, b. Dec. 25, 1887; d. Sept. 17, 1888.
8. Cecilia Emma, b. Aug. 2, 1889.
9. Charles Brush, b March 17, 1891.
10. Walter Howell, b. Dec. 20, 1892.
11. Lottie Bell, b. May 23, 1894.

III. MARGARETTA BELL,[8] b. June 29, 1854; unmarried.
IV. CORNELIA,[8] b. June 14, 1857; d. unmarried about 1880.

562.

SAMUEL CLARK[7] CHURCHILL (SAMUEL,[6] SAMUEL,[5] BENJA-
MIN,[4] JOHN,[3] ELIEZER,[2] JOHN[1]). Born at Augusta, Me., July 11,
1827. Married 1st, July 8, 1861, at Augusta, ELIZA J. MORRILL.
Married 2d, March 30, 1872, at Augusta, ANNA J. McCLURE.

Children of First Wife.
  I. NETTIE ELIZA,[8] b. July 7, 1862.
 II. HARRIET ELIZABETH,[8] b. Nov. 8, 1863.

Child of Second Wife.
III. MAUDE M.,[8] b. May 7, 1877.

565.

CYRUS[7] CHURCHILL (JOHN,[6] JOHN,[5] JOSEPH,[4] JOHN,[3] ELIE-
ZER,[2] JOHN[1]). Born in New Portland, Me., May 21, 1823. Married ELIZA MELLEN.

Children.
  I. ELLA MARIA,[8] b. July 7, 1853; m. GEORGE HASKIN, July 12, 1876.
 II. GEORGE W.,[8] b. Dec. 23, 1857; m. IDA FRANK THOMPSON; no
     children.

566.

JASON[7] CHURCHILL (JOSEPH,[6] JOHN,[5] JOSEPH,[4] JOHN,[3]
ELIEZER,[2] JOHN[1]). Born April 24, 1819. Married, April 9, 1845,
JANE GUNN, who was born Oct. 20, 1822.

Children.
        I. SOPHIA,[8] b. March 22, 1846; m. EDWARD McGRECHIN.
       II. MARTHA J.,[8] b. Sept. 20, 1847; d. Aug. 8, 1848.
      III. SARAH E.,[8] b. Oct. 27, 1848; died August, 1849.
       IV. MARY,[8] b. Jan. 21, 1852; m. HOMER DE WITT.
1027   V. JASON,[8] b. Jan. 24, 1854; m. CATHARINE MANNING.
       VI. SARAH JANE,[8] b. Dec. 13, 1860.

568a.*

DIADEMA[7] CHURCHILL (SANFORD,[6] JOHN,[5] JOSEPH,[4] JOHN[3]
ELIEZER,[2] JOHN[1]). Born in Embden, Me., July 29, 1822. Died in
Solon, Me., Dec. 4, 1900. Married, at Stark, Nov. 16, 1849, WILLIAM
H. NOTTAGE, of Stark, a farmer. They lived at Stark and Bingham,
and had children born at Stark.

Children.
  I. SANFORD J. NOTTAGE,[8] b. July 23, 1852; m. ADA E. STEWARD.
     Live in Bingham, Me.
 II. MARY L. NOTTAGE,[8] b. June 9, 1854; m. GEORGE HENDERSON,
     June 15, 1881. Live in Solon, Me.

* NOTE. These records, from No. 568a to 571, and also 572a, were received by the kindness of Mrs. Serena Perkins, but too late to be printed in the regular form, under No. 264, and
so are placed in order here.

III. LIBBY G. NOTTAGE,[5] b. March 26, 1856; m. CAD JOICE. Live in
 Bingham.
IV. HENRY NOTTAGE,[5] b. Feb. 14, 1858; m. SARAH GILMAN. Live in
 Bingham.
 V. JOAN S. NOTTAGE,[5] b. April 8, 1861; m. CHARLES G. FRENCH.
 Live in Solon, Me.
VI. JOHN NOTTAGE,[5] b. Aug. 16, 1862; m. BELLE A. SQUIRE. Live in
 Solon, Me.

568b.

IRENA W.[7] CHURCHILL (SANFORD,[6] JOHN,[5] JOSEPH,[4] JOHN,[3]
ELIEZER,[2] JOHN[1]). Born in Stark, Me., Sept. 29, 1823. Died Aug.
25, 1887. Married, at New Sharon, Me., JAMES CHAPMAN. They
lived in New Sharon, where he was a farmer. They had no children·

569.

CYRUS[7] CHURCHILL (SANFORD,[6] JOHN,[5] JOSEPH,[4] JOHN,[3]
ELIEZER,[2] JOHN[1]). Born in Stark, Me., April 3, 1825. Married, at
Stark, Me., BETSEY SEEMAN, daughter of Alexander and Mercy
(Young) Seeman, of Stark. He served three years in the Civil War.
He was a farmer. They had six children, of whom we have no record.

570.

HOLLIS HUTCHINS[7] CHURCHILL (SANFORD,[6] JOHN,[5]
JOSEPH,[4] JOHN,[3] ELIEZER,[2] JOHN[1]). Born in Stark, Me., June 24,
1826. Married, at Stark, NANCY W. SEEMAN, daughter of Alexander and Mercy (Young) Seeman, of Stark. He was a farmer.

They had Children born in Stark.

 I. CHARLES S.,[8] b. March 30, 1849; m. EMMA E. WENTWORTH, at
 Wilton, Me., March 20, 1875; d. Dec. 16, 1890.
 II. LORENZO L.,[8] b. June 8, 1852; m. MARY WITHEE, at Augusta, Me.,
 Oct. 22, 1881. Live in Stark.
III. MANLEY,[8] b. May 2, 1859; m. SARA M. SMITH, at Stark, Dec. 9,
 1890.

570a.

SERENA EAMES[7] CHURCHILL (SANFORD,[6] JOHN,[5] JOSEPH,[4]
JOHN,[3] ELIEZER,[2] JOHN[1]). Born in Stark, Me., Feb. 16, 1828.
Married, at Norridgewock, 1853, JOHN W. PERKINS, son of Joseph
and Rachel (Matthews) Perkins. He was a farmer, at Industry and
Wilton, Me.

Children born at Industry, Me.

 I. JOSEPH W[8] PERKINS, b. Dec. 4, 1853. Living unmarried in
 Wilton. Me. (1903).
 II. HATTIE J.[8] PERKINS, b. May 5, 1855; m. NATHAN FOGG. Live in
 Industry, Me.
III. CLEVELAND W.[8] PERKINS, b. Jan. 18, 1858; m. SERENA E. LOOK,
 at South Dakota, June 25, 1882. They live in Groton, South
 Dakota.

570b.

LUCINDA B.[7] CHURCHILL (SANFORD,[6] JOHN,[5] JOSEPH,[4] JOHN,[3] ELIEZER,[2] JOHN[1]). Born in Stark, Me., Nov. 22, 1829. Married, at Stark, Me., ALVIN S. CHAPMAN, of Stark. He was a farmer. They lived in Stark and Industry, Me., and had children.

Children.

I. EMERY[8] CHAPMAN, b. Jan. 26, 1861; m. GEORGIA A. WING, Aug. 27, 1887.
II. SYLVESTER[8] CHAPMAN, b. June 20, 1863; m. OCTAVIA O. SAFFORD, Jan. 7, 1887.
There were eight or nine children, of whom we can obtain no record.

571.

JOHN[7] CHURCHILL (SANFORD,[6] JOHN,[5] JOSEPH,[4] JOHN,[3] ELIEZER,[2] JOHN[1]). Born in Stark, Me, Feb. 27, 1831. Married at Stark, Me., LOVERNA GREENLEAF, daughter of John and Lydia. They lived at Stark. He was a farmer.

Children born in Stark.

I. ROSE,[8] m. ALEXANDER HORTON. They live in Stark.
II. OLIVE,[8] b. Nov. 10, 1874; m. TAVEY GRANT, Nov. 10, 1892, at Anson.
III. ZOE,[8] b. March 21, 1878; m. JOHN HUTCHINSON, of Stark, and live there.

572.

ELIAS HUTCHINS[7] CHURCHILL (SANFORD,[6] JOHN[5] JOSEPH,[4] JOHN,[3] ELIEZER,[2] JOHN[1]). Born in Stark, Me., July 25, 1833. Lived in New Sharon and Stark, Me. This information from Mrs. Nancy G. Churchill, of Stark, Me., 1903. Married, at Stark, Me., Sept. 21, 1850, NANCY GREENLEAF. Mr. Churchill died Oct. 7, 1902.

One Child born in Stark, Me.

I. ALZADA,[8] b. Oct. 6, 1860; m. FREDERICK W. SMITH, of New Sharon, Me., in 1887, and had two children: (1) Harry E. Smith, b. Feb. 27, 1890; (2) Robert H. Smith, b. April 14, 1893.

572a.

MARCIA ANN[7] CHURCHILL (SANFORD,[6] JOHN,[5] JOSEPH,[4] JOHN,[3] ELIEZER,[2] JOHN[1]). Born in Stark, Me., March 18, 1835. Married BENJAMIN F. GREENLEAF, at Stark, Me. They had five children whose names we have not been able to obtain.

579.

JOHN W.[7] CHURCHILL (WILLIAM,[6] WILLIAM,[5] JOSEPH,[4] JOHN,[3] ELIEZER,[2] JOHN[1]). Born in New Portland, Sept. 13, 1835. He died Nov. 21, 1890. Married 1st, HANNAH BAILEY. Married 2d, MARY LUCE.

Children of First Wife.

    I. ESTELLE,[8] m. JOHN JORDAN. Had two children: (1) Clarence Jordan; (2) Ross Jordan.
    II. HANNAH,[8] unmarried.

Children of Second Wife.

1028   III. EDWARD,[8] m. MABEL PORTER. One son.
    IV. BELLE,[8] m. FRANK TRASK. Had a son and daughter.
    V. EFFIE.[8]
    VI. CLINTON.[8]
    VII. CORA.[8]
    VIII. HARRIET.[8]

580.

WILLIAM TILSON[7] CHURCHILL (TILSON[6] WILLIAM[5] JOSEPH,[4] JOHN,[3] ELIEZER,[2] JOHN[1]). Born in New Portland, Me., Sept. 30, 1833, and lived there. Married ABIGAIL LUCE. She died Sept. 8, 1899.

Children born in New Portland.

1029   I. DELBERT,[8] b. July 31. 1862; m. SARAH F. FLETCHER. One child, Merrill E. Churchill, b. Aug. 12, 1897.
1030   II. ALVARUS.[8] b. Oct. 31, 1865; m. IDA THOMPSON, Dec. 24, 1891. One child, Florence, b. Jan. 14, 1897.

581.

ALBERT[7] CHURCHILL (DANIEL,[6] DANIEL,[5] JOSEPH,[4] JOHN,[3] ELIEZER,[2] JOHN[1]). Born at the Forks of the Kennebec, Me., Oct. 29, 1829. Died March 25, 1902. Married IRENA BERRY, 1854.

Children.

    I. IRENA,[8] m. J. H. DAVIS, of Skowhegan, Me.

Children.

    1. Albert L. Davis.   3. John Davis.
    2. Fannie Davis.   4. Mahlon Davis.

    II. CAROLINE A.,[8] m. ALMON H. CARL, Madison, Me.

Children.

    1. Daisy May Carl.   3. Maud Carl.
    2. Vesta Carl.   4. Alice Carl.

1031   III. ABEL.[8]
    IV. LULU,[8] m. MILTON PHILLIPS.
    V. ALICE.[8]

582.

ABEL[7] CHURCHILL (DANIEL,[6] DANIEL,[5] JOSEPH,[4] JOHN,[3] ELIEZER,[2] JOHN[1]). Born at the Forks of the Kennebec River, May 3, 1833. Married LYDIA M. BERRY, 1854.

Children.

  I. JULIA MAY,[8] m. REV. F. W. SHERWIN.
  II. CARRIE VIOLA,[8] m. C. H. MEAD.
  III. ALICE,[8] m. GEORGE WOOD.

584.

DANIEL FOSTER[7] CHURCHILL (DANIEL,[6] DANIEL,[5] JOSEPH,[4] JOHN,[3] ELIEZER,[2] JOHN[1]). Born at the Forks of the Kennebec River, Jan. 6, 1842. Married LUCENA I. DAME.

Children.

1032   I. ALBERT.[8]
1033 II. ANDREW.[8]
1034 III. MILTON.[8]

585.

WARREN[7] CHURCHILL (DANIEL,[6] DANIEL[5] JOSEPH,[4] JOHN,[3] ELIEZER,[2] JOHN[1]). Born in Solon, Me., Sept. 6, 1846. He died April 20, 1900. Married 1st, CLARA E. WOODBERRY; 2d, ADA HILL.

Child.

1035   I. BERTRAM DANIEL,[8] m. SARAH PERKINS. Probably other children, but names not received.

586.

JOHN[7] CHURCHILL (ASA,[6] DANIEL,[5] JOSEPH,[4] JOHN,[3] ELIEZER,[2] JOHN[1]). Born at Moose River, or Embden, Me., June 6, 1836. Removed to the West, and, in April, 1901, was living at Augusta Kan. Married, Sept. 27, 1870, HARRIET L. PARKER.

Child.

1036   I. ASA EMERY,[8] b. Dec. 3, 1873.

587.

HARRISON[7] CHURCHILL (ASA,[6] DANIEL,[5] JOSEPH[4] JOHN,[3] ELIEZER,[2] JOHN[1]). Born at Moose River, May 2, 1841. Mr. Churchill was living at Dewey, Mont., April, 1901. Married, at New Diggings, Wis., March 12, 1886, DORA OLIVER.

Children.

1037   I. WARREN O.,[8] b. Oct. 30, 1887.
1038 II. RUSSELL H.,[8] b. April 6, 1889.
    III. MILDRED H.,[8] b. Feb. 15, 1891.
    IV. MARJORIE M.,[8] b. April 27, 1893.

588.

HORATIO[7] CHURCHILL (ASA,[6] DANIEL,[5] JOSEPH,[4] JOHN,[3] ELIEZER,[2] JOHN[1]).   Born at Moose River, Me., April 1, 1843.   He was adopted by Ozias McFaden, of Embden, Me., and brought up in that town.   He went West and settled at Buda, Ill., April 4, 1867. He has carried on the brick and drain-tile business many years. He has been somewhat in public office and is a Past-master in Free masonry.   Mr. Churchill and family were living in Buda, Ill., April, 1901.   Married 1st, Sept. 12, 1874, MELINDA H. KEALIHER of York, Neb.   Married 2d, Sept. 8, 1881, MARY H. HODGETTS, of Kewanee, Ill.   First wife died Feb. 7, 1881.

Children of First Wife.

1039   I. DANIEL LEWIS,[8] b. Feb. 3, 1876.
1040   II. OSCAR WARREN,[8] b. May 20, 1877.

Children of Second Wife.

III. NELLIE MAY,[8] b. Sept. 12, 1883.
IV. BESSIE E.,[8] b. Jan. 16, 1885.
V. HAZEL M.,[8] b. May 5, 1890.

589.

HARTWELL[7] CHURCHILL (ASA,[6] DANIEL,[5] JOSEPH[4] JOHN,[3] ELIEZER,[2] JOHN[1]).   Born at Moose River, Me., Feb. 2, 1845.   He is a minister of the Baptist fellowship, and, Feb. 22, 1901, lived at Ashland, Mich.   Married, Jan. 13, 1870, at Skowhegan, LYDIA E. PRATT, of Skowhegan, Me.

Children.

I. BERTHA L.,[8] b. June 20, 1871.
II. L. MYRTELLA,[8] b. Nov. 6, 1873.
III. LULU A.,[8] b. March 28, 1879.
IV. LILLIAN P.,[8] b. Oct. 5, 1880.
V. ADDIE E.,[8] b. Oct. 11, 1883.
VI. GRACE M.,[8] b. Oct. 17, 1886.

591.

AMOS[7] CHURCHILL (AMOS,[6] DANIEL,[5] JOSEPH,[4] JOHN,[3] ELIEZER,[2] JOHN[1]).   Born in Madison, Me., Sept. 5, 1845.   Lived at Symco, Wis.   He died June 23, 1883.   Married, at Symco, Wis., Sept. 18, 1866, MARY CAROLINE CHURCHILL, daughter of Daniel, No. 269.   After Mr. Churchill's death his widow married again as noted below.

Children.

1041   I. WILLIAM O.,[8] b. Oct. 8, 1867.
        II. GLADYS M.,[8] b. Aug. 7, 1873; d. Aug. 14, 1884.
1042   III. LESLIE L.,[8] b. Aug. 16, 1877.
1043   IV. FLOYD W.,[8] b. July 5, 1880.
1044   V. AMOS R.,[8] b. May 29, 1883; d. Oct. 3, 1883.
        MRS. MARY CAROLINE CHURCHILL married 2d, January, 1886, CHARLES A. JENKINS.   See No. 269.

603.

CHARLES[7] CHURCHILL (JESSE,[6] BENJAMIN,[5] JOSEPH,[4] JOHN,[3] ELIEZER,[2] JOHN[1]). Born 1844. Married VILLA A. BOYNTON.

Children.

1045   I. BION,[8] b. 1866.
1046   II. ALTON,[8] b. 1868.

606.

JOHN[7] CHURCHILL (CALEB,[6] JOHN,[5] EBENEZER[4] WILLIAM,[3] WILLIAM,[2] JOHN[1]). Born at Chittenden, Vt., Dec. 12, 1790. Lived in Brandon, Vt. He was a farmer. He died at Goshen, Vt., Feb. 26, 1867. Married, Nov. 26, 1818, LOIS LATHAM, born at Springfield, Vt., 1797, and died at Goshen, Dec. 8, 1875.

Children of John and Lois (Latham) Churchill, born àt Brandon, Vt.

      I. HARVEY G.,[8] b. Dec. 1, 1820. He was a farmer. Died at Goshen, Vt., unmarried, April 17, 1894.
1047   II. ALVIN J.,[8] b. Aug. 22, 1822; m. 1st, MARIETTA E. DAVISON, Nov. 21, 1849; m. 2d, MRS. HANNAH WIGGIN.
         He was a physician, and died at Udall, Kan., Oct. 30, 1888.
1048 III. SIMEON L.,[8] b. Nov. 2, 1824; m. MARY MARCELLA DAVISON, of Pittsford, Vt., Jan. 8, 1851. She was born at Ludlow, Vt., and died at Goshen, April 8, 1868. He was a farmer

Children born in Brandon.

      1. Marion A., b. June 12, 1856; m. 1st, William B. Catlin, of Ticonderoga, N.Y., Sept. 5, 1874. He died at Goshen, Vt., Dec. 22, 1883; m. 2d, G. W. Holdridge, of Wichita, Kan., March 8, 1899.
      2. Ida M., b. Oct. 3, 1859; m. Orrel T. Severy, Aug. 30, 1881. They lived in Goshen, and had children: (1) Walter H. Severy, b. Oct. 1, 1882; (2) Ralph T. Severy, b. Aug. 2, 1886.

    IV. BETSEY L.,[8] b. Jan. 20, 1827; m. ISAIAH CARLISLE, of Goshen, Jan. 8, 1851. She died in Randolph, Wis., Feb. 6, 1862.
     V. LOIS C.,[8] b. Jan. 22, 1829; died young.
    VI. A DAUGHTER, not named, b. Feb. 24, 1830; died in infancy.
1049 VII. CALEB W.,[8] b. April 6, 1831; m. ANNA H. PETERS, Feb. 18, 1867. They lived at Salt Lake City. No further record received.
1050 VIII. LEWIS C.,[8] b. April 6. 1836; m. JULIA NORTON, at Ticonderoga, N.Y., March 21, 1864.

Children born, three at Goshen, Vt., and the youngest at Leicester, Vt.

      1. John A., b. March 5, 1865; m. Florence Friend, of Butler, Mo., at Udall, Kan., April 16, 1890. They removed to Oklahoma, in 1894, where he is a farmer. They have children: (1) Alma B.; (2) Velma W.; (3) Vera B.; (4) Lewis M.
      2. Berton L., b. Aug. 15, 1866; m. Minnie M. Elliott, of Pittsford, Sept. 29, 1887. Children: (1) Roy W.; (2) Curtis B.; (3) Clarence E.; (4) Percival L.
      3. Mary L., b. May 23, 1868; m. Lincoln A. Schoppe, at Udall, Kan., Jan. 24, 1888. She died at Udall, Jan. 23, 1898, leaving two sons and two daughters.
      4. Winnifred C., b. in Leicester, May 4, 1871.

IX. COLUMBIA L..[8] b. March 25, 1838; m REV. JOHN BLANCHARD, April 27, 1887.

Mr. Blanchard was born at Roxbury, Mass., in 1823. She died at Goshen, Aug. 10, 1898.

X. A DAUGHTER, not named, b. Jan. 21, 1841; d. in infancy.

607.

CALEB[7] CHURCHILL, JR. (CALEB,[6] JOHN,[5] EBENEZER,[4] WILLIAM,[3] WILLIAM,[2] JOHN[1]). Born in Chittenden, Vt., Dec. 15, 1794. He lived in Chittenden, a farmer. Married, Dec. 19, 1832 MIRIAM PARMELEE.

Children born at Chittenden, Vt.

 I. JOANNA MIRIAM,[8] b. Sept. 8, 1833; d. unmarried, aged 17 years.
 II. ALMIRA PARMELEE.[8] b. September, 1834; d. unmarried, aged 31 years.
1051 III. EDWIN RUTHVEN,[8] b. June 13, 1836; m. CLARA RECORD, in Bethany, Mo., Dec. 25, 1867. He served as private in the Civil War in Company H, First Vermont Cavalry, from November, 1863, to the close of the war. He then settled first in Bethany, Mo., and later in Kearney, Neb., where he was living in 1903. He was a teacher in the public schools for many years, and is also a mechanic. He lived awhile at Mankato, Kan.

Children of Edwin R. and Clara (Record) Churchill.

 1. William T., b. at Bethany, Mo., Oct. 23, 1869; d. there Dec. 17, 1878.
 2. Thirza P., b. at Bethany, Mo., July 17, 1871; m. Erastus Fairchild, April 4, 1895.

Children of Erastus and Thirza (Churchill) Fairchild, born at Kearney, Neb.

  (1) Cecil M. Fairchild, b. Jan. 17, 1896; (2) Harold E. Fairchild, b. Jan. 30, 1899; (3) Zoe Fairchild, b. Oct. 30, 1900; (4) Ovillin P. Fairchild, b. March 3, 1903.
 3. Althea M., b. at Bethany, Mo., Sept. 3, 1872; m. David M. Taton, Aug. 13, 1890.

Children born, two at Cheyenne, Wyoming, and the last at North Platte, Neb.

  (1) Hettie L. Taton, b. Sept. 20, 1891; (2) Althea S. Taton, b. Oct. 15, 1893; (3) Helen M. Taton, b. Sept. 25, 1899.
 4. Charlotte H., b. March 11, 1875; m. Charles W. Hollingshed, at Kearney, Neb., Feb. 10, 1890. They lived at Henderson, Ky., in 1903. No children.
 5. Norah M.. b. Jan. 5, 1877, at Bethany, Mo.; d. at Mankato, Kan., Aug. 29, 1879.
 6. Grace C., b. at Mankato, Kan., Oct. 20, 1879; m. Silas E. Pickeral, at Kearney, Neb., Dec. 20, 1898. They live at Kearney, Neb., and have children: (1) Beulah M. Pickeral, b. Jan. 22, 1899; (2) Onie E. Pickeral, b. April 1, 1900; (3) Ethel H. Pickeral, b. Oct. 30, 1902.
 7. Mary A., b. at Mankato, Kan., Oct. 2, 1882; m. Thomas E. Jeffres, Aug. 20, 1900. They live at North Platte, Neb., and have (1) Genevieve M. Jeffres, b. Nov. 14, 1901.
 8. Charles E., b. at Mankato, Kan., March 13, 1885.
 9. Harry C., b. at Mankato, Kan., May 25, 1888.
 10. John R., b. at Kearney, Neb., Feb. 18, 1891.

IV. WILSON BARLOW,[8] b. Jan. 5, 1838; m. 1st, at Brandon, Vt., MARY
S. WRIGHT, who died July 1, 1896; m. 2d, MATTIE SMITH, July
28, 1897. Mr. Churchill served nine months in the Civil War, in
the Fourteenth Regiment, Vermont Volunteers. Enlisted in
1862. They live in Brandon, Vt.

Children of Wilson B. and Mary S. (Wright) Churchill.

1. Eugene, b. at Chittenden, Vt., Jan. 8, 1861; m. Ella J. Nutting,
at Merrill, Wis., March 28, 1884. They live in Idaho.
2. Lillian V., b. at Brandon, Vt., Jan. 12, 1863; m. A. J. Jones,
at Brandon, Aug. 15, 1893.
3. Clayton,⎫ b. March 10, 1867, at Sparta, Wis.; d. there, aged
⎬ one month.
4. Carlton, ⎨ b. March 10, 1867, at Sparta, Wis.; d. there, aged
⎭ six months.
5. Delmont O., b. Sept. 14, 1875, at Sparta, Wis.; m. 1st, Ada
Easton, at Brandon, Vt., July 29, 1897, who d. at Castleton,
Vt., Feb. 14. 1900; m. 2d, Susie Walker, of Benson, Vt.
They live at West Granville, N.Y., and have one child, (1)
Alma L., b. at Castleton, Vt., Jan. 7, 1900.

V ANGELINE J.,[8] b. at Chittenden, Vt., Sept. 14, 1840; m. WILLIAM
R. JOHNSON, at Chittenden, Oct. 26, 1857. Mr. Johnson was
born at Massena, N.Y., Nov. 5, 1836. He enlisted at Fairhaven,
Vt., Aug. 8, 1862, in Company C, Eleventh Regiment, Vermont
Volunteer Infantry, but was later transferred to the Heavy
Artillery, and was discharged at Burlington, Vt., July 6, 1865.
He is a mechanic. To Mrs. Angeline J. (Churchill) Johnson the
credit is due for the complete and accurate account which has
been furnished the editor of this volume. While she has been in
somewhat frail health for years, her interest has not failed and
her labors, in research and correspondence, have been unremit-
ting and exceedingly appreciative of the material needed. The
present residence of this family is Holden, Vt.

Children of William R. and Angeline (Churchill) Johnson.

1. Abbie M. Johnson, b. at Chittenden, Sept. 20, 1858; m. Denni-
son R. Fassett, at Forestdale, Vt., March 19, 1876.
2. Nellie E. Johnson, b. in Brandon, Vt., July 27, 1861; m. William
A. Nutter, at New York City, Feb. 12, 1887. They lived in
Brooklyn, N.Y., where she d. July 10, 1897.
3. Bertha D. Johnson, b. in Chittenden, March 20, 1868; m. Ernest
J. Whitcomb, of Chittenden, at Forestdale, Vt., Dec. 31,
1888. She d. May 14, 1896.
4. Oliver E. Johnson, b. in Chittenden, Dec. 6, 1870; d. at
Brandon, Vt., Feb. 23, 1876.
5. Mabel A. Johnson, b. in Brandon, Nov. 13, 1873; m. Herbert
A. Ingalls, at Chittenden, April 22, 1891. They lived at
Pittsford, Vt, on a farm.
6. Leon H. Johnson, b. at Rochester, Vt., Jan. 2, 1879; m. Caroline M. Howard, at Rutland, Vt., April 12, 1902. They live
at Chittenden, Vt.

VI. CHARLES HENRY,[8] b. at Chittenden, Vt., Feb. 10, 1843; m. 1st,
AMANDA M. CHURCHILL, dau. of Azem (610), at Sudbury, Vt.,
Jan. 2, 1868; m. 2d, MRS. HARRIET M. (GRAHAM) TOMLINSON,
at Pittsford, Vt, Nov. 12, 1900. She was the dau. of John
Graham.
Mr. Charles H. Churchill enlisted in Company H, First Ver-
mont Cavalry, Nov. 30, 1863, and served till the close of the Civil
War. They live in Holden on a farm, and have children.
Mr. Churchill has been deeply interested in the progress of this
volume, and has given much valuable assistance in compiling this
branch.

Children.

1. Azem B., b. in Chittenden, Feb. 1, 1869; d. July 1, 1884.
2. Charles H., Jr., b. at Sudbury, Vt., May 25, 1871; m. Laura
   F. Herrick, at Danby, Vt , Feb. 23, 1892. They have children ·
   (1) Edna L., (2) Ruth E., (3) Reba, (4) Ella, (5) Lena,
   (6) Vina, (7) Kate.
3. Bela, b. at Sudbury, Vt., Dec. 4, 1872; m. Alice Huntoon, at
   Rutland, Vt., Dec. 8, 1896. They live on a farm in Chittenden, Vt., and have children: (1) Pearl A., (2) Azem C.,
   (3) Warren L.

1054 VII. COLUMBUS CALEB,[8] b. in Chittenden, Vt., March 12, 1844; m.
ELMIRA L. BUMP, at Middlebury, Vt., Sept. 10, 1866. She was
b. Jan. 27, 1846. He was educated at the public schools and two
years at an academy.

He served in the army in the Civil War, two years, in Company
K, Twenty-Second Regiment, New York Volunteers, and then re-
enlisted Nov. 30, 1863, in Company C, Tenth Vermont Volunteers,
and remained in service till the close of the war. He was taken
prisoner at the second battle of Bull Run in 1862, was exchanged
and returned to his regiment in the field. He was severely
wounded at the battle of Cedar Creek, Oct. 19, 1864. After marriage he settled on a farm in Chittenden for twenty years, but in
1887 entered the ministry as an itinerant Methodist preacher,
which calling he followed for ten years, retiring to his farm in
1897, on account of failing health. He gave interest and help to
this volume.

Children born in Chittenden, except last.

1. Emma L., b. March 13, 1868; m. Charles J. Wheeler, at Hague,
   N.Y., Dec. 31, 1889. She d. at Pittsford, Vt., May 19, 1896,
   leaving children: (1) Fred A. Wheeler, b. at Pittsford,
   Dec. 29, 1890; (2) Grace E. Wheeler, b. at Pittsford, Aug. 9,
   1892.
2. Waldo H., b. July 31, 1869; m. Mary M. Brewster, of West
   Rutland, Vt., Jan. 22, 1896. They live at Rutland, and have
   (1) John B., b. Oct. 26, 1896.
3. Lewis B., b. Feb. 10, 1872; m. Fanny Dudley, at Bath, N.Y.,
   Nov. 2, 1898. He is a minister at Houghton, N.Y., and they
   have two children: (1) Leslie D., b. Nov. 18, 1899; (2) Mary
   A., b. Dec. 8, 1901.
4. Anna B., b. Jan. 22, 1876; m. Rev. Willard C. Boardman, at
   Houghton, N.Y., July 24, 1895. They sailed from New York
   Feb. 5, 1902, for Sierra Leone, as missionaries, and he died
   there March 27, 1902, soon after his arrival. Mrs. Anna
   (Churchill) Boardman remains at Sierra Leone as a mis
   sionary.
5. Martha M., b. May 19, 1880; m. Jerome Fuller, of Rochester,
   Vt., at Warren, Vt., Sept. 18, 1899. He is a farmer at
   Rochester.
6. Miriam L., b. Dec. 27, 1881.
7. Abbie L., b. at Johnsburgh, N.Y., Aug. 10, 1889.

1055 VII. OLIVER ERASTUS,[8] b. Dec. 4, 1846; m. Mary R. Sherburn, at
Bolton, Vt., March 31, 1871.

He enlisted in Company C, Eleventh Regiment Vermont Volunteers, Aug. 1, 1862, and served until the close of the Civil War. In
1867 he removed to Missouri, where he remained some years, but
later settled in Illinois. He was a teacher in the public schools for
many years, working as a mechanic in vacations. They lived in
Libertyville, Ill., in 1903, and have children.

Children.

1. Alfred H., b. at Bethany, Mo., June 21, 1873; m. Daisy A.
   Gaylord. He is a physician in Oswego, Ill.
2. Rolla W., b. at Bethany, Mo., June 10, 1875. He is a lawyer
   in Chicago.
3. Nola E., b. at Bethany, Mo., Sept. 10, 1877; m. Dr. William J.
   McQuaig, and they live in Chicago, Ill.; have one child: (1)
   Malcolm C. McQuaig.
4. George S., b. at Ringwood, Ill., March 24, 1880; d. there Feb.
   18, 1882.
5. Flora A., b. at Libertyville, Ill., Dec. 29, 1889.

1056   IX. JOHN QUINCY,[8] b. Feb. 20, 1848; m. ELECTA D. DURGY, Aug. 22,
        1868, at Chittenden, Vt. They live at Brandon, Vt. He is a
        mechanic.

They have Children.

1. George M., b. July 22, 1869, at Chittenden; m. Grace Delphy,
   of Lincoln, Vt., Jan. 3, 1896.
2. Clara J., b. at Chittenden, Vt., May 29, 1871. She is superintendent of nurses at Mary Fletcher Hospital, Burlington, Vt.
3. John Q., b. at Brandon, Vt., March 9, 1874; m. Susan Stevens,
   at West Rutland, Vt. They live at Brandon, Vt., and have
   one child: (1) Ruth E., b. Jan. 4, 1900.
    X. FLORA AMELIA,[8] b. Nov. 12, 1851; m. 1st, CHARLES F. SEGAR, at
        Brandon, Nov. 24, 1874. Mr. Segar served as a soldier in the
        Civil War, and died at Marengo, Ill., Feb. 6, 1878, and Flora M.
        (Churchill) Segar m. 2d, REV. JAMES R. WYLIE, July 2, 1888,
        at Chittenden, Vt. He is now (1903) pastor of the Methodist
        Church in Dyke, N.Y.

Child of Charles F. and Flora A. (Churchill) Segar.

1. Carrie M., b. in Chittenden, May 1, 1876; m. Elmer Franks, of
   Ontario, N.Y., March 17, 1898. They live at Williamson
   N.Y., where he is a farmer.

608.

ZACCHEUS H.[7] CHURCHILL (CALEB,[6] JOHN,[5] EBENEZER,[4]
WILLIAM,[3] WILLIAM[2] JOHN[1]). Born in Chittenden, Vt, March 29,
1799. Of Zaccheus and his family we have been able to learn very
little. Mrs. Johnson, of Holden, has tried to get the record, but up
to the time of this account going to press we have received very
little. He married HANNAH N. BACON, Dec. 4, 1827, and removed
to Pennsylvania. Mrs. Johnson has a letter received from her
brother, Edwin R., years ago, in which he says that "when I visited
Uncle Zaccheus Churchill, in 1866, he was living some twenty-five
miles south of Erie, Penn., and had five children." There were two
sons and two daughters, and one other, he did not remember
whether a son or daughter. He remembered the names of two of
the children, the oldest son, Simeon, who was married and had eight
children. The youngest son was Azem. All the children were
married.

609.

NATHAN HAWLEY[7] CHURCHILL (CALEB,[6] JOHN,[5] EBENE-
ZER,[4] WILLIAM,[3] WILLIAM,[2] JOHN[1]). Born in Chittenden (then
called Philadelphia), Vt., June 11, 1803. He was a farmer and
settled first in Chittenden, but about 1840, after his second marriage,
he removed to Brandon, and took up a new section of seventy-two
acres of land, upon which he built a rough log-house at first. Being
a shrewd and industrious man, he began to speculate a little, in land
and cattle at first, and later in lumber and various commodities.
He set up a distillery for getting out " Winter-Green Oil," and afterwards built a saw-mill and conducted a wheelwright and blacksmith
establishment. He died at Brandon, Jan. 12, 1884. Married 1st,
at Reading, Vt., Oct. 4, 1825, DOROTHY SHELDON, daughter of
Jacob, of Reading. She was born at Reading, Vt., Jan. 19, 1804,
and died March 10, 1838. Married 2d, March 10, 1839, at Pitts
ford, Vt., NANCY LYON, daughter of John and Polly Carry Lyon.
Nancy was born Dec. 9, 1819, and died Oct. 18, 1901.

Children of First Wife.

     I. DOROTHY CHARLOTTE,[8] b. Oct. 20, 1826; d. Oct. 28, 1827.
    II. JOSEPH LORENZO,[8] b. Oct. 4, 1828; d. Jan. 7, 1852, unmarried, on
        the voyage to the Sandwich Islands.
   III. JULIA CAROLINE,[8] b. June 18, 1830; m. 1st, CALEB BRIGGS, about
        1852. He went to California, never returned. She obtained
        a divorce, and m. 2d, B. G. CLOW, of Reno, Nevada, April 14,
        1871.
1057 IV. GERMAN SHELDON,[8] b. Oct. 15, 1832; m. MARIETTA F. SWAIN, of
        So. Reading, Mass., 1857. He was a druggist at Wakefield,
        Mass., and died in 1864.
1058   V. JOHN A.,[8] b. July 20, 1835; m. MARY ANN CONLON, Dec. 25, 1860.
        They lived at Council Bluffs, Iowa. He was a merchant. Two
   children, Dorothy, d. at 9 years and a son d. in infancy.

Children of Second Wife, Nancy (Lyon) Churchill.

    VI. DOROTHY CHARLOTTE,[8] b. May 27, 1840; d. Dec. 19, 1845.
1059 VII. NATHAN W.,[8] b. Dec. 9, 1842; m. FRANCES L. ROGERS, of Brandon,
        Dec. 9, 1866.
        He served from Sept. 15, 1864, to June 21, 1865, in the Civil War,
      in Company H, First Vermont Cavalry; d. July 5, 1886. He was a
      farmer and carpenter at Brandon, Vt.

Children.

     1. John R., b. Jan. 2, 1870; m. at Council Bluffs, Iowa, but wife's
        name not obtained. He was a dentist, and died Feb. 22, 1896,
        at Los Angeles, Cal., leaving one child, Barbara.
     2. Nathan H., Jr., b. Dec. 5, 1871. He married and lives in San
        Francisco, Cal., but we have no further information of him,
        except that he was a horsedealer.
  VIII. JANE L.,[8] b. March 15, 1844; m. HORACE SMITH, April 2, 1864.
    Mrs. Smith d. June 30, 1887.

Children born in Virginia City, Nevada.

1. Grant H. Smith, b. April 13, 1865; m. and lives in Salt Lake City.
2. Stuart Smith, b. June, 1869. He is a banker in San Francisco,
3. Herbert L. Smith, b. Dec. 27, 1871. An architect, Oxnard, Cal.
4. Jay Miles Smith, b. Aug. 28, 1874. Lives near San Francisco.
5. Hawley Smith, b. Oct. 5, 1880. Lives near San Francisco.

1060   IX. ROYAL M.,⁸ b. Oct. 27, 1846; m. ABBIE E. JOHNSON, Oct. 27, 1866.
     They lived in Brandon, Vt. He served in the war of the Rebellion three years, 1862 to 1865, in Company H, Eleventh Regiment, Vermont Volunteers, enlisting when fifteen years old. He was a moulder by trade, also a lumberman. He d. May 24, 1880.

Children.

1. Nancy J., b. at Brandon, June 14, 1870; m. Henry H. Horner, April 9, 1886, and d. Jan. 12, 1900.
2. Joseph R., b. at Brandon, May 25, 1874. He is a grocer in Brandon, Vt.
3. Grace F., b. in Chittenden, June 22, 1876; d. in Brandon, June 13, 1888.
4. Hugh H., b. in Chittenden, May 2, 1878; m. Annette I. Smith, April 3, 1901, in Fitchburg.
5. Daisy A., b. in Chittenden, Aug. 16, 1879; m. George J. Bacon, of Brandon, Sept. 15, 1902.

1061   X. RILEY V.,⁸ b. May 13, 1851; m. MARY A. PHILLIPS, June 28, 1887.
     He went West and worked in the mines and quartz-mills in California, Nevada, and Utah, but finally settled in Neola, Iowa, as a farmer.

Children.

1. George H., b. Dec. 30, 1887.
2. Riley V., Jr., b. Aug. 21, 1889.
3. Amelia M., b. Dec. 30, 1890.
4. Howel E., b. Feb. 2, 1892.
5. Phillips V., b. Oct. 24, 1894.
6. Victoria, b. March 25, 1897; d. April 20, 1897.

1062   XI. GEORGE H.,⁸ b. Dec. 27, 1852; m. M. J. SARGENT, dau. of Dr. A. J. and Ruth (Edmunds) Sargent, Oct. 4, 1876. She was born in Danby, Vt., Dec. 7, 1852.
     They lived on the old homestead of Nathan Hawley Churchill, in the present town of Forest Dale, Vt. Mr. Churchill is a farmer, lumberman, and manufacturer.

Children.

1. Fred W., b. Sept. 3, 1877; m. Ida V. Le Rean. He is a druggist, Brandon, Vt.
2. Leo R., b. Nov. 2, 1881.
3. Ruth Fern, b. Jan. 6, 1889; d. Feb. 5, 1889.
4. Andrew Hawley, b. Aug. 19, 1891.

610.

AZEM⁷ CHURCHILL (CALEB,⁶ JOHN,⁵ EBENEZER,⁴ WILLIAM,³ WILLIAM,² JOHN¹). Born in Chittenden, Vt., Nov. 13, 1805. He was a farmer in Chittenden, Vt. He died Sept. 11, 1877. Married, Aug. 29, 1831, MERCY M. MANLEY, born at Chittenden, Jan. 19, 1814, daughter of Seth. She died at Chittenden, May 27, 1873.

Children born at Chittenden.

I. JANET H.,[8] b. Dec. 28, 1832; m. CYRUS BARNARD, of Chittenden, Jan. 15, 1851. He was in the army, lost at sea from transport while enroute from New Orleans to New York, Dec. 22, 1863.

Children.

1. Eugene A. Barnard, b. May 1, 1853; m. Annie E. Wetmore, Aug. 18, 1880.
2. Nettie A. Barnard, b. Dec. 8, 1854; m. John Tarbel, at Pittsford, Vt., Dec. 8, 1872.

II. SYLVIA,[8] b. Sept. 11, 1833; m. NELSON PARMELEE, of Pittsford, March 13, 1860. They settled first in Pittsford, but removed in a few years to Fon du lac, Wis., and later to Grand View, Tenn., where Mr. Parmelee d. Aug. 5, 1899.

Children.

1. Mertie A. Parmelee, b. Feb. 24, 1862; m. E. T. Phillips, Grand View, Tenn., July 16, 1882.
2. John A. Parmelee, b. March 24, 1871. Lives at Iron Mountain, Minn.

III. ELSIE A.,[8] b. June 22, 1835; m. HOMER M. HEWITT, Nov. 12, 1853. They lived at Chittenden and Pittsford, Vt., where he d. April 12, 1899.

Children.

1. Merritt H. Hewitt, b. June 23, 1856; d. Sept. 13, 1859.
2. Elmer E. Hewitt, b. Jan. 27, 1861; m. Millie J. Wood, June 12, 1889.
3. Ella A. Hewitt, b. Jan. 15, 1872; d. Feb. 22, 1885.

IV RACHEL M.,[8] b. June 16, 1837; m. SYLVESTER C. TARBEL, March 10, 1864, at Whitehall, N.Y.

Children.

1. Wilson H. Tarbel, b. Feb. 3, 1867; m. Hattie M. Cotting, Aug. 17, 1890.
2. Mercy M. Tarbel, b. July 16, 1868; m. Elam French, Jan. 15, 1903, at Chittenden, Vt.

V LUCELIA M.,[8] b. Nov. 30, 1839; m. ALBERT FLETCHER, of Pittsford, Vt., at Hampton, N.Y., Sept. 1, 1864. They settled first in Pittsford, Vt., but removed some time after 1879 to Aberdeen, So. Dakota.

Children.

1. Azem O. Fletcher, b. Nov. 18, 1866; d. in So. Dakota, Oct. 17, 1886.
2. Bertha M. Fletcher, b. April 26, 1869; m. C. E. Douglas, Feb. 17, 1895.
3. Emma L. Fletcher, b. Oct. 25, 1872; d. in So. Dakota, Nov. 6, 1894.
4. Guy C. Fletcher, b. June 28, 1879; m. Mary Oleson, Sept. 4, 1899, at Aberdeen, So. Dakota.

VI. AMANDA M.,[8] b. April 22, 1841; m. third son of Caleb, Jr., CHARLES H. CHURCHILL, JR., Jan. 2, 1868.

1063 VII. AZEM B.,[8] b. Jan. 8, 1843.
He was a member of Company G, Twelfth Regiment, Vermont Volunteers, and died of fever, at Wolf Shoals Run, Va., April 12, 1863.

VIII. ALZINA,[8] b. Dec. 19, 1844; m., April 27, 1873, REV. GEORGE NILES, who d. in Brandon, Feb. 27, 1889. She d. April 26, 1885. No record of children received.

IX. ADELIA E.,[8] b. March 31, 1854, d. Oct. 19, 1854.

612.*

WILLIAM[7] CHURCHILL (WINSLOW,[6] ISAAC,[5] EBENEZER,[4] WILLIAM,[3] WILLIAM,[2] JOHN[1]). Born in Chittenden, Vt., Aug. 16, 1797, attended Nine Mile Creek school. A farmer, and lived at Camillus, N.Y., later at Glen Ellyn. No further account of this family has been obtained. Married at Camillus, MRS. POLLY HAND.

Children.

    I. DIANA.[8] She married several times, it is said, but we have not been able to obtain any further account. She was living in Des Moines, Iowa, and her address was given as Mrs. Diana Coffin, but no answer was received.

    II. CHRISTIANA.[8]

1064 III. ISRAEL,[8] d. young.

    IV. MARTHA.[8]

    V. MARY.[8]

613.

SETH[7] CHURCHILL (WINSLOW,[6] ISAAC,[5] EBENEZER,[4] WILLIAM,[3] WILLIAM,[2] JOHN[1]). Born at Camillus, N.Y., May 25, 1805. He was reared on the farm, attended the common school, and settled on a farm in his native town, but removed later to Babcock's Grove, Ill., and there took up a claim and settled a farm. Married, at Jordan, N.Y., Oct. 9, 1828, ROXANA WARD.

Children born, the first three at Camillus, the others at Babcock's Grove.

    I. MARY JANE,[8] b. 1829; m. ERASTUS KETCHUM, JR.

1065 II. HORACE,[8] b. Dec. 9, 1831; m. MATILDA CRUM, March 24, 1851, at York, Ill.
He was a farmer at Milton Township, Ill., but started for California in the spring of 1852, and was never heard from afterwards.

One Child.

    1. Horace Albert, born Dec. 10, 1852; m. Lucy Idella Headly, of Toulon, Ill., Dec. 31, 1876. They lived in 1884 at 331 Illinois street, Chicago, and had then two children: (1) Ada S., b. at Prospect Park, Ill., Jan. 16, 1878; (2) Horace Alexander, b. at same place, Oct. 29, 1880.

1066 III. MYRON,[8] b. April 23, 1834; m. HANNAH DRISCOL.
He died near Fort Carney, on his way to California.

    IV. EMILY,[8] b. Aug. 17, 1838; m. OSCAR JOHNSON, in 1861.

1067 V. HENRY WILLIAM,[8] b. July 17, 1840; m. MRS. MATILDA (CRUM) (CHURCHILL) SHERMAN.
She was the widow of his brother Horace, and, later, widow of Hiram Sherman.

614.

MAJOR[7] CHURCHILL (WINSLOW,[6] ISAAC,[5] EBENEZER,[4] WILLIAM,[3] WILLIAM,[2] JOHN[1]). Born in Camillus, N.Y., July 8, 1807. Reared as a farmer's boy, he remained a farmer. Educated in the

---

* Nothing has been obtained concerning Isaac,[7] No. 611, nor of William[7], mentioned on page 153, and, by mistake, numbered there, 612.

common schools. He settled at Somerset, Niagara County, N.Y. He died at Ridgeway, N.Y., April 4, 1888. Married, at Yates, Orleans County, N.Y., Dec. 31, 1835, MARY A. DELINE, daughter of John and Anna (Lott) Deline.

Children born in Somerset, Niagara County, N.Y.

I. JANE E.,[8] b. Nov. 20, 1836; m. 1st, ROBERT BAWDEN; m. 2d, WILLIAM D. HOYT, Jan. 20, 1881.

Children by First Husband born in Medina, N.Y.
1. Willie Bawden, b. Nov. 10, 1861; d. July 2, 1862.
2. Anna W. Bawden, b. Aug. 5, 1864; d. Nov. 15, 1882.

II. LAVINIA,[8] b. March 4, 1840; m. MATHEW CORSER. They lived at Somerset, Niagara County, N.Y. He was a farmer and school-teacher.

Children born at Somerset.
1. Clara Corser, b. 1863; m. 1st, George Lobbett; m. 2d, Robert Perfit.
2. Robert Corser.
3. Willie Corser, m. Addie Perfit.

III. NELSON,[8] b. Sept. 29, 1843; d. aged 3 years.
IV. MERCY,[8] b. July 11, 1849; m. THEODORE MERCHANT, July 4, 1868; d. without issue, Feb. 7, 1869.

1068 V. WELLINGTON M.,[8] b. Aug. 16, 1851; m. ELVIRA CHASE, of Middleport, N.Y., Jan. 3, 1877.
She was the daughter of Ansel and Almira (———) Chase. They lived at North Ridgeway, N.Y. He was a farmer. They had two children.

Children.
1. Jessie, b. Nov. 1, 1877.
2. Roy, b. Oct. 22, 1885.

VI. ROSE,[8] b. April 25, 1855; m. WILLIAM J. LOBBETT, at North Ridgeway, N.Y., Dec. 20, 1876.
He was the son of Joseph H. and Blessing B. (Gardner) Lobbett, was a farmer and they lived at North Ridgeway.

615.

WINSLOW[7] CHURCHILL, JR. (WINSLOW,[6] ISAAC,[5] EBEN-EZER,[4] WILLIAM,[3] WILLIAM,[2] JOHN[1]). Born in Camillus, N.Y., June 13, 1812. Removed with his father's family to Milton Township, now Glen Ellyn, Ill. Settled later at Downer's Grove, and lived there and at Lombard, Ill., afterwards. He was a farmer. He died May 28, 1899. Married 1st, at Glen Ellyn, May 5, 1838, JULIETTE MORTON, she died May 29, 1853; married 2d, at Glen Ellyn, Nov. 10, 1853, SARAH ANN NICHOLS, who died Oct. 25, 1858; married 3d, Dec. 25, 1858, MARGARET WILLARD, who died Nov. 1, 1882; married 4th, June 4, 1885, ELIZABETH EVANS.

Children, all born in Lombard, Ill.

I. OLIVE,[8] b. April 20, 1839; m. HARVEY CHURCH, at Lisle, Ill., Dec. 16, 1874. They lived at Wichita, Iowa.
II. ORSON,[8] b. June 12, 1840; d. at Lombard, Nov. 1, 1854.
III. ORSCENA,[8] b. Jan. 16, 1842, unmarried. Lived at Downer's Grove, Ill.

ISAAC BRADFORD CHURCHILL AND WIFE.

(No. 616, page 277.)

IV. ESTHER,⁸ b. July 12, 1844; d. Feb. 20, 1845.
V. PHILINDIA,⁸ b. July 4, 1846; m. EDWARD LAWRENCE, July 25, 1872, at Lisle, Ill. She died at Aurora, Ill., Oct. 28, 1874.
VI. HARRIET,⁸ b. May 28, 1849; m. SAMUEL GRANIS. Lived at Lombard, Ill.
VII. ELVIRA,⁸ b. March 6, 1851; m. FRANK STADEBAKER, Feb. 16, 1878, Aurora, Ill.

Children of Second Wife.

1069 VIII. HENRY W.,⁸ b. Nov. 22, 1854; m. JULIA DAVIS, Aurora, Ill., Nov. 2, 1878. Lived at Aurora, Ill.
1070 IX. JAMES W.,⁸ b. Sept. 23, 1856; m. MAGDALENE MAYER, at Iowa, Oct. 13, 1887. Lived at Lamberton, Minn.
1071 X. ISAAC B.,⁸ b. Oct. 24, 1858; m. MATILDA TIMPKIE, at Downer's Grove, 1887. Lived at 244 W. Huron street, Chicago, Ill.

Children of Third Wife.

XI. ORILLA,⁸ b. Oct. 27, 1859; m. ASA TOWNSEND, at Lisle, Dec. 25, 1878. Lived at Downer's Grove.
XII. ROSELLA,⁸ b. Oct. 27, 1859; m. FRANK LACEY, April 16, 1884, at Downer's Grove. Lived at Lisle, Ill.
XIII. ANNIS H.,⁸ b. Oct. 3, 1862; unmarried. Lived at 118 Cortlandt street, Chicago.
XIV. LOUISA C.,⁸ b. Dec. 25, 1864; m. CHARLES SMITH, at Downer's Grove, Dec. 22, 1886. Lived at 118 Cortlandt street, Chicago.

616.

ISAAC BRADFORD⁷ CHURCHILL (WINSLOW,⁶ ISAAC,⁵ EBENEZER,⁴ WILLIAM,³ WILLIAM,² JOHN¹). Born in Camillus, N.Y., April 22, 1818, and was brought up on his father's farm. He attended the common schools of his native town, and at the age of sixteen removed with his father to the West, and settled in what was then Milton Township, now Glen Ellyn, Ill., and there, when he was of age, he entered upon a claim next to his father's, which he now lives upon, and which at the present time is a well-improved farm of two hundred and thirty acres. He is a man of well-earned prosperity and influence, and has been interested and very helpful in the compiling of this volume. Married, Sept. 15, 1841, ANGELINA BARKER, daughter of Zelotus and Margaret (Mason) Barker.

Children born at Glen Ellyn.

1072 I. AMOS,⁸ b. March 29, 1842; m., Nov. 26, 1866, MARILLA BRONSON, dau. of David and Rhoda (Page) Bronson, of Naperville, Ill., where she was born, March 10, 1846.
Amos Churchill spent his early years on the farm, and received a common school education and prepared for college. He enlisted in Company D, Eighth Illinois Cavalry, Sept. 1, 1861, and was sent forward to Washington soon after. His regiment joined the army of the Potomac under General C. McLellan, arriving at Hampton in time to witness the battle between the "Monitor" and "Merrimac." Mr. Churchill was engaged in all the battles of the Army of the Potomac, from March 1, 1862, to June, 1863. He served as orderly to General Sumner up to the battle of Chancellorsville. He was engaged in the great battles of South Mountain, Antietam, Chancellorsville.

On June 1, 1863, he was severely wounded in the arm in a desperate skirmish with the enemy, near Beverly's Ford, and his horse was shot, but lived long enough to bear him to the hospital at Brandy Station. Mr. Churchill's wound was so severe that he was discharged, and arrived home Oct. 1, 1863. He resumed his studies and entered Wheaton College, until the spring of 1864, when the President called for recruits for one hundred days, and he enlisted in Company H, One Hundred and Forty-first Regiment, Illinois Volunteers, and was elected lieutenant of the company. His command was used mainly for garrison duty to relieve veteran troops, at Columbus, Cairo, and Paducah, Ky. On Oct. 10, 1864, Lieutenant Churchill, with his company, was mustered out at Chicago, and immediately resumed his studies until the spring of 1865, when upon the call of the President, he raised a company, and took them to camp, where they were mustered in, but on account of his wounded arm the surgeons would not pass him at the muster, and he returned again to his studies. He served in many offices of trust in his native town, on the board of education and in other relations. He engaged in farming and dealing in grain, etc., and in 1883 formed a partnership with W. H. Luther, in the coal and grain and agricultural tools business, which business in 1890 was dissolved, and continued by Mr. Churchill under the firm name of Churchill & Newton. Mr. Churchill has been always a self-reliant worker, a public spirited and influential citizen. He is a past commander of Post No. 513, G.A.R., and deacon of the Congregational Church.

Their children, born at Glen Ellyn.

1. Jessie M., b. June 19, 1868; m. Benj. B. Curtis, June 19, 1886. One child: (1) Esther M. Curtis, b. Nov. 28, 1899.
2. Jennie E., b. Sept. 14, 1870; m. Lewis D. Townsend, April 22, 1891. One child: (1) Richard D. Townsend, b. March 27, 1902.
3. Josie M., b. Nov. 29, 1872; m. George H. Whittle, June 2, 1891. Twins, Marilla B. and Harriett J. Whittle, b. Aug. 6, 1902.
'. Julia Almeda, b. May 21, 1875; d. Aug. 23, 1875.
. Adeline Barker, b. Dec. 19, 1877.
6. Fannie Bell, b. Dec. 9, 1880; m. Clarence A. Rowland, June 18, 1901. One child: (1) Ora E. Rowland, b. June 17, 1902.
7. Rhoda V., b. Oct. 2, 1885.
8. Amos, b. Dec. 28, 1888.

II. WEALTHY IRENA,[8] b. Dec. 5, 1843; m. 1st, MANLY BROWN; m. 2d, STEPHEN STANDISH, Feb. 11, 1867.

1073 III. ANDREW ZELOTUS,[8] b. March 1, 1846; m. CELIA KERNAN, Dec. 21, 1870.
They live at Oak Park, Ill. Mr. Churchill's boyhood and youth were spent on the home farm, and in attendance upon the public school. He enlisted as a private in the Civil War, May 15, 1864, and was discharged with his company, Oct. 10, 1864.

Children born in Oak Park

1. Angeline Edna, b. Dec. 27, 1872; m. Bert C. Davison, Oct. 18, 1893.
2. Arthur Bradford, b. July 10, 1879; d. Jan. 7, 1902.
He was in the high school in his native town when the Spanish War broke out, and enlisted in the Illinois Naval Reserves, and was mustered May 24, 1898, upon the U.S.S. "Fern," and was present at the battle of Santiago. After returning from the war he took a course at a business college, and then for two years filled a position in a large firm with credit, when his health failed, and for recovery he was sent to Arizona, but he died there, at Tucson, early in January, 1902. His body was embalmed and brought

AMOS CHURCHILL.
(No. 1072, page 277.)

home, where a public funeral was held Jan. 14, 1902. He was a fine and promising young man, and popular with all the community.

   3. Florence Celia, b Jan. 5, 1884.

IV. ISAAC BRADFORD, JR.,[8] b. Feb. 14, 1849; d. Sept. 15, 1850.

V. GEORGE PERRY,[8] b. Sept. 29, 1851. Killed by the cars at Wheaton, Feb. 24, 1868.

VI. NETTIE,[8] b. July 29, 1855; m. JOSEPH CLARKE, at Glen Ellyn, Nov. 24, 1881. They lived at Glen Ellyn and had children.

Children.

1. Nellie Louise Clarke, b. Oct. 5, 1882; d. 1884.
2. Bessie Marilla Clarke, b. April 1, 1884; m. L. W. McDonald, Feb. 8, 1901.
3. Perry J. Clarke, b. July 17, 1886.
4. Agnes Ellen Clarke, b. June 25, 1889.
5. Isaac Bradford Clarke, b. Feb. 27, 1893.
6. Ruth Nettie Clarke, b. Aug. 8, 1895.

VII. HATTIE,[8] b. Dec. 8, 1857; m. CHARLES WEINPRESS, Dec. 22, 1880.

One Child.

1. Margaret Weinpress, b. June 24, 1882.

617.

HIRAM[7] CHURCHILL (WINSLOW,[6] ISAAC,[5] EBENEZER[4] WILLIAM,[3] WILLIAM,[2] JOHN[1]). Born at Camillus, N.Y., April 7, 1820. He was brought up on the farm, and attended the common school. Removed with his father's family to Illinois in 1834. He learned and followed the trade of carpenter. Lived at Milton, Ill., till May, 1852, when he started for California, overland, in a company which included Horace Churchill, son of Seth. Neither of these was heard from after passing Council Bluffs, and it is supposed that they were attacked and killed by the Indians near Fort Carney. Married, at Glen Ellyn, Nov. 1, 1840, DRUSILLA MILLER, b. Sept. 22, 1820.

Children born at Glen Ellyn.

I. MERCY,[8] b. Aug. 23, 1841; m. FRANK WADSWORTH, 1870.

One daughter.

1. Mamie Clara Wadsworth.

II. WELLINGTON,[8] b. Jan. 5, 1843; d. unmarried, in the army, June 30, 1862.

III. SARAH LUCINDA,[8] b. July 3, 1844; d. Aug. 24, 1844.

1074 IV. BYRON,[8] b. March 6, 1846; m. RHODA MILES, Jan. 11, 1868.

1075 V. JAMES EDWIN,[8] b. July 12, 1848; m. MARY GREEN, March 17, 1871.

VI. HIRAM WALLACE,[8] b. Dec. 3, 1850; d. April 14, 1858.

618.

BRADFORD[7] CHURCHILL (SETH,[6] ISAAC,[5] EBENEZER,[4] WILLIAM,[3] WILLIAM,[2] JOHN[1]). Born at Chittenden, Vt., Aug, 23, 1800. Moved to Leroy, N.Y., in 1830, to Dane County, Wis., in 1845, and thence, about 1865, to Fort Dodge, Iowa. He died in Iowa, March 31, 1881. Married, March 23, 1825, MARY ADAMS.

Children.

    I. ENOS,[8] b. March 26, 1826; d. in infancy.
    II. EUNICE ROSETTA,[8] b. March 29, 1829; living unmarried in 1900.
1076   III. ENOS ALBERT,[8] b. Sept. 24, 1831; m. LAURA J. POWERS, Feb. 1,
          1855. Their only surviving child is Dr. C. H. Churchill, b. in
          Dane County, Wis., May 21, 1858. Educated at Cornell College
          and Rush Medical College, in practice at Fort Dodge; m. Cora
          A. Bond, 1880, and they have children: (1) Charles P. B., b.
          Oct. 20, 1887. (2) Glenwood B., b. Aug. 15, 1890.
    IV. SARAH JERUSHA,[8] b. Oct. 19, 1835; living unmarried in 1900.
    V. JUDITH ANN,[8] b. Dec. 11, 1839; living unmarried in 1900.

619.

ENOS[7] CHURCHILL (SETH,[6] ISAAC,[5] EBENEZER,[4] WILLIAM[3] WILLIAM,[2] JOHN[1]). Born at Chittenden, Vt., March 13, 1807, and lived there, and died Oct. 21, 1884. Married, in 1826, NANCY SEARLES.

Children.

    I. SARAH,[8] b. April 13, 1831; d. in infancy.
    II. MARY,[8] b. June 26, 1834; d. at the age of 16 years.
    III. EUNICE,[8] b. Oct. 23, 1839; m. HIRAM COREY, July 4, 1859.

620.

ELISHA BRADFORD[7] CHURCHILL (ELISHA,[6] ISAAC,[5] EBENEZER,[4] WILLIAM,[3] WILLIAM,[2] JOHN[1]). Born in Swanton, Vt, June 14, 1807, and lived in Burlington, Vt. Married, at Burlington, Vt., 1833, MIRANDA BARBER.

Children born at Burlington, Vt.

1077   I. JOHN BRADFORD,[8] b. May 23, 1834; m. SUSAN M. ABBOTT, Nov.
          18, 1857; married at Northampton, Mass. He died about 1878.
    II. CHLOE ALVINA,[8] b. Aug. 30, 1835; m. DR. HENRY R. HOLMAN,
          July 16, 1856. They lived at Cincinnati, O., Kansas City, Mo.,
          and Denver, Col., and in 1884 at Worcester, Mass.

Children.

      1. Fred. Augustus Churchill Holman, b. Cincinnati, June 11, 1857;
         d. at Kansas City, June 25, 1859.
      3. Carrie Maud Holman, b. Kansas City, Sept. 2, 1859; m. F. W.
         Marshall, Worcester, Mass., Jan. 29, 1884.
      3. Frank Foster Holman, b. Kansas City, Oct. 17, 1861; d. March
         2, 1862.
      4. Charles Henderson Holman, b. Kansas City, Dec. 2, 1862; m.
         Ida Louise Bessel, New York, February, 1896.
      5. Frederick Ralph Holman, b. Denver, Col., March 15, 1874.

    III. ELLEN ELIZA,[8] b. June 15, 1838; d. Aug. 11, 1856.

622.

HORACE[7] CHURCHILL (ELISHA,[6] ISAAC,[5] EBENEZER,[4] WILLIAM,[3] WILLIAM,[2] JOHN[1]). Born in Swanton, Vt., Dec. 14, 1814, and died at Milwaukee, Wis., Oct. 28, 1849. Married, 1835, in Sheldon, Vt., ALSISTA ITALY BOWEN, who died June 28, 1848.

Children born in Michigan and Wisconsin.

I. HORACE W.,[8] b. April 23, 1836; drowned Sept. 9, 1860, on Lake Michigan, in the wreck of the " Lady Elgin."

II. MARY ITALY,[8] b. April 17, 1838; m. I. T. BRANCH, Sept. 25, 1857. They lived in Milwaukee, Wis., where she died Dec. 27, 1864, leaving two sons.

Children born in Milwaukee, Wis.

1. Walter Tenney Branch, b. July 25, 1859; m. Millie Belle Campbell, July 28, 1863. They live in Denver, and have two sons, Carlton and Walter.

2. Vernon Harris Branch, b. Feb. 3, 1863; m. Luella Brown, Oct. 20, 1885. They live in Wichita, Kan., 1903, and have one child, Hazel Branch, b. at Concordia, Kan., Oct. 1, 1886.

Mr. Branch, the father, married again, and in 1886, was living in Orwell, Vt.

III. EUNICE C.,[8] b. May 16, 1841; d. 1862.

IV. WARREN,[8] b. Feb. 10, 1846; d. in Racine, Wis., 1878.

623.

SETH WARREN [7] CHURCHILL (ELISHA [6] ISAAC,[5] EBENEZER,[4] WILLIAM,[3] WILLIAM,[2] JOHN [1]). Born at Swanton, Vt., May 17, 1821. Reared at Swanton, and received a common school education in his native town. He removed West, and settled at Milwaukee, Wis., where he kept a hotel from 1844 to 1852. He was a passenger on the " City of Pittsburg," through the Straits of Magellen. The ship was burned in the harbor of Valparaiso, Chili, Oct. 24, 1852, and Mr. Churchill took passage to Panama by steamer, and thence to San Francisco, Dec. 14, 1852. He removed to San José, Cal., in 1864, and there kept the " Auzerais House " for twelve years, since which he has been engaged in the insurance business with his residence at San José. Mr. Churchill has been interested in the progress of this volume, and has helped very much in the compiling in his own life. Married, at Marysville, Cal., Dec. 31 1854, SOPHIA J. MAY, daughter of George and Sophia (Smith) May, born Feb. 3, 1835.

Children.

I. CLARA ISABELLA,[8] b. at Marysville, Cal., Oct. 30, 1855.

II. MAY,[8] } b. at Young's Hill, Cal., Jan. 11, 1857; d. Feb. 7 and 21,
III. MARY,[8] } 1857.

1078 IV. HARRY HOWARD,[8] b. Oct. 5, 1859, at Marysville; m. MARY J. MEIGS, Jan. 9, 1886, at San Francisco. Died at San José, Dec. 29, 1896.

1079 V. GEORGE MAY,[8] b. at Marysville, Sept. 6, 1861; m. NELLIE WOODWARD, at San Diego, Oct. 22, 1888. They had children, but the names have not been received.

VI. LUCY,[8] b. at San José, Aug. 12, 1865.

VII. JENNIE,[8] b. at San José, March 7, 1868; m. MILO S. BAKER, San José, July 14, 1897.

1080 VIII. SETH WARREN, JR.,[8] b. San José, July 24, 1871; m. MARIAN D. BURT, at San José, Dec. 5, 1898.

Child.

1. Florence May, b. Jan. 22, 1899.

IX. ADA MAY,[8] b. at San José, Jan. 22, 1876; m. ROMAYNE S. HUNKINS, of San José, Jan. 1, 1900.

624.

HENRY [7] CHURCHILL (ELISHA,[6] ISAAC,[5] EBENEZER [4] WILL-IAM,[3] WILLIAM,[2] JOHN [1]). Born in Swanton, Vt., Sept. 23, 1823 and died May 19, 1879. Married, Sept. 28, 1847, MIRANDA GATES, who died March 4, 1899.

Children.

1083   I. HELEN LUCRETIA,[8] b. July 28, 1848; d. Dec. 16, 1852.
         II. AUGUSTUS WARREN,[8] b. June 3, 1850.
             He lived in Chico, Cal., in 1885.
        III. SETH ERASTUS,[8] b. Feb. 9, 1852; unmarried in 1885.
         IV. CLARA,[8] b. June 1, 1856; m. WILLIAM SINGER.
          V. FRED,[8] b. Jan. 15, 1860; d. Sept. 21, 1884.
1084   VI. FRANK.[8] In 1885 was at Rocklin, Cal.

625.

ANDREW JACKSON [7] CHURCHILL (ANDREW,[6] JOSHUA [5] EBENEZER,[4] WILLIAM,[3] WILLIAM,[2] JOHN [1]). Born June 12, 1821. He lived in West Peru, Me. The date of the marriage of his parents, Andrew [6] Churchill and Polly Aldham, as given on page 156, is incorrectly given. Married NANCY WYMAN.

Children.

         I. NANCY,[8] b. May 7, 1849; d. Oct. 2, 1864.
        II. PHEBE,[8] b. July 3, 1850; m. A. L. GOWD, April 4, 1870.
1085   III. ANDREW J., JR.,[8] b. Dec. 12, 1852.

627.

SAMUEL [7] CHURCHILL (EZRA,[6] JOSHUA,[5] EBENEZER,[4] WILLIAM,[3] WILLIAM,[2] JOHN [1]). Born in Sumner, Me., Aug. 15, 1810. Settled first in Sumner, but removed to Montville, Me. Married 1st, April, 1834, ACHSAH CHURCHILL, daughter of Joshua (No. 285), who was born in Salem, Mass., Sept. 2, 1808, and died May 27, 1866. Married 2d, March 15, 1868, NANCY PENNEY.

Child of First Wife born in Sumner, Me.

         I. MARIA M.,[8] b. April 29, 1837; m. GEORGE H. THOMPSON, of
             Searsport, Me. One child, Leslie G. Thompson, b. in Searsmont,
             Me., May 12, 1861.

Child of Second Wife, Nancy Penney.

1086   II. ULYSSES GRANT,[8] b. in Montville, Me., Oct. 23, 1869.

632.

IVORY [7] CHURCHILL (ELIAS,[6] DAVID,[5] DAVID,[4] WILLIAM,[3] WILLIAM,[2] JOHN [1]). Born at Plympton, March 18, 1799. Married, June 30, 1823, MARY E. BLAKE, of Boston.

Children.

1087   I. HENRY CUSHMAN,[8] b. Jan. 26, 1825; m. MARY D. ALLEN, of Brookfield, Mass.

1088   II. EDWARD BLAKE,[8] b. Dec. 18, 1828; m. ARAVESTA SMITH, of Lynn, May 28, 1852.

  III. SARAH SIMPSON,[8] b. Feb. 27, 1832; accidentally killed, May, 1851.

  IV. SUSAN ANN,[8] b. May 30, 1839; m. SAMUEL ——, March 30, 1859.

635.

OTIS[7] CHURCHILL (DAVID,[6] DAVID,[5] DAVID,[4] WILLIAM,[3] WILLIAM,[2] JOHN [1]). Born in Plympton, Jan. 12, 1805. Lived in Ashfield, Mass., till 1811, then went to New York in the family of his step-father, Captain Warren; fled with them from the British and Indians in 1812, in the war on the borders, which robbed the families of homes and property. He remained with his step-father until twenty-one years of age, and then worked at carpenter trade and wagon-making for eighteen years. In 1845 he moved to Niagara Falls, and engaged in house building for eight years, and then moved to Milwaukee, Wis., in 1854. He settled soon in Brookfield, Wis. Finally he with his two boys took up 80-acre lots in Rock Elm, Wis., and settled down to farming. He died Sept. 16, 1886. Married 1st, May 30, 1831, MARY RUSSELL, born Jan. 5, 1813; she died May 10, 1842. Married 2d, Dec. 14, 1842, BELINDA RUSSELL, born Sept. 16, 1820; died June 18, 1859, daughters of Joseph and Ruth. Married 3d, Dec. 17, 1862, MRS. MARY L. (CALKINS) POMEROY, widow of Charles B., born Oct. 5, 1832.

Children of First Wife, born at Lewiston, N.Y.

  I. ELIZA,[8] b. June 2, 1832, at Lewiston, N.Y.; d. unmarried at Niagara Falls, Feb. 20, 1855.

  II. DAVID HENRY,[8] b. Sept. 13, 1834; d. Nov. 14, 1862, in the hospital at Baltimore.

  III. MARY JANE,[8] b. Jan. 20, 1837; d. July 12, 1841.

  IV. RUTH ANN,[8] b. Sept. 30, 1838; d. July 19, 1841.

1089   V. JAMES,[8] b. Feb. 20, 1842; m. HATTIE M. BARNES, in Brookfield, Wis., July, 1860.

He is a railroad official, So. Minneapolis, Wis. They had six children. Names not obtained.

Children of Second Wife, born at Niagara Falls and in Wisconsin.

1090   VI. WILLIAM OTIS,[8] b. Jan. 25, 1844; m. SARAH E. PUTNEY, in Waukesha, Wis., Dec. 7, 1871.

He is a farmer at Rock Elm, Wis. They have two children.

1091   VII. WESLEY RUSSELL,[8] b. Aug. 30, 1845; m. CARRIE E. POMEROY.

He is a physician. In 1887 was at Reedsburg, Wis. Has one child, Altie P. Churchill, b. 1879.

  VIII. MARY SOPHIA,[8] b. Oct. 17, 1847; d. June 21, 1854.

  IX. SARAH JANE,[8] b. Oct. 28, 1849; d. Sept. 6, 1856.

  X. HARRIET MELLISSA,[8] b. Aug. 21, 1852; d. Sept. 20, 1853.

1092   XI. FRANKLIN B.,[8] b. Aug. 26, 1854; m. FLORENCE N. DAWSON, Nov. 14, 1884.

A farmer, and owns a sawmill. Has fine stock of cattle and horses. No children. Lives at Rock Elm.

1093 XII. WILBUR T.,[8] b. Jan. 27, 1857; m. JENNIE WHIPP, Oct. 7, 1886, Rock Elm, Wis.
Has a general merchandise store and a small farm.

636.

LEVI[7] CHURCHILL (LEVI,[6] DAVID,[5] DAVID,[4] WILLIAM,[3] WILLIAM,[2] JOHN [1]). Born in Hingham, May 5, 1803 and lived there. Married, Sept. 10, 1828, LUCRETIA KEEN, of East Bridgewater. She died Jan. 1, 1897, aged 90 years.

Children.

    I. CELIA,[8] b. Feb. 4, 1830; d. 1833.
    II. CYNTHIA MARIA,[8] b. Sept. 7, 1832; d. 1833.
1094 III. WARREN KEEN,[8] b. Feb. 24, 1834; m. ELIZABETH H. JOSSELYN, Nov. 19, 1863.
They lived at Elmwood, Plymouth County, Mass., where he was a grocer, and had held the position of postmaster from the time it was established in 1863 until his death, March 2, 1898. He was the oldest living past master of Fellowship Lodge of Freemasons in Bridgewater. He was an influential and respected citizen. He helped about this volume.

Children.

    1. George M., b. Jan. 8, 1874.
    2. Asaba W., b. July 5, 1875.
    IV. BETHIA,[8] b. Aug. 10, 1838; unmarried.
    V. ANDREW,[8] b. Nov. 9, 1841; d. April 8, 1844.
1095 VI. NEWTON,[8] b. April 7, 1844; m. ABBY W. WHITE.

Children.

    1. Harry N., b. Sept. 14, 1868; d. August, 1878.
    2. Percy M., b. Jan. 5, 1873.
    VII. ASABA,[8] b. June 16, 1846; d. 1848.

637.

LUTHER[7] CHURCHILL (LEVI,[6] DAVID,[5] DAVID,[4] WILLIAM,[3] WILLIAM,[2] JOHN [1]). Born in Hingham, April, 1805. Married EVELINE BLANCHARD.

Children.

1096   I. LUTHER, JR.,[8] b. March 2, 1828.
1097   II. BENJAMIN F.,[8] b. Jan. 22, 1832.
1098 III. ELIAS P.,[8] b. Oct. 24, 1836.
1099 IV. CALEB S.,[8] b. 1840.
1100   V. THOMAS J.,[8] b. 1842.
    VI. LIZZIE T.[8] b. 1846.
  VII. EVALINE,[8] b. 1848.

638.

ABISHA S.[7] CHURCHILL (LEVI,[6] DAVID [5] DAVID [4] WILLIAM,[3] WILLIAM,[2] JOHN [1]). Born in Hingham, Oct. 13, 1807; died Dec. 9, 1890. Married MERCY L. WHITMAN.

Children.

    I. HATTIE P.,[8] m. GEORGE BENSON, June 18, 1850.

Children.

1. George H. Benson, b. July 14, 1851.
2. Fred L. Benson, b. Sept. 2, 1855.
3. Walter L. Benson, b. Aug. 5, 1858.

1101 II. FREDERICK S.,[8] b. Nov. 19, 1838; m. FRANCELIA A. WHITE, Oct. 8, 1863.

He was a shoe manufacturer in Boston, and died in Neponset, Sept. 23, 1897.

Children.

1. Hattie P., b. April 23, 1865.
2. Viola S., b. Nov. 22, 1876.

640.

ETHAN STETSON[7] CHURCHILL (LEVI,[6] DAVID[5] DAVID,[4] WILLIAM,[3] WILLIAM,[2] JOHN[1]). Born Jan. 11, 1835, at East Bridgewater, Mass. He was a piano-maker. Lived at Dedham. He served in the Civil War, as a musician in a band. He died at Dedham, March 19, 1896. Since passing this name, on page 160, we have received new information. Married, at Weymouth, September, 1859, ANNIE MATILDA COOK, daughter of Samuel and Mary (Hunt) Cook. Mrs. E. S. Churchill died at Dedham, April 13, 1902.

Children born at Weymouth.

I. GRACE A.,[8] b. Oct. 9, 1861; m. 1st, CHAUNCEY S. CHURCHILL, of Dedham; m. 2d, WALDO CHASE.
II. M. GERTRUDE,[8] b. April 3, 1863; m. CLEVELAND COX, April 4, 1883.

One Child.

1. Harold Augustus Cox, b. June 27, 1884.

641.

JESSE[7] CHURCHILL, JR. (JESSE,[6] DAVID,[5] DAVID,[4] WILLIAM,[3] WILLIAM,[2] JOHN[1]). Born in Hingham, Jan. 30, 1806. Died Oct. 24, 1870. Married 1st, Oct. 20, 1833, CHRISTIANA CUSHING, daughter of Elnathan. She died Nov. 13, 1840, aged 23. Married 2d, BETSEY A. JENKINS, of Boston, Nov. 7, 1841. She died in Hingham, Jan. 13, 1867. Married 3d, MRS. SOPHRONIA W. (BEAL) LOW.

First Wife's Children born in Hingham.

I. CATHARINE CUSHING,[8] b. Nov. 15, 1834; m. SILAS H. COBB.
II. CHRISTIANA,[8] b. Nov. 30, 1837; m. HENRY S. EWER.

Second Wife's Children.

III. SUSAN LINCOLN,[8] b. March 15, 1843; m. JOHN W. ELDRIDGE, Feb. 3, 1864.
IV. MARTHA ANN,[8] b. July 4, 1847; m. CHARLES DANIELS.

642.

JAMES[7] CHURCHILL (JESSE,[6] DAVID,[5] DAVID[4] WILLIAM,[3] WILLIAM,[2] JOHN[1]). Born in Hingham, Feb. 5, 1808. He died in Hingham, Feb. 17, 1869 or '70. Married CYNTHIA HUMPHREY FRENCH. On page 160 surname is incorrect. She died in Hingham, Jan. 20, 1866.

Children born in Hingham.

1102   I. JAMES THOMAS.[8]
       II. CYNTHIA,[8] m. (———) MURCH.
       III. EMMELINE.[8]

643.

THOMAS C.[7] CHURCHILL (JESSE,[6] DAVID,[5] DAVID,[4] WILLIAM,[3] WILLIAM,[2] JOHN[1]). Born in Hingham, Feb. 5, 1808, and lived there. He enlisted in the Civil War, and died at Harrison's Landing, Va., Aug. 7, 1862. Married, at Hingham, Sept. 13, 1829, SARAH SPRAGUE, born in Hingham Oct. 23, 1810; died April 13, 1891.

Child.

I. AMELIA SPRAGUE,[8] b. October, 1831; m. DR. JAMES M. DALY, of Boston, March 11, 1852.

Children.

1. Grace A. Daly, b. January, 1853; d. September, 1853.
2. James Harlow Daly, b. June 30, 1855; m. Clara Bussey Kendrick, April 23, 1881. They have children: (1) Harlow B., b. Dec. 1, 1883. (2) Clara E., b. July 4, 1886.

644.

CHARLES[7] CHURCHILL (JESSE,[6] DAVID,[5] DAVID,[4] WILLIAM,[3] WILLIAM,[2] JOHN[1]). Born in Hingham, July 10, 1810. Married 1st, Oct. 20, 1833, MEHITABLE GILL. She died May 25, 1835. Married 2d, November, 1838, SARAH NICHOLS, who was born at Boston, Sept. 7, 1812.

Child of First Wife.

I. HELEN MARIA,[8] b. Sept. 12, 1834; m. SIDNEY SPRAGUE, of Hingham.

Children of Second Wife.

       II. CHARLES E.,[8] b. in Boston, 1839; d. unmarried.
1103   III. WILLIAM HENRY,[8] b. Feb. 16, 1841; m. ROSAMOND JANETTE. Lived in Boston and had children: (1) Edwin Francis; (2) Nettie E.; (3) Janette; (4) William H.; and (5) Elmer Ware.
       IV. EDWIN,[8] died in infancy.

645.

RUFUS[7] CHURCHILL (JESSE,[6] DAVID,[5] DAVID,[4] WILLIAM[3] WILLIAM,[2] JOHN[1]). Born in Hingham, April 23, 1815. Married, Aug. 18, 1845, MRS. LUCY A. (BURR) KIMBALL. He died April 11, 1872.

Children.

I. IMOGENE.[8]
1105 II. MOSES.[8]

646.

THADDEUS[7] CHURCHILL (JESSE,[6] DAVID,[5] DAVID,[4] WILLIAM,[3] WILLIAM,[2] JOHN[1]). Born in Hingham, Feb. 27, 1823. Lived in Boston. Married 1st, MARGARET M. GREEN, b. Jan. 7, 1837. Married 2d, MARY J. HERSEY.

Child of First Wife.
I. MARGARET SIDERS,[8] m. MR. CHANDLER.

Child of Second Wife.
1106 II. RUSSELL THAYER,[8] b. Aug. 6, 1872.

647.

ZADOCK[7] CHURCHILL (SAMUEL,[6] WILLIAM,[5] DAVID,[4] WILLIAM,[3] WILLIAM,[2] JOHN[1]). Born July 13, 1780. Married BETSEY PALMER.

Child.
I. BETSEY,[8] m. BARNABAS BRYANT.

648.

SAMUEL[7] CHURCHILL (SAMUEL[6] WILLIAM,[5] DAVID,[4] WILLIAM,[3] WILLIAM,[2] JOHN[1]). Born May 24, 1804. Lived in Halifax, Mass. Married 1st, SABA CHURCHILL, daughter of No. 296. Married 2d, April 30, 1837, SARAH STURTEVANT

One Child by Second Wife.
1107 I. EDMUND W.,[8] b. March 13, 1838. Lives in Halifax, Mass.

649.

JOSEPH[7] CHURCHILL (JOSEPH,[6] WILLIAM,[5] DAVID,[4] WILLIAM,[3] WILLIAM,[2] JOHN[1]). Born in Plympton, Aug. 10, 1788. Married MRS. REBECCA (DUNHAM) MOREY, of Plymouth.

Children.
I. REBECCA,[8] m. REUBEN DICKEY.
II. EUNICE,[8] unmarried.
1108 III. JOSEPH.[8]
1109 IV. GEORGE HENRY,[8] m. MARY NESS.
V. SEBRINA.[8]

650.

HOSEA[7] CHURCHILL (JOSEPH,[6] WILLIAM,[5] DAVID,[4] WILL-
IAM,[3] WILLIAM,[2] JOHN[1]).   Born in Plympton, Aug. 24,1792. Married EUNICE MOREY, of Plymouth, 1811.

Children born in Plymouth.

1110	I.	HOSEA,[8] b. 1813.
	II.	BETSEY W.,[8] b. 1815.
1111	III.	SILAS M.,[8] b. 1817.
1112	IV.	BARTLETT,[8] } twins, b. 1822.
1113	V.	HENRY,[8]
1114	VI.	JOHN CLARK,[8] b. 1827.

653.

GEORGE[7] CHURCHILL (JOSEPH,[6] WILLIAM[5] DAVID,[4] WILL-
IAM,[3] WILLIAM,[2] JOHN[1]).   Born in Plympton, Oct. 29, 1802.
Married LYDIA MORTON.

Children.

1114a   I. WILLIAM,[8] b. 1822; m. ARKAM DICKEY.
        They removed to California.   No record received of any
        children.
        II. MADISON,[8] b. 1827; never married.
1114b   III. JONATHAN,[8] b. 1835; m. NELLIE M. CATE.

Children.

1. Fannie, b. 1866; m. Walter R. Terry.   Lives in Flandreau,
   So. Dakota.
2. Percy, b. 1874.   Lives in Flandreau, So. Dakota.

1114c   IV. THOMAS,[8] b. 1838; m. MARY ELLEN TOWER, in Belmont, Me.

Children.

1. Helen L., b. March 30, 1862; d. at 3 years.
2. Fred T., b. Dec. 6, 1866.

1114d   V. WESLEY,[8] b. in Corinna, Me., March 11, 1841; m. ADELIA HEALE,
      of Lincolnville, Me., 1865.   She d. April 1, 1896.
      They lived in Swanville, Minn.   He was a farmer.

One Child.

1. William, b. in Hancock, Minn., Sept. 1, 1881.

654.

JOHN[7] CHURCHILL (JOSEPH,[6] WILLIAM,[5] DAVID,[4] WILLIAM[3]
WILLIAM,[2] JOHN[1]).   Born in Plympton, Aug. 15, 1804.   Married
MARY ANN TILDEN.

Children.

	I.	MARY ANN,[8] b. 1824; m. BENJAMIN ALBEE.
	II.	SARAH,[8] b. 1826.
1115	III.	JOHN,[8] b. 1830; m. THANKFUL SCAMMON.
1116	IV.	DANIEL,[8] b. Aug. 4, 1832; m. CARRIE B. TOWER.
1117	V.	ELBRIDGE F.,[8] b. 1834; m. FRANCES A. CLARK.
1118	VI.	JAMES F.,[8] b. April 23, 1836; m. (———) TOWER.

1119 VII. Elihu T.,[8] b. 1839; m. Harriet M. Clark.
1120 VIII. Henry,[8] b. 1841.
    IX. Adrianna,[8] b. 1842; d. aged 17 years.
    X. Lydia,[8] b. 1844; m. (———) Dudley.

655.

WILLIAM[7] CHURCHILL (William,[6] William,[5] David, William,[3] William,[2] John [1]). Born in Bainbridge, N.Y., May 22, 1795. Married Minerva Luther. She was born March 1, 1800.

Children.

      I. Betsey,[8] b. Oct. 30, 1818; m. John Stag.
1121 II. Leroy W.,[8] b. Dec. 8, 1820; m. Isabel Cuthbert; no children.
    III. Catherine,[8] b. Sept. 16, 1822; m. James Wells.
1122 IV. William,[8] b. Nov. 15, 1823; m. Sarah A. Kenyon.
    V. Lorentine,[8] b. July 16, 1826; d. April 1, 1828.
    VI. Margaret,[8] b. Sept. 1, 1828; m. James Port.
    VII. Anson,[8] b. May 29, 1830; d. next day.
1123 VIII. Jackson V.,[8] b. May 1, 1831; m. Mary Roman.
    IX. Clerentine,[8] b. May 30, 1833; d. Aug. 16, 1843.
    X. Daniel,[8] b. April 9, 1835; d. July 1, 1839.
    XI. Eliza,[8] b. July 15, 1838; m. Richard Evans.
    XII. Frances,[8] b. April 12, 1841; d. Sept. 18, 1841.
    XIII. Morilla,[8] b. May 25, 1844; m. Thomas Stone.

656.

OLIVER[7] CHURCHILL (Oliver,[6] James,[5] David,[4] William,[3] William,[2] John [1]). Born in Plympton, Nov. 19, 1794. Married 1st, 1826, Sally Bradford. No children. She died 1826. Married 2d, Mary A. Loring, daughter of Ezekiel. She died 1873.

Children of Second Wife.

1124 I. Thomas Loring,[8] b. April 3, 1834; m. Helen H. Briggs, Dec. 20, 1864.
    He died Dec. 17, 1900.
    One child: (1) Alice Bradford, b. May 2, 1866.
1125 II. James Oliver,[8] b. July 5, 1835.
    III. Mary Hudson,[8] d. at Plympton, Oct. 11, 1868.

657.

ISAIAH[7] CHURCHILL (Oliver,[6] James,[5] David,[4] William,[3] William,[2] John [1]). Born in Plympton, Oct. 10, 1806. Married 1st, Polly Stevens Parker, daughter of Jonathan. Married 2d, Jane Bradford Hayward. Married 3d, Angeline Standish, daughter of John.

Children of First Wife.

    I. Charlotte Parker,[8] b. June 6, 1835; m. David S. Plummer, Meredith, N.H.
1126 II. Granville Mellen,[8] b. Sept. 24, 1836.
    III. Mary Granville,[8] b. Oct. 10, 1838.

1127   IV. FREDERICK STEPHEN,[8] b. March 18, 1840. He served in Company
           H., Third Regiment, Mass. Volunteers, and later Eighteenth Regi-
           ment, and was killed at second battle of Bull Run, Aug. 30, 1862.
1128   V. ISAIAH FREDERICK,[8] b. Feb. 21, 1842; m. ANNIE K. LORING,
           March 23, 1868. He served two terms of enlistment in the Civil
           War.
1129   VI. EDMUND FINDLEY,[8] b. Feb. 21, 1842. He served in Eighteenth
           Mass. Regiment in the Civil War; was color bearer.
1130   VII. THEODORE PARKER,[8] b. May 3, 1844. He served in Company A,
           Thirty-third Mass. Regiment, in the Civil War, and died in camp
           near Fredericksburg, Va., Dec. 14, 1862.

659.

LOUIS[7] CHURCHILL (LEWIS,[6] NATHANIEL,[5] NATHANIEL,[4]
WILLIAM,[3] WILLIAM,[2] JOHN[1]). Born in Cornish, N.H., January,
15, 1802. Removed to the West and lived in Iowa. Married
ROSAMOND RECORD. We have the names of two children only.
No further record.

Children.

1131   I. WILLIAM.[8]
1132   II. LUTHER.[8]

661.

BARKER BREWSTER[7] CHURCHILL (LEWIS,[6] NATHANIEL,[5]
NATHANIEL,[4] WILLIAM,[3] WILLIAM,[2] JOHN[1]). Born Feb. 4, 1815.
Born in Cornish, N.H. . He was a carpenter by trade, and removed
from the old homestead to Cornish Flat in 1861. He enlisted for
the Civil War Aug. 29, 1864, and was honorably discharged Sept.
11, 1865. After the war he continued at his trade until his death,
Oct. 15, 1879. He married 1st, MARY A. ANGIER, 1842 ; 2d, Jan.
31, 1867, MRS. MARY J. (WESTGATE) BRITTON.

Children of First Wife.

1133   I. EDGAR A.,[8] b. Aug. 29, 1847; unmarried.
           He is a farmer; lives in Cornish. Served in the Civil War. Has
           been selectman of his native town several terms.

       II. MARY E.,[8] b. April 20, 1850; m. LOVELL B. GEORGE, of Newport,
           N.H., Aug. 29, 1874.

Children.

           1. Jennie B. George, b. July 20, 1875; m. John C. Wiggins, Aug.
              29, 1894.
              They lived in Sunapee, N.H., and have children: (1) Her-
              man L., b. July 20, 1895; (2) Edgar J., b. July 23, 1896;
              and Harold J., b. Sept. 1, 1898.
           2. Albert W. George, b. March 5, 1879; m. Alice B. Reed, Jan.
              13, 1901.
              One child : Blanche May George, b. Sept. 4, 1902.

       III. JENNIE,[8] b. Dec. 31, 1855 ; m. WILLIAM F. WAITE, of Worcester,
            July 11, 1876. She died May 25, 1891. He died Sept. 19, 1889.

Children.

1. Rosie May Waite, b. May 22, 1877; d. Nov. 23, 1893.
2. Nettie Bell Waite, b. Feb. 13, 1879.
3. Kate J. Waite, b. Nov. 5, 1880; m. William C. Smith, 1901.
   And have one child: Ethan Allen Smith.
4. Frank E. Waite, b. Oct. 23, 1882.
5. Ernest W. Waite, b. Feb. 28, 1889.

Child of Second Wife.

IV NETTIE B.,[8] b. Feb. 20, 1868; m. M. B. LINDSAY, of Cornish, Sept. 27, 1896.

Child.

1. Helen M. Lindsay, b. July 25, 1898.

663.

LEVI[7] CHURCHILL (LEVI,[6] NATHANIEL,[5] NATHANIEL,[4] WILLIAM,[3] WILLIAM,[2] JOHN[1]). Born in Croydon, N.H., Oct. 17 1802. Married, March 28, 1827, NANCY ANN SPRAGUE, who was born May 27, 1804.

Children.

1134 I. JAMES MILLER,[8] b. Feb. 19, 1828; m. NANCY JONES.
1135 II. DAVID RIPLEY,[8] b. Jan. 26, 1830; m. SOPHIA G. BROWN, May 2, 1857. She was born May 6, 1836.
      III. LUCY ANN,[8] b. June 28, 1834.
1136 IV. LEVI,[8] b. Aug. 7, 1837; m. ELIZABETH J. FORBS.
      V. LYDIA,[8] b. Aug. 7, 1837; d. Nov. 24, 1851.
1137 VI. THOMAS SPRAGUE,[8] b. Dec. 25, 1842; died at the age of 21 years.

664.

DAVID RIPLEY[7] CHURCHILL (LEVI,[6] NATHANIEL,[5] NATHANIEL,[4] WILLIAM,[3] WILLIAM,[2] JOHN[1]). Born in Stowe, Vt., 1805. Settled in Knox County, Ohio. Married, April 24, 1829, in Ohio, POLLY PEREW, b. Oct. 7, 1807.

Children born in Knox County, Ohio.

      I. ROSAMOND,[8] b. July 25, 1830; m. ALEXANDER SCOTT, Sept. 17, 1848.
1138 II. LEVI,[8] b. April 27, 1833; m. REBECCA CLEMENS, June 18, 1858.
1139 III. HENRY,[8] b. Feb. 7, 1836; m. SARAH BROWN, at Highland, Kan., Oct. 25, 1866.
      Went to school at Fillmore, Mo. He served in the Union army, a private, three years and eight months. He is a farmer and lives at Phillipsburg, Kan.

Children all born in Highland, Kan., except Charles R. and Hattie E., born Phillipsburg. Kan.

1. Mary F., b. Aug. 4, 1867; m. G. H. Tucker, Jan. 27, 1889.
2. George F., b. March 27, 1869; m. Minnie A. Runnion, Feb. 13, 1900.

3. Annie M., b. Dec. 13, 1870; m. Edward Newton, Aug. 14, 1887;
   d. Dec. 16, 1888.
4. William L., b. April 16, 1873; m. Mary Cobbey, March 7, 1900.
5. Vinnie L., b. Jan. 11, 1875; m. Yalman Ferguson, Dec. 17, 1895.
6. Charles R., b. Sept. 21, 1876.
7. Clarence E., b. Nov. 4, 1878; d. Nov. 18, 1883.
8. Hattie E., b. Feb. 23, 1881.

     IV. MELISSA JANE,⁸ b. Feb. 15, 1839; d. June 14, 1839.
1140   V. GEORGE,⁸ b. March 14, 1845; m. RUTH CRAIG.

666.*

NATHANIEL⁷ CHURCHILL (JOSEPH,⁶ NATHANIEL,⁵ NA
THANIEL,⁴ WILLIAM,³ WILLIAM,² JOHN¹). Born in Thompson,
Conn., April 23, 1810. They lived in Vienna, Oneida County, N.Y.,
for a short time, and afterwards in Annsville, same county. He
died September, 1868. Married, in Annsville, N.Y., Oct. 24, 1833,
NANCY MOWERS, b. in Danube, Herkimer County, N.Y., Sept. 1,
1805, and died August, 1880.

Children.

I. RHODA A.,⁸ b. Oct. 4, 1834; m. 1st, Oct. 17, 1854, JOHN LEONARD
BREWSTER, b. in Parish, N.Y., April 2, 1831; d. Sept. 16, 1857;
m. 2d, Feb. 6, 1867, ROBERT STACE, b. in England, Jan. 7, 1827;
d. 1898.

Children of First Husband.

1. George Henry Brewster; b. Sept. 12, 1855.
2. Marietta Brewster, b. Dec. 12, 1857.

Children of Second Husband.

3. Nellie Stace, b. Nov. 26, 1867; d. Dec. 12, 1867.
4. Cynthia Stace, b. Oct. 28, 1868; d. Jan. 19, 1885.
5. Melvin Stace, b. July 17, 1870.
6. Aaron James Stace, b. March 9, 1873.
7. Anna Stace, b. Jan. 10, 1876.

  II. MARTHA,⁸ b. Sept. 4, 1836; d. April 21, 1839.
1141 III. WILSON B.,⁸ b. Nov. 9, 1838; m. ANNETTA RAINE, in Oriskany,
N.Y., Jan. 4, 1865.
He was living in 1899, in Camden, N.Y.

Four Children.

1. Nora.   3. Frank.
2. Jessie.   4. Howard.

*Mrs. Deborah (Churchill) Hyde, sister of Nathaniel, appears on page 165, but much information has been found since which deserves place here. She married Asa Waterman Hyde, in Glenmore, N.Y., Oct. 28, 1834. He was born Sept. 28, 1808, and died June 16, 1860. They lived in Glenmore. Their children were: (1) Ezra J. Hyde, b. November, 1835. He was a soldier and died at Gettysburg, just after the battle, unmarried. (2) Asa Niles Hyde, b. Aug. 11, 1838; m. Hannah Seaton, Dec. 29, 1860, and d April 12, 1864, in the army, leaving one child, Celia Hyde, b. April 7, 1863; d. Sept. 13, 1865. (3) Celia M. A. Hyde, b. March 27, 1842; m. Schuyler Bemis, April 10, 1865, and had one child, Nettie Bemis. (4) Harriet L. Hyde, b. May 21, 1844; m. Eugene Barber, April 4, 1875, and had two children, Frederick W. and Lena May Barber. (5) Joseph Asher Hyde, b. May 21, 1851; m. Delphine McKee, and had one child, George C. Hyde.

667.

ORRIN[7] CHURCHILL (JOSEPH,[6] NATHANIEL[5] NATHANIEL, WILLIAM,[3] WILLIAM,[2] JOHN[1]). Born in Thompson, Conn., Dec. 18, 1812. Lived in Annsville, N.Y. He died Oct. 16, 1894. Married SARAH E. SPRAGUE, who was born Oct. 17, 1821, and died April 15, 1896.

Children born in Annsville, N. Y.

   I. THEODOSIA,[8] b. June 7, 1844.
   II. EMMA EMOGENE,[8] b. June 15, 1847.
1142 III. IRA SPRAGUE,[8] b. May 23, 1849.
   IV. JENNIE,[8] b. October, 1851; d. Feb. 2, 1875.
1143 V. FREDERICK,[8] b. Feb. 13, 1856.

668.

GEORGE[7] CHURCHILL (JOSEPH,[6] NATHANIEL[5] NATHANIEL, WILLIAM,[3] WILLIAM,[2] JOHN[1]). Born in Thompson, Conn., June 7, 1815. He died Oct. 29, 1895. Married .1st, April, 1842, SARAH POWERS CLARK. Married 2d, MRS. LUCINA MONELL, 1846. She died April, 1894.

Child by First Wife.

   I. SARAH POWERS,[8] b. May 12, 1843; m. ALEXANDER S. BENNETT, March 27, 1862.

Children by Second Wife.

   II. CAROLINE AMELIA,[8] b. 1847; m. DAVID CURTIS, of Oswego, N.Y.
   III. HANNAH JANE,[8] b. 1851; m. CHARLES T. CROFT, of Oswego.

669.

EDWIN LEWIS[7] CHURCHILL (JOSEPH,[6] NATHANIEL,[5] NATHANIEL,[4] WILLIAM,[3] WILLIAM,[2] JOHN[1]). Born in Annsville, N.Y., in 1825. Living at Half Day, Lake County, Ill., in December, 1900. Married CHARITY COLLINS, of Annsville, N.Y.

Children.

144 I. JOSEPH W.[8]
   II. JOSEPHINE.[8]

674.

CHARLES[7] CHURCHILL (CORNELIUS[6] EBENEZER[5] ICHABOD,[4] WILLIAM,[3] WILLIAM,[2] JOHN[1]). Born in Plympton, July 16, 1807. Lived in Abington, Mass. Married, Aug. 22, 1829, MARY B. WALES.

Children born in Abington.

   I. JOHN B.,[8] b. June 24, 1831; d. Dec. 16, 1864.
   II. ELIZA A.,[8] b. Dec. 7, 1832; m. LIVINGSTON LOUD, Dec. 11, 1857.
   III. MARY C.,[8] b. July 10, 1835; m. CHARLES H. WILLIAMS, Dec. 10, 1856.

1145 IV. CHARLES O.,[8] b. July 16, 1838; m. BETSEY A. HOLBROOK, June 5,
1857.
V. ELVIRA H.,[8] b. March 3, 1841.
VI. EMMA D.,[8] b. April 13, 1844.

676.

ANSEL [7] CHURCHILL (ANSEL,[6] EBENEZER [5] ICHABOD,[4] WILL-
IAM,[3] WILLIAM,[2] JOHN [1]). Born Dec. 23, 1809. Married SARAH
P. DELANO.

Children.

1146 I. NATHAN DELANO,[8] b. 1852; m. HELEN A. TOWER, dau. of Lorenzo,
b. Nov. 15, 1852. Lived in Middleboro', Mass., in 1889.

Children.

1. Carrie Delano, b. April 6, 1875.
2. Frank Wilson, b. April 5, 1879.
II. SARAH,[8] m. CHARLES A. WRIGHT. Lived in Milford, Mass.

677.

HENRY [7] CHURCHILL (ANSEL,[6] EBENEZER,[5] ICHABOD,[4] WILL-
IAM,[3] WILLIAM,[2] JOHN [1]). Born Jan. 13, 1813. Married ESTHER
SHAW.

Children.

1147 I. HENRY.[8]
1148 II. THOMAS.[8]
1149 III. GEORGE L.[8]
1150 IV. OTIS.[8]

678.

JAMES [7] CHURCHILL (ANSEL,[6] EBENEZER,[5] ICHABOD,[4] WILL-
IAM,[3] WILLIAM,[2] JOHN [1]). Born July 5, 1815. Married REBECCA
CROCKER.

Child.

1151 I. EDWIN.[8]

679.

GEORGE LEWIS [7] CHURCHILL (ANSEL,[6] EBENEZER,[5] ICHA-
BOD,[4] WILLIAM,[3] WILLIAM,[2] JOHN [1]). Born Sept. 15, 1817. Mar
ried, Jan. 2, 1843, LOUISE BONNEY.

Children.

1152 I. WILLIAM L.[8]
II. GEORGIANNA M.[8]
III. LOIS.[8]
1153 IV. SAMUEL H.[8]
1154 V. GEORGE H.[8]

680.

ORAMEL H.⁷ CHURCHILL (ZEBEDEE,⁶ ICHABOD,⁵ ICHABOD,⁴ WILLIAM,³ WILLIAM,² JOHN ¹). Born at Woodstock, Vt., May 20, 1825. Married, Sept. 28, 1846, SARAH C. SMITH, of Middleboro'

Children.

1154a I. EDWIN H.,⁸ b. Aug. 30, 1849; m. LAURA E. DARLING.
     II. ALICE,⁸ b. Feb. 17, 1854; m. GEORGE U. WASHBURN.
     III. CHARLES A. Y.,⁸ b. Jan. 18, 1863; unmarried.

681.

ICHABOD SYLVESTER ⁷ CHURCHILL (SETH W.,⁶ ICHABOD ⁵ ICHABOD,⁴ WILLIAM,³ WILLIAM,² JOHN ¹). Born in Woodstock, Vt., 1817. Married, May 30, 1839, ADALINE DICKERMAN, of Chicopee, Mass.

Children.

     I. FRANCES.⁸
     II. HELEN H.,⁸ b. in Springfield, Aug. 23, 1844.
1155 III. FREDERICK A.,⁸ b. in Springfield, Jan. 20, 1847; m. ELLEN GEERS.
1156 IV. FRANKLIN PIERCE,⁸ b. in Chicopee, Aug. 10, 1853.
     V. MARY.⁸

682.

JOSEPH HENRY ⁷ CHURCHILL (SETH W.,⁶ ICHABOD,⁵ ICHABOD,⁴ WILLIAM,³ WILLIAM,² JOHN ¹). Born in Woodstock, Vt., Sept. 18, 1820. Married, in Springfield, Mass., Jan. 29, 1843, CAROLINE SIKES.

Child born in Chicopee.

1157 I. CHARLES HENRY,⁸ b. Sept. 26, 1845.

683.

SETH DOTEN ⁷ CHURCHILL (SETH W.⁶ ICHABOD,⁵ ICHABOD,⁴ WILLIAM,³ WILLIAM,² JOHN ¹). Born in Woodstock, Vt., May 5 1823. Married ELIZA TINKHAM, of Springfield.

Children.

     I. IDA,⁸ m. W. W. CASE; lives in the West.
   *II. DANIEL.⁸
   *III. HENRY.⁸
     IV. ASA TIDD.⁸

---

* These two brothers lived unmarried in Chicago, and afterwards in Davenport, Iowa. None of the brothers had issue.

685.

ZACCHEUS[7] CHURCHILL (Zaccheus,[6] Thomas,[5] Ichabod [4] William,[3] William,[2] John[1]). Born in Salem in 1799. Lived in Salem, and died Aug. 30, 1833. Married, in Salem, Oct. 31, 1819, Eliza Gilbert.

Children born in Salem.

1158	I.	Addison Gilbert,[8] b. May 9, 1820.
1159	II.	John Gilbert,[8] b. Sept. 5, 1821.
	III.	Augustus,[8] b. June 20, 1823; d. in infancy.
	IV.	Augustus,[8] b. Sept. 30, 1825.
	V.	Eliza Ann,[8] b. Aug. 25, 1827; m. (———) Tufts.
1160	VI.	William Henry,[8] b. in 1832; unmarried.

686.

WILLIAM[7] CHURCHILL (Zaccheus,[6] Thomas [5] Ichabod [4] William,[3] William,[2] John[1]). Born in Salem, June 16, 1807. Married, Jan. 30, 1828, Sarah L. Curtis, who was born Feb. 28, 1807.

Children born in Salem.

	I.	Sarah,[8] b. Dec. 25, 1828.
	II.	Abigail,[8] b. July 8, 1834.
1161	III.	William,[8] b. July 14, 1837.
	IV.	Laura,[8] b. March 16, 1841.
	V.	Charles H.,[8] b. June 15, 1844; d. in infancy.
1162	VI.	Charles H.,[8] b. Feb. 28, 1848.

690.

LEMUEL PIERCE[7] CHURCHILL (Pelham,[6] Josiah,[5] Isaac,[4] Isaac,[3] William,[2] John[1]). Born April 2, 1831, at Newport, R.I. Lived at Brockton, Mass. Married Priscilla F. Perkins.

Children.

1163	I.	Frank P.,[8] b. Jan. 7, 1854; m. Ida Estes, Dec. 24, 1884.
	II.	Matthew,[8] b. November, 1857; d. Sept. 10, 1858.
1164	III.	Henry A.,[8] b. Feb. 17, 1865.

702.

ASAPH[7] CHURCHILL (Asaph,[6] Zebedee,[5] Perez,[4] Benjamin,[3] William,[2] John[1]). Born in Milton, April 20, 1814. Was fitted for college at Milton Academy and Day's Academy in Wrentham, and at the age of thirteen entered Harvard College, where he graduated in 1831. He studied law in his father's office and at the Harvard Law School, was admitted to the Norfolk County bar in 1834, at the age of twenty. He immediately opened an office at Dorchester Lower Mills, and held his Milton and Dorchester practice as long as he lived, though he opened an office in Boston in 1856, and from that time had his office in that city.

He was always a resident of Dorchester, after his marriage, in 1838. He was an able lawyer and a very influential man in the affairs of his town. He was one of the original promoters, and later president and director, of the Milton Branch (now Shawmut Branch) of the Old Colony Railroad, was director and president of the bank, now the Blue Hill National, holding one or both these offices for twenty-eight years. He was State senator from Norfolk County in 1856, and held other positions of trust and responsibility. He died Nov. 29, 1892, at Milton. Married 1st, in Dorchester, May 1, 1838, MARY BUCKMINSTER BREWER, daughter of Darius and Harriet (Buckminster) Brewer, of Dorchester; married 2d, in Milton, June, 1862, MARY ANNE WARE, daughter of Dr. Jonathan and Mary Anne (Tileston) Ware, of Milton, who died May 5, 1886.

Children of Asaph Churchill and First Wife, born in Dorchester.

1165 I. GARDNER ASAPH,[8] b. May 26, 1839; m. ELLEN BRASTOW BARRETT, dau. of Nathan and Harriet (Ware) Barrett, and born in Boston, Sept. 2, 1839. Married in Wrentham, April 16, 1862, and died Aug. 20, 1896.

Mr. Churchill was educated in the public schools of Dorchester. In his youth he went on several voyages as a sailor, part of the time in a ship engaged in the East Indian trade. He gained experience and studied navigation, so that he was fitted to fill a position of trust; and when, during the Civil War, he enlisted in the navy, he was appointed, Dec. 15, 1862, acting ensign. After a period of training in gunnery on board the ship "Macedonian" he was assigned to duty on board the United States ship "Release," and served as sailing-master of that vessel, and afterwards, in the same capacity, on the United States steamers "Memphis" and "Shawmut," and (with an interval of a few months' furlough on account of sickness) he served until the surrender of General Lee, when, in 1865, he resigned.

He was a gallant officer, and on one occasion, by his coolness and prompt action, saved the "Memphis" from destruction by a rebel torpedo ram, in the North Edisto river, March 6, 1864.

After the war Mr. Churchill engaged in the business of printing with the firm of Rockwell & Rollins, and on the death of Mr. Rollins, in 1869, he became the junior partner of the firm of Rockwell & Churchill, in which progressive and prosperous house he remained till his death. He had excellent taste in all matters pertaining to the business, was of quick perception and good judgment in all matters in which he took an interest.

He served with credit for two terms, 1875–1876, as representative to the Legislature from Dorchester, and was a trustee of the Insane Asylum at Danvers three years. He was a member of the Masonic fraternity, of the Grand Army of the Republic, and of several patriotic societies, among others the Society of Colonial Wars, and the Sons of the American Revolution. He was interested in history and genealogy, was an active member of the New England Historical and Genealogical Society. He had for many years been interested in gathering material for a genealogy of the Churchill family, and in company with Mr. N. W. Churchill had, at the time of his death, nearly completed an account of the Plymouth branch of the family, to which his own line belonged, to the seventh generation, and it was in pursuance of his intention that his family decided to publish the volume which has grown to include the three great .branches, and eight or nine, instead of six, generations of one branch. In 1887 Mr. Churchill compiled and published a genealogy of his. own line in a neat pamphlet of eighteen pages. for private distribution. After his marriage and return from the war Mr. Churchill lived at Wrentham for some years, and then removed to Milton Lower Mills, in Dorchester, where he lived till 1884, when he removed to Alban street, Ashmont.

Children of Gardner A. and Ellen (Barrett) Churchill.

1. Mary Brewer, b. in Wrentham, Dec. 31, 1864; m. Franklin A. Wyman, of Dorchester, Feb. 9, 1898, and has one child: (1) Dorothy Churchill Wyman, b. July 3, 1899.
2. Asaph, b. in Wrentham, Aug. 18, 1866; m. Helen Olivia French, dau. of William Abrams and Olivia (Chapman) French of Jamaica Plain, June 14, 1900. They reside at Milton, and have one child: (1) Olivia. b. Oct. 28, 1901.

    Mr. Churchill fitted for college at the Roxbury Latin School, and graduated at Harvard in 1888. He fitted himself for the wholesale paper business, and in 1901 established himself in that business in Boston. Upon the death of Colonel Rockwell, in 1902, he was appointed trustee of the Rockwell & Churchill printing concern.
3. Ellen Barrett, b. in Dorchester, May 19, 1877

II. FANNY BUCKMINSTER,[8] b. in Dorchester Aug. 11, 1841; m. JOSEPH H. LOCKE, of Louisville, Ky., March 19, 1861.

Children.

1. Hersey Goodwin Locke.
2. Fanny Morey Locke.
3. Christine Seward Locke.
4. Harriet Buckminster Locke.

1166 III. JOSEPH RICHMOND,[8] b. in Dorchester, July 29, 1845; m. MARY CUSHING, of Dorchester, Feb. 21, 1871.

He was educated in Dorchester and Milton and Harvard College, where he graduated in 1867, and at the Harvard Law School 1869. He was admitted to the bar June 12, 1869, and began practice in Boston the following October with his father under the firm name A. & J. R. Churchill. Jan. 9, 1871, he was appointed by Governor Claflin a justice of the Municipal Court, Dorchester District of Boston. Much leisure was devoted to botanical study and the formation of a large herbarium. In 1887 by request of the editors of the " History of the Town of Milton" he compiled a history of the trees and plants growing naturally in Milton, forming a part of Chapter 18 of that book. He was appointed, in 1900, by Harvard College to visit the Botanical Gardens at the University. Has published several papers on botanical subjects in " Rhodora." Jan. 1, 1901, on the completion of thirty years' service as justice of the Municipal Court, he was presented by members of the bar with a silver service, in appreciation of his long and able administration of that office.

Children born in Dorchester.

1. Richmond, b. July 20, 1874; d. 1880.
2. Edward Cushing, b. July 11, 1877; d. in 1880.
3. Anna Quincy, b. May 31, 1884.

IV. MARY,[8] b. April 4, 1847; m. JOHN HARROD FOSTER, of Brookline, Mass., Dec. 12, 1872.

JUDGE JOSEPH R. CHURCH LL,
DORCHESTER, MASS.
(No. 1166, page 298.)

Children.

1. John Harrod Foster.
2. Helen Mason Foster.
3. Reginald Foster.

V. HARRIET BREWER,⁸ b. Jan. 7, 1855.

1167 VI. JOHN MAITLAND BREWER,⁸ b. Jan. 18, 1858.
He fitted for college in the Boston Latin School, and graduated at Harvard in 1879. He entered the Harvard Law School, but was hindered in his course by frail health. He was admitted to the bar in July, 1884, and began practice in the office of his father and brother in Boston. He died at the Isles of Shoals, where he had been some time on account of his failing health, July 29, 1900.
Married, in Dublin, N.H., June 15, 1898, FLORENCE MAY WINDSOR, daughter of Gershom. They had one child: (1) John Maitland Brewer.

Child by Second Wife of Asaph, Mrs. M. A. (Ware) Churchill.

VII. WINSLOW WARE,⁸ b. July 5, 1873.

703.

JOSEPH McKEAN⁷ CHURCHILL (ASAPH,⁶ ZEBEDEE,⁵ PEREZ,⁴ BENJAMIN,³ WILLIAM,² JOHN¹). Born in Milton, April 29, 1821. He graduated at Harvard College in 1840, and Harvard Law School in 1845. He was a delegate to the Constitutional Convention in 1853, representative from Milton to the Massachusetts Legislature for 1858 and 1859. He was a member of the council of Governor Banks in 1860–61. He enlisted in the Forty-fifth Regiment of Massachusetts Volunteers, for nine months, and was made captain of Company B of that regiment, which arrived in Newbern, N.C., Nov. 5, 1862, and was discharged July 8, 1863. He served on the board of Norfolk County Commissioners from 1868 to 1871. Appointed special justice in 1867, he was later made one of the associate justices of the Municipal Court of Boston, which office he held at the time of his death. He died suddenly of heart failure, in Milton, March 23, 1886. Married, June 6, 1861, AUGUSTA PHILLIPPS GARDNER, of Richmond, Va.

Children born in Milton.

I. MARY GARDNER,⁸ b. May 19, 1864; d. in infancy.
II. McKEAN GARDNER,⁸ b. March 7, 1866; d. Feb. 12, 1883.

704.

CHARLES MARSHALL SPRING⁷ CHURCHILL (ASAPH,⁶ ZEBEDEE,⁵ PEREZ,⁴ BENJAMIN,³ WILLIAM,² JOHN¹). Born in Milton, May 1, 1825. Fitted for college at Milton Academy and at Needham, with the late Rev. Daniel Kimball. Graduated at Harvard 1845, and at Harvard Law School 1848. In the winter of 1845 to 1847 Mr. Churchill travelled extensively in Europe, Asia, and Africa, visiting the islands of the Ægean Sea, Smyrna, Constanti-

nople, then to Egypt and up the Nile to Luxor, to Thebes, back to
Cairo, and across the desert with a camel-train to Suez and along
the shore to the Gulf of Akaba, and thence to Mt. Sinai, and through
Palestine and its historic places, and to Baalbec and Damascus.
In this journey Mr. Churchill's fellow-travellers were the late Dr.
Howard Crosby, of New York, the eminent scholar and minister,
and his family. He completed his travels with a tour through
Greece, Italy, a pedestrian tramp through Switzerland, then Ger-
many, and up the Rhine, stopping awhile at Heidelberg, and then
to Paris to attend lectures on the French civil law and the Code
Napoleon. Returning home he completed his course at Harvard
Law School and was admitted to the Suffolk bar Oct. 8, 1850, and
began practice in Dorchester and Milton. He has lived in Milton
on a part of the old Churchill estate. Mr. Churchill is a Unitarian,
a life-long member of the Third Religious Society in Dorchester.
Married, in Dorchester, April 6, 1853, SUSAN ELIZABETH SPOONER,
daughter of Dr. John Phillips and Abby Elizabeth (Tuckerman)
Spooner, of Dorchester.

Children born in Milton.

      I. ELIZABETH TUCKERMAN,[8] b. Jan. 10, 1854. Living in Milton, un-
          married.
1168   II. CHARLES EDWARD,[8] b. Dec. 30, 1855. Living in Milton, un-
          married. He is engaged in business in Boston.
1169 III. JOHN PHILLIPS SPOONER,[8] b. Feb. 16, 1858; m. HENRIETTA ADELE
          FAY, Boston, Nov. 21, 1894. He is a lawyer in Boston, and
          resides in Milton. They have one child.

Child.

      1. Louise Fay, b. in Boston, March 29, 1896.

1170   IV HOWARD CROSBY,[8] b. Feb. 11, 1860; m. CATHERINE MANNING.

Children.

      1. Joseph Howard, b. in Anthony, Kan., Oct. 24, 1889; d. in St.
          Paul, Minn., Nov. 8, 1890.
      2. Mary Elizabeth, b. in St. Paul, April 12, 1891.
      3. Joanna, b. in Montana, Dec. 31, 1892.
      4. John Spooner, b. in Havre, Mont., May 14, 1895; d. in St. Paul,
          Minn., Jan. 25, 1896.
      5. Bernard Francis, b. in Des Moines, Ia., Dec. 25, 1897.

1171   V. JOHN RUSSELL,[8] b. Sept. 1, 1862; m. HARRIET KRUEGER, Milwau-
          kee, Wis., Nov. 9, 1897.
1172 VI. FRANK SPOONER,[8] b. Aug. 28, 1864; m. LUCRETIA MOTT HALLI-
          WELL, West Medford, Dec. 31, 1894. They live in Chicago.

They have Children born in Chicago, Ill.

      1. Richard Halliwell, b. Jan. 11, 1896; d. Jan. 14, 1896.
      2. Lucretia Mott, b. Nov. 16, 1898.
      3. Winthrop, b. Sept. 23, 1900.

1173 VII. WILLIAM WINTHROP,[8] b. Nov. 28, 1866. In business in Boston.
    VIII. GEORGE PHILLIPS,[8] b. March 6, 1870; d. Jan. 31, 1874.
     IX. MARY GARDNER,[8] b. Oct. 31, 1874. A teacher.

705.

GEORGE ATWOOD[7] CHURCHILL (ASAPH[6] PEREZ[5] PEREZ,[4] BENJAMIN,[3] WILLIAM,[2] JOHN[1]). Born in Middleboro', Sept. 26, 1819. Lived in Salem, Mass., and was a machinist by trade. Married, in Middleboro', March 2, 1842, AMARANTHA BURGESS, daughter of William and Lucy (Pierce) Burgess, born March 24, 1824.

Children.

    I. ELLEN M.,[8] b. in Middleboro', Aug. 12, 1843; d. aged 11 years.
    II. LUCY A.,[8] b. in Lowell, July 29, 1846; m. EDWARD ROCKWOOD, of Worcester, July 7, 1865. She died in Boston, Dec. 7, 1881. No children.
    III. EDGAR L.,[8] b. in Salem, Nov. 12, 1848; d. Feb. 8, 1866. Served in the army near the close of the Civil War.
1174   IV. HORACE F.,[8] b. in Salem, April 7, 1851; m. SARAH A. HERSEY, April 7, 1870.

Children born in Salem.

    1. Arthur C., b. April 6, 1871.
    2. William T., b. May 10, 1872.
    3. Lillian G., b. May 15, 1878.
    4. Horace A., b. April 15, 1893.

1175   V GEORGE LEFOREST,[8] b. Nov. 12, 1853; m. MARTHA MILLETT HERSEY, April 19, 1870. They lived at Salem and Lowell, and had seven children.

Children.

    1. Bertha Irene, b. April 26, 1872.
    2. Benjamin Atwood, b. March 19, 1874.
    3. George LeForest, b. May 10, 1875.
    4. Harrie Greenleaf, b. Nov. 25, 1877.
    5. Nellie L., b. Dec. 1, 1879.
    6. Millie, } twins, b. Feb. 15, 1888.
    7. Mabel,   }
1176   VI. ORLANDO,[8] b. Dec. 20, 1856.
    VII. IDA E.,[8] b. Nov. 28, 1857; m. WILLIAM L. DUNTLEY, Nov. 30, 1882. They lived in Lynn, Mass., and had children.

Children.

    1. Joseph I. Duntley, b. June 17, 1884.
    2. George E. Duntley, b. Aug. 22, 1885.
    3. Edgar L. Duntley, b. Nov. 4, 1886.
    VIII. FLORENCE A.,[8] b. Aug. 24, 1863.

706.

CHARLES ASAPH[7] CHURCHILL (ASAPH,[6] PEREZ[5] PEREZ[4] BENJAMIN,[3] WILLIAM,[2] JOHN[1]). Born in Middleboro', Nov. 6, 1835. He settled first in Middleboro', but later removed to Brockton, where he was engaged in shoemaking. While his children were young he left his family and has not been heard from since. Married, June 4, 1859, HANNAH D. DRINKWATER.

Children.

I. RHODA MELVINA,[8] m. FRED BRETT, of Brockton.
II. ARDELLA SAVERY,[8] m. J. MITCHELL, of Brockton.
   She is now (1903) a widow, and has three children.

708.

ZEBEDEE P.[7] CHURCHILL (ZEBEDEE,[6] ISAAC,[5] PEREZ,[4] BEN-JAMIN,[3] WILLIAM,[2] JOHN[1]). Born in Pomfret, Vt., May 15, 1818. Lived in Pomfret and Woodstock, Vt. Married 1st, June 1, 1846, ORLENA BOUTWELL. She died June 26, 1854. Married 2d, Feb. 25, 1855, EMILY ORDWAY.

Children by First Wife.

I. ELLEN E.,[8] b. March 30, 1847; d. Dec. 8, 1875.
II. ALBERT B.,[8] b. Jan. 31, 1849; d. March 3, 1851.
III. OLIVE O.,[8] b. Nov. 15, 1851; m. WEBSTER L. SAWYER, Feb. 23, 1875.

Child.

1. Dora E. Sawyer, b. Dec. 22, 1875.

IV. HANNAH E.,[8] b. Feb. 10, 1854; d. March 22, 1864.

Children by Second Wife.

V. EMILY M.,[8] b. March 6, 1856; m. FRANK L. HOISINGTON, Sept. 21, 1875.

Children.

1. Ella A. Hoisington, b. Oct. 30, 1876.
2. Ella L. Hoisington, b. Aug. 31, 1879.
   Mrs. Emily M. Hoisington died April 27' 1880.

1177 VI. MARK Z.,[8] b. July 30, 1858.
VII. ETTA A.,[8] b. Jan. 24, 1861; d. June 13, 1874.
VIII. ADDIE B.,[8] b. Nov. 4, 1863; m. EDGAR D. CROWELL, June 18, 1885.

Children.

1. Arthur E. Crowell, b. July 15, 1886.
2. A son, name not given, b. Nov. 30, 1888.

IX. EDNA M.,[8] b. Aug. 13, 1866; m. FRANK W. BRADLEY, May 16, 1888.
X. LUCY I.,[8] b. May 5, 1870.

713.

WILLIAM[7] CHURCHILL (SPRAGUE,[6] JOSEPH,[5] PEREZ,[4] BEN-JAMIN,[3] WILLIAM,[2] JOHN[1]). Born in Paris, Me., Sept. 5, 1813. Lived in Sumner, Me. He died Jan. 2, 1889. Married, Oct. 30, 1840, MARY LIBBY, who was born Jan. 13, 1821.

Children.

I. NANCY,[8] b. Aug. 20, 1841; m. WILLIAM S. DUNHAM.
II. HARRIETT,[8] b. March 15, 1843; m. B. R. DOBLE. They live in Weymouth and have children.

Children.

1. Albert L. Doble, b. Feb. 19, 1861.
2. Isaac Loring Doble, b. Jan. 27, 1863.
3. E. Francis Doble, b. Feb. 12, 1865.
4. Eolus Randall Doble, b. Sept. 24, 1867.

III. ADELINE,[8] b. Jan. 24, 1845; m. SAMUEL E. LOUD, Sept. 28, 1868.

Children.

1. Cora Loud, b. 1870.
2. Eugene Coolidge Loud, b. 1879.

1178   IV. WILLIAM,[8] b. April 19, 1848; m. FLORA MERRILL.
1179   V. ALMON,[8] b. Nov. 24, 1861; m. ANNA H. FLETCHER.

Children.

1. Alma Fletcher, b. Aug. 30, 1884; d. Aug. 19, 1888.
2. Annie Beryl, b. April 27, 1891.
3. Lovel Israel, b. Dec. 31, 1895.

714.

KINGMAN[7] CHURCHILL (SPRAGUE,[6] JOSEPH,[5] PEREZ[4] BEN-JAMIN,[3] WILLIAM,[2] JOHN[1]). Born in Paris, Me., June 18, 1823. Lived in Paris, on the old homestead farm. Married LORETTA ANDREWS, daughter of Daniel.

Children.

I. FANNIE W.,[8] b. June 26, 1852.
II. EMMA A.,[8] b. June 27, 1856.
III. ABBIE J.,[8] b. Aug. 16, 1859.
1180   IV. CHARLES.[8]
       V. ELLEN.[8]

716.

JOSEPH[7] CHURCHILL (WILLIAM,[6] JOSEPH,[5] PEREZ,[4] BENJA-MIN,[3] WILLIAM,[2] JOHN[1]). Born Feb. 2, 1828. A merchant tailor. Lived at Bryant's Pond and Norway, Me. Died at Norway, Aug. 16, 1881. Married 1st, BETSEY MOODY, of Casco, Me. She died Oct. 20, 1853. Married 2d, Sept. 3, 1855, VIANA PERHAM, daughter of Joel, of Woodstock.

One Child by Second Wife.

1181   I. WALTER,[8] b. Dec. 6, 1858, at Bryant's Pond; m. LINDA RAWSON, of Paris, Me., Sept. 6, 1891, and have one child.

Child.

1. Walter Albert, b. June 14, 1893, at Portland, Me.

717.

WILLIAM[7] CHURCHILL (WILLIAM,[6] JOSEPH,[5] PEREZ,[4] BEN-JAMIN,[3] WILLIAM,[2] JOHN[1]). Born in Buckfield, Me., Jan. 22, 1837. He died at Norway, Sept. 26, 1873. Married MARY PENLEY, of Norway.

Children.

    I. Cora,[8] b. March 26, 1859; d. April 29, 1861.
   II. Harry,[8] b. June 19, 1865; d. Jan. 9, 1881.
  III. Mary,[8] b. Feb. 13, 1871; d. May 7, 1898.

720.

WILLIAM H.[7] CHURCHILL (Jabez,[6] Jabez,[5] Benjamin[4] Benjamin,[3] William,[2] John[1]). Born in Hallowell, Me., Oct. 10, 1841. He removed West and settled at Stockton, Minn. Married, but wife's name not received.

Children born in Stockton, Minn.

        I. J. Louise,[8] b. April 8, 1869.
1182   II. Arthur,[8] b. Sept. 2, 1872.
1183 III. Harry M.,[8] b. Feb. 28, 1874.

721.

THOMAS WILSON[7] CHURCHILL (William,[6] William,[5] Benjamin,[4] Benjamin,[3] William,[2] John[1]). Born in Wayne, Me., June 28, 1821, and lived there until after 1842, when he removed to Presque Isle, Me., where he spent his life. He was a farmer, an upright and respected man. He died Jan. 1, 1900. Married 1st, at Presque Isle, Me., June, 1849, Sarah Ireland, daughter of Silas and Celia (Chubbuck) Ireland. Married 2d, Mrs. Elizabeth Frost.

Children by First Wife, born in Presque Isle, Me.

    I. Emily,[8] b. Dec. 28, 1849; m. Sylvanus S. Richardson, Presque Isle, May 11, 1876. He was the son of Samuel and Lydia (Stover) Richardson, of Sullivan, Me. They live in Presque Isle (1903), where he is a farmer.

Children born in Presque Isle.

    1. Ida M. Richardson, b. March 19, 1877; m. Rufus W. Fenlason, Caribou, Me., Dec. 8, 1897.
    2. Olive Richardson, b. June 3, 1879.
    3. Lucille M. Richardson, b. Aug. 8, 1885.

   II. William,[8] b. 1851; d. Jan. 13, 1852.
  III. Annette,[8] b. 1853; m. Daniel Chase, December, 1887, Presque Isle; d. July, 1879.
1184 IV. Frank,[8] b. 1855; m. Sarah Maria Frost, Presque Isle, 1880. She is dead.
      They lived on his father's homestead at South Presque Isle. Four children.

Children.

    1. Harry.   3. Harvey.
    2. Lizzie.   4. Edward.

1185 V. Floraman,[8] b. 1857; m. Elsie Clark, Peacham, Vt., September, 1898.

Child.

1. Francis.
VI. NELLIE,[8] b. Jan. 16, 1859; m. DARIUS McGUIRE, Presque Isle, August, 1883.
VII. ALMA,[8] b. May, 9, 1861; d. September, 1870.
VIII. HATTIE,[8] b. March 26, 1863; m. GEORGE W. THOMPSON, Presque Isle, 1882.

Child.

1. Flora Thompson.
IX. ALBERT,[8] b. May, 1865; d. Jan. 19, 1887, at Richmond, Me.
X. KATIE,[8] b. June 8, 1869.
1186   XI. ELMER,[8] b. March, 1872; m. MABEL E. BROWN, Presque Isle, May, 1891.
The wife died, leaving two children.

Children.

1. Albert. | 2. Harold.

722.

LEWIS[7] CHURCHILL (WILLIAM,[6] WILLIAM,[5] BENJAMIN,[4] BENJAMIN,[3] WILLIAM,[2] JOHN[1]). Born in Wayne, Me., March 2, 1823. Attended the schools in his native town until about thirteen years old, when he went to live in Winthrop, his mother having sold the farm. He attended school in Winthrop two years, and then lived at his sister Florinda's, in Leeds, until twenty-one years old. Lives at Leeds, a farmer. Married at Leeds, Me., Feb. 19, 1850, RUTH PETTINGILL. They had no children born to them, but adopted two, who took the Churchill name, viz.

    1. Mary A. Cushman, who took the name Churchill, b. March 7, 1855, being adopted by Lewis and Ruth, when seventeen months old. Married Wesley Welch, at Wayne, Me., April 30, 1877. They live at Oakland, Me., where he is a marble cutter and engraver. Their children born at Leeds, Me., are: (1) Carrie Alice Welch, b. July 31, 1878; m. Bert Haley, at Oakland, Me., May 10, 1899; (2) Lewis Churchill Welch, b. Aug. 11, 1880; (3) Mary Louise Welch, b. at North Anson, Feb. 13, 1882; d. Feb. 21, 1902; (4) Annabel Welch, b. at Leeds, April 30, 1884; (5) William W. Welch, b. March 1, 1886; (6) Gerald Cushman Welch, b. June 19, 1888; (7) Earle Dunham Welch, b. Jan. 28, 1893; d. Feb. 18, 1899, at Oakland.

    2. Loring Lyman, who took the name Churchill, b. July 14, 1871, being adopted when an infant; m. Maria A. Gulliver, Readfield, Me., Nov. 24, 1892. They live in Leeds with the parents by adoption, and have three children (in 1903): (1) Harriet Ruth Churchill, b. Sept. 18, 1894; (2) Merton Edwards Churchill, b. Nov. 7, 1897; d. Oct. 19, 1899; (3) Stella May Churchill, b. Sept. 1, 1899.

724.

ADDISON H.[7] CHURCHILL (NATHAN,[6] WILLIAM,[5] BENJAMIN,[4] BENJAMIN,[3] WILLIAM,[2] JOHN[1]). Born April 23, 1836, in Avon, Me. We have not succeeded in obtaining anything further in regard to

the children of this family. Married, September, 1867, MARY
TEBBETTS, of Avon, Me.

Children.

1187   I. GEORGE.[8]
         II. FLORA.[8]
         III. LYDIA.[8]
         IV. ALTA.[8]
1188   V. WILLIAM.[8]
1189   VI. ADDISON.[8]

725.

WILLIAM W.[7] CHURCHILL (NATHAN,[6] WILLIAM [5] BENJAMIN,[4]
BENJAMIN,[3] WILLIAM,[2] JOHN[1]). Born in Avon, Me., Oct. 1, 1846.
He was a mill-man and lived in Phillips, Me. Married, Jan. 1,
1878, CORA M. RANGER, of Weld, Me.

Children.

1190   I. HARRY,[8] b. Nov. 18, 1878.
1191   II. ERNEST,[8] b. Dec. 12, 1879.
         III. MARY A.,[8] b. Sept. 17, 1881.
1192   IV. FRANK A.,[8] b. Aug. 30, 1888.

725b.

ABRAHAM[7] CHURCHILL (WILLIAMS,[6] JOSEPH [5] BENJAMIN,[4]
BENJAMIN,[3] WILLIAM,[2] JOHN[1]). Born in Herrick, Pa., Jan. 16,
1821. Lived at Lenoxville, Pa. Married, in Susquehanna County
Pa., Feb. 26, 1845, MARGARET CLARKSON, born Feb. 2, 1825.

Children.

1193   I. CARVASSO,[8] b. Dec. 5, 1845.
         II. ABRAHAM WILLIAMS,[8] b. Aug. 22, 1847; d. July 30, 1850.
1194   III. WOOSTER BEACH,[8] b. Oct. 11, 1849.
             He was living at Tresco, Pa., in 1899.
         IV. ISABELLA BATHSHEBA,[8] b. Jan. 18, 1852.
1195   V. ABRAHAM WILLIAMS,[8] b. Dec. 22, 1855.
         VI. MALVINA ELLA,[8] b. Feb. 3, 1864; d. May 8, 1872.

725c.

JOSHUA WILLIAMS[7] CHURCHILL (WILLIAMS [6] JOSEPH [5]
BENJAMIN,[4] BENJAMIN,[3] WILLIAM,[2] WILLIAM[1]). Born Dec. 31,
1825, at Herrick, Pa., lived at Clark's Green, Pa., a farmer. He is
a strong temperance man, and an active worker for the cause. A
member of the Methodist church for sixty-eight years, up to May,
1903. Married 1st, 1850, SARAH GILL; she died 1855. Married 2d,
1859, LOUISA R. TREAT, who died 1879.

Children by First Wife.

1196   I. NORMAN E.,[8] married, and it is said has four children, but we have
             no account of them. Lives, in 1903, at Puget Sound, Wash.
1197   II. MARTIN,[8] married, it is said, and has a family in Wyoming County,
             Pa.

725d.

ELISHA[7] CHURCHILL (NATHANIEL,[6] NATHANIEL,[5] LEMUEL,[4] BARNABAS,[3] JOSEPH,[2] JOHN[1]). Born at Herrick, Pa., Dec. 28, 1827, and died at Tunkhannock, July 23, 1886. They lived at Tunkhannock, Pa. He was a contractor and builder. Married, at Brook lyn, Pa., Oct. 7, 1831, SARAH C. BAKER, daughter of Daniel and Juliette (Case) Baker.

Children, first three born at Herrick.

     I. CORA A.,[8] b. Sept. 18, 1854; m. G. H. SHELDON, Lynn, Pa., May 1, 1875.
     II. ROSE E.,[8] b. Nov. 28, 1856; m. IRWIN DUCE, Lynn, Pa., Sept. 27, 1876.
     III. ADA E.,[8] b. Nov. 17, 1858; m. EUGENE BARTREE, Tunkhannock, March 24, 1880.
1198   IV. FRANK N.,[8] b. in Sullivan County, Pa., May 7, 1862; m. FLORA OWEN.
1199   V. NORMAN E.,[8] b. in Tunkhannock, June 27, 1868; m. LENA SAUNDERS.
1200   VI. CARL,[8] b. Nov. 19, 1877, in Lynn, Pa.

725f.

CHARLES[7] CHURCHILL (WILLIAMS,[6] JOSEPH,[5] BENJAMIN[4] BENJAMIN,[3] WILLIAM,[2] JOHN[1]). Born in Herrick, Pa., June 12, 1834, and lived at Herrick and Susquehanna, Pa., where he was proprietor of the Marble and Granite Works. Married, at Susquehanna, Pa., Oct. 11, 1860, ESTHER JANE ROGERS, daughter of John and Esther (Smith) Rogers.

Children born at Herrick, Pa.

     I. VERNA ASENATHA,[8] b. Oct. 27, 1861; m. ANTON A. GARNER. They lived at Binghamton, N.Y.
1201   II. JESSE L.,[8] b. Dec. 10, 1864; m. MAUD A. PLATT, June 24, 1896.
        Mr. Churchill was educated in the public schools of Susquehanna, and entered his father's business. In 1887 he established the Horseheads Monumental Works, at Horseheads, N.Y., of which he is proprietor. He is a Freemason of prominence and ability They have one child.

Child.

     1. Rogers Platt Churchill, b. Sept. 14, 1902.
     III. LOUISA MAY,[8] b. May 18, 1872; d. March 27, 1875.

725g.

SILAS OWEN[7] CHURCHILL (WILLIAMS,[6] JOSEPH,[5] BENJAMIN,[4] BENJAMIN,[3] WILLIAM,[2] JOHN[1]). Born in Herrick, Pa., July 15, 1844. A farmer, lived on the old homestead, now Uniondale, Pa. Married, March 10, 1868, HELEN E. CARPENTER, who was born Nov. 21, 1849.

Children born at Uniondale.

1202 I. Ira S.,[8] b, June 9, 1869; m. Mary J. Carpenter, April 23, 1890. They live at Uniondale, Pa.
1203 II. Albert M.,[8] b. Dec. 28, 1871; m. Edith Curtis, Nov. 30, 1898. They live in Lestershire, N.Y.
III. Jennie A.,[8] b. Nov. 16, 1873; m. Joseph F. Fletcher, May 24, 1898. They live at Forest City, Pa.
IV. Edith M.,[8] b. Aug. 16, 1878; m. Frank R. Dickey, Nov. 28, 1895. They live at Burnwood, Pa.
1204 V. Harry W.,[8] b. March 29, 1883.
1205 VI. Clarence F.,[8] b. May 21, 1892.

727.

CHANDLER[7] CHURCHILL (Nelson[6] Nelson[5] Benjamin,[4] Benjamin,[3] William,[2] John[1]). Born in Coleraine, July 23, 1826. Married, in Charlemont, Nov. 8, 1849, Lucy Flagg.

Children.

1206 I. Ashley T.,[8] b. 1850.
II. Lucy E.,[8] b. 1853; d. 1860.
III. Angie B.,[8] b. 1861.

728.

HORACE[7] CHURCHILL (Alvin,[6] Nelson,[5] Benjamin[4] Benjamin,[3] William,[2] John[1]). Born in Coleraine, Mass., Jan. 1, 1833. Married, Sept. 18, 1862, Cynthia J. Chaffin, of Heath, Mass.

Child.

I. Anna R.[8]

729.

FREDERICK[7] CHURCHILL (Alvin[6] Nelson,[5] Benjamin,[4] Benjamin,[3] William,[2] John[1]). Born in Charlemont, Nov. 8, 1839. Married, Dec. 30, 1870, Josephine Willis, at Charlemont, Mass.

Children.

1207 I. Charles Sumner,[8] b. Feb. 23, 1874.
1208 II. Wallace Eugene,[8] b. Feb. 8, 1877.
1209 III. Arthur Walton,[8] b. Aug. 2, 1879.
IV. Bertha Philena,[8] b. Feb. 1, 1882.
1210 V. Merritt Hilton,[8] b. July 13, 1885.

730.

ANSON IRVING[7] CHURCHILL (Alvin,[6] Nelson,[5] Benjamin,[4] Benjamin,[3] William,[2] John[1]). Born in Charlemont, Nov. 2, 1849. Married, at Charlemont, Nov. 28, 1874, Anna Cilley.

Children.

1211   I. Fred Alvin,[8] b. Aug. 8, 1875.
1212 II. George Edward,[8] b. March 10, 1877.
1213 III. Henry Anson,[8] b. Feb. 10, 1879.
     IV. Nellie Bell,[8] b. Feb. 2, 1881.
1214 V. Bert Horace,[8] b. July 25, 1884.

731.

SAMUEL [7] CHURCHILL (Shepard [6] Jabez,[5] Jabez,[4] Josiah,[3] William,[2] John [1]). Born April 1, 1809, in Buckfield, and lived there, a farmer. Married Lovina Packard.

Children.

     I. Cordelia,[8] b. Aug. 31, 1833.
1215 II. Ezra F.,[8] b. March 23, 1839. Enlisted in the army in the Civil War, and died in service.
   III. Charles C.,[8] b. Dec. 23, 1840. He was in the Civil War.
   IV. Elizabeth E.,[8] b. Jan. 7, 1846.
    V. Julia,[8] b. Sept. 13, 1849.

732.

MARTIN [7] CHURCHILL (Shepard,[6] Jabez,[5] Jabez,[4] Josiah,[3] William,[2] John [1]). Born in Buckfield, April 12, 1811, and lived there. Married Betsey Churchill, daughter of Asaph [5] (No. 143, *q.v.*).

Children born in Buckfield.

1216   I. Nathaniel,[8] b. April 6, 1834; m. Anna Barnes. (No issue.)
   II. Hannah,[8] b. Jan. 24, 1836; m. Seth B. Dudley, Dec. 24, 1854.

Children born in Buckfield.

1. Nellie M. Dudley, b. July 31, 1856.
2. Jennie Dudley, b. March 28, 1858; m. James Lewis, May 8, 1880.
3. Cyrus K. Dudley, b. Jan. 23, 1860.
4. Albert C. Dudley, b. March 10, 1863.
5. Minerva Dudley, b. Nov. 19, 1865; d. Aug. 20, 1892.
6. Harry Dudley, b. Sept. 10, 1867.
7. John Dudley, b. Nov. 24, 1870.
8. Perien Dudley, b. Nov. 20, 1874.
9. Herbert Dudley, b. April 8, 1877.

  III. Emily,[8] b. Dec. 16, 1838; m. Simon Dudley.
     They had two children, names not received.
  IV. Amanda,[8] b. Aug. 15, 1840; m. Ezekiel Burns, of Oxford.
   V. Martin V. B.,[8] b. Aug. 1, 1842; d. Jan. 4, 1849.
  VI. Clara,[8] b. March 4, 1845; m. Millett Shedd.

Children.

1. Charles Shedd.
2. Silas Shedd.

1217 VII. Asaph,[8] b. March 4, 1848; m. Fannie Murch, Dec. 4, 1870. He was born in Buckfield, and lived there.

Children born in Buckfield.

1. Fannie M., b. Nov. 3, 1871.
2. Asaph C., b. Feb. 3, 1874.
3. Jennie M., b. Oct. 26, 1875.

    4. Howard L., b. July 25, 1877.
    5. Ernest B., b. Nov. 11, 1880.
    6. Fred C., b. Nov. 25, 1882.
    7. Harriet L., b. Feb. 9, 1885.
    8. Flora Belle, b. April 2, 1887.
    9. Lizzie, b. Dec. 23, 1888.
VIII. ROSE,[8] b. April 16, 1850; m. JAMES ROWLEY.
    Lived at Provincetown, Mass.

Children.

    1. Ernest Rowley, b. Aug. 28, 1872.
    2. Ada Rowley, b. July 5, 1877.
    3. Flora Rowley, b. June 20, 1878.
    4. Mildred Rowley, b. Oct. 24, 1894.
IX. FLORA,[8] b. Dec. 28, 1851; m. CHARLES HANNAFORD.
    Lived at North Bridgton, Me.

Child.

    1. Frederick Hannaford.
X. REUBEN,[8] b. Sept. 12, 1856; d. March, 1858.
XI. MARY,[8] b. July 18, 1858; unmarried.

733.

NATHAN[7] CHURCHILL (SHEPARD,[6] JABEZ[5] JABEZ,[4] JOSIAH,[3] WILLIAM,[2] JOHN[1]). Born in 1819, and lived in Buckfield, Me. A farmer. Married HARRIET THOMAS.

Children.

    I. ALMIRA.[8]
    II. ANNETTE,[8] m. GEORGE MASON.
1218 III. EDWIN.[8]
1219 IV. ALBERTON.[8]
    V. A CHILD.

734.

JOSIAH[7] CHURCHILL (SHEPARD,[6] JABEZ[5] JABEZ,[4] JOSIAH,[3] WILLIAM,[2] JOHN[1]). Born in Buckfield, Me., Dec. 4, 1825, and lived in South Paris. Married TRYPHENA HOLT.

Children.

    I. NELLIE,[8] m. CALEB DUDLEY.
1220 II. CLIFFORD.[8]

737.

JAMES N. D.[7] CHURCHILL (MATTHEW,[6] JABEZ,[5] JABEZ,[4] JOSIAH,[3] WILLIAM,[2] JOHN[1]). Born in Falmouth, Me., March 15, 1815. Married 1st, April 7, 1836, ORPHIA CHURCHILL, daughter of Bela, No. 348. Married 2d, HANNAH KEENE WHITE.

Children of First Wife.

I. PHEBE,[8] m. RUEL PHILLIPS, of Auburn, Me., 1860. He died Dec. 29, 1891.

Children.

1. Orlando Phillips, b. Dec. 27, 1863; d. Oct. 21, 1882.
2. Ida S. Phillips, b. June 3, 1868; m. Robert O. Dunning, Oct. 19, 1887. Three children: (1) Orland Dunning. (2) Grace Dunning. (3) Ralph Dunning.

1221   II. BELA,⁸ removed to Pennsylvania, and married, and in 1902 was living with his family in Pine Mills, Texas, but did not answer our letters of inquiry.

1222   III. ELISHA P.,⁸ b. in Raymond, April 28, 1845; m. HANNAH G. TORREY, of Dixfield, Me., Oct. 16, 1866.

Children.

1. Henry P., b. Dec. 31, 1867; m. Jennie M. Littlefield; lives in Strong, Me.
2. Elury D., b. June 9, 1869; d. in infancy.
3. Elury W., b. Oct. 27, 1871; d. July 9, 1892.
4. Clara L., b. June 1, 1887, in Hallowell.

1223   IV   DEMERIC SWAN,⁸ b. July 3, 1847; m. MINNIE A. BLAKE, June 17, 1877. Lived at Mechanics Falls, Me.

Children.

1. Harry Wilber, b. June 9, 1878.
2. Nellie Isabel, b. Jan. 7, 1880.
3. Eva Maria,   } b. Aug. 23, 1881.
4. George Lewis,   }
5. Orphia, b. March 18, 1884.
6. Arthur, b. March 23, 1886.
7. Winfield, b. Oct. 11, 1888.

V. DENNIS,⁸ unmarried.

Children of Second Wife.

VI. ORPHIA,⁸ b. May 12, 1856; m. 1st, HARRY WELLS; no children; m. 2d, MINOT FAUNCE.

Children by Second Husband.

1. James E. Faunce.
2. Maurice F. Faunce.

1224   VII. REUBEN,⁸ b. Oct. 28, 1858; m. ALICE CAMPBELL, of Pictou, August, 1886.

Child.

1. Ernest, b. Oct. 30, 1887.

738.

SILAS H.⁷ CHURCHILL (MATTHEW,⁶ JABEZ,⁵ JABEZ,⁴ JOSIAH,³ WILLIAM,² JOHN¹). Born in Raymond, Jan. 19, 1817. Settled in Raymond at first, and later in life in New Gloucester. A farmer and teacher in the public schools. He died Oct. 4, 1898. Married, April 10, 1853, ARDELLA H. TOBIE, of New Gloucester, daughter of Thomas H. and Mary (Harris) Tobie.

Children born in Raymond.

1225   I. FREDERICK TOBIE,⁸ b. April 10, 1854; m. 1st, LAURA E. VERRY, Mt. Vernon, Ohio. 1889; m. 2d, HARRIET E. CLARK. They live in New Gloucester. He is a farmer. They have two children.

Children.

1. Cecil Verry, b. at Kearney, Neb., 1890.
2. Velina D., b. in Raymond, Me., 1894.

II. ROSILLA TOBIE,[8] b. Nov. 2, 1855; d. in Raymond, Sept. 16, 1858.

1225a III. WALTER E.,[8] b. May 8, 1858; m. IDA L. BLODGET, Colebrook, N.H., 1884. She was the daughter of James and Emily Blodget. They lived in Berlin, N.H., and had three children, viz.:

Children.

1. Peleg Walter, b. July, 1885.
2. Wendell H., b. October, 1887.
3. Sally, b. October, 1895.
   Mr. Walter E. Churchill is a merchant.

IV LEROY,[8] b. July 16, 1860; m. ALICE A. ATHERTON, of Colebrook, N.H. She was the daughter of Edward and Mary Atherton. They lived at Colebrook, N.H. He was postmaster there. Died in 1893. Their children were:

Children.

1. Eva Hammond, b. in Colebrook.
2. Blaine Leroy.

1226 V. WENDELL A.,[8] b. April 20, 1863; unmarried in 1901, and lived in Des Moines, Iowa.

739.

MATTHEW [7] CHURCHILL (MATTHEW,[6] JABEZ,[5] JABEZ,[4] JOSIAH,[3] WILLIAM,[2] JOHN [1]). Born in North Raymond, Jan. 11, 1821. He died April 3, 1883. Married, in Boston, Nov. 13, 1851, SARAH ABIGAIL ADAMS, who was born in North Boothbay, Me.

Children.

1227 I. RALPH,[8] b. Sept. 5, 1852; m. NELLIE M. MOODY, in Winchester, Mass., Nov. 29, 1872.

II. CYNTHIA ADAMS,[8] b. March 4, 1855; m. ARTHUR FESSENDEN ELLIS, of Hyde Park, Mass., Nov. 17, 1875. No children.

740.

JOSEPH WARREN [7] CHURCHILL (MATTHEW,[6] JABEZ,[5] JABEZ,[4] JOSIAH,[3] WILLIAM,[2] JOHN [1]). Born in Raymond, Me., Aug. 9, 1829. Lived in his native town. A farmer, educated in the public school at home. Married, at Raymond, July 8, 1849, MARY JOHNTHENA DOANE, daughter of John Randall and Lucy Doane.

Children born at North Raymond.

I. JEANETTE BAILEY,[8] b. Oct. 13, 1850; m. ORRIN PETERSON, at Harrison, Me., March 28, 1866.

Children.

1. Edgar S. Peterson, b. Poland, Sept. 11, 1866.
2. Mabel M. Peterson, b. Auburn, March 6, 1868.
3. Josephine M. Peterson, b. Upton, Mass., June 20, 1872.
4. Matthew A. Peterson, b. Upton, Aug. 31, 1874.
5. Arvilla P. Peterson, b. Upton, Sept. 12, 1877.
6. Alice B. Peterson, b. Holliston, Oct. 5, 1879; d. Oct. 7, 1883.

1228   II. John Randall,[8] b. Nov. 10, 1851; m. 1st, Hattie E. Sheldon, April 5, 1884; m. 2d, Clemina M. Darst, Jan. 7, 1895.

Children of First Wife, born at Kearney, Neb.

1. Mary Pearl, b. April 3, 1885.
2. George Warren, b. Dec. 2, 1887.

Children of Second Wife.

3. Ruth Floe, b. at Perry, Oklahoma Territory, Oct. 12, 1895.
4. Jeanette Modes, b. Nov. 13, 1897.
5. Darrell Dale, b. at Pedee, Oklahoma Territory, May 28, 1900.
Mr. Churchill is a farmer at Pedee.

    III. Josephine Bonaparte,[8] b. Oct. 16, 1854; m. Charles Franklin Nickerson, of Lewiston, Me., 1873.

    IV. Matthew,[8] b. March 28, 1857; d. at Raymond, May 28, 1874.

1229   V. Warren Levi,[8] b. March 24, 1860; m. Elizabeth Parker, April 26, 1884.

    VI. Jennie Small,[8] b. at New Gloucester, June 24, 1867; m. James W. Krepps, at Boston, April 3, 1889. They live in Brooklyn, N.Y. No children.
Mrs. Krepps has assisted much in the compiling of this Raymond family.

1230 VII. George Samuel,[8] b. Feb. 21, 1873; m. Mary Ellen Ballard, Lynn, Mass., 1894.

741a.

JOSIAH [7] CHURCHILL (Josiah,[6] Josiah,[5] Jabez,[4] Josiah,[3] William,[2] John [1]). Born in New Gloucester, Me., May 22, 1809, and lived there and at Raymond, and Harrison, Me.

Children.

    I. Sarah,[8] b. in New Gloucester, Me., Oct. 10, 1833; m. Nicholas Jordan.

    II. Lydia,[8] b. Nov. 13, 1834, in New Gloucester.

1231 III. Joseph Fessenden,[8] b. in Raymond, Me., July 1, 1838; m. 1st, Sarah Smith, of Auburn, Me.; m. 2d, Emma F. Latham, of New Gloucester.

Children of Joseph F. and Emma (Latham) Churchill.

1. Walter F., b. March 30, 1875.
2. Edith, b. 1877.
3. Olive, b. 1881.
4. Ralph, b. 1887.

    IV. Hannah,[8] b. in Raymond, Aug. 21, 1839.

    V. Marshall,[8] b. Sept. 25, 1842; d. March 10, 1843.

    VI. Loann,[8] b. May 26, 1844.

  VII. Maria.[8]

VIII. Lida A.,[8] b. in Harrison, Me. Unmarried.
Miss Churchill removed in childhood to New Gloucester, and there received the usual common-school instruction, but being of studious habits and high ambition she gained far more than the usual common-school education. By the diligent pursuit of her purpose to attain literary ability, she has overcome many obstacles and achieved an honorable place among the leading authors of Maine. Besides her brilliant and popular society sketches in various magazines she has published two volumes, entitled "My Girls" and "Interweaving." She is now, 1902, on the editorial staff of the "Success" magazine in New York City.

742.

RICHARD FOSS[7] CHURCHILL (ASAPH,[6] ASAPH,[5] JABEZ,[4] JOSIAH,[3] WILLIAM,[2] JOHN[1]). Born in Minot, Me., Jan. 28, 1828. Lived in Lowell, Mass. Married, April 19, 1854, SARAH DANIELS, who was born in Dover, N.H., Nov. 28, 1830. He died Feb. 14, 1875.

Children born in Lowell.

I. EDWARD,[8] b. June 15, 1856; d. Aug. 19, 1858.
II. EMMA J.,[8] b. April 3, 1859; d. July 26, 1859.
III. ANNIE L.,[8] b. July 9, 1860, d. Dec. 9, 1862:
IV. WILLIAM A.,[8] b. Feb. 21, 1864; d. March 6, 1864.
V. ——— A.,[8] b. at Lawrence, Mass., Dec. 19, 1866; d. Dec. 27, 1868.
VI. LILLA,[8] b. at Lowell, Mass., Jan. 31, 1870.

743.

GEORGE[7] CHURCHILL (ASAPH,[6] ASAPH[5] JABEZ[4] JOSIAH,[3] WILLIAM,[2] JOHN[1]). Born Sept. 4, 1837. Married, Dec. 12, 1866, ANNIE H. DWYER; she was born June 3, 1845.

Children.

1232 I. GEORGE ARTHUR,[8] b. Jan. 29, 1868.
1233 II. WALTER ASAPH,[8] b. May 27, 1875; d. Oct. 27, 1875.

747.

GEORGE HIRAM[7] CHURCHILL (HIRAM,[6] ASAPH,[5] JABEZ,[4] JOSIAH,[3] WILLIAM,[2] JOHN[1]). Born in Charlestown, Mass., Oct. 4, 1864. Married, at Charlestown, Dec. 29, 1886, ELLA CONNOR.

One Child.

I. FRANCES GERTRUDE, b. Nov. 10, 1887.

748.

FREDERICK AUGUSTUS[7] CHURCHILL (HIRAM,[6] ASAPH,[5] JABEZ,[4] JOSIAH,[3] WILLIAM,[2] JOHN[1]). Born in Charlestown, Mass., Dec. 21, 1867. Married, at Charlestown, March 24, 1888, MARGARET MAY TUFTS.

One Child.

I. GRACE VIVIAN, b. Aug. 30, 1889.

750.

REV. ROGER WILLIAMS[7] CHURCHILL (NATHANIEL,[6] ASAPH,[5] JABEZ,[4] JOSIAH,[3] WILLIAM,[2] JOHN[1]). Born at Emery's Mills, York County, Me., Aug. 30, 1848. Studied law in the office of Copeland Edgerly, Great Falls, N.H., and was admitted to the bar, but took a course at Bates Theological Seminary, and became minister of the Free Baptist Church at Richmond, Me. Married, at

Mechanics Falls, Me., Dec. 13, 1883, MAGGIE A. ARCHIBALD. We have not been able to obtain any further record.

759.

WILLIAM HENRY[7] CHURCHILL (JOHN,[6] JOHN,[5] ISRAEL,[4] JOSIAH,[3] WILLIAM,[2] JOHN [1]). Born April 11, 1844. Mr. Churchill was living July 26, 1887, when he wrote this account of his family from Woburn P.O., Ontario. Married, Dec. 11, 1866, ALICE TITUS, who was born Jan. 30, 1848.

Children.

	I.	MINERVA,[8] b. March 21, 1868.
1234	II.	FREDERICK,[8] b. July 22, 1870.
	III.	CHRISTIANA,[8] b. March 28, 1872.
1235	IV.	WILLIAM,[8] b. Aug. 27, 1874.
	V.	JENNIE,[8] b. Nov. 27, 1875; d. Feb. 28, 1886.
	VI.	HARRIET,[8] b. Aug. 28, 1877.
	VII.	MABEL,[8] b. Aug. 3, 1879; d. Aug. 12, 1881.
	VIII.	LILLA,[8] b. Dec. 14, 1882.
	IX.	JOHN HAROLD,[8] b. Dec. 22, 1884; d. Feb. 24, 1886.

760.

GEORGE FREDERICK[7] CHURCHILL (JOHN,[6] JOHN,[5] ISRAEL, JOSIAH,[3] WILLIAM,[2] JOHN [1]). Born in Oshawa, Canada, Dec. 19, 1854. Married, Oct. 10, 1876, LIZZIE M. ADDY, of Chicago.

Child.

1236   I. EDWARD PAYSON,[8] b. June 27, 1878, in Chicago.

764.

CURTIS M.[7] CHURCHILL (WILLIAM T.,[6] JACOB,[5] JOSEPH,[4] JOSIAH,[3] WILLIAM,[2] JOHN [1]). Born in Vermont, May 3, 1815. In 1884 he lived at 590 Ashland avenue, St. Paul, Minn. A builder and contractor. Married 1st, Sept. 20, 1838, JANE ANN GILCHRIST, who died May, 1847. Married 2d, July 27, 1848, MARY C. BUNNELL.

Children of First Wife.

I. OPHELIA VIOLA,[8] b. Oct. 9, 1839; m. JEROME CLOSSER, LaPorte, Ind.
II. EVELYN AUGUSTA,[8] b. Oct. 15, 1845. Unmarried. She is an M.D.
III. LOUISE,[8] d. in infancy.
IV. JANE ANN,[8] d. in infancy.

Children of Second Wife.

V. FLORA,[8] d. in infancy.
VI. LOUISA EVANZA,[8] b. May 7, 1853.
VII. FREDERICK WILLIAM,[8] b. 1857. Drowned Oct. 11, 1873, at Hastings, Minn., aged 16.
1237 VIII. WARNER LEMAN,[8] b. Sept. 18, 1868.

765.

JOEL GILBERT [7] CHURCHILL (WILLIAM T.,[6] JACOB,[5] JOSEPH,[4] JOSIAH,[3] WILLIAM,[2] JOHN [1]). Born, July 26, 1819. Married, August, 1842, 1st, MARGARET HEWETT, who was born April 15, 1824, and died Aug. 7, 1857. Married 2d, MARY JOPLIN.

Child by First Wife.

I. MARY ELIZABETH,[8] b. July 11, 1844; m. 1st, GEORGE A. PATTERSON, April 20, 1860; m. 2d, JEREMIAH S. WRIGHT, Jan. 29, 1878.

By Second Wife.

II. ISABEL,[8] b. Oct. 1, 1863; m. JOHN PATTERSON, 1886.

766.

CARMI D.[7] CHURCHILL (ARTEMUS,[6] JACOB,[5] JOSEPH,[4] JOSIAH,[3] WILLIAM,[2] JOHN [1]). Born in Oswego County, N.Y., Dec. 7, 1821. Settled in Scriba, N.Y. A farmer. Married, Feb. 10, 1850, CELIA KIMBALL, in Hannibal, Oswego County, N.Y.

Children.

I. ALICE,[8] b. May 26, 1853; m. JOHN SNELLER, of Cicero, N.Y.
II. LAURA,[8] b. March 10, 1855; m. GEORGE WHITFORD. She died June 5, 1884.
1238   III. HENRY C.,[8] b. July 9, 1857; unmarried in 1887. Lived at Binghamton, N.Y. He was engaged in a fruit raising, cooperage, and wholesale produce business.
IV. ATWOOD M.,[8] b. Dec. 25, 1860; d. unmarried, May 3, 1886, in Scriba.

767.

CHARLES R.[7] CHURCHILL (ARTEMUS,[6] JACOB,[5] JOSEPH,[4] JOSIAH,[3] WILLIAM,[2] JOHN [1]). Born in Kingsbury, N.Y., Nov. 24, 1824. He was a carpenter. He was a soldier in the Civil War in 1861. He died May 31, 1883. Married, May 10, 1854, MARY J. ASSELTINE, in Briton, Canada.

Children.

I. ARTEMUS A.,[8] d. at 16 years.
1239   II. MATTISON.[8]
1240   III. CHARLES.[8]

769.

JULIUS B.[7] CHURCHILL (ARTEMUS,[6] JACOB,[5] JOSEPH [4] JOSIAH,[3] WILLIAM,[2] JOHN [1]). Born in Kingsbury, March 5, 1832. He lived in Scriba, N.Y., where he is a fruit farmer and hop-raiser Married, June 18, 1859, ELIZA KNIGHT.

Children.

I. CARRIE M.[8]
II. GENEVIEVE LEONA.[8]

771.

HENRY PALMER[7] CHURCHILL (PALMER,[6] JACOB,[5] JOSEPH,[4] JOSIAH,[3] WILLIAM,[2] JOHN[1]). Born Aug. 11, 1830. Married 1st, June, 1853, MARIA BROWN; married 2d, Dec. 18, 1879, CLARISSA MEADE.

Children by First Wife.

1241   I. CHARLES,[8] b. December, 1854.
1242   II. WILLIAM,[8] b. July, 1856.
       III. IDA,[8] b. July 12, 1861; m. WALTER PLASTRIDGE, January, 1880.
1243   IV. EDWIN,[8] b. June 10, 1863.
       V. DORA,[8] b. July 27, 1867.
       VI. BELLE,[8] b. April 1, 1870.

772.

FRANK ALANSON[7] CHURCHILL (OTIS,[6] JACOB,[5] JOSEPH,[4] JOSIAH,[3] WILLIAM,[2] JOHN[1]). Born Aug. 9, 1838. Lived in Sandy Hill, N.Y., and South Adams, Mass. Married, Oct. 4, 1864, MARY L. SHAFFER.

Children.

       I. ETTA M..[8] b. in South Adams, Mass., Aug. 18, 1865.
1244   II. GEORGE,[8] b. in Sandy Hill, N.Y., May 16, 1867.

773.

CHARLES PALMER[7] CHURCHILL (JACOB,[6] JACOB,[5] JOSEPH,[4] JOSIAH,[3] WILLIAM,[2] JOHN[1]). Born in Kingsbury, Washington County, N.Y., July 26, 1832. Enlisted in the army in the Civil War in 1861, and served three years as a drummer. He was in thirteen battles; was wounded twice. Discharged April 29, 1865. He came home, and died May 12, 1867. Married, in Hartford, N.Y., July 3, 1854, EMELINE BEEBE. No further record.

774a.

CHARLES HAMILTON[7] CHURCHILL (ERASTUS,[6] BENJAMIN[5] JOSEPH,[4] JOSIAH,[3] WILLIAM,[2] JOHN[1]). Born at Manlius, N.Y., but removed to Waukesha with his father. Lived at Clear Lake, Wis. Married ELIZABETH REGULAR.

Children.

       I. ISADORA,[8] d. young.
1245   II. CHESTER.[8]

774b.

HIRAM DeFORREST[7] CHURCHILL (ERASTUS,[6] BENJAMIN,[5] JOSEPH,[4] JOSIAH,[3] WILLIAM,[2] JOHN[1]). Born at Manlius, N.Y. Living, in April, 1900, at AuClaire, Wis. Married MARY ANN HOWARD.

Children.

I. LYDIA.[8]
II. JENNIE.[8]
III. IDA.[8]
IV. FANNY.[8]
1246   V. HIRAM.[8]

774c.

WILLIAM NELSON[7] CHURCHILL (ERASTUS, BENJAMIN,[5] JOSEPH,[4] JOSIAH,[3] WILLIAM,[2] JOHN[1]).   Born at Manlius, N.Y. Married, at Waukesha, Wis., May 14, 1862, ELIZABETH S. TAYLOR, born at Waukesha, Nov. 18, 1847.

Children.

I. NETTIE IRENE,[8] b. July 10, 1863; m. 1st, WILLIAM BAGGS (she was divorced from Baggs); and m. 2d, J. H. PHILLIPS.

First Husband's Children.

1. Georgiana Baggs, b. Feb. 22, 1882.
2. Charles W. Baggs, b. Aug. 24, 1883.

Second Husband's Children.

3. Ervin James Phillips, b. 1888.
4. Elsie Pearl Phillips, b. May 6, 1894.
5. Adelbert Harold Phillips, b. Feb. 1, 1900.

II. ALICE MAE,[8] b. Feb. 5, 1879.   She lives at Waukesha, and has furnished the account of the family of Erastus, her grandfather.
III. MABEL,[8] b. Oct. 23, 1881; died.
1247   IV. WARREN NORMAN,[8] b. Nov. 1, 1884.

774d.

CHARLES HAWLEY[7] CHURCHILL (CHARLES P.,[6] BENJAMIN,[5] JOSEPH,[4] JOSIAH,[3] WILLIAM,[2] JOHN[1]).   Born Feb. 20, 1835. He died in the Hospital of St. Helena, Ark., March 8, 1863.   Married, March 1, 1857, SARAH VAN SHEICK.

Children born in Waukesha, Wis.

I. FRANCES MARION,[8] b. Aug. 7, 1858.
1248   II. WILLIAM ELLSWORTH,[8] b. Nov. 5, 1860.
1249   III. CHARLES HAWLEY,[8] b. March 21, 1863; m. MARY ALTA ROGERS, Aug. 1, 1888.   She was born near Marengo, Ill., June 15, 1869.

774f.

ALPHONZO T.[7] CHURCHILL (CHARLES P.,[6] BENJAMIN[5] JOSEPH,[4] JOSIAH,[3] WILLIAM,[2] JOHN[1]).   Born at Waukesha, Wis., March 13, 1858.   Mr. Churchill completed his education at the

State Normal School, River Falls, Wis. He was a teacher for some years, and for two years a professor at Deer Park, Wis. He then established the " Clear Lake Herald," a large weekly newspaper. He is now (1900) editor and publisher of " The River Falls Times," at River Falls, Wis. Married, at Deer Park, Wis., LULU RICHMERE.

774g.

MELBOURNE[7] CHURCHILL (LAFAYETTE,[6] ALVA,[5] JACOB,[4] JOSIAH,[3] WILLIAM,[2] JOHN[1]). Born in Pennsylvania, Sept. 12, 1856. Married, Feb. 25, 1879, BRIDGET CUSTY, who was born Dec. 14, 1860.

Children.

I. SUSAN AGNES,[8] b. May 13, 1880; d. July I, 1880.
II. NELLIE MAE,[8] b. Nov. 21, 1882.
III. JENNIE EDNA,[8] b. May 29, 1887.
1250 IV. FRANCIS MELBOURNE,[8] b. June 17, 1889.
V. ANNA,[8] b. Sept. 10, 1892.
VI. MARGARET CATHARINE,[8] b. Oct. 13, 1895.
VII. JOSEPHINE,[8] b. Sept. 4, 1900.

774h.

ELMER[7] CHURCHILL (LAFAYETTE,[6] ALVA,[5] JACOB,[4] JOSIAH,[3] WILLIAM,[2] JOHN[1]). Born in Pennsylvania, July 31, 1868. Married, April 15, 1890, IGNATIA STORRS, who was born Feb. 26, 1872.

Children.

1251 I. ELLERY LAFAYETTE,[8] b. Sept. 12, 1891.
II. MINNIE DORA,[8] b. Feb. 5, 1893.
III. CARRIE BLANCHE,[8] b. Aug. 9, 1895.
IV. VESTA GRACE,[8] b. March 16, 1899.

774i.

JOHN PITT[7] CHURCHILL (ROSWELL P.,[6] SEYMOUR,[5] JACOB,[4] JOSIAH,[3] WILLIAM,[2] JOHN[1]). Born Dec. 13, 1858. Married ELIZABETH PHREUN.

Children.

1252 I. EDWARD PALMER,[8] b. Oct. 9, 1878.
II. CAMELIA,[8] b. Nov. 14, 1882.
1253 III. HARRY GARFIELD,[8] b. March 24, 1885.

776.

REV. GEORGE W.[7] CHURCHILL (EBENEZER,[6] GEORGE,[5] EBENEZER[4] JOHN,[3] JOHN,[2] JOHN[1]). Born in Middletown, O., June 27, 1830. Received his education in the public schools. He became a Baptist preacher, and, in succession, preached at Columbiana, Marietta, Beverly, Brookfield, Cumberland, and Cambridge, in Ohio, at the latter place eight years, his longest pastórate. In 1880 he removed to Leon, Kan., where he preached, as also at Augusta and Derby in the same State, and later at Pawnee and Perkins, Oklahoma, where he died, Dec. 18, 1896. Married 1st, Sept. 28, 1850, ELIZABETH GEORGE, born Sept. 14, 1830; died at Leon, Kan., Feb. 27, 1880. Married 2d, at Leon, Kan., Nov. 2, 1880, MRS. ELIZA-BETH GALLIHER; died Dec. 10, 1898.

Children, all of First Wife.

1254   I. JOHN F.,[8] b. Columbiana, O., Sept. 18, 1851; m. EMMA A. BLACK, of Cambridge, O., Oct. 27, 1874.
He was a photographer at Leon, Kan.; d. 1898. Children: (1) Mary, (2) Minnie, (3) Frank. The two daughters live at their grandfather Black's, in Cambridge, O. The son is somewhere in the far West.

II. MELVINA,[8] b. at Columbiana, June 10, 1853; m. JOHN ALBRIGHT.
She died at Fredericktown, O., 1890. They had one son, (1) George Albright, b. in 1879. In 1902 the father and son lived at Hillsboro.

III. LIBBIE,[8] b. at Columbiana, Sept. 30, 1855; m. REV. N. EDGAR BENNETT, Bethel, O., Jan. 5, 1880.
They live at Wilmington, O. He is a minister of twenty-two years' standing.

1255   IV. JONATHAN K.,[8] b. Marietta, O., April 20, 1858; m. CALLIE McCOY, Dallas, Texas, 1886.
They live at Kansas City, Mo. He is a book-keeper for the Appletons.

1256   V. EDWIN S.,[8] b. Beverly, O., May 17, 1860; m. ORRA HUTCHINS, in the State of Washington.
He is now (1902) in Douglas, Alaska. He is a mine inspector.

VI. GEORGE HARLAN,[8] b. Beverly, O., July 10, 1863; d.Jan. 16, 1880, at Leon, Kan.

VII. MARY C.,[8] b. Brookfield, O., Jan. 6, 1866; m. A. T. GRAY, New Richmond, O., Jan. 6, 1886.
They live at Crawfordsville, Ind. Two children: (1) Helen Gray, b. 1889, (2) Charles Gray, b. 1897.

1257 VIII. WARREN RICHARD,[8] b. Cumberland, O., Oct. 9, 1869; m. IVAH JONES, Chicago, Ill.
They live at Chicago, Ill. He is a book-keeper.

777.

BENJAMIN PEABODY[7] CHURCHILL (EBENEZER[6] GEORGE,[5] EBENEZER,[4] JOHN,[3] JOHN,[2] JOHN[1]). Born in Middletown, O., Aug. 4, 1832. Married, 1854, EVELENE E. BRADFIELD, of East Fairfield, O.

Children.

I. GEORGE J.[8] In 1887 he was living in Pittsburgh, Penn., but we could get no answer to our letters, so we have no further record of this last family of the line of the youngest son of John and Hannah (Pontus) Churchill, and the last son, so far as known, in this junior line, in the Plymouth branch.

THE CONNECTICUT BRANCH

OF

THE CHURCHILL FAMILY

———

DESCENDANTS OF JOSIAH CHURCHILL
OF WETHERSFIELD

FIRST GENERATION.

1.

JOSIAH [1] CHURCHILL * (or Churchell, as he himself spelled the name) makes his first appearance in Wethersfield, Conn., on the occasion of his marriage. He may have been there some time before that event, and probably had been, but we have found no evidence of his presence until then. We have found no evidence of his parentage, birthplace, or previous condition. There is no evidence that he was related to either John of Plymouth, who was near his own age, nor to William, the ancestor of the New York branch of the family. Some hints or suggestions of a possible solution of the question of his nativity will find mention in the prefatory part of this volume, but since they are purely speculative, we do not place them here.

The first entry relating to his real estate in Wethersfield is the following record:

> The 2d month & 28th daie 1641 the lands of Josias Churchell lying in Wethersfield on Connecticutt river.
> One pece whereon his howse standeth con: six acrs more or less. The ands (the ends) abutt against the hie waie west & great Mea: east. The sids against the waie into the great mea: South & the house of John Jessiope (Jessup) North. (Town Records, B. 1, p. 204.)

This homestead was on the east side of High street, on the north corner of an ancient road leading to the "Great Meadow," and the river. It faced the southern extremity of the Common, which stretched north from his house to the river. But he did not reside here all his life, for, under the date December, 1659, we find this entry in the records:

> The Hom lot of Josias Churchell which he bought of Mr. Tantor (Taintor) which was Gildersleeves formerly living in Weathersfield, on Connecticot River. (Town Records, B. 1, p. 205.)

This homestead of Richard Gildersleeve was on the west side of High street, a few doors south of Mr. Churchill's earlier home.

---

* The old records have the name Churchell for the first three generations, but we have adopted the later, general form, in this and in other names.

It is difficult to glean biographical material from the meagre and matter-of-fact records of our forefathers. In Hinman's genealogical account of the early Connecticut settlers, he says of Josiah Churchill, "He was a gentleman of more than a medium estate for the time in which he lived, and of reputation in the Colony." He was active and useful in public affairs, though not holding the highest positions. He was a juror of the Particular Court in 1643, 1649, and 1651, at the Quarter Court, 1664 and 1665, and at the County Court, 1666, 1670, and 1675. He was chosen a constable in 1657 and 1670, and was elected one of the two town surveyors in 1666 and 1673.

He executed his will on the 17th of November, 1683, and died before January, 1687. The inventory of his estate was taken Jan. 5, 1687, by James Treat and John Buttolph, selectmen of Wethersfield, and was found to amount to 618 pounds 12 shillings and 6 pence. This inventory shows that at his death he owned two home lots and two hundred and ten acres of land. He left his son Joseph "that house and home lott he now lives on," together with "all other buildings thereon." He left to Joseph also several other pieces of land, and a fifty-acre lot, "at ye west end of Weathersfield bounds," in the newly settled tract which later became the parish of Newington. He left to his son Benjamin a number of pieces of land, and the old homestead, at the decease of his mother. According to the custom of the times his daughters were given certain shares of "moveable estate." Among the items in the inventory are "a great chist," and "2 bibells and other books." This "great chist" probably reappears in the inventory of his son Joseph, which specifies a chest with the initials "J. C.," as well as a piece of "turkic work."

Mention is made of his children Joseph, Benjamin, Mary Church, Elizabeth Buck, Anne Rice, and Sarah Wickham.

JOSIAH CHURCHILL, above mentioned, married ELIZABETH FOOTE, daughter of Nathaniel and Elizabeth (Deming) Foote, who died at Wethersfield, Sept. 8, 1700, aged about eighty-four years.

Children of Josiah and Elizabeth (Foote) Churchill, born in Wethersfield.

I. MARY,[2] b. March 24, 1639; m. SAMUEL CHURCH, son of Richard, of Hadley, Mass. They settled in Hadley about 1659. He died April 13, 1684. She died in 1690.

Children of Samuel and Mary (Churchill) Church.

1. Mary Church, b. Jan. 23, 1665; m. Samuel Smith.
2. Samuel Church, b. Aug. 19, 1667. He lived in Hadley.
3. Richard Church, b. Dec. 9, 1669; m. Sarah Bartlett, Jan. 24, 1696. He was slain by the Indians, Oct. 15, 1696.

4. Mehetabel Church, b. Jan. 11, 1672; m. Nehemiah Dickinson.
5. Josiah Church, b. April 10, 1673; married, it is said, and had a family at Hadley, but we have no records.
6. Joseph Church, b. May 26, 1678; d. unmarried in 1721.
7. Benjamin Church, b. Sept. 1, 1680. Lived in Hadley. No record.
8. John Church, b. Dec. 24, 1682. Perhaps he is the settler at E. Hadley.

II. ELIZABETH,[2] b. May 15, 1642; m. HENRY BUCK, of Wethersfield, Oct. 31, 1660. Mr. Buck was the youngest of two brothers who came to Wethersfield in 1647. He was born in England in 1626, as we learn from the record of his death, July 7, 1712, at the age of eighty-six years. He was granted lands in Wethersfield in 1658, and acquired quite an estate later on, and became a citizen of influence and ability, filling the town offices, and being elected a deputy to the General Assembly in 1667.

Children of Henry and Elizabeth (Churchill) Buck, born in Wethersfield.

1. * Henry Buck, b. 1662; m. Rachel (————).
2. Samuel Buck, b. Feb. 2, 1664; m. Sarah Butler, Jan. 23, 1690.
3. Martha Buck, b. Oct. 15, 1667; m. Jonathan Deming, Oct. 27, 1687.
4. Elizabeth Buck, b. June 6, 1670.
5. Mary Buck, b. March 12, 1673; m. Benjamin Smith, March 14, 1700.
6. Sarah Buck, b. July 25, 1678.
7. Ruth Buck, b. Dec. 4, 1681.
8. Mehitable Buck, b. Jan. 4, 1684; m. Ebenezer Alexander.

III. HANNAH,[2] b. Nov. 1, 1644; m. SAMUEL ROYCE, of New London, January, 1667. She died early, leaving no children.
IV. ANN,[2] b. 1647; m. MR. RICE, as shown by her father's will.
   We have found no further mention of her -
2 V. JOSEPH,[2] b. Dec. 7, 1649; m. MARY (————), May 13, 1674.
3 VI. BENJAMIN,[2] b. May 16, 1652; m. MARY (————).
   VII. A SON, who died, aged one year.
   VIII. SARAH,[2] b. Nov. 11, 1657; m. MR. (————) WICKHAM.
   The name of her husband is upon the authority of her father's will. Hinman says she married Thomas Wickham, but Mr. E. S. Welles, an expert genealogist, has investigated the records, and finds that the wife of Thomas Wickham, and the mother of six of his children, was named Mary.

---

* Henry and Rachel Buck removed with the " Fenwick Colony," about 1692, and settled in Fairfield, Salem County, N.J. Their son, Jeremiah Buck, had a wife, Mary, and a son, John Buck, who married Lorana Whitacor, about June, 1761, and these parents had a daughter, Mary Buck, who married Samuel Westcott, and their son, George B. Westcott, married Mary A. Hynson, and had a daughter, Harriet Louisa Westcott, born Oct. 3, 1838, who married Thomas Hill, of Baltimore, Md. They have three children: (1) Anna Byrant Hill, (2) Malcolm Westcott Hill, and (3) Norman Alan Hill. Mrs. Thomas Hill is State Regent of the Maryland Daughters of the Revolution, and the above information is furnished by her.

SECOND GENERATION.

2.

JOSEPH [2] CHURCHILL (Josiah [1]). Born in Wethersfield,
Conn., Dec. 7 1649. He was one of the beneficiaries named in the
will of his maternal grandmother, Elizabeth (Deming) (Foote),
widow of Governor Thomas Welles. In an indenture dated Nov.
30, 1668, he is styled "husbandman." He lived in Wethersfield,
on land inherited from his father; probably the home lot described
December, 1659, as belonging to Josiah Churchill, in terms as follows:

On pece a hom lot wheare on a house standeth containing three ac (acres)
more or less the ends abutt against the streat east and Mr. Wells weast the sids
against the Hom lot of Sam Welles South and John Hubburd North.

In the inventory of his estate his home lot is mentioned as con-
sisting of three acres, which would indicate that he passed his life
on the homestead bequeathed by his father. That he was a man
of ability and influence is shown by his gradual advancement to
places of trust and influence. The Wethersfield Records show that
at the age of thirty he was chosen one of the town surveyors; three
years later he was one of the assessors, and next year, 1684, he was
made collector of taxes; in 1689 was chosen constable, assessor
again in 1695, and at the annual meeting, held Dec. 27, 1697,
"Sergt." Joseph Churchell was chosen "Selectman," and again re-
elected in 1698, and was still holding that office when he died, April
1, 1699, at the age of forty-nine years. The above date of death
appears in the heading of the inventory. His estate was valued at
four hundred and sixty-one pounds, and his heirs, according to a
memorandum at the end of the inventory, were the relict, Mary,
Nathaniel, Mary Edwards, Elizabeth Butler, Dinah, Samuel, Joseph,
David, Jonathan, and Hannah.

Married, at Wethersfield, May 13, 1674, MARY (———). Long
and diligent search by many different investigators has not brought
to light the surname of Joseph Churchill's wife. She survived him
and lived to advanced age. She is mentioned as "Widow Mary,
Senior," in the settlement of her son, Nathaniel's, estate, April 2,

1728. An estate, apparently hers, was inventoried July 4, 1738. This indicates that she died that year.

Children of Joseph and Mary Churchill.

I. MARY,[3] b. April 6, 1675; m. JOSIAH EDWARDS, April, 1699.
   Mr. Edwards died some time before the birth of the twins.

Children of Josiah and Mary (Churchill) Edwards.

1. Josiah Edwards, b. March 17, 1700.
2. Churchill Edwards, b. April 17, 1703.
3. Jonathan Edwards, b. Jan. 13, 1704.
4. William Edwards, b. 1706.
5. David Edwards, b. April 6, 1707
6. Mercy Edwards, b. Sept. 24, 1710.
7. Nathaniel Edwards, b. April 12, 1713.
8. Mary Edwards, b. April 12, 1713; m. Capt. Zebulon Peck, of
   Bristol, Conn., July 10, 1735. They lived in Bristol, where
   he died Jan. 13, 1795, and she died May 23, 1790.

4   II. NATHANIEL,[3] b. July 9, 1677; m. MARY HURLBUT.
    III. ELIZABETH,[3] b. 1679; m. RICHARD BUTLER.
    IV. DINAH,[3] b. 1680; m. JACOB DEMING, Nov. 3, 1709.
        They lived at Wethersfield and had children born there.

Children.

1. Dinah Deming, b. Oct. 18, 1710; d. Nov. 13, 1710.
. Joseph Deming, b. Nov. 24, 1711.
. Jacob Deming.
4. Moses Deming; m. Sarah Norton, and lived at New Briton,
   Conn.
. Anne Deming.
5. Lucy Deming.
   We are not sure of the order of birth of the last four children.

5   V. SAMUEL,[3] b. 1688; m. MARTHA BOARDMAN, June 26, 1717.
6   VI. JOSEPH,[3] b. 1690; m. LYDIA DICKERMAN, Jan. 12, 1714.
7   VII. DAVID,[3] b. 1692; m. DOROTHY (———).
8   VIII. JONATHAN,[3] b. 1692; m. MRS. SARAH DEMING.
     IX. HANNAH,[3] b. 1696; d. unmarried.

3.

LIEUT. BENJAMIN[2] CHURCHILL (JOSIAH[1]). Born in Wethersfield, May 16, 1652, and lived there. The records of his native town show that Mr. Churchill was early recognized as of ability and enterprise. At the age of twenty-three he was elected a surveyor, and soon after held successively the offices of collector, assessor, and constable. At the age of thirty-seven years he was chosen selectman, and for years served in that office. He was a surveyor of some note beyond his own town and often served on committees of survey for other towns by appointment of the General Assembly. May 8, 1701, he was elected lieutenant of the "Trainband," for the north precinct of Wethersfield. He was living in April, 1728, but the tax-list of 1730 does not contain his name, and the probability is that he died before 1730, though the date of his death is not found on the records. Married, July 6,

1676, MARY (————). The surname of the wife of Benjamin as well as that of his brother Joseph's wife has been a matter of much careful research without avail.

Children of Benjamin and Mary Churchill.

9   I. JOSIAH,[3] b. Jan. 8, 1676/7; m. ELIZABETH TOUSEY, May 8, 1706.
      II. PRUDENCE,[3] b. July 2, 1678; m. COL. DAVID GOODRICH, of
          Wethersfield, Dec. 1, 1698.
          Colonel Goodrich was born May 4, 1667. He was a very able
          and enterprising man, especially prominent in military affairs, in
          the Indian troubles from 1701 on. He was advanced successively
          from sergeant to captain, and in the Indian war of 1709 he was
          actively engaged as captain, adjutant; and quartermaster of the
          troops raised for the relief of Hampshire County. Again in 1723
          he commanded a company, and was a member of the Colonial War
          Committee. In 1725 he ranked as colonel. He was a justice of
          peace and, except for a year, he represented Wethersfield as deputy
          to the General Court from 1716 to 1740. He died Jan. 23, 1755.
          Prudence, his wife, died May 9, 1752.

Children of Col. David and Prudence (Churchill) Goodrich.

      1. Hezekiah Goodrich, b. Jan. 28, 1700.
      2. Prudence Goodrich, b. June 8, 1701.
      3. Sarah Goodrich, b. March 12, 1703.
      4. Mary Goodrich, b. Dec. 15, 1704.
      5. Hannah Goodrich, b. Aug. 7, 1707.
      6. Jeremiah Goodrich, b. Sept. 9, 1709.
      7. Anne Goodrich, b. Feb. 14, 1712.
      8. Zebulon Goodrich, b. Nov. 22, 1713.
      9. Benjamin Goodrich, b. Nov. 13, 1715.
      10. Abigail Goodrich, b. Jan. 18, 1718.
      11. Charles Goodrich, b. Aug. 7, 1720.
      12. Millicent Goodrich, b. Jan. 23, 1723.

      III. ABIGAIL,[3] b. Feb. 18, 1680; m. THOMAS WRIGHT, Nov. 3, 1715.
          No issue.
      IV. ANNE,[3] m. BENJAMIN BELDEN, Jan. 29, 1713/14.

Children.

      1. Mary Belden, b. Dec. 9, 1715.
      2. Benjamin Belden, b. Feb. 9, 1717/8.
      3. Charles Belden, b. March 13, 1719/20.

THIRD GENERATION.

4.

NATHANIEL[3] CHURCHILL (JOSEPH,[2] JOSIAH[1]). Born in Wethersfield, July 9, 1677. He lived in Old Wethersfield until about 1719, when he removed with his family to the westermost precinct of the town, near Farmington bounds. He was active in public matters, in the land interests particularly in that locality, and his name is found on petitions to the General Court in 1715, and as member of a committee of citizens April 7, the same year. His will was probated later in 1715. He left a double portion to his son Nathaniel, viz., one hundred and thirty pounds, and to his younger sons, John, Daniel, and Josiah, sixty-five pounds. The inventory of his estate, Feb. 28, 1716, showed its value to be three hundred and seventy-one pounds. He died some time in the fall of 1715. The distribution of his estate was made April 2, 1728. Married, Oct. 9, 1701, MARY HURLBUT, daughter of Jonathan and Mary (Deming) Hurlbut, of Middletown, Conn., born June 9, 1679, and died in 1738, when her estate was administered by her son Daniel and her husband's brother, Samuel.

Children of Nathaniel and Mary (Hurlbut) Churchill.

      I. MARY,[4] b. Oct. 11, 1702; d. in infancy.
10   II. NATHANIEL,[4] b. Oct. 29, 1703; m. REBECCA GRISWOLD.
11   III. JOHN,[4] b. Jan. 19, 1706; m. BETHIA STOCKING.
12   IV. DANIEL.[4] b. Nov. 3, 1710; m. ABIGAIL WHITE.
     V. JOSIAH,[4] bapt. Aug 8, 1714; m. MARTHA GILL, of Middletown, dau. of Ebenezer and Lydia (Cole) Gill.
          They had no children who lived to maturity, if any issue at all. His will, dated March 1, 1770, makes his nephew Benjamin, son of his brother Daniel, his sole heir.

5.

ENSIGN SAMUEL[3] CHURCHILL (JOSEPH,[2] JOSIAH[1]). Born in Wethersfield, 1688. He settled in Newington parish, where he bought land of Joseph Allen in 1712, fifty-two acres, adjoining land of Capt. Robert Wells and Jonathan Deming. He lived in a house on the hillside just south of the present house in which Miss Mary Churchill lives (1903). Like his father and grandfather he was

active in public affairs in town and church. His name appears very
frequently in the records of the Newington society, where he served
on the Prudential and School Committees, and in other minor
affairs, like repairs on the meeting-house, school-house, etc. One vote
of the society, taken June 26, 1721, in anticipation of the settlement
of the Rev. Elisha Williams, is of interest, viz. :

Voted and agreed as followeth :

Samuel Hunn, Jabezeth Whittlesey, Richard Borman, and Samuel Churchel,
shall undertake to make twenty thousand bricks for Mr. Elisha Williams, to
take the care and provide the hands and all things for said work.

In one of the Wethersfield deeds he is called " Smith," indicating
his trade. In 1746 the General Assembly appointed him ensign of
the local military company, and he bore the title afterwards, and
has been designated in the family ever since as " Ensign Samuel."
He died in Newington Parish, July 21, 1769, and lies buried in the
churchyard. Married, June 26, 1717, MARTHA BOARDMAN, born
Dec. 19, 1695, daughter of Daniel and Hannah (Wright) Boardman,
of Wethersfield, and granddaughter of Samuel Boardman, of Cley-
don, England, one of the first settlers, and for many years one of the
most prominent citizens of Wethersfield. Mrs. Martha (Boardman)
Churchill died Dec. 14, 1780, in Newington.

*Children of Ensign Samuel and Martha (Boardman) Churchill, born in the
Newington Parish.*

13   I. GILES,[4] b. June 11, 1718; married and settled in Stamford, N.Y.
14   II. SAMUEL,[4] b. April 27, 1721; m. THANKFUL (HEWIT) SEAGER.
15   III. CAPT. CHARLES,[4] b. Dec. 31, 1723; m. LYDIA BELDEN, Nov. 19,
             1747.
16   IV. JESSE,[4] b. Aug. 31, 1726; m. 1st, JERUSHA GAYLORD; m. 2d, SARAH
             CADY; m. 3d, ELIZABETH BELDEN.
17   V. BENJAMIN,[4] b. April 10, 1729; m. 1st, ABIGAIL BARNES; m. 2d,
             HULDA BEECHER.
18   VI. WILLIAM,[4] b. Nov. 6, 1732; m. 1st, RUTH TRYON, and m. 2d, ABIAH
             WILDMAN.

6.

JOSEPH [3] CHURCHILL (JOSEPH,[2] JOSIAH [1]). Born in 1690.
Settled in Bolton, Conn., in 1725. He was one of the leading men
of the town, and was a selectman 1728–1734, and held many other
offices of responsibility. He died in Bolton, Feb. 12, 1768. Married, January, 1714, LYDIA DICKERMAN, daughter of John, of Hatfield, Mass. We have record of only the following:

Children born in Bolton.

19   I. JOSEPH,[4] b. Nov. 23, 1714; m. (———) (———).
        II. MARTHA,[4] b. 1717; m. DR. JUDAH STRONG, 1740.

Child.

1. Judah Strong, b. 1742; m. Martha Alvord, dau. of Samuèl. One child, (1) Joseph Churchill Strong, b. Oct. 3, 1778, in Bolton. He was educated as a physician, and became an assistant surgeon in the United States Army. He settled at Knoxville, Tenn. Dr. Joseph C. and Martha (Alvord) Strong had two sons. Robert Nelson Strong, M.D., and Benjamin Rush Strong M.D. — both well-known physicians, the latter at Tuscumbia, Ala.

7.

DAVID⁸ CHURCHILL (JOSEPH,² JOSIAH¹). Born 1692. Settled in Glastonbury, Conn. Died in Glastonbury, April 16, 1782, aged ninety years. Married DOROTHY (————).

Children.

    I. DOROTHY,⁴ b. Oct. 3, 1726; m. RICHARD FOX, March 20, 1745.
    II. ELIZABETH,⁴ b. Feb. 1, 1729; d. June 19, 1729.
    III. BETTY,⁴ b. June 9, 1731; d. unmarried May 24, 1754.
20   IV. DAVID,⁴ b. Oct. 16, 1733; d. Jan. 10, 1755.
    V. ANNE,⁴ b. Oct. 23, 1737; m. BENJAMIN ANDRUS, Oct. 30, 1760.

Children.

1. Anne Andrus, b. Sept. 19, 1762.
2. Loraina Andrus, b. Jan. 13, 1765; d. May 3, 1768.
3. Thankful Andrus, b. March 29, 1767.

21   VI. JOSEPH,⁴ b. May 31, 1743; m. ELIZABETH ANDRUS, Jan. 25, 1764. No further record of this couple has been obtained.

8.

JONATHAN³ CHURCHILL (JOSEPH,² JOSIAH¹). Born 1692, twin brother of David. Married MRS. SARAH DEMING.

Children.

22   I. JONATHAN,⁴ b. 1724; m. LYDIA SMITH.
    II. DORCAS,⁴ b. 1724.
23   III. WILLIAM,⁴ b. Nov. 5, 1727; m. CHLOE BROWN.
    IV. BENJAMIN,⁴ ⎫
    V. HEZEKIAH,⁴ ⎬ twins, b. Sept. 22, 1731, and both died soon.

9.

JOSIAH⁸ CHURCHILL (BENJAMIN,² JOSIAH¹). Born Jan. 28, 1676/7. He died Aug. 22, 1751. Married, May 8, 1706, ELIZABETH TOUSEY, who was the daughter of Thomas Tousey. She died Oct. 28, 1751.

Children.

    I. ARMINELL,⁴ b. Feb. 26, 1708/9; m. DANIEL BUTLER, May 14, 1730.

Children.

1. Elizabeth Butler, b. March 11, 1731.
2. Mary Butler, b. Oct. 18, 1732.
3. Sarah Butler, b. Sept. 11, 1734.

4. Abigail Butler, b. Feb. 10, 1737.
5. Eunice Butler, b. July 26, 1739.
6. Prudence Butler, b. Oct. 21, 1741.
7. George Butler, b. Dec. 26, 1743; d. Jan. 4,
8. Samuel Butler, b. Feb. 19, 1746.
9. Lydia Butler, ⎱ twins, b. April 12, 1748.
10. Hannah Butler, ⎰
11. George Butler, b. Feb. 22, 1750.

II. PRUDENCE,[4] b. Dec. 20, 1710; m. WILLIAM DEM
III. HEZEKIAH,[4] b. Aug. 20, 1712; d. June 24, 1714.
IV. MARY,[4] b. Oct. 6, 1714; m. JONATHAN WARNER
V. SARAH,[4] b. June 15, 1716; m. THOMAS BUTLER,

Children.

1. Chloe Butler, b. Jan. 31, 1739.
2. Huldah Butler, b. Feb. 15, 1741.
3. Rhoda Butler, b. Jan. 7, 1743.
4. Josiah Butler, b. Nov. 12, 1745.
5. Sarah Butler, b. Feb. 1, 1747.
6. Elisha Butler, b. Dec. 2, 1748.
7. Elizabeth Butler, b. Aug. 19, 1753.

24   VI. JOSIAH,[4] b. June 28, 1720; m. EUNICE DEMING,

FOURTH GENERATION.

10.

NATHANIEL[4] CHURCHILL (NATHANIEL,[3] JOSEPH,[2] JOSIAH [1]). Born Oct. 29, 1703. Married REBECCA GRISWOLD.

Children.

   I. ABIGAIL,[5] b. Sept. 28. 1727.
   II. MARY,[5] b. Aug. 22, 1729; d. in infancy.
25   III. NATHANIEL,[5] b. June 25, 1731; m. 1st, ELIZABETH SAGE; m. 2d, JANE BUSHNELL.
   IV. REBECCA,[5] b. Feb. 10, 1734.
   V. LUCY,[5] b. May 3, 1736.
26   VI. JANNA,[5] b. Feb. 20, 1739; m. MRS. SARAH (MIX) FOSTER, widow of Thomas.
27   VII. AMOS,[5] b. March 5, 1743; m. LYDIA COWLES, Feb. 4, 1768.
   VIII. MARY,[5] b. June 30, 1746.
27a   IX. JOSIAH,[5] b. July 1, 1748; m. (———) (———); no children.
   X. HANNAH,[9] b. July 15, 1750.

11.

JOHN[4] CHURCHILL (NATHANIEL,[3] JOSEPH,[2] JOSIAH [1]). Born in Wethersfield, Jan. 19, 1706. Went to Middletown with his father in 1719. Settled in Portland, Conn., about 1725. He was one of the organizers of the Congregational Church, in Portland. Married, at Middletown, June 8, 1727, BETHIA STOCKING, who was the daughter of George and Elizabeth Stocking, of Middletown, and was born April 12, 1703, and died July 20, 1779.

Children born in Portland.

   I. MARY,[5] b. March 18, 1728; m. GEORGE COOPER.
      He was the son of Thomas and Abigail (Whitmore) Cooper, of Middletown. She died July 30, 1798.

Children.

      1. Abigail Cooper, bapt. June 9, 1749; d. 1751.
      2. Abigail Cooper, bapt. June 7, 1752.
      3. George Cooper, bapt. Jan. 20, 1754.
      4. Mary Cooper, bapt. May 23, 1756.
      5. Elizabeth Cooper, bapt. Nov. 11, 1766.

   II. JOHN,[5] bapt. Jan. 25, 1730; d. June 2, 1753. No record.
   III. HANNAH,[5] bapt. April 11, 1731; m. JOSIAH PELTON, of Saybrook, son of John and Jemima, b. 1714/15, and died Feb. 2, 1792. She died June 12, 1810.

Children.

1. Jemima Pelton, bapt. 1751.
2. Josiah Pelton, bapt. Jan. 21, 1753.
3. Prudence Pelton, bapt. April 9, 1755.
4. Hannah Pelton, bapt. 1760.
5. Moses Pelton, bapt. 1762.
6. Phebe Pelton, bapt. July 28, 1764.
7. A child, bapt. March 30, 1765.
8. Marchall Pelton, bapt. Oct. 16, 1768.
9. Josias Pelton, bapt. April 5, 1772.
10. John Pelton, bapt. April 5, 1772.

28   IV. JOSEPH,[5] bapt. Jan. 27, 1734; m. PRUDENCE TRYON, Sept. 4, 1754.
         V. LYDIA,[5] bapt. May 23, 1737; d. in infancy.
        VI. ELIZABETH,[5] bapt. June 16, 1747.
       VII. LYDIA,[5] bapt. June 16, 1747; m. NATHANIEL OLCOT, Feb. 4, 1767.
      VIII. PRUDENCE,[5] bapt. June 16, 1747.
        IX. SARAH,[5] b. 1744; d. Sept. 11, 1828; m. ELISHA HURLBURT, Feb. 16,
             1761, son of David, Jr., and Ruth (Belden) Hurlburt.

Children.

1. Jehiel Hurlburt, bapt. Sept. 10, 1762.
2. Asa Hurlburt, bapt. Feb. 19, 1769.
3. Charles Hurlburt, bapt. Feb. 19, 1769.
4. John Churchill Hurlburt, bapt. July 5, 1772.
5. Seth Hurlburt, bapt. May 21, 1775.
6. Sarah Hurlburt, bapt. June 1, 1777.
7. Bethia Hurlburt, bapt. April 23, 1780.
8. Jared Hurlburt, bapt. Oct. 13, 1782.

12.

DANIEL[4] CHURCHILL (NATHANIEL,[3] JOSEPH,[2] JOSIAH[1]).
Born in Middletown, Conn., Nov. 3, 1710. Settled in Chatham.
Removed to Exeter, Otsego County, N.Y., arriving May 10, 1795.
Married, June 16, 1735, ABIGAIL WHITE, daughter of Nathaniel.

Children.

   I. RUTH,[5] b. Oct. 20, 1736; m. STEPHEN WHITE.
      He was probably son of Deacon Joseph and Abigail (Butler)
      White, who was born Jan. 17, 1731, and died 1813, having outlived
      all her children.

      Child of Ruth Churchill and Stephen White.

      1. Dr. Joseph White, b. Sept. 26, 1763; m. 1st, Olive Hall, 1787, b.
         Oct. 15, 1768; d. Sept. 20, 1792; m. 2d, Deborah Hall (sister),
         b. Feb. 21, 1774; d. Aug. 23, 1821.

      Children of Dr. Joseph White and Olive, his wife.

      1. Dr. Delos White, b. Oct 20, 1788.
      2. Dr. Menzo White, b. Oct. 19, 1793.
      3. Leventia White, b. Nov. 15, 1795; m. Jacob Livingston.
      4. Joseph White, b. Sept. 3, 1801.
      5. George W. White, b. Aug. 27, 1810.

  II. SARAH,[5] b. April 5, 1739; d. April 30, 1739.
 III. ABIGAIL,[5] b. March 16, 1740; d. March 29, 1743.
  IV. ELISHA,[5] b. Aug. 24, 1742.
   V. WILLIAM,[5] b. March 2, 1745; d. July 4, 1749.

29   VI. BENJAMIN,[5] b. Feb. 5, 1747; m. ELIZABETH HURLBUT.
30   VII. DANIEL,[5] b. Oct. 2, 1750; m. EUNICE SAXTON.
      VIII. ABIGAIL,[5] b. May 2, 1753; never married.
       IX. SARAH,[5] b. Nov. 25, 1757; m. BENJAMIN HODGE, April 9, 1780.

         He was born in Chatham, Conn., Jan. 1, 1753. He served in the Revolution. They lived in Glastonbury until 1793, when he moved to Richfield, N.Y.

Children born in Glastonbury, except three last.

   1. William Hodge, b. July 2, 1781.
   2. Clarissa Hodge, b. Sept. 25, 1782; d. Jan. 20, 1790.
   3. Philander Hodge, b. Oct. 26, 1784; drowned Dec. 11, 1808, in French Creek, Penn.
   4. Alfred Hodge, b. Jan. 26, 1787; d. Dec. 9, 1789.
   5. Lorin Hodge, b. April 6, 1789.
   6. Sarah Hodge, b. Oct. 29, 1791; d. Feb. 28, 1792.
   7. Clarissa Hodge, b. Dec. 26, 1792; m. Mr. Aylesworth.
   8. Alfred Hodge, b. in Richfield, N.Y., May 9, 1795; m. Sophia English.
   9. Benjamin Hodge, b. April 26, 1797; m. Mrs. Davis.
  10. Velorus Hodge, b. March 26, 1800.

13.

GILES[4] CHURCHILL (SAMUEL,[3] JOSEPH,[2] JOSIAH[1]). Born June 18, 1718. He settled about 1751 on the forks of the Delaware river, upon the grant made to William Penn. Died in Florida, N.Y., 1771. We have not ascertained the name of his wife.

Children born at the forks of the Delaware river.

31   I. ELIJAH,[5] b. Sept. 4, 1755; m. ELINOR NOONEY, March 10, 1777.
32   II. STEPHEN,[5] b. April 15, 1758; m. ESTHER LLOYD, Dec. 14, 1780.
    III. SARAH.[5]
    IV. OLIVE,[5] m. JOSEPH STEEL.
     V. GILES.[5]

14.

SAMUEL[4] CHURCHILL (SAMUEL,[3] JOSEPH,[2] JOSIAH[1]). Born in the West Parish of Wethersfield, now Newington, April 27, 1721. He settled first in Sheffield, Mass., about 1746, where he married next year, and labored industriously at his farm as well as occasionally at the making of shoes. Here he remained until his family had increased to ten children, six sons and four daughters, when he removed to Vermont. The story of his subsequent career in the new home and his stirring adventures in the border warfare in the Revolution has been published many years ago by his grandson, Amos Churchill, son of Joseph, in sketches of the history of Hubbardton, Vt. (The sketches were published first in the "Vermont Historical Gazetteer," Vol. III.) We quote the account from the time of the removal from Sheffield.

    My grandfather having a large family, most of them boys, and some married and beginning to have families, he was anxious to provide for them farms if possible. And, as land was cheap in the then new State of Vermont, he sold his farm in Sheffield, estimated at three thousand dollars ($3,000), to a man by the name of Hickok (who pretended to own a large quantity of land in the town of Hubbardton, Rutland County, Vt.), and took a quitclaim deed of three thousand (3,000) acres of land lying in Hubbardton aforesaid. He had previously been through the town with Hickok and others. The next season he came on with his surveyor, and located his three thousand (3,000) acres in a different part of the town, chose his place of residence, cleared a piece of land,· built a log house, and moved on in the spring of 1775, and went to clearing up his farm. He had been in possession for a little more than two years, and was still attending to his business, when a detachment of soldiers arrived on the morning of the 7th of July, 1777, warning him of danger, and advising him to escape. They were two miles north of Warren's encampment. Upon receiving the information they started off as fast as possible, the women and children mounted on three horses and the men on foot. They had gone but a little on their way when the firing commenced. They all pushed on as fast as possible until they were among the bullets, and two of their horses were wounded. The old lady, when she saw that her horse was wounded, jumped from his back, exclaiming, "I wish I had a gun, I would give them what they want." They all retreated except John and Silas who were in the battle. Silas was taken prisoner, but John made his escape and went back to their house. Here they were all surprised, and were taken prisoners by a Tory captain named Sherwood, with a party of painted Tories and Indians who had been lurking on the hills east of the house during the battle. After plundering the house of all the provisions, most of the clothing, and everything else that they could make use of, the barbarous wretch ordered the women and children to leave the house or he would burn the whole together; at any rate the house should be burnt. One of the young women taking her bed in her arms proceeded with a heavy heart to the door, let it fall, saying, "You have taken all our men prisoners, and all our provisions, and now how can you be so cruel as to burn our house?" So saying she fainted. This, with the tears and entreaties of the others, so softened his savage heart that he left them their shelter, but deprived them of their provisions and much of their clothing. My grandfather was taken some distance from the house into the woods by the Indians and tied to a tree and dry brush piled around him, they often saying to him, "Tell us where your flour is, you old rebel." Sherwood suspected that he had some concealed which they had not yet found. After keeping him here for two or three hours, questioning him about his flour, threatening and taunting him, and he constantly asserting that he had none, that they had taken it all, etc., and while in the act of setting fire to the brush, Sherwood came forward and ordered them to desist, being thoroughly convinced that he had none. His cattle and hogs were all killed and all such parts as they could use were taken, each one being ordered to take as much as he could carry. William was lame, having cut his foot a few days before, and could not travel, and they released him. Ezekiel being a small boy, they sent him back. The others were marched off to Ticonderoga. The prisoners, inhabitants of Hubbardton, were Samuel Churchill, the father, John and Silas, his sons, Messrs. Uriah Hickok, Henry Keeler, and Elijah Kellogg. The women and children being left destitute of provisions could not remain there. The British Tories and Indians being south, they feared to take a southern direction. One of their horses being lame from the wound he had received, could not travel. They, with what clothing they had left, started off as well as they could with their two horses. The company consisted of four women, two boys (one thirteen years old being lame, and the other eleven years old), two small children (one three years old, and the other but a few months). Those who could not walk were mounted on the two horses with what baggage they had. Thus equipped, this desolate family started off on their dreary and wearisome journey for the place of their former residence in Sheffield. But, instead of taking a southern direction through Bennington, etc., which they feared to do on account of the enemy, they took an eastern direction through the wilderness, across the Green Mountains to the Connecticut river at No. 4, now Charlestown, N.H.; then down the river south to Springfield, then across the mountains again to Sheffield, the place of their former residence, a distance as they travelled of more than three hundred and fifty (350) miles. Most of the way there were no roads, and but few inhabitants. Their progress was slow and distressing, but the old lady, being a resolute woman, generaled the expedition with much fortitude and perseverance. The first night they stopped at Col. Benjamin Cooley's, in Pittsford. He was very kind, and refreshed them with such as his log house afforded.

The second day they arrived at the fort in Rutland. Here they were furnished with some provisions. The third night they encamped in the woods on the mountain. The fourth night they arrived at Captain Coffin's, in Cavendish. Here they stopped two days, and were the recipients of his hospitality. And so on, from place to place, until in about three weeks they arrived safely at the place of their destination, among their friends in Sheffield.

The men, prisoners at Ticonderoga, were put to work in the daytime where they could be with safety, and at night were confined in cells. My grandfather and Mr. Hickok were set to boating wood across the lake. At first, for a while, a number of British soldiers would go with them, but they, working faithfully and manifesting no discontent, were at length sent off with but one soldier. They persuaded him to go with them, and fastening their boat on the eastern shore of the lake they all left. My grandfather and Mr. Hickok went to their places of residence in Hubbardton. Here they found nothing but desolation and putrefaction. On the floor of Mr. Hickok's house lay the putrid body of a dead man. That they buried, and then, proceeding over the battle-ground, they could discover nothing but a promiscuous mass of scattered fragments of men, clothing, firearms, and direful desolation. Proceeding still further to the place of my grandfather's house where he had left his family, and all that he held dear on earth, what a heart-rending scene did he behold! Nothing was to be seen but death, desolation, and destruction. Here, where a few weeks before was a happy family, and all in health and prosperity, now no living creature could be found. The carcasses of his animals were lying here and there in a state of putrefaction; his harvest had ripened and was perishing; and nothing was left but what was heart-sickening to the sensitive feelings of two escaped, hungry, weary, and desponding searchers of consolation. The whole town was searched, and not a solitary being was left of whom to inquire. They left this dreary, heart-sickening scene, and proceeded to Castleton. Here Mr. Hickok found his family, but my grandfather, not finding his, and gaining no intelligence of them, wended his weary way, on foot and alone, to the south, one hundred and thirty (130) long miles, through dangers that beset him on every side, to the place from which he had formerly moved. Here he found, with a grateful heart, that they had arrived some days before, safe and all in good health. His two sons, John and Silas, remained prisoners until October, when Silas was retaken by Colonel Brown. In the fall, after the capture of Burgoyne, my grandfather moved his family back to Castleton, ten miles from his home. He saved some of his corn and potatoes, cut and laid up some poor hay for his horses, and in the winter moved to his place. Here he remained without interruption until the close of the war. When the town began to be infested with land claimants almost as destructive as the Tories and Indians, on examining his title, he found it worthless, as the man of whom he bought it had no good title to any land in the town. He had given his children each a lot of one hundred (100) acres, and on ten lots they had made a beginning. These were held by the "quieting act." Six more he bought the second time. The rest were given up. He built the first frame barn and the second frame house. The boards for the barn were drawn twelve and one-half miles on an ox sled, and the nails were picked up from the ruins of Fort Ticonderoga after it was burnt. His children, all but one, settled in the town, where they all lived until after his death, except Samuel, who died before. After settling his children, he retired from business and lived a number of years, enjoying a competence, to the advanced age of eighty years.

Married, 1747, THANKFUL (HEWIT) SEAGER, the young widow of Joseph, of Newington.

Children of Samuel and Thankful Churchill.

I. MARTHA,[5] b. Jan. 14, 1748; m. ABDIEL WEBSTER.
　　They are reported to have had two sons and a daughter, but the names have not been received. Mrs. Webster died in Hubbardton, at advanced age, having been a widow for many years.

34　　II. JOSEPH,[5] b. Feb. 14, 1750; m. AMY STILES, Dec. 7, 1773.

  III. LYDIA,[5] b. June 1, 1751; m. ABNER ASHLEY.
    They are said to have had a son and six daughters, whose names
    we have not ascertained. Lydia (Churchill) Ashley died in Bethany,
    N.Y., a widow, aged eighty-two years.
  IV. LOIS,[5] b. May 30, 1753; m. DAVID BALDWIN.
    They are said to have had three sons and two daughters, whose
    names we have not obtained. Lois (Churchill) Baldwin died in
    New Marlborough, Mass., aged eighty-three years.
  V. THANKFUL,[5] b. March 7, 1755; d. unmarried at great age.

35 VI. SAMUEL,[5] b. May 20, 1756; m. ANNA CAMP.
36 VII. JOHN,[5] b. March 12, 1758; m. MARTHA BALDWIN.
37 VIII. SILAS,[5] b. June 18, 1760; m. ELIZABETH CULVER. No children.
38 IX. WILLIAM,[5] b. Feb. 10, 1763; m. EUNICE CULVER.
39 X. EZEKIEL,[5] b. June 24, 1765; m. ELIZABETH DYER.

15.

CAPT. CHARLES[4] CHURCHILL (SAMUEL,[3] JOSEPH[2] JOSIAH[1]). Born in Newington Parish, Dec. 31, 1723, and died there Oct. 29, 1802. A detailed sketch of the life of Capt. Charles Churchill would be almost the same as a history of the Newington Parish for the last half of the eighteenth century. He was notably a leading citizen in the parish, of high patriotic spirit and excellent abilities. For thirteen years in succession he was a member of the Newington Society Committee, and after 1781 he was the presiding officer until 1801, the year before his death. To many public offices of trust and responsibility was added that of deacon of the church, to which he was chosen Aug. 31, 1786. At the session of the General Assembly, May, 1762, he was appointed captain of the Tenth Company or "trainband," in the Sixth Connecticut Regiment, which office he filled for twenty years.

At the beginning of the Revolutionary War he was on the first committee appointed at the town meeting convened June 16, 1774, to consider the resolution passed by the Colonial House of Representatives, on the second Thursday of May preceding, concerning the impending war.

In all the stirring events following, he was among the foremost of the citizens in his unselfish endeavors and sacrifices for the good of his people and country. The records of the town, and traditions in the family, show that he was untiring in his efforts to raise men for the service and to procure food and clothing for them, and for their families while they were in the field.

It is related that he several times entertained his company at his fine old house, and on these occasions the five great baking ovens were kept going at once, and that in the largest oven, in the cellar, they roasted a whole ox.

In the "Record of Connecticut Men in the War of the Revolution" he is listed as captain of one of the militia companies which turned out

SAMUEL CHURCHILL.
(No. 42, page 354.)

MRS. MERCY (BOARDMAN) CHURCHILL.
(Wife of No. 42, page 354.)

THE CAPT. CHARLES CHURCHILL
HOUSE, NEWINGTON, CONN., 1740.

(No. 15, page 338.)

to repel Tryon's invasion of New Haven, July 5, 1779, and he also
appears in his office as captain in active service in the Sixth Regiment, but unfortunately we have no other particulars of his service
in the field, evidently much of his time in active service. It is
related that at one time when he was in camp with three of his
sons, his wife wrote him of the difficulty she found in carrying on
the farm without their aid. " But," answered the captain, " I have
left you Joseph and Benjamin," meaning his youngest sons, Silas
and Solomon, and showing the spirit of the loyal patriot.

During the last twenty years of his life, his name appears on the
records of the Society with the title " Esquire," showing that he
had taken up the dignity and duties of a justice of the peace, in
place of his military duties. He collected a library of law books as
a necessary adjunct to his practice, some of which are still in existence. His will, a document of considerable length, is entirely in his
own hand. His estate was appraised at $3,834.80, by Abel Andrus
and Lemuel Whittlesey. Besides managing a farm of one hundred
and twenty acres, Captain Churchill conducted a tannery, which in
the tax lists was liberally assessed as a " faculty," or trade.

It is to be regretted that there are no portraits of Captain Charles
or of his wife. Enough is known of him, however, to give the picture of a strong, brave, and manly life, forceful and efficient in all
that made for a free and righteous government. The place he made
for himself in the community of his day, the family he reared, the
good name he left, and the things he accomplished, make his general
character portrait, while the details may in part be filled in by
hints here and there of peculiar traits or eccentric tendencies, — the
touch of humor in likening his sons to Jacob's, in the answer to his
wife quoted above, and the tradition that in his family devotions he
always prayed standing in front of the " bowfat" cupboard, in the
north room, as the wainscotted parlor in his house was called. Of
his wife, Mr. George D. Seymour, a descendant, writes :

Some leaves sewed into a little book, found with other papers in Samuel
Churchill's house, contain the following entry which, in a way, takes the place of
other portraiture. I do not identify the handwriting, and the entry is incomplete,
but from the context I feel sure that these tributes were written by one of
Samuel Churchill's children :

" March 25, 1805. Feb. 10th, Sunday, Grandmother came over to our
house, said she did not feel very well, & wanted that I should make her some
tea, most of the family had gone to meeting. I was very glad to please her in
anything that she required, because that she was always so very good to us all —
she drank some tea, thanked me for my trouble and went home. I think that
was the last time that ever she came into our house ; she was taken sick pretty
soon after; she died March 19. She never spoke after Sunday afternoon till she
died, Tuesday night (three o'clock) but was in the utmost distress that could
be. Grandmother had six children 39 grandchildren and great grandchildren
when she died. Oh may all follow her pious example, and walk in the paths of
virtue as she walked, whose loss we mourn. O what a kind, kind mother we

have lost. I think she was as tender of her grandchildren as own mothers are. Oh how often have I experienced her goodness, but not only me but all of her dear offspring. Oh how often has she spoken kindly to me, — and took my hand and told me, that I was born to hard fortune. (She said my hands indicated hard labor.) I think I shall never forget my dear Grandmother, nor my Grandfather neither, — I think of him many times, — and particularly I have heard him read,— and in his prayers — he used to have that passage ' Man Loveth Darkness rather than light because' his deeds are evil,' and many more passages, when I hear mentioned brings my Grandfather to mind. Oh that his Children were as good, as kind, as Charitable to the poor as their parents were. It is striking that they had six Children living at their death, & only one that ever made any public profession of Religion, that one a minister, altho a minister he will not save his brethren from "

The writing here breaks off. The minister referred to was the Rev. Silas. The intimation of the grandmother's interest in palmistry gives a natural touch to this simple and affectionate picture of her last days.

Capt. Charles Churchill married, Nov. 19, 1747, LYDIA BELDEN, born May 1, 1730, daughter of Josiah and Mabel (Wright) Belden, and a lineal descendant of Richard Belden, of Wethersfield, the emigrant, while her paternal grandmother was Dorothy Willard, a descendant of Major Simon .Willard, one of the founders of Concord, Mass., and notable as a magistrate, and a military officer, in the early annals of the Colony of Massachusetts. They were married as above, by the Rev. Joshua Belden, a kinsman of hers, of Newington. She died March 19, 1805.

Children of Capt. Charles and Lydia (Belden) Churchill, born in Newington.

      I. HANNAH,[5] b. Jan. 11, 1749; d. aged three days.
40   II. LEVI,[5] b. May 20, 1752; m. ELIZABETH HURLBUT, daughter of Joseph, Jr.
     III. MARY,[5] b. Sept. 22, 1753; d. Sept. 27, 1753.
41   IV. CHARLES, JR.,[5] b. May 3, 1755; m. a southern woman, name not received.
42   V. SAMUEL,[5] b. April 5, 1757; m. MERCY BOARDMAN, March 31, 1806.
     VI. HANNAH,[5] b. Dec. 28, 1758; m. 1st, SETH KILBOURN, April 27, 1786. He died Oct. 27, 1802; m. 2d, STEPHEN WEBSTER, June 8, 1806. She died Jan. 25, 1838;
43   VII. SOLOMON,[5] b. July 29, 1764; m. 1st, LUCRETIA MARSH, of New Hartford;' m. 2d, CHLOE DEMING.
44   VIII. REV. SILAS,[5] b. April 5, 1769; m. 1st, RHODA BELDEN, Oct. 12, 1797; m. 2d, SARAH SARGENT.

16.

JESSE[4] CHURCHILL (SAMUEL,[3] JOSEPH,[2] JOSIAH [1]). Born in Newington, Aug. 31, 1726. Lived in Newington (except for a short time, when he was at Bristol) until 1775, when he removed to Hubbardton, Vt., and there took up a farm, and began clearing it, built a log-house, and with several of his children settled near by, prepared to make this his permanent home. When the war of the Revolution, in 1777, involved Vermont, he, being too old to engage actively, withdrew to Wethersfield, his former home. He was

deacon of the First Church in Newington many years; a farmer,
prosperous and respected.   He died in Wethersfield (Newington
Parish), May 7, 1806, aged eighty years.   Married 1st, in Farmington, Conn., Nov. 8, 1750, JERUSHA GAYLORD, of Farmington.   Married 2d, Nov. 29, 1769, SARAH (BOARDMAN) CADY, widow of
Nicholas, and daughter of Sergt. Nathaniel and Ruth (Parker) Boardman.   Married 3d, June 15, 1778, ELIZABETH (———) BELDEN.   No
children by this marriage.   Norman Churchill writes, in 1880, that
his grandfather " married the rich widow Belden."   She died July
3, 1794, at the age of fifty-eight years.

Children of First Wife, born in Newington.

I. MARTHA,[4] b. Oct. 1, 1751; m. BENAIJAH BOARDMAN, Dec. 22, 1774.
   She was his second wife (the first, Lucy Price, of Wethersfield,
   m. 1772, who d. soon after, May 17, 1773).   Mr. Boardman was
   born at Newington, May 14, 1749, son of Isaac.   He settled first at
   Newington, but removed some time before July, 1777, to Hubbardton, Vt.   In the battle at Hubbardton, on July 7, 1777, it is said
   that the soldiers of the British force (largely made up of Tories
   and Indians) took possession of that part of the town in which their
   house was situated, and Mrs. Boardman, having been left alone in
   the house with two small children, concealed herself with them under a feather bed on the floor.   The house was soon made a temporary hospital for the wounded soldiers, and "she suffered so
   much from fright and the smothering and heat that afterwards she
   lost many of her fingernails."   Mr. Boardman was a soldier in the
   Revolution, was a sergeant in the company of Capt. Elijah Wright,
   Col. Enos' Regiment.
      He was in service on the Hudson in 1781, engaged for three
   months.
      About 1788 he removed to Ovid, N.Y., where he built a saw-
   mill in 1793, the first saw-mill in that town.   He afterwards removed
   to Canoga, N.Y., where he built the first saw-mill in that town.   He
   was widely known and very influential in his time.
      Children, the first two born at Newington, and the four eldest
   were baptized there, the two youngest of these were said to have
   been "brought down from Arlington," probably Vermont.

Child of the First Wife.

1. Meekins Boardman, b. May 17, 1773.

Children of the Second Wife.

2. Samuel Boardman, b. Feb. 17, 1780; m. 1st, Julia Ward; m.
   2d, Lydia Kirby.
3. Jesse Churchill Boardman, b. Aug. 20, 1781; m. 1st, Mary
   Rungar; m. 2d, Mrs. Elizabeth Larned.
4. Rebecca Meekins Boardman, b. June 10, 1783; m. William
   Hall, 1798.
5. Jerusha Boardman, b. May 22, 1785; m. James Huff, Sept. 15,
   1804.
6. Elizabeth Boardman, b. Feb. 11, 1787; d. at Fayette, N.Y.,
   Sept. 22, 1801.
7. Sarah Boardman, b. April 17, 1789; m. Daniel Tooker, December, 1804.
8. Lucy Boardman, b. Nov. 23, 1791; m. Ganet Arnold, May 22,
   1813.
9. Benaijah Boardman, Jr., b. Oct. 14, 1793; m. Laura A. Hurd
      Benaijah, Jr., was the first white child born between the
   Seneca and Cayuga lakes.

45   II. SAMUEL,[5] b. June 7, 1753; m. REBECCA WOODRUFF.
            They lived in Wethersfield. Had no children. He was born in
            Newington. Removed with his father to Hubbardton, where he
            took up and began clearing a farm. He was in the battle of Hub-
            bardton, after which he returned permanently to Wethersfield.
        III. ELIZABETH,[5] b. March 29, 1755; m. FRANCIS DEMING, Aug. 21,
            1782.
            They lived in Wethersfield. No children reported.
46   IV. JESSE, JR.,[5] b. March 18, 1757; m. 1st, HANNAH BOARDMAN; m.
            2d, OLIVE TILDEN; m. 3d, MRS. ANNA EGGLESTON.
47   V. LEVI,[5] b. Dec. 15, 1759; m. HANNAH BELDEN.
        VI. JERUSHA,[5] b. Nov. 6, 1761; m. BENJAMIN BOARDMAN.
       VII. GILES,[5] b. Dec. 17, 1763; died in youth.

Children by Second Wife.

48   VII. ITHAMAR,[5] b. Nov. 1, 1772; m. SARAH BLINN.
        IX. SALLY,[5] m. CYRUS RANGER.
            They lived in Hubbardton many years, but removed finally to
            Oswego Village, N.Y.

Children.

        1. Orilla Ranger.
        2. Sally Ranger; m. Mr. Connor, and lived in Woodville, Wis.

49   X. NATHANIEL CADY,[5] b. Oct. 20, 1776.

17.

BENJAMIN[4] CHURCHILL (SAMUEL,[3] JOSEPH,[2] JOSIAH[1]).
Born in Newington Parish, April 10, 1729. He died in Southington, and in his will mentions his wife Hulda, daughter of Lydia
Churchill and Abigail Way; sons Asahel, Benjamin, Ira, Jedediah,
and grandsons, Chauncy, Joseph, and Anson, sons of Jedediah; and
Major, son of Ira. Married 1st, April 19, 1753, ABIGAIL BARNES;
married 2d, HULDA BEECHER.

Children by First Wife.

50   I. ASAHEL,[5] b. May 1, 1754; m. EUNICE PINEY.
        II. LYDIA,[5] b. Sept. 13, 1756.
51   III. BENJAMIN,[5] b. March 16, 1759.
52   IV. SAMUEL,[5] b. Aug. 7, 1761; m. HANNAH BARNES, Feb. 22, 1787.
53   V. IRA,[5] b. April 9, 1764; m. EUNICE PAYNE.
54   VI. JEDEDIAH,[5] b. May 27, 1766.
       VII. ABIGAIL,[5] b. Aug. 15, 1770; m. (———) WAY.

Children.

1. Philena Way.   6. Lydia Way.
2. Fannie Way.   7. Anna Way.
3. Levi Way.   8. Henry Way.
4. Abigail Way.   9. Franklin Way, d. in infancy.
5. Joseph Way.

18.

WILLIAM[4] CHURCHILL (SAMUEL,[3] JOSEPH[2] JOSIAH[1]).
Born at Newington Parish, Nov. 6, 1732. Lived at Farmington,
Conn., until about 1769, when he removed with the large numbers

who settled in the Wyoming Valley, Pa. He was there with his family in the time of the massacre in 1778, but escaped, and reached what is now Elmira, N.Y., and thence to New Jersey, and there made their home. Married 1st, Sept. 25, 1760, in Farmington, Conn., RUTH TRYON, who died, 1776; married 2d, ABIAH WILDMAN.

Children of First Wife, born in Farmington, Conn.

    I.   JEMIMA,[5] b. April 15, 1761; never married; d. April 13, 1836.
55 II.   DAVID,[5] b. Dec. 20, 1762; m. SARAH ALCOTT.
    III. PHEBE,[5] b. April 27, 1764; m. SAMUEL MARTIN, of Coventry, N.Y.
56 IV. LEMUEL,[5] b. March 4, 1766; m. PATIENCE GILDERSLEEVE.
    V.   RUTH,[5] b. Dec. 13, 1767; m. LUCIUS COOKE, of Wallingford, Conn.
    VI. MARTHA,[5] b. Oct. 25, 1769; m. 1st, CHARLES TRYON; m. 2d, BEN-
         JAMIN DEMING.
57 VII. WILLIAM,[5] b. Dec. 26, 1771; m. JANE DELL.
    VIII. MARY,[5] b. July 6, 1773; m. LUCIUS ATWATER, of Berlin, Conn.
         They lived in Bristol or Berlin. He died in Berlin, in 1867, aged
         ninety-four years.

Children.

1. Carlos Atwater, b. Feb. 2, 1797; m. Hannah Larkin.
2. Lucius Atwater, b. April 24, 1798; m. Angeline Norton, of Bristol, Conn.
3. Rhoda Atwater, b. Nov. 16, 1800; m. Allen Burnell, of Burlington, Conn.
4. Nelson Atwater, b. Aug. 10, 1803; unmarried; d. July 21, 1872.
5. Mary Atwater, b. Dec. 4, 1805; m. Sheldon Twichell, of Oxford, Conn.
6. Emily Atwater, b. June 25, 1808; m. Coe Hart, of Litchfield, Conn.
7. Julia Atwater, m. John Crandall, of Burlington, Conn.
8. William Atwater, m. Elizabeth (———).

Children by Second Wife.

58 IX. SAMUEL,[5] b. May 22, 1778; m. ANNA McCARTHY.
59 X.   ASA,[5] b. July 12, 1780; m. HANNAH NORTON.
    XI. ABIAH,[5] b. Dec. 17, 1782; m. 1st, HEMAN ROOT; m. 2d, SILAS HUB-
         BELL.

Children by First Husband.

1. Eliza B. Root, b. 1811; m. Alpheus Strong, Jr., 1828.
      Children: (1) Elias Strong, b. 1831; m. Jerusha A. Perkins, 1852; (2 and 3) Twins, Eliza and Alpheus Strong, b. May 9, 1838. Eliza m. George D. Hannon in 1856; and Alpheus d. in 1864; (4) Ellen J. Strong, b. Dec. 17, 1843; m. Rufus W. Robinson, 1859.
2. Betsey Maria Root, b. at Montgomery, Mass., May 10, 1822; d. April 10, 1840.
3. Silas Root Hubbell, son of second husband, b. at Montgomery, Mass., April 17, 1826.

19.

JOSEPH[4] CHURCHILL (JOSEPH,[3] JOSEPH,[2] JOSIAH[1]). Born in Bolton, Conn., Nov. 23, 1714. Married, but the name of his wife is not found by us.

One Child reported.

60 I. JOSEPH,[5] b. 1750; m. RHODA GOODRICH, dau. of Benjamin, b. March 25, 1750, and married Sept. 11, 1777.

22.

JONATHAN ⁴ CHURCHILL (JONATHAN ³ JOSEPH,² JOSIAH ¹).
Born at Wethersfield, Conn., 1724. Married LYDIA SMITH.

Children.

        I. OLIVER,⁵ b. Feb. 14, 1748; d. Jan. 2, 1749.

63   II. JONATHAN,⁵ b. Nov. 25, 1749; m. 1st, SARAH BURGESS; m. 2d, COMFORT WOODCOCK.

64   III. HEZEKIAH,⁵ b. Feb. 2, 1752; m., name of wife not received.

    IV. JOSIAH,⁵ b. Feb. 25, 1754. Died during the war of the Revolution.

     V. LYDIA,⁵ b. July 5, 1756.

65   VI. MOSES,⁵ b. Dec. 1, 1759; m. MARY CROSBY.

66   VII. OLIVER,⁵ b. April 15, 1762; m. EUNICE BARNES.

  VIII. REBECCA,⁵ b. July 20, 1764; m. SOLOMON RANNEY.

    IX. ABIGAIL,⁵ b. Dec. 2, 1766; died at four years of age.

67   X. AMOS,⁵ b. Oct. 19, 1769; m. DEBORAH THORNTON.

23.

WILLIAM ⁴ CHURCHILL (JONATHAN ³ JOSEPH,² JOSIAH ¹).
Born Nov. 5, 1727. Lived, it is said, at Litchfield, Conn. Married
CHLOE BROWN.

Children.

68   I. WILLIAM,⁵ b. 1766; m. POLLY MERRIMAN, at Wallingford, Conn.

69   II. DAVID,⁵ b. March 17, 1768; m. ZERVIAH LEACH, March 6, 1797.

70   III. STEPHEN.⁵

    IV. CHLOE,⁵ m. DAVID DOUGAL.

Child.

    1. Truman Dougal.

71   V. EDWIN.⁵

72   VI. SAMUEL,⁵ b. April 18, 1775; m. REBECCA ST. JOHN, Feb. 22, 1798.

73   VII. LEVI,⁵ b. 1777; m. MARY HAVEN.

  VIII. ANNA,⁵ m. AMBROSE PERO. No children.

    IX. LUCINDA,⁵ m. JOSEPH GRANT.

FIFTH GENERATION

25.

NATHANIEL[5] CHURCHILL (NATHANIEL,[4] NATHANIEL[3] JOSEPH,[2] JOSIAH[1]). Born June 25, 1731. Married 1st, Sept. 25, 1755, ELIZABETH SAGE; married 2d, JANE BUSHNELL.

Children of First Wife.

77   I. NATHANIEL,[6] b. March, 2, 1756; m. MRS. LYDIA (OSGOOD) PEN-FIELD.
     II. BETTY,[6] b. Nov. 18, 1757; m. STEPHEN WILLIAMS, Feb. 18, 1781.
     III. ABIGAIL,[6] b. Dec. 5, 1759.

Children of Second Wife.

78   IV. STEPHEN,[6] b. Nov. 19, 1761; m. POLLY DE WOLFE.
79   V.   SAGE,[6] b. Dec. 13, 1763; m. ELIZABETH MATHER, dau. of David and Hannah.
80   VI. JOHN,[6] b. March 20, 1765.
81   VII. SOLOMON,[6] b. April 24, 1767; m. SALINA HART.
     VIII. SARAH,[6] b. April 24, 1767; m. REUBEN PECK.
     IX. JANE,[6] b. Jan. 17, 1769/70; m. WILLIAM STEDMAN.
     X.   MEHITABLE,[6] b. Jan. 3, 1773; m. APPLETON WOODRUFF, Dec. 24, 1792.
     XI. ALMA,[6] b. April 28, 1776; d. young.
     XII. ANNA,[6] b. April 14, 1778; m. JESSE NICKERSON.

26.

JANNA[5] CHURCHILL (NATHANIEL,[4] NATHANIEL,[3] JOSEPH,[2] JOSIAH[1]). Born at Middletown, Conn., Feb. 20, 1739. Settled, first, it is said in Lenox, Mass., but in 1783 removed to Hubbardton, Vt., and thence about 1793 to Georgia, Vt. He was a farmer. Died in Georgia, Vt., in 1815. Married MRS. SARAH (MIX) FOSTER, widow of Thomas Foster.

Children of Janna and Sarah Churchill.

     I.   SARAH JANE.[6]
82   II.   THOMAS FOSTER,[6] b. Feb. 26, 1780; m. MARY STRONG.
83   III. JOSIAH,[6] b. March 9, 1784; m. 1st, CHARLOTTE RUMSEY, Feb. 11, 1808; m. 2d, HARRIET WIGHTMAN.
84   IV.   JANNA,[6] b. Feb. 18, 1786; m. ELIZABETH PARSONS, Jan. 10, 1810.
     V.   OLIVE,[6] m. WALKER RUMSEY.
     VI.   RACHEL,[6] m. ELISHA LINCOLN.
     VII. LAURA,[6] d. unmarried.
     VIII. LUCY,[6] m. SAMUEL BRIGHAM.

27.

AMOS[5] CHURCHILL (NATHANIEL,[4] NATHANIEL,[3] JOSEPH,[2] JOSIAH[1]). Born in Wethersfield, March 5 1743; settled in Middle town, where he was a justice of the peace, and deacon of the Orthodox church in 1779, but changed to the Baptists later. He removed, sometime later, to Broadalban, Montgomery County, N.Y. Married, Feb. 4, 1768, LYDIA COWLES, of Meriden, Conn.

Children born mostly in Middletown, Conn.

I. LYDIA,[6] b. April 16, 1769; m. ELIJAH ROBERTS, of Middletown, Conn. Settled in Mayfield, N.Y.
II. AMOS,[6] b. May 20, 1771; d. April 15, 1774.
III. HULDAH,[6] b. March 29, 1773; m. ELIJAH BACON, of Middletown. Settled in Mayfield, N.Y.
85   IV. AMOS, JR.,[6] b. April 14, 1775; m. OLIVE WILCOX, of Middletown. Settled in Broadalban, N.Y.
86   V. ROSWELL,[6] b. April 4, 1777; m. ABIGAIL ROBERTS of Middletown, July 1802.
VI. LUCY,[6] b. Jan. 10, 1780; m. 1st, AMOS EDWARDS; m. 2d, ISAAC CORNWELL, of Middletown. Moved to Mayfield, N.Y.

Children.

1. Amos C. Cornwell, m. Lovina Bemus, of Mayfield, N.Y.
2. Isaac Cornwell.
3. Lucy Cornwell, m. Alanson Churchill.

87   VII. JESSE,[6] b. June 2, 1782; m. CATHERINE SMITH, of Middletown.
VIII. OLIVE,[6] b. Sept. 19, 1784.

28.

JOSEPH[5] CHURCHILL (JOHN,[4] NATHANIEL,[3] JOSEPH,[2] JOSIAH[1]). Baptized in Portland, Conn., Jan. 27, 1734. He was a captain in the Revolution under Colonel Sage, and served at New York City and on Long Island, from June to December, 1776. He was in the battles at Harlem and White Plains. He died Dec. 19, 1797. Married, Sept. 4, 1754, PRUDENCE TRYON. She was the daughter of John and Esther Tryon, of Wethersfield, born Jan. 25, 1731, died May 1, 1799.

Children.

I. PRUDENCE,[6] b. May 13, 1755; d. Feb. 21, 1808; m. GEORGE BUSH, of Portland, Conn., Sept. 9, 1779.
He was the son of Moses and Susanna (Johnson) Bush, b. June 11, 1756.

Children.

1. John Churchill Bush, b. Aug. 10, 1780.
2. Joseph Bush, bapt. June 24, 1789.
3. Prudence Bush, } twins, bapt. April, 1790.
4. Lucy Bush,   }

88   II. JOHN,[6] b. Jan. 8, 1757.
III. BETHIAH,[6] b. Feb. 19, 1759; m. BENJAMIN GOODRICH, Jan. 26, 1784. Settled in Schenectady, N.Y.
IV. MARY,[6] b. April 10, 1761; d. 1833; m. JESSE PLUM, July 2, 1777, of Middletown.

Children.

1. Jesse Plum, b. Feb. 7, 1779.
2. Elijah Tryon Plum, b. Nov. 5, 1786.
3. Bethiah Plum, b. April 1, 1794.

89   V. JOSEPH,[6] b. May 20, 1763; m. ANNA LOWDEN, Oct. 28, 1790.
90   VI. ASEL,[6] bapt. June 21, 1765; d. May 19, 1768.
91   VII. ASAHEL,[6] bapt. May 21, 1768.
92   VIII. CHARLES,[6] b. June 12, 1769; m. RUTH CHIPMAN, Oct. 29, 1788.
93   IX. DAVID,[6] b. May 16, 1771.

29.

BENJAMIN [5] CHURCHILL (DANIEL,[4] NATHANIEL,[3] JOSEPH,[2] JOSIAH [1]). Born Feb. 5, 1747, in Chatham, Conn. Settled in Salisbury, Conn. Perhaps he is the soldier who served in Capt. James Stoddard's Company at Peekskill, 1777. Married ELIZABETH HURLBURT.

Children.

          I. ELISHA,[6] never married.
94   II. EBENEZER,[6] m. SABRINA TUPPER.
95   III. CHARLES,[6] b. June 5, 1793; m. LOIS BALDWIN.
         IV. AUGUSTUS,[6] never married.
          V. SARAH.[6]
         VI. SOPHIA,[6] m. Mr. Peck.
        VII. BENJAMIN,[6] died young.

30.

DANIEL [5] CHURCHILL (DANIEL,[4] NATHANIEL,[3] JOSEPH [2] JOSIAH [1]). Born at Chatham, Conn., Oct. 2, 1750. He enlisted at Middletown, Conn., in the Fourth Company, Second Regiment, under the command of Captain Meigs. Served from May 10, 1775, to Dec. 17, 1775. Private. Stationed at Roxbury, Mass. He removed to Richfield, N.Y., April, 1795. He died at Richfield, N.Y., Dec. 12 1812. Married, 1779, EUNICE SAXTON.

Children born at Chatham, Conn.

          I. NANCY,[6] b. Oct. 22' 1781; m. ANDREW MARTIN, of Richfield, N.Y.
              They lived at Richfield, Kingston, Canada, and Tonawanda, N.Y.

Children.

1. Daniel Martin, b. in Richfield.
2. Cynthia Martin, b. in Kingston, Canada.
3. Lydia A. Martin, b. in Kingston, Canada, Feb. 2, 1804.
4. Alfred Martin, b. in Kingston, Canada.
5. Selden Martin, b. in Kingston, Canada.
6. Philemon Martin, b. in Tonawanda, N.Y.

96   II. SELDEN,[6] b. Dec. 14' 1783; m. 1st, MARY DUEL; m. 2d, LUCRETIA CLEMENTS.
        III. PHILEMON,[6] b. May 20, 1785. Died unmarried.
97   IV. ALFRED,[6] b. Aug. 29, 1790; m. EMMA DERBYSHIRE.

31.

ELIJAH[5] CHURCHILL (GILES,[4] SAMUEL,[3] JOSEPH,[2] JOSIAH[1]). Born Sept. 5, 1755. Served as corporal, Fourth Company Light Dragoons, from Enfield. Enlisted May 7, 1777. A carpenter. Five feet nine inches high, dark complexion, gray eyes, dark hair. They lived, in 1784, in Enfield. Married, March 10, 1777, ELINOR NOONEY, born in Simsbury, Conn., April 7, 1756. She died Oct. 9, 1846.

Children.

    I. SOPHIA,[6] b. Feb. 8, 1782; d. Feb. 18, 1782.
    II. ELIJAH,[6] b. April 21, 1784; d. Sept. 4, 1796. From the records of town of Enfield.
98   III. JAMES,[6] b. Nov. 11, 1785; m. BETSEY GILBERT.
    IV. ELEANOR,[6] b. Nov. 14, 1788; d. Jan. 1, 1790.
    V. ELEANOR,[6] b. July 7, 1790; m. LYMAN DAVIS, of Stamford, N.Y., March 2, 1815.

Children.

1. Sophie Davis.
2. Eunice Davis.
3. Edgar Davis.
4. Abigail Davis.
5. Nancy Davis.
6. Tina Davis.

99   VI. GILES,[6] b. July 28, 1793; m. ABIGAIL HASKINS.
100 VII. CHARLES,[6] b. Feb. 16, 1796; m. HANNAH PERCIVAL, Nov. 4, 1819.
    VIII. SOPHIA,[6] b. Jan. 30, 1798; m. JESSE JOHNSON, Chester, Mass.

32.

STEPHEN[5] CHURCHILL (GILES,[4] SAMUEL,[3] JOSEPH,[2] JOSIAH[1]). Born April 15, 1758, at the forks of the Delaware river. Married, Dec. 14, 1780, ESTHER LLOYD.

Children.

    I. MARY,[6] b. Sept. 7, 1781; m. MR. HUTCHINS. She d. Oct. 9, 1859.
    II. PHEBE,[6] b. Jan. 3, 1784; m. MR. STODDARD. She d. Jan. 4, 1857.
101 III. GILES,[6] b. March 12, 1786; m. ABIGAIL TOOKER.
    IV. ESTHER,[6] b. July 25, 1788; m. MR. WEBB.
102 V. SAMUEL,[6] b. Sept. 16, 1790; m. 1st, SALLY NEWCOMB; m. 2d, SALLY SHAFER.
    VI. STEPHEN,[6] b. May 13, 1793; d. unmarried 1809.
103 VII. ELIJAH,[6] b. Feb. 23, 1797; m. SARAH A. BENEDICT.
104 VIII. JOSEPH,[6] b. May 9, 1799; m. CLARA LYON. He d. June 23, 1868.
    IX. MELINDA,[6] b. July 22, 1801.

34.

JOSEPH[5] CHURCHILL (SAMUEL,[4] SAMUEL,[3] JOSEPH,[2] JOSIAH[1]). Born in Sheffield, Mass., Feb. 3, 1748 (according to the town records). He settled in his native town and remained there until after the close of the Revolutionary War. In 1783 he removed to Hubbardton, Vt., where his father had settled in 1774/5. He served in the Revolution in Capt. Enoch Noble's Company, from

Sheffield, Oct. 23, 1780, to Nov. 7, 1780, sixteen days. Marched to
Bennington, Vt. Married, Dec. 7, 1773, AMY STYLES, born March
2, 1755. He died March 20, 1821.

Children born in Sheffield.

105   I. AMOS,[6] b. Oct. 1, 1774; m. 1st, NABBA HAVEN; m. 2d, CHLOE
         SMITH.

106   II. WORTHY LOVELL,[6] b. May 13, 1776; m. 1st, RUHAMA WHELPLEY;
         m. 2d, SOPHIA KINGSLEY.

       III. LOVISA,[6] b. March 19, 1779; m. EPHRAIM HENDEE, June, 1802.
         They settled at first in Sudbury, Vt., but about 1810 removed to
         Avon, N.Y.

Children.

1. Hannah Hendee, b. March 12, 1803; m. Jonas Howes, Nov. 7,
   1830.
2. Amy Lovisa Hendee, b. Feb. 18, 1805; m. Hiram Pearson,
   Oct. 23, 1827.
3. Joseph Hendee, b. Nov. 14, 1808; m. Mary Clark, Feb. 28,
   1839.
4. Ruby Hendee, b. 1810; m. Addison Ransom, Nov. 2, 1840.
5. Ephraim Churchill Hendee, b. Jan. 15, 1812; m. Hannah Merrill, March 29, 1839.
6. A. Alonzo Hendee, b. June 16, 1815.

       IV. SYLVIA,[6] b. Aug. 24' 1781; m. THOMAS KETCHAM. They settled
         in Sudbury, Vt.

Children born there.

1. Isaac Ketcham, settled in Sudbury, Vt.
2. Joseph C. Ketcham, settled in Illinois.
3. Allan Ketcham, settled in Whiting.
4. Sarah A. Ketcham.
5. Roxana Ketcham.
6. Eliza Ketcham.
7. Sylvia Ketcham, settled in Hubbardton, Vt.
8. Lucy Ketcham.
9. Thomas Ketcham, a physician.

107   V. CYRUS,[6] b. Feb. 9, 1783; m. RACHEL HUSTLER.

       VI. HULDA,[6] b. Nov. 12, 1785; m. DAVID PEARSON,* of Avon, N.Y.,
         Feb. 11, 1811.
         He was born in the town of Wells, Vt., March 27, 1785. They
         lived on a farm one-half a mile from East Avon.

Children born at East Avon, N. Y.

1. Ruhama Pearson, b. Nov. 30, 1811; m. S. D. Halsey, in Avon,
   Feb. 11, 1835.
   They removed, in 1837, to Grand Blanc, Mich. Of their
   three children, two, viz. : D. P. Halsey and Mrs. S. J. Case, are
   now (1901) living in Flint, Mich. The father and mother died
   in Michigan.
2. Margaret Pearson, b. April 13, 1813; d. Sept. 4, 1865.
3. Adelia Pearson, b. June 30, 1815; m. John Smith, Oct. 2, 1835.
   They had one son who lives in Flint, Mich., and two daughters
   live in Grand Blanc.
4. Anna J. Pearson, b. Oct. 29, 1816; m. John Bainbridge, Oct.
   21, 1847.
   She is a widow and lives in Santa Barbara, Cal.

---

* The sons of David Pearson changed their name to Pierson.

5. Charles Churchill Pearson, b. Jan. 18, 1818; m. Martha A. Dutton, Dec. 19, 1849.
They live in Flint, Mich., and have three sons and three daughters, all married, and five of them living in Flint. All have children, in all sixteen grandchildren. Mr. and Mrs. Pearson celebrated their fiftieth anniversary in 1899, and have a family gathering every Christmas. Mr. Pearson (Pierson) is a produce merchant in Flint, Mich., now (December, 1901) at the age of eighty-four years.
6. Jane L. Pearson, b. Oct. 9, 1819; m. Delgren Lacy, July 3, 1849.
They moved to Seattle in 1875, and died there, leaving one daughter.
7. Mary Pearson, b. May 13, 1821; m. 1st, Dr. F. Drake, Feb. 10, 1859; m. 2d, J. Johnson, 1868.
She died in Flint, Mich., without children.
8. Laura Pearson, b. May 6, 1823; m. Bertrand E. Rust, July 5, 1851.
She is a widow, no children, and lives in Atlas, Mich. (1901).
9. Ephraim Pearson (Pierson), b. Feb. 24, 1825; m. Sarah Merrill, Sept. 27, 1849.
They live in Flint. Mrs. Pierson died in 1900. No children.
10. Andromeda Pearson, b. July 6, 1827; m. E. Day. No children. Both dead.
11. Delos D. Pearson, b. July 6, 1827; m. Philena Douglas, Jan. 1, 1855.
They live in Flint, and have three sons living on farms in Goodrichville, Mich.

108   VII. CHARLES,[6] b. Dec. 10, 1787; m. POLLY HYDE.
      VIII. ROXANA,[6] b. Nov. 19, 1789; d. unmarried December, 1813.
109   IX. DANIEL,[6] b. Jan. 4, 1792; m. 1st, SUBMIT HAWES, in Stafford, N.Y.; m. 2d, MRS. MILLER, in Chillicothe, O. He died July 20, 1833.
110   X. ALVAH,[6] b. May 15, 1794; m. NANCY HOLMES.
111   XI. JOSEPH,[6] b. Sept. 9, 1796; m. POLLY HENNIGAN.
      XII. AMY,[6] b. Oct. 10, 1799; m. ALANSON RICHARDSON.
      They settled in Concord, Erie County, N.Y.

Children.

1. Worthy L. Richardson. | 3. Ruth Richardson.
2. Cyrus Richardson. | 4. Betsey Richardson.

35.

SAMUEL [5] CHURCHILL (SAMUEL,[4] SAMUEL,[3] JOSEPH,[2] JOSIAH [1]). Born in Sheffield, Mass., May 20, 1756. Removed to Hubbardton in the winter of 1785. He died in Hubbardton, in 1797, aged about forty-one years. We have not been able to get an account of this family. Married ANNA CAMP, of Salisbury, Conn.

Children.

112   I. PHILO.[6]
113   II. ZENAS,[6] m. (———) CASTLE. Lived in Attica, N.Y.
114   III. DAVID,[6] b. in Hubbardton, May 29, 1786; m. 1st, name unknown; m. 2d, SARAH PRESCOTT, Feb. 23, 1829.
115   IV. RUFUS,[6] m. (———) STRONG, Alexander, N.Y.
      V. ESTHER,[6] m. MOSES DISBROW, in Vermont.

36.

JOHN[5] CHURCHILL (SAMUEL,[4] SAMUEL,[3] JOSEPH,[2] JOSIAH[1]). Born at Sheffield, March 12, 1758, and lived there until his father's removal to Hubbardton in 1775. We have seen that he was in the battle at that place on July 7, the same year, and was taken prisoner and carried to Ticonderoga where he was kept until October, when he returned to Castleton, Vt., whither his father had returned with his family after Burgoyne's surrender. It is possible that he served later in the war in the company of Capt. Roger Alden, of Lebanon, Conn., Jan. 1 to Dec. 31, 1781. After the war he cleared up his farm in Hubbardton and lived there until 1805, when he removed to Tully, N.Y. Married MARTHA BALDWIN.

Children, all but the youngest born in Hubbardton, Vt.

116   I. JOHN,[6] b. April 13, 1787; m. MARY HOUSE, at Homer, N.Y., 1813.
117   II. SYLVESTER,[6] b. Oct. 7, 1788; m. THEODOSIA HOUSE, at Homer, N.Y., 1816.
     III. ANNICE,[6] b. Oct. 14, 1790; m. CHESTER SHARP.

Children of Chester and Annice (Churchill) Sharp.

1. John W. Sharp. | 2. Mary Sharp. | 3. George E. Sharp.

    IV. ELECTA,[6] b. Dec. 19, 1792; m. CLARK TOWN.
118   V. ALVIN,[6] b. Nov. 7, 1794; m. SALLY SEELY.
    VI. SYLVINA,[6] b. Aug. 25, 1796.
   VII. JOAB,[6] b. Nov. 10, 1798; d. Nov. 4, 1816.
  VIII. SARAH,[6] b. Jan. 4, 1801; m. JOHN BACON, at Spafford, N.Y., 1825. They lived at Scott and later at Spafford, N.Y., and had children born at Scott.

Children.

1. Warren Bacon, b. 1826; d. in 1852.
2. David Bacon, b. June 13, 1828; m. 1st, Ruth House, Westfield, N.Y., 1855. She d. 1894; m. 2d, Jessie Follansbee, Hot Springs, Ark., 1897.
3. Almon Bacon, b. April 25, 1830; m. Harriet Tripp.
   He was a graduate of Rochester Seminary, founded Baptist Seminary for educating Indians in the Indian Territory at Muscogee, and was a professor there twenty years.
4. Irena Bacon, b. 1835; d. at the age of two years.
5. Philena Bacon, b. 1835; m. Isaac Gilson, at Petoskey, Mich.; d. March, 1900.
6. Harrison Bacon, b. 1842; m. Frances Churchill, of Spafford, 1874.

    IX. IRENA,[6] b. Oct. 8, 1802; m. LUCIUS VAIL.
119   X. JOTHAM,[6] b. Dec. 29, 1804; m. (———) RANDELL.
120   XI. CHAUNCEY,[6] b. at Tully, N.Y., Oct. 3, 1808; m. CATHARINE MERRY, March 17, 1834.

38.

WILLIAM[5] CHURCHILL (SAMUEL,[4] SAMUEL,[3] JOSEPH,[2] JOSIAH[1]). Born in Sheffield, Mass., Feb. 10, 1763. Settled first in Hubbardton, Vt.; about 1806 removed to Champlain, N.Y. He was with his mother in the battle at Hubbardton.   Married, March 26, 1787, EUNICE CULVER, born Dec. 31, 1762.

Children.

  I. RUSSELL,[6] b. Dec. 21, 1787; d. in youth.
  II. CLARISSA,[6] b. Sept. 28, 1789; m. (———) PHILLIPS, of Chazy, N.Y.
  III. PAMELIA,[6] b. Oct. 2, 1791; m. (———) NORTH, of Champlain, N.Y.
121 IV. DARIUS,[6] b. April 25, 1793; m. TRYPHENIA ADELINE NEWTON.
122 V. WILLIAM, JR.,[6] b. March 23, 1795; m. ISABELLA JOHNSON, Dec. 24, 1822.
123 VI. SAMUEL,[6] b. Aug. 2, 1797; d. in New Orleans, in 1820.
124 VII. EZEKIEL,[6] b. July 15, 1799.
125 VIII. JULIUS,[6] b. March 20, 1802; m. NANCY FILMORE.
126 IX. JAMES,[6] b. Nov. 9, 1804; m. ELIZA JOHNSON.
  X. EUNICE,[6] b. May 20, 1807.

·39.

EZEKIEL[5] CHURCHILL (SAMUEL,[4] SAMUEL,[3] JOSEPH,[2] JOSIAH[1]). Born June 24, 1764, in Sheffield, Mass. Settled in Hubbardton, Vt., until about 1704, when he removed to Alexander, N.Y. He was a farmer. He died Feb. 12, 1813. Married, 1786 ELIZABETH DYER. She was born Aug. 30, 1766, and died Oct. 25, 1843.

Children.

  I. INFANT CHILD,[6] b. Jan. 30, 1787; d. same day.
127 II. EZEKIEL,[6] b. Dec. 27, 1787; m. HANNAH BAKER, April 5, 1810.
  III. SARAH,[6] b. March 24, 1790; m. ELIAS PERSONS, March 5, 1807. She died Dec. 17, 1825.

Children.

1. Hanson Persons.	6. Elias Persons.
2. Leverett W. Persons.	7. Sally Persons.
3. Charlotte Persons.	8. Almaria Persons.
4. Franklin Persons.	9. Columbus Persons.
5. Eunice Persons.	10. Lucinda Persons.

 IV EUNICE,[6] b. Feb. 24, 1792; m. THOMAS DEMARY, of New Hampshire, Oct. 12, 1817.

Children.

  1. Josiah Newton Demary, d. unmarried.
  2. Diantha Demary, d. young.
  3. Nancy B. Demary, b. June 5, 1822; m. Harry Cooley.
  4. Lurany Demary, b. May 27, 1824; m. Hanford A. Conger.
  5. Almaria Demary, b. Feb. 27, 1827; m. Jonas Ellis.
  6. Adaline Demary, b. June 1, 1829; m. Mortimer Wadsworth.
  7. Olivia Demary, d. young.
  8. Mary Ann Demary, m. Leonard Demary.

 V. DIANTHA,[6] b. Nov. 14, 1793; m. GEN. JOSIAH NEWTON, Feb. 14, 1811.

Children.

  1. Arabella Newton, m. (———) Moore, of Rochester, N.Y.
  2. Earl Newton, d. unmarried.
  3. Danforth Newton.

VI. A CHILD,⁶ b. July 24, 179̃5; d. same day.
128 VII. SILAS,⁶ b. June 13, 1796; m. ESTHER PARMELEE.
VIII. PRUDENCE,⁶ b. May 21, 1798; d. Aug. 14, 1814.
IX. WEALTHY,⁶ b. May 1, 1800; m. JEREMIAH BALDWIN.

Children.

1. Harriet Baldwin, m. (――――) Cooley.
2. Gilman Baldwin.
3. Henry Baldwin.

X. LEVI,⁶ b. Sept. 11, 1802; d. July 25, 1803.
129 XI. LEVI WILLIAM,⁶ b. May 10, 1804; m. SOPHRONIA FRISBEE, November, 1824.
XII. HENRY,⁶ b. Aug. 12, 1806; d. Feb. 12, 1813.
XIII. HARRIET CORDELIA,⁶ b. Sept. 2, 1808; m. WILLIAM DANIELS, November, 1834.

Children.

1. Elizabeth Daniels.	5. John T. Daniels.
2. Almaria Daniels.	6. Henry A. Daniels.
3. Caroline Daniels.	7. Frances Daniels.
4. Evelene Daniels.	

130 XIV. CULLEN DYER,⁶ b. March 1, 1811; m. CAROLINE BROWN, Feb. 25, 1836.
131 XV. EZEKIEL HENRY,⁶ b. June 29, 1813; m. CAROLINE H. COGSWELL, Nov. 23, 1837.

40.

LEVI⁵ CHURCHILL (CHARLES,⁴ SAMUEL,³ JOSEPH,² JOSIAH¹). Born at Wethersfield, Conn., May 28, 1752. He lived at Newington until 1802, when he removed with his family to Booneville, N.Y., where he settled. He died Feb. 12, 1836. Married 1st, Oct. 30, 1771, ELIZABETH HURLBUT, daughter of Joseph; married 2d, RUTH MERRILLS.

Children of First Wife, born at Newington.

I. ELIZABETH,⁶ b. June 27, 1773; m. LEONARD HUBBARD, Feb. 18, 1799, as his first wife, and had one child, Abigail Deming Hubbard.
II. LYDIA,⁶ b. July 14, 1776; m. MR. SMITH.
132 III. NOBLE,⁶ b. Nov. 11, 1779; m. OLIVE STODDARD, Oct. 12, 1801.

Children of Second Wife.

133 IV. CHARLES BELDEN,⁶ b. Sept. 27, 1785; m. ELIZABETH HUBBARD, Feb. 4, 1807.
V. OCTAVIA,⁶ b. Dec. 14, 1786; m. JOSIAH B. CHURCHILL (No. 141).
VI. CALVIN,⁶ b. Dec. 14, 1786.
VII. SILAS,⁶ b. Sept. 9, 1790.
134 VIII. CAROLUS,⁶ bapt. in Newington, Jan. 5, 1800; d. in Galesburg, Ill.
135 IX. BENJAMIN,⁶ b. May 3, 1792.
X. HANNAH.⁶
XI. SOPHIA.⁶
XII. MARY.⁶

41.

CHARLES⁵ CHURCHILL (CHARLES,⁴ SAMUEL,³ JOSEPH,² JOSIAH¹). Born in Newington, Conn., May 3, 1755. Lived near Newbern, N.C., at Chappell Hill. He died Sept. 16, 1818. The family later removed to New Orleans, La. Married a Southern woman, name not obtained.

Children.

136   I. CHAPPELL McCLURE,[6] b. in Newbern, N.C.
137   II. CLAUDIUS BELDEN,[6] m. LOUISIANA HOLLIDAY
       III. CLINTON GREENE.[6]
        IV. CONSTANTINE WOODS.[6]
138   V. CRISPEN OSBORNE.[6]
        VI. CLEOPAS WASHINGTON.[6]

42.

SAMUEL[5] CHURCHILL (CHARLES,[4] SAMUEL,[3] JOSEPH,[2] JOSIAH[1]). Born in Newington, April 5, 1757, and died there Dec. 10, 1834. He was a farmer, and lived across the road from his father's, in a house built for him by his father. He was a man eminent for his piety, with which, perhaps, was mingled a sense of quiet humor; for instance, it is said that he was accustomed to read oftener than any other the Psalm which reiterates " For his mercy endureth forever," Mercy being the name of his wife. Married, July 16, 1778, MERCY BOARDMAN, daughter of Jonathan and Martha (Hurlbut) Boardman, born in Rocky Hill, Conn., Aug. 2, 1757, and died Jan. 24, 1834.

Children.

139   I. CHISLIEU,[6] b. Dec. 4, 1779; m. CELINDA HURLBUT, March 31, 1806.
        II. *MARY ANN,[6] b. Aug. 25, 1782; d. unmarried Feb. 18, 1848.
140   III. JOHN,[6] b. April 11, 1785; m. LAURA WELLS, Sept. 9, 1811. He died Sept. 17, 1823.
141   IV. JOSIAH B.,[6] b. Aug. 29, 1787; m. 1st, OCTAVIA CHURCHILL (see No. 41); m. 2d, PHEBE MARIA THOMPSON.
142   V. CHARLES,[6] b. Sept. 12, 1790; m. MATILDA JOHNSON.
        VI. *MERCY,[6] b. Nov. 10, 1792; d. unmarried May 7, 1866, aged seventy-three.
       VII. SAMUEL,[6] b. Nov. 10, 1792; d. in infancy.
      VIII. *CHARLOTTE,[6] b. Dec. 3, 1795; d. unmarried April 7, 1864, aged sixty-nine.
        IX. *HARRIET,[6] b. Feb. 12, 1798; d. unmarried July 12, 1825.
         X. *LUCY,[6] b. Feb. 6, 1801; d. unmarried March 30, 1883, aged eighty-two years.

43.

SOLOMON[5] CHURCHILL (CHARLES,[4] SAMUEL,[3] JOSEPH,[2] JOSIAH[1]). Born in Newington, July 29, 1764, and spent his life there. He was a farmer, a man of excellent character and standing in the community. Though he did not make profession of religion until late in life, he was of undoubted piety and especially strict in

---

* These sisters formed a quintet of maiden ladies who lived and died on their father's homestead. Of the number Charlotte is said to have been in every way the most accomplished. She was what the people in her day called a " dressy " person, and seems to have been a woman of unusual charm and good breeding. Lucy, the youngest, lived on alone at the old home, with " no one to lean on," as she was accustomed to say.

his regard for the Sabbath. It is said that he forbade even "the cracking of nuts" on the Lord's day, and a grove of butternut trees near his house gives a touch of probability to the tradition. With him regular attendance on divine worship was one of the chief concerns of life, and he would face the fiercest snow-storms of the winter, which blocked in even good Parson Belden, who, on one occasion, discovered Mr. Churchill in front of the parsonage on horseback, floundering in the snow-drifts, and shouted the question, "Where are you going, Mr. Churchill?" "To meeting," replied the sturdy parishioner. "Well, come in here, then," answered the parson, "as I am not going out in this storm." His grandson, Leonard Churchill Hubbard, in 1903, describes him thus, as he appeared about 1820 : "He was of medium height, a rather stocky-looking man, round face, kind-spoken, and jovial for one of his years." He died June 16, 1842. Married 1st, Oct. 28, 1789, LUCRETIA MARSH, daughter of Job, of New Hartford. She died, Nov. 2, 1811, aged forty-eight years, and he married 2d, CHLOE DEMING, a maiden lady of fifty years.

Children of Solomon and Lucretia (Marsh) Churchill.

1. JULIA,[6] b. May 31, 1792; d. unmarried, Sept. 16, 1822.

This woman deserves more than the notice of birth and death. In the family she was long ago canonized as its saint. Every family tradition testifies to her pure piety and her fortitude in affliction, as she was a life-long invalid. Her voluminous journal, running through many years, records her gentle and pious character. It holds little except her account of the sermons, heard from Sunday to Sunday, and her own religious experiences. Some valuable references occur here and there, like her statement as to the beginning of the Newington Sunday-school, on June 20, 1819, at which time she writes: "Attended church in the daytime and in the evening. This day hath been solemn. A Sabbath-school was established in this place. Four little children were committed to my care to instruct on the Sabbath. O Lord, help me to do my duty toward them, and wilt thou touch their young and tender minds by the influences of thy Spirit!" In August, the same year, she writes that her class has increased to seven, and notes in her prayer that they are only four and five years old. Nov. 4, 1819, she writes: "The Sunday-school is now out, and this day the scholars received their premiums. I commit my little class to thee, O Lord. Bless them, I pray thee, O Lord; prepare them for Heaven."

These brief extracts, Mr. Seymour says, are a fair sample of the journal of this devout and devoted woman and illustrate the spirit which animated her, and probably the other founders of the Sunday-school. She has been described as "fervently prayerful." She also wrote verses addressed to different members of the family, and elegies lamenting the death of local worthies. The making of verses, indeed, seems to have been characteristic of the Newington Churchills of this generation, and, apparently, was one of the few diversions allowed by the stern Calvinism of the times. A pamphlet of the semi-centennial celebration of the Wethersfield and Berlin Sunday-school Union states that, "The Sunday-school in Newington, in its beginning, was the voluntary enterprise of some young ladies of the church."

II. NANCY,[6] b. March 17, 1795; m. LEONARD CHESTER HUBBARD, of
Newington, April 23, 1826. Mr. Hubbard was the son of Timothy and Abigail (Deming) Hubbard, born May 9, 1793, and
died Sept. 20, 1838. For his first wife he married Elizabeth
Churchill, daughter of Deacon Levi, whose only child died
young. Nancy, the second wife, was a person of very strong
individuality. After her mother's death she was forced to assume the chief duties of the household, her older sister, Julia,
being an invalid, until the time of her marriage. Mr. Seymour,
to whom we are indebted for most of the biographical matter relating to the family of Capt. Charles Churchill, says that "she
was a woman of great decision of character, brought up her
family in the fear of God, and lived to great age. In her later
years she was tenderly cared for by her family, but she never re-
linquished her authority, nor gave up the strict Sabbath day observance to which she had been bred in her father's household." He
describes her as having "jet black eyes and hair and unusually
white skin." He recalls one Sabbath he passed in the home of her
son Leonard, with whom she was living, and well remembers the
austere character of the day, all secular conversation being
avoided, and the reading of the Bible occupying the chief attention. She seemed to him like an ancient prophetess.
They lived at Newington until after the birth of their children,
when they removed to Berlin.

Children born at Newington.

1. Leonard Churchill Hubbard, b. Jan. 15, 1828; m. Mary J. Arnold, at Berlin, Oct. 6, 1859.
Mr. Hubbard was educated at Wesleyan Academy, Wilbraham,
Mass. Lived at Berlin, Conn., a farmer. Sometime deacon
of the Congregational Church at Berlin.

Children.

(1) Leonard Clarence Hubbard, b. Jan. 24, 1865, m. Louisa
Junge, of New York, March 19, 1898; (2) Eleanor Arnold Hubbard, b. March 1, 1870.

2. Kasson Hubbard, b. Dec. 6, 1831; d. April 6, 1834.
3. Elizabeth Hubbard, b. Jan. 25, 1835; m. Henry Francis, Dec.
6, 1855.
They lived at New Britain, Conn., and had children.

Children.

(1) James H. Francis, b. Nov. 1, 1860; (2) Grace E. Francis, b. April 9, 1862; m. John D. Garvie, of New Britain.

4. Abigail Hubbard, b. Oct. 31, 1837; d. at New Britain, April 20,
1898.

143   III. CHESTER,[6] b. May 6, 1798; m. LUCRETIA OLMSTED, Aug. 24,
1826.
IV. CYNTHIA,[6] b. Oct. 30, 1801; m. CYRUS WEBSTER, of Newington,
Nov. 22, 1822. They settled at first at Newington, where their
children were born, but later removed to Berlin, where he was a
farmer. She died at Berlin, May 11, 1869.

Children of Cyrus and Cynthia (Churchill) Webster.

1. Chester Churchill Webster, b. Nov. 10, 1825; m. Marilla Richards, and had children.

Children.

(1) David C. Webster, (2) Oliver Webster, (3) Charles Webster, (4) Nellie Webster.

2. Chauncy Webster, b. May 26, 1828; m. Mary Johnson, 1853, at Canton, Ill.
3. Charles Selah Webster, b. Nov. 22, 1834; m. Julia S. Higgins, Oct. 12, 1853.

Children.

(1) Harriet Churchill Webster, b. at Berlin, March 20, 1870; m. Hon. Frank L. Wilcox, of Berlin. Jan. 19, 1898; (2) Cyrus Webster, b. Sept. 3, 1874; d. at Berlin, Sept. 5, 1891.

V   JEMIMA,[6] b. Nov. 19, 1805, and died unmarried, at New Britain, June 9, 1899, while on a visit to her niece, Mrs. Francis. She was born in the "Great House" built by her grandfather, Capt. Charles Churchill, and had many stories of the old days. She lived a useful life spent mostly in the families of her sisters. Mr. Seymour remembers her as "a very smart" old lady, erect in carriage, prim without severity, scrupulous as to the details of her old-fashioned dress, and pleasant-spoken. Like her father, she set great store on divine worship, and rarely failed to go to meeting to the end of her days.

44.

REV. SILAS[5] .CHURCHILL (CHARLES,[4] SAMUEL,[3] JOSEPH,[2] JOSIAH[1]). Born in Newington, Conn., April 5, 1769. Graduated at Yale College in the class of 1787, studied theology with his father-in-law to be, and settled in the ministry in the Presbyterian church in New Lebanon, N.Y. He served in this, his only pastorate, faithfully for almost fifty years. He died in New Lebanon, March 1, 1854. Married 1st, Oct. 12, 1797, RHODA BELDEN, daughter of Rev. Joshua, of Newington. She was born May 29, 1766, and died May 28, 1823. He married 2d, SARAH SARGENT, 1825.

Children of First Wife, born in New Lebanon, N.Y.

　I. JOSHUA BELDEN,[6] b. Nov. 2, 1798. He was a farmer in Oregon; d. there, unmarried, 1874.
144　II. SILAS,[6] b. June 5, 1800; m. 1st, CLARISSA AVERY, Oct. 27, 1825; m. 2d, CORNELIA S. LYNDES, Oct. 27, 1836.
　III. CLARISSA,[6] b. May 2, 1802; died aged four years.
　IV. MARY ANN,[6] b. 1804; unmarried.
　V. RHODA,[6] b. 1806; m. REV. E. A. BEACH.
145　VI. CHARLES,[6] b. Sept. 2, 1808.

Children of Second Wife.

　VII. SARAH,[6] b. May, 1829.
　VIII. JOHN,[6] b. 1832.

46.

REV. JESSE[5] CHURCHILL (JESSE,[4] SAMUEL,[3] JOSEPH,[2] JOSIAH[1]). Born in Wethersfield, Conn., March 18, 1757. The tradition in the family is that, at the outbreak of the Revolution, he tried to enlist, but was rejected at first on account of his boyish appearance, but he succeeded later, and served in the company of Capt. Jonathan Hale, of Glastonbury, and was stationed at Boston January to March, 1776. He reënlisted in the company of Captain

Welles, and served in New York. His regiment was at the battles of Long Island and White Plains. He evidently acquired a fair education, and perhaps became a teacher in the succeeding years. After his first marriage he settled for a time in Glastonbury, where his first child was born. About 1790 he removed to Hubbardton and occupied the farm which his father had taken up in 1775, but had abandoned when Vermont became involved in the border warfare. He lived for some years in the old log-house built by his father. On this old homestead his seven children by the first wife were born, and here she died, leaving him with a family of seven children. Mr. Churchill then fitted himself for the ministry. It is said that he studied at Andover Theological School, and by his Church Covenant, dated at Andover, June 2, 1784, now in possession of a grandson, J. W. Hull, of Pittsfield, it seems that he was then a student. He probably took a special course. His son Norman writes us, in 1885: "After the death of my mother my father took an abbreviated course in theology, was ordained in 1807, and began to preach as a Congregational minister." He removed to Litchfield, N.Y., the same year. He was settled awhile at New Lebanon, N.Y.

He was chaplain of the Twenty-seventh Regiment, New York militia, from 1810 to 1822, and served in the War of 1812, under Colonel Bellinger, in the Black River campaign, his son Norman going with him as his waiter. His last pastorate was at Winfield, N.Y. He died at Morrisville, N.Y., Sept. 29, 1828, and was buried at Winfield.

He married 1st, in Wethersfield, Nov. 2, 1786, HANNAH BOARDMAN, daughter of Charles and Abigail (Stillman) Boardman. She died at Hubbardton, Dec. 10, 1804. Married 2d, Aug. 28, 1807, OLIVE TILDEN, daughter of John, and sister of Elam Tilden, the father of Samuel J. Tilden, the Democratic presidential candidate of 1876. Married 3d, March 23, 1823, MRS. ANNA EGGLESTON, in Batavia, N.Y. She was a widow with a family of children, one of whom Norman Churchill married.

Children of Rev. Jesse Churchill and First Wife, first two born at Glastonbury, the others at Hubbardton.

I.   ELIZABETH,[6] b. Dec. 1, 1787; m. ELIJAH WOODRUFF, son of Elijah, b. at Farmington, Conn., Sept. 9, 1778. Married at Winfield, N.Y., Feb. 21, 1817. Lived at Sheldon, N.Y. He was a farmer, and died Feb. 28, 1828. She died at Buffalo, N.Y., March 22, 1848.

Children of Elijah and Elizabeth (Churchill) Woodruff, born in Sheldon, N. Y.

1. Mary Woodruff, b. Nov. 23, 1817; m. Benjamin Zimmermann, May 27, 1840, and lived in Grinnell, Iowa.
2. Almira Woodruff, b. June 15, 1822; d. unmarried, at Tabor, Iowa, Oct. 22, 1897.
3. Aurelia Stillman Woodruff, b. Feb. 1, 1825; m. John Hallam, at Tabor, Iowa.

4. Corinna Woodruff, b. Aug. 25, 1827; m. Charles Hobart, at
   Buffalo, Oct. 22, 1845. Lived at Sterling, Ill.
   They have four children: (1) Charles W. Hobart, (2) George
   C. Hobart, (3) Henry M. Hobart, (4) Mary Hobart.

[I. GEORGE,[6] b. Oct. 11, 1789. Never married. He died at Troy, Ill.,
   Aug. 11, 1872. He was brought up on the old farm in Hubbardton, and received the common school education in his native town.
   On the removal of his father's family to New York State, he
   went to Albany, and became an apprentice in a printing office,
   served his time, and then worked as a journeyman printer until
   he was able to purchase a half interest in a small printing office,
   which he soon after sold out, and started West. He obtained a
   situation in Louisville, Ky., in the " Courier " office, and worked
   there a while, and, in 1817, located in St. Louis, Mo., and being
   attracted by the fertile lands of Illinois, bought a tract of land a
   few miles southeast of Edwardsville, in that State, where he
   lived the remainder of his life. In order to raise money for the
   improvement of his farm, he worked at his trade in the office of
   the " Missouri Gazette," in St. Louis. While connected with
   that paper he wrote a series of articles, advocating the admission
   of Missouri as a free State. He assisted in establishing a
   newspaper, in Edwardsville, " The Spectator," and was a constant contributor to its columns, especially in 1822–1824, while
   the contest was on to make Illinois a slave State. In the final
   defeat of this attempt he bore a prominent part. He was elected
   to the General Assembly of Illinois in 1822, and was reëlected
   in 1824, showing that the people approved his course. He served
   by reëlection till 1832, and in the Senate in 1838, and again in the
   House in 1844, serving in all sixteen years. He was well
   versed in the English language and literature. A diligent collector of historical documents.

III. GILES,[6] b. Dec. 26, 1791, at Hubbardton, Vt. He removed to the
   West, and taught school; and, about 1817, went South to New
   Orleans, it is said. No account of his subsequent career has come
   to us.

147   IV. WILLIAM BOARDMAN,[6] b. March 4, 1794; m. 1st, ALMIRA HUMES;
   m. 2d, MRS. JANE (——) KINGSTON; m. 3d, MRS. LURA (HILL)
   ROBERTS.

   V. POLLY,[6] b. April 12, 1796; m. LEWIS WEEKS, at Litchfield, N.Y.,
   by her father, Rev. Jesse Churchill, Feb. 1, 1816. Mr. Weeks
   was born Aug. 7, 1790. They lived at Shelden, N.Y., where
   seven of their children were born; but before 1835 removed
   West, and settled at Ridge Prairie, Ill. She died at Afton, Iowa,
   Nov. 28, 1881. He died at Galesburg, Ill., Nov. 10' 1864.

Children of Lewis and Polly (Churchill) Weeks.

1. George Churchill Weeks, b. Sept. 13, 1817; d. at Ridge Prairie,
   Ill., Aug. 9, 1835.
2. Hannah Amelia Weeks, b. Nov. 5, 1819; m. James R. Perrigo,
   Jan. 26, 1842.
3. Horace Belknap Weeks, b. March 14, 1822; m. 1st, Diadema
   (Hyde) Sharman; m. 2d, Mary A. Daniels, September, 1856.
4. William Wallace Weeks, b. June 11, 1823; m. Ruth Vaughn,
   Jan. 25, 1848.
5. John Lewis Weeks, b. Sept. 14, 1827; m. Emily Finch, Galesburg, Sept. 7, 1849; d. Oct. 31, 1849.
6. Charles Boardman Weeks, b. Jan. 29, 1830; m. Elizabeth J.
   Alexander, Oct. 1, 1860.
7. Mary Churchill Weeks, b. May 13, 1832; m. Jonathan C. Gar-
   wood, Oct. 18, 1852.
8. Cyrus Edward Weeks, b. at Ridge Prairie, Ill., Feb. 4, 1836; d.
   Aug. 26, 1838.

148   VI. NORMAN,[6] b. Nov. 5, 1799; m. ANNA EGGLESTON, in Batavia, N.Y.
        VII. LEVI GAYLORD,[6] b. July 28, 1802; d. unmarried, in Troy, Ill., Dec.
             3, 1851. He is buried at Collinsville, Ill.

Child of the Second Wife, Olive (Tilden) Churchill.

        VIII. LUCENA ANN,[6] b. at New Lebanon, N.Y., Jan. 31, 1809; m.
              CHARLES WILLIAMS HULL, Sept. 10, 1834. He was the son of
              Jeremiah and Keturah (Williams) Hull, b. at Stonington, Conn.,
              Dec. 3, 1798. They were married at New Lebanon, N.Y., by
              Rev. Silas Churchill. After her father's death, Lucena was taken
              to live with her uncle, Elam Tilden, until her marriage. She d.
              April 5, 1890.

*Children of Charles Williams and Lucena Ann (Churchill) Hull, born at New
Lebanon, N.Y.*

        1. Charles Williams Hull, b. Aug. 5, 1836; m. Julia Tubbs, at
           Brattleboro, Vt., Oct. 3, 1869.
        2. George Frederick Hull, b. June 14, 1838; m. Amy Doty, of
           Hancock, Mass., Oct. 16, 1862.
        3. Edwin Augustus Hull, b. March 3, 1840. Soldier in Civil War,
           Company B, Forty-fourth Regiment, N.Y. Volunteers. Died
           at Alexandria, Va., July 25, 1862. Unmarried.
        4. James Wells Hull, b. Sept. 20, 1842; m. Helen Edwards
           Plunkett, Pittsfield, Mass., in 1876.
           They live in Pittsfield, Mass., where he is secretary of Berk-
           shire Life Insurance Company. Member of Massachusetts
           Board of Health from 1893. They have five children, born in
           Pittsfield: (1) Helen Edwards Hull, b. Nov. 3, 1877; (2) Rosa-
           mond Hull, b. April 29, 1879; (3) Norman Churchill Hull, b.
           Aug. 5, 1881; (4) Edward Boltwood Hull, b. Feb. 3, 1884; (5)
           Carolyn Kellogg Hull, b. Sept. 19, 1891.
        5. Henrietta Tilden Hull, b. Oct. 8, 1846; d. at New Lebanon,
           April 25, 1848.
        6. Anna Lucena Hull, b. Sept. 14, 1848; unmarried.

47.

LEVI[5] CHURCHILL (JESSE,[4] SAMUEL,[3] JOSEPH,[2] JOSIAH[1]).
Born at Newington, Dec. 15, 1759. Lived at Wethersfield. Married, Jan. 5, 1785, HANNAH BELDEN.

Children born at Wethersfield.

          I. JERUSHA GAYLORD,[6] b. April 7, 1786; d. unmarried July 1, 1849.
         II. SAMUEL,[6] b. Jan. 3, 1788; d. Feb. 17, 1791.
149   III. SIMEON,[6] b. Jan. 3, 1788; m. ANNA COLEMAN.
         IV. MABEL,[6] b. Jan. 9, 1790; d. unmarried, 1879.
          V. REBECCA,[6] b. Oct. 4, 1792; d. unmarried, Sept. 16, 1865.
         VI. ELIZABETH,[6] b. Jan. 29, 1795; m. JACOB GRISWOLD, January, 1818.
150   VII. LEVI BELDEN,[6] b. March 24, 1797; m. ABIGAIL GRISWOLD, June
              27, 1816.
        VIII. SALLY,[6] b. Oct. 14, 1799; m. SAMUEL COLEMAN.
          IX. HANNAH BELDEN,[6] b. July 17, 1805; m. CAPT. JOHN HANMER, Jan.
              14, 1833. Captain Hanmer was born in Wethersfield, Feb. 11,
              1801.

Additional Note on Rev. Jesse Churchill. — Our authority for statements above
are letters of Norman Churchill, of Galesburg, Ill., his son; letters from
Professor Comstock, of Galesburg, Ill.; Mrs. Lucena A. (Churchill) Hull,
his youngest daughter, in the application of James W. Hull, her son, for
membership in the Sons of the American Revolution, in 1889; Conn. Hist. Society Collections, Vol. 8, p. 137; "Connecticut Men in the Revolution," p. 385;
Military Minutes of Council of Appointment of New York. In 1814 his regiment
was stationed at Fort Pike, near Sackett's Harbor.

Children of Capt. John and Hannah Belden (Churchill) Hanmer.

1. Caleb J. Hanmer, b. Nov. 25, 1833; m. Ellen N. Dix, May 3,
   1859.
   Children: (1) Lizzie Hanmer, b. Aug. 16, 1860; d. March
   26, 1863. (2) Nellie N. Hanmer, b. Sept. 2, 1862; m. Eugene
   Kendall, May 26, 1887. (3) Frederick C. Hanmer, b. Oct. 24,
   1864; m. Nellie T. Ridgeway, Oct. 25, 1892. (4) Gertrude M.
   Hanmer, b. June 13, 1870; m. John L. Way, Oct. 15, 1891.
2. Elizabeth Hanmer, b. Oct. 18, 1835; unmarried.
3. Mary Ann Hanmer, b. Aug. 8, 1837; m. Elijah Stillman Goodrich, Oct. 9, 1859.
   Children: (1) James Raymond Goodrich, b. Aug. 20, 1860;
   m. Lizzie Horton Judd, Feb. 4, 1897, and had two children,
   James Stillman and William Judd. (2) Mabel Edith Goodrich,
   b. May 3, 1867; m. George Hills Gilman, of Hartford, April
   20, 1898.
4. Charles Henry Hanmer, b. Oct. 18, 1839; m. Clara E. Way, of
   Gilead, Conn., November, 1865.
   Children: (1) Alfred Wells Hanmer, b. May 13, 1867; m.
   Nellie E. Talcott, Sept. 10, 1890. (2) Charles Henry Hanmer,
   b. Nov. 5, 1869; m. Lila Case. (3) John Way Hanmer, b.
   Nov. 26, 1872; d. February, 1896. (4) Edward Shaw Hanmer,
   b. Feb. 21, 1876. (5) William Ellis Hanmer, b. Oct. 7, 1879..
5. Felicia Hemans Hanmer, b. Sept. 6, 1842; m. Dudley Wells,
   Oct. 15, 1862.
   Children: (1) Mary Anna Wells, b. Oct. 9, 1865; m. Hosmer
   B. Redfield, June 13, 1888. (2) Hannah Churchill Wells, b.
   April 11, 1868. (3) Gideon Wells, b. April 4, 1871; m. Adah
   Adams, Oct. 27, 1897. (4) James Dudley Wells, b. May 3,
   1875.
6. John Hanmer, b. May 16, 1849; m. Fannie R. Buckley, Jan.
   28, 1874.
   Children: (1) Alice Elizabeth Hanmer, b. Nov. 6, 1874; (2)
   Fannie Buckley Hanmer, and (3) Mary Goodrich Hanmer,
   twins, b. Oct. 6, 1878.

48.

ITHAMAR [5] CHURCHILL (JESSE,[4] SAMUEL,[3] JOSEPH,[2] JOSIAH [1]).
Born at Newington, Nov. 1, 1772. About 1793 he removed to Hubbardton and occupied the house and lot which had been abandoned
by his brother Samuel. He removed to Pennsylvania about 1818.
He died Sept. 24, 1852. Married, Sept. 12, 1797, SARAH BLINN,
born May 12, 1774, and died Aug. 17, 1831·

Children born in Hubbardton, Vt

151   I. JAMES,[6] b. Aug. 17, 1798; m. PHEBE MARVIN, April 3, 1828.
      II. HARRIET,[6] b. July 7, 1801; m. JOHN PELL, 1821.
152   III. HORACE,[6] b. Oct. 20, 1806; m. REBECCA BROWN.
153   IV. LORENZO,[6] b. Dec. 6, 1809; m. NANCY M. WRIGHT.
       V. LAURA,[6] b. March 9, 1812; unmarried. In January, 1889, she was
          living in the family of her nephew, Almond, in Woonsocket,
          Dakota.
154   VI. LEVI B.,[6] b. Nov. 26, 1816; m. LOUISA NORTHRUP, May 26, 1842.

50.

ASAHEL [5] CHURCHILL (BENJAMIN,[4] SAMUEL,[3] JOSEPH,[2]
JOSIAH [1]). Born May 1, 1754. He died Dec. 25, 1839. Married,

at Southington, Conn., Nov. 12, 1778, EUNICE PINEY, who was born June 25, 1750, and died Oct. 18, 1839.

Children.

155   I. ISAAC,[6] b. Sept. 8, 1779; married, but name of wife not obtained.
        II. ABEL K.,[6] b. April 22, 1781; d. Oct. 18, 1805.
       III. ASAHEL,[6] b. June 21, 1783.
156   IV. IRA,[6] b. May 27, 1785; m. SARAH HYDE, at Whitestown, N.Y., June 6, 1809.
         V. SALMON,[6] b. March 1, 1787; d. April 14, 1811.
157   VI. BENJAMIN,[6] b. Dec. 11, 1789. He was last heard of in 1858, in Newbern, N.C.
       VII. OREN,[6] b. July 8, 1791; m. BETSEY COREY.
            They lived at Pierpont, O., where he died April 14, 1871, and she in 1869. No children.
      VIII. JONATHAN,[6] b. Nov. 9, 1793; d. March 9, 1814..
        IX. LYDIA,[6] b. Oct. 7, 1796; m. ALPHEUS WILSON.
            They lived at Watertown, N.Y., and had the following children born there:

Children.

            1. Rich B. Wilson, b. Nov. 22, 1822; m. Lucy A. Collins, March 13, 1850, and had children.
               Children: (1) May E. Wilson, b. May 13, 1854; d. Nov. 9, 1860. (2) John R. Wilson, b. Sept. 5, 1857. (3) Norah M. Wilson, b. June 8, 1866; m. George Goutremont, May 14, 1893.
            . Joel Wilson, b. May 18, 1825; d. young.
            . Huldah Wilson, b. July 13, 1827.
            ♀. Buckley Wilson, b. July 29, 1830; m. Mary Barney. He d. July 31, 1893
158   X. ELISHA,[6] b. Aug. 16, 1798.
        XI. POLLY,[6] b. Sept. 25, 1800.

52.

SAMUEL[5] CHURCHILL (BENJAMIN,[4] SAMUEL[3] JOSEPH,[2] JOSIAH[1]). Born at Bristol, Conn., Aug. 7, 1761, and died in Moreau, N.Y., March 26, 1817. He removed sometime before 1800, it is said, to Moreau, N.Y., where he afterwards lived. Married, Feb. 22, 1787, HANNAH BARNES, who was born March 4, 1765, and after Mr. Churchill's death married a Mr. Hamlin, and lived at Glenn's Falls, N.Y.

Children of Samuel and Hannah (Barnes) Churchill, born, five at Bristol and the others at Moreau.

159   I. CHESTER,[6] b. Feb. 22, 1788; m. MERCY CARL.
        II. NANCY,[6] b. Sept. 14, 1790; m. GEORGE SHOEMAKER, at Moreau, N.Y., Jan. 9, 1814.
            They lived in Moreau till about 1820, when they moved to Greenfield, N.Y. He died April 8, 1838, and she died April 23, 1868.

Their Children, the first three born in Moreau, the rest in Greenfield.

            1. Walter Shoemaker, b. Nov. 2, 1814; m. Nellie B. Crandel, Jan. 2, 1837.
               They had two children: (1) George E. Shoemaker, m. Mary

Williams, and (2) Jennie L. Shoemaker, m. Mr. Ellis, of
Boston.

2. George Shoemaker, Jr., b. Jan. 13, 1817; d. unmarried, July
19, 1842.

3. Ann Eliza Shoemaker, b. March 13, 1819; m. Robert Gillis,
Jan. 2, 1840. They had children.
Children: (1) George H. Gillis, (2) Harriet Gillis, (3) John
R. Gillis, (4) a daughter, d. young.

4. Hiram Shoemaker, b. April 7, 1822; m. Mary E. Ford, at
Milton, N.Y., Sept. 17, 1848.
They removed West, and settled in Neenah, Wis., the same
month of their marriage, and have lived there. They had children.
Children: (1) Henry Kirk Shoemaker, b. July 19, 1849. He
fitted for the ministry and began his work, but died at the age of
twenty-two years, Feb. 17, 1872.   (2) Ella Jane Shoemaker, b.
Jan. 24, 1853. She became a teacher of music, but died, unmarried, Jan. 2, 1875. Mrs. Mary (Ford) Shoemaker died Sept.
26, 1885. Mr. Hiram Shoemaker has assisted the editor greatly
in getting this account of the family of Samuel Churchill.

5. Charles Shoemaker, b. Feb. 12, 1826; m. Lucy Y. Towle, at
Saratoga, March 2, 1846.
These parents died leaving two sons and two daughters,
names not obtained.

6. Maria Shoemaker, b. Nov. 8, 1829; m. Daniel Curtis, at Saratoga, N.Y. She d. June 6, 1858, leaving one son, Rev.
Charles H. Curtis, of Watervliet, N.Y.

160   III. DANEY,[6] b. Nov. 24, 1792; m. MINERVA BURNHAM.

     IV. HANNAH,[6] b. Aug. 8, 1794; m. WILLIAM BILLINGS.
They lived in Western New York, and had a son and daughter,
names not obtained.

     V. ELECTA,[6] b. May 22, 1797; m. JOSEPH MERRILL.
They lived in Michigan, where she died March 1, 1868, leaving
children, of whom only one name is obtained, viz., Eveline Merrill,
who married Mr. Horton.

161   VI. CHARLES,[6] b. Oct., 17, 1800; m. LAURA CURTIS.
162   VII. SAMUEL, JR.,[6] b. July 4, 1804; m. ELIZA CULVER.
163   VIII. ITHUEL,[6] b. Aug. 2, 1806; m. 1st, RUTH ARMINDA WHITMAN; m.
2d, LYDIA MARSTON.

164   IX. PHILO CLARK,[6] b. Jan. 11, 1812; m. 1st, SOPHRONIA WHEDON; m.
2d, ANNA ALDRICH; m. 3d, MRS. ELIZABETH (JOHNSON) TITUS.

53.

IRA[5] CHURCHILL (BENJAMIN,[4] SAMUEL,[3] JOSEPH,[2] JOSIAH[1]).
Born at Bristol, Conn., April 9, 1764. Lived there until 1820,
when he removed and settled in Greene, O., of which township
he was among the early settlers. He cleared and worked a homestead farm. Two sons with their families settled near him in the
new township. He died June 14, 1834. Married, at Bristol, Conn.,
June 17, 1790, LOIS MUNSON, born in Southington, Conn., March
25, 1770, and died in Greene, Trumbull County, O., Feb. 27,
1845.

Children born in Bristol, Conn.

165   I. BARNABAS,[6] b. March 21, 1791; m. POLLY ROOT, Dec. 25, 1815.
166   II. MAJOR,[6] b. Sept 6, 1792; m. EUNICE PAYNE, April 17, 1818.
167   III. BRYAN,[6] b. March 11, 1795; m. MARY P. HADSELL, April 24, 1817.
168   IV. IRA, JR.,[6] b. Dec. 19, 1796; m. BETSEY MATTHEWS.
     V. MARTIN,[6] b. July 25, 1801; d. Aug. 21, 1801, at Bristol, Conn.
     VI. AMMI,[6] b. Sept. 30, 1802; d. unmarried, in Pennsylvania, July 8,
1822.

VII. Lois Delta,[6] b. Feb. 2, 1805; m. John Hickok, in Greene, O.,
Jan. 1, 1824. Mr. Hickok was born in Franklin, N.Y., Feb. 24,
1798, and d. at Greene, O., Aug. 12, 1869. They settled first
at Mecca, O., but later on the farm with Mrs. Churchill's
parents, and at their death inherited the homestead. Mrs. Hickok
died Feb. 6, 1880.

Children.

1. Ammi Leoline Hickok, b. at Mecca, O., April 28, 1826; m. Mary
Underwood, March 2, 1848. They lived at Colebrook, O.
No children. She d. at Greene, March 25, 1876.
2. Bethunia Eunetia Hickok, b. Nov. 21, 1831, at Mecca, O.; m.
Jepthah Gorham.
3. Aurilla Almarine Hickok, b. at Greene, O., Sept. 6, 1844; m.
George Clark, May 31, 1862. She d. March 23, 1869, at Greene,
leaving two boys who went West with their father, and were
lost trace of by the mother's family.

169 VIII. Ceylon Munson,[6] b. June 10, 1812; m. Frances Richards,
October, 1848.

54.

JEDEDIAH[5] CHURCHILL (Benjamin,[4] Samuel,[3] Joseph,[2]
Josiah[1]). Born May 27, 1766, probably at Southington, Conn.
We have not succeeded in getting any complete account of this
family. Married, at Southington, July 24, 1791, Sarah Hayford.

Children.

I. Orrin,[6] d. young.
II. Ruth,[6] m. Gates Miller, April 23, 1823. She d. June 26, 1856.
He d. April 16, 1881.

Children.

1. William Henry Miller, b. Sept. 25, 1824; d. Aug. 16, 1840.
2. Mary Olive Miller, b. June 2, 1835; m. John Becker.

III. Chauncy,[6] b. 1796. He was a sailor, and was lost at sea, it is
supposed.
IV. Lydia,[6] m. Henry N. Halsted.
170   V. Joseph Hayford,[6] b. Aug. 6, 1803; m. Sarah Lovina Stevens, of
Rutland, Vt.
171   VI. Anson J.[6]
VII. Infant,[6] d. soon.

55.

DAVID[5] CHURCHILL (William,[4] Samuel,[3] Joseph[2]
Josiah[1]). Born in Farmington, Conn., Dec. 20, 1762. Lived in
Bristol, Conn. Was by occupation a tin peddler, and very widely
known. Married Sarah Alcott, daughter of Jesse.

Children born in Bristol, Conn.

I. Ruth,[6] b. Aug. 31, 1787; d. unmarried.
II. Clara,[6] b. Jan. 8, 1789; d. young.
III. Ithamar,[6] b. May 15, 1790; d. without issue.
172   IV. Lewis,[6] b. Oct. 8, 1793; m. Sarah Caroline Tuttle.
V. Polly,[6] b. Aug. 29, 1795.
VI. Sally,[6] b. July 3, 1798.

VII. Milton,[6] b. 1801.
173 VIII. Alfred,[6] b. May 12, 1804; m. Rosetta Alcott.
IX. Almira,[6] b. May 12, 1804.
X. Albert,[6] b. May 12, 1804; d. Aug. 16, 1804.

56.

LEMUEL[5] CHURCHILL (William,[4] Samuel,[3] Joseph[2] Josiah[1]). Born March 4, 1766, at Farmington, Conn. Went to the Wyoming Valley with his father's family, and shared their experiences there. We have not been able to find any further information in regard to this family. He died Aug. 27, 1848. Married, Oct. 25, 1791, Patience Gildersleeve, born April 24, 1766. She died May 31, 1836.

Children.

I. Susannah,[6] b. Nov. 8, 1793; d. April 7, 1807.
174 II. William Tryon,[6] b. March 23, 1795; m. Elizabeth Hopper, Jan. 15, 1820.
III. Jemima,[6] b. June 19, 1796; d. Sept. 22, 1799.
175 IV. Asa Gildersleeve,[6] b. March 11, 1798; m. Lucy Clark.
176 V. John L.,[6] b. June 13, 1800; m. 1st, Pamelia Chase; m. 2d, Maria Hazlet.
177 VI. Charles,[6] b. Dec. 5, 1802; m. Elizabeth Butler Cornell, April 25, 1831.
VII. Ruth,[6] b. May 14, 1805; m. Luke Clark.
VIII. Julia Ann,[6] b. March 9, 1807.

57.

WILLIAM[5] CHURCHILL (William,[4] Samuel,[3] Joseph,[2] Josiah[1]). Born in the Wyoming Valley, Dec. 26, 1771. Went with his father's family to New Jersey. About 1798 he moved to Homer, N.Y., and then to Scipio, Cayuga County, N.Y., where he lived fourteen years, then settled near Marietta, O., for nineteen years, and then to Michigan, and lived there until his death. He was a deacon in the Baptist church for fifty years. He died March 4, 1863, aged ninety-one years. Married, 1796, in New Jersey, Jane Dell. She died April 1, 1839.

Children.

178 I. Joseph Dell,[6] b. July 29, 1797; m. Lucretia Bocock, March 28, 1827. He d. Aug. 9, 1851.
II. Ruth,[6] b. April 29, 1799; d. Aug. 6, 1823, unmarried.
III. Anna,[6] b. March 11, 1801; d. March 9, 1814.
179 IV. Silas,[6] b. Feb. 5, 1803; m. Elizabeth Gray, Feb. 7, 1829.
V. Lydia,[6] b. Aug. 16, 1804; d. Sept. 15, 1804.
180 VI. Adna,[6] b. Aug. 24, 1805; m. Sallie A. Hamilton.
VII. A Son,[6] b. Aug. 24, 1805; d. same day.
VIII. Martha,[6] b. Nov. 19, 1807; d. March 9, 1814.
181 IX. Randell,[6] b. Nov. 2, 1809; m. Jane Hamilton, May 14, 1834.
X. William Hubbard,[6] b. Dec. 13, 1811; d. March 16, 1814.
XI. Asa,[6] b. Jan. 27, 1815; d. July 10, 1816.
XII. Rhoda,[6] b. May 19, 1817; m. William F. Arnold, May 15, 1834. She d. Oct. 7, 1854.

Children.

1. Lydia Arnold, b. Feb. 28, 1835; d. Nov. 28, 1842.
2. Lucy Arnold, b. Sept. 1, 1836; d. Oct. 7, 1854.
3. Cornelia Arnold, b. Dec. 16, 1838.
4. Sarah Arnold, b. Jan. 12, 1841.
5. Philo Arnold, b. July 4, 1843.
6. Edwin P. Arnold, b. April 20, 1845.
7. Frank M. Arnold, b. Sept. 7, 1847.
8. James O. Arnold, b. Oct. 6, 1850; d. March 21, 1872.

182 XIII. JAMES,[6] b. April 18, 1819; m. MAILA HARWOOD, May 4, 1846.

58.

SAMUEL[5] CHURCHILL (WILLIAM,[4] SAMUEL,[3] JOSEPH,[2] JOSIAH [1]). Born in the Wyoming Valley, May 22, 1778. He was about two months old when the Indians and Tories, under Major Butler, drove the people from their pleasant and prosperous homes. He was brought up in New Jersey. Married ANNA MCCARTHY.

Children.

183   I. ALBERT,[6] b. Jan. 6, 1802; m. 1st, HARRIET DRESSER; m. 2d, ANNA
       FOSDICK.
      II. ANNA,[6] b. April 9, 1804; m. DANIEL HOPKINS, Jan. 9, 1820.

Children.

1. Anna Hopkins, b. Sept. 29, 1821.
2. Lovina Hopkins, b. Aug. 14, 1823.
3. Phebe Hopkins, b. Sept. 18, 1825.
4. Daniel Hopkins, b. April 3, 1828.
5. Charles Hopkins, b. March 21, 1831.
6. Mary Ann Hopkins, b. July 27, 1834.
7. Martha M. Hopkins, b. April 4, 1837.
8. Morton Hopkins, b. July 27, 1839.
9. Wilson S. Hopkins, b. July 11, 1842.
10. Edward Hopkins, } twins, b. Nov. 30, 1844.
11. Edgar Hopkins, }

184   III. SAMUEL,[6] b. Aug. 8, 1806; m. MARY FOSDICK.
185   IV. ASA,[6] b. Jan. 16, 1809; m. (———) DORRELL.
         V. MARY,[6] b. Oct. 29, 1811; m. JOEL BUTTS.
        VI. CINDERILLA,[6] b. May 22, 1814; m. SAMUEL BRASS.
186   VII. THOMAS,[6] b. Aug. 5, 1815; m. AURELIA WOODWARD.
      VIII. MEHITABLE,[6] b. June 17, 1819; m. GREEN PARKER.
187   IX. JOHN HUBBARD,[6] b. May 23, 1821; m. LUCY FOSDICK.
188   X. TRUMAN,[6] b. March 21, 1823; m. CHARLOTTE DAVIS.
        XI. LAURA,[6] b. April 21, 1826; m. BARNARD CRAM.

59.

ASA [5] CHURCHILL (WILLIAM,[4] SAMUEL,[3] JOSEPH,[2] JOSIAH [1]). Born in New Jersey, July 12, 1780. Married, 1802, HANNAH NORTON, of Bristol, N.Y.

Children.

I. NANCY,[6] b. March 27, 1804; m. EDWARD JONES, of Meredith, N.Y.

Child.

1. Almira Jones; m. (———) Stebbins.

　　II. JOEL NORTON,[6] b. Oct. 21, 1805; m. ABIGAIL ALLEN, of Bristol.
　　　　No issue.
189　III. WILLIS,[6] b. March 10, 1810; m. AMELIA BRADLEY, Aug. 21, 1834.
　　IV. MELINDA,[6] b. May 14, 1812; m. SAMUEL BROWN, of Harwinton,
　　　　Conn.

Children.

　　1. Ellen Melinda Brown, b. May 30, 1833; m. John E. Lewis.
　　2. Antoinette Brown, b. Sept. 15, 1835; m. Lewis Humphrey.
　　3. Edgar Julius Brown, b. Oct. 1, 1837; m. Mary C. Alfred.
　　4. Belden Samuel Brown, b. Feb. 27, 1839; m. Adeline Alfred.
　　5. Juliette Brown, b. March 10, 1841; m. DeWitt Hull.

　　V. ALEXANDER,[6] b. Nov. 19, 1814; d. Sept. 26, 1815.
190　VI. LEVI,[6] b. March 26, 1817; m. 1st, MARY CAMP, dau. of Johnson;
　　　　m. 2d, MRS. CYNTHIA TAYLOR.
　　VII. CHARLES,[6] b. May 26, 1820; d. Oct. 26, 1821.

60.

JOSEPH [5] CHURCHILL (JOSEPH,[4] JOSEPH,[3] JOSEPH,[2] JOSIAH [1]).
Born in Newington, 1750, and lived there in the old " Red House,"
known as the "Dowd House" later. He owned and operated a
grist-mill, and his sons followed him in that business. He died
April 26, 1812. Married, Sept. 11, 1777, RHODA GOODRICH, born
March 25, 1750. She was the daughter of Benjamin, and she died
Feb. 24, 1827, aged seventy-seven.

Children born in Newington.

　　I. SARAH,[6] b. 1778; m. CHARLES ALCOTT.

Children.

　　1. Sallie Alcott, b. October, 1809; d. in infancy.
　　2. Calvin Alcott, b. Nov. 22, 1815; d. young.
　　3. Sarah Jane Alcott, b. June 26, 1819; m. Harrison O. Gillette.

191　II. JOSEPH,[6] b. 1780; m. ANNA ALLEN JUDD, 1804.
192　III. JAMES,[6] b. March 28, 1782; m. CLARISSA STEEL, dau. of David.

63.

JONATHAN [5] CHURCHILL (JONATHAN,[4] JONATHAN,[3] JOSEPH [2]
JOSIAH [1]). Born at Woodbury, Conn., Nov. 25, 1749. Served in
the Revolutionary War, in Capt. Hezekiah Leach's Company. A
letter dated November, 1776, is preserved among his descendants,
which he wrote from "Saw-pits in Rye," meaning "rifle-pits" in a
rye-field. Married 1st, SARAH BURGESS; 2d, COMFORT WOODCOCK.

Children of First Wife

　　I. SALLY,[6] b. June 18, 1775; d. Oct. 8, 1795.
193　II. JOSIAH, [6] b. Jan. 11, 1777; m. OLIVE ODELL.
　　III. LUCY,[6] b. May 11, 1779; unmarried.
194　IV. LEMAN,[6] b. Dec. 6, 1780; m. POLLY DEMILLS.
　　V. POLLY,[6] b. April 8, 1784; m. 1st, DAVID TAYLOR; m. 2d, AMASA
　　　　COOK. No children reported of either marriage.
　　VI. IRENE,[6] b. Feb. 14, 1786; m. PHINEAS COOK.
　　VII. PHEBE,[6] b. Feb. 28, 1791; m. DANIEL TAYLOR.

Children of Second Wife.

195   VIII. DANIEL,[6] b. Nov. 14, 1798; m. CATHARINE DAVIS.
    IX. ABIGAIL,[6] born July 26, 1806; unmarried.
    X. PATTY EMILY,[6] b. May 13, 1808; never married, probably.

64.

HEZEKIAH [5] CHURCHILL (JONATHAN,[4] JONATHAN,[3] JOSEPH,[2] JOSIAH [1]). Born at Woodbury, Conn., Feb. 2, 1752. Settled in Bethlehem, Conn. Married, but we have not received the name of his wife.

Child.

196   I. SAMUEL,[6] who married a wife whose name is not obtained, and they
    had a daughter who married THOMAS SPROUL, and we have no
    further record of the family.

65.

MOSES [5] CHURCHILL (JONATHAN,[4] JONATHAN,[3] JOSEPH,[2] JOSIAH [1]). Born at Woodbury, Conn., Dec. 1, 1759. Married MARY CROSBY.

Children.

    I. MARY ANN,[6] b. 1787; m. SAMUEL CURTIS.
    II. BETSEY,[6] b. 1789; m. BENJAMIN SPARKS.
197   III. MOSES, JR.,[6] b. 1791; m. ANNA HUBBARD.
    IV. LUCY,[6] b. 1793; m. (———) SAMPSON.
    V. MAJOR,[6] b. 1795; d. in infancy.
    VI. POLLY,[6] b. 1797; m. SOLOMON PHILLIPS.
    VII. REBECCA,[6] b. 1799; d. at the age of fourteen years.
    VIII. INFANT DAUGHTER,[6] b. 1801; d. at Cornwall.
    IX. SAMUEL,[6] b. 1803; d. single, 1838, aged thirty-five years.

66.

OLIVER [5] CHURCHILL (JONATHAN,[4] JONATHAN,[3] JOSEPH,[2] JOSIAH [1]). Born at Bethlehem, Conn., April 15, 1762. He lived at Pawlet, Vt., the greater part of his life. Married, 1788, EUNICE BARNES, daughter of Abel, born at Litchfield, Conn., 1764. She died at Pawlet, Vt., June 14, 1809. Married 2d, in 1810, LYDIA GOODRICH.

Children of First Wife.

198   I. GILBERT,[6] b. Sept. 25, 1789; m. ABIGAIL DAVIS, of Bergen, N.Y.

Children of Second Wife, born at Pawlet, Vt

199   II. WILLIAM,[6] b. March 6, 1812; m. CHARITY RUSSELL, of Monroe, N.Y.
    III. ALMINA,[6] b. Nov. 15, 1814.
    IV. MARY,[6] b. Jan. 10, 1817; m. WILLIAM COOK. Mrs. Cook d. Jan.
    15, 1870. Mr. Cook d. Feb. 26, 1867.

Children.

    1. Ebenezer Cook, b. Feb. 21, 1840; d. April 23, 1841.
    2. Ebenezer Cook, b. Aug. 14, 1842.
    3. Amy Cook, b. June 17, 1845.

4. Stephen Cook, b. March 24, 1848; d. young.
5. Charles Cook, b. May 22, 1851; d. Jan. 24, 1852.
6. Lydia Cook, b. July 10, 1853; d. March 21, 1865.
7. David Cook, b. Dec. 25, 1855; d. March 13, 1865.
8. Seth Cook, b. July 11, 1858.
9. Eunice Cook, b. Nov. 28, 1861.

	V.	LAURA,[6] b. Aug. 20, 1818; m. THEODORE CRANMER. No issue.
200	VI.	OLIVER,[6] b. June 21, 1821.
201	VII.	HIRAM,[6] b. March 25, 1825; unmarried. A school teacher.
202	VIII.	CHARLES,[6] b. May 20, 1828; d. at Bergen, N.Y., Dec. 25, 1849.

67.

AMOS[5] CHURCHILL (JONATHAN,[4] JONATHAN,[3] JOSEPH,[2] JOSIAH[1]). Born at Bolton, Canada, Oct. 19, 1769. Lived in Bolton, Canada, and Bedford, Mass. He owned and worked a stone-quarry. An honest and straightforward man. He died May 8, 1857. Married, Oct. 25, 1795, DEBORAH THORNTON, who was born Dec. 26, 1776, and died Feb. 25, 1860.

Children.

	I.	ELECTA,[6] b. Dec. 14, 1796.
203	II.	LEMAN,[6] b. May 6, 1798; m. MINERVA ANDERSON.
204	III.	HIRAM,[6] b. Dec. 5, 1800; m. ABIGAIL BETSEY INGALLS.
	IV.	CONSTANT,[6] b. Nov. 2, 1802.
205	V.	OLIVER,[6] b. Jan. 28, 1805; m. a MISS CLARK, it is said, and had a son Charles, b. in 1839, who m. a Blanchard.
	VI.	HARRIET,[6] b. March 6, 1808, and d. June 18, 1879. No further record.
206	VII.	OTIS,[6] b. May 28, 1810; m. SUSAN P. RAYMOND, May 4, 1837
	VIII.	DEBORAH,[6] b. May 6, 1812.
	IX.	HARLOW,[6] b. Aug. 12, 1814.
207	X.	AMOS,[6] b. Dec. 31, 1816; m. LUCRETIA ROWE, Sept. 27, 1842.

68.

WILLIAM[5] CHURCHILL (WILLIAM,[4] JONATHAN,[3] JOSEPH[2] JOSIAH[1]). Born at Litchfield, Conn., 1766. Settled in Fairfax, Vt., about 1798, but removed, in 1812, to Randolph, Portage County, Ohio. Married, at Wallingford, Conn., 1794, POLLY MERRIMAN.

Children.

208	I.	STEPHEN MAJOR,[6] b. Dec. 4, 1796; m. MARIA BEACH.
	II.	DIANA,[6] m. WILLIAM HYLIAR.
	III.	POLLY,[6] d. unmarried.
	IV.	JULIA,[6] m. (———) DESTHICK.
	V.	ESTHER,[6] m. ISAAC HARGETT.
	VI.	CHARLOTTE,[6] m. JOHN McGOWAN.
209	VII.	PHILO,[6] m. ELECTA MERRIMAN.
	VIII.	EMILY,[6] m. TRUMAN CASE.
	IX.	CLARISSA,[6] m. 1st, HIBBARD CASE; m. 2d, ALMON CARLTON.
210	X.	LYMAN,[6] m. EMILY ADAMS.

69.

DAVID[5] CHURCHILL (WILLIAM,[4] JONATHAN,[3] JOSEPH,[2] JOSIAH[1]). Born at Litchfield, Conn., March 17, 1768. Married ZERVIAH LEACH, March, 1797. She was born Oct. 14, 1772.

Children.

I. MATILDA,[6] b. January. 1798; m. DAVID T. NORTON.
211   II. CARMEL,[6] b. June 4, 1799; m. ELIZABETH STOAT.
212   III. DAVID,[6] b. Feb. 2, 1801; m. ZOA EGGLESTON, 1828.
IV. HANNAH,[6] b. October, 1802; m. WILLIAM YOUNG.
213   V. CYRUS,[6] b. July 6, 1804; m. MARY PHELPS, Sept. 4, 1827.
214   VI. LEVI,[6] b. Aug. 24. 1806; m. MARY PINE, March 4, 1830.
VII. SALLY,[6] b. Nov. 20, 1807; m. 1st, MILES CODY, Dec. 9, 1832; m. 2d, RUFUS WELTHY, Aug. 15, 1850.

Children, all by First Husband.

1. Lyman Cody, b. April 14, 1834.
2. Joseph Cody, b. April 30, 1837.
3. Elijah Cody, b. March 13, 1840.
4. Philo Cody, b. Oct. 5, 1842.
5. Warren Cody, b. Oct. 26, 1846.

215 VIII. TRUMAN,[6] b. April 21, 1809; m. CHARLOTTE CHADWICK.
IX. WILLIAM,[6] b. 1810; d. aged eight months.
216   X. WILLIAM,[6] b. Aug. 24, 1812; m. SUSAN PINE.
217   XI. JOHN,[6] b. March 17, 1814; m. ANNE WALKER.
XII. CHARITY SOPHIA,[6] b. Oct. 29, 1815; m. 1st, DANIEL PINE, July 5, 1835; m. 2d, JOHN MONROE, Oct. 14, 1849.

Children of First Husband.

1. Levi Churchill Pine, b. July 20, 1838.
2. Infant, d. without name.
3. Mary Matilda Pine. b. July 29, 1841; m. Mr. Hall.
4. Malvina Pine, b. June 11, 1844.
No record of children of second husband.

72.

REV. SAMUEL[5] CHURCHILL (WILLIAM,[4] JONATHAN[3] JOSEPH,[2] JOSIAH[1]). Born at Litchfield, Conn., April 18, 1775. He early showed a strong desire for a liberal education, and at fourteen years attracted the attention of Dr. Rice, of Litchfield, who took him to his home where his education was completed. He became a fine scholar, especially in the classic languages and Hebrew. He was ordained to the Baptist ministry in 1797 and preached several years in Connecticut, before his settlement in Whiting, Vt. Somewhere about 1814 he removed to Elizabethtown, N.Y., where he preached thirteen years. In 1827 he removed to Williamsville, N.Y., and thence, in a year, to the town of Louth. Canada, and thence two years later to Springfield, Pa., and thence in 1838 to Hayfield, where he filled out his last pastorate, and died, Feb. 18, 1842. Married, at Norwalk, Conn., Feb. 22, 1798, REBECCA ST. JOHN, daughter of Peter St. John, of Norwalk, Conn. She died in Louth Canada, Oct. 29, 1828.

Children.

I. BETSEY,[6] b. April 1, 1799; m. ANSEL KNAPP, May, 1816.

Children.

1. Samuel Knapp, b. August, 1817.
2. Alanson Knapp, b. September, 1821; d. 1832.
3. Almira Knapp, b. September, 1825; d. June, 1833.
4. Sophronia Knapp, b. October, 1827; m. Andrew Williams, 1845.
5. Horace Knapp, b. October, 1837; m. Jane Thompson.

II. EZEKIEL ST. JOHN,[6] b. 1802; d. in 1811, aged nine years.
III. ALMIRA,[6] b. Nov. 26, 1804; m. REV. PAUL SCOTT RICHARDS, July 8, 1824.

Children.

1. Almira Richards, b. April 10, 1827.
2. Clarkson Howard Richards, b. May 10, 1829.

218   IV. JAMES HOIT,[6] b. Dec. 7, 1806; m. 1st, LENA SKELLEY, March 9, 1830; m. 2d, LOVISA ADAMS, March 24, 1836.
V. REBECCA,[6] b. April 22, 1809; m. JOHN W. SENCHORD, March, 1828. They had no children; she died in 1833.
VI. IRENE RICH,[6] b. May 3, 1813; m. WILLIAM CARRINGER, Jan. 25, 1838.

Children.

1. Philena Elizabeth Carringer, b. Oct. 31, 1838; m. John S. Green, April 8, 1863
2. Phidelia Churchill Carringer, b. Nov. 8, 1840; m. Andrew Patrick, Oct. 9, 1858.
3. Almira Lucy Carringer, b. Jan. 11, 1843; m. Hiram A. Knapp, March 21, 1862.
4. Olive Maria Carringer, b. Nov. 16, 1845; m. Andrew Patrick, March 14, 1865

VII. SARAH ANN,[6] b. Nov. 3, 1816; d. July 21, 1835; unmarried.
VIII. NANCY JUDSON,[6] b. June 3, 1819; m. ALLAN HARROUN, Oct. 29, 1839.
She was born in Elizabethtown, N.Y., June 3, 1819. She was educated in the schools of her native town, with a year at Mrs. Norman Nicholson's Seminary, and a private academy at Williamsville, N.Y. In 1828 she went with her father's family to Louth, Canada, where her mother died, and she soon after went to live with her older sister, Mrs. Richards, at Forestville, N. Y., where she finished her schooling at the private academy of Mrs. Charles Labatte. In the fall of 1833 she returned to her father's home, then at Sheakleyville, Pa. Here she began her experience in school-teaching, which lasted until her marriage. Her husband was the son of Capt. Eliott Harroun, of Pembroke, N.Y., where he was born. Two children were born to Mrs. Harroun here, but died in infancy. They removed to Wisconsin in 1844, and settled in the township of Rosendale, being the fourth family to settle there, but within a few months were joined by a score of families, mostly from the East. They removed a little later to Sparta, Wis. Here they prospered, as the town grew rapidly, and Mr. Harroun, being a carpenter, found profitable employment; but the fever of the West was still strong and so they removed again, in 1856, to Kansas, with their four children, the oldest about thirteen years. They found themselves in the midst of the war of " Border Ruffian-ism," and after two years were glad to get back to the North, and settle among civilized people, in Dodge County, Wis. Here their eldest boy died, and the husband met with an accident which ren-dered him unfit for work for some years, so that Mrs. Harroun was forced to resort to teaching again for her family's support. This teaching she continued twelve years, while her children grew up and became helpful as teachers, and her husband recovered in part, and the family prospered again. Mr. Harroun died April 23, 1889. Mrs. Harroun has been a diligent helper in the compilation of her grandfather's line of the family.

Children of Allan and N. J. (Churchill) Harroun.

1. Child, name not given, died in infancy.
2. Child, name not given, died in infancy.
3. Levi Clarkson Harroun, b. Jan. 12, 1842; d. in Wisconsin, Nov. 18, 1857.
4. James Ansel Harroun, b. in Wisconsin, Oct. 4, 1845; m. Katie McKay, June 26, 1878.   He is in business in Luverne, Minn. He has one child: (1) Ella Harroun, b. May 26, 1883.
5. Alpha Harroun, b. Nov. 4, 1848; m. Morris Welliver, Nov. 4, 1868.
6. Olive Adele Harroun, b. April 14, 1852; m. Henry Bowen, Nov. 28, 1872.

219   IX. ADONIRAM JUDSON,[6] b. July 15, 1821; m. CELESTIA ANTHONY, May, 1849.

X. SAMUEL STILLMAN,[6] b. May 1, 1825; d. unmarried in 1854.

73.

LEVI[5] CHURCHILL (WILLIAM,[4] JONATHAN,[3] JOSEPH,[2] JOSIAH[1]). Born, probably, in Litchfield, Conn., 1777. Married MARY HAVEN.

Children.

220   I. LEVI,[6] m. MARGARET CROMWELL.
II. LUCINDA,[6] m. DAVID LEACH.

SIXTH GENERATION

77.

NATHANIEL[6] CHURCHILL (NATHANIEL,[5] NATHANIEL,[4] NATHANIEL,[3] JOSEPH,[2] JOSIAH[1]). Born March 2, 1756. Married, April 2, 1783, MRS. LYDIA (OSGOOD) PENFIELD, widow of Nathaniel Penfield.

Children.

221   I. NATHANIEL,[7] b. March 20, 1784; m. SARAH RAY, 1806. *[handwriting]*
222   II. JEREMIAH.[7]
223   III. ELISHA.[7]
        IV. LYDIA,[7] m. HERMAN RAY.
        V. NAOMI,[7] m. NORMAN ELDER.
224   VI. JOHN SAGE,[7] b. July 20, 1798, in Hubbardton, Vt.; m. NARCISSA WHITE.
225   VII. PHINEAS PENFIELD,[7] b. Sept. 14, 1804; m. MARILLA GREGORY, Nov. 27, 1827.

78.

STEPHEN[6] CHURCHILL (NATHANIEL,[5] NATHANIEL,[4] NATHANIEL,[3] JOSEPH,[2] JOSIAH[1]). Born Nov. 19, 1761. Settled in New Canaan, Conn. The following meagre record, with no dates of birth, but dates of marriage with few names of persons, is all we have been able to obtain. Married, Sept. 7, 1787, POLLY DeWOLFE.

Children.

    I. FANNY FULLER,[7] m. MR. SEDGWICK, Jan. 12, 1812.
    II. RHODA,[7] m. LEACH IRELAND, Jan. 29, 1812.
226   III. JESSE,[7] m., name not given, Feb. 20, 1814.
    IV. CYNTHIA.[7] m. MR. ALDEN, Jan. 26, 1818.
227   V. PUTNAM,[7] m. 1st, CALISTA A. TAYLOR, March 28, 1820; m. 2d name not given, Feb. 21, 1831.
    VI. MARY,[7] m. MR. ALDEN, Nov. 23, 1825.
228   VII. WILLIAM HENRY,[7] m., name not given, Dec. 26, 1826.
    VIII. HULDA,[7] m. PRICE LAKE, Aug. 26, 1827.
    IX. MEHITABLE,[7] m., name not given, Jan. 12, 1831.

79.

SAGE[6] CHURCHILL (NATHANIEL,[5] NATHANIEL,[4] NATHANIEL,[3] JOSEPH,[2] JOSIAH[1]). Born at New Canaan, Conn., Dec. 13, 1763. Lived in Cornwall, Vt., till 1800, when he removed to Elizabethtown N.Y. He was a farmer. Died Feb. 27, 1813, at Lake Champlain. Married ELIZABETH MATHER, daughter of David and Hannah (Dunham) Mather.

(373)

Children born in Cornwall, Vt., but no dates of birth found. The church records show the first four baptized Oct. 6, 1793.

	I. AARON,[7] d. young.
229	II. BUSHNELL.[7]
	III. ELIZABETH,[7] m. ROBERT D. LINDSAY.

Children.

1. James E. Lindsay. Lived at Davenport, Ia.
2. Margaret L. Lindsay, m. (———) Pond, lived at Crown Point, N.Y.
3. Martha E. L. Lindsay, m. (———) Tompkins, and lived at Neillsville, Wis.
4. Freeman D. Lindsay.

IV. ROXANA,[7] m. MR. WHITCOMB. Mrs. Roxana Whitcomb died in Randolph, Vt. Children: We have received the names of three sons. Charles Whitcomb, who in 1890 was living in Middlebury, Pa., William Whitcomb, and Horace Whitcomb.

230 V. JESSE MATHER,[7] b. Nov. 18, 1796, in Cornwall; m. MARTHA McCAULEY, June 31, 1822.

231 VI. ELDREDGE.[7] Mr. James E. Lindsay wrote in 1890 that his uncle Eldredge died a few years before, leaving two sons, John M. then living in Marysville, Mo., and N. B., then at Florence, No. Dakota.

232 VII. JOHN.[7]

81.

SOLOMON [6] CHURCHILL (NATHANIEL,[5] NATHANIEL,[4] NATHANIEL,[3] JOSEPH,[2] JOSIAH [1]). Born at New Canaan, Conn., April 24, 1767. Settled in Berlin, Conn. Married, Dec. 30, 1790 SELINA HART, daughter of Elijah and Sarah (Gilbert) Hart, born Oct. 30, 1770.

Children.

234	I. SOLOMON,[7] b. Oct. 20, 1791; m. CANDACE GILBERT, Dec. 1, 1812.
235	II. AMZI,[7] b. Dec. 11, 1793; m. MARIA WHITE, Newton, L.I.
	III. PRUDENTIA,[7] b. 1795; d. Sept. 24, 1798.
236	IV. CYRUS,[7] b. Dec. 15, 1797; m. CLARISSA BRADLEY, Guilford, Conn.
	V. SELINA HART,[7] b. 1799; d. Nov. 17, 1799.
	VI. SELINA HART,[7] b. March 5, 1801; m. ANDREW RAPELYE, of Long Island, March 15, 1823.

Children.

1. Andrew Rapelye, b. Aug. 23, 1824.
2. Helen Selina Rapelye, b. Aug. 9, 1827.

VII. PRUDENTIA,[7] b. July 15, 1804; m. ALBERT WEBSTER, of West Hartford

VIII. LOUISA.[7] b. Nov. 20, 1807; d. June, 1808.

IX. LOUISA,[7] b. Feb. 8, 1809; m. EBENEZER EVANS, of Southington. She died soon, without children.

X. JAMES BUSHNELL,[7] b. May 20, 1810; m. EBENEZER EVANS, of Southington (as 2d wife).

237 XI. JOHN,[7] b. 1813, m. 1st, EMELINE CLEVELAND, Canton, Mass., in Wallingford, Conn.; m. 2d, LUCY R. FRENCH, of Litchfield, Conn.

82.

THOMAS FOSTER[6] CHURCHILL (JANNA,[5] NATHANIEL,[4] NATHANIEL,[3] JOSEPH,[2] JOSIAH[1]). Born in Georgia, Vt., Feb. 20, 1780. He settled in Georgia, Vt., where he was a farmer and lumber dealer. He operated a saw-mill, and was also interested in vessels on Lake Champlain. He was drowned Feb. 17, 1827, while crossing the lake on the ice, with a heavy horse-team. He was then living in Georgia, Vt. Married MARY STRONG, born at Southampton, Mass. She died in Ellenboro, Grant County, Wis., Nov. 6, 1864.

Children, all born (probably) in Georgia, Vt.

	I.	TIMOTHY PICKERING,[7] d. in infancy (at three months).
238	II.	TIMOTHY CLAPP,[7] m. and lived at Muscoda, Wis.; d. there, 1848, leaving one child, Lucy.
	III.	CANDACE STRONG,[7] b 1813; m. 1st. HERVEY SMITH; m. 2d, E. J. DRAKE. She d. at Plattsville, Wis., May 15, 1850, and left no children.
239	IV.	EBEN DORMAN,[7] b. at Georgia, Vt., Nov. 6, 1815; m. MARTHA E. STORY, July 17, 1851, at Plattsville, Wis.
	V.	STEPHEN MIX,[7] b. 1818; d. unmarried at Plattsville, N.Y., Aug. 6, 1850.
	VI.	MARY,[7] d. in Richmond, Pa., aged eighteen years.
	VII.	JOSIAH NOBLE,[7] b. 1824; d. unmarried, at Plattsville, Aug. 11, 1850.
240	VIII.	JAMES ALFRED,[7] b. Aug. 24, 1825; m. JULIA ANN BUTLER, Aug. 18, 1853.

83.

JOSIAH[6] CHURCHILL (JANNA,[5] NATHANIEL,[4] NATHANIEL,[3] JOSEPH,[2] JOSIAH[1]). Born March 9, 1784. Removed with his father in 1793 to Georgia, Vt. He was adopted by his uncle Josiah, who removed to Elmore, Lamoille County, Vt. Josiah removed West, and settled at Bethany, Genesee County, N.Y., where he became a man of influence. He served in the War of 1812, on the frontier. He was a surveyor of note, and was a justice of the peace, and town supervisor, and was representative two years. He died August 19, 1853. Married 1st, Feb. 11, 1808, CHARLOTTE RUMSEY. She died March 17, 1826. Married 2d, in 1827, HARRIET WIGHTMAN, born June 28, 1803.

Children of First Wife.

241	I.	WILLIAM R.,[7] b. Dec. 22, 1808; m. FIDELIA BUSHNELL, Oct. 31, 1833.
242	II.	JAMES M.,[7] b. Nov. 15, 1810; m. ELIZABETH SPERRY, Feb. 8, 1844 He lived in Fulton County, Ill., a trader. He wrote this account of his father's family. They had no children, and both died in Avon, Ill.
	III.	CHARLOTTE R.,[7] b. May 6, 1813; m. WILLIAM H. VAN EPPS, Jan. 4, 1836. She was thrown from a carriage, soon after birth of her only child, and killed by the fall, Aug. 23, 1848.

Child.

1. William H. Van Epps, Jr., b. 1848.

243   IV. JOSIAH,[7] b. Sept. 28, 1818; d. in infancy.
          V. ALTA MARIA,[7] b. June 27, 1821; m. 1st, NATHANIEL PECK, Feb. 10,
              1841; m. 2d, ELEAZER CHURCHILL, Oct. 27, 1851.
              She d. in Akron, N.Y., 1894.

Child of Second Husband.

1. Louise E. Churchill, b. Oct. 4, 1861; m. Orlando Kellogg
   Parker, Oct. 8, 1885.

Children of Second Wife.

          VI. ANN ELIZABETH,[7] b. Oct. 18, 1828; m. GEORGE G. DIXON, Oct. 3,
              1850.
              They had one child d. in infancy. Mrs. Dixon d. March, 1852.
         VII. OLIVE AMELIA,[7] b. Aug. 11, 1832; m. ALBERT G. DeSHON, Feb.
              11, 1858.
              They had no children.
        VIII. CHARLES H.,[7] b. Dec. 10, 1836; d. July 3, 1850.
244   IX. ALBERT J.,[7] b. Oct. 2, 1842; m. MARY E. MAILLIARD, Oct. 31, 1866.

84.

JANNA [6] CHURCHILL (JANNA,[5] NATHANIEL,[4] NATHANIEL,[3]
JOSEPH,[2] JOSIAH [1]). Born in Hubbardton, Vt., Feb. 18, 1786. He
removed and settled in New York, probably in Genesee County,
where he was a farmer. He died June 11, 1861. Married, Jan. 10,
1810, ELIZABETH PARSONS, of Bennington, Vt. She died Aug. 7,
1863.

Children.

          I. ADALINE L.,[7] b. Feb. 14, 1811; m. SAMUEL T. ADAMS, Sept. 12
             1835.

Children of Samuel T. and Adaline L. (Churchill) Adams.

1. John Q. Adams, b. Jan. 26, 1836; m. Susan Randall.
2. E. Marie Adams, b. May 13, 1838.
3. Helen L. Adams, b. Nov. 27, 1840; m. Henry Whitman, and
   d. May 3, 1883.
4. Charles C. Adams, b. May 23, 1843; d. Dec. 23, 1853.
5. Charlotte C. Adams, b. Sept. 23, 1847; m. Sanford Fleming.
6. Tyner Hall Adams, b. Aug. 26, 1849; m. Julia Paul.

          II. ELIZA M.,[7] b. Sept. 2, 1812; m. ELIJAH C. ADAMS.
245   III. MARCELLUS C.,[7] b. March 3, 1814; m. ABBY PAGE.
246   IV. CHARLES P.,[7] b. Sept. 6, 1815; m. 1st, HARRIET AUSTIN; m. 2d,
              HARRIET PERKINS.
           V. LUCY Z.,[7] b. Aug. 16, 1817; d. aged seven years.
247   VI. JULIUS M.,[7] b. May 7, 1825; m. 1st, ELMIRA ROBERTS; m. 2d,
              SARAH BADGLEY.
         VII. CHARLOTTE,[7] b. Sept. 3, 1826; unmarried.

85.

AMOS [6] CHURCHILL (AMOS,[5] NATHANIEL,[4] NATHANIEL,[3]
JOSEPH,[2] JOSIAH [1]). Born in Middletown, Conn., April 14, 1775.
Removed with his father's family to Broadalbin, N.Y. They lived

at Broadalbin.   Married, in Middletown, Conn., about 1795, OLIVE
WILCOX.

Children born at Broadalbin.

I. OLIVE,[7] m. JAMES BELL, of Providence, N.Y.

Children of James and Olive (Churchill) Bell.

1. Sarah Bell.	6. Amos C. Bell.
2. Ann Bell.	7. Harriet C. Bell.
3. Fanny Bell.	8. James H. Bell.
4. Maria Bell.	9. Jared Bell.
5. William H. Bell.	10. Olive Eliza Bell.

248   II. DR. AMOS,[7] b. May 12, 1805, m. 1st, ANN MARIA DOWNING; m.
2d, LUCY HALE.

III. HARRIET,[7] b. Nov. 15, 1807; d. unmarried, at Broadalbin, Oct 24,
1842.

IV. GILES WILCOX,[7] b. June 27, 1811; d. without issue, June 5,
1871.

249   V. DR. CHARLES W.,[7] b. Oct. 10, 1814; m. LOUISA SIGISON, of New
York, Aug. 22, 1843.

VI. ELIJAH W.,[7] b. Sept. 27, 1817; m. ELIZA JUDSON, of Mayfield, N.Y.

86.

ROSWELL[6] CHURCHILL (AMOS,[5] NATHANIEL,[4] NATHANIEL,[3]
JOSEPH,[2] JOSIAH[1]).   Born at Middletown, Conn., April 4, 1777.
Settled at Mayfield, N.Y., where he was a manufacturer of merino
cloth.   He imported the first merino sheep sometime before 1812,
and received from the State a large silver punch bowl in recognition
of his manufacture of the finest merino cloth produced in the State.
He was a man of fine presence and dignified manners.   He was a
justice of the peace in Mayfield.   He removed from Mayfield to
Albany, and later to New York City.   Died April, 1835.   Married
1st, July, 1802, at Middletown, ABIGAIL ROBERTS, of that town,
daughter of Ebenezer and Abigail (Dobell) Roberts.   She died 1811.
Married 2d, ABIGAIL COVELL, of Providence, N.Y.   She died 1854.

Children.

I. LORENA,[7] b. at Middletown, Conn., Dec. 11, 1803; m. REV. LEMUEL
COVELL.

One Child.

1. Adelia Covell.

II. CAROLINE,[7] b. at Mayfield, N.Y.; m. SOLOMON WHIPPLE, Dec. 20,
1826.

Children.

1. Harriet Fidelia Whipple, b. Feb. 25, 1828; m. Robert Thompson, Nov. 19, 1855.
2. Frances Emily Whipple, b. March 30, 1830; d. unmarried, 1887.
3. William Wirt Whipple, b. July 4, 1832; d. unmarried, 1887.
4. Mary Whipple, b. Aug. 20, 1834.   Was living March, 1902.
5. Daniel Thornton Whipple, b. May 3, 1837; d. 1887.
6. Henry Churchill Whipple, b. May 3, 1839; m. Julia Wood.
7. Abigail Whipple, b. Dec. 6, 1841; d. 1887.

8. Francis Marvin Whipple, b. April 17, 1843; d. 1887.
9. Caroline Ella Whipple, b. March 10, 1845; d. 1887.
10. Alanson Edgar Whipple, b. Jan. 3, 1849; d. 1887.

III. EMMELINE,[7] b. at Mayfield, N.Y.; m. ERASTUS McKENNY.
IV. ABIGAIL,[7] b. at Mayfield, N.Y.; d. unmarried, at Albany, aged eighteen years.

Children of Second Wife.

251   V. ALANSON COVELL,[7] b. 1813; m. LUCY CORNWALL.
252   VI. ERASMUS DARWIN,[7] b. Nov. 7, 1815; m. SARAH E. FINCH, b. Jan. 27, 1817.
     VII. WILLIAM HENRY,[7] b. 1817; m. MARY PEARSON .
²52a VIII. RENSELLAER EMMET,[7] b. Jan. 20, 1820; m. GERTRUDE RAMSEY.
252b   IX. CHARLES R.,[7] m. LYDIA BOWDEN.
     X. JAMES EDWIN.[7] Never married.

87.

JESSE[6] CHURCHILL (AMOS,[5] NATHANIEL[4] NATHANIEL,[3] JOSEPH,[2] JOSIAH[1]). Born at Middletown, June 2, 1782. Removed to Broadalbin, N.Y., before 1809, and died there March 29, 1842. Married, 1804, CATHERINE SMITH, of Middletown, Upper Houses. She died 1846.

Children born, first two at Middletown, the rest at Broadalbin.

253   I. WILLIAM ELIOTT,[7] b. Feb. 22, 1805; m. 1st, SARAH E. COWLES; m. 2d, LOUISA TERRY.
254   II. HENRY,[7] b. Feb. 17, 1807; m. 1st, SELINA BURR, at Gloversville, Fulton County, 1831; m. 2d, SYBIL E. ROBERTS, at Albany, N.Y., June 1, 1852.
255   III. TIMOTHY GRIDLEY,[7] b. April 28, 1809; m. PATIENCE LAWRENCE, of New York.
     IV. MARY ANN,[7] b. Sept. 8, 1812; m. at Hartford, Feb. 19, 1850, H. S. SMITH, of Gloversville, N.Y., and lived there. They had no children.
     V. LUCY MARIA,[7] b. July 16, 1813; m. PETER M. REYNOLDS, of Johnstown, N.Y.
     VI. JANE ELIZA,[7] b. about 1816; m. GEORGE W. ROOT, of Hartford, June 6, 1854. No children.
256   VII. ALLEN COWLES,[7] b. July 17, 1820; m. CAROLINE C. WARNER, at Gloversville, Oct. 28, 1840.
257   VIII. CHARLES BROCKWAY,[7] b. Feb. 26, 1828; m. CAROLINE SMITH, of New York City.

89.

JOSEPH[6] CHURCHILL (JOSEPH,[5] JOHN,[4] NATHANIEL,[3] JOSEPH,[2] JOSIAH[1]). Born May 20, 1763. He lived for a time at Cornwall, N.S., but later returned to Chatham (now Portland), Conn. Married, Oct. 28, 1790, ANNA LOWDEN, at Cornwall, N.S.

Children.

     I. PRUDENCE,[7] b. at Cornwall, N.S., Aug. 27, 1793; m. JOSEPH WADE, of Granville, N.S. They had no children.
258   II. SAMUEL,[7] b. at Chatham, Conn., Aug. 2, 1795; m. ELIZA WILLET, of Granville, N.S.

92.

CHARLES.[6] CHURCHILL (JOSEPH,[5] JOHN,[4] NATHANIEL,[3] JOSEPH,[2] JOSIAH [1]). Born in Chatham, Conn., June 12, 1769. He was a ship-builder and for some years owned the ship-yard at Chatham, Conn., and lived there. He died April 21, 1840. Married, Oct. 29, 1788, RUTH CHIPMAN, daughter of Ebenezer. She was born Jan. 4, 1768, and died Jan. 11, 1849.

Children born in Chatham, Conn.

259   I. JOHN,[7] b. July 28, 1789; m. EMILY WILCOX, July 1, 1809.
     II. MELANTHA,[7] b. Sept. 11, 1791; m. BENJAMIN GOODRICH.

Children.

1. Jeremiah J. Goodrich.
2. Lauretta Goodrich.
3. Frances Eliza Goodrich.
4. Benjamin Goodrich.
5. Jackson Goodrich.
6. Ralph Goodrich.
7. Alfred Goodrich.
8. Watson Goodrich.
9. Ruth Goodrich.
10. Elizabeth Goodrich.

260   III. ALFRED,[7] b. Jan. 26, 1794; m. SALLY HALL, dau. of David, of Portland, Conn., Oct. 3, 1813.
     IV. LAURA,[7] b. July 25, 1797; d. June 20, 1815.
     V. RUTH,[7] b. Aug. 29, 1799; d. Dec. 30, 1818.
261   VI. CHARLES,[7] b. Jan. 29, 1802; m. LUCY TAYLOR, of Glastonbury.
     VII. JOSEPH BUSH,[7] b. July 5, 1804; d. Aug. 11, 1805.
     VIII. JOSEPH BUSH,[7] b. Feb. 21, 1807; d. Feb. 16, 1824.
     IX. PRUDENCE,[7] b. Dec. 23, 1809; m. Feb. 26, 1829, ERASMUS GLADWIN, the son of James and Margaret (Tripp) Gladwin, of Haddam, Conn., b. Oct. 19, 1801.

Children.

1. Joseph Churchill Gladwin, b. June 24, 1830.
2. Laura Gladwin, b. Jan. 13, 1833.
3. Frederick Erasmus Gladwin, b. March 20, 1839.

93.

CAPT. DAVID[6] CHURCHILL (JOSEPH,[5] JOHN,[4] NATHANIEL,[3] JOSEPH,[2] JOSIAH [1]). Born in Portland, Conn., May 16, 1771. Died May 19, 1821. Married 1st, Oct. 14, 1792, JERUSHA UFFORD, daughter of Eliakim and Christian (White) Ufford, of Portland. She was born April 25, 1771; died Oct. 6, 1805. Married 2d, BETSEY GRIFFIN.

Children of First Wife.

     I. GEORGE WASHINGTON,[7] b. Sept. 28, 1793; d. May 9, 1801.
     II. MARIA,[7] b. Sept. 29, 1795; d. May 3, 1796.
262   III. HENRY UFFORD,[7] b. June 30, 1797; m. EMILY GREEN HALL, June 30, 1817.
263   IV. DAVID DICKINSON,[7] b. Jan. 31, 1800; m. ESTHER PATTEN PAYNE, July 21, 1831.
     V. MARY,[7] b. May 2, 1803; d. March 27, 1868; m. SAMUEL COOPER HALL, of Middletown, Conn., June 25, 1826. He was the son of William C. and Olive (Cooper) Hall; b. Sept 8, 1799; d. October, 1852. No children.
264   VI. GEORGE,[7] b. Sept. 6, 1805; m. SARAH PECK.

Children of Second Wife.

VII. EBENEZER,[7] b. 1807; d. Sept. 10, 1815.
VIII. WILLIAM,[7] b. 1811; d. Oct. 15, 1815.
IX. ELIZABETH PRUDENCE,[7] b. Jan. 27, 1814; m. LUCIUS SMITH, Brooklyn, L.I., December, 1840. He was b. Aug. 27, 1813. She d. Oct. 24, 1875.

Children of Lucius and Elizabeth (Churchill) Smith.

1. Sidney Churchill Smith, b. Jan. 6, 1842.
2. Virginia Eloise Smith, b. Sept. 18, 1844.
3. Eben Griffin Smith, b. Aug. 11, 1846; d. July 22, 1875.
4. Dan Danielson Smith, b. Jan. 3, 1849.
5. Elizabeth Milo Smith, b. Oct. 20, 1850.
6. Charles Carroll Smith, b. July 4, 1855; d. Aug. 5, 1855.

X. ANNA MARIA,[7] b. Sept. 17, 1817; d. June 7, 1865; m. JOHN FRELINGHUYSEN SCHENCK, M.D., Oct. 9, 1850. He was of Flemington, N.J.; b. June 6, 1799.

Children.

1. Griffin Churchill Schenck, b. April 10, 1852.
2. Charles Edward Schenck, b. April 20, 1855; d. April 10, 1856.
3. Mary Elizabeth Schenck, b. Sept. 21, 1858.

94.

EBENEZER [6] CHURCHILL (BENJAMIN,[5] DANIEL,[4] NATHANIEL,[3] JOSEPH,[2] JOSIAH [1]). Born in Salisbury, Conn., April, 1791. He was a cattle dealer. Settled first in Edmundston, N.Y., and later in Sherburne, N.Y., and died there April, 1822; married SABRINA TUPPER, of an Irish family of quality.

One Child born in Sherburne, N. Y.

265   I. EBENEZER DELOS,[7] b. Feb. 11, 1822; m. HANNAH LEMOYNE ATKINS, Oct. 2, 1849.

95.

CHARLES [6] CHURCHILL (BENJAMIN,[5] DANIEL,[4] NATHANIEL [3] JOSEPH,[2] JOSIAH [1]). Born in Salisbury, Conn., June 5, 1793. Lived in Utica, N.Y., where he was a lumber dealer. An upright man. Married LOIS BALDWIN, daughter of Isaac, born in New Milford, Conn., March 11, 1785.

Children.

I. CHARLES BALDWIN,[7] b. April 20, 1821; d. in Chatham, Conn., 1851.
II. ELIZABETH EDMISTON,[7] b. July 14, 1822. Living (1901) unmarried.
III. CORNELIA M.,[7] m. WILLIAM BARTON.

Children.

1. Charles Barton, d. 1882.
2. Lena Barton, d. 1875.

96.

SELDEN [6] CHURCHILL (DANIEL,[5] DANIEL,[4] NATHANIEL,[3] JOSEPH,[2] JOSIAH [1]). Born in Chatham, Conn., Dec. 14, 1783 and removed with his father to Richfield, N.Y., in 1795. About 1800 he became a fur-trader at Davenport, Iowa, but his health being broken down by rheumatism, he returned to the old farm at Richfield, N.Y., to which his father had migrated from Chatham, Conn. He was a man of more than ordinary ability, a student of Shakespeare, and a humorist of local note. He was very tall of stature. Died in 1866. Married 1st, MARY DUEL, daughter of Daniel, of New York; married 2d, LUCRETIA CLEMENTS.

Children of First Wife.

266   I. DR. ALONZO,[7] b. Jan. 20, 1811; m. JANE MORGAN, Feb. 10, 1834.
        II. NANCY,[7] m. ROBERT BARNES.
267   III. DANIEL,[7] m. MARY ELMINA HULL.

Children of Second Wife.

     IV. LUCRETIA.[7]
     V. MALVINA,[7] never married.
     VI. ADELAIDE.[7]

97.

ALFRED [6] CHURCHILL (DANIEL [5] DANIEL,[4] NATHANIEL [3] JOSEPH,[2] JOSIAH [1]). Born in Chatham, Conn., Aug. 29, 1790. Settled in Utica, N.Y., Oct. 28, 1828, and became a very prosperous and influential citizen of that city. He was proprietor at one time of the celebrated hostelry of an earlier day known as "Bagg's Hotel." He died in Utica, Jan. 10, 1865. Married EMMA DERBYSHIRE, of Hartwick, N.Y.

Children.

268   I. ALFRED DERBYSHIRE,[7] b. in Hartwick, N.Y., Sept. 30, 1826; d. single, Dec. 27, 1843.
269   II. GEORGE CLARENCE,[7] b. in Utica, N.Y., April 14, 1829; m. ANNIE BRAYTON.
     III. CHARLOTTE D.,[7] b. Feb. 21, 1831; d. Feb. 26, 1834.

98.

JAMES [6] CHURCHILL (ELIJAH,[5] GILES,[4] SAMUEL,[3] JOSEPH,[2] JOSIAH [1]). Born, Chester, Mass., on the old homestead, Nov. 11, 1785. They lived in Stamford, N.Y. He died at Stamford, N.Y. Sept. 5, 1843. Married, March 2, 1815, BETSEY GILBERT, who was born in Stamford, July 4, 1792, and died July 13, 1878, at Stamford, N.Y.

Children born in Stamford.

270   I. Charles Gilbert,[7] b. Dec. 2, 1817; m. Ruth P. Ackley.
        II. Sally Ann,[7] b. Oct. 12, 1821; d. Aug. 9, 1829.
        III. Elijah,[7] b. May 5, 1824; d. Jan. 8, 1848. No family.
        IV. James, Jr.,[7] b. May 28, 1826; d. Jan. 9, 1853. No family.
271   V. George,[7] b. March 2, 1830; m. Sarah Fuller.
272   VI. Andrew L.,[7] b. Feb. 6, 1833; m. Amelia Ackley, Jan. 4, 1855.
273   VII. Addison J.,[7] b. May 1, 1836; m. Elizabeth Houghtaling.

99.

GILES[6] CHURCHILL (Elijah,[5] Giles,[4] Samuel,[3] Joseph,[2] Josiah[1]). Born in Middlefield, Mass., July 28, 1793, and lived there. Died Feb. 7, 1864, aged seventy-five years. Married Abigail Haskins, born Sept. 26, 1796, in Simsbury, Conn.

Children born in Middlefield, Mass.

274   I. William,[7] b. April 18, 1816.
274a   II. Elijah Lyman,[7] b. 1819.
        III. Abigail,[7] b. 1821.
        IV. Laura,[7] b. 1824.

100.

CHARLES[6] CHURCHILL (Elijah[5] Giles,[4] Samuel,[3] Joseph,[2] Josiah[1]). Born in Middlefield, Feb. 16, 1796. Lived in Chester, Mass. He died Aug. 22, 1865. Married 1st, Nov. 4, 1819, Hannah Percival, who was born Oct. 6, 1799, died Dec. 17, 1835. Married 2d, April 1, 1841, Dolly W. Davis.

Children born in Chester, Mass.

    I. Lucy Sophia,[7] b. Sept. 5, 1820; m. Lyman Johnson, Oct. 4, 1849. She d. Sept. 25, 1900.

Children.

    1. Jane Lucy Johnson, b. Sept. 19, 1851.
    2. George Lyman Johnson, b. June 14, 1855

    II. Hannah Maria,[7] b. Dec. 19, 1822; m. Baxter Johnson, March 2, 1844.

Children born in Hinsdale, Mass.

    1. Ellen Sarah Johnson, b. Aug. 29, 1846; m. Charles B. Canfield, Oct. 21, 1869.
    2. Clara Maria Johnson, b. July 10, 1853; m. Clark Durant Noble, April 29, 1880. Both married in Hinsdale.

    III. Sarah,[7] b. Nov. 6, 1824; d. Nov. 15, 1843.
    IV. Anna,[7] b. July 14, 1828; m. Zadock Ingalls, of Chester, Mass; April 4, 1850.

Children.

    1. Hannah DeEtte Ingalls, b. Nov. 28, 1851.
    2. Charles Zadock Ingalls, b. April 4, 1854.
    3. Sarah Ann Ingalls, b. Oct. 17, 1855.
    4. Myra Phelps Ingalls, b. Oct. 2, 1862.
    5. James Thompson Davis Ingalls, b. Feb. 28, 1864.
    6. Clara Belle Ingalls } b. May 8, 1867.
    7. Carrie Belle Ingalls }

274b   V. CHARLES ELIJAH,[7] b. April 9, 1833; m. MARTHA WRIGHT, Dec. 8, 1863; d. Jan. 2, 1864. No further record obtained.

      VI. CLARISSA E.,[7] b. April 9, 1833; m. MILO MILTON WENTWORTH, April 9, 1861. She was his second wife, and d. Nov. 14, 1871, at the birth of fourth child.

Children.

  1. Ella Maria Wentworth, b. Dec. 19, 1864; m. Luther Wadsworth Bridges, Oct. 16, 1894.

  2. Emma Jane Wentworth, b. Jan. 5, 1865; d. Jan. 19, 1865, aged two weeks.

  3. Arthur Milton Wentworth, b. Sept. 4, 1870.

  4. Ada Lillian Wentworth, b. Nov. 14, 1871.

   VII. HARRIET,[7] b. Nov. 29, 1835; d. Feb. 18, 1838·

Child by the Second Wife.

  VIII. HARRIET ELIZA.[7] b. Dec. 28, 1846; m. GEORGE CONE, of Chester, Mass., Jan. 13, 1872, at Warren, Mass. Lived at Chester.

Children born at Chester.

  1. Clayton Bishop Cone, b. Oct. 25, 1874.

  2. Lewis Nelson Cone, b. June 13, 1876; d. Aug. 29, 1883.

  3. Harriet Eliza Cone, b. Jan. 28, 1881.

101.

DR. GILES[6] CHURCHILL (STEPHEN,[5] GILES,[4] SAMUEL,[3] JOSEPH,[2] JOSIAH[1]). Born in Cherry Valley, N.Y., March 12, 1786. He was a physician in the town of Concord, Erie County,. N.Y. He died Sept. 26, 1873, in Concord, N.Y. Married, Feb. 7, 1813, ABIGAIL TOOKER, born in Lyme, Conn., Aug. 22, 1788; died March 12, 1863.

Children born in Concord.

     I. ELIZA ANN,[7] b. in Concord, N.Y., Dec. 9, 1813; m. PRENTICE STANBRO. They lived in Springville, N.Y., where she died Aug. 22, 1869.

    II. EMMELINE,[7] b. Jan. 20, 1816; d. Feb. 17, 1816

275 III. STEPHEN GILES,[7] b. Aug. 30, 1817; m. MARGARET WIDRIG, 1844.

276 IV. MARCUS B.,[7] b. Nov. 9, 1825; m. AMANDA VAN CAMP, Dec. 18, 1849.

102.

SAMUEL[6] CHURCHILL (STEPHEN,[5] GILES,[4] SAMUEL,[3] JOSEPH,[2] JOSIAH[1]). Born in Harpersfield, N.Y., Sept. 16, 1790. Died June 26, 1857. Lived awhile in Harpersfield, but removed later to Meredith N.Y. Married 1st, in Harpersfield, N.Y., Oct. 11, 1818, SALLY C. NEWCOMB, born Oct. 13, 1790. Married 2d, in Andes, N.Y., May 22, 1844, SALLY SHAFFER.

Children by First Wife.

     I. MARY,[7] b. Nov. 12, 1819; m. AUGUSTUS CHAFFE.

277 II. STEPHEN,[7] b. July 10, 1821; m. CAROLINE GAYLORD.

278 III. NEWCOMB GAYLORD,[7] b. Sept. 22, 1823; m. THIRZA GATES.

279   IV. SAMUEL STODDARD,[7] b. Aug. 18, 1825; m. 1st, EMILY DRUMMOND; m. 2d, LOUISA J. GATES.
      V. HARRY,[7] b Aug. 17, 1827.
280   VI. WILLIAM,[7] b. Feb. 24, 1831; m. CORINTH ABBOTT.
281   VII. JEDEDIAH,[7] b. June 5, 1832; m. ADELINE FRANTZ, b. Nov. 26, 1837.

103.

DEACON ELIJAH [6] CHURCHILL (STEPHEN,[5] GILES,[4] SAM-UEL,[3] JOSEPH,[2] JOSIAH [1]). Born in the town of Harpersfield, Delaware County, N.Y., Feb. 3, 1797, and died there, March 24, 1878. From a brief memoir, published by some of his children in 1878, which has come into the hands of the editor of this volume since the printing of the family of his grandfather and father, we gather a few traditions, which adds a little to our knowledge of them. Giles Churchill, about 1751, settled on the Delaware river, in what is now the town of Cochecton, N.Y., though he may have chosen the west bank, as that was within the boundary of William Penn's grant. Here, in an unbroken wilderness, he built a small log-cabin, and thither, in a short time, brought his wife, and his children were born, and his cleared farm began to give back goodly harvests, while other families were settling around him Here, in 1758, Stephen, the father of Deacon Elijah, was born. The rapid settlement of the lands, and, doubtless, the undue encroachments of the white men, aroused the hostility of the Indians to the desperate resolve of driving out or destroying the invaders. Although Penn's purchase was supposed to be exempt, it was not deemed to be a sure protection to any, when once the native hordes started on their raids; so that when it was found, in 1765, that the tribes were gathering, the settlers fled, leaving their homes and farms, to find safety in the older settlements. Stephen was then seven years old, and remembered some facts concerning the flight. The Indians burned their house while they were yet within sight of the smoke of its burning. The family had a horse upon which the mother and younger children rode, while their only provisions, a bag of meal, was laid on the back of their one cow. Under such conditions they pursued their flight till they reached the limits of Massachusetts, and probably located near relatives of the husband or wife, it is not known in what town. The tradition is that the old wilderness home was " at the forks of the Delaware river," but Cochecton is seen to be a long distance below the forks. Stephen Churchill, father of Deacon Elijah, now grown to manhood, located and married at some place unknown to us, but appears with a small family, about 1785, at Harpersfield, Delaware County, N.Y., cleared up and improved a farm, and there spent his life. Here Deacon Elijah was born, as above noted. He suffered the great privations of

frontier farm-life in his early years; but despite his limited means
for schooling, he obtained a better than the ordinary education, and
began to teach school at an early age, working on the farm except
in winter, when he was teaching.　His father died when he was
about fifteen years of age, and his older brother carried on the farm
for some years, when his younger brother, Joseph, married and took
the farm for a while, and then, at his mother's desire, Elijah bought
out the interests of his brothers and sisters and settled down on the
homestead farm.　His sister Esther married a Mr. Webb and settled
in Andes, and here, when he was about thirty-three years old, he
married his wife.　He was a strong and able man, a good citizen.
He was a leading influence in public affairs, a consistent Christian,
and an earnest promoter of education.　He was very popular in the
community.　In his younger days was captain of the local militia.
He was an ardent Whig, and became an earnest Republican.　He
knew how to be a good father without repressing or punishing his children, and also knew how to make a Christian home and a Christian
life pleasant and attractive.　He joined the First Presbyterian
Church in Stamford, with many others from Harpersfield, June,
1834, at its organization, and was then elected elder, or deacon, an
office which he held during his life.　His funeral sermon was
preached in the Presbyterian Church in Stamford, N.Y., by his
pastor, Rev. L. E. Richards, March 24, 1878.　This discourse was
published in connection with the memoir above mentioned.　Married,
at Andes, N.Y., May 12, 1830, SARAH A. BENEDICT, of Andes.

Children.

    I.　CALVIN B.,[7] b. Sept. 3, 1831; m. ADELINE HITCHCOCK.　No issue.

282   II.　EPENETUS W.,[7] b. Aug. 25, 1833; m. ANNIE WILCOX, June 1, 1863.

   III.　SARAH A.,[7] b. Nov. 25, 1838.　Unmarried.

   IV.　DR. STEPHEN ELIJAH,[7] b. Sept. 7, 1841.　Unmarried.
       Lived in Stamford, N.Y.　Proprietor of the noted Churchill
       Hall, a summer hotel in Stamford.　He was also a practising
       physician.

   V.　FRANCES A.,[7] b. June 14, 1844; m. C. L. McCRACKEN.　No issue.
       He was the writer of a memoir of Deacon Elijah.　He died June
       29, 1898.

   VI.　ESTHER M.,[7] b. Aug. 12, 1847; m. NATHAN COE, Dec. 17, 1872.

Children.

    1.　Louis Sumner Coe, b. Oct. 6, 1873; m. Gertrude Hart, Nov.
      9, 1901.　Both of Springfield.
    2.　Frances Irene Coe, b. July 9, 1884.

   VII.　ADDIE VESTA,[7] b. June 19, 1856; m. CHARLES H. WIBERLY, Oct.
      29, 1885.

Children.

    1.　Irving Churchill Wiberly, b. July 29, 1890.
    2.　Maurice Calvin Wiberly, b. March 24, 1892; d. Aug. 27, 1892.
    3.　Edna Lillian Wiberly, b. July 9, 1893.
    4.　Marion Drummond Wiberly, b. July 18, 1896.

105.

AMOS[6] CHURCHILL (JOSEPH,[5] SAMUEL,[4] SAMUEL,[3] JOSEPH,[2] JOSIAH[1]). Born in Sheffield, Mass., Oct. 1, 1774. He went with his father's family, in 1783, to Hubbardton, Vt. His advantages for school were very limited. He wrote himself, " I had no chance at school until the winter after I was fifteen, when I went to school in the back room of a log-house, to a very ordinary teacher. I never studied any books at school but the New England Primer and Dilworth's Spelling-book ; these I learned by heart." In spite of all these limitations he acquired a fair education for his day and place. He was a man of more than common ability and intelligence, a shrewd observer of men and events, a lover of history. He had great facility in rhyming, and his brother, Rev. Alvah, used to receive long letters from him, written in verse, and in his articles prepared for the " Gazetteer," mentioned below, several pieces of verse appear, touched up here and there with quaint humor. When upward of seventy-six years, he compiled a series of articles on the history of Hubbardton, for the " Vermont Historical Gazetteer," in 1851, but from notes collected many years before. These articles were later published in book form, rare copies of which can be found. The history, from his grandfather down, is fairly accurate, but before that generation he depended upon tradition, and his reckoning is altogether erroneous. The account on pages 335–337 is quoted from his work. Mr. Churchill settled first in Pittsford, Vt., less than a mile from his father's house in Hubbardton, but on May 21, 1821, removed to Hubbardton, and spent his days there. He was a good citizen, an active member of the Baptist Church in Hubbardton. He was physically a strong man, and a very diligent worker, even to old age. He was active in promoting public improvements, and instrumental in raising the monument on the Hubbardton battleground to the memory of the patriots who fought there July 7, 1777, and on the occasion of the celebration, July 7, 1859, the anniversary of the battle, he was one of the speakers. Mr. Churchill lived to the advanced aged of ninety-one years, and died March 2, 1865. Married 1st, Jan. 29, 1799, NABBA HAVEN, of Sandisfield, Mass., daughter of Nathan. She was born May 23, 1778, and died Sept. 2, 1842. Married 2d, CHLOE SMITH, of Brandon, Vt., March 29, 1846. She was born Dec. 26, 1784.

Children of Amos and Nabba (Haven) Churchill.

I. LOUISA,[7] b. Oct. 21, 1799; m. EBENEZER COOK, January, 1822.
They settled in Pittsford, Vt., where he died Oct. 2, 1841.

Children.

1. Orilla Cook, m. Chauncey W. Fray, of Pittsford. Two chil
dren: (1) Suzina Fray, and (2) Adoniram J. Fray.
2. Amos Cook, d. aged about eighteen years.
3. Elisha Cook, m. Minerva Flag.
4. Adoniram J. Cook, d. young.

283   II. SAMUEL S.,[7] b. Nov. 26, 1800; m. MARY RICHARDSON.
      III. ORRILLA,[7] b. Sept. 23, 1802; d. Aug. 4, 1803.
284   IV. ISAAC NEWTON,[7] b. July 17, 1805; m. MARGARET PERRY.
       V. ALZINA,[7] b. July 1, 1812; d. the same day.

106.

GEN. WORTHY LOVELL [6] CHURCHILL (JOSEPH,[5] SAMUEL,[4] SAMUEL,[3] JOSEPH,[2] JOSIAH [1]). Born in Sheffield, Mass., May 13, 1776. He went with his father, in 1783, to Hubbardton, Vt., and there grew to manhood, working on the farm and attending, in winter, the primitive schools then procurable. He worked on the farm like other boys and young men of his day, and doubtless shared the general ambitions of young men to make good and prosperous farmers. About the time he came of age, the conditions of land settlement in Vermont had changed. The fathers of families owned all the farms, or their creditors held them by mortgage. Young men must buy except the few who remained on the homestead with their fathers. Mr. Churchill married in 1797, and began life in his native town, where he remained for several years, till three of his children were born.

Then the Holland Purchase in Western New York opened up a vast tract of fertile land, and thither, with many others from Vermont, young Churchill went. From lists of settlers, and casual references in Turner's "History of the Holland Purchase," as well as from correspondence with members of General Churchill's family, the editor has been able to glean a few facts of the busy and eventful life of this typical pioneer of the early West.

In the first list of settlers in the Holland Purchase, in Batavia Township, No. 12, Range 1, the name of Worthy L. Churchill stands first, and next William Rumsey, the names following in the order in which the land grants were assigned, so that these two were the first proprietors recorded, and the first settlers. Batavia Village was soon the centre of pioneer settlers, and the Land Office was established there and a town government formed. The first tavern was opened there. Mr. Churchill bought a large tract of land in that part of Batavia which became the town of Stafford.

At the first town meeting held in Batavia, March 1, 1803, " Lovell Churchill," as he is there named, was chosen one of the overseers of the highways; and in the following June, when a court of law was organized and the first grand jury empanelled, Mr. Churchill was a member, and next year on the traverse jury, and in 1807, at the first murder trial in the new county, that of James McLean, for the murder of William Orr, he was a juror, and with his full name, Worthy L. Churchill. In the primitive organization of the militia of the county he was active and efficient, and had passed through all the minor offices before 1812, for at the beginning of the war that year we find him in command of a regiment with the rank of colonel. He undoubtedly had part as an officer in the opening events and skirmishes along the frontiers, on the Niagara river, in the disastrous autumn compaign of 1812. A year later, December, 1813, he was in command of his regiment in the army of defence at Buffalo, and, in the battle on December 29th and 30th, in the absence of General Hopkins, the command devolved upon Colonel Warren and Colonel Churchill. The orders had been given them to attempt the impossible, to capture a strong battery, defended by a large force of well-drilled British regulars. The American troops consisted of untrained and poorly armed recruits, but they made a brave assault in the face of a deadly fire from the heavy British guns, and driven back once, they were led on in a second desperate charge, only to be overwhelmed again, and this time to be pursued and out-flanked by a large body of fresh troops and Indian allies who had unexpectedly arrived at the British lines. In the disastrous retreat which followed, the villages of Buffalo and Black Rock were de-stroyed, the houses burned to ashes, and all who could not escape were brutally massacred by the Indian allies of the British. Again in July, 1814, Colonel Churchill had a part in the defence of Fort Erie, at the head of the Niagara river. Here the tide of battle was turned by the Genesee County Militia under General Porter who gathered to protect the garrison of American regulars who were in danger of being surrounded and cut-off. By a daring and skilful outflanking move General Porter led a large body of his troops through the woods and came down unexpectedly with such an impetuous assault upon the British flank and rear that they were forced to retire from the field and the investment of the fort. In this battle Colonel Churchill was severely wounded and taken prisoner, and carried to Canada, but soon after exchanged. He was colonel of the Sixty-fourth Regiment, New York State Militia, but afterwards attained the rank of major general of the State Militia.

Colonel Churchill was a surveyor of land and an extensive land-owner and dealer in land, while cultivating a large farm. He was active and influential in public affairs, and was sheriff of Genesee County from 1820 to 1825. He died May 25, 1839. Married 1st,

in Hubbardton, Vt., 1797, RUHAMA WHELPLEY, who died in 1802. Married 2d, in Batavia, N.Y., 1804, SOPHIA KINGSLEY, born Sept. 4, 1781, in Rutland, Vt., but removed with her father's family to Genesee County, N.Y., and died at Lake Mills, Wis., March 6, 1867.

Children of First Wife, born in Vermont.

      I. BEULAH,[7] b. in 1798; m. MR. DOWNING. No children.

285   II. ALFRED,[7] b. May 8, 1800; m. SUSAN D. WILSON, September, 1821. She was b. 1800.

286   III. JOSEPH WHELPLEY,[7] b. Nov. 15, 1801; m. DELIA S. WILSON, 1829. She was b. 1808.

Children of Second Wife.

    IV. LOVELL KINGSLEY,[7] b. 1804; d. unmarried, in 1822.
     V. SOPHIA,[7] b. May, 1807; m. JOHN WEBBER, Nov. 11, 1828. Mr. Webber was born in Devonshire, Eng., near Taunton, 1796. Came to America in 1817, and was the first of the large and flourishing colony of natives of England who settled in Stafford. This colony gave the town a distinctively English character and society. She d. June 10, 1881.

Children born in Stafford.

    1. Worthy Lovell Webber, b. Dec. 12, 1828; m. Mary Fox, of Niagara Falls, March 15, 1860; and died in Syracuse, N.Y., Nov. 3, 1874.
    2. Mary Sophia Webber, b. Feb. 8, 1832; m. Charles L. Gillette, March 8, 1854. She died in Batavia, Nov. 15, 1900, leaving children, who were b. in Batavia, (1) Isaac W. Gillette, b. 1856; m. Harriet Swift. (2) Henry L. Gillette, b. 1860; m. Marietta Winn, 1891. (3) Sophia E. Gillette, b. 1863. (4) Rudolph W. Gillette, b. 1867; m. Mary Showerman, 1893. (5) John F. Gillette, b. 1868; d. soon. (6) John H. Gillette, b. 1874; d. 1897.
    3. Julia Augusta Webber, b. 1834; d. unmarried, Nov. 15, 1864.
    4. John Herschell Webber, b. April 15, 1837; m. Mary Jane Radley, of Stafford, Dec. 19, 1867. They lived in Stafford. He was a prosperous farmer. They had children b. in Stafford: (1) Nellie Churchill Webber, b. Sept. 30, 1871; (2) Charles Radley Webber, b. Sept. 19, 1873; (3) Clara Elizabeth Webber, b April 2, 1880.
    5. George Follett Webber, b. May 17, 1847; d. Feb. 18, 1865.

    VI. JANE E.,[7] b. 1811; m. ZECHARIAH LOTHROP. No issue.

287 VII. JAMES W.,[7] b. April 8, 1814; m. VIENA THOMPSON, of Norwich, Conn.

  VIII. ALTA C.,[7] b. 1817; m. REV. ALMON WHITMAN, May 28, 1848.
    IX. CAROLINE,[7] b. 1819; m. REV. ALMON WHITMAN, Jan. 26, 1841. Caroline, the first wife, died March 20, 1845, and Alta C. died at Newark, Wis., May 24, 1875.

Children by Second Wife, Alta C.

    1. Lovell D. Whitman, b. Feb. 28, 1849; d. Feb. 28, 1864.
    2. Caroline D. Whitman, b. Oct. 10, 1851; m. William L. Porter, Jan. 1, 1885.
    3. Judson F. Whitman, b. Nov. 12, 1856.
    4. Irving A. Whitman, b. April 21, 1858.
    5. Sophia C. Whitman, b. April 4, 1860.

    X. DEMIS MARIA,[7] b. April 21, 1821; d. of consumption, 1842.
    XI. MORILLA C.,[7] b. Dec. 6, 1824; m. ENOCH BROWN FARGO, Nov. 10, 1844.
      Mr. Fargo was born in Colchester, Conn., Feb. 18, 1821, and died at Lake Mills, Wis., Nov. 2, 1892. At the age of eleven he

removed with his father's family to Stafford, N.Y., and was brought up on the farm which he with his seven brothers helped to clear in the new country. The public schools and a few terms at Wyoming Academy was his fitting for his career. Entering upon trade in a small way with a brother, they later established a store at Churchville, N.Y., but in 1845 they removed their business to Lake Mills, Wis., where, in 1848, Mr. Fargo, with partners, built the largest machine works in the State west of Milwaukee. In a few years he bought out the whole plant and several hundred acres of land about the village, which he cut up into house lots and sold as fast as the demand came. He also had a large farm upon which he conducted a creamery, and besides these branches he had a large general store. While active in these varied interests he was always public-spirited and alert for his personal duties as a good citizen. The village grew up around his business, and the people were largely in his employ, and he had great power over their welfare, which he ever exercised with wisdom and kindness.

Children of Enoch B. and Morilla (Churchill) Fargo, born at Lake Mills, Wis.

1. Frank Brown Fargo, b. April 25, 1845; m. 1st, Emma M. Jenne, Nov. 19, 1867; m. 2d, Louise M. Mears, Jan. 11, 1893, at Oshkosh, Wis. Mr. Fargo received a good education in the public schools and Wisconsin University, besides his business training under his father. He established the largest plant for producing dairy supplies in the United States, and besides this he owns and operates a stock and dairy farm of several hundred acres. Mrs. Emma M. (Jenne) Fargo died April, 1891, leaving one child, (1) Fannie Maria, who was born July, 1868; m. John L. Crump, at Lake Mills, and has one child, Roland Fargo Crump.
   Children of F. B. and Louise M. (Mears) Fargo, all born at Lake Mills: (1) Dorothy Morilla Fargo, b. July 11, 1894; (2) Stuart Mears Fargo, b. Oct. 8, 1897; (3) Frank Barber Fargo, b. June 3, 1900.
2. Sarah Fargo, b. Oct. 14, 1847; m. Levi W. Ostrander, Nov. 19, 1867. She was educated at Galesburg Female College. They removed to Olympia, Washington, where he was a banker. She died at Olympia, Aug. 8, 1894, leaving one child, (1) Harry Fargo Ostrander, b. May, 1876.
3. Enoch James Fargo, b. March 14, 1850; m. 1st, Mary Rutherford, January, 1876. She was born March 1, 1857, and died March 5, 1895, at Lake Mills, Wis.; m. 2d, Addie Hoyt, who d. June 19, 1901; m. 3d, Mattie Hoyt, Feb. 17, 1902. Mr. E. J. Fargo, educated at a commercial school, engaged at first with his father in general trade, and afterwards joined his brother, F. B., in the dairy goods business. He has also a large farm, where all branches of farming go on in up-to-date methods. He is an active and influential citizen. Children of E. J. Fargo, all by first wife: (1) Elsie Rutherford Fargo, b Dec. 1, 1876; (2) Myrtie Churchill Fargo, b. June 23, 1878; d. Feb. 9, 1887; (3) Mattie Pauline Fargo, b. Sept. 14, 1883.
4. Isaac Latimer Fargo, b. Oct. 22, 1851; d. May 9, 1901. He received a liberal education, finishing up at Chicago University. He started out upon what promised to be a successful dramatic career upon the stage, but frail health prohibited the pursuit of this profession, and he was taken into the business with his brother as chemical superintendent of the color department, until ill health forced his removal to Redlands, Cal., where he died, May 9, 1901. He m. 1st, Kate L. Hoyt, Oct. 30, 1877, who died Nov. 5, 1878, without issue; m. 2d, Kate A. Mills, Dec. 25, 1883, and by her had one child, (1) Marjorie Vale Fargo, b. June 16, 1886.

5. Corydon Thompson Fargo, b. May 10, 1855; m. Emma Edgerton, Jan. 8, 1879. He was educated at the State University
at Madison, Wis., and engaged in farming with all modern
methods and improvements, combining the up-to-date dairy
and stock-raising business, on a grand scale. Children of C. T.
and Emma E. Fargo : (1) Gertrude Evelyn Fargo, b. July 7,
1880; (2) George Edgerton Fargo, b. June 16, 1882; (3)
Marion Vienna Fargo, b. Jan. 7, 1885; (4) Jeannette Fargo,
b. June 16, 1887; (5) Howard Corydon Fargo, b. Aug. 5,
1890.

6. Florence Jane Fargo, b. Oct. 13, 1865; m. Calvin Larison, at
Olympia, Wash. They live at Seattle, where he is an official
on the Northern Pacific R.R. They have two children, (1)
Winifred Larison, b. 1891; (2) Margaret Larison, b. 1893.

VII. SARAH L.,[7] b. June 6, 1826; m. JOHN GILBERT, of Albion, N.Y.,
a farmer.
They had two sons, and she died of consumption, in 1863.
One of the sons died soon after from the same disease. The other,
Richard Gilbert, married and lives in Albion, N.Y.

107.

CYRUS[6] CHURCHILL (JOSEPH,[5] SAMUEL,[4] SAMUEL[3]
JOSEPH,[2] JOSIAH[1]). Born in Hubbardton, Vt., Feb. 9, 1783, and
died at Ypsilanti, Mich., Aug. 18, 1860. He lived in Stafford,
Lewiston, and Cambray, N.Y., for some years, but settled finally in
Ypsilanti, Mich. Married, Feb. 23, 1813, RACHEL HUSTLER,
daughter of Thomas. Her father was a soldier in the English
army, but during a battle deserted to the Americans and served in
their army to the end of the war, rising to the rank of major in the
Continental Army. Rachel (Hustler) Churchill died Oct. 1, 1844.

Children.

I. AMY K. R.,[7] b. Dec. 11, 1813; never married, but lived and
cared for her parents, and occupied the old home until her
death, Feb. 6, 1886.

288   II. JOSEPH T. H.,[7] b. Dec. 28, 1815; m. HARRIET (HUBBARD)
ARNOLD, widow of John.

III. SYLVIA A. J.,[7] b. Aug. 5, 1824; m 1st, DANIEL LOCKWOOD;
m. 2d (——) LACY; m. 3d (——) (——-). Died March
18, 1892. No children.

289   IV. LEWIS MARQUIS,[7] b. Oct. 3, 1827; m. REBECCA CORDELIA
MAPES; lived at Duck Creek, Wis., about 1860. No children.

V. ELIAS CASS,[7] b. May 8, 1829; m. JENNIE TERWILLIGER, lived at
Carson City.

290   VI. ALFRED WILSON,[7] b. May 10, 1832; m. (——) (——-). No
children.
He died from a wound received at the battle of Cedar Creek,
Va., Oct. 19, 1864.

108.

·CHARLES[6] CHURCHILL (JOSEPH[5] SAMUEL,[4] SAMUEL,[3]
JOSEPH,[2] JOSIAH[1]). Born in Hubbardton, Vt., Dec. 10, 1787.
Settled in Stafford, Genesee County, N.Y. He was killed by the
Indians in the battle at Black Rock, Dec. 31, 1813. Married
POLLY HYDE. They had one child, who died young.

109.

DANIEL⁶ CHURCHILL.(JOSEPH,⁵ SAMUEL,⁴ SAMUEL,³ JOSEPH,²
JOSIAH¹). Born in Hubbardton, Vt., Jan. 4, 1792. Settled in
Stafford, Genesee County, N.Y. He removed from there to Illinois,
and lived near Sparta, Ind. He was a bridge-builder, and moved
from place to place as his contracts called him. He died of cholera,
at Chillicothe, O., July 20, 1833.

Married 1st, in Stafford or Batavia, N.Y., about 1814, SUBMIT
HAWES, who was born March 23, 1785, and died Sept. 15 1827;
married 2d, in Chillicothe, O., MRS. MILLER.

Children of First Wife.

I. JEANNETTE,⁷ b. in Stafford, N.Y., Dec. 15, 1815; m. MARTIN
POWELL, in Sparta, Dearborn County, Ind., April 12, 1838. He d.
Dec. 5, 1883, and she d. April 2, 1892.

Children born in Dearborn County, Ind.

1. William Powell, b. March 16, 1839; m. Margarette Shankland,
March, 1863. He lives at Mount Vernon, Mo.
2. Thomas C. Powell, b. Aug. 25,1840; m. Margaret Logan, March
16,1869. He lives at Williamsport, Ind. His wife d. Dec.
18, 1889.
3. John Powell, b. Jan. 31, 1842; d. unmarried, Feb. 1, 1872.
4. Mary A. Powell, b. Sept. 1, 1843; unmarried, lives in Chadron,
Neb.
5. Alvah Marion Powell, b. Dec. 30, 1845; m. Mattie Shankland.
6. Daniel Churchill Powell, b Jan. 25, 1848; d. April 23,1864.
7. Eliza J. Powell, b. Feb. 2, 1850; m. George Logan, Dec. 28,
1870.

NOTE.—Mrs. Mary A. Stewart, who has been my chief informant in relation to
Daniel Churchill, her father, relates that her mother went from Brattleboro,
Vt., to Stafford, N.Y., in the family of General Worthy L. Churchill, and
there, at his brother's house, Daniel met and married her. They lived a few
years in Stafford, and then in company with his brother Alvah, Daniel went to
the West. They took their families along, Daniel his wife and one child, and
Alvah the same. Like many of the early pioneers, they floated down the Ohio
river on a flat boat which held all their earthly possessions. When they
reached Aurora, Ind., their brother, Joseph, who had been settled some years at
Sparta, happened to be at Aurora on business, and recognized them, and running down to the shore hailed them, and all stopped over with him for the time.
Alvah settled two years in Kentucky, and then returned to Sparta. Daniel took
up a farm in Edwards County and lived there several years, and then engaged in
building bridges, mostly over the Erie canal. He was a natural mechanic, and
skilful with tools even as a boy. There are pieces of furniture and spinning-
wheels still in existence, it is said, which he made in his youth. Mrs. Huldah
Piersons, Mrs. Stewart says, had a stand which he constructed when a boy of
sixteen years. Sometime before 1827 he removed with his family to Tusca-
rawas, O., and there his first wife died. His second wife, Mrs. Miller, was a
widow with a large family, but only the youngest daughter, about twelve years
of age, came to live in Mr. Churchill's home. His death was quite sudden, and
his family was left poor, the prairie farm was sold for taxes, and the children
found homes for a time with strangers, but afterwards with relatives. The
above information, and the account of the family of Jeannette (Churchill)
Powell, have been given me by Mrs. Stewart and Miss Mary A. Powell, the
latter of Chadron, Neb. — EDITOR.

291 II. JULIUS,[7] b. in Edward County, Ill., Dec. 20, 1820; m. PIRELLA M. FALKNER.

   III. MARY ANN,[7] b. in Edward County, Oct. 15, 1823; m. DR. S. S. STEWART, Cincinnati, Nov. 16, 1852. Dr. Stewart d. Jan. 18 1873. They had no children. Mrs. Stewart lives now (1903) in Moore's Hill, Ind.

110.

REV. ALVAH[6] CHURCHILL (JOSEPH,[5] SAMUEL,[4] SAMUEL,[3] JOSEPH,[2] JOSIAH[1]). Born in Hubbardton, Vt., May 15, 1794. He grew up on the farm, and lived the sturdy life of the farmer boys of his day. He attended school in winter and worked the rest of the year. He managed to acquire a more than ordinary education, as he was a diligent student of such books as he could procure. He never saw a grammar until after he had finished at the district schools, and bought the first one he saw. He learned the trade of carriage-maker, and was a good carpenter. He was in service for a time during the War of 1812, but we have no definite account of the circumstances. For a few years after his marriage he lived in Hubbardton; but in the spring of 1819 started West, and with his wife and child joined his brother Daniel at General Churchill's, in Stafford, N.Y., and with him proceeded to their future home in the far West, as has been related in the account of his brother Daniel's journey. An opportunity to teach school opening in Lexington, Ky., he went there from Sparta and taught two years, then returned to Sparta and lived with his brother, who was then unmarried; but took up a land claim and cleared a farm meantime, within a short distance of his brother Joseph's. On his return from Kentucky, he was ordained as a Baptist minister, and began as a volunteer preacher to the isolated and poor in the outlying settlements, riding away on Saturday on horseback, with saddle-bags filled with books and tracts, preaching in some church or school-house on Sunday, and returning home on Monday, while the wife with her small family managed the home, enduring the many hardships of pioneer life. His missionary work was voluntary and free. After years of this rough life, he removed to Wilmington, Ind., in order to secure better school advantages for his children There he built a church, and filled the pulpit until the people were able to hire a pastor. He engaged also in carriage-making. He was public spirited, and very active in school affairs. He was an ardent patriot in the years preceding and during the Civil War. He was a faithful minister, an influential and upright citizen, a self-sacrificing and loyal friend of all. He was not entirely successful in his business, and never accumulated property. Although of a strong family, his strenuous hard work and exposure in early and middle life told upon his

health in his later years.   He died May 15, 1867. Married 1st, at
Hubbardton, Vt., in 1816, NANCY HOLMES, who was born Sept. 1,
1793, and died Oct. 2, 1836, in Wilmington, Ind.   Married 2d, at
Wilmington, Ind., in 1841, ELMIRA SMITH, who survived her husband.

Children of Rev. Alvah and Nancy (Holmes) Churchill.

I.   MARIETTE,[7] b. Jan. 25, 1817; m. 1st, NATHAN MERRILL TENNEY,
from Maine, Nov. 19, 1836; m. 2d, ALEXANDER LOWE.   He died
Jan. 18, 1854; m. 3d, R. J. B. ROBERTS, May 21, 1855.
She died in Delaware, Ind., September, 1869.

Children of First Husband.

1.   Harriet Tenney, d. young.
2.   Jane Tenney, d. young.

Children of Second Husband.

3.   Alexina Lowe, m. Flavius C. Fox, Dec. 25, 1880.
Lived at Solida, Col.   Child: (1) Marie Churchill Fox, m.
Maurice Blockmore Lewis, April 23, 1902.
4.   Judson Lowe, d. aged sixteen years.

Children of Third Husband.

5.   Holmes Churchill Roberts; m., but wife's name not obtained.
They lived at Cincinnati, O. (1016 West 9th street).   Chil-
dren: (1) Abbie Roberts; (2) Bessie Roberts; (3) William
Roberts.

II.   ESTHER ANN,[7] b. Lexington, Ky., Oct. 3, 1819; m. 1st, JOHN
BLACKMORE, Sept. 3, 1840; m. 2d, R. J. ROBERTS, Wilmington,
Nov. 4, 1869.
They lived at Wilmington and Delaware, Ind.   He was a farmer.

Children by First Husband.

1.   Alvah R. Blackmore, b. Wilmington, Ind., Oct. 4, 1841; m.
Mary Sage, Delaware, Ind., Aug. 3, 1865.
2.   Eliza Blackmore, b. Delaware, Ind., March 17, 1845; m. T. B.
Louis, Delaware, Ind., Nov. 10, 1863.
Mr. Louis was the son of Jacob and Barbara (Smith) Louis,
and was a merchant at Logansport, Ind.   Mrs. Olive A. (Blackmore) Louis was educated at Moore's Hill College.

Children born at Logansport, Ind.

(1)   Charles Harvey Louis, b. Aug. 22, 1864; d. Oct. 3, 1864.
(2)   Effie V. Louis, b. Nov. 19, 1866; m. Robert W. McIl-
vaine, Lafayette, Ind., Aug. 12, 1897.
(3)   Jeanette A. Louis, b. Nov. 9, 1869; m. W. J. Rosebery,
Dec. 18, 1896.
(4)   Maurice Blackmore Louis, b. April 17, 1873; m. Marie
Churchill Fox, Richmond, Ind., April 23, 1902.

3.   Olive A. Blackmore, b. Delaware, Ind., Jan. 30, 1853; m. J. J.
Lansing, Delaware, Ind., Sept. 17, 1874; d. Dec. 9, 1886.

292   III.   JOHN RANSOM,[7] b. Dec. 3, 1821; m. SARAH MAYHEW, Jan. 1, 1852.
IV.   NANCY ORILLA,[7] b. at Sparta, Ind., March 6, 1824; m. ROBERT
DELOS BROWN, Aug. 17, 1841.   She d. April, 1847.

Children.

1. Emma Brown, m. Mr. Fiddler.   Lives 119 Ramsay ave., Indianapolis, Ind.
2. Latham Brown.   Lives at Mitchell, Ind.

V   OLIVE M.,[7] b. at Sparta, Ind., April 5, 1827; m. THOMAS BLACKMORE, April 5, 1849.   They lived at Elizabethtown, O.

Children.

1. Son, b. Feb. 15, 1851; d. in infancy.
2. Alice Blackmore, b. March 18, 1852.
2. Cora Blackmore, b. April 8, 1854; m. Charles Curtis, Feb. 26, 1884.   Child: Roy Churchill Curtis.
4. Alta Holmes Blackmore, b. Nov. 4, 1856.
5. Ida Blackmore, b. May 4, 1859.

VI.   WILLIAM HARVEY,[7] b. near Wilmington, Ind., Oct. 28, 1829; d. at Aurora, Aug. 18, 1866.   He acquired a good education, and was a school-teacher for some years, until 1852, when he enlisted in the regular army as a private, at Newport, Ky., in the fifth cavalry, made up mostly of Southern men.   Sidney Johnson was colonel and Robert E. Lee, lieutenant-colonel of the regiment, which was stationed in Texas when the Civil War broke out.   His officers joined the South, and he was given leave to get out of the State in a certain time.   He came North and served through the war on the Union side.   He was orderly-sergeant in General Grant's cavalry escort for two years, was wounded and sent home once on furlough.   He rose from the ranks to the rank of brevet major, with rank of captain.   After the war, and while stationed at Warrington, Ind., his horse reared and fell upon him while on parade, and he died from the injuries received.   He was a brave soldier and a loyal patriot and true friend.

VII.   CAROLINE L.,[7] b. near Wilmington, Ind., Dec. 2, 1831; m. 1st, CHARLES WEBBER, Aug. 2, 1857; m. 2d, DANIEL STANTON, Nov. 22, 1877.   Mr. Webber was born at Aurora, Ind., Oct. 4, 1824, son of Jona and Sarah White Webber, and died at Aurora, April 28, 1861.   Mr. Stanton was born near Lynchburg, Va., April 6, 1805, son of Latham and Huldah Butler Stanton; d. at Richmond, Ind., July 15, 1894.   His parents were originally from Nantucket, Mass.

One Child of First Husband.

1. Mary Davis Webber, b. at Aurora, Ind., June 1, 1858; m. Clayton B. Hunt, at Richmond, Ind., Oct. 12, 1893.   Mr. Hunt was b. at Richmond, Ind., Nov. 23, 1845.

VIII.   SUSAN JANE,[7] b. near Wilmington, Ind., Feb. 21, 1884; m. REV. S. J. KAHLER, July 21, 1859.   She was thrown upon her own resources at an early age, owing to the failure of her father's health and business.   She was obliged to work hard and economize, and study diligently to acquire what her ambition demanded, a liberal education.   Teaching to pay her own way, studying hard and living with close economy, she was able to graduate, in 1858, at Moore's Hill College, with the highest honors in her class. She was appointed instructor in the Preparatory Department. Mr. Kahler was professor of mathematics at the college, having graduated from the State University of Kansas in 1858.   After one year's association on the college faculty, these two were married, and after three years in the college, Mr. Kahler began the work of an itinerant Methodist minister, which he followed eight year's in Indiana and eight years in Kansas.   In 1883 he was forced to retire from the ministry on account of the failure of his voice.   They removed to California, and now reside at Fernando.   Mrs. Kahler has furnished the editor of this volume the facts concerning her father's life.

' *Children.*

1. Elmer E. Kahler, b. at Moore's Hill, Ind., May 31, 1861; d. Aug. 24, 1862.
2. Carrie W. Kahler, b. at Star City, Kan., Nov. 3, 1863; d. Jan. 20, 1864.
3. Eugene W. Kahler, b. July 30, 1866; d. Aug. 14, 1866.

IX. ALVAH MARION,[7] b. June 8, 1836, and d. July 5, 1837.

111.

JOSEPH [6] CHURCHILL (JOSEPH,[5] SAMUEL,[4] SAMUEL,[3] JOSEPH,[2] JOSIAH [1]). Born at Hubbardton, Vt., Sept. 9, 1796, and was there brought up on the farm. He went to the West in 1818. Stayed the first winter in Cincinnati, and the next spring located a land-claim at what is now Sparta, Ind. He became a prosperous farmer, and was engaged somewhat in laying out and building roads and turnpikes. He was a much respected and upright citizen, and was greatly interested in the development of his farm and his stock, which was the finest in the county. Mr. James O. Churchill, of Cheyenne, Wyo., Miss Jessie Kelsey, Moore's Hill, Ind., and Miss Minnie Roberts, of Pierceville, Ind., have assisted the editor much in the compiling of this family. He died in Sparta, Dec. 9, 1859. Married, at Napoleon, Ind., Dec. 15, 1822, MARY HENIGAN.

Children born at Sparta.

I. EVALINE,[7] b. Nov. 6, 1823; m. LEANDER HOOPER KELSEY, Sparta, June 21, 1846. They lived at Sparta, Ind., Aurora, Ind., and Moore's Hill, Ind. He was a teacher and a farmer. His parents were John and Suky (Taylor) Kelsey.

Children.

1. Oscar Kelsey, b. at Sparta, May 10, 1847; m. Tirzah E. Copeland, Dec. 26, 1875.
2. Joseph Kelsey, b. at Sparta, March 14, 1849; d. Aug. 5, 1849.
3. Ernest Kelsey, b. Aurora, Dec. 25, 1850; m. Laura B. Dillon, Council Bluffs, Iowa, Aug. 30, 1876.
4. Marion Kelsey, b. Aurora, Jan. 21, 1852; m. Kate Holbrook, Newport, Ky., Feb. 29, 1879.
5. Curt Kelsey, b. Sparta, June 14, 1854; m. Mollie Sayles, Loveland, Ia., Jan. 28, 1883.
6. Jessie Kelsey, b. Moore's Hill, June 18, 1856.

293   II. CHARLES,[7] b. June 24, 1825; m. 1st, MARTHA HUSTIN, Dec. 25, 1847; m. 2d, MARY A. HINDS, Jan. 29, 1852.
III. DOLLY,[7] b. April 16, 1827; m. BENJAMIN BURLINGAME, at Wilmington, Ind., Dec. 19, 1861. They lived at first at Wilmington, Ind., and after 1865/6, at Sparta. He was a farmer and wagon-maker. He held the office of commissioner of Dearborn County for six years. They lived on the old farm settled by Joseph Churchill in 1819.

Children.

1. Mary A. Burlingame, b. Wilmington, Feb. 7, 1864; d. Aug. 2, 1864.

2. Harry Stewart Burlingame, b. Wilmington, July .21, 1865; m.
Minnie L. Houston, dau. of John and Margaret (Beathe)
Houston, Sparta, Sept. 22, 1886. He was a graduate of
Moore's Hill College, and is a farmer and school teacher.
Lives at Sparta. Their children: (1) Franklin Stewart, b.
Jan. 27, 1889; (2) Olive Dorothy, b. Nov. 18, 1890.
3. Caroline Wood Burlingame, b. at Sparta, Nov. 4, 1867; m.
Joseph E. Allen, of Sparta.

IV. BURKE,[7] b. July 28, 1828. Left home in his youth and all trace of
him was lost.
V. HARRIET,[7] b. Nov. 28, 1829; m. JOSEPH RICHARDSON, Dec. 28,
1853. They lived at Sparta, Ind., where he was a cooper.

Children born at Sparta.

1. Emma Richardson; m. C. Annible, of Arkansas.
2. William Richardson.

VI. ROXANNA,[7] b. April 29, 1831; m. D. R. Taylor, July 1, 1849. He
was the son of Aaron and Mary (———) Taylor. They lived
at Sparta, Ind., and he was there engaged in coopering. Mr.
Taylor served three years in the Civil War, in Company K,
Sixty-eighth Regiment Indiana Volunteers.

Children born at Sparta.

1. Joseph Taylor, b. July 6, 1850.
2. Irving C. Taylor, b. March 19, 1852; d. March 13, 1868.
3. Minnie A. Taylor, b. March 30, 1854; m., at Sparta, Samuel
Roberts, April 29, 1891. He was the son of Jefferson and
Matilda (Hodges) Roberts. They live (1902) at Pierceville,
Ind. He is a farmer and poultry-raiser. He served in the
Civil War three years, in Company F, Thirty-seventh Regi-
ment Indiana Volunteers.

Child born at Versailles.

(1) Roxanna C. Roberts, b. Sept. 10, 1892.
4. Ella T. Taylor, b. Aug. 19, 1856.
5. Charles V. Taylor, b. Aug. 29, 1859; d. December, 1862.
6. Oscar F., b. Nov. 2, 1865; m. Maggie Ramsay, Aurora, April
28, 1892.

294 VII. GEORGE VERNON,[7] b. Nov. 20, 1832; m. EMILY A. DAVIS.
VIII. RHODA,[7] b. Aug. 20, 1835; m. F. M. JOHNSON, September, 1855;
no children.
IX. ALTA,[7] b. July 5, 1838; m. HARVEY COMSTOCK, at Santa Cruz,
Dec. 21, 1876. He was the son of Louis and Elizabeth (Latin)
Comstock, and was a farmer at Santa Cruz, where they lived.
They had children born there.

Children.

1. Paul W. Comstock, b. Nov. 8, 1877; d. May 11, 1891.
2. Mary Josephine Comstock, b. Feb. 4, 1879; d. Dec. 24, 1889.
3. Dollie H. B. Comstock, b. March 1, 1881; d. May 20, 1891.

X. AUGUSTA JEANNETTE,[7] b. Nov. 9, 1840; m. GEORGE GOULD, 1861.
295 XI. JOHN F.,[7] b. Aug. 21, 1847; m. ANNA GARNER, January, 1870.

112.

PHILO[6] CHURCHILL (SAMUEL,[5] SAMUEL,[4] SAMUEL,[3] JOSEPH,[2]
JOSIAH[1]). Born in Massachusetts, and brought up in Hubbardton,
whither his father moved when he was a child. We have not
been able to obtain much information of him or his descendants, ex-

cept the reference made by Amos Churchill, noted below (see 114), and other casual mention. It is said that two of his sons were merchants in Alexander, N.Y., in 1834. Mr. Henry E. Churchill, of Middletown, N.Y., wrote, in 1890, that Philo lived and died in Alexander. Married (———) Castle, a sister of his brother Zenas' wife, and had

Children.

    I. ALMOND.[7]
    II. CASTLE.[7]
  III. PHILO, JR.[7]
  IV. SARAH.[7]

113.

ZENAS[6] CHURCHILL (SAMUEL,[5] SAMUEL,[4] SAMUEL,[3] JOSEPH,[2] JOSIAH[1]). Born in Hubbardton, Vt. Removed to Genesee County, N.Y. Married (———) CASTLE. They lived awhile in Attica, N.Y. but in 1846 were living in Kane County, Ill. We have as yet no further record of the family, except that Henry E. Churchill, above mentioned, says that they had a son, CASTLE.

114.

DAVID[6] CHURCHILL (SAMUEL,[5] SAMUEL,[4] SAMUEL,[3] JOSEPH,[2] JOSIAH[1]). Born in Hubbardton, Vt., May 29, 1786. Mr. Amos Churchill, No. 105, the chronicler of the Hubbardton family, says that David, with his brothers, went West, and settled in Attica and Alexander, N.Y., and afterwards went to Kane County, Ill. We have not found any further account of them. Married 1st, name not obtained. Married 2d, Feb. 23, 1829, SARAH PRESCOTT, who was born April 24, 1798.

Children of First Wife.

     I. ELVIRA,[7] b. Nov. 2, 1813; m. SOLOMON SHERWIN.
    II. POLLY,[7] b. Dec. 27, 1815; d. young.
  III. MARIAH,[7] b. Dec. 1, 1816; never married.
  IV. ELIZA,[7] b. Sept. 5, 1820; m. JOHN A. WATERMAN.
    V. NANCY,[7] b. June 25, 1822; m. 1st, AZRO WATERS; m. 2d, WILLIAM HUBBARD.
  VI. WILLIAM,[7] b. Nov. 21, 1824; m., it is said, late in life; no children.
 VII. DAVID H.,[7] b. Oct. 5, 1826; d. at age of six months.

Children of Second Wife.

VIII. ESTHER,[7] b. Aug. 16, 1831; m. R. S. A. TARBELL, July 1, 1855.

Children.

  1. Lillie R. Tarbell, b. July 9, 1856; m. D. F. Rockhold, March 11, 1876.
  2. Myrta A. Tarbell, b. Oct. 9, 1858; m. Buzzell Wells, Feb. 26, 1880.
  3. Reuben J. Tarbell, b. June 24, 1861; m. Laura Wood, Dec. 30, 1887.
  4. Robert A. Tarbell, b. Aug. 13, 1862.

5. Menzo E. Tarbell, b. May 12, 1864; m. Emma Reagle, May 6, 1886.
6. Marquis De La F. Tarbell, b. May 30, 1866.
7. Amy Tarbell, b. Oct. 16, 1868.
8. Amanda Tarbell, b. May 9, 1871.

296   IX. GEORGE W.,[7] b. April 20, 1833; m. ADDIE E. WILLIAMS, 1865/6.
297   X. M. DE LAFAYETTE,[7] b. Feb. 8, 1835; m. MARY J. CAMPBELL, July, 1, 1855.
298   XI. OSCAR C.,[7] b. March 4, 1837; m. MARY I. DUNBAR, July 3, 1876.
      XII. ORSON,[7] b. Oct. 3, 1839; d. March 3, 1841.
      XIII. AMANDA,[7] b. March 14, 1841; m. HEMAN GOODNOUGH.
299   XIV. MENZO,[7] b. Dec. 13, 1843; m. S. V. CLARK, Nov. 3, 1870.

115.

RUFUS[6] CHURCHILL (SAMUEL,[5] SAMUEL,[4] SAMUEL[3] JOSEPH,[2] JOSIAH[1]). Born in Hubbardton, Vt., and was brought up there. Removed to Alexander, N.Y., and there married (——) STRONG. In 1846 they were in Kane County, Ill., but we have no further account of the family.

116.

JOHN[6] CHURCHILL (JOHN,[5] SAMUEL,[4] SAMUEL,[3] JOSEPH,[2] JOSIAH[1]). Born at Hubbardton, Vt., April 15, 1787. Removed first to Homer, N.Y., and thence to Portland, N.Y. He was a farmer and lived, mostly, at Westfield, N.Y. Married, at Homer, N.Y., 1813, MARY HOUSE, daughter of Deacon John.

Children.

I. PHEBE,[7] b. at Homer, 1815; m. HAMILTON CHERRY, in Portland, N.Y. They settled near Buffalo, N.Y, became perosperous and wealthy. She died in 1896. He died 1891.
   They had three sons and one daughter, it is said.
II. MARTHA M.,[7] b. at Portland, N.Y., 1818; d. 1826.

117.

SYLVESTER[6] CHURCHILL (JOHN,[5] SAMUEL,[4] SAMUEL,[3] JOSEPH,[2] JOSIAH[1]). Born at Hubbardton, Oct. 7, 1788. Came to Portland, N.Y., soon after marriage, and with his brother John, whose wife was his wife's sister, settled there, Deacon House, the father-in-law, having settled in the adjoining town of Westfield. Mr. Churchill was a farmer. In 1835 he sold out his property in Portland, and removed to Munson, O. Married, at Homer, N.Y., January, 1816, THEODOSIA HOUSE, daughter of Deacon John.

Children born at Portland, N. Y.

300   I. ISAIAH,[7] b. Nov. 1, 1816; m. EUNICE MORRIS, Franklin, O., April, 1839; d. 1851.
301   II. ORVILLE S.,[7] b. Oct. 18, 1818; m. SARAH VANNANKEEN, Chardon, O., 1842.
302   III. DANIEL,[7] b. July 16, 1820; m. JULIA HOUSE, Westfield, N.Y., 1841; d. 1896.

303　　IV. Levi,[7] b. Dec. 21, 1822; m. Sally A. Hintston, Munson, O., Oct.
　　　　　　8, 1851.
　　　　　V. Martha,[7] b. Jan. 4, 1826; m. George Warner, March 4, 1847.
　　　　　　They lived in Vida, Minn., it is said.
　　　　VI. Mary,[7] b. May 11, 1827; m. Moses Cluff, 1848.
　　　　　　They lived in Olmsted County, Minn., we have been told.

118.

ALVIN [6] CHURCHILL (John,[5] Samuel,[4] Samuel,[3] Joseph,[2] Josiah [1]). Born in Hubbardton, Nov. 7, 1794. Removed and settled in Scott, N.Y. Alvin, the father, died March 26, 1878. The mother died June 23, 1864. Married Sally Seeley, born in Pompey, N.Y., Dec. 17, 1805.

Children born in Scott, N. Y.

　　　I. Fidelia,[7] b. in Scott, N.Y., Nov. 21, 1824; m. Edwin W. Pratt,
　　　　　March 17, 1858. They live at Homer, N.Y. No children.
　　　II. Clarissa,[7] b. June 26, 1826; m. Peter Curtis, April, 1856.

Children.

　　　　1. Adelbert Curtis, b. March, 1857.
　　　　2. Leonardus Curtis, b. October, 1858.
304　　III. Orville,[7] b. July 3, 1829; m. Mary Jane Rigles.
　　　IV. Philena,[7] b. May 28, 1831; d. May 16, 1833.
305　　V. Samuel Lyman,[7] b. Feb. 15, 1834; m. Mrs. Mary A. (Alvord)
　　　　　Randall, Aug. 27, 1858.
　　　VI. Nelson,[7] b. April 20, 1841.
　　　　　Enlisted in the Union Army for the Civil War, was taken pris-
　　　　　oner at the battle of Gettysburg, and confined at Belle Isle prison;
　　　　　was at last exchanged, but died in the hospital at Annapolis, Md.

119.

JOTHAM [6] CHURCHILL (John,[5] Samuel,[4] Samuel,[3] Joseph,[2] Josiah [1]). Born in Hubbardton, Vt., Dec. 29, 1804. Removed with his father's family, to Tully, N.Y., and lived there until his marriage. Married Miss Randell, and, it is said, had a large family of children, three of whose names have come to us from Mr. Sylvester C. Churchill, of Tula, N.Y., son of Chauncey, brother of Jotham. The family settled in Iowa.

Three of their Children.

　　　　I. Silas.[7]
　　　　II. William.[7]
　　　　III. John.[7]

120.

CHAUNCEY [6] CHURCHILL (John,[5] Samuel,[4] Samuel,[3] Joseph,[2] Josiah [1]). Born at Tully, N.Y., Oct. 3, 1808. He was a farmer and lived at East Scott, Cortland County, N.Y. Married, March 17, 1834, Catharine Merry, daughter of John and Clarinda (Davis) Merry.

Children born at Scott, N. Y.

I. SYLVESTER C.,[7] b. Dec. 20, 1834; m. HELEN DOWD, Otisco, N.Y., March 28, 1866.
   They lived at Tula, Cortland County, N.Y. He is a farmer. They had two adopted children, Burdette A. Rust and Inez E. Anthony. He has helped us about this family.

II. JOHN W.,[7] b. Aug. 13, 1836; m. ALICE P. MARTINIE.

III. OLIVE C.,[7] b. Feb. 16, 1838; d. May 11, 1838.

IV. SYLVANUS A.,[7] b. Nov. 26, 1839; m. 1st, CAROLINE EADIE, Nov. 21, 1867; m. 2d, SARAH E. WOODWORTH, Sept. 7, 1892.

V. OLIVER CLINTON,[7] b. March 22, 1841; m. DELPHINE ROE, at Preble, N.Y., Oct. 26, 1865.

VI. MARTHA ASENATH,[7] b. Nov. 24, 1842; m. JAMES SHAWHAN, Champaign County, Ill., Nov. 8, 1871.

Child.

1. Walter Shawhan, b. Jan. 18, 1873; d. Aug. 28, 1873.
   Martha Asenath, the mother, died Dec. 12, 1893; James, the father, died Dec. 25, 1891.

VII. OLIVE C.,[7] b. Aug. 6, 1844; m. WILLIAM S. KELLOGG, Nov. 10, 1864.
   They lived at Homer, N.Y., where he was employed in a manufactory.

Children.

1. Olin Clay Kellogg, b. at South Spafford, N.Y., April 20, 1870; m. Effie Wheelock.
   He is a graduate of Syracuse University, 1892. In 1901 instructor in North Western University, Evanston, Ill., A.B. and Ph.D.

2. Alice Lydia Kellogg, b. at Homer, N.Y., Oct. 20, 1874.

VIII. LA FAYETTE M.,[7] b. March 17, 1846; m. ELIZA PRATT, Preble, N.Y., March 9, 1870.

IX. CHLOE I.,[7] b. Oct. 4, 1847; m. WILLIAM A. KELLOGG, East Scott, N.Y., Nov. 18, 1869.
   They lived at Homer, N.Y., and later in New York City. They had four children.

Children.

1. Gertrude Amanda Kellogg, b. 1870; m. Orrie P. Cummings.
2. Edward Leland Kellogg.
3. Olive Catharine Kellogg.
4. William Kellogg.

X. CATHARINE HELEN,[7] b. April 10, 1849; m. GEORGE BURROUGHS, March 28, 1871.
   They lived at South Spafford, Onondaga County, N.Y. He is a farmer.

Child.

1. Walter L. Burroughs, b. at East Scott, March 11, 1877; m. Nina Gilbert, Homer, N.Y., July, 1897.

XI. CALEB W.,[7] b. Nov. 27, 1850; m. 1st, ACHSIE EADIE, Spafford, N.Y., March 28, 1881; m. 2d, MINNIE BROWN, Champaign County, Ill., Nov. 6, 1884.

XII. BENJAMIN F.,[7] b. July 30, 1852; m. CARRIE CHURCHILL, Spafford, N.Y., May 21, 1878.

XIII. JASON M.,[7] b. April 2, 1855; m. JENNIE FRENCH, of Spafford, N.Y., Sept. 25, 1878.

121.

DARIUS⁶ CHURCHILL (WILLIAM,⁵ SAMUEL⁴ SAMUEL,³ JOSEPH,² JOSIAH¹). Born in Hubbardton April 25, 1793. He removed with his father's family to Champlain, N.Y., about 1807, and lived there. Married, at Shoreham, Vt., about 1816, TRYPHENIA ADELINE NEWTON, daughter of Liberty and Asintha (North) Newton, born Oct. 1, 1796, at Shoreham, Vt.; died at Champlain, N.Y., June 28, 1835.

Children born in Champlain, N.Y.

313   I. GEORGE,⁷ b. March 22, 1818; m. JANE JACKSON.
        II. CAROLINE,⁷ b. Dec. 10, 1819; d. May 29, 1842; unmarried.
314   III. SAMUEL,⁷ b. March 28, 1823; m. JEMIMA D. JACKSON, Sept. 3, 1846.
315   IV. WILLIAM,⁷ b. Sept. 5, 1827; m. OLIVE REMINGTON.

122.

WILLIAM⁶ CHURCHILL, JR. (WILLIAM,⁵ SAMUEL,⁴ SAMUEL,³ JOSEPH,² JOSIAH¹). Born in Hubbardton, Vt., March 23, 1795. Removed with his father's family to Champlain, Clinton County, N.Y., about 1807. Married, Dec. 24, 1822, ISABELLA JOHNSON, born Oct. 9, 1796.

Children born in Clinton, N.Y.

316   I. WASHINGTON,⁷ b. March 19, 1824; m. MARY LUCINDA CONVERSE, Feb. 25, 1847.
        II. ELEANOR,⁷ b. July 30, 1826; m. GEORGE F. CONVERSE, Oct. 12, 1843.

Children.

    1. Albert Benson Converse, b. Oct. 18, 1844; m. Maggie J. Taylor, April 11, 1864.
    2. Samuel C. Converse, b. June 12, 1847; m. Helen M. Churchill, Oct. 24, 1869.
    3. Isabella L. Converse, b. May 21, 1850; m. Edward Baker, Jan. 1, 1871.
    4. Viola J. Converse, b. Jan. 19, 1854; d. Sept. 19, 1855.
    5. Clara E. Converse, b. Nov. 23, 1856; m. James Linton, Jan. 3, 1874.
    6. Chloe A. Converse, b. July 13, 1859.

       III. CLARISSA,⁷ b. April, 1828; m. ROYAL W. CONVERSE, Sept. 19, 1861.

Children born in Clinton, N.Y.

    1. William P. Converse, b. March 22, 1865.
    2. Effie Elsie Converse, b. Nov. 27, 1868.

317   IV. BENJAMIN,⁷ b. Feb. 22, 1831; m. HANNAH E. PRATT.
318   V. WILLIAM HENRY,⁷ b. Dec. 18, 1834; m. JANE ANN BARKER.
       VI. JAMES EDWARD,⁷ b July 14, 1837; d. Aug. 21, 1838.

125.

DR. JULIUS[6] CHURCHILL (WILLIAM,[5] SAMUEL,[4] SAMUEL,[3] JOSEPH,[2] JOSIAH [1]). Born in Hubbardton, Vt., March 20, 1802. Died in Champlain, N.Y., Feb. 7, 1881. He was only four years old when his father removed with his family to Champlain, N.Y., then a small hamlet surrounded by an almost unbroken wilderness. William Churchill, his father, bought a hundred acres of woodland and cleared a farm, known in late years as the old "Junior Churchill Place," situated on the road to Chazy. The father was a large and athletic man, and a great worker, as were his six sons. They were all able men physically and mentally. Dr. Julius stayed at home working on the farm, and attending school in the winter, until the age of twenty-one, and then against the wishes and advice of his father he started out alone to acquire a medical education. He chopped wood and taught school to get money to pursue his studies. He studied with Dr. Miles Stevenson, of Chazy, and Dr. Benjamin Moore, of Champlain. In 1826–1827 he attended lecture courses at the Medical University at Castleton, Vt., and on Aug. 28, 1828, received a diploma from the Clinton County Medical Society to practise "Physic and Surgery," and soon began practice in Champlain Village. In those days of wretched roads and sparse settlements, his practice soon extended over a wide range, which had to be traversed on horseback with saddlebags holding his stock of medicines. He was strong, enthusiastic, and skilful, and soon became popular, and had a very large clientage. He was fond of fine horses, and had the best in the country round. For some ten years, and up to 1840, he was postmaster of Champlain. He was an exceedingly active man, and fond of using tools, and about 1840 built himself an office with his own hands, and used this same office in his practice till his death. He was somewhat eccentric, a great collector of curiosities of all sorts, pictures, ancient arms and armor, minerals, fossils, and in one addition to his office, a sort of green-house, he had a wonderful variety of flowering plants, cactus-plants, one of which at his death was thirty-eight years old, and ten feet in height. In this greenhouse he kept, also, a lot of singing birds. Dr. Churchill was versatile, was a lover of music, and played well on the violin, cornet, and clarionet. He was intensely interested in physical science, especially geology and mineralogy, and when Sir Charles Lyell, the eminent English geologist, visited America, Dr. Churchill accompanied him in his exploration of the Mississippi Valley and was of great help to him, and they were always after-wards warm friends. How he found time for all his work and his extensive reading and valuable collection of books was a wonder to his friends, who knew he never neglected any of his home or professional duties. He was always up in the morning at four o'clock, and never idle. He was active and influential in public matters, and a popular and honored member of the County Medical Association. His scientific studies led him to very advanced convictions in regard to religion. He was indeed a very pronounced advocate of free thought. He was opposed and denounced by many as an atheist, and some of the more bigoted church-people honestly sought to ostracize him socially as well as to boycott his practice; but the more they persecuted and railed, the firmer he became in his convictions about religion. Theodore Parker lectured in Champlain, and the doctor found that he was in accord with the great preacher's liberal thought, and they became friends, and continued for some years to correspond. He was one of the first thinking men in America, to accept the theory of evolution. The unreasoning and ignorant bigotry of many of his friends, who, as Christian believers, turned against him, made him somewhat bitter at times, though not for long. The limits of this sketch will not admit of a full account of a very wonderful man, one of the ablest and best of all who have borne the name of Churchill. An essay on the " Life of Dr. Julius Churchill, Physician, Philosopher, and Pioneer in Rational Thought," was read before the Association for Moral and Spiritual Education, at Brooklyn, N.Y., March, 1884, by Edward J. Moore, and later published in pamphlet form. The above facts and comments have been gathered from the sketches above mentioned by the editor of this volume, who feels that so notable a member of the Hubbardton line ought to be brought to the acquaintance of his kinsfolk throughout America. The postmaster at Champlain wrote me in 1900 that none of the doctor's family remained in the town, and he knew not whether any were living or not. I have, however, just discovered his daughter, Mrs. Cornelia Traver who furnished the memoirs above noted, in 1886, and is now living in Chicago, and gives further help about her own and her brother's families. Married, in Champlain, N.Y., 1831, NANCY FILLMORE, daughter of Capt. Cepta Fillmore, and a cousin of Millard Fillmore, the thirteenth president of the United States. She was born Jan. 29, 1804, and died April 24, 1866, at Springfield, Ill.

Children born in Champlain, N. Y.

I. ASTLEY COOPER,[7] b. July 6, 1832; d. July 21, 1833.
319   II. RUSSELL,[7] b. July 14, 1833; m. MARY TURNER.
319a   III. CORNELIA SCHUYLER,[7] b. Nov. 21, 1835; m. DOLPHIN TRAVER, June 15, 1853.
320   IV. JOHN FILLMORE,[7] b. Dec. 28, 1837; m. CATHERINE WISEMAN, Dec. 2, 1863.
     V. MATILDA,[7] b. Dec. 20, 1840; d. January, 1875.

126.

JAMES[6] CHURCHILL (WILLIAM,[5] SAMUEL[4] SAMUEL,[3] JOSEPH,[2] JOSIAH[1]). Born in Hubbardton Vt., Nov. 9, 1804. Married ELIZA JOHNSON.

Child.

321   I. JOSEPH E.,[7] b. Oct. 22, 1829; m. JULIA BULL.

127.

EZEKIEL DYER[6] CHURCHILL (EZEKIEL,[5] SAMUEL,[4] SAMUEL,[3] JOSEPH,[2] JOSIAH[1]). Born at Hubbardton, Vt., July 15, 1787. Moved with his father's family to Alexander, N.Y., in 1804. He died from accidentally cutting his knee while hewing a piece of timber, Dec. 2, 1810. Married, April 3, 1810, HANNAH BAKER.

Child born after Father's Death

I. AMANDA,[7] b. 1811; m. FIDELLO TAYLOR. No children.

128.

SILAS[6] CHURCHILL (EZEKIEL,[5] SAMUEL,[4] SAMUEL,[3] JOSEPH[2] JOSIAH[1]). Born at Hubbardton, Vt, June 13, 1796. Removed with his father's family to Alexander, N.Y., in 1804. He died in Yorkshire, N.Y., Aug. 9, 1885. Married 1st, Nov. 5, 1818, ESTHER PARMELEE; died April 28, 1844. Married 2d, Oct. 23, 1844, DIANTHA BELKNAP; died March 18, 1879.

Children of First Wife.

I. DORLISKA,[7] b. Dec. 14, 1819.
II. ARABELLA,[7] b. June 14, 1822; d. Oct. 15, 1852.
III. EMILIUS,[7] b. Jan. 14, 1824; d. 1846.
322   IV. PEMBROKE,[7] b. April 29, 1826; m. CAROLINE M. CLEMENTS, Nov. 2, 1853.
V. HOMER,[7] b. June 29, 1828.
VI. EL ROY,[7] b. Sept. 14, 1830.
323   VII. DELOSS,[7] } b. Oct. 14, 1832.
324   VIII. DE FOREST,[7] }
IX. CECILIA,[7] b. May 15, 1835.
X. OCTAVIA,[7] b. April 3, 1837; d. June 13, 1876.
325   XI. EUGENE,[7] b. Oct. 14, 1840.

Child of the Second Wife.

326   XII. PULASKI,[7] b. March 24, 1846; d. March 18, 1879.

129.

LEVI WILLIAM[6] CHURCHILL (EZEKIEL,[5] SAMUEL,[4] SAMUEL,[3] JOSEPH,[2] JOSIAH[1]). Born in Alexander, N.Y., May 10, 1804. Died in Michigan in 1892. Married SOPHRONIA FRISBEE, November, 1824.

Child.

326a   I. CULLEN.[7]

130.

CULLEN DYER [6] CHURCHILL (EZEKIEL,[5] SAMUEL,[4] SAMUEL,[3] JOSEPH,[2] JOSIAH [1]).   Born at Alexander, N.Y., March 1, 1811. Lived there and at Ellington, N.Y. Died at Ellington, N.Y., Feb. 7, 1893. Married 1st, Feb. 25, 1836, CAROLINE BROWN. She died May 2, 1845. Married 2d, July 22, 1845, SARAH RUBLEE. She died Nov. 21, 1848. Married 3d, Feb. 8, 1849, EUNICE VAN DUSER. She died Jan. 3, 1859. Married 4th, Jan. 5, 1860, JANE PLATNER.

Children of First Wife.

    I. EUNICE ELIZABETH,[7] b. Dec. 9, 1836; m. MARCUS THACHER, of Ellington, N.Y. They had no children.
    II. DELPHINE LOVISA,[7] b. Feb. 3, 1838; m. CHARLES W. HEALD, Aug. 2, 1859.

Children.

    1. Charles Roderick Brigham Heald, b. Nov. 27, 1862.
    2. Mary Lizzie Heald, b. in Moline, Ill., July 20, 1864.
    3. Charles Cassimer, b. June 6, 1867.

326b III. CHARLES CARROLL,[7] b. April 30, 1839; m. CHARITY PERSON, of Ellery, Feb. 6, 1869.
    IV. CASSIMER PULASKI,[7] b. Oct 20, 1840. He was killed in the Civil War.
327 V. ALBRO RUTHVEN,[7] b. Sept. 13, 1843; m. MARY J. McLEES, of Davisburg, Mich., Feb. 26, 1877.

Child of Second Wife.

328 VI. HOMER CULLEN,[7] b. Nov. 14, 1848; m. RHODA WEEGAR, of Randolph, N.Y., December, 1876

Children of Third Wife.

    VII. EVELYN CLINTON,[7] b. Nov. 29, 1849; d. unmarried, at Randolph N.Y., Oct. 15, 1876.
    VIII. ALICE OPHELIA,[7] b. May 28, 1851; m. FRANCIS C. BATES, May, 1871. Children: (1) Mirth Bates, b. 1876; m. Willis Calkins, Oct. 12, 1897. (2) Florence Bates, b. 1885. (3) Ormal Bates, b. 1886.
    IX. LEICESTER ELROY,[7] b. Oct. 9, 1852; unmarried.
    X. HARRIET CORDELIA,[7] b. Nov. 12, 1854; m. JOEL D. TORRANCE, of Randolph, N.Y., September, 1876. No children. They lived at Randolph, where she died Jan. 19, 1894.
    XI. FRANCES MARION,[7] b. Sept. 17, 1858; d. Sept. 30, 1859.

Children of Fourth Wife.

    XII. LIZZIE EUDORA,[7] b. Oct. 29, 1860; d. June 26, 1864, of scarlet fever.
    XIII. BARDEN D.,[7] b. May 22, 1862; d. June 27, 1864, of scarlet fever.
328a XIV. WILLIS FLETCHER,[7] b. July 8. 1864; m. 1st, ALICE B. LORD, Jan. 25, 1893; m. 2d, JENNIE JOHNSON, Feb. 13, 1895.

131.

HENRY EZEKIEL [6] * CHURCHILL (EZEKIEL,[5] SAMUEL,[4] SAMUEL,[3] JOSEPH,[2] JOSIAH [1]).   Born, Alexander, N.Y., June 29, 1813.

* He changed his name, at his marriage, to Henry Ezekiel.

They lived in Alexander and Attica, N.Y. He was a dry goods merchant. Married, Nov. 23, 1837, at Alexander, CAROLINE HOLMES COGSWELL.

Children born in Alexander, and the last in Attica.

I. ORANGE CLARK,[7] b. Dec. 28, 1838; d. in Aspinwall, New Granada, S.A., April 13, 1860.
II. EVELYN ADAMS,[7] b. Aug. 16, 1842; m. GEORGE S. DREW, Dec. 31, 1862. Children: (1) Charles H. Drew, b. Sept. 20, 1863; (2) Eva Caroline Drew, b. Jan. 4, 1865; m. Dr. Gifford, in June, 1891.
III. OCTAVIA GOODALE,[7] b. Oct. 11, 1852; m. RICHARD M. RORTY, May 27, 1874, in Attica, N.Y., and lived in Middletown, N.Y.

Children.

1. Malcolm Churchill Rorty, b. May 1, 1875.
2. Philip Adams Rorty, b. Aug. 25, 1876.
3. Marian Helen Rorty, b. Dec. 11, 1878.
4. Richard Mackay Rorty, b. May 18, 1882.
5. Bertha Cogswell Rorty, b. Sept. 17, 1883.
6. Eva Winifred Rorty, b. Sept. 29, 1886.
7. James Mackay Rorty, b. March 30, 1890.

132.

NOBLE[6] CHURCHILL (LEVI,[5] CHARLES,[4] SAMUEL,[3] JOSEPH,[2] JOSIAH[1]). Born at Newington, Conn., Nov. 11, 1779. Settled first in New York, but removed to what is now Eaton, Preble County, O., about 1830. Died at Eaton, O., Jan. 28, 1866. Married, Oct. 12, 1801, OLIVE STODDARD.

Children of Noble and Olive (Stoddard) Churchill.

I. CANDACE,[7] b. Oct. 9, 1804; m. JONATHAN HOLCOMB.
Mrs. Holcomb is said to have been a very highly gifted woman and brilliant writer. Died June, 1866.

Children.

1. Son, name not known.
2. Lurania Holcomb; m. Dr. (———) Munday.
Mrs. Munday was, like her mother, highly cultured, and a gifted writer.

II. ELIZABETH,[7] b. Oct. 29, 1806; m. JOHN ADAMS.
Mrs. Elizabeth Adams died in 1877.

Children.

1. John Adams, Jr.
2. George W. Adams.
He lived in Oxford, O., a prosperous business man. One child: (1) Laura Adams.

III. EMMELINE,[7] b. April 6, 1809; m. JEREMIAH GUILD.
Mrs. Guild died in 1871.

Child.

1. Julia Guild.
IV. LAURA W.,[7] b. April 18, 1812; m. PROF. EBENEZER BISHOP.
Mrs. Bishop died in 1872.

Children.

1. Georgia Bishop, m. Mr. Schaub, of Hamilton, O.
2. Alice Bishop, m. Mr. Mason, San Diego, Cal.
V. JULIA ANN,[7] b. June 12, 1814; m. 1st, AARON WESTON, of Westboro,
Mass.; m. 2d, GEORGE GLASS.
She was highly gifted and brilliant. She died in Toledo, O.,
1871.

Children of First Husband.

1. Son, died in infancy.
2. Julia Weston, m. William Blake.
Mrs. Blake was a fine actress; at one time with Fanny Davenport, and later starred with a company of her own.

Children.

1. William Blake.   3. Ida Blake.
2. Charles Blake.   4. Lillie Blake.
The sons live in St. Louis. Ida lives in Ohio, and Lillie in
Chicago, with her cousin, Mrs. Powell.
329   VI. GILBERT W.,[7] b. April 23, 1817; m. JANE BLACK.
330   VII. CHESTERFIELD L.,[7] b. Feb. 1, 1820; m. ANNE STARKWEATHER,
May, 1850.
331   VIII. JOHN EDWIN,[7] b. August, 1822; m. JENNIE PRESTON.
332   IX. CHARLES CLINTON,[7] b. Dec. 16, 1825; m. MARY ASHE RIVERS.

133.

CHARLES BELDEN[6] CHURCHILL (LEVI,[5] CHARLES,[4] SAM-
UEL,[3] JOSEPH,[2] JOSIAH[1]). Born at Newington, Conn., Sept. 27,
1785. He removed to Boonville, N.Y., the day of their marriage,
and lived there. They made their home in their later years with
their son Charles B. Mr. Churchill served in the War of 1812, and
received a pension for years before his death, Sept. 17, 1878. Mar
ried, in Connecticut, Feb. 4, 1807, ELIZABETH HUBBARD, born in Bur-
lingtou, Conn., May 6, 1787. She died July 21, 1867.

Children born in Boonville, N. Y.

I. ETTA MARIA,[7] b. April 8, 1808; m. WILLIAM CLEVELAND.

Child.

1. Alonzo Cleveland.
333   II. LEVI MERRILL,[7] b. Feb. 8, 1811; m. HARRIET PROTHROUGH, Sept.
18, 1838.
334   III. CHARLES BELDEN,[7] b. April 25, 1813; m. LOUISA HURLBURT.
IV. ABIGAIL,[7] b. Aug. 20, 1815.
335   V. WILLIAM STEWART,[7] b. March 4, 1818.
336   VI. LEONARD HUBBARD,[7] b. April 28, 1820.
337   VII. CHESTER BECKLEY,[7] b. April 14, 1824.
VIII. ELIZABETH,[7] b. April 14, 1826.
338   IX. MARTIN LA FAYETTE,[7] b. Sept. 1, 1832.

134.

CAROLUS [6] CHURCHILL (LEVI,[5] CHARLES,[4] SAMUEL,[3] JOSEPH,[2] JOSIAH [1]). Born in Newington, Conn., April 24, 1791. Lived in New York City and Boonville, Oneida County, N.Y. Removed some time between 1831 and 1836 to Trumbull, O. Married, at German Flats, N.Y., 1811, POLLY ROWLAND.

Children born in New York, except those noted.

339   I. CARMI,[7] b. Feb. 25, 1813; m. SARAH STOWE, and d. May 9, 1892.
340   II. JOHN,[7] b. Aug. 13, 1814; m. ELEANOR BERTRAM, of East Trumbull, O.; d. April 6, 1897.
       III. PHILINDA,[7] b. Dec. 14, 1816; m. JOSHUA SMITH, and d. in Mercer County, Ill., Sept. 12. 1854.
341   IV. NICHOLAS,[7] b. 1818, in Oneida, N.Y.; m. LYDIA ANN ROWLAND, of Joliet, Ill.
342   V. CALVIN WEBSTER,[7] b. 1820, in Oneida, N.Y.; m. SARAH BUGBEE, 1840.
343   VI. GEORGE,[7] b. Oct 6, 1825; m. MARGARET CAMPBELL.
344   VII. BENJAMIN M.,[7] b. May 1, 1827; m. SARAH ROWLAND, Peoria. Ill.
       VIII. ARTIMISSA,[7] b. April 27, 1829; m. 1st, JOHN PALMER, Knox County, Ill.; m. 2d, BENJAMIN ORUM, Warren County, Ill.
       IX. MARY,[7] b. March 25, 1831; m. HEZEKIAH WITT, of Knox County, Ill.
       X. ABIGAIL,[7] b. Nov. 14, 1836, in East Trumbull, O.; m. 1st, VAN DOREN AMY, Sept. 27, 1854; m. 2d, CALVIN ROUTH, March 10, 1880.
       Mr. Amy served in the Civil War, and died in Galliton, Tenn., Jan. 22, 1863. He was in the One Hundred and Second Regiment Illinois Volunteers. They lived at Henderson, and later at Alexis, Ill. Mrs. Routh gave us the above account of her father's family.

Children of First Husband, born at Henderson.

1. Charles S. Amy. b. July 30, 1855; m. Viola Rees, April 3, 1879, at Iona. Ill.
2. William A. Amy. b. Nov. 1, 1859; d. June 6, 1876.
3. John W. Amy, b. Dec. 18, 1861; d. June 29, 1863.

135.

BENJAMIN [6] CHURCHILL (LEVI,[5] CHARLES,[4] SAMUEL,[3] JOSEPH,[2] JOSIAH [1]). Born in Newington, Conn., May 3, 1792. Moved with his parents to Boonville, Oneida County, N.Y., in 1802. Died Aug. 23, 1893, aged 102 years 3 months 23 days. Married, July 15, 1824, CATHARINE STRATER, of Martinsburg, N.Y. She died Jan. 3, 1880, aged 69 years 6 months.

Children.

345   I. CALVIN WEBSTER,[7] m. MARIETTA STRATER.
       II. MARIAN,[7] m. GEORGE HARRIS, of Boonville.
       III. CAROLINE,[7] m. ELIAKIM B. WILLIAMSON, Boonville, N.Y.
346   IV. DANIEL,[7] m. CAROLINE CONANT, in Alexis, Ill.
       V. ELIZABETH,[7] m. HIRAM PAGE, in Galesburg, Ill.
347   VI. LEVI HENRY,[7] m. MARIAN ELIZA WILLIAMSON.

348   VII. HARVEY,⁷ m. NANCY ROUTH, in Hopkins, Mo.
       VIII. MINERVA,⁷ m. JOHN BROWN, of Galesburg.
       IX.   CATHARINE L.,⁷ m. DAVID A. COLLINS.
       X.   MARIETTA,⁷ b. March 23, 1829; m. MARTIN HOGAN.
       XI.   ANNE,⁷ d. at the age of fourteen years.

137.

DR. CLAUDIUS BELDEN⁶ CHURCHILL (CHARLES,⁵ CHARLES,⁴ SAMUEL,³ JOSEPH,² JOSIAH ¹). Born in Newbern, N.C. The information about Dr. Churchill is very meagre, we have not been able to learn where he was educated or where he practised, or resided during his active life. He probably removed sometime in the "forties" to New Orleans. His oldest son was born in North Carolina, his youngest in Louisana. He died in 1864, in New Orleans. Married LOUISANA HOLIDAY.

Children.

352   I.   CHARLES HOLIDAY,⁷ b. about 1830; m. MARTHA THORN, October, 1864.
353   II. SYLVESTER BROWN,⁷ m. MALVINA BERMUDIZ.
       III. CLAUDIA ISABELLA,⁷ m. JAMES A. FERGUSON, of Whately, Mass.

Child.

       1. Louisiana F. Ferguson, m. Peter G. Riddell.
          One child, (1) James F. Riddell. They live (1902) in So. Africa.

354   IV. WYLIE CROOME,⁷ m. CORA BELLE MARINER.
355   V.   THOMAS HOLIDAY,⁷ m. LAURA K. STIRLING.
       VI. HANNAH BROWN,⁷ b. in New Orleans; m. DR. ALEX CHASTANT, of New Orleans.
356   VII. ZACHARY TAYLOR,⁷ b. in New Orleans, about 1850. Died unmarried in 1874.

139.

CHISLIEU⁶ CHURCHILL (SAMUEL,⁵ CHARLES,⁴ SAMUEL,³ JOSEPH,² JOSIAH ¹). Born in Newington, Conn., Dec. 4, 1779, and lived there, a farmer. He died July 9, 1857. Married, March 31, 1806, CELINDA HURLBUT, born Jan. 12, 1788, and died Nov. 27, 1865.

Children born in Newington.

357   I.   CHAUNCY,⁷ b. Feb. 8, 1808; m. ABIGAIL WEBSTER.
358   II. CALVIN,⁷ b. March 18, 1810; m. MARY GILSTRAP, Aug. 9, 1832.
       III. SARAH,⁷ b. Sept. 6, 1812; m. JOHN SHEPARD, April 2, 1856. No issue.
       IV. MARY ANN,⁷ b. April 26, 1814; m. FLAVEL WIER, Nov. 26, 1834.
       V.   CLARISSA,⁷ b. Jan. 20, 1818; m. TRUMAN WIER, Oct. 28, 1838.
359   VI. SAMUEL SEYMOUR,⁷ b. Feb. 28, 1825; m. LOUISA HUNT, Nov. 11, 1846.

140.

JOHN⁶ CHURCHILL (SAMUEL,⁵ CHARLES,⁴ SAMUEL,³ JOSEPH,² JOSIAH ¹). Born in Newington, April 11, 1785, and died there, Sept. 17, 1823, of fever, on his way home to New Hartford,

from the South. After marriage he bought a farm in New Hartford, where his wife's brother lived, and they settled there. Mr.
Churchill was of quiet manners, medium in stature, and rather
slender in build. His portrait, painted in 1812, shows that he was
of attractive personality. Married, in Newington, at " Ten Rod,"
the home of the bride's father, by the Rev. Joab Brace, LAURA
WELLES, daughter of Absalom and Lorraine (Patterson) Welles, of
Newington, where she was born, July 23, 1789. She died in
Bristol, July 3, 1877, and is there buried. She was a descendant,
in the seventh generation, from Governor Thomas Welles. Her
portrait, painted at twenty-three, shows a face, not of great beauty,
but full of force and animation. She was an accomplished rider and
made two journeys on horseback, before her marriage, to Lebanon,
N.Y., to visit her uncle Stephen Patterson's family. She was also
accomplished in dancing, and used to tell of her experience in her
youth, and how, one evening, she wore through two pairs of satin
slippers dancing. Her father was proud of her accomplishments,
and was much more liberal in his ideas of religion than many of his
neighbors, and certainly more so than her husband's people, who
were very strict Calvinists. Her home was at " Ten Rod," and was
a place of pleasant social life and generous hospitality. Left a widow
when young, with only the farm in New Hartford, and with a family
of five children to bring up, she showed unusual courage and re-
source. Some seven years after her husband's death she removed
with her family to Bristol, where her oldest daughter had settled
upon her marriage. Mrs. Churchill was a woman of high spirit, and
proud of her Welles and Patterson ancestry, and while genial in
disposition and forceful in character, she preserved the simple
manners and quiet dignity of an earlier day.

Children of John and Laura (Wells) Churchill.

    I. LAURA,[7] b. July 23, 1812; m. LORA WATERS, of Bristol, Oct. 21,
        1833.
        They lived in Bristol: no children. She died at Bristol, Oct. 11,
        1892. They adopted and brought up, from infancy, her own cousin,
        Sophia Wells.

360   II. JOHN,[7] b. Sept. 16, 1814; m. ELIZA ANN HENDRICK.
    III. ELECTA,[7] b. April 5, 1818; m. HENRY ALBERT SEYMOUR.
        They were married at Bristol, Conn., July 28, 1844, at the home
        of her sister, Mrs. Waters, by Rev. R. H. Seely. Mr. Seymour
        was a lineal descendant of Richard Seymour, who settled in Hart-
        ford, as early as 1639, and he was born at New Hartford, Jan. 22,
        1818. They lived at New Hartford until 1846, when they removed
        to Bristol. Mr. Seymour was a man of ability and energy, and
        soon after he came to Bristol became prominent in public affairs,
        and held many places of trust. Upon the incorporation of the
        Bristol Savings Bank he became president, and held the office till
        his death, on April 6, 1897. Electa Churchill is described as having
        a brilliant complexion, dark blue eyes, and very dark brown hair.

She was vivacious and witty in conversation, a loyal, hospitable, and gracious woman, greatly beloved by her own family circle and neighbors.

Children, the first born at New Hartford, the rest at Bristol.

1. Laura Electa Seymour, b. April 5, 1846.
2. Henry Albert Seymour, b. April 2, 1847; m. Mary Marilla Leggett, Washington, D.C., Oct. 30, 1872.
   He was educated at Williston Academy, and Columbian Law School, Washington, D.C. Removed to Washington in 1870. He has been for years a principal examiner in the Patent Office, and law-clerk to the commissioner of patents.
   Their children, born in Washington : (1) Laura Leggett Seymour, b. Nov. 11, 1873; (2) Rae Mortimer Seymour, b. Aug. 24, 1877; (3) Helen Welles Seymour, b. Dec. 18, 1878.
3. Mary Harriet Seymour, b. July 22, 1849; m. Miles Lewis Peck, Oct. 18, 1871.
   Children, born at Bristol, Conn. : (1) Josiah H. Peck, b. March 5, 1873; (2) Howard S. Peck, b. May 17, 1874; (3) Hilda M. Peck, b. April 19, 1881; (4) Rachel K. Peck, b. Jan. 6, 1883; (5) Mary M. L. Peck, b. Jan. 22, 1895.
4. Lilla Welles Seymour, b. May 10, 1852; d. Nov. 7, 1854.
5. John Churchill Seymour, b. June 5, 1853; d. the same day.
6. Grace Ella Seymour, b. July 13, 1856; m. William Shurtleff Ingraham, Oct. 11, 1881.
   Children, born at Bristol, Conn.: (1) Faith Allen Ingraham, b. April 30, 1886; (2) Edward Ingraham, b. Dec. 20, 1887; (3) Dudley Seymour Ingraham, b. Aug. 14, 1890.
7. George Dudley Seymour, b. Oct. 6, 1859.
   Educated at Hartford public schools. Graduated from the high school in 1878, and from the Columbian University Law School in 1880. Engaged in his brother's office at Washington until 1883, when he opened an office in New Haven. He devotes himself exclusively to patents and patent law practice. He is interested in literature and the fine arts, and family history. He is (1903) secretary of the Society of Colonial Wars in Connecticut. Mr. Seymour is unmarried.
8. Helen Welles Seymour, b. Jan. 29, 1864; d. July 12, 1866.

361 IV. ABSALOM WELLES,[7] b. March 29, 1820; m. HARRIET MASON PORTER.
362 V. CHARLES,[7] b. May 25, 1822; m. ALICE PHILLIPS.

141.

JOSIAH BELDEN[6] CHURCHILL (SAMUEL[5] CHARLES,[4] SAMUEL,[3] JOSEPH,[2] JOSIAH[1]). Born in Newington, Conn., Aug. 28 1787, and was there brought up, but removed, probably about 1806, to Boonville, N.Y., where he settled near his uncle Levi Churchill whose daughter he married. He lived in Boonville until the death of his first wife, when, I learn from an account written for me by his daughter, Mrs. Wonser, in October, 1900, he took his children to Newington, and there they were placed in different homes among Mr. Churchill's former friends and relatives, so that they attended the same school. After his second marriage he removed to Sempronius and later to Summerhill, N.Y., and then in 1837 he removed with the younger portion of his family to Troy, Erie County, Penn. He died April 18, 1852. He served in the War of 1812. Married, in Boonville, N.Y., Oct. 14, 1808, OCTAVIA CHURCHILL, daughter of Levi and Ruth (Merrills) Churchill, born in Newington, Dec. 14, 1786, and died in Boonville, N.Y., July 20, 1820. Mrs. Wonser writes of her mother, " As I was but seven years old when mother died, I have only a child's recollection of her, but as I remember her she was of medium size, with very fair complexion and mild black eyes; I thought then and think now that she was a very handsome woman." Married 2d, PHEBE MARIA THOMPSON, March 11, 1824 She was born Jan. 31, 1800.

Children of First Wife born in Boonville, N. Y.

I. CELINA CASSON,[7] b. Aug. 4, 1809; m. ROBERT POOLE, Summerhill, N.Y.
   She died in Cazenovia, N.Y. No further record received.

II. MARCIA BOARDMAN,[7] b. Feb. 26, 1811; m. EVELYN WOODFORD, Summerhill, N.Y.
   She was brought up in the family of her aunt, ElizabethHubbard, of Berlin, Conn. Her sister, Mrs. Wonser, describes her as resembling her mother, and very handsome. There seems to have been something of a romance in her story which is sad in its close. She was very much beloved by her relatives and friends, and especially by her aunt Elizabeth's family; and all were bitterly opposed to the man whom she chose for a husband, but in spite of their opposition she married him. Evelyn Woodford was a tailor and was not apparently successful. After some years of futile efforts he heard of an opening in Texas, and, leaving his wife, he went ahead to get a home ready. The wife with her two small children, one an infant, followed soon after on a small schooner, that being then the only available conveyance. A terrible storm swept down on them, lasting many woful days, lasting the young mother lay in her small cabin-bunk, seasick, homesick, and heartsick, with her babies, one on each arm; but after many days they arrived at their port and found the husband. The baby died soon after, and the mother's health was completely shattered. She lived only a year or two, another child being born to her. She died at Matagorda Bay, Texas, Nov. 22, 1838, and her husband soon after married a Texas woman.

Children of Evelyn and Marcia (Churchill) Woodford.

1. Milton Mozart Woodford, b. Nov. 26, 1834; m. Juliana Hitchcock, Dec. 25, 1855.
   He shared the perilous voyage to Texas, with his mother, and after her death his step-mother, it is said, sent him off on a return voyage, after a few years, to his uncle Samuel C., who, with other relatives, provided for him, after a fashion, until he was eighteen.
   Children: (1) Carrie L. Woodford, b. July 2, 1857; (2) Charlton M. Woodford, b. Jan. 2, 1861; (3) Arthur F. Woodford, b. Nov. 3, 1866; (4) Helen Marcia Woodford, b. May 21, 1869; (5) Bernet Woodford, b. June 25. 1871; d. Sept. 10, 1871; (6) Robert Hawley Woodford, b. May 23, 1876.
2. Barnard Woodford, b. 1837 and d. Jan. 7, 1838.

III. RUTH MERRILLS,[7] b. March 12, 1813; m. M. G. WONSER, Summerhill, N.Y., Aug. 12, 1832.
   Mrs. Wonser writes in October, 1900, being then in her 87th year, " My mother, Octavia, was a very religious and conscientious woman, and a few days before her death, wanted us children to be baptized, so we stood up in a row by her bedside, and a preacher sprinkled some water upon our heads and said some words which we did not

then understand, but took it as a sort of compact that we were to be good." I regret that I do not find anywhere among the letters of Mrs. Wonser any account of her own girlhood. Married at the age of nineteen and a half years, she lived a life full of activity and showed herself a woman of remarkable force and ability. They lived a few years at Milan and Summerhill, N.Y., and then removed West and settled at Ellisville, Ill., and later at Erie, Ill., where Mrs. Wonser was living with her youngest daughter Ruth, in October, 1900. In July, 1880, she wrote, "I have had a very active life, practised medicine for twenty years, but one year ago I fell and broke my hip, which has laid me up for a year, and will probably make me a cripple for life." She says, "In religion, I am a Bible-Spiritualist, and on the 30th of September, 1867, the society to which I then belonged granted me the privilege of speaking to the people and solemnizing marriages." A copy of this certificate is before the editor of this volume as he writes. It is a regular recognition and fellowship of her as a lawful minister. Dated at Geneseo, Ill., Sept. 30, 1867, and signed by Samuel McHose, President, and John C. Moody, Secretary.

Children of M. G. and Ruth M. (Churchill) Wonser.

1. Octavia L. Wonser, b. at Milan, N.Y., June 7, 1833; m. 1st Daniel Tift, Erie, Ill., Oct. 20, 1852; m. 2d, Joseph Medhurst, Galesburg, Ill.
2. Annette E. Wonser, b. at Summerhill, N.Y., Oct. 16, 1835; m. 1st, C. E. Coburn, St. Louis, Oct. 20, 1851; m. 2d, Edward Fenton; lives in California.
3. F. J. Mortimer Wonser, b. at Ellisville, Ill., May 5, 1838; m. Julia Weaver, Erie, Jan. 1, 1859.
    Mr. Wonser is a prosperous lawyer at Tama, Iowa, and has the following children : (1) William W. Wonser, b. Dec. 1, 1859; m. Bertie Lamb, at Sterling, Ill., Sept. 7, 1881, and has two children, Ferne and Marjorie; (2) Charles J. Wonser, b. July 19, 1862; m. Josephine Patterson, at St. Olaf, Iowa, March 26, 1889; (3) Flora C. Wonser, b. Feb. 5, 1865; (4) Charlotte E. Wonser, b. Nov. 18, 1866; (5) Louis Wonser, b. March 12, 1869, d. Jan. 6, 1870; (6) Fred Wonser, b. June 4, 1871; (7) Ernest Wonser, b. July 24, 1873; d. Sept. 8, 1874; (8) Vera Wonser, b Oct. 18, 1878.
4. Marcia W. Wonser, b. March 7, 1840, at Ellisville; m. John Fenton, at Erie, March 14, 1859.
5. Charles Wonser, b. at Ellisville, Feb. 16, 1842; d. Oct. 20, 1843.
6. Mileden Wonser, b. at Ellisville, May 16, 1844; d. in Erie, Ill., Sept. 27, 1845.
7. Charlotte E. Wonser, b. at Ellisville, May 16, 1846; d. in Erie, Ill., Sept. 12, 1850.
8. Kate L. Wonser, b. at Erie, Ill., April 20, 1848; m. John Bushee, Oct. 1, 1866.
9. Colonel D. Wonser, b. at Erie, Ill., Oct. 6, 1850; m. Marcia Kelly, Oct. 3, 1869.
10. Ruth R. Wonser, b. at Erie, Ill., Jan. 3, 1853.

363   IV. SAMUEL CICERO,[7] b. Jan. 30, 1815; m. 1st, EMILY NORTH, Aug. 30, 1840; m. 2d, SOPHIA G. GUNN, March 27, 1843.

V   CHARLOTTE.[7] b. Feb. 24, 1817; m. LEVINUS SPERRY, April 6, 1845.
    She graduated from Groton Seminary, N.Y., where she remained for several years as a teacher. Mr. Sperry was a public-spirited man, an ardent Abolitionist, and very active in that direction, an excellent Christian in practical works as well as in his faith. Mrs. Wonser writes of him : "If the world were full of souls like him, it would be a beautiful world to live in." They lived at, or near, Galesburg, Ill., and later at Bushnell, Ill., where she died Feb. 2, 1856. He died April 10, 1893. In his later years he lived in Pueblo, Col.

Children.

1. Oriana J. Sperry, b. Jan. 3, 1846; d. Feb. 8, 1848.
2. Levinus Mentor Sperry, b. Feb. 16, 1849; m. 1st, Julia
   Churchill, dau. of Norman, June 25, 1874; m. 2d, Sarah J.
   Shields, Aug. 10, 1880.
   He graduated at Knox College, June, 1874, and on the same
   day, June 25, married his first wife, who lived only a year.
3. Charlotte Emma Sperry, b. Nov. 1, 1850; m. 1st, Miles Hubbard,
   Nov. 28, 1880; m. 2d, Fremont Getman, Feb. 1, 1891.
4. Lewis Belden Sperry, b. Aug. 30, 1852; m. Bertha A. Magehe.
   Feb. 16, 1888.
5. Ira Peck Sperry, b. Feb. 16, 1854; d. Sept. 5, 1854.
6. Lydia Orilla Peck Sperry, b. Dec 23, 1855.
VI. JULIA,[7] b. Oct. 4, 1818; d. Oct. 18, 1818.
VII. NANCY,[7] b. April 26, 1820, and died the same day.

Children of the Second Wife.

VIII. GEORGE THOMPSON,[7] b. Nov. 26, 1824, at Sempronius, N.Y.; m.
   1st, ALMINA LAWRENCE, Aug. 27, 1847; m. 2d, SARAH C. LAW-
   RENCE, Jan. 15, 1852.
IX. JOSIAH HUBBARD,[7] b. July 2, 1826, at Summerhill, N.Y. He enlisted in the army, in the Civil War, and was killed at Fredericksburg, in the battle, Dec. 13, 1862.
X. CHARLES,[7] b. Jan. 12, 1829, at Summerhill, N.Y. He enlisted in
   the Seventy-fifth Regiment Illinois Volunteers, and served over
   three years, and returned home broken in health. In 1900 he was
   living in Morrison, Ill.

142.

CHARLES[6] CHURCHILL (SAMUEL,[5] CHARLES,[4] SAMUEL,[3]
JOSEPH,[2] JOSIAH.[1]) Born at Newington, Sept. 12, 1790. He went
South, and settled first in Irdell County, and later in Fayette County,
Tenn. He died Jan. 29, 1845, in Tennessee. Married, in Irdell
County, N.C., Sept. 11, 1828, MATILDA JOHNSON, daughter of James
and Cassandra (Northcroft) Johnson, b. Nov. 24, 1812, and died July
23, 1887, in Independence County, Ark.

Children born in Irdell County, N.C.

365   I. SAMUEL BOARDMAN,[7] b. Jan. 2, 1831; m. SARAH E. HISTON.
      II. HARRIET JULIA,[7] b. Jan. 13, 1833; m. ISRAEL McGRADY PICKENS,
          of Fayette County, Tenn., Oct. 13, 1852. Mr. Pickens was killed
          in the Civil War.

Children born in Fayette County, Tenn.

1. Charles P. Pickens, b. Sept. 4, 1854; m. Emma C. McDonald,
   Independence County, Ark., Sept. 25, 1879.
2. John W. Pickens, b. Aug. 23, 1856; m. Phebe J. Summers,
   Independence County, Ark., Aug. 15, 1878.
3. James McGrady Pickens, b. Sept. 21, 1858; m. Lulu E. Bennett,
   Independence County, Ark., Jan. 22, 1880.
4. Lulu A. V. Pickens, b. April 9, 1861.
5. Cora Katie Pickens, b. Feb. 27, 1863.

366   III. JAMES NORTHCROFT,[7] b. Jan. 12, 1835; m. CHARLOTTE T. HOGAN.
367   IV. WILLIAM PRICE.[7] b. Dec. 24, 1836; m. MARY E. RUSSELL.
368   V. CURTIS JOHNSON,[7] b. Dec. 11, 1838; m. AMANDA A. HOGAN.
       VI. MARY ANN,[7] b. Feb. 2, 1841. Never married.
     VIII. MARCIA MATILDA VICTORY,[7] b. July 24, 1843; m. WILLIAM H.
          WALDEN, of Fayette County, Tenn., Nov. 8, 1865.

Children.

1. Ella A. Walden, b. Jan. 6, 1867.
2. Charles Henry Walden, b. Jan. 12, 1869.
3. George Curtis Walden, b. July 15, 1871.
4. James William Walden, b. Nov. 1, 1875.
5. Mary Theodosia Walden, b. Sept. 27, 1878.
6. Edgar Eldridge Walden, b. March 5, 1883.

143.

CHESTER[6] CHURCHILL (SOLOMON,[5] CHARLES,[4] SAMUEL[3] JOSEPH,[2] JOSIAH[1]). Born in Newington parish, May 6, 1798. He acquired a common school education in his native village and started out for himself at the age of eighteen. He went to Boonville, N.Y., and taught school the next year, but a little later he engaged in trade. At first he began by carrying merchandise to sell in the South, but succeeded so well that some ten years later he was able to establish a warehouse in Hartford, whence he shipped invoices of goods to different points in the South for sale. He showed great ability and with his untiring energy a successful career was assured, but his health failed so that he was obliged to spend his winters South. On his way to Augusta, Ga., for his winter sojourn, he was taken sick at Rappahannock, Va., and died there Nov. 7, 1837, and was there buried. His nephew, Leonard Churchill Hubbard, says of him : " He was of medium build, well proportioned, pleasing in address, active and attractive." Married, Aug. 24, 1826, LUCRETIA OLMSTED, daughter of Francis and Nancy (Judd) Olmsted, of West Hartford. She was a very accomplished person, far better educated than most women of her day, having studied Latin, surveying, navigation, etc., under the well-known Dr. Strong, of Hartford. She was a teacher of Latin and the higher branches in a select school in Hartford, having seventy pupils, at one time, under her tuition. After the death of her husband she resumed her former vocation for some time in Newington. She was a woman of great energy of mind, and possessed a wonderful memory. She survived her husband more than thirty-seven years, and died in Newington, Conn., March 8, 1875.

Children of Chester and Lucretia (Olmsted) Churchill.

I. FRANCIS,[7] b. July 23, 1828; d. Jan. 24, 1834.
II. JULIA,[7] b. Nov. 3, 1831; m. JAMES WATKINS, ESQ., in the South. She was a lady of fine culture and beautiful person. She went to the South, after her father's death, to look after his landed interests, which were quite extensive, and there married. She died in Tennessee, without children, Feb. 17, 1870.
III. MARY,[7] b. Oct. 28, 1836. She is living (in 1903), unmarried, in Newington, in the house built by Capt. Charles Churchill for his son Samuel.

144.

DEACON SILAS [6] CHURCHILL (Rev. Silas,[5] Charles [4] Samuel,[3] Joseph,[2] Josiah [1]). Born in New Lebanon, N.Y., June 5, 1800. He lived in New Lebanon, a respected and influential citizen. Died at New Lebanon, Aug. 9, 1878. Married 1st, at New Lebanon, N.Y., Oct. 27, 1825, Clarissa Avery, daughter of William T. and Phebe (Troop) Avery, born Oct. 31, 1793; died March 13, 1836. Married 2d, Oct. 27, 1836, Cornelia S. W. Lynde, at Hartford, Conn., where she was born May 5, 1806. She died August, 1896.

Children born at New Lebanon, N. Y.

369   I. Francis Elliott,[7] b. Sept. 12, 1826; m. Katharine Whitmore, Aug. 16, 1852.

     II. Mary Cornelia,[7] b. April 21, 1829; m. Rev. William Decker, New Lebanon, June 16, 1857, and died at Turin, N.Y., in 1899. One child, a daughter, born in Florida, N.Y.

370   III. William Thomas,[7] b. Dec. 25, 1830; m. Alice Summers, April 25, 1883.

371   IV. Silas Payson,[7] b. Nov. 12, 1832; m. Mary Amelia Hoyt, Sept. 15, 1863.

     V. Ellen Clarissa,[7] b. Aug. 26, 1835; d. unmarried, June 8, 1857.

Second Wife's Children.

     VI. Martha Octavia,[7] b. Sept. 1, 1838; m. Jerome McWilliams at New Lebanon, N.Y., Nov. 28, 1866. They lived on the old homestead.

371a   VII. Joseph Lynde,[7] b. Jan. 30, 1840; m. (———) (———) at Oakland, Ore., June 6. 1874.

     VIII. Alfred Whittlesey,[7] b. Jan. 25, 1842; d. in the army in the Civil War, April 9, 1864.

     IX. Abbie Elizabeth,[7] b. April 26, 1844; d. May 30, 1856.

     X. Anna Rhoda,[7] b. Aug. 1, 1846; m. Charles Cooper, Cleveland, O., Oct. 23, 1872. They lived in Watertown, N.Y.

147.

WILLIAM BOARDMAN [6] CHURCHILL (Jesse,[5] Jesse,[4] Samuel,[3] Joseph,[2] Josiah [1]). Born at Hubbardton, Vt., March 4, 1794. From all that I can learn of Mr. Churchill, he seems to have been either unfortunate or a poor manager. They lived at Ridge Prairie, Ill., until 1840. His wife's mother lived with them, and her brother near by. In 1840 her brother moved to Wisconsin, and she, taking her five children, with her mother, went with them, leaving her husband behind. Yet she is said to have been a good and noble woman. The separation was final, however, and she settled and passed her life at Monroe, Wis. She was a faithful mother, despite her desperate step. He died at Collinsville, Ill., Dec. 9, 1856, after two later marriages, by which no children are reported. Married 1st, Aug. 3, 1823, Almira Humes, born in

Portsmouth, N.H., April 5, 1806, and died in Monroe, Wis., April 23, 1893. Married 2d, Mrs. Jane (———) Kingston. Married 3d, Mrs. Lura (Hill) Roberts.

Children born at Ridge Prairie, Ill.

   I. Caroline E.,[7] b. June 26, 1824; m. John Augustine Bingham, in Monroe, Wis., Nov. 25, 1843. He was born in Morristown, N.Y., Feb. 27, 1819.

Children born in Monroe, Wis.

    1. Helen Maria Bingham, b. Oct. 10, 1845.
    2. Horace Bingham, b. Feb. 5, 1848; d. Dec. 28, 1849.
    3. Alice Bingham, b. May 4, 1851; m. Herbert Edson Copeland, Sept. 7, 1872.
       Children: (1) Edwin B. Copeland, b Sept. 30, 1873; member Company H, First Regiment, Wisconsin Volunteers, in Spanish War of 1898; (2) Herbert B. Copeland, b. July 24, 1875.
    4. Ada Bingham, b. Feb. 6, 1854; unmarried.
    5. Homer William Bingham, b. February, 1856; m. Addie Ludlow, July 20, 1897, at Denver, Col., and lived there, and had child, Helen Ludlow Bingham, b. in Denver, Col., Dec. 18, 1897.
    6. John Herbert Bingham, b. Jan. 14, 1859; d. Jan. 23, 1881.

372   II. Jesse Norman,[7] b. Jan. 26, 1826; m. Ann E. Sherman, Feb. 22, 1854.
372a   III. George,[7] b. May 19, 1830; m. 1st, Olive Brown, Oct. 25, 1857; m. 2d, Emma Summeril, May 28, 1876.
    IV. Lucena Ann,[7] b. Feb. 14, 1833; m. William Sykes, Sept. 1, 1858.

Children.

    1. George Quigley Sykes, b Aug. 7, 1859; m. May Ivy, June 4, 1890.
    2. Frederick Sykes, b. May 7, 1861; d. Feb. 7, 1863.
    3. Frank Sykes, b. Sept. 17, 1864.
    4. Jennie Sykes, b. Dec. 18, 1866; m Louis Erhard, Sept 9, 1897.

    V. Maria,[7] b. April 7, 1835; m. Jeremiah Kelley, July 7, 1856.

148.

NORMAN[6] CHURCHILL (Jesse,[5] Jesse,[4] Samuel,[3] Joseph,[2] Josiah[1]). Born at Hubbardton, Vt., Nov. 5, 1799, and lived there until he was eight years old, and held many incidents of his early school-days there in memory. In 1807, his mother having died in 1804, he went with his father's family to Litchfield, N.Y., where his father had settled in the ministry. Here and at the other places of his father's settlement he received a good common school education, mainly by his own efforts, and he was especially well versed in the phraseology of the Bible, having a retentive memory. He wrote many letters, from 1880 to 1886, to the early compilers of this volume, and to some of his kindred who have forwarded the same to us; and these letters, made up of notes and comments on the family, give a vast deal of information about others of the name, but not enough about himself. His notes are written in a quaint, and often

half humorous style, but always with the purpose of imparting the
facts.   His many shrewd though kindly comments upon his relatives, living and dead, would be of much interest to his kindred, but
the editor would not feel at liberty, even if there were space, to publish the notes in this volume.   He was with his father, who served
as chaplain in the army in the War of 1812, and was his father's
orderly, or servant.   July 3, 1880, he wrote: "Sixty-five years ago I
was a soldier at Sackett's Harbor."   He learned the trade of carpenter and also that of hatter and also sleigh-maker.   He had the
Yankee faculty of doing well nearly everything that pertains to the
construction of houses.   He lived in Winfield, N.Y., the last parish
of his father's ministry, until 1839, when he removed with his family, his wife and six children, to Galesburg, Ill., having joined
the colony of settlers two years before, by the purchase of a lot of
land.   He spent there the remainder of his honorable, kindly, and
useful life.   He became an influential member of the Old First
Church, Presbyterian, was chosen an elder in 1846, and held that
office till his death.   He was a man of great strength of character,
decidedly original and independent in thought, and quaint of speech,
but conscientious and faithful in all the relations of life, a consistent Abolitionist, and an earnest promoter of all good institutions.
He died in Galesburg, Sept. 20, 1886.   Married, in Winfield
N.Y., March 5, 1826; ANNA EGGLESTON.   She was the daughter of
his father's third wife by a former husband, and was born at
Batavia, N.Y., Jan. 24, 1806, and died at Galesburg, Ill., March 1,
1882.

*Children of Norman and Anna (Eggleston) Churchill, the first six born at Win-
field, N. Y., the others at Galesburg, Ill.*

I. EMILY AMELIA,[7] b. May 17, 1827; m. REV. JAMES HENRY WARREN,
   D.D., at Galesburg, Ill., June 27, 1850.
   Mr. Warren graduated at Knox College in 1847, and was pastor
   of the Congregational Church at Nevada City, 1851 to 1858, and
   leaving that to become editor of "The Pacific," the first religious
   newspaper on the coast; four years then pastor at San Mateo, and
   then he became superintendent of the Home Missions of California
   for nearly thirty years.   Mrs. Emily (Churchill) Warren was educated at Monticello Academy, and was afterwards a teacher in
   Knox College.   In June, 1899, they were living at 1544 Taylor
   street, San Francisco, Cal.   A letter from Mrs. Warren at that
   time gives this account of her family.

Children of Rev. James H. and Emily (Churchill) Warren.

1. Anna Churchill Warren, b. in San Francisco, Feb. 21, 1851.
   Educated at Laurel Hall, San Mateo.   A teacher many years.
   Lives at home.
2. Mary Stuart Warren, b. July 2, 1853, in Nevada City, Cal.; m.
   Dr. Marcel Pietryzchi, and lives in Dayton, Wash.
3. Clarence Harrison Warren, b. March 6, 1856, in Nevada City,
   Cal.   He graduated from the University of California,

became a journalist, and is city editor of one of the leading dailies of California; m. Bessie Staniford, June 25, 1882.

    4. Eleanor Warren, b. in Nevada City, Feb. 21, 1858. She is an artist.

373   II. GEORGE,[7] b. April 2, 1829; m. 1st, CLARISSA AMELIA HURD; m. 2d, ADALINE HELETIA HAYES; m. 3d, ELLEN MARIA SANBORN.

    III. CORNELIA ANN,[7] b. March 17, 1831; m., in Galesburg, Ill., July 30, 1851, MILTON LEMMON COMSTOCK, who was born in New Haven, O., Oct. 19, 1824.

He graduated at Knox College, Galesburg, Ill., of which institution he held the professorship of mathematics from 1858 to 1898, and is professor emeritus since. Cornelia (Churchill) Comstock was educated at, and was afterwards teacher in, Cherry Grove Academy. They lived at Burlington and Kossuth, Iowa, and from 1858 Galesburg, Ill.

Children of Prof. Milton L. and Cornelia (Churchill) Comstock.

    1. Flora Ardelle Comstock, b. Sept. 20, 1852; d. Sept. 4, 1854.
    2. George Erastus Comstock, b. July 4, 1854; d. May 11, 1857.
    3. Cornelia Belle Comstock, b. at Kossuth, Iowa, March 12, 1858; m. William W. Hammond. They live at Peoria, Ill., and have children: (1) Harry C. Hammond, (2) Clara Hammond.
    4. Clara Emily Comstock, b. Nov. 12, 1860, at Galesburg, Ill.
    5. Clarence Elmer Comstock, b. May 5, 1866; m. Gary Driggs, Dec. 27, 1900. He is professor of mathematics, in the Polytechnic Institute, Peoria, Ill.
    6. Ada Heletia Comstock, b. Feb. 2, 1869.

374   IV. NORMAN,[7] b. July 16, 1833; m. ANN HINSEY, Nov. 21, 1860.

    V. JULIA,[7] b. April 3, 1836; m. LEVINUS MENTOR SPERRY, June 25, 1874.

He was the grandson of Josiah Belden and Octavia (Churchill) Churchill. Julia (Churchill) Sperry died July 1, 1875.

    VI. MARY VICTORIA,[7] b. Aug. 26, 1838; d. Aug. 4, 1841.
    VII. ELVIRA,[7] b. Oct. 17, 1841; unmarried.
    VIII. WILBERFORCE,[7] b. Nov. 4, 1843; d. in the army hospital at Vicksburg, Miss., Feb. 7, 1863.
    IX. ISABEL,[7] b. Jan. 6, 1846.

149.

SIMEON[6] CHURCHILL (LEVI,[5] JESSE[4] SAMUEL,[3] JOSEPH,[2] JOSIAH[1]). Born in Wethersfield, Jan. 3, 1788. Lived at Wethersfield. No further facts in relation to this family than herein stated. Married ANNA COLMAN.

Children.

    I. MARTHA ANN,[7] b. Oct. 6, 1817.
    II. SIMEON,[7] b. June 9, 1819.
    III. MARY,[7] b. Oct. 11, 1822.

150.

LEVI BELDEN[6] CHURCHILL (LEVI,[5] JESSE,[4] SAMUEL,[3] JOSEPH,[2] JOSIAH[1]). Born at Wethersfield, March 24, 1797. They lived at Griswoldville, Conn., in 1832. Married, June 27, 1816, ABIGAIL GRISWOLD.

Children.

375   I. Justus G.,[7] b. Nov. 5, 1816; m. Abigail Harris, Jan. 28, 1844.
       II. Prudence Wells,[7] b. April 11, 1819; m. James S. Griswold, Sept. 1, 1841.
376   III. Levi,[7] b. April 24, 1824; m. Mary Jane Blinn, April 10, 1861.
377   IV. Stephen Belden,[7] b. June 21, 1830; m. Abigail Mario, May 5, 1857.
       V. Abigail M.,[7] b. Oct. 12, 1832; m. John Newton Standish, April 4, 1855.
           He was the son of James Tryon Standish, of Wethersfield, and was for several years captain of the Governor's Horse Guards. He died at Fairfield, Conn., May 18, 1888.

Children of John N. and Abigail (Churchill) Standish.

    1. John Newton Standish, b. Feb. 3, 1856; m. Mary S. Simpson.
    2. Miles Stephen Standish, b. Oct. 9, 1857; m. Florence May Bouton.
    3. Rose Maria Standish, b. Dec. 13, 1860; unmarried, lives at Fairfield, Conn.
    4. Harriet Isabella Standish, b. Nov. 30, 1863; m. Arthur Griswold, Jan. 15, 1885.
    5. George Welles Standish, b. Aug. 14, 1865; m. Margaret Hearn.
    6. Frank Ernest Standish, b. Nov. 25, 1869; d. in Bridgeport, Conn., Feb. 19, 1881.

    VI. Harriet Elizabeth,[7] b. Oct. 1, 1836; m. Bart Elisha Blinn, Nov. 18, 1856.

151.

JAMES[6] CHURCHILL (Ithamar,[5] Jesse,[4] Samuel,[3] Joseph,[2] Josiah[1]). Born in Hubbardton, Vt., Aug. 17, 1798. He settled in Mount Vernon, Knox County, O., a farmer, and lived there until about 1844, when he removed to Illinois, and later to Iowa. He died Oct. 15, 1868. Married, in Knox County, O., April 3, 1828, Phebe Marvin, born Dec. 1, 1808; died March, 1850.

Children.

378   I. Cyrus,[7] b. March 17, 1829; m. Susannah Wagner, Dec. 24, 1854.
379   II. Matthew M.,[7] b. Dec. 1, 1830; m. Nancy Blosser.
380 III. Almon I.,[7] b. April 7, 1834; m. Mrs. Sarah E. (Hathaway) Lee, Jan. 30, 1869.
381 IV. Henry J.,[7] b. April 4, 1836; m. Margaret Ann Dugger, May 27, 1863.
       V. Levi D.,[7] b. Sept. 26, 1845; d. April 8, 1860.

153.

LORENZO[6] CHURCHILL (Ithamar,[5] Jesse,[4] Samuel,[3] Joseph,[2] Josiah[1]). Born in Hubbardton, Vt., Dec. 6, 1809. Removed with his father's family to Pennsylvania in 1818, and later to Ohio. He died Sept. 17, 1857. Married, in Tioga County, N.Y., 1835, Nancy M. Wright, of Delaware County, O. She was born Jan. 17, 1818, in Putnam County, N.Y.; daughter of Elijah and Adah (Evans) Wright.

Children.

382   I. NORMAN W.,[7] b. Feb. 13, 1837; m. DULAMA F. CONNELLY.
    II. IRA L.,[7] b. Sept. 13, 1840; unmarried.
    III. CHARLES P.,[7] b. Jan. 8, 1844; d. Aug. 16, 1874; unmarried.
    IV. SARAH M.,[7] b. Sept. 25, 1851; d. Dec. 31, 1852.
    V. MARY J.,[7] b. June 26, 1855; unmarried.

154.

LEVI BLINN[6] CHURCHILL (ITHAMAR,[5] JESSE[4] SAMUEL,[3] JOSEPH,[2] JOSIAH[1]). Born in Hubbardton, Vt., Nov. 26, 1816. Re moved to Pennsylvania, with his father's family. Married, May 26, 1842, LOUISA NORTHRUP, born Nov. 12, 1821.

Children.

    I. LAURA HELEN,[7] b. March 3, 1843; d. Aug. 13, 1846.
    II. LORENZO LENT,[7] b. March 4, 1845; d. Dec. 28, 1857.
    III. MARY LIBBIE,[7] b. March 17, 1857; m. CHARLES EDGAR BARTLETT, of Sacramento, Cal., Nov. 24, 1880.
383   IV. LAUREN BLINN,[7] b. Jan. 16, 1861.
    V. LILLIAN VESTA,[7] b. Dec. 31, 1862.

155.

ISAAC[6] CHURCHILL (ASAHEL,[5] BENJAMIN,[4] SAMUEL,[3] JOSEPH,[2] JOSIAH[1]). Born (perhaps at Southington, Conn.) Sept. 8 1779. Settled "in the Black River Country," Jefferson County, N.Y. Married, but the name of his wife has not been obtained, nor have we been able to get any definite account of this family. He died Feb. 6, 1851.

Children.

384   I. MERRITT,[7] m. late in life and had one son, name not obtained.
    II. CYNTHIA,[7] m. MR. SAULSBURY.

Children.

    1. Artie Saulsbury, m. John Kimball.
    2. Isola Saulsbury.

    III. MERINDA,[7] m. PETER MONROE. No children.
    IV. ARTIE,[7] m. MR. ROSE, and had three sons and one daughter, names not received.

156.

ARA[6] CHURCHILL (ASAHEL,[5] BENJAMIN,[4] SAMUEL,[3] JOSEPH[2] JOSIAH[1]). Born in Connecticut, May 27, 1785. (The name is given erroneously on page 362.) Settled in Batavia, N.Y., about 1809, and lived there until 1820, and then in Alexander. He was a farmer. He served in the War of 1812. An honest, quiet, and lovable Christian man, and his wife was a fit "helpmeet," and a bright and capable homekeeper; both were fond of music, and good singers. They were Baptists in faith, strong for temperance, and he was a loyal Republican in politics. Both were proud of their lineage and fond of their family. He died Jan. 26, 1871. Married 1st, at Whitestone, N.Y., June 6, 1809, SARAH HYDE, daughter of Simon and Pamelia (Vaughan) Hyde, of Whitestone, N.Y. Married 2d, Dec. 1, 1858, MARY BELINDA RANDALL, daughter of Rev. Joseph and Lydia (Chapman) Randall.

Children born in Batavia, the last five in Alexander.

I. INFANT,[7] b. June 23, 1810; d. the same day.
II. EUNICE,[7] b. Feb. 14, 1812; m. 1st, NATHAN MEADE, June 5, 1842; m. 2d, MILTON GRAY, Sept. 28, 1847.
   Mrs. Eunice (Churchill) Gray died in Toledo, O., Jan. 13, 1894. Mr. Meade was in the army in the Civil War under General Butler, and later under General Ord.

Child of First Husband.

1. Charles Nathan Don Meade, b. in Batavia, Dec. 5, 1843; m. Freedom J. Holton, at Batavia, Oct. 7, 1868. They lived in Syracuse, N.Y., and Toledo, O., and had children, (1) Robert H. Meade, b. Jan. 27, 1872; (2) Florence M. Meade, b. May 10, 1876, in Syracuse; (3) Alice C. Meade, b. May 30, 1882, d. July 12, 1882; (4) Orel F. Meade, b. Oct. 30, 1883, d. June 13, 1885; (5) Kittie Lou Meade, b. in Toledo, June 13, 1886; d. Nov. 6, 1887.

385   III. CHARLES HYDE,[7] b. April 28, 1814; m. 1st, JANE INNES, Oct. 25, 1841; m. 2d. MARY B. RANDALL, Dec. 1, 1858.
IV. PAMELIA,[7] b. June 24, 1816; m. WILLIAM ENNIS, of Alexander, N.Y.
   They lived at Brooklyn, Mich., and had children born there.

Children.

1. Ara Churchill Ennis.
2. Edward Ennis, m. Frances Vest.
3. Jennie Ennis, m. Park Hart, Brooklyn, Mich.

V. CUTLER LUTHER,[7] b. May 15, 1818; d. March 12, 1820.
VI. SARAH ANN,[7] b. July 26, 1820; m. SUNDERLAND P. GARDNER, Dec. 28, 1842, at Alexander. She died Oct. 4, 1861.
   They lived at Batavia and Oakfield, N.Y., and had children.

Children.

1. William Earl Gardner, b. Feb. 1, 1844, at Batavia; m. Belle Lovett, of East Penfield, Dec. 10, 1873, and had Albert, Fred, Florence E., and Lottie May Gardner.
2. Ara Dan Gardner, b. July 8, 1845; d. unmarried at Allegan, Feb. 11, 1868.
3. Charles L. Gardner, b. May 28, 1848; d. June 8, 1848, at Oakfield.
4. Sarah A. Gardner, b. May 18, 1850; m. Dr. J. F. Tubbs, of Oakfield, Sept. 2, 1871.
   They live at Fairport, N.Y., and have two children, viz., Alma S. Tubbs and Belle F. Tubbs.

386   VII. ARA DAN,[7] b. Jan. 21, 1825; m. BETSEY R. STIMERS, Jan. 8, 1851.
        VIII. MARY ELIZABETH,[7] b. Sept. 3, 1828; m. 1st, HENRY GETTEN, Al-
        exander, N.Y., Dec. 17, 1846; m. 2d, ALPHEUS SPRING, of Alex-
        ander, Aug. 5, 1876.
            They lived at Bethany, N.Y., and had children.

Children.

1. Oscar Fernando Getten, b. March 20, 1849; d. Aug. 29, 1865,
   at Alexander.
2. Helen Viletta Getten, b. Aug. 6, 1851; m. John S. Baldwin,
   Jan. 7, 1874, at Alexander, N.Y., where they had two children, of whom the (1) died in infancy; (2) Howard Getten
   Baldwin, b. Feb. 10, 1888.
       The mother died at West Bethany, Dec. 23, 1899.

   IX. TRYPHOSA,[7] b. Feb. 7, 1832; m. 1st, HIRAM CADY, in 1851; m. 2d,
   R. B. CADY.
       They lived at Batavia, and had one child.

Child.

1. Almon Cady, b. April, 1852; d. 1854.

157.

BENJAMIN [6] CHURCHILL (ASAHEL,[5] BENJAMIN,[4] SAMUEL [3]
JOSEPH,[2] JOSIAH [1]).   Born near Hartford, Conn., Dec. 11, 1789.
Removed first to the Black River Country, N.Y., and thence, about
1818, to Newbern, N.C.   The account of this family has come to
the editor since the mention of Benjamin, on page 362.   Married
HENRIETTA WOOD.

Children, first four born in New York, the rest in North Carolina.

	I.	HARRIET.[7]
	II.	CALVIN,[7]
	III.	CAROLINE,[7] } Twins. m. LEWIS WOOLTEN.
386a	IV.	JAMES,BRYAN,[7] b. April, 1817; m. SARAH HALL, 1838.
387	V.	ORIN,[7] b. Oct. 19, 1819; m. 1st, SARAH REID, Dec. 12, 1839. She
		d. Sept. 12, 1846; m. 2d, RHODA ANN SHACKFORD, Jan. 7, 1847.
	VI.	ELIZA,[7] m. JOSEPH YOUNG.
	VII.	ALMIRA.[7]
	VIII.	MARY ANN,[7] d. early.
	IX.	GEORGE WASHINGTON HAYMAN.[7]
	X.	POLLY ANN,[7] b. 1835; m. ARMISTEAD SHACKFORD.

158.

ELISHA [6] CHURCHILL (ASAHEL,[5] BENJAMIN [4] SAMUEL [3]
JOSEPH,[2] JOSIAH [1]).   Born Aug. 16, 1798, in the Black River Country, N.Y.   Married someone whose name we have not received.

Children.

   I. LOVINA,[7] m. 1st, ALFRED GOWDY, of Jefferson County, N.Y.; m.
   2d, ALLEN BENEDICT, of Fairport, N.Y.

Child.

1. Josephine Gowdy, m. Frank Hadcock; no children.

II. OLIVE,[7] m. GUSTAVUS CHAMPLAIN.

Child.

1. Ernest Champlain; d. young.

159.

CHESTER [6] CHURCHILL (SAMUEL,[5] BENJAMIN,[4] SAMUEL,[3] JOSEPH,[2] JOSIAH [1]). Born in Bristol, Conn., Feb. 22, 1788. Lived in Batavia, N.Y., about three miles west of "the village." He was at one time proprietor of a boat on the Mississippi river, and lost his life there. About 1833 he was owner of two stores at Kinderhook, Pike County, Ill., and had a large trade with the Indians and frontier farmers. Married, in Batavia, N.Y., MERCY CARL.

Children.

388　　I. CHESTER.[7]
389　　II ALMOND.[7]

160.

DANEY [6] CHURCHILL (SAMUEL,[5] BENJAMIN [4] SAMUEL [3] JOSEPH,[2] JOSIAH [1]). Born in Bristol, Conn., Nov. 24, 1792. Lived at Moreau and Portland, N.Y. He died at Portland, N.Y., Dec. 8, 1856. Married, Nov. 7, 1816, at Moreau, N.Y., MINERVA BURNHAM. She died at Portland, N.Y., Aug. 5, 1886.

Children.

I. MARIA,[7] b. Jan. 3, 1818; m. 1st, JOHN M. BROWN, Oct. 19, 1836, who d. Dec. 24, 1879; m. 2d, JASON BIGELOW, Nov. 24, 1887.

Children of First Husband.

1. Minerva C. Brown, b. at Portland, N.Y., Feb. 7, 1838; m. 1st, at Wheeling, Va., Oct. 19, 1859, George W. Artis, who died March 21, 1867; and she m. 2d, at Hanley, Mich., April 15, 1883, William Whipple. They live (March, 1900) at Hendersonville, Mich.

2. Sarah M. Brown, b. at Portland, Aug. 26, 1843; m. 1st, at Portland, N.Y., Eleazer Swetland, April 10, 1862. He d. in the army, 1864, and she m. 2d, Willard Taylor, at Grand Rapids, Mich., Sept. 12, 1872. They live (March, 1900) at Manton, Mich.

3. Harriet J. Brown, b. at Portland, Nov. 1, 1844; d. September, 1845.

4. Ella Maria Brown, b. at New Hamburg. Penn., Dec. 11, 1848. Lived (March, 1900) in Portland, N.Y.

5. Virginia Bell Brown, b. at Wheeling, Va., March 20, 1860; m. at Hanley, Mich., Frank B. Fay, March, 1878. Living (March, 1900) at Swartz Creek, Mich.

390   II. George,[7] b. July 26, 1821; m. Eliza J. Wade Fletcher, May 17, 1852.
III. John Harvey,[7] b. Dec. 27, 1826; d. at Portland, May 1, 1843.
IV. Mary Jane,[7] b. Jan. 23, 1830; d. at Portland, Sept. 28, 1857.

161.

CHARLES[6] CHURCHILL (Samuel,[5] Benjamin,[4] Samuel,[3] Joseph,[2] Josiah[1]). Born in Moreau, N.Y., Oct. 17, 1800. He was a tailor. Settled first near Lake George, N.Y., where he lived for some sixteen years, but moved later to Bloomfield, Oakland County, Mich., in June, 1837. Here he purchased a farm, about three and a half miles from Pontiac, and went there to live with his family. In the fall of 1864 he sold his farm, and removed to Pontiac, where he bought a residence. In August, 1837, he joined the Congregational Church in Pontiac, of which he was a worthy and beloved member until his death, caused by falling from a load of wood, in his own door-yard. He died Dec. 31, 1866. He was an exemplary Christian man, a wise and devoted husband and father. Married 1st, at Glens Falls, N.Y., Dec. 30, 1821, Laura Curtis, daughter of Thomas and Mary (Andrews) Curtis. She died in 1854. Married 2d, Mrs. Sarah M. Chipman, of Fenton, N.Y., March, 1855.

Children of First Wife.

I. Isabella,[7] b. in Chester, N.Y., May 30, 1823; m. Hon. A. C. Baldwin, of Pontiac, Mich. Mr. Baldwin was an eminent jurist and statesman, and one of the most prominent citizens of Pontiac, and all that section of the State, as lawyer, teacher, Congressman, and judge, for some forty years. Mrs. Baldwin was a fine, cultured, and beautiful woman, a worthy wife of a noble man. She died June 6, 1894. Their daughter, Augusta Isabella Baldwin, born Nov. 21, 1866, married Dr. Edmund A. Christian, Jan. 24, 1894.
II. Charlotte,[7] b. in Ticonderoga, July 27, 1825; m. Albert A. Hubbard, Bloomfield, Mich., Jan. 9, 1849, and d. Aug. 16, 1850.
III. Lovisa Maria,[7] b. in Schroon, N.Y., April 10, 1828; d. in Bloomfield, Mich., Sept. 11, 1851.

162.

SAMUEL[6] CHURCHILL (Samuel,[5] Benjamin,[4] Samuel,[3] Joseph,[2] Josiah[1]). Born at Moreau, N.Y., July 4, 1804. Settled first at Batavia, N.Y. About 1835 he went West with his brother, Philo Clark, and found their brother Chester, at his stores at Kinderhook, Ill. After some months they returned and settled down at Salem Cross-roads, N.Y. We have heard that there were other children in this family, but after long and persistent effort we find only two names. Married Eliza Culver.

Children born at Batavia, N. Y.

391   I. DARIUS DANA,[7] b. Oct. 24, 1827; m. EMILY SHADBOLT, March 30,
            1850.
391a   II. WALTER H.,[7] b. April 27, 1838.

163.

ITHUEL[6] CHURCHILL (SAMUEL,[5] BENJAMIN,[4] SAMUEL,[3]
JOSEPH,[2] JOSIAH[1]). Born in Moreau, N.Y., Aug. 21, 1806. He was
early set to hard work, and had to win his way in the world. He
became a strenuous, thrifty, and prosperous man. He stood for all
good enterprises, and was a generous helper of all who seemed to
him to need help. He was very strong in his convictions, and conscientious in his decisions. He was successful in his management,
and acquired what was, for his day, wealth. A generous supporter
of the church, a public-spirited citizen, and ever ready to help
others; and yet the mystery and tragedy of his casting off his wife,
a good, capable, and faithful woman, by divorce, — by which act the
wife of his home and mother of his children was sent out into
the world to make her way, and live her life alone, — stands out
in strange contrast to his good and kindly deeds, and his strong
Christian character. The fault was, perhaps, the rigid will, that
could not bend from a decision once made. One of his children
wrote to me some years since, that it was a mystery to her, and she
thought it the one great mistake of his life, for her mother was an
intelligent and capable woman, a mother whom "her children rose
up and called blessed." He settled first in Portland, N.Y., as a
farmer, but in 1854 sold out his several farms and removed to Pontiac, Mich., and died there Sept. 5, 1861. Married 1st, at Batavia,
N.Y., March, 1831, RUTH ARMINDA WHITMAN, daughter of James
and Sabrina Whitman, of Batavia. They were divorced September,
1842, and she died in Ellington, N.Y., July 9, 1874. He married
2d, LYDIA MARSTON.

Children of First Wife.

I. JULIA ANN,[7] b. at Batavia, Dec. 3, 1831; m. OLIVER HOPSON, in
     Portland, N.Y., October, 1850. They moved to Corunna, Mich.,
     in 1857. She died Jan. 12, 1890.

Children.

1. Leslie N. Hopson, b. Dec. 19, 1851; m. Mahala Smith.
2. James A. Hopson, b. Nov. 12, 1853; m. Ellen Butcher.
3. Frank C. Hopson, b. July 5, 1855; m. Maria Cram.
4. Carrie Hopson, b. May 30, 1856; m. James Warren.
5. Nettie Hopson, m. Levi Cram.
6. Minnie Hopson, m. George Butcher.
7. Arthur Hopson, d. 1870, aged three and one-half years.

II. FRANCES EVELINE,[7] b. in Portland, N.Y., June 13, 1835; m. 1st,
HENRY C. DAVIS, Oct. 10, 1853; d. in army, 1860; m. 2d, THOMAS
DAVIS, 1863. They lived in Ellington, N.Y. She died April 9,
1889.

Children.

1. Ella Davis, b. October, 1854; m Fred Day.
2. Mary Davis, b. May, 1856; m. William Alverron.
3. Lillian Davis, b. May, 1858; m. Frank Waith.
4. Herman Davis, b. 1860.

Children of Second Husband.

5. Grace Davis, b. July, 1867; m. A. C. Randall. Lives in Duluth,
Mich.
6. Wayne Davis, b. 1870.
7. Belle Davis, b. 1873.
8. Lulu Davis, b. 1876.

III. LUCY MARIA,[7] b. at Portland, N.Y., Dec. 7, 1839; m. 1st, in Portland, N.Y., Nov. 23, 1857, JOHN QUINN. Divorced in December,
1868; m. 2d, in Corunna, Mich., June 14, 1870, WILLIAM BALL.
Lived in Portland for some years, and then moved to Neenah,
Wis., and from 1870 to 1894 she lived in Duluth, Minn., and in
1899 in Walla Walla, Wash.

Children of First Husband.

1. Eva L. Quinn, b. in Portland, N.Y., April 7, 1857; m. Robert
Trefry, in Duluth, Dec. 17, 1879. Their children: (1) Son,
b. Dec. 31, 1881; d. next day; (2) Edwin K. Trefry, b. Aug.
25, 1884; d. March, 1887; (3) Ethel M. Trefry, b. June 13,
1886; (4) Ada Mary Trefry, b. Sept. 5, 1889. In December,
1899, this family was living in Argentine, Kan.
2. Marian Churchill Quinn, b. in Neenah, Wis., Feb. 14, 1866; m.
in Duluth, December, 1891, Philip Lage, and lived in Argentine, Kan.

Children by Second Husband born in Duluth.

3. Edna B. Ball, b. June 18, 1871; m., June 18, 1891, William
Barrett, in Duluth. Children: (1) William Ball Barrett, b.
June 15, 1892; (2) Paul Verne Barrett, b. Dec. 3, 1894; (3)
Ruth Edna Barrett, b. Aug. 19, 1896; (4) Harry Neal Barrett,
b. Aug. 13, 1899; d. Nov. 3, 1899.
This family was living, in 1899, in Walla Walla, Wash.
4. Alice C. Ball, b. Aug. 23, 1874.
5. Lucie B. Ball, b. Aug. 6, 1875.

Children of Ithuel and Lydia (Marston) Churchill.

IV. OLIVE ADELL,[7] b. in Portland, N.Y., Oct. 8, 1846.
392   V. JOHN HARVEY,[7] b. in Portland, N.Y., Dec. 18, 1848; m. ESTELLA
L. HART, May 7, 1882.

164.

PHILO CLARK [6] CHURCHILL (SAMUEL,[5] BENJAMIN,[4] SAM-
UEL,[3] JOSEPH,[2] JOSIAH [1]). Born at Moreau, Saratoga County,
N.Y., Jan. 11, 1812. His father died when he was six years old.
His mother afterward married and removed to Glens Falls, N.Y.,
and at twelve years he was apprenticed to his brother Charles, to
learn the tailor's trade. The boy went by stage from Moreau to White-

hall, and thence by a small sailing-boat to his brother's place, near Lake George, — a very rough passage, and a walk alone, over a high mountain. He remained with his brother until he was twenty-one years old, and then sought out a place for himself, trying various places, but after a few years, with his brother Samuel, then living at Batavia, N.Y., he went by canal and on foot to the Ohio river, and thence by boat to St. Louis, and up the Missouri river to Council Bluffs, working their way by helping to load the steamers with wood. They finally arrived at Kinderhook, Pike County, Ill., where their eldest brother, Chester, had two trading-stores for trade with the Indians and surrounding farmers. After some· time spent at Chester's, they returned to New York State and settled at Salem Cross-roads, where he became acquainted with a young girl who was from the northern part of the State, but attending school, boarding at her brother's. This girl's name was Sophronia Whedon, and after a year's acquaintance and correspondence they were married, and lived, at first, at the home of Samuel, in Batavia, N.Y., and in September, 1838, they started with a span of horses and emigrant wagon for Illinois, overland. They were both prostrated by chills and fever, at Canton, Ill., and on partial recovery found that the doctor's bill had absorbed one horse and the wagon, leaving them helpless. The brother Chester, warned of their plight by letter, came for them and took them to his home. Clark, as he was called by his family, entered the employ of his brother as clerk, until Chester died soon after, and he then settled down to farming. Eight years after his wife died, leaving three children, the youngest three months old. He married a second wife a year afterwards, who died Nov. 2, 1859. He married his third wife in 1860, and removed to near Peoria, Ill. His removal was on account of the persecution of the border ruffians from Missouri, who raided the farms of Northern union men. He made his home at or near Peoria, until 1880, when he purchased a farm at Keosauqua, Iowa, where he remained until his death, April 16, 1889. Mr. Churchill was a member, and for forty years deacon, in the Baptist Church.

Married 1st, May 10, 1838, SOPHRONIA WHEDON, born March 10, 1820, and died Jan. 10, 1846, at Kinderhook, Ill.; married 2d, 1847, ANNA ALDRICH, who died Nov. 2, 1859; married 3d, June 24, 1860, Mrs. ELIZABETH (JOHNSON) TITUS, daughter of William Johnson, born Oct. 22, 1837, near Zanesville, O.

Children of First Wife born in Kinderhook, Ill.

393   I.   EDWIN,[7] b. Sept. 18, 1839; m. CARRIE WEST, of Greenwood, Ind.
394   II.   DANEY JABEZ,[7] b. Jan. 10, 1841; m. MARTHA GATES, April 13, 1863.
395   III.   FRANCIS WAYLAND,[7] b. Oct. 24, 1845; m. ELLA SHAFFER, March 1, 1871.

Child of Third Wife.

396   IV. ROBERT CLARK,[7] b. at Hilton, Ill., June 4, 1866; m. MIRIAM LEOTA PARK, at Leando, Iowa, Feb. 26, 1890.

165.

BARNABAS[6] CHURCHILL (IRA,[5] BENJAMIN,[4] SAMUEL,[3] JOSEPH,[2] JOSIAH[1]). Born in Bristol, Conn., March 21, 1791, and lived there until the fall of 1820, when he removed to Ohio. The journey with his household goods, his wife and two small children, was made in an ox-cart, and took six weeks on the road. They stopped a few months in Bristol, O., and then in the spring of 1821 reached Greene, where he bought a farm and made a permanent home. He was a public-spirited citizen, a zealous member of the Congregational Church, — of strong anti-slavery principles, and active in upholding what he believed was right. He was a tanner, shoemaker, and farmer. He served in the War of 1812. He died in Greene, May 18, 1867. Married, at Farmington, Conn., Dec. 25, 1815, POLLY ROOT, daughter of Salmon and Sarah (Finney) Root. Barnabas Churchill and his wife and all their descendants who have died in Greene are buried in the family cemetery on the old farm.

Children.

397   I. RICHARD MARTIN,[7] b. in Bristol, Conn., March 16, 1817; m. ISABEL MILLER, Dec. 2, 1843.
    II. ROBERT BARNABAS,[7] b. in Bristol, Conn., Feb. 27, 1819; d. at Fort Wayne, Ind., Sept. 22, 1861.
398   III. SALMON ROOT,[7] b. in Bristol, O., Feb. 25, 1821; m. SARAH HOAGLAND.
    IV. SARAH,[7] b. in Greene, O., Dec. 15, 1822; unmarried; d. in Greene, April 7, 1882.
    V. BETSEY,[7] b. in Greene, O., Dec. 2, 1824; m. MARTIN COATS, Jan. 8, 1846.

Children born at Mecca, O., and Greene, O.

1. Ellen Clara Coats, b. May 2, 1847; m. George Moore, August, 1866.
    They lived at Forest City, Minn., where she died March 12, 1876.
2. Albert B. Coats, b. Sept. 27, 1849, at Greene.
    He was a clergyman, at Akron, O., in 1901.
3. Frank Coats, b. Sept. 12, 1852, at Mecca.

    VI. ROXY,[7] b. at Greene, Aug. 17, 1826; d. Aug. 24, 1826.
    VII. IRA RODNEY,[7] b. at Greene, Sept. 30, 1827; d. Jan. 27, 1868.
    VIII. HANNAH,[7] b. at Greene, Sept. 15, 1829; m. SOLOMON GUNN, at Greene, O., March 31, 1852.
    They settled in Greene upon the old farm where Mrs. Gunn was born, and cared for the old father and mother, and an invalid brother and sister. Mrs Gunn was living there in March, 1901, with her daughter, Mrs. Winans, it being now in the town of Kenilworth, O. Mr Gunn was educated at the Grand River Institute, Austinberg, O., and died in 1898. Mrs. Gunn helped the editor greatly in this account of her father's family.

Children of Solomon and Hannah (Churchill) Gunn.

1. Arthur Rollin Gunn, b. Dec. 7, 1853; d. June 7, 1864.
2. Bertha May Gunn, b. Oct. 20, 1865. Living with her mother at Kenilworth, 1901.
3. Edith Jane Gunn, b. Dec. 23, 1869; m. William W. Winans, at Greene, O., Dec. 24, 1890 They live on the old homestead, and have children: (1) Mabel Maude Winans, b. in Mecca, O., Jan. 2, 1892; (2) Walter William Winans, b. in Greene, May 5, 1896; (3) Alice Verna Winans, b. in Greene, Aug. 3, 1897; (4) Almer Arthur Winans, b. in Greene, July 12, 1900.

IX. ROMEO,[7] b. at Greene, O., Dec. 31, 1831. He enlisted for service in the Civil War, in Company C, Twenty-ninth Regiment, Ohio Volunteer Infantry, and died at Harper's Ferry, Jan. 13, 1863.

166.

MAJOR[6] CHURCHILL (IRA,[5] BENJAMIN,[4] SAMUEL,[3] JOSEPH[2] JOSIAH[1]). Born in Bristol, Conn., Sept. 6, 1792. Served for several months in the War of 1812. Was engaged in the expedition above Fort Erie. He settled at first in his native town, but some time about 1818–19, perhaps in company with his brother Barnabas, he made a journey to Ohio, took up a claim of land, and then returned to Connecticut for his family. The greater part of his journey was made on foot. It was in the winter of 1820, probably, that he again set out for the West, this time with oxen and sleds, taking along his father and mother and their younger children, Lois Delia and Ceylon M. The distance from Bristol, Conn., across New York State to Buffalo, in direct line, is about three hundred miles. Their journey, made with the clumsy ox-teams, probably covered in its roundabout course nearer four hundred miles. All possible of their household furnishings and provisions for themselves they carried with them. When they arrived at Buffalo the snow was nearly gone, so that they were forced to take to the ice on Lake Erie, and then, when they came to Geneva, the ice had so melted away from the shore that they had great difficulty to get to land. The rest of their journey was made by land to Greene Township, Trumbull County, O. Here they cleared and cultivated farms, and in this town and vicinity they and their children have lived honorable and useful lives. Major Churchill was a well-educated man for his day, was an upright and influential citizen. He was postmaster of Greene for eighteen years. He died in Greene, Sept. 8, 1874. Married, at Bristol, Conn., April 17, 1818, EUNICE PAYNE, daughter of Solomon and Mary (Clark) Payne.

Children.

I. CALISTA,[7] b. in Bristol, Conn., Oct. 28, 1820; m. 1st, ALBERT PERCY, Oct. 20, 1836; m. 2d, WATSON T. CHAPMAN, Dec. 28, 1842.

Child of First Husband.

1. Lauren A. Percy, b. at Greensburg, O., May 3, 1838; m. Charlotte Clark, 1861.
Served through the Civil War in Company B, One Hundred and Fifth Regiment, Ohio Volunteer Infantry, in Fourteenth Army Corps.

Children of Second Husband, born in Wayne, O.

2. Eunice May Chapman, b. Nov. 8, 1849; m. F. E. Dwight, of Marshalltown, Ia.
3. W. B. Chapman, b. Nov. 18, 1852; m. Sarah R. Mohler, Marshalltown, Ia.

II. MARY PAYNE,[7] b. in Greene, O., May 24, 1822; m. REV. EDWIN WAKEFIELD, May 22, 1845.
Mr. Wakefield was born in Greene, O., Oct. 24, 1818. He was educated at the Western Reserve Seminary, entered the ministry, and he served faithfully for forty years. Mrs. Mary P. Wakefield died Oct. 29, 1888, at Greensburg.

Children born at Greensburg.

1. Edmund Barrett Wakefield, b. Aug. 27, 1846; m. Martha A. Sheldon, Aug. 23, 1870.
He was educated at Bethany and at Hiram College. Served in Company G, Ohio Volunteer Infantry, Twenty-third Army Corps, in all the later actions of that corps, in the Civil War. He was a member of the Geological Survey under Dr. Hayden, and has been professor of law and political science in Hiram College since 1890.
2. Dora M. Wakefield, b. May 27, 1852; m. Robert P. Crane.

III. CLARISSA ADALINE,[7] b. in Greene, O., June 15, 1824; m. WILLIAM HORTON, Dec. 29, 1841.
They lived at Greene or Greensburg, where he was a farmer and carpenter. Both now living there (March, 1901).

Children.

1. Maria A. Horton, b. May 22, 1843; m. 1st, Anson M. Peabody, March 24, 1861. He died in the army, 1862; m. 2d, Philander Wollcott, April 22, 1869. He was killed by a bull in 1883.
2. Mary Emma Horton, b. Dec. 27, 1848; m. Alfred Lamphear, Aug. 13, 1868.
3. Milton Burgess Horton, b. May 24, 1851; m. Ida M. Greenwood, April 17, 1875.
4. Minnesota Horton, b. Sept. 10, 1856; m. George W. Irwin, Nov. 29, 1876; d. Sept. 1, 1877.
5. William D. Horton, b. Dec. 7, 1858; m. Carrie I. Hillman, Nov. 25, 1882.

IV. MILTON AMMI,[7] b. Dec. 11, 1828; d. July 3, 1840.
V. HESTER EUNICE,[7] b. Jan. 2, 1834; d. May 12, 1884.

167.

BRYAN[6] CHURCHILL (IRA,[5] BENJAMIN,[4] SAMUEL,[3] JOSEPH,[2] JOSIAH[1]). Born in Bristol, Conn., March 11, 1795. He settled in Connecticut, probably in Bristol, and lived afterwards at Plainville, Conn. Mrs. Morse, his daughter, gave us the dates and names, but nothing more. He died June 23, 1875, at Plainville. Married, April 24, 1817, MARY P. HADSELL, born Oct. 8, 1795. She died Sept. 1, 1878.

Child.

I. MARY ELIZABETH,[7] b. July 10, 1823; m. LEWIS MORSE, Sept. 1, 1844.
They lived (in 1886) in Plainville, Conn.

Children.

1. Lewis C. Morse, b. June 12, 1852; m. Jane E. Belden, Oct. 2,
1873.
   One child, (1) a daughter, name not given, b. May 15, 1875.
2. Bryan E. Morse, b. Oct. 2, 1860; m. Wealthy Pardee, March
20, 1884.

168.

IRA[6] CHURCHILL (IRA,[5] BENJAMIN,[4] SAMUEL,[3] JOSEPH,[2]
JOSIAH[1]). Born in Bristol, Conn., Dec. 19, 1796, and always lived
in that town. In 1886 he was living, at the age of eighty-nine years,
at Forestdale, a part of Bristol, with his wife, aged eighty-seven, in
the same house where they began housekeeping at marriage, sixty-
two years before. We have received no more than this meagre account of the family. He died at Forestdale Oct. 15, 1886. Married,
in Bristol, 1824, BETSEY MATTHEWS. They had two children, a
son and daughter, but we have not received the names, and ·have
learned that they died years ago, before the date above mentioned,
1886.

169.

CEYLON MUNSON[6] CHURCHILL (IRA,[5] BENJAMIN,[4] SAM-
UEL,[3] JOSEPH,[2] JOSIAH[1]). Born in Bristol, Conn., June 10, 1812.
Removed with his parents, in 1820, to Greene, O. He lived in
Trumbull County, not far from the old home, his last residence
being Bazetta Township, near Cortland. He was a mechanic and
artist. He died in Bazetta, O., March 4, 1887. Married, at Orwell,
O., October, 1848, FRANCES RICHARDS, who was born Oct. 27, 1819,
and died July 4, 1888.

Children.

I. DELIA FLORINE,[7] b. July 20, 1850; m. WASHINGTON HYDE, June,
1872.
   They lived at Warren, O., where she died, September, 1873.
399   II. OTTO BURCHARD,[7] b. June 16, 1852; m. MARY JANE CRAFT,
March 18, 1877.

170.

JOSEPH[6] HAYFORD (JEDEDIAH,[5] BENJAMIN,[4] SAMUEL,[3]
JOSEPH,[2] JOSIAH[1]). Born at Bristol, Conn., Aug. 30, 1803. He
lived in New Hartford, Oneida County, N.Y., but spent last days in
Kirkland, N.Y. He died May 11, 1880. Married, June 7, 1831,
SARAH LOVINA STEVENS, of Rutland, Vt., where she was born Nov.
8, 1813, and died in New Hartford, N.Y., Jan. 3, 1869.

Children born in New Hartford, N.Y.

400   I. Edwin Jerome,[7] b. July 18, 1833; m. Ellen M. Cook, Sept. 21, 1858.
401   II. Henry Clay,[7] b. April 25, 1835.
          III. George W..,[7] b. Oct. 18, 1837; d. May 6, 1843.
          IV. Joseph Chauncey,[7] b. July 18, 1840.
402   V. Benjamin W.,[7] b. July 6, 1843; m. Ellen M. Crumb, June 7, 1865.
          VI. Martha Jane,[7] b. Nov. 9, 1849; d. April 9, 1885.

171.

ANSON J.[6] CHURCHILL (Jedediah,[5] Benjamin,[4] Samuel,[3] Joseph,[2] Josiah[1]). Born in Winsted, Conn. (probably). Lived, in 1886, at West Vienna, Oneida County, N.Y. Married Sarah Malory.

Children.

403   I. Jay A.[7]
404   II. William H.[7]
405   III. Joseph.[7]
406   IV. George E.,[7] m. Gertrude Nickerson.
406a   V. Lovina,[7] m. John Washburn.

172.

LEWIS[6] CHURCHILL (David,[5] William,[4] Samuel,[3] Joseph,[2] Josiah[1]). Born in Bristol, Conn., Oct. 8, 1793. Married Sarah Caroline Tuttle.

Children.

I. Eliza,[7] d. in infancy.
II. Sarah,[7] d. in infancy.
III. Finette,[7] m. (———) Brackett. No children.
IV. Sophronia,[7] m. Luther Piper.

Children.

1. Emma Piper; m. Frank Hale.
2. Eleanor Piper.

V. William Milton,[7] b. in Walcott, Conn., Dec. 22, 1831; m. Julia M. Doolittle, of Cheshire, Conn. No children.
407   VI. Franklin Dwight.[7] b. in Bethany, Conn., Feb. 14, 1834; m. Jane L. Blakeslee, of Prospect, Conn.

173.

ALFRED[6] CHURCHILL (David,[5] William,[4] Samuel,[3] Joseph,[2] Josiah[1]). Born in Bristol, Conn., May 12, 1804. Our information relating to this family is very meagre So far as we can learn, there were no grandchildren. Married 1st, Rosetta Alcott; 2d, Samantha Dayton, in Litchfield.

Children, all by First Wife.

I. Eveline,[7] b. Oct. 3, 1830.
408   II. Newell,[7] b. July 11, 1833.
409   III. Dennis,[7] b. Feb. 5, 1837.

174.

WILLIAM TRYON [6] CHURCHILL (Lemuel,[5] William,[4] Samuel,[3] Joseph,[2] Josiah [1]). Born near Elmira, N.Y., March 23, 1795. He lived there until 1824, when he removed to Tioga County, Penn., and settled in an almost unbroken wilderness, near Crooked Creek. They endured the many privations incident to pioneer life. He died in 1832, leaving a widow and five children, and the sixth was born a few months after. Married, in Tioga County, N.Y., Jan. 15, 1820, Elizabeth Hopper. After Mr. Churchill's death his widow married Mr. Joseph Neal. She died in 1887, in her eighty-sixth year.

Children born, the first two in New York, the rest in Pennsylvania.

    I. John,[7] b. Oct. 19, 1821; m. Jane Goodell; no children.
   II. Olive,[7] b. June 2, 1823; m. Nehemiah French.
  III. Ruth,[7] b. Sept. 16, 1825; m. George Champlin, April 8, 1852.

Children.

    1. Marion Champlin, b. Dec. 31, 1853; m. David Paris, November, 1875.
    2. Emma Champlin, b. Sept. 29, 1855; m. Volney Gillet, July 2, 1879.
    3. Nellie Champlin, b. Feb. 11, 1858; m. Joseph Allen, July 27, 1878.
    4. Lizzie Champlin, b. May 24, 1860; m. William Tuttle, November, 1879.

   IV. Esther,[7] b. Nov. 25, 1827; m. George Freeman.
    V. Elisha,[7] b. April 11, 1829; d. in infancy.
411   VI. William H.,[7] b. Feb. 27, 1833; m. Louisa Nichols, Jan. 7, 1861.

175.

ASA GILDERSLEEVE [6] CHURCHILL (Lemuel,[5] William,[4] Samuel,[3] Joseph,[2] Josiah [1]). Born near Elmira, N.Y., March 11 1798. Mr. Churchill seems to have settled with his first wife at Wellsboro, Tioga County, Penn., where several children were born, and where he had a good farm, it is said. Some time before 1860 he started from his home on a journey, his first wife having died. He had become quite a local celebrity, from his faculty of ready rhyming upon all sorts of events and topics. He went on foot to Niagara Falls, making and reciting his rhymes along the way, to get his food and lodging, and it is said that he was generally welcome to the farmers' homes, where he would gather a company of young and old about him, and amuse them by reciting poetical legends, mostly his own, or composing new ones for the locality where he happened then to be. Business advertisements in rhyme were a specialty, and obituaries, and doleful, or heroic, or tragic, or comic events were treated "to order," and in this way he earned his living, it is said. The Huntsville, Ont., "Forester" gives a sketch of his eccentric character, unique career, and tragic end. He was known in Huntsville as "the Muskoka poet," or otherwise as the "Old Poet Churchill." It is said that he intended to return home after visiting Niagara Falls, but that he evidently found his wandering way of life pleasant, and kept on into Canada. After several years he located at Collingwood, Ont., where he married a second wife, a widow, and soon after removed to Parry Sound, where he took up and settled upon a farm, on which he lived until his second wife died, when he returned again to Huntsville, where he married, for his third wife, a German widow by the name of Albert, who, in her turn, died some five years later. In all these years the old man had not returned to, nor yet heard from, any of his children or relatives in the States. Some six weeks before his death occurred, this old man of ninety-four years started on foot from Huntsville to revisit his children, if he could find them, at Wellsboro, Penn., and had actually arrived within a few miles of his old home when he was run down by an express train, while walking on the New York, Pennsylvania, & Ohio Railroad track.

It is to be regretted that we have failed to obtain answers to repeated appeals to the daughters to give their own dates and families.

Married 1st, in Tioga County, Penn., LUCY CLARK ; 2d, at Collingwood, Ont., MRS. (———) (———) ; 3d, at Huntsville, Ont., MRS. (———) ALBERT.

Children of First Wife.

   I. MARY ANN,[7] m. FRANK CLEMENS.
  II. ROXANA,[7] m. WILLIAM CLEMENS. They were living in East Charlton, Penn., a few years ago.
 III. WILLIAM.[7] Died in the army in the Civil War.
 IV. LEMUEL.[7] Left home in his youth; nothing further known.

176.

JOHN LEMBERSON[6] CHURCHILL (LEMUEL,[5] WILLIAM,[4] SAMUEL,[3] JOSEPH,[2] JOSIAH[1]). Born near Elmira, N.Y., June 13, 1800. Lived twenty-eight miles north of Pittsburgh. A lawyer of some repute, location not given. A poet of no mean ability, and a shrewd speculator, but we have no further account. He died Aug. 7, 1879. Married 1st, PAMELIA CHASE ; 2d, MARIA HAZLET daughter of Rev. Samuel. She died Oct. 6, 1872

Children of First Wife.

   I. JERUSHA BENNETT,[7] m. JOHN FERGUSON, in Indiana, Penn., 1846, and d. March 31, 1901.

II. Julia Ann,[7] m. H. Leslie.
III. Samuel,[7] killed in battle in Civil War.
IV. Clarissa,[7] m. Isaac Empfield.
V. Mary,[7] m. Samuel Moorhead.

Children of Second Wife.

412　　VI. John Wesley,[7] b. in Indiana, Penn., June 10, 1840; m. Jennie
　　　　　　L. Keiber.
　　　VII. Philander,[7] d. young.
　　VIII. Pamelia Jane,[7] m. Mr. Kerl.
413　　IX. James Templeton.[7]
　　　　X. Sarah Elizabeth,[7] b. July 29, 1852; m. George W. Thompson.
　　　　XI. Beulah Melissa.[7] She was at Oswego Normal School in 1886,
　　　　　　and wrote a long letter, but gave no information about the
　　　　　　family.

177.

CHARLES[6] CHURCHILL (Lemuel,[5] William,[4] Samuel,[3] Joseph,[2] Josiah[1]). Born near Elmira, N.Y., Dec. 5, 1802. His father's family seems to have located in Pennsylvania later on, and he settled in Tioga County, where, his son Clark writes, " He was a sort of a country doctor, a speculator in timber-lands, etc." Later in his life he resided with his son, George W. Churchill, at Bucyrus, O., whence, on his seventy-sixth birthday, he wrote to his brother, William Tryon, Dec. 5, 1878. Married, April 25, 1831, Elizabeth Butler Cornell.

Children.

414　　I. Josiah Butler,[7] b. Dec. 4, 1831; m. Catharine Kissel, Sept. 21,
　　　　　　1865.
　　　II. Hamilton,[7] b. May 26, 1834.
415　III. Clark,[7] b. June 17, 1836; m. Margaretha Schmidt, Oct. 12,
　　　　　　1864. They had no children.
　　　　　　He went to the Pacific coast in early life, located first in Cali-
　　　　　　fornia, where he studied law, and was admitted to the bar in 1862.
　　　　　　He settled in Virginia City, Nev., and became a successful prac-
　　　　　　tising lawyer. Was chosen city solicitor in 1865. In 1880 he was
　　　　　　appointed adjutant-general of Arizona Territory, and in 1885
　　　　　　became attorney-general of the territory. He has lived in Arizona,
　　　　　　at Prescott, and Phœnix.
416　　IV. George Washington,[7] b. Nov. 16, 1838.
　　　　V. Marian,[7] b. Jan. 23, 1831; m. Charles Palmer.
　　　　VI. Emily M.,[7] b. March 11, 1844.

178.

JOSEPH DELL[6] CHURCHILL (William,[5] William,[4] Samuel,[3] Joseph,[2] Josiah[1]). Born near Jersey City, N.J., July 29, 1797. When about twenty-three years old he " went West," and settled in Arkansas, on the White river, some forty miles from Little Rock, at Pineville, Izard County. He died Aug. 9, 1851. Married, March 28, 1827, Lucretia Bocock, born Oct. 28, 1803.

Children.

417   I. JOHN SILAS,[7] b. Nov. 24, 1828; m. SUSAN JANE TAYLOR, Dec. 30, 1851.

418   II. JAMES JEFFREY,[7] b. Dec. 30, 1829; m. MARTHA ANN SCOTT, Aug. 31, 1859.

III. MARY CAROLINE,[7] b. May 24, 1831; m. HARTLEY STEPHENS, July 4, 1848. She died in Lance County, Ark., in 1863.

IV. LAVINIA,[7] b. Feb. 9, 1833; m. CRAWFORD McALISTER, 1871. They lived in Pope County, Ark. P.O. address, Rondo, Ark.

V. JANE,[7] b. May 9, 1836; single.

VI. LUCY ANN,[7] b. Feb. 24, 1838; m. NATHAN J. LANGSTON, Sept. 1 1851. They lived in Wideman, Izard County, Ark.

419   VII. WILLIAM WALKER,[7] b. Aug. 14, 1840; m. DELPHINE McALISTER, 1874.

VIII. DEMPSIA WHITE,[7] b. Aug. 14, 1842; d. unmarried, 1862.

IX. INFANT,[7] b. Dec. 20, 1843; received no name; d. soon.

420   X. JOSEPH A.,[7] b. Nov. 22, 1846; m. NANCY ANN DUVALL, January, 1871.

179.

SILAS[6] CHURCHILL (WILLIAM,[5] WILLIAM,[4] SAMUEL,[3] JOSEPH,[2] JOSIAH[1]). Born at Scipio, Cayuga County, N.Y., Feb. 5, 1803. Moved to near Marietta, O., with his father's family, when eleven years old. In August, 1884, he wrote N. W. Churchill a long letter, which gave much information about his uncles and brothers, but very little about himself. He says he was married the second time, but does not mention the second wife's name, or that of his youngest daughter, nor that of his son, his only child by his second wife. He was living, in 1884, with Mrs. Ferguson, Janesville, Iowa. Married 1st, Feb. 7, 1829, ELIZABETH GRAY, "who was raised near Washington, Penn.," and died in Ohio, in 1843. Married 2d, 1848. Her name not received.

Children.

I. MARTHA JANE,[7] m. JOHN FERGUSON.
They had eleven children, but we have no names or dates.

II. ELIZABETH,[7] m. ROBERT FAIRBURN.
They had six children, but we have no names.

III. A DAUGHTER,[7] name not received.

Child by Second Wife.

IV. A SON,[7] name not received; d. about 1880; unmarried.

180.

ADNA[6] CHURCHILL (WILLIAM,[5] WILLIAM,[4] SAMUEL[3] JOSEPH,[2] JOSIAH[1]). Born at Scipio, N.Y., Aug. 24, 1805. Removed with his father's family to near Marietta, O., in 1814. Lived at Fabius, Mich. He died Oct. 4, 1884. Married, May 26, 1829, SALLIE A. HAMILTON, born Dec. 17, 1806.

Children.

I. ELIZABETH J.,[7] b. April 20, 1830; m. MR. JEWELL.
They lived at Wexford, Mich., but we have not received the names of her children.

421　II. WILLIAM A.,[7] b. Dec. 13, 1831; m. MATILDA D. RUMSEY, Oct. 31, 1858. She was born May 18, 1837.

422　III. JOHN H.,[7] b. April 5, 1834; unmarried in 1888. Lived at Eagle Creek, Ore.

IV. LETITIA,[7] b. Nov. 13, 1836; m. JOHN CORRINE, March 14, 1858. He was born July 6, 1824, at Coxsakie, N.Y
They lived at Leonidas, Mich.

Children.

1. Sarah O. Corrine, b. Jan. 6, 1859; m. Leland Millard, Jan. 6, 1876.
2. Horace A. Corrine, b. Oct. 1, 1860; m. Isabelle M. Shank, June 19, 1881.
3. Byron F. Corrine, b. Aug. 19, 1862.
4. George W. Corrine, b. July 29, 1864.
5. Leonard T. Corrine, b Sept. 1, 1866; d. May 31, 1868.
6. Anne M. Corrine, b. June 8, 1868; m. Levi Strong, May 24, 1884.
7. John M. Corrine, b. Oct. 27, 1870.
8. Marietta Corrine, b. Nov. 1, 1873; d. Sept. 6, 1883.
9. Earl Corrine, b. Sept. 24, 1875; d. June 4, 1876.
10. Matilda Corrine, b. Sept. 5, 1877.

V. JOSEPH ADNA,[7] b. Oct. 24, 1839; d. Jan. 9, 1840.
VI. RUTH,[7] b. April 26, 1841; d. next day.
VII. RHODA ANN,[7] b. June 20, 1845; d. Sept. 8, 1847
VIII. SARAH LUCRETIA,[7] b. Sept. 16, 1850; d. in 1851.

181.

RANDELL[6] CHURCHILL (WILLIAM,[5] WILLIAM,[4] SAMUEL,[3] JOSEPH,[2] JOSIAH[1]). Born in Scipio, N.Y., Nov. 2, 1809. Removed with his father's family to near Marietta, O., in 1814. He died Oct. 5, 1865. Married, May 14, 1834, JANE HAMILTON, born 1811.

Children.

423　I. THOMAS H.,[7] b. March 3, 1835; m. REBECCA HEBRON, Nov. 27, 1866.
424　II. WILLIAM R.,[7] b. Dec. 18, 1836; m. MARY WELCH, Oct. 5, 1870.
425　III. JOSEPH N.,[7] b. Feb. 5, 1839; m. SARAH BOYD, Aug. 26, 1866.
426　IV. JOSHUA P.,[7] b. March 18, 1844; m. MARTHA T. STAMP, March 16, 1879.

V. MARY,[7] b. July 21, 1849; m. GEORGE W. COLLINS, Nov. 11, 1866.

Children.

1. Millard Collins.
2. Randell Collins.
3. Roscoe Collins.

VI. LOREN E.,[7] b. July 15, 1852; unmarried.
He lives at Waterloo, Blackhawk County, Iowa, and is county superintendent of schools.

182.

JAMES[6] CHURCHILL (WILLIAM,[5] WILLIAM,[4] SAMUEL,[3] JOSEPH,[2] JOSIAH [1]). Born in Scipio, N.Y. April 18, 1819. He evidently went to the West, and settled in Michigan. Died July 20, 1885. Married, in St. Joseph County, Mich., May 4, 1846, MAILA HARWOOD, who was born June 4, 1819.

Children.

427   I. HIRAM WILLIAM,[7] b. March 13, 1847; m. ELIZABETH RUSHING, Oct. 27, 1868.
        II. ALBERT WEBSTER,[7] b. Feb. 12, 1849; d. May 9, 1849.
       III. SYLVIA JANE,[7] b. March 23, 1850; m. JOHN ROBERTSON, July 27, 1867. They lived, in 1902, at Rowena, South Dakota, but we have no further account.
        IV. MAILA R.,[7] b. Jan. 26, 1853; m. ISAAC SMITH, Jan. 4, 1872. They lived at Webster City, Iowa, in 1902. Mrs. Maila Smith wrote this account of her father's and her own families.

Children of Isaac and Maila R. (Churchill) Smith.

        1. Isabel E. Smith, b. Nov. 19, 1874; m. Charles Pierce, Jan. 22, 1894. One child, (1) Floyd S. Pierce. He lived with his grandparents, Smith. She died Feb. 24, 1899. Mr. Smith died a few weeks earlier
        2. Sarah M. Smith, b. July 9, 1876; m. Franklin Seamands, March 29, 1899.
        3. Emma E. Smith, b. Nov. 28, 1882; m. Edward Brewer, Dec. 26, 1900

183.

ALBERT[6] CHURCHILL (SAMUEL,[5] WILLIAM,[4] SAMUEL[3] JOSEPH,[2] JOSIAH [1]).. Born, probably in New Jersey, Jan. 6, 1802. Nothing more than the following list of children has been received. Married 1st, HARRIET DRESSER ; 2d ANNA FOSDICK.

Children.

428   I. WILLIAM.[7]
429   II. ASA.[7]
430   III. JOHN.[7]
        IV. PATIENCE.[7]
431   V. AMOS,[7] b. in Newburg, O., July 25, 1837.
        VI. CHILD,[7] no name.
       VII. ELECTA.[7]
432 VIII. MILO.[7]
        IX. ARMITTA.[7]
         X. SARAH.[7]

189.

WILLIS[6] CHURCHILL (ASA,[5] WILLIAM,[4] SAMUEL[3] JOSEPH,[2] JOSIAH [1]). Born in Westfield, Mass., March 10, 1810. Lived for many years at Newark, N.J., but his business was in New York City, 493 Greenwich street. I find by an account received since page

366 was printed, that Asa Churchill, the father of Willis, was born
at Westfield, Mass., instead of New Jersey. He manufactured
knives and forks at Farmington, Conn., in 1812, but afterwards
moved to Bristol and carried on blacksmithing, and died there
1833. Willis died June 4, 1880. Married, Aug. 21, 1834, AMELIA
BRADLEY, of Hamden, Conn. Mrs. Amelia Churchill was living at
Newark with her daughters in 1899.

Children.

   I. MARY,[7] b. Sept. 8, 1835; unmarried.
433 II. CHARLES,[7] b. July 8, 1837, in Hamden, Conn.; m. CHARLOTTE
   LOUISE LEWIS, March 19, 1861.
  III. ELLEN,[7] b. April 30, 1839.
  IV. DAVID B.,[7] b. Jan. 10, 1842; d. Feb. 2, 1842.
   V. EMMA,[7] b. Dec. 4, 1843; d. Aug. 25, 1847
  VI. AMELIA,[7] b. May 27, 1851; m. REV. DELEVAN DEWOLF, April 21,
   1875.
  VII. ALICE,[7] b. Aug. 30, 1853.

190.

LEVI[6] CHURCHILL (ASA,[5] WILLIAM,[4] SAMUEL,[8] JOSEPH,[2]
JOSIAH[1]). Born in Bristol, Conn., March 26, 1817. Lived at
Chester, and later at Haddam, Conn. Married 1st, at Southbury,
Conn., MARY CAMP, daughter of Johnson Camp, of Southbury
She died Sept. 13, 1868. Married 2d, MRS. CYNTHIA TYLER, of
Haddam, Conn. She died Sept. 9, 1883.

191.

JOSEPH[6] CHURCHILL (JOSEPH[5] *). Born in Newington,
1780. He lived in Newington, and for some years carried on the
business left by his father, in company with his brother, and then
sold out to his brother. He died Feb. 28, 1829. Married, 1804,
ANNA ALLEN JUDD. She was born in New Britain, 1781; died
July 27, 1823.

Children born in Newington.

   I. LAURA,[7] b. 1805.
   II. RHODA,[7] b. 1808.
434 III. WILLIAM ALLEN,[7] b. May 10, 1810; m. ELIZA JANE FRANCIS, of
   New Britain, 1835.
  IV. MARIA,[7] b. 1812.

---

  * We are obliged here to make an abrupt correction in the descent of
Joseph,[5] by reason of a late discovery in the records of Bolton, Conn., to the
effect that Joseph,[4] son of Joseph[3] and Lydia Dickerman, of Bolton, was
drowned Jan. 31, 1737, and could not therefore have been the father of Joseph,[5]
who was born in 1750, and married Rhoda Goodrich in 1777. The theory of
descent was accepted by our senior compiler, N. W. Churchill, and apparently
by the family, until the discovery of the record of the death above noted. As
the family of Joseph,[5] No. 60, and Rhoda Goodrich is already printed, we let it
stand, and begin the line with them, until the true descent is discovered.

192.

JAMES⁶ CHURCHILL (JOSEPH⁵). Born in Newington, March 28, 1782. He lived on the old homestead, where he operated the grist mill, which he owned for a time, with his brother Joseph, but finally bought out his interest. He died March 22, 1848. Married, Nov. 27, 1816, CLARISSA STEEL, daughter of David, of Berlin, Conn., where she was born Aug. 29, 1793, and died April 7, 1879 The note referring to No. 191 applies to James.

Children born in Newington.

    I. JAMES,⁷ b. 1817; d. Sept. 7, 1883; unmarried.
    II. CLARISSA,⁷ b. 1819; m. ALMOND GOODWIN. They had no children. She died in Newington, aged sixty years.
435   III. LOREY,⁷ b. June 20, 1821; m. LUCY STEEL.
436   IV. SAMUEL W.,⁷ b. June 28, 1828; m. ELLEN L. HUBBARD, Dec. 26, 1855.

193.

JOSIAH⁶ CHURCHILL (JONATHAN,⁵ JONATHAN,⁴ JONATHAN,³ JOSEPH,² JOSIAH¹). Born in Litchfield, Conn., Jan. 11, 1777. Settled in Franklin, Susquehanna County, Penn., as a farmer, soon after his marriage. He was a man of good business ability and methods. A good citizen. Married, in Litchfield, Conn., OLIVE ODELL.

Children born in Franklin, Penn.

    I. CLARISSA,⁷ b. June 28, 1803; m. SAMUEL .BAKER, April 7, 1825, b. in Susquehanna, Penn., April 11, 1795.

Children, all born in Franklin, Penn.

    1. Olive Baker, b. June 22, 1827; m. Kerby French.
    2. Sarah Emeline Baker, b. Dec. 3, 1830; m. Conrad Burgh.
    3. Benjamin Josiah Baker, b. Sept. 15, 1832.
    4. Joseph Martin Baker, b. March 4, 1837.
    5. Clarissa Baker, b. April 20, 1839; m. Isaac McKeeley.
    6. Phebe Lucretia Baker, b. Sept. 25, 1845; m. Wallace Haywood.

    II. LUCRETIA,⁷ b. 1805; m. AARON VAN VORCE, 1825.

Children.

    1. Mary Van Vorce, m. Henry J. Carew.
    2. John Van Vorce, b. Oct. 8, 1829; m. Sarah M. Bellman.
    3. Francis Van Vorce, b. April 1, 1836; m. John Park, of Binghamton, N.Y., Feb. 24, 1857.
    4. Ellen A. Van Vorce, b. Sept. 30, 1838; m. John R. Laird, of Williamsport, Penn., Oct. 8, 1861.

Child.

    (1) Herbert R. Laird, m. Mary Wilson, and had (1) Samuel Wilson Laird, and (2) Ellen Churchill Laird

437   III. AMOS,⁷ b. Jan. 23, 1808; m. ABIGAIL HOLLY, March 4, 1829.

194.

LEMAN[6] CHURCHILL (JONATHAN,[5] JONATHAN,[4] JONATHAN[3] JOSEPH,[2] JOSIAH[1]). Born in Litchfield, Conn., Dec. 6, 1780. He went with his brother, and settled and lived in Franklin, Penn., a farmer. He spelled his name with an "e" mostly. His name is put Lemon Churchell, on his gravestone, at Upsonville, Penn. He died July 25, 1823. Married, Nov. 4, 1810, POLLY DEMILLS, daughter of Garrett and Delmer, born in Pougkeepsie, N.Y., March 6, 1785; died Dec. 19, 1822.

Children born in Franklin, Penn.

I. MARY EMMELINE,[7] b. Nov. 2, 1811; d. Feb. 15, 1815.
II. IRENE,[7] b. July 8, 1814; m. JOHN V. CASHORONS, Dec. 26, 1831.
　　She died March 20, 1833, leaving no children.
438　III. JONATHAN,[7] b. June 10, 1816.
439　IV. FREEBORN,[7] b. Sept. 15, 1817; 'm. ELIZA J. CLEMENS, March 6, 1850.
V. SARAH,[7] b. Sept. 16, 1820; m. HENRY BEEBE, June 2, 1847. Mr. Beebe was born in Windsor, N.Y., Nov. 16, 1821. They lived in Franklin, Penn., and had children born there.

Children.

1. Eliza Jane Beebe, b. Oct. 26, 1851.
2. Laura Amanda Beebe, b. May 20, 1856.

195.

DANIEL[6] CHURCHILL (JONATHAN,[5] JONATHAN,[4] JONATHAN,[3] JOSEPH,[2] JOSIAH[1]). Born in Litchfield, Conn., Nov. 14, 1798. Married CATHERINE DAVIS, born April 10, 1810; died Feb. 5, 1869.

Children.

I. HANNAH ELIZABETH,[7] b. Feb. 29, 1829; m. JAMES PLACE.
II. LUCY,[7] b. March 10, 1834; m. 1st, EDGAR HALLOCK; m. 2d, LEWIS KING.
III. MARY,[7] b. Nov. 20, 1836; m. 1st, LUCIAN WILSON; m. 2d, JOSEPH GILMORE.
IV. JOHN M.,[7] b. March 10, 1839; unmarried.
V. ELLEN,[7] b. Feb. 11, 1841; d. June 19, 1843.
VI. ANNIE,[7] b. Nov. 20, 1843; m. CHARLES BLACKINSON.
VII. DAVID L.,[7] b. Feb. 16, 1846; d. unmarried, July 17, 1863, in the army.
VIII. CHARLES,[7] b. June 14, 1848; d. Aug. 6, 1864.
IX. ELIZA,[7] b. Dec. 7, 1850.

197.

MOSES[6] CHURCHILL, JR. (MOSES,[5] JONATHAN,[4] JONATHAN[3] JOSEPH,[2] JOSIAH[1]). Born June 30, 1791. He seems to have lived at Litchfield, Conn., and Sheffield, Mass. He died Aug. 30, 1862. Married ANNA HUBBARD. She died March 12, 1884.

Children.

I. Lucretia,[7] b. Dec. 24, 1816; m. Stephen Harrison, Nov. 23,
1852. Mr. Harrison was born Oct. 7, 1804, and died Dec. 2,
1880.

One Child.

1. Anna Sophia Harrison, b. Dec. 29, 1853.

II. Elizabeth,[7] b. Oct. 16, 1818; m. John Gordon, Feb. 15, 1841.
Mr. Gordon was born Jan. 25, 1807, and died Feb. 15, 1872.

Children, born in Sheffield, Mass.

1. Edward J. Gordon, b. April 9, 1842.
2. Henry A. Gordon, b. July 14, 1843.
3. Pamelia E. Gordon, b. June 21, 1845; d. Nov. 11, 1880.
4. Albert Gordon, b. Oct. 15, 1848; d. Sept. 18, 1856.

III. Sophia,[7] b. March 21, 1821; m. George Berry, June 3, 1854, and
died July 1, following, less than one month after marriage,
and Mr. Berry married her sister Mary A. Churchill.

IV. Jonathan,[7] b. June 21, 1824; d. unmarried, July 1854.

440 V. Norman W.,[7] b. April 25, 1826; m. Betsey M. Sheldon, Nov. 25,
1855.

VI. George,[7] b. Feb. 15, 1828; d. single, Sept. 7, 1862.

VII. Mary A.,[7] b. July 9, 1831; m. George J. Berry, March 27, 1856,
as his second wife. Mr. Berry was born in London, Eng., June
10, 1829.

They had Children, born in Sheffield, Mass.

1. Sophia E. Berry, b. June 9, 1857; d. August, 1862.
2. Jesse J. Berry, b. Oct. 20, 1861.

VIII. Pamelia,[7] b. Nov. 29, 1837; unmarried. She lived in Litchfield,
Conn.

198.

DR. GILBERT [6] CHURCHILL (Oliver,[5] Jonathan,[4] Jonathan,[3] Joseph,[2] Josiah [1]). Born in Bethlehem, Conn., Sept. 25,
1789. Removed with his father's family to Pawlet, Vt. I find no
correspondence or notes giving any information of Dr. Churchill,
his education or residence, or death. Married 1st, Abigail Davis,
of Bergen, N.Y.; married 2d, Oct. 29, 1851, Mrs. Harriet (Griswold) Williams, daughter of Rev. John Griswold. No children by
second wife.

Children by First Wife.

I. Eunice,[7] b. May 21, 1819; d. Sept. 3, 1821.
II. Eunice Barnes,[7] b. Sept. 9, 1824; m. George W. Miner, Aug.
24, 1854. Mr. Miner died Feb. 24, 1856.
III. Abigail,[7] b. April 28, 1826; d. Oct. 20, 1838.
IV. Louisa,[7] b. May 11, 1829; m. Artemas Gale, Sept. 30, 1851.
V. Gilbert Barnes,[7] b. Sept. 22, 1833; d. June 8, 1853.
VI. Sarah Briggs,[7] b. Oct. 25, 1836; d. Sept. 23, 1850.

199.

WILLIAM [6] CHURCHILL (Oliver,[5] Jonathan,[4] Jonathan,[3]
Joseph,[2] Josiah [1]). Born in Pawlet, Vt., March 6, 1812. Married
Charity Russell, daughter of Elansing Russell, of Monroe County,
N.Y.

Children born in Monroe County, N. Y.

I. HELEN LUCY,[7] m. MR. KNAPP.
   They lived at Logansport, Ind. She died in St. Louis, in 1873, while on a trip to California. No further account.

441 II. GEORGE WILLIAM,[7] b. 1843; m. MARY J. PETERSON, 1871.

III. IRVING ELANSING.[7]
   He was a herder, and died in Montana in 1894.

441a IV. FLAVIUS,[7] married and lived in Ohio, but no further record.

V. FRANCES JANE,[7] b. Jan. 2, 1849; m. ROWLAND SAUNDERS, Dec. 12, 1867.
   They lived at Mason, Mich., and had children.

Children.

1. Lucy Saunders, b. Feb. 28, 1869; m. 1st, Willard Kent, May 9, 1885; m. 2d, Gordon S. Aldrich, June 22, 1896.
2. Artie Saunders, b. March 28, 1872; m. John Pinkerton, Dec. 11, 1888.
3. George Rowland Saunders. b. Aug. 6, 1874.
4. Sexton Saunders, b. Aug. 2, 1876; d. young.
5. Chloe Saunders, b. Dec. 11, 1878.
6. Frances Saunders, b. Jan. 13, 1881.
7. Wesley Saunders, b. Sept. 4, 1884.
8. Mary P. Saunders, b. Nov. 2, 1886.
9. Charles Saunders, b. Jan. 12, 1889; d. Feb. 28, 1894.
10. Fred Saunders, b. June 17, 1891.

200.

OLIVER[6] CHURCHILL (OLIVER,[5] JONATHAN,[4] JONATHAN,[3] JOSEPH,[2] JOSIAH[1]). Born at Pawlet, Vt., June 21, 1821. He was living, about 1881, at Loyal, Wis. Married and had a family, it is said.

203.

LEMAN[6] CHURCHILL (AMOS,[5] JONATHAN,[4] JONATHAN,[3] JOSEPH,[2] JOSIAH[1]). Born at Fairfax Vt., May 6, 1798. They lived in Bolton, Cardwell County, Ont., Can. Married, 1822, MINERVA ANDERSON, who was born April 8, 1800.

Children born in Bolton, Ont., Can.

442   I. JONATHAN THORNTON,[7] b. May 10, 1825; m. EMILY E. LEONARD.
443 II. ELIAS D.,[7] b. May 18, 1827.
III. ZILPHA L.,[7] b. June 9, 1829.
IV. PERSIS L.,[7] b. March 27, 1832
V. ANISE M.,[7] b. Nov. 15, 1833.
444 VI. RICHARD H.,[7] b. Aug. 22, 1835; m. SUSAN RUDDLE.

204.

HIRAM[6] CHURCHILL (AMOS,[5] JONATHAN,[4] JONATHAN,[3] JOSEPH,[2] JOSIAH[1]). Born at Bolton, Can., Dec. 5, 1800. He lived at Bolton, Can., and later, at North Fairfax, Vt. He was a farmer. He died Dec. 5, 1875. Married, in St. Albans, Vt.,

ABIGAIL BETSEY INGALLS, of St. Albans, Vt. She died June 11, 1869.

Children born at Bolton, Can.

    I. CONSTANCE,[7] d. young.
    II. ABIGAIL,[7] m. JUDSON BROWN, North Fairfax; no children.
445   III. HIRAM PARKER,[7] b. March 28, 1826; m. 1st, MARY WARNER THOMPSON; m. 2d, PAULINA (LEONARD) STORY.
446   IV. OLIVER JOSEPH,[7] b. Oct. 17, 1827; m. MARY ANN KIMBALL, June 15, 1853.

206.

OTIS [6] CHURCHILL (AMOS,[5] JONATHAN,[4] JONATHAN,[3] JOSEPH,[2] JOSIAH [1]). Born at Bolton, Can., May 28, 1810. We have received no further account. He died March 2, 1884. Married 1st, May 4, 1837, SUSAN P. RAYMOND; 2d, Nov. 7, 1874, MRS. A. (PITMAN) GIBBS.

Children.

447   I. HIRAM W.,[7] b. Feb. 8, 1838.
    II. SUSAN R.,[7] b. Feb. 22, 1843; d. March 22, 1843.
    III. WILLIAM H.,[7] b. Feb. 13, 1844; d. Sept. 9, 1844.

207.

AMOS [6] CHURCHILL (AMOS,[5] JONATHAN,[4] JONATHAN,[3] JOSEPH,[2] JOSIAH [1]). Born at West Bolton, Can., Dec. 31, 1816. Removed to Vermont when young, and at twenty-one years came to Medford and learned the stone-cutter's trade. He removed to Quincy in '1849' and engaged in the stone-cutting business, later establishing the firm of Churchill & Hitchcock. He lived in Quincy until his death, March 31, 1901. Married, in Medford, Sept. 27, 1842, LUCRETIA ROWE, daughter of Alexander and Sally (Bean) Rowe, of Campton, N.H. She died Feb. 27, 1901.

Child born in Medford, Mass.

    I. ELLEN BELINDA,[7] b. Oct. 18, 1845; m. J. HENRY EMERY, Oct. 1, 1868, in Quincy, Mass. He was the son of Jonathan and Nancy Emery. He is engaged in the leather business in Boston, and lives in Quincy.

Children born in Quincy, Mass.

    1. Alice Jacobs Emery, b. July 5, 1871; m. William Edwards, Oct. 22, 1891.
    2. Florence Raymond Emery, b. Nov. 22, 1877.

208.

STEPHEN MAJOR [6] CHURCHILL (WILLIAM,[5] WILLIAM,[4] JONATHAN,[3] JOSEPH,[2] JOSIAH [1]). Born at Fairfax, Vt., Dec. 4, 1796. Removed to Randolph, O., with his father's family in 1812 and lived there. We learn that his brother Philo had two sons and a daughter, but no names given; and that his brother Lyman had one son, who died at the age of ten years. Married, at Randolph, O., May 23, 1821, MARIA BEACH, born Aug. 8, 1803.

Children born in Randolph, O.

448   I. ORWELL S.,[7] b. Feb. 25, 1822; m. CLARISSA COLTON, June 5, 1843.
       II. OLIVE L.,[7] b. Feb. 8, 1824; m. CALVIN HUDSON, Sept. 4, 1845, at Randolph. They lived at Randolph and Edinburgh, O.

Children, first two born at Randolph, others at Edinburgh.

        1. Mina S. Hudson, b. Dec. 10, 1846; m. J. S. Gunder, April 19, 1866. Two children: (1) Josie E. Gunder, b. Oct. 27, 1867 · m. Clayton M. Barnard, Nov. 16, 1893, and has Mina M. Barnard. (2) Frank E. Gunder, b. Feb. 12, 1870; m. Miss Harold, Nov. 25, 1896, and has Thelma Gunder.
        2. Milford C. Hudson, b. Nov. 24, 1862; m. (———) (———), and has Roy M. Hudson, b. Sept. 18, 1883; and Clyde E. Hudson, b. May 23, 1891.
     III. MARY M.,[7] b. March 10, 1826; m. JOSEPH E. JEROME, Feb. 17, 1850.

Children born in Randolph, O.

        1. Amelia L. Jerome, b. May 6, 1856; m. Herman Harper, Jan. 1, 1895.
        2. Nettie J. Jerome, b. Dec. 1, 1861; d. July 16, 1884.
        3. Jessie M. Jerome, b. September, 1865.
        4. Elgin J. Jerome, b. Aug. 14, 1867.
     IV. WILLIAM B.,[7] b. Aug. 27, 1828; d. July 26, 1854, at Randolph.
449   V. JULIUS R.,[7] b. June 16, 1832; m. LUCINDA E. SAINT, December, 1857.
     VI. AMELIA M.,[7] b. May 25, 1837; d. Nov. 24, 1858, at Randolph.

211.

CARMEL[6] CHURCHILL (DAVID,[5] JONATHAN,[4] JONATHAN,[3] JOSEPH,[2] JOSIAH[1]). Born June 4, 1799, in Fairfax, Vt. Moved to Zora, Ont., with his father's family. We have not been able to get any further account of this family than what is found below. Married, in Westminster, Ont., ELIZABETH STOAT.

Children.

450   I. ABRAHAM,[7] b. 1827.
      II. LUCINDA,[7] m. ETHAN SQUIRE. No children.
     III. SAMUEL,[7] d. at five years.
     IV. ALMIRA,[7] d. young.
     V. NAOMI,[7] m. ETHAN SQUIRE (as second wife).
450a   VI. ELIAS,[7] m. MARY GRIMSHAW.
     VII. JAMES,[7] d. at fourteen years.

212.

DAVID[6] CHURCHILL (DAVID,[5] JONATHAN,[4] JONATHAN,[3] JOSEPH,[2] JOSIAH[1]). Born at Fairfax, Vt., Feb. 2, 1801. Lived at Zora, Can., till about 1835, when he removed to Berlin, Mich. Married, 1828, ZOA EDGERTON.

Children, three born at Zora, Can., and five at Berlin, Mich.

451   I. PETER,[7] b. Jan. 3, 1829; m. CHARITY E. CLARK, at Romeo, Mich.
452   II. WARREN D.,[7] b. March 4, 1831.
         III. LOUISA A.,[7] b. Feb. 19, 1834; d. at Berlin, Mich., Sept. 21, 1875.
453   IV. NELSON,[7] b. Berlin, Mich., April 8, 1836.
          V. N. JUDSON,[7] b. Berlin, Mich., July 15, 1838; d. Jan. 11, 1865.
         VI. CYRUS,[7] b. Berlin, Mich., March 26, 1843; d. March 14, 1844.
454   VII. NORVILLE F.,[7] b. Berlin, Mich., June 11, 1846.
        VIII. ERMINA L.,[7] b. Berlin, Mich., Feb. 16, 1849.

213.

REV. CYRUS [6] CHURCHILL (DAVID,[5] JONATHAN,[4] JONATHAN,[3] JOSEPH,[2] JOSIAH [1]). Born July 6, 1804, in Fairfax, Vt. He settled first in Zora, Ont., and in 1837 in Almont, Mich., where he died Nov. 4, 1857. He was a farmer and a preacher. The account of this family was written for us in 1889. Married, Sept. 4, 1827, MARY PHELPS, born in Brantford, Ont., Dec. 11, 1806, and died in Almont, Mich., October, 1889.

Children born at Zora, Ont.

455   I. JAMES D.,[7] b. July 6, 1828; m. FRANCES P. WARNER, Sept. 27, 1856.
          II. LYDIA,[7] b. Sept. 22, 1829; m. SAMUEL CARPENTER, March 17, 1847.
         III. AUGUSTA,[7] b. July 26, 1831; m. ROBERT DURHAM, March 31, 1850.
          IV. URSULA,[7] b. April 10, 1833; m. PHILO GIBBS, 1876.
           V. HENRY,[7] b. Feb. 7, 1835; d. June 5, 1838.

Children born at Almont, Mich.

         VI. ORPHIA,[7] b. Sept. 12, 1838; d. Nov. 1, 1838.
        VII. IRENE,[7] b. Oct. 8, 1840; d. 1846.
       VIII. CAROLINE,[7] b. Feb. 28, 1842. Lived at Thornville, Mich. Un-married.
         IX. ANGELINE,[7] b. May 10, 1846; m. EDGAR BRISTOL, October, 1864.
          X. MARY LINA,[7] b. April 1, 1850; m. CHARLES HOUGH, February, 1871.

214.

LEVI [6] CHURCHILL (DAVID,[5] JONATHAN,[4] JONATHAN,[3] JOSEPH,[2] JOSIAH [1]). Born at Fairfax, Vt., Aug. 24, 1806. Removed with his father's family to Zora Ont., and sometime about 1837 settled in Lapeer County, Mich. Our information about this family is meagre. Married, March 4, 1830, MARY PINE.

Children's names, perhaps not in order of birth.

456   I. JOHN.[7]
          II. MALINDA.[7]
457   III. CYRUS,[7] d. young.
458   IV. LUCIUS,[7] d. young.
459   V. CHARLES.[7]
          VI. ELIZA.[7]
         VII. ORPHA JANE.[7]
460   VIII. THEODORE.[7]

215.

TRUMAN [6] CHURCHILL (DAVID,[5] WILLIAM,[4] JONATHAN,[3] JOSEPH,[2] JOSIAH [1]). Born in Rutland County, Vt., April 21, 1809. Died in Almont, Mich., Jan. 7, 1870. He removed to Ontario, and settled in Middlesex County, and lived there until 1836, when he removed to Lapeer County, Mich. Married, in 1829, in Ontario, CHARLOTTE CHADWICK, born in St. Catherine's, Ont., Nov. 11, 1813.

Children born in Ontario.

461   I. BARNEY,[7] b. July 22, 1832.
          Lived at Imlay City in 1889.
462   II. DAVID,[7] b. Nov. 11, 1833; m. MARY J. REYNOLDS, 1857.
463   III. WILLIAM L.,[7] b. Oct. 26, 1839.
          Lived at Atlanta, Mich., 1889.
464   IV. WASHINGTON,[7] b. May 1, 1846.
          Lived at Almont, Mich., 1889.
    V. SARAH M.,[7] b March 26, 1854; m. MARTIN PATTON, 1869; d. in Almont, Mich., Oct. 4, 1886.
    VI. JULIA E.,[7] b. June 13, 1857; m. MR. SCHELL.
          They were living at Deanville, Mich., 1889.

216.

WILLIAM [6] CHURCHILL (DAVID,[5] JONATHAN,[4] JONATHAN,[3] JOSEPH,[2] JOSIAH [1]). Born at Fairfax, Vt., Aug. 24, 1812. Re moved with his father's family to Zora, Ont. Married, in Ontario, Aug. 24, 1834, SUSAN PINE, daughter of John.

Children born, the first in Ontario, the rest in Imlay City, Mich.

465   I. WALTER B.,[7] b. March 27, 1837; m. MARIA J. BEST, Aug. 8, 1858.
    II. JOHN H.,[7] b. Dec. 9, 1838; d. Dec. 10, 1838.
    III. ANNIE PAMELIA,[7] b. March 22, 1840; m. THOMAS RIDLEY, Oct. 6, 1860.
          They lived in Imlay City, Mich., where she died April 20, 1897.
466   IV. ALBERT,[7] b. Oct. 3, 1841. He served in the Civil War as a scout, was captured and killed by the enemy somewhere in Virginia.
    V. WILLIAM EDWARD,[7] b. Aug. 15' 1843; d. May 30, 1844.
    VI. WILLIS,[7] b. July 10, 1845; d. the same day.
467   VII. DANIEL,[7] b. June 8, 1846; m. CLEMANTHA CLARK, Sept. 29, 1868.
468   VIII. CALVIN P.,[7] b. July 28, 1848; m. EMILY KILBRETH, March, 1869.
    IX. MARY M.,[7] b. Dec. 29, 1850; m. REV. NEWMAN BENNETT STEELE, Sept. 29, 1868.
          They lived at Imlay City and many other places whither his ministry called him.

Children.

1. Lewis Steele, b. June 10, 1869; m. Carrie B. Farnsworth, and had one child, Zola Steele, b. May 6, 1897.
2. D. Howard Steele, b. May 30, 1871; d. Jan. 6, 1891.
3. Julia A. Steele, b. June 14, 1873; d. July 28, 1886.
4. Gertrude Steele, b. Aug. 1, 1876; m. Walter J. West, and had Evelyn Steele West, b. Sept. 10, 1903.

> 5. Newman B. Steele, Jr., b. Oct. 13, 1879; graduated from Kala-
>   mazoo College, June, 1903.
> 6. Blanche A. Steele, b. July 6, 1881; d. Sept. 18, 1881.
> 7. Bessie M. Steele, b. Feb. 3, 1884; d. April 26, 1884.
> 8. Marion Steele, b. Aug. 1, 1886.

469   X. WILLIAM J.,[7] b. May 8, 1853; m. HARRIET FITCH.
        XI. EMILY EVA,[7] b. Aug. 24, 1854; m. GEORGE KINNEE.
       XII. CHARLOTTE ADELE,[7] b. Dec. 19, 1856; d. Feb. 16, 1891.
469a   XIII. NEWMAN,[7] b. July 5, 1859; m. ROSA TUNK.

218.

JAMES HOIT[6] CHURCHILL (SAMUEL,[5] JONATHAN,[4] JON-
ATHAN,[3] JOSEPH,[2] JOSIAH [1]). Born at Whiting, Vt., December,
1806. Removed with his father's family to New York State, and
thence, in 1827, to Louth, Canada. He received a good education,
finishing up at the seminary at Elizabethtown. He did not go to
Pennsylvania with his father's family, but remained in Canada and
taught school, first at Beansville, where he married his first wife.
Later he located at Hamilton, Can., and, in 1853, removed to
Dowagiac, Mich., where he bought a farm, and there spent the remainder of his busy and useful life. He died July 3, 1866. Married 1st, at Beansville, Can., March 9, 1830, LENA SKELLEY, b.
May 14, 1812, daughter of Deacon Skelley; and she died Aug. 10,
1834. Married 2d, March 24, 1836, MRS. LOVISA ADAMS BARBER.
(Notice the error on page 371, where the name is given Adams, which
evidently was a slip of the eye of the painstaking compiler. Two of
James' children, independently, give the name Barber.) She was
born March 9, 1816.

Children of First Wife, born in Canada.

    I. ROBERT,[7] b. Dec. 29, 1831; d. July 29, 1833.
   II. ALMIRA,[7] b. April 15, 1834; m. HENRY RUTH, April 26, 1853.
    They lived at Elkwood, No. Dak.

Children.

> 1. William Hervey Ruth, b. Nov. 7, 1854.
> 2. Walter Henry Ruth, b. March 8, 1857; d. Feb. 28, 1863.
> 3. Jane Ruth, b. Jan. 21, 1859.
> 4. Salem E. Ruth, b. Sept. 19, 1861; d. Feb. 2, 1863.
> 5. Augusta Ruth, b. Jan. 4, 1864.
> 6. Frank Jacob Ruth, b. July 16, 1866.
> 7. Ella Elizabeth Ruth, b. May 4, 1868.
> 8. Lena Zell Ruth, b. Oct. 31, 1870.
> 9. Harry Eugene Ruth, b. Sept. 18, 1872.

Children of Second Wife.

470   III. LEWIS A.,[7] b. Aug. 16, 1837; m. EUNICE S. FLANDERS.
471   IV. FRANCIS L.,[7] b. Aug. 8, 1839; m. LYDIA DIXON, Jan. 3, 1862.
      V. OLIVIA,[7] b. Nov. 3, 1842; m. JOHN GRAHAM, May 4, 1859.
     This family lived, in 1903, in Otsego, Mich.

Children.

1. L. Orley Graham, b. Aug. 6, 1860; m. Carrie Hinckley, May 19, 1886, and had (1) Gladys Graham, b. Sept. 24, 1887; (2) Greta Graham, b. Nov. 13, 1888.
2. Arthur R. Graham, b. Jan. 7, 1864; m. Rose Brooks, and had Rex A. Graham, b. Dec. 29, 1887.

472   VI. O. EUGENE,[7] b. May 1, 1849; m. ABBIE D. STURR, April 29, 1873.
473   VII. CLARENCE C.,[7] b May 26, 1854; m. JANE STURR, Feb. 28, 1879. They had no children to live. They resided, in 1903, in Dowagiac, Mich.

219.

ADONIRAM JUDSON [6] CHURCHILL (REV. SAMUEL,[5] JONATHAN,[4] JONATHAN,[3] JOSEPH,[2] JOSIAH[1]). Born July 15, 1821, in Elizabethtown, N.Y. Removed with his father's family in their various moves·until his death in Hayfield, Penn., in 1842, when he went West, and settled in Fond Du Lac County, Wis. In 1903 he was living in Spring Valley, Minn. Married, May 1, 1849, in Eldorado, Wis., CELESTIA ANTHONY.

Children born in Eldorado, Wis.

I. SAMANTHA LOUISA,[7] b. Jan. 29, 1850; m. MAJOR GEORGE ANDRUS, Dec. 25, 1871. One child reported, Roy Andrus, b. Feb. 22, 1877.
II. GILBERT ANTHONY,[7] b. Dec. 10, 1851. Unmarried.
474 III. FRANK DELASON,[7] b. Aug. 28, 1853; m. HARRIET ALLEN, May, 1884.
475 IV. CYRUS WILLIAM,[7] b. Sept. 5, 1855; m. JENNIE BAILEY, March, 1882.
V. CAROLINE CELESTIA,[7] b. Sept. 28, 1857; m. FRANK BUSHNELL, April 22, 1880. One son (1) Arthur Bushnell, b. Dec. 22, 1886.
476 VI. GEORGE HARVEY,[7] b. May 7, 1860; m. MAGGIE LOUKS, March 19, 1884.
476a VII. ALBERT NATHAN,[7] b. Dec. 16, 1865.

SEVENTH GENERATION.

221.

NATHANIEL [7] CHURCHILL (NATHANIEL,[6] NATHANIEL,[5] NATHANIEL,[4] NATHANIEL,[3] JOSEPH,[2] JOSIAH [1]). Born March 20, 1784, in Newington, Conn. Removed to Hubbardton, Vt., with his father's family, and thence to Poultney, Vt., but settled in Genesee County, N.Y., and was living about 1850 in Stafford, of that county. Married 1st, 1806, SARAH RAY, born Feb. 3, 1786, and died Sept. 16, 1830. Married 2d, October, 1832, HARRIET BOSTWICK.

Children.

477   I. DENNIS,[8] b. March 3, 1807; m. LIVONIA P. KINGSLEY.
      II. LURANA,[8] b. Aug. 21, 1808; m. IRA OSGOOD.
478   III. ELIEZER,[8] b. July 1, 1810; m. ELVIRA BERRY, April, 1834.
      IV. LYDIA,[8] b. Feb. 3, 1815; m. GILES MINOT.
479   V. WILLIAM,[8] b. Dec. 9, 1817; m. CAROLINE WHEELER, of Alexandria.
      VI. JOHN F.,[8] b. March 7, 1820.
480   VII. GEORGE W.,[8] b. Oct. 21, 1822; m. CATHARINE HARVEY.

Child by Second Wife.

      VIII. SARAH,[8] b. Oct. 20, 1837; m. CHARLES LOTHROP.

222.

JEREMIAH [7] CHURCHILL (NATHANIEL,[6] NATHANIEL [5] NATHANIEL,[4] NATHANIEL,[3] JOSEPH,[2] JOSIAH [1]). Born in Hubbardton, Vt. Lived in Essex, N.Y. He was a farmer. Married, at Elmore, Vt., April 7, 1812, MEHITABLE BODFISH.

Child born in Elmore, Vt.

    I. JAMES ADDISON,[8] b. Feb. 11, 1814; m. ZILPHA E. STROUD, of Willsborough, N.Y., Aug. 5, 1832, at Essex Village. He was a safe-maker, and lived in Bethany, N.Y., Plymouth, Mich., and finally settled at Oshkosh, Wis., where he died Sept. 18, 1870. They had no children.

224.

JOHN SAGE [7] CHURCHILL (NATHANIEL,[6] NATHANIEL,[5] NATHANIEL,[4] NATHANIEL,[3] JOSEPH,[2] JOSIAH [1]). Born in Hubbardton, Vt., July 20, 1798. He was a pattern designer in foundries in Poultney, Vt., until 1852, when he removed to Rockford, Ill., and then in 1870 went to Nebraska City, Neb., and thence to Lincoln, Neb., in 1880, in same business. Died May 1, 1880. Married, in Troy, N.Y., Sept. 11, 1831, NARCISSA WHITE, of Poultney, Vt.

Children.

I. MARY JANE,[8] b. June 9, 1832; m. 1st, CHARLES SEVITZ; m. 2d, WILLIAM ADAMS.

481 II. JOHN NATHANIEL,[8] b. Sept. 10, 1835; m. SOPHIA DEMAS THAYER, Sept. 21, 1857. She was born at Chittenden, Vt., May 8, 1834. He went West with his father in 1852, and settled in Rockford, Ill., where he lived till the opening of the Civil War, when he enlisted and served until 1863, when his capture by the enemy and confinement in Libby prison disabled him for service and he was sent home. Before the war he was engaged first in building windmills and afterwards in farming. In 1869 he removed to Nebraska City, and was employed by the Marsh Manufacturing Company, till their failure in 1884. Then he removed to Dakota, and became a real estate agent, at Canton, Dak., where he was living in August, 1884. They had one son.

Child.

1. Edmund John, b. Dec. 10, 1864.

225.

PHINEAS PENFIELD[7] CHURCHILL (NATHANIEL,[6] NATHANIEL,[5] NATHANIEL,[4] NATHANIEL,[3] JOSEPH,[2] JOSIAH [1]). Born Sept. 14, 1804, in Hubbardton, Vt. Removed West, and settled at Rockford, Ill. He was a prosperous farmer. Married 1st, Nov. 27, 1827, MARILLA GREGORY, who died. Married 2d, Oct. 6, 1831, in Orwell, Vt., AMANDA WRIGHT, who was born Oct. 7, 1804.

One Child by First Wife.

I. HENRY,[8] died in infancy.

Children by Second Wife, born at Rockford, Ill.

II. MARY MARIA ISABEL,[8] b. July 16, 1832; m. ALTA GILBERT CHAPMAN, May 22, 1853. They lived at Cedar Falls, Ia.

III. INFANT SON,[8] b. Jan. 9, 1834; d. on the tenth day.

IV. HENRY C.,[8] b. Nov. 21, 1838; d. Oct. 21, 1840.

V. DANIEL W.,[8] b. Aug. 27, 1841; d. March 22, 1844.

VI. MINERVA R.,[8] b. April 14, 1844; never married.

VII. AMANDA A.,[8] b. April 15, 1846; m. JOHN P. KETTLEWELL, Oct. 27, 1874, in Exeter, Neb., and lived there.

227.

PUTNAM[7] CHURCHILL (STEPHEN,[6] NATHANIEL,[5] NATHANIEL,[4] NATHANIEL,[3] JOSEPH,[2] JOSIAH [1]). Born in New Canaan, Conn. Date of birth not received. Married 1st, March 23, 1820, CALISTA A. TAYLOR. Married 2d, Feb. 2, 1831. (Name of wife not received.)

Child by First Wife.

I. ELIZABETH,[8] m. MARK Z. LAMPRY.

Children by Second Wife.

482   II. WILLIAM SUMNER.[8]
            III. AUGUSTA.[8]
            IV. MARIA,[8] b. August, 1835.
            V. JANE BUSHNELL,[8] b. 1837.

228.

WILLIAM HENRY[7] CHURCHILL (STEPHEN,[6] NATHANIEL,[5] NATHANIEL,[4] NATHANIEL,[3] JOSEPH,[2] JOSIAH[1]).   Born in New Canaan, Conn., Jan. 1, 1816.   Lived in Hartford, Farmington, and Meriden, Conn.   Married, Jan. 6, 1842, SARAH ANN SEDGWICK.

Children, first three born in Hartford.

I. EDWARD W.,[8] b. Oct. 24, 1842.
II. WILBER S.,[8] b. Nov. 25, 1844; d. unmarried, Oct. 25, 1875.
III. WILLIS E.,[8] b. Jan. 20, 1847; m. JANE S. PLUMMER, of Rowley.

Children of Willis and Jane Churchill.

1. Lydia Mason, b. Dec. 11, 1878.
2. Mehitabel Helen, b. April 5, 1881.
3. Lizzie Willard, b. April 5, 1881.
4. William Everett, b. June 5, 1883.
5. Anna Frances, b. Jan. 17, 1886.

IV. DAVID H.,[8] b. July 18, 1849, in Farmington, Conn.; d. Oct. 23, 1881.
V. FLORENCE JOSEPHINE,[8] b. March 5, 1852, in Meriden, Conn.; d. 1853.
VI. HELEN AUGUSTA,[8] b. Jan. 6, 1858, in Meriden, Conn.
VII. JOSEPH BRACE,[8] b. Dec. 31, 1860, in West Hartford, Conn.
VIII. LEVI HENRY,[8] b. Jan. 31, 1863; m. MRS. (SCHWINK) HOAGLAND. They lived in Waterbury, Conn.

230.

JESSE MATHER[7] CHURCHILL (SAGE,[6] NATHANIEL,[5] NATHANIEL[4] NATHANIEL,[3] JOSEPH,[2] JOSIAH[1]).   Born at Cornwall, Vt., Nov. 18, 1796.   He settled in Elizabethtown, N.Y., but removed later to Canandaigua, N.Y., and in 1837 to Chicago, Ill. In the War of 1812 he served with credit in the Elizabethtown Regiment of the State Militia, through the Plattsburg campaign.   At the battle of Plattsburg the captain of his company was shot, and he was put in command of the company.   Probably he was an ensign or lieutenant previous to that.   He was soon after commissioned as captain, which office he held until Aug. 25, 1830, when he resigned as captain in the Thirty-seventh Regiment, Fortieth Brigade, Eleventh Division, State Militia.   The acceptance of his resignation

MR. JEROME CHURCHILL,

YREKA, CAL.

(No. 486, page 455.)

and his honorable discharge, signed by Brig. Gen. Joseph S. Weed, is now in the possession of his family. He died at Riverside, Ill., at the home of his eldest child, Mrs. Wesencraft, April 5, 1887. Married, at Elizabethtown, N.Y., Jan. 31, 1822, MARTHA McCAULEY. She died May 11, 1886.

Children born in Elizabethtown, N. Y.

    I. JANE,[8] m. MR. WESENCRAFT. Their daughter, Lotta A., in 1902, lived at Riverside, Ill.
    II. CAROLINE,[8] m. MR. SWARTOUT.
    Lived, in 1903, in Orlando, Fla., where she died June 1, 1898.
486 III. JEROME,[8] b. in Elizabethtown, N.Y., Feb. 11, 1826. He removed with his parents to Canandaigua, N.Y., and in 1837 to Chicago, where he received a common school education. He was self-supporting from sixteen years on, and did much to help in the support of his father's family. In May, 1849, he joined the pioneers in the rush to the "land of gold." He started with the overland company from St. Joseph and arrived in the Sacramento Valley on Sept. 11, 1849. Mr. Churchill was at this time twenty-three years old, of strong and fine physique, and both mentally and morally equipped for winning the eminent position which he gained for himself and still holds in business and society. In May, 1851, he located at Yreka, Cal., making that the centre of his trade as a merchant, while he established branch stores at various mining-camps which he supplied by pack-trains of mules, a somewhat hazardous method at that time on account of the Indians. In 1859, after eight years of hard work, he was able to retire with a good competency, and investing his money in profitable enterprises, by degrees drifted into the banking business, while he has a chief interest in several large stock-ranches. He was largely interested in establishing the Yreka Railroad, of which he is president, as well as of the Siskiyou County Bank. Married, in Waukegan, Ill., Nov. 14, 1861, JULIA PATTERSON, who was born in Lockport, N.Y. Her great-grandfather on her mother's side was Ethan Allen, hero of Ticonderoga. Mrs. Churchill was educated at Rockford Female Seminary, Ill., and occupies a position of influence in the women's associations in California. She has furnished us with this account of the Churchill family, of her husband and his father.

Children born in Yreka.

1. Carrie May, b. May 24, 1863; d. July 22, 1864.
2. Jerome Percy, b. March 1, 1866. He was educated at the California State Pharmacy and the Philadelphia College of Pharmacy, and is a chemist and druggist by profession. Married, June 10, 1891, Josephine Wheeler of Oakland, Cal. Children: (1) Percy Wheeler, b. Aug. 7, 1895; (2) Jerome, Jr., b. May 5, 1899.
3. Jesse Warren, b. April 3, 1868. Took a course at the Worcester, Mass., School of Technology; is an electrician by profession, though engaged chiefly with his father's banking and stock-raising interests. Married, Feb. 24, 1892, May V. Wheeler, of Oakland, Cal., sister of his brother's wife, and they have one child, Dorothy May, b. Feb. 27, 1895.

    IV. ELIZA,[8] b. Jan. 11, 1830; m. GEORGE WRIGHT PATTERSON, in Chicago, Ill., Sept. 15, 1846.
    They lived at Michigan City, Ind., where he was a shoe dealer and hotel keeper.

Children born at Michigan City, Ind.

1. Martha Corinna Patterson, b. Feb. 27, 1850; m. James E. Lathrop.
2. Jerome L. Patterson, b. July 4, 1852; d. March 31, 1855.
3. George Henry Patterson, b. Jan. 31, 1856.
4. Carrie May Patterson, b. May 12, 1859

234.

SOLOMON[7] CHURCHILL (SOLOMON,[6] NATHANIEL,[5] NATH-ANIEL,[4] NATHANIEL,[3] JOSEPH,[2] JOSIAH[1]). Born, probably in Berlin, Conn., Oct. 20, 1791. He died May 11, 1834. Married, Dec. 1, 1812, Berlin, Conn., CANDACE GILBERT, born July 12, 1791, and was the daughter of Hooker and Candace (Sage) Gilbert. Died June 9, 1835.

Children.

	I.	LAURA,[8] b. Dec. 26, 1813.
483	II.	WILLIAM,[8] b. Jan. 6, 1816.
	III.	SARAH.[8]
	IV.	EMELINE.[8]
484	V.	GILBERT.[8]
485	VI.	CYRUS,[8] b. Dec. 11, 1826.

235.

AMZI[7] CHURCHILL (SOLOMON,[6] NATHANIEL,[5] NATHANIEL,[4] NATHANIEL,[3] JOSEPH,[2] JOSIAH[1]). Born, probably in Berlin, Conn., Dec. 11, 1793. Married, July 4, 1819, MARIA WHITE, of Newton, L.I., who was born Feb. 4, 1795.

Children.

I. CATHARINE SELINA,[8] b. July 26, 1820; m. SAMUEL COCHRAN, July 3, 1837.
II. MICHAEL WHITE,[8] b. Dec. 19, 1825; d. young.
III. HANNAH MARIA,[8] b. Dec. 20, 1828; m. HENRY CONKLIN, July 3, 1847.

236.

CYRUS[7] CHURCHILL (SOLOMON,[6] NATHANIEL,[5] NATHANIEL,[4] NATHANIEL,[3] JOSEPH,[2] JOSIAH[1]). Born at Berlin, Conn., Dec. 15, 1797. Removed to New Haven, 1848. He was a carriage maker. He was highly respected for his strict integrity and unfailing goodness. He died May 15, 1864, at New Haven. Married, April 18, 1833, at Guilford, CLARISSA BRADLEY, of Guildford, Conn., born Sept. 17, 1804, and died at New Haven, July 27, 1900.

Children.

I. SARAH CORNELIA,[8] b. Feb. 5, 1834, in Springfield, Mass.; unmarried. Lived in New Haven, Conn.
II. MARY JANE,[8] b. March 23, 1837; m. HIRAM A. GRAY, Oct. 2, 1880, at Cambridge, Mass. He died at Hartford, Conn., Dec. 27, 1891.

RES DENCE OF JEROME CHURCH LL YREKA CAL

III. **Benjamin Bradley,**[9] b. July 25, 1841; d. Aug. 13, 1844.
IV. **Charles Benjamin,**[8] b. July 25, 1847; m. **Corinne Hosford,** daughter of Dr. Willard and Harriet (Hosford) Hosford, of Orford, N.H., Nov. 16, 1870. She was born Sept. 10, 1842. Mr. Churchill was born at Guilford, Conn., and removed with his father's family in 1848. He was fitting for college at the Hopkins School, in New Haven, when his father's death compelled him to relinquish his purpose of a college course, and he began a business career instead in the store of his uncle, Benjamin Bradley, of Boston, a well-known old-time merchant. Later he became connected with the New Haven Clock Company and the New England Watch Company of Waterbury, Conn.

Children of Benjamin B. and Corinne (Hosford) Churchill.

1. Lillian, b. at Orford, N.H., Sept. 30, 1871. Graduated from Smith College, 1895. Died at Waterbury, Jan. 31, 1900. She was a beautiful and accomplished young woman.
2. Katharine Corinne, b. at Boston Highlands, Mass., Jan. 24, 1873. She is an accomplished musician and teacher of music.

237.

JOHN[7] CHURCHILL (**Solomon,**[6] **Nathaniel,**[5] **Nathaniel,**[4] **Nathaniel,**[3] **Joseph,**[2] **Josiah**[1]). Born at Berlin, Conn., Aug. 10, 1813. Married 1st, at Wallingford, Conn., **Emeline Cleveland,** of Canton, Mass. Married 2d, **Lucy R. French,** of Litchfield, Conn. In 1866 lived in Winsted, Conn.

One Child by First Wife.

I. **Henry,**[8] b. Jan. 1, 1834; m. **Ellen Catlin.**
One son, John, married and had a son who, in 1886, lived in Meriden, Conn., a telegraph operator. Name not obtained.

239.

EBEN DORMAN[7] CHURCHILL (**Thomas Foster,**[6] **Janna,**[5] **Nathaniel,**[4] **Nathaniel,**[3] **Joseph,**[2] **Josiah**[1]). Born in Georgia, Vt., Nov. 6, 1815. At the age of twelve he left Vermont and went West to Cuyahoga Falls, later to Galena, Ill., and finally settled at Platteville, Wis. He was a farmer and a miner. He died on Dec. 14, 1871. Married, at Platteville, July 17, 1851, **Martha E. Story,** who was born at Underhill, Vt., and removed to Platteville, Wis., in 1846.

Children born in Platteville, Wis.

I. **Frances Ann,**[8] b. May 6, 1852; m. **Francis A. Bartle,** Jan. 1, 1870.
In 1886 they lived in Hurley, S. Dakota.
II. **Mary Ellen,**[8] b. May 23, 1854; m. **Frank M. Bonson,** Platteville, April 3, 1877.
489 III. **Thomas Foster,**[8] b. Jan. 15, 1856; m. **Catharine Robinson.**
He was a farmer and lived at Blue Earth City, Minn., in 1896.

Children.

1. Martha V., b. at Minneapolis, Dec. 16, 1894.
2. Thomas Stanley, b. at Blue Earth City, Sept. 11, 1896.

IV. CORA ELIZA,[8] b. Jan. 29, 1858; d. May 27, 1860.
V. RALPH ELMER,[8] b. May 3, 1860; m. GERTRUDE SLIVER, Jan. 17, 1886.
   They lived at Los Angeles, Cal.
VI. JENNIE CORA,[8] b. Jan. 24, 1862; m. WILLIS TOWNSEND, Nov. 1, 1884.
   They lived at Bosberg, Wash.
VII. JOHN CHARLES,[8] b. March 23, 1865; unmarried.
   He graduated at the State Normal School of Wisconsin in 1889.
   He studied law, and entered upon the practice at Lancaster, Wis.
   He was clerk of courts for several years for Grant County, Wis.
VIII. FRANK LESLIE,[8] b. July 31, 1867; m. FLORENCE CAMPBELL, daughter
   of Samuel H. and Henrietta (Freed) Campbell, at Washington,
   D.C., July 17, 1895.
   He graduated at Wisconsin State Normal School, 1890, and at
   Columbian University, Washington, D.C., and from the Law School,
   LL.B., in 1895. He was employed in the Civil Service Depart-
   ment until 1896, when he removed to Lancaster, Wis., and began
   the practice of law.

Children of Frank L. and Florence Churchill.

1. Martha Ella, b. July 4, 1896.
2. Frank Campbell, b. Oct. 31, 1898.
IX. LUCY MARTHA,[8] b. Sept. 23, 1871; m. WILLIAM MCBRIDE.
   They lived at Platteville, Wis.

240.

JAMES ALFRED [7] CHURCHILL (THOMAS FOSTER,[6] JANNA,[5]
NATHANIEL,[4] NATHANIEL,[3] JOSEPH,[2] JOSIAH [1]). Born in Georgia, Vt.,
Aug. 24, 1825. Settled in Ellenboro, Grant County, Wis., where
he was a farmer. Married, at Waterloo, Wis., Aug. 18, 1853,
JULIA ANN BUTLER, daughter of Drury and Matilda (Coon) Butler,

Children born in Ellenboro.

I. MARY ETTA,[8] b. June 29, 1854; m. A. D. FINNEY, April 19, 1881.
   at Platteville. She died June 10, 1889, at Lima, Wis.
II. LAURA,[8] b. Nov. 29, 1856.
   Lived in Cassville, Wis.
III. ELLA FLORENCE,[8] b. Jan. 10, 1860.
IV. ALVARETTA,[8] b. Aug. 4, 1863; d. at Ellenboro, Nov. 29, 1863.
V. IDA MATILDA,[8] b. March 20, 1865.
   Lived, February, 1901, Hartington, Neb.
VI CLARA ALICE,[8] b. Aug. 23, 1867; m. FRANK A. FLORINE, at Ellen-
   boro, Jan. 24, 1894.
   Lived at Cuba City, Wis.
VII. MARTHA OLIVE,[8] b. April 17, 1870; m. CHARLES J. MCCORMICK.
   Lived at Patchgrove, Wis.
493 VIII. JAMES ADELBERT,[8] b. Nov. 4, 1873.
   Lived at Platteville, Wis.
IX. THODE STEPHEN,[8] b. April 13, 1879.
   Lived at Hartington, Neb.

241.

WILLIAM RUMSEY [7] CHURCHILL (JOSIAH,[6] JANNA [5]
NATHANIEL,[4] NATHANIEL,[3] JOSEPH,[2] JOSIAH [1]). Born at Batavia,
N.Y., Dec. 22, 1808. He settled in Portland, Mich., where he was
a merchant. He died in Portland, about 1887. Married 1st, Oct.
31, 1833, FANNIE FIDELIA BUSHNELL, b. 1816; 2d, ANNA KNOX.

Children of First Wife.

I. FRANCES AMELIA,⁸ b. Aug. 24, 1835; m. CHARLES HENRY, Sept. 28, 1856.
II. EMILY MARIA,⁸ b. March 29, 1837; d. at sixteen years.
III. INFANT,⁸ not named.
IV. INFANT,⁸ not named.
V. ADELAIDE CAROLINE,⁸ b. 1843; d. young.
494 VI. JAMES,⁸ b. Aug. 27, 1845; m. CLARA WHITLOCK, b. June 7, 1852.
VII. EVELINA,⁸ d. young.

Children of Second Wife.

VIII. ANNA,⁸ d. young.
IX. HARRIET,⁸ d. young.
X. WILLIAM,⁸ d. young.
XI. HELEN,⁸ d. young.
XII. CAROLINE,⁸ m. MR. WOODWORTH.
XIII. MARA,⁸ m. FRANK SPROUL.

244.

ALBERT J.⁷ CHURCHILL (JOSIAH,⁶ JANNA,⁵ NATHANIEL,⁴ NATHANIEL,³ JOSEPH,² JOSIAH¹). Born at East Bethany, N.Y., Oct. 2, 1842. He settled at Avon, Ill., where he was a dealer in dry goods, notions, boots and shoes, jewelry, and silver ware, but later was engaged in the firm of Tompkins Brothers, of Avon. Married, Oct. 31, 1866, at Avon, Ill., MARY E. MAILLIARD, daughter of one of the French retainers who came to America with Joseph Bonaparte.

Children.

495 I. JULIAN,⁸ b. Sept. 14, 1868; m. LULÙ MINGS, Oct. 12, 1892.

Children.

1. Marguerite, b. Oct. 6, 1894.
2. Ross A., b. March 7, 1898.
3. Herbert Winston, b. Aug. 3, 1900.

II. ANNIE EUGENIE,⁸ b. May 22, 1870; m. DR. W A. NEECE, Jan. 25, 1899.
They lived at Alexis, Ill.

Children.

1. Marjorie Neece, b. Jan. 6, 1900.
2. Bret C. Neece, b. Feb. 10, 1903.

III. CLARA L.,⁸ b. Feb. 19, 1874; m. REV. B. G. CARPENTER, June 8, 1899.

Child.

1. Kenneth Carpenter, b. June 8, 1899.

IV. FANNIE E.,⁸ b. July 16, 1881.

245.

MARCELLUS C.⁷ CHURCHILL (JANNA,⁶ JANNA,⁵ NATHANIEL,⁴ NATHANIEL,³ JOSEPH,² JOSIAH¹). Born in St. Albans, Vt., March 13, 1814. We have been unable to get any satisfactory account of this family. Married ABBIE B. PAGE.

Children.

I. FANNIE,[8] m. GILBERT MOFFATT.
II. ELIZABETH,[8] m. GEORGE MAYER.

One Son.

1. Durand Churchill Mayer.

III. FLORENCE,[8] m. ARTHUR FRANCIS, of England. They lived at
Englewood, and had one child, a son, d. young.
IV. CLAUDE NEWMAN,[8] d. young.
V. SARAH,[8] m. WILLIAM PAGE.

246.

CHARLES P.[7] CHURCHILL (JANNA,[6] JANNA,[5] NATHANIEL,[4] NATHANIEL,[3] JOSEPH,[2] JOSIAH[1]). Born in St. Albans, Vt., Sept. 6, 1815. Removed to Genesee County, N.Y., with his father's family, but settled later in Buffalo. Married 1st, Sept. 2, 1844, HARRIET AUSTIN, born Dec. 21, 1818. Married 2d, April 7, 1852, HARRIET PERKINS.

Children of First Wife.

496   I. MARCELLUS AUSTIN,[8] b. 1845; m. 1st, JENNIE HOYT, of Pen Yan,
N.Y., 1874, who died in Japan, December, 1875; m. 2d, NELLIE
CHESTERWOOD, in Buffalo, 1878. In 1893 he lived in Buffalo,
N.Y.

Child of First Wife.

1. Charles Hoyt, b. June 10, 1875.

Children of Second Wife.

2. Mary Alice, b. August, 1879.
3. Susie, b. 1882.
4. Bessie, b. March, 1884.

II. ARTHUR EUGENE,[8] b. Jan. 7, 1849; d. in infancy.

Children of Second Wife.

III. MARY ALICE,[8] b. Dec. 27, 1852; m. EDWARD CARVER, June 12,
1883. No children. Lived in Marshalltown, Ia., in 1893.
496a   IV. EDWARD DUDLEY,[8] b. Sept. 11, 1854; m. (———) (———),
August, 1882. They lived in Buffalo, and had four children
names not obtained.
V. MARTHA,[8] b. March 25, 1856; d. at four years of age.
VI. CHARLES P., JR.,[8] b. Dec. 25, 1857; unmarried.
VII. JENNIE C.,[8] b. Sept. 9, 1859; m. FRANK DARROW. Lived in Minneapolis, and had two children.

Children.

1. Gertrude Charlotte Darrow, b. April 21, 1879.
2. Clayton Churchill Darrow, b. Feb. 7, 1884.

VIII. HARRIETTE LAVANCH,[8] b. April 7, 1862; unmarried.
497   IX. HERBERT HADDOCK,[8] b. April 7, 1862; m. JOSEPHINE BUTLER,
August, 1883. Mrs. Josephine Churchill died May 26, 1888.

Children.

1. Harriette M., b. Sept. 18, 1884.
2. Marie Josephine, b. April 26, 1888.

248.

DR. AMOS[7] CHURCHILL (AMOS,[6] AMOS,[5] NATHANIEL,[4] NATHANIEL,[3] JOSEPH,[2] JOSIAH[1]). Born at Broadalbin, N.Y., March 12, 1805. He studied medicine, and practised in New York City, and died there Jan. 17, 1840. Married 1st, ANN MARIA DOWNING, of New York City, who died without issue. Married 2d, LUCY HALE, of Wethersfield, Conn.

One Child by Second Wife.

I. HARRIET,[8] b. in 1838; m. MR. BIRDSALL. They lived some time in Sheffield, Mass.

249.

DR. CHARLES W.[7] CHURCHILL (AMOS,[6] AMOS,[5] NATHANIEL,[4] NATHANIEL,[3] JOSEPH,[2] JOSIAH[1]). Born at Broadalbin, N.Y., Oct. 10, 1814. He was a physician, and practised medicine at 91 St. Marks Place, New York City, from 1838. Married, Aug. 22, 1843, LOUISA SIGISON, of New York.

They had Two Children whose Names we have received.

I. LOUISA JANE,[8] b. March 25, 1846.
II. OLIVE EMMA,[8] b. Oct. 28, 1849.

250.

ELIJAH WILCOX[7] CHURCHILL (AMOS,[6] AMOS,[5] NATHANIEL[4] NATHANIEL,[3] JOSEPH,[2] JOSIAH[1]). Born at Broadalbin, N.Y., Sept. 27, 1817. Lived for some years at Broadalbin, but some time before 1855 removed to Wisconsin and settled at Waupaca. He died Oct. 8, 1876. Married ELIZA JUDSON, of Mayfield, N.Y.

Children of Elijah and Eliza (Judson) Churchill.

I. HARRIET A.,[8] b. June 2, 1844; d. Aug. 24, 1845.
II. CHARLES J.,[8] b. at Broadalbin, N.Y., Dec. 24, 1846. Removed with his father's family to Waupaca, Wis. He was educated at Waupaca public schools and commercial college. He studied and practised law at Waupaca. He was clerk of Circuit Court for Waupaca County from 1870 to 1883, and has held other public offices. He was chosen president of the Waupaca County National Bank in 1890, and still holds the position in 1904. He married, at Waupaca, Nov. 20, 1868, ANN E. WALKER, daughter of Fred W. and Mary (Martin) Walker.

Children.

1. Lucy May, b. Nov. 19, 1869; m. Frank S. Baldwin, Sept. 8, 1891.
2. Frederick, b. July 17, 1871.
3. Herbert, b. July 9, 1875; m. Jessie Hollenbeck, Sept. 2, 1901.
4. Ned J., b. Nov. 3, 1879.
5. C. Lloyd, b. March 5, 1883.
6. Richard, b. Jan. 26, 1891.

III. EDWIN L.,[8] b. March 15, 1848; d. March 4, 1851.

IV. SARAH L.,[8] b. April 19, 1850; d. March 8, 1851.
V. SYLVANUS A.,[8] b. July 4, 1853; m. CLARA HART, at Appleton, Wis.,
   July 11, 1873.
   He was a farmer at Waupaca and Bloomville.

Children.

1. Fannie M., b. May 7, 1877.
2. Adelbert H., b. Jan. 12, 1879.
3. Irma A., b. May 2, 1884.
4. Charles B., b. April 9, 1889.
5. Ethel L., b. Nov. 28, 1891.

VI. EDWARD LOTHROP,[8] b. March 22, 1858; m. ALICE E. HUMPHREY,
   at Amsterdam, N.Y., June 15, 1884.
   He was a carpenter. They lived at Binghamton, N.Y.

Children.

1. Lucy May, b. May 19, 1888.
2. Mildred E., b. April 25, 1893.

251.

ALANSON COVELL[7] CHURCHILL (ROSWELL,[6] AMOS,[5]
NATHANIEL,[4] NATHANIEL,[3] JOSEPH,[2] JOSIAH[1]). Born, probably,
at Mayfield, N.Y., 1813. In a letter to G. A. Churchill, April 29,
1886, Mr. Churchill signs his name Alansing, but we hold to the
regular form of the name. In this letter he gives much information
upon various points, but fails to give the most important items about
his own family. He says that his father, Roswell, kept a hotel at
the " village of Fondasbush," until about 1825, when he moved to
Albany and kept a hotel there until 1840, when he went to New
York City and kept a hotel there until his death. This is much
different from the account received from his younger brother,
Charles R. Churchill, who says nothing about the hotels, but magni-
fies the cloth business. The facts seem to be that he achieved the
sheep-raising and cloth-making before engaging in hotel keeping.
Alanson says he died in New York City, at the age of seventy-six
years, which would show that the year given on page 377 should be
1853. At the time of this letter Alanson lived in Cedar Rapids,
Ia., and writes on paper which has his business head, " A. C. Churchill and Son, Dealers in Hardware, Cutlery, Nails, etc., Acorn Stoves
and Ranges, 25 South First Street." The junior member of the
firm is H. N. Churchill. Married LUCY CORNWALL, daughter of
Isaac and Lucy (Churchill) Cornwall, his own cousin. No dates of
marriage or birth of children are given. He gives his record as
follows: "I have one son and two daughters. One daughter lives
in Omaha, Neb., and has three children. One son and daughter
live here." The letter-heads show that the son's name is H. N.
Churchill, and at the date of the letter, neither the son or the
daughter at home were married. We have no later information of
the family.

252.

ERASMUS DARWIN[7] CHURCHILL (Roswell,[6] Amos,[5] Nathaniel,[4] Nathaniel,[3] Joseph,[2] Josiah [1]). Born in Mayfield, N.Y., Nov. 7, 1815. He settled in Stillwater N.Y., and died there. Married Sarah E. Finch, who was born Jan. 27, 1817.

Children.

        I. Erasmus D.,[8] b. Dec. 8, 1838; d. unmarried.
498   II. Judson,[8] b. Oct. 19, 1841; m. Sophia H. Pulkamus, June 24, 1868. She was b. March 14, 1845. No further record obtained.
       III. Sarah Emily,[8] b. July 27, 1844; d. young.
499   IV. Wickliff E.,[8] b. July 27, 1847; m. Alice Spotts. No further record obtained.
       V. Howard,[8] b. Dec. 22, 1850; unmarried.

252.*

WILLIAM HENRY[7] CHURCHILL (Roswell [6] Amos [5] Nathaniel,[4] Nathaniel,[3] Joseph,[2] Josiah [1]). Born in Mayfield, N.Y., 1817. He lived in San Francisco, Cal., in 1886, and, Alanson says, had two or three sons and two daughters. Married Mary Pearson.

252a.

RENSELLAER EMMET[7] CHURCHILL (Roswell,[6] Amos,[5] Nathaniel,[4] Nathaniel,[3] Joseph,[2] Josiah [1]). Born in Mayfield, N.Y., Jan. 20, 1820. Lived in Albany, N.Y. Married Gertrude Ramsey.

Children.

       I. John Roswell.[8]
       Three daughters, it is said.

252b.

CHARLES ROSWELL[7] CHURCHILL (Roswell,[6] Amos,[5] Nathaniel,[4] Nathaniel,[3] Joseph,[2] Josiah [1]). Born in Mayfield. He filled out one of the early blanks for G. A. Churchill, but gave no information about himself or his family. The blank was sent to him Sept. 29, 1885, but he does not give his residence, or the date of his reply, or date of his birth or marriage. He married Lydia Bowden. We have received nothing further.

253.

WILLIAM ELLIOTT[7] CHURCHILL (Jesse,[6] Amos,[5] Nathaniel,[4] Nathaniel,[3] Joseph,[2] Josiah [1]). Born at Middletown, Conn., Feb. 22, 1805. Removed to Broadalbin, N.Y., with his

---

* This number and the two following numbers were not reported at the first enumeration.

father's family previous to 1809, and became a merchant in New
York City, No. 9 East Twenty-Second street. Married 1st, at
Meriden, Conn., July, 1832, SARAH M. COWLES, of Meriden, Conn.,
daughter of Major E. A. Cowles ; 2d, 1852, LOUISA TERRY, of Hartford, Conn., daughter of Eliphalet Terry, Esq.

Children, all of First Wife.

I. JOHN COWLES,⁸ b. 1834; d. 1838.
II. CATHERINE R.,⁸ b. 1836.
III. SARAH N.,⁸ b. 1838.
IV. LUCY C.,⁸ b. 1840; d. 1874.

254.

HENRY⁷ CHURCHILL (JESSE,⁶ AMOS,⁵ NATHANIEL,⁴
NATHANIEL,³ JOSEPH,² JOSIAH¹). Born at Middletown, Feb. 17,
1807. Settled at Gloversville, N.Y. Held the office of provost-
marshal during the Civil War. Married 1st, at Gloversville, N.Y.
1830, SELINA BURR, born March 15, 1808 ; died March 13, 1851; 2d,
at Albany, N.Y., June 1, 1852, SYBIL E. ROBERTS.

Children of First Wife, born at Gloversville.

I. WILLIAM SCOTT,⁸ b. March 28, 1831 ; d. April 12, 1835.
II. HELEN,⁸ b. Jan. 12, 1837 ; m. GEORGE C. ROOT, April 29, 1859.
III. ALICE,⁸ b. Feb. 8, 1839 ; m. HENRY D. MOORE.
IV. CAROLINE,⁸ b. July 10, 1841 ; m. WARNER MILLER, July, 1865.
        He was of Herkimer, N.Y., United States Senator from New York
        State.
500   V. HENRY,⁸ b. June 15, 1844; m. ELLA GILCHRIST.
        Lived in Herkimer, N.Y., in 1886, and was engaged in paper
        manufacture in the firm with his brother-in-law, Senator Warner
        Miller.

Children of Second Wife.

VI. SELINA BURR,⁸ b. September, 1855 ; d. 1876.
VII. JESSIE,⁸ b. June, 1857; m. MR. EGGLESTON.
VIII. CORA,⁸ b. March, 1861.

255.

TIMOTHY GRIDLEY⁷ (JESSE,⁶ AMOS,⁵ NATHANIEL,⁴ NATH-
ANIEL,³ JOSEPH,² JOSIAH¹). Born April 28, 1809, at Broadalbin,
N.Y. Married, June 15, 1836, PATIENCE LAWRENCE, daughter of
John, of New York City.

Children born at Broadalbin.

I. ANNA P.,⁸ b. May 9, 1837.
II. JANE LAWRENCE,⁸ b. June 9, 1839 ; m. REV. HENRY Y. SATTERLEE,
        D.D., June 29, 1866.
III. JOHN LAWRENCE,⁸ b. Nov. 14, 1842. He was a member of the
        Seventh Regiment, New York City, and enlisted in the Civil
        War, became a lieutenant, and afterwards colonel of a regi-
        ment. He was taken prisoner and suffered so severely from
        the hardships of his captivity that he never recovered his health.

He was a man of excellent military ability and high character. After his death a mural tablet to his memory was placed in the Seventh Regiment Armory, New York City. He died in Natchez, November, 1868.

IV. WILLIAM ELIOT,⁸ b. July 15, 1845; d. May 12, 1847.

V. EMILY VIRGINIA,⁸ b. Dec. 13, 1848; m. DR. CLARENCE SATTERLEE.

256.

ALLEN COWLES⁷ CHURCHILL (JESSE,⁶ AMOS,⁵ NATHANIEL,⁴ NATHANIEL,³ JOSEPH,² JOSIAH¹). Born at Broadalbin, N.Y., July 17, 1820. They lived at Gloversville. Married, at Gloversville, N.Y., Oct. 28, 1840, CAROLINE C. WARNER, of that town. She was born Dec. 29, 1820.

Children born at Gloversville.

  I. SARAH LOUISA,⁸ b. July 9, 1843; d. December, 1843.
  II. EMILY LOUISE,⁸ b. Nov. 3, 1844; m. EUGENE HILL, May 7, 1867.
501 III. WILLIAM ELIOT,⁸ b. Feb. 5, 1848; m. EMMA JOHNSON, November, 1868.
  IV. CLARA BELLA,⁸ b. April 13, 1852; m. ARTHUR SALISBURY, December, 1868.
502 V. ALLEN COWLES,⁸ b. about 1854.
  VI. STELLA LOUISA,⁸ b. about 1856.
502a VII. LOUIS WARNER,⁸ b. about 1858.

257.

CHARLES BROCKWAY⁷ CHURCHILL (JESSE,⁶ AMOS,⁵ NATHANIEL,⁴ NATHANIEL,³ JOSEPH,² JOSIAH¹). Born at Broadal bin, Feb. 26, 1828. Married CAROLINE SMITH, of New York City, daughter of Leonard K. Smith.

Children.

  I. CHARLES BROCKWAY, JR.,⁸ b. June, 1859.
  II. FLORENCE,⁸ b. 1865; d. 1879.
  III. LEONARD K.,⁸ b. June, 1867; d. 1871.

258.

SAMUEL⁷ CHURCHILL (JOSEPH,⁶ JOSEPH,⁵ JOHN,⁴ NATHANIEL,³ JOSEPH,² JOSIAH¹). Born at Chatham, Conn., Aug 2, 1795. We have letters, written in 1885, from his sons Joseph and Charles, and his daughter, Mrs. Loring, and I think Mr. N. W. Churchill, our senior compiler, visited the Lorings, at Shrewsbury, as he is urged in their letters to do, and we have much more particular records than appear in the letters, and their letters state that they have the "old Bible record." From these letters we learn something more about Joseph (No. 89) than appears on page 378. The old marriage certificate corrects name of wife and place of marriage and gives date and shows that Joseph Churchill married Anna Loudon, the 21st of October, 1790, at Cornwallis, N.S., by William

Manning, Rector of St. John's Church. These letters say that Joseph was a sea captain, and in 1797 sailed out of Halifax in command of the English ship "Earl of Dublin," which it is supposed was captured by pirates, and all on board destroyed, as nothing was ever heard of ship or crew afterwards. His widow was living at Chatham, Conn., with his people at the time, but got homesick, and returned to Nova Scotia, where she afterwards married and lived at Granville. Samuel was brought up at Granville, N.S., and became a tanner and currier, and lived at Cornwallis and Annapolis, until about 1840 he removed to Massachusetts and settled at Salem, where he died June 4, 1861. Married, at Granville, N.S., June 24, 1817, ELIZA WILLET, daughter of Walter, of Granville. She died at Durham, N.H., Nov. 2, 1884.

Children born, all but the last, in Nova Scotia.

503   I. JOSEPH,[8] b. in Cornwallis, N.S., July 17, 1819; m. FRANCES A. TAYLOR, of Digby, N.S. He was adopted and brought up by his aunt, Mrs. Prudence Wade, who had no family of her own. Mrs. Wade died many years ago, but Mr. Wade, in 1885, was living at the age of almost a hundred years. Joseph became a merchant and extensive ship-owner at Digby, N.S., where he was living in August, 1885, when he wrote his letter. He says, in closing his letter, "I have two daughters and one son." Unfortunately he does not give their names or dates of birth.

    II. ABIGAIL ANN,[8] b. Aug. 25, 1821; m. STEPHEN SAUNDERS, of Manchester, N.H.

    III. PRUDENCE SHAW,[8] b. June 24, 1824; m. HIRAM WOODBURY, of Salem, N.H.

504   IV. CHARLES SUMNER,[8] b. Aug. 3, 1826; m. 1st, PHEBE RODIMOND, of Haverhill, N.H.; m. 2d, HENRIETTA FOSTER, of Granville, N.S., in Salem, Mass., in 1858. He was living in Rock Bottom. Mass., in 1885, a farmer.
He lived at different times in Salem, Waverley, and Stowe, Mass.

Child of First Wife.

1. Annie E., d. in Waverley, Mass., 1871.

Children of Second Wife.

2. Charles H., b. in Salem, Mass., June 27, 1860. He was a merchant in Boston in 1885.
3. Robert B., b. in Waverley, Mass., in 1867.
4. Kitty C., b. in Waverley, Mass., in 1869.
5. Samuel Lawrence, b. in Waverley, Mass., 1873.
6. Richard Foster, b. in Stowe, Mass., in 1879.

    V. MARY,[8] b. May 10, 1829; m. CHARLES BUTLER, of Methuen, Mass. She died leaving one son, John Butler.

    VI. WILLIAM LAWRENCE,[8] b. Oct. 14, 1831; m. SARAH BROCK. He was killed accidently while raising a steamer off Sandy Hook, leaving one daughter who, in 1885, lived with her mother in New York City. Name not received.

    VII. MARGARET,[8] b. April 8, 1833; m. JOHN COE. She died in Philadelphia, leaving one child who died in infancy.

    VIII. GILBERT WILLET,[8] b. May 8, 1836; d. Feb. 4, 1856.

    IX. ARABELLA LOUISA,[8] b. Aug. 27, 1838; m. HIRAM LORING, Shrewsbury, Mass.

X. HARRIET SOPHIA,[8] b. Sept. 30, 1840; m. JOSEPH WILLIAM COE, of Durham, N.H. He was a prosperous farmer at Durham. They had five children, names not received.

XI. MELINDA SHAW,[8] b. Nov. 23, 1842; m. WALTER WILLET, of Digby, N.S.
They lived at Digby in 1885.

259.

JOHN [7] CHURCHILL (CHARLES,[6] JOSEPH,[5] JOHN [4] NATHANIEL [3] JOSEPH,[2] JOSIAH [1]). Born in Portland, Conn., July 28, 1789. He was employed in his father's shipyards until the closing of that business, when he removed from Portland, Conn., to Richfield, O., and there worked at his trade of general carpentry. He died Feb. 27, 1874. Married, in Portland, Conn., July 1, 1809, EMILY WIL-COX, daughter of Asahel and Lucy (Crittenden) Wilcox, b. June 17, 1792, and died at Richfield, Sept. 13, 1879.

Children born, all except the youngest, in Portland, Conn.

I. JOHN, JR.,[8] b. May 2, 1810; m. LOVINA GRIMMONS, b. at Chatham, Conn., m. at Portland, Conn., Sept. 30, 1832.
Mr. Churchill was a carpenter and farmer, and settled first at Richfield, O., but afterwards, at Hinckley, O., where he died Dec. 24, 1883. Lovina, his wife, d. Dec. 1, 1871.

Children born, the first at Richfield, the others at Hinckley.

1. Jane Elizabeth, b. Sept. 23, 1833; m. William S. Parker, Aug. 12, 1850.
Their children : (1) Clara M.; (2) Sumner E.; (3) Nellie A · (4 and 5) Leon and Stella L., twins.
2. David, b. Aug. 20, 1835; d. March 30, 1836.
3. Ann Amelia, b. March 26, 1837; m. Walter Scott Waitt, Dec. 13, 1857.
4. Mary Ellen, b. March 6, 1839; d. Aug. 17, 1885; unmarried.
5. Lucy Lovina, b. Nov. 4, 1842.
She was living unmarried in West Richfield, O., in 1887, and furnished an excellent account of her grandfather's line.
6. Charles Adelbert, b. Sept. 3, 1844; m. Louise J. Myers, May 24 1868, at Pleasanton, Mich.
They lived at Bear Lake, Mich. Children: (1) Alfred F.; (2) Mary A.; (3) John A.; (4) Otis K.; (5) Bert, d. soon; (6) Charles B.
7. Ruth Helen, b. April 30, 1848; d. soon.
8. Ruth Sophia, b. July 14, 1851.

II. FREDERICK AUGUSTUS,[8] b. Aug. 21, 1812; m. EVELINE BEACH, of Hinckley, O., at Richfield, Oct. 15, 1832. He died at Galva, Ill., July 11, 1876. She died February, 1880.

Children of Frederick A. and Eveline (Beach) Churchill.

1. Charles H., b. Aug. 1, 1833; m. Josephine (———).
They lived at Mountain Grove, Mo., and Nortonville, Kan., and had children : (1) Charles Sumner; and (2) Eva Laura.
2. Ruth, d. unmarried, Dec. 11, 1852.
3. Scott. He was married and had a family, it is said.
He was living in Scandia, Kan., in 1889, but we have no answer from him.

III. SYLVESTER,[8] b. Oct. 31, 1814; m. ELIZABETH PATCH, of Hinckley,
   O., Jan. 1, 1835. She was born at Bennington, Vt., June 23,
   1813, and was the daughter of Samuel and Martha (Nichols)
   Patch. Sylvester was graduated at the Ohio Medical School, in
   1838. He practised in Ohio, Texas, and Indiana, but settled
   down finally in Kirkwood, Ill., where he was living June, 1885,
   and filled out a blank for Mr. G. A. Churchill. Sylvester died
   at Kirkwood, Ill., Jan. 18, 1886, and his wife died at Crawfordsville, Ind., 1873.

Children of Dr. Sylvester and Elizabeth (Patch) Churchill.
   1. Sanford Lewis, b. Dec. 4, 1836; d. Aug. 14, 1839.
   2. Lucy Martha, b. April 1, 1838; m. John Eaton, Feb. 19, 1861.
      He died Feb. 3, 1874. Children: (1) Ida O. Eaton, b. March
      30, 1862; (2) Viola May Eaton, b. June 13, 1865; (3) Law-
      rence Joseph Eaton, b. July 14, 1873.
   3. John Sanford, b. March 25, 1841; m. Rose E. Dummer, White
      Rock, Kan., Jan. 3, 1867. They had children: (1) Clara
      Frances Churchill, b. Sept. 28, 1868; d. April 7, 1869; (2)
      William Leonard, b. Feb. 2, 1871; (3) Minnie Elizabeth, b.
      Sept. 16, 1873; (4) Laura Iona, b. Jan. 14, 1877.
   4. Lydia Ann, b. Jan. 8, 1843; m. Joseph J. Barrett, of Nolan,
      Tex.
   5. Francis Marion, b. May 7, 1845; m. Mary Miller, of Saline
      City, Ind.
   6. Emily Melissa, b. July 21, 1851; m. William Quillen, of Round
      Hill, Ind.
   7. Joseph Sylvester, b. April 4, 1856; m. Cora A. Blanat, about
      1879. They had one son, who died with its mother soon after
      the birth.

IV LAURA EMILY,[8] b. May 10, 1816; m. FREDERICK HARMON GRAVES,
   Aug. 15, 1832. She died April 26, 1879, and her husband, Mr.
   Graves, died March 28, 1878. They lived at Richfield, O.

They had Children.
   1-2. Edward Sherman and Edwin Harmon Graves, b. Nov. 28,
      1833; Edwin d. March 11, 1835.
   3. Edmund Augustine Graves, b. Nov. 30, 1835.
   4. Emily Maria Graves, b. Aug. 16, 1837.
   5. Enoch Harmon Graves, b. Nov. 9, 1839.
   6. Elbert Lewis Graves, b. July 29, 1842.
   7. Elmore John Graves, b. Aug. 2, 1845; d. March 30, 1846.
   8. Elvin Francis Graves, b. April 28, 1847; d. Dec. 7, 1847.
   9. Martha Alice Graves, b. Sept. 29, 1848.
   10. Alfred Austin Graves, b. May 20, 1851.
   11. Frank Ferdinand Graves, b. Feb. 3, 1854.
   12. Eva Agnes Graves, b. June 13, 1856; d. Nov. 28, 1860, at
      Shelbyville, Mo.
      The father of this family, Frederick H. Graves, d. March 28,
      1878; the mother, Laura Emily Graves, d. April 26, 1879.
      Edward S. Graves, the oldest son, d. July 3, 1880. Miss Lucy
      Lovina Churchill gave the above account in 1887.

V. LUCY,[8] b. Oct. 31, 1818; d. unmarried, Dec. 18, 1837.
VI. RUTH,[8] b. May 21, 1821; m. HENRY INGERSOLL, of Hinckley, O., at
   Richfield, O., Dec. 24, 1845. They lived at Hinckley, O.

Children.
   1. Helen Augusta Ingersoll, b. October, 1846; m. George Town-
      send, at Shelbina, Mo., in the fall of 1871, and d. there July,
      1872.
   2. Charles Ingersoll, b. July 16, 1848, and d. in Cleveland, O.,
      July, 1864.
      Mrs. Ruth Ingersoll d. on the day of her son's birth. Her
      husband, Henry Ingersoll, d. in Cleveland, O., July, 1870.

509   VII. JOSEPH BLAKE,[8] b. March 28, 1824; m. MARY JANE CLIFFORD, of
Richfield, O., April 25, 1847. They lived at Richfield, O., where
he d. Jan. 17, 1883, and his wife Mary Jane d. there, Oct. 7,
1882. We have no report of any children.

VIII. EMMELINE PULSIFER,[8] b. July 24, 1826; m. HENRY WISMER, of
New York, at Richfield, O., Feb. 24, 1847. She d. at Richfield,
O., Nov. 29, 1847, leaving no children.

IX. EUNICE VIENNA,[8] b in Richfield, O., April 4, 1832. Unmarried.

260.

CAPT. ALFRED[7] CHURCHILL (CHARLES,[6] JOSEPH,[5] JOHN,[4]
NATHANIEL,[3] JOSEPH,[2] JOSIAH[1]). Born in Chatham, Conn., Jan.
26, 1794. Married, Oct. 3, 1813, SALLY HALL, daughter of David
and Lucia, of Portland, Conn., born 1795, and died Sept. 9, 1864.

Children.

I. SALLY MARIA,[8] d. July 14, 1836.

510   II. WILLIAM H.[8]
In 1888 we had a letter from Mr. William Hamilton Churchill,
who said he was the son of William Henry, and his grandfather
Capt. Alfred David Churchill, but we have received nothing further.

261.

CHARLES[7] CHURCHILL (CHARLES,[6] JOSEPH,[5] JOHN,[4] NATH-
ANIEL,[3] JOSEPH,[2] JOSIAH[1]). Born at Chatham, Conn., Jan. 29,
1802. It is much to be regretted that we have not received more
of this family. Married LUCY TAYLOR, of Glastonbury, Conn.

Children.

I. MARY HANNAH,[8] d. Oct. 25, 1824.

511   II. CHARLES RUSSELL.[8]

512   III. EDWIN FRANKLIN.[8]

IV. HANNAH.[8]

513   V. JOSEPH MILES.[8]

262.

CAPT. HENRY UFFORD[7] CHURCHILL (DAVID,[6] JOSEPH,[5]
JOHN,[4] NATHANIEL,[3] JOSEPH,[2] JOSIAH[1]). Born June 30, 1797, in
Chatham, Conn. Died March 30, 1868. Married, June 30, 1817,
EMILY GREEN HALL, daughter of Joel and Lucy (Brown) Hall, of
Portland, Conn. She was born June 3, 1797, and died July 9,
1874.

Children.

I. JERUSHA UFFORD,[8] b. April 1, 1818.

II. EMILY HALL,[8] b. Dec. 25, 1819.

III. MARY BROWN,[8] b. Jan. 24, 1822.

IV. FRANCES MATILDA GERTRUDE,[8] b. Oct. 12, 1823.

V. DAVID,[8] b. March 31, 1826; d. Dec. 2, 1847.

VI. JOEL HALL,[8] b. March 5, 1828; d. Sept. 22, 1845.

VII. LUCY HALL,[8] b. Nov. 2, 1829.

515   VIII. WILLIAM HENRY,[8] b. Nov. 28, 1831. Married, but wife's name
not obtained.

Children.

1. Henry C., m. Amelia Lugden, of Middletown, 1877.
2. John H., m. Clarissa Alice Zimmerman, at Dodge City, Kan., 1884.
3. Richard Gerard, m. Annie Whitney, of Cambridge, Mass., 1886.
4. Mary E., m. F. L. Kelsey, Middletown, Conn., 1884.
5. Wesley B.

IX. GEORGE ATWOOD,⁸ b. Oct. 22, 1833; d. June 13, 1856.

263.

CAPT. DAVID DICKINSON ⁷ CHURCHILL (DAVID,⁶ JOSEPH,⁵ JOHN,⁴ NATHANIEL,³ JOSEPH,² JOSIAH ¹). Born at Chatham, Conn., Jan. 31, 1800. He died Aug. 21, 1844. Married, July 21, 1831, ESTHER PATTEN PAYNE, daughter of John and Hannah (Hall) Payne, of Portland, Conn.

Children.

I. JULIA MARIA,⁸ b. Sept. 12, 1833; d. Oct. 18, 1844.
II. WILLIAM PAYNE,⁸ b. April 19, 1835; d. Dec. 1, 1835.
III. ELLA,⁸ b. Jan. 15, 1837.
IV. MARGARET,⁵ b. April 10, 1839.
V. ELIZABETH,⁸ b. June 28, 1841; d. Aug. 28, 1846.
VI. DAVID DICKINSON,⁸ b. April 16, 1844; d. Dec. 23, 1873.

264.

GEORGE ⁷ CHURCHILL (CAPT. DAVID,⁶ JOSEPH,⁵ JOHN,⁴ NATHANIEL,³ JOSEPH,² JOSIAH ¹). Born at Chatham, Conn., Sept. 26, 1805. He followed the sea, and was captain of the ship "Bingham," in 1832. The home was at New London, Conn. He died Dec. 16, 1840, at sea. Married, August, 1830, SARAH PECK, daughter of Lyman and Betsey (Mason) Peck, of New London, born Dec. 5, 1807; died July 12, 1837.

Children born at New London.

I. ELIZABETH PECK,⁸ b. February, 1832; d. May 10, 1833.
II. SARAH ELIZABETH,⁸ b. Jan. 1, 1834; d. June 28, 1861.
516 III. HENRY LYMAN,⁸ b. Aug. 26, 1836; m. EMMA V. LATIMER, Sept. 17, 1862, at New London, Conn.
Mr. Churchill served as acting assistant engineer in the U.S. Navy, on the U.S. warship "Memphis," in 1862, and also in 1864-1865 on the gunboats "Port Royal," "Monongahela," and "Circassian." He died March 16, 1874.

Children of Henry L. and Emma V. (Latimer) Churchill.

1. Franklin Peck, b. March 13, 1864.
2. Ellen Bartlett, b. Dec. 1, 1866; d. Dec. 19, 1868.
3. Harry Latimer, b. Jan. 24, 1869; d. Feb. 25, 1869.
4. May Hall, b. Aug. 7, 1872; d. March 26, 1877.

265.

EBENEZER DELOS ⁷ CHURCHILL (EBENEZER,⁶ BENJAMIN,⁵ DANIEL,⁴ NATHANIEL,³ JOSEPH,² JOSIAH ¹). Born in Sherburne, N.Y., Feb. 11, 1822. His father died when he was six weeks

EBENEZER DELOS CHURCHILL.
(No. 265, page 470.)

old, and his mother married a second husband, who was so cruel to him that when he was eight years old he left his home and went away among strangers, where he suffered many privations, but managed to get on and work his way, and get some schooling, until about fifteen he found some good friends in the family of Elias Ward, of Gloversville, N.Y., with whom he lived as a son, until he was twenty-one years old. His Churchill kindred supposed that he was dead, but some property title requiring proof, his uncle, Charles Churchill, of Utica, after a long search, found him engaged in glove-making, and now grown to be a tall and sturdy young man. He was soon established in his uncle's office and lumber business at Utica. Later he became a purchasing agent for the firm, and located at Vienna, Can., for a time. His Uncle Charles, his good friend and a noble man, died in 1850; but Mr. Churchill still remained purchasing agent till 1857, when he removed with his family to Madison, Wis. They lived there for nine years. Mr. Churchill built and operated a gristmill near Madison for several years, but in 1866 removed, with several of his friends and their families of Madison, to Chenoa, Ill., then a small hamlet, but located at the crossing of two thriving railroads, and a fertile and promising spot. He resumed his old business of lumber dealing for a few years, then engaged in the grain business, in which he prospered, and has built up to extensive proportions, in which now his sons, grown up and educated at school and college, are his partners. He is a public-spirited and widely influential citizen. He is a liberal and loyal member of the Presbyterian Church in Chenoa, helpful in many local charities, "a self-made man" in the best sense of that much abused phrase. Married, Oct. 2, 1849, HANNAH LEMOYNE ATKINS, born Jan. 13, 1832.

Children, first three born at Vienna, Can.

I. ANNA ELIZABETH,[8] b. July 17, 1850; unmarried.

517 II. CHARLES FORDYCE,[8] b. Nov. 29, 1852; m. LORA M. ELDER, Oct. 19, 1876.
She was born Aug. 10, 1857. Married in Bloomington, Ill.

Children of Charles F. and Lora M. Churchill.

1. Lena Lemoyne, b. May 20, 1878.
2. Edward Delos, b. Jan. 18, 1881; d. July 30, 1882.
3. Harriet Josephine, b. Aug. 3, 1884.
4. Guy Fordyce, b. May 18, 1886.

518 III. EBENEZER DELOS, JR.,[8] b. Oct. 23, 1854; m. MARIA A. FARNS-WORTH, June 12, 1879.
She was born Nov. 15, 1854. Married at Sheboygan, Wis.

Children of Ebenezer D. and Maria A. Churchill.

1. Frank Hebert, b. Oct. 17, 1881.
2. Clarence Farnsworth, b. Aug. 17, 1891.
3. Edward Fordyce, b. Dec. 25, 1895.

519   IV. Francis Lemoyne,[8] b. Feb. 11, 1860, in Madison, Wis.; m. Lillie
A. McDowell, April 5, 1893.
She was born June 22, 1866.

Children of Francis Lemoyne and Lillie A. Churchill.

1. Fred Weaver, b. May 12, 1896.
2. Woodford McDowell, b. Oct. 23, 1897.
3. James Delos, b. Jan. 15, 1899.
4. Mildred, b. Dec. 11, 1901.

266.

DR. ALONZO[7] CHURCHILL (Selden,[6] Daniel[5] Daniel,[4]
Nathaniel,[3] Joseph,[2] Josiah[1]).   Born at Richfield, N.Y., Jan.
20, 1811.   Educated at Richfield Public School, Fairfield Academy, Albany Medical School, Bellevue, N.Y.   Surgeon in Tenth
Regiment, N.Y. Volunteers, in the Civil War.   Held the largest
medical and surgical practice in Utica, and was surgeon in
all the principal hospitals of Utica.   He represented Utica in the
Legislature in 1867.   He was six feet one inch in height, and
weighed two hundred and ten pounds.   He died at Utica, N.Y.,
Dec. 28, 1896.   Married, at Richfield, N.Y., Feb. 10, 1834, Jane
Morgan, daughter of Walter and Delia Leach (Derbyshire) Morgan.

Children.

I. Charlotte Jane,[8] b. Jan. 20, 1842, in Richfield; m. James
Edward Carmalt, at Utica, Sept. 9, 1865.
He was the son of Caleb and Sarah (Price) Carmalt.   They lived
at Glenburn and Morton, Penn.

Children born at Morton, Penn.

1. Dr. Churchill Carmalt, b. June 15, 1866.
Educated at the Utica Public Schools, Scranton, Penn., Private
School, Harvard Coll., A.B. Columbia University.   Surgeon,
N.Y. City.
2. William Kelley Carmalt, b. 1867; d. 1871.
3. Raymond Walter Carmalt, b. 1868; d. 1869.
4. Sarah Price Carmalt, b. July 3, 1870; m. Theodore Starr,
Utica, Feb. 10, 1901.
5. James Walter Carmalt, b. Oct. 24, 1872.

II. Emma Derbyshire,[8] b. at Cherry Valley, N.Y., 1850; unmarried.
In January, 1897, she was living in Utica, in the old home.

267.

DANIEL[7] CHURCHILL (Selden,[6] Daniel,[5] Daniel,[4]
Nathaniel,[3] Joseph,[2] Josiah[1]).   Born at Richfield, N.Y.   The
information about this family is very scant.   Of Daniel's half sisters
we learn that Lucretia married a Henry (————), and Adelaide
married Rev. Austin Craig.   He married Mary Elmina Hull.

Children.

I. Selden A.[8]
II. Alfred D.[8]

269.

GEORGE CLARENCE[7] CHURCHILL (ALFRED,[6] DANIEL,[5] DANIEL,[4] NATHANIEL,[3] JOSEPH,[2] JOSIAH [1]). Born in Utica, N.Y. April 14, 1829. He is a lawyer at Utica, N.Y. He has been much interested and very helpful in the account of his line of the Connecticut branch. Married, in Utica, March 20, 1861, ANNIE SEDGWICK BRAYTON, of Utica.

Children born at Utica.

I. ALFRED,[8] b. Feb. 6, 1862; d. Nov. 11, 1863.
II. ANNIE BRAYTON,[8] b. Oct. 30, 1863.
III. GERTRUDE EMMA,[8] b. Jan. 7, 1866; d. Jan. 30, 1869.
IV. GEORGE BRAYTON,[8] b. July 5, 1868; d. Sept. 24, 1868.
V. ISABELLA,[8] b. July 25, 1870; d. Aug. 6, 1882.

270.

CHARLES GILBERT[7] CHURCHILL (JAMES,[6] ELIJAH,[5] GILES,[4] SAMUEL,[3] JOSEPH,[2] JOSIAH [1]). Born in Stamford, N.Y., Dec. 2, 1817. Married RUTH P. ACKLEY.

Children.

I. ELIJAH P.[8]
   In 1901 he was living in Prattsville, N.Y.
II. MILLA FRANCES,[8] m. WILMOT RICHTMYER, Bristol, Cónn.
III. LYDIA AUGUSTA,[8] m. JOHN SMITH.
   They live at Cairo, N.Y.
IV. MARY ELIZABETH,[8] m. 1st, FRED CLARK, who died; m. 2d, DAVID BEEBE.

271.

GEORGE[7] CHURCHILL (JAMES,[6] ELIJAH,[5] GILES,[4] SAMUEL,[3] JOSEPH,[2] JOSIAH [1]). Born in Stamford, N.Y., March 2, 1830. Married SARAH FULLER.

Two Children.

I. JOHN.[8]
   In 1901 was living in Stamford, N.Y.
II. CHILD,[8] name not received.

272.

ANDREW LIVINGSTON[7] CHURCHILL (JAMES,[6] ELIJAH,[5] GILES,[4] SAMUEL,[3] JOSEPH,[2] JOSIAH [1]). Born in Stamford, N.Y., Feb. 6, 1833. Lived in Stamford, N.Y., on a farm of one hundred and fifty acres, with the summer boarding house (noted below). In 1885 he was the proprietor of the summer hotel, the Cold Spring House, at Stamford, N.Y. Married, Jan. 4, 1855, AMELIA ACKLEY.

Children born in Stamford, N. Y.

I. MARY EVA,[8] b. 1858; deceased.
II. JULIA ADELAIDE,[8] b. 1865.
III. ELIZA BELL,[8] b. 1868; deceased.
IV. FREDERICK H.,[8] b. 1872; m. (———) (———).
   In 1901 lived in Stamford.

273.

ADDISON JESSE[7] CHURCHILL (James,[6] Elijah,[5] Giles,[4] Samuel,[3] Joseph,[2] Josiah[1]). Born in Stamford, N.Y., May 1, 1836. Lived for a time in Durham, then at Prattsville, N.Y.; but later located in New York City, where he was, in 1902, proprietor of Hotel St. George, on Broadway and Twelfth street. Married, Jan. 18, 1856, Mary Elizabeth Houghtaling, b. July 28, 1839; daughter of John Staats and Mary Ann (Fiero) Houghtaling.

Children of Addison J. and Mary E. (Houghtaling) Churchill.

520   I. John Staats,[8] b. in Durham, N.Y., Dec. 7, 1859; m. Katharine Gilfillian, April 19, 1893.

    II. Mary Elizabeth,[8] b. at Prattsville, N.Y., Oct. 23, 1861; m. Emory A. Chase, June 30, 1885. He was born Aug. 31, 1854.

Children.

1. Jesse Churchill Chase, b. Jan. 13, 1887.
2. Albert Woodworth Chase, b. April 30, 1890.

521   III. Frank G.,[8] b. in Prattsville, Jan. 19, 1863; m. Nellie Gilfillian, Oct. 19, 1887.

522   IV. James E.,[8] b. in Prattsville, June 11, 1868.

274.

WILLIAM M.[7] CHURCHILL (Giles,[6] Elijah,[5] Giles,[4] Samuel,[3] Joseph,[2] Josiah[1]). Born in Middlefield, Mass., April 18, 1816. We have obtained very little in regard to the children of Giles Churchill. We learn from a brief letter from his son, James H. Churchill, of Springfield, written March 23, 1885, that his father was then living in New York, but he gave no further account of the family, nothing of his mother or other children of his parents except to say that he had a brother in the Civil War, and gives his own name. So the record stands.

Children.

    I. William M.,[8] b. May 24, 1844; served in Company G, Tenth Massachusetts Volunteers, and d. March 3, 1863.

    II. James H.,[8] served three years in Civil War in Company G, Thirty-first Regiment, Massachusetts Volunteers.

James H. adds that his uncle, Elijah Lyman Churchill, "lives in Middlefield on the old homestead, aged sixty-six years," and a letter from Elijah L. himself, March 23, 1885, gives the names of his grandfather and father, but nothing more, and he does not say whether he is married or not.

275.

STEPHEN GILES[7] CHURCHILL (Dr. Stephen G.,[6] Stephen,[5] Giles,[4] Samuel,[3] Joseph,[2] Josiah[1]). Born in Concord, N.Y., Aug. 30, 1817. Married, 1840, Margaret Widrig.

Children.

523   I. HARRISON TYLER,[8] b. March 10, 1841; m. SUSAN E. SEAVEY in 1866.

Children.

1. Harold. | 2. Bertha. Lives in Wisconsin.

II. LEWIS MILTON,[8] b. Dec. 27, 1842; d. young.
III. GEORGE MILTON,[8] b. March 19, 1844; d. young.
524 IV. CLARK EUGENE,[8] b. Oct. 24, 1847; m. ELLA L. FERRIN, Dec. 9, 1873, at Springville, N.Y. He was postmaster of Arcade, N.Y., in 1901.
V. MARCUS GILES,[8] b. Dec. 8, 1850; d. young.
VI. EMMA EMMELINE,[8] b. Dec. 13, 1853; m. CHARLES WOODWARD, in 1879. They live in Wisconsin and have two children.
VII. FLORA G.,[8] b. Feb. 20, 1861; m. ALBERT WELLS, 1885. They live in Wisconsin, and have two children.

276.

MARCUS B.[7] CHURCHILL (DR. GILES,[6] STEPHEN,[5] GILES,[4] SAMUEL,[3] JOSEPH,[2] JOSIAH [1]). Born in Concord, N.Y., Nov. 9, 1825. Lived in Concord nearly all his life, but later in Springville, N.Y., where he died Dec. 5, 1897. Married, Dec. 24, 1849, AMANDA VAN CAMP, who was born in Onondaga County, N.Y., June 30, 1832, and died in Springville, N.Y., Feb. 21, 1896.

Children born in Concord, N.Y.

I. LIBBIE,[8] b. Jan. 27, 1853; m. J. F. CLARK, June 3, 1874.
525 II. CHARLES W.,[8] b. July 24, 1859; m. JENNIE L. ADAMS, Jan. 1, 1878. They lived in Springville, N.Y., in 1891.

Children.

1. Charlotte A., b. in Springville, Dec. 8, 1881.
2. Warren H., b. in Springville, Sept. 1, 1888.

III. EMMA,[8] b. April 2, 1861; m. J. S. WIDRIG, May 1, 1879.

278.

NEWCOMB GAYLORD[7] CHURCHILL (SAMUEL,[6] STEPHEN,[5] GILES,[4] SAMUEL,[3] JOSEPH,[2] JOSIAH [1]). Born in Meredith, N.Y., Sept. 22, 1823. Lived in Springville, N.Y., in 1888. A letter, dated at Springville, N.Y., April 30, 1888, was written for him, "per Alta L. Churchill," but gives no account of any children. Married, May 13, 1851, THIRZA S. GATES, of Bennington, N.Y.

279.

SAMUEL STODDARD[7] CHURCHILL (SAMUEL,[6] STEPHEN,[5] GILES,[4] SAMUEL,[3] JOSEPH,[2] JOSIAH [1]). Born at Meredith, N.Y., Aug. 18, 1827. Married 1st, March 29, 1851, EMILY DRUMMOND. Married 2d, Dec. 10, 1857, LOUISA J. GATES, b. June 27, 1825.

Children of First Wife.

I. SARAH ALICE,[8] b. July 25, 1852; m. GEORGE RUSSELL, Dec. 23,
1872.

Children.

1. Agnes May Russell, b. May 25, 1874.
2. Frank L. Russell, b. July 21, 1887.

II. ESTHER HELEN,[8] b. June 1, 1856; m. EUGENE FARRINGTON, Nov. 16,
1887.

Children of Second Wife.

526   III. FREDERICK E.,[8] b. Sept. 13, 1859; m. ABBIE D. SANFORD. They
lived at Osborne Hollow.
527   IV. AUGUSTUS,[8] b. Dec. 4, 1860; m., Nov. 27, 1884, ADDIE M. CATOR,
b. Oct. 14, 1862. They lived at Osborne Hollow, N.Y.

Child.

1. Louisa M., b. Jan. 19, 1889.

528   V. JOSEPH TRACY,[8] b. Dec. 22, 1863; m. MAGGIE A. REYNOLDS, b.
Aug. 22, 1862. They lived at Osborne Hollow, N.Y., in 1889.
No children.

282.

EPENETUS W.[7] CHURCHILL (DEA. ELIJAH,[6] STEPHEN,[5] GILES,[4]
SAMUEL,[3] JOSEPH,[2] JOSIAH[1]). Born in Harpersfield, N.Y., Aug. 25,
1833. Married, June 1, 1863, ANNA WILCOX.

One Child.

I. ALICE.[8]

283.

SAMUEL SUMNER[7] CHURCHILL (AMOS,[6] JOSEPH,[6]
SAMUEL,[4] SAMUEL,[3] JOSEPH,[2] JOSIAH[1]). Born at Hubbardton, Vt.,
Nov. 26, 1800. He was a farmer and wool grower, and lived at
Pittsford, Vt. He was industrious and economical, and starting
with only his good health and courage, and an excellent wife, to
whom he was married at the age of twenty, he succeeded in winning
a fair competency in the rugged hills of Vermont, reared a family
of ten children to strong and self-reliant manhood and womanhood.
The mother of this family was a typical New England wife and
mother of an earlier day, wise, strong, and capable. She spun,
wove, and made the garments her children as well as herself and
her husband wore, and taught her daughters the same home arts.
Both Mr. and Mrs. Churchill were highly respected in their community. He was deacon in the Baptist Church in Hubbardton,
and died Jan. 23' 1845. The mother died in Sudbury, Vt., Jan. 8,
1862, aged fifty-nine years and six months. Married, March 22,
1820, MARY RICHARDSON, Hubbardton, Vt., where she was born,
June 15, 1802.

Children born at Pittsford, Vt.

I. MARY,[8] b. Dec. 27, 1820; m. at Hubbardton, May 2, 1843, CHAUNCEY WASHINGTON BROUGHTON, of Brandon, Vt., who was b. July 22, 1813.

They settled in Brandon.

He was a miller by occupation, until he removed, in 1844, from Brandon to Kaneville, Ill., where he was among the first settlers to take up a section of public land. By dint of hard work and great sacrifice he accumulated a large property, and, in 1854, sold out and removed to Fayette, Iowa, but next year he returned to Illinois and settled in DeKalb County, where he bought a large tract of land and built a fine house, and here they spent the rest of their days. She died in DeKalb County, Ill., May 4, 1860. Mr. Broughton m. for his second wife, his wife's sister Caroline, the eighth child of S. S. C., *q. v.*

One child born at Brandon, Vt.

1. Charles Preston Broughton, b. Feb. 23, 1844; m. Etta Beers, Dec 22, 1875.

He grew up in the new country on the farm, but received an excellent education. In December, 1867, he started out for himself and bought a large tract of land in Allen County, Kans., but in 1871 returned to assist his father in the management of his extensive farms in Illinois. In 1877 he removed to Lee's Summit, where he bought a large tract of land, and became one of the most prosperous and wealthy farmers of that region.

One child, (1) Chauncy Preston, b. Feb. 24, 1890; d. June 6, 1890.

II. ELIZABETH,[8] b. April 28, 1822; m. FRANKLIN WARD, of West Rutland, 1841. He was the son of Aaron and Olive (Southworth) Ward.

They lived for a time on the old Churchill homestead, as he was appointed administrator under the will of his wife's father, but after 1850 became manager of slate quarries in West Rutland and Fairhaven, Vt, but in 1856 he sold out and purchased a dairy farm in Oswell, Vt., where he spent the rest of his life. Mrs. Ward was well educated at Brandon Seminary, and was a successful teacher. She died June 15, 1859.

Children.

1. Adelaide J. Ward, b. Oct. 10, 1842; m. Hiram B. Scott, Sept. 4, 1866.
2. Helen Ward, b. 1843; d. in infancy.
3. Annette Ward, b. Jan. 24, 1845; m. William E. Thorp.
4. Evaline, b. July 16, 1853; d. February, 1854.
5. Emaline, b. July 16, 1853; d. Dec. 17, 1866.

III. JOHN BOWER PRESTON,[8] b. Feb. 4, 1824; d. Dec. 25, 1844.

He was a fine and promising young man, with bright hopes and a brave future.

IV. SYLVIA,[8] b. May 29, 1826; m. FAYETTE HOLMES, eldest son of Pliny and Vesta (Caldwell) Holmes, and a descendant of Governor Bradford of the Plymouth Colony, it is said.

They lived in Hubbardton, and later in Sudbury, Vt., where he had a large sheep farm, until 1898, when he removed to Joliet, Ill., where he continued the business, and next year went to Russell, Kan. She d. in Denver, Aug. 19, 1894.

Children born in Hubbardton and Sudbury, Vt.

1. Julia Sylvia Holmes, b. July 10, 1849; m. Hiram Smith, Aug. 11, 1874.

They settled at Cameron, Mo., where he was a lawyer with good practice.

Two children: (1) Sherman Edwin Smith; (2) Fayetta Lois Smith.

2. **Willard Clay Holmes**, b. Nov. 8, 1851; m. Harriet M. Amidon, of Whiting, Vt.

They live in Gibbon, Kan. He is engaged in sheep raising. Five children: (1) Louie R. Holmes; (2) Robert W. Holmes; (3) Florence S. Holmes; (4) Howard R. Holmes; (5) Cora L. Holmes.

3. **Carry Mary Holmes**, b. Oct. 16, 1853; m. Albert Smith, at Russell, Kan., July 16, 1884.

She was an invalid nearly all her life. They removed to Denver, where she died Aug. 12, 1894.

4. **Cora Elizabeth Holmes**, b. Nov. 14, 1860, at Sudbury, Vt.

She was a fine scholar and a natural teacher. She was for many years the patient and loving nurse of her mother and sisters, and later she became a trained nurse in Joliet, Ill. Un married.

V. **Louisa**,[3] b. Jan. 14, 1828; m. CHARLES E. WARD, of West Rutland, Vt., April 25, 1848.

She was ambitious and resolute, and gained an excellent education, and began teaching school at sixteen years. Mr. Ward was born in West Rutland, March 3, 1824. They settled first on a farm in West Rutland, but, in 1852, removed to DeKalb County, Ill., and took up a farm on new land. Two years afterward he sold out his farm and bought out a large saw and planing mill, in which he carried on a thriving business for some twenty-three years, when the whole plant was burned, and though his loss was very severe, he built up again within a year, and resumed business. He was a trusted and influential citizen. He died Sept. 4, 1877. His widow was living in Joliet in 1901.

Children born in Joliet, Ill.

1. **Abbie Churchill Ward**, b. Feb. 14, 1855; m. Ferdinand W. Schroeder, at Joliet, July 31, 1883.

They lived at Joliet, and had six children: (1) Charles Ward Schroeder, b. May 8, 1884; (2) Helen Theresa Schroeder, b. June 6, 1886; (3) Pearl F. Schroeder, b. May 10, 1888; (4) Raymond Churchill Schroeder, b. July 6, 1889; (5) Glen Wilson Schroeder, b. Oct. 11, 1891; (6) Lloyd Schroeder, b. Feb. 7, 1898.

2. **Cora Louisa Ward**, b. Jan. 19, 1860; m. Joseph Handwerk, at Joliet, Sept. 6, 1882.

He is a prosperous hardware merchant in Joliet. They have no children.

3. **Frank Emerson Ward**, b. April 8, 1866; m. Alice Sandiford, at Joliet, Ill., April 17, 1899.

He is professor of mechanics and superintendent of the machine shops at the Kansas State University, Lawrence, Kan. They have three children: (1) Charles E. Ward; (2) Dorothy Sandiford Ward; (3) Winifred Emily Ward.

4. **Ralph Rollo Ward**, b. June 12, 1870; m. Alma Rogers, at Syracuse, Kan., Dec. 24, 1895.

He graduated at Park College, Mo., June 8, 1893, and from McCormick Theological Seminary in 1896. Ordained to the Presbyterian ministry at Albion, Ind., where he preached till 1898. In 1902 he is pastor of the church at Arkansas City, Kans. No children reported.

VI. **Alzina Maria**,[3] b. Jan. 20, 1830; m. GEORGE C. KNAPP, at Castleton, Vt., Sept. 6, 1855.

Mrs. Knapp's life has been varied and full of deep interest. Inspired with a desire for an education more than the common schools afforded, she was left fatherless at the age of fifteen, but fitted herself for teaching in the home schools, and began at the age of

seventeen years. Thus enabled to attend Castleton Seminary,
where, in the last half of her graduating year, a fall on the ice disabled her for near two years. Her class standing was maintained,
however, and, on recovery, she returned to Castleton Seminary as
a teacher. There, Sept. 6, 1855, she married Rev. Mr. Knapp, and
with him went to Turkey to share his labors as a missionary.
They were settled in Bitlis, Armenia, the pioneers in this benight-
ed city. They remained forty years in the work there, the last
fifteen years devoted to a training school for young men fitting for
Christian teachers and preachers. Mr. Knapp died in Bitlis,
March 12, 1895, and in 1896 Mrs. Knapp returned to America,
but leaving a son and daughter still working as missionaries in
Turkey. Mrs. Knapp now lives in Colorado Springs, Col., 1901.

Children born in Bitlis, Armenia.

1. Arthur Churchill Knapp, b. Nov. 8, 1859; d. Oct. 18, 1862.
2. Mary Elizabeth Knapp, b. Feb. 23, 1861; d. Oct. 16, 1863.
3. George Perkins Knapp, b. June 13, 1863; m. Anna J. Hunt,
   July 2, 1890.
   He worked as a missionary teacher in Armenia, and in 1901
   was in Harpoot, Turkey, with his family, after a sojourn of a
   few years in America. Their children, born in Bitlis, are:
   (1) Winifred Hunt Knapp, b. March 8, 1892; (2) Addison
   Ely Knapp, b. Nov. 2, 1894; (3) Margaret Washburn Knapp, b.
   Sept. 7, 1896.
4. John Herbert Knapp, b. Oct. 24, 1865; m. Helen Hastings, of
   Colorado Springs.
   He was sent to America to receive his education; became a
   civil engineer, and located at Colorado Springs, where he was
   living in 1901. Children: (1) Agnes Churchill Knapp, b. Oct.
   24, 1892; (2) Charlotte Hastings Knapp, b. April 2, 1894; (3)
   Helen Louisa Knapp, b. Dec. 22, 1895. Mrs. Helen Knapp, the
   mother, died Aug. 6, 1896.
5. Grace Higley Knapp, b. Nov. 21, 1870.
   She remained in Bitlis, Armenia, as a missionary teacher,
   when her mother came back to America.
6. Edith Alzina Knapp, b. Nov. 4, 1874.
   She came to America when quite young, and was educated in
   Joliet, Ill., and Massachusetts. She lived with her brother
   Herbert and her mother in Colorado Springs, in 1901. A teacher
   of fine ability.

VII. SARAH LUCINDA,[6] b. Jan. 14, 1832; m. JAMES RODNEY PEARSON,
      at Joliet, Ill., Nov. 21, 1855.
      She was born in Pittsford, Vt. She acquired a good education in
      the home schools and Brandon Seminary. She was a fine singer.
      She went to Joliet, Ill., in 1854, to visit her sister's family; met
      there Mr. Pearson, and was married as above noted. He was born
      in Rutland, Vt., April 27, 1830, and went to Joliet in 1854. He
      was foreman in the planing-mill of C. E. Ward for about twenty-
      three years. He removed to Lee's Summit, Mo., and settled on a
      farm adjoining his wife's brother, S. J. Churchill, in 1867, but in
      1872 moved back to Joliet, where he was living in 1901.

Children of J. R. and Lucinda (Churchill) Pearson.

1. Charles Royce Pearson, b. Sept. 11, 1858, at Joliet, Ill.; m.
   Nellie E. Porter, at Joliet, July 15, 1878.
   He received a good education. He became an engineer.
   They have children: (1) Clara Louisa Pearson, b. April 15,
   1879; (2) George Edward Pearson, b. March 3, 1880; (3) Will-
   iam Nutt Pearson, b. Sept. 22, 1882; (4) Royce Eugene
   Pearson, b. March 7, 1884.

    2. Fred William Pearson, b. May 20, 1866, at Joliet, Ill.; m.
Jennie Johnson, in Joliet, Ill., Jan. 25, 1884.

    He was captain of Company B, of Illinois National Guard,
Fourth Infantry, and with his company, May 7, 1898, joined the
army, in the Third Regiment, Illinois Volunteers. They served
in the Spanish War, and his regiment was assigned to service in
Porto Rico until Nov. 11, 1898. Children: (1) Charles Harold
Pearson, b. Aug. 21, 1887; (2) Fred Richard Pearson, b. March
26, 1889.

VIII. CAROLINE COOK,[8] b. March 23, 1838; m. CHAUNCEY W. BROUGH-
TON, whose first wife was Caroline's oldest sister, with whom she
had lived in Illinois from eight years old to sixteen. She then
returned to Vermont, and lived with her sister Sylvia, and taught
school until she was sent for to care for Mrs. Broughton in her
last sickness, and after her death, May 4, 1860, she married Mr.
Broughton, in Joliet, Ill., Jan. 30, 1861, as his second wife, and
he who had been a kind father to her in her girlhood was now
a devoted husband. They had five children, and she died two
days after the birth of her fifth child, May 27, 1871.

Children.

    1. William A. Broughton, b. Feb. 18, 1863; d. Jan. 6, 1866.
    2. Ella Broughton, b. Jan. 26, 1865; m. John Woods, Jan. 30, 1895.
They had children: (1) Carrie May Woods; (2) Addie Mary
Woods; (3) Ruth Ella Woods; (4) Alta Rose Woods.
    3. May Broughton; b. May 7, 1867; m. J. J. Kingsley, in Joliet,
Ill.
They lived in DeKalb, on a farm.
    4. Judson K. Broughton, b. April 18, 1869; d. Oct. 26, 1869.
    5. Ben. Broughton, b. May 25, 1871; m. Alice Belle Cleveland,
in Carlton, Ill.
They lived on a farm at Lake View, Iowa. They have one
child, Lois Marie Broughton, b. Feb. 22, 1897.

  IX. ROXANNA,[8] b. at Hubbardton, Vt., March 27, 1841; m. MORTON J.
KINNEY, of Hydeville, Vt., Nov. 16, 1859.

    She received a good education at the home schools and at Bran-
don Seminary. She taught school very successfully. She died
June 16, 1866, leaving no children.

529   X. SAMUEL JOSEPH,[8] b. in Hubbardton, Vt., Nov. 1, 1842; m. 1st,
ADELIA HOLMES, at Sudbury, Vt., May 4, 1864. She died at
Pleasant Hill, Kan., March 31, 1877, and he m. 2d, at Council
Grove, Kan., Aug. 4, 1879, LOUANA GRANT, b. Feb. 26, 1844, at
Cooperstown, N.Y.

    Mr. Churchill's father died when he was two years old, and his
early life was full of hardships, and his school privileges very limited. At fourteen he started out for himself, and soon made better
opportunities by his own exertions. In August, 1861, he enlisted
as private in Battery G, Second Illinois Light Artillery, and took
part in the battle of Fort Donaldson, and afterwards in the important campaigns under Generals Grant and Logan, in Tennessee and
Mississippi. His battery was among the first to enter Vicksburg,
July 4, 1863. Mr. Churchill reënlisted in April, 1864, and receiving his "veteran furlough," returned to his old home in Sudbury,
Vt., and married the girl of his choice, to whom he was engaged in
1860. He returned to his battery, then at Memphis, Tenn. He
was promoted to a corporal's rank, and served with distinction in
his place to the close of the war; participated in nineteen battles,
and at Nashville won a medal of honor from the government for
gallant conduct. Mr. Churchill has prepared an interesting sketch
of his own line of the Churchill family, in which he gives a very
full account of his services in the war, and of his subsequent very
creditable career. The limits of this volume will not admit of a

more full account, but will refer to the book which he published in
1901, pertaining to his own immediate line. Mr. Churchill was an
excellent soldier, and since the war has proved himself a strenuous
and honorable citizen. In 1901 he was living in Lawrence, Kan.,
and occupies a place of high honor in the Grand Army of the Re.
public.

Children of Samuel J. and Adelia (Holmes) Churchill.

1. Adelia May, b. June 1, 1867; m. Alva Leslie Sloan, Nov. 7,
   1890, in Portland, Ore.   She graduated at the Kansas State
   University with high rank, and was a successful teacher.   Mr.
   Sloan was an inspector and assistant engineer on the Santa Fé
   System of Railroads.
   They have two children: (1) Winifred Newlin Sloan, b. Dec.
   25, 1891; (2) Della Marion Sloan, b. Dec. 7, 1893.
2. Frank Holmes, b. Sept. 8, 1868; d. in Lawrence, Kan., Jan. 18,
   1891.
3. Estella Maud, b. Feb. 26, 1870; d. Aug. 9, 1870.
4. Winifred Grace, b. July 23, 1873; m. James Owen, Nov. 5, 1896,
   in Lawrence, Kan.   Mr. Owen is a lawyer, with a large practice at Cripple Creek, Col.
   They had Margaret Owen, b. July 25, 1899.
5. Lena Blanche, b. Oct. 12, 1874; d. July 8, 1898, after three
   years of hard struggle against disease, painful at times, but
   borne with fortitude and patience.   She was finely educated;
   a promiseful and precious life.

284.

DEACON ISAAC NEWTON [7] CHURCHILL (Amos,[6] Joseph,[5]
Samuel,[4] Samuel,[3] Joseph,[2] Josiah [1]). Born in Hubbardton, Vt.
July 7, 1805.   Lived in his native town until after the death of his
father and the settling up of the estate, when he sold out and
bought a farm near Fairhaven, Vt., but just across the State line,
in the borders of New York.   He was a farmer and well-to-do, a
deacon in the Baptist Church, a good and benevolent man.   He
died Jan. 14, 1892.   He held the valuable manuscripts of his father's
historical notes, and I find several letters from him written in 1891,
in answer to questions from our senior compiler, N. W. Churchill,
who, I think, visited him in that year.   Married Margaret Ann
Perry in 1832.

Children.

531   I. Milton Perry,[8] b. March 15, 1833; m. 1st, Emma E. Cutts, Oct.
      4, 1860, who d. without issue Jan. 29, 1864; and he m. 2d, Abbie
      Perry, of Canton, N.Y., Oct. 17, 1864.
      They lived on a farm near Fairhaven, Vt.   The old manuscripts
      of his grandfather Amos were in his possession.

Children by Second Wife.

1. Corianna, b. July 10, 1865; d. in 1867.
2. Jay, b. 1871; d. the same year.

II. Eliza Ann,[8] b. Dec. 5, 1841; d. April 20, 1858.

285.

ALFRED[7] CHURCHILL (WORTHY L.,[6] JOSEPH,[5] SAMUEL,[4] SAMUEL,[3] JOSEPH,[2] JOSIAH[1]). Born in Hubbardton, May 8, 1800. Removed with his father's family to Batavia, N.Y., 1802, and was brought up there. He died Oct. 8, 1868, in Illinois. Married, September, 1821, at Batavia, N.Y., SUSAN D. WILSON, born Sept. 24, 1800. She died Aug. 4, 1867.

Children.

I. FAYETTA,[8] b. at Batavia, June 16, 1824; m. DAVID HANCHETT, Nov. 28, 1848, at Kaneville, Ill.

Children.

1. Louisa C. Hanchett.
2. Alfred P. Hanchett.
3. William H. Hanchett.
4. Francis G. Hanchett.
5. Charles S. Hanchett.
6. John Lovell Hanchett.
7. James Churchill Hanchett.

Mrs. Fayetta Hanchett was living at La Porte City, Iowa, January, 1894.

II. ELIZA Y.,[8] b. May 21, 1828, at Stafford, N.Y.; m. SAMUEL HOUGH, March 12, 1861, at King's Point, Mo., and d. at Astor, Iowa, Feb. 18, 1904.

Children.

1. Fayetta R. Hough. | 2. May Emma Hough.

III. DELIA S.,[8] b. Oct. 22, 1831, at Stafford; m. GILBERT BARBER, Oct. 2, 1857, at Rockford, Ill., and d. at Rutland, Vt., Feb. 26, 1873.
IV. SUSAN D.,[8] b. Jan. 12, 1833, at Colesville, N.Y.; d. at Batavia, June 29, 1850.
V. FANNIE L.,[8] b. July 6, 1835, at Warrensville, Ill.; m. OTTO GERSTING, of St. Paul, Minn., Dec. 18, 1861.
She was living in St. Paul, in March, 1899.
VI. EMMA,[8] b. Sept. 15, 1839, at Geneva, Ill.; m. JOHN BARBER, at Kaneville, Ill., June 4, 1865.

Children.

1. Agnes Barber. | 2. Clara Barber.

286.

JOSEPH WHELPLEY[7] CHURCHILL (WORTHY L.,[6] JOSEPH,[5] SAMUEL,[4] SAMUEL,[3] JOSEPH,[2] JOSIAH[1]). Born in Hubbardton, Vt. Nov. 15, 1801. Removed in his infancy, with his father's family, to Batavia, N.Y., and brought up on the then frontier of the United States. He was able to secure a college preparation, and graduated at Middlebury College, and studied law with Gen. Ethan B. Allen, and settled down to a successful practice of his profession in Batavia. In 1838 Mr. Churchill moved West, and settled in Kane County, Ill., at a place which he named Batavia, after his home in New York. Here he practised for sixteen years, serving several terms in the Legislature with Douglas and Lincoln, and other leaders of that day, with all of whom he was on terms of intimate comradeship.

He was successful and popular, but in 1854, having lost the use of one eye, he decided to give up the practice of the law, and to turn to stock-raising, in which his father had formerly engaged quite extensively. He moved to Davenport, Iowa, and opened a law office, however, and practised until 1864, when he removed to Bremer County, Iowa, opened up a farm and did well for four years, then sold out and moved back to Scott County, and settled on a farm in Pleasant Valley, until 1882, when he moved back to Davenport. Mr. Churchill was a man of thorough education, strict integrity, and great natural ability. He died at Davenport, Oct. 2, 1884. Married, in Batavia, Sept. 29, 1829, DELIA S. WILSON, born in 1808.

Children of Joseph W. and Delia (Wilson) Churchill.

    I. GEORGIA D.,[8] b. May 3, 1836; unmarried,

531a   II. WORTHY L.,[8] b. Dec. 14, 1839 ; m. MILLIE MONTGOMERY, of Chicago, 1866.

Child.

    1. Florence, b. 1876.

531b III. HOBERT D.,[8] b. Feb. 15, 1848; m. ELLEN HYDE, of Pleasant Valley, Iowa, 1875.

Child.

    1. Howard Lee, b. 1879.

287.

JAMES W.[7] CHURCHILL (WORTHY L.[6] JOSEPH[5] SAMUEL,[4] SAMUEL,[3] JOSEPH,[2] JOSIAH[1]). Born in Stafford, N.Y., April 8, 1814. He received a good education at the home schools and at Wyoming Academy. He was a successful school teacher in the winter terms of the public schools, and also a prosperous farmer. In 1852 he removed with his family to Lake Mills, Wis., where he resided until his death. He was an excellent scholar and much respected citizen and beloved friend. Married, at Bethany, N.Y., 1843, VIENNA THOMPSON, of Norwich, Conn.

Children born in Stafford, N.Y.

    I. MARY VIENNA,[8] b. Dec. 3, 1844; m. at Madison, Wis., REV. JOHN LANGDON DUDLEY, of Milwaukee, Wis., Oct. 15, 1872. He died in Boston, Mass., about 1896. They had no children. Mrs. Dudley is well known in the literary world, under the pseudonym, Marion V. C. Dudley, and in March, 1899, was at Jackson, Fla.

    II. MARTHA JANE,[8] b. Jan. 4, 1850; m. JULIUS HYDE KEYES, of Watertown, Wis., Oct. 25, 1873. He d. about 1892, at Eau Claire, Wis.

Children of J. H. and Martha J. (Churchill) Keyes.

    1. Donald Churchill Keyes, b. Jan. 6, 1882.

    2. Dudley Hyde Keyes, b. Dec. 17, 1883.

        In 1899 Mrs. Keyes was living with her sons, at Madison, Wis.

288.

JOSEPH THOMAS HUSTLER[7] CHURCHILL (CYRUS,[6] JOSEPH,[5] SAMUEL,[4] SAMUEL,[3] JOSEPH,[2] JOSIAH[1]). Born in Hub bardton, Vt., Dec. 28, 1815. Removed with his father's family to Ypsilanti, Mich. He left home in early manhood and went to Wisconsin, where he engaged in the lumber business for some years. At Oconto Falls he helped to construct the first saw-mill built on the Oconto river, where he was living in 1845, and to which place he had come from Chicago, by boat, to Kewanee, Wis., and thence through the forests, by way of Green Bay. After his marriage he removed to the banks of the Wisconsin river, to the vicinity of Steven's Point, in the central part of the State, and here, for a time, engaged in lumbering. In 1848, in the fall, he removed to St. Louis, floating down the Wisconsin and Mississippi rivers on a lumber-raft, with his household goods, his wife, and eldest son. From St. Louis he went to Beardstown, Ill., and thence, soon after back to his old home, Ypsilanti, Mich. Thence, after a short stay, he, in company with his brother Lewis, removed to Brockway, Mich., and settled upon a tract of land in the woods, cleared up a farm which after four years they sold, and removed to Grand Traverse, Mich., where they lived for a year and then moved again to Kaneville, Ill., whence after a few months they went to Green Bay, Jan. 1, 1858, and have lived in that vicinity ever since.

These experiences of one of the sturdy pioneers, as kindly furnished me by his son Robert H., give a picturesque view of the indomitable energy and persistence of the early New Englanders, who planted the West with the pregnant seeds of the New Puritan civilization. Mr. J. T. H. Churchill was still living (1901) at Abrams, Oconto County, Wis., in hale and hearty old age. Never prominent in political or ecclesiastical matters, he had for many years been a consistent member of the Baptist Church, and a public-spirited and useful citizen. Married, at Oconto Falls, Wis., Dec. 20, 1845, HARRIET (HUBBARD) ARNOLD, widow of John. She was born July 25, 1819, and died Dec. 18, 1881.

Children of J. T. H. and Harriet (Hubbard) Churchill.

532   I. ROBERT HAZARD,[8] b. on the banks of the Wisconsin river, not far from Steven's Point, Wis., April 10, 1847, and shared the hardships and novelties of the family's removals from place to place. He learned the business of machinery manufacture in the Marinette Iron Works Company, and in 1894 set up in the saw-mill machinery and mill supply business for himself, in which he was still prosperously engaged in 1903. Mr. Churchill has been greatly interested in the genealogy of the Churchill family, and has made a diligent search in his own line, and has furnished us with all information in his power. Married AMANDA AMELIA

MOORE, at Marinette, Wis., April 14, 1874. She was born at
Manitowoc Rapids, Wis., Sept. 18, 1850. Both Mr. and Mrs.
Churchill are respected members of the First Baptist Church in
Marinette, and active members in the cause of temperance.

Children of Robert H. and Amanda (Moore) Churchill.

1. Arthur Moore, b. Sept. 5, 1876.
2. Myron Robert, b. Sept. 9, 1879.
3. Sarah Harriet, b. Aug. 29, 1881.
4. Florence Ethel (adopted), b. April 27, 1887.

II. HASWELL B.,[8] b. at Ypsilanti, Mich., Oct. 24, 1850. He was living
in Marinette, unmarried, in 1902.
III. LUDROVICK M.,[8] b. at Brockway, Mich., June 15, 1852; m. SARAH
JANE VAUGHN, Jan. 13, 1878. She was born Jan. 13, 1855.

Children of Ludrovick and Sarah (Vaughn) Churchill.

1. Alen H., b. June 26, 1879.
2. Eva L., b. April 18, 1881.
3. Amy L., b. May 28, 1883.
4. Harold B., b. Feb. 21, 1886.
5. Robert R., b. March 21, 1888.
6. Myrtle C., b. April 27, 1890.
7. Loyal M., b. Sept. 12, 1892.
8. Laura S., b. Nov. 27, 1894.
9. Harriet S., b. March 27, 1899.

IV. EVELINE ELIZABETH,[8] b. at Brockway, Mich., July 31, 1856; m.
GEORGE A. WILSON, Oct. 19, 1882. They lived, in 1902, at
Abrams, Wis. They had no children.
V. ANGELINE A.,[8] b. at Fort Edward, Wis., June 15, 1858; m. SAMUEL
A. WOOD, July 23, 1887; d. March 5, 1889, leaving no children.

291.

JULIUS[7] CHURCHILL (DANIEL,[6] JOSEPH,[5] SAMUEL,[4] SAMUEL,[8]
JOSEPH,[2] JOSIAH[1]). Born in Edwards County, Ind., Dec. 20, 1820.
Settled at Cold Spring, Ind., where he took up land and made a
farm, beginning with nothing except his hands, his courage, and
integrity ; he gained a competency and a high position in his community, for his upright dealing and honorable character. He was
devoted to his family, and especially so in the training and education of his daughters, by whom he was beloved as few fathers have
been. At the time of his death he left a fine farm in perfect order,
and well-stocked, besides a handsome personal property. In early manhood he was for years a teacher in the public schools. This account
of the family was furnished by Mrs. Alice Churchill Huntington, of
Moore's Hill, Ind., and shows conditions up to Dec. 14, 1902. Married, at Cold Spring, Ind., 1842, PIRELLA M. FALKNER, daughter of
Cornelius and Lucinda (Halsted) Falkner.

Children born in Cold Spring, Ind.

I. ANN JEANNETTE,[8] b. Dec. 11, 1843; m. GEORGE C. COLUMBIA, May
10, 1877.
They lived in Sparta some years, where three children were born
to them, the two eldest of whom died. Mr. Columbia was appointed

recorder for Dearborn County, Ind., and removed to Lawrenceburg, where Mrs. Columbia died, Oct. 26, 1881. One daughter, Emma Columbia, survived her mother. She was born in 1879, and resided in Lawrenceburg.

II. HARRIET S.,[8] b. Dec. 30, 1845; m. J. L. SHEPARD, Oct. 18, 1868, at Cold Spring, Ind. They lived awhile at Cold Spring, but later removed to Booth, Kan.

Children born at Cold Spring.

1. Stella Shepard, m. Charles McMurray, at Hutchinson, Kan.
2. George M. Shepard, married, and lives at Hutchinson, Kan.
3. Irving Shepard, lives unmarried at Booth, Kan.

III. MARY H.,[8] b. Jan. 11, 1847; d. July 24, 1849.

Children.

1. Margaret Bossong, b. 1879; m. Charles Robinson, Moore's Hill, 1901.
2. Churchill Bossong, b. Jan. 12, 1886.

IV. LYDIA FRANCES,[8] b. Jan. 28, 1849; m. JOSEPH M. BOSSONG, Cold Spring, Oct. 27, 1875. They lived at Cold Spring, Ind., where he was a farmer.

V. SARAH L.,[8] b. Jan. 24, 1852; m. MILTON EVANS, Dec. 25, 1878. Lived at Cold Spring.

Children.

1. Minnie Evans, d. in infancy.
2. Benjamin Evans, b. about 1882.

VI. ALICE C.,[8] b. Jan. 13, 1854; m. G. W. HUNTINGTON, Dec. 27, 1878. They live at Moore's Hill, Ind., and have had no children.

292.

JOHN RANSOM[7] CHURCHILL (ALVAH,[6] JOSEPH,[5] SAMUEL,[4] SAMUEL,[3] JOSEPH,[2] JOSIAH[1]). Born at Sparta, Ind., Dec. 3, 1821. He served two years in the war with Mexico. Died July 12, 1853. Married Jan. 1, 1852, at Delaware, Ind., SARAH MAYHEW, of Maine, daughter of James and Mira (Allen) Mayhew.

One Child born in Delaware, Ind.

533   I. WILLIAM HOLMES,[8] b. Oct. 20, 1853, m. 1st, ANNA BELLE DENLEY, Oct. 28, 1884; m. 2d, ANNA JONES, at Kansas City, Apr. 30, 1902. They lived at Kansas City, Mo. (1904), and he was a railroad conductor.

Children.

1. Charles L., b. Sept. 18, 1885; m. Gertrude Frisby, at Fort Scott, Kan., Dec. 15, 1901.
2. Henry Edward, b. Aug. 22, 1887.
3. Clifford Notman, b. Nov. 6, 1889.
4. Willis Ransom, b. Feb. 27, 1903.

293.

CHARLES C.[7] CHURCHILL (JOSEPH,[6] JOSEPH,[5] SAMUEL,[4] SAMUEL,[3] JOSEPH,[2] JOSIAH[1]). Born in Sparta, Ind., June 24, 1825 and lived there till 1862, when he settled in Benville, Ind. He was proprietor of a saw-mill. He died from the effects of an accident, a heavy log having rolled upon him, injuring his spine, Feb. 13, 1872. Married 1st, Dec. 25, 1847, MARTHA HUSTIN, who died July 5, 1849, and he married 2d, Jan. 29, 1850, MARY A. HINDS, daughter of James and Mary (Brumbly) Hinds.

Child of First Wife.

I. INFANT,[8] d. soon after birth.

Children of Second Wife, five born at Sparta, the rest at Benville, Ind.

II. MARY J.,[8] b. Dec. 6, 1853; m. JOHN W. JONES, at Benville, Ind., Oct. 22, 1873.
    She died at Spring Creek, Mo., Dec. 26, 1900, leaving seven children, but we have not obtained the names.

III. ANNIE F.,[8] b. June 18, 1855; d. at Benville, Ind., March 12, 1860.

IV. SARAH ANGELINE,[8] b. Feb. 27, 1857; m. EDWARD P. DELAY, Jan. 1, 1879, at Benville, Ind.
    He was the son of Thomas and Keturah (Cupples) Delay. They lived at New Marion, Ind., where he was a farmer.

Children.

1. Rosa A. Delay, b. Nov. 27 1879.
2. Lenora B. Delay, b. March 19, 1881.
3. Nellie F. Delay, b. June 30, 1884.
4. Emma G. Delay, b. May 3, 1886.
5. Thomas V. Delay, b. June 5, 1888.
6. Martha G. Delay, b. June 3, 1890.
7. Charles F. Delay, b. May 27. 1894.
8. Claudia Carmen Delay, b. July 28, 1900, and died Aug. 22, 1900.
    Two other children were born, but died in infancy unnamed.

V. NETTIE F.,[8] b. Feb. 15, 1859; d. Aug. 2, 1861, at Benville, Ind.

IV. EMMA C.,[8] b. April 6, 1860; m. CHARLES R. ADAMS, April 7, 1880.
    They lived at Benville and Connersville, Ind., and had children.

Children.

1. Minnie Isabel Adams, b. Feb. 1, 1881.
2. Clara Mabel Adams, b. Aug. 27, 1882.
3. Cora Esther Adams, b. Sept. 24, 1887.
4. Edna Florence Adams, b. Feb. 16, 1895.

VII. CHARLES J.,[8] b. Oct. 20, 1862.

VIII. GEORGE C.,[8] b. March 10, 1865; accidentally killed at his father's mill, April 12, 1869.

534 IX. HENRY T.,[8] b March 20, 1867; m. 1st, ELIZABETH STEVENS, of Moore's Hill, Ind., Nov. 30, 1886; m. 2d, ELLEN SMITH, of West Lake, La., Sept. 26, 1900. Lived at West Lake, La., in 1902.

One Child by First Wife.

1. Laura M., b. at Connersville, Ind., May 25, 1889. Lived there, unmarried, in 1902.

535 X. MORTON C.,[8] b. at Connersville, May 8, 1869; m. ELLEN SHELDON, of Marble Corner, Ind., June 12, 1892.
    They lived at Connersville and Rexville, Ind., where he was a farmer. They had children.

Children.

1. Goldie L., b. at Connersville, Nov. 11, 1894.
2. Wildie G., b. at Rexville, Dec. 14, 1900.

XI. MARTHA L.,[8] b. March 31, 1872; m FRANK X. WILLERT, Conners ville, June 17, 1894. They lived in Connersville in 1902.

Children.

1. John J. Willert, b. Aug. 16, 1895; d. aged four weeks.
2. Charles V. Willert, b. March 30, 1900, and d. Sept. 28, 1900.

294.

GEORGE VERNON [7] CHURCHILL (Joseph,[6] Joseph,[5] Samuel,[4] Samuel,[3] Joseph,[2] Josiah [1]). Born in Sparta, Ind., Nov. 20, 1832. Lived at Moore's Hill, a farmer. Prof. J. O. Churchill and Mrs. Delay have assisted greatly in compiling the account of this family. Married, at Wilmington, Ind., Nov. 25, 1852, Emily Davis, daughter of Noah and Sallie (———) Davis.

Children born at Moore's Hill.

  I. Edgar F.,[8] b. Sept. 27, 1853; unmarried. He was a stenographer at Moore's Hill, in 1887.
536 II. Frank D.,[8] b. March 13, 1855; m. Emma C. Edwards, dau. of Rev. A. C. Edwards.
      He was educated at Franklin College, Indiana. In 1887 he was superintendent of public schools in Aurora, Ind. He died at Oakland City, Ind., 1893.
537 III. James O.,[8] b. Jan. 23, 1857; m. Minnie Russell, dau. of Rev. A. W. and Martha (Buchanan) Russell, of Cheyenne, Wyo., June 7, 1887.
      He was educated at the public schools and Moore's Hill College, Indiana. They lived at Cheyenne. He is superintendent of City Schools, and secretary of State Board of Examiners, and trustee of State University.

Children born in Cheyenne.

1. Vernon, b. 1888. | 2. Emily, b. 1891.

  IV. Eva,[8] b. July 23, 1859. Living unmarried at Moore's Hill in 1887.
   V. Fannie,[8] b. June 6, 1863; m. O. E. Remy, Oct. 17, 1883, and d. July 24, 1886. No children reported.
  VI. Mary,[8] b. Oct. 4, 1864; m. J. E. Schooley. They lived at Moore's Hill, Ind. No children reported.
538 VII. Noah F.,[8] b. Sept. 14, 1869; m. Sadie Slater, 1888. He was a farmer near Moore's Hill, Ind. No children reported.

295.

JOHN F.[7] CHURCHILL (Joseph,[6] Joseph,[5] Samuel,[4] Samuel,[3] Joseph,[2] Josiah [1]). Born in Sparta, Ind., Aug. 21, 1847. He was an engineer and lived in Osawatomie, Kan. Married, January, 1870, Anna Garner. Said to have had a family of three children, but we have not the names.

295a.*

ALMOND [7] CHURCHILL (Philo,[6] Samuel,[5] Samuel,[4] Samuel,[3] Joseph,[2] Josiah [1]).

* We refer to Almond [7] Churchill, son of No. 112, in order to make some additions and corrections from new information just received, after pages 397 to 399 were in print. This information comes from Enos [8] Churchill, son of Zenas,[7]

295h.

ENOS[7] CHURCHILL (ZENAS,[6] SAMUEL,[5] SAMUEL,[4] SAMUEL,[3] JOSEPH,[2] JOSIAH [1]). Born in Erie County, N.Y., Oct. 14, 1828. Removed West in early life, and lived in Cortland, De Kalb County Ill. Served in the Civil War, in Company F, Thirteenth Regiment Illinois Volunteer Infantry, with rank of sergeant. Lived in Illinois. Sometime after 1866 he removed to California, and settled for awhile at Hollister, and later at Stockton, where he was living January, 1904. Married 1st, in Cortland, Ill., Sept. 29, 1850, OLIVE ANN MEEKER, who died June 1, 1860, in Illinois. Married 2d, in De Kalb County, Ill., Aug. 26, 1866, ASENATH O. WILMARTH, who died at Stockton, Cal., Aug. 29, 1903.

Children of First Wife, born in Illinois.

I. FLORETTA T.,[8] b. March 8, 1855; m. M. M. BURNETT, at Hollister, Cal., March 20, 1872.

---

and now resident in Stockton, Cal. The name of the wife of Philo Churchill, No. 112, was Sally Castle, and his children were as given on page 398, except the second was named Thaddeus C., and a fifth child was Julia. These five children, it is said, lived and died in Alexander, N.Y., where the widow of Thaddeus C. was living, the last my informant heard. He gives the family of Zenas Churchill, his father, which I will include in this note, referring to No. 113. ZENAS[6] CHURCHILL was born March 12, 1784; married ALMIRA CASTLE, Nov. 29, 1805. She was born in Rutland County, Vt., Oct. 4, 1785.

Children of Zenas[6] and Almira (Castle) Churchill.

295d   I. DAVID,[7] b. in Rutland, Vt., Oct. 12, 1806; m. MARIA PARKER, and had Hanmer D. and Jasper Churchill; and David, the father, d. March 2, 1854, on the Isthmus of Panama.

II. ANN,[7] b. April 5, 1808; m. HARVEY ANDREWS, in Erie County, N.Y., and d. in Tulare County, Cal., July 4, 1883.

III. SALLY,[7] b. in New York, Feb. 5, 1810; m. HARRIS BURBECK, and d. in Iowa, Nov. 27, 1875.

295e   IV. CASTLE,[7] b. Aug. 12, 1813; m. 1st, PATTY CROSSETT; m. 2d, CAROLINE SMITH; left one daughter, and d. in Tulare County, Cal., Sept. 14, 1885.

295f   V. DANIEL,[7] b. New York, Feb. 20, 1815; m. ANTOINETTE JOSLYN, and d. in De Kalb County, Ill., Oct. 13, 1844, leaving one daughter.

VI. ANGELINE,[7] b. New York, Nov. 28, 1817; m. MARCENAS HALL. Living, in 1904, in Oklahoma.

295g   VII. ZENAS, JR.,[7] b. New York, Nov. 2, 1819; m. MARION PARKER, and d. in San Benito, Cal., Feb. 3, 1897. Children: (1) Herman, m. Bertha Imbley; (2) David; (3) Ella M., m. J. M. Slinkhard.

VIII. ALMIRA,[7] b. New York, Nov. 17 1821; m. ELIAS- HARTMAN, and d. Dec. 20, 1902.

IX. MALINDA M.,[7] b. New York, Feb. 6, 1823; d. April 1, 1825. (Two children died in infancy.)

295h   XII. ENOS,[7] b. in Erie County, N.Y., Oct. 14, 1828. (See in proper order.)

N.B. The five sons of Zenas take the numbers 295d to 295h. The name of the wife of RUFUS[7] CHURCHILL (115) was LOIS STRONG. They had one child, Andrew, who served in the Civil War, in the One Hundred and Fifth Illinois Regiment, and was killed in the army by the kick of a mule. Rufus and wife lived with Elvira Sherwin, their niece, near Cortland, Ill., and died there. DAVID[6] CHURCHILL (114) died Aug. 14, 1860, and his wife, SARAH, died Oct. 26, 1872.

538a II. FRANK B.,[5] b. Aug. 26, 1859; m. 1st, LEONA BAGLEY; m. 2d, SUE BAINTER.

Children.

1. Clyde.
2. Leland.

3. Raymond.

Child of Second Wife, born at Hollister, Cal.

III. CAROLINE M.,[8] b. Nov. 13, 1870; d. July 11, 1892.

296.

GEORGE W.[7] CHURCHILL (DAVID,[6] SAMUEL,[5] SAMUEL,[4] SAMUEL,[3] JOSEPH,[2] JOSIAH[1]). Born at Attica, N.Y., April 20, 1833. He was a carpenter; learned the trade of his uncle, Timothy Churchill, but later became a machinist of note and ability and a millwright. He served in the Civil War over three years, Company K, Sixty-fifth Regiment Illinois Volunteers. Served under General Sherman in Georgia. They lived at Sycamore, Ill. He died May 25, 1894. Married, in Cortland, Ill., March 11, 1866, ADDIE E. WILLIAMS, born at Plymouth, N.Y., May 1, 1846. She was the daughter of Rev. Benjamin S. and Eunice M. (Wood) Williams. She, with her mother, were living in Sycamore, Ill., November, 1903, and aided this account.

Children.

I. CORA E.,[8] b. Sept. 21, 1867, in Cortland, Ill.; m. LECONTE MORRIS, at Sycamore, Ill., Dec. 25, 1898. They lived at Traverse City, Mich. Children: (1) Cornelia E. Morris; (2) Bertha B. Morris. Mr. Morris is a jeweller.
II. MERRITT,[8] b. June 10, 1869, at Sycamore, Ill.; d. Oct. 6, 1870, at Sycamore, Ill.
III. BERTHA A.,[8] b. May 7, 1871, at Sycamore, Ill. Living in Sycamore, unmarried, November, 1903, in the old home, with her mother and her aged grandmother Williams.
539 IV. GEORGE PAUL,[8] b. Nov. 18, 1875, at Sycamore, Ill.; m. BESSIE LEACH, at Sycamore, Dec. 25, 1899. They live at Sycamore. He is in the telephone business. One child: George Byron Churchill.

297.

MARQUIS DE LAFAYETTE[7] CHURCHILL (DAVID,[6] SAMUEL,[5] SAMUEL,[4] SAMUEL,[3] JOSEPH,[2] JOSIAH[1]). Born in Attica, N.Y., Feb. 8, 1835. They lived in Pampas township, Ill. He died March 13, 1865. Married, at Pampas township, at same time and place as his sister Esther, July 1, 1855, MARY JANE CAMPBELL.

Children born in Pampas, Ill.

I. ELLA FLORENCE,[8] b. June 28, 1858.
540 II. DAVID JAY,[8] b. Oct. 31, 1860.
541 III. GEORGE E.,[8] b. Sept. 8, 1864.

298.

OSCAR C.⁷ CHURCHILL (DAVID,⁶ SAMUEL,⁵ SAMUEL,⁴ SAMUEL ³ JOSEPH,² JOSIAH ¹). Born March 4, 1837. He served in the Army of the Cumberland, in the Civil War, in the Twentieth Corps, Third Division, First Brigade, under Gen. Benjamin Harri son and Gen. Joseph Hooker, commanding corps. Mr. Churchill lived in Albany, Ore., a hotel keeper. Married, July 9, 1870, MRS. MARY (BAKER) DUNBAR, at Sycamore, Ill.

Children.

542   I. FLOYD K.,⁸ b. in Republic County, Kan., Feb. 27, 1872; m. LAURA STARR, Salem. Ore., August. 1894.
   II. ESTELLA,⁸ b. in Republic County, Kan.; m. PROF. W. M. SMITH, Salem, Ore.
542a   III. RICHARD C.,⁸ b. in Republic County, Kan., Jan. 23, 1877; m. JULIA W. PERRY, Salem, Ore., April 29, 1901.
542b   IV. WALTER E.,⁸ b. in Humeston, Iowa, 1879; m. ETHEL RICHEY, 1903, at Albany, Ore.
542c   V. FRANK E.,⁸ b. in Humeston, Iowa, 1882.
543   VI. HOWARD E.,⁸ b. in Salem, Ore.

299.

MENZO ⁷ CHURCHILL (DAVID,⁶ SAMUEL,⁵ SAMUEL,⁴ SAMUEL,³ JOSEPH,² JOSIAH ¹). Born Dec. 13, 1843, in Pampas township, Ill. He lived in Liberty and Summit, Kan., and in St. Catharine, Mo. He helped us very greatly in his own and his father's family record in 1889, having the old Bible record. Married, at Liberty, Kan., Nov. 3, 1870, SARAH VIOLETTA CLARK, born in Cedar Rapids, Ia.

Children.

   I. ELMER ELLSWORTH,⁸ b. Feb. 17, 1872, in Liberty, Kan.
   II. NELLIE MAUD,⁸ b. Feb. 24, 1874, in Liberty, Kan.
544   III. NORMAN LESTER,⁸ b. March 11, 1876, in Liberty, Kan.
   IV. SILVIA GERTRUDE,⁸ b. July 1, 1878, in Liberty, Kan.; d. Feb. 6, 1879.
545   V. ARTHUR NUD,⁸ b. Jan. 1, 1880, in Liberty, Kan.
   VI. LAURA MAY,⁸ b. May 15, 1882, in Liberty, Kan.
   VII. VERNA BELL,⁸ b. May 8, 1884, in Summit, Kan.
   VIII. AMANDA,⁸ b. May 13, 1886, in St. Catharine, Mo.; d. Oct. 20, 1886.
546   IX. EARL,⁸ b. March 23, 1888, in St. Catharine, Mo.

302.

DANIEL ⁷ CHURCHILL (SYLVESTER,⁶ JOHN,⁵ SAMUEL,⁴ SAMUEL,³ JOSEPH,² JOSIAH ¹). Born in Portland, N.Y., July 16, 1820. Lived at Portland and Westfield, N.Y., and died in 1896. He was a farmer. Married, at Westfield, N.Y., 1841, JULIA HOUSE, daughter of David and Nabby House.

Children born at Portland, N. Y.

547   I. LEROY,⁸ b. 1842; m. NANCY JANE WALKER.
   II. AMY R.,⁸ b. 1848; d. June 19, 1867.
   III. LILLIE M.,⁸ b. 1853; m. JOHN VANBERG, at Portland, 1890.

303.

LEVI[7] CHURCHILL (Sylvester,[6] John,[5] Samuel,[4] Samuel,[3] Joseph,[2] Josiah [1]). Born at Portland,.N:Y., Dec. 21, 1822. They lived in Chardon, O. Married; at Manson, O., Oct. 8, 1851, Sarah A. Hintston.

Child.

I. Sarah J.,[8] m. Mr. Sanders, and was living at Munson, O., and wrote us July 20, 1901, but gave no information about her father's or her own family, except that Levi Churchill was her father.

304.

ORVILLE[7] CHURCHILL (Alvin,[6] John,[5] Samuel,[4] Samuel,[3] Joseph,[2] Josiah.[1]). Born July 3, 1829. Married, Mary Jane Rigles.

Children.

548 I. Adelbert.[8]
II. Francella.[8]
III. Ella.[8]
549 IV. Miles.[8]
V. Harriet.[8]

305.

SAMUEL LYMAN[7] CHURCHILL (Alvin,[6] John,[5] Samuel,[4] Samuel,[3] Joseph,[2] Josiah [1]). Born in Scott, N.Y., Feb. 15, 1834. He lived in Spafford, N.Y., and was a farmer and cooper. Married 1st, April 27, 1858, Mary A. (Alvord) Randall, born in Decatur N.Y., May 6, 1827; died April 6, 1862. Married 2d, July 11, 1862, at Florence, N.Y., Harriet A. Russell, born July 25, 1843.

Child by First Wife.

550 I. Seymour L.,[8] b. Jan. 5, 1861.

Children by Second Wife.

551 II. Jason C.,[8] b. April 13, 1863.
552 III. Abraham L.,[8] b. Aug. 9, 1866.
553 IV. Irving L.,[8] b. May 24, 1871.
V. Mary V.,[8] b. May 7, 1873.
554 VI. Ernest M.,[8] b. Feb. 26, 1875. He served in the war with Spain, Third Missouri Regiment. Graduated at Wesleyan University; professor in Canfield College, Owatoma, Mo.
VII. Martha V.,[8] b. Jan. 8, 1877; d. June 3, 1882.
VIII. Alice May,[8] b. July 14, 1884.

306.

JOHN W.[7] CHURCHILL (Chauncy,[6] John,[5] Samuel,[4] Samuel,[3] Joseph,[2] Josiah [1]). Born at Scott, N.Y., Aug. 13, 1836. Educated in district school. Removed and settled a farm at Long View, Champaign County, Ill., in 1859. Married 1st, at Raymond, Cham-

SYLVANUS CHURCHILL,
TULA, N.Y.
(No. 307, page 493.)

paign County, Ill., April 13, 1871, ALICE P. MARTINIE, daughter of
David and Mary (Triplet) Martinie. She died Aug. 1, 1886. Married 2d, March, 1890, CATHERINE WATSON.

Children born in Raymond, Champaign County, Ill.

I. MARY C.,[8] b. May 26, 1872; m. H. B. STEVENS, at Philo, Ill., September, 1892.
They lived, 1899, on the old Churchill homestead, at East Scott,
N.Y. They have four children. Names not given.
555   II. CHARLES F.,[8] b. Jan. 1, 1876.
556   III. ETHELBERT C.,[8] b. Jan. 23, 1882.

307.

SYLVANUS A.[7] CHURCHILL (CHAUNCY,[6] JOHN,[5] SAMUEL[4]
SAMUEL,[8] JOSEPH,[2] JOSIAH [1]). Born at Scott, Cortland County, N.Y.
Nov. 26, 1839. Educated in the common schools and the acad
emy at Homer, N.Y., and lived in his native town, a farmer. Married 1st, Nov. 22, 1867, CAROLINE EADIE, died Sept. 2, 1888. She
was the daughter of John and Abigail (Doty) Eadie. Married 2d,
Sept. 7, 1892, SARAH ERMINNIE WOODWORTH, daughter of Cyrenus
and Charlotte (Manton) Woodworth.

Children born at East Scott, N.Y.

557   I. HERMAN,[8] b. Oct. 9, 1869; m. CORA FRENCH, June 15, 1898, at
Menominie, Wis.
Herman Churchill attended the public schools until fourteen years
of age, then graduated at Homer Academy, in 1887, and from Syracuse University with degree of A.B., in 1894, member of Phi Beta
Kappa Society. Mr. Churchill has been a successful teacher in
several of the high grade schools in New York and Wisconsin, and
in the Madison, Wis., High School, but for several years has
spent his summers in postgraduate work at the universities of Wisconsin and Chicago. He received A.M. from University of Wisconsin, 1902, and is now (1904) instructor in North Western
University

They have One Child.

1. Irving Lester Churchill, b. at Madison, Wis , April 9, 1901.

II. EDITH,[8] b. Aug. 20, 1875.
558   III. EADIE,[8] b. Aug. 20, 1875; m. MAY S. CROSLEY, Dec. 4, 1902, and
have one

Child.

1. Doris May, b. Oct. 5, 1903.

Children of Second Wife.

559   IV. SYLVANUS W.,[8] b. July 14, 1894.
560   V. LEO,[8] b. April 29, 1896.
VI. GLADYS ERMINNIE,[8] b. May 8, 1902.

308.

OLIVER CLINTON [7] CHURCHILL (CHAUNCY,[6] JOHN,[5] SAMUEL,[4] SAMUEL,[3] JOSEPH,[2] JOSIAH [1]). Born at Scott, N.Y., March 22, 1841. He was educated at public schools and at Homer Academy, N.Y. Served in the Union Army in the Civil War. Lived at Homer, N.Y., where he was a grocer. Married, at Preble, N.Y., Oct. 26, 1865, DELPHINE ROE.

One Child, born at Homer, N. Y.

I. ALICE LOUISE,[8] b. Oct. 1, 1872.

309.

LAFAYETTE M.[7] CHURCHILL (CHAUNCY [6] JOHN,[5] SAMUEL,[4] SAMUEL,[3] JOSEPH,[2] JOSIAH [1]). Born at Scott, N.Y., March 17, 1846. Educated in the common schools. Married, at Preble, N.Y., March 9, 1870, ELIZA PRATT, daughter of Orrin and Ruth E. (Capron) Pratt.

Children.

       I. CHARLES P.,[8] b. in Scott, N.Y., June 6, 1871; d. at Raymond, Ill., Aug. 21, 1880.
561   II. LESLIE M.,[8] b. in Scott, N.Y., March 6, 1873.
      III. CATHARINE A.,[8] b. in Scott, N.Y., May 21, 1875; m. CLARENCE WILLIAMS, Dec. 24, 1894, in Philo, Ill.
      IV. OLIVE C.,[8] b. in Raymond, Ill., March 19, 1880; m. ROYAL COLE, June 20, 1899, at Philo, Ill.
      V. RUTH E.,[8] b. in Raymond, Ill., July 17, 1882.
562   VI. MELVIN C.;[8] b. in Raymond, Ill., Sept. 26, 1885.
563   VII. CLINTON S.,[8] b in Raymond, Ill., Dec. 10, 1888.
      VIII. HELEN A.,[8] b. in Raymond, Ill., April 5, 1891.

310.

CALEB WASHINGTON [7] CHURCHILL (CHAUNCY,[6] JOHN,[5] SAMUEL,[4] SAMUEL,[3] JOSEPH,[2] JOSIAH [1]). Born at Scott, Cortland County, N.Y., Nov. 27, 1850, and has lived there, a farmer, since. That part of Scott is now (1899) Tula, his post-office address. He was educated in the public schools and at Homer Academy, N.Y. Married 1st, at Spafford, N.Y., March 28, 1871, ACHSAH EADIE, daughter of John and Abigail (Doty) Eadie. Married 2d, Nov. 6, 1884, MINNIE A. BROWN, in Champaign County, Ill.

First Wife's Children, born in South Spafford.

564   I. WILLIE J.,[8] b. Dec. 8, 1872.
      II. BERTHA EUPHEMIA,[8] b. Oct. 11, 1874.
565   III. FLOYD LEROY,[8] b. Jan. 8, 1878.

Children of Second Wife, born at Tula, N. Y.

      IV. ACHSAH MINNIE,[8] b. March 27, 1886.
566   V. ARCHIBALD CALEB,[8] b. March 9, 1888.

PROF. HERMAN CHURCHILL.

(No. 557, page 493.)

567   VI. NEIL S.,[8] b. Aug. 21, 1889.
    VII. BLANCHE ELIZABETH,[8] b. Jan. 12, 1891.
    VIII. NELLIE KATE,[8] b. Dec. 25, 1892.
    IX. LULA MARGARET,[8] b. June 19, 1895.
568   X. HAROLD LINSLEY,[8] b. June 1, 1897.

311.

BENJAMIN FRANKLIN[7] CHURCHILL (CHAUNCY,[6] JOHN,[5] SAMUEL,[4] SAMUEL,[3] JOSEPH,[2] JOSIAH[1]). Born at Scott, Cortland County, N.Y., July 30, 1852, educated in the public schools, lived at Onondaga Valley, N.Y. He was a grocer and postmaster, town clerk, and member of the school board of the town. Married, at Spafford, N.Y., May 21, 1878, CARRIE CHURCHILL, daughter of James.

Children.

    I. ETHEL ANN,[8] b. June 24, 1879.
    II. HELEN MAY,[8] b. July 14, 1883.
569   III. LEON BENJAMIN,[8] b. June 30, 1888.

312.

JASON M.[7] CHURCHILL (CHAUNCY[6] JOHN,[5] SAMUEL,[4] SAMUEL,[3] JOSEPH,[2] JOSIAH[1]). Born in Scott, N.Y., April 2, 1855. Completed his education in Homer Academy, N.Y. Taught school several terms. Settled after marriage at Philo, Champaign County, Ill. A farmer. Married, Sept. 25, 1878, at Spafford, N.Y., JENNIE E. FRENCH, daughter of Jason C. and Emily (Rice) French.

Children born at Raymond, Ill.

    I. LOTTIE J.,[8] b. June 26, 1880.
    II. AGNES E.,[8] b. Nov. 21, 1884.
570   III. EUGENE J.,[8] b. at Crittenden, Ill., April 3, 1892.

313.

GEORGE[7] CHURCHILL (DARIUS,[6] WILLIAM,[5] SAMUEL,[4] SAMUEL,[3] JOSEPH,[2] JOSIAH[1]). Born in Champlain, N.Y. March 22, 1818. Died March 30, 1875. We have obtained no facts in regard to Mr. Churchill's residence or occupation. Married, Feb. 13, 1842, LOUISA JANE JACKSON, born at Peru, N.Y., Sept. 10, 1819, daughter of Israel and Esther (Allen) Jackson, of Plattsburgh, N.Y. She died in South Bombay, N.Y., April 11, 1885.

Children.

    I. WALLACE,[8] b. Nov. 15, 1842. He enlisted in the army and died in
        the service in the Civil War, at New Orleans, July 30, 1864.
    II. RUSSELL,[8] b. Sept. 18, 1844; m. ABBIE KIRBE, Nov. 5, 1877. They
        lived at Burlington, Vt.
    III. CAROLINE,[8] b. Nov. 23, 1845; m. JONAS PHELPS, Oct. 15, 1874.
        They lived in South Bombay, N.Y.

IV. TRYPHENIA A.,⁸ b. March 12, 1847; d. Aug. 15, 1858.
 V. MARY E.,⁸ b. May 13, 1849; m. ALEXANDER JOHNSTON, Nov. 18
    1869. They lived in Helena, N.Y.
VI. LYDIA A.,⁸ b. Oct. 16, 1851; m. FRANK YADOW, Oct. 26, 1889.
    They lived at South Bombay, N.Y.
VII. PHEBE E.,⁸ b. May 16, 1853; m. 1st, BETHUEL ALLEN, April 12,
    1876; m. 2d, ALLEN DRAPER, in 1895. They lived in Philadel-
    phia, N.Y.
VIII. ESTHER J.,⁸ b. Aug. 28, 1855; d. Aug. 25, 1870.
IX. THERESA A.,⁸ b. June 8, 1858; d. Dec. 13, 1877.

314.

SAMUEL⁷ CHURCHILL (DARIUS,⁶ SAMUEL,⁵ SAMUEL,⁴ SAM-
UEL,³ JOSEPH,² JOSIAH ¹). Born March 28, 1823, in Champlain, N.Y.
When he was twelve years old his mother died, and he went to live
with Abijah North, of Champlain, and later went to Keeseville,
N.Y., and learned the blacksmith trade of John Dunning. He settled, first as a farmer and blacksmith, in Chazy, N.Y., but in 1852
moved to Avon, N.Y., and set up as a wagon-maker, but soon
changed and kept a general store, until 1879, when he went West,
first to Leadville, Col., and then to Aspen, Col., in 1881, where he
died Feb. 18, 1897. Mr. Churchill served in the Civil War, in the
Thirteenth Regiment, New York Volunteer Infantry, and in the
Eighth New York Cavalry. Married, at Plattsburgh, N.Y., Sept.
3, 1846, JEMIMA DEUEL JACKSON, daughter of Israel and Esther
(Allen) Jackson, born in Peru, N.Y., May 13, 1825. Died in Avon,
N.Y., April 6, 1880.

Children, first three born in Chazy, the rest in Avon, N.Y.

 I. DARIUS P.⁸ (Charles J. North), b. May 13, 1847.
    The name "Charlie North" became so fastened upon him in boy-
    hood, when he left home to live among strangers, that he later
    adopted the name Charles J. North, and had the same legally con-
    firmed by order of the court at Buffalo, N.Y., 1881. Mr. North
    has been greatly interested in the work of the compilers of this vol-
    ume, and has from time to time contributed much in aid of his own
    line. He has paid some attention to genealogy and history, is
    treasurer of the Buffalo Historical Society, member of the N.Y.
    Society, Sons of the American Revolution, and also of the New
    York Society of Mayflower Descendants, and has also been active
    and influential in political reform movements, inaugurated by the
    Republican party in New York. This account is from his letter to
    the editor, in 1903, but we have much helpful correspondence with
    him, dating back to 1885, and in nearly every year since. From
    1884, perhaps earlier, for many years Mr. North was in the insur-
    ance business in Buffalo, under the firm name of North & Vedder,
    West Seneca street, but in 1903 his address is 283 Ellicott square. He
    married DORA C. BRIGGS, dau. of Horace and Catherine (Morse)
    Briggs, June 30, 1881.
 II. HARMINIA ERNESTINE,⁸ b. Aug. 6, 1848; m. FREDERICK AMOS
    HAILE, at Rochester, N.Y., Sept. 21, 1868.
    He was the son of John C. and Celia F. Haile, born at Edwards,
    N.Y., June 21, 1843. They lived in Avon, N.Y., until 1885, when
    they removed to Aspen, Col.

Children born in Avon, N. Y.

1. Minnie Lutheria Haile, b. Nov. 27. 1869; m. Andrew Jackson Pickrell, Oct. 9, 1889, at Aspen, Col.
2. Frederick Churchill Haile, b. Dec. 27, 1872. He graduated at the School of Pharmacy, at the University at Buffalo, N.Y.

III. LUTHERA H.,[8] b. May 14, 1852; d. unmarried at Avon, N.Y., Oct. 25, 1870.

571   IV. ORVILLE S.,[8] b. Feb 13, 1855; m. LEILA C. ROBERTS, at Pitkin, Col. They lived at Aspen, Col., and had one child.

Child.

1. Marjorie E., b. Feb. 14, 1885.

V. SARAH ELIZA,[8] b. Oct. 11, 1859; m. JOHN T. SHUMATE, at Aspen, Col., April 26, 1887.
They lived at Glenwood Springs, Col., where he was a lawyer and, in 1899, held the office of district attorney.

Children.

1. Churchill Shumate, b. April 2, 1888.
2. John Edward Shumate, b. Aug. 19, 1897; d. June 19, 1897.
3. Ruth Shumate, b. June 1, 1899.
4. Bailey Shumate, b. Aug. 14, 1900.

VI. ESTHER J.,[8] b. Aug. 28, 1861; d. July, 1862.

315.

WILLIAM[7] CHURCHILL (DARIUS,[6] WILLIAM,[5] SAMUEL,[4] SAMUEL,[3] JOSEPH,[2] JOSIAH[1]). Born in Champlain, N.Y., Sept. 5, 1827. He learned the trade of wagon-maker, and when a young man went to Rochester and worked in the Cunningham Carriage Factory, but later removed to Henrietta, N.Y., where for some time he had a small farm, and also carried on a general wheelwright business. About 1865 he moved West, and it is not known in what place he located. Married, in Henrietta, N.Y., OLIVE REMINGTON, daughter of Thomas.

One Child reported, perhaps there were others.

I. NEWTON.[8]

316.

WASHINGTON[7] CHURCHILL (WILLIAM,[6] WILLIAM,[5] SAMUEL,[4] SAMUEL,[3] JOSEPH,[2] JOSIAH[1]). Born in Clinton, N.Y., March 19, 1824. In 1886 they lived in Eau Claire, Wis., as we learn from Joseph E. Churchill (No. 321). Married, Feb. 25, 1847. MARY LUCINDA CONVERSE.

Children.

572   I. JULIUS C.,[8] b. Dec. 22, 1848; m. CLARA F. PARISH, Sept. 19, 1872.

Children.

1. Oroh Hope, b. Aug. 13, 1875.
2. Marian J., b. July 12, 1883.
3. Julius C. Churchill, d. June 28, 1887.

II. HELEN M.,[8] b. Feb. 18, 1851; m. SAMUEL C. CONVERSE, Oct. 24, 1869.

Children.

1. Samuel Otis Converse, b. May 17, 1871; d. July 11, 1871.
2. Washington F. Converse, b. Dec. 8, 1872; d. Feb. 1, 1873.
3. Lillian Helen Converse, b. April 19, 1875.
4. Ralph C. Converse, b. Jan. 27, 1884; d. Nov. 14, 1884.

573   III. EDWARD W.,[8] b. Nov. 6, 1853; m. CLARA E. GRIFFIN, March 10, 1874.

Children.

1. Arthur C., b. July 26, 1875.
2. Mary W., b. Sept. 14, 1878.
3. Hattie L., b. Dec. 17, 1883.

IV. MELINDA A.,[8] b. April 21, 1856; m. ABRAM BINDER, Nov. 5, 1874.

Children.

1. Lena P. Binder, b. Oct. 24, 1877.
2. Lloyd W. Binder, b. Feb. 17, 1880
3. Leroy Jeffrie Binder, b. Dec. 27, 1885.

574   V. GEORGE S.,[8] b. Nov. 1, 1858; d. March 10, 1859.
VI. ELLA LUCINDA,[8] b. Aug. 21, 1860; d. Nov. 21, 1860.
575   VII. PERIN W., [8] b. Nov. 6, 1862; m. CARRIE HADDOCK, Nov. 20, 1884.
576   VIII. GILBERT C.,[8] b. June 16, 1866; d. Dec. 27, 1866.
577   IX. DARIUS W.,[8] b. June 23, 1868.
578   X. BIRNEY A.,[8] b. Dec. 6, 1873.

317.

BENJAMIN J.[7] CHURCHILL (WILLIAM,[6] WILLIAM,[5] SAMUEL,[4] SAMUEL,[3] JOSEPH,[2] JOSIAH[1]). Born in Clinton, N.Y., Feb. 22 1831. Mr. Churchill in 1886 prepared a careful and very full record of the family of his father and of the families of his brothers and sisters, but failed to give residences or occupations. He lived in Eau Claire, Wis., in 1886. We regret that we have not later infor mation. Married, Oct. 25, 1856, HANNAH E. PRATT.

Children.

I. JENNIE A.,[8] b. June 25, 1858; m. WILLIAM A. SEVERN, Oct. 10, 1883.
II. HATTIE E.,[8] b. May 24, 1862; d. June 18, 1865.
579   III. CHARLES W ,[8] b. Oct. 18, 1864.
IV. CORA E.,[8] b. April 7, 1867.
580   V. HOMER E.,[8] b. Aug. 27, 1869.

318.

WILLIAM HENRY[7] CHURCHILL (WILLIAM[6] WILLIAM[5] SAMUEL,[4] SAMUEL,[3] JOSEPH,[2] JOSIAH[1]). Born in Clinton, N.Y., Dec. 13, 1834. We have no later information of this family than that furnished by Benjamin J. Churchill, in 1886, when they lived in or near Eau Claire, as we learn from Joseph E. Churchill, of Columbus. Married, Sept. 6, 1860, JANE ANN BARKER.

Children.

    I. MARY L.,[8] b. July 31, 1861.
    II. JESSIE E.,[8] b. July 8, 1864.
   III. LIZZIE J.,[8] b. June 11, 1868; d. July 23, 1868.
   IV. LIBBIE P.,[8] b. April 26, 1871.
581   V. WILLIAM H.,[8] b. Oct. 2, 1878.

319.

RUSSELL [7] CHURCHILL (JULIUS,[6] WILLIAM [5] SAMUEL,[4] SAMUEL,[3] JOSEPH,[2] JOSIAH [1]). Born July 14, 1833, at Champlain, N.Y. Removed and settled at Springfield, Ill., where he died June 14, 1875. Married, April 14, 1858, MARY TURNER, born Aug. 13, 1832. She was of Scituate Harbor, Mass.

Children.

    I. ISABEL,[8] b. June 18, 1860.
    II. JESSIE,[8] b. Nov. 5, 1863.
   III. EDGAR RUSSELL,[8] b. June, 1867; d. at two years.

320.

JOHN FILLMORE [7] CHURCHILL (DR. JULIUS [6] WILLIAM,[5] SAMUEL,[4] SAMUEL,[3] JOSEPH,[2] JOSIAH [1]). Born in Champlain, N.Y. Dec. 28, 1837. Died at Kalamazoo, Mich., Oct. 12, 1873. Married at Kalamazoo, Mich., Dec. 2, 1863, CATHERINE WISEMAN.

Children.

    I. CATHERINE E.,[8] b. March 9, 1866.
582   II. CHARLES W.,[8] b. Aug. 27, 1868.

321.

JOSEPH E.[7] CHURCHILL (JAMES,[6]* WILLIAM,[5] SAMUEL,[4] SAMUEL,[3] JOSEPH,[2] JOSIAH [1]). Born Oct. 22, 1829. He was living in Columbus, Wis., December, 1903, engaged in a commission business. Married, in Columbus, Wis., Oct. 30, 1877, JULIA BULL.

Child.

    I. RODNEY J.,[8] b. 1879; unmarried in December, 1903. Living in Columbus, Wis.

---

* From Mrs. Helen E. (Churchill) Anderson, of Columbus, Wis., we have just received information (Dec. 20, 1903) enabling us to add materially to the record of her father (No. 126), viz.: James Churchill moved to Champlain, N.Y., with his father's family in 1806. Learned the trade of carpenter and millwright. Married ELIZA JOHNSON, March 10, 1826, at Champlain, N.Y. They lived in Champlain until 1849, when Mr. Churchill went to California, where he spent ten years, and died in 1859, at Nevada City, Cal. His family removed to Columbus, Wis., in 1854, and his widow died there March 3, 1903, aged ninety-four years six months. Children: (1) Pamelia L., b. June 20, 1828; d. May 8, 1841; (2) Joseph E. (No. 321, *q. v.*); (3) Cynthia, b. March 24, 1832; d. July 9, 1832; (4) Helen E., b. Feb. 23, 1835; m. C. B. Anderson, at Columbus, Wis., Dec. 8, 1867; (5) James H., b. June 14, 1838; d. May 9, 1841.

322.

PEMBROKE[7] CHURCHILL (SILAS,[6] EZEKIEL,[5] SAMUEL,[4] SAMUEL,[3] JOSEPH,[2] JOSIAH[1]). Born April 29, 1826. Mr. Churchill lived in Warren, Mass., later for a time in Milton, Pa., but in 1885 in Webster, Mass., since which last date we have no news from the family. Married, Nov. 2, 1853, CAROLINE M. CLEMENTS.

Children born, three in Warren, Mass., and one in Milton, Pa.

    I. EDDIE,[8] b. March 19, 1860; d. two days after.
    II. FLORENCE,[8] b. March 1, 1861; d. Oct. 2, 1861.
583   III. DURAND LEON,[8] b. Aug. 27, 1862.
    IV. WALTER EDGAR,[8] b April 30, 1873; d. June 10, 1873.

326a.

CULLEN[7] CHURCHILL (LEVI W.,[6] EZEKIEL,[5] SAMUEL,[4] SAMUEL,[3] JOSEPH,[2] JOSIAH[1]). Born, probably, in Alexander, N.Y. He married, but we have not received the name of his wife.

One Child.

    I. CULLEN.[8] No further record.

326b.

CHARLES CARROLL[7] CHURCHILL (CULLEN D.,[6] EZEKIEL,[5] SAMUEL,[4] SAMUEL,[3] JOSEPH,[2] JOSIAH[1]). Born April 30, 1839, probably at Alexander, N.Y. Married, Feb. 6, 1869, CHARITY PERSON, of Ellery, N.Y.

Child.

    I. MARY M.,[8] b. 1872; m. CHARLES H. WHITE, of Jamestown, N.Y., July 21, 1897.
       They were living in 1902, in Conewango Valley, Chant County N.Y.

327.

ALBRO RUTHVEN[7] CHURCHILL (CULLEN D.,[6] EZEKIEL,[5] SAMUEL,[4] SAMUEL,[3] JOSEPH,[2] JOSIAH[1]). Born Sept. 13, 1843, probably at Alexander. Married, Feb. 26, 1877, MARY J. McLEES, of Davisburg, Mich.

Children.

    I. EVELYN,[8] b. 1883.
    II. ANNA,[8] b. 1887.

328.

HOMER CULLEN[7] CHURCHILL (CULLEN D.,[6] EZEKIEL,[5] SAMUEL,[4] SAMUEL,[3] JOSEPH,[2] JOSIAH[1]). Born Nov. 14, 1848. Married, December, 1876, RHODA WEEGAR, of Randolph, N.Y.

Children.

I. ELVA S.,[8] b. 1878; m. ELMER WYMAN, of Stramburg, N.Y:, Feb. 17, 1898.
They live in Springfield, Mass.

584   II. CASSIMER,[8] b. 1881.

328a.

WILLIS FLETCHER[7] CHURCHILL (CULLEN D.,[6] EZEKIEL,[5] SAMUEL,[4] SAMUEL,[3] JOSEPH,[2] JOSIAH[1]). Born July 8, 1864. Married 1st, Jan. 25, 1893, ALICE B. LORD. She died Feb. 3, 1894. Married 2d, Feb. 13, 1895, JENNIE JOHNSON.

Children of Second Wife.

I. RUTH E..[8] b. December, 1895.

585   II. HAROLD,[8] b. Jan. 23, 1898.

329.

GILBERT WILLIAM[7] CHURCHILL (NOBLE,[6] LEVI[5] CHARLES,[4] SAMUEL,[3] JOSEPH,[2] JOSIAH[1]). Born April 23, 1817, in New York State. He lived at Eaton, O., and was by occupation an undertaker. We have not been able to reach his children. He died Sept. 6 1890. Married JANE BLACK, of Pittsburg, Penn.

Children.

586   I. ALBERT.[8] Lived in Iowa, and was a physician.
587   II. CHARLES,[8] m. and lived in Eaton, O.
588   III. CALVIN,[8] m. and lived in Eaton, O.
       IV. OLIVE,[8] m. MR. KENNEY. They lived in Eaton, O., in 1890.

330.

CHESTERFIELD LEONARD[7] CHURCHILL (NOBLE,[6] LEVI,[5] CHARLES,[4] SAMUEL,[3] JOSEPH,[2] JOSIAH[1]). Born Feb. 1, 1820, later authority states, in Ohio. Perhaps his father removed to Ohio in 1820. Chesterfield settled in California, and became a physician and an eminent surgeon in the. San Francisco hospitals, California. He was also a fine painter and expert musician. Died in San Diego, in 1874. Married, May, 1850, ANNE STARKWEATHER.

Children.

I. EMMA,[8] m. MR. GREGG.
II. A DAUGHTER,[8] m. JOSEPH ALLISON, of San Diego, Cal.
III. AGNES,[8] m. MR. LA TOURETTE, Portland, Ore.

331.

JOHN EDWIN[7] CHURCHILL (NOBLE,[6] LEVI,[5] CHARLES,[4] SAMUEL,[3] JOSEPH,[2] JOSIAH[1]). Born August, 1822. He acquired a good education, but was of eccentric nature and Bohemian habits

and tastes. He was a painter of ability, a poet and a lecturer of
some note, and also a fine musician and toured the country with Ole
Bull about the time of the Civil War. About 1871 he wandered
away from his family, and was last heard of in Savannah, Ga., with
Sidney Lanier, painting his portrait, but was very ill. That was in
1881. Married, at Le Roy, N.Y., 1862, JENNIE PRESTON. Mrs.
Jennie P. Churchill was a fine singer, and lived with her daughter until
her death in 1888.

Children.

    I. DOLLIE ZENOBIA,[8] b. at Cleveland, O., 1863; m., name of husband
        not received. In 1899 she lived at Chicago, a widow, no children.
    II. EVANGELINE,[8] b. at Pontiac, Mich., 1866; m. RICHARD POWELL, a
        prosperous business man of Chicago. They had two children
        who died in infancy.

332.

DR. CHARLES CLINTON[7] CHURCHILL (NOBLE,[6] LEVI,[5]
CHARLES,[4] SAMUEL,[3] JOSEPH,[2] JOSIAH[1]). Born at Eaton, O., Dec.
26, 1825. See page 407. His father's removal to Ohio was probably in 1820 instead of 1830, but to Eaton in 1830. Graduated at
the College of Surgeons, Philadelphia. He lived in Memphis, and
later California. A man of high culture and noble character.
While on a visit to his son, he died at Memphis, Tenn., Nov. 28
1898. Married 1st, at Memphis, MARY ASHE RIVERS, of Memphis.
Married 2d, in Memphis, 1878, MRS. ELIZABETH DUNNING.

Child.

588a   I. CHARLES NOBLE,[8] b. in Memphis, Jan. 4, 1861; m. KATE E. CHISM,
        of Francis Point, Miss., April 13, 1887. He is a member of the
        firm of Chism, Churchill & Co., wholesale grocers, Memphis,
        Tenn.

333.

LEVI MERRILL[7] CHURCHILL (CHARLES BELDEN,[6] LEVI,[5]
CHARLES,[4] SAMUEL,[3] JOSEPH,[2] JOSIAH[1]). Born in Boonville, N.Y.,
Feb. 8, 1811. At the age of eleven years he went to live in the
family of his aunt Elizabeth, wife of Leonard Hubbard, and was by
them brought up to the age of twenty-one years. In this kindly
Puritan household was another adopted relative of the Hubbards, his
cousin, Marcia Boardman Churchill, between whom and himself was
a very strong cousinly attachment. He went to South Carolina at
the age of twenty years, and lived there for thirty-eight years. The
most of this time he lived in South Carolina, but carried on business
in Augusta, Ga. During the Civil War he made a fortune, but lost
it when the war closed. In 1868 he moved to Illinois, and settled
at or near Canton in that State. In the lists of his children and
grandchildren he unfortunately omits the names of many who died

young.   Married, in South Carolina, Sept. 18, 1838, HARRIET
PROTHROUGH, of Augusta, Ga.

Children born in Edgefield, S.C.; two, who died young, not named.

    I. ELMINA E.,[8] m. T. J. HOWARD, of Edgefield, S.C.
          They lived at Wood, Ga., and had five children, names not
          given. Mrs. Howard died in 1886.
    II. MARTHA MINERVA,[8] m. DANIEL PERRINE, at Canton, Ill.
          In 1902 they lived in Bedford, Ind., and had one son, name not
          given.
    III. MARY ZYLPHA,[8] m. DAVID PERRINE, of Canton, Ill.
          In 1902 they lived in Texarkana, Ark., and had one daughter,
          name not given.

589   IV. CHARLES NATHANIEL,[8] b. March 11, 1845; m. MITTIE COLLIN. at
          Augusta, Ga.
          He was a farmer in 1902, at Wood, Ga. They have two sons,
          names not received.

590   V. JAMES PAGE,[8] b. Oct. 6, 1848; m. 1st, MATTIE BUSSEY, Memphis,
          Mo.; m. 2d, NELLIE BENNINGTON, Mount Pleasant, Iowa.
          In 1902 he was living in Roseville, Ill., a farmer, and at that
          time helped us about his family account. Child of first wife: (1)
          Jessie Lou, b. July 15, 1872; m. John Cady. Children of second
          wife: (2) James Forest, b. Sept. 8, 1881; (3) George Levi, b.
          Jan. 19, 1891; (4) Nellie Columbia, b. Jan. 29, 1893.

590a   VI. LEVI MERRILL,[8] b. April 2, 1850; m. SOPHIE BURGETT, at Lewis-
          ton, Ill.
          They lived at Minneapolis in 1902, and had a son and daughter,
          names not obtained. Mr. Churchill was a merchant.
    VII. HARRIET EUGENIA,[8] m. JACK SUTER, at Wyaconda, Mo., and they
          lived there, and had three sons, two of whom died in infancy.
    VIII. ISABELLA,[8] b. Sept. 30, 1856; m. CHARLES F. MARINER, at Canton,
          Ill.
          They lived, in 1902, in Galesburg, Ill., and had one son and one
          daughter, names not obtained.

334.

CHARLES BELDEN[7] CHURCHILL, JR. (CHARLES B [6]
LEVI,[5] CHARLES,[4] SAMUEL,[3] JOSEPH,[2] JOSIAH[1]). Born April 25,
1813, in Boonville, N.Y. Moved to Canton, Ill., in 1837, taking
with him his father and mother and four younger brothers and a
sister. They settled on a farm in Putnam Township, and, in 1842,
bought and planted a new farm in Canton Township. In 1845 he
engaged in trade, and travelled through the South and in Canada in
pursuit of his enterprise. In 1850 he returned to Illinois, and settled on his farm in Canton, and became a prosperous and influential
citizen. Married, Nov. 26, 1850, LOUISA E. HURLBURT, born in
Boonville, N.Y., and a daughter of Mary (Churchill) Hurlburt. Mrs.
Louisa E. Churchill was a woman of education and culture.

Children born in Canton, Ill.

    I. SARAH J.,[8] b. Aug. 23, 1851; unmarried in 1885.
    II. A DAUGHTER,[8] d. unnamed.
    III. ABBIE A,[8] b. June 22, 1853; m. FRANK MARR, of Hagerstown, Md.,
          June 11, 1879.
          They lived in New Tacoma, Wash., in 1885, and had children:
          (1) Rosa B. Marr; (2) Lucile H. A. Marr.

IV. A son,[8] d. unnamed.
V. ELIZABETH,[8] b. Feb. 27, 1856; m. NORTON H. CHURCHILL, Dec. 22,
    1879. He is the son of No. 345.
VI. CHARLES B.,[8] b Aug. 1, 1859; d. in 1865.
591 VII. FRANKLIN S.,[8] b. Feb. 2, 1865; m. FINVOLA CAMPBELL, Nov. 9,
    1887.

339.

CARMI [7] CHURCHILL (CAROLUS,[6] LEVI,[5] CHARLES,[4] SAMUEL,[3] JOSEPH,[2] JOSIAH [1]). Born in Boonville, N.Y., Feb. 25, 1813. (We learn since printing page 409, that Carolus [6] Churchill and Polly Rowland were married at New Berlin, N.Y., March 14, 1812, and that he enlisted at Boonville, September, 1814, and served in "the War of 1812," until his discharge, at Sackett's Harbor, November, 1814.) Carmi settled in Ashtabula County, Ohio, first, but later lived in Canton and Henderson, Ill., and in Rome, Iowa, where he died May 9, 1892. Married 1st, SALLIE STOWE; 2d, in Ohio, ELVIRA CONANT; 3d, in Rome, Iowa, Mrs. FRANCES JACKSON.

Children of First Wife.

591a   I. HORACE,[8] b. in Ashtabula County, Ohio; m. 1st, CORNELIA DALEY,
        in Henderson, Ill.; 2d, MARGARET WILLEY, in Henderson, Ill.
    II. ROXANNA,[8] b. in Ashtabula County, Ohio; m. SWAZY HITT, in
        Henderson, Ill.
    III. JANE,[8] b. Canton, Ill.; m. JOHN CONANT, in Henderson, Ill.

Children of Second Wife.

    IV. ELIZABETH,[8] b. in Henderson, Ill.; m. WILLIAM DRIFFILL, at
        Alexis, Ill.
    V. HARRIET,[8] b. at Galesburg, Ill.; m. MR. BROWN, in Rome, Iowa.
    VI. EMMA,[8] b. in Henderson. Ill.; m. WILLIAM KELLEY, at Perry, Iowa.
591b VII. HARDY,[8] b. in Henderson, Ill.; m. (name not given) at Perry, Iowa.
    VIII. HARRY,[8] b. in Andover, Ill. Killed in a railroad accident in
        Missouri.

Child of Third Wife.

    IX. BETHIA,[8] b. in Rome, Iowa.

340.

JOHN [7] CHURCHILL (CAROLUS [6] LEVI,[5] CHARLES,[4] SAMUEL,[3] JOSEPH,[2] JOSIAH [1]). Born in New York State, Aug. 13, 1814. He removed to Ohio and lived at East Trumbull. He was a dairy farmer. Married ELEANOR BERTRAM, of East Trumbull, Ohio, born Jan. 1, 1820. He died April 6, 1897, and she died April 19, 1886.

Children born at East Trumbull.

    I. ADELINE,[8] b. April 8, 1844; m. HENRY KELLOGG, and died in July,
        1866.
    II. WARREN,[8] b. Dec. 29, 1846. Enlisted in the Civil War, in 1863,
        and died soon after his return home, from effects of sickness and
        exposure.

340a.

PHILINDA [7] CHURCHILL (CAROLUS,[6] LEVI,[5] CHARLES,[4] SAMUEL,[3] JOSEPH,[2] JOSIAH [1]). Born in Oneida County, N.Y., Dec. 14, 1816. Married JOSHUA SMITH. They lived in Ashtabula, Ohio, and Rock Island, Ill., where she died, Sept. 12, 1850.

Children born in Ohio.

  I. MEHITABEL [8] SMITH, b. Feb. 13, 1837; m. JAMES REYNOLDS, in Monmouth, Ill.
  II. - HANNAH [8] SMITH, m. ROYAL SCOTT, in Monmouth, Ill.
  III. SAMUEL [8] SMITH.
  IV. JEANNETTE [8] SMITH, m. AUGUSTUS CHURCHILL, of Monmouth, Ill.
  V. CHARLES [8] SMITH.

341.

NICHOLAS [7] CHURCHILL (CAROLUS,[6] LEVI,[5] CHARLES,[4] SAMUEL,[3] JOSEPH,[2] JOSIAH[1]). Born in 1818 in Oneida, N.Y. He removed to the West and lived in Canton, Ohio, and Henderson, Ill., and later in Monmouth, Kan. Married in Joliet, Ill., LYDIA ANN ROWLAND, daughter of Nicholas and Polly Rowland. Married 2d, IDA CURTIS, in Rockland, Ill. He was a farmer and died in Marshall County, Kan., Feb. 19, 1901.

Children born, the first in Fulton, the rest in Henderson, Ill.

591c I. AUGUSTUS,[8] m. JEANNETTE CHURCHILL, in Monmouth, Ill.
591d II. FAYETTE,[8] m. HELEN JENNINGS, in Henry County, Ill.
591e III. FRANCIS.[8]
591f IV. JAMES.[8]
       V. ALFREDA.[8]
591g VI. WILLIAM.[8]

342.

CALVIN WEBSTER [7] CHURCHILL (CAROLUS,[6] LEVI,[5] CHARLES,[4] SAMUEL,[3] JOSEPH,[2] JOSIAH[1]). Born in Oneida, N.Y., in 1820. He removed West and settled first in Ohio, but later lived in Alexis, Ill., and later in Aurora, Neb. He was a farmer. He died in Nebraska. Married 1st, SARAH BUGBEE. Married 2d, JOANNA RAFFERTY.

Children of First Wife.

  I. and II. TWIN BOYS, unnamed, died in infancy.
  III. LURINDIA,[8] b. 1843; m. TIMOTHY RAFFERTY, at Alexis, Ill.
  IV. HANNAH,[8] b. in Ohio, in 1844; d. at Galesburg, Ill., March 10, 1848.
  V. MILLIE,[8] b. in Henderson, Ill., in 1854; m. HARVIE CHURCHILL.
  VI. ORVILLA O.,[8] m. REUBEN H. CONANT, Monmouth, Ill.
  VII. INEZ,[8] m. JONATHAN WELSH, at Alexis, Ill.

Children of Second Wife.

591h VIII. FRANCIS MARION;[8] m. 1st, CLARA WILLIS, who died in Nebraska; m. 2d, MARTHA BREMERSTED; 3d, NETTIE MOORE. They lived in Missouri.

IX. LILLA E.,[3] b. 1856; m. CLEMENT WALFORD.
X. JOHN,[8] m. ANNA BREMERSTED.
XI. MAUD,[8] m. EDWARD NEWCOME. They live in Nebraska.

343.

GEORGE[7] CHURCHILL (CAROLUS,[6] LEVI,[5] CHARLES,[4] SAMUEL,[3] JOSEPH,[2] JOSIAH[1]). Born in Boonville, N.Y., Oct. 6, 1825. Re moved West and settled in Castana, Iowa; a farmer. Married in Bureau County, Ill., MARGARET CAMPBELL.

Children born in Bureau County, Ill.

    I. MARIA.[8]
    II. ANGELINE.[8]
591i   III. OREN,[8] m. EVA BRAMBLE.
    IV. MAY,[8] m. REUMAN BIGELOW, in Monona County, Iowa.
591j   V. CHARLES,[8] m. RACHEL RILEY, in Ute, Iowa.
    VI. JOHN,[8] m. RENA RILEY, in Ute, Iowa.
    VII. ANNA,[8] m. 1st, ISAAC MULNIX; and 2d, MR. MITCHELL, Ute, Iowa.

344.

BENJAMIN[7] CHURCHILL (CAROLUS,[6] LEVI,[5] CHARLES,[4] SAM-UEL,[3] JOSEPH,[2] JOSIAH[1]). Born in Boonville, N.Y., May 1, 1827. Removed with his father's family to the West, and settled in Alexis, Ill. Married in Peoria, Ill., in 1846, SARAH ROWLAND, daughter of Nicholas and Polly Rowland.

Children.

    I. EMILY J.,[8] b. in Peoria; d. young at Henderson, Ill.
    II. INFANT BOY, b. at Henderson; died unnamed.
    III. JOSEPHINE A.,[8] b. May 26, 1850; m. 1st, PERRY HINES, of Wood-hull, Ill., Sept. 9, 1872; 2d, JOHN DRIFFELL, Alexis, Ill., Sept. 9, 1876. She died Jan. 25, 1897, leaving a son, Benjamin Hines, and two daughters of second husband.
    IV. ESTHER L.,[8] b. Jan. 29, 1852; m. EDMUND WIXON, Sept. 7, 1876, at Alexis, Ill. They have a son and daughter.

344a.

ARTIMISSA[7] CHURCHILL (CAROLUS,[6] LEVI,[5] CHARLES[4] SAM-UEL,[3] JOSEPH,[2] JOSIAH[1]). Born in Oneida, County, N.Y., April 27, 1829. Removed with her father's family to the West. Lived after marriage in Henderson, and near Alexis, Ill. Married 1st, JOHN PALMER, in Knox County, Ill., a farmer. Married 2d, BENJAMIN ORUM, a bookkeeper in a mercantile house in Galesburg, Ill. Artimissa (Churchill) Orum died Oct. 27, 1885.

Children of First Husband.

    I. G. W.[8] PALMER, b. in Victoria, Ill., July 20, 1847; m. H. M. LEVALLEY, Victoria, Ill.
    II. ELIZABETH[8] PALMER, b. in Ionia, Ill., Sept. 17, 1851.
    III. JOHN[8] PALMER, b. in Kelley Township, Ill., Feb. 3, 1853.

IV. JAMES F.⁸ PALMER, b. in Kelley Township, Ill., May 10, 1854; m. SARAH CHURCHILL, in Canton, Ill.
V. EDWARD⁸ PALMER, b. in Kelley Township, Ill., April 8, 1857; m. CORA FANSTOCK, in Galesburg. Ill.
VI. ABEL⁸ PALMER, b. in Kelley Township, Ill., Feb. 12, 1859; m. BELLE CUNNINGHAM, in Canton, Ill.
VII. CHARLES L.⁸ PALMER, b. in Kelley Township, Ill., Sept. 21, 1860; m. 1st, HETTIE WITT; 2d, NETTIE McMULLIN.

Children of Second Husband born in Kelley Township, Ill.

VIII. MARY J.⁸ ORUM, b. Aug. 13, 1866; m. FRED SUYDAM.
IX. FANNIE⁸ ORUM, b. Dec. 27, 1869; m. LEE STANNARD.
X. BENJAMIN⁸ ORUM, d. aged about one year.

344b.

MARY⁷ CHURCHILL (CAROLUS,⁶ LEVI,⁵ CHARLES,⁴ SAMUEL,³ JOSEPH,² JOSIAH¹). Born in Oneida County, N.Y., March 25, 1831. Removed with her father's family to the West, and lived after marriage in Henderson and Monmouth, Ill. Married at Henderson, in 1849, HEZEKIAH WITT.

Children born at Henderson and Monmouth, and as noted.

I. JOHN⁸ WITT, b. Jan. 19, 1850.
II. ADELINE⁸ WITT, b. Feb. 21, 1851; m. THOMAS LONGSHORE at Monmouth.
III. RUTH⁸ WITT, b. May 7, 1853; m. WILLIAM JONES, at Monmouth.
IV. GEORGE⁸ WITT, b. Aug. 12, 1855; m. GEORGIANNA OSTROM, at Monmouth.
V. LAURA⁸ WITT, b. at Galesburg, Ill., Dec. 20, 1857; m. CHARLES McGLAFLIN, at Monmouth.
VI. LILLIE⁸ WITT, b. Dec. 9, 1860; m. WALTER ADAMS, at Monmouth.
VII. HETTIE⁸ WITT, b. July 13, 1861; m. CHARLES PALMER, at Keokuk, Iowa.
VIII. DELLIA⁸ WITT, b. Dec. 25, 1863; m. EDWARD RICHARDS, at Monmouth.
IX. EDWARD⁸ WITT, b. May 24, 1871; m. ANNIE STEVENSON, at Atchison, Kan.
X. IDA⁸ WITT, b. at Oquawka, Ill., Dec. 29, 1869; d. there Feb. 3, 1870.

345.

CALVIN WEBSTER⁷ CHURCHILL (BENJAMIN,⁶ LEVI,⁵ CHARLES,⁴ SAMUEL,³ JOSEPH,² JOSIAH¹). Born in Boonville, N.Y. Married MARIETTA STRATER.

Children.

I. NORTON M.,⁸ m. ELIZABETH CHURCHILL. He is a farmer. They live near Mt. Ayr, Ia., and have two children.

Children.

1. Charles B. | 2. Louisa E.

II. EARL,⁸ m. HARRIET ACKWORTH.
III. LELAND,⁸ m. EMMA GOLD.

IV. ANNIE,[8] m. MARION LYONS.
V. ROSELLA,[8] m. CHARLES ROCKWELL.
VI. CHARLES,[8] m. HARRIET WALKER.
VII. LURA,[8] m. FRED VAN ORMAN
VIII. CHILD,[8] d. in infancy

346.

DANIEL[7] CHURCHILL (BENJAMIN,[6] LEVI,[5] CHARLES,[4] SAMUEL,[3] JOSEPH,[2] JOSIAH[1]). Born in Boonville, N.Y. Married, in Alexis, Ill., CAROLINE CONANT.

Said to have been Children, of whom the following Six lived to be Married.

I. EDWIN A.,[8] m. EMMELINE GREEN.
II. HERBERT,[8] m. MISS DAVIS.
III. EVA,[8] m. HERBERT BESWICK.
IV. RICHARD,[8] m. MISS MCLANE.
V. CAROLINE.[8]
VI. GOLDIE.[8]

347.

LEVI HENRY[7] CHURCHILL (BENJAMIN,[6] LEVI,[5] CHARLES,[4] SAMUEL,[3] JOSEPH,[2] JOSIAH[1]). Born in Boonville, N.Y. Married, in Georgetown, Mo., July 4, 1860, MARIAN ELIZA WILLIAMSON, of Boonville.

Children.

I. EUNICE MAHALA,[8] m. EMERY W. JOHNSTON, of Bedford, Ia.
II. ELLEN F.,[8] d. in infancy.
III. KATE.[8] m. LESTER S. HIBBARD, of Hopkins, Mo.
IV. CHLOE A.,[8] m. SENECA BALL, of Hopkins, Mo. They had two

Children.

1. Jesse S. Ball, d. in infancy.
2. Ira S. Ball, d. in infancy.
V. MAUD ANNETTE,[8] unmarried.
VI. RUBY IRENE,[8] m. WILL R. TAME.
     Three other children died in infancy.

348.

HARVEY A.[7] CHURCHILL (BENJAMIN[6] LEVI,[5] CHARLES[4] SAMUEL,[3] JOSEPH[2] JOSIAH[1]). Born in Boonville, N.Y. Married 1st, in Galesburg, Ill., MILLIE CHURCHILL. Married 2d, in Galesburg, Ill., NANCY J. ROUTH.

Child of First Wife.

I. ISHMAEL,[8] m. MARY BARKS.

Children of Second Wife.

II. EFFIE,[8] m. NOAH BARKS.
III. DELOS,[8] m. CAROLINE ROBERTSON.
IV. BERTHA,[8] m. ELMER HUNT.

V. SELDEN,[8] unmarried.
VI. PEARL,[8] m. GEORGE WRAY.
VII. LILLIE,[8] d. in infancy.
VIII. LLOYD,[9] unmarried.
IX. GLADYS,[9] unmarried.

352.

CHARLES HOLIDAY [7] CHURCHILL (DR. CLAUDIUS B.,[6] CHARLES,[5] CHARLES,[4] SAMUEL,[3] JOSEPH,[2] JOSIAH [1]). Born about 1830, in Newburne, N.C. Lived in New Orleans, La., a hardware merchant. Died April 28, 1868. Married, October, 1864, MARTHA THORN.

Children born in New Orleans.

I. CHARLES ROBERT,[8] b. 1870. He is a graduate of Tulane University, New Orleans, 1889. In January, 1904, is a dealer in electrical and sugar machinery in New Orleans and unmarried.
II. IDA FRANCES,[8] m. J F. THOMAS, JR.

Child.

1. Ida Churchill Thomas.

353.

SYLVESTER BROWN [7] CHURCHILL (DR. CLAUDIUS B.,[6] CHARLES,[5] CHARLES,[4] SAMUEL,[3] JOSEPH,[2] JOSIAH [1]). Born in Newburne, N.C. Died in 1890. Married MALVINA BERMUDIZ.

Children born in New Orleans, La.

I. WILLIAM GOODRICH.[8]
II. SYLVESTER B.,[8] m. MISS MOORE.
III. MARY,[8] m. AMBROSE A. MOORE.
IV. JAMES FERGUSON,[8] d. early.
V. EDWARD EVERETT.[8]

354.

WYLIE CROOME [7] CHURCHILL (DR. CLAUDIUS B.,[6] CHARLES,[5] CHARLES,[4] SAMUEL,[3] JOSEPH,[2] JOSIAH [1]). Born, probably, in New Orleans. Married CORA BELLE MARINER.

Children.

I. CHARLES HOLIDAY.[8]
II. ALFRED MARINER,[8] m. MISS MOORE.
III. CORA BELLE.[8]
   She was adopted by a family living in Little Rock, Ark.

355.

THOMAS HOLIDAY [7] CHURCHILL (DR. CLAUDIUS B. [6] CHARLES,[5] CHARLES,[4] SAMUEL,[3] JOSEPH,[2] JOSIAH [1]). Born in New Orleans, and lived there. He was a clerk or bookkeeper. Died in 1889. Married LAURA K STIRLING.

Children born in New Orleans.

I. CLAUDIUS BELDEN.[9]
II. THOMAS HOLIDAY.[8]
    He was collector at New Orleans.
III. EMILY GREEN [8]
IV. ROMEO.[8]

357.

CHAUNCY[7] CHURCHILL (CHISLIEU,[6] SAMUEL,[5] CHARLES,[4] SAMUEL,[3] JOSEPH,[2] JOSIAH[1]). Born Feb. 8, 1808, in Newington Conn. He died June 23, 1868. Married, Nov. 5, 1836, ABIGAIL SMITH WEBSTER.

Children.

I. HENRY ANDROS,[8] b. Feb. 28, 1837; d. Feb. 25, 1842.
II. EDWARD CHESTER,[8] b. May 12, 1840; d. June 19, 1840.
III. SARAH VIRGINIA,[8] b. March 11, 1842.
592   IV. EDWARD HENRY,[8] b. July 14, 1844.

358.

CALVIN[7] CHURCHILL (CHISLIEU,[6] SAMUEL[5] CHARLES[4] SAMUEL,[3] JOSEPH,[2] JOSIAH[1]). Born March 1810. He removed to the South and was a Methodist minister, in Georgia, and died on his return, June 23, 1868. Married, Aug. 9, 1832, MARY GILSTRAP.

Children.

I. HENRY GILSTRAP,[8] b. July 4, 1833; d. Aug. 28, 1835.
II. MARY ELIZABETH,[8] b. July 11, 1836; d. July 19, 1840.
III. ANGELINA VIRGINIA,[8] b. Aug. 29, 1838.

359.

SAMUEL SEYMOUR[7] CHURCHILL (CHISLIEU,[6] SAMUEL,[5] CHARLES,[4] SAMUEL,[3] JOSEPH,[2] JOSIAH[1]). Born Feb. 28, 1825, in Newington, Conn., and lived there, a farmer. He died April 2, 1900. Married, Nov. 11, 1846, at Vernon, Conn., LOUISA HUNT, of Vernon, Conn. She was the daughter of Erastus and Tryphena (Clark) Hunt, born Jan. 23, 1825; died Sept. 19, 1894.

Children.

I. HENRY DWIGHT,[8] b. May, 5, 1849; unmarried.
593   II. GEORGE EDWARD,[8] b. Dec. 11, 1858; m. ANNA WICKHAM, dau. of William F., of East Hartford, Aug. 23, 1888. Mr. Churchill is one of Newington's representative citizens, and has held many public offices of honor and trust, member of the General Assembly in 1899, and delegate to the Constitutional Convention in 1902. Children: (1) Almeron, b. July 27, 1889; (2) Louisa, b. Sept. 12, 1898.

360.

JOHN[7] CHURCHILL (JOHN,[6] SAMUEL,[5] CHARLES,[4] SAMUEL,[3] JOSEPH,[2] JOSIAH[1]). Born in New Hartford, Conn., Sept. 16, 1814. Lived on the farm until about sixteen, when he removed with his mother to Bristol. He was a man of large frame, slow in movement, and deliberate in thought and speech; a student of nature, a lover of plants and flowers. He was also an extensive collector of native Indian implements. Retiring in disposition he took no part in public matters, while he was of sterling character and sound judgment, and a loyal Freemason. He at one time had a Daguerrean room and took pictures. His wife was a woman of more than usual intellectual force, a reader of the best literature, especially royal biography. In later life she was a strong advocate of woman suffrage. She died at Bristol, Dec. 20, 1892, aged seventy years. He died at Bristol, June 28, 1887, and was buried with Masonic honors. Married, at Bristol, Nov. 4, 1841, ANN ELIZA HENDRICK.

Children born at Bristol.

I. ELECTA,[8] b. Sept. 7, 1843; m. AUSTIN DAVID THOMPSON, Sept. 13, 1865. He was born at Barnard, Vt., and was the son of Nathan P. and Elvira (Ellis) Thompson. He served in the army three years during the Civil War. They lived at Bristol, Conn., and had two children: (1) Eva Mae Thompson, b. Oct. 26, 1866; (2) Austin Churchill Thompson, b. Sept. 4, 1871; m. Julia Edna Booker, of Torrington, Conn.
II. ANN ELIZA,[8] b. 1847; and d. Oct. 12, 1856, aged nine years.
III. LUCY AUGUSTA,[8] b. Jan. 8, 1850; unmarried.
IV. JOHN,[8] b. Feb. 27, 1859; m. ELLA STEELE, of New Britain, Conn., Nov. 16, 1898. She was the dau. of Jefferson and Mary (Steele) Steele.

360a.

ELECTA[7] CHURCHILL (JOHN,[6] SAMUEL,[5] CHARLES,[4] SAMUEL[3] JOSEPH,[2] JOSIAH[1]). The account of her family on pages 411 and 412, being incomplete there, is continued here to remedy the defects. Her eldest son, Henry Albert Seymour after graduation at the Columbian Law School at Washington, D.C., became a clerk in the U.S. Census office at Washington, then an examiner in the Patent Office, and subsequently law clerk to the Commissioner of Patents, and a principal examiner in the Patent Office. Afterwards he began practice in Washington as a patent lawyer and has had a successful and brilliant career. He has been extensively engaged in electric litigation. He is a member of the New York Yacht Club, and of the Metropolitan and Cosmos Clubs of Washington, D.C. Mrs. Mary Marilla (Leggett) Seymour, his wife, was the daughter of General Mortimer Dormer Leggett, a very distinguished Union officer in the Civil War. and his wife, Marilla (Wells) Leggett. Mrs. Seymour was born at Warren, Ohio, 2 August, 1853. Their residence is Washington, D.C.

It is noted of the eldest daughter of Grace Ella (Seymour) Ingraham, that, christened Faith, she afterwards learned that an ancestress of hers named " Faith Allen " was hung for witchcraft on Gallows Hill, Salem, along with Rev. George Burroughs, and thereupon assumed for herself the name Faith *Allen* Ingraham.

And I wish to express here the debt of gratitude which I, as editor, and largely compiler, of these later generations, owe to Mr. George Dudley Seymour, for the constant and kindly help he has found time to give in the work of compiling and revising and advising, whenever appealed to, in the midst of his pressing business and social duties, in his busy life, as secretary of the Colonial War Society of Connecticut, member of the Century Club, of New York, the Cosmos Club, of Washington D.C., and the Graduates Club, of New Haven, and numerous other organizations which claim his time and attention.

361.

ABSALOM WELLES[7] CHURCHILL (John,[6] Samuel,[5] Charles,[4] Samuel,[3] Joseph,[2] Josiah[1]). Born March 29, 1820, at New Hartford, Conn. He removed in early manhood to Massachusetts, and lived first at Harvard, then at Groton, and later at Nashua, N.H., where he had a farm, and represented the town in the Legislature of 1855. Later he lived at what is now Ayer Junction, and at Shirley, Mass. In September, 1862, he enlisted in the Fifty-third Massachusetts Regiment, and was appointed to a position in the quartermaster's department, and remained there through his year of service. He was of genial nature, fine courtesy, and distinguished bearing, commanding the respect of all, and holding the affection of his friends. He was a life-long Unitarian in theology, but with strict Calvinistic ideas of home habits, and especially Sunday observance. He was a Mason and an Odd Fellow. He died at Shirley Village, Mass., April 10, 1875. Married, at Littleton, Mass., April 2, 1844, Harriet Mason Porter, daughter of John Mason and Harriet (Whitcomb) Porter, of Littleton.

Children.

I. Harriet Welles,[8] b. in Harvard, Mass., April 6, 1845; m. Charles L. Bailey, of Manchester, N.H., Nov. 30, 1869. In 1903 the family lived at Waltham, Mass.

Children born at Shirley, Mass.

1. Annie Mason Bailey, b. March 20, 1872.
2. Joseph Wells Bailey, b. April 4, 1874.

II. AUGUSTA PORTER,[8] b. in Groton, Mass , July 10, 1847; unmarried.
III. MARY KENDALL,[8] b in Nashua, N.H., Oct 12, 1851; m. HENRY
RICHARDSON, Oct. 30, 1879, in Waltham, Mass.

Children born in Waltham.

1. Wells Churchill Richardson, b. Aug 26, 1880.
2. Amy Porter Richardson, b. July 9, 1886.

IV. CLARENCE MASON,[8] b. in Nashua, N.H., Oct. 6, 1853; d. in Bristol,
Conn., July 12, 1855.
594   V. JOHN MASON,[8] b. in Ayer, Mass . April 8, 1862; m. LAURA A.
LINSCOTT, of Maplewood, Me., Nov. 26, 1883. They lived in
Waltham in 1889.

Children.

1. Laura Waters Churchill, b. July 23, 1884.
2. Harriet Mason Churchill, b. June 8, 1887.

362.

CHARLES[7] CHURCHILL (JOHN,[6] SAMUEL,[5] CHARLES,[4] SAM-
UEL,[3] JOSEPH,[2] JOSIAH [1]). Born in New Hartford, Conn., May 25,
1822. He was a man of active physical habit, ready and witty
in conversation, tall and well-knit in figure, and bearing, it is
said, in later years, a close resemblance to the actor, Joseph Jefferson. He was a lumber merchant at Bristol. He died at Bristol,
Nov. 16, 1891. Married, at Middletown, Conn., May 3, 1843, ALICE
C. PHILLIPS, daughter of Otis and Celestia (Taylor) Phillips; she
was born at Canton, Conn., Jan. 3, 1826, and died at Bristol, Oct.
20, 1899. She was a noble, home-loving mother, and the shock of
the loss of their soldier son was very severe, and saddened the
whole after lives of both the father and mother.

Children born in Bristol, Conn.

I. CHARLES,[8] b. Aug. 27, 1844. At the age of eighteen years he
enlisted in the Sixteenth Regiment, Company K, Connecticut
Volunteers, went to the front, participated in the battle of
Antietam, was there taken prisoner, and, after nearly two years
of terrible suffering and privation, died in prison at Florence,
S.C., Nov. 3, 1864. He was a handsome, manly youth of rare
personal attractions and endowments, and popular with all. His
loss was deeply mourned.
II. LAURA WATERS,[8] b. June 10, 1846; m. CHARLES LEVI FRISBIE, of
Plainville, Conn., Nov. 6, 1866. They lived in Plainville, and
had children: (1) Nellie Alice Frisbie, m. 1st, Elmore C. Whitman, of Bristol, and had a son, Harry Churchill Whitman. Then
was divorced from Whitman, and m. 2d, A L. Bradley, of New
Marlborough, Mass., and had a son, Churchill Frisbie Bradley.
(2) Charles Churchill Frisbie, m. Annie C. Wirtz, of Naugatuck,
Conn., and had Churchill Roswell Frisbie, b. in Naugatuck, and
d. in New Britain in 1902, aged six years; and second son,

Charles Churchill Frisbie, b. in Naugatuck, and d. in New
Britain, aged four years; and third son, Howard Frisbie, b. in
New Britain in 1900.

III. ALICE ELECTA,[8] b. June 8, 1848; m. WILLIAM W. RUSSELL, at
Bristol, April 17, 1872.

Children.

1. William Walter Russell, d. young.
2. Ernest Churchill Russell, b. Nov. 17, 1882; m. Annie Meyer,
May 6, 1903, at Los Angeles, Cal., and live there.

IV. JOHN WELLES,[8] b. June 18, 1851; d. 1856.
V. MARY CHARLOTTE,[8] b. Dec. 18, 1856; m. ERWIN H. PERKINS, Dec.
14, 1882. He was born Feb. 15, 1841, son of Elias and Mary
(Botsford) Perkins.
VI. ARTHUR CLARENCE,[8] b. June 5, 1858; d. June 13, 1861.
VII. ANNIE CHARLIEU,[8] b. June 12, 1861; m. ROSWELL O. BEACH, May
18, 1887. He was the son of Isaac W. and Ellen S (Olmsted)
Beach, b. Sept. 28, 1861, and d. Dec. 13, 1895.

363.

SAMUEL CICERO[7] CHURCHILL (JOSIAH B.,[6] SAMUEL,[5]
CHARLES,[4] SAMUEL,[3] JOSEPH,[2] JOSIAH[1]). Born in Boonville, N.Y.,
Jan. 30, 1815. When five years old his mother died and his
father took the family to Newington, where they were taken into
the families of the relatives. Samuel C. went to live with his
grandfather until the age of eleven, when, his father having married
again, he went to live with him at Sempronius, N.Y., and worked on
the farm, and later in the woolen mills at Summerhill, N.Y. He
had but limited advantages at school until after he came of age, when
he was able to attend several terms at the academy at Groton, N.Y.,
and fitted himself as best he could for his life work. He became a
minister of the Methodist fellowship, and labored faithfully on
several circuits in Western New York and Pennsylvania, from 1842
to 1849. He was an able, active, and consecrated Christian
minister, a devoted husband and father, extending a wide and be-
neficent influence. On account of bronchial trouble he was obliged
to give up constant preaching and engaged in farming in Nebraska.
He died at Hamilton, Neb., Aug. 2, 1891. Married 1st, Aug. 30,
1840, EMILY NORTH, of Berlin, Conn., who died Aug. 25, 1841.
Married 2d, March 27, 1843, SOPHIA G. GUNN, daughter of William,
of Mt. Upton, N.Y.

Child of First Wife.

I. SAMUEL CICERO,[8] b. at Akron, O., June 5, 1841, and d. in infancy.

Children of Second Wife.

596   II. BERNARD FISK,[8] b. at Clarion, Penn., July 4, 1844; m. JANE WAT-
TENPAUGH, of Elgin, Ia., April, 1874. In 1880 he was settled
on a farm of two hundred acres, in Nuckles, Neb.
III. EMILY JANE,[8] b. Nov. 1, 1845, at Ellington, N.Y.; m. PHILO R.
WOODS, at Fayette, Ia., Oct. 24, 1867.
Mr. Woods and his wife were educated in the Upper Iowa Uni-
versity, from which institution he enlisted Sept. 15, 1861, in Com-

pany C, Twelfth Regiment Iowa Volunteers, and served until his discharge, Jan. 26, 1866. He had the rank of sergeant. After the war he returned to the university and finished his course of study, and was later appointed an instructor in the same school.

Children of Philo R. and Emily J. (Churchill) Woods.

1. Herbert Carlton Woods, b. Aug. 26, 1871; m. Mary M. Dickson, at Luana, Ia., Dec. 28, 1893.
2. Paul Churchill Woods, b. Sept. 10, 1876; m. Amy L. Luther, at New Albin, Ia., Dec. 1, 1898.

IV. WILLIAM SAMUEL,[8] b. at Dayton, N.Y., Aug. 29, 1848; d. at Harding, Ia., 1857.

V. ADDISON COWPER,[8] b. at Forestville, N.Y., July 2, 1850.
Educated at the Upper Iowa University, where he graduated in the scientific course in 1876, and took A.M. degree in 1878. He is unmarried, a farmer and stock-raiser at Nuckles, Neb.

VI. MARY SOPHIA,[8] b. at Wattsburg, Penn., Sept. 11, 1853; m. 1st, EDWARD L. MONTGOMERY, at Fayette, Ia., Sept. 11, 1871, and m. 2d, REV. L. MORRISON, at Hardy, Neb., Aug. 13, 1895.

364.

GEORGE THOMPSON[7] CHURCHILL (JOSIAH B.,[6] SAMUEL,[5] CHARLES,[4] SAMUEL,[3] JOSEPH,[2] JOSIAH[1]). Born at Sempronius, N.Y., Nov. 26, 1824. His residence was Erie, Penn., in 1880, when he wrote us an account of his father's and his own family, and I find no further record than is given below. Married 1st, Aug. 27, 1847, ALMINA LAWRENCE, born Dec. 16, 1825; died June 28, 1849. Married 2d, Jan. 15, 1852, SARAH C. LAWRENCE, born Dec. 29, 1832.

Child of First Wife.

I. ALMINA JANE,[8] b. Sept. 7, 1848; d. June 28, 1849. The mother died same day.

Children of Second Wife.

597   II. JOSIAH WILLIS,[8] b. Feb. 27, 1853; m. ALICE D. WITLER, b. July 5, 1856.

Children.

1. Lucile Witler, b. Jan. 31, 1879.
2. Harold Witler, b. Nov. 7, 1885.

III. ALMINA ELLA,[8] b. Jan. 20, 1857; d. Oct. 16, 1861.
IV. ALICE MARIA,[8] b. Nov. 12, 1858; m. CHARLES S. CLARK, Jan. 15, 1880.

598   V. GEORGE SILAS,[8] b. April 23, 1863.

365.

SAMUEL BOARDMAN[7] CHURCHILL (CHARLES,[6] SAMUEL,[5] CHARLES,[4] SAMUEL,[3] JOSEPH,[2] JOSIAH[1]). Born in Iredell County, N.C., Jan. 2, 1831. He removed West and settled first in Texas and died there Nov. 10, 1882. Married, at Bastrop, Texas, Sept. 5, 1855, SARAH E. HISTON.

Children.

I. JOHN O. B.,[8] b. July 4, 1856.
II. MARY VIRGINIA,[8] b. April 13, 1858.
III. CHARLES WILLIAM,[8] b. Oct. 13, 1860.

366.

JAMES NORTHCROFT[7] CHURCHILL (CHARLES,[6] SAMUEL,[5] CHARLES,[4] SAMUEL,[3] JOSEPH,[2] JOSIAH[1]). Born in Iredell County N.C., Jan. 12, 1835. He removed to Arkansas and settled. Married, in Independence County, Ark., May 12, 1858, CHARLOTTÉ T. HOGAN, who was born in Henry County, Tenn., Sept. 4, 1835.

Children born in Independence County, Ark.

I. CHARLES DAVID,[8] b. Aug. 1, 1859; m. CALLIE LINN, Dec. 16, 1880. They had two children living in 1888. The mother died Oct. 20, 1887.

Children.

1. Daisy Pauline, b. Sept. 21, 1881.
2. Oscar Linn, b. June 19, 1883.

II. MARY MATILDA,[8] b. March 28, 1861; m. W. J. WARD, Dec. 1, 1886.
III. JAMES CURTIS,[8] Sept. 11, 1863; m. AMANDA SORRELLS, Jan. 22, 1885.
IV. LUCY CHARLOTTE BOARDMAN,[8] b. Nov. 10, 1868; m. R. C. DORR, Sept. 18, 1886.

Child.

1. Claudius Goldman Dorr, b. Nov. 14, 1887.

367.

WILLIAM PRICE[7] CHURCHILL (CHARLES,[6] SAMUEL,[5] CHARLES,[4] SAMUEL,[3] JOSEPH,[2] JOSIAH[1]). Born in Iredell County, N.C., Dec. 24, 1836. Removed to Arkansas, and settled. Married, in Independence County, Ark., Feb. 15, 1863, MARY C. RUSSELL. She was born in Jackson County, Ala., May 14, 1847.

Children born in Independence County, Ark.

I. WILLIAM,[8] b. Nov. 7, 1863; m. MINERVA T. WATTS, Nov. 11, 1880.

Children.

1. John Lacy, b. Feb. 4, 1882.
2. Bertha L., b. May 25, 1887.

II. JOHN CHARLES,[8] b. April 8, 1866.
III. SARAH MATILDA,[8] b. Feb. 11, 1869.
IV. HARRIET L.,[8] b. July 24, 1871.
V. JAMES CURTIS,[8] b. Oct. 14, 1873.
VI. SAMUEL H.,[8] b. Oct. 14, 1873; d. June 16, 1874.
VII. DAVID POE,[8] b. April 11, 1876.
VIII. ROBERT LEE,[8] b. Jan 14, 1879.
IX. CHARLOTTE O.,[8] b. July 18, 1883.
X. A CHILD, unnamed, d. in infancy.

368.

CURTIS JOHNSON [7] CHURCHILL (CHARLES,[6] SAMUEL,[5] CHARLES,[4] SAMUEL,[3] JOSEPH,[2] JOSIAH [1]). Born in Iredell County N.C., Dec. 11, 1838. Removed to Independence County, Ark., and lived there. He died April 7, 1884. Married, in Independence County, Ark., Jan. 28, 1869, AMANDA A. HOGAN.

Children.

I. FREDERIC,[8] b. Nov. 5, 1869.
II. LOUISA H.,[8] b. Sept. 25, 1870.
III. MATILDA A.,[8] b. Jan. 12, 1872.
IV. MARY H.,[8] b. Aug. 13, 1873.

369.

FRANCIS ELLIOTT [7] CHURCHILL (SILAS,[6] SILAS [5] CHARLES,[4] SAMUEL,[3] JOSEPH,[2] JOSIAH [1]). Born in New Lebanon, N.Y., Sept. 12, 1826. Lived in Hartford, Conn., a short time, and then went to New York, where he served an apprenticeship with Fahnestock & Co., wholesale druggists. He removed to Cleveland, O., and engaged in the drug business there till about 1867, when he purchased land in Waterloo, Ia. In 1874 he removed to Burlington, Ia., where he was engaged in the wholesale drug business until his death, April 26, 1896. Married, at Cleveland, O., Aug. 16, 1852, KATHERINE WHITMORE, daughter of John and Amy (Harvey) Whitmore, of London, Eng.

Children born in Cleveland, O.

I. ALICE BELL,[8] b. July 16, 1855; m. A. J. ARTHUR, June, 1882, Burlington, Ia.
II. ELLEN CLARISSA,[8] b. April 28, 1857; m. CHARLES H. STRONG, March 15, 1881, at Burlington, Ia.

Child.

1. Arthur Churchill Strong.

599 III. FRANCIS SAMUEL,[8] b. May 8, 1859; m. LAURA NELSON, June 15, 1892, at Burlington. She was the daughter of John R. and Elizabeth (Schramm) Nelson. He was educated at Cleveland, O., and Waterloo, Ia., and is engaged in the wholesale drug business at Burlington, Ia.
600 IV. ARTHUR TEMPLE,[8] b. Jan. 24, 1862; m. JOSEPHINE NEWMAN, June 27, 1888.

370.

WILLIAM THOMAS [7] CHURCHILL (SILAS,[6] SILAS,[5] CHARLES,[4] SAMUEL,[3] JOSEPH,[2] JOSIAH [1]). Born in New Lebanon, N.Y., Dec. 25, 1830, but moved to Hartford, Conn., at the age of sixteen, and has lived there ever since; a merchant 1904. Married, April 25, 1883,

ALICE SUMNER WOODBRIDGE, daughter of Christopher A. and Mary Sumner Woodbridge, of Portland, Me., born in Manchester, Conn., 1843. No children. The name given us by first informant was as it appears on page 317, but it is here corrected.

371.

SILAS PAYSON[7] CHURCHILL (SILAS,[6] SILAS,[5] CHARLES,[4] SAMUEL,[3] JOSEPH,[2] JOSIAH[1]). Born in New Lebanon, N.Y., Nov. 12, 1832. Lived in Cleveland, O. Married, at La Fayette, Ind., Sept. 15, 1863, MARY AMELIA HOYT.

Children.

	I.	INFANT,[8] b. Oct. 11, 1866; d. same day.
	II.	EDITH EMMA,[8] b. March 14, 1868; d. March 18, 1868.
601	III.	ALFRED PAYSON,[8] b. Sept. 8, 1870.
602	IV.	EUGENE HOYT,[8] b. Aug. 10, 1873.
603	V.	STILES COLLINS AVERY,[8] b. Sept. 27, 1878.

371a.

JOSEPH LYNDE[7] CHURCHILL (SILAS,[6] SILAS,[5] CHARLES,[4] SAMUEL,[3] JOSEPH,[2] JOSIAH[1]). Born in New Lebanon, N.Y., Jan. 30, 1840. He has been a stock-raiser and farmer, and, in 1904, he had been postmaster at Cole's Valley, Ore., seventeen years. Married MILLIE ANN EMMITT, at Cole's Valley, Ore., and they have one

Child.

I. JOHN FRANCIS.[8]

372.

JESSE NORMAN[7] CHURCHILL (WILLIAM BOARDMAN,[6] JESSE,[5] JESSE,[4] SAMUEL,[3] JOSEPH,[2] JOSIAH[1]). Born Jan. 26, 1826, at Ridge Prairie, Ill. He received a common school education, and learned enough of mechanical construction to become an efficient millwright, in which business he was engaged at Monroe, Wis., where he settled. After 1854 he dropped the "Jesse" from his name and was afterwards known as Norman, and his letters to us are signed "N. Churchill." His sister, Caroline E. Bingham,* and her daughter, have been loyal helpers in the compilation of this line of the family. He died May 9, 1901. Married, in Monroe, Feb. 22, 1854, ANNE E. SHERMAN. She was born in Erie County, Penn., in June, 1831.

---

* Of Mrs. Bingham's family, Helen M. graduated at Boston University Medical School in 1881, and practised in Milwaukee eight years, and later removed to Denver; her sister, Ada, graduated at the same school in 1878, and practised in Monroe, but later removed to Denver, where their brother Homer also lives, in 1902, a lumber dealer. Alice (Bingham) Copeland's son, Edwin B., received a liberal education, and received from Halle, Germany, Ph.D., in 1896; was, in 1902, professor of botany in West Virginia University. Now, 1904, he is with the Philippine Commission in Manila. (See ante p. 418.)

Children born in Monroe, Wis.

607   I. CHARLES BOARDMAN,⁸ b. Feb. 19, 1855; m. AMELIA WOOD, dau. of Joseph and Elizabeth Wood, b. in Monroe, Aug. 5, 1857, and married Sept. 8, 1883.

Mr. Churchill carried on a large business under the firm name of Churchill & Co., plumbers, pipe-fitters, etc., with drain tile and other extensive departments. They lived in Monroe, and had children born there.

Children.

1. Edith E., b. June 30, 1885.
2. Charlotte A., b. June 11, 1887.
3. Joseph N., b. Dec. 22, 1893.
4. Helen P., b. Jan. 4, 1896.
5. Norma, b. Aug. 14, 1897.

II. DOLLIE,⁸ b. May 1, 1862; d. Dec. 15, 1864.
III. KITTIE,⁸ b. May 1, 1862; d. Oct. 7, 1865.
608   IV. WILLIAM WILBERFORCE,⁸ b. Jan. 6, 1867; m. 1st, PEARL DADMUN, of Dorchester, Mass., Sept. 29, 1894. She was the daughter of Joseph Dadmun, of Boston (Jamaica Plain), Mass., b. Feb. 22, 1871, and d. Jan. 7, 1896, in New York City; m. 2d, LETTIE E. WOOD, at Monroe, Wis., June 25, 1901.

Mr. Churchill was foreman of the department of mechanical engineering in the firm of Westinghouse, Church, Kerr & Co., of New York City, and, it is said, was chief engineer in the construction of the South Terminal Station in Boston, Mass.

V. MINNIE BEATRICE,⁸ b. April 8, 1869; m. DR. GEORGE WILLIAM COLE, Jan. 21, 1891. He was a physician; at Guerneville, Cal., in 1900.

Child.

1. Margaret, b. June 2, 1892.

VI. ERNI NORMAN,⁸ b. Nov. 25, 1872; m. EDITH D. HARRIS, at Postville, Ia., June 19, 1900. They lived in Monroe, Wis. He is a plumber.

372a.

GEORGE⁷ CHURCHILL (WILLIAM BOARDMAN,⁶ JESSE,⁵ JESSE⁴ SAMUEL,³ JOSEPH,² JOSIAH¹). Born at Ridge Prairie, Ill., May 19, 1830. Married 1st, Oct. 25, 1857, OLIVE BROWN, who died May 1, 1874. Married 2d, May 28, 1876, EMMA SUMMERIL. Mr. Churchill is part proprietor and manager of a planing mill. They live in Monroe, Wis., in 1904.

Child of First Wife.

I. ALICE,⁸ b. Oct. 6, 1859; d. March 16, 1899.

373.

GEORGE⁷ CHURCHILL (NORMAN,⁶ JESSE⁵ JESSE,⁴ SAMUEL,³ JOSEPH,² JOSIAH¹). Born at Winfield, N.Y., April 2, 1829. He removed with his father's family to Galesburg, Ill., in 1839. He received a thorough training in the preparatory department at Knox College, entered the regular course in 1847, and graduated in 1851.

After some years spent in study and teaching, he visited Europe, and while in Germany studied the system of schools, which made him later the efficient leader in the establishment of the graded schools in Galesburg, Ill.   In 1855 he began his real life-work as principal of the Academic Department of Knox College, with the title "professor," which position he held until his death, Sept. 10, 1899. Genial, thorough, and conscientious, he made a deep and lasting impression upon the thousands of students who came under his instruction during his forty years of service.   But his influence was by no means limited to his college work, for he was alderman of Galesburg four years, city engineer for twenty-two years, besides serving on the board of education, the park commission, the library board, and director of the Mechanics and Loan Association for eighteen years.   In the First Church in Galesburg he was a member from 1847, deacon for thirty-six years, leader of the choir and superintendent of the Sunday school for twenty-five years.   He was a true friend, a beloved and honored teacher, and a noble man. Married 1st, Aug. 7, 1855, CLARISSA AMELIA HURD, daughter of Elisha and Harriet W., born in Castile, N.Y., Dec. 23, 1830, and died in Galesburg, Ill., Sept. 27, 1857.   Married 2d, Aug. 23, 1858, at Arlington, Vt., ADALINE HELETIA HAYES, born Aug. 11, 1831, and died in Galesburg, April 24, 1869.   Married 3d, Dec. 22, 1869, MRS. ELLEN MARIA (SANBORN) WATKINS, daughter of David, born in Brimfield, Ill., March 17, 1841.

Child of Professor George and Clarissa A. (Hurd) Churchill, born at Galesburg, Ill.

609   I. MILTON ERASTUS,[8] b. Sept. 5, 1856; m. IDA POST, in Waverley, Neb., Sept. 19, 1883.
She was the daughter of Edwin and Mary (Doolittle) Post, born in Galesburg, Ill., Sept. 19, 1856. Prof. M. E. Churchill had a very thorough training, as shown by the following degrees received by him, viz.: A.B., Knox College, 1877; A.M., 1880; B.D., Yale University, 1883; instructor in Latin and Greek, Knox College, 1878-80 and 1885-87; principal Emerson Institute, Mobile, 1883-85; professor of Latin, Blackburn University, 1887-91; studied in Germany, 1891; professor of Greek and German in Illinois College from 1891. They lived in Jacksonville, Ill., 1903, and had children: (1) Jessie Lucinda, b. Dec. 1, 1885; (2) George Milton, b. Aug. 27, 1888; (3) Delia Post, b. Feb. 14, 1892.

Children of Second Wife.

II. MARY HAYES,[8] b. March 28, 1860; d. July 7, 1863.
III. CHARLES EDWARD,[8] b. Aug. 24, 1862; m. MARGARET SCHRAMM, at Hudson, Wis., May 17, 1890. She was b. Feb. 8, 1867, in Brooklyn, N.Y.
They lived in Chicago, 1899. He was a lawyer; office, 108 Dearborn street.

610   IV. GEORGE B.,[8] b. Aug. 16, 1865; m. 1st, Jan. 17, 1894, MARTHA
LOUISE O'CONNOR, b. in Galesburg, Ill., Nov. 28, 1869,
and she d. Dec. 7, 1894, leaving no children. He m. 2d, CLARA
SCOTT BABCOCK, March 12, 1896. She was b. Oct. 5, 1872.
He was a prosperous hardware merchant in Galesburg. They
lived at Galesburg, and had

Children.

1. Lake George, b. Jan. 10, 1899.
2. Marjorie Pauline, b. Dec. 6, 1900.

V. FANNIE FASSETT,[8] b. May 4, 1867; d. Sept. 11, 1867.

Child of Third Wife.

VI. WILLIAM DAVID,[8] b. Dec. 13, 1876; d. July 8, 1882.

374.

NORMAN[7] CHURCHILL, JR. (NORMAN,[6] JESSE,[5] JESSE,[4]
SAMUEL,[3] JOSEPH,[2] JOSIAH[1]). Born in Winfield, N.Y., July 16,
1833. Removed with his father's family to Galesburg, where he
was brought up, and lived there. He died Sept. 14, 1901. Married,
in Galesburg, Nov. 21, 1860, ANN E. HINSEY, who was born in
Tazewell County, Ill., Feb. 8, 1838.

Children.

611   I. FRED WARREN,[8] b. in Galesburg, Sept. 13, 1861
II. CLARA ADELLE,[8] b. in Henry County, April 20, 1867.
III. JENNIE HINSEY,[8] b. in Galesburg, July 9, 1876; m. GEORGE INNESS,
April 4, 1901, and they had child: (1) Sybil Inness, b. in Gales-
burg, Oct. 5, 1902.

375.

JUSTUS GRISWOLD[7] CHURCHILL (LEVI B.,[6] LEVI,[5] JESSE,[4]
SAMUEL,[3] JOSEPH,[2] JOSIAH[1]). Born at Griswoldville, Conn., Nov.
5, 1816. He died Aug. 22, 1874. Married, Jan. 28, 1844, ABIGAIL
HARRIS.

Children.

612   I. CHARLES M.[8]
II. CLARA,[8] m. SAMUEL ASHWELL, of Rock Hill. Conn.
613   III. FRANK S.,[8] m ELLA F. WILLIAMS, Rock Hill, Conn.
IV. PRUDENCE,[8] m. W. R. GRISWOLD, Rock Hill, Conn.
614   V. WINFIELD S.,[8] m. SARAH W. ROBINSON, Rock Hill, Conn.
VI. BELLE,[8] d. in her fourteenth year.

377.

STEPHEN BELDEN[7] CHURCHILL (LEVI B.,[6] LEVI,[5] JESSE,[4]
SAMUEL,[3] JOSEPH,[2] JOSIAH[1]). Born at Griswoldville, Conn., June
21, 1830. Married, May 5, 1857, ABIGAIL MARIO.

Children.

   I. ALICE AMELIA,⁸ b. July 11. 1858; m. EDMOND S. SMITH.
  II. ELIZABETH MARIA,⁸ b. July 11, 1858; m. CLIFFORD E. CLARK.
 III. EMMA ABIGAIL,⁸ b. Aug. 24, 1862; m. WILLIAM S MORRIS.
615 IV. LEVI BELDEN,⁸ b. Oct. 10, 1864; m. GRACE WATROUS BERRY.
616 V. STEPHEN,⁸ b. Nov. 30, 1867; m. LILLIAN PRUDENCE GRISWOLD, June 15, 1892.
617 VI. FREDERICK GRISWOLD,⁸ b. May 16, 1870; m. ALICE GERTRUDE WOOLEY.
 VII. NELLIE MAY,⁸ b. July 30, 1872; m. EDWARD MCDONOUGH, Oct. 21, 1896.
VIII. HATTIE MABEL,⁸ b. Oct. 28, 1875; m. HIRAM F. SHEPARD, Oct. 21, 1896.

378.

CYRUS B.⁷ CHURCHILL (JAMES,⁶ ITHAMAR,⁵ JESSE,⁴ SAMUEL,³ JOSEPH,² JOSIAH¹). Born in Bloomfield, Morrow County, O., March 17, 1829. They lived in Boon County, Ill., and later at Berrien Springs, Mich. In 1889 Mr. Churchill was conducting a watchmaker and jewelry store, with subscription and news depot, at Berrien Springs, Mich. Married, in Buchanan, Mich., Dec. 24, 1854, SUSANNAH WAGNER, born in Buchanan Feb. 23, 1834.

Children born in Boon County, Ill.

  I. MARY F.,⁸ b. April 3, 1856; unmarried.
 II. IDA,⁸ b. Feb. 23, 1858; m. WIGHTMAN F. SAVAGE, who was b. in New Buffalo, Mich., Dec. 6, 1858.

Children born in New Buffalo.

1. Frank P. Savage, b. Dec. 7, 1880.
2. Irving P. Savage, b. May 14, 1883.
3. Fannie A. Savage, b. Feb. 10, 1887.

379.

MATTHEW MARVIN⁷ CHURCHILL (JAMES,⁶ ITHAMAR,⁵ JESSE,⁴ SAMUEL,³ JOSEPH,² JOSIAH¹). Born in Bloomfield, O., Dec. 1, 1830. He lived in Gladbrook, Ia., in 1884, but removed to Rushville, Neb., in 1886, and was living there in January, 1889, when he wrote this family record in a clear hand. Married NANCY BLOSSER.

Children.

   I. LILLA M.,⁸ b. April 25, 1866.
  II. EMMA A.,⁸ b. April 24, 1868.
 III. LAURA A.,⁸ b. Aug. 17, 1870.
 IV. CRURA A.,⁸ b. Sept. 9, 1873.
618 V. ISAAC,⁸ b. May 23, 1876.
 VI. ELLEN,⁸ b. Aug. 10, 1879.
 VII. FANNIE,⁸ b. May 30, 1881.
VIII. PHEBE,⁸ b. Feb. 26, 1884.

380.

ALMOND ITHAMAR[7] CHURCHILL (JAMES,[6] ITHAMAR,[5] JESSE,[4] SAMUEL,[3] JOSEPH,[2] JOSIAH[1]). Born at Mt. Vernon, O., April 7, 1834. Lived for many years at Toledo, Ia. He was there a cabinet maker and painter, but removed later to South Dakota and lived at Woonsocket He was a county magistrate there. Married, Jan. 30, 1869, MRS. SARAH E. HATHAWAY LEE, born July 9, 1840. She was the widow of Horace R. Lee, who died Dec. 1, 1867. She was born in Lewis County, N.Y

Children.

I. GEORGE HATHAWAY,[8] b. Jan. 1, 1870; d. June 14, 1872.
II. LYDIA HATHAWAY,[8] b. Nov. 29, 1874; d. Aug. 14, 1875.
III. BERNICE L.,[8] b. Sept. 9, 1881; m., Jan. 16, 1901, RALPH P. HARDY. They lived at Oelwein, Ia., in December, 1903.

381.

HARRY J.[7] CHURCHILL (JAMES,[6] ITHAMAR,[5] JESSE,[4] SAMUEL,[3] JOSEPH[2] JOSIAH[1]). Born at Mt. Vernon, O., April 4, 1836. He was living at Keswick, Ia., in 1888. Married, May 27, 1863, MARGARET ANN DUGGER, born May 30, 1837, daughter of James.

Children.

I. ZELLA I.,[8] b. March 19, 1864, at Toledo, Ia.; m. RUSSELL MARTIN, at Hedrick, Ia.
II. LAURA DELL,[8] b. June 7, 1870, and d. at Cuba, Mo., Feb. 20, 1903; m. T. W. NETTERFIELD, Keswick, Ia., June 28, 1891.

Children.

1. Byron A. Netterfield, b. Oct. 4, 1893.
2. Meredith Netterfield, d. in infancy.
3. Pansy Grace Netterfield, b. Oct. 29, 1900.

619   III. JAMES ANDREW,[8] b. Sept. 22, 1873; m. ORA HARDING, at Keswick, Ia., June 30, 1896.

Children.

1. Margaret Lucille, b. Jan. 12, 1898.
2. Clara Waunita, b. Dec. 18, 1899.
3. Doris Gail, b. May 7, 1902.

620   IV. NORMAN ALMOND,[8] b. June 15, 1877; unmarried in 1903.
621   V. EDMOND ORSEMUS.[8] b. Jan. 13, 1881; m. LILLIAN SUTTON, at Gunnison, Col., April 20, 1903.

385.

CHARLES HYDE[7] CHURCHILL (ARA,[6] ASAHEL,[5] BENJAMIN,[4] SAMUEL,[3] JOSEPH,[2] JOSIAH[1]). Born at Batavia, N.Y., April 28, 1814. Lived at Alexander, a farmer, a quiet and somewhat retiring man, but an excellent and respected citizen. An interesting feature of his was that one of his eyes was light gray, while the other was a keen black, the sight of each equally good. He died Jan. 21, 1893. Married 1st, at Alexander, N.Y., Oct. 25, 1841, JANE INNES, daughter of Henry and Nancy (Van de Bogart) Innes. Married 2d, MARY B. RANDALL, Dec. 1, 1858, daughter of Joseph and Lydia (Chapman) Randall.

Children born at Alexander.

    I. JANE ROSETTE,[8] b. July 7, 1843; d. unmarried at Alexander, March 4, 1891. A great sufferer for long years, but patient and uncomplaining; a sweet and beautiful soul.
    II. DELIA ANN,[8] b. Nov. 22, 1845; d. Nov. 11, 1851.
    III. MARTHA LOUISE,[8] b. Dec. 16, 1847; unmarried. She helped us to get a correct account of her father's family, and was living, in March, 1901, on the old homestead at Alexander, where she was born, but with post-office address at Batavia.
622   IV. JOHN HENRY,[8] b. July 5, 1852; m. HARRIET A. WITTER at Alexander, Dec. 29. 1881. She was the daughter of William and Mary (Perkins) Witter.
        They lived at Batavia, on a farm, and had one son, viz.: (1) Charles Witter, b..Nov. 2, 1882.

386.

ARA DON [7] CHURCHILL (ARA,[6] ASAHEL,[5] BENJAMIN,[4] SAMUEL,[3] JOSEPH,[2] JOSIAH [1]). Born at Alexander, Jan. 21, 1825, and settled first as a farmer, afterwards a grocer, and finally a hardware merchant at Fairport, N.Y. He had an excellent voice and was a successful singing-school teacher, until the death of his daughters from diphtheria, a severe blow from which he could not recover. A genial and kindly man, a respected citizen. Died Oct. 23, 1891, at Fairport, N.Y. Married, at Darien, N.Y., Jan. 8, 1851, BETSEY ROOT STIMERS, daughter of George and Lydia (Root) Stimers.

Children born at Alexander.

    I. EDITH ELIZABETH,[8] b. Jan. 19, 1852; d. April 6, 1866.
    II. APHIA MAY,[8] b. Dec. 22, 1859; d. April 9, 1866
    III. SARAH LYDIA,[8] b. Nov. 9, 1865; m. AUDOBON FRANK WARREN, Fairport, N.Y., May 10, 1888.

386a.

JAMES BRYAN [7] CHURCHILL (BENJAMIN [6] ASAHEL,[5] BENJAMIN,[4] SAMUEL,[3] JOSEPH,[2] JOSIAH [1]). Born April 18, 1817. Lived for some time in Madison, N.C., and was a tinman by trade and prosperous in earlier days. In 1899 he was living with his daughter, Mrs. Jones. Married, 1838, SARAH HALL, of North Carolina.

Children.

623   I. JOHN HENRY,[8] b. Jan. 3, 1839; d. about 1882; m. MARY CATHERINE
BROWER, daughter of Fletcher and Catherine Brower, at
Greensboro', N.C., January, 1860. They lived at Pittsboro,
where he was a lumberman.

Children born in Pittsboro.

1. Lulu Catherine, b. Nov. 30, 1861; m. William Francis Jones,
   June 10, 1878, at Farmington, N.C. No children.
2. Thomas Benjamin, b. in 1862; d. in 1864.
3. Henry Lewis, b. 1864.
4. Virginia Brown, b. 1866; m. Frank B. Ward, January, 1893,
   at Farmington, N.C., and died there, November, 1893

624   II. BENJAMIN LUTHER,[8] b. at Newbern, Sept. 9, 1840; d. about 1886;
m. SUSAN GREEN, at Newbern, N.C., in 1864. They lived in
Newbern.

Children born in Newbern.

1. Lee.
2. Thomas.
3. Benjamin.
   These three sons grew to manhood and died unmarried.
4. Katherine, m. Charles McGehe, at Newbern, N.C.

III. MARTHA ANN,[8] b. March 20, 1842; m. 1st, EDWARD JONES, in 1859,
He was killed in the Civil War in 1861; m. 2d, H. S. PRATT, in
1863. They lived at Madison, N.C. Four children it is said,
but names not obtained.
IV. ELIAS S.,[8] b. Aug. 10, 1845; d. in infancy.
V. CORNELIA LEE,[8] b. April 8, 1847; m. M. F. PERRY, of Ridgeway,
N.C., and lived there in 1899. No children.
625   VI. JOSEPH MARTIN,[8] b. Jan. 9, 1849; d. about 1871, at Ridgeway.
VII. SAMUEL W.,[8] b. May 20, 1850; d. in infancy.
VIII. ANNIE ELIZA,[8] b. Nov. 24, 1853; m. JERRY HUDSON, who died in
the fall of 1889 leaving the widow with six children, the oldest,
Annie Eulalia Hudson, the rest of the names not mentioned.
Lived at Winston, N.C., in 1899.
IX. MARY ESTELLE,[8] b. Jan 5, 1856; m. GEORGE O. JONES, Oct. 26,
1873. Mr. Jones was a wholesale tobacco-merchant at Ridgeway,
Va.

Children.

1. George Byron Jones, b. Jan. 9, 1877.
2. John B. Jones, b. July 8, 1879.
3. Thomas King Jones, b. July 31, 1881.
4. James Benjamin Jones, b. Oct. 17, 1883.
5. Mary Churchill Jones, b. April 15, 1886.
6. Daisy Jones, b. Oct. 6, 1888.
7. Gertrude Osborn Jones, b. Dec. 27, 1890.
8. Samuel Paul Jones, b. June 19, 1893, and d. March 14, 1894.

X. SUSAN WALKER,[8] b. Sept. 14, 1860; m. GEORGE I. GRIGGS, Nov. 10,
1878.

Children.

1. Katie Wills Griggs, b. Sept. 4, 1879.
2. Maggie Hall Griggs, b. Dec. 25, 1881.
3. Susan Churchill Griggs, b. Dec. 12, 1884.
4. Mary Bud Griggs, b. May 4, 1887.
   The above family live in Ridgeway, Va.

387.

REV. ORRIN[7] CHURCHILL (Benjamin,[6] Asahel,[5] Benjamin,[4] Samuel,[3] Joseph,[2] Josiah[1]). Born in Newbern, N.C., Oct. 19, 1819. He was a Baptist minister. They lived in Moncure, N.C., where all the children were born. Mr. Churchill himself gave his family record, but gave no marriages or other information concerning his children than we give below. Married 1st, Dec. 12, 1839, Sarah Reid, who died Sept. 12, 1846. Married 2d, Jan. 7, 1847, Rhoda Ann Shackford. He died Sept. 20, 1895.

Children of First Wife.

 I. Caroline,[8] b. Oct. 19, 1842.
626 II. John Robinson,[8] b. Sept. 2, 1844.
 III. Mary Ann,[8] b. July 23, 1846; d. in infancy.

Children of Second Wife.

 IV. Sarah A.,[8] b. Oct. 22, 1848.
627 V. James Benjamin,[8] b. June 17, 1849; d. June 30, 1888.
628 VI. Sidney Daniel,[8] b. June 22, 1853.
 VII. Martha Jane,[8] b. May 31, 1856; d. in infancy.
 VIII. Annie H.,[8] b. Aug. 7, 1858.
629 IX. Thomas W.,[8] b. July 27, 1860; m. Emma Harris, at Haywood, N.C., Dec, 20, 1882.
 They lived at Haywood. In January, 1904, he gave me his own family, but nothing more.

Children born at Haywood.

 1. Ernest Coin, b. Oct. 30, 1883.
 2. Mary Line, b. Aug. 20, 1885.
 3. Clara Baine, b. Aug. 20, 1887.
 4. Rosa Emma, b. Feb. 14, 1889.
 5. Orin Henry, b. July 27, 1890; d. July 27, 1890.
 6. Marguerite, b. Aug. 9, 1891.
 7. Lessie, b. July 17, 1893.

630 X. Charles S.,[8] b. Sept. 21, 1863.

388.

CHESTER R.[7] CHURCHILL * (Chester,[6] Samuel,[5] Benjamin,[4] Samuel,[3] Joseph,[2] Josiah[1]). Born in Batavia, N.Y. He removed West and settled in Barry, Ill.; a farmer. Married in 1853, at Batavia, N.Y., Maria Horner.

* Information received from Mrs. Cordelia (Churchill) Clark, of Kinderhook, Ill., since page 425 was printed, adds somewhat to our meagre account of the family of Chester[6] Churchill, No. 159, on that page. We can give here the names of his children in the order of birth, but without dates: I. Mahala; II. Almon S.; III. Melvin B.; IV. Mariette; V. Chester R.; VI. Samuel; VII Albert; VIII. Cordelia, and IX. Cornelia. The last two were twins. All the information given me by Mrs. Clark, besides this list, is found in the numbers from 388 to 389c inclusive.

Children born at Barry, Ill.

I. CHARLES.[8]
II. CLARA.[8]
III. SOPHIA.[8]
IV. ELMER.[8]
V. CHESTER.[8]
VI. IDA.[8]

389.

ALMON S.[7] CHURCHILL (CHESTER[6] SAMUEL,[5] BENJAMIN,[4] SAMUEL,[3] JOSEPH,[2] JOSIAH[1]). Born in Batavia, July 28, 1813. Lived in Batavia, N.Y., and later in Kinderhook, Ill. He was a farmer. Married LOUISIANA SMITH, in Batavia, N.Y.

Children, the first born in Batavia, the rest in Kinderhook.

I. JAMES A.,[8] m. LOUISA MORRIS.
II. EDWARD,[8] m. MARY CARR.
III. HIRAM S.,[8] m. MARTHA SMITH.
IV. NANCY M.,[8] m. J. R. FOX.

389a.

MELVIN B.[7] CHURCHILL (CHESTER,[6] SAMUEL,[5] BENJAMIN,[4] SAMUEL,[3] JOSEPH,[2] JOSIAH[1]). Born in Batavia, N.Y. Settled in Kinderhook, Ill. Married SARAH HORNER.

Children born in Kinderhook.

I. HENRY.[8]
II. AMANDA.[8]
III. HELEN.[8]
IV. EMMA.[8]
V. CHESTER.[8]
VI. SARAH.[8]

389b.

CORDELIA[7] CHURCHILL (CHESTER,[6] SAMUEL[5] BENJAMIN,[4] SAMUEL,[3] JOSEPH,[2] JOSIAH[1]). Born in Batavia, N.Y. Settled and lived at Kinderhook, Ill. Married, May 18, 1846, ASA CLARK, farmer, then of Batavia, N.Y.

Children born in Kinderhook,

I. HERBERT C. CLARK, b. May 6, 1854; m. ELLA WAGG.
II. LIBBIE C. CLARK, b. Jan. 28, 1860; m. AARON BONNIFIELD.
III. MARY A. CLARK, b. Jan. 4, 1863; m. CHARLES WAGG.
IV. FRANK A. CLARK, b. Feb. 6, 1865; m. ETTA TALBOT.

389c.

CORNELIA[7] CHURCHILL (CHESTER,[6] SAMUEL,[5] BENJAMIN,[4] SAMUEL,[3] JOSEPH,[2] JOSIAH[1]). Born in Batavia, N.Y. Lived and died in Corfu, N.Y. Married JOHN HUNN.

Child born in Corfu, N. Y.

   I. Isabelle[8] Hunn, died young, in Corfu.

390.

GEORGE[7] CHURCHILL (Daney,[6] Samuel,[5] Benjamin,[4] Samuel,[3] Joseph,[2] Joseph[1]). Born in Portland, N.Y., July 26, 1821, and lived there. Married, at Portland, May 17, 1852, Eliza J. Wade Fletcher.

One child born at Portland, N. Y.

   I. George Daney,[8] b. March 22, 1860; d. Aug. 11, 1864.

391.

*DARIUS DANA[7] CHURCHILL (Samuel,[6] Samuel,[5] Benjamin,[4] Samuel,[3] Joseph,[2] Josiah[1]). Born in Batavia, N.Y., Oct. 24, 1827. Settled in Batavia, N.Y., a farmer. In 1904 he was living in Daws, N.Y., and Mrs. Churchill filled out blanks which enabled me to give the following account of the family. Married, in Leroy, N.Y., March 30, 1850, Emily Shadbolt, daughter of Robert and Abbie (Wilder) Shadbolt, born March 27, 1833. The record below is corrected up to 1904.

Children born in Batavia, N. Y.

   I. Almeda,[8] b. Oct. 24, 1851; m. John O. Higley, March 11, 1874. They lived at Batavia, where he was a farmer. One child, (1) Homer D. Higley, b. Aug. 30, 1880.
  II. Emily,[8] b. Jan. 19, 1854; m. Cleveland Wilber, Nov. 24, 1871. They lived at Batavia, where he was a farmer.

Children.

   1. George Sanford Wilber, b. July 17, 1873.
   2. Earl Dana Wilber, b. Nov. 10, 1877.
631 III. George B.,[8] b. Nov. 14, 1862; m. Clara B. Edgerton, Nov. 28, 1883. They lived at Elba, N.Y. He was a farmer.

---

  * We have additional data relating to No. 162 since page 427 was printed, and in this note the six children of Samuel,[6] whose names we had not then received, are included with such record as we have now obtained. To Darius Dana,[7] No. 391, and Walter H.,[7] No. 391a, we add: II. Sarah,[7] b. June 1, 1830; m. 1st, Amasa E. Dorman, Feb. 19, 1852, at Batavia. He d. July 2, 1866, and she m. 2d, March 23, 1893, Simeon W. Hosmer, who d. December 31 of the same year. Child by first husband, (1) George E. Dorman, b. March 29, 1854, and m. Nettie Howe, March 29, 1879. III. Martha,[7] b. Jan. 18, 1834; m. John Kern, Aug. 14, 1853. IV. Walter H.; see 391a. V. Elizabeth,[7] b. May 1, 1840; m. Joseph Adams, at Batavia, Aug. 28, 1861. VI. Harriet,[7] b. Sept. 3, 1842; m. William Walker, Sept. 3, 1862. VII. Ellen,[7] b. March 7, 1846; m. Henry Walker, March 23, 1864. VIII. Mary,[7] b. March 3, 1850; m. Otis G. Elliot, July 9, 1870.

Children.

1. Clark B., b. Sept. 9, 1884.
2. Walter H., b. Feb. 28, 1886.
3. John S., b. Sept. 30, 1887.
4. Charles R., b. Nov. 8, 1889.
5. Emily J., b. Dec. 22, 1891.
6. Mary Meda, b. Aug. 13, 1894.
7. Sarah R., b. Nov. 21, 1896.
8. Darius D., b. July 5, 1899.
9. Hazel, b. Dec. 20, 1901.
10. A son, b. Jan. 2, 1903; d. unnamed.

632   IV. HOWARD D.,[8] b. Sept. 6, 1866; m. PHILOLA EDGERTON, March 21, 1888. They live at Elba, N.Y., where he is a farmer. Child, (1) Helen E., b. Dec. 19, 1897.

633   V. ROBERT SAMUEL,[8] b. July 8, 1872; m. CARRIE S. HUBBARD, Jan. 14, 1892. They live at Batavia, where he is a farmer. Child, (1) Ruth M., b. Dec. 4, 1893.

391a.

WALTER H.[7] CHURCHILL (SAMUEL,[6] SAMUEL,[5] BENJAMIN,[4] SAMUEL,[3] JOSEPH,[2] JOSIAH [1]). Born in Batavia, N.Y., April 27, 1838. He lived in Batavia until about 1869, when he removed to Michigan and settled at Shelby, where he spent the rest of his useful life. He was judge of probate of Oceana County, Mich., for years. He died June 23, 1900. Married 1st, in Batavia, N.Y., Jan. 24, 1859, JANE GREEN, who died June 10, 1868, in Shelby, Mich. Married 2d, in 1869, LUCADA A. CARTER, who died Dec. 23, 1872, in Shelby, Mich. Married 3d, at Whitehall, Mich., Dec. 25, 1874, SARAH A. HAMLIN, who was living in Shelby, Mich., 1903.

Children of First Wife, born in Batavia, N. Y.

I. IDA,[7] d. young.
II. WILLIAM H.,[8] d. young.

Children of Second Wife, born in Shelby, Mich.

634   III. CHARLES L.,[8] b. Nov. 16, 1870; m. MOLLIE PURCELL, at Grand Rapids, Mich., Nov. 12, 1891. They lived at Shelby, and had children born there.

Children.

1. Lucada G., b. Dec. 2, 1892.
2. Walter H., b. Dec. 18, 1897.
3. Charles L., b. March 1, 1900.
4. Robert C., b. Feb. 13, 1901.

IV. WALTER H.,[8] b. in 1872; d. in 1873.

392.

JOHN HARVEY[7] CHURCHILL (ITHUEL,[6] SAMUEL,[5] BENJA-MIN,[4] SAMUEL,[3] JOSEPH,[2] JOSIAH [1]). Born in Portland, N Y., Dec. 18, 1848. Removed with his father's family to Pontiac, Mich. In

1886 he was living at Battle River, Custer County, Dakota, when
his letter-head was " Dr. H. J. Churchill, dealer in drugs, groceries,
notions, etc." His signature was Harvey John Churchill. In 1899
we received his address as " Hermosa, South Dakota," but our letter
was not answered, and we have no news since. Married, at Dewitt,
Mich., 7 May, 1882, ESTELLA L. HART.

393.

EDWIN [7] CHURCHILL (PHILO C.,[6] SAMUEL [5] BENJAMIN,[4] SAM
UEL,[3] JOSEPH,[2] JOSIAH [1]). Born at Kinderhook, Pike County, Ill.,
Sept. 18, 1839. After receiving what instruction he could get at
the home school, he went to Greenwood, Ind., to attend the school
there, working for his board. In the spring of 1861 he enlisted
among the first of the Volunteers, in Company D, Seventeenth Indiana Regiment, and served under General Rosencrantz, in General
Sherman's corps, and was engaged in many battles in that fighting
division during his three years of service. At the end of his term
he reënlisted and after a furlough at home, during which he married
and spent some time recruiting for his regiment, he was commissioned Second Lieutenant, and rejoining his regiment at the front,
served to the end of the war, going with Sherman's army " from
Atlanta to the Sea." After the war he returned to Greenwood and
taught school and " farmed it " for awhile, and then moved to Wolcott, Ind. He was an earnest and consistent Christian man and did
much good in the churches in Wolcott. He died March 15, 1875.
Married, in Greenwood, Ind., Feb. 11, 1864, SARAH CARRIE WEST,
born Dec. 29, 1844. She was the daughter of John and Keren H.
(Hendricks) West.

Children born, three in Greenwood and two in Wolcott, Ind.

635 I. WILLIAM C.,[8] b. Nov. 20, 1867 ; m. MAUDE BURTON, at Goodland,
    Ind., April 21, 1896. They lived at Wolcott, Ind. (1904). He
    was a builder and contractor.

Child.

   1. Donald Glenn, b. at Wolcott, Ind., May 15, 1900.

 II. KATIE A.,[8] b. Oct. 23, 1869; d. May 26, 1886.
III. HAPPY C.,[8] b. Sept. 18, 1871; m. O. C. PECK, at Wolcott, Oct. 10,
   1894.

Children.

   1. Virgil Peck, b. November, 1895; d. April 30, 1896, aged five
    months.
   2. Fannie Peck, b. Feb. 3, 1898.
   3. Harley Peck, b. Oct. 16, 1900.

 IV. DAISIE L.,[8] b. July 16, 1873; m. JOHN W. DUNLOP, at Wolcott,
   Oct. 2, 1889.

Children.

1. Charles Dunlop, b. Dec. 14, 1890.
2. Carrie Dunlop, b. Aug. 12. 1892.
3. Flora Dunlop, b. Feb. 21, 1893.
4. Virgil Dunlop, b. May 26, 1895.
5. Helen M. Dunlop, b. Jan. 2, 1902.

636   V. JOHN EDWIN,[8] b. Feb. 13, 1875; m. MARGARET COLLINS, at Reynolds, Ind., Nov. 15, 1898.

394.

DANEY JABEZ[7] CHURCHILL (PHILO C.,[6] SAMUEL,[5] BENJAMIN,[4] SAMUEL,[3] JOSEPH,[2] JOSIAH[1]). Born in Kinderhook, Pike County, Ill., Jan. 10, 1841. He was an artist and music teacher. He died in St. Joseph, Mo., Nov. 22, 1893. Married, April 13, 1863, MARTHA GATES. He is said to have married twice, later, but we have not the record.

Children of First Wife.

637   I. ELMER.[8]
638   II. OTTO.[8] Said to have been living in St. Joseph, Mo., in 1902, but we received no answer to our letters and circulars.

395.

FRANCIS WAYLAND[7] CHURCHILL (PHILO CLARK,[6] SAMUEL,[5] BENJAMIN,[4] SAMUEL,[3] JOSEPH,[2] JOSIAH[1]). Born in Kinderhook, Ill., Oct. 24, 1845. He was a baker by trade and was located at Kansas City, Mo., in 1904. Married at Bedford, Iowa, March 1, 1871, ELLA SHAFFER.

Children.

I. RUBY P.,[8] b. in Bedford, Iowa, February, 1872.
II. ERNEST,[8] b. in Columbus, Kan., 1875; d. unmarried in 1896.
III. DANEY,[8] b in Albany, Mo., April, 1877.
IV. OSTIA,[8] b. in St. Joseph, Mo., 1887.
V. MINNIE,[8] b. in St. Joseph, 1889

396.

ROBERT CLARK[7] CHURCHILL (PHILO CLARK,[6] SAMUEL[5] BENJAMIN,[4] SAMUEL,[3] JOSEPH,[2] JOSIAH[1]). Born in Hilton, Ill., June 4, 1866. He was educated at the common school, and learned stenography, and, at the age of twenty, went to St. Louis to try his hand at the work, but soon abandoned it, and tried various other forms of clerical work in St. Louis, and finally found employment in Keosauqua, where he worked until his marriage, when he went to farming in Iowa, for a year or more, and then removed to Oregon,

and, after trying several localities like Medford and Williams in
that State, finally settled at Selma, where he has a farm of one
hundred and sixty acres of land, conducts a store, and is postmaster.
Mr. Churchill has taken an interest in our work and helped along
upon his own line.   Our last letter from him was on Jan. 21, 1902.
Married, at Leando, Iowa, Feb. 26, 1890, MIRIAM LEOTA PARK.

Children.

	I. JESSIE A.,[8] b. Dec. 17, 1890, at Keosauqua, Iowa.
639	II. CARL B.,[8] b. June 23, 1893, at Selma, Ore.
640	III. EMMET C.,[8] b. May 16, 1895, at Selma, Ore.
	IV. FLORENCE,[8] b. Jan. 30, 1898, at Selma, Ore.
641	V. SAMUEL C.,[8] b. March 24, 1900, at Selma, Ore.
642	VI. OTTO,[8] b. Dec. 9, 1901, at Selma, Ore.

397.

RICHARD MARTIN [7] CHURCHILL (BARNABAS,[6] IRA,[5] BENJA-
MIN,[4] SAMUEL,[3] JOSEPH,[2] JOSIAH [1]).   Born in Bristol, Conn., March
16, 1817.   Removed with his father's family to Greene, Ohio, in
1820.   He died at Vineland, N.J., May 27, 1880.   Married at
Mecca, Ohio, Dec. 2, 1843, ISABEL MILLER.

Children.

I. CHARLES FRANKLIN,[8] b. in Greene, Ohio; d. before 1901.
II. HORACE CARTER,[8] d. in Wayne County, Ohio.
III. HUBERT,[8] d. in Wayne County, Ohio.
IV. LUCY ADELLA.[8]
V. MARY ISABEL,[8] m. MR. NEWTON, and lived some time in Oneonta,
N.Y., but we received no answers to our inquiries.

398.

SALMON ROOT [7] CHURCHILL (BARNABAS,[6] IRA,[5] BENJAMIN,[4]
SAMUEL,[3] JOSEPH,[2] JOSIAH [1]).   Born in Bristol, Ohio, Feb. 25, 1821.
Lived in New Brighton, Minn., where he died March 14, 1890.   We
have not received answers to letters of inquiry sent to a daughter,
said to have lived at New Brighton in 1901.   Married, at Greene
Ohio, September, 1850, SARAH HOAGLAND.

Children.

I. LAPORTE.[8]
II. AGNES.[8]
III. EMILY.[8]
IV. AMY.[8]

399.

OTTO BURCHARD [7] CHURCHILL (CEYLON,[6] IRA,[5] BENJAMIN [4]
SAMUEL,[3] JOSEPH,[2] JOSIAH [1]).   Born in Bristol, Ohio, June 16, 1852.
He was reared and received his education and has always lived in or

near Cortland, Ohio, where in 1901 he was a prosperous wholesale dealer in country produce and was one of the directors of the First National Bank in Cortland. Married at Cortland, Ohio, March 18, 1877, MARY JANE CRAFT, who was born in Mecca, Ohio, March 8, 1856.

Children born in Cortland.

 I. MARY FLORINE,[8] b. Jan. 12, 1878.
 II. BESSIE EVE,[8] b. June 24, 1882.
 III. ALDA BURR,[8] b. Dec. 5, 1884.
643 IV. FRANK R.,[8] b. Nov. 5, 1886.
644 V. SEALY J.,[8] b. July 14, 1889.

400.

EDWIN JEROME [7] CHURCHILL (JOSEPH H.,[6] JEDEDIAH,[5] BENJAMIN,[4] SAMUEL,[3] JOSEPH,[2] JOSIAH [1]). Born in New Hartford, N.Y., July 18, 1833. Lived there and later in Kirkland, N.Y. Mr. Churchill wrote us in 1890 that his brother, Henry C., lived in Norfolk, Va., and his brother, Joseph C., in Alto, Mich., but we could not reach either by letter. Married, Sept. 21, 1858, ELLEN M. COOK.

Children born in New Hartford, N.Y.

 I. JOSEPHINE ESTELLA,[8] b. July 3, 1859; d. Nov. 29, 1885.
 II. NETTIE GERTRUDE,[8] b. Sept. 24, 1861.
645 III. EDWIN PLATT,[8] b. June 27, 1869.
 IV. ALLANTHEN COOK,[8] b. April 16, 1872; d. July 27, 1872.

402.

BENJAMIN W.[7] CHURCHILL (JOSEPH H.,[6] JEDEDIAH,[5] BENJAMIN,[4] SAMUEL,[3] JOSEPH,[2] JOSIAH [1]). Born in New Hartford, N.Y., July 6, 1843. This family was living, in March, 1890, in Whitesboro, N.Y., and Mr. Churchill then wrote us the account of his family. Married, June 7, 1865, ELLEN M. CRUMB, born Nov. 30, 1845.

Children.

 I. MARION L.,[8] b. Feb. 21, 1866; m. F. A. MOULTON, Oct. 16, 1889.
646 II. FRANKLIN F.,[8] b. Aug. 7, 1867.
647 III. JOSEPH G.,[8] b. Jan. 21, 1869.
 IV. SARAH J.,[8] b. Sept. 20, 1871.
 V. WILLIAM D.,[8] b. Sept. 18, 1873; d. March 21, 1875.
648 VI. BENJAMIN W.,[8] b. June 26, 1876.
 VII. ETHEL MAY,[8] b. July 16, 1885.

403.

JAY A.[7] CHURCHILL (ANSON J.,[6] JEDEDIAH,[5] BENJAMIN,[4] SAMUEL,[3] JOSEPH,[2] JOSIAH [1]). Born, probably at West Vienna, N.Y., but June 16, 1886, was living at Whitestone, L.I., and wrote us a letter, but gave only the names of his father and brothers and their addresses at that time. William H., West Vienna, who, he says, was a soldier all through the Civil War, Rev. Joseph, who was then at West Vienna, N.Y., George E. whose address was in doubt.

In December, 1904, I learned from the postmaster at West Vienna, N.Y., that the family have all gone from that town and, as well as he could learn, the father, Anson J., married Sarah Mallory, and that Jay A. is married and is a minister in the New York Conference, that Rev. Joseph lived at Sheepshead Bay, L.I., but our letter to that address was returned unclaimed; that George E. married Gertrude Dickinson; that William H. is dead; that Mrs. Lovina Washburn's address was Oil City, Penn., but my letter to her was also returned unclaimed, so that this is all the account we have been able to obtain of the family.

407.

FRANKLIN DWIGHT[7] CHURCHILL (Lewis,[6] David,[5] William,[4] Samuel,[3] Joseph,[2] Josiah[1]). Born in Bethany, Conn., Feb. 14, 1834. This family live (1902) in Southington, Conn. Married JANE L. BLAKESLEE, of Prospect, Conn.

Children.

      I. Arthur James,[8] b. Dec. 20, 1861; unmarried.
649   II. Frank Blakeslee,[8] b. Sept. 26, 1864; m.

Children.

   1. Maud.   2. Clyde.
650 III. William Dwight,[8] b. Jan. 8, 1877.

411.

WILLIAM H.[7] CHURCHILL (William T.,[6] Lemuel[5] William,[4] Samuel,[3] Joseph,[2] Josiah[1]). Born, Feb. 27, 1833, in Tioga County, Penn. His father died a few months before he was born. When three years old he was taken and brought up by people outside his family, his mother having married a second husband. He lived in Rensselaer, Ind., in 1886. Married, Jan. 7, 1861, Louisa Nichols, born Jan. 12, 1835. This record was obtained in 1886.

Children.

651   I. William Augustus,[8] b. Oct. 1, 1862.
652   II. Marcus Austin,[8] b. May 22, 1864.
653 III. Thomas Corwin,[8] b. Aug. 30, 1865.
654 IV. Fenton Orris,[8] b. Jan. 18, 1867.
655   V. Luther Ellsworth,[8] b. Jan. 24, 1869.
656 VI. Marion Atwood,[8] b. May 17, 1870.
      VII. Cheney Oscar,[8] b. Feb. 16, 1872; d. May 2, 1872.
657 VIII. Herman Hoyt,[8] b. Aug. 7, 1875.

414.

JOSIAH BUTLER[7] CHURCHILL (Dr. Charles[6] Lemuel,[5] William,[4] Samuel,[3] Joseph,[2] Josiah[1]). Born Dec. 4, 1836. Mr. Churchill was living in Lawrence, Kan., March 4, 1886, and gave us this account of his family.. Married, Sept. 21, 1865, Catherine Kissel.

Children.

I. Bessie May,[8] b. May 1, 1868.
658   II. Carlie Dio,[8] b. June 26, 1874.

417.

JOHN SILAS[7] CHURCHILL (Joseph D.,[6] William,[5] William,[4] Samuel,[3] Joseph,[2] Josiah[1]). Born, Nov. 24, 1828, at Pineville, Izard County, Ark. Married, Dec. 30, 1851, Susan Jane Taylor.

Children.

659   I. George Washington,[8] b. July 26, 1852; m. Kesiah Morgan.

Children.

1. Rebecca, b. Sept. 23, 1875.
2. John Thomas, b. Dec. 30, 1876.
3. Mary Lovina, b. May 23, 1879
4. Olive Jane, b. Dec. 19, 1881.
5. William Ambrose, b. Feb. 18, 1887.

II. Christy Ann,[8] b. July 1, 1854; d. Sept. 22, 1876.
III. Sarah Elizabeth,[8] b. May 29, 1856; m. Jacob Henry Fitzhugh.

Children.

1. John Fitzhugh, b. Jan. 22, 1877.
2. Tildia Fitzhugh, b. Aug. 8, 1881.
3. Alexander Fitzhugh, b. July 3, 1887.

IV. Louisa Jane,[8] b. Sept. 4, 1858; m. De Leon Laport Coplin.

Children.

1. John Wesley Coplin, b. Dec. 24, 1877.
2. Albert Washington Coplin, b. Dec. 13, 1879.

V. William Martin,[8] b. Nov. 19, 1860; d. Aug. 4, 1868.
660   VI. Henry Price,[8] b. July 13, 1863.
VII. Rebecca,[8] } b. July 7, 1869 { d. Nov. 20, 1871.
VIII. Lavinia,[8] } { d. September, 1869.

418.

JAMES JEFFREY[7] CHURCHILL (Joseph Dell,[6] William,[5] William,[4] Samuel,[3] Joseph,[2] Josiah[1]). Born at Pineville, Ark., Dec. 30, 1829. He was a farmer and house builder, and lived at different times at Russellville, Glassvillage, and Appleton, Ark., and 1904, Leta, Ark. Married, at Pineville, Ark., Aug. 31, 1859, Martha Ann Scott. She was the daughter of George W. and Mary (Hill) Scott.

Children.

660a   I. JOSEPH WILLIAM,⁸ b. Sept. 9, 1860; m. 1st, ELIZABETH CACKS; m. 2d, LETHY COFFMAN.
   II. JAMES JEFFREY,⁸ b. July 23, 1862; d. at Russellville, Ark., 1864.
   III. MARY CHRISTIA,⁸ b. Jan. 27, 1866; m. MARION EDWARD COFFMAN.
660b   IV. GEORGE WASHINGTON,⁸ b. Feb. 13, 1868; m. MARTHA E. AKINS.
   V. JOHN GREEN,⁸ b. Feb. 2, 1870; d. at Glassvillage, Ark., March 2, 1872.
660c   VI. HENRY AMBROSE,⁸ b. Jan. 24, 1871; m. MARY VAUGHN.
   VII. ALFRED ALLEN,⁸ b. Aug. 11, 1873; d. at Glassvillage, Ark., Feb. 11, 1874.
   VIII. REV. JASPER NEWTON,⁸ b. Jan. 21, 1875; m. MARY FRANCES BRUNCE.
   IX. MONROE KING,⁸ b. Oct. 17, 1877; m. EDA KANSAS STORY.
   X. ANDREW JACKSON,⁸ b. Feb. 9, 1879; m. RONA MAY VOSS.
   XI. SAMUEL DAVID,⁸ b. Feb. 19, 1880; d. at Appleton, Ark., Feb. 17, 1902.

419.

WILLIAM WALKER⁷ CHURCHILL (JOSEPH DELL,⁶ WILLIAM,⁵ WILLIAM,⁴ SAMUEL,³ JOSEPH,² JOSIAH¹). Born at Pineville, Ark., Aug. 14, 1840. He was a farmer at Galley Rock, Ark., and Whitt, Texas, from 1875 or 1876. Still living at Whitt, with wife Delphine, in 1904. Married 1st, at Galley Rock, Ark., December, 1869, LYDIA MATTHEWS, died, 1873; married, 2d, at Clinton, Ark. January, 1874, DELPHINE MCALISTER.

Child of First Wife born at Galley Rock, Ark.

660d   I. ELTON LEETH,⁸ b. Jan. 16, 1872; m. LAURA MORELAND, at Whitt, Texas, Feb. 8, 1891.

Children born at Whitt, Texas.

1. Lydia Ann, b. March 30, 1892.
2. James Albert, b. Jan. 10, 1895.
3. Jarrel Eli, b. Dec. 16, 1896.
4. Robert Raymon, b. July 3, 1900.

Children of Second Wife born at Whitt, Texas.

660e   II. JOSEPH CRAFFORD,⁸ b. Dec. 4, 1877; m. BERTHA LUSK, at Whitt, Texas, July 15, 1898.

Children born at Whitt, Texas.

1. Cula Clare, b. June 30, 1900.
2. Veracue Gladys, b. April 3, 1902.
   III. SANORA FLORENCE,⁸ b. Oct. 14, 1880; m. J. O. TAYLOR, at Whitt, Texas, July 29, 1899. They live at Valley Creek, Texas; he is a farmer.

Children.

1. Pearlie Beatrice Taylor, b. May 27, 1902.
2. Barbara Alice Taylor, b. Dec. 21, 1903.
   IV. DEMPSEY MONROE,⁸ b. July 7, 1882; d. July 20, 1885.
   V. PEARLEY ARMINDA,⁸ b. July 10, 1885.
660f   VI. WILLIAM WALKER, JR.,⁸ b. Sept. 30, 1888.
660g   VII. FREDERIC LAFAYETTE,⁸ b. Sept. 22, 1890.
   VIII. AVA RILLA ANGELINE,⁸ b. July 3, 1895.

420.

JOSEPH A.[7] CHURCHILL (JOSEPH DELL,[6] WILLIAM [5] WILL
IAM,[4] SAMUEL,[3] JOSEPH,[2] JOSIAH [1]). Born at Pineville, Ark., Nov.
22, 1846. Lived at Oran, Texas, in 1904. He was a farmer. Married at Galley Rock, Ark., January, 1871, NANCY A. DUVALL,
daughter of John and Elizabeth Duvall.

Child.

660h	I. JOHN WILLIAM,[8] b. at Galley Rock, Ark., Dec. 15, 1870; m. LAURA
FOSTER, at Whitt, Texas, Jan. 8, 1893.

421.

WILLIAM A.[7] CHURCHILL (ADNA,[6] WILLIAM,[5] WILLIAM,[4]
SAMUEL,[3] JOSEPH,[2] JOSIAH[1]). Born Dec. 13, 1831, near Marietta,
Ohio, but removed with his father's family to Fabius, Mich.,
and lived there, and at Leonidas, Mich., from which latter place
he wrote us May 4, 1888. Married in Fabius, Mich., Oct. 31, 1858,
MATILDA D. RUMSEY, born May 18, 1843.

Children born in Fabius, Mich.

I. EMMA ANN,[8] b. March 7, 1860; m. MONROE H. SMITH, at Leonidas,
Mich., Oct. 10, 1882. They lived at Leonidas, and Meerdon,
Mich.

Children.

1. Lloyd Smith, b. July 6, 1884.
2. Mildred V. Smith, b. May 25, 1886.
3. Linnie M. Smith, b. Dec. 8, 1891.
4. Carroll M. Smith, b. June 8, 1894.

661	II. JOHN MARCELLUS,[8] b. Oct. 9, 1861; m. ZETHA M. ARNOLD April
25, 1888, daughter of James and Sophia (Robinson) Arnold, of
Leonidas, Mich.

One Child.

1. Louis A. Churchill, b. March 8, 1889.

III. WILBUR ADNA,[8] b. Jan. 24, 1870; d. Oct. 25, 1872.
IV. MINNIE MYRTELLE,[8] b. Aug. 24, 1875; m. FRANK PECK, at Center-
ville, Mich., May 13, 1895. They lived, 1904, at Moorepark,
Mich.

Children.

1. Bertha R. Peck, b. April 1, 1896.
2. Verne Peck, b. Feb. 5, 1901.
3. Leon Peck, b. March 3, 1903.

424.

WILLIAM R.[7] CHURCHILL (RANDELL,[6] WILLIAM,[5] WILLIAM,[4]
SAMUEL,[3] JOSEPH,[2] JOSIAH[1]). Born Dec. 18, 1836, probably near
Marietta, Ohio. Married, Oct. 5, 1870, MARY WELCH.

Children.

    I. ANNIE.[8]
662 II. WILLIAM.[8]
    III. MARTHA.[8]

425.

JOSEPH N.[7] CHURCHILL (RANDELL,[6] WILLIAM [5] WILLIAM [4] SAMUEL,[3] JOSEPH,[2] JOSIAH[1]). Born Feb. 5 1839, probably near arietta, Ohio. Married, Aug 26, 1866, SARAH BOYD.

Children.

    I. JANE MARY.[8]
663 II. FRED D.[8]
    III. MARY M.[8]

426.

JOSHUA P.[7] CHURCHILL (RANDELL,[6] WILLIAM,[5] WILLIAM [4] SAMUEL,[3] JOSEPH,[2] JOSIAH[1]). Born March 18, 1844. In 1888 he was living in Winslow, Iowa. Married, March 16, 1879, MARTHA T. STAMP.

Children.

664 I. RALPH L.,[8] b. April 7, 1880.
    II. GRACE,[8] b. June 8, 1883.

427.

HIRAM WILLIAM [7] CHURCHILL (JAMES,[6] WILLIAM,[5] WILLIAM,[4] SAMUEL,[3] JOSEPH,[2] JOSIAH[1]) Born in Newberg, Mich., March 13, 1847. Settled first in Finchford and Parkersburg, Iowa, but later removed to Boulder, Col., and from there, March, 1901, removed to Salt Lake City, Utah, where he died July 17, 1903. He was a farmer. Married at Newberg, Mich., Oct. 27, 1863, ELIZABETH RUSHING, daughter of William and Mary (Stevenson) Rushing. Mrs. Churchill, in 1904, lived in Salt Lake City.

Children, the first born in Finchford, the rest in Parkersburg, Iowa.

    I. ESTELLA MAILA,[8] b. Jan. 31,1867; died at Parkersburg, Dec. 31, 1881.
    II. BLANCHE ELIZA,[8] b. Aug. 21, 1872; died at Parkersburg, April 17, 1873.
    III. MAUD ESTHER,[8] b. June 8, 1874; died at Parkersburg, July 8, 1874.
    IV. ETTA IDELL,[8] b. March 30, 1875; m. DAVID C. GIBSON, of Boulder, Col., Feb. 3, 1904. They lived in Salt Lake City 1904.

433.

CHARLES [7] CHURCHILL (WILLIS,[6] * ASA,[5] WILLIAM,[4] SAMUEL,[3] JOSEPH,[2] JOSIAH[1]). Born in Hamden, Conn., July 8, 1837. He

---

*From a daughter of Willis Churchill we learn something more of his brother Levi (No. 190) whose, children were: 1 Jane,[8] m. William Lee, and had children. one of whom was William H. Lee, living in December, 1903, at Providence, R.I.; 2, Martha A,[8] m. Walter Clark, and 3, Henry.[8] All three born at Hamden, Conn. Willis Churchill's widow, with their daughter, Mary, are living at 12 Vanderpool Street, Newark, N.J., in December, 1903.

CHARLES CHURCHILL,
LONDON, ENG.
(No. 433, page 538.)

lived there until the removal of his father's family to Newark, N.J., in 1861, and was educated in the public schools, and in his father's business of exporting American tools and machinery. He removed to London, Eng., in 1862, and there in 1865 established the house of Charles Churchill & Co., engineers and importers of American machine tools, which in 1903 was at 9--15 Leonard street, Finsbury. He has made frequent visits to America. Married, March 19, 1861, CHARLOTTE LOUISE LEWIS, born in Sing Sing, N.Y., in 1836.

Children born in London.

664a   I. CHARLES HENRY,[8] b. April 1, 1864; m. MARGARET SARAH JAMES,
dau. of John and Amelia, July 1, 1891.

Children born in London.

1. Harold Edwin, b. July 16, 1892.
2. Enid Margaret, b. May 25, 1896.

665   II. WILLIS CLARK,[8] b. May 5, 1868.
665a   III. ARTHUR LYMAN,[8] b. June 12, 1872; m. MARY MINNIE GUTHRIE, dau.
of John Buchanan and Mary (Cree) Guthrie, of London, Sept. 3, 1898.

Children.

1. Audrey Mary, b. July 9, 1899.
2. Daphne Louise, b. Nov. 7, 1902.

IV. ALICE LOUISE,[8] b. Oct. 12, 1878.

434.

WILLIAM ALLEN[7] CHURCHILL (JOSEPH,[6] JOSEPH[5]). Born in Newington, Conn., May 10, 1810. He received a common school education, and became apprenticed to William B. North, the first goldsmith and jeweler of New Britain, and himself afterwards developed and built up a great business in the same line, and which, owing to his genius and fine taste, became one of the finest houses in the country ; indeed, as Elihu Burritt, in his memorial address, said of him, " He founded here in New Britain a normal school of æsthetic culture for beautifying homes with the best artistry of nature." He had a great influence in the community by his example, first, perhaps, in making his own house and grounds beautiful, but in many other ways of wise citizenship and generous public spirit. The Centre Church at New Britain is a lasting monument to his devotion, taste, and genius, while in many other directions the public welfare received his loyal service. He died May 28, 1874. Married 1st, in New Britain, Conn., Sept. 14, 1835, ELIZA JANE FRANCIS, who died Jan. 23, 1837 ; 2d, in Wethersfield, Conn., Dec. 4, 1838, SARAH WELLS BLINN.

One child by First Wife.

I. ELIZA JANE,[8] b. Aug. 24, 1836; m. COL, EMORY FOOTE STRONG, of
Bridgeport, as his second wife, July 28, 1858. No children mentioned. Mrs. Strong died in November, 1892

Children of Second Wife.

II. SARAH AUGUSTA,[8] b. July 8, 1841; m. FRANK LOUIS HUNGERFORD,
Dec. 21, 1869. They lived at New Britain, Conn.

Children.

1. Wm. Churchill Hungerford, b. Feb. 26, 1871; m. Charlotte
Olmstead of New York City, Nov. 2, 1898.
2. Florence Hungerford, b. Nov. 25, 1874; d. Nov. 24, 1876.
3. Frank Mills Hungerford, b. Sept. 14, 1878; d. July 14, 1893.
4. Belle Hungerford, b. Dec. 15, 1881; d. Sept. 11, 1887.

III. JULIA ISABELLA,[8] b. Aug. 14, 1843; m. JOHN B. POWELL. No
children.

666   IV. WILLIAM WALCOTT,[8] b. Sept. 22, 1845. Unmarried.
667   V. FREDERICK HOSEA,[8] b. March 27, 1848; m. ANNIE LOUISE SMITH,
dau. of William H., born in New Britain, Conn., Nov. 5,
1874. He graduated at the high school in 1867 and at the Sheffield Scientific School, Yale College, in 1870. He then spent
several years in the study of the law, and graduated from the Law
School of Harvard University in 1874. He began practice in
New Britain, and was very successful, but turned his attention
to the study of electrical science and with intense application
devoted himself to the purpose of forming an electric company in New Britain. The strain of this extra study and work,
added to his increasing professional labors, undoubtedly over-
taxed the rather slender constitution and exceedingly sensitive,
nervous temperament, till reason was temporarily unbalanced and
in a moment, by his own hand, he took his own life, so prized in
the community, so precious to his family. In every direction he
had all, it seemed, that any one could have to live for. His
home and family relations were the happiest possible, and in his
business and social life all was promiseful and good; and he was
very happy in all ways, especially in his beautiful home. He
was a man of generous impulses, and strict integrity, and his
untimely loss, just in the beginning of his prime of manhood,
was widely and deeply mourned. He died March 4, 1881.

Children born in New Britain.

1. May, b. Sept. 2, 1875; m. George Sherman Talcott, June 9,
1897, who was born in New Britain, Conn., July 27, 1879, a
graduate of Yale College 1891. Child (1) Lucy Talcott, b.
April 10, 1899.
2. William, b. Nov. 3, 1876; graduated at Yale College in 1897.
3. Rose, b. June 3, 1878.

VI. ANNIE FLORENCE,[8] b. Feb. 4, 1853; d. March 14, 1858.

435.

LOREY [7] CHURCHILL (JAMES,[6] JOSEPH [5]). Born in Newington,
Conn., June 20, 1821. He lived many years in Baltimore, Md.
He died in New Haven at the house of his father, Samuel, May 7,
1876. Married, July 18, 1841, LUCY STEEL.

Children, probably all born in Baltimore, Md.

　　I. LOUISA,[8] b. March 11, 1844.
668　II. ALONZO,[8] b. March 11, 1846; d. young.
　III. LOREY,[8] b. Oct. 5, 1847; d. young.
　IV. LUCY,[8] b. Dec. 20, 1848.
　　V. JAMES,[8] b. April 13, 1850; d. very soon.
669　VI. JAMES,[8] b. Sept. 8, 1851. Married, and in 1899 was living in Baltimore, Md., but we have no further record.

436.

SAMUEL W.[7] CHURCHILL (JAMES,[6] JOSEPH[5]*). Born in Newington, Conn., June 18, 1828. He grew up on the old homestead at Newington, and for a time operated the old grist-mill. About 1855 he bought a farm in New Britain, Conn., in that part known as the "Stanley Quarter." Later he became engaged as a contractor with the firm of O. B. North & Co., of New Britain, and, in 1861, removed to New Haven. In 1890 he removed to Milford, Conn., where he lived with his wife and daughter, Ruby, until 1903, when the family returned to New Haven. Married, Dec. 26, 1855, ELLEN L. HUBBARD, born Dec. 12, 1836, at New Britain, Conn., daughter of Henry E. Hubbard.

Children.

670　I. CHARLES S.,[8] born in New Britain Conn., Sept. 22, 1856; m. in New Britain, Nov. 11, 1885, ANNA D. GREEN, dau. of ROBERT C. of Pottsville, Penn.
　　Mr. Churchill was educated at New Haven and at Yale University, where he graduated from the Sheffield Scientific School in 1878. Entered the railway service as civil engineer in 1879, and has been engaged continuously in that profession since, in the projection and construction of some important lines in Connecticut, Pennsylvania and Virginia, West Virginia and Ohio, and is at present (1904) chief engineer of the Norfolk and Western R.R. Office at Roanoke, Va. The family live at Roanoke, Va. Mr. Churchill is a member of the American Society of Civil Engineers, and of other important railway and technical societies.

Children.

　1. Mary E., b. in Pottsville, Sept. 30, 1886.
　2. Ethelind, b. in Roanoke, Va., Feb. 1, 1889.
　3. Robert C., b. in Roanoke, Va., Oct. 20, 1890.
　4. Helen E., b. in Roanoke, Va., Jan. 6, 1893.

　II. IDA N.,[8] b. in New Britain, Conn., April 23, 1859; m. 1st, HARRY CHAFFEE, Oct. 13, 1875. Mr. Chaffee died Dec. 2, 1880, leaving two children. Mrs. Chaffee m. 2d, CHRISTOPHER T. LANGLEY.

---

　* My search for the father of Joseph [5] has been diligent and persistent, but up to this time I have found no positive proof. A tradition, coming directly from his oldest daughter, born in 1778, that her father's family was driven from their home at a place called "Three Rivers," by the Indians, seems to point to Giles Churchill, who left Newington, and in 1751 settled at the Forks of the Delaware river and was driven off with his family and died in Florida, N.Y., 1771. He had five children born at the "Forks," but we think he had others before settlement there, of whom one was Joseph. See note in Appendix.

Children of First Husband.

1. Herbert Chaffee, b. Aug. 26, 1877.
2. Hattie May Chaffee, b. Oct. 4, 1879; d. March 1890.

Children of Second Husband.

3. Frederick D. Langley, b. Aug. 17, 1886.
4. Nellie D. Langley, b. Nov. 1, 1887.
5. Raymond Langley, b. Feb. 2, 1889; d. young.
6. Ruth C. Langley, b. Jan. 31, 1891.
7. Edwin H. Langley, b. Jan. 11, 1893; d. young.

III. HATTIE,[8] b. in New Britain, Conn., Oct. 8' 1860; d. in New Haven,
Dec. 2, 1877.

671 [V.: VIRGIL,[8] b, in New Haven, Nov. 3, 1865; m. JENNIE E. HUBBELL,
New Haven, Nov. 17, 1886.
They live in New Haven. He is a watchman and inspector
(1904).

Children.

1. Louise Estelle, b. May 14, 1887.
2. Frank Virgil, b. in Milford, Conn., Oct. 27, 1891.
3. Charles S., b. Skelton, Conn., Aug. 3, 1893.
4. Calvin Downs, b. in New Haven, July 12, 1895.
5. Elsie May, b. July 21, 1900, in New Haven.

V. RUBY J.,[8] b. in New Haven, May 5, 1878; unmarried in 1904.
Living with her parents in New Haven, Conn.

437.

AMOS [7] CHURCHILL (JOSIAH,[6] JONATHAN,[5] JONATHAN,[4] JONA-
THAN,[3] JOSEPH,[2] JOSIAH [1]). Born in Bridgewater, Penn., Jan. 23
1808. He inherited the paternal homestead in Bridgewater, in that
section which afterwards became Franklin. His father died when
he was a child, and he was placed under a guardian, who taught him
to spell his name Churchell, and this form was handed down to his
children, but we retain the common form. He died in Franklin,
Oct. 22, 1850. Married, at Bridgewater, March 4, 1829, ABIGAIL
HOLLEY, born near White Hall, N.Y., and died at Franklin, Penn.,
Oct. 7, 1890.

Children born in the old home above noted.

I. LOUISA,[8] b. Jan. 15, 1831; m. MILES J. HADSELL, April 2, 1863.

One Child.

1. Albert Josiah Hadsell, b. Oct. 26, 1864.

672 II. EDWARD,[8] b. June 5, 1833; m. JANE A. THOMAS, April, 1872.
He died in Franklin, Penn., Aug. 5, 1876. No children.

673 III. Dr. Albert,[8] b. March 17, 1836; m. Mary A. Guthrie, March 31, 1861.
She was born at Carthage, Mo., Feb. 7, 1844. He was educated as a physician, and at the beginning of the war was in Missouri, and was in the midst of stirring scenes during the years of its continuance, in which time he "drifted" into Texas, and located for some years in Fannin and Grayson Counties, in that State. In 1867 he settled in Nevada, Mo., and has since, up to 1904, lived there. Dr. Churchill is active in other ways than his profession, and has taken great interest in many reform movements, local and general. He is an outspoken and forceful writer and has thus exerted a wide influence.

Children.

1. May Bell, b. Feb. 3, 1862, in Newton County, Mo.; m. Wm. F. Norman, Oct. 10, 1883.
Children: (1) Clyde Churchill Norman, b. Oct. 27, 1884. (2) Glenn Erwin Norman, b. July 2, 1886.
2. Mary Alice, b. in Warren, Tex., Dec 10, 1863.
3. Ella Louisa, b. in Grayson County, Tex., Apr. 22, 1866.
4. Lula Viola, b. in Nevada, Mo., July 25, 1870.
5. William Albert, b. in Nevada, Mo., Sept. 14, 1872.
6. Edwin Ross, b. in Nevada, Mo., Aug. 23, 1875
7. Frank Lee, b. in Nevada, Mo., Feb. 6, 1879.

IV Almira,[8] b. July 11, 1839; m. Orlando J. Ross, May 1, 1860.
They lived in Binghamton, N.Y. Mrs. Ross has been much interested and has helpfully aided in compiling this branch of the family.

Children.

1. Jennie Alice Ross, b. Aug. 30, 1865.
2. William Henry Ross, b. Aug. 31, 1868, d. Mar. 23, 1871.
3. Timothy Amos Ross, b. Oct. 30, 1870, d. Jan. 8, 1871.

V Lucy Maria,[8] b. June 22, 1844; m. Dr. Watson Hull, Nov. 20, 1865.
They lived in Monroeton, Penn. Mrs. Hull has been, for many years, an efficient and kindly helper in the work of compiling this genealogy.

Child.

1. Jennie Lucy Hull, b. July 13, 1867, at Vestal Centre, N.Y.

439.

FREEBORN [7] CHURCHILL (Leman,[6] Jonathan,[5] Jonathan,[4] Jonathan,[3] Joseph,[2] Josiah [1]). Born in Franklin, Penn., Sept. 15, 1817. Lived at Great Bend, Penn. Married, March 6, 1850, in Bridgewater, Penn., Eliza Jane Clemens, born Sept. 20, 1824, in New Preston, Conn.

Children born at Great Bend, Penn.

674 I. Leman Augustus,[8] b. April 29, 1852.
II. Kate Amelia,[8] b. April 15, 1859.
675 III. Elmer Judson,[8] b. Dec. 5, 1861.

440.

NORMAN W.[7] CHURCHILL (Moses, Jr.,[6] Moses,[5] Jonathan,[4] Jonathan,[3] Joseph,[2] Josiah[1]).   Born in Sheffield, Mass., April 25 1826.   Lived for a time in Virginia, but returned later and lived at Sheffield, Mass.   Married, in Newark Valley, N.Y., Nov. 25, 1855, Betsey M. Sheldon, born in New Marlboro', Mass., Jan. 16, 1832.

Children.

676   I. George H.,[8] b. at Louisa Court House, Va., Aug. 30, 1856; m. Mary R. Lincoln, Nov. 26, 1876; d. Nov. 19, 1882; and he married 2d, Clara E. Frisbie, of Huron, Dakota, June 25, 1885.

Child of First Wife.

1. Mabel L., b. at Kirkville, Mo., Aug. 9, 1877.

Child of Second Wife.

2. Clyde, b. Sept. 4, 1886.

677   II. Robert S.,[8] b. at Sheffield, Mass., Feb. 9, 1866.   Unmarried in 1887.   In 1887 he was living in Highmore, Dakota, and wrote us.

III. Wilfred N.,[8] b. at Sheffield, Mass., Oct. 15, 1867; d. Aug. 2, 1868, at Hudson City, N.Y.

441.

GEORGE WILLIAM[7] CHURCHILL (William,[6] Oliver,[5] Jonathan,[4] Jonathan,[3] Joseph,[2] Josiah[1]).   Born in Munroe County, N.Y., 1843.   He was "bound-out," when a boy, to the age of twenty-one, with a man in Churchville, N.Y.   He removed to Illinois, and in 1863 enlisted in the army as second lieutenant.   In 1901 he lived at Plattsville, Ill., a retired farmer.   Married, in Kendall County, Ill., 1871, Mary J. Peterson.

Children.

678   I. Rufus J.,[8] born in 1874; m. Edna E. McCloud, in 1897.
679   II. Clarence G.,[8] b. in 1876; m. Mary A. Heap, 1896.

III. Nora Mae,[8] b. in 1884; unmarried.   Living at home in Plattsville in 1901.

442.

JONATHAN THORNTON[7] CHURCHILL (Leman,[6] Amos,[5] Jonathan,[4] Jonathan,[3] Joseph,[2] Josiah[1]).   Born in Bolton, Canada, May 10, 1825.   The family was living in Canton, N.Y., in 1890.   Married, Oct. 19, 1847, Emily E. Leonard.

Children, the first three born in Westford, Vt., the rest in Canton, N. Y.

680   I. ALBA LEMAN,[8] b. July 2, 1849; m. 1st, ABBIE M. AUSTIN; 2d,
           MARY JANE EDWARDS. This family lived in West Brookfield,
           Mass., January, 1890. No children reported
681   II. CHARLES H.,[8] b. Dec. 23, 1851.
682 III. ADDISON E.,[8] b. March 21, 1854.
683   IV. JONATHAN A.,[8] b. Oct. 6, 1855.
       V. EMMA E.,[8] b. Dec. 17, 1857.
684   VI. RICHARD E.,[8] b. Oct. 8, 1859.
685 VII. OMER V.,[8] b. Jan. 18, 1862.
686 VIII. AMOS A.,[8] b. Sept. 10, 1864.
      IX. ELLA E.,[8] b. May 4, 1866.
       X. ALICE A.,[8] b. Nov. 5, 1868.
      XI. ADA I.,[8] b. January, 1871.

443.

ELIAS D.[7] CHURCHILL (LEMAN[6] AMOS[5] JONATHAN,[4] JONA-
THAN,[3] JOSEPH,[2] JOSIAH[1]). Born in Bolton, Ont., May 18, 1827.
In 1891; it is said, lived in Fredericksburg, Iowa. He was married
and had two sons and two daughters, but we have not received any
further news of the family.

444.

RICHARD H.[7] CHURCHILL (LEMAN,[6] AMOS,[5] JONATHAN,[4]
JONATHAN,[3] JOSEPH,[2] JOSIAH[1]). Born in Bolton, Canada, Aug.
22, 1835. Married SUSAN RIDDLE.

Children.

    I. JOHN L.,[8] b. 1860; d. in 1886.
   II. SUSIE A.,[8] b. 1863; m. MR. HOLROYD. They lived in Geneva, Ill., in
       1891
687 III. FRANK BURR,[8] b. 1871; m. Wife's name not received.

Child.

    1. Paul, b. in Flanigan, Ill., 1891.

445.

HIRAM PARKER[7] CHURCHILL (HIRAM,[6] AMOS,[5]
JONATHAN,[4] JONATHAN,[3] JOSEPH,[2] JOSIAH[1]). Born at Bolton,
Canada, March 28, 1826. He was a farmer. Lived at North
Brookfield, Mass., and North Fairfax, Vt. Married, at North Brook-
field, Mass., Dec. 19, 1850, MARY WARNER THOMPSON, daughter
of Chauncey. 2d, at North Fairfax, Vt., March 29, 1864, MRS.
PAULINA (LEONARD) STORY, daughter of Heman Leonard.

Children, first two born in North Brookfield, the others in Fairfax, Vt.

688   I. George O.,[8] b. Dec. 7, 1854 ; m. Gertrude B. Locke, Grand Island, Neb. They lived in Fairmont and Hastings, Neb. He was a photographer.

Children.

1. Leslie Parker, b. April 7, 1881.
2. Clarence Montague, b. Nov. 10, 1882.
3. Frank Oliver, b. September, 1884.
4. Leroy Edmund, b. April 3, 1886.
5. Robert Julius, b. March 25, 1889.

II. Henry E.,[8] b. Aug. 13, 1857; d. at South Fairfax, Vt., June 14, 1867.

III. Sarah A.,[8] b. July 13, 1863 ; d. at South Fairfax, September, 1866.

Children of Second Wife.

689   IV. William L.,[8] b. April 23, 1865; m. Jennie King, of Georgia, Vt., Oct. 14, 1901.
690   V. Frank E.,[8] b. Feb. 29, 1868.
         VI. Hattie E.,[8] b. Sept. 11, 1870; m. Elmer Judd, of North Fairfax, April 7, 1891.
691   VII. Hervey A.,[8] b Sept. 11, 1870; m. 1st, Kate Rankin; 2d, Jennie Brigham.
692   VIII. Myron L.,[8] b. July 23, 1881.

446.

. OLIVER JOSEPH [7] CHURCHILL (Hiram [6] Amos,[5] Jonathan,[4] Jonathan,[3] Joseph,[2] Josiah[1]).   Born at Bolton, Canada, Oct. 17, 1827. Lived at North Fairfax, Vt., and was a farmer. Married, at North Brookfield, Mass., June 15, 1853, Mary Ann Kimball, daughter of Benjamin and Abigail (Irving) Kimball.

Children born at North Fairfax, Vt.

I. Anna Elizabeth,[8] b. May, 1854; m. Walter G. Mandell, Sept. 16, 1875.

693   II. Warren Augustus,[8] b. February, 1858; d. unmarried at North Brookfield, Nov. 17, 1871.

III. Ella Adelaide,[8] b. April 11, 1862; m. Arthur J. Goddard, Feb. 6, 1883.

694   IV. Elmer Addison,[8] b. April 11, 1862; m. Eudora F. Browning, at Rutland, Mass., July 29, 1886. She was the daughter of George Porter and Arvilla H. (Baker) Browning. Residence in North Brookfield, where Mr. Churchill is foreman in a shoe manufactory. They have had one child.

1. Leon Elmer, b. at North Brookfield July 31, 1887; d. July 31, 1894.

695   V Herbert Hiram,[8] b. Jan. 2, 1866; m. Carrie E. Darling, West Brookfield, June 15, 1892. She was daughter of George A. and Amelia H. (Mosier) Darling.

Children born at North Brookfield.

1. Roy Oliver, b. Dec. 28, 1893.
2. Merle A., b. March 12, 1895.
3. Warren E., b. Dec. 21, 1897.
4. Leon A., b. June 13, 1901.

448.

ORWELL[7] CHURCHILL (STEPHEN M.,[6] WILLIAM[5] WILL-
IAM,[4] JONATHAN,[3] JOSEPH,[2] JOSIAH[1]). Born in Randolph, Ohio
Feb. 25, 1822. He was a farmer at Randolph. Married, at
Randolph, June 4, 1843, CLARISSA COLTON, daughter of Chesley
and Polly Colton.

Children born at Randolph.

I. MARVIN W.,[8] b. May 6, 1844; m. MALITTA MERRIMAN, Dec. 26
1865.
696 II. EDWARD J.,[8] b. Dec. 1, 1848; m. ELLEN TODD, March 20, 1867, at
Edinburgh.

Children born at Rootstown and Randolph.

1. Alice B., b. May 4, 1870; m. Charles L. Gouldin, Dec. 24,
1890, Rootstown, O. They have one child, Gladys I. Gouldin, b. at Ravenna, Oct. 3, 1891.
2. Ellen L., b. Sept. 6, 1875.
3. Walter O., b. at Randolph, Nov. 26, 1878; m. Dorothea
Kemp, Dec. 25, 1901, at Ravenna.

III. CLARA A.,[8] b. Nov. 19, 1856; m. FRANK MORRISON, Sept. 5, 1879,
at Ravenna.

One Child.

1. Frank Morrison, b. Aug. 29, 1888, at Rockcreek, Ohio.

449.

JULIUS RALPH[7] CHURCHILL (STEPHEN M.,[6] WILLIAM,[5]
WILLIAM,[4] JONATHAN,[3] JOSEPH,[2] JOSIAH[1]). Born at Randolph,
Ohio, June 16, 1832. He lived at Lime, Ohio, where he was a tanner. Married, Dec. 22, 1857, LUCINDA E. SAINT, daughter of Levi
and Mary M. (Miller) Saint.

Children born at Lime

I. MELVIN,[8] died in infancy.
II. LAURA M.,[8] b. April 21, 1861; m. CHARLES M. MELHORN, Oct. 13,
1881, at Westminster, Ohio.
697 III. JULIUS A.,[8] b. Oct. 12, 1862; m. FLORENCE JENNINGS, Oct. 18, 1887,
at Crookston, Minn.
698 IV. CLIFFORD B.,[8] b. Aug. 25, 1864; m. CARRIE B. FARAT, June 6, 1899,
at Lime.
699 V. LEE PORTER,[8] b. Jan. 1, 1867.
700 VI. STEPHEN M.,[8] b. Sept. 27, 1873; m. MILDRED KEIL, Sept. 7, 1898,
at Lime.

451.

PETER[7] CHURCHILL (DAVID,[6] DAVID,[5] JONATHAN,[4] JONA-
THAN,[3] JOSEPH,[2] JOSIAH[1]). Born in Zora, Ont., Jan. 3, 1829.
Removed with his father's family to Berlin, Mich., in 1839. He

lived at Novesta, Mich.   Married, at Romeo, Macomb County, Ont., CHARITY E. CLARK.

Children.

701   I. LOREN N.,[8] b. March 19, 1860; m. 1st, NELLIE ADELAIDE PHILLIPS, Dec. 26, 1892, who died July 12, 1895; m. 2d, MRS. MARY E. McNUTT, March 27, 1899.

Child of First Wife.

1. Eveline May, b. Nov. 6, 1893.

Child of Second Wife.

2. Eliott Glenn, b. April 8, 1900.

702   II. JASON N.,[8] b. Oct. 21, 1862.   Lived at Novesta, Mich., in 1902.
       III. VIOLA ISOLA,[8] b. July 23, 1864; m. SAMUEL J. MITCHELL, Dec. 19, 1894.   They lived at Shabbona, Mich.

Children.

1. Gladys E. Mitchell, b. Jan. 13, 1897.
2. Harry S. Mitchell, b. May 18, 1898.

IV. EVA,[8] b. April 20, 1868; m. ALBERT W. KITCHIN, March 18, 1891, at Novesta, Mich.   They lived at Cass City, Mich.

Children.

1. Jason A. Kitchin, b. May 18, 1893.
2. Ray E. Kitchin, b. June 30, 1895.
3. Alice E. Kitchin, b. Jan. 16, 1897; d. Aug. 23, 1898.

703   V. WILLARD D.,[8] b. Nov. 12, 1870; m. JENNIE I. HENDERSON, June, 13, 1894.

Children.

1. Lillie M., b. July 11, 1895.
2. Daniel P., b. June 21, 1897.

704   VI. WILLIAM H.,[8] b. Nov. 12, 1870.
705   VII. WARREN H.,[8] b. April 20, 1876; m. LILLIAN MAUD MILTON, at Novesta, June 18, 1902.
       VIII. ERMINA MAY,[8] b. Feb. 10, 1878; m. IRA R. HOWEY, at Novesta, June 18, 1902.   They lived at Novesta, Mich.

455.

JAMES D.[7] CHURCHILL (CYRUS,[6] DAVID,[5] JONATHAN[4] JONATHAN,[3] JOSEPH,[2] JOSIAH[1]).   Born at Zora, Can., July 6, 1828. He removed with his father's family in 1837 to Almont, Mich., and lived there.   Married, at Almont, Mich., Sept. 27, 1856, FRANCES P. WARNER.

Children born at Almont, Mich.

I. BELLE,[8] b. Nov. 11, 1857; m. WILLIAM SPANGLER, of Almont July 12, 1883.

Children.

1. Neva B. Spangler, b. July 18, 1886.
2. Roy Churchill Spangler, b. May 26, 1888.

706   II. CYRUS J.,⁸ b. Nov. 27, 1859.
         III. FRANCES A.,⁸ b. Oct. 7, 1861.
         IV. FLORA L.,⁸ b. May 8, 1864; d. May 20, 1865.
707   V. ROBERT D.,⁸ b. June 11, 1867.
708   VI. FRED M.,⁸ b. May 17, 1831.

462.

DAVID⁷ CHURCHILL (TRUMAN,⁶ DAVID,⁵ WILLIAM⁴ JONATHAN,³ JOSEPH,² JOSIAH¹). Born in Middlesex County, Ont. Nov. 11, 1833. Removed with his family to Lapeer County, Mich., in 1836. The latest news from this family was given by Mr. David Churchill himself, dated at Imlay City, Mich., Nov. 18, 1889, and given below. Married, in 1857, MARY J. REYNOLDS, who was born in Northumberland County, Ont., 1840.

Children.

    I. VIOLETTA,⁸ b. March 21, 1858; m. DUNCAN McNEVIN, in 1879.
    II. EMMA J.,⁸ b. March 30, 1860; m. J. C. WILLIS, in 1879.
    III. ANNA E.,⁸ b. May 20, 1838; m. W. H. TERRY, in 1882.
    IV. LUCY,⁸ b. June 24, 1871; m. F. H. McCLISH, 1888.
709   V. FRANK G.,⁸ b. June 3, 1878.

465.

WALTER B.⁷ CHURCHILL (WILLIAM,⁶ DAVID,⁵ JONATHAN, JONATHAN,³ JOSEPH,² JOSIAH¹). Born in Oxford County, Can March 27, 1837. Removed with his father's family, soon after his birth, to Lapeer County, Mich. He received a common school education. He engaged in business in Imlay City, Mich. He was a prosperous and influential citizen. He served in various public offices, among which were township supervisor for sixteen years, and county treasurer four years. Married, at Imlay City, May 8, 1858, MARIA J. BEST, daughter of John P. and Catherine (Walker) Best, of Imlay City.

Children born at Imlay City.

710   I. GEORGE H.,⁸ b. Oct. 24, 1870; m. ISALINE VAIL, at Almont, Mich., Sept. 3, 1896.
         II. MAUD P.,⁸ b. Jan. 8, 1883; m. AUSTIN LORD, Aug. 3, 1901.

470.

LEWIS ABRAHAM⁷ CHURCHILL (JAMES H.,⁶ SAMUEL⁵ JONATHAN,⁴ JONATHAN,³ JOSEPH,² JOSIAH¹). Born Aug 16, 1837, in Bearsville, Can. Removed to Michigan about 1860. Mr. Churchill wrote us Feb. 17, 1890, and then lived at Pine Grove, but post-office address, Gobleville, Mich. Married, in Townsend, Can., West, 1859, EUNICE FLANDERS, born "on Nottaway Prairie," St. Joseph's County, Mich., Aug. 17, 1840.

Children.

- I. FLORENCE IDELLE,[8] b. in Volinia, Mich., Aug. 26, 1860; m. WM. W. PATRICK, June 1, 1887.
- 711 II. FRANK F.,[8] b. in Pine Grove, Mich., Oct. 6, 1865; m. EVA M. VOORHEES, Dec. 25, 1886.
  He was a music teacher in the State Normal School; 1903 lived in Plattsville, Mich.

Children born there.

1. Floyd, b. Dec. 13, 1887.
2. Bessie, b. Jan. 1, 1889.

- 712 III. CHARLES CLAUDE,[8] b. Feb. 30, 1877.

471.

FRANCIS LEVI[7] CHURCHILL (JAMES H.[6] SAMUEL[5] JONATHAN,[4] JONATHAN,[3] JOSEPH,[2] JOSIAH[1]). Born in Norfolk County, Ont., Aug. 8, 1839. Removed to Michigan and lived there. He died March 22, 1872. Married, Jan. 3, 1862, LYDIA DIXON, of Volinia, Mich.

Child.

- 712 I. DIXON J.,[8] b. Nov. 12, 1864; married, but name of wife not obtained.
  He finished his education at Ann Arbor University, Mich., and settled at Plattsville, where he was a professor of music for eight years. He died, leaving a widow and one son. After his death his widow, with her husband's mother, Mrs. Lydia Churchill, and the boy, removed to California, where, in 1903, they lived on a fruit-farm.

472.

ORLAND EUGENE[7] CHURCHILL (JAMES H.,[6] SAMUEL,[5] JONATHAN,[4] JONATHAN,[3] JOSEPH,[2] JOSIAH[1]). Born in Norfolk County, Ont. May 1, 1849. He was a teacher and later a farmer, and lived at Penn., Mich., in 1890. Married, April 29, 1873, ABBIE D. STURR, daughter of Joseph, of Volinia, Mich.

Children.

- 713 I. JOSEPH S.,[8] b. Feb. 3, 1875.
  He was a teacher in Cass County, Mich., in 1903.
- 714 II. FRED PEARSE,[8] b. May 14, 1878.
  He was a farmer in 1903. His mother was then living with him.

474.

FRANK DELASON [7] CHURCHILL (ADONIRAM J.,[6] SAMUEL,[5] JONATHAN,[4] JONATHAN,[3] JOSEPH,[2] JOSIAH [1]). Born in Eldorado, Wis., Aug. 28, 1853. Lived in Bushnell, South Dakota, in 1904; a school teacher and farmer. Married, in Webster, South Dakota, May, 1884, HARRIET ALLEN, daughter of Lucian and Rhoda Allen.

Children born in Bushnell.

I. RHODA CELESTIA,[8] b. March 28, 1885.
II. LUCIAN ALLEN,[8] b. Sept. 15, 1887.

475.

CYRUS WILLIAM [7] CHURCHILL (ADONIRAM J.,[6] REV. SAMUEL,[5] JONATHAN,[4] JONATHAN,[3] JOSEPH,[2] JOSIAH [1]). Born in Fon du Lac County, Wis., Sept. 5, 1855. Removed West and settled in Brookings County, South Dakota, a farmer. Married, at Spring Valley, Minn., March 12, 1882, JENNIE L. BAILEY, born in Illinois March 10, 1865.

Children born in Brookings County, South Dakota.

I.   MYRTLE LOUISE,[8] b. Aug. 4, 1883.
II. MAUDE ETHEL,[8] b. Sept. 16, 1884.
715 III. CHARLES JUDSON,[8] b. Jan. 1, 1891.
IV. LYLA FERN,[8] b. Feb. 27, 1900.

476.

GEORGE HARVEY [7] CHURCHILL (ADONIRAM JUDSON,[6] REV. SAMUEL,[5] JONATHAN,[4] JONATHAN,[3] JOSEPH,[2] JOSIAH[1]). Born in Eldorado, Wis., May 7, 1860. Lived in South Dakota and at Spring Valley, Minn., where he was a farmer. Married at Spring Valley, March 19, 1884, MAGGIE LOUCKS, daughter of Harmon and Eve Ann (———) Loucks.

Children.

I.   HARRIETT,[8] b. Sept. 22, 1885, in Rondell, South Dakota.
II. IRENE C.,[8] b. Oct. 22, 1887, in Groton, South Dakota.
III. JAY E.,[8] b. Nov. 5, 1889, in Spring Valley, Minn.
IV. GLEN R.,[8] b. April 21, 1892, in Frankford, Minn.
V.   CHARLES W.,[8] b. June 2, 1897, in Spring Valley, Minn.
VI. DORIS L.,[8] b. Oct. 2, 1899, in Spring Valley, Minn.

477.

ALBERT NATHAN [7] CHURCHILL (ADONIRAM JUDSON,[6] REV. SAMUEL,[5] JONATHAN,[4] JONATHAN,[3] JOSEPH,[2] JOSIAH[1]). Born in

Eldorado Wis., Dec. 6, 1865. Lived at Spring Valley, Minn., a farmer. Married, at Cherry Grove, Minn., Nov. 9, 1898, ANNA KAVANAGH, daughter of William and Jane (————) Kavanagh.

Child.

I. DALE K.,[3] b. at Spring Valley, June 20, 1900.

THE MANHATTAN BRANCH

OF

THE CHURCHILL FAMILY

DESCENDANTS OF WILLIAM CHURCHILL
OF MANHATTAN

FIRST GENERATION.

1.

WILLIAM[1] CHURCHILL, the progenitor of the Manhattan branch of the Churchill family in America, appears first publicly mentioned on the occasion of his marriage in 1672. It has been conjectured that he was the son of Joseph Churchill of London, but we have found no evidence to show such relation, or that Joseph of London had any family, or, in fact, anything about him further than the mention of his name as a merchant who was trading with merchants in Salem and elsewhere in the early times of the Massachusetts colony. The compilers have found no evidence of William's parentage, birth-place, or previous condition. It seems probable that he may have been a soldier, from his after career. When, in 1689, the revolution in England placed William of Orange on the throne, the provinces immediately repudiated the royal officers of James II., and the citizens organized for self government, pending the action of the new king. This citizens' party included the common people, with many of the most respectable Protestant citizens, while the officers and magistrates appointed by James still adhered to him. Jacob Leisler, a German by birth, and senior captain of one of the five train-bands of the town, commanded by Colonel Bayard, was commissioned by King James. Leisler was a zealous opponent of the Roman Catholics, a merchant of wealth, and a man of great energy and determination. The five companies of militia and a great crowd of citizens gathered about Leisler, and clamored for him to become leader of the party until news could be received from the new king; so he assumed the place of power. William Churchill was appointed lieutenant, and Joost Stoll ("a dram-man") was chosen ensign. Leisler was chosen ruler of the town for the time, while Nicholson and the other officers of the province took refuge at Albany. Lieutenant Churchill became the chief military officer, and figured prominently in the conduct of affairs, under Lieut.-Governor Leisler, as he was chosen and called by the people, and after the new royal governor was sent over, and Leisler, by the devices of his enemies, was seized, condemned, and executed without the authority of the king, whose cause he had so

faithfully served ; Churchill shared his overthrow, but after temporary imprisonment was released.   The New York Historical Collections, in the volume for 1868, contain full details of the Leisler
administration, with his subsequent arrest, trial, and execution,
with the trial of his adherents.   Lieutenant Churchill was tried, and
the judge, in his charge referring to him, said he was " apparently
illiterate," and his own testimony and conduct show him to have
been an honest, fearless, and popular man, however uneducated, and
his independent spirit was not broken by arrest or threats by the
governing powers, for in 1696 he was summoned before the court
because he refused to appear at muster in arms on a training-day,
being enrolled as a " Sentinell " (i.e., private) in Captain Tudor's
Company, and being summoned and "commanded by the Lieut.
Coll, in his own person," did give him " insolent language."   " Said
Churcher," when brought before the court martial, "did alledge
that he had a commission for a lieutenant under Leisler, and did
then say that he would not appear in arms in any inferior station,
that being sufficient to discharge him."   But the court did not con-
cur in his opinion, and, for contempt aforesaid, did fine him ten
pounds or six months' imprisonment.   In 1698 William Churcher,
bricklayer, was admitted freeman at New York.   The lot of land
in New York City upon which William Churchill lived was granted
May 13, 1668, to Samuel Drissons, by Deputy Governor Richard
Nicolls, and deeded by his widow Feb. 14, 1682, to Mr. Churchill.
The description of this lot shows that it contained a " Spring of
Water."   Widow Susannah Churchill, Dec. 3, 1714, conveyed this
same lot to William Prevoorst.   This property is said to have been
located on what is now Wall street.   In the General Index to Land
Records of New York is a description of a survey of land laid out
to William Churchill, in 1676, eighty acres on the north west side of
Staten Island, with six acres of salt meadow fronting said lot, and
four acres fresh meadow in the cove, to the north of Daniel
Perrin's lot.   It is said that he removed to Jamaica, Long Island,
about 1690, but the editor has found no authority for the statement.
Mr. Churchill made a will Sept. 19, 1702, in which he gave the bulk,
perhaps all, his property to his wife Susannah, but when this was
offered for probate the authorities for some reason declared it
invalid, and by the custom of the English law, his estate passed to
his eldest son, Charles, who it seems was a mariner, and on Sept. 25,
1714, executed a deed, conveying the property to his mother according to the terms of his father's will.
     William Churchill married at Manhattan, after March 10, 1672,
SUSANNAH BRAYSER, or BRASYER.   The record of the New York

licenses for marriage reads "William Churcher and Susannah Brasyer, March 10, 1672·

Children born in Manhattan, now New York City.

   I. ANNE,[2] b. September, 1673; d. May 15, 1691, aged 17¾ years. See
       gravestone in Trinity Churchyard, New York.

2   II. CHARLES,[2] b. May, 1675; m but wife's name not known.

   III. RICHARD,[2] b. March, 1676; d. Aug. 5, 1681, aged 5½ years.

3   IV. ROBERT,[2] m. SARAH (————————).

4   V. EDWARD,[2] b. 1679; m. WENTJE RYDER.

SECOND GENERATION.

2.

CHARLES [2] CHURCHILL (WILLIAM [1]). Born in New York, 1675. He was a mariner and we have the account of his dealing with his mother in restoring to her the rights of property under his father's will which the law gave to him. Married (——————).

*Children.**

I. A DAUGHTER, said to have married and settled in King's County (Brooklyn), but no further record of her is known.

5   II. JOHN,[3] b. about 1725/6; m. MARY TAYLOR.

III. ANNA,[3] m. 1st, ROBERT COKER; m. 2d, EDWARD ABEIL.

Children baptized in the Reformed Dutch Church.

1. Robert Coker, bapt. June 4, 1715.
    The witnesses to this christening were Charles Churcher, Abiah Brazyer, and Susannah Churcher.
2. William Coker, bapt. Oct. 9, 1717.
    Witnesses, Hendrik Bras and Susannah Play.

By Second Husband.

3. Edward Abeil, bapt. Dec. 25, 1719
    Witnesses, Timothy Tilley and Janetje Pouwell.

3.

ROBERT [2] CHURCHILL (WILLIAM [1]). Born in Manhattan, now New York City. Settled at or near Fairfield, Conn. His will of Nov. 3, 1733, gives his property to his children, fifty shillings to Nehemiah, lands to Robert and daughters Elinor and Patience. Married, about 1693/4, Sarah (——————).

Children born at or near Fairfield, Conn.

I. ABIGAIL,[3] bapt. Feb. 17, 1695.

II. SARAH,[3] bapt. Feb. 17, 1695.

III. ELINOR,[3] bapt. Oct. 20, 1695; m. (——————) SHERWOOD.

6   IV. NEHEMIAH,[3] bapt. March 21, 1698; m. MARTHA GREEN May 3, 1716.

7   V. EDWARD,[3] b. about 1718; m. ESTHER HULL, near Walesburg, New Haven County, Conn.

7a   VI. ROBERT.[3]

VII. PATIENCE,[3] m. (——————) OSTERBANK.

---

*It is probable that Charles Churchill had other children, but we have not found any positive evidence.

4.

EDWARD [2] CHURCHILL (WILLIAM [1]). Born in 1679 in Manhattan, now New York City, and was there brought up. Settled first in Jamaica, L.I., and May, 1839, at Rombout, now Fishkill on the Hudson. He became an extensive land owner and a prominent citizen. He died between April 13 and May 13, 1757. His will, a very clear and strong document, is a type of the documents of the time and place, and gives some indication of the character and disposition of the man.

THE WILL OF EDWARD CHURCHILL.

In the name of God, Amen! I Edward Churchill of Rombout precinct, in the county of Dutchess and province of New York, being weak in body but of sound mind and memory and understanding, thanks be given to God for the same, and considering my life in danger, do make this my last Will and Testament as followeth:

FIRST: I commit my precious and immortal soul to God who gave it, hoping for pardon and remission of all my sins through the merits of Jesus Christ, my blessed Saviour and Redeemer, and my body to the earth, there to be buried in such christianlike and decent manner as to my executors hereafter named shall seem meet and convenient.

Item. I will that all my just debts and funeral charges be duly paid and satisfied.

Item. I bequeath to Wentje, my dearly and well beloved wife, an honorable maintenance out of my real estate, and one of the small back rooms of my house for her to live in.

Item. I give and bequeath to my well beloved son Abel, the sum of five pounds and cut him off from any farther or other right to my estate both real and personal.

Item. I give and bequeath to my well beloved son John all my Real Estate during his natural life, and, after his decease I give it to his sons Joseph and Edward Churchill, to them their heirs and assigns forever, to be equally divided between, both as to quantity and quality. I give also to my son John my Wagon and Tackling belonging to it, and my great coat, and the Book of Acts of Assembly of the Province of New York, and order that any of my children if they need may freely peruse said Book of Acts.

Item. I give to my beloved son Robert, all and singular, my wearing clothes and apparel and my pleasure slay, and a bond he has given me, to be returned back to him again.

Item. I give to my beloved daughter Anna, widow, relick of Isaac Coffin, the sum of forty-five pounds, to be deposited in the hands of my executors to be applied to her use as she shall need.

Item. I give to my beloved daughter Levina, wife of John Totten, the sum of forty-five pounds. These Legacies to be paid out of my movable estate.

Item. I give to my son John's son John the sum of five pounds.

Item. After all these Legacies are paid; I will and order that in case anything remains of my personal estate that the said overplus shall be equally divided among my present grandchildren.

Item. Lastly, I do nominate, constitute and appoint my son Robert Churchill, my son-in-law John Totten, and William Roe, executors of this my last Will and Testament.

In witness whereof I, the said Edward Churchill, have hereunto set my hand and seal the thirteenth day of April in the thirtieth year of his Majesty's reign, and the year of our Lord one thousand seven hundred and fifty seven.

EDWARD CHURCHILL, L. S.

Signed, sealed, published and declared by the said Edward Churchill to be his last Will and Testament in the presence of us who hereunto subscribe our names as witnesses in his presence.

CHAUNCY GRAHAM.
DIECK BRINKERHOFF.
JOSEPH WRIGHT.

DUTCHESS COUNTY ss.

Be it remembered that on the thirteenth day of May in the year of our Lord one thousand seven hundred and fifty-seven, personally appeared before us, Jacobus Terbos Esqr., one of the Judges of the court of common pleas for the county assigned, and Henry Terbos and John Bailey, Esqrs., Justices of the peace in said county, Chauncy Graham and Dieck Brinkerhoff, two of the witnesses of the within last will and testament of Edward Churchill, and declared on the holy Evangelist of Almighty God that the within named Edward Churchill executed the within written instrument as his last Will and Testament by signing, sealing, and publishing it to be his last will and testament in their presence, and that the said testator was of sound and perfect mind and memory according to the best of their judgment, and that Dieck Brinkerhoff further deposes and says that he saw Joseph Wright, the other witness of the said within last will and testament of the said Edward Churchill, sign his name as a witness in presence of the said testator.

Sworn before us the day and year first above written.

JACOBUS TERBOS.
HENRY TERBOS.
JOHN BAILEY.

Sir Charles Hardy, Knight, Captain General and Governor-in-chief in and over the province of New York and the Territories depending thereon in America, Vice Admiral of the same, and Rear Admiral of the Blue Squadron of his Majesty's Fleet:

To all to whom these presents shall come or may concern:

Greeting:

Know ye that at Dutchess county, on the thirteenth day of May Instant before Jacobus Terbos, Esqr., one of the Judges of the Superior Courts of common pleas for the said county, assisted by Henry Terbos and John Bailey, Esqrs., justices of the peace for said county, and at the city of New York on the day of the date hereof before John Goldby, being thereunto delegated and appointed, the last Will and Testament of Edward Churchill, deceased, (a copy whereof is hereunto annexed) was proved, and now approved and allowed of by me. The said deceased having whilst he lived and at the time of his death Goods, Chattels and Credits within this Province by means whereof the proving and registering the said will, and the granting administration of all and singular the said goods, chattels and credits of the said deceased and any way concerning his will was granted unto John Totten, one of the executors in the said will named, being first sworn well and faithfully to administer the same and to make and exhibit a true and perfect Inventory of all and singular the said Goods, Chattels and Credits, and also to render a just and true account thereof when thereunto required.

In testimony whereof I have caused the Prerogative seal of the Province of New York to be hereunto affixed the seventeenth day of May one thousand seven hundred and fifty-seven.

GEORGE BANYAR, *D. Secry.*

Edward Churchill, married, at Jamaica, L.I., March 1, 1714, WENTJE (or WANCH) RYDER said to have been the daughter of a Quaker from Rhode Island, who settled on Long Island and married a Dutch wife.

Children born, probably at Jamaica, L.I.

8   I. ABEL,[3] b. 1716.
9   II. JOHN,[3] m. 1st, HANNAH HINCKE; 2d, REBECCA SUDRED.
      III. ANNA,[3] m. ISAAC COFFIN.
      IV. LAVINA,[3] m. JOHN TOTTEN.
10   V. ROBERT.[3]

THIRD GENERATION.

5.

JOHN [3] CHURCHILL (CHARLES,[2] WILLIAM [1]). Born about 1725-6. Married MARY TAYLOR, who was born Aug 10, 1731, and died Sept. 19, 1826, aged 95 years 1 month and 9 days.

Children.

11   I. JAMES,[4] b. Jan. 15, 1761; m. HANNAH DOBBS.
     II. STACIA,[4] b. Feb. 2, 1770; d. unmarried Oct. 27, 1807.
     III. ELIZABETH,[4] b. 1772; m. JOHN APPLEBEE, 1793.

Children.

    1. Elizabeth Applebee, b. 1794; m. Jasper Sherwood, 1818.
      Children: (1.) Eliza Jane Sherwood, b. 1819; m. A. M. Morton. (2.) Caroline Matilda Sherwood, b. 1821; m. A. M. Jacobs. (3.) Andrew J. Sherwood. b. Oct 14, 1828.

6.

NEHEMIAH [3] CHURCHILL (ROBERT,[2] WILLIAM [1]). Born at or near Fairfield, Conn., where he was baptized March 21, 1698. We have no further account of this family, except as below. Married May 3, 1716, MARTHA GREEN.

Child.

    I. ABIGAIL,[4] b. Feb. 17, 1718.

7.

EDWARD [3] CHURCHILL (ROBERT [2] WILLIAM [1]). Born about 1718. They lived in Greenwich, Conn. Married, in Walesburg, New Haven County, Conn., 1741, ESTHER HULL, daughter of Abijah and Abigail.

Children born in Greenwich, Conn.

    I. JAMES,[4] b. Dec. 25, 1742; d. in infancy.
12   II. JOHN,[4] b. June 3, 1744; m. 1st, (———) ALLEN; m. 2d, SARAH (———).
     III. ESTHER,[4] b. May 11, 1746.
13   IV. EDWARD,[4] b. Sept. 4, 1748; m. (——— ———).
     V. SARAH,[4] b. 1750; m. GABRIEL ALLEN in West Haven.

    They had ten children, but we have not been able to obtain all the names. There were six sons and four daughters. From several letters written by one of the sons, Dr. Hull Allen, of Milford,

Conn., in 1889, when he was in his ninety-third year, we glean a
few of the names. Several died in childhood. We give those we
have, but perhaps not in order. Hull Allen, b. 1797; m. and had
one son and two daughters. Betsey Allen, m. 1st, William Platt;
2d, James Hitchcock, but had no children. Sally Ann Allen, m.
Isaac Tibbals, no children. Joseph Allen died away from home.
William Allen was a merchant in Westport, Conn. Edward Allen,
a clergyman in New Jersey, left two sons who became physicians.

8.

ABEL ⁸ CHURCHILL (EDWARD,² WILLIAM ¹). Born at Jamaica, L.I., probably 1716. He settled in his native place, Jamaica
L.I. Married (wife's name not ascertained).

Child.

14   I. JOHN,⁴ m. RACHEL DAVIS, Nov. 30, 1769.

9.

JOHN ³ CHURCHILL (EDWARD,² WILLIAM ¹). Born at Jamaica, L.I , 1718. Lived in Dutchess County, N.Y. Nov. 8, 1764,
his name appears in a list of witnesses against the administration of
Mathew Dubois. Married 1st, HANNAH HINCKE; married 2d,
Dec. 10, 1755, REBECCA SUDRED.

Children born in Dutchess County, N.Y.

          I. HANNAH,⁴ b. Aug. 19, 1744; d. in infancy.
         II. HINCKE,⁴ b. Nov. 28, 1745; d. young.
15   III. JOHN,⁴ b. Jan. 25, 1746/7; m. JEMIMA KANE.
16   IV. EDWARD,⁴ b. Feb. 2, 1749; m. MARY ELIZA CHESSMAN.—
          V. REBECCA,⁴ b. Dec. 7, 1750; m. ———.
17   VI. JOSEPH,⁴ b. Nov. 24, 1752.
        VII. ISAAC,⁴ b. April 29, 1754; d. on the ninth day after.

Children of the Second Wife.

        VIII. HANNAH,⁴ b. June 2, 1757; m. PAUL NELSON.
18   IX. ISAAC,⁴ b. June 28, 1758; m. NANCY PHILLIPS.
          X. PHEBE,⁴ b. Nov. 29, 1759; d. in infancy.
19   XI. JONAS,⁴ b. Aug. 21, 1760.
        XII. PHEBE,⁴ b. Nov. 29, 1761.
20   XIII. HENRY,⁴ b. March 6, 1763; m. CYNTHIA VAN TASSAL.
21   XIV. BENJAMIN,⁴ b. Oct. 30, 1765; m. 1st, CORNELIA VAN TASSAL; m.
                2d, CATHERINE BLAINE.
         XV. MARY,⁴ b. Dec. 14, 1766.
22   XVI. OLIVER,⁴ b. July 2, 1770.

10.

ROBERT ³ CHURCHILL (EDWARD,² WILLIAM ¹). Born at
Jamaica, L. I. (probably). Settled near Poughkeepsie. Married——.

Child.

23   I. ROBERT,⁴ m. JEMIMA RAMUS.

FOURTH GENERATION.

11.

JAMES [4] CHURCHILL (JOHN,[3] CHARLES [2] WILLIAM [1]). Born in Tarrytown, N.Y., Jan. 15, 1761. Removed to Rensalaer County before 1804, and in 1816 to Onondaga County, N.Y., and settled in Spafford, on a farm. He died March 8, 1821, in Spafford. Married HANNAH DOBBS, born Dec. 23, 1771, in Westchester County, N.Y., and died June, 1842.

Children.

	I.	BETSEY ANN,[5] b. Sept. 1, 1793; m. SIDNEY BROWNELL. They lived in Dowagiac, Mich
24	II.	JOHN,[5] b. Aug. 3, 1795; m. MARY PALMER.
25	III.	PETER,[5] b. May 29, 1798; m. 1st, LUCINDA CRANE; m. 2d, CHARITY WILLIAMSON.
26	IV.	JAMES, JR.,[5] b. June 15, 1801; m. AMANDA WILLARD.
27	V.	FREDERICK W.,[5] b. April 15. 1804; m. TABITHA WILLARD.
28	VI.	WILLIAM,[5] b. June 14, 1806; m. CELINDA FISHER, Feb. 16, 1832. He died Aug. 15, 1882, and she died March, 1877. No children.
29	VII.	ALEXANDER M.,[5] b. April 20, 1809; m. 1st, LYDIA MCKAY; m. 2d, JANE ROBERTSON.
30	VIII.	ANSON,[5] b. Nov. 31, 1813; m. IZABENDA BEARSE.
31	IX.	GILBERT W.,[5] b. Sept. 21, 1815; m. 1st, ELEANOR RAINEY, who d. 1851; m. 2d, HARRIET LITTLEFIELD.

12.

JOHN [4] CHURCHILL (EDWARD,[3] ROBERT,[2] WILLIAM [1]). Born in Greenwich, Conn., June 2, 1744. Lived in Milford, Conn. He died Nov. 15, 1815. Married 1st, —— ALLEN; married 2d, SARAH ——, born 1748.

First Wife's Children born in Milford, Conn.

32	I.	JOHN,[5] b. Aug. 3, 1770; m. RUHAMA ORTON.
	II.	SARAH,[5] b. March 30. 1772; m. SAMUEL OVIATT.
33	III.	TIMOTHY,[5] b. June 23, 1776; m. DOROTHY KILBORN, Feb. 24, 1803.
34	IV.	WILLIAM,[5] b. April 8, 1781; m. KETURAH MORSE.
35	V.	ELIAS,[5] b. Feb. 15, 1783; d. unmarried Sept. 10, 1828.

Second Wife's Children.

36	VI.	HULL,[5] b. June 17, 1787.
37	VII.	GARRETT D.,[5] b. April 8, 1793; m. ELIZABETH M. ROOT.

13.

EDWARD[4] CHURCHILL (EDWARD,[3] ROBERT,[2] WILLIAM[1]). Born in Greenwich, Conn., Sept. 4, 1748. He lived in West Haven, Conn., and was a cooper by trade, and died in early manhood, leaving two children. Married, but we have not learned the name of his wife.

Children born at West Haven, Conn., probably.

38   I. EDWARD, JR.,[5] b. 1773; m. 1st, MARGERY MORSE, 1797; m. 2d, MARTHA MORSE.

     II. ABIGAIL,[5] b. Feb. 5, 1774; m. ELIJAH LAKE.

He died in 1835. She died Aug. 26, 1851. He was a farmer, and about 1811 settled in Millerton, N.Y., where Miss Louisa Lake, who furnished this account of her grandmother's family, was still living in 1902.

Children born in Millerton, N. Y.

1. Rebecca Lake, b. March 8, 1797; m. Daniel Mosher.
2. Edward Lake, b. Jan. 17, 1800.
3. Israel Lake, b. Sept. 13, 1803; d. March, 1805.
4. Abigail Lake, b. Aug. 24, 1805; m. Edmond Eldridge, of Millerton.
5. Israel E. Lake, b. Oct. 8, 1808; m. Cornelia Van Densen, Nov. 10, 1841.

    Children: (1) Sarah Jane Lake, b. Sept. 8, 1842; d. Aug. 31, 1856; (2) Laura E. Lake, b. Sept. 17, 1843; m. William E. Hamilton; d. Feb. 11, 1890, at Chapinville, Conn.; (3) Eliza Ann Lake, b. Nov. 6, 1845; d. April 20, 1847; (4) Louisa Lake, b. Oct. 1, 1846; (5) Emma Lake, b. Aug. 28, 1850; (6) Lydia M. Lake, b. Jan. 9, 1853; (7) Henry I. Lake, b. June 1, 1855; d. unmarried in Millerton, N.Y., Sept. 19, 1882; (8) Martha G. Lake, b. Feb. 21, 1858; m. Charles S. Davis, in Millerton, Dec. 21, 1892.

6. Hannah Lake, b. May 7, 1811; d. in Millerton, Oct. 19, 1822.
7. Elijah Lake, Jr., b. Dec. 23, 1813; m. in Wisconsin: name of wife not received.
8. Phebe E. Lake, b. March 29, 1816; m. Josiah Wells, of Tioga County, N.Y.
9. Leonard A. Lake, b. May 26, 1819; m. Sarah Twiss.

14.

JOHN[4] CHURCHILL (ABEL,[3] EDWARD,[2] WILLIAM[1]). Born at Jamaica, L.I. He joined the militia and went to Derby, Conn. Married, at Derby, Conn., Nov. 30, 1769, RACHEL DAVIS, daughter of Gen. John Davis; married by Rev. Richard Mayfield.

Children.

39   I. WILLIAM,[5] b. Nov. 1, 1770.

     II. ABEL,[5] b. Feb. 10, 1774.

This man changed his surname to Church, so that we follow his line no further.

15.

JOHN[4] CHURCHILL (JOHN,[3] EDWARD,[2] WILLIAM[1]).   Born in
Dutchess County, N.Y., Jan. 25, 1746.   They removed to Fairfield,
Herkimer County, and he became there a prominent citizen, justice
of the peace, etc.   Married JEMIMA KANE, born Aug. 9, 1746.

Children.

   I. REBECCA,[5] b. April 3, 1769; d. in infancy.
   II. JOHN, JR.,[5] b. May 3, 1770; d. in infancy.
40 III. ISAAC,[5] b. Oct. 1, 1772; m. HULDAH PHILLIPS.
41 IV. JOHN,[5] b. Sept. 4, 1774; m. and had seven or eight children.
   V. REBECCA,[5] b. Oct. 4, 1776; m. PHILIP KANE.

Children.

  1. John Kane, b. 1829; m. Betsey Nelson.
   Children: (1) Nelson Kane; (2) Albert Kane; (3) Eliza Kane.

  2. William Kane.
  3. Nancy Kane.
  4. Charles Kane.
  5. Archibald Kane.
  VI. CATIE,[5] b. Feb. 16, 1779; m. EBENEZER WATKINS.
  VII. NANCY,[5] b. Oct. 1, 1780; m. JOHN PICKERT.

Children.

  1. Maria Pickert, b. Oct. 29, 1800; m. Manning Todd.   Lived at
   Fairfield, N.Y.
  2. Catherine Pickert, b. Oct. 6, 1802.
  3. Levenus Pickert, b. Nov. 14, 1804.
  4. Lysander Pickert, b. Oct. 16, 1806.
  5. Nancy Pickert, b. Sept. 6, 1809; m. Mr. Wooster.
  6. Emilius Pickert, b. Aug. 8, 1812.
  7. Sarah Pickert, b. March 29, 1815.
  8. Lucina Pickert, b. July 12, 1818.

  VIII. ABRAHAM,[5] b. June 9, 1782; never married.
   IX. JEMIMA,[5] b. March 31, 1785; m. JACOB LOUCKS.
   X. PHILIP,[5] b. Aug. 25, 1787; never married.
   XI. SARAH,[5] b. July 29, 1790; m. BENJAMIN BECKLEY.

16.

EDWARD[4] CHURCHILL (JOHN,[3] EDWARD,[2] WILLIAM[1]).
Born in Dutchess County, Feb. 2, 1749.   Married MARY ELIZA
CHESSMAN.

Children.

42 I. EDWARD,[5] b. 1777; m. PHEBE FERRIS.
   II. POLLY,[5] b. 1779; m. CALEB VAN WIE.
43 III. ROBERT,[5] b. April 6, 1781; m. REBECCA VAN REDSENBERG.
   IV. LOVINA,[5] m. CAPT. (———) PEARCE.
   V. REBECCA,[5] m. LEWIS TATOR.
   VI. PHEBE,[5] m. JACOB BACKMAN.

18.

ISAAC⁴ CHURCHILL (JOHN,³ EDWARD,² WILLIAM¹). Born at Fishkill, N.Y., June 28, 1758. He served in the War of the Revolution, and was a pensioner. He lived near Little Falls, N.Y., over fifty years. Married NANCY PHILLIPS in 1760; died April 13, 1847, aged 87 years. He died June 14, 1843.

Children.

	I.	REBECCA,⁵ m. JOHN LOUX.
	II.	CATHERINE,⁵ m. ABIAL SHETLIFF.
44	III.	JOHN S.,⁵ b. 1784; m. ANN NEELY, b. 1787.
45	IV.	ISAAC,⁵ b. Aug. 6, 1786; m. BETSEY PARKER.
	V.	NANCY,⁵ m. JACOB PETRIE.
	VI.	POLLY,⁵ m. THOMAS BUCHANAN.
46	VII.	BENJAMIN PHILLIPS,⁵ b. June, 1797; m. CATHERINE WETHERWAX, Dec. 17, 1817.
47	VIII.	REUBEN,⁵ b. March 5, 1800; m. PHEBE TUCKER.
48	IX.	HENRY,⁵ b. Jan. 5, 1804; m. LYDIA WETHERWAX.

19.

JONAS⁴ CHURCHILL (JOHN,³ EDWARD,² WILLIAM¹). Born at Fishkill, N.Y., Aug. 21, 1760. Removed to Little Falls soon after the close of the Revolutionary War, and lived and died there. Married POLLY SUTTON.

Children born in Little Falls, N.Y.

49	I.	OLIVER,⁵ m. POLLY FOSTER.
	II.	HANNAH,⁵ m. GEORGE PARKER.
	III.	OLIVE,⁵ m. MR. CATOR.
50	IV.	JONAS,⁵ m. (——— ———), late in life.
	V.	ANNA,⁵ m. ADAM BIDLEMAN.
	VI.	ELIZABETH,⁵ b. May 10, 1801; m. SAMUEL MILLER.

20.

HENRY⁴ CHURCHILL (JOHN,³ EDWARD,² WILLIAM¹). Born at Fishkill, N.Y., March 6, 1763. Married CYNTHIA VAN TASSAL.

Children born at Fishkill.

51	I.	BENJAMIN,⁵ b. Jan. 7, 1783; m. 1st, DEBORAH VAIL, Nov. 1, 1806· 2d, REBECCA WEBB.
	II.	MARIA,⁵ b. Nov. 5, 1792; m. WILLIAM ROBINSON, Jan. 30, 1813. They lived in Matteawan, where she died Feb. 23, 1879.

Children.

1. Emmeline Robinson, b. Nov. 28, 1813; m. A. W. Lester, Oct. 4, 1842.

    She died June 18, 1844, leaving child (1) William R. Lester, b. Aug. 25, 1843.

2. Cynthia Robinson, b. March 26, 1816; m. David Ackerman,
   Nov. 30, 1838.
   Mrs. Ackerman was living near Fishkill, N.Y., in 1891. No
   children.
3. Henry Robinson, b. Nov. 24, 1819; m. Sarah Colville, June 5,
   1851.
   They lived at the old homestead in Matteawan.
   Children: (1) Annie Robinson, b. May, 1852; (2) Carrie
   Robinson, b. September, 1856.
4. Mary Elizabeth Robinson, b. Sept. 9, 1821; died unmarried.
5. John Peter Robinson, b. May 4, 1825; m. Mary Low, of Patterson, N.J., Oct. 11, 1854.
   Children: (1) Ida Robinson, b. 1855; (2) William Robinson,
   b. 1857; d. 1872; (3) Frank Robinson, b. 1860; d. October, 1875;
   (4) Mary Robinson, b. 1864; (5) John Peter Robinson, died in
   infancy.
6. Helen Louise Robinson, b. Dec. 3, 1827; m. Augustus Lester,
   of Troy, N.Y., May 23, 1848. Mr. Lester died in 1870.
   Children: (1) Augustus V. Lester, b. Feb. 14, 1849; d.
   March 22, 1850; (2) Frederic A. Lester, b. April 6, 1851; living,
   unmarried, in Philadelphia in 1891; (3) Marie Louise Lester,
   b. April 10, 1853; m. 1st, E. S. Wheeler, d. 1883; m. 2d, Judson A. Brown, Oct. 11, 1888, and by the latter had child, Judson
   L. Brown, b. 1889; (4) George W. Lester, b. May 5, 1855;
   d. April 16, 1858; (5) Annie Lester, b. May 15, 1857; d. Nov.
   12, 1860; (6) Carrie Lester, born March 4, 1860; d. Dec. 4,
   1862.

52   III. HENRY,[5] b. Dec. 1, 1794; m. HELEN MOTT.
53   IV. JOHN,[5] b. April 1, 1799; m. ROSANNA LYON.
        V. HANNAH,[5] m. DANIEL MOORES.
        VI. REBECCA,[5] b. 1801; m. DANIEL PHILLIPS.

Child.

1. Rebecca Phillips, m. Thomas L. Lester, of Matteawan.
   Children: (1) Henry M. Lester; (2) Mary L. Lester; (3)
   Adelia D. Lester; (4) Elizabeth Lester; (5) Anna R. Lester;
   (6) Kittie S. Lester; (7) Cornelia Lester.
   VII. ELIZABETH,[5] m. MOSES NICHOLS.
   VIII. PHEBE,[5] m. ISAAC VAN NOSTRAND.

21.

BENJAMIN[4] CHURCHILL (JOHN,[3] EDWARD,[2] WILLIAM[1]).
Born in Dutchess County, N.Y., Oct. 30, 1765. Lived in Oppenheim, N.Y. He died Nov. 26, 1862. Married 1st, CORNELIA VAN
TASSAL. Married 2d, CATHERINE BLAINE, who was born Feb. 14,
1781, and died Jan. 30, 1868.

Children of First Wife, born at Oppenheim, N.Y.

I. REBECCA,[5] m, JOHN YOURAN, of Oppenheim, N.Y.

Children, perhaps not in order of birth.

1. Catherine Youran, m. Adam Deifeldorf.
2. Anna Youran, unmarried.
3. John Youran.
4. Sylvester Youran.
5. Benjamin Youran.

II. WILLIAM.[5]
III. POLLY,[5] b. Dec. 20, 1792, m. NATHAN BROWN, who was the son of
       Josiah and Elizabeth (Dodge) Brown, and was born at Williams-
       town, Mass., Jan. 23, 1787, and died at Oppenheim, March 23,
       1856. Mr. Brown was a widely known, prosperous, and highly
       respected business man. He was one of the most active of the
       forwarding merchants in the early days of the settlement of West-
       ern New York, and during the War of 1812 was extensively
       engaged in forwarding supplies and munitions of war. After the
       opening of the Erie Canal he became one of the proprietors of the
       Pilot line of boats, and at the great celebration of the completion
       of the canal Governor Clinton was conveyed in one of his boats
       and under his personal direction from Buffalo to Albany. He
       continued the active business agent of the company till 1830,
       when he retired to his farm in Oppenheim, and engaged exten-
       sively in agriculture. He filled many public offices of trust
       with credit, and was a lifelong and earnest worker in the cause
       of temperance. In his private as well as public life he was a
       good, noble, and generous man.

Children of Nathan and Polly (Churchill) Brown, born at Oppenheim, N. Y.

1. Elizabeth Brown, b. July 16, 1812; m. Dr. L. G. Haskins, at
   Oppenheim, N.Y., Sept. 4, 1834. She died at Newport, N.Y.,
   Feb. 5, 1896.
2. Jeanette Brown, b. June 5, 1819; m. Erastus Heath.
   She died in Rochester, N.Y., March 28, 1886.
3. Celestia Brown, b. May 3, 1821; m. Richard Hewitt.
   They lived in Johnstown, N.Y., where she died Feb. 6, 1904.
4. Mary Brown, b. Jan. 17, 1823; m. Addison Lamberson, Dec. 11,
   1845.
   They lived in Dolgeville, N.Y., where she died Oct. 24, 1899.
5. Ophelia Brown, b. Dec. 12, 1826; m. John W. Cook.
   She died in New Hartford, N.Y., Dec. 27, 1900.
6. Josephine Brown, b. July 4, 1829; m. 1st, Asa Snell; 2d,
   James Brockett.
   She died in Dunkirk, Ind., April 22, 1903.
7. Stephen W. Brown, b. Oct. 4, 1835; m. Electa Clark, Nov. 21,
   1854.
   He died in Gloversville, N.Y., Sept. 5, 1898.

IV. HENRY,[5] m. MISS FARLING, of Oppenheim, N.Y.
V. LANEY,[5] m. EVALIN BROWN.

Children of Second Wife, Catherine (Blaine) Churchill.

VI. ARCHIBALD,[5] b. March 22, 1804; d. April 2, 1808.
VII. ENOCH N.[5] b. Nov. 5, 1805; m., but wife's name not received.
        They settled in Illinois first, but later in California, where he
        died. No children.
VIII. PHEBE,[5] b. Sept. 3, 1807; m. DANIEL MOSHER.
        They had two sons and a daughter, names not received. Moved
        West, and all trace of the family lost.
IX. ARVILLA,[5] b. March 7, 1808; m. 1st, JAMES GORDON, Nov. 5, 1828;
       m. 2d, MR. PERKINS.
       They lived in Oppenheim on a farm.

Children, all by First Husband.

1. William Gordon, b. Aug. 8, 1829; d. July, 1840.
2. Caroline Gordon, b. March 1, 1831; m. Geo. Wilson in 1854.
3. Hiram Gordon, b. July 21, 1833; d. July, 1840.
4. Rebecca Gordon, b. March 11, 1836; d. July, 1840.
5. Armina Gordon, b. July 24, 1838; d. July, 1840.

      6. Mary Catherine Gordon, b. Nov. 1, 1840; m. I. G. Horne, September, 1863.

          Was living in Bradford, Penn., May, 1904.

      7. Benj. Gordon, b. April 7, 1843. Lost in the Civil War.

      8. John Gordon, b. July 3, 1845; m. Matilda Seaman.

      9. Robert Gordon, b. Oct. 4, 1847; m. Terrene Robinson, 1874.

    10. Melissa Arvilla, b. Sept. 9, 1849; m. Geo. Malony, Jan. 1, 1868.

53a   X. JOSEPH,[5] b. Jan. 8, 1811; m. LUCY PANGBURN, Jan. 14, 1840.

     XI. ADALINE,[5] b. Aug. 31, 1813; m. 1st, a man who deserted his wife and child, Juliette Churchill; m. 2d, Mr. WILLIAMS and had two children, names not received.

    XII. RHODA ANN,[5] b. Sept. 8, 1815; m.(——————).

Child.

      1. Marie Antoinette, m. Mr. Hastings, and they have two daughters, names not obtained.

    XIII. BENJAMIN,[5] b. Oct. 17, 1817, unmarried. About 1856 he went to California, where he became a respected and influential citizen, holding important town and county offices.

53b XIV. JOHN B.,[5] b. Nov. 7, 1819; m. 1st, MARGARET GETMAN; 2d name not obtained.

     XV. ALMINA JANE,[5] b. Aug. 27, 1822; m. 1st, WILLIAM SHELDON STEWART, at Oppenheim, March 3, 1840. Mr. Stewart was the son of William and Abigail (Sheldon) Stewart, and was b. March 4, 1810, and d. Dec. 19, 1884. He was a contractor and farmer, a man of ability and influence, a citizen respected and honored. The family resided at Oppenheim, N.Y. Mrs. Stewart m. 2d, ROBERT KLOCK, in 1887. He d. May 26, 1899.

Children.

      1. Stephen S. Stewart, b. Jan. 26, 1841; m. S. Fanny Lassell, Dec. 16, 1868.

      2. Margaret M. Stewart, b. Oct. 2, 1843; m. Charles A. Kibbe, May 12, 1868.

      3. Willard Nelson Stewart, b. March 4, 1846; m. Mary M. Klock, Sept. 9, 1868.

      4. John C. Stewart, b. April 3, 1847; m. Josephine Lassell, Sept. 15, 1868.

      5. Abigail E. Stewart, b. May 7, 1849; m. Philo E. Johnson, Jan. 1, 1879.

      6. Adelia C. Stewart, b. Oct. 21, 1853; m. Oscar W. Krause, Aug. 25, 1880.

      7. William Benjamin Stewart, b. June 17, 1856; m. Delia Healy, Dec. 6, 1882.

   XVI. ELIZA C.,[5] b. Aug. 27, 1822; d. May 2, 1823.

23.

ROBERT[4] CHURCHILL (ROBERT,[3] EDWARD[2] WILLIAM[1]). Born in Jamaica, L.I. (probably). Married JEMIMA RAMUS.

Children born in Dutchess County, N.Y.

54   I. ZEPHENIAH,[5] m. HANNAH DATES.

55   II. STEPHEN W.,[5] b. June 8, 1791; m. MARGARET DATES.

     III. ELIZA,[5] m. MINNARD FRAZER.

    IV. SARAH,[5] m. 1st, Mr. PERKINS; m. 2d, JAMES MAJOR. They lived in Poughkeepsie, N.Y.

Child by First Husband.

1. Abner Perkins.

Child by Second Husband.

2. Mary Jane Major.

56   V.   ABNER,[5] m. ABBEY BENAWAY; no issue.
57   VI. ROBERT,[5] m. MARY VARNEY.

FIFTH GENERATION.

24.

JOHN [5] CHURCHILL (JAMES,[4] JOHN [3] CHARLES,[2] WILLIAM [1]).
Born Aug 3, 1795. Lived at or near Auburn, N.Y. He died
Feb. 4, 1867. Married MARY PALMER, born April 9, 1798. Died
May 31, 1858.

Children born at or near Auburn, N. Y.

I. BETSEY ANN,[6] b. Sept. 23, 1819; m. THOMAS SWAN, Dec. 25, 1843.

Children born in Auburn, La Grange County, N. Y.

1. Maria Josephine Swan, b. July 30, 1844; d. Sept. 29, 1848.
2. George Anson Swan, b. Aug. 8, 1846.
3. Mary Ella Swan, b. May 5, 1851.
4. Ernest Swan, b. Jan. 28, 1856.
5. Sarah Eva Swan, b. March 25, 1861; d. May 2, 1884.

II. ADELIA MARIA,[6] b. Feb. 12, 1821; m. DANIEL C. GRAY, Nov. 26,
1846.

Child.

1. William Henry Gray, b. in Cayuga County, June 10, 1862.

58   III. GEORGE WASHINGTON,[6] b. Feb. 9, 1823; m. HANNAH CAPRON,
Jan. 1, 1850.
59   IV. FITZ HENRY,[6] b. Feb. 22, 1827; m. JANE LITTLEFIELD, July, 1850.
60   V. WILLIAM OSCAR,[6] b. Aug. 21, 1829; m. MORGIANNA DILL.
VI. MARY ELIZA,[6] b. April 16, 1833; m. ALLEN DEAN, Dec. 2, 1859.

Children born in Cayuga, N. Y.

1. Charles Henry Dean. | 2. William Oscar Dean.

61   VII. JAMES VARNUM,[6] b. Sept. 25, 1835; m. ANN CRONIN, Oct. 2, 1859.
VIII. JOHN WESLEY,[6] b. June 28, 1838; d. unmarried, July, 1866.

25.

PETER [5] CHURCHILL (JAMES,[4] JOHN,[3] CHARLES,[2] WILLIAM [1]).
Born, probably at Tarrytown, N.Y., May 29, 1798. Lived at
Spafford, N.Y.; a blacksmith and farmer. Married 1st, in 1825
LUCINDA CRANE, who died Feb. 20, 1832; married 2d, in 1833,
CHARITY WILLIAMSON, who died March 1, 1869.

Children of First Wife born in Spafford, N. Y.

61a   I. JAMES,[6] b. July 2, 1826; m. CHLOE ANN CARR.
61b   II. GEORGE,[6] b. May 4, 1829; m. EVALINE NORTON.
Lived in Borodino, N.Y., in 1886.

Children of Second Wife born in Spafford, N. Y.

III. CAROLINE,[6] b. March 20, 1835; m. THEODORE GALE.
      Lived in Summerville, Mich., in 1904, with her daughter (1)
      Lillian Gale; m. Kelley Patcher. No children.
IV.   LOVILLIE,[6] b. March 15, 1843; m. GEORGE A. PATTEN, Nov. 26,
      1868.
      He was the son of William and Elizabeth Patten. George A.
      Patten was a farmer and lived in Spafford and Zealand, N.Y. He
      served three years in the Union Army during the Civil War

Children.

1. Alton W. Patten, b. in Spafford, N.Y., Oct. 23, 1869.
2. Flora E. Patten, b. in Spafford, Oct. 11, 1872; m. E. L. Gordon,
    of Spafford, Sept. 21, 1892.

26.

JAMES[5] CHURCHILL, JR. (JAMES,[4] JOHN,[3] CHARLES,[2]
WILLIAM [1]). Born June 15, 1801. Married AMANDA WILLARD.

Children.

I. ANGELINE,[6] m. HARRIE BARMSON.
II. HARRIET,[6] m. JONATHAN DAVIS.
     They lived at Dowagiac, Mich., it is said.

27.

FREDERICK W.[5] CHURCHILL (JAMES,[4] JOHN,[3] CHARLES [2]
WILLIAM [1]). Born in Renssalaer County, N.Y., April 15, 1804.
In 1887 Frederick and his wife were living with their daughter,
Mrs. Andrew, in Dowagiac, Mich. Married TABITHA WILLARD,
born in Otsego County, 1803.

Children.

62   I.   WILLARD D.,[6] b. April 15, 1829; m. LAURIETTE BARROWS.
63   II. MARCUS D.,[6] b. Nov. 29, 1831; m. PHIDELIA HALL.
64   III. PETER P.,[6] b. June 30, 1833; m. LUCY ANN BISHOP, and died
          Jan. 20, 1860.
     IV. MARY MARIA,[6] b. Feb. 10, 1840; m. WM. H. BESSON. She died
          Feb. 10, 1867.
     V.   ESTHER ANN,[6] b. March 15, 1841; d. June, 1841.
     VI. CORDELIA B.,[6] b. Oct. 8, 1842; m. LUMAN ANDREW.
          This family lives in Dowagiac, Mich.

Children.

1. Lottie B. Andrew, b. Sept. 30, 1863.
2. Arthur Andrew, b. June 19, 1865.

29.

ALEXANDER M.[5] CHURCHILL (JAMES,[4] JOHN,[3] CHARLES,[2]
WILLIAM[1]). Born in Renssalaer County, N.Y., April 20, 1809. He

was a farmer and lived in Spafford, N.Y. Married 1st, LYDIA McKAY, born March 30, 1819, and died June 13, 1843. She was the daughter of Augustin McKay. Alexander M. married 2d, JANE ROBERTSON, born 1817, married 1848, and died Nov. 5, 1850.

Child of First Wife.

I. ALLAVESTA,[6] m. H. B. SWETLAND, Jan. 31, 1866, and d. Oct. 23, 1900.

Child.

1. Milton A. Swetland, b. June 17, 1870; m. Dora Stanton, Oct. 21, 1891, and has in March, 1904, two children, Madge Swetland, aged ten years, and Marion Swetland, aged four years

Child of Second Wife, born in Otisco, N. Y.

II. JANE,[6] b. 1850; m. ORLANDO GRINNELL. He was the son of Seymour and Eliza Grinnell. They lived in Spafford, N.Y., where he was a farmer.

Children born in Spafford.

1. Lena Grinnell, b. July, 1872; m. William Willetts.
2. Isabel Grinnell b. August, 1874; m. Walter Tishop of Otisco, N.Y.
3. Milo A. Grinnell, b. July, 1876.
4. Marvin Grinnell, b. April, 1878.
5. Miles S. Grinnell, b. August, 1880.
6. Ira M. Grinnell, b. August, 1882.
7. Nellie F. Grinnell, b. February, 1885.
8. Alton Grinnell, b. February, 1888.
9. Ernest Grinnell, b. March, 1890.
10. Raymond Grinnell, b. May, 1892.

30.

ANSON[5] CHURCHILL (JAMES,[4] JOHN,[3] CHARLES,[2] WILLIAM [1]). Born in Onondaga County, N.Y., Nov. 31, 1813, and lived there, a blacksmith by trade. He died Oct. 25, 1849. Married, at Spafford, IZABENDA BEARSE, daughter of Aaron and Phebe (Smith) Bearse.

Child born at Spafford.

I. JENNIE,[6] b. Aug. 17, 1847; m. Erastus E. Brown, Dec. 3, 1866, at Borodino, N.Y. He was the son of Russel and Laura Brown. Mr. Erastus Brown is a lawyer, and in 1904 is settled in Lincoln, Neb., but lived formerly in Moravia, N.Y.

Child born in Moravia.

1. Anson C. Brown, b. Aug. 2, 1867; died Aug. 2, 1868.

31.

GILBERT W.[5] CHURCHILL (JAMES,[4] JOHN,[3] CHARLES,[2] WILLIAM [1]). Born in Rensselaer County, Sept. 21, 1815. Removed with his father's family to Spafford, N.Y., when one year old and lived there. He learned the carpenter's trade, and worked at it several years, but later bought a farm and made that his business. Died Oct. 1, 1899. Married 1st, ELEANOR RAINEY, who died in 1851; married 2d, HARRIET LITTLEFIELD.

Children of First Wife.

I. MORTIMER,[6] b. Dec. 20, 1843; d. in Raleigh, N.C., July 25, 1873; m. CORNELIA RUTZCH, but left no children.

II. MARY,[6] b. July 18, 1847; m. T. J. WIARD.

Child.

1. Ward Wiard, b. Nov. 2, 1870.

Children of Second Wife.

III. ALVIRA,[6] b. April 1, 1854; m. DAVID WILSON.

Children.

1. Jessie Wilson, b. Sept. 26, 1881.
2. Sarah Wilson, b. Sept. 27, 1884.
3. Marion Wilson, b. June 8, 1891.

65 IV. ANSON W.,[6] born June 14, 1856; m. JENNIE BURROUGHS.

V. ELEANOR,[6] b. Feb. 28, 1858; m. ORIN ROOT.

Children.

1. Bruce Root, b. Sept. 24, 1889.
2. Neva Root, b. April 19, 1892.
3. Harriet Root, b. Aug. 31, 1895.
4. Churchill Root, b. Oct. 21, 1898.

VI. JESSIE L.,[6] b. Nov. 11, 1861; unmarried.

32.

JOHN [5] CHURCHILL (JOHN,[4] EDWARD,[3] ROBERT,[2] WILLIAM [1]). Born in Milford, Conn., Aug. 3, 1770. Settled in Litchfield, Conn. He was a shoemaker by trade, and, about 1810, removed to the "Northfield Society," in the southeast part of the town, where he spent the rest of his life. Married, in Litchfield, Dec. 16, 1801, RUHAMA ORTON, of Litchfield.

Children born in Litchfield.

I. JEANNETTE,[6] b. Sept. 8, 1803; m. GEORGE PALMER, at Litchfield May 19, 1822.
They lived in Le Roy, N.Y., where Mr. Palmer was a tailor.

Children born in Le Roy, N.Y.

1. Andrew Palmer, b. March 27, 1823; m. Elizabeth Hull, in Constantine, Mich.
2. Mary J. Palmer, b. Feb. 8, 1827; m. James L. Dixon, in Constantine, Mich., May 20, 1849.
   Children: (1) Emily W. Dixon, b. in Constantine, Mich., June 7, 1853; m. Heman H. Smith; (2) Minnie Jennet Dixon, b. at Lake City, Minn., Sept. 4, 1860; m. William F. Shaw, at Red Wing, July 3, 1898; (3) George Edward Dixon, b. at Lake City, Minn., Nov. 17, 1865; d. at Lake City, March 20, 1885.

66   II. HIRAM,[6] b. Dec. 30, 1804; m. NAOMI NETTLETON.
  III. CHARLES,[6] b. Nov. 11, 1806.
  IV. ANNA,[6] b. Aug. 28, 1809; m. NATHANIEL C. ALVORD.
    They lived at Le Roy, N.Y., till after the birth of second child, when they removed to Trenton, Mich., and settled. He was a carpenter and farmer.

Children.

1. Emily Alvord.	4. John Alvord.
2. Hobart Alvord.	5. George Alvord.
3. Nathaniel C. Alvord, Jr.	6. Anna Alvord; m. Martin Foy.

67 V. JOHN,[6] b. Feb. 15, 1811; m. CAROLINE PECK.
68 VI. DANIEL CANFIELD,[6] b. Feb. 17, 1813; m. 1st, ESTHER TURNER; m. 2d, (———) McKINNON.
  VII. SARAH ANN,[6] b. July 27, 1815; m. JAMES COON.

Child.

  1. James Churchill Coon. (Was of Detroit, Mich., December, 1887.)

69 VIII. HENRY,[6] b. March 30, 1818; m. URANIA MATTHEWS.
70 IX. HOMER,[6] ⎰ b. June 10, 1822 ⎰ m. JULIA IVES.
71 X. HOBART,[6] ⎱   ⎱ m. JANE BALDWIN.

33.

TIMOTHY[5] CHURCHILL (JOHN,[4] EDWARD,[3] ROBERT[2] WILLIAM[1]). Born in Litchfield, Conn., June 23, 1776. He lived in Litchfield and was a shoemaker by trade. This account was furnished by William Willard Churchill and Mrs. Julia A. (Churchill) Beebe, in 1884. He died Aug. 11, 1842. Married in Litchfield County, Feb. 24, 1803, DOROTHY KILBOURN, of Litchfield Conn. She died May 22, 1854, in Rochester, N.Y.

Children born in Litchfield, Conn.

72 I. LEWIS KILBOURN,[6] b. Dec. 14, 1803; m. OLIVE BRADLEY.
73 II. GEORGE,[6] b. April 7, 1806; m. MARY ADDIS.
74 III. WILLIAM,[6] b. April 20, 1808; m. MARY H. WILLARD.
  IV. MARY A.,[6] b. July 20, 1811; m. ELLIOT HITCHCOCK.
  V. SOPHIA PAGE,[6] b. Dec. 17, 1814; m. JOSEPH H. BUELL, of Holly, N.Y., at Litchfield, Conn , Oct. 20, 1839.

Children.

  1. Daniel Hand Buell, b. Aug. 10, 1844.
  2. Frances Maria Buell, b. Oct. 17, 1847; m. John B. Fuller, of Holly, N.Y., Oct. 20, 1875, and has four children:
    (1) William B.; (2) Francis I.; (3) Jennie S.; and (4) Julia C.
  3. Henry Joseph Buell, b. March 6, 1854; m. Mary McCargo, of Holly, N.Y., Sept. 12, 1878 and has children:
    (1) Ann Sophia Buell, b. Nov. 26, 1879; (2) Frederick Churchill Buell, b. July 26, 1881.

  VI. MARIA L.,[6] b. March 10, 1818; m. NELSON TOMLINSON.
  VII. JULIA ADELAIDE,[6] b. Aug. 27, 1820; m. ARAM BEEBE, of Holly, N.Y. He died at St. Johns, Mich., April 15, 1882; m. at Litchfield, Conn., Nov. 27, 1843.

Children.

1. Horace Aram Beebe, b. June 5, 1846; d. Feb. 12, 1848.
2. William Churchill Beebe, b. Dec. 12, 1859; d. Jan. 6, 1860.

VIII. EMMELINE,[6] b. July 11, 1823; d. young.
IX. CHARLES H.,[6] b. July 31, 1826; d. young.

34.

WILLIAM [5] CHURCHILL (JOHN,[4] EDWARD,[3] ROBERT,[2] WILLIAM [1]). Born in Milford, Conn., April 8, 1781. Settled in Northfield, on a farm, and built the house there in which he lived and died. Died in Northfield, Conn., Sept. 10, 1828. Married, at Northfield, Conn., Dec. 24, 1800, KETURAH MORSE, born Feb. 20, 1785, and died Nov. 2, 1868.

Children born in Northfield, Conn.

I. SALLY,[6] b. April 26, 1802; m. SYLVESTER HINE, son of Andrew, of Milford, Conn., Dec. 31, 1824. She died Feb. 23, 1878.

Children.

1. William J. Hine.
2. Albert J. Hine.
3. Eliada O. Hine.
4. Polly Sarah Hine; m. Andrew Lounsbury.
5. Catharine Emily Hine; m. Mr. Slade.
6. Julia Tyler Hine.
7. Adaline Clarinda Hine; m. John Blakeslee.
8. Samuel David Hine.

75   II. DAVID MORSE,[6] b. Sept. 26, 1804; m. SALLY MARIA HINE, June 3, 1827.
III. ALMIRA,[6] b. Dec. 3, 1806; m. JOSEPH HINE, Aug. 6, 1826, at Northfield. She died July 30, 1885, at Fairhaven, Conn.
IV. EUNICE,[6] b. Dec. 27, 1808; m. JEREMIAH SMITH, June 26, 1831, at Harwinton, Conn.

Children.

1. Israel Jordan Smith.
2. Emma Jane Smith; m. Henry Riggs. ✓
3. Clark Smith, who enlisted in the army in the Civil War, and died there.

V. KETURAH JULIA,[6] b. Aug. 18, 1811; m. JESSE WASHINGTON TYLER, March 25, 1837, at Burlington, Conn.
VI. EMILY,[6] b. April 22, 1813; m. ASAPH HUMISTON BLAKESLEE, Plymouth, Mass., 1833.
VII. LUCY,[6] b. Sept. 7, 1816; d. Nov. 3, 1832.
VIII. SAMUEL BUEL,[6] b. Aug. 3, 1818; d. March 3, 1819.
IX. MARIA BUEL,[6] b. Jan. 5, 1821; m. 1st, EZRA DOWD, of Burlington, 1849; m. 2d, LORENZO CLEVELAND, of Torrington.

Child of First Husband.

1. Stanley Ives Dowd.

Child of Second Husband.

2. Edna Cleveland; m. Clark Bronson.

75a   X. ASHBEL WESSELS,⁶ b. Jan. 28, 1823; m. 1st, EVELINE BRONSON, Burlington; m. 2d, ALMA HARRISON, of East Morris.

XI. CHLOE ELIZABETH,⁶ b. Sept. 21, 1827; m. HENRY DEARBORN DAVIS, at Northfield, Oct. 1, 1847. He was the son of Jabez and Cynthia (Thwing) Davis, b. Sept. 10, 1824.

Children born at Northfield.

1. Frederick Jefferson Davis,. b. October, 1848; m. Harriet Folant in 1873.
2. Henrietta Davis, b. Jan. 20, 1851; d. Oct. 12, 1873.
3. Cynthia Isabelle, b. in Torrington, April 23, 1859; m. William H. Folant, Nov. 27, 1879.

37.

GARRETT D.⁵ CHURCHILL (JOHN,⁴ EDWARD,³ ROBERT,² WILLIAM ¹). Born in Litchfield, Conn., April, 1793. Removed and settled on the west shore of Seneca Lake in 1832. Married ELIZABETH M. ROOT, who was born in Kent, Litchfield County, Conn Sept. 16, 1794, and died in Tyrone, N.Y., Feb. 1, 1879, aged 85 years.

Children born near Litchfield, Conn.

77   I. JOSEPH,⁶ b. Oct. 8, 1818; m. ABIGAIL MATHER.

II. LAVINA,⁶ b. May 10, 1822; m. LEWIS CLARK. They lived in Altay, N.Y., in 1890.

Children.

1. Serena Clark; m. Joseph Danmarter. They lived in Wisconsin and had four children.
2. Lewis Clark, d. unmarried in Wichita, Kans.
3. Ira Clark, unmarried.
4. Myron Clark; m. Ellen Cushing.
5. Emma Clark, living unmarried in Altay, N.Y., 1890.
6. Emmet Clark (twin brother of Emma); m. Nettie Tuttle, and lived in Binghamton, N.Y., and had two children.
7. George Clark, m. Mary Mattison, and lived at Dundee, N.Y., in 1890.

78   III. JOHN,⁶ b. Nov. 18, 1824; m. LOUISA TOWNSEND.
79   IV. NEWTON,⁶ b. Oct. 10, 1828; m. NANCY J. SMITH.

V. BETSEY M.,⁶ b. Jan. 31, 1830; m. GRIFFIN B. WALTON, of Dundee, N.Y.

Children.

1. Griffin B. Walton, Jr. 2. William Franklin Walton.
G. B. Walton, Jr., gave us an account of his grandfather's family in 1890. He married Emma Douglas of Hammondsport, N.Y., and had (1) Flora M. Walton; (2) Mabel Walton; (3) John J. Walton; (4) Albert D. Walton.
W. F. Walton m. Clara Patterson, of South Bradford, N.Y. Children: (1) Grace Walton; (2) Cora Walton; (3) Griffin B. Walton; (4) Frank Walton.

VI. JANE,⁶ b. Feb. 1, 1833; m. SIMEON FORMAN. They lived in Monticello, Iowa.

Children.

1. Lillie M. Forman, b. March 11, 1857, at Castle Grove, Iowa; m. Joseph T. Minnis, Nov. 14, 1886.
2. William T. Forman, b. May 3, 1860, at Castle Grove, Iowa.

38.

EDWARD[5] CHURCHILL, JR. (EDWARD,[4] EDWARD,[3] ROBERT,[2] WILLIAM[1]). Born at Hartford, or West Haven, Conn., about 1773. We have two distinct accounts, one from his son John (born 1813), living in 1884, when he wrote us, in Springville, N.Y. He says, " My father's parents died when he was an infant; he had one sister, his senior, by the name of Abigail. He was bound out to a Mr. Buckingham, and suffered many hardships in his early days. In 1830 he removed to Boston, Erie County, N.Y. and there died, aged one hundred years. He was a very temperate man, honest and upright in his dealings, a Baptist in his religious faith. He lived to see five generations of his descendants. My mother died fifty-eight years ago (1826), and my father married her sister Martha." The other account is from Edward's grandson, Byron A. Churchill, of Buffalo, N.Y., who gives the date of his birth as about 1767, and his death 1867, and his first wife's death as 1819. He also says that his grandfather was a farmer and shoemaker, of very small stature, never weighing more than one hundred and thirty pounds, but very energetic, even to old age, for when he was ninety-two years old he rode a horse forty-five miles in one day, and without a saddle. He accumulated a property of near $20,000. Married 1st, in Litchfield, Conn., in 1797, MARGERY MORSE, who died before 1826; married 2d, in Boston, N.Y., in 1826, MARTHA MORSE, who died in 1865.

Children.

I. SARAH,[6] b. Sept. 17, 1799; m. 1st, NATHAN HUMPHREY; m. 2d, WHEELER DRAKE.
   They lived in Concord, N.Y., from 1832 to her death in 1867. It is said that there were two children of the first husband and three of the second, but our diligent inquiries at Concord and Boston, N.Y., have failed to find any of them.
II. MARTHA,[6] b. Dec. 1, 1800; m. BENJAMIN GREGORY.
   They lived in Bangall, N.Y. Mr. Charles Gregory of that town gave us the following account in 1886.

Children born in Bangall.

1. Mary E. Gregory, b. Oct. 19, 1817; never married.
2. Charles Gregory, b. Oct. 23, 1820; m. Mary J. Creed.
3. Eliza Gregory, b. Jan. 23, 1823; unmarried.
4. Amy A. Gregory, b. Sept. 27, 1826; m. Jarvis C. Robinson.
5. Edward B. Gregory, b. Aug. 10, 1829; m. Julia A. Mosher.

III. ABIGAIL,[6] b. Oct. 20, 1802; m. ADAM GENSMAN.
   They lived in Concord, N.Y., up to about 1866, when they
   removed to Brighton, Mich. They are said to have had four
   children, but the names have not been received.
80   IV. EDWARD, JR.,[6] b. Feb. 25, 1805; m. NAOMI FARQUHARSON.
81   V. LEVI MORSE,[6] b. July 10, 1807; m. 1st, JULIANA BOWMAN; m. 2d,
      ELIZA SMITH.
   VI. LAURA,[6] b. Dec. 20, 1808; m. GEORGE DECKER.
   She is said to have died at Juda, Wis., whither they had removed,
   in 1864. They had seven children, it is said, but names have
   not been received.
   VII. ACHSIE MARIA,[6] b. April 29, 1811; m. JOHN ANTHONY, April 29,
      1829, at Canajoharie, N.Y.
   He was a farmer at Boston, N.Y., town-clerk and justice of the
   peace. Mrs. Anthony died Oct. 11, 1890; Mr. Anthony died Aug.
   21, 1890.

Children.

   1. Elizabeth Anthony, b. Feb. 3, 1830; m. Milo Canfield, Sept. 7,
      1848.
   2. Martha Anthony, b. Feb. 28, 1832; m. Walter D. Smith,
      June 8, 1853.
   3. Gorham Anthony, b. Nov. 25, 1837; died in infancy.
   4. Almina Anthony, b. Sept. 25, 1839; m. Edwin W. Randall,
      May 30, 1860.
   5. George Anthony, b. July 1, 1842; m. Helen Horton, Aug. 28,
      1861.
   6. Mary Josephine Anthony, b. Oct. 1, 1844; m. Lauren J.
      Drake, Dec. 22, 1863.
   7. Carlos Emmons Anthony, b. Nov. 16, 1846; d. July 21, 1886.
   8. Margery Gertrude Anthony, b. Jan. 20, 1849; unmarried.
   9. John Anthony, Jr., b. April 20, 1851; m. Adelaïde F. Good-
      speed, April 24, 1872.
   10. Achsie Maria, b. Jan. 4, 1855; m. Tibbetts J. Soule, Feb. 5,
      1873.
82   VIII. JOHN,[6] b. Dec. 17, 1813; m. LAURA WELLINGTON.
83   IX. STEPHEN,[6] b. April 30, 1816; m. 1st, ORPHA PAYNE; 2d, JANE
      PALMERTON.
84   X. LUMAN B.,[6] b. March 3, 1819; m. Oct. 19, 1842, MARY AGARD,
      Concord, N.Y.
   XI. MARGERY,[6] b. June 5, 1821; died in infancy.

Child of Second Wife.

   XII. OLIVE,[6] m. REUBEN DYE.
   They had three sons who survived them, it is said, but we have
   not been able to get the names.

40.

ISAAC[5] CHURCHILL (JOHN,[4] JOHN,[3] EDWARD,[2] WILLIAM [1]).
Born in Dutchess County, Oct. 1, 1772. We have not been able to
obtain any further information than the names given below. Married HULDA PHILLIPS.

Children.

      I. CALISTA.[6]
85   II. VARNUM.[6]
     III. JULIA ANN.[6]
86   IV. MORGAN.[6]
87   V. RILEY.[6]
88   VI. EDGAR.[6]
89   VII. GAYLORD.[6]

41.

JOHN[5] CHURCHILL (John,[4] John,[3] Edward,[2] William [1]). Born Sept. 4, 1774, in Dutchess County, N.Y. Married; name of wife not received.

Children.

    I. Betsey.[6]
    II. Nancy.[6]
    III. Rosina.[6]
    IV. Almira.[6]
90   V. Ira.[6]
91   VI. Henderson.[6]
92   VII. Jerome.[6]
    VIII. Catharine.[6]

42.

EDWARD[5] CHURCHILL (Edward,[4] John,[3] Edward,[2] William [1]). Born 1777. Lived in New York State. Married Phebe Ferris.

Children.

93   I. John,[6] m. Julia McLoud.
    II. Abraham,[6] never married.
·94   III. James,[6] m. but name of wife not ascertained.
    IV. Charles;[6] he was adopted out of the family and took another name.
95   V. William,[6] m. Mary McCloud.
    VI. Maria,[6] m. Col. Daniel Stinson; no children.
    VII. Amy Eliza,[6] b. May 18, 1810, m. Jesse Ketchum, of New York. They removed to Mt. Pleasant, Iowa, where they lived, and she died there Sept. 7, 1899.

Children.

1. Julianna Ketchum, b. July 6, 1831; m. Joshua D. Loving, April 7, 1850.
    Children: (1) Harriet Loving; (2) William Loving; (3) Edward Loving; (4) Mary Frances Loving, b. Feb. 14, 1862; m. 1st, William George Mast, Dec. 24, 1878, who died May 19, 1884, leaving children: George Winfield Mast, b. Oct. 8, 1879; Jesse Ketchum Mast, b. Sept. 30, 1881; and Mabel Claire Mast, b. Aug. 13, 1883.
    Julianna m. 2d, Dr. W. W. Hipolite, of De Vall's Bluff, Ark., whence Mabel Claire Mast, in July, 1903, sent the editor this account of her grandmother Amy Eliza (Churchill) Ketchum's family.
2. Frank H. Ketchum.
3. Jesse Ketchum.
4. Leander Ketchum.
5. Winfield Ketchum.
6. William Ketchum.
7. Lyde Ketchum.
8. Harriet Ketchum.
9. Oscar Ketchum.
10. Albert Ketchum.
11. Edward Ketchum.

    VIII. Sarah,[6] m. George Morris.
    IX. Catherine,[6] m. John Rowe.

43.

ROBERT [5] CHURCHILL (EDWARD,[4] JOHN,[3] EDWARD,[2] WILL-IAM [1]). Born April 6, 1781. Married at Rhinebeck, Aug. 29 1802, REBECCA VAN VRADENBERG, born July 8, 1785.

Children.

96   I. PHILIP B.,[6] b. Jan. 11, 1805; m. LUCINDA BRIGGS.
97   II. WILLIAM,[6] b. Sept. 29, 1806; m. JANE CARPENTER.
       III. LEWIS,[6] b. Nov. 4, 1808; never married.
       IV. LUCIUS,[6] b. Sept. 8, 1810; d. May 31, 1811.
98   V. THOMAS T.,[6] b. Oct. 6, 1812; m. CATHERINE L. ASHER.
       VI. BLONDINA,[6] b. May 28, 1814; m. WILLIAM ASHER.
      VII. MARGARET,[6] b. Dec. 28, 1817; m. WALTER JOYCE.
    VIII. ABRAM,[6] b. Jan. 12, 1820; never married.
      IX. MARY,[6] b. Sept. 12, 1823; m. JOHN S. HOBBS, Oct. 29, 1846.

Children born in Red Hill, Dutchess County, N.Y.

     1. Mary Ann Hobbs, b. July 30, 1847.
     2. Rebecca Hobbs, b. Oct. 2, 1849; d. Sept. 3, 1876.
     3. William Hobbs, b. Oct. 21, 1852.
     4. John Hobbs, b. Aug. 10, 1854.
     5. Ida Hobbs, b. Aug. 21, 1857; unmarried.
     X. LAVINA,[6] b. April 5, 1825; d. July 20, 1825.
     XI. JOHN HENRY,[6] b. Jan. 1, 1828; d. young.
    XII. JANE ANN,[6] b. Sept. 26, 1830; m. GEORGE COWLES.

44.

JOHN S.[5] CHURCHILL (ISAAC,[4] JOHN,[3] EDWARD,[2] WILLIAM [1]). Born near Little Falls, N.Y., 1784. They lived near or in Herkimer, and at Little Falls, and Boonville, N.Y. He died in Boonville. Married ANN NEELY, born 1787. She died in Boonville, N.Y.

Children.

99   I. MORGAN NEELY,[6] b. November, 1809; m. CATHARINE MANETON.
100   II. HENRY MORTIMER,[6] b. May 29, 1811; m. CAROLINE McMASTERS.
      III. NANCY,[6] b. 1812; m. TRUMAN YALE.
     IV. SUSAN,[6] b. 1814; m. CHAUNCY PLATT.
101   V. REUBEN,[6] b. 1816; m. 1st, AUGUSTA PECK; m. 2d, MARY TYLER; m. 3d, ANN WILLIAMS.
      VI. MARY,[6] b. 1818; m. GEORGE HAMMOND.
     VII. CATHERINE,[6] b. 1821; m. CHANDLER PHELPS.
102 VIII. JOHN,[6] b. 1824; m. ELIZA RICH.

45.

ISAAC [5] CHURCHILL, JR. (ISAAC,[4] JOHN,[3] EDWARD,[2] WILL-IAM [1]). Born Aug. 6, 1786. He died July 1, 1867. Married BETSEY PARKER, born May 26, 1787. She died Aug. 18, 1865.

Children.

103   I. ISAAC P.,[6] b. Jan. 8, 1807; m. MARY BILLINGER.
      II. HARRIET,[6] b. Sept. 16, 1809; m. ISAAC BARNES.
     III. MARY ANN,[6] b. Oct. 18, 1810; m. —— YALE; d. May 29, 1849.
     IV. EMMELINE,[6] b. Sept. 24, 1812; m. ARTEMAS BURT.

104   V. JAMES,[6] b. Jan. 30. 1815; m. CAROLINE STARIN.
     VI. SALLY,[6] b. April 18, 1817; m. DANIEL PARKS.
    VII. NANCY,[6] b. Dec. 1, 1820; m. JOHN CALVIN.
  VIII. CATHERINE,[6] b. Feb. 16, 1824; m. AUDREY WATSON.
    IX. ELIZABETH,[6] b. Nov. 16, 1827; m. WILLIAM GWELLNER.

46.

BENJAMIN PHILLIPS[5] CHURCHILL (ISAAC,[4] JOHN,[3] ED
WARD,[2] WILLIAM[1]). Born June, 1797. This family lived at Little
Falls, N.Y. Married, Dec. 17, 1817, CATHERINE WETHERWAX.

Children born at Little Falls, N. Y.

105   I. ALBERT,[6] b. June 10, 1818; m. SUSAN BROWNING.
    II. CATHERINE,[6] b. April 10, 1822; unmarried.
       This lady, in 1885, gave information of her father's family.
   III. MARGARET,[6] b. May 2, 1828; m. THEOPHILUS EVANS.
   IV. CORDELIA,[6] b. March 22, 1831; m. DANIEL ARNOLD.
    V. GEORGE,[6] b. March 1833; unmarried.
106   VI. JACOB,[6] b. Feb. 29, 1838; m. HARRIET WEEKS.

47.

REUBEN[5] CHURCHILL (ISAAC,[4] JOHN,[3] EDWARD,[2] WILLIAM[1]).
Born March 5, 1800. Married PHEBE TUCKER, of Little Falls, N.Y.

Children born at Little Falls.

107   I. NORMAN A.,[6] b. Feb. 21, 1831.
    II. SOPHIA LANG,[6] b. Feb. 17, 1835; unmarried.
   III. CORNELIA,[6] }
   IV. CORDELIA,[6] } (twins), b. Nov. 14, 1836; unmarried.
    V. ELIZABETH,[6] b. April 8, 1839; m. JOAB SMALL.
   VI. HENRIETTA,[6] b. June 20, 1841; m. NICHOLAS BUTLER.

48

HENRY[5] CHURCHILL (ISAAC,[4] JOHN,[3] EDWARD,[2] WILLIAM[1]).
Born at Little Falls, N.Y., Jan. 5, 1804, and died April 12, 1881.
He was an upright and respected citizen. His son, Henry P., writes
an account of him, but omits to mention the place where he lived
and died, and gives no date of death. Married LYDIA WETHERWAX,
born April 5, 1805.

Children.

    I. CHARLOTTE ELEANOR,[6] b. July 17, 1832; unmarried.
    II. JULIA,[6] b. April 4, 1838; unmarried.
108   III. HENRY PHILLIPS,[6] b. June 27, 1844; m. LILLIE CUYLER LACEY,
      Sept. 6, 1870. She was born April 11, 1849. They lived from
      1884 to 1891 in Kansas City, Mo., where he was president of
      the "Safe Deposit and Savings Bank." We have numbers of
      letters from him to N. W. Churchill showing that he was greatly
      interested in the work and was willing to contribute to the ex-
      penses of a research in England if thought advisable. He
      visited Europe several times on business, and N. W. had evi-
      dently visited him in Kansas City. He makes no mention of
      having children, so that his father's line stops here.

51.

BENJAMIN [5] CHURCHILL (HENRY,[4] JOHN,[3] EDWARD,[2] WILL-
IAM [1]). Born at Fishkill, Jan. 7, 1783. Married, Nóv. 1, 1806,
DEBORAH VAIL.

Child.

108a   I. WILLIAM HENRY,[6] b. Sept. 11, 1807; m. PAMELIA CLARK WIGHT,
           April 29, 1830.

52.

HENRY [5] CHURCHILL (HENRY,[4] JOHN,[3] EDWARD,[2] WILLIAM [1]).
Born at Matteawan (Fishkill), Dec. 1, 1794. Married, April 1, 1817,
HELEN MOTT, born Oct. 22, 1798.

Children born at Matteawan.

109   I. WILLIAM DOLOWAY,[6] b. June 17, 1818.
        II. SARAH ELIZABETH,[6] b. Oct. 17, 1822.
       III. HENRY MOTT,[6] b. March 21, 1826; d. in infancy.
110   IV. HENRY HEYER,[6] b. Oct. 7, 1831.
         V. HELEN LOUISE,[6] b. July 3, 1834.
111   VI. COLWELL DEWITT,[6] b. Jan. 16, 1837.

52a.

JOSEPH [5] CHURCHILL (BENJAMIN,[4] JOHN [3] EDWARD,[2] WILL-
IAM [1]). Born at Oppenheim, N.Y., June 11, 1811. He removed to
Illinois and remained until 1847, when, with his wife and two
children, he crossed the plains in the company of Supt. Joel Palmer,
and settled on a claim near Hubbard, Marion County, Ore. He
went to the gold mines in California, but returned after much hard-
ship to Marion County, where they remained until 1861, when they
removed to Salem, Ore. November, 1861, Mr. Churchill enlisted in
Company B, First Regiment Oregon Cavalry, and served three years.
He also served in the war against the Indians in the Oregon country.
He died at Salem, Ore., Sept. 22, 1892. Married in Boone County,
Ill., Jan. 14, 1840, LUCY PANGBURN, who was born June 2, 1818,
and died in Salem, Jan. 4, 1900.

Children.

111a   I. ENOCH CHESTER,[6] b. in Boone County, Ill., Sept. 16, 1841; m. 1st,
           MARIA ALVIRA THOMAS, Nov. 1, 1868, who died July 7, 1883; m.
           2d, SARAH E. MCKENNEY, April 1, 1885.
111b   II. CLARK NELSON,[6] b. in Boone County, Ill., March 20, 1845; m.
           ISABELLA LONG, Oct. 9, 1876.
      III. LYDIA JANE,[6] b. in Marion County, Ore., Jan. 14, 1848; m. N. BIER,
           Salem, Ore., July 28, 1868. She died in Salem, Oct. 14, 1891,
           leaving children.

Children.

1. Almond A. Bier, b. Oct. 2, 1871; d. Oct. 18, 1873.
2. Lena P. Bier, b. Oct. 4, 1873.
3. Charles E. Bier, b. Nov. 4, 1875.

IV. JANETTA M.,[6] b. in Marion County, Ore., Dec. 8, 1850; d. Nov. 11, 1851.

V. MARY J.,[6] b. in Marion County, Ore., Sept. 21, 1852; m. GEORGE F. SMITH, at Portland, Ore., Aug. 19, 1882.

Children.

1. Frank Smith, }
2. Fred Smith, } (twins), b. July 7, 1883.
　　Fred died Jan. 29, 1884, and Frank died May 30, 1884.
3. Chester O. Smith, b. Feb. 6, 1886.

VI. MARETTE S.,[6] b. in Marion County, Ore., Feb. 14, 1855; m. ANDREW D. SMITH, at Portland, Ore.. Aug. 19, 1882.

Children.

1. Eva E. Smith, b. April 29, 1883.
2. Frank L. Smith, b. Dec. 18, 1885.

VII. JOHN J.,[6] b. in Salem, Ore., Nov. 7, 1861; d. Sept. 13, 1863.

53.

JOHN [5] CHURCHILL (HENRY,[4] JOHN,[3] EDWARD,[2] WILLIAM [1]). Born in Matteawan, N.Y., April 1, 1799, and died Dec. 9, 1849. They lived at Matteawan, Little Britain, and New Windsor, N.Y. This account was given in 1884, by Miss Cynthia E. Churchill, 19 Spencer place, Brooklyn, N.Y.　Married, Nov. 19, 1819, at Jersey City, ROSANNA BAILEY LYON, born Dec. 2, 1802, the daughter of Aaron Lyon, of Jersey City, N.J.　She was born Dec. 22, 1802, and died July 27, 1870.

Children.

I. SAMUEL HALSEY,[6] b. in Matteawan, November, 1820; d. November, 1841, unmarried.

II. ELIZABETH LYON,[6] b. in Matteawan, Jan. 27, 1822; d. unmarried, June 17, 1872.

112　III. AARON LYON,[6] b. in Matteawan, January, 1824; m. ADALINE BRETT, of Fishkill, N.Y.

IV. HARRIET,[6] b. at Little Britain, 1827; d. 1830.

V. MARGARET WILMARTH,[6] b. at Little Britain, April 3, 1830; m. 1st, WILLIAM DUMISTON; m. 2d, ROBERT McDONALD.

113　VI. WILLIAM WILMARTH,[6] b. at Matteawan, April 24, 1832; m. CHAR-LOTTE BRADLEY, and died May 24, 1882.

VII. CYNTHIA EMMELINE,[6] b. at Matteawan, Dec. 29, 1835; unmarried.

VIII. MARIA ROBINSON,[6] b. at Matteawan, July 13, 1839; m. WM. H. BARRETT, of Cornwall, and died at Philadelphia, Penn., April 9, 1884, leaving four children.

IX. HARRIET McMARTIN,[6] b. at New Windsor, N.Y., November, 1841; m. REV. ALVIN BAKER, and died at Otisco, N.Y., Sept. 21, 1869, leaving no children.

114　X. JOHN AUGUSTUS,[6] b. at New Windsor, N.Y., Feb. 28, 1844; m. HARRIET S. HYEL, Oct. 24, 1867.

55.

STEPHEN W.[5] CHURCHILL (ROBERT,[4] ROBERT,[3] EDWARD [2] WILLIAM [1]). Born June 8, 1791, in Dutchess County, N.Y. They lived near Poughkeepsie. He was a farmer. After the death of his wife he lived with some one of his children from time to time, mostly with Zaccheus, at whose house, at Harbor Creek, Penn., he died. Married, near Poughkeepsie, Dec. 9, 1812, MARGARET DATES, who was born June 2, 1793, and died Jan. 27, 1891.

Children born at or near Poughkeepsie, N. Y.

I. ELIZABETH,[6] b. Aug. 10, 1813; m. EBENEZER WORDEN, at Manchester, Oct. 5, 1831.
They lived at Poughkeepsie, where he was a shoemaker.

Children.

1. Charles Constantine Worden, b. March 4, 1833; d. Feb. 7, 1836.
2. William Henry Worden, b. July 30, 1835. He enlisted in the War of the Rebellion and d. July 4, 1863, in the army.
3. Charles Brodhead Worden, b. April 23, 1840. Enlisted in the war and died in the army June 10, 1864.
4. George Worden, b. Sept. 6, 1842; d. May 2, 1883.
5. James Edward Worden, b. March 16, 1846. Served three years in the Union Army, in the Civil War.
6. Stephen Worden, b. June 13, 1852.
7. Mortimer Worden, b. Sept. 16, 1854.
8. David Worden, b. Sept. 16, 1854. Lived at Harbor Creek, Penn., in 1904.

II. CHARLOTTE,[6] b. Feb. 8, 1815; m. GEORGE WHEELER, Jan. 29, 1833.
They lived in Dutchess County, N.Y.

Children born in Dutchess County.

1. Henry E. Wheeler, b. Sept. 20, 1835; m. Elizabeth Sherman.
2. Orville A. Wheeler, b. May 16, 1838; m. Elizabeth Ridley, of Wayne County, N.Y.
3. Margaret E. Wheeler, b. Dec. 19, 1840; m. Edward Tage, Erie, Penn.
4. Albert P. Wheeler, b. July 8, 1843; m. Mary E. Hannan, St. Clair County, Mich., Jan. 1, 1860.

115 III. GEORGE R.,[6] b. Sept. 5, 1817; m. ELIZA (———).
IV. DORINDA,[6] b. at Manchester, N.Y., Oct. 20, 1819; m. JOSEPH B. STEVENS, at Manchester, Jan. 4, 1849.
They lived in New York City, Erie County, Penn., and Dekalb County, Ill. Mr. Stevens d. Nov. 28, 1864. She d. March 11, 1896.

Children.

1. Amasa B. Stevens, b. Jan. 17, 1850; m. Laura B. Pfeil, Erie, Penn., Feb. 3, 1875.
2. Samuel Stevens, b. June 17, 1851; d. Jan. 17, 1852.
3. William W. Stevens, b. Nov. 30, 1854; m. Amelia Foster.
4. Sarah A. Stevens, b. May 1, 1857; m. Frank J. Town, Erie, Penn., Jan. 5, 1876.

V. SARAH,[6] b. Nov. 20, 1821; m. THOMAS H. FOWLER, April 6, 1852, at Poughkeepsie. He was the son of Richard R. and Martha (Purdy) Fowler, and was a farmer at Holley, N.Y. He was a school-teacher in early life.

Children born in Holley.

1. Rosella E. Fowler, b. April 23, 1854; m. at Holley, Dec. 28, 1875, Andrew Bowman.
2. Charity M. Fowler, b. March 8, 1857; m. Adelbert Knicker-bocker, Oct. 25, 1876, at Holley.
3. K. Adelaide Fowler, b. Jan. 8, 1859.
4. Richard R. Fowler, b. Oct. 28, 1864; m. Elizabeth Boyce, Nov. 10, 1893, at Kendall's Mills, N.Y.

115a   VI. ZACCHEUS,[6] b. Jan. 23, 1824; m. SARAH JANE BEARDSLEY, Sept. 10, 1844.

     VII. CORNELIA,[6] b. March 22, 1826; m. BARNARD LEWIS, at New York City.

They lived in New York City, Rochester, and Poughkeepsie.

Children.

1. Margaret E. Lewis, b. Nov. 25, 1853; unmarried.
2. Phebe E. Lewis, b. July 11, 1855; m. Ira Serren, April 14, 1879.
3. James B. Lewis, b. Aug. 11, 1858; m. Jennie Bayldon, Nov. 18, 1883.
4. George W. Lewis, b. May 25, 1860; m. Mary Lather, Nov. 23, 1884.
5. Ella M. Lewis, b. May 12, 1865; m. Jerome M. Sleigler, Sept. 2, 1896, at Yonkers, N.Y.

   VIII. CATHERINE,[6] b. Oct. 23, 1828; m. ALLEN MCNAMEE.

They lived at Bellville, Kan. No further record received.

   IX. MARGARET,[6] b. Feb. 5, 1832; d. Feb. 3, 1835.

   X. JOHN PETER,[6] b. Nov. 23, 1836; d. March 4, 1838.

57

ROBERT[5] CHURCHILL (ROBERT,[4] ROBERT,[3] EDWARD,[2] WILL-IAM [1]). Born in Dutchess County, N.Y. The meagre information about this family is obtained from Mr. A. B. Stevens, of Erie, Penn., in 1904. Married MARY VARNEY.

Children.

   I. JAMES,[6] removed to Michigan; unmarried in 1904.
   II. ARTHUR,[6] living unmarried in Erie, Penn., in 1904.
   III. JOHN,[6] m. NANCY BACKUS.

They were living in Erie County, Penn., in 1904, and said to have had two sons, but the names not obtained.

SIXTH GENERATION.

58.

GEORGE WASHINGTON[6] CHURCHILL (JOHN,[5] JAMES,[4] JOHN,[3] CHARLES,[2] WILLIAM[1]). Born at or near Auburn, N.Y. Feb. 9, 1823. Married, Jan. 1, 1850, HANNAH CAPRON.

Children born in Cayuga County, N. Y.

116	I. FRANKLIN HARVEY[7]
	II. MARY ANGELINE.[7]
117	III. WILLARD CAPRON.[7]
118	IV. CHARLES HENRY.[7]
	V. GERTRUDE MARIA.[7]

59.

FITZ HENRY[6] CHURCHILL (JOHN,[5] JAMES,[4] JOHN,[3] CHARLES,[2] WILLIAM[1]). Born at or near Auburn, N.Y., Feb. 22, 1827. Married, July, 1850, JANE LITTLEFIELD.

Children born at Seneca Falls, N. Y.

119	I. JOHN MILTON,[7] b. May 8, 1851.
	II. LAURA ANN.[7]

60.

WILLIAM OSCAR[6] CHURCHILL (JOHN,[5] JAMES[4] JOHN[3] CHARLES,[2] WILLIAM[1]). Born at or near Auburn, N.Y., Aug. 21, 1829. Married MORGIANNA DILL.

Children born in Cayuga County, N. Y.

120	I. WILLIAM.[7]
121	II. BENJAMIN.[7]
	III. EMMA.[7]

61.

JAMES VARNUM[6] CHURCHILL (JOHN,[5] JAMES,[4] JOHN,[3] CHARLES,[2] WILLIAM[1]). Born at or near Auburn, N.Y., Sept. 25, 1835. Married, Oct. 2, 1859, ANN CRONIN.

Children born in Auburn, N. Y.

122	I. JOHN LEWIS,[7] b. March 27, 1860.
123	II. EDWARD SEYMOUR,[7] b. March 23, 1862.
124	III. WILLIAM HENRY,[7] b. June 3, 1866.

61a.

JAMES [6] CHURCHILL (PETER,[5] JAMES,[4] JOHN,[3] CHARLES,[2] WILLIAM [1]). Born at Spafford, N.Y., July 2, 1826. He attended the public schools at Spafford. He lived at Spafford, Onandaga Valley, and Syracuse, N.Y., a merchant. This family, for some reason, spelled their surname with an *e*, but we retain the regular form. He died May 21, 1898. Married, at Vesper, N.Y., Feb. 7, 1854, CHLOE ANN CARR, daughter of Almon and Arethusa (Morse) Carr.

Children born, the first at Mottville, the rest at Spafford.

　　　I. CARRIE E.,[7] b. July 25, 1856; m. BENJAMIN FRANKLIN CHURCHILL, May 21, 1878. See Connecticut branch No. 311.
124a　II. HARLIE J.,[7] b. June 17, 1858; m. LILLIAN CADY, Oct. 21, 1890.
　　　III. NELLIE A.,[7] b. May 15, 1863; m. FRANK E. FREEMAN, Sept. 16, 1886.
　　　　　She died in Syracuse, N.Y., Dec. 3, 1902.
　　　IV. JENNIE M.,[7] b. Jan. 16, 1865; m. GEORGE G. NORRIS, Sept. 15, 1891.

62.

WILLARD. D.[6] CHURCHILL (FREDERICK W.,[5] JAMES,[4] JOHN,[3] CHARLES,[2] WILLIAM [1]). Born April 15, 1829. In 1887 he lived in Breckenridge, Col., but we have no further account than below. Married LAURIETTE BARROWS.

Child.

　　　I. MOLLIE.[7]

65.

ANSON [6] CHURCHILL (GILBERT W.,[5] JAMES,[4] JOHN,[3] CHARLES,[2] WILLIAM [1]). Born June 14, 1856. This family lived in Borodino, N.Y., where Mr. Churchill is proprietor of the " Churchill House." Married, at Vesper, N.Y., Aug. 30, 1883, JENNIE BURROUGHS, daughter of Seymour H. and Betsey Ann Burroughs.

Children.

　　　I. IVA,[7] b. June 7, 1884.
　　　II. NINA,[7] b. May 5, 1888.
　　　III. RUBY K.,[7] b. Jan. 12, 1895.

66.

HIRAM [6] CHURCHILL (JOHN,[5] JOHN,[4] EDWARD,[3] ROBERT,[2] WILLIAM [1]). Born in Litchfield, Conn., Dec. 30, 1804. He was a shoemaker and settled in business at or near New Haven. (This is on the authority of Mr. Myron Osborne, of Litchfield, who wrote us in 1886.) Married NAOMI NETTLETON.

Child.

124b   I. Asa.[7]

He was a physician at Meriden, Conn., but we have not been able to get any further information about him.

67.

REV. JOHN [6] CHURCHILL (John,[5] John,[4] Edward,[3] Robert,[2] William [1]). Born in Litchfield, Conn., Feb. 15, 1811. He fitted at Amherst College for Yale, in 1832 and 1833. Studied medicine at Yale 1833–1835 and then changed, and took the course in theology and graduated in 1839. He preached the rest of that year at Watertown, Conn., until April 22, 1840, when he was ordained as minister of the North Church in Woodbury, Conn., which office he filled until June 25, 1869, when he became acting pastor of the church in Oxford, Conn. He was a man of wide influence, and a preacher of ability. He received the degree of M.A. from Yale in 1844, and in 1868 delivered the annual address to the Alumni, which was published. He took deep interest in public questions and was elected to represent Woodbury in the Legislature in 1867 and again in 1868. He died at Woodbury, Dec. 29, 1880, after two years of failing health. Married, at New Haven, Oct. 20, 1840, Caroline Peck, daughter of Nathan and Mehitabel (Tibbals) Peck.

Children born in New Haven.

I. Harriette,[7] b. May 18, 1843; m. Willis A. Strong, at Woodbury, Oct. 11, 1882.

They lived at Woodbury, where Mr. Strong was a druggist. He died there Sept. 11, 1894.

Children born at Woodbury, Conn.

1. Caroline Julia Strong, b. Jan. 10, 1885.
2. Willis A. Strong, b. May 19, 1887.

II. Nathan Peck,[7] b. July 1, 1845; unmarried.

68.

DANIEL CANFIELD [6] CHURCHILL (John,[5] John,[4] Edward,[3] Robert,[2] William [1]). Born in Litchfield, Conn., Feb. 17, 1813. He was a shoemaker by occupation, and settled in Northfield, Conn. He was also quite noted as a teacher of music. Married 1st, in Northfield, Conn., Esther Turner. Married 2d, in Bethlehem, Conn., Lucy M. Kasson.

Children born in Northfield.

I. Gertrude Charlotte,[7] b. Feb. 3, 1867; m. Corydon C. Griswold, of North Woodbury, and lived there. He was a farmer.

Children born at North Woodbury.

1. Julia Churchill Griswold.
2. Homer Churchill Griswold.
3. Walter Emerson Griswold.
4. John Hobert Griswold.

II. JOHN KASSON,[7] b. July 15, 1868; d. at Brunswick, Ga., May 19, 1892.
III. ANNA LUCRETIA,[7] b. Sept. 24, 1870; m. DE LOSS D. PLATT, at Waterbury, Conn., Feb. 26, 1895.
   They lived at West Cheshire, Conn.   He was a metallurgist.

Children.

1. Clayton Churchill Platt, b. in Brooklyn, N.Y., Oct. 2, 1896.
2. Richard Orville Platt, b. at South Coventry, Conn., June 17, 1898.

IV. CARRIE MAUDE,[7] b. March 20, 1872.
V. ELIZABETH KASSON,[7] b. Aug. 1, 1874; m. GEORGE E. PRATT, at Buffalo, N.Y., Sept. 22, 1898.

Children.

1. Harold Samuel Pratt, b. in Buffalo, N.Y., July 23, 1899.
2. Mary Helen Pratt, b. in Buffalo, Dec. 24, 1900.
3. Ralph Wilbur Pratt, b. in Titusville, Penn., March 24, 1903.

69.

HENRY [6] CHURCHILL (JOHN,[5] JOHN,[4] EDWARD,[3] ROBERT,[2] WILLIAM [1]). Born in Litchfield, Conn., March 30, 1818. Lived in Waterbury, Conn. He was a railroad contractor. Married URANIA H. MATTHEWS, daughter of Zeba and Joanna (Allen) Matthews, born July 29, 1825, at Goshen, Conn.

Child born at Waterbury, Conn.

I. FLORENCE C.,[7] b. July 2, 1846; m. ALONZO B. AKINS.
   She was a graduate of Lake Erie College, Painesville, Ohio. Mr. Akins was the son of Henry and Mercy M. (Wilkinson) Akins. He served in the Union Army in the Civil War of 1861, in First Ohio Light Artillery.

Children born at Columbia, Ohio.

1. William Akins, b. March 27, 1869; m. Jane G. Mitchener, June 19, 1902.
2. Joseph H. Akins, b. April 28, 1872.
3. Charles F. Akins, b. Feb. 21, 1877.
4. Florence Gertrude Akins, b. Feb. 9, 1879.
5. Mercy Urena Akins, b. June 8, 1883.
6. Homer Churchill Akins, b. June 3, 1891.

70.

HOMER [6] CHURCHILL (JOHN,[5] JOHN,[4] EDWARD,[3] ROBERT,[2] WILLIAM [1]). Born June 10, 1822. He was a manufacturer of church organs in Middletown, Conn. They lived in Middletown and he died there. Married, Oct. 13, 1846, JULIA IVES.

Child born in Middletown.
I. EMMA A.,[7] b. Dec. 25, 1847; unmarried.

71.

HOBART [6] CHURCHILL (JOHN,[5] JOHN,[4] EDWARD,[3] ROBERT,[2] WILLIAM [1]). Born June 10, 1822. We have heard that this family was living in Waterbury, Conn., in 1902. Married, in Seymour, Conn., April, 1851, JANE BALDWIN.

Children.
I. GERTRUDE A.,[7] b. Dec. 9, 1855; d. May 25, 1866.
II. HENRY B.,[7] b. March 30, 1866; unmarried.

72.

LEWIS KILBOURN [6] CHURCHILL (TIMOTHY,[5] JOHN,[4] EDWARD,[3] ROBERT,[2] WILLIAM [1]). Born in Litchfield, Dec. 14, 1803. He was a hatter by trade. Married OLIVE M. BRADLEY, of Litchfield, Conn.

Children.
I. MARY A.,[7] b. Nov. 15, 1831; m. O. A. HUBBELL, Oct. 13, 1853.

Children.
1. Cornelia Churchill Hubbell.
2. Florence Sophia Hubbell.
125   II. WILLIAM,[7] b. April 5, 1840; m. 1st, NELLIE FEARING; 2d, MATTIE HOSFORD.
125a   III. CHARLES H.,[7] b. Sept. 28, 1843; m. ADELAIDE BUFFINTON.

73.

GEORGE [6] CHURCHILL (TIMOTHY,[5] JOHN,[4] EDWARD,[3] ROBERT, WILLIAM [1]). Born April 7, 1806. Married MARY ADDIS.

Child.
126   I. GEORGE,[7] b. 1833; m. SARAH SHEPARD.

74.

WILLIAM [6] CHURCHILL (TIMOTHY,[5] JOHN,[4] EDWARD,[3] ROBERT,[2] WILLIAM [1]). Born in Litchfield, April 20, 1808. Learned the mason's trade and went to Rochester, N.Y, in 1828, where, after a few years, he engaged in the lumber business. He was prosperous and influential in the affairs of the growing city, and was for ten years president of the Monroe Company Savings Bank, and was for several years an alderman in the city. Married, at Troy, N.Y., Nov. 2, 1837, MARY HUNTER WILLARD, of Stockbridge, Mass.

Children born in Rochester, N. Y.

  I. MARY FRANCES,[7] b. Aug. 20, 1842.
127 II. WILLIAM WILLARD,[7] b. March 30, 1852.
128 III. FREDERICK LEVI,[7] b. July 29, 1855.
  IV. JULIA JANE,[7] b. April 5, 1858; m. CHARLES P. FORD, Jan. 19, 1882.

75·

DAVID MORSE[6] CHURCHILL (WILLIAM,[5] JOHN,[4] EDWARD,[3] ROBERT,[2] WILLIAM[1]). Born in Northfield, Conn., Sept. 26, 1804. Married SALLY MARIA HINE, of Milford, Conn., June 3, 1827.

Children.

  I. ANNA,[7] m. CHARLES CATLIN.

Children.

1. Luther Catlin.	4. David Catlin.
2. Warren Catlin.	5. Anna Catlin.
3. Charles Catlin.	6. Frank B. Catlin.

  II. ALMA B.;[7] m. 1st, ANDREW SMITH, who died; 2d, WELLS W DAVIS, Sept. 21, 1862.

Child of First Husband.

  1. Henry L. Smith, b. Aug. 17, 1857.

Child of Second Husband.

  2. William C. Davis, b. May 24, 1867.

  III. LUCY,[7] b. Nov. 11, 1833; m. DANIEL MANSFIELD.
  IV. ALVIN H. D.,[7] d. at twelve years.
  V. JERRY SMITH,[7] d. in infancy.
  VI. PERRY OLIVER,[7] m. SARAH WOODRUFF (no children).
128a VII. CHARLES CARROLL,[7] b. Sept. 7, 1840; m. ALICE F. DILLON.
  VIII. EMILY M.,[7] d. in infancy.
  IX. SYDNEY M.,[7] d. in infancy.

77.

JOSEPH[6] CHURCHILL (GARRETT D.[5] JOHN,[4] EDWARD,[3] ROBERT,[2] WILLIAM[1]). Born near Litchfield, Conn., Oct. 8, 1818. Removed with his father's family to New York State and settled at Bradford, in Steuben County, where he was a farmer. In 1890 he wrote giving the names of his children. In 1904 his second daughter, Mrs. Robinson of Addison, N.Y., answered my inquiry with a little further information. Joseph died January, 1903, at South Bradford. Married, at Barrington, N.Y., Oct 3, 1839, ABIGAIL MATHER, who died in South Bradford, 1885.

Children.

  I. DANIEL,[7] b. May 20, 1841; d. in infancy.
  II. JULIA MARIA,[7] b. Dec. 8, 1843; m. CHARLES SWARTHOUT.
   They removed to Michigan, where she died, leaving two sons and a daughter, whose names are not received.

III. MARY ELIZABETH,[7] b. Nov. 2, 1846; m. GILBERT ROBINSON, at Bath, N.Y., 1875.

Mrs. Robinson received a good education, and was a school-teacher for many years before her marriage. She has lived at Addison, N.Y., where her husband is a farmer.

Children born in Addison, except the first.

1. Adelbert Robinson, b. in Bath, N.Y., Aug. 9, 1878.
2. Myrtie Robinson, b. June 13, 1879; m. William Rice, in 1897.
3. Claude Robinson, b. Oct. 10, 1882.
4. Eddie Robinson, b. April 7, 1884; d. Sept. 5, 1889.

129   IV. HEMAN,[7] b. Jan. 20, 1850; m. 1st, ETTA MATHER, 1874, in Lawrenceville, Penn.; 2d, LYDIA LEONARD.

Child by First Wife.

1. Mary; she lived, in 1904, in Wellsboro, Penn.

130   V. MERRITT,[7] b. Jan. 12, 1856; m. AMANDA GREEK, of Glenora, N.Y.

He lived, it is said, near Dundee, N.Y., in 1904. One child, a daughter, who lived, in 1904, near Watkins, N.Y.

78.

JOHN [6] CHURCHILL (GARRETT D.,[5] JOHN,[4] EDWARD,[3] ROBERT,[2] WILLIAM [1]). Born near Litchfield, Conn., Nov. 18, 1824. They lived in Watkins, N.Y. The account of this family was given by Mr. G. B. Walton, of Dundee, N.Y., in 1890. Mr. and Mrs. Churchill were then deceased. Married LOUISA TOWNSEND, of North Hector, N.Y.

Children.

I. IDA,[7] m. WILLIAM W. BATTY.
They lived in Watkins, N.Y., and had no children.
II. JOHN,[7] lived in Watkins, N.Y.; unmarried, 1890.
III. EVA,[7] m. SMEDLY EVARTS.
They lived in Watkins, N.Y., and had no children, in 1890.
IV. FRED,[7] unmarried; lived in Newark, N.J., 1890.
V. ALBERT,[7] unmarried; lived in Watkins, N.Y., 1890.
VI. WILLIAM,[7] unmarried; lived in Watkins, 1890.
VII. KITTIE,[7] unmarried; lived in Watkins, N.Y., 1890.

79.

NEWTON [6] CHURCHILL (GARRETT D.,[5] JOHN,[4] EDWARD,[3] ROBERT,[2] WILLIAM [1]). Born near Litchfield, Conn., Oct. 10, 1828. Married 1st, NANCY J. SMITH.

Children.

131   I. GEORGE,[7] m. (———) BAKER, of Middleville, Mich.
They lived, in 1890, at Grand Rapids, Mich. Two children it is said, but names not received.
132   II. WARREN,[7] m. ADELLA CANLEY, of Watkins, N.Y.
They lived, in 1890, at Altay, N.Y. One daughter, name not received.
133   III. LEROY,[7] m. ZADA PRESTON, of Monterey, N.Y.
They lived, in 1890, at Reading, Schuyler County, N.Y.
IV. IDA MAY,[7] m. JAMES SHEA.
They lived, in 1890, at Dundee, N.Y.

Children.

1. Grace Shea.   2. Leroy Shea.   3. Bessie Shea.

80.

EDWARD [6] CHURCHILL JR. (EDWARD,[5] EDWARD,[4] EDWARD [3]
ROBERT,[2] WILLIAM [1]).   Born at Bangall, N.Y., Feb. 26, 1805.
Lived, in the latter part of his life, in Springville, N.Y.   He was a
carpenter and lived after marriage at Boston, N.Y., and also West
Fales, N.Y. He died in Springville, N.Y., Aug. 19, 1889.   Married,
at Cherry Valley, N.Y., April 25, 1825, NAOMI FARQUHARSON,
daughter of James and Hannah (Cross) Farquharson.

Children.

I. MARGERY J.,[7] b. in Montgomery County, N.Y., Jan. 26, 1826; m.
    WILLIAM M. SIBLEY, M.D., at Boston, N.Y., Sept. 23, 1846.
    They lived at Collins Centre, N.Y., where he was a physician.
    He died Jan. 17, 1867.

Children born at Collins Centre.

1. Margery Adaline Sibley, b. Aug. 27, 1847; d. April 12, 1850.
2. William Edward Sibley, b Jan. 23, 1849; m. Louisa Shehan, in
   Wisconsin, 1880.
   Children : (1) Edward Sibley, b. at Chicago, April 30, 1881;
   (2) Joseph Sibley, b. at Chicago, Dec. 23, 1883; (3) Paul Sib-
   ley, b. at Watertown, Dakota, Jan. 13, 1886.
3 Irving Augustine Sibley, b. June 27, 1852; m. Cora Curtis, at
   Buffalo, N.Y., Jan. 3, 1872. They lived at Chicago, Ill., and
   South Bend, Ind.
   Children : (1) Irving A. Sibley, Jr., b. Sept. 30, 1878; (2)
   William C. Sibley, b. Sept. 24, 1881; (3) Frank Sibley, b. Feb.
   29, 1892.

II. HANNAH ALMIRA,[7] b. March 29, 1829; m. WILLIAM H. FREEMAN,
     April, 1848.

Child.

1. Helen Freeman; m. Sewell E. Glazier, of Boston, N.Y.

III. CYRUS DOWNS,[7] b. Dec. 4, 1836; d. in infancy.
134   IV. BYRON A.,[7] b. March 10, 1841; m. 1st, MARION S. GLAZIER, March
           30, 1859; m. 2d, OLIVE A. SMITH, Oct. 25, 1866.

81.

LEVI MORSE [6] CHURCHILL (EDWARD, JR.,[5] EDWARD,[4]
EDWARD,[3] ROBERT,[2] WILLIAM [1]).   Born at Stamford, Dutchess
County, N.Y., July 10, 1807.   Removed to Green County, Wis., in
1847.   Married 1st, JULIANA BOWMAN, born at Schoharie, N.Y.
Married 2d, ELIZA SMITH.

Children.

135   I. CHARLES BOWMAN,[7] b. at Schoharie, N.Y., Jan. 22, 1829; m.
          BETSEY ANN STEPHENS.
136   II. HARVEY,[7] m. ELIZA CHAMBERLAIN.
137   III. EDWARD,[7] m. ELLEN JOBES.
      IV. MARY,[7] m. JOHN CLYMER.

138   V. MASON M.,[7] b. Sept. 23, 1839; m. LUCY ROBINSON, 1863.
    VI. URIAH B.,[7] b. April 19, 1842.
        Served in Civil War, from Green County, Wis. Enlisted Aug. 7, 1862. Killed at Resaca, May 15, 1864. Was in Libby Prison a while.
139   VII. ARTHUR SMITH,[7] b. Feb. 2, 1844; m. ORLENA C. MURPHY, Feb. 2, 1879.
140 VIII. HOWELL,[7] b. May 13, 1849; m. EMMA ROBINSON.
    IX. HARRIETT E.,[7] b. Dec. 25, 1853; m. MARSHALL OGG, 1872.
    X. SALLY M.,[7] b. Aug. 19, 1856; m. EDGAR SCARBOROUGH.

82.

JOHN [6] CHURCHILL (EDWARD,[5] EDWARD,[4] EDWARD,[3] ROBERT,[2] WILLIAM [1]). Born in Bangall, N.Y., Dec. 14, 1813. He was living in Springville, Erie County, N.Y., Oct. 1, 1884, and wrote a letter and filled out a blank giving account of his father's and his own families. Married LAURA WELLINGTON. She died May 26, 1884.

Children.

141   I. JOHN OZRO,[7] b. Oct. 1, 1837; m. HARRIET POTTER.
142   II. GEORGE MORSE,[7] b. April 1, 1840; m. FRANCES MORRIS.
    III. LAURA MARTHA,[7] b. Oct. 28, 1842; m. SALMON STOCKER.
    IV. LOVINA MARIA,[7] b. Oct. 28, 1844; d. March 28, 1846.
    V. EDWARD,[7] b. May 14, 1848; d. March 19, 1850.
    VI. GERARD,[7] b. July 25, 1851; d. Oct. 22, 1865.
    VII. GERALDINE,[7] b. Feb. 24, 1854; m. HENRY E. WAITE.

83.

STEPHEN [6] CHURCHILL (EDWARD,[5] EDWARD,[4] EDWARD,[3] ROBERT,[2] WILLIAM [1]). Born April 30, 1816. We were unable to find any descendants from whom we could obtain information. Married 1st, 1835, ORPHA PAINE. Married 2d, 1848, JANE PALMERTON.

Children of First Wife.

143   I. ELBERT.[7] In 1886 lived in Columbus, Wis., a prosperous dentist. No further account.
144   II. LUMAN B.[7] In 1886 lived in Springville, N.Y., a miller. No account obtained
    III. DAUGHTER,[7] d. in infancy.

Children of Second Wife.

145   IV. EDWARD.[7]
    V. ADELAIDE.[7]
146   VI. CARLOS.[7]
147 VII. WARD.[7]

97.

WILLIAM [6] CHURCHILL (ROBERT,[5] EDWARD [4] JOHN,[3] EDWARD,[2] WILLIAM [1]). Born at Rhinebeck, N.Y., Oct. 29, 1807. The meagre information below was given by Mrs. Emily Churchill Tripp, of Bangall, N.Y., in 1890. Married JANE CARPENTER, born 1807.

Children.

   I. THIRSYETTE,[7] b. 1828; m. SOLOMON GRITMAN.
   II. MARY JANE,[7] b. 1830; d. young, unmarried.
   III. ELIZABETH,[7] b. 1833; m. PETER SEISM.
       They lived in Madison County, N.C., in 1890.
   IV. EMILY,[7] b. March 30, 1836; m. JOHN P. TRIPP.
       They lived at Bangall, N.Y., in 1890.
148   V. BENJAMIN,[7] b. June 8, 1839; m. SARAH CHURCHILL (cousin).
       They lived at Bullshead, N.Y., in 1890.
149   VI. WALTER E.,[7] b. Sept. 22, 1844; m. MARY WEEKS.
       They lived at Little Rest, N.Y., in 1890.
150   VII. PHILETUS,[7] b. May 15, 1847; m. HANNAH KINNEY.

98.

THOMAS TILOTSON [6] CHURCHILL (ROBERT,[5] EDWARD,[4] JOHN,[3] EDWARD,[2] WILLIAM [1]). Born Oct. 6, 1812. He died May 19, 1882. Married, April 20, 1834, CATHERINE L. ASHER.

Children.

   I. CEDELIA,[7] b. Dec. 16, 1835; m. JOHN W. HEUZEN.

Children.

   1. Emma Heuzen. | 3. William Heuzen.
   2. Lavina Heuzen. | 4. Robert Heuzen.
          5. Sheridan Heuzen.

151   II. CHARLES,[7] b. April 19, 1838; m. ANNIE MARIA WAGNER 1863.
   III. ROBERT P.,[7] b. July 1, 1840; d. June 14, 1863.
   IV. MARY JANE,[7] b. Oct. 9, 1842; m. JOHN KRAPSER.

Children born in Dutchess County.

   1. Emma Krapser. | 3. Nettie Krapser.
   2. Ira Krapser. | 4. Edward Krapser.
          5. John Krapser.

152   V. JOHN WILLIAM,[7] b. Sept. 17, 1844; unmarried.

99.

MORGAN NEELY [6] CHURCHILL (JOHN S.,[5] ISAAC,[4] JOHN,[3] EDWARD,[2] WILLIAM [1]). Born Nov. 4, 1804, at Little Falls, Herkimer County, N.Y., and when four years old removed with his father's family to Boonville, N.Y., where he lived until about 1856, when he removed to Cortland, N.Y. We have received no record of children by first wife, probably there were none to live. He died Jan. 9, 1878. Married 1st, CATHERINE MANSTON. Married 2d, March 6, 1834, ELIZA MORGAN, born April 5, 1812.

Children of Second Wife.

153   I. JAMES MONROE,[7] b. July 26, 1835.
   II. MARTHA JANE,[7] b. May 3, 1839; m. DWIGHT FOSTER.
   III. ANNA ELIZA,[7] b. Aug. 11, 1841; m. MR. TERRELL.
       They lived, in 1886, at Cortland, N.Y. She wrote this account of the family.
   IV. GEORGE WASHINGTON,[7] b. Oct. 24, 1844; d. June 14, 1845.
   V. CHARLOTTE MARY,[7] b. Nov. 20, 1846; d. Oct. 31, 1862.
   VI. JEROME NEELY,[7] b. Aug. 31, 1849; d. March 24, 1851.

100.

HENRY MORTIMER [6] CHURCHILL (JOHN S.[5] ISAAC,[4] ·JOHN,[3] EDWARD,[2] WILLIAM [1]). Born May 29, 1811, in Herkimer, N.Y. Lived first in Boonville, N.Y., but removed about 1856 to Chautauqua County. He was a farmer. He died March 13, 1868, in Fredonia, N.Y. Married, in Boonville, N.Y., CAROLINE McMASTER, born Oct. 16, 1824, in Trenton, N.Y.

Children, five born in Boonville, N. Y.

  I. DEMARIS L.,[7] b. Sept. 25, 1843; m. 1st, ALBERT LUKE; m. 2d, JOHN YOUNG, of Burnhams, N.Y. She died Jan. 21, 1898, in Burnhams, N.Y.
  II. ANNA R.,[7] b. Jan. 18, ·1845; died in Fredonia, N.Y., July 28, 1866.
154 III. FRANK M.,[7] b. Oct. 28, 1848; m. EVA C. TUCK, of Portland, N.Y.
  IV. GEORGE H.,[7] b. Jan. 6, 1853; unmarried.
   He was a prosperous hardware merchant in Bloomington, Ill. Died there April 1, 1889.
155 V. WALTER S.,[7] b. June 29, 1855; m. STELLA SIGGINS of Bradford, Penn.

Four Children of H. M. Churchill born in Pomfort, Chautauqua County, N. Y.
156 VI. ROSELL,[7] b. Aug. 1, 1858; m. MRS. EMMA OGILVIE, of Decatur.

Child.

  1. Delmer D., b. in Bloomington, Ill., May 11, 1895.
  VII. LILLIE J.,[7] b. April 10, 1861; m. FRANK BILLINGS, of Portland, N.Y.

Children born in Portland, N. Y.

  1. A daughter, d. in infancy.
  2. Edith Billings, b. April 1, 1889.
  3. Ethel Billings, b. April 1, 1889; d. May 16, 1889.
  VIII. KATIE,[7] b. Feb. 23, 1863; unmarried, lives in Portland, N.Y., with her mother.
  IX. HERMAN,[7] b. Jan. 27, 1865.

101.

REUBEN [6] CHURCHILL (JOHN S.,[5] ISAAC,[4] JOHN,[3] EDWARD,[2] WILLIAM [1]). Born 1816, at Boonville, N.Y., and died at Little Falls, N.Y., before 1901. Mr. Louis R. Noble, of Mattoon, Ill., wrote this account .of the family and tried to get further information, but could get no answers to his letters, nor any dates. Married 1st, AUGUSTA PECK; married 2d, MARY TYLER; married 3d, ANN WILLIAMS.

Children of First Wife.

  I. LORETTE,[7] m. —— PLATTE, of Alden Creek, N.Y.
  II. LORANA.[7]

Child of Second Wife.

  III. MARY TYLER,[7] b. 1857; m. LOUIS R. NOBLE, b. 1854.

Children of Third Wife.

IV. RHODA.[7]
157   V. CLINTON.[7]
      VI. KATHARINE.[7]
158   VII. REUBEN.[7]

104.

JAMES [6] CHURCHILL (ISAAC, JR.,[5] ISAAC,[4] JOHN,[3] EDWARD,[2] WILLIAM[1]). Born Jan. 30, 1815. Married CAROLINE STARIN, born 1817.

Children born at Little Falls, N. Y.

I. JANE.[7]
II. JOSEPHINE.[7]
III. SUSAN,[7] b. Nov. 24, 1842; m. ROBERT McCHESNEY, Jan. 9, 1868.

Children.

1. James McChesney, b. March 9, 1870.
2. Nellie McChesney, b. Jan. 9, 1872; m. STEPHEN C. WATERS, Feb. 8, 1889.

160   IV. JAMES H.,[7] b. Feb. 11, 1845.
      V. CHARLES S.,[7] b. April 11, 1848; d. Feb. 19, 1873.
      VI. PETER ADAM,[7] b. Sept. 1, 1852; d. May 23, 1888.

We have received no further record of the above family of James.

105.

ALBERT [6] CHURCHILL (BENJAMIN P.,[5] ISAAC,[4] JOHN,[3] EDWARD,[2] WILLIAM [1]). Born at Little Falls, N.Y., June 10, 1818. Married SUSAN BROWNING.

Children.

I. CORNELIA,[7] b. July 6, 1840; m. GEORGE P. RUSS.
II. JULIA,[7] b. March, 1842; m. JOHN DE RYTHER.
III. EMMA,[7] m. WILLIAM BELDEN.
IV. FANNIE,[7] m. GEORGE WATERS.
161   V. FREDERICK,[7] b. June 21, 1851; m. SUSAN AGNES WARD.

106.

JACOB [6] CHURCHILL (BENJAMIN P.,[5] ISAAC,[4] JOHN,[3] EDWARD,[2] WILLIAM[1]). Born in Little Falls, N.Y., Feb. 29, 1838. Married HARRIET WEEKS.

Children.

162   I. FRANK,[7] b. April 10, 1863; m. ROSE SHULL.
163   II. WARD,[7] b. Aug. 7, 1864.
      III. EDITH,[7] b. Jan. 2, 1867.
164   IV. GEORGE,[7] b. Aug. 28, 1871.

108a.

WILLIAM HENRY [6] CHURCHILL (BENJAMIN,[5] HENRY,[4] JOHN,[3] EDWARD,[2] WILLIAM [1]). Born Sept. 11, 1807. Married, April 29, 1830, PAMELIA CLARK WIGHT. She died Dec. 22, 1883.

Children of William H. and Pamelia C. (Wight) Churchill.

       I. DEBORAH ANN,[7] b. July 17, 1831.
164a   II. GEORGE HENRY,[7] b. Oct. 4, 1832.
      III. CLARISSA WIGHT,[7] b. March 4, 1834.
      IV. ADDISON BRISTO,[7] b. Aug. 7, 1835; d. March 31, 1857.
164b   V. CHARLES,[7] b. April 3, 1838.
      VI. FRANCIS AUGUSTUS,[7] b. Nov. 13, 1840; d. June 11, 1843.
     VII. SARAH HARRISON,[7] b. Feb. 25, 1841; d. Feb. 19, 1872.
   VIII. HARRIET DECKER,[7] b. July 14, 1843; d. April 5, 1853.
      IX. PAMELIA,[7] b. May 9, 1847; d. May 4, 1853.
164c   X. WILLIAM HENRY,[7] b. Sept. 18, 1849.

109.

DR. WILLIAM DOLOWAY[6] CHURCHILL (HENRY,[5] HENRY,[4] JOHN,[3] EDWARD,[2] WILLIAM[1]). Born at Matteawan, June 17, 1818. He was a physician and the family lived at Matteawan (Fishkill), N.Y. Married, Nov. 2, 1843, MARY JACKSON, born Dec. 24, 1823.

Children born at Matteawan.

165   I. SYDNEY FOWLER,[7] b. Sept. 18, 1844; m. but name of wife not received.

          Children.

      1. Minnie Estelle, b. in New Haven, Conn , June 22, 1869.
      2. Helen Adah, b. in Newburgh, N.Y., May 26, 1873.
    II. MARY ADAH,[7] b. Dec. 17, 1846; m. 1st, JOHN GREEN; m. 2d, HENRY (———).

111.

COLWELL DEWITT[6] CHURCHILL (HENRY,[5] HENRY,[4] JOHN,[3] EDWARD,[2] WILLIAM[1]). Born at Matteawan, Jan. 16, 1837. The meagre account below is all we could obtain. Married MARY FERGUSON.

Children born at Matteawan.

166   I. HENRY LEWIS,[7] b. May 31, 1857; m. SUSIE FREELIGH, Feb. 28, 1882. No children.
     II. ALICE DELL,[7] b. March 25, 1862.
   III. LOUISE OAKLEY,[7] b. Oct. 19, 1867.
   IV. JOSEPH BURTIS PEARY,[7] b. Sept. 1, 1872; d. Nov. 1, 1875.
167   V. FRANK M.,[7] b. Jan. 19, 1879.

111a.

ENOCH CHESTER[6] CHURCHILL, (JOSEPH,[5] BENJAMIN,[4] JOHN,[3] EDWARD,[2] WILLIAM[1]). Born in Boone County, Ill., Sept. 16, 1841. Removed with his father's family to Oregon, in 1847. Married 1st, in Salem, Ore., Nov. 1, 1868, MARY ALVIRA THOMAS, who died July 7, 1883. Married 2d, SARAH E. MCKINNEY, April 1, 1885.

Children of First Wife.

     I. INEZ,[7] b. May 28, 1871; d. June 20, 1873.
167a II. ARTHUR,[7] b. Jan. 28, 1875.
    III. CLARA,[7] b. March 16, 1877.
    IV. ORVILLE,[7] b. June 6, 1879; d. Oct. 18, 1879.

Child of Second Wife.

    V. INFANT DAUGHTER, b. Oct. 2, 1886; d. the same day.

111b.

CLARK NELSON [6] CHURCHILL (JOSEPH,[5] BENJAMIN,[4] JOHN,[3] EDWARD,[2] WILLIAM [1]). Born in Boone County, Ill., March 20, 1845. Removed with his father's family, in 1847, to Oregon. Married Oct. 9, 1876, ISABELLA LÓNG.

Children.

167b I. ALLEN J.,[7] b. Nov. 26, 1877.
167c II. RALEIGH,[7] b. July 3, 1880.

114.

JOHN AUGUSTUS [6] CHURCHILL (JOHN,[5] HENRY,[4] JOHN,[3] EDWARD,[2] WILLIAM [1]). Born at New Windsor, N.Y., Feb. 28, 1844. He was a man of ability, integrity, and well merited prosperity. He died after a long illness, Feb. 19, 1902. Married, Oct. 24, 1867, HARRIET S. HYEL.

Children.

    I. GERTRUDE,[7] b. Aug. 30, 1868; d. aged two and one-half years.
168 II. GEORGE HYEL, b. Oct. 19, 1869; m. MARY FRANKLYN KING.
    III. MARIE,[7] b. Aug. 3, 1872; m. HAROLD HERMAN JOHN BARING, of London, at New York City, at St. Thomas' Church, Oct. 24, 1898. Mr. Baring has been M.P. of London, Eng. They live at High Beach, Loughton, Essex County, Eng., at the old home of Mr. Baring's father. No children.

115.

GEORGE R.[6] CHURCHILL (STEPHEN W.,[5] ROBERT,[4] ROBERT,[3] EDWARD,[2] WILLIAM [1]). Born near Poughkeepsie, N.Y., Sept. 5, 1817, and lived in 1889 at Arlington, N.Y., but we failed to get from him a full account of his family. Died Dec. 26, 1898. Married ELIZA (———). She died January, 1904.

Children.

    I. MARGARET,[7] b. about 1841; m. MR. WALKER. They lived in Poughkeepsie in 1904.
    II. MARY,[7] b. 1843; m. WARREN LYONS. They lived in Freehold, N. J., in 1904.
    III. JOHN.[7] No further information obtained.
    IV. CORNELIA,[7] b. about 1852.

115a.

ZACCHEUS NEWCOMB [6] CHURCHILL (STEPHEN W.,[5] ROBERT,[4] ROBERT,[3] EDWARD,[2] WILLIAM [1]). Born at Poughkeepsie, N.Y., Jan. 23, 1824, removed to Harbor Creek, Penn., and settled there, and later at Erie, Penn. He served in the Civil War of 1861 65 in the Navy, under Capt. John Bumont, of the gunboat " Mackinaw." Married, Sept. 10, 1844, SARAH JANE BEARDSLEY, born July 12, 1824.

Children.

      I. EMILY,[7] b. May 17, 1846; m. JOHN SCHMEHL, Erie, Penn.
     II. ORREYETTE,[7] b. March 8, 1848.
168a   III. CHARLES B.,[7] b. June 5, 1850; m. HARRIET ANNA SIBBETTS, Port Gibson, Dec. 18, 1869.
    IV. CORNELIA R.,[7] b. April 1, 1851.
     V. AGNES,[7] b. July 12, 1856; m. JOHN ANDERSON, Erie, Penn., March 27, 1895.
168b   VI. WALTER G.,[7] b. July 8, 1860; m. VIOLA E. RUCK, Feb. 28, 1889.
   VII. MARY ARVESTA,[7] b. July 11, 1866; m. KIRK OLIVER.

SEVENTH GENERATION.

126.

GEORGE⁷ CHURCHILL (GEORGE,⁶ TIMOTHY,⁵ JOHN,⁴ EDWARD,³ ROBERT,² WILLIAM ¹). Born in Litchfield, Conn., 1833. Married SARAH SHEPARD.

Children.

168c   I. ALVORD.⁸
168d   II. GEORGE.⁸

128a.

CHARLES CARROLL⁷ CHURCHILL (DAVID M.⁶ WILLIAM,⁵ JOHN,⁴ EDWARD,³ ROBERT,² WILLIAM ¹). Born near Litchfield, Conn., Sept. 7, 1840. Married, July 1, 1869, ALICE F. DILLON.

Children.

168e   I. EDWARD,⁸ b. June 14, 1870.
     II. ALMA P.,⁸ b. March 15, 1878; d. in infancy.
168f   III. DAVID A.,⁸ b. Feb. 10, 1880.

134.

BYRON A.⁷ CHURCHILL (EDWARD,⁶ EDWARD,⁵ EDWARD ⁴ EDWARD,³ ROBERT,² WILLIAM ¹). Born 1841. He lived in Boston, Erie County, N.Y. He was a man of prominence, and was twice elected to the county office of Justice of the Sessions. Married 1st, March 30, 1859, MARION S. GLAZIER; she died Sept. 22, 1864. Married 2d, Oct. 25, 1866, OLIVE A. SMITH.

Child of First Wife.

   I. RINDA MAY.⁸

Children of Second Wife.

168g   II. JAMES A.,⁸ b. Aug. 11, 1867.
     III. H. ALMIRA,⁸ b. Jan. 26, 1869.

139.

ARTHUR SMITH⁷ CHURCHILL (LEVI MORSE,⁶ EDWARD, JR.,⁵ EDWARD,⁴ EDWARD,³ ROBERT,² WILLIAM¹). Born in Erie County, N.Y., Feb. 2, 1844. Removed with his father's family to Green County, Wis., in 1847. Enlisted in the Army, for the Civil

War, in the Twenty-second Regiment, Wisconsin Volunteers, Aug. 7, 1862. Was confined in Libby prison. Studied several years at the University of Chicago, and was admitted to the bar in 1878, when he removed to Atlantic, Cass County, Iowa, and practised his profession until 1885, when he settled at Omaha, Neb., Feb. 25, 1885. He wrote us this account, and we have nothing further in relation to the family. Married, Feb. 2, 1869, OLENA C. MURPHY.

Children.

I. AMY E.,⁸ b. Nov. 16, 1869.
II. ZITTA B.,⁸ b. Nov. 17, 1872.

141.

JOHN OZRO⁷ CHURCHILL (JOHN,⁶ EDWARD,⁵ EDWARD,⁴ EDWARD,³ ROBERT,² WILLIAM¹). Born Oct. 1, 1837. He lived in Boston, Concord, and Springville, N.Y. Married, Oct. 28, 1858, HARRIET SARAH POTTER.

Children.

I. ELLA ADEL,⁸ b.. in Boston, Erie County, N.Y.; m. ELMER ORMAL LELAND, January, 1887.

Children.

1. Rachel Harriet Amanda Leland, b. in Springville, June 18, 1890.
They live in Buffalo, N.Y

168h   II. JESSE EDWIN STANCLIFT,⁸ b. in the town of Concord, N.Y., Dec. 14, 1864; m. MAUD HOVEY, Oct. 21, 1897. Mr. Churchill is a Methodist minister.

Child.

1. Doris, b. Aug. 2, 1898.

III. MARY BLANCHE,⁸ b. in Springville, N.Y., Aug. 20, 1869; d. July 29, 1896.
IV. MARTHA BELLE,⁸ b. in Springville, N.Y., Oct 12, 1871.
She graduated from Syracuse University in 1896, and in 1899 was a teacher in the Vail-Deane School at Elizabeth, N.J.
V. LULU WELLINGTON,⁸ b. at Concord, N.Y., March 2, 1875.
She lived in 1899 at Springfield with her parents, unmarried.

152.

CHARLES⁷ CHURCHILL (THOMAS T.,⁶ ROBERT,⁵ EDWARD,⁴ JOHN,³ EDWARD,² WILLIAM¹). Born April 9, 1838. Married ANNIE MARIA WAGNER.

Children born in Dutchess County, N.Y.

    I. MARTHA.⁸
169 II. HENRY.⁸
    III. MARY.⁸
170 IV. RICHARD ⁸
171 V. ROBERT.⁸
    VI. GERTRUDE.⁸
172 VII. JOHN.⁸

161.

FREDERICK[7] CHURCHILL (ALBERT,[6] BENJAMIN P.,[5] ISAAC,[4] JOHN,[3] EDWARD,[2] WILLIAM[1]). Born at Little Falls, June 21, 1851. He died in New York City. Married, Jan. 14, 1869, SUSAN AGNES WARD, born Feb. 7, 1851.

Child born in Little Falls.

172   I. CARL FRED,[8] b. March 12, 1872.

164a.

GEORGE HENRY[7] CHURCHILL (WILLIAM HENRY,[6] BENJAMIN,[5] HENRY,[4] JOHN,[3] EDWARD,[2] WILLIAM[1]). Born Oct. 4, 1832. Married, but wife's name not obtained.

Children.

173   I. FRANK HENRY,[8] b. Feb. 6, 1860.
174   II. EDITH,[8] b. Jan. 18, 1862.

164c.

WILLIAM HENRY[7] CHURCHILL (WILLIAM HENRY,[6] BENJAMIN,[5] HENRY,[4] JOHN,[3] EDWARD,[2] WILLIAM[1]). Born Sept. 18, 1849. Married, but wife's name not obtained.

Children.

   I. JOHN A,[8] b. Sept. 21, 1873, d. May 4, 1881.
   II. GRACE L.,[8] b. Oct. 9, 1876.
175   III. ALEXANDER,[8] b Feb. 28, 1881.

168.

GEORGE A.[7] CHURCHILL (JOHN A.,[6] JOHN,[5] HENRY,[4] JOHN,[3] EDWARD,[2] WILLIAM[1]). Born Oct. 19, 1869. Married, in New York City, Nov. 21, 1894, MARY FRANKLYN KING.

Child.

176   I. GEORGE KING,[8] b. in New York City, Jan. 6, 1897.

168a.

CHARLES BEARDSLEY[7] CHURCHILL (ZACCHEUS,[6] STEPHEN W.,[5] ROBERT,[4] ROBERT,[3] EDWARD,[2] WILLIAM[1]). Born at Poughkeepsie, N.Y., June 5, 1850. Lived at Geneva, Port Gibson, and East Syracuse, N.Y. He was a general mechanic by occupation. Married, Dec. 18, 1869, at Port Gibson, N.Y., HARRIET ANNA SIBBETTS, daughter of Jonathan and Caroline (Smith) Sibbetts.

Children.

    I. Mary Sibbetts,[8] b. at Geneva, Jan. 1, 1871; m. A. R. Goodwin,
        Nov. 30, 1892.
    II. Winnifred,[8] b. at Waterloo, April 8, 1873; m. Charles C.
        Rumrill, November, 1899.
177   III. Oscar Benjamin,[8] b. at Port Gibson, March 15, 1875; m. Minnie
        McGowin, Sept. 12, 1899. They live (1904) at East Syracuse,
        N.Y.

Children.

    1. Ivan Floyd, b. Nov. 24, 1900.
    2. Mildred Winnifred, b. July 25, 1902.
    3. Earl, b. Feb. 28, 1904.

168b.

WALTER GEORGE[7] CHURCHILL (Zaccheus,[6] Stephen W.,[5]
Robert,[4] Robert,[3] Edward,[2] William[1]). Born at Erie, Penn., July
8, 1860. Lived in his native town. Married, at Erie, Penn., Feb.
28, 1889, Viola Emily Ruck, daughter of Jacob L. and Margaret
L. (Blair) Ruck.

Children born at Erie.

178   I. Carl Walter,[8] b. Jan. 7, 1890.
179   II. Blair Bennett,[8] b Jan. 10, 1892.
180   III. Boyd Thomas,[8] b. July 5, 1894.

APPENDIX

APPENDIX TO THE CHURCHILL FAMILY IN AMERICA.

In this volume, as well as in nearly all extensive genealogies there are found some lines bearing the family name which we have not been able to connect with ancestors in either of the great branches. Neither time nor money has been spared in our efforts to find the connection of the following unassigned families. We place each under the branch to which it probably belongs.

PLYMOUTH BRANCH.

Jacob Churchill and Abigail Bosworth, both of Halifax were married by Rev. Abel Richmond, of that town, June 3, 1811. Diligent inquiries, as early as 1889, with correspondence with their descendants in the far West failed then to establish the parentage of Jacob, but later information gives the birth of Abigail Bosworth, daughter of David and Patience, born in Halifax, Oct. 22, 1793. The editor had a transcript of the Churchill items on the Halifax town records made by the clerk, in 1900, from which we learn that a Jacob Churchill married, Nov. 2, 1790, Joanna Bosworth, and that Oct. 15, 1787, another Jacob Churchill, of Plympton, married Eunice Sturtevant. The latter is identified as No. 305 of the Plymouth branch. Of Jacob and Joanna we have no further information. In the town records of Halifax for March 1, 1812, Jacob Churchill was chosen highway surveyor, and April 6, 1812, Jacob Churchill was chosen to keep and sweep the meeting-house for the ensuing year. It is possible that either of the above may have been the father of Jacob who married Abigail Bosworth. (See No. 305, p. 166.) Jacob and Abigail (Bosworth) Churchill removed to Ohio some time before 1823, when they lived at Point Harmer, near Marietta, O. He was a blacksmith, and died about 1825. His wife Abigail later married Benjamin Racer.

Children of Jacob and Abigail (Bosworth) Churchill.

I. Eunice, m. Rev. Charles Dana, of Newport, O.
   Their son, Rev. Watson Dana, was living in Newport, O., in 1889.
II. Lydia, m. Mr. Wright.

III. JACOB, no further record received.
IV.. JAMES M., b. at Point Harmer, O., Feb. 13, 1823; m. CORDELIA
PAULINE TILLSON, at Point Harmer, O , 1846.
They lived at Hudson and Newport, O., and at River Falls, Wis.,
and Hastings, Minn., and later in Minneapolis. He was a tailor
by occupation. He had no interest in this matter of family history
and could not remember the name of his grandfather.

Children of James M. and Cordelia (Tillson) Churchill.

1. Elizabeth Racer, b. Jan. 6, 1848.
2. Jacob M., b. at Newport, O., April 23, 1851; m. Elmira Burrell Gordon.
They lived at River Falls, Wis. He was a farmer.

Children of Jacob M. and Elmira B. (Gordon) Churchill.

(1.) Ellen Maude, b. Jan. 4, 1874; d. March 7, 1877.
(2.) Abbie Elizabeth, b. Feb. 19, 1876.
(3.) Lucy Cordelia, b. April 14, 1878; d. Feb. 10, 1879.

3. Watson Dana, b. at Newport, O.
4. James Watson, b. at Newport, O.
5. Samuel Reigney, b. at Newport, O.
6. Robert Sheldon, b. at Hudson, O., Nov. 22, 1860.
In 1889 was living at Minneapolis, a printer by occupation.
7. Edward Derby, b. at Hastings, Minn., Feb. 25, 1864.

CONNECTICUT BRANCH.

(*Explanatory Note.*)

Referring here to my note under No. 436 (p. 541), I may now add
that diligent research has been continued up to this time with no
additional result as to the parentage of " Joseph, the Miller," of
Newington. In this search I have been generously assisted by Mr.
Charles S. Churchill, of Roanoke, Va., a descendant of Joseph,
through his son James (No. 192). All possible sources of evidence
have been tried, and much time and money expended upon this
problem by the editor in the last two years, in addition to the efforts
of the compilers years ago. Our senior compiler, N. W. Churchill,
corresponded with Mrs. Sarah (Alcott) Gillette, born in 1819 (granddaughter of Joseph and Rhoda), who wrote him that her mother
had often told her about her father's family, but never mentioned
Bolton as their old home ; on the other hand, she said that her
grandfather (*i.e.*, Joseph, the Miller) used to tell that his father's
family settled at a place called "Three Rivers," and were driven
away by the Indians when the children were young. Mr. Churchill
did not give this tradition much credit, not having then received the
account of the same tradition from another branch of the family.
And so the only solution seemed to be that the father of Joseph,
the Miller, was the son of Joseph (No. 6) and Lydia Dickerman ;
and that account I received from him, and arranged and published

(see pp. 330 and 343). A more careful final examination of all his
letters, papers, and manuscripts, after his decease, with letters received by me from other sources, led to the reëxamination of the
Bolton records by the genealogist of Newington, E. Stanley Welles,
who found that the Joseph whom we had adopted from Bolton had
been drowned Jan. 31, 1837, so that he could not have been the
father of our Joseph, who was born, his gravestone in Newington
shows, in 1750. I found in the Memoir of Deacon Elijah Churchill,
of Stamford, N.Y., published in 1878, that his grandfather, Giles
Churchill, son of Ensign Samuel, of Newington, left Newington
and settled somewhere near Stamford, N.Y., and there married, and
in 1751 removed to the forks of the Delaware river with a few other
settlers, and made a rude home in the wilderness; five children
were born there. The story of the Indian invasion is told on page
384, of this volume.

Putting this story with the assertion of Mrs. Gillette's mother, I
am led to the conviction, in the absence of any other clue, that
Giles Churchill had children older than those born at "the Forks,"
and my theory is that one of these was Joseph, born 1750, who
married Rhoda Goodrich. I have found no positive evidence of
this theory, though I have diligently sought from town clerks,
county clerks, ministers of the oldest churches in the region
around Stamford, N.Y., and Florida, N.Y., at which place, it is said,
Giles lived in 1771. I have found no proof of this last statement
of his residence, but, on the other hand, the Memoir of Deacon
Elijah states that he came with his family after the Indian raid
and "located in some part of Massachusetts." None of the
descendants of Joseph, the Miller, have been able to give any
information as to his parentage, while all have had the general
impression that he was closely connected with the Newington
line, and that his grandfather was Samuel. Again, the descendants
of Capt. Charles Churchill, son of Ensign Samuel, have always
considered the family of Joseph, the Miller, as cousins.

BRANCH NOT KNOWN.

DANIEL CHURCHILL settled in Locke, Cayuga County, N.Y., early
in the last century, cleared up a farm and married a woman named
Clarke, whose sister married a neighbor, Lawrence Wormer.
Researches, begun by the compilers in 1885 and diligently continued
up to the present time, have failed to reveal his parentage or place
of birth. From several letters written in 1888 I am able to glean
a few references which may serve as hints to his descendants if they

wish to investigate further. Mr. David Curtice of La Grange,
O., son of Hosea, writes, in 1889, that his father moved from
Hawley, Mass., to Pompey, N.Y., about 1795 and removed to Locke,
Cayuga County, in 1803. Mr. Curtice says: "I remember Daniel
Churchill very well, but I do not know where he came from, or
when he came to Locke. His farm joined my father's, and they
were good friends. My father, Hosea Curtice, was born in Massachusetts Feb. 13, 1774, and I think Daniel Churchill was six or eight
years younger than my father, and he was a captain in the War of
1812. I remember Daniel Churchill from 1816 to 1826, and I think
he died about the latter date. He had four girls and three boys."
Philo A. Churchill, son of Daniel and Nancy (Clarke) Churchill,
writes from Keeneyville, Penn., 1889, that his father said that his
grandfather, Daniel Churchill, was adopted when a small boy by
a man named Lowden Priest, and was brought up by him. David
Curtice also speaks of Lowden Priest, who, with Daniel Churchill
visited Curtice at La Grange, O. Mr. Seymour B. Clarke, of
Moravia, N.Y., a nephew of Daniel Churchill, wrote in 1888 giving
testimony in agreement with that above, but giving the additional
information that Daniel Churchill married a Clarke, and that the
Clarke family came from Stonington, Conn., to Cayuga County,
N.Y. The above material, collected by the compilers of this volume,
is given in addition to the following notes furnished by Mr. Wilbur
Churchill, of Sabinsville, Penn., in 1899, in the hope that the
descendants may be helped by it to clear up the birth-place and
parentage of their ancestor Daniel and find his proper connection
in the Churchill family. Wilbur Churchill's notes are mostly without dates or proper order of births, but contain the names in the
families from Daniel to the present generation.

ACCOUNT WRITTEN BY WILBUR CHURCHILL.

First Generation.

1. DANIEL CHURCHILL lived in Cayuga County, N.Y. A
farmer, and was a captain in the War of 1812. I cannot learn who
he married or when. (See testimony of authorities above that his
residence was Locke, N.Y., that his wife's name was Clarke, and
that he was brought up by Lowden Priest.)

Children born at Locke, N.Y.: 2. PHILO; 3. DAVID A.
4. ELIZA, married Rev. Theodore McElhenney, of Watkins, N.Y.,
a presiding elder in the Methodist communion and raised a large
family at Watkins; 5. LAWRENCE; 6. LUCY, married William
Hallenbeck and settled in Iowa; 7. SALLY, married Jacob B. Doan,

of Chatham township, Penn., and her children were: (1) Andrew J. B. Doan; (2) Sylvester .Doan; (3) Mary Doan; (4) Eliza Doan; (5) Sally Doan and (6) Jacob Doan; 7a. POLLY, married a Baptist minister and removed to the West

Second Generation.

2. PHILO, son of Daniel, lived in Jamestown, N.Y. and Chatham township, Penn.; a farmer. Died in Keeneyville, Penn. Married Sallie Maria Craft, of Cayuga County, N.Y. Children: 8. DANIEL; 9. REBECCA, born at Jamestown, N.Y., married Lyman Stowell, of Tioga County, Penn., and lived at Keeneyville, Penn., no chil dren; 10. RANDOLPH; 11. JAMES; 12. MARY, born in Chatham, Penn., married Mr. Heath, of New York State, no children; 13. FRANK; 14. RUTH, born in Chatham, married William Stevens of Keeneyville, a farmer, and lived there, one child, a daughter; 15. ELIZA, born in Chatham, Penn., married Francis Church, two chil dren, sons, names not given; 16. RILEY, married and had one daughter, but no names received.

3. DAVID A., son of Daniel, born in Locke, N.Y.; he was a farmer and shoemaker, and a man of good judgment and ability, holding several important local offices in Chatham, Penn., where he settled in 1843. Married Martha Buchanan, of Oneida County, N.Y. David A. and Martha (Buchanan) Churchill died at Marion, Wis. Children: 17. CLARK LATHAM; 18. JAMES BUCHANAN; 19. JEROME BONAPARTE; 20. WILBUR; 21. WILLIAM (these two last twins); 22. MARTHA JANE, born in Locke, N.Y., married in Chatham, Penn., E. R. Burley, and had children : (1) Clark Burley; (2) Ida Burley; (3) Helen Burley; (4) Mary Burley; (5) Emmett Burley; (6) Ebenezer Burley; (7) Edith Burley. 23. DAVID CORDON; 24. DANIEL; 25. LUNETTE, died aged three years.

5. LAWRENCE, son of Daniel, born in Locke, N.Y., settled in Oswego County, married and had a family, but we have no further account.

Third Generation, Descendants of Daniel Churchill.

8. DANIEL, son of Philo, born in Jamestown, N.Y.; in 1899 lived in Keeneyville, Penn., a farmer and dairyman. Married Nancy Clark of Chatham, Penn. Children: 26. PHILO; 27. CHAD; 28. CHARLES; 29. MORGAN. These four sons of Daniel lived at Keeneyville, Penn., in 1899.

10. RANDOLPH, son of Philo, born in Jamestown, N.Y. Settled at Chatham Valley, Penn., a farmer. Married Fanny Cloose, of Chat-

ham. Children: 30. FRANCIS, born in Chatham, Penn. Married
Emma Strong, of Chatham. Child, Anna Churchill. 31. WILLIS,
born in Chatham. Married Dolly Stevens, of Keeneyville, Penn.
One child, name not received.

11. JAMES, son of Philo, born in Jamestown, N.Y. Served in
the Civil War. Removed to Nebraska. Married and has family,
but no names of wife or children obtained.

13. FRANK, son of Philo, born in Chatham, Penn. Lived in
Keeneyville. Married Miranda Avery, of Chatham. Child: 32.
BYRON, born at Middlebury. Married Miss Starkey of same town.

17. CLARK LATHAM, son of David A., born in Cortland County,
N.Y. Married Sophia Catlin, of Charleston, Penn. Children: 33.
HENDERSON, died young; 34. EMMET, born in Wellsville, N.Y.
Married and had six children, but names not received.

18. JAMES BUCHANAN, born in Cortland County, N.Y. Married
Elizabeth Hayman. He served in the Civil War in a Wisconsin
regiment. Lived in 1899 in Marion, Wis. No children.

19. JEROME BONAPARTE, born in Milan, N.Y. Married Mary
J. G. Burney, of Ontario, Can. Lived for twenty-five years in
Canada and then moved to Sabinsville, Penn., where he died September, 1897, and his wife died Jan 7, 1898. Children: 35. DAVID
A., born in Canada. Married Lottie Spaulding, of Wellsfield, Penn.
Lived at Brooklyn, Penn. Child: Areta Churchill; 36. ELIZA;
37. CHARLES; 38. WILLIAM; 39. ERWIN. No further acccount
of these last four children of Jerome B. Churchill.

20. WILBUR, son of David A. and Martha (Buchanan) Churchill,
born in Locke, N.Y., April 17, 1835. Settled in Tioga County,
Penn., with his father's family, in 1843. Mr. Churchill enlisted
in February, 1864, at Sabinsville, Penn., as a private in Company F, Eleventh Regiment, Pennsylvania Volunteer Cavalry. He
was promoted to Brigade Saddler later. At the battle of 'Reams'
Station he was seriously injured, and was at the hospital for several
months, but in the spring of 1865 was detailed as Chief Saddler at
Brigade Headquarters, at Aiken's Landing, on the James river, and
participated later in the battles at Blackwater and Jarrett Station,
and was honorably discharged at Richmond, Va., Aug. 13, 1865. After
the war he settled in Sabinsville, Penn., and engaged in the oil and gas
business, in which he is still (1899) engaged, being a director and
one of the heaviest stockholders in the Sabinsville Company. Married, May 22, 1858, Sophia Octavia Beatty, born in Otsego County,
N.Y., Oct. 12, 1840, daughter of John and Amanda (Walling)
Beatty.

Children of Wilbur and Sophia Churchill.

40. CHARLES CLARENCE, born at Sabinsville, Penn., married Sarah J. Cooper, of Little Marsh, Penn. Children: (1) Clarence Laverne; (2) Thomas, died young; (3) Jason E.; (4) Mildred; (5) Arthur B.; (6) Emma J., died young. 41. EMMA JANE, born at Sabinsville, Penn., married Fayette Briggs, of Gurnee, Penn., and lived there. Child: (1) Hattie May Briggs. 42. WILBUR DANIEL CHURCHILL, born at Sabinsville, married Henrietta Cisco, of Sabinsville. Three children: (1) Frank Wilbur; (2) Tressie May; (3) Neva Janette. 43. CLARK LAVERNE, born at Sabinsville, married Almeda Douglass, of same town. Children: (1) Clara E. and (2) Douglass.

21. WILLIAM, son of David A. and Martha (Buchanan) Churchill, and twin brother of Wilbur, born at Locke, N.Y., April 17, 1835, married Betsey Sandow, in Chatham Valley, in 1858. He enlisted in the One Hundred and Forty-ninth Regiment, Pennsylvania Volunteer Infantry. Served two years. Was wounded in the battle of the Wilderness. Settled in Marion, Wis., in 1868 and was living there in 1899. Children: 44. LUNETTE; 45. MARY; 46. ANNA; 47. LAVERNE; 48. VINNA; 49. HENRY; 50. JAMES. We have no further account of this family

23. DAVID CORDON, son of David A. and Martha (Buchanan) Churchill, born in Chatham Valley, Penn. Married Harriet Short, of Chatham. Served in the Civil War in a Pennsylvania regiment. They lived in 1899 in Marion, Wis. Children: 51. WILLIAM; 52. RAY.

24. DANIEL, son of David A. and Martha (Buchanan) Churchill, born at Chatham Valley, Penn. Served in the Civil War in a New York regiment and died in the service in the Peninsula Campaign.

ANOTHER UNASSIGNED FAMILY.

In May, 1903, in searching for the descendants of Michael Churchill (p. 153, No. 281), I came upon Mr. Van Buren Churchill, of Elmdale, N.Y., who gave me the following account of his father's family. I am inclined to think that this family is connected with the Manhattan branch, as the grandfather first appears at Poughkeepsie, N.Y.

SOLOMON CHURCHILL married Elizabeth Wiley, lived near Poughkeepsie. Children: *1.* MARK; *2.* JOHN; *3.* EZRA; *4.* BARTHOLOMEW.

4. BARTHOLOMEW CHURCHILL, born in Poughkeepsie. Married Sarah Taylor. They settled at Nyash, N.Y., where he was a farmer.

Children of Bartholomew and Mary (Taylor) Churchill.

5. BENJAMIN F., born Jan. 29, 1829. Married Emily Parker
Oct. 23, 1853, at Macomb, N.Y. They lived at Macomb, where he
was a farmer.

> *Children of Benjamin F. and Emily (Parker) Churchill.*
>
> (1.) Van Buren, b. May 23, 1856; m. Maggie C. Lockie, at
>   Gouverneur, N.Y., Feb. 12, 1880. He is a farmer at above
>   place (1903). No children.
> (2.) Sarah Churchill, b. Sept. 23, 1858; m. Mr. Osborn.
> (3.) John F., b. March 4 1860; m. Maggie Partridge.
> (4.) Jennie, b. Feb. 23, 1864; m. A. Hosmer.
> (5.) Estella, b. Nov. 13, 1865; m. Noel Aldoes.
> (6.) N. H., b. Oct. 20, 1867.

6. NANCY, born May 14, 1837. Married William Partridge.

7. THANKFUL, born Sept. 27, 1843. Married T. S. Atkins.

NOTES OF ADDITION AND CORRECTION, PLYMOUTH BRANCH.

Page 256, No. 1007. Children of John and Martha J. (Bagnell)
Churchill·

1. Emma F., born 1850, died in infancy; *2.* George, born 1851,
died in 1855; *3.* John West, born 1853; *4.* Nellie Louise, born
1856; *5.* George, born 1858; *6.* Charles G., born 1861.

Page 277, No. 1072. Children and grandchildren of Amos and
Marilla (Bronson) Churchill:

1. Jessie M., born June 19, 1868. Married B. B. Curtis, June
19, 1886. Children: (1) Ruby B. Curtis, born Aug. 23, 1887, died
Jan. 27, 1888; (2) Arthur B. Curtis, born June 25, 1889, died Sept.
29, 1890; (3) Clarence R. Curtis, born Nov. 23, 1891; (4) Willard
C. Curtis, born Dec. 17, 1895, died Jan. 25, 1896; (5) Esther M.
Curtis, born Nov. 28, 1899.

2. Jennie E., born Sept. 14, 1870. Married Lewis D. Townsend,
April 22, 1891. Children: (1) Julia V. Townsend, born May 13,
1892; (2) Rhoda M. Townsend, born July 28, 1893, died Feb. 5,
1894; (3) Douglas C. Townsend, born Oct. 8, 1894, died Feb. 9,
1895; (4) Lyle B. Townsend, born May 27, 1896; (5) Richard D.
Townsend born March 27, 1902.

3. Josie M., born Nov. 29, 1872. Married George H. Whittle
June 2, 1891. Children: (1) Marie Whittle, born April 20, 1892·
(2) Amos M. Whittle, born Jan. 19, 1894; (3) Margaret H. Whittle;
born Nov. 12, 1895; (4) and (5) Marilla B. and Harriet H. Whittle,
twins, born Aug. 6, 1902.

6. Fannie Bell, born Dec. 9, 1880; married Clarence A. Rowland,
June 18, 1901. Children: (1) Ora Elizabeth Rowland, born June
17, 1902; (2) Clarence A. Rowland, born Oct. 4, 1903.

ADDITIONAL CORRECTIONS.

Page 12, under No. 32. *For* WORCESTER, *read* FOSTER.

Page 25, under No. 98. *For* JOSIAH,[5] *read* JOSIAH.[4]

Page 32, under No. 45. *For* No. 214, *read* No. 294.

Page 36, under No. 55. Add to children of JOSEPH[4] and ANNE DAGGETT, WILLIAM.[5] See *page 90,* under No. 149.

Page 41, under No. 166. *For* CLARA EDDY MEACHAM, *read* CLARA (MEACHAM) EDDY.

Page 45, under No. 186. *For* ANN E. GOVE, *read* ANN LANGDON GOVE.

Page 49, second paragraph. *For* Francis Porter, *read* Frances Porter. The surname of their children is Francis.

Page 51, under No. 202. *For* ELIZABETH HOLMAN, *read* ELIZA (HOLMAN) NORRIS.

Page 53, under No. 84. Marriage of Charles[6] an error. See *page 60,* No. 238.

Page 56, under No. 215. *For* MARIA, *read* MARCIA J. HOLMES.

Page 76, under No. 310. *For* Colwell, *read* Caswell.

Page 77, under No. 127. NANCY,[6] marriage and family an error. See *pages 61* and *62,* under No. 103. Last line on page 61.

Page 81, under No. 330. *For* ARVILLA GROW, *read* ARVILLA (GROW) WATKINS.

Page 89, under No. 145. *For* ABIGAIL HANLEY, *read* ABIGAIL HAWLEY.

Page 102, under No. 170. Correct by No. 406a, etc., page 211.

Page 106, second line. *For* Brownson, *read* Brown.

Page 106, under No. 416. *For* SARAH JANE CARVER, *read* S. J. CANN.

Page 111, under No. 428. *For* ANNA HOOLE, *read* WELTHA A. (JENKINS) HOOLE.

Page 115, under No. 189. *For* HYRONA, *read* IRENE FOLSOM PURINTON.

Page 128, under 488. *For* DIMON, *read* DAMON.

Pages 144 and *260.* The number of John,[7] born Dec. 8, 1810, should be 556a.

Page 158, under No. 632. *For* CLARK, *read* BLAKE.

Page 160, under No. 644. *For* MORGIANA, *read* MEHITABLE.

Page 160, under No. 640. *For* ADALINE WRIGHT, *read* ANNIE M. COOK.

Page 160, under No. 642. *For* CYNTHIA HUMPHREY, *read* CYNTHIA HUMPHREY FRENCH.

Page 162, under No. 295. *For* JOANNA TILTON, *read* MARGARET TILTON.

Page 162, under No. 654. *For* MARGARET, *read* MARY ANN, TILDEN.

Page 162, under No. 296. SABA [7] m. SAMUEL instead of JAMES CHURCHILL.

Page 176 under No. 714. *For* dau. of David, *read* dau. of Daniel.

Page 177, under No. 717 *For* MARY PERLEY, *read* MARY PENLEY.

Page 180, under No. 340, in ninth line of sketch. *For* wife's mother, *read* wife's brother.

Page 183, under No. 734. *For* MARY HOLT, *read* TRYPHENA HOLT.

Page 203, under No. 389, fourth line. *For* MARGETTE, *read* MARIETTE.

Page 204, under No. 393. *For* ALMON, *read* ALMOND M.

Page 211, under No. 406, seventh line. *For* CATHERINE, *read* MARY C.

Page 214, under No. 406c. *For side numbers* 406d, etc., *read* 829a, 829b, etc.

Page 238, under No. 474, third line. *For* EVELINE, *read* EMELINE.

Page 250, under No. 992. ELEAZER's child, Mary A., married. *For* 1863, *read* 1868.

Page 276, third and fourth lines. *For* DELINE, *read* DELANO.

Page 298. To eighteenth line add second child (2) Barbara Ellen Churchill, born Nov. 21, 1903.

Page 342, under No. 53. *For* EUNICE PAYNE, *read* LOIS MUNSON.

Page 373, under No. 228. *Read* b. Jan. 1, 1816; m. SARAH ANN SEDGWICK, Jan. 6, 1842.

Page 374, under No. 81, fifth line from bottom of page. *For* JAMES, *read* JANE.

Page 377, under No. 85. Give No. 250 to ELIJAH W. [7]

Page 378, under No. 87. *For* SARAH E., *read* SARAH M.

Page 399, under No. 298. *For* MARY I., *read* MARY (BAKER) DUNBAR.

Page 423, eighth line. Leave out second marriage. See 385 below.

Page 447, under 212. *For* EDGERTON, *read* EGGLESTON.

Page 486. Place Bossong children below their parents.

Page 488, foot-note, last line on page. *Read* Enos [7] Churchill, son of Zenas.[6]

' *Page 507*, under 345. *For* NORTON M., *read* NORTON H.

Page 534, fifth line. *For* 1904, *read* 1903.

Page 540, under No. 435, next to last line. *For* father, *read* brother.

Page 576, under side number 68. *For* MCKINNON, *read* LUCY M. KASSON.

Page 582, side number 99. *For* MANETON, *read* MANSTON.

Page 604. Head number 152 should be 151.

Page 605, under No. 168. *For* GEORGE A., *read* GEORGE H. CHURCHILL.

ADDED ITEMS.

The Churchill Family of Virginia has not been published in this volume as it is known that they have a well-kept record and correct genealogy mostly published in Virginia and Kentucky local histories. William Churchill, the emigrant ancestor, came from Northampton in Oxfordshire, and settled about 1669 upon the south bank of the Rappahannock river, Va. He was a gentleman of large estate and fine culture, held an honorable position in the State in his time, and founded a family which has ever been held in good repute in the later times.

There are some Churchill families whose connection with either of the branches collated by us we have not been able to find, but presume that these may be descended from the lines which have eluded our search, and it is probable that a few of the name may have been late comers through Canada and the provinces.

A William Churchill, said to have lived in St. Johnstown, N.Y., and to have died at the age of nearly one hundred years, had sons, William, John, and Henry, and a daughter who married Mr. Zimmerman. Henry, born 1794, married Polly Faling and had five children : (1) Archibald M.; (2) Cornelia; (3) Polly ; (4) Elizabeth; (5) John. The son of Archibald, Cyrus W. Churchill, was living in Carson City in 1900, and gave us some information.

INDEX OF NAMES

INDEX OF NAMES.

EXPLANATORY NOTE. — In this index Roman numerals iii to xv refer to Editor's Preface; pages from 1 to 320 refer to the Plymouth branch of the Churchill Family; pages 321 to 552 refer to the Connecticut branch; pages 553 to 606 refer to the Manhattan branch; and pages 607 to 619 refer to the Appendix.

Abbott, Corinth, 384.
Susan M., 280.
Abeil, Anna(Churchill-Coker), 558.
Edward, 558.
Abernath, 93, 197.
Abercrombie, Jane B. (Churchill), 198.
Ned, 198.
Ackerman, Cynthia (Robinson), 568.
David, 568.
Ackley, Amelia, 382, 473.
Ruth P., 382, 473.
Ackworth, Harriet, 507.
Adams, Adah, 361.
Adaline L. (Churchill), 376.
Adeline (Churchill), 176.
Alice (Perry), 175.
Annette, 175.
Arabella E. (Churchill), 175.
Austin V., 175.
Celestia, 175.
Charles C., 376.
Charles R., 487.
Charlotte C., 376.
Clara Mabel, 487.
Cora Esther, 487.
E. Marie, 376.
Edgar A., 175.
Edna Florence, 487.
Effie (Dana), 175.
Elijah C., 376.
Eliza M. (Churchill), 376.
Elizabeth (Churchill), 407, 528.
Emily, 369.
Emma C. (Churchill), 487.
Flora, 118, 235.
Frank, 174.
George W., 407.
Helen L., 376.
James D., 175.
Jennie L., 475.
John, 136, 407.
John, Jr., 407.
John Q., 376.
John S., 136.
Joseph, 528.
Julia Paul, 376.
Laura, 407.
Lillie (Witt), 507.
Lovisa, 371, 450.
Martha A., 175.
Martha L., 174.
Martin V., 175.
Mary, 155, 279.
Mary A. (Churchill), 174.
Mary J.(Churchill-Sevitz), 453.
Maverick, 176.

Adams, continued.
Millard O., 175.
Milo P., 174.
Minnie Isabel, 487,
Nancy E. (Churchill), 136.
Obed, 175.
Ollie (Norcross), 175.
Oscar C., 136.
Owen O., 175.
Samuel T., 376.
Sarah Abigail, 185, 312.
Sarah (Gibbs), 175.
Susan (Randall), 376.
Tynor Hall, 376.
Ursula, 156.
Walter, 507.
Wealthy B., 174.
William, 453.
Willis C., 175.
Zenas, 174.
Addis, Mary, 576, 592.
Addy, Lizzie M., 188, 315.
Agard, Mary, 580.
Akerman, Alonzo, 154.
Elbyron, 154.
Erastus, 154.
John D., 154.
Lurana (Churchill), 154.
Mary J. (Cox), 154.
Miles, 154.
Pamelia (Holmes), 154.
Winslow, 154.
Akins, Alonzo B., 591.
Charles F., 591.
Florence C. (Churchill), 591.
Florence Gertrude, 591.
Henry, 591.
Homer Churchill, 591.
Jane E. (Mitchener), 591.
Joseph H., 591.
Martha E., 536.
Mercy M. (Wilkinson),591.
Mercy Urena, 591.
William, 591.
Albee, Benjamin, 288.
Mary A. (Churchill), 288.
Albert, 436.
Albertson, Jacob, 53.
Martha, 53.
Albright, George, 320.
John, 320.
Melvina (Churchill), 320.
Alcott, Calvin, 367.
Charles, 367.
Jesse, 364.
Rosetta, 365, 434.
Sallie, 367.
Sarah, 343, 364, 610.
Sarah (Churchill), 367.
Sarah Jane, 367.
Alden, 373.
Cynthia (Churchill), 373.

Alden, continued.
Deborah (Churchill), 53.
Eliezer, 53.
Gideon S., 37.
Isaac, 53.
Lewis, 53.
Mary (Churchill), 373.
Rebecca, 53.
Roger, Capt., 351.
Aldoes,Estella(Churchill), 616.
Noel, 616.
Aldrich, Anna, 363, 429.
Gordon S., 445.
Lucy(Saunders-Kent), 445.
Alesworth, Clara Matilda, 198.
Alexander, Ebenezer, 325.
Elizabeth J., 359.
Mehitable (Buck), 325.
Alfred, Adeline, 367.
Mary C., 367.
Alger, Isaac, 40.
Priscilla (Lothrop-Robinson), 40.
Allen, 562, 564.
Abigail, 367.
Bethuel, 496.
Betsey, 563.
Caroline W. (Burlingame), 397.
Edward, 563.
Ella M., 229.
Esther, 495, 496.
Ethan, 455, 482.
Gabriel, 562.
Grace M., 255.
Harriet, 451, 551.
Hull, Dr., 562, 563.
Joanna, 591.
Joseph, 329, 435, 563.
Joseph E., 397.
Leah, 20, 44.
Letitia (Churchill), 253.
Lucian, 551.
Maria, 55.
Maria (Claflin), 90.
Mary D., 283.
Matilda, 105, 218.
Mira, 486.
Nellie (Champlin), 435.
Pasco, 253.
Phebe E. (Churchill), 496.
Rhoda, 551.
Sally Ann, 563.
Sarah, 149.
Sarah (Churchill), 562.
Susan, 138, 258.
Thomas, 218.
Van, 90.
William, 563.
Allerton, Isaac, 230.
Allison, Abigail W. (Churchill), 203.
Charles, 203.

Bell, *continued.*
Fanny, 377.
Harriet C., 377.
James, 84, 377.
James A., 251.
James H., 377.
Jared, 377.
Maria, 377.
May C. (Crosby), 251.
Olive (Churchill), 377.
Olive Eliza, 377.
Ruth (Churchill), 84.
Sarah, 377.
Thomas, 84.
William H., 377.
Bellinger, Col., 358.
Bellman, Sarah M., 442.
Bemis, Celia M. A. (Hyde), 292.
Nettie, 292.
Schuyler, 292.
Bemus, Lovina, 346.
Benaway, Abbey, 571.
Benedict, Allen, 424.
Lovina (Churchill-Gowdy), 424.
Sarah A., 348, 385.
Bennett, Alexander S., 293.
Almira (Churchill), 220.
Andrew, J., 159.
Carrie Morton, 54.
Cynthia (Churchill), 159.
Edwin Scott, 159.
Elizabeth C. (Vose), 54.
Elizabeth Churchill, 54.
Emily, 214, 215.
George W., 159.
Gilbert, 220.
James H., 159.
Joshua, 159.
Libbie (Churchill), 320.
Lulu E., 415.
Maria Miles, 159.
N. Edgar, Rev., 320.
Samuel, 54.
Sarah P. (Churchill), 293.
Bennington, Nellie, 503.
Benson, Celestia (Churchill), 35.
Charlotte M. (King), 170.
Ellen, 190.
Fred L., 285.
Frederick, 256.
George, 284.
George H., 285.
Hattie P. (Churchill), 284.
Jepthah, 35, 87.
Lucy (Churchill), 256.
Maria, 35, 85.
Mariette L. (not Margette), 96, 203, 618.
Sally, 35, 86.
Walter L., 285.
Bent, Jemima (Billington), 7.
Joseph, 7.
Bentley, 22.
Olive (Churchill), 22.
Benway, Arthur L., 164.
Lemuel, 164.
Lucy E., 164.
Sarah (Churchill), 164.
Sarah J. (Tandy), 164.
Berkeley, Matilda Fontain, 120.
Bermudiz, Malvina, 410, 509.
Berry, Elvira, 452.
Emily E. (Robbins), 183.
Florence, 67.
George, 444.
Grace Watrous, 522.
Irena, 147, 264.
Jesse J., 444.
John T., 183.
Lydia M., 147, 265.
Mary A. (Churchill), 444.

Berry, *continued.*
Sophia (Churchill), 444.
Sophia S., 444.
Bertram, Eleanor, 409, 504.
Besse, 35.
Celestia (Churchill), 35.
Bessel, Ida Louise, 280.
Bessey, Charity, 87.
John, 87.
Joshua, 87.
Mahala, 87.
Silence (Churchill), 87.
Besson. Mary M. (Churchill), 573.
Wm. H., 573.
Best, Catherine (Walker), 549.
John P., 549.
Maria J., 449, 549.
Beswick, Eva (Churchill), 508.
Herbert, 508.
Betts, Delilah, 89, 189.
Bicknell, Brownell M., 177.
John, 86.
Marcena (Churchill), 86.
Philena H. (Churchill), 177.
Bidleman, Adam, 567.
Anna (Churchill), 567.
Bier, Almond A., 585.
Charles E., 585.
Lena P., 585.
Lydia J. (Churchill), 584.
N., 584.
Bigelow, 86.
Harriet, 86.
Jason, 425.
Maria (Churchill-Brown), 425.
May (Churchill), 506.
Polly (Churchill), 86.
Reuban, 506.
Billings, Abbie, 78.
Bertha, 258.
Edith, 598.
Elizabeth (Churchill), 258.
Ethel, 598.
Frank, 598.
Grace Holmes, 258.
Hannah (Churchill), 363.
Henry B., 258.
Jesse, 258.
Lillie J. (Churchill), 598.
Lucy (Swan), 184.
Mary Ellen, 258.
William, 363.
Billinger, Mary, 582.
Billington, Abigail, 7.
Abigail (Churchill), 7.
Constant, 7.
Francis, 7.
Jemima, 7.
Joseph, 7.
Sarah, 7.
Sukey, 7.
Binder, Abram, 498.
Lena P., 498.
Leroy Jeffrie, 498.
Lloyd W., 498.
Melinda A. (Churchill), 498.
Bingham, Ada, 418, 518.
Addie (Ludlow), 418.
Alice, 418, 518.
Arthur, 220.
Caroline E. (Churchill), 418, 518.
Clara (Churchill), 220.
Helen Ludlow, 418.
Helen Maria, 418, 518.
Homer William, 418, 518.
Horace, 418.
John Augustine, 418.
John Herbert, 418.
Bird, Albert H., 257.

Bird, *continued.*
Angie, 86.
Arthur S., 224.
Asaph, 35.
Benjamin, 35.
Eliza A. (Churchill), 257.
George Emerson, 224.
John, 35.
Julia E. (Churchill), 224.
Lyman, 35.
Polly, 81, 176.
Polly (Churchill), 35.
Birdsall, 461.
Harriet (Churchill), 461.
Bisbee, Abigail, 15, 31.
Abigail (Churchill), 15, 31.
Abner, 15.
America, 176.
Ansel, 15, 31.
Bathsheba (Palmer), 15.
Clara (Churchill-Tuttle), 176.
Hannah, 15, 31.
Hannah (Churchill), 15.
Hopestill, 15, 31.
Issachar, 15.
Joanna, 30, 70.
Joanna (Brooks), 15.
John, 15, 170.
Josiah, 15, 31.
Levi, 15, 31.
Lydia (Cushman), 32.
Mary (Harlow), 15.
Priscilla (Ripley), 170.
Reuben, 32.
Sally, 78, 170.
Sarah, 15.
Susanna, 31.
Susannah, 15.
Sylvanus, 15, 31.
Bishop, Alice, 408.
Ebenezer, Prof., 408.
Georgia, 408.
Laura W. (Churchill), 408.
Lucy Ann, 573.
Bitts, Rachel, 36.
Black, Emma A., 320.
J. B., Dr., 217.
Jane, 408, 501.
Rebecca (Churchill), 217.
Blackinson, Annie (Churchill), 443.
Charles, 443.
Blackmer, Branch, 1, 7.
Blackmore, Alice, 395.
Alta Holmes, 395.
Alvah R., 394.
Cora, 395.
Eliza, 394.
Esther A. (Churchill), 394.
Ida, 395.
John, 394.
Mary (Sage), 394.
Olive A., 394.
Olive M. (Churchill), 395.
Thomas, 395.
Blackwell, Abiah, 7, 11.
Martha, 17, 34.
Samuel, 34.
Blaine, Catherine, 563, 568.
Emma, 222.
Blair, Margaret L., 606.
Blaisdell, Elizabeth Ann, 45.
Martha C. (Hood), 45.
Mary (Churchill), 45.
Mary Melvina, 45.
Nicholas, 45.
Robinson, 45.
Blake, Anna A. (Churchill), 256.
Charles, 256, 408,
Ida, 408.
Julia (Weston), 408.
Lillie, 408.

Churchill, *continued:*
Ellen, 39, 64, 114, 119, 145, 149, 177, 187, 219, 303, 441, 443, 522, 528.
Ellen A., 188.
Ellen Annette, 228.
Ellen B. (Barrett), 297.
Ellen Barnes, 247.
Ellen Barrett, 298.
Ellen Bartlett, 470.
Ellen Belinda, 446.
Ellen (Benson), 190.
Ellen (Catlin), 457.
Ellen (Chase), 69, 149.
Ellen Clarissa, 417, 517.
Ellen Covington, 241.
Ellen E., 302.
Ellen Eliza, 280.
Ellen F., 508.
Ellen F. (Strong), 122, 237.
Ellen (Geers), 295.
Ellen (Hyde), 483.
Ellen (Jobes), 595.
Ellen L., 547.
Ellen L. (Hatch), 203.
Ellen L. (Hubbard), 442, 541.
Ellen M., 301.
Ellen M. (Cook), 434, 533.
Ellen M. (Crumb), 434, 533.
Ellen M. (Sanborn), 420.
Ellen M. (Sanborn-Watkins), 520.
Ellen Maria, 116.
Ellen Maude, 610.
Ellen (Sand), 128.
Ellen (Sheldon), 487.
Ellen (Smith), 487.
Ellen Sophia, 172.
Ellen (Todd), 547.
Ellen (Webster), 228.
Ellery La Fayette, 319.
Ellinor G., 233.
Ellinor M., 233.
Ellis, 24, 25, 60, 136, 156.
Elmer, 194, 305, 319, 527, 531.
Elmer Addison, 546.
Elmer Ellsworth, 491.
Elmer Judson, 543.
Elmer Ware, 286.
Elmina E., 503.
Elmira, 249.
Elmira B. (Gordon), 610.
Elmira (Caliss), 145.
Elmira L. (Bump), 270.
Elmira (Roberts), 376.
Elmira (Smith), 394.
Elmira (Williams), 210.
El Roy, 405.
Elsie A., 274.
Elsie (Clark), 304.
Elsie Jane (White), 145.
Elsie May, 542.
Eisie (Murphy), 135, 255.
Elson, 260.
Elton Leeth, 536.
Elury D., 311.
Elury W., 311.
Elva S., 501.
Elvira, 68, 176, 182, 277, 398, 420, 489.
Elvira (Berry), 452.
Elvira (Chase), 276.
Elvira (Conant), 504.
Elvira D. (Howard), 214.
Elvira H., 294.
Emeline, 456.
Emeline (Beebe), 191, 317.
Emeline (Cleveland), 374, 457.
Emeline H. (Knapp) (not Eveline), 123, 238, 618.
Emeline R., 252.

Churchill, *continued.*
Emery, 68.
Emery S., 146.
Emilius, 405.
Emily, 70, 79, 96, 105, 127, 164, 176, 179, 182, 275, 304, 309, 369, 488, 528, 532, 577, 596, 597, 602.
Emily A., 179.
Emily A. (Davis), 397, 488.
Emily (Adams), 369.
Emily Amanda, 192.
Emily Amelia, 419.
Emily (Bennett), 214, 215.
Emily (Crosby), 219.
Emily (Drummond), 381, 475.
Emily E. (Leonard), 445, 544.
Emily Eva, 450.
Emily F., 248.
Emily G. (Hall), 379, 469.
Emily Green, 510.
Emily Hall, 469.
Emily Howard, 243.
Emily J., 203, 506, 529.
Emily Jane, 514.
Emily (Kilbreth), 449.
Emily (King), 253.
Emily Louise, 465.
Emily M., 302, 437, 593.
Emily Maria, 459.
Emily Melissa, 468.
Emily (North), 414, 514.
Emily (Ordway), 175, 302.
Emily (Parker), 616.
Emily (Shadbolt), 427, 528.
Emily (Tribble), 133, 247.
Emily Virginia, 465.
Emily (Wilcox), 379, 467.
Emily (Willis), 84, 183.
Emma, 149, 220, 235, 441, 475, 482, 501, 504, 527, 588, 599.
Emma A., 303, 522, 592.
Emma A. (Black), 320.
Emma A. (Wooley), 149.
Emma Abigail, 522.
Emma Adelia, 260.
Emma Ann, 537.
Emma (Blaine), 222.
Emma (Boise), 69, 150.
Emma (Bowen), 114, 231.
Emma C., 487.
Emma C. (Edwards), 488.
Emma D., 294.
Emma Derbyshire, 472.
Emma (Derbyshire), 347, 381.
Emma E., 545.
Emma E. (Cutts), 481.
Emma E. (Wentworth), 262.
Emma Emmeline, 475.
Emma Emogene, 293.
Emma F., 616.
Emma F. (Latham), 313.
Emma Frances, 200.
Emma Franklin, 244.
Emma (Gold), 507.
Emma (Harris), 526.
Emma Irene, 115.
Emma J., 314, 549, 615.
Emma Jane, 615.
Emma (Johnson), 465.
Emma L., 270.
Emma (Lake), 237.
Emma Louise, 208.
Emma (Ogilvie), 598.
Emma Olivia, 216.
Emma (Robinson), 596.
Emma (Rose), 250, 251.
Emma (Strong), 614.
Emma (Summeril), 418, 519.

Churchill, *continued.*
Emma T., 232.
Emma V. (Latimer), 470.
Emmeline, 181, 286, 378, 383, 407, 577, 582.
Emmeline Amelia, 123.
Emmeline (Burgess), 217.
Emmeline E. (Dodge), 203.
Emmeline (Green), 508.
Emmeline (Pope), 49, 118.
Emmeline Pulsifer, 469.
Emmeline S. (Bailey), 46, 116.
Emmeline V., 254.
Emmet, 614.
Emmet C., 532.
Enid Margaret, 539.
Enoch Chester, 584, 600.
Enoch N., 569.
Enos, 24, 56, 127, 155, 242, 280, 488, 489, 619.
Enos Albert, 280.
Epenetus W., 385, 476.
Ephraim, 12, 20, 24, 25, 59, 60, 134, 135, 167.
Ephraim E., 250.
Ephraim F., 248.
Ephraim Finney, 134, 248.
Erasmus D., 463.
Erasmus Darwin, 378, 463.
Erastus, 90, 182, 191.
Ermina L., 448.
Ermina May, 548.
Ernest, 116, 306, 311, 531.
Ernest B., 310.
Ernest Coin, 526.
Ernest M., 198, 492.
Ernest T., 200.
Erni Norman, 519.
Ernst, 221.
Erwin, 614.
Esbon, Dr., 210.
Estella, 491, 616.
Estella L. (Hart), 428, 530.
Estella M., 238.
Estella Maila, 538.
Estella Maud, 481.
Estelle, 229, 264.
Estelle Maria, 116.
Esther, 55, 158, 207, 277, 348, 350, 369, 385, 898, 435, 490, 562.
Esther Ann, 394, 573.
Esther Annette, 228.
Esther (Brooks), 49, 118.
Esther (Harlow), 138, 257.
Esther Helen, 476.
Esther (Hull), 558, 562.
Esther J., 496, 497.
Esther J. (Rogers), 181, 307.
Esther L., 506.
Esther (Lloyd), 335, 348.
Esther M., 385.
Esther P. (Payne), 379, 470.
Esther (Parmelee), 353, 405.
Esther (Shaw), 167, 294.
Esther (Shepard), 158.
Esther (Turner), 576, 590.
Ethan S., 160, 243, 285.
Ethel 259.
Ethel Ann, 495.
Ethel Austin, 228.
Ethel L., 462.
Ethel May, 260, 533.
Ethel (Richey), 491.
Ethelbert C., 493.
Ethelind, 541.
Etta A., 302.
Etta Idell, 538.
Etta M., 317.
Etta Maria, 408.

Churchill, *continued*.
Etta (Mather), 594.
Etta Myrtilla, 234.
Eudora F. (Browning), 546.
Eugene, 269, 405.
Eugene Hoyt, 518.
Eugene J., 495.
Eulala, 226.
Eunice, 32, 39, 74, 77, 78, 96, 101, 133, 149, 161, 209, 256, 280, 287, 352, 423, 444, 577, 609.
Eunice (Badger), 39, 96.
Eunice Barnes, 444.
Eunice (Barnes), 344, 368.
Eunice C., 281.
Eunice (Churchill), 32, 74, 161.
Eunice (Corington), 59, 133.
Eunice (Culver), 338, 352.
Eunice (Deming), 332.
Eunice (Durkee), 71, 155.
Eunice (Dyer), 111.
Eunice Elizabeth, 406.
Eunice Ellen, 113.
Eunice (Finney), 59.
Eunice (Follansbee), 119, 235.
Eunice J., 207.
Eunice (King-Hoyt), 45, 112.
Eunice (Kinney), 41, 100.
Eunice (Lewis), 73, 160.
Eunice Mahala, 508.
Eunice (Morey), 162, 288.
Eunice (Morris), 399.
Eunice (Payne), 363, 431.
Eunice (Piney), 342, 362.
Eunice R., 169.
Eunice Ripley, 79.
Eunice (Ripley), 16, 32.
Eunice Rosetta, 280.
Eunice S. (Flanders), 450, 550.
Eunice (Saxton), 335, 347.
Eunice (Shaw), 34, 84.
Eunice (Sturtevant), 76, 166, 609.
Eunice T. (Simmons), 78, 170.
Eunice (Van Duser), 406.
Eunice Vienna, 469.
Eunice (York), 69, 150.
Eva, 207, 226, 488, 508, 548, 594.
Eva Belden, 234.
Eva (Bramble), 506.
Eva C., 218.
Eva C. (Tuck), 598.
Eva Hammond, 312.
Eva L., 485.
Eva Laura, 467.
Eva M., 227.
Eva M. (Voorhees), 550.
Eva Maria, 311.
Eva (Upton), 257.
Evalin (Brown), 569.
Evaline, 284, 396.
Evaline (Norton), 572.
Evangeline, 502.
Evelina, 459.
Eveline, 434.
Eveline (Beach), 467.
Eveline (Blanchard), 159, 284.
Eveline (Bronson), 578.
Eveline E. (Bradfield), 195, 320.
Eveline Elizabeth, 485.
Eveline May, 548.
Evelyn, 500.
Evelyn Adams, 407.

Churchill, *continued*.
Evelyn Augusta, 315.
Evelyn B., 248.
Evelyn Clinton, 406
Everett, 199.
Experience, 25.
Experience (Ellis), 7, 12.
Experience (Hale), 96, 203.
Experience (Stafford), 37, 91.
Ezekiel, 89, 336, 338, 352, 405.
Ezekiel Henry, 353, 406.
Ezekiel St. John, 371.
Ezra, 19, 36, 41, 42, 72, 79, 80, 89, 103, 104, 106, 126, 138, 156, 171, 184, 216, 217, 218, 241, 258, 615.
Ezra, Jr., 157.
Ezra F., 309.
Ezra Rhodes, 241.
Fabyan, 186.
Faith, 27.
Fannie, 236, 250, 254, 255, 288, 460, 488, 522, 599.
Fannie Bell, 278, 616.
Fannie E., 459.
Fannie Fassett, 521
Fannie G., 238.
Fannie Hart, 171.
Fannie L., 482.
Fannie M., 309, 462.
Fannie (Murch), 309.
Fannie (Tinkham), 255.
Fannie W., 303.
Fanny, 41, 191, 192, 318.
Fanny Buckminster, 298.
Fanny (Cloose), 613.
Fanny (Davenport), 90, 191.
Fanny (Dudley), 270.
Fanny Fuller, 373.
(Farling), 569.
Fayetta, 482.
Fayette, 505.
Fenton Orris, 534.
Ferguson, 187.
Fidelia, 175, 400.
Fidelia (Bushnell), 375, 458.
Finette, 434.
Finvola (Campbell), 504.
Fitz Henry, 572, 588.
Flavilla V. (Kellogg), 202.
Flavius, 445.
Flora, 149, 306, 310, 315.
Flora A. 271.
Flora (Adams), 118, 235.
Flora Amelia, 271.
Flora Belle, 310.
Flora G., 475.
Flora G. (Jack), 228.
Flora L., 549.
Flora (Merrill), 303.
Flora (Owen), 307.
Floraman, 304.
Florence, 220, 242, 259, 264, 460, 465, 483, 500, 532.
Florence A., 301.
Florence Aline, 171.
Florence C., 591.
Florence (Campbell), 458.
Florence Celia, 279.
Florence Ethel, 485.
Florence (Friend), 267.
Florence (Harris), 216.
Florence (Hubbard), 218.
Florence Idelle, 550.
Florence (Jennings), 547.
Florence Josephine, 454.
Florence M. (Windsor), 299.
Florence May, 234, 281.
Florence N. (Dawson), 283.

Churchill, *continued*.
Floretta T., 489.
Florinda, 180.
Florinda W., 178.
Flossie Estelle, 205.
Floyd, 550.
Floyd K., 491.
Floyd Leroy, 494.
Floyd W., 266.
Forest F., 151.
Forest White, 258.
Francelia, 149.
Francelia A. (White), 285.
Francella, 492.
Frances, 162, 219, 238, 289, 295, 351.
Frances A., 385, 549.
Frances A. (Clark), 288.
Frances A. (Taylor), 466.
Frances A. C. (McKin), 57, 128.
Frances Amelia, 459.
Frances Ann, 457.
Frances Caroline, 199.
Frances (Dervan), 252.
Frances E. (Richardson), 49, 118.
Frances Eveline, 428.
Frances Gertrude, 314.
Frances Ilsley, 116.
Frances (Jackson), 504.
Frances Jane, 445.
Frances L. (Rogers), 272.
Frances Lenore, 213.
Frances Maria, 175, 216.
Frances Marion, 200, 318, 406.
Frances (Marshall), 201.
Frances Mary, 210.
Frances Matilda Gertrude, 469.
Frances (Morris), 596.
Frances P. (Warner), 448, 548.
Frances (Richards), 364, 433.
Frances V., 198.
Francis, 25, 57, 126, 130, 186, 244, 305, 416, 505, 614.
Francis Augustus, 600.
Francis C., 243.
Francis Elliott, 417, 517.
Francis Gerald, 202.
Francis Gorton, 201.
Francis H., 242.
Francis Henry, 192.
Francis L., 450, 550.
Francis Lemoyne, 472.
Francis Marion, 468, 505.
Francis Melbourne, 319.
Francis Samuel, 517.
Francis Vennell, 129. 243.
Francis Wayland, 429, 531.
Francis Worcester, Capt., 58, 129.
Frank, 116, 197, 220, 231, 242, 244, 282, 292, 304, 320, 599, 603, 614.
Frank A., 232, 306.
Frank Alanson, 191, 317.
Frank Albert, 132.
Frank B., 490.
Frank Blakeslee, 534.
Frank Burr, 545.
Frank Campbell, 458.
Frank D., 488.
Frank Delason, 451, 551.
Frank E., 207, 491, 546.
Frank F., 550.
Frank G., 474, 549.
Frank Giles, 228.
Frank H., 192, 203.
Frank Henry, 605.
Frank Herbert, 471.

Churchill, *continued.*
Frank Holmes, 481.
Frank Homer, 260.
Frank Lee, 543.
Frank Leslie, 458.
Frank M., 205, 257,'598,'600.
Frank N., 307.
Frank Oliver, 546.
Frank P., 226, 296.
Frank R., 221, 533.
Frank S., 233, 521.
Frank Spooner, 300
Frank Virgil, 542.
Frank Wilbur, 615.
Frank Wilson, 294.
Franklin, 128, 247.
Franklin B., 283.
Franklin Dwight, 434, 534.
Franklin F., 533.
Franklin Green, 132.
Franklin Harvey, 588.
Franklin Hunter, 99.
Franklin Newton, 171.
Franklin Peck, 470.
Franklin Pierce, 295.
Franklin S., 504.
Fred, 282, 594.
Fred Alvin, 309.
Fred C., 310.
Fred D., 538.
Fred H., 197.
Fred Lee, 128, 242.
Fred Loring, 258.
Fred M., 549.
Fred Pearse, 550.
Fred S., 232.
Fred Sylvester, 258.
Fred T., 288.
Fred W., 273.
Fred Warren, 521.
Fred Weaver, 472.
Frederic, 122, 517.
Frederic Lafayette, 536.
Frederick, 48, 183, 189, 198, 218, 241, 242, 293, 308, 315, 461, 599, 605.
Frederick A., 128, 295.
Frederick A., Jr., 225.
Frederick Arthur, 229, 244.
Frederick Augustus, 111, 117, 128, 187, 225, 234, 314, 467.
Frederick E., 476.
Frederick Ellis, 247.
Frederick Griswold, 522.
Frederick H., 473.
Frederick Hosea, 540.
Frederick Levi, 593.
Frederick Meecham, 98.
Frederick S., 285.
Frederick Seward, 94.
Frederick Stephen, 290.
Frederick Tobie, 311.
Frederick W., 564, 573.
Frederick William, 315.
Freeborn, 443, 543.
Freeman, 108, 220.
Freeman Grozier, 79, 171.
Gamaliel, 20.
Gardner, 90.
Gardner Asaph, iii, iv, v, vi, vii, ix, x, 230, 297, 462, 463, 468.
Garrett D., 564, 578.
Garth, 202.
Gaylord, 580.
Genevieve Leona, 316.
George, xiii. xv, 37, 92, 103, 106, 118, 126, 131, 136, 160, 162, 165, 186, 193, 214, 218, 219, 221, 234, 235, 240, 256, 288, 292, 293, 306, 314, 317, 359, 379, 382, 402, 409, 418, 420, 426, 444, 470, 473, 495,

Churchill, *continued.*
506, 519, 528, 572, 576, 583, 592, 594, 599, 603, 616.
George, Capt., 94, 200.
George, Rev. 217.
George A., 112.
George Albert, 111, 224.
George Arthur, 314.
George Atwood, 173, 301, 470.
George B., 521, 528.
George Bacon, 200.
George Bosworth, 171.
George Boyer, 213, 214.
George Brayton, 473.
George Byron, 490.
George C., 487.
George Charles Spencer, Duke, xv.
George Clarence, 381, 473.
George Clinton, 119, 235.
George Daney, 528.
George E., 203, 251, 434, 490, 534.
George Edward, 309, 510.
George Ernst, 221.
George F., 291.
George Francis, 132, 246.
George Frederick, 188, 216, 315.
George H., 273, 294, 544, 549, 598.
George Harlan, 320.
George Harris, 112, 227.
George Harvey, 451, 551.
George Hathaway, 523.
George Henry, 287, 600, 605.
George Hiram, 187, 314.
George Hyel (not George A.), 601, 605, 619.
George J., 320.
George King, 605.
George Knox, 257.
George L., 221, 294.
George Lathrop, 103.
George LeForest, 301.
George Levi, 503.
George Lewis, 167, 294, 311.
George M., 146, 271, 284.
George May, 281.
George Milford, 208.
George Milton, 475, 520.
George Morse, 596.
George O., 546.
George Paul, 490.
George Perry, 279.
George Phillips, 300.
George Quincy, 171.
George R., 586, 601.
George Rollin, 204.
George S., 271, 498.
George Samuel, 313.
George Silas, 515.
George Spencer, Duke, xiv, xv.
George Sumner, 245.
George Teylor, 198.
George Thompson, 415, 515.
George Vernon, 397, 488.
George W., 122, 237, 238, 249, 250, 253, 259, 261, 399, 434, 452, 490.
George W., Rev., 195, 319.
George W. C., 168.
George W. D., 145.
George Warren, 313.
George Washington, 128, 132, 217, 379, 437, 535, 536, 572, 588, 597.
George Washington, Dr., 58, 133.
George Washington Hayman, 424.

Churchill, *continued.*
George Webster, 131.
George William, 197, 445, 544.
Georgie, 218, 244.
Georgia D., 483.
Georgia E., 227.
Georgianna, 219.
Georgianna M., 294.
Geraldine, 596.
Gerard, 596.
German Sheldon, 272.
Gershom, 17.
Gertrude, 216, 246, 601, 604.
Gertrude A., 592.
Gertrude A. (Taylor), 132, 246.
Gertrude B. (Locke), 546.
Gertrude Charlotte, 590.
Gertrude (Dickinson), 534.
Gertrude Emma, 473.
Gertrude (Flint), 134, 251.
Gertrude (Frisby), 486.
Gertrude Maria, 588.
Gertrude (Nickerson), 434.
Gertrude (Ramsey), 378, 463.
Gertrude (Silver), 458.
Gilbert, 57, 121, 236, 456.
Gilbert, Dr., 368, 444.
Gilbert Anthony, 451.
Gilbert Barnes, 444.
Gilbert C., 498.
Gilbert F., 250.
Gilbert W., 408, 501, 564, 574.
Gilbert Willet, 466.
Giles, xiii, 330, 335, 342, 348, 359, 382, 384, 474, 541, 611.
Giles, Dr., 348, 383.
Giles Wilcox, 377.
Gladys, 509.
Gladys Erminnie, 493.
Gladys Ferguson, 228.
Gladys M., 266.
Glen R., 551.
Glenwood B., 280.
Goldie, 508.
Goldie L., 487.
Grace, 538.
Grace A., 243, 285.
Grace A. (Churchill), 243, 285.
Grace C., 268.
Grace Cora, 224.
Grace D., 254.
Grace (Delphy), 271.
Grace Edna, 234.
Grace Ethel, 243.
Grace F., 273.
Grace Huntington, 199.
Grace L., 605.
Grace M., 266.
Grace M. (Allen), 255.
Grace (Tylle), xiii
Grace Vivian, 314.
Grace W. (Berry), 522.
Granville Mellen, 289.
Gustavus, 126.
Gustavus Vasa, 128.
Guy, 235.
Guy Fordyce, 471.
Guy Lester, 228.
H. Almira, 603.
H. N., 462.
Hamilton, 437.
Haumer D., 489.
Hannah, 3, 5, 7, 9, 15, 17, 24, 25, 26, 30, 31, 35, 41, 57, 60, 61, 63, 66, 69, 71, 73, 74, 82, 89, 102, 108, 128, 135, 136, 143, 158, 165, 184, 186, 219, 221, 249, 253, 255,

Churchill, *continued.*

Henry, 54, 94, 112, 125, 131, 144, 156, 167, 176, 198, 217, 220, 221, 225, 240, 242, 250, 282, 288, 289, 291, 294, 295, 353, 378, 448, 453, 457, 464, 527, 538, 563, 567, 568, 569, 576, 583, 584, 591, 604, 615, 619.
Henry, Dr., 217.
Henry A., 296.
Henry Ambrose, 536.
Henry Andros, 510.
Henry Anson, 309.
Henry B., 592.
Henry C., 238, 316, 453, 470.
Henry Clay, 204, 434, 533.
Henry Cushman, 283.
Henry D., 249, 252.
Henry Dwight, 510.
Henry E., 398, 546.
Henry Edward, 486.
Henry Ezekiel, 406.
Henry Franklin, 244.
Henry Gilstrap, 510.
Henry Harrison, 203.
Henry Heyer, 584.
Henry Hill Boody, 111.
Henry J., 421, 523.
Henry L., 198, 240.
Henry Lewis, 525, 600.
Henry Lyman, 470.
Henry Melville, 258.
Henry Mortimer, 582, 598.
Henry Mott, 584.
Henry P., 311.
Henry Palmer, 191, 317.
Henry Perket, 256.
Henry Phillips, 583.
Henry Price, 535.
Henry T., 487.
Henry Ufford, Capt., 379, 469.
Henry W., 226, 277.
Henry William, 275.
Hepsibah, 82.
Herbert, 116, 198, 248, 461, 508.
Herbert C., 117.
Herbert H., 228.
Herbert Haddock, 460.
Herbert Hiram, 546.
Herbert Leon, 228.
Herbert R., Jr., 260.
Herbert Remson, 260.
Herbert Winston, 459.
Herman, 489, 493, 598.
Herman Hoyt, 534.
Hervey A., 546.
Hervey Shaw, 182.
Hester Eunice, 432.
Hetty, 143.
Hezekiah, 331, 332, 344, 368.
Hincke, 563.
Hiram, 56, 88, 95, 155, 162, 187, 279, 318, 369, 445, 576, 589.
Hiram DeForrest, 192, 317.
Hiram Noah, 95.
Hiram Parker, 446, 545.
Hiram S., 527.
Hiram W., 446.
Hiram Wallace, 279.
Hiram William, 440, 538.
Hobart, 576, 592.
Hobert D., 483.
Hollis, 46, 183.
Hollis Hutchins, 146, 262.
(Holmes), 247.
Homer, 405, 576, 591.
Homer Cullen, 406, 500.
Homer E., 498.
Hope E., 203.
Horace 156, 183, 199, 275, 279, 280, 308, 361, 504.

Churchill, *continued.*

Horace A., 301.
Horace Albert, 275.
Horace Alexander, 275.
Horace Carter, 532.
Horace F., 301.
Horace H., 205.
Horace M., 97.
Horace Mann, 234.
Horace P., 177.
Horace W., 281.
Horatio, 149, 266.
Hosea, 75, 162, 163, 288.
Howard, 292, 463.
Howard Crosby, 300.
Howard D., 260, 529.
Howard E., 491.
Howard Kellogg, 202.
Howard L., 310.
Howard Lee, 483.
Howard Malcolm, 257.
Howard K., 204.
Howel E., 273.
Howell, 596.
Hubert, 532.
Hugh H., 273.
Hulda, 50, 349, 373.
Hulda (Beecher), 330, 342.
Hulda (Brown), 22, 49.
Huldah, 346.
Huldah Jane, 182.
Huldah (Phillips), 566, 580.
Hull, 564.
(Hurll), 128, 242.
Ichabod, 11, 15, 19, 20, 32, 39, 44, 74, 76, 77, 95, 161.
Ichabod D., 46, 117.
Ichabod F., 117.
Ichabod Sylvester, 168, 295.
Ida, 221, 295, 317, 318, 522, 527, 529, 594.
Ida C. (Lilley), 240.
Ida C. (Matthews), 202.
Ida (Curtis), 505.
Ida E., 301.
Ida (Estes), 296.
Ida F. (Thompson), 261.
Ida Frances, 509.
Ida (Hall), 132.
Ida L. (Blodget), 312.
Ida M., 267.
Ida M. (Thompson), 147.
Ida Matilda, 458.
Ida May, 594.
Ida N., 541.
Ida (Post), 520.
Ida (Thompson), 264.
Ida V. (Le Rean), 273.
Idella Francis, 172.
Iguatia (Storrs), 194, 319.
Imogene, 287.
Inez, 505, 601.
Inez E. (Anthony), 401.
Inez (Lent), 250.
Ira, 342, 362, 363, 581.
Ira, Jr., 363, 433.
Ira L., 422.
Ira Rodney, 430.
Ira S., 308.
Ira Sprague, 293.
Irena, 90, 115, 264, 351.
Irena (Berry), 147, 264.
Irene (or Irena W.), 146, 150, 233, 262, 367, 443, 448.
Irene C., 551.
Irene F. (Purington) (not Hyrona), 45, 115, 617.
Irene G. (Canfield), 116, 233.
Irene (Grant), 207.
Irene Rich, 371.
Irene Sophronia, 192.
Irene (Walton), 69, 150.
Irma A., 462.

Churchill, *continued.*

Irving Elansing, 445.
Irving F., 251.
Irving L., 492.
Irving Lester, 493.
Isaac, 6, 8, 9, 11, 16, 17, 19, 20, 25, 30, 32, 34, 41, 42, 43, 58, 71, 78, 80, 81, 100, 144, 146, 153, 175, 247, 260, 275, 362, 422, 522, 563, 566, 567, 580, 582.
Isaac B., 277.
Isaac Bradford, ix, 154, 155, 277.
Isaac Bradford, Jr., 279.
Isaac Covington. 133, 247.
Isaac Newton, Deac., 387, 481.
Isaac O., 174.
Isaac P., 582.
Isabel, 199, 202, 316, 420, 499.
Isabel (Cuthbert), 289.
Isabel (Gilbert), 89, 189.
Isabel Lovejoy, 205.
Isabel (Miller), 430, 532.
Isabel (Rodney), 532.
Isabella, 221, 223, 230, 426, 473, 503.
Isabella Bathsheba, 306.
Isabella (Johnson), 352, 402.
Isabella (Long), 584, 601.
Isabella (Van Osdall), 205.
Isabelle, 233.
Isadora, 317.
Isadora D., 243.
Isadore, 207.
Isaiah, 74, 101, 162, 208, 209, 289, 399.
Isaiah Frederick, 290.
Isaiah Jenkins, 171.
Isaiah Thomas 171.
Isaline (Vail), 549.
Ishmael, 508.
Israel, 17, 35, 71, 101, 108, 209, 275.
Israel Gerow, 210.
Israel Harding, 255.
Israel L., 253.
Ithamar, 342, 361, 364.
Ithuel, 363, 427.
Iva, 589.
Ivah (Jones), 320.
Ivan Floyd, 606.
Ivory, 158, 282.
Izabenda (Bearse), 564, 574.
Izana, 183.
J. Allen, 207.
J. Louise, 304.
Jabez, 17, 28, 34, 35, 81, 82, 85, 86, 142, 177, 186.
Jabez, Jr., 65, 142.
Jackson V., 289.
Jacob, 17, 36, 76, 81, 89, 90, 108, 126, 166, 176, 191, 221, 583, 599, 609, 610.
Jacob M., 610.
Jacob Miles, 37, 91.
James, 9, 24, 34, 60, 67, 74, 90, 105, 145, 160, 162, 163, 167, 176, 181, 193, 217, 256, 283, 286, 294, 348, 352, 361, 366, 367, 381, 405, 421, 440, 442, 447, 459, 495, 499, 505, 541, 562, 564, 572, 581, 583, 587, 589, 599, 616, 613, 614, 615, 618.
James, Capt., 31, 74.
James, Jr., 382, 564, 573.
James, Lieut., 17, 34.
James A., 157, 527, 603.
James Addison, 452.

Heuzen, *continued*.
John W., 597.
LaVina, 597.
Robert, 597.
Sheridan, 597.
William, 597.
Hewett, Margaret, 190, 316.
Hewit, Thankful, 330, 337.
Hewitt, Anna, 36, 88.
Celestia (Brown), 569.
Ella A., 274.
Elmer E., 274.
Elsie A. (Churchill), 274.
Homer M., 274.
Merritt H., 274.
Millie J. (Wood), 274.
Richard, 569.
Hibbard, Asenath, 59, 134.
Kate (Churchill), 508.
Lester S., 508.
Nancy (Churchill), 42.
Samuel, 42.
Hickok, Ammi Leollue, 364.
Aurilla Almarine, 364.
Bethunia Eunetia, 364.
John, 364.
Lois D. (Churchill), 364.
Mary (Underwood), 364.
Uriah, 336, 337.
Hicks, Lydia (Doane), 6.
Robert, 6.
Samuel, 6.
Sarah, 5, 6.
Higginbotham, Katherine, 201.
Higgins, Ella, 131.
John C., 181.
Julia S., 357.
Mary (Churchill), 181.
Richard, 1, 3.
Higley, Almeda (Churchill), 528.
Homer D., 528.
John O., 528.
Hill, Maj.-Gen., xiii.
Ada, 148, 265.
Anna Bryant, 325.
Emily L. (Churchill), 465.
Eugene, 465.
Harriet L. (Westcott), 325.
Lura, 359, 418.
Lydia (Churchill), 168.
Malcolm Westcott, 325.
Mary, 535.
Norman Alan, 325.
Roswell, 168.
Thomas, 325.
Hillman, Carrie I., 432.
Alexander, 69.
Jane (Churchill), 69.
Hilton, Bradford R., Capt., 220.
Katharine, 186.
Margery A. (Churchill), 220.
Hincke, Hannah, 561, 563.
Hinckley, Carrie, 451.
Jabez, 139.
Ruth, 63, 139.
Hinds, James, 487.
Mary A., 396, 487.
Mary (Brumbly), 487.
Hine, Adaline Clarinda, 577.
Albert J., 577.
Almira (Churchill), 577.
Andrew, 577.
Catharine Emily, 577.
Eliada O., 577.
Joseph, 577.
Julia Tyler, 577.
Polly Sarah, 577.
Sally (Churchill), 577.
Sally Maria, 577, 593.
Samuel David, 577.
Sylvester, 577.
William J., 577.

Hines, Benjamin, 506.
Josephine A. (Churchill), 506.
Perry, 506.
Hinman, 324.
Hinsey, Ann, 420, 521.
Hintston, Sally A., 400, 492.
Hipolite, Julianna (Ketchum), 581.
W. W., Dr., 581.
Histon, Sarah E., 415, 515.
Hitchcock, 446.
Abigail, 122, 237.
Adeline, 385.
Betsey (Allen-Flatt), 563.
Elliot, 576.
James, 563.
Juliana, 413.
Mary A. (Churchill), 576.
Hitt, Roxanna (Churchill), 504.
Swazy, 504.
Hoagland, Sarah, 430, 532.
(Schwink), 454.
Hobart, Charles, 359.
Charles W., 359.
Corinna (Woodruff), 359.
George C., 359.
Henry M., 359.
Mary, 359.
Hobbs, Ida, 582.
John, 582.
John S., 582.
Mary Ann, 582.
Mary (Churchill), 582.
Rebecca, 582.
William, 582.
Hobson, Ambrose, 215.
Edith (Phillips), 215.
Hodgdon, Alfred Lyman, 185.
Elizabeth, 185.
Ellen, 185.
Fannie (McNally), 185.
Lucy, 185.
Mabel, 185.
Persis M. (Churchill), 185.
Samuel, 185.
Hodge, Alfred, 335.
Benjamin, 335.
Clarissa, 335.
(Davis), 335.
Elizabeth, 258.
Lorin, 335.
Philander, 335.
Sarah, 335.
Sarah (Churchill), 335.
Sophia (English), 335.
Velorus, 335.
William, 335.
Hodges, Matilda, 397.
Hodgetts, Mary H., 149, 266.
Hogan, Amanda A., 415, 517.
Charlotte T., 415, 516.
Marietta (Churchill), 410.
Martha (Perry), 108.
Martin, 410.
T. R., 108.
Hogle, Almira (Churchill), 89.
David, 89.
Hoisington, Ella A., 302.
Ella L., 302.
Emily M. (Churchill), 302.
Frank L., 302.
Holbrook, Betsey, 28.
Betsey A., 294.
Ella G., 132, 246.
Kate, 396.
Lucretia, 182.
Holcomb, Candace (Churchill), 407.
Charles S., 193.
Dean, 193.
Hollis, 193.
Jonathan, 407.
Lurania, 407.

Holcomb, *continued*.
Luna, 90, 193.
Lura M., 193.
Lutilda (Churchill), 193.
Sadie (Mott), 193
Tyra, 194.
Holden, Mary, 69, 148.
Holdridge, G. W., 267.
Marion A. (Churchill-Catlin), 267.
Holland, Annette, 124.
Hollenbeck, Jessie, 461.
Holley, Arminda E., 49.
Curtis D., 49.
Eliza (Churchill), 49.
Erastus, 49.
Frances E., 49.
Marietta, 49.
Holliday, Louisiana, 354, 410.
Hollingshed, Charles W., 268.
Charlotte H. (Churchill), 268.
Holly, Abigail, 442, 542.
Holman, Carrie Maud, 280.
Charles Henderson, 280.
Chloe A. (Churchill), 280.
Eliza (not Elizabeth), 51, 120, 617.
Frank Foster, 280.
Fred. Augustus Churchill, 280.
Frederick Ralph, 280.
Henry R., Dr., 280.
Ida L. (Bessel), 280.
Holmes, 70, 247.
Abner, 10.
Adelia, 480.
Allen, 94.
Allen Turner, 94.
Almira, 138.
Barnabas, 61.
Bathsheba, 10.
Bathsheba (Holmes), 10.
Bethia, 25, 60.
Bethia (Churchill), 37, 61.
Betsey, 61.
Betsey (Rogers), 26.
Caleb, 74.
Carry Mary, 478.
Cora Elizabeth, 478.
Cora L., 478.
Desire, 6, 10, 42.
Eleazer, 11, 18, 26.
Eliezer, 74.
Elisha, 10.
Elkanah, 10.
Elnathan, 10.
Ephraim, 62, 7.
Esther, 74, 94.
Fayette, 477.
Florence S., 478.
Frank, 94.
Gamaliel, 74.
George, 77.
Gideon F., 139.
Hannah, 10, 209.
Hannah F. (Churchill), 94.
Harriet, 74, 81, 176.
Harriet M. (Amidon), 478.
Helen A. (Drew), 139.
Howard R., 478.
Jane, 10.
Joanna (Churchill), 79.
John Calderwood, 37.
Jonathan, 10, 74.
Joseph, 10, 27, 256.
Julia Sylvia, 477.
Lemuel, Capt., 176.
Louie R., 478.
Lydia, 11, 18, 74, 77.
Lydia (Churchill), 11.
M. F., 139.
Marcia J. (not Maria), 56, 127, 617.

704 INDEX OF NAMES

West, *continued.*
Walter J., 449.
Westbrook, Mary B., 239.
Westcott, Eliza Ann, 22.
George B., 325.
Harriet Louisa, 325.
Mary A. (Hynson), 325.
Mary (Buck), 325.
Samuel, 325.
Westgate, Mary J., 164, 290.
Westinghouse, 519.
Weston, Aaron, 408.
Abner, 16.
Almira, 27.
Benjamin, 27, 247.
Betsey, 27.
Betsey H. (Churchill), 247.
Betsey (Lanman), 27.
Charles, 167.
Clarissa (Churchill), 158.
David, 16.
Dorcas (Churchill), 107.
(Eldredge), 107.
Elinor, 107.
Eliza E. (Churchill), 158.
Elizabeth (Hatfield), 107.
Esther (Churchill-Morton), 158.
Florence White, 192.
Frederick, 107.
George, 27, 107, 192.
Hannah, 27.
Hannah (Churchill), 158.
Harvey, 27, 138.
Ida M. (White), 192.
Jabez, 16.
Jacob, 107.
Joanna (Washburn), 27.
Julia, 408.
Julia A. (Churchill), 408.
Lemuel, 107.
Leoni (Kelley), 107.
Lewis, 27, 158.
Lucy, 27, 167.
Lucy Ann, 42.
Lucy (Churchill), 27.
Lucy (Harlow), 27.
Lydia E., 107.
Martha B. (Drew), 27.
Martha (Jenkins), 107.
Mary, 16.
Mary (Churchill), 27.
Mary (Coffran), 42.
Matilda, 107.
Mercy M., 167.
Mercy S. (Churchill), 167.
Nathan, 107.
Norman J., 107.
Otis, 158.
Patty, 28.
Polly, 27.
Polly (Holmes), 27.
Rebeckah, 16.
Robert, 42, 107, 167.
Rufus, 16, 158.
Sally (Churchill), 138.
Samuel, 158.
Sarah (Churchill), 27.
Sophie (Jenkins), 107.
Susannah (Churchill), 16.
William, 27, 167.
Capt. William, 27.
Zadoc, 107.
Westwood, Frank G., 132.
Jennie C. (Swift), 132.
Wethern, B. T., 68.
Mary W. (Churchill), 68.
Micah Delmont, 69.
William Corydon, 69.
Wetherwax, Catherine, 567, 583.
Lydia, 567, 583.
Wetmore, Annie E., 274.
Whalen, Mary, 188.

Whaley, Mary, 215.
Wharff, Lydia Ann, 58, 133.
Whedon, Sophronia, 363, 429.
Wheeler, Albert P., 586.
Caroline, 452.
Charles J., 270.
Charlotte (Churchill), 586.
E. S., 568.
Edward Churchill, 141.
Elizabeth (Ridley), 586.
Elizabeth (Sherman), 586.
Emma L. (Churchill), 270.
Fred A., 270.
George, 586.
Grace E., 270.
Henry E., 586.
James Snow, 141.
Joseph F., 141.
Joseph Franklin, 141.
Josephine, 455.
Margaret E., 586.
Marie L. (Lester), 568.
Mary E. (Hannan), 586.
May V., 455.
Melissa (Churchill), 141.
Orville A., 586.
Wheelock, Effie, 401.
Fannie, 202.
Whelpley, Ruhama, 349, 389.
Whipp, Jennie, 284.
Whipple, Abigail, 377.
Alanson Edgar, 378.
Caroline (Churchill), 377.
Caroline Ella, 378.
Celestia (Adams), 175.
Daniel Thornton, 377.
Frances Emily, 377.
Francis Marvin, 378.
Harriet Fidelia, 377.
Henry Churchill, 377.
Julia (Wood), 377.
Mary, 377.
Minerva C. (Brown-Artis), 425.
Morillo M., 175.
Solomon, 377.
William, 425.
William Wirt, 377.
Whitacor, Lorana, 325.
Whitcomb, 374.
Bertha D. (Johnson), 269.
Charles, 374.
Ernest J., 269.
Harriet, 512.
Horace, 374.
John, Col., 52.
Millicent, 58, 129.
Roxana (Churchill), 374.
William, 374.
White, Abby W., 284.
Abigail, 329, 334.
Abigail (Butler), 334.
Charles H., 500.
Christian, 379.
Cornelius L., 258.
Deborah (Hall), 334.
Delos, 334.
Ebenezer, Col., 33.
Eliza T., 43.
Elizabeth (Hodge), 258.
Elsie Jane, 145.
Francelia A., 285.
George W., 334.
Hannah, 184, 310.
Ida May, 192.
Joseph, 334.
Joseph, Deac., 334.
Joseph, Dr., 334.
Leventia, 334.
Lillie C., 258.
Lucinda, 31.
Marcellus, 192.
Maria, 374, 456.
Mary (Churchill), 192.

White, *continued.*
Mary M. (Churchill), 500.
Menzo, Dr., 334.
Nancy, 72.
Narcissa, 373, 453.
Nathaniel, 334.
Olive (Hall), 334.
Orphia, 101.
Ruby, 72.
Ruth (Churchill), 334.
Sarah, 395.
Stephen, 334.
Whitfield, Amelia M. (Atkins), 101.
Charles W., 41.
Charles Watts, 101.
Frederick John, 101.
George Frederick, Dr., 101.
Henry Allen, 101.
James Carr, 101.
John Isaiah, 101.
Julia (Wood), 101.
Kate (Knapp), 101.
Mariah, 101.
Minnie (Wead), 101.
Nathaniel Churchill, 101.
Orphia (White), 101.
Phebe (Brant), 101.
Phebe (Fletcher), 101.
Rebecca Carr, 101.
Susannah (Churchill), 101.
Thomas Nice, 101.
Zenas Elliot Bliss, 101.
Whitford, Adelia (Churchill), 191.
Daniel, 191.
George, 316.
Laura (Churchill), 316.
Whiting, Azariah, 10.
Betsey D., 59.
Betsey (Morton), 28.
Comfort, 125.
Deborah (Churchill), 125.
Eveline T., 43.
Franklin T., 108.
George W., 108.
Hannah W. (Churchill), 108.
Ida J., 108.
Ida (Sprague), 108.
Joanna, 76.
Joseph, 28.
Louisa (Glover), 108.
Martha H., 134, 248.
Martha (Pratt), 108.
Olive F., 108.
Rebecca (Churchill-Holmes), 10.
Rosilla E., 108.
Sarah M., 108.
Warren T., 108.
William H., 108.
Whitlock, Clara, 459.
Whitman, Almon, Rev., 389.
Alta C. (Churchill), 389.
Caroline (Churchill), 389.
Caroline D., 389.
Elmore C., 513.
Harry Churchill, 513.
Helen L. (Adams), 376.
Henry, 376.
Henry J., 147.
Irving A., 389.
Jacob, Rev., 107.
James, 427.
Jonathan, 30.
Judson F., 389.
Leah, 30.
Lovell D., 389.
Mary, 107.
Martha S. (Churchill), 147.
Mercy L., 159, 284.
Nellie A. (Frisbie), 513.
Phebe, 42.

CPSIA information can be obtained
at www.ICGtesting.com
Printed in the USA
LVOW05s1218020117
519400LV00008B/677/P

9 781333 549565